EDITION **5**

Gateways to Democracy

An Introduction to American Government

John G. **Geer**
VANDERBILT UNIVERSITY

Richard **Herrera**
ARIZONA STATE UNIVERSITY

Wendy J. **Schiller**
BROWN UNIVERSITY

Jeffrey A. **Segal**
STONY BROOK UNIVERSITY

Australia • Brazil • Canada • Mexico • Singapore • United Kingdom • United States

Gateways to Democracy: An Introduction to American Government, **Fifth Edition**
John G. Geer, Richard Herrera,
Wendy J. Schiller, Jeffrey A. Segal

SVP, Higher Education & Skills Product:
  Erin Joyner

VP, Higher Education & Skills Product:
  Thais Alencar

Product Director: Laura Ross

Product Manager: Lauren Gerrish

Product Assistant: Martina Umunna

Marketing Director: Neena Bali

Senior Marketing Manager: Valerie Hartman

Senior Content Manager: Laura Hildebrand

Learning Designer: Erika Hayden

Digital Delivery Lead: Dana Edmunds

Senior In-House Subject Matter Expert,
  Emily Hickey

Manufacturing Planner: Ron Montgomery

IP Analyst: Deanna Ettinger

IP Project Manager: Carly Belcher

Production Service: MPS Limited

Compositor: MPS Limited

Art Director: Sarah Cole

Text Designer: Sarah Cole

Cover Designer: Sarah Cole

Cover Image: smartboy10/DigitalVision
  Vectors/Getty Images

For product information and technology assistance, contact us at
Cengage Customer & Sales Support, 1-800-354-9706 or
support.cengage.com.

For permission to use material from this text or product,
submit all requests online at
www.cengage.com/permissions.

Library of Congress Control Number: 2020916815

Student Edition:
ISBN: 978-0-357-45921-8

Loose-leaf Edition:
ISBN: 978-0-357-45930-0

Cengage
200 Pier 4 Boulevard
Boston, MA 02210
USA

Cengage is a leading provider of customized learning solutions with employees residing in nearly 40 different countries and sales in more than 125 countries around the world. Find your local representative at **www.cengage.com.**

To learn more about Cengage platforms and services, register or access your online learning solution, or purchase materials for your course, visit **www.cengage.com.**

Printed at CLDPC, USA, 01-21

Brief Contents

Contents

Letter to Instructors

Dear American Politics Instructor:

As teachers and scholars of American government, we have come together to write a textbook that engages students in both the process and the policy outcomes of the U.S. government. We present an updated lens through which we can examine the theoretical and structural foundations of American democracy and the resulting political process that demands an active and informed citizenry. To help students understand American democracy and see how they can be involved in their government, we peel back the layers of the political system to expose its inner workings and to examine how competing interests can both facilitate and block the people's will. In doing so, we use the conceptual framework of gateways. We contend that there are gates—formal and informal—that present obstacles to participation and empowerment. But there are also gateways that give students a chance to influence the process and to overcome the obstacles. The gateways framework helps students conceptualize participation and civic engagement—even democracy itself. Our book is both realistic and optimistic, contending that the American system can be open to the influence of students and responsive to their hopes and dreams—if they have information about how the system works. But we avoid cheerleading by also pointing out the many gates that undermine the workings of government. Although the size and complexity of the American constitutional system is daunting, it is imperative to prepare for the demands of democratic citizenship. This has never been truer than today, when we have a rapidly changing demographic balance within our population. Today groups that have been systematically disempowered in American politics and society, such as African Americans and second- and third-generation Latinos, are asserting their power in our politics. It is our hope that this textbook can awaken students and motivate them not only to learn about politics but to also participate actively throughout every stage of their lives.

In keeping with the theme of gates and gateways in American politics, we also open each chapter with a **vignette** that tells the story of an individual who has successfully navigated his or her own way in politics. The important role of the vignette for the instructor is to show the students how people have made a difference in American political and social life; our vignette subjects vary by historical era, career choice, gender, race, ethnicity, and party affiliation. We also include landmark **Supreme Court cases** related to every chapter's subject to show students the continuous and vital role the Court plays in both upholding and knocking down gates to policy implementation and political participation. We include **policy features** in each chapter to illustrate how the chapter's core content operates on a real-time, real-life basis. We also have an **Election 2020 feature** in each chapter. To prepare students to evaluate the vast amounts of data present in today's political discourse, we include a **Political Analytics feature** in each chapter, which asks students to look closely at visual representations of data and to think critically about what they see.

New to This Edition

- An even greater focus on diversity and participation that reflects both the changing demographic infrastructure in America today and the many protests that dotted the American landscape during 2020 and perhaps beyond.
- Expanded information about Donald Trump's presidency including extensive policy coverage as well as analysis of the Republican Party under Trump.
- Discussion of the COVID-19 pandemic's effects on the workings of American government.
- Coverage of the 2018 congressional elections and the 2020 presidential and congressional elections.
- An expanded section on protest politics, including #MeToo, Black Lives Matter, and gun policy social movements.
- Discussion of the reconfigured Supreme Court with new Justices Neil Gorsuch, Amy Coney Barrett, and Brett Kavanaugh, and the tenure of John Roberts as Chief Justice.

- New information about recent Supreme Court cases and their ramifications, such as *Bostock v. Clayton County* (2020) and *Department of Homeland Security v. Regents of the University of California* (2020).
- New opening chapter vignettes featuring Alexandria Ocasio-Cortez, Mayor Pete Buttigieg, and Dr. Anthony Fauci.
- Explanatory text to accompany all figures to help students interpret data.

MindTap: Your Course Stimulus Package

As an instructor tool, **MindTap** is here to simplify your workload, organize and immediately grade your students' assignments, and help you to customize your course with current events videos and news sources as you see fit. Through deep-seated integration with your learning management system (LMS), grades are easily exported, and analytics are pulled with the click of a button. MindTap can be used fully online with its interactive e-book for *Gateways to Democracy*, or in conjunction with the printed text.

Teaching American government remains a vitally important but constantly challenging task for all of us. We know that there are many books to choose from to use in your course. We believe that *Gateways to Democracy* has an innovative approach in reaching and engaging students across a range of backgrounds and enables instructors to more easily achieve their pedagogical goals in American government courses. We have seen it work for our students, and we know it will work for yours.

Sincerely,

John G. Geer, john.g.geer@vanderbilt.edu
Richard Herrera, herrera@asu.edu
Wendy J. Schiller, Wendy_Schiller@Brown.edu
Jeffrey A. Segal, jeffrey.segal@stonybrook.edu

Letter to Students

Dear Student:

Our book begins with a simple question: How does anyone exert political influence in a country of more than 330 million people? Students in American government classrooms across the country are grappling with this question as they develop an appreciation of their role in American public life. In our own classrooms, students ask us: What is my responsibility? Can I make a difference? Does my participation matter? How can I get my opinions represented? These are gateway questions that probe the opportunities and limits on citizen involvement in a democracy. For that reason, we not only provide you with essential information about the American political system but also show you how to become a **more powerful advocate for yourself** within that system. It is not enough to know what you want your government and society to be—you must learn how to make it happen. This course shows you how people from all walks of life have opened gateways to influence public policy, and it shows you the relevance of government in your life. It is our hope that this information motivates you not only to learn about politics but also to participate actively throughout every stage of your life.

In keeping with the theme of gates and gateways in American politics, we open each chapter with a vignette that tells the story of someone who has successfully navigated his or her way in politics. These are people like you who have different gender, ethnic, racial, and partisan backgrounds and who have made a difference in American political and social life. We also include other features focusing on the Supreme Court, public policy, the 2018 and 2020 elections, and data analysis that show you how politics plays out in the United States. All of these special features are designed to relate specifically to you—the student—to give you a blueprint with which to navigate the political system. What makes *Gateways to Democracy* different?

- Streamlined learning objectives and outcomes help you better understand the material and prepare for the graded assignments in the course. We have key terms and guide questions throughout each chapter.
- A focus on diversity reflects the changing demographic infrastructure in America, especially among young people, by providing new coverage of the politics and issues affecting all Americans in every chapter.
- Updated accounts of people who are changing American politics today are included.
- Current policy case studies are included on issues such as voter ID laws, fracking, drone warfare, government surveillance of citizens' communications, the Black Lives Matter social movement, and the impact of the COVID-19 pandemic.

The Benefits of Using MindTap as a Student

As a student, the benefits of using MindTap with this book are endless. With automatically graded practice quizzes and activities, an easily navigated learning path, and an interactive e-book, you will be able to test yourself in and outside the classroom with ease. The accessibility of current events coupled with interactive media makes the content fun and engaging. On your computer, phone, or tablet, MindTap is there when you need it, giving you easy access to flashcards, quizzes, readings, and assignments.

As teachers, our main goal both in this book and in the classroom is to empower you as active participants in American democracy. We know that you balance a lot of competing demands for your time, from other classes, to work, to family responsibilities. This book provides you with the core information you need to succeed in your American government classes, and just as important, to knock down the gates that may stand in your way to achieve your goals within the political system.

Sincerely,

John G. Geer, john.g.geer@vanderbilt.edu
Richard Herrera, herrera@asu.edu
Wendy J. Schiller, Wendy_Schiller@Brown.edu
Jeffrey A. Segal, jeffrey.segal@stonybrook.edu

Resources

Students

Cengage Unlimited

Cengage Unlimited is the first-of-its-kind digital subscription that empowers students to learn more for less. Students get total access to everything Cengage has to offer on demand—in one place. That's 20,000 e-books, 2,300 digital learning products, and dozens of study tools across 70 disciplines and over 675 courses. Currently available in select markets. Details at www.cengage.com/unlimited.

MindTap

Access *Gateways to Democracy* 5e resources by visiting **www.cengage.com**. If you purchased MindTap access with your book, click on **"Register a Product"** and then enter your access code.

The Cengage Mobile App

Complete course work on the go with the *Cengage Mobile App*, which delivers a seamless course experience on a smartphone or tablet. Read or listen to your textbook, whether online or offline, and study with the help of flashcards, practice quizzes, and instant feedback from your instructor. You can receive due date reminders and complete assignments from the convenience of your mobile device!

Instructors

Access *Gateways to Democracy* 5e resources via **www.cengage.com/login.** Log in using your Cengage Learning single sign-on username and password or create a new instructor account by clicking on **"New Faculty User"** and following the instructions.

MindTap for
Gateways to Democracy, 5e

Printed Access Card ISBN: 9780357459263
Instant Access Code ISBN: 9780357459256

MindTap for *Gateways to Democracy*, 5e, is an immersive, outcomes-driven online learning experience built upon Cengage content and correlated to a core set of learning outcomes. MindTap is the platform that gives you complete control of your course to craft unique learning experiences that challenge students, build confidence, and elevate performance.

MindTap introduces students to core concepts from the beginning of your course using a simplified learning path that progresses from understanding to application. Built upon proven learning research and theory, auto-graded assessments and content are paired in a visually captivating side-by-side format.

A variety of activity types enable students to flex their critical thinking muscles while soaking in key concepts. Learners are encouraged to read with close attention, write persuasively with logic, interpret data, consider and articulate their own positions on key topics, and much more. You can further engage students with polling questions that spark discussion and activate learning.

MindTap also provides ample opportunities for students to check themselves for where they need extra help, as well as allowing faculty to measure and assess student progress. With the Cengage Mobile App, you also give your students the power to read, listen and complete activities on their mobile devices, so they're empowered to learn on their own terms.

Instructor Companion Website for *Gateways to Democracy*, 5e

ISBN: 9780357459225

This Instructor Companion Website is an all-in-one multimedia online resource for class preparation, presentation, and testing. Accessible through **www.cengage.com/login** with your faculty account, you will find available for download: book-specific Microsoft PowerPoint® presentations; a Test Bank compatible with multiple learning management systems; an Instructor's Manual, and more.

The Test Bank, offered in Blackboard, Moodle, Desire2Learn, and Canvas formats, contains learning objective–specific multiple-choice and essay questions for each chapter. Import the test bank into your LMS to edit and manage questions and to create tests.

The Instructor's Manual includes information about all of the activities and assessments available for each chapter and their correlation to specific learning objectives, an outline, key terms with definitions, a chapter summary, and several ideas for engaging with students with discussion questions, ice breakers, case studies, and social learning activities that may be conducted in an on-ground, hybrid, or online modality.

The Microsoft PowerPoint presentations are closely tied to the Instructor's Manual, providing ample opportunities for generating classroom discussion and interaction. They offer ready-to-use, visual outlines of each chapter which may be easily customized for your lectures. A guide to teaching online presents technological and pedagogical considerations and suggestions for teaching an introduction to American government course when you can't be in the same room with students.

Cognero for *Gateways to Democracy*, 5e

ISBN: 9780357459287

Cengage Learning Testing Powered by Cognero is a flexible online system that allows you to author, edit, and manage test bank content from multiple Cengage Learning solutions, create multiple test versions in an instant, and deliver tests from your LMS, your classroom, or wherever you want. The test bank for *Gateways to Democracy* 5e, contains learning objective–specific multiple-choice and essay questions for each chapter.

Acknowledgments

Writing the fifth edition of an introductory textbook requires a dedicated and professional publishing team. We were extremely fortunate to continue to work with a number of excellent people at Cengage Learning, including Lauren Gerrish and Erika Hayden who led comprehensive revisions, and Emily Hickey, who was an outstanding developmental editor. Laura Hildebrand has been a top notch manager who has elevated our work in this significantly revised edition with a greater focus on the vital role that traditionally underrepresented groups, such as African Americans and Latinos, play in forcing open gates that stand in the way of participation. Lori Hazard has been a vigilant director of the production process and Haripriya Lakshminarasiman has been terrific at updating our photos and images. We also want to thank our longtime Marketing Manager, Valerie Hartman, and the entire sales force at Cengage Learning for their tireless efforts to promote *Gateways to Democracy*.

Our gratitude goes to all those who worked on the various supplements offered with this text, especially the test bank and Instructor's Manual.

By definition, an American government textbook is a sweeping endeavor, and it would not be possible to succeed without our reviewers. They provided truly constructive input throughout the review and revision process. We list their names on the following page, and we are grateful to them for their contributions to this material's development.

Each of us would also like to thank the individuals who supported us throughout the project.

JOHN G. GEER: I would like to extend special thanks to Grayson Hoffman for her hard work and insights in pulling together new material for the fifth edition. As each edition goes into print, my debt to Jeff, Rick, and Wendy gets larger and larger. They are tremendous coauthors and even better friends. I am so lucky to work with them on this project. My deepest and most heartfelt appreciation goes to Beth Prichard Geer. Beth makes every part of my life better and supports me in all endeavors. It is a true joy to have a partner on life's amazing journey. For that, I will be forever grateful.

RICHARD HERRERA: I appreciate the opportunity to expand my contributions to *Gateways*. The author team continues to be supportive. John, Wendy, and Jeff are an exciting and thoughtful group of scholars with whom to work. The creative process that produced this edition has been a wonderful experience. Their support and suggestions have been essential to honing my ideas and contributions. I would also like to thank Marian Norris for her support, patience, and encouragement throughout this adventure. Finally, I thank all of the students I have taught over the years for helping me understand how to improve the textbook.

WENDY J. SCHILLER: I would like to express my appreciation for continued collaboration with John, Jeff, and Rick who are each excellent scholars and colleagues. I would also like to thank my husband, Robert Kalunian, who provides an endless supply of patience, support, and perspective.

JEFFREY A. SEGAL: I thank my coauthors, John, Wendy, and Rick, for once again making the endeavor of the new edition a totally enjoyable experience. My professional colleagues, both at Stony Brook and beyond, have cheerfully answered innumerable queries from me. I appreciate their assistance.

Reviewers

We would like to thank the instructors who have contributed their valuable feedback through reviews of the fourth edition in preparation for this fifth edition:

Amy Colon, SUNY Sullivan
Virginia Haysley, Lone Star College
Ellen Key, Appalachian State University
Greg Rabb, Jamestown Community College

We would also like to thank the following instructors whose feedback was instrumental in shaping recent prior editions:

Jennifer Danielle Bachan, Houston Community College
Robert Ballinger, South Texas College
Anthony Daniels, University of Toledo
Matthew Dunne, Housatonic Community College
Jared Farley, New Mexico Military Institute
Chad Hankinson, Oklahoma State University
Kara Lindaman, Winona State University
Lisa Lawrason, Delta College
Kristina Mitchell, Texas Tech University
Ryane Straus, College of Saint Rose

About the Authors

John G. **Geer**

(PhD, Princeton University) is Ginny and Conner Searcy Dean of the College of Arts and Sciences, Professor of Political Science, and codirects the Vanderbilt Poll. Geer has published widely, including *In Defense of Negativity*, which won the Goldsmith Prize from the Shorenstein Center at Harvard University. Geer has been a visiting scholar at Harvard University and Princeton University. Geer teaches Introduction to American Politics, as well as specialty courses on elections and campaigns. His teaching has drawn much note, winning numerous teaching awards at both Arizona State University and Vanderbilt University. Geer is a frequent commentator in the press, with appearances on all the major networks (e.g., Fox News, CBS Evening News, CNN), and he has been quoted in newspapers ranging from *The New York Times* to *The Washington Post* to the *Los Angeles Times*. He has done interviews for major international outlets as well, such as BBC and Al Jazeera.

Richard **Herrera**

(PhD, University of California, Santa Barbara) is Professor Emeritus of Political Science in the School of Politics and Global Studies at Arizona State University. He directed the ASU Capital Scholars Washington, DC, Summer Internship program for fifteen years and taught American government for thirty years. He has contributed articles to the *American Political Science Review*, *Journal of Politics*, *Legislative Studies Quarterly*, and *State Politics and Policy Quarterly*. His current research interests are focused on U.S. governors, their ideology, policy agendas, and representative functions. He taught courses in American Politics, American Political Parties, and American Politics and Film.

Wendy J. **Schiller**

(PhD, University of Rochester) is the Royce Family Professor of Teaching Excellence in Political Science, Professor of International and Public Affairs, and Chair of the Department of Political Science at Brown University (Twitter acct @profwschiller). She was legislative assistant for Senator Daniel P. Moynihan, a federal lobbyist for Governor Mario M. Cuomo, a Guest Scholar and PhD Fellow at the Brookings Institution, and a post-doctoral fellow at Princeton University. She has published *Electing the Senate: Indirect Democracy Before the Seventeenth Amendment* (2015) with Charles Stewart III, *The Contemporary Congress* (2003, 2005, 2015, 2017) with Burdett Loomis, and *Partners and Rivals: Representation in U.S. Senate Delegations* (2000). She teaches courses on a wide range of American politics topics, including Introduction to the American Political Process, The American Presidency, Congress and Public Policy, Parties and Interest Groups, and The Philosophy of the American Founding.

Jeffrey A. **Segal**

(PhD, Michigan State University) is SUNY Distinguished Professor in the Political Science Department at Stony Brook University. He has served as Visiting Senior Research Scholar at Princeton University, visiting Professor of American Government at Harvard University, and held a Guggenheim Fellowship. Segal is best known, with Harold Spaeth, as the leading proponent of the attitudinal model of Supreme Court decision making. Segal has twice won the Wadsworth Award for a book (with Spaeth) or article ten years or older with lasting influence on law and courts. He has also won the Lifetime Achievement Award from the Law and Court Section of APSA. His work on the influence of strategic factors on Supreme Court decision making won the Franklin Burdette Award from the American Political Science Association. With Lee Epstein, Kevin Quinn, and Andrew Martin, he won Green Bag's award for exemplary legal writing. He has also won a national award sponsored by the American Bar Association for innovative teaching and instructional methods and materials in law and courts.

Career Opportunities: Political Science

Introduction

One of the most important decisions a student has to make is the choice of a major; many consider future job possibilities when making that call. A political science degree is useful for a successful career in many different fields, from lawyer to policy advocate, pollster to humanitarian worker. Employer surveys reveal that the skills that most employers value in successful employees—critical thinking, analytical reasoning, and clarity of verbal and written communication—are precisely the tools that political science courses should be helping you develop. This guide is intended to spark ideas about careers you might pursue with a political science degree and the types of activities you can engage in now to help you secure one of those positions after graduation.

Careers in Political Science

Law and Criminal Justice

Do you find that your favorite parts of your political science classes are those that deal with the Constitution, the legal system, and the courts? Then a career in law and criminal justice might be right for you. Traditional jobs in the field range from lawyer or judge to police or parole officer. In the past decade, there has also been tremendous growth in homeland security, including jobs in mission support, immigration, travel security, and prevention and response. A former political science student of at least one of the authors is now an FBI agent.

Public Administration

The many offices of the federal government combined represent one of the largest employers in the United States. Flip to the bureaucracy chapter and consider that each federal department, agency, and bureau you see looks to political science majors as future employees. A partial list of such agencies would include the Department of Education, the Department of Health and Human Services, and the Federal Trade Commission. This does not even begin to account for the multitude of similar jobs in state and local governments that you might consider.

Campaigns, Elections, Polling, and Elected Office

Are campaigns and elections the most exciting part of political science for you? Then you might consider a career in the growing industry based around political campaigns. From volunteering and interning to consulting, marketing, and fundraising, there are many opportunities for those who enjoy the competitive and high-stakes electoral arena. For those looking for careers that combine political knowledge with statistical skills, there are careers in public opinion polling. Pollsters work for independent national organizations such as Gallup and YouGov or as part of news operations and campaigns. For those who are interested in survey methodology, there are also a wide variety of nonpolitical career opportunities in marketing and survey design. You might also consider running for public office yourself.

Interest Groups and International and Nongovernmental Organizations

Is there a cause that you are especially passionate about? At least one interest group is likely working to see progress made on that issue. Many of the positions that one might find in for-profit companies also exist in their non-profit interest group and nongovernmental organization counterparts, including lobbying and high-level strategizing. Don't forget that there are also major international organizations—such as the United Nations, the World Health Organization (WHO), and the International Monetary Fund (IMF)—where a degree in political science could be put to good use. While competition for those jobs tends to be fierce, interest in and knowledge about politics and policy will give you an advantage.

Foreign Service

Does a career in diplomacy and foreign affairs, complete with the opportunity to live and work abroad, sound exciting to you? Tens of thousands of people work for the State Department, both in Washington,

D.C., and in consulates throughout the world. They represent the diplomatic interests of the United States abroad. Entrance into the Foreign Service follows a process, starting with the Foreign Service Officers Test—an exam given three times a year that includes sections on American government, history, economics, and world affairs. Being a political science major is a significant help in taking the FSOT.

Journalism

Much of the content of online, newspaper, and television news concerns politics. Expert knowledge in the world of politics plus the ability to write well can land students in journalism positions where they can make a difference. Famous examples are *Washington Post* journalists Bob Woodward and Carl Bernstein, who uncovered the Watergate scandal, and *Boston Globe* reporters Robby Robinson, Michael Rezendes, and Sacha Pfeiffer, who helped uncover the priest child-abuse scandal in Boston. Public speaking ability can then make radio or television careers more likely.

Graduate School

While not a career, graduate school may be the next step for you after completing your undergraduate degree. Earning a PhD or master's degree in political science could open additional doors to a career in academia as well as many of the professions mentioned here. If a career as a researcher in political science interests you, you should speak with your advisers about continuing your education.

Preparing While Still on Campus

Internships

One of the most useful steps you can take while still on campus is to visit your college's career center with regard to an internship in your field of interest. Not only does it give you a chance to experience life in the political science realm, but it can also lead to job opportunities later down the road and add experience to your résumé.

Skills

In addition to your political science classes, these skills will prove useful as a complement to your degree:

Writing: Like anything else, writing improves with practice. Writing is one of those skills that is applicable regardless of where your career might take you. Virtually every occupation relies on an ability to write clearly, concisely, and persuasively.

Public Speaking: Presenting your ideas clearly and effectively is a vital skill in the modern economy. You can practice this skill in a formal class setting or through extracurricular activities that get you in front of a group.

Quantitative Analysis: As massive amounts of information are collected digitally, the nation is facing a drastic shortage of people with basic statistical skills to interpret and use these data. A political science degree can go hand in hand with courses in introductory statistics.

Foreign Language: One skill that often helps a student or future employee stand out in a crowded job market is the ability to communicate in a language other than English. Solidify or set the foundation for your verbal and written foreign language communication skills while in school.

Student Leadership

One attribute that many employers look for is "leadership potential," which can be tricky to indicate on a résumé or cover letter. What can help is a demonstrated record of involvement in clubs and organizations, preferably in a leadership role. While many people think immediately of student government, most student clubs allow you the opportunity to demonstrate leadership skills.

Conclusion

We hope that reading this has sparked some ideas about potential future careers. As a next step, visit your college's career placement office to further explore what you have read here. You might also visit your college's alumni office to connect with graduates who are working in your field of interest. Political science opens the door to a lot of exciting careers—have fun exploring the possibilities!

1 Gateways to American Democracy

> **"*Change will not come if we wait for some other person, or if we wait for some other time. We are the ones we've been waiting for. We are the change that we seek.*"**[1]

Shown on the next page, the gates of Columbia University where Barack Obama earned his undergraduate degree.

BARACK OBAMA
Columbia University

It is an American story. Barack Obama was not born into wealth or privilege, yet he secured fame and success. There are not many countries where it is possible for someone of humble origins to rise to the pinnacle of power and influence in the world. But in America it is possible because of the many gateways open to citizens.

Obama's life was not just one of modest beginnings but one shaped by diversity—an ever-increasing aspect of American life in the twenty-first century. Obama is multiracial, with a white mother and a black father. He spent his formative years in Indonesia following the divorce of his parents and his mother's remarriage. At age 10, Obama went to live with his grandparents in Hawaii, where he experienced many different cultures.

Obama faced his share of hardships growing up. Not having his father around was difficult, and the moves he made to Indonesia and Hawaii were inevitably unsettling. But his family focused on securing him a good education, which was part of the motivation for his moving back to the United States in the early 1970s.

In 1979, Obama enrolled at Occidental College in Los Angeles. During this time he became active in student organizations opposing South Africa's practice of apartheid—his first effort at using a gateway to influence public policy. After his sophomore year, Obama transferred to Columbia University in New York, completing a bachelor's degree in political science. His interest in politics and the pursuit of gateways of influence continued. After graduating, Obama moved to Chicago to work as a community organizer in Chicago's largely poor and black South Side.

Eventually, Obama enrolled in Harvard Law School, where he became the first African American president of the Harvard Law Review. This recognition drew national media attention and a contract from Random House to write a book about race relations, ultimately titled *Dreams from My Father: A Story of Race and Inheritance*. This memoir touched on themes of race and racial identity. It was also during Obama's stint at Harvard that he met Michelle Robinson, a Chicago South Side native and fellow lawyer who worked for the firm where he completed a summer internship. They married in 1992 and decided to live in Chicago to raise their family.

Obama immersed himself in the African American community in Chicago. He directed the Illinois Vote project, which increased Black turnout in the 1992 election and registered hundreds of thousands of people to vote. Obama continued to pursue the gateway offered by elections. In 1996, Obama ran for and won an Illinois state senate seat, representing the 13th District of Illinois.

During his time as a state senator, Obama worked with both Republicans and Democrats. He helped to pass substantial amounts of legislation on issues ranging from health care and welfare reform to a bipartisan effort to monitor racial profiling in police activity.

Obama decided to run for U.S. Congress against Chicago alderman and incumbent congressman Bobby Rush in the 2000 Democratic primary. But Obama was not nearly as well-known as Rush, and he lost by 30 percentage points in the Democratic primary. It was a stinging defeat, yet it did not deter Obama. Four years later, he ran for an even bigger prize—the U.S. Senate. This time the well-known and potentially well-financed Democrats chose not to run, making it possible for him to win the primary. Obama's luck continued when the GOP nominee, Jack Ryan, faced a scandal involving his ex-wife and sex clubs, forcing him out of the race. That development opened wide a gate for Obama to win the Senate seat.

As he ran for Senate in 2004, he continued to gain national attention, so much so that he was invited to deliver the keynote address at the 2004 Democratic National Convention. On this huge stage, he gave an inspirational speech that propelled him to the top ranks of possible presidential candidates in 2008. He made the most of that opportunity, running a successful campaign that beat the formidable Hillary Clinton in the primaries and then went on to defeat the Republican nominee and war hero, Senator John McCain.

Holding aside one's personal beliefs about President Obama, his story is compelling, speaking directly to how the U.S. political system can work. You can be born into modest circumstances and yet, with grit, determination, and resilience, have a chance to do great things. Not everyone will become president, but everyone can make a real difference by getting involved just as Obama did. Obama's career is proof that the steps you take as a student to be involved in your community can take you places you cannot even imagine right now. The key is to start by walking through one of the many gateways of American politics.

Sandra Baker/Alamy Stock Photo

Gateways: Evaluating the American Political System

LO 1-1 Identify the successes we have achieved and the obstacles we face in establishing a "more perfect union"

This text, *Gateways to Democracy*, explains how citizen involvement has expanded American democracy and how each of you can also influence the political system. We call the avenues of influence "gateways." This text serves as a handbook for democratic citizenship by peeling back the layers of American government to reveal the ways you can get involved and to explain the reasons you should do so. The American political system is complicated, large, and sometimes frustrating. As the term *gateways* implies, there are also *gates*—obstacles to influence, institutional controls that limit access, and powerful interests that seem to block the people's will. We describe these as well because to be a productive and influential member of American society, you need to understand how the hurdles and portals of American politics work.

The COVID-19 crisis underscores that some hurdles we face arise from events outside of the control of any individual or government. Nearly all Americans have been affected by this pandemic. It has caused us to change our behavior and led local, state, and national governments to act, in an effort to solve the problem. As you read this book, we will make, where appropriate, links to our gates and gateways theme and this global health crisis.

Key Questions

Have you encountered any recent political gates or gateways tied to COVID-19?

If you step back and look at American democracy, there are many successes tied to the involvement of our citizens:

- Our institutions have proven stable, even under the worst crises (e.g., a civil war, terrorist attacks, global pandemics).
- Our government has had peaceful transitions of power.
- Citizens are able to protest those policies they oppose.
- Americans enjoy substantial freedom.
- American society has offered over our nearly 250 years a gateway to millions of immigrants.
- Americans exhibit more commitment to civic duty than do citizens in nearly all other major democracies.[2]
- Americans' support of marriage equality has surged over the past few years, underscoring a broadening commitment to civil rights.

Now, these successes do not mean that there are not problems:

- The government does not always respond to public opinion.
- Racial tensions persist across the country and have worsened lately.
- There are growing disparities in wealth among our citizens, yielding increasing inequality in the country.[3]
- The public's trust in the formal institutions of government has never been so low.[4]
- The rate of turnout tends to be the lowest among major democracies, although turnout in 2020 was at record highs.
- Distrust of some religious minorities, such as Muslims and Mormons, remains.[5]
- America has sought at times to erect gates (e.g. walls) to keep certain groups out.

- Political polarization is on the rise, limiting the chance for genuine deliberation among our citizens.[6]
- The U.S. national debt will be more than $40 trillion by 2024.[7]

To solve these and other problems and achieve the "more perfect Union" promised in the Constitution, the nation's citizens must be vigilant and engaged. We have framed our text with the goal of demonstrating the demands and rewards of democratic citizenship. As we explore the American political system, we place special emphasis on the multiple and varied connections among citizenship, participation, institutions, and public policy. Our focus is on the following gateway questions:

Image 1.1 The death of George Floyd sparked protests around the country.

- How can you get yourself and your opinions represented in government?
- How can you make government more responsive, and responsible, to citizens?
- How can you make American democracy better?

The laws that regulate the American economy, social issues, and even political participation are examples of **public policy**—the actions by government to achieve a goal. In the arena of public policy, we determine who gets what, when, and how, and with what result. In each chapter of this book, we will examine a major public policy issue related to the topic. You will find that the public policy process is often divided into the following five stages:

1. Identifying the problem
2. Placing the problem on the agenda of policy makers
3. Formulating a solution
4. Enacting and implementing the solution
5. Evaluating the effectiveness of the solution

These stages combine to form an ideal model of the process; however, this process does not always unfold so neatly. You will also find that individuals, organizations, and political institutions all work together to determine public policies: Congress, the president, the executive branch agency that deals with the issue, the courts, political parties, interest groups, and interested citizens. In each chapter, you will learn about an important public policy, analyze who the stakeholders are and how the policy is formed, evaluate the policy, and, finally, construct your own solution (see Public Policy and Gateways to Democracy).

public policy: *Intentional actions of government designed to achieve a goal.*

Image 1.2 The United States has great wealth, but far too many citizens face poverty and homelessness.

Democracy and the American Constitutional System

LO 1-2 Analyze how the constitutional system balances liberty and order

Today democracy is presumed to be a good form of government, and most would say it is the best form. Democracy is the type of government to which many nations aspire, but this has not always been true. Only in the past two centuries—partly through the example of the United States—has democracy gained favor. Let us sketch some of the fundamental aspects of American democracy.

Liberty and Order

democracy: *System of government in which the supreme power is vested in the people and exercised by them either directly or indirectly through elected representatives.*

self-government: *Rule by the people.*

majority rule: *Idea that a numerical majority of a group should hold the power to make decisions binding on the whole group; a simple majority.*

liberty: *Political value that cherishes freedom from an arbitrary exercise of power that constricts individual choice.*

order: *Political value in which the rule of law is followed and does not permit actions that infringe on the well-being of others.*

rule of law: *Legal system with known rules that are enforced equally against all people.*

minority rights: *Idea that the majority should not be able to take certain fundamental rights away from those in the minority.*

constitutional system: *System of government in which people set up and agree on the basic rules and procedures that will govern them.*

Literally and most simply, **democracy** is rule by the people, or **self-government**. In a democracy, the citizens hold political authority, and they develop the means to govern themselves. In practice, that means rule by the majority, and in the years before American independence, **majority rule** had little appeal. In 1644, John Cotton, a leading clergyman of the colonial period, declared democracy "the meanest and worst of all forms of government."[8] Even after American independence, Edmund Burke, a British political philosopher and politician, wrote that a "perfect democracy is . . . the most shameless thing in the world."[9] At the time democracy was associated with mob rule, and mobs were large, fanatical, ignorant, and dangerous. If the mob ruled, the people would suffer. There would be no **liberty** or safety; there would be no **order**. Eighteenth-century mobs destroyed private property, burned effigies of leaders they detested, tarred and feathered their enemies, and threatened people who disagreed with them. In fact, such events occurred in the protests against British rule in the American colonies, and they were fresh in the minds of those who wrote the Declaration of Independence and the Constitution.

John Adams, a signer of the Declaration of Independence and later the nation's second president (1797–1801), was not a champion of this kind of democracy. "Democracy," he wrote, "is more bloody than either aristocracy or monarchy. Remember, democracy never lasts long. It soon wastes, exhausts, and murders itself. There is never a democracy that did not commit suicide."[10] Adams knew about mobs and their effects firsthand. As a young lawyer before the Revolution, he agreed to defend British soldiers who had been charged with murder for firing on protesters in the streets of Boston. The soldiers' cause was unpopular, for the people of Boston detested the British military presence. But Adams believed that, following British law, the soldiers had a right to counsel (a lawyer to defend them) and to a fair trial. In later years, he considered his defense of these British soldiers "one of the best pieces of service I ever rendered my country."[11]

Why? In defending the soldiers, Adams was standing up for the **rule of law**, the principle that could prevent mob rule and keep a political or popular majority under control so it could not trample on **minority rights**. An ancient British legal principle, the rule of law holds that all people are equal before the law, all are subject to the law, and no one is above it. Adams and the others who wrote America's founding documents believed in a **constitutional system** in which the people set up and agree on the basic rules and procedures that will govern them. A constitutional system is a government of laws, not of men. Without a constitution and rule of law, an unchecked majority could act to promote the welfare of some over the welfare of others, and society would be torn apart.

The American constitutional system, therefore, serves to protect both liberty and order. The Constitution sets up a governmental structure with built-in constraints on power (gates) and multiple points of access to power (gateways). It also has a built-in means for altering the basic rules and procedures of governance through amendments. As you might expect, the procedure for passing amendments comes with its own set of gates and gateways.

The Constitution as Gatekeeper

"If men were angels," wrote James Madison, a leading author of the Constitution and later the nation's fourth president (1809–17), "no government would be necessary. . . . In framing a government which is to be administered by men over men," he continued, "the great difficulty lies in this: You must first enable the government to control the governed; and in the next place oblige it to control itself" (see *Federalist* 51 in the Appendix). Madison and the other **Framers** of the Constitution recognized that the government they were designing had to be strong enough to rule but not strong enough to take away the people's rights. In other words, the Constitution had to serve as a gatekeeper, both allowing and limiting access to power at the same time.

Thomas Jefferson, James Madison, Alexander Hamilton, and the other **Founders** had read many of the great political theorists. They drew, for example, on the ideas of the British political philosophers Thomas Hobbes and John Locke in perceiving the relationship between government and the governed as a **social contract**. If people lived in what these philosophers called a state of nature, without the rule of law, conflict would be unending, and the strong would destroy the weak. To secure order and safety, individuals come together to form a government and agree to live by its rules. In return, the government agrees to protect life, liberty, and property. Life, liberty, and property, said Locke, are **natural (unalienable) rights**—rights so fundamental that government cannot take them away.

But these ideas about government as a social contract were untested theories when Madison and others began to write the Constitution. There were no working examples in other nations. The only model for self-government was ancient Athens, where the people had governed themselves in a **direct democracy**. In Athens, citizens met

Image 1.3 Paul Revere printed this famous engraving of the Boston Massacre in 1770. Emphasizing the shedding of innocent blood—five colonists died—it rallied Bostonians to resist British tyranny. Evidence at the trial of the soldiers indicated that they were provoked by the mob with taunts, clubs, and stones. Lawyer John Adams argued for the defense.

Key Questions

According to political philosophers, people agree to social contracts in forming a government like the one in the United States. What do you agree to do as part of that social contract?

Framers: *The people who were involved in writing the Constitution.*

Founders: *The people who were involved in establishing the United States, whether at the time of the Declaration of Independence or the writing of the Constitution.*

social contract: *Theory that government has only the authority accorded it by the consent of the governed.*

natural (unalienable) rights: *Rights that every individual has and that government cannot legitimately take away.*

direct democracy: *Form of democracy in which political power is exercised directly by citizens.*

Image 1.4 Alexander Hamilton, a key player in this nation's founding, has risen to fame in modern day since the release of the hit Broadway musical about his life and legacy. The show's impact on popular culture is a reminder of the importance of highlighting lesser-known histories in innovative ways.

Public Policy and Gateways to Democracy

The Gap Between Minimum Wage and Living Wage

The first federal minimum wage requirement was signed into law by President Franklin Delano Roosevelt in 1938 as part of the Fair Labor Standards Act; it set the minimum wage at 25 cents per hour and established a 44-hour workweek. States could mandate pay levels above the federal minimum wage, but they could not go below it. While he was lobbying Congress and the public on behalf of the bill, President Roosevelt said that the United States should give "all our able-bodied working men and women a fair day's pay for a fair day's work."[12] Others have also argued that individuals, families, and communities must be able to earn a living wage in order to rise above the poverty level, which would in turn give them more time and energy to participate in the democratic process.

Today the federal minimum wage is set at $7.25, although more than twenty-five states require employers to pay more than that wage.[13] Still, even at that wage, working full time leaves these workers well below what is called a "living wage." A living wage is not an extravagant level of income. Rather it involves the ability to provide the necessities of life, such as food, shelter, and health care. Given that standard, many workers in this country are well below the poverty level. Table 1.1 shows the gap between the minimum wage and the living wage in each state and the District of Columbia. In forty-seven states, the formal minimum wage is below a wage that would allow these workers to climb out of poverty. In the three states where the minimum wage is higher than the living wage, it is only by less than one dollar. In cases like the state of Arkansas, the gap is about 60 cents (which is still about $1,200 a year). In Virginia, the gap is $6.92 which yields an income difference of about $13,800. These data underscore why there have been numerous calls for increasing the minimum wage. The case becomes even more compelling when you consider these data only consider workers as supporting themselves. If they are supporting a family, the gap grows considerably.

Even with the data from Table 1.1, there are reasons not to raise the minimum wage. The central argument of opponents of raising the minimum wage is that most of these jobs are located in small businesses that cannot afford to pay the higher wages. Employers cannot hire more workers at a higher rate, and in fact they may be forced to fire existing workers if the minimum wage is increased. The demands of maintaining profitability could force such actions. Those who oppose raising the minimum wage also argue that open trade policies have given an unfair advantage to foreign manufacturers that can hire workers at very low wages, and so produce and sell goods for less.

It is difficult, however, to assess the impact of raising the minimum wage on job growth or trade imbalances because there are so many other factors that affect the economy. For example, the last raise in the federal minimum wage occurred in 2009 in the midst of a major recession caused by a crash in the housing market. How many jobs were lost due to the recession, and how many resulted from the hike in the minimum wage? It is possible that the increased minimum wage contributed to a decline in jobs, but it is also possible that the increase had no effect at all in the larger context of an economic downturn. Economists and other experts have not reached a consensus on this question. This issue takes on greater significance in the coming years as the American economy recovers from the massive jobs losses triggered by the COVID-19 pandemic.

In making a policy choice, you must judge what President Franklin Roosevelt called a "fair day's pay for a fair day's work." In the context of the American democracy, the minimum wage debate raises fundamental questions about the government's role in guaranteeing equality of economic opportunity. This debate over the government's role in supporting a basic level of income has taken on much greater importance in light of the COVID-19 crisis. Consider the March 2020 coronavirus

Table 1.1   Minimum Wage vs. Living Wage by State

	Wage Gap	Living Wage (1 adult)	Minimum Wage		Wage Gap	Living Wage (1 adult)	Minimum Wage
Alabama	$4.08	$11.33	$7.25	Montana	$2.73	$11.38	$8.65
Alaska	$2.70	$12.89	$10.19	Nebraska	$2.02	$11.02	$9.00
Arkansas	$0.62	$10.62	$10.00	Nevada	$2.26	$11.26	$9.00
Arizona	$0.32	$11.68	$12.00	New Hampshire	$5.04	$12.29	$7.25
California	$1.61	$14.61	$13.00	New Jersey	$2.92	$13.92	$11.00
Colorado	$1.19	$13.19	$12.00	New Mexico	$2.25	$11.25	$9.00
Connecticut	$1.13	$13.13	$12.00	New York	$4.01	$15.09	$11.80
DC	$2.76	$17.76	$15.00	North Carolina	$4.54	$11.79	$7.25
Delaware	$3.43	$12.68	$9.25	North Dakota	$3.87	$11.12	$7.25
Florida	$3.61	$12.17	$8.56	Ohio	$2.08	$10.78	$8.70
Georgia	$7.31	$12.46	$5.15	Oklahoma	$3.70	$10.95	$7.25
Hawaii	$5.63	$15.73	$10.10	Oregon	$1.12	$13.12	$12.00
Idaho	$3.79	$11.04	$7.25	Pennsylvania	$4.20	$11.45	$7.25
Illinois	$2.77	$12.77	$10.00	Rhode Island	$1.85	$12.35	$10.50
Indiana	$3.82	$11.07	$7.25	South Carolina	$4.30	$11.55	$7.25
Iowa	$3.64	$10.89	$7.25	South Dakota	$1.08	$10.38	$9.30
Kansas	$3.71	$10.96	$7.25	Tennessee	$3.50	$10.75	$7.25
Kentucky	$3.57	$10.82	$7.25	Texas	$4.23	$11.48	$7.25
Louisiana	$4.03	$11.28	$7.25	Utah	$4.33	$11.58	$7.25
Maine	$0.09	$11.91	$12.00	Vermont	$1.61	$12.57	$10.96
Maryland	$4.08	$15.08	$11.00	Virginia	$6.92	$14.17	$7.25
Massachusetts	$1.21	$13.96	$12.75	Washington	$0.20	$13.30	$13.50
Michigan	$1.64	$11.29	$9.65	West Virginia	$2.09	$10.84	$8.75
Minnesota	$1.87	$11.87	$10.00	Wisconsin	$4.16	$11.41	$7.25
Missouri	$1.69	$11.14	$9.45	Wyoming	$5.95	$11.10	$5.15
Mississippi	$3.79	$11.04	$7.25				

Sources: Amy K. Glasmeier, "Living Wage Calculator," Massachusetts Institute of Technology, accessed February 11, 2020, http://livingwage.mit.edu, and "State Minimum Wages: 2020 Minimum Wages by State," National Conference of State Legislatures, accessed February 11, 2020, https://www.ncsl.org/research/labor-and-employment/state-minimum-wage-chart.aspx#Table.

stimulus bill, Families First Coronavirus Response Act, passed by Congress and signed by President Trump. The bill provided for direct payments made to Americans to help navigate the economic fallout of the country largely closing down to mitigate the crisis. Most individuals earning less than $75,000 could expect a onetime cash payment of $1,200. Married couples would each receive a check, and families would get $500 per child. That means a family of four earning less than $150,000 could expect about $3,400. The government sought to provide a base level of income for a large swath of the public.[14]

together to debate and to vote. That was possible because only property-owning males were citizens, and they were few in number and had similar interests and concerns.[15]

But the new United States was nothing like the old city-state of Athens. It was an alliance of thirteen states—former colonies—with nearly 4 million people spread across some 360,000 square miles. Direct democracy was impractical for such a large and diverse country, so those who wrote the Constitution created a **representative democracy** in which the people elect representatives who govern in their name. Some observers, including the Framers, call this arrangement a **republic**, a form of government in which power derives from the citizens, but their representatives make policy and govern according to existing law.

Could a republic work? No one knew, certainly not the Framers. The government they instituted was an experiment, and they developed their own theories about how it would work. Madison, for example, rejected the conventional view that a democracy had to be small and homogeneous so as to minimize conflict. He argued that size and diversity were assets because competing interests in a large country would balance and control—or check—one another and prevent abuse of power. Madison called these competing interests **factions**, and he believed that the most enduring source of faction was "the various and unequal distribution of property. Those who hold, and those who are without property, have ever formed distinct interests in society," he wrote. "Those who are creditors, and those who are debtors, fall under a like discrimination. A landed interest, a manufacturing interest, a mercantile interest, a monied interest, with many lesser interests, grow up of necessity in civilized nations, and divide them into different classes, actuated by different sentiments and views" (see *Federalist* 10 in the Appendix).

In a pure democracy, where the people ruled directly, Madison expected that passions would outweigh judgments about the common good. Each individual would look out for himself, for his self-interest, and not necessarily for the interests of society as a whole, which is what we might call **civic interest**. In a republic, however, the people's representatives would of necessity have a broader view. Moreover, they would, Madison assumed, come from the better educated, a natural elite. The larger the republic, the larger the districts from which the representatives would be chosen, and thus the more likely that they would be civic-minded leaders of the highest quality. More important, in a large republic, it would be less likely that any one faction could form a majority. In a small seaside republic, for example, it would be possible for fishing interests to form a majority that could pass laws to the detriment of non-fishing interests. In another small republic, a religious sect could form a majority. But in a large and diverse republic, such narrow minded majorities would not be possible. Interests would balance each other out, and selfish interests would actually be checked by majority rule.

Balance, control, order—these values were as important to the Framers as liberty. So while the Constitution vested political authority in the people, it also set up a governing system designed to prevent any set of individuals, any political majority, or even the

representative democracy: *Form of democracy in which citizens elect public officials to make political decisions and formulate laws on their behalf.*

republic: *Form of government in which power derives from citizens, but public officials make policy and govern according to existing law.*

faction: *Defined by James Madison as any group that places its own interests above the aggregate interests of society.*

civic interest: *Concern for the well-being of society and the nation as a whole.*

Key Questions

Is it in your self-interest to participate in politics? How do you make most political choices, with your heart or with your mind? How did Madison think most people made political decisions?

Legislative Branch

Makes the laws

Executive Branch

Executes the laws

Judicial Branch

Interprets the laws

Figure 1.1 The Three Branches of Government

Within the federal government, power is divided into three separate branches.

government itself from becoming too powerful. The Framers purposely set up barriers and gates that blocked the excesses associated with mob rule.

Consequently, although the ultimate power lies with the people, the Constitution divides power both horizontally and vertically. Within the federal government, power is channeled into three different branches—the **legislative branch** (Congress), which makes the laws; the **executive branch** (the president and the government departments, or bureaucracy), which executes the laws; and the **judicial branch** (the Supreme Court and the federal courts), which interprets the laws (see Figure 1.1). This horizontal division of power is referred to as the **separation of powers**. To minimize the chance that one branch will become so strong that it can abuse its power and harm the citizenry, each branch has some power over the other two in a system known as **checks and balances**. The Constitution also divides power vertically, into layers, between the national government and the state governments. This arrangement is known as **federalism**. In a further division of powers, state governments create local governments.

The American constitutional system thus simultaneously provides gateways for access and gates that limit access. The people govern themselves, but they do so indirectly and through a system that disperses power among many competing interests. This textbook explores both the gateways and the gates that channel and block the influence of citizens.

American Political Culture

LO 1-3 Describe the political values and ideologies Americans share

As an experiment, the American republic has been open to change in the course of the nation's history. Despite their theorizing, the Framers could not have anticipated exactly how it would develop. Madison was right, however, about the enduring influence of factions. The people quickly divided themselves into competing interests and shortly into competing **political parties**, groups organized to win elections. The process by which competing interests determine who gets what, when, and how is what we call **politics**.[16]

Madison was right, too, about the sources of division, which are often centered in the unequal distribution of property and competing ideas about how far government should go to reduce inequality. Public opinion about such matters is sometimes described along a scale that ranges from left to right, and when people have a fairly consistent set of views over a

legislative branch: *The branch of the federal government that makes the laws.*

executive branch: *The branch of the federal government that executes the laws.*

judicial branch: *The branch of the federal government that interprets the laws.*

separation of powers: *Government structure in which authority is divided among branches (executive, legislative, and judicial), with each holding separate and independent powers and areas of responsibility.*

checks and balances: *Government structure that authorizes each branch of government (executive, legislative, and judicial) to share powers with the other branches, thereby holding some scrutiny of and control over the other branches.*

federalism: *System of government in which sovereignty is constitutionally divided between national and state governments.*

political parties: *Broad coalitions of interests organized to win elections in order to enact a commonly supported set of public policies.*

politics: *Process by which people make decisions about who gets what, when, and how.*

political ideology: *Set of coherent political beliefs that offers a philosophy for thinking about the scope of government.*

range of policy choices, they are said to have a **political ideology**—that is, a coherent way of thinking about government—a philosophy, so to speak. In contrast, **party identification**, or partisanship, is a psychological attachment to a particular party. This attachment is related to political ideology, but it tends to be more personal than philosophical.

A person's ideology can be a strong clue as to what he or she thinks about politics. On the left end of the scale are **liberals** who favor government efforts to increase equality, including higher rates of taxes on the wealthy than on the poor and greater provision of social benefits, such as health care, unemployment insurance, and welfare payments to support those in need. **Conservatives**, on the right, believe that lower taxes will prompt greater economic growth that will ultimately benefit everyone, including the poor. Thus, liberals support a large and active government that will regulate the economy, while conservatives fear that such a government will suppress individual liberty and create a dependency that actually harms those it aims to help. Figure 1.2 captures this ideological dimension.

The left-right division is not just about economics, however. For social issues, liberals generally favor less government interference, while conservatives favor rules that will uphold traditional moral values. Conservatives are, therefore, more likely to oppose abortion and same-sex marriage, while liberals are more likely to favor a woman's right to make decisions over reproductive matters as well as the right of same-sex couples to wed.

Although terms such as *conservative* and *liberal* are often used to label American political attitudes, it is often more complicated because of the mix of economic and social issues. In addition, Americans are often not ideologically consistent in their orientation to politics. They are likely to take positions on various issues, leaning left on some and right on others. In fact, many Americans are **moderates**, not seeing themselves as ideologically extreme. A sizable number of Americans also describe themselves as **libertarians**, believing that government should not interfere in either economic matters or social matters. Others take a **populist** perspective, opposing concentrated wealth and adhering to traditional moral values.

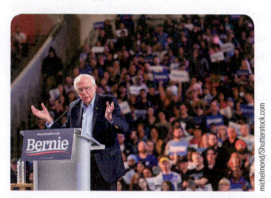

michelmond/Shutterstock.com

Image 1.5 Bernie Sanders led a movement that sought to transform American politics. While he was unable to capture the Democratic nomination for president, he did reinvigorate the progressive wing of the party.

party identification: *Psychological attachment to a political party; partisanship.*

liberals: *Individuals who have faith in government to improve people's lives, believing that private efforts are insufficient. In the social sphere, liberals usually support diverse lifestyles and tend to oppose any government action that seeks to shape personal choices.*

conservatives: *Individuals who distrust government, believing that free markets offer better ways than government involvement to improve people's livelihood. In the social sphere, conservatives have more faith in government's ability to enforce traditional values.*

These ideological frameworks start to crystallize when people are in their early twenties, especially as they start to learn more about politics and come across competing perspectives. College can be an especially formative period when people start to forge their ideological lenses.

Despite the diversity of American **political culture**, we generally favor **individualism** over communal approaches to property and poverty, especially in comparison to the industrialized democracies of Europe and elsewhere in the world. The United States spends less on government programs to help less-well-off people than many other countries, and it has historically refrained from assuming control of business enterprises, such as railroads and banks, except

LEFT (LIBERAL):
Greater faith in a large and active government to promote economic growth.

RIGHT (CONSERVATIVE):
Greater preference for a small and limited government to promote economic growth.

Figure 1.2 **American Political Ideology**

Political ideology has been described in many ways. In one popular version, political thought is plotted on a continuum from left (liberal) to right (conservative).

in times of crisis. The United States tends to favor **capitalism**, an economic system in which business enterprises and key industries are privately owned, as opposed to **socialism**, in which they are owned by government. Yet, to prevent the worst abuses of capitalism, which can arise as businesses pursue profit to the detriment of citizens, Congress has passed laws that regulate privately owned businesses and industries. For example, government monitors banks and financial markets, ensures airline safety, and protects workers from injury on the job.

These regulations tend to moderate vast inequalities in wealth as well. Though prizing individualism, American political culture also has a long-standing tradition of **egalitarianism**. Americans rejected kings in the Revolution and titles of nobility in the Constitution. They also rejected British inheritance laws, which gave virtually all property to the eldest male. With estates divided more equally, and with a vast frontier that allowed land ownership to spread broadly, property in the United States was never as concentrated in the hands of a few as it had been in Europe. This greater equality, in turn, produced a political culture that values each individual's ability to achieve wealth and social status through hard work, not inheritance, and supports a free enterprise economic system, within limits. These observations were first made by Alexis de Tocqueville, one of the many Europeans who traveled to the United States in the nineteenth century to investigate the American experiment. His *Democracy in America* (1835) is a classic study of American institutions and culture. It remains insightful today for its thoughtful observations of American politics and character.

De Tocqueville was impressed by the extent to which individual Americans participated in political life. In a republic, policy making should reflect the will of the people expressed through their elected representatives and interest groups. Madison envisioned that the people's representatives managing the policy-making process would be an elite—well-educated people of "merit." But if the people divide into different classes, as Madison also envisioned, there is a danger to democracy if the people's representatives are an elite who represent only their own interests and not civic-minded leaders who consider the common good. In the early 1950s, the sociologist C. Wright Mills in fact wrote about a narrow **power elite** made up of leaders from corporations, government, and the military who controlled the gates and gateways to power. But a few years later, the political scientist Robert Dahl took issue with Mills and argued that policy making is more **pluralist**, with authority held by different groups in different areas. In this view, coal companies, as stakeholders, have a large say in coal policy, and farmers, as stakeholders, have a large say in farm policy, rather than a single power elite controlling both policy areas. While it is true, for example, that the coal industry pursues its interests vigorously, so do other industries. Elected representatives seek to balance these various interests even as they seek to do what is best for their constituents. The fact that no one group has a monopoly on power suggests that a more **majoritarian** policy-making process is in the making, in which those with a numerical majority hold the authority.

moderates: *Individuals who are in the middle of the ideological spectrum and do not hold consistently strong views about whether government should be involved in people's lives.*

libertarians: *Those who generally believe that government should refrain from acting to regulate either the economy or moral values.*

populists: *Those who oppose concentrated wealth and adhere to traditional moral values.*

political culture: *A shared way of thinking about community and government and the relationship between them.*

individualism: *Set of beliefs holding that people, and not government, are responsible for their own well-being.*

capitalism: *Economic system in which businesses and key industries are privately owned and in which individuals, acting on their own or with others, are free to create businesses.*

socialism: *Economic system in which the government owns major industries.*

egalitarianism: *Belief in human equality that disdains inherited titles of nobility and inherited wealth.*

power elite: *Small handful of decision makers who hold authority over a large set of issues.*

pluralist: *A political arrangement where power is spread across groups and individuals that yields shared governing.*

majoritarian: *System of policy making in which those with a numerical majority hold authority.*

Responsiveness and Equality: Does American Democracy Work?

LO 1-4 Evaluate American democracy in terms of responsiveness and equality

Does American democracy work? That is a question we will be asking in every chapter of this text, and we invite you to start working on an answer. As citizens, you have both a right and a responsibility to judge the government because it is *your* government.

Image 1.6 President Trump's rhetoric and behavior have rocked the political world by tapping into the anger and frustration many Americans felt about the political system and then challenging long held norms.

Darren McCollester/Getty Images News/Getty Images

To guide your thinking, we focus on two basic themes, **responsiveness** and **equality**. Is government responsive to the needs of its citizens? Do all citizens have an equal chance to make their voices heard? We ask you to keep these themes in mind as you learn about the U.S. political system. To give you a basis for making a judgment, we inform you of the findings of political scientists who have been asking and answering these questions for decades. Throughout this text, we present the latest data that speak to these broad issues. It is important to remember that we are not offering our opinions about government; instead, we are putting forward the most compelling evidence and theories, from a variety of perspectives, over the past fifty or so years. It is up to you to consider them and form your own conclusions.

responsiveness: *Idea that government should implement laws and policies that reflect the wishes of the public and any changes in those wishes.*

equality: *Idea that all individuals are equal in their moral worth and so must be equal in treatment under the law and have equal access to the decision-making process.*

monarchy: *System of government that assigns power to a single person who inherits that position and rules until death.*

autocracy: *System of government in which the power to govern is concentrated in the hands of an individual ruler.*

oligarchy: *System of government in which the power to govern is concentrated in the hands of a powerful few, usually wealthy individuals.*

public goods: *Goods or benefits provided by government from which everyone benefits and from which no one can be excluded.*

One way to begin to evaluate American democracy, and to appreciate it, is to look briefly at alternative models of government. In a **monarchy**, an **autocracy**, and an **oligarchy**, a single person or a small elite rules society. Such systems are by definition undemocratic. Rulers in these systems have little reason or need to be responsive to the people. They hold most of the power and are not generally accountable to those they rule. They may try to satisfy the people with programs that meet basic needs for food and safety, but they do so to ensure control. These rulers have little regard for the opinions of the people and do not want them to be engaged in public life. In these systems, the rulers tend to be excessively wealthy, and the people are likely to be impoverished. To maintain order, the rulers typically rely on a strong army or a secret police force to keep the people in line through fear and intimidation. Rulers in such systems are overthrown when dissatisfaction rises to a level at which citizens are willing to risk their lives in open revolt, as they did in Iran in 2018, or when the army or police conspire to replace one ruler with another.

In contrast, a democracy asks its citizens to be actively engaged in their own governance, for the benefit of all. As the preamble to the U.S. Constitution states, the people create government (agree to a social contract) to "establish Justice, insure domestic Tranquility, provide for the common defence, promote the general Welfare, and secure the Blessings of Liberty to ourselves and our Posterity." The American system of government fundamentally provides protection from foreign enemies and from internal disorder; it also strives to meet the common needs of all citizens.

To promote the general welfare, the government develops public policy, as we have seen. Through incentives, it can alter the actions of individuals that lead collectively to bad outcomes. Consider the following example. If everyone drives to work, pollution increases and more resources are consumed. If a few people then decide to take the bus, those decisions, while admirable, do not yield a cleaner environment or save many resources. But if government incentives, such as making buses free, encourage lots more people to take public transportation, the result is a cleaner environment and saving of resources.

The government often has a stake in pursuing what economists call **public goods**, goods from which everyone benefits. The core idea is that no one can be excluded. We all get the benefits of clean air, even if we have been driving cars and not taking buses. The fact that people cannot, by definition, be denied access to public goods creates disincentives for people to contribute to their provision. Government can require people to contribute to public goods through taxation. This is a primary justification for government. **Private goods**, by contrast, can be extended to some individuals and denied to others. When a government awards a contract to build a new library, the firm that wins the contract gets private goods (that is, money) from the government. The firms that lost the bid are denied that chance.

Who determines what goods, whether private or public, the government should provide, at what levels, and how to pay for them? These are core public policy problems. There are competing interests at every point in determining who gets what, when, and how. Politics is the process by which the people determine how government will respond. And it is in evaluating the basic fairness of government's response, and the basic equality of the people's general welfare that is thus secured, that we see whether American democracy is working.

Representative democracy succeeds when there is constant interaction between the people and the government. Government must be responsive to the needs and opinions of the people, and the public must find ways to hold government accountable. Government officials who are unresponsive to the people need to be removed from office. Elections provide the most common way to remove elected officials and are the primary mechanism for forging responsiveness. But unelected officials are also responsive to the public. The president appoints Supreme Court justices, with the advice and consent of the Senate, and those justices generally issue judgments that are consistent with public opinion. The bureaucrats who are hired to work in government departments carry out laws that the people's representatives have passed and the president has signed. In addition, work in government is always subject to review and investigation by other branches of government, by the media, and by citizen watchdog groups.

Perhaps complicating the government's requirement to be responsive is the changing nature of policy demands made by its citizens. In 2014, a majority of kindergartners were nonwhite—the first time in American history.[17] In just a few years, those kindergartners will be of voting age, helping to redefine the American electorate. Figure 1.3 confirms this observation. By 2045, whites will no longer represent a majority of the voting population.[18] To be sure, nonwhites share many issues that are of concern to white Americans, such as a strong economy. But even so, this change will alter American politics in fundamental ways. People with different racial and ethnic backgrounds may hold views about the role of government and about specific policies that may be different than other groups.

For a government to respond fairly to citizens, all citizens must have an opportunity to participate in it. Each citizen must have a chance to have his or her voice heard, either by voting or by participating in the political process and public life. These ideas form the basis of **political equality**. If citizens are not treated equally by the government, with the same degree of fairness, then the foundation of democratic government is weakened. Simply put, democracy requires political equality, and political equality requires democracy.

The notion of equality was enshrined in the Declaration of Independence: "We hold these truths to be self-evident: That all men are created equal; that they are endowed by their Creator with certain unalienable rights; that among these are life, liberty, and the pursuit of happiness." But this ringing statement did not announce an enforceable right, and government under the Constitution has in the course of the nation's history involved profound inequalities, most notably permitting slavery and a severe restriction of the civil rights of the African American minority for nearly two centuries. The American constitutional system was nearly a century and a half old before it guaranteed women the right to vote. Other racial and

private goods: *Goods or benefits provided by government in which most of the benefit falls to the individuals, families, or companies receiving them.*

Key Questions

What do the changing demographics of the United States mean for our national political discussions? What is the difference between equality of opportunity and equality of outcome?

political equality: *The idea that people should have equal amounts of influence in the political system.*

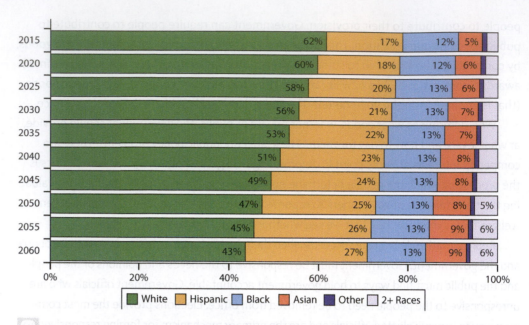

Figure 1.3 **Increasing Minority Population in the United States**

The growing Latino and Asian populations will likely make the United States a minority-majority country within three decades.

Note: Numbers may not add to 100% because of rounding.

Source: https://www.brookings.edu/blog/the-avenue/2018/03/14/the-us-will-become-minority-white-in-2045-census-projects/.

ethnic minorities have had to challenge the system to secure their rights, and, as the next chapters demonstrate, civil rights are still evolving. One way to evaluate American democracy is to evaluate the degree to which political equality has been achieved.

An example of the ongoing fight for civil rights can be seen in the recent 2018 Georgia gubernatorial race, which sparked allegations of illegal efforts to shrink the number of eligible voters. There are still gates in place to exclude specific citizens from voting through methods like voter suppression and passage of laws that make it harder, especially for the poor, to vote. In 2019, Georgia removed over 300,000 voters in what officials called routine removals of inactive voters. Voting rights advocates, including Stacey Abrams' nonprofit, Fair Fight, see these purges as a type of voter suppression that disenfranchises mostly Democratic low-income voters, young voters, and voters of color.[19] It is important to keep recent events like this in mind when evaluating political equality in America.

equality of opportunity:
Expectation that citizens may not be discriminated against based on race, gender, or national background and that every citizen should have an equal chance to succeed in life.

There are other aspects of equality. **Equality of opportunity** is one aspect—the expectation that citizens will be treated equally before the law and have an equal opportunity to participate in government. Does equality of opportunity also mean that citizens have an equal opportunity to participate in the economy (to get a job, to get rich) and in social life (to join a club, to eat at a restaurant)? And what about **equality of outcome**, the expectation that incomes will level out or that standards of living will be roughly the same for all citizens? In the United States, equality of outcome, or results, might entail the proportional representation of groups that have experienced discrimination in the past; that is, for full equality of outcome in Congress or on corporate boards, the number of African Americans would have to be equal to their proportion in the overall population, about 13 percent. What can, or should, government do to ensure equality of opportunity, or equality of outcome? These questions are hotly contested (see Supreme Court Cases: *Plyler v. Doe*), especially efforts to forge equality of outcome. We return to these issues in the final section of this introductory chapter.

equality of outcome:
Expectation that equality is achieved if results are comparable for all citizens regardless of race, gender, or national background or that such groups are proportionally represented in measures of success in life.

One way to think further about equality is to contrast America with countries in Europe, which, as we have seen, have more communal approaches to property and poverty than does the United States and spend more on social programs. European governments, particularly as they exist in Scandinavian countries, limit extreme wealth through tax policies, and the result is greater income equality than in the United States. But the political culture of these nations does not prize individualism as highly as does the political culture of the United States, and the equality of results valued in democratic-socialist systems is nothing like American egalitarianism, which prizes individual effort and rejects Europe's rigid class divisions and inherited titles and wealth.

If the Declaration of Independence announced equality as a natural right of human-kind, then the American democratic experiment has taken a long time to work out what that equality means. In 2015, the Supreme Court made marriage equality the law of the land, extending the right to marry to same-sex couples in the landmark case *Obergefell v. Hodges*.[20] Just a few years earlier, the election of Barack Obama as president was another significant achievement for American racial equality. Many observers thought it would be decades before the country elected an African American president.[21] That view reflected the long history of discrimination in this country. But Obama's swearing in as president, not just once but twice, sent an undeniable signal about equality in America.

In 2016, Hillary Clinton broke more barriers by becoming the first woman to be nominated for president by a major party. In 2020, the country saw a gay man in a same-sex marriage, Pete Buttigieg, compete with success for the Democratic nomination, winning the Iowa caucuses. We challenge you to join these twenty-first-century pioneers. This text will give you the information you need to understand the way American government works and to recognize the gates and the gateways. We also invite you to think critically about American democracy, to engage in a class-wide and nationwide conversation about how well it is working, to offer ideas for making it work better, to influence the decision makers who make public policy, and even to become one of them.

The Demands of Democratic Government

LO 1-5 List the responsibilities of individuals in a democracy

American democracy is not a spectator sport. It does not mean choosing sides and rooting for your team from the sidelines or from the comfort of your living room. It requires more than being a passive fan; you need to get into the game. But politics is much more than a game. It shapes your life on a day-to-day basis. As a result, you have both rights and responsibilities. While the specific reasons to be involved in public life may vary, the need to participate does not.

Self-Interest and Civic Interest

The first reason to be involved is **self-interest**. You want government to serve your needs. Those needs, of course, range widely, depending on your stage of life, personal circumstances, and values. Some individuals prefer that the government stay out of people's lives as much as possible, and others prefer governmental assistance for the causes they hold dear. As a student, you may want the government to invest more in higher education and job creation; as a parent, you may want more aid for child care and school construction; as a

self-interest: *Concern for one's own advantage and well-being.*

Supreme Court Cases

Plyler v. Doe (1982)

QUESTION: Does the equal protection clause prohibit states from charging children of undocumented workers tuition in order to attend public school?

ORAL ARGUMENT: December 1, 1981 (listen at http://www.oyez.org/cases/1980-1989/1981/1981_80_1538)

DECISION: June 15, 1982 (read at http://caselaw.lp.findlaw.com/cgi-bin/getcase.pl?court=us&vol=457&invol=202)

OUTCOME: Texas violates the equal protection clause when it charges tuition to public school students who cannot prove U.S. citizenship (5–4).

In response to the increasing costs of educating children who were not citizens of the United States, Texas passed a law in 1975 stating that it would not reimburse local school districts for any of those costs. The law also relieved local school districts of any obligation to educate such children.

The parents of unnamed Mexican children who were denied access to the Tyler Independent School District filed suit. They claimed that the law deprived their children of the equal protection of the law as guaranteed by one of the clauses of the Fourteenth Amendment to the Constitution.

The Supreme Court ruled with the parents, noting first that while the subjects filing the lawsuit were not citizens of the United States, the Fourteenth Amendment prohibits states from denying the equal protection of the law to all "persons" under its jurisdiction, a term that does not distinguish between citizens and non-citizens. In reaching this part of the decision, the Court relied on a speech by Congressman John Bingham, one of the authors of the Fourteenth Amendment: "Is it not essential to the unity of the Government and the unity of the people that all persons, whether citizens or strangers, within this land, shall have equal protection in every State in this Union in the rights of life and liberty and property?"

The Supreme Court's equal protection decisions set different standards of review depending on the group being discriminated against in the law. The toughest standard, "strict scrutiny," applies to laws that discriminate on account of race or discriminate against aliens who are legally in the country. The parents bringing the suit admitted that they could not establish that the children were in the country legally. This distinction meant that the Court would only apply is lowest standard of review, "minimal scrutiny." Under strict scrutiny, Texas would have to show that it had a vital or "compelling interest" in passing the law, a difficult hurdle to pass. However, under minimal scrutiny, Texas only had to show a rational justification for the law.

Texas argued that it had a rational justification for the law, protecting the state's budget. It argued that without such a rule, undocumented workers would flood Texas, and the state's citizens would be required to pay more in taxes to educate them.

A majority of justices rejected that argument. They noted that the law places a lifetime hardship on the children, that undocumented workers come to Texas for a variety of reasons, and that prohibiting the employment of undocumented workers would be far more effective in protecting Texas's budget than denying education to their children.

A public education is a gateway for individuals to a higher-paying job, a fuller life, and a more active role in the democratic system. Providing equal access to education is one of the central ways we ensure equality of opportunity in the United States.

Thinking Critically

1. Can you identify reasons unrelated to prejudice that would lead Texas to want to deny education funds to the students in this case?

2. Should the Supreme Court treat cases involving legal immigrants (strict scrutiny) differently from cases involving undocumented residents (minimal scrutiny)?

working person, you may view health care as the most important government responsibility. Whatever way you define your self-interest, by getting involved you send signals to elected officials, and if enough people agree with you, the government will likely act.

The second reason, what we called earlier *civic interest*, is more complex. The idea is that people get involved in the process because they want to be part of the voluntary organizations that make up the **civil society** that enables communities to flourish. They want to help others, improve their neighborhoods, and create an even better nation. Groups of interested people can accomplish things that individuals acting alone cannot. Sometimes these activities supplement governmental action; for example, neighborhood watch groups keep communities safe, and soup kitchens feed the hungry. Sometimes the activities aim at getting more out of government—more funding for roads or for new sports arenas, for example. By working together, people can encourage greater responsiveness from government. In so doing, they are better able to communicate their needs to a government that, in turn, becomes more responsive.

As gains in civic interest lead to broader public involvement, they also advance equality. In a democracy, the power of individual acts can be amplified, as Obama's actions demonstrate. Sometimes this amplification takes place through the courts; lawsuits arising from an alleged injustice experienced by one person can result in broad rulings that affect a great many. There are spillover effects to activism that can benefit everyone. Several examples come from the civil rights movement, in which students and others successfully sought to desegregate lunch counters, interstate buses, and local schools.[22]

Today's students are more likely to be civic-minded than college students in previous generations. If you were born between about 1981 and 1996, you are part of the generation that social science researchers have identified as the **Millennials**. If you were born in 1997, onward, you are part of **Generation Z**. This newest generation appears to be loyal, caring, accountable, focused, and thoughtful, according to one recent study. Millennials are more likely to be optimistic and practical, and to identify as political independents. They tend to hold more liberal social views and are more likely religiously unaffiliated.[23] Many Millennial and Generation Z students have started new waves of youth civic engagement with social movements like Black Lives Matter, Students Demand Action, #MeToo, and international climate strikes. This youth involvement mirrors student involvement and protests during the Civil Rights Movement and Vietnam War.

Participation in the public sphere serves the larger civic interest. Voting is the most obvious political act. In addition, people express their views and ideas to public officials by volunteering in political campaigns, attending rallies, writing letters, and organizing meetings. E-mail, websites, blogs, podcasts, social networking, text messages, and uploading of videos on YouTube offer additional means of joining the debate about politics and having an influence on government. Those who control the levers of power need to know your views so they can respond. With all the new technologies, the interface between people and politicians is now easier than ever.

Politics and the Public Sphere

Your generation has the power to shape the future in which you will live. Will America continue to be a land of opportunity? The following three issues represent some of the important concerns that you and the nation face. Working on these problems is reason enough to take part in the nation's civic life.

Educational Opportunity.   Because you are attending college, education policy affects you every day and is important to your future. Education has long been considered

civil society: *Voluntary organizations that allow communities to flourish.*

Millennials: *Generation born between 1981 and 1996.*

Generation Z: *Generation born from 1997, onward.*

both a fundamental component of democratic society and a stepping-stone to economic advancement. But what does it take to get a college degree, and who should bear the burden?

These are important questions because the cost of a college education continues to rise. Private colleges are increasingly expensive, and during times of economic decline, as state and local governments have faced budget cuts, public institutions of higher learning have also raised tuition (see Figure 1.4). The consequence of these increases is that students are taking on more and more debt to pay for these higher costs. This debt imposes a greater financial burden on you and begins to hurt just when you may also be thinking about having a family and buying a house.

If an educated public is necessary to democracy, and if the entire nation benefits from the contributions of college-educated individuals, does the federal government have an obligation to promote educational opportunity? Congress has decided it does and authorizes the Department of Education to spend some $32 billion annually to fund financial aid for higher education, including Pell Grants, work-study programs, and supplemental education opportunity grants. In response to deficit concerns, however, Pell Grants in general have been decreasing—from $41 billion in 2012 to $22 billion for the fiscal year 2020 budget.[24]

College affordability is a concern of all college students and deserves to be a concern for the nation generally. Yet Americans do not hear much discussion about education in the news media; even President Obama's proposal to make community college free did not

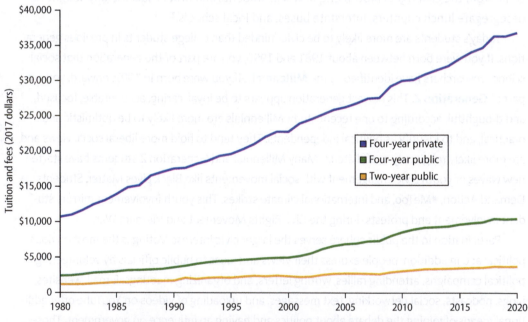

Note: The amounts shown are the list or published tuition and fees, not what students actually pay. Most undergraduates receive grant aid. The amounts shown are "sticker price" and do not account for grant aid. The College Board estimates them by weighting published tuition and fees by full-time undergraduate enrollment. They are deflated using the Consumer Price Index.

Figure 1.4 College Costs, 1980–2020

College costs have been increasing at a steady rate over the past four decades, drawing the interest of policy makers over the past few years.

Source: College Boards Trends in Higher Education, Table 2 accessed February 13, 2020, http://trends.collegeboard.org/college-pricing/figures-tables/published-prices-national.

Note: The amounts shown are the list or published tuition and fees, not what students actually pay. Most undergraduates receive grant aid. The amounts shown are "sticker price" and do not account for grant aid. The College Board estimates them by weighting published tuition and fees by full-time undergraduate enrollment. They are deflated using the Consumer Price Index.

garner much attention. In the election of 2020, several candidates such as Bernie Sanders and Elizabeth Warren made college costs a major issue of their campaigns, but it still typically garners only limited coverage by television, cable, websites, and radio stations.[25] Does the lack of media attention pose a barrier to getting educational opportunity on the policy agenda? What can you do to make government responsive to concerns about education? Education policy is examined in more detail in Chapter 3, Federalism.

Economic Opportunity.   Educational opportunity is linked to economic opportunity because the more education you have, the more you are likely to earn. And the differences over the course of a lifetime can be millions of dollars in personal income (see Figure 1.5). Even so, you still have to ask whether you be able to find a good job after graduation. This is an important question as you continue your education.

Key Questions
What value do you place on earning a college degree? Should college education be free?

Having a population of educated citizens who have good-paying jobs and who make a contribution to society is surely important for the entire nation. But does the government have an obligation to create economic opportunity? Should it intervene in business and the marketplace to equalize opportunity or to preserve competition, or should government allow the economy to be shaped by market forces? Should government step in to assist when a non-economic shock, like a pandemic or a foreign war, leads to massive unemployment and curtailment of economic activity? This last question has taken on new meaning in light of the COVID-19 crisis and the massive infusion of money by the federal government to help workers, small businesses, corporations, state and local governments, and hospitals. Government was not correcting a problem with the economy. It was responding to an external event that lead to widespread economic dislocation. There was nearly unanimous support by both parties for this unprecedented intervention by the government to address the COVID-19 crisis. It will be interesting to see how this crisis recasts this long-standing debate about the role of government. Despite relief at the start of the pandemic, the Republican-controlled Senate and President Trump defeated every attempt at COVID-19 relief packages from the House Democrats through late October 2020.

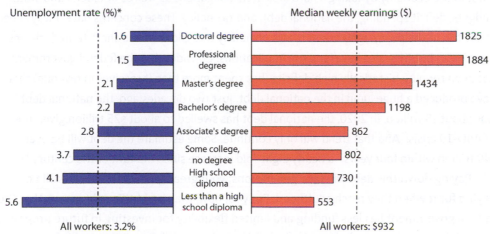

Note: *These estimates are prior to the surge in unemployment tied to COVID-19.

Figure 1.5 Earnings and Unemployment Rates by Educational Attainment

The benefits of a college education are clear: You can expect to earn about twice as much per week with a college degree than with only a high school degree.

Source: Bureau of Labor Statistics, accessed February 13, 2020, https://www.bls.gov/emp/chart-unemployment-earnings-education.htm.

A Changing and Frustrated Electorate

All elections present candidates and parties with the challenge of gauging voters' preferences across a variety of issues. The 2020 election was no exception as Donald Trump's and Joe Biden's campaigns used focus groups and surveys to try to get a handle on what voters cared about and how best to reach the hearts and minds of the voters. The 2016 election seemed to be an election that spoke to the anger of the American public—something Trump tapped into. Two years later, the anger was directed at President Trump when the Democrats captured control of the House of Representatives. The battle for the Democratic nomination in 2020 continued to underscore a frustration by many voters about the actions and statements of President Trump. Much of this unhappiness can be tied to the changing demographics of the United States, and with those shifts come more complicated sets of policy demands from voters. (See Figure 1.3 and the discussion in Section 1.4.)

These changes in the electorate also are fueling reactions by white Americans. One manifestation of that is the anger registered by this part of the electorate (see also Figure 1.6). There were notable partisan differences in 2016, with Republican white voters angrier than their Democratic counterparts. But anger can cut many ways.

In 2020, the Democrats led by Joe Biden were motivated and turned out in record numbers. When all the votes were counted, President Trump lost by more than 4 percentage points nationally (or about 6 million votes). His mishandling of the pandemic and willingness to invoke racist rhetoric gave many Americans reason to vote him out of office. The task now facing President Biden is to unify a nation beset by crises, anger, and disagreement.

Because of the fundamental importance of this question, we examine the role of government in the economy by taking a hard look at its obligations as well as at federal and state budgets, deficit spending, the national debt, and tax policy. These concerns have always been at the top of the policy agenda and that is obviously true today. These short-term decisions are critical, but they also have long run implications. Consider that the federal government has been running historically high deficits (has spent more than it receives in revenue) that have produced a huge jump in the national debt. Just two decades ago, the national debt was about $5 trillion. In 2020, the national debt has swelled to about $25 trillion given the COVID-19 crisis. And that trend will only continue. Some estimate the debt will be over $40 trillion within four years—a nearly eight-fold increase since the turn of the century.[26]

Paying down this debt will take generations; your great-grandchildren will still be paying for it when they reach adulthood. For you, now, the size of this debt means that the federal government has less funding and limited flexibility for investing in future programs that might create economic opportunity, such as education, job training, and infrastructure projects. How the government pays off this debt affects you, too, especially changes in the tax system that may alter your future income and job prospects. Thus, the federal budget and its ability to expand economic opportunity will directly affect your quality of life and standard of living. But given the experience of the COVID-19 crisis, the conversation about those long-term costs is more in the background than normal.

Participation Opportunity.   How can you make your voice heard on education policy and economic policy issues that matter to you? Your first obligation is to learn about the issues and then to vote in a way that advances both your self-interest and your civic interest. You can also make your voice heard by joining groups that advocate your position. The U.S. Constitution guarantees rights of free speech and assembly, and both are fundamental gateways in any democracy.

Over a decade ago, citizens formed the *Tea Party movement* to express their opinions that the government was not being responsive to their interests. The Tea Party movement grew out of localized groups of citizens who believed that the federal government has become too big, too expensive, and too intrusive. In the first set of elections after they formed, members of the Tea Party aligned themselves with Republicans. The members of the Tea Party often clashed with more establishment Republicans. But with Trump in the White House, the Tea Party movement ebbed. Trump transformed the party in his image and found a way to marginalize more establishment Republicans. Most leaders in the GOP went along with Trump's every move, save for a few like former Senators Corker (R-TN) and Flake (R-AZ) and current Senator Mitt Romney (R-UT).

Regardless of your opinions about the Tea Party or Trump, the value of participation and the value of free expression of opinion in American democracy is critical. Political movements can alter the political landscape by shifting the policy agenda and the direction of public discourse. As individuals and groups make their voices heard with energy and commitment, they fulfill a vital role in making our government more responsive and, hence, more democratic.

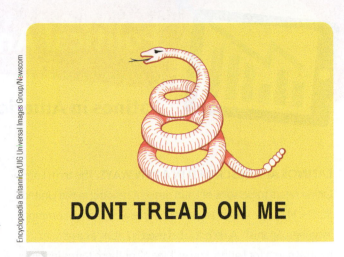

DONT TREAD ON ME

Image 1.7   The "Don't Tread on Me" slogan adopted by the Tea Party movement has a long association with resistance and protest. The movement adopted its central symbol, the snake, to represent the colonies in the era of the American Revolution.

Your Gateway to American Democracy

James Madison, a key member of the Founding Fathers, offers an important final thought: "Knowledge will forever govern ignorance; and a people who mean to be their own governors, must arm themselves with the power which knowledge gives."[27] To govern yourself, you will need to understand your government, to be informed about issues you care about, to participate in politics, and to be engaged in the nation's civic life. As Madison and all those who wrote the nation's founding documents understood, an engaged public is the best check on excesses of power that threaten fair and just government. If the people do not meet the demands of democratic citizenship, if they do not fulfill their responsibilities, they will lose the freedoms they cherish.

Image 1.8   The Black Lives Matter movement set an important tone on many campuses about the need to foster a greater commitment to inclusion, equity, and diversity and those efforts continue today.

Latinos in American Politics

LATINOS ARE DESCRIBED IN A FEW WAYS. The term Latino/Latina refers to persons of Latin descent residing in the United States. Hispanic is often used for people who share a common language, Spanish. A recent label used is Latinx as a gender neutral name for Latino. You will see all of these terms in this book and others, as well as in the media. It is important to note that all of these terms describe an ethnicity, not a race. Therefore, it is possible that some Latinos identify as white, while others may be black, and still others are of mixed race. All of these terms are broad and may mask important distinctions among Latinos.

In the United States, about two-thirds of Latinos are of Mexican descent, known as Mexican-Americans. Others are of Cuban, Puerto Rican, or Dominican heritage. Latinos may also be from Central or South America. The political attitudes and preferences may vary in important ways when we begin to explore the so-called Latino vote. Recall from Figure 1.3 that the Latino population has been growing at a rapid rate. Figure 1.6a shows the growth of Latinos since 1980 and their

projected numbers by 2050. The percentage of Americans who are Latinos has almost tripled in the last forty years.

While the growth of the Latino population is impressive, another way to assess the group's political importance is to see how many are in the electorate. That is, how many are eligible voters? In 2016, 27.3 million Latinos were eligible to vote. In 2020, that number grew to 32 million Latinos. Most of that 5 million voter increase is due to Latinos turning 18 years old. Figure 1.6b shows the growth of the Latino electorate as a share of the total electorate. The 2020 election will represent the first election in which Latinos are the second largest percentage of the eligible voters, surpassing African Americans. Moreover, Latinos' share of eligible voters is largest in California, Texas, Florida, Arizona, and New Mexico, important states for presidential candidates.

The population of Latinos in the United States is growing, and their share of the electorate is projected to reach over

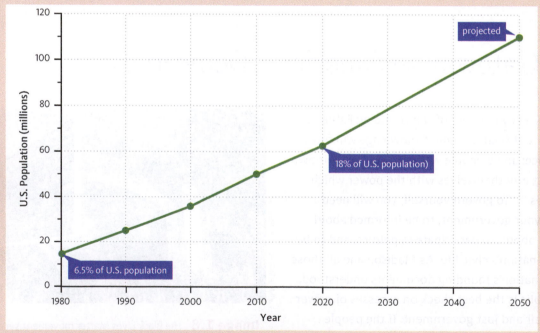

Figure 1.6A **Latino Population Growth**

Source: U.S. Census Bureau, Population Projection Databases, https://www.census.gov/programs-surveys/popproj/data/datasets.All.html.

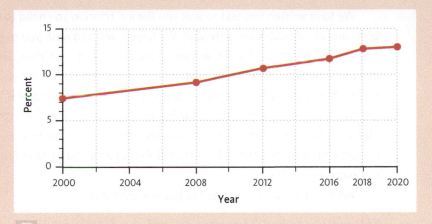

Figure 1.6B Latino Share of U.S. Electorate

Source: https://www.pewresearch.org/fact-tank/2020/01/31/where-latinos-have-the-most-eligible-voters-in-the-2020-election/ft_2020-01-31_latinovoters_01/

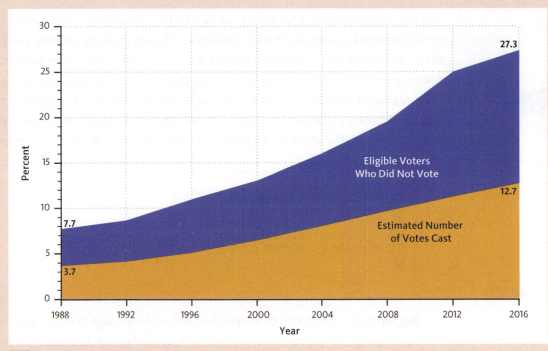

Figure 1.6C Latino Voters and Nonvoters

Source: https://www.pewresearch.org/fact-tank/2017/05/12/black-voter-turnout-fell-in-2016-even-as-a-record-number-of-americans-cast-ballots/ft_17-05-10_voter-turnout_latino/

13 percent. One may conclude that their political power is substantial. Latinos, however, have historically punched below their political weight. Though they are a sizeable minority of voters, only half of them are eligible to vote. Of those who are eligible to vote, less than 50 percent actually vote. Figure 1.6c shows that since the 1996 presidential election, eligible Latinos who did not vote exceeded those who did by 4 million in 1996 and by over 14 million in 2016.

Thinking Critically

1. The 2020 election provided Latinos an opportunity to make a difference in the outcome. How might you use data from that election to assess how Latinos contributed to the results?

2. There are a number of reasons why Latinos have not voted in as large a percentage as white or African American voters. What might be some of those reasons?

We have written this text to give you the information you need to understand your government—its gates and gateways. We hope it will also push you to evaluate whether government is working for you and for all the nation's citizens. How democratic are we? How can we be better? One thing is certain: We will not be better unless you are involved. The only way to make American democracy more responsive and more equal is by participating.

We, therefore, invite you—actually, we urge you—to enter the gateways to democracy. These gateways are open to you as an American. They empower you, as a citizen, to play an important role in American civic life, and they enable you to experience the amazing arena of American politics.

We look forward to sharing the journey with you.

What you need to know about your text and online study tools to study efficiently and master the material

Learning about American government can be your first step through the gateway. Each chapter of *Gateways to Democracy* is built to maximize efficient studying and help you get the most out of your course in American government. But these study materials are just part of the guidance for learning that *Gateways to Democracy* provides. Study aids start on the first page of every chapter, with a list of learning outcomes Each outcome is keyed to a major section of the chapter. Then, at the end of the chapter, you'll find the outcomes and a summary of the main ideas associated with each. Use this Learning Outcomes chart as a chapter review.

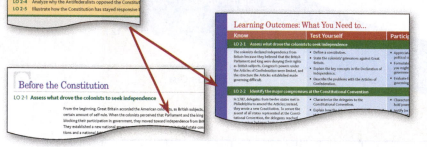

Key Terms are boldfaced in the chapter text, defined on the page, and amplified at the end of the chapter with questions that will let you test your comprehension. In Chapter 1, however, definitions are consolidated to serve as essential vocabulary that you can refer to throughout the course.

Understanding the workings of American government and your role as a citizen involves more than mastering content. Throughout the chapter, margin questions—called Key Questions—ask you to think for yourself about the role and responsiveness of government, the meaning of citizen equality, and the gates and gateways in American democracy.

Gateways to Democracy also offers an online learning package called MindTap. Through interactive assignments,

including videos, graphs, and assessments, you can master the essential concepts of American government and understand how they apply to real life. With MindTap, you learn more, are better prepared to participate in class, and improve your grade. MindTap also includes an eBook. Get instant access via CengageBrain (http://www.cengagebrain.com) or via a printed access card in your bookstore.

Chapter Review

Key Terms

Use the list of key concepts for this chapter as a glossary for this course. Each of the following entries includes the page numbers on which a particular concept is introduced, and most list later chapters in which the concept is discussed. A full glossary of key concepts is also included at the end of this text.

autocracy (p. 14). System of government in which the power to govern is concentrated in the hands of an individual ruler.

capitalism (p. 12). Economic system in which businesses and key industries are privately owned and in which individuals, acting on their own or with others, are free to create businesses.

checks and balances (p. 11, Chapter 2). Government structure that authorizes each branch of government (executive, legislative, and judicial) to share powers with the other branches, thereby holding some scrutiny of and control over the other branches.

civic interest (p. 10, Chapter 11). Concern for the well-being of society and the nation as a whole.

civil society (p. 19). Voluntary organizations that allow communities to flourish.

conservatives (p. 12, Chapter 6). Individuals who distrust government, believing that free markets offer better ways than government involvement to improve people's livelihood. In the social sphere, conservatives have more faith in government's ability to enforce traditional values.

constitutional system (p. 6). System of government in which people set up and agree on the basic rules and procedures that will govern them.

democracy (p. 6). System of government in which the supreme power is vested in the people and exercised by them either directly or indirectly through elected representatives.

direct democracy (p. 7). Form of democracy in which political power is exercised directly by citizens.

egalitarianism (p. 13). Belief in human equality that disdains inherited titles of nobility and inherited wealth.

equality (p. 14). Idea that all individuals are equal in their moral worth and so must be equal in treatment under the law and have equal access to the decision-making process.

equality of opportunity (p. 16, Chapter 15). Expectation that citizens may not be discriminated against based on race, gender, or national background and that every citizen should have an equal chance to succeed in life.

equality of outcome (p. 16, Chapter 5). Expectation that equality is achieved if results are comparable for all citizens regardless of race, gender, or national background or that such groups are proportionally represented in measures of success in life.

executive branch (p. 11, Chapter 13). The branch of the federal government that executes the laws.

faction (p. 10, Chapter 8). Defined by James Madison as any group that places its own interests above the aggregate interests of society.

federalism (p. 11, Chapters 2, 3). System of government in which sovereignty is constitutionally divided between national and state governments.

Founders (p. 7, Chapters 2, 16). The people who were involved in establishing the United States, whether at the time of the Declaration of Independence or the writing of the Constitution.

Framers (p. 7). The people who were involved in writing the Constitution.

Generation Z (p. 19). Generation born from 1997, onward.

individualism (p. 12). Set of beliefs holding that people, and not government, are responsible for their own well-being.

judicial branch (p. 11). The branch of the federal government that interprets the laws.

legislative branch (p. 11). The branch of the federal government that makes the laws.

liberals (p. 12, Chapter 6). Individuals who have faith in government to improve people's lives, believing that private efforts are insufficient. In the social sphere, liberals usually support diverse lifestyles and tend to oppose any government action that seeks to shape personal choices.

libertarians (p. 12). Those who generally believe that government should refrain from acting to regulate either the economy or moral values.

liberty (p. 6, Chapter 2). Political value that cherishes freedom from an arbitrary exercise of power that constricts individual choice.

majoritarian (p. 13). System of policy making in which those with a numerical majority hold authority.

majority rule (p. 6). Idea that a numerical majority of a group should hold the power to make decisions binding on the whole group; a simple majority.

Millennials (p. 19, Chapter 6). Generation born between 1981 and 1996.

minority rights (p. 6). Idea that the majority should not be able to take certain fundamental rights away from those in the minority.

moderates (p. 12, Chapter 6). Individuals who are in the middle of the ideological spectrum and do not hold consistently strong views about whether government should be involved in people's lives.

monarchy (p. 14). System of government that assigns power to a single person who inherits that position and rules until death.

natural (unalienable) rights (p. 7, Chapter 4). Rights that every individual has and that government cannot legitimately take away.

oligarchy (p. 14). System of government in which the power to govern is concentrated in the hands of a powerful few, usually wealthy individuals.

order (p. 6). Political value in which the rule of law is followed and does not permit actions that infringe on the well-being of others.

party identification (p. 12, Chapter 6). Psychological attachment to a political party; partisanship.

pluralist (p. 13). A political arrangement where power is spread across groups and individuals that yields shared governing.

political culture (p. 12). A shared way of thinking about community and government and the relationship between them.

political equality (p. 15). The idea that people should have equal amounts of influence in the political system.

political ideology (p. 12, Chapter 6). Set of coherent political beliefs that offers a philosophy for thinking about the scope of government.

political parties (p. 11, Chapters 2, 9). Broad coalitions of interests organized to win elections in order to enact a commonly supported set of public policies.

politics (p. 11). Process by which people make decisions about who gets what, when, and how.

populists (p. 12). Those who oppose concentrated wealth and adhere to traditional moral values.

power elite (p. 13). Small handful of decision makers who hold authority over a large set of issues.

private goods (p. 15). Goods or benefits provided by government in which most of the benefit falls to the individuals, families, or companies receiving them.

public goods (p. 14). Goods or benefits provided by government from which everyone benefits and from which no one can be excluded.

public policy (p. 5, Chapter 16). Intentional actions of government designed to achieve a goal.

representative democracy (p. 10). Form of democracy in which citizens elect public officials to make political decisions and formulate laws on their behalf.

republic (p. 10, Chapter 2). Form of government in which power derives from citizens, but public officials make policy and govern according to existing law.

responsiveness (p. 14). Idea that government should implement laws and policies that reflect the wishes of the public and any changes in those wishes.

rule of law (p. 6, Chapter 4). Legal system with known rules that are enforced equally against all people.

self-government (p. 6, Chapter 3). Rule by the people.

self-interest (p. 17, Chapters 6, 11). Concern for one's own advantage and well-being.

separation of powers (p. 11, Chapter 2). Government structure in which authority is divided among branches (executive, legislative, and judicial), with each holding separate and independent powers and areas of responsibility.

social contract (p. 7). Theory that government has only the authority accorded it by the consent of the governed.

socialism (p. 13). Economic system in which the government owns major industries.

Learning Outcomes: What You Need to...

Know	Test Yourself	Participate
LO 1-1 Identify the successes we have achieved and the obstacles we face in establishing a "more perfect union"		
American democracy offers many gateways to participation because, at its core, American government is about individuals and self-governance. There are also gates against public participation—obstacles to influence, institutional controls that limit access, and powerful interests that seem to block the people's will. To be an engaged and productive citizen, you need to take advantage of the gateways but also know how to navigate around the gates.	• List the successes of American democracy. • Identify challenges we face in achieving "a more perfect union."	• Begin evaluating American democracy based on the concepts you have learned in this chapter.

Know	Test Yourself	Participate

LO 1-2   Analyze how the constitutional system balances liberty and order

Democracy is self-government. In the American constitutional system, the people set up and agree on the basic rules and procedures that will govern them. The American constitutional system works to protect both liberty and order. The Constitution sets up a governmental structure with built-in constraints on power (gates) and multiple points of access to power (gateways). Power in American government is divided among three branches (executive, legislative, and judicial) and between the national government and the states.	• Make a connection between minority rights and democratic rule. • Define social contract. • Analyze how the Constitution divides power.	• Understand the tension that surrounds issues related to government responsiveness and citizen equality.

LO 1-3   Describe the political values and ideologies Americans share

American political culture favors individualism, and the U.S. economic system favors capitalism. American citizens may lean conservative or liberal, but most are moderates. With a government designed to constrain power and the popular will, and a citizenry divided into different perspectives and prizing individualism, the development of public policy is difficult and complex.	• Assess the importance of political ideology. • Distinguish between liberalism and conservatism. • Identify the political values that most Americans share.	• Figure out what political beliefs you hold and where you stand within the spectrum of political ideologies.

LO 1-4   Evaluate American democracy in terms of responsiveness and equality

One way to evaluate whether public policy is serving the people of the United States and to judge whether American democracy is working is to measure government responsiveness and citizen equality.	• Identify the functions of government as defined by the Preamble. • Contrast the role of citizens in a democracy to their role in other forms of government. • Explain the differences between equality of opportunity and equality of outcome.	• Consider what political goals you think the government should set for itself regarding responsiveness and equality.

LO 1-5   List the responsibilities of individuals in a democracy

Civic interest pushes people to help others and become active participants in a democracy. Education is a fundamental component of democratic society and a stepping-stone to economic advancement.	• Compare self-interest to civic interest. • Describe public policies that encourage you to participate in American democracy.	• Recognize all the options for participation and their importance.

2

The Constitution

> *"In New York, in Washington, they don't understand our problems. They don't know about the 3 million Mexicans who live in the Southwest. Let us pray to God that we triumph, that the nation's Supreme Court agrees with us."*

Shown on the next page, the University of Texas at Austin where Gus Garcia completed his undergraduate studies.

GUS GARCIA
University of Texas at Austin

Gus Garcia, high school valedictorian and star of the debate team at the University of Texas at Austin, grew up observing the social and legal discrimination against Latinos in Texas. It was the 1940s. Like Thurgood Marshall, the famed civil rights attorney and the first African American on the Supreme Court, Garcia wanted to fight for the rights of his people. Garcia followed his undergraduate years at the University of Texas with law school there. After serving in the Judge Advocate General Corps in the military, Garcia returned to Texas where he worked as legal counsel for the League of United Latin American Citizens (LULAC) and helped create the American GI Forum, a veterans group for Latinos, in 1948.

He also ran for the Board of Education in San Antonio, Texas, in 1948, joining forces with a local African American businessman. Their white opponents took out an ad in the local paper on the day before the election declaring, "It is your duty to keep racial and sectional strife out of your schools by electing experienced people who can work together in harmony. . . . Among the other candidates is a Negro undertaker [and] an active member of LULAC"[1]

(i.e., Garcia). Garcia won the election, becoming the first Latino to serve on the San Antonio School Board.

In 1948, Garcia won a federal district (trial) court case on behalf of Minerva Delgado and others seeking to deny the state of Texas the authority to segregate Latino public school students as a violation of the Fourteenth Amendment, which guarantees equal protection of the law.[2] This decision, without recognition from higher courts, was largely ignored within the state of Texas. As Garcia continued the struggle for Latino civil rights, Thurgood Marshall requested access to the *Delgado* case file from the attorneys in that case as part of his battle against racial discrimination.[3]

In 1952, Garcia began work on the case of *Hernandez v. Texas*.[4] The case would arguably become the most important constitutional decision by the Supreme Court regarding the Latino community in the United States.

Changes to the meaning of the Constitution can come about in two ways. First, there are constitutional amendments, twenty-seven of which have been enacted since 1791. Constitutional interpretation by the Supreme Court provides a second, and far more frequently used, gateway to updating the meaning of the Constitution.

Learning Outcomes

LO 2-1 Assess what drove the colonists to seek independence

LO 2-2 Identify the major compromises at the Constitutional Convention

LO 2-3 Explain how the structure of the Constitution protects liberty

LO 2-4 Analyze why the Antifederalists opposed the Constitution

LO 2-5 Illustrate how the Constitution has stayed responsive to changing needs

The *Hernandez* case involved the murder conviction of Pedro Hernandez by an all-white jury in Texas. It was the first time that the Supreme Court dealt with a case involving issues related to Latinos as well as the first time a Latino attorney had argued before the Supreme Court. Texas argued that the equal protection clause applied only to African Americans, not other ethnic groups. Garcia, alternatively, argued that within Texas, Mexican Americans were treated as "a class apart" from the white community and should receive the protections of the equal protection clause of the Fourteenth Amendment. The fact that Latinos still had separate schools and bathrooms, and did not sit on juries, convinced a unanimous Supreme Court that "the constitutional guarantee of equal protection of the laws is not directed solely against discrimination between whites and Negroes."[5] The justices were convinced that under the social and legal system in Texas, Mexican Americans were treated as "a separate class"[6] and as such deserved full constitutional protection from the equal protection clause, and that Texas denied Hernandez that protection by excluding Latinos from serving on juries. The Court, which had already heard but not yet decided the *Brown v. Board of Education* case, was interested enough in Garcia's argument that it gave him unscheduled extra time during oral argument, an extremely rare gesture. The Supreme Court reversed the conviction of Hernandez. That reversal allowed Texas to retry Hernandez by a jury that did not exclude Latinos. Hernandez was found guilty again.

Nevertheless, Gus Garcia's legal victory led to a fundamental change in how the U.S. Constitution is interpreted with regard to discrimination against Latinos, granting them legal security under the equal protection clause of the Fourteenth Amendment. Garcia used the constitutional system of the United States to create new rights for the Latino community. Moreover, just two weeks after the *Hernandez* decision, the Supreme Court struck down segregated schools in *Brown v. Board of Education*, a case in which Garcia had been a supporter.

In this chapter, we examine the governing documents prior to the Constitution, particularly the Articles of Confederation and its deficiencies. We also track the debates at the Constitutional Convention and afterward, as the people of the United States decided whether to ratify the new Constitution. They did ratify it, but almost immediately they amended it. After we examine the structure and philosophy behind the new Constitution, we consider its responsiveness, through both amendment and less formal procedures, to changing times.

Source: The information from this vignette comes from the Salinas article cited in the first footnote as well as A Class Apart: A Mexican American Civil Rights Story, *PBS Home Video, 2009, from which we pulled the opening quote.*

Before the Constitution

LO 2-1 Assess what drove the colonists to seek independence

From the beginning, Great Britain accorded the American colonists, as British subjects, a certain amount of self-rule. When the colonists perceived that Parliament and the king were blocking their participation in government, they moved toward independence from Britain. They established a new national government under documents that included state constitutions and a national Articles of Confederation. In this section, we trace that process.

The British Constitution

constitution: *Document or set of documents that establishes the basic rules and procedures for how a society shall be governed.*

A **constitution** is the fundamental law undergirding the structure of government. In a modern democracy, a constitution sets forth the basic rules and procedures for how the people shall be governed, including the powers and structure of the government, as well as the rights retained by the people.

Unlike many constitutions today, the British constitution is not a single document but rather a series of documents. Beginning with the Magna Carta in 1215, the British constitution defined the rights of the people and Parliament and limited the powers of the king. Following the so-called Glorious Revolution of 1688–89, Parliament asserted the power to suspend the law, to levy taxes, and to maintain a standing army. By the eighteenth century, British subjects believed that the British constitution guaranteed them certain rights, including the right not to be taxed without their consent and the right to be tried by a jury of their peers.

Toward Independence

Key Questions

Should the colonists have had the same rights as other British subjects? What rights do you think you have as an American? When did you last think about those rights?

The American colonists believed they had all the rights of British subjects. Thus, they objected when, following the French and Indian War (1754–63), Great Britain tried to recoup some of the costs of defending the colonies by imposing regulations and taxes on them. The Sugar Act of 1764 set forth a long list of items that could be exported only to Great Britain, limiting competition for the colonists' goods. The Stamp Act of 1765 established a tax on virtually all forms of paper used by the colonists. Although Britain had previously levied import and export taxes on the colonies, this was the first direct tax by Britain on the colonists on products made and sold in America.

The colonists reacted angrily, forming trade associations to boycott, or refuse to buy, British goods. They also published pamphlets denouncing the loss of liberty. Led by Patrick Henry, they challenged not just the taxes themselves, but Parliament's authority to pass such measures. "Give me liberty," proclaimed Henry before the Virginia House of Burgesses, "or give me death." Soon enough, riots broke out against Stamp Act collectors, making enforcement impossible.

Britain repealed the Stamp Act in 1766 but replaced it with the Townshend Acts, which imposed new taxes on imports. The colonists mobilized against these new import taxes. Led by Samuel Adams, the Massachusetts legislature issued a letter declaring the Townshend Acts unconstitutional because they violated the principle of "no taxation

THE STAMP ACT RIOTS AT BOSTON.

Image 2.1 American Colonists protest the British Stamp Act.

without representation." The colonists thus began to insist that they had the right to participate in the political decisions that affected them.

The British had a more limited view of both participation and representation. At the time, only about one in six British adult males had the right to vote for Parliament, whereas two-thirds of free American adult males could vote for their colonial representatives.[7] Moreover, while most British cities did have representation in Parliament, some—just like the colonies—did not. Rather, representation in Parliament was based on historical population centers, so large new cities such as Manchester and Birmingham sent no representatives to Parliament, while the town of Dunwich continued to send a representative even though storms and erosion had swept it into the North Sea centuries earlier.

The British justified their lack of representation by claiming that all English citizens were represented by all members of Parliament, who purportedly acted in the common good. As political thinker and politician Edmund Burke wrote, "Parliament is a *deliberative* assembly of *one* nation, with *one* interest, that of the whole."[8] The colonists, however, rejected this view.

Aggrieved by taxation without representation, the colonists continued to resist the Townshend Acts through boycotts of taxed goods. Britain responded by dissolving the Massachusetts legislature and seizing a ship belonging to John Hancock, one of the leaders of the resistance. Britain also sent troops to quell the resistance, but the presence of soldiers during peacetime aggravated tensions. British soldiers fired on a threatening crowd in 1770, killing five colonists and wounding six others in what became known as the Boston Massacre. With boycotts of British goods costing Britain far more than the taxes raised, Parliament rescinded all of the Townshend Act taxes except the one on tea. In 1773, Parliament granted the East India Company the exclusive right to sell tea to the colonies, and the

Key Questions

How did the American view of representation differ from the British view?

Table 2.1   Events Leading to the Revolution

Year	Event	Description
1764	Sugar Act	Required colonists to export certain items only to Britain
1765	Stamp Act	Imposed taxes on almost all paper products; boycotts and riots followed
1766	Townshend Act	Imposed new taxes on imports; led to rallying cry "no taxation without representation"
1770	Boston Massacre	Five colonists killed by British soldiers; led Parliament to repeal all Townshend Act taxes except for tea tax
1773	Boston Tea Party	Colonists dumped taxed tea into Boston Harbor
1774	Coercive Act	Restricted political freedoms in Massachusetts
1774	Quartering Act	Required colonists to house British soldiers in their homes
1774	First Continental Congress	Rejected reconciliation with Britain and sent grievances to King George III
1775	Second Continental Congress	Acted as the national government of states, 1775–81; approved Declaration of Independence and appointed George Washington as commander of the army

Key Questions

What do modern social movements have in common with the Boston Tea Party?

company then granted local monopolies in the colonies. Angered by both the tax and the monopoly, colonists once again took action. Disguised as Native Americans, they dumped a shipload of tea into Boston Harbor (see Table 2.1).

In 1774, Britain responded to the Boston Tea Party with the Coercive Acts, which, among other things, gave the royal governor the right to select the upper house of the Massachusetts legislature. The Coercive Acts also denied Massachusetts the right to try British officials charged with capital offenses. Further legislation, the Quartering Act, required colonists to house British soldiers in their private homes, even during times of peace.[9] These acts convinced many colonists that their liberty was at stake and that rebellion and independence were the only alternatives to British tyranny.

In an attempt to present a more united front about colonial grievances, Benjamin Franklin proposed a congress, or assembly of representatives. The First Continental Congress, with delegates chosen by the colonial legislatures, met in Philadelphia in 1774. It rejected a reconciliation plan with England and instead sent King George III a list of grievances. It also adopted a very successful compact among the colonies not to import any English goods. Finally, it agreed to meet again as the Second Continental Congress in May 1775. This Second Continental Congress acted as the common government of the states between 1775 and 1781.

In April 1775, following skirmishes with British troops in Lexington and Concord, outside of Boston, the Second Continental Congress named George Washington commander of a new Continental Army. In 1776, with hostilities under way, Thomas Paine penned his influential pamphlet *Common Sense*, which called for independence from Britain. "There is something very absurd, in supposing a continent to be perpetually governed by an island," he argued.[10] *Common Sense* was the most widely distributed pamphlet of its time, and it helped convince many Americans that independence was the only way they could secure their right to self-government.

The Declaration of Independence

In June 1776, the Continental Congress debated an independence resolution but postponed a vote until July. Meanwhile, it instructed Thomas Jefferson and others to draft a **Declaration of Independence**. Congress approved the Declaration of Independence on July 4. Jefferson's Declaration relied in part on the writings of John Locke in asserting that people had certain natural (or unalienable) rights that government could not take away, including the right to life and liberty (see Chapter 1, Gateways to American Democracy). For Locke's reference to property, Jefferson substituted "the pursuit of happiness."

The Declaration that Jefferson penned was a radical document. It established the right of the people to alter or abolish governments that do not meet the needs of the people; it declared the colonies independent from Britain; and it contained a stirring call for equality, human rights, and public participation in government that, although not legally enforceable at the time, has inspired generations of Americans seeking to make these ideas a reality.

> *We hold these truths to be self-evident: That all men are created equal; that they are endowed by their Creator with certain unalienable rights; that among these are life, liberty, and the pursuit of happiness; that, to secure these rights, governments are instituted among men, deriving their just powers from the consent of the governed; that whenever any form of government becomes destructive of these ends, it is the right of the people to alter or to abolish it, and to institute new government, laying its foundation on such principles, and organizing its powers in such form, as to them shall seem most likely to effect their safety and happiness.*

The Declaration went on to list grievances against King George III, including suspending popularly elected colonial legislatures, imposing taxes without representation, and conducting trials without juries. It then declared the united colonies to be thirteen "free and independent states." (The full text of the Declaration of Independence is in the Appendix.)

Even before the Declaration, the Continental Congress advised the colonies to adopt new constitutions "under the authority of the people." Reacting against the limitation on rights imposed by the British monarch and by royal governors in the colonies, these new state constitutions severely limited executive power but set few limits on legislative authority. At the same time, Americans made little effort to establish a national political authority, as most Americans considered themselves primarily citizens of the states in which they

Key Questions

Was the American Revolution about: taxation or something else? What evidence do you have for your conclusion?

Declaration of Independence: *The 1776 document declaring American independence from Great Britain and calling for equality, human rights, and citizen participation.*

Key Questions

What has the Declaration of Independence's statement on equality meant to Americans? How are Americans equal, and not equal, today?

Francis G. Mayer/Fine Art/Corbis

Image 2.2 Members of the Second Continental Congress voted to approve the Declaration of Independence on July 4, 1776, though only John Hancock, president of the Congress, signed it that day.

lived. Nevertheless, the Continental Congress needed legal authority for its actions, and, in 1777, its members proposed a governing document called the **Articles of Confederation**.

The Articles of Confederation

The Articles required unanimous consent of the states for adoption, which did not occur until 1781, just a few months before American victory in the Revolutionary War. They formally established "the United States of America," in contrast to the Declaration, which was a pronouncement of "Thirteen United States of America." According to the Declaration, each of the thirteen independent states had the authority to do all "acts and things which independent states may of right do," such as waging war, establishing alliances, and concluding peace. These were thirteen independent states united in a war of independence. With the Articles, the states became one nation with centralized control over making war and foreign affairs. But due to the belief that Great Britain had violated fundamental liberties, the Articles emphasized freedom from national authority at the expense of order. Thus, the states retained all powers not expressly granted to Congress under the Articles.

Moreover, those expressly granted powers were extremely limited. Congress had full authority over foreign, military, and Indian affairs. It could decide boundary and other disputes between the states, coin money, and establish post offices. But Congress did not have the authority to regulate commerce or, indeed, any authority to operate directly over citizens of the United States. For example, Congress could not tax citizens or products (such as imports) directly; it could only request (but not demand) revenues from the states.

In addition to limiting powers, the Articles made governing difficult. Each state had one vote in Congress, with the consent of nine of the thirteen required for most important matters, including borrowing and spending money. Amending the Articles required the unanimous consent of the states. In 1781, tiny Rhode Island, blocking an amendment that would have set a 5 percent tax on imports, denied the whole nation desperately needed revenue. Moreover, the Articles established no judicial branch, with the minor exception that Congress could establish judicial panels on an ad hoc basis to hear appeals involving disputes between states and to hear cases involving crimes on the high seas. There was no separate executive branch, but Congress had the authority to establish an executive committee along with a rotating president who would manage the general affairs of the United States when Congress was not in session.[11]

These deficiencies led to predictable problems. With insufficient funds, the nation's debts went unpaid, hampering its credit. Even obligations to pay salaries owed to the Revolutionary War troops went unfulfilled. Without a centralized authority to regulate commerce, states taxed imports from other states, stunting economic growth. Lack of military power allowed Spain to block commercial access to the Mississippi River. Barbary pirates off the shores of Tripoli captured American ships and held their crews for ransom.

While the government of the United States suffered from too little authority, James Madison, Thomas Jefferson, and others came to believe that the governments of the states possessed too much authority. Popularly elected legislatures with virtually no checks on their authority passed laws rescinding private debts and creating trade barriers against other states. They also began taking over both judicial and executive functions. As Jefferson declared, this aggregation of power was no more acceptable if done by a plural legislature than if done by a unitary executive: "173 despots would surely be as oppressive as one."

Key Questions

Why didn't the Articles of Confederation work as a governing document?

Though the legislature was chosen by the people, "An *elective despotism* was not the government we fought for."[12]

With the United States in desperate financial straits, James Madison proposed a convention of states to consider granting the national government the power to tax and to regulate trade. Only five states showed up at this 1786 Annapolis Convention, preventing it from accomplishing much.

As the Annapolis Convention took place, word spread of a revolt in western Massachusetts that made the weakness of the national government all too clear. Revolutionary War hero Daniel Shays and several thousand distressed farmers forced courts to close and threatened federal arsenals. Not until February 1787 did Massachusetts put down Shays's Rebellion. The revolt helped convince the states that, on top of the Articles' other problems, the document provided for too much freedom and not enough order. The Annapolis Convention thus issued an invitation to all thirteen states to meet in Philadelphia in May 1787 to consider revising the Articles of Confederation. This time only Rhode Island declined the invitation.

Bettmann/Corbis

Image 2.3 Daniel Shays led a protest movement of debt-ridden farmers facing foreclosures on their homes and farms. Demanding lower taxes and the issuance of paper money, they engaged in mob violence to force the Massachusetts courts to close.

The Constitutional Convention

LO 2-2 Identify the major compromises at the Constitutional Convention

The delegates who met in Philadelphia were charged with amending the Articles of Confederation so that the national government could work more effectively. Almost immediately, however, they moved beyond that charge and began debating a brand-new constitution. To complete that newly proposed constitution, the delegates needed to reach compromises between large and small states over representation, between northern and southern states over issues related to slavery, and between those who favored a strong national government and those who favored strong state governments. The document they created, which was then sent to the states for ratification, is, with subsequent amendments, the same Constitution we live by today. (The full text of the Constitution of the United States is in the Appendix.)

The Delegates

The fifty-five delegates to the **Constitutional Convention** of 1787 represented large (Virginia) and small (Delaware) states. They represented states in the South with large slave populations (South Carolina, 43 percent of total population), states in the North with small slave populations (Connecticut, 1 percent of population), but only one state (Massachusetts)

Constitutional Convention: *Meeting in 1787 at which twelve states intended to revise the Articles of Confederation but ended up proposing an entirely new Constitution.*

John Jay (1745–1829) of New York was a delegate to the First Continental Congress and president of the Second, though he was not present when the Declaration of Independence was signed. He was U.S. minister to Spain from 1780 to 1782 and a negotiator of the peace treaty with Britain in 1783. He was an author of the *Federalist Papers* and the first chief justice of the United States.

John Adams (1735–1826) of Massachusetts was a delegate to the First and Second Continental Congresses and, with his cousin Samuel, a Signer of the Declaration of Independence. He was a diplomat to France in 1778–79, a negotiator of the peace treaty with Britain in 1783, and U.S. minister to Britain in 1785–88. He was vice president under George Washington and president from 1797 to 1801.

Thomas Jefferson (1743–1826) of Virginia was a delegate to the Second Continental Congress and drafted the Declaration of Independence. He was U.S. minister to France in 1785–89, vice president under John Adams, and president from 1801 to 1809.

Benjamin Franklin (1706–90) was born in Boston but moved to Philadelphia. He was a delegate to the Second Continental Congress and helped draft the Declaration of Independence. He was a diplomat to France in 1776–85 and a negotiator of the peace treaty with Britain in 1783. He was a member of the Constitutional Convention.

James Madison (1751–1836) of Virginia was a delegate to the Second Continental Congress. He was an influential member of the Constitutional Convention and an author of the *Federalist Papers,* and he was instrumental in drafting the Bill of Rights. He was president from 1809 to 1817.

George Washington (1732–99) of Virginia was a delegate to the First and Second Continental Congresses and was commander of the Continental Army. He presided over the Constitutional Convention and was president from 1789 to 1797.

Alexander Hamilton (1755–1804) was born in the West Indies but attended college in New York, and served on General Washington's staff during the Revolution. At the Constitutional Convention, he advocated a strong central government. He was an author of the *Federalist Papers* and the first secretary of the treasury.

Figure 2.1   **Founders of the United States and Framers of the Constitution**

The Founders were the leaders of the American Revolution and the new United States. The Framers were those who wrote the Constitution. All Framers were Founders, but not all Founders were Framers. Only some of the Founders were Signers, the people who signed the Declaration of Independence.

The Granger Collection, NYC; RMN-Grand Palais/Art Resource, NY; Wim Wiskerke/Alamy Stock Photo; Fine Art Premium/Corbis; GL Archive/Alamy Stock Photo; Christie's Images/Corbis; Alexander Hamilton (1755–1804). Oil on canvas, c1792, by John Trumbull/The Granger Collection, New York

with no slaves.[13] Not all the delegates were rich, but none were poor. All were white, and all were male. Most were in their thirties or forties, and a majority had legal training.[14] Not surprisingly, the delegates' behavior at the Convention substantially reflected their interests and the statewide interests they represented.[15] The delegates included prominent men, such as James Madison, who would draft much of the Constitution (see Figure 2.1).

The Convention's rules granted each state one vote, regardless of the size of the state or the number of delegates it sent. To secure the assent of all states represented at the Convention, compromises had to be reached that would satisfy the various interests represented there. To keep the gateways to compromise open, the delegates voted to keep their deliberations secret until they completed their work. This decision also created a gate that limited popular influence.

Large Versus Small States

Upon the opening of the Philadelphia Convention in May 1787, Edmund Randolph of Virginia presented the delegates with James Madison's radical proposal for a new government. Known as the Virginia Plan, Madison's proposal included a strong central government that could operate directly on the citizens of the United States without the states acting as intermediaries. The legislative branch would consist of two chambers: a lower chamber elected by the people and an upper chamber elected by the lower chamber. Each chamber would have representation proportional to the populations of the states: the larger the population, the more representatives a state would have. The legislature would have general authority to pass laws that would "promote the harmony" of the United States and could veto laws passed by the states. The Virginia Plan proposed a national executive and a national judiciary, both chosen by the legislature. A council of revision, composed of the executive and judicial members, would have final approval over all legislative acts.

Madison's proposals astonished many of the delegates from the smaller states and some from the larger states as well. To counter the Virginia Plan, on June 15, 1787, William Patterson of New Jersey presented the Convention with the New Jersey Plan, which strengthened the Articles by providing Congress with the authority to regulate commerce and to directly tax imports and paper items. It also proposed a national executive chosen by the legislature and a national judiciary chosen by the executive.[16] Each state would retain equal representation in Congress.

The choice between proportional or equal representation generated enormous controversy. Madison insisted that proportional representation for both chambers was the only fair system, and the small states insisted that they would walk out if they lost their equal vote. Roger Sherman of Connecticut proposed what became known as the **Connecticut Compromise**. The makeup of the lower chamber, the House of Representatives, would be proportional to population, but the upper chamber, the Senate, would represent each state equally.

Nation Versus State

While the question of representation threatened the Convention, there was substantial agreement over the role of the national government. The delegates rejected the New Jersey Plan, which would have continued government under the Articles.

The delegates also did not approve the Virginia Plan in full, but the plan substantially influenced the proposed Constitution. Under the new Constitution, the government had the authority to operate directly on the citizens of the United States. Congress was not granted general legislative power, but rather **enumerated powers**—that is, a list of powers it could employ. Among its enumerated powers were the authority to tax to provide for the general welfare; to regulate commerce among the states and with foreign nations; to borrow money; to declare war, raise armies, and maintain a navy; and to make all laws "necessary and proper for carrying into Execution the foregoing Powers." The tax and commerce powers were among those missing from the Articles.

Congress did not receive the authority to veto state laws, but the Constitution declared that national law would be supreme over state law, bound state judges to that decision, and created a national judiciary that would help ensure such rulings. Moreover, the Convention set explicit limits on state authority, prohibiting the states from carrying on foreign relations, coining money, and infringing on certain rights. Finally, the Convention approved a national executive (that is, the president) who could serve as a unifying force throughout the land. Table 2.2 presents the components of the Virginia Plan, the New Jersey Plan, and the proposed Constitution.

Connecticut Compromise:
Compromise on legislative representation whereby the lower chamber is based on population, and the upper chamber provides equal representation to the states.

enumerated powers:
Powers expressly granted to Congress by the Constitution.

Key Questions
Were the delegates to the Constitutional Convention more concerned about liberty or about order?

Table 2.2 **The Virginia and New Jersey Plans Compared to the Constitution**

Issue	Virginia Plan	New Jersey Plan	Constitution
Operation	Directly on people	Through the states	Directly on people
Legislative structure	Bicameral and proportional	Unicameral and equal	Bicameral, with lower chamber proportional and upper chamber equal
Legislative authority	General: power to promote the harmony of the United States	Strict enumerated powers of the Articles of Confederation, plus power to regulate commerce and limited power to tax	Broad enumerated powers
Check on legislative authority	Council of revision	None	Presidential veto, with possibility of a two-thirds override
Executive	Unitary national executive chosen by legislature	Plural national executive chosen by legislature	Unitary national executive chosen by Electoral College
Judiciary	National judiciary chosen by legislature	National judiciary chosen by executive	National judiciary chosen by president with advice and consent of Senate

North Versus South

Resolving the question of nation versus state proved less difficult than resolving the question of representation. More difficult still were questions related to slavery. Although slavery existed in every state except Massachusetts, the overwhelming majority of slaves, nearly 95 percent, were in the southern states, from Maryland to Georgia.[17] As Madison put it, "The States were divided into different interests not by their difference of size, but principally from their having or not having slaves."[18] Not all northern delegates at the Convention opposed slavery, but those who were abolitionists, including Benjamin Franklin, wanted an immediate ban on importing slaves from Africa, prohibitions against the expansion of slavery into the western territories, and the adoption of a plan for the gradual freeing of slaves. Delegates from Georgia and South Carolina, whose states would never accept the Constitution on these terms, wanted guaranteed protections for slavery and the slave trade and no restrictions on slavery in the territories. To secure a Constitution, compromises were necessary.

Many supporters of slavery recognized the horrors of the foreign slave trade, and by 1779 all states except North Carolina, South Carolina, and Georgia had banned it. Leaving the authority to regulate the foreign slave trade to Congress would inevitably have resulted in its being banned everywhere and probably would have kept those three states from joining the union. Thus, a slave trade compromise prohibited Congress from stopping the slave trade until 1808.

A second compromise involved how slaves should be counted when calculating population for purposes of representation. Madison's Virginia Plan based representation on the number of free inhabitants of each state, whereas the southernmost slave states wanted slaves to be fully counted for purposes of representation. Delegates from the northern states, on the other hand, argued that slave states, which by definition denied the humanity of slaves, should not benefit by receiving extra representation based on the number of slaves that they had. Under the Articles, taxes requested of the states were based on the population of each state, with five slaves counting as three people. The Convention agreed to use this

Key Questions
What would have resulted had the delegates not compromised on slavery?

three-fifths formula not just for representation but also for whatever direct or population taxes the national government might choose to levy. This **three-fifths compromise** had a significant impact on representation in the House of Representatives,[19] as Figure 2.3 demonstrates.

A third compromise involved slavery in the western territories, and it came not from the Convention but from the government under the Articles, which passed the Northwest Ordinance in July 1787. This ordinance, which established the means for governing the western lands north of the Ohio River (eventually the states of Ohio, Indiana, Illinois, Michigan, and Wisconsin, and parts of Minnesota), prohibited slavery in this territory but also provided that fugitive slaves who escaped to the territory would be returned to their owners. The Constitution incorporated these provisions. With the precedent of prohibiting slavery in the Northwest Territory established in the Northwest Ordinance, the Convention gave Congress the right to regulate the territories of the United States without mentioning whether slavery could be allowed or prohibited.

Gates Against Popular Influence

Compared to the British constitutional system, the 1787 Constitution provided direct and indirect gateways for popular involvement (see Figure 2.2). Nevertheless, the Framers did not trust the people to have complete control over choosing the government. In two important ways—the election of the president and the election of the Senate—the Constitution limited popular control (see Figure 2.2).

Originally, state legislatures selected U.S. senators. The Framers feared that a Congress elected directly by the people would be too responsive to the popular will. The indirect election of senators was thus intended to serve as a check on the popular will. In 1913, the Seventeenth Amendment granted the people the right to elect senators directly.

Another gate against the people's participation was the election of the president through the **Electoral College**. Rather than directly electing the president through a popular vote, the Constitution established an Electoral College, in which electors actually choose the president. Each state receives a number of electors equal to its number of representatives plus senators, and each state legislature chooses the manner for selecting the electors from its state—by popular vote or legislative selection. State legislatures used to select electors. Today, each state legislature allows the people of the state to choose that state's electors, but in the early days of the **republic**, many state legislatures kept that right for themselves. Yet, the Electoral College remains in effect as a gate against direct popular control, as in the 2016 presidential election, when Democrat Hillary Clinton won the popular vote but lost the Electoral College vote to Republican Donald Trump.

three-fifths compromise: *Compromise over slavery at the Constitutional Convention that granted states extra representation in the House of Representatives based on their number of slaves at the ratio of three-fifths.*

Key Questions

What compromises made the Constitution possible? Is compromise, as a political strategy, good or bad for democracy? Why is it out of favor today?

Key Questions

Why did the delegates to the Constitutional Convention set up gates against citizen participation? Whose participation did they not consider at all? What effect did this have?

Electoral College: *The presidential electors, selected to represent the votes of their respective states, who meet every four years to cast the electoral votes for president and vice president.*

republic: *Form of government in which power derives from citizens, but public officials make policy and govern according to existing law.*

Freedom — Articles of Confederation — Constitution — British rule — Order

Figure 2.2 Relative Balance of Freedom and Order

This figure shows how the Constitution remedied various flaws from the Articles of Confederation. While the Articles lasted only four years, the Constitution has endured for over two hundred years.

Political Analytics

Impact of the Three-Fifths Compromise

THE THREE-FIFTHS COMPROMISE REACHED at the Constitutional Convention had consequences for how states were represented in the House of Representatives. But how did it actually work after the first census? More than 675,000 slaves lived in the United States in 1790, spread across all of the original states except Massachusetts. More than 90 percent of all slaves lived in the five southern states (Georgia, Maryland, North Carolina, South Carolina, and Virginia).

Figure 2.3 shows how the number of slaves in each of the states translated into "persons" as a result of the three-fifths compromise. The southern states rose in

population by close to 400,000 people as a result of the compromise; thus, they had more representation in the House of Representatives than if slaves had not been counted as persons at all. Note the percentage increase in population the states gained by counting each slave as three-fifths of a person rather than not at all. If slaves had been counted as full persons instead, the southern states' population would have grown by more than 600,000 people.

Examine the graph. Notice the total number of citizens and slaves in the United States at the start of the republic as well as where most slaves lived.

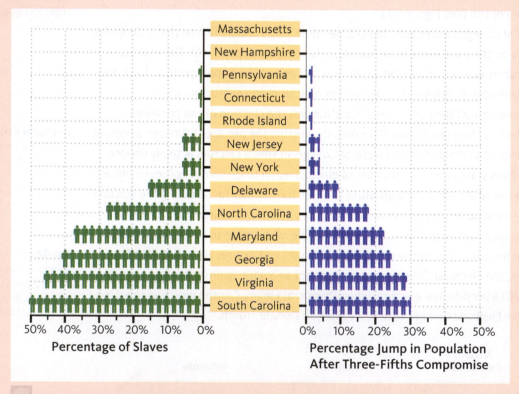

Figure 2.3A **Percentage of Slaves in the States and the Results of the 3/5 Compromise**

Sources: U.S. Census Bureau, Historical Statistics of the United States, Colonial Times to 1970. Chapter XIV Statistics of Slaves, http://www2.census.gov/prod2/decennial/documents/00165897ch14.pdf; U.S. Census, Census of Population and Housing, 1790, http://www.census.gov/prod/www/decennial.html. Accessed March 7, 2016.

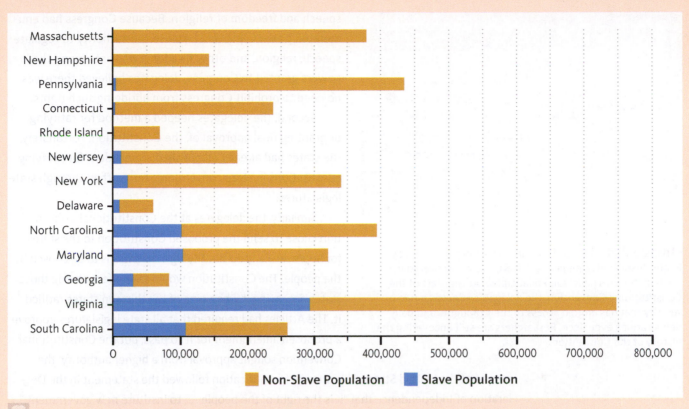

Figure 2.3B Slave and Non-Slave Populations in the Original Thirteen States, 1790

Thinking Critically

1. Keeping in mind that the Constitution called for one representative per 30,000 in population, if the three-fifths compromise had not been reached, and slaves had not been counted at all as persons, how would the states have been affected in the House of Representatives?

2. What information can be interpreted from Figure 2.3 about total state populations and the number of slaves in these states?

Popularly elected state legislatures often passed unjust and confusing laws. What Madison called "a spirit of *locality*" often superseded the common interest, allowing single-chamber legislatures to yield to sudden and violent passions that swept the nation.[20] Others shared Madison's fear. To make the point, George Washington used an analogy. "Why do you pour that coffee into your saucer," he asked Thomas Jefferson. "To cool it," replied Jefferson. "Even so," said Washington, "we pour legislation into the senatorial saucer to cool it."[21]

The Ratification Process

With agreements reached on representation in Congress, federal or national power, and slavery, the delegates made a few final decisions. First, despite the urging of George Mason of Virginia, the delegates chose not to include a **Bill of Rights**—a listing of rights retained by the people that Congress did not have the authority to take away, such as freedom of

Key Questions
Did the delegates trust the people?

Key Questions
Do the people today retain the right to institute new government?

Bill of Rights: *First ten amendments to the Constitution, which provide basic political rights.*

Image 2.4 This draft of the Constitution, written by Pennsylvania delegate James Wilson, was rediscovered in 2010 in Wilson's papers in Philadelphia. At the start of the Constitutional Convention, the delegates adopted a rule of secrecy that has limited access to their thoughts and daily deliberations ever since. Researchers are still uncovering the history of the Convention.

speech and freedom of religion. Because Congress had enumerated powers only, and because the authority to regulate speech, religion, and other freedoms was not among the powers granted to Congress, delegates believed there was no need to prohibit Congress from abridging such rights.

Second, the delegates needed a method for ratifying, or granting final approval of, the Constitution. Fortunately, the states had already established a precedent for ratifying constitutions in state conventions, rather than through state legislatures.

Similarly, the delegates at the Constitutional Convention chose to send the proposed Constitution to the states for approval via special ratifying conventions to be chosen by the people. The Constitution would take effect among those states approving it when nine of the thirteen states ratified it. The Articles had required that all state legislatures approve a proposed amendment for it to pass, but the Constitutional Convention sought approval from a higher authority: the people of the United States. This process for ratification followed the statement in the Declaration of Independence that "it is the right of the people . . . to institute new government." Hence, the Constitution's preamble establishes the Constitution in the name of "We the People of the United States."

In September 1787, with these final steps taken, delegates to the Constitutional Convention believed they had produced a constitution that remedied the deficiencies of the Articles (see Table 2.3), and they voted on the final document. Some of the delegates had

Table 2.3 Deficiencies of the Articles of Confederation and Constitutional Remedies

Deficiency in the Articles of Confederation	Remedy in the Constitution
Legislative branch could not regulate commerce	Congress can regulate commerce "among the states"
Legislative branch could only request taxes from states	Congress can directly raise taxes from individuals
Approval of nine of thirteen states needed for passage of major legislation	Approval of a majority of both legislative chambers needed for passage of all legislation; a two-thirds majority needed to override presidential vetoes
No permanent executive branch	A "President of the United States"
No permanent judicial branch	A Supreme Court plus other inferior courts that Congress can establish
Unanimity for constitutional amendments	Approval of two-thirds of each Congressional chamber plus three-fourths of the states
Few limits on state authority, mostly over foreign affairs	States limited in foreign affairs, plus could not suppress certain rights through bills of attainder, *ex post facto* laws, and so on

left by September, but thirty-nine signed the document, with only three refusing to do so. Crucially, given Convention rules, a majority of the delegates from each of the states voted yes.

Government Under the Constitution

LO 2-3 Explain how the structure of the Constitution protects liberty

The final document sent to the states for ratification laid out a structure of democratic government and proposed mechanisms whereby the Constitution could be amended. It also reflected the Framers' attempt to establish a government powerful enough to ensure public order yet contain enough gateways to guarantee individual liberty.

The Structure of Government

The Constitution established three branches of government: the legislative, the executive, and the judicial.

The Legislative Branch.　The legislative branch, as explained in Chapter 1, makes the laws. The Constitution established a bicameral Congress, consisting of two chambers. The lower chamber, the House of Representatives, is proportioned by population (until the Thirteenth Amendment, the slave population was added to the free population according to the three-fifths formula described previously). Members of the House are elected for two-year terms directly by the people, with voting eligibility determined by each state. Representatives have to be at least 25 years old, residents of the state they serve, and U.S. citizens for at least the previous seven years.

The upper chamber, the Senate, consists of two senators from each state, regardless of size. Designed to serve as a check on the popular will, as well as a remnant of states' rights in the Articles, which would be expressed in the House of Representatives, state legislatures chose senators until 1913 when the Seventeenth Amendment granted the people of each state the exclusive right to do so.[22] A six-year term also serves to limit responsiveness to popular whims, and an age minimum of 30 presumably provides more mature and level-headed thinking. Senators also have to be residents of the state in which they serve and U.S. citizens for nine years or more.

Bills to levy taxes must originate in the House, but other bills may originate in either chamber. To become law, a bill must pass each chamber in identical form and is then presented to the president for his signature. If the president signs the bill, it becomes law, but if he disapproves, he can **veto** the bill. Congress can then override the veto by a two-thirds majority in each chamber.

veto: *Authority of the president to block legislation passed by Congress. Congress can override a veto by a two-thirds majority in each chamber.*

Article I, Section 8, of the Constitution limits Congress's authority to an eighteen-paragraph list, or enumeration, of certain powers. The first paragraph grants Congress the authority "to Collect Taxes . . . to pay the Debts and provide for the common Defence and general Welfare of the United States." Paragraphs 2 through 17 grant additional powers such as borrowing and coining money, regulating commerce, and raising an army. Then paragraph 18 grants Congress the authority to pass all laws "necessary and proper for carrying into Execution the foregoing Powers."

Additionally, the Constitution gives the House the authority to impeach—to bring charges against—the president and other federal officials for "treason, bribery or other high crimes and misdemeanors." As Alexander Hamilton explained in *Federalist* 65, "The subjects of its jurisdiction are those offenses which proceed from the misconduct of public men, or, in other words, from the abuse or violation of some public trust. They are of a nature which may with peculiar propriety be denominated POLITICAL [emphasis in original], as they relate chiefly to injuries done immediately to the society itself." This seemingly suggests that criminal activity is not a requirement for impeachment, rather, that political activities against the public trust may be sufficient.

The Senate has the sole authority to try cases of impeachment, with a two-thirds vote required for removal from office. The Senate also has the sole authority to ratify treaties, which also require a two-thirds vote, and to confirm executive and judicial branch appointments by majority vote.

During the summer of 2019, an unnamed whistleblower reported to Congress that President Trump was withholding vital military aid to Ukraine, which was defending itself from an attack by both Russia and Russian separatists, unless the president of Ukraine announced an investigation into former vice president Joe Biden. At the time, Biden was considered the front runner for the Democratic nomination and the candidate with the best chance to defeat Trump in November. House Democrats argued that the president was using his authority to advance his personal political agenda. They voted to open an impeachment inquiry without the support of a single Republican member of the House. During the inquiry, Trump refused to allow any of his White House staff to testify or provide documentary evidence. The House eventually supported two articles of impeachment against Trump: the first charge was abuse of power; the second charge, obstruction of Congress.

The Senate that tried Trump consisted of fifty-three Republicans, forty-five Democrats, and two independents (including Bernie Sanders) who caucus with the Democrats. All votes in impeachment trials except removal are by a simple majority. Thus, the Republicans were easily able to stop Democratic Party requests to hear witnesses and obtain new evidence from White House documents. In the final vote, all Democrats voted to convict on both counts, and all Republicans voted to acquit on the obstruction of Congress charge while Republican Mitt Romney, alone among Republicans, voted to convict on the abuse of power charge. This put the Democrats far short of the sixty-seven votes they needed to remove Trump.

The Executive Branch.   The executive branch of government consists of a unitary president, chosen for a four-year term by an Electoral College. The Electoral College itself is chosen in a manner set by the legislature of each state. Eventually, every state gave the people the power to vote for its electors (as discussed earlier). A president must be at least 35 years of age (by Inauguration Day), a resident of the United States for the previous fourteen years, and either a natural-born citizen of the United States or a citizen of the United States at the time of the adoption of the Constitution.

As far as legislative and executive powers go, because the Framers believed that the legislative branch would naturally be stronger than the executive branch, they did not feel the need to enumerate the executive powers as they did the legislative powers. Recall that

Election 2020

Although the Constitution of 1787 was more democratic than any other Constitution of its time, it still imposed numerous gates on public participation. Among these gates was the Electoral College, which would choose the president. As we will see in Chapters 3 (Federalism) and 11 (Voting and Participation), Alexander Hamilton favored more gates to limit participation, while Thomas Jefferson favored more gateways to public involvement.

As for the Electoral College, which clearly limited public influence in the selection of the president, Alexander Hamilton wrote in *Federalist* 68 that the electors would be the "men most capable of analyzing the qualities adapted to the station and acting under circumstances favorable to deliberation, and to a judicious combination of all the reasons and inducements which were proper to govern their choice." Alternatively, James Madison, who would help form the Democratic-Republican Party with Thomas Jefferson, proposed at the Constitutional Convention the direct election of the president by the people. Madison lost that battle as the convention decided that the president would be selected by an Electoral College that would be designated by the legislature of each state.

The first so-called faithless elector, an elector who does not cast his ballot for the candidate to whom he was pledged, occurred in the 1796 election, when Samuel Miles, a John Adams elector from Pennsylvania, voted instead for Thomas Jefferson. The faithless elector received the following criticism in a letter to a local paper: "What, do I choose Samuel Miles to determine for me whether John Adams or Thomas Jefferson shall be president? No! I choose him to act, not to think."[23] Between the 1800 election and the 2012 election, twelve electors cast ballots for a candidate other than the candidate to whom they were pledged. In the 2016 election, seven electors did so. (Three more attempted to do so but they were replaced by their states before their ballots were counted.)

Three of the seven were Democratic electors from the state of Washington, which imposed a $1,000 fine for voting for a candidate other than the statewide winner; three more were from the state of Colorado, which required electors to vote for the candidate who received the most votes in the state. (The Washington and Colorado electors filed suit in federal court claiming that the Constitution prohibited any limits on their free choice, much as Hamilton suggested.)

Image 2.5A and B The state of Washington fined Bret Chiafalo $1,000 for not casting his Electoral College vote for Hillary Clinton. Polly Baca sued the state of Colorado to block enforcement of its law requiring presidential electors only to vote for the candidate to whom they are pledged. Both won their cases in the Supreme Court.

Due to the COVID-19 crisis, the Supreme Court was not holding regular sessions when their court date arrived. Rather, oral arguments were held by teleconference. The oral arguments, which were live streamed by C-SPAN, showed a concern by the justices for chaos to ensue in a close election if electors could be bribed or induced into switching their votes.

In the end, the Court ruled, unanimously, that states were free to require Electors to vote for the candidate who won that state and to punish Electors who did not do so.

Congress does not have a general legislative authority, but only those legislative powers granted under the Constitution. In contrast, the Constitution provides the president with a general grant of "the executive Power" plus certain specific powers, including the right to veto legislation and grant pardons. The president also is commander in chief of the armed forces. With the advice and consent of the Senate, the president makes treaties and appoints ambassadors, judges, and other public officials. The president can be removed from office either via impeachment or, under the Twenty-Fifth Amendment, a vote by the vice president and a majority of the cabinet that the president is unable to discharge his duties.

Key Questions

Why did the delegates establish three branches of government?

The Judicial Branch.   The Constitution vests the judicial authority of the United States in one Supreme Court and other inferior courts that Congress might choose to establish. The president appoints judges with the advice and consent of the Senate. They serve "during good Behaviour," which, short of impeachment, means a life term.

The Constitution extends the authority of the federal courts to hear cases involving certain classes of parties to a suit—cases involving the United States, ambassadors, and other public ministers; suits between two or more states or citizens from different states—and certain classes of cases, most notably cases arising under the Constitution, laws, and treaties of the United States. In the historic case *Marbury v. Madison* (1803), the Supreme Court took this authority to hear cases arising under the Constitution of the United States to establish the power of **judicial review**, the authority of the Court to strike down any law passed by Congress when the Court believes the law violates the Constitution (see Supreme Court Cases: *Marbury v. Madison*).[24]

judicial review: *Authority of courts to declare laws passed by Congress and acts of the executive branch to be unconstitutional.*

The Amendment Process

amendment: *Formal process of changing the Constitution.*

The Constitution provides two paths for changing the Constitution via **amendment**. The first path requires a two-thirds vote in each chamber of Congress, followed by the approval of three-fourths of the states. That statewide approval can be attained either through the state legislatures or through state ratifying conventions, as directed by Congress. The second path allows two-thirds of the states to request a national constitutional convention that could propose amendments that would go into effect when approved by three-fourths of the states (see Figure 2.4). Again, this approval could be obtained through state legislatures or through state ratifying conventions. Additionally, the Constitution prohibits amendments that would deny any state an equal vote in the Senate or any amendment that would have allowed a banning of the foreign slave trade before 1808.

Both paths for amending the Constitution are complex and difficult, which has kept the Constitution from being modified over popular but short-lived issues. Recently, these have included proposed amendments that would require a balanced federal budget, allow the federal or state governments to prosecute those who burn the American flag, and

Passage by two-thirds in both chambers of Congress

Constitutional convention called by Congress at the request of two-thirds of state legislatures

Ratified by legislatures in three-fourths of the states

Ratified by conventions in three-fourths of the states

→ Most common method

→ Method used once for ratification of the Twenty-First Amendment (the repeal of Prohibition)

→ Possible methods that have never been used

Figure 2.4 Amending the Constitution

An amendment can be proposed by two-thirds of each chamber of Congress or by a constitutional convention called by two-thirds of state legislatures. Either way, ratification requires three-quarters of the states to approve the amendment. Why do you think the methods indicated by the blue arrows have never been used?

prohibit states from recognizing same-sex marriages. In 1917 Congress proposed and in 1919 the states ratified the temporarily popular Prohibition amendment (the Eighteenth Amendment), which banned the manufacture, sale, and transportation of alcohol, only to have it repealed in 1933 (the Twenty-First Amendment) in the face of massive civil disobedience.

The states have never called a constitutional convention to amend the 1787 Constitution, but Senator Marco Rubio (R-FL) has called for a constitutional convention that would limit the size of the national government.[25] It is not clear, though, that a convention called for a particular purpose could be limited to that purpose. Recall that the 1787 Constitutional Convention was originally called merely to amend the Articles of Confederation. Over the years many politicians have called for such conventions without success. Congress, though, has sent thirty-three proposed amendments to the states for ratification. Other than the Twenty-First Amendment (the repeal of Prohibition), which Congress sent to state ratifying conventions, all other proposed amendments went directly to the state legislatures. Of the thirty-three amendments that Congress proposed, twenty-seven have received the required assent of three-fourths of the states. These include the Bill of Rights (the First through the Tenth Amendments), which passed within two years of the adoption of the Constitution, and three Civil War amendments (the Thirteenth through the Fifteenth Amendments) that abolished slavery and attempted to protect the rights of former slaves. We further discuss these and other amendments to the Constitution later in this chapter.

Key Questions

Why did the delegates make it hard to amend the Constitution? Do you think this was the right choice?

Supreme Court Cases

Marbury v. Madison (1803)

QUESTION: Does Congress have the authority to expand the Supreme Court's original jurisdiction beyond that granted by the Constitution?

ORAL ARGUMENT: February 10, 1803

DECISION: February 23, 1803 (read at http://www.law.cornell.edu/supremecourt/text/5/137)

OUTCOME: No, thus establishing the power of judicial review (4–0)

It is hard to imagine a more momentous decision resulting from what the historian John A. Garraty called, this "trivial squabble over a few petty political plums."* In the closing days of President John Adams' administration, the Federalist Adams nominated William Marbury to the position of justice of the peace for the District of Columbia, and the Federalist Senate confirmed the nomination. But in the hectic final hours of Adams' administration, Secretary of State John Marshall neglected to deliver the commission. When Democratic-Republican Thomas Jefferson became president, his new secretary of state, James Madison, refused to deliver the commission, thus keeping Marbury from assuming his office.

Marbury filed suit at the Supreme Court, believing that the Judiciary Act of 1789 expanded the Court's original jurisdiction to give the Court the authority to hear cases involving writs of *mandamus* (orders to government officials to undertake specific acts) as an original matter—that is, as a trial, and not just as an appeal.

The Supreme Court declared that because the Constitution precisely specified which types of cases the Supreme Court could hear as an original matter, the section of the Judiciary Act that expanded the Court's original jurisdiction conflicted with the Constitution. Moreover, if a law conflicts with the Constitution, either the law is supreme over the Constitution, or the Constitution is supreme over the law. The Court ruled that it must be the case that the Constitution is supreme over the law. Finally, the Court declared that the judiciary would decide such issues. "It is emphatically the province and duty of the judicial department to say what the law is," wrote John Marshall, who in the closing days of the Adams administration had been nominated and confirmed as chief justice of the United States. The Supreme Court would not order Madison to deliver the commission to Marbury. Marbury presumably had the right to get the commission from a different court but never sought to do so. Instead, he returned to his highly successful banking career.

The Court in *Marbury* granted itself the momentous authority of judicial review, the power to strike down laws passed by Congress and state legislatures on the grounds that those laws violate the Constitution. Although the Court did not frequently use this power in the early days of the republic, citizens filing lawsuits would later use it to get the Court to strike down, among other things, segregated schools (*Brown v. Board of Education*, 1954), antiabortion statutes (*Roe v. Wade*, 1973), and prohibitions on same-sex marriages (*Obergefell v. Hodges*, 2015).

Thinking Critically

1. How does judicial review provide a gateway to participation in the political system?
2. Why is it the judiciary's job to determine whether a law is unconstitutional?

*"The Case of the Missing Commissions," in John A. Garraty, ed., *Quarrels That Have Shaped the Constitution* (New York: Harper and Row, 1964), 13

The Partition of Power

In attempting to explain and justify the constitutional structure, James Madison wrote of "the necessary partition of power among the several departments as laid down in the constitution" (see *Federalist* 51 in the Appendix). He acknowledged that elections serve as the primary means of ensuring that the government is responsive to the wishes of the people. If it is not, the people can vote for a new government. Under the Constitution, the people have direct authority to elect the House of Representatives. But to prevent the majority from imposing oppressive laws on the minority, the rest of the government was chosen indirectly, as we have seen.

Lest the people not be sufficient to keep government under control, however, the Constitution had built in "auxiliary precautions," as Madison called them, to make sure government could not concentrate power. Thus, **federalism** splits power between nation and state, **separation of powers** divides the powers that remained with the national government among the three branches of government, and **checks and balances** give each branch some authority over the powers of the other branches. Even after all this, the Constitution places additional limits on both federal and state powers.

Federalism. The first means of preventing a concentration of power was to divide authority between the national and state governments. Rather than provide Congress with a general power to legislate in the national interest, the Constitution granted Congress enumerated powers. All powers not granted to Congress remained with the states. This division of power is made explicit in the Tenth Amendment to the Constitution: "The powers not delegated to the United States by the Constitution, nor prohibited by it to the States, are reserved to the States respectively, or to the people."

Separation of Powers. Madison believed that "the accumulation of all powers, legislative, executive, and judiciary, in the same hands, whether of one, a few, or many, and whether hereditary, self-appointed, or elective, may justly be pronounced the very definition of tyranny."[26] Thus, after dividing power between the national and state governments, the Constitution separates those powers that it grants to the national government among the three branches. Under the Constitution, all legislative powers granted belong to Congress, the executive power vests in the president of the United States, and the judicial authority resides in a Supreme Court, plus any lower courts Congress might choose to establish. Moreover, because the "legislative authority . . . necessarily, predominates" in a republican government (*Federalist* 51), legislative power was further separated into two distinct chambers, a House and a Senate, each with different manners of election and terms of office.

Checks and Balances. Under the Constitution, balance among the branches was achieved by giving each one some authority to counteract, or check, the authority of the other two (see Figure 2.5). Thus, the president has the authority to propose legislation to Congress and to veto bills passed by Congress; Congress can override that veto by a two-thirds majority of each chamber. The president has the authority to pardon people convicted of crimes. The president also nominates federal judges, subject to the advice and consent of the Senate. The Senate also advises and consents to high-ranking executive branch appointments, such as ambassadors and cabinet officials. The House can impeach

federalism: *System of government in which sovereignty is constitutionally divided between national and state governments.*

separation of powers: *Government structure in which authority is divided among branches (executive, legislative, and judicial), with each holding separate and independent powers and areas of responsibility.*

checks and balances: *Government structure that authorizes each branch of government (executive, legislative, and judicial) to share powers with the other branches, thereby holding some scrutiny of and control over the other branches.*

> **Key Questions**
> Why does the Constitution divide and separate power?

> **Key Questions**
> Has the division of power between the national government and the states hindered or advanced democracy?

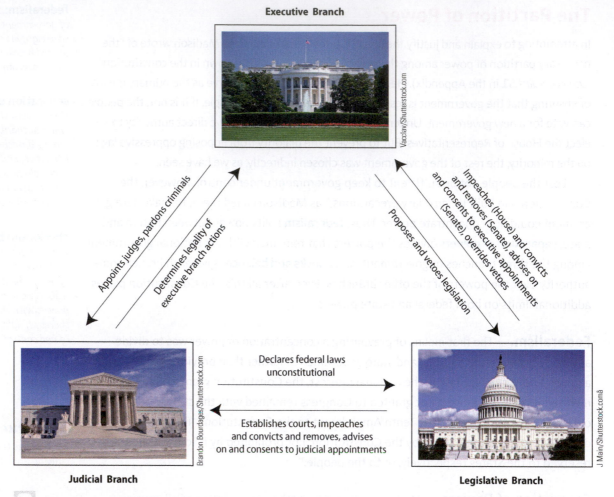

Executive Branch

Appoints judges, pardons criminals

Determines legality of executive branch actions

Impeaches (House) and convicts and removes (Senate), advises on and consents to executive appointments (Senate), overrides vetoes

Proposes and vetoes legislation

Declares federal laws unconstitutional

Establishes courts, impeaches and convicts and removes, advises on and consents to judicial appointments

Judicial Branch

Legislative Branch

Figure 2.5 **Checks and Balances**

The Constitution provides each branch of government with a partial control over the workings of the other two branches.

executive and judicial appointees, and the Senate can convict and remove impeached officials from office by a two-thirds majority. Congress, subject to presidential veto, has the authority to establish lower courts and set their jurisdiction (decide what cases they can hear). It also has the authority to set the Supreme Court's appellate jurisdiction. The appellate jurisdiction is the Supreme Court's authority to hear cases on appeal from lower courts and is the heart of the Supreme Court's judicial power. Congress has this authority over the courts; the courts, on the other hand, can decide the constitutionality of laws passed by Congress. While the Constitution does not explicitly grant this power of judicial review to courts, judicial review has been largely unchallenged since announced by the Supreme Court in *Marbury v. Madison*. The courts also have the authority to review the legality of actions taken by executive branch officials.

Limits on Powers.   The delegation of powers to Congress, and the reservation of all remaining powers to the states, would have given states the same authority to pass oppressive laws that they had under the Articles. To prevent that, the Constitution limits state authority in several ways. First, it makes federal law supreme over state law. Second, it guarantees that the states establish a republican form of government. Third, the Constitution sets limits on the sort of legislation states can pass. They also cannot pass bills of attainder (legislative acts declaring people guilty of crimes) or prosecute individuals under *ex post facto* laws, which make behavior illegal after individuals have engaged in it. In a provision indicative of American egalitarianism, the Constitution denies states the power to grant titles of nobility. While not embracing the notion of equality announced in the Declaration of Independence, the Framers did make it clear that they rejected the British system of inherited social status. The Constitution also prohibits states from passing laws that would allow individuals to disregard the obligation of contracts, such as laws negating debts.

The Constitution also expressly limits the authority of Congress. Like the states, Congress can pass neither bills of attainder nor *ex post facto* laws. It also cannot suspend the writ of *habeas corpus*—a guarantee that incarcerated people can go before a judge to have the legality of their confinement determined—except in cases of invasion or rebellion.

The Ratification Debates

LO 2-4 Analyze why the Antifederalists opposed the Constitution

With the proposed Constitution to be accepted or rejected by the people of the various states, the state ratification debates largely ignored the question of representation that led to the Connecticut Compromise and the three-fifths compromise. Instead, most of the debate concerned the extent of national power under the Constitution, with many expressing fears about the consolidation of federal authority over the states, the scope of executive and legislative power, and the lack of a bill of rights.

Federalists and Antifederalists

By the time the state ratifying conventions started meeting, two distinct camps had formed. Those who supported the Constitution cleverly named themselves **Federalists**, even though they were really more nationalist than federalist. ("Federal," according to Madison, meant "a Confederacy of sovereign states,"[27] which better described the Articles of Confederation, or even the New Jersey Plan, than the new Constitution.) Those who opposed the Constitution, whose leaders included the outspoken Revolutionary leader Patrick Henry of Virginia, became known as the **Antifederalists**.

Madison, along with John Jay, who later became the first chief justice of the United States, and Alexander Hamilton, who later founded the Federalist Party and served as the first secretary of the treasury, wrote eighty-five essays, today known as the *Federalist Papers*, that attempted to convince the citizens of New York to ratify the Constitution. They wrote anonymously under the pen name "Publius," taken from an early leader in the ancient Roman Republic. Madison's essays, especially, are still read today as a leading source for understanding the Constitution. We quoted from them earlier in this chapter and in Chapter 1, and two of the most famous essays, numbers 10 and 51, are in the Appendix. The Antifederalists published their attacks under anonymous pen names as well, most notably

Federalists: *Initially, those who supported the Constitution during the ratification period; later, the name of the political party established by supporters of Alexander Hamilton.*

Antifederalists: *Those who opposed the new proposed Constitution during the ratification period.*

Key Questions

Were the Antifederalists more concerned about liberty or about order?

"Brutus"—another leader of the ancient Roman Republic—and "Old Whig," named after the English political party that opposed the monarchy.

Consolidation of Federal Authority

The Antifederalists found much to disapprove of in the proposed Constitution. They argued that the Constitutional Convention had violated the Articles by moving beyond mere amendment and proposing a new government, one that did not require the unanimous consent of the states. They worried that because sovereignty, the ultimate lawmaking authority, could not be split, and because national law was supreme over state law, a national government under the Constitution would inevitably consolidate its authority over the state governments.

The Federalists answered both of these charges by claiming that sovereignty rested not in the legislature, as had typically been believed, but in the people, as the preamble to the Constitution suggested. Therefore the people could propose any new form of government they wished. And if the people were sovereign, they could split their grant of lawmaking authority between the national and state governments as they saw fit.

The Scope of Executive Authority

Other concerns centered on the scope of executive authority. With no term limits on the executive in the original Constitution, the Antifederalists feared that the president would turn into a monarch, and of the worst type—an elected one. George Mason, who was one of three delegates not to sign the proposed Constitution, also worried that "the President of the United States has the unrestrained Power of granting Pardon," which could be used to instigate crimes and then cover them up by pardoning his criminal partners. Alexander Hamilton responded in *Federalist* 69 with an explanation of the limits on the executive: elections, whereby the president could be voted out of office; impeachment, whereby the president could be removed from office for "high crimes and misdemeanors"; and the limited veto power, which could be overridden. The president of the United States, Hamilton concluded, was much closer in power to the governor of New York than to the king of England.

The Scope of Legislative Authority

general welfare clause: *Gives Congress the power to tax to provide for the general welfare (Article I, Section 8).*

necessary and proper clause: *Gives Congress the power to pass all laws necessary and proper to the powers enumerated in Article I, Section 8.*

Two provisions in Article I, Section 8, of the Constitution, which specified the powers of Congress, particularly alarmed the Antifederalists: the **general welfare clause** and the **necessary and proper clause**. Section 8 of the Constitution begins by stating that "Congress shall have Power to lay and Collect Taxes . . . to . . . provide for the . . . general Welfare of the United States." It concludes by stating that Congress has the power "to make all Laws which shall be necessary and proper for carrying into Execution the foregoing Powers." Antifederalist Brutus contended that "the legislature under this constitution may pass any law which they may think proper."[28] Brutus further wrote that the necessary and proper clause, labeled "the sweeping clause" by the Antifederalists, granted the government "absolute and uncontroulable power, legislative, executive and judicial."[29] James Monroe, who would later serve as the fifth president (1817–25), told the Virginia ratifying convention that the sweeping clause gave Congress "a general power . . . to make all laws that will enable them to carry their powers into effect. There are no limits pointed out. They are not restrained or controlled from making any law, however oppressive in its operation, which they may think necessary to carry their powers into effect."[30]

Madison responded in *Federalist* 41 that the power to tax "to provide for the general Welfare" was not a general grant of power to tax for any purpose whatsoever but, rather, a power to tax for the enumerated powers that followed. "Nothing is more natural nor common than first to use a general phrase, and then to explain and qualify it by a recital of particulars."[31] To Madison, Article I, Section 8, granted the right to tax to provide for the general welfare and then listed various other powers that defined the full scope of the general welfare clause.

Similarly, the Federalists argued that the necessary and proper clause was not a general grant of authority to pass all laws that were necessary and proper, but rather, as the clause explicitly stated, the authority to pass all laws that were "necessary and proper for carrying into Execution the foregoing [that is, previously listed] Powers." Thus, if a law is necessary and proper for borrowing money, or raising an army, or establishing a post office, Congress may pass such a law, for those powers are among the "foregoing Powers" granted Congress. This explicit restriction of the necessary and proper clause to the other powers was absent, however, in the general welfare clause. To Madison, the restriction was obviously implied; to the Antifederalists, it was a threat to limited government.

Nevertheless, to clarify that the Constitution did not provide general powers to Congress, the Federalists agreed to an amendment to the Constitution declaring that "The powers not delegated to the United States by the Constitution, nor prohibited by it to the States, are reserved to the States respectively, or to the people." Interestingly, the amendment parallels a similar provision from the Articles that declared that the states retained all powers not "expressly delegated" to the national government. By limiting congressional authority to those powers delegated to it, rather than the stricter standard of those powers expressly delegated to it, the Constitution creates a somewhat greater authority for **implied powers**.

The Lack of a Bill of Rights

The most serious charge against the Constitution was that it did not contain a bill of rights. Patrick Henry, who had famously proclaimed "Give me liberty or give me death" in 1765, told the Virginia ratifying convention in 1788 that if the state gives up its powers "without a bill of rights, you will exhibit the most absurd thing to mankind that ever the world saw— [state] government that has abandoned all its powers—the powers of direct taxation, the sword, and the purse. You have disposed of them to Congress, without a bill of rights—without check, limitation, or control."[32]

In contrast, the Federalists argued that a bill of rights was not necessary because Congress had only those powers granted by the Constitution. If Congress was not granted the authority to, say, abridge freedom of the press, it was unnecessary to say that Congress could not abridge freedom of the press. The Federalists, specifically Alexander Hamilton in *Federalist* 84, went further to claim that a bill of rights could be dangerous because listing some rights but not others could imply that the rights not listed could be abridged.

Consider two documents. The first one states that Congress has the right to regulate commerce between the states, to tax to provide for the general welfare, and to raise armies. Under this document, does Congress have the right to abridge the right to assemble? The Federalist answer was no because Congress has enumerated powers only, and the right

Key Questions
Why were the Antifederalists opposed to a strong executive?

Key Questions
How would you define "the general welfare" for which Congress is supposed to provide? What elements of the Antifederalist argument do you detect in political arguments today?

implied powers: *Powers not expressly granted to Congress but added through the necessary and proper clause.*

Image 2.6 A 1787 engraving depicting the conflict between the Federalists and Antifederalists in Connecticut. The Federalists are portrayed as representing trading interests while the Antifederalists are shown as favoring farming interests.

to limit freedom of assembly is not one of them. The Antifederalist answer was yes because the power was not prohibited.

Now consider a second document that states that Congress has the right to regulate commerce between the states, to tax to provide for the general welfare, and to raise armies. In addition, it states that Congress may not abridge freedom of the press. May Congress abridge the right to assemble? The Federalists argued that the potential for Congress to regulate the right to assemble is greater in the second document than in the first. That is, in the second case, Congress could say "we are prohibited from abridging freedom of the press, but we are not prohibited from abridging the right to assemble, so we are allowed to do that." By listing certain rights, the Constitution could be interpreted as allowing Congress to limit those freedoms not listed.

It is hard to imagine people concluding from the Federalist argument that rights would be safer without a bill of rights. Not only is this a complicated argument, but combining the necessary and proper clause with the broad powers granted Congress under the Constitution—such as regulating interstate commerce and taxing to provide for the general welfare—probably means that Congress could have found ways to pass laws abridging freedom of assembly, freedom of speech, and other freedoms. The Federalists eventually gave in to the Antifederalist argument, agreeing that amending the Constitution to provide a bill of rights would be among the first items of business under a newly ratified Constitution. To prevent the listing of certain rights to create an assumption that Congress could abridge other rights not listed, the Bill of Rights included the Ninth Amendment: "The enumeration in the Constitution, of certain rights, shall not be construed to deny or disparage others retained by the people."

Despite the Antifederalist arguments about excessive national power, the lack of a bill of rights, and a too-powerful executive, states began ratifying the new Constitution. By June 1788, ten states had ratified, one more than needed to establish the new Constitution. Yet some states delayed. North Carolina and Rhode Island did not ratify until after George Washington was elected president.

The Responsive Constitution

LO 2-5 Illustrate how the Constitution has stayed responsive to changing needs

The government the Framers devised has lasted more than two hundred years. As in 1787, it still has three branches of government, Congress still consists of two chambers, and the Electoral College still chooses the president. But other parts of the U.S. constitutional system have changed substantially, some to fix flaws and some to respond to new circumstances and developing ideas about the nature of equality. Some of these changes, such as the Bill of Rights, came through the formal amendment process. Others were the result of changing interpretation by the Supreme Court about what the Constitution means. Still others are what some call "extraconstitutional." That is, they affect the way the constitutional system operates even though the Constitution itself has not been amended to reflect them. Most prominent is the development of political parties (see Chapter 9, Political Parties).

The Bill of Rights

As part of the fight over ratification, the Federalists agreed that they would propose a Bill of Rights after the new Constitution was ratified, and some states' ratifying conventions forwarded proposals for specific amendments. The states then ratified ten of the amendments in 1791 as a Bill of Rights that became part of the Constitution. Many of these amendments stated rights that had been guaranteed under British law or had been abridged by the British during the decade before the Revolution, causing the Americans to demand independence.

Key Questions

The Articles of Confederation, once ratified, did not last a decade. Why has the Constitution lasted for more than two centuries?

The First Amendment guarantees major political rights, including freedom of speech, press, and assembly, and the free exercise of religion. It also prohibits establishing a national religion or, more precisely, any law "respecting an establishment of religion." The Second Amendment protects the right to bear arms; the Third Amendment prohibits the quartering of soldiers in one's home in times of peace. The Fourth, Fifth, Sixth, and Eighth Amendments protect rights relating to criminal procedure, including the right at trial to the assistance of an attorney and the right to a trial by jury (Sixth). The Seventh Amendment protects the right to a trial by jury in civil cases over $20. The criminal procedure amendments also prohibit unreasonable searches and seizures (Fourth); compulsory self-incrimination (Fifth); double jeopardy, or being tried a second time for a crime after one is found not guilty (Fifth); and cruel or unusual punishments (Eighth). The Fifth Amendment also prohibits deprivations of life, liberty, or property without due process of law, and it prohibits the government from seizing private property for a public use without fair or "just" compensation. We examine the meanings of these amendments in Chapter 4, Civil Liberties.

The Civil War Amendments

Following the Civil War, Congress proposed and the states ratified three amendments. The Thirteenth Amendment (1865) prohibits slavery. The Fourteenth Amendment (1868), aimed at protecting the newly emancipated slaves, makes all people born in the United States citizens of the United States. It also prohibits states from denying anyone due process of law, the equal protection of the law, as demonstrated in *Plyler v. Doe* (see Chapter 1, Gateways to American Democracy), and the privileges or immunities of citizens of the United States. The Fifteenth Amendment (1870) prohibits states from denying anyone the right to vote on account of race or prior status as a slave. All three amendments give Congress the authority to enforce the measures by appropriate legislation, thus adding to Congress's enumerated powers. These amendments radically changed the structure of the federal government by giving the national government

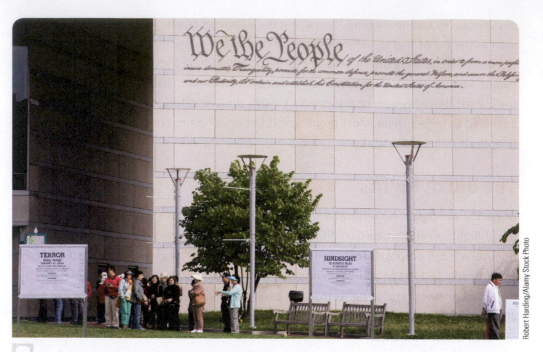

Image 2.7 After more than two hundred years, Americans love the Constitution and are interested in learning about it. The original is in a sealed case at the National Archives in Washington, D.C., but visitors to the National Constitution Center in Philadelphia, shown here, enjoy exhibits that tell the story of the Constitution and its contemporary relevance.

authority over internal matters of the states. We deal with these civil rights more extensively in Chapter 5, Civil Rights.

Amendments That Expand Public Participation

Other amendments have extended the gateways to public participation in government by giving the people the right to vote for their senators directly (Seventeenth, 1913), guaranteeing women the right to vote (Nineteenth, 1920), allowing residents of the District of Columbia to vote in presidential elections (Twenty-Third, 1961), prohibiting states from setting poll taxes as a requirement of voting in federal elections (Twenty-Fourth, 1964), and guaranteeing the right to vote for those age 18 or older (Twenty-Sixth, 1971). For a summary of all the amendments, see Figure 2.6.

The Equal Rights Amendment

In 1972, Congress proposed and sent to the states the Equal Rights Amendment. That amendment simply declares "equality of rights under the law shall not be denied or abridged by the United States or by any state on account sex." Twenty-two out of the required thirty-eight states ratified the amendment in 1972. Eight more ratified in 1973. At that point, conservative political activist Phyllis Schlafly began a campaign against the amendment. The campaign was very effective: only three states ratified in 1974, one in 1975, and none in 1976.[33] When the original deadline for ratification passed, Congress extended the deadline. Still, the states did not meet the new deadline. Congress then

Key:	Criminal Procedure	Participation	Equality	Structure	Miscellaneous

First	1791	Prohibits abridging freedoms of religion, speech, press, assembly, and petition
Second	1791	Prohibits abridging the right to bear arms
Third	1791	Prohibits involuntary quartering of soldiers in one's home during peacetime
Fourth	1791	Prohibits unreasonable searches and seizures
Fifth	1791	Affirms the right to indictment by a grand jury and the right to due process; protects against double jeopardy, self-incrimination, and taking of property without just compensation
Sixth	1791	Affirms rights to speedy and public trial, to confront witnesses, and to counsel
Seventh	1791	Affirms right to jury trials in civil suits over $20
Eighth	1791	Prohibits excessive bail, excessive fines, and cruel and unusual punishments
Ninth	1791	Declares that the enumeration of certain rights does not limit other rights retained by the people
Tenth	1791	Reserves the powers not granted to the national government to the states or to the people
Eleventh	1798	Prevents citizens from one state from suing another state in federal court
Twelfth	1804	Requires that electors cast separate votes for president and vice president and specifies requirements for vice presidential candidates
Thirteenth	1865	Prohibits slavery in the United States
Fourteenth	1868	Makes all persons born in the United States citizens of the United States and prohibits states from denying persons within its jurisdiction the privileges or immunities of citizens, the due process of law, and equal protection of the laws; apportionment by whole persons
Fifteenth	1870	Prohibits states from denying the right to vote on account of race
Sixteenth	1913	Grants Congress the power to tax income derived from any source
Seventeenth	1913	Gives the people (instead of state legislatures) the right to choose U.S. senators directly
Eighteenth	1919	Prohibits the manufacture, sale, or transportation of intoxicating liquors
Nineteenth	1920	Guarantees women the right to vote
Twentieth	1933	Declares that the presidential term begins on January 20 (instead of March 4)
Twenty-First	1933	Repeals the Eighteenth Amendment
Twenty-Second	1951	Limits presidents to two terms
Twenty-Third	1961	Grants Electoral College votes to residents of the District of Columbia
Twenty-Fourth	1964	Prohibits poll taxes
Twenty-Fifth	1967	Specifies replacement of the vice president and establishes the position of acting president during a president's disability
Twenty-Sixth	1971	Guarantees 18-year-olds the right to vote
Twenty-Seventh	1992	Sets limits on congressional pay raises

Figure 2.6 Amendments to the Constitution

Following the specific protections of the first eight amendments to the Constitution, many subsequent amendments have corrected structural problems in the operation of government. Others have expanded participation and equality.

Image 2.8 and 2.9 Conservative political activist Phyllis Schlafly launched a campaign against the proposed equal rights of women in 1972. Due to her efforts, the amendment fell three states short of ratification. Since then a few states have ratified, with Virginia providing the thirty-eighth needed state in 2020.

Key Questions
How has the Constitution changed, and why?

eliminated the deadline. Early in 2020, Virginia became the thirty-eighth state to ratify the amendment. Given the ups and downs of passage, and the fact that some states have rescinded their ratification, federal courts will now decide the validity of the amendment.

Constitutional Interpretation

The Constitution has also changed through interpretation by the Supreme Court (see Public Policy and the Constitution: The Death Penalty). Following the explicit establishment of judicial review in *Marbury v. Madison,* the Court has exercised the authority to determine what the Constitution means. Under that authority, the powers of Congress have grown enormously. During the Great Depression of the 1930s, the Court began to interpret Congress's power to tax to provide for the general welfare as extending beyond the enumerated powers. Rather, in line with the interpretation of the general welfare clause that the Antifederalists feared, the Court now holds that Congress can tax and spend for virtually any purpose that is not expressly prohibited.

Key Questions
What is the significance of judicial review?

Additionally, Congress's authority to regulate commerce between the states is now so grand that it covers virtually all commercial activity, including wheat grown by a farmer for consumption by livestock on that farmer's land because of the effect that all similarly situated wheat could have on national grain markets.[34] But in 2012, the Supreme Court held that the commerce clause did not give Congress the right to mandate that individuals purchase health insurance, upholding that requirement under the taxing part of the general welfare clause.[35]

The growth of national authority confirms that the Antifederalists were correct to insist on a Bill of Rights. Although Congress has not been granted the explicit right to abridge freedom of speech or freedom of the press, it would have the authority to do so under current readings of the commerce, taxing, and various other clauses, were it not for the Bill of Rights.

Future Amendments

Many of the formal changes in the Constitution since the Bill of Rights have centered on greater direct participation: direct voting for senators; no poll taxes; no abridgments of rights to vote on account of race, sex, or age so long as one is 18; and no exclusion of residents of the District of Columbia from voting for president. District residents do not have representation in Congress, however, because the Constitution declares that "The House of Representatives shall be composed of Members chosen every second Year by the People of the several States," and the District of Columbia is not a state. District residents are always hopeful that a constitutional amendment will give them representation. As they overwhelmingly vote for Democrats, the Democratic Party supports such an amendment, but Republicans oppose it. It is unlikely that three-quarters of the states would approve, given the partisan consequences of such a change.

Members of Congress introduced eighty-two proposed constitutional amendments during the 113th Congress. Seven of these proposed changes related to the Supreme Court's 2010 decision *Citizens United v. Federal Election Commission*, which gave corporations the same rights as individuals to make independent campaign expenditures for or against political candidates (see Chapter 8, Interest Groups, for more on the *Citizens United* case and Chapter 10, Elections and Campaigns, for more on campaign financing). Four of the proposed amendments would require term limits for members of Congress and six would limit federal spending. The rest were distributed over a wide variety of topics.[36] Not one of the proposed amendments received a vote in either chamber.

Alex Wong/Getty Images News/Getty Images

Image 2.10 Eleanor Holmes Norton is now in her sixteenth term as a nonvoting delegate to Congress from the District of Columbia. The Constitution gives Congress authority over the District of Columbia, and residents were not able to vote for president until 1961. The position Norton holds as a nonvoting delegate was made permanent only in 1971.

Institutional Changes

Not all changes to the Constitution occur via amendment or interpretation. Fundamental changes to the U.S. constitutional system have occurred through the establishment of new institutions, most notably **political parties**. They began to emerge during Washington's first term as president. When Secretary of the Treasury Alexander Hamilton pushed for aggressive use of the necessary and proper clause to allow the national government to regulate the economy, James Madison and Thomas Jefferson rose in opposition (see Chapter 9, Political Parties). These early divisions between political elites laid the groundwork for the emergence of the first set of opposing political parties.

The rise of political parties has meant that the president and vice president run as members of a political party, not as individuals. In Congress, representatives and senators organize themselves by parties, with members of the majority party having most of the power. The struggle that James Madison envisioned between the different branches of government, with Congress and the president checking each other, really exists only when the president and the majority party in Congress represent different parties—a situation known as divided government. When Congress and the president are from the same party, checks by Congress are curtailed. Members of the president's party in

Key Questions
What new amendments to the Constitution would you like to see passed?

political parties: *Broad coalitions of interests organized to win elections in order to enact a commonly supported set of public policies.*

The Death Penalty

The Constitution contains some degree of ambiguity about the death penalty. In several places, it seems to allow capital punishment. The Fourteenth Amendment's due process clause says that states may not deprive people of life, liberty, or property without due process of law, thus suggesting that life, liberty, and property may be taken so long as the states follow due process. Similarly, the Fifth Amendment declares that no person shall be held for a capital crime without indictment by a grand jury. In contrast, the Eighth Amendment prohibits "cruel and unusual" punishments.

Before 1972, most states allowed capital punishment and did so by declaring crimes for which capital punishment could be imposed (usually murder, but sometimes also rape) and then leaving it up to the jury to decide whether capital punishment should be inflicted in a specific case. In 1972, the Supreme Court put a temporary halt to capital punishment, declaring that the process of complete jury discretion was cruel and unusual in that it led to an arbitrary and unequal imposition of the death penalty.[37] According to one justice in this sharply divided case, who received the death penalty and who did not was as arbitrary as who gets hit by lightning. (Figure 2.7 shows the fluctuations in the number of executions per year.)

Various states responded to this decision by requiring juries to follow certain guidelines before imposing the death penalty. In 1976, the Supreme Court ruled 7–2 that the death penalty with such guidelines did not constitute cruel and unusual punishment under the Constitution.[38] Currently, thirty-one states permit capital punishment.[39] In 2016, the Supreme Court struck down Florida's capital punishment system, where the judge and not the jury had the final word on whether the defendant shall be put to death.[40]—Congress allows it for certain federal crimes, including terrorist acts that result in death, murder for hire, kidnappings that result in murder, and murder related to the smuggling of aliens.[41] Dzhokhar Tsarnaev, one of the Boston Marathon bombers, was sentenced to death on May 15, 2015, making him the first person sentenced to death by the federal government since the terrorist attacks on September 11, 2001.[42]

Although the Supreme Court has attempted to limit the unequal application of the death penalty, one clear finding from studies is the effect of the race of the victim: Juries are far more likely to impose the death

Figure 2.7 Annual Executions in the United States, 1960–2019

The number of executions each year dropped significantly in the years before the Supreme Court's temporary halt of capital punishment in 1972, but public support for capital punishment remained high. After the Court reinstituted capital punishment in 1976, the number of executions rose. The number later dipped, as DNA evidence revealing that some death row inmates had been wrongly convicted made the public wary about the death penalty.

Source: Death Penalty Information Center, accessed February 17, 2020, https://deathpenaltyinfo.org/documents/FactSheet.pdf.

penalty when the victim is white than when the victim is black.[43] The Supreme Court has ruled that, even if this were the case overall, someone challenging a death sentence based on such statistics would have to prove that the jury intentionally discriminated in his or her particular case.[44]

The Supreme Court has put limits on who can be sentenced to death. Offenders who were under the age of 18 when their crimes were committed and those convicted of rape, even the rape of a child, cannot receive the death penalty.[45]

Some states have begun to limit their own use of this punishment. The Innocence Project, a group dedicated to reversing convictions of people who were innocent, reports 337 death penalty cases in which DNA testing demonstrated that the wrong person was convicted of the crime.[46] This finding has led many states to reduce the number of death penalty sentences. It has also led many, but not all, states to allow convicted

criminals access to DNA evidence, though the Supreme Court does not require them to do so.[47] Illinois was the first state to suspend the use of the death penalty because the evidence in several death penalty cases was shown to be insufficient in establishing guilt, and the newest scientific methods using DNA exonerated several death row inmates.

In considering how well policy making works in the constitutional system, it is worth noting the inconsistent use of the death penalty across states. If two individuals commit the same crime in different states, one might be put to death and the other might be allowed to live. Should states have their own policies on capital punishment, or should the federal government impose a uniform policy on them? The inconsistent use of the death penalty raises questions about equality under the constitutional system and serves as one of the most important examples of the unintended consequences of our federalist constitutional design.

Construct Your Own Policy

1. Draft a constitutional amendment that would eliminate the death penalty in all fifty states, and include an alternative sentence for crimes that might otherwise qualify for the death penalty.
2. Draft a set of five requirements for the imposition of the death penalty that would apply in all fifty states.

Congress are more likely to be loyal to the president than they are to their own branch of government.[48]

Political parties also allow for greater responsiveness of politicians to the national welfare. In the early pre-party days of the United States, a representative had little incentive to care about national conditions. A voter could decide whether he (virtually all voters were male then) liked or disliked the job that his representative was doing for his district and could vote accordingly, but he had little way of knowing whether the representative was responsible for the state of the nation. With political parties, however, voters can hold a representative of the party in power accountable not just for the job that the representative is doing for the district but also for the job that the government is doing for the nation. Thus, the representatives of the people are more likely to be responsive to the interests of the people.

The Constitution and Democracy

Government under the 1787 Constitution would today be considered severely lacking in both democracy and equality. The government allowed some of the people, mostly white males with property, to choose one chamber of the legislative branch of their government but did not grant the people a direct vote for the other chamber of the legislature or for the chief executive. And a government that allowed slavery would today be a pariah, an outcast, among the nations of the world.

Moreover, in 1787, states regulated the right to vote. Slaves were not allowed to vote, but states differed as to whether women, free blacks, and men without property could vote. In 1790, Georgia, South Carolina, and Virginia prohibited free blacks from voting. South Carolina required voters to believe in God, heaven, and hell. Only New Jersey granted women the right to vote, a right that lasted until 1807. Every state except Vermont required some form of tax payment for voter eligibility.[49]

Yet, compared to the despots and monarchs who had long ruled other countries, the government of 1787 established numerous gateways for participation by the common person. By giving voters a direct say in their state legislatures and at least indirect influence in all branches of the national government, the 1787 Constitution was a striking break with the past, even if it did not live up to the Declaration's statement that "all men are created equal."

Participation is much more widespread today than in 1787. Although the Electoral College continues to play its role every four years, each state allows the people to choose their electors. In addition, amendments to the Constitution have widened the gateways to democracy. Due to the Seventeenth Amendment, the people today directly choose their senators, making that body directly responsive to public wishes. Moreover, voting equality is guaranteed in various ways: Poll taxes are illegal (Twenty-Fourth Amendment), and voting rights, which are now guaranteed to those 18 years old and older (Twenty-Sixth Amendment), may not be abridged due to race (Fifteenth Amendment) or sex (Nineteenth Amendment).

Although the 1787 Constitution allowed the national government to exercise direct control over the citizenry, the tiny size of the national government left the people with far more control over their daily lives than they have today. But it is also the case that today the people have more control over the government. In addition to new constitutional gateways, opportunities for participation are greater than ever, with the Internet relaying information virtually instantly. It is much easier for representatives to be responsive to their constituents' desires when they can easily learn what their constituents believe, and constituents can readily learn what their representatives have done.

Chapter Review

Key Terms

amendment (p. 48). Why did the Framers make amending the Constitution so difficult?

Antifederalists (p. 53). What were the Antifederalist arguments against the proposed Constitution?

Articles of Confederation (p. 36). What were the deficiencies of the Articles of Confederation?

Bill of Rights (p. 43). What are the basic protections in the Bill of Rights?

checks and balances (p. 51). Why does government need checks and balances?

Connecticut Compromise (p. 39). What did the Connecticut Compromise accomplish?

constitution (p. 32). Why is a constitution needed instead of ordinary laws that can say the same things?

Constitutional Convention (p. 37). What were the major compromises reached at the Constitutional Convention?

Declaration of Independence (p. 35). What are the basic principles of the Declaration of Independence?

Electoral College (p. 41). Why does the Constitution provide for an Electoral College?

enumerated powers (p. 39). Why are Congress's powers enumerated?

federalism (p. 51). What does a federal system try to do?

Federalists (p. 53). Who were the Federalists?

general welfare clause (p. 54). What does the general welfare clause do?

implied powers (p. 55). Does the Constitution grant implied powers?

judicial review (p. 48). What is judicial review?

necessary and proper clause (p. 54). What does the necessary and proper clause do?

political parties (p. 61). What role did political parties have under the Constitution?

republic (p. 41). What distinguishes a republic from other forms of government?

separation of powers (p. 51). Why do governments chosen by the people still need a separation of powers?

three-fifths compromise (p. 41). What were the problems of the three-fifths compromise?

veto (p. 45). Why is the president given veto power?

Learning Outcomes: What You Need to...

Know	Test Yourself	Participate

LO 2-1   Assess what drove the colonists to seek independence

Know	Test Yourself	Participate
The colonists declared independence from Britain because they believed that the British Parliament and king were denying their rights as British subjects. Congress's powers under the Articles of Confederation were limited, and the structure the Articles established made governing difficult.	• Define a constitution. • State the colonists' grievances against Great Britain. • Explain the key concepts in the Declaration of Independence. • Describe the problems with the Articles of Confederation.	• Appreciate American political culture. • Formulate grievances you might have about the government today. • Evaluate the impact of governing documents.

LO 2-2   Identify the major compromises at the Constitutional Convention

Know	Test Yourself	Participate
In 1787, delegates from twelve states met in Philadelphia to amend the Articles; instead, they wrote a new Constitution. To secure the assent of all states represented at the Constitutional Convention, the delegates reached compromises between large and small states over representation, between northern and southern states over issues related to slavery, and between those who favored a strong national government and those who favored strong state governments in the balance of power between the two. This newly proposed Constitution was then sent to the states for ratification, and it is, with subsequent amendments, the same Constitution Americans live by today.	• Characterize the delegates to the Constitutional Convention. • Explain how the interests of the large and small states differed. • State why the convention rejected the Virginia Plan. • Explain how the interests of the northern states and the southern states differed. • Describe how the 1787 Constitution protected against too much popular influence. • Recall who would ratify the new Constitution.	• Characterize the people who hold power today. • Justify (or critique) equal representation in the Senate. • Evaluate compromise as a tool for governing.

LO 2-3   Explain how the structure of the Constitution protects liberty

Know	Test Yourself	Participate
The Constitution lays out the structure of democratic government and the means by which the Constitution can be amended. It reflects the Framers' attempt to establish a government powerful enough to ensure public order yet restrained enough to guarantee individual liberty.	• Describe the basic structure of the U.S. Constitution. • Explain how amendments get proposed and ratified. • Evaluate why power is partitioned.	• Evaluate whether the Constitution provides gateways for, or gates against, public participation. • Determine whether the amendment process is too difficult. • Evaluate the dangers of unified power.

Know	Test Yourself	Participate
LO 2-4 Analyze why the Antifederalists opposed the Constitution		
Debates over the ratification of the Constitution centered on a fear of consolidated federal authority over the states, the scope of executive and legislative power, and the lack of a bill of rights. To achieve ratification, the Federalists gave in to Antifederalist demands for a bill of rights, passing one as the first ten amendments to the Constitution.	• Characterize the Federalists and Antifederalists. • Compare competing arguments over who was sovereign under the Constitution. • Explain why the Antifederalists believed the president had too much power. • Explain why the Antifederalists believed Congress had too much power. • Recall which problem in the proposed Constitution the Federalists agreed to correct.	• Identify these positions in politics today. • Argue whether the national government or the people are sovereign today. • Evaluate the extent of presidential power. • Evaluate the extent of congressional power.
LO 2-5 Illustrate how the Constitution has stayed responsive to changing needs		
Subsequent amendments ended slavery, protected the rights of African Americans, and generally extended public participation in government while also expanding federal authority over the states. The constitutional system established in 1787 has also been changed by constitutional interpretation and its operation altered by the development of political parties.	• List the major rights protected by the Bill of Rights. • List the major rights protected by the Civil War amendments. • Explain how amendments have expanded the gateways to public participation. • Describe how the meaning of the Constitution can change without formal amendments. • Discuss potential future changes to the Constitution. • Identify the informal practices that have changed how the Constitution operates.	• Propose new rights that you would like to see constitutionally protected. • Contrast the gateways to public participation that exist today and those that existed in 1787. • Examine the evolution of constitutional meaning, and judge whether it is valid.

3 Federalism

> **"What gets me up in the morning . . . is that I can be a voice for those that don't have one . . . There's no better place to fight for working families than the governor's chair."**[1]

Sewall Hall at the University of Colorado at Boulder, shown on the next page, is a feature of the campus where Governor Brown completed her undergraduate studies.

KATE BROWN
University of Colorado at Boulder

When Kate Brown took her oath of office as governor in February 2015, she became Oregon's second and the thirty-sixth female governor in American history. She also became the first openly bisexual governor in the United States. While her sexuality may have presented a gate to her political ambitions, it proved to be nothing more than a headline.

Brown made her sexual identity public as the result of a news story in the *Oregonian*, the most prominent newspaper in Oregon.[2] As a result of that "outing," she talked about the process of coming out to her legislative colleagues: "Representative Bill Markham, who is over 70 years old, extremely conservative, and a legislator for more than 20 years comes to join me. Over lunch he looks up to say, 'Read in the *Oregonian* a few months ago you were bisexual. Guess that means I still have a chance?!'"[3] It is clear that her colleagues judged and valued her legislative professionalism more than her sexual identity. She joins an increasing number of high-level elected officials across the nation who identify as gay or bisexual. In January 2020, there were seven members of Congress and one U.S. senator, for example, who so identified.[4]

After earning her bachelor's degree from the University of Colorado at Boulder in 1981 in environmental studies and women's studies, Brown pursued a law degree at Lewis and Clark Law School in Portland. She practiced family and juvenile law and began working with two nonprofit organizations the Juvenile Rights Project and the Oregon Women's Health and Wellness Alliance.

Brown began her political career when she was appointed to the Oregon state House of Representatives in 1991. The following year, she won her first election to that seat by a mere seven votes. After serving for six years in the Oregon House, she successfully ran for the state Senate and, in 2008, became the state's first woman to serve as senate majority leader.

In her seventeen years in the Oregon legislature, Brown led the effort to pass Oregon's Family and Medical Leave Act. This legislation made Oregon one of the first states to allow parents to stay home with their sick children without jeopardizing their jobs. She was instrumental in advancing Oregon as the first state to require insurance companies to cover preventive health screenings for women. She also helped pass the Oregon Equality Act prohibiting discrimination in employment and housing on the basis of sexual orientation and was involved in securing Oregon's Family Fairness Act, which legally recognizes committed same-sex relationships as domestic partnerships.[5]

In 2009, Brown was elected Oregon's secretary of state. Oregon does not have a lieutenant governor, who might serve as the sort of state-level vice president. Instead, if there is a vacancy in the governor's office, the secretary of state ascends to that office. In 2015, Governor John Kitzhaber (D) resigned amidst a political scandal, and Brown became governor. In her first years in office, Brown was ambitious in her policy priorities of education, economy, equity, and safety preparedness on Oregon school and college campuses.[6] She proposed and then signed legislation that calls for a gradual rise of the minimum wage to $13.25.

In some ways, Brown's political career has been a matter of being in the right place at the right time. She has been appointed to office twice. Another way to see these events is that Brown pursued gateways when they opened. She was in a position to be appointed to her first elected office as a result of her activities as an attorney and involvement in community organizations. Voting and campaign activities are the most obvious gateways to participating in civic life, but charitable organizations and nonprofits also offer opportunities to get involved. Brown's education put her in a position to walk through gateways, much like many video games have levels that, once achieved, open new portals. Brown's story is one of finding her passions and being ready to accept opportunities as they arise.

She ran successfully for election in 2016, securing the office in her own right with 51 percent of the vote. Kate Brown earned a full four-year term as governor of Oregon with her successful reelection in 2018.

Stephen Finn/Alamy Stock Photo

Why Federalism?

LO 3-1 Explain why the Framers chose a federal system

The delegates to the 1787 Constitutional Convention in Philadelphia recognized that the system of government established by the Articles of Confederation was failing. Congress did not have the authority to regulate commerce or to raise money by taxing citizens or imports; it could only request revenues from the states. Thus, the nation's debts went unpaid, and its credit was sinking. Moreover, trade barriers erected by states against other states impeded commerce. Something had to be done. If the delegates were not able to fix the problems caused by the Articles, James Madison and others feared that the union could disintegrate.[7]

The Granger Collection, NYC

Image 3.1 Benjamin Franklin published this political cartoon in his *Pennsylvania Gazette* on May 9, 1754, shortly after hostilities began in the French and Indian War. It shows New England as one segment and leaves out Delaware and Georgia altogether. Later, during the Revolution, it was a powerful symbol of American unity.

Why Unify?

Federalism presupposes some form of union, so the answer to the question "why federalism?" first requires an answer to the question "why unify?"

The primary answer to the unification question is that some form of union allows smaller political entities to pool their resources to fight a common enemy. The colonists could not have won the Revolutionary War if they had not banded together to fight the British. Benjamin Franklin published his famous "Join, or Die" cartoon to represent the need for the colonists to stick together in military battles in the French and Indian War (1754–63).[8] By the late 1760s, though, the cartoon had come to symbolize the need for united action against British rule. After the Revolution, common threats remained not only from England but also from France and various American Indian tribes.

Beyond military necessity, many colonists considered themselves to be part of a common nation with Americans in the other states. A nation is said to exist when people in a country have a sense of shared identity due to a common origin, history, or ancestry, all of which the colonists shared. This sense of common identity made some form of union not only a military necessity but also a political advantage. The American people, however, also had strong loyalties to their states, an attachment that would have made eliminating states politically impossible. This strong loyalty to the states made the American people wary of awarding too much power to the national government. How strong the national government would be was the subject of heated debate at the Constitutional Convention.

Key Questions
Today the people of the United States no longer share a common origin, history, or ancestry. What are some implications of that lack of a common history?

Confederal, Unitary, and Federal Systems

A **confederal system** had existed under the Articles of Confederation. In a confederal system, independent states grant powers to a national government to rule for the common good in certain limited areas such as defense. The independent states that make up the confederation usually have an equal vote, and the confederation might require unanimous consent or other supermajorities (for example, two-thirds or three-quarters) to pass legislation. The confederal organization usually acts through the states that constitute it rather than acting directly on the citizens of those states (see Figure 3.1).

But the Framers who met in Philadelphia in 1787 were not inclined to continue the confederal system. A majority of the delegates believed that the New Jersey Plan, which would have strengthened the national government but still granted each state one vote and still required a supermajority to pass most important issues, did not go far enough. They knew that the United States needed a stronger national government.

If a confederal system gives hardly any power to the national government, a **unitary system** of government gives it virtually every power. State or regional governments might still exist under a unitary system, but their powers and, in fact, their very existence are entirely up to the national government. The authority of a state or regional government in a pure unitary system is similar to the relationship between a state government today and the cities and counties that exist under the state's jurisdiction. Counties can make local decisions, but they exist only because their state established them, and a county has only the authority the state grants to it.

A confederal system was too weak for the United States, and an overly strong central government would pose its own set of problems. The Framers particularly feared that too much power in any government could lead to tyranny. Freedom would be better guaranteed by dividing governmental powers, rather than by concentrating them in a central government.

confederal system: *System of government in which ultimate authority rests with the regional (for example, state) governments.*

unitary system: *System of government in which ultimate authority rests with the national government.*

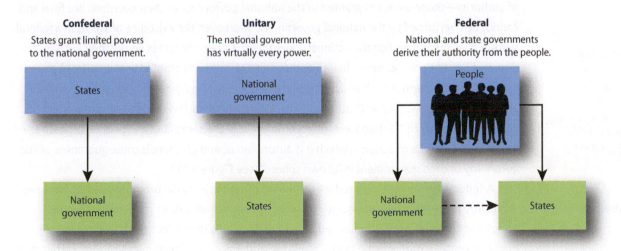

Figure 3.1 Confederal, Unitary, and Federal Systems of Government

Political authority is derived from different sources in these three forms of government. In the U.S. federal system, the people provide political authority to the states and the national government.

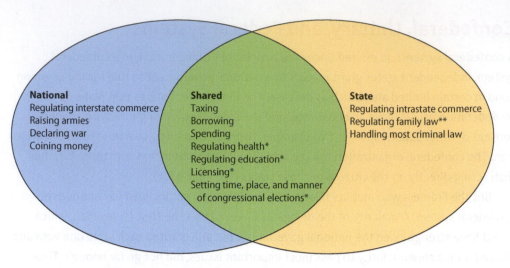

National
Regulating interstate commerce
Raising armies
Declaring war
Coining money

Shared
Taxing
Borrowing
Spending
Regulating health*
Regulating education*
Licensing*
Setting time, place, and manner
   of congressional elections*

State
Regulating intrastate commerce
Regulating family law**
Handling most criminal law

*These were once reserved powers of the states, but the growth of federal authority means that they are now regulated by both.
**Federal courts have eliminated the right of states to prohibit same-sex marriages. See later in this chapter as well as Chapter 5.

Figure 3.2 **Examples of National, State, and Shared Powers**

State governments and the national government exercise political power in several areas, and in some areas, the two levels of government overlap in their authority. For example, both the national and state governments have the power to tax.

federalism: *System of government in which sovereignty is constitutionally divided between national and state governments.*

The Framers thus established a new system of government, **federalism**. A federal system, like that of the United States, mixes features of confederal and unitary governments. The Constitution created one legislative chamber chosen by the people and based on population, and another chosen by the states and based on equal representation. Within the states' areas of authority—those areas not granted to the national government—their decisions are final and cannot be overturned by the national government. Moreover, the existence of states in a federal system does not depend on the national government; rather, the states derive their authority directly from the people. Nevertheless, within areas of authority granted to the national government, or areas of authority shared by the states and the national government, the national government reigns supreme. Political scientist William Riker defines federalism as a system of government in which "(1) two levels of government rule the same land and people, (2) each level has at least one area of action in which it is autonomous, and (3) there is some guarantee of the autonomy of each government in its own sphere" (see Figure 3.2).[9]

Key Questions

Which government has the biggest impact on your day-to-day life—the federal government or your state government? Which government do you know more about?

A federal system not only reduces the risks of tyranny; it also promotes self-government. While any representative democracy involves **self-government**, or government by the people, self-government is enhanced when the decisions that affect the citizens' lives are made by representatives who are local, closer to them, and more similar to them, rather than by representatives who live far away and are dissimilar. Thus, self-government is enhanced when people in Massachusetts, to the extent possible, make rules for the people who live in Massachusetts, while people in Texas make rules for the people who live in Texas.

self-government: *Rule by the people.*

The Framers' choice of a federal system of government was innovative because virtually all of the world's governments at the time were either unitary or confederal. Madison's Virginia Plan did not propose a pure unitary system—Congress could not eliminate the states. However, by giving Congress a complete veto over laws passed by the states and by granting Congress the general authority to pass laws that would promote "the harmony" of the United States,[10] it would have moved the United States in that direction. The American system was an experiment, and its evolution has been shaped by the tensions, even conflicts, inherent in a system in which power is both divided and shared. Since 1787, about two dozen other nations have ordered themselves as federal systems.

Constitutional Framework

LO 3-2 Summarize how the Constitution institutes the federal system

The Constitution lays the framework of the U.S. federal system in a variety of ways. First, the Constitution grants specified powers to the national government, reserving all remaining powers to the states or the people. Second, the Constitution sets limits on both the powers granted to the federal government and the powers reserved to the states. Third, the Constitution lays out the relationships among the several states as well as between the states and the federal government.

Grants of Power

The Constitution lists the grants of power to Congress in Article I, Section 8. These **enumerated powers** include several powers that could only lie in a national government: raising armies, declaring war, and establishing rules for citizenship. The enumerated powers also grant powers that the central government under the Articles of Confederation did not have, including the power to tax to provide for the general welfare, to borrow money, and to regulate interstate and foreign commerce. To the list of powers in Article I, Section 8, the Framers added one final power that would substantially strengthen the national government: the power to make all laws that are "necessary and proper" for carrying out the enumerated powers.

    The **necessary and proper clause** does not grant Congress the authority to pass any law that it desires. Rather, the clause requires that the law be necessary and proper to one of the listed powers, such as collecting taxes or regulating commerce.

    The original Constitution does not list the powers of the state governments, as the states retained all powers that were not prohibited by the Constitution. But to ease the concerns of the Antifederalists who wanted this relationship spelled out in the Constitution, the Tenth Amendment declares that "the powers not delegated to the United States by the Constitution, nor prohibited by it to the States, are reserved to the States respectively, or to the people" (see Figure 3.3 for the amendments that pertain to federalism). The **reserve powers** of the states, sometimes referred to as the police powers, include powers to protect the safety, health, and welfare of their citizens, although the federal government now regulates many of these activities. During the COVID-19 outbreak, for example, some governors exercised police powers in the areas of health and safety by issuing states of emergency, stay-at-home orders, and shelter-in-place requirements. These steps were taken to limit exposure of the contagious virus to residents and "flatten the curve."

enumerated powers: *Powers expressly granted to Congress by the Constitution.*

necessary and proper clause: *Gives Congress the power to pass all laws necessary and proper to the powers enumerated in Article I, Section 8.*

> *Key Questions*
>
> Are there any state powers you think the federal government should have? Are there any federal powers you think should belong to the states?

reserve powers: *Powers retained by the states under the Constitution.*

| Key: | Criminal Procedure | Participation | Equality | Structure | Miscellaneous |

Fifth	1791	Affirms the right to indictment by a grand jury and right to due process; protects against double jeopardy, self-incrimination, and taking of property without just compensation
Tenth	1791	Reserves the powers not granted to the national government to the states or to the people
Eleventh	1798	Prevents citizens from one state from suing another state in federal court
Thirteenth	1865	Prohibits slavery in the United States
Fourteenth	1868	Makes all persons born in the United States citizens of the United States and prohibits states from denying persons within its jurisdiction the privileges or immunities of citizens, the due process of law, and equal protection of the laws; apportionment by whole persons
Fifteenth	1870	Prohibits states from denying the right to vote on account of race
Sixteenth	1913	Grants Congress the power to tax income derived from any source
Seventeenth	1913	Gives the people (instead of state legislatures) the right to choose U.S. senators directly

Figure 3.3 Constitutional Amendments That Pertain to Federalism

These amendments to the Constitution specifically affect federalism in the United States. For example, the Thirteenth Amendment abolished slavery in all states, taking away individual states' ability to decide whether slavery would be allowed in their borders.

However, marriage and divorce laws, insurance regulations, and professional licensing (of teachers and electricians, for example) remain almost exclusively within state authority, though subject to national requirements that states provide due process and equal protection. States have authority to define and prosecute most crimes, but the federal government may do so too, with the most prominent examples including federal laws relating to guns, drugs, bank robbery, and terrorism.

Many powers belong to both the state and national governments. These **concurrent powers** include taxing, borrowing and spending money, making and enforcing laws, establishing court systems, and regulating elections. Many areas that were once exclusively within state authority, such as health care, education (see Public Policy and Federalism: Public Education), and occupational licensing, are now regulated by both the state and the federal governments (see Figure 3.3).

concurrent powers: *Powers held by both the national and state governments in a federal system.*

Limits on Power

The Constitution grants only specified powers to the national government, but even those powers are limited. The Constitution prohibits Congress from suspending the writ of *habeas corpus*, the right of individuals who have been arrested and jailed to go before a judge who determines whether their imprisonment is legal. The Constitution also bars the passage of any law that declares an individual guilty of a crime (a bill of attainder) and any law that makes an act illegal after the fact (an *ex post facto* law).

Following concerns expressed by Antifederalists during the state ratification debates that the proposed Constitution granted the national government too much power, one of the first orders of business for the First Congress was a proposed bill of rights. The first ten amendments to the Constitution created associational freedoms (speech, press, assembly, and religion) that Congress could not abridge; limited the authority of governmental prosecutions against alleged criminals by restricting searches and seizures and guaranteeing the right to counsel and to public trials; and protected certain additional rights, including the right to bear arms and the right to jury trials in civil suits over $20 (see Chapter 4, Civil Liberties, for more details on these rights). The Bill of Rights originally applied only to the national government, not to the states.

The Constitution contains its own set of limits on the state governments. Like the national government, states cannot pass bills of attainder or *ex post facto* laws or create titles of nobility. Moreover, states cannot coin money or enter into treaties or alliances with foreign nations. The Constitution also limits the authority of states to tax imports and exports.

The guarantee clause of the Constitution (Article IV, Section 4) guarantees that states shall have a "Republican Form of Government," meaning that a state cannot establish a pure **direct democracy** (although New England towns sometimes run along these lines), a monarchy, or a dictatorship (here the term *republican* has nothing to do with the Republican Party but refers to representative democracy). In *Federalist* 39, Madison defined a republican form of government as one that "derives all its powers directly or indirectly from the great body of the people; and is administered by persons holding their offices during pleasure, for a limited period, or during good behavior."[11] That is, as long as the people who run the government are selected directly (as in the House of Representatives) or indirectly (as in the Electoral College) by the people, and those officeholders either have limited terms of office (as do the president and members of Congress) or can be removed for not meeting the standards of "good behavior" (as in the judiciary), the government can be considered republican.

direct democracy: *Form of democracy in which political power is exercised directly by citizens.*

The Fourteenth (1868) and Fifteenth (1870) Amendments limit state authority further. The Fourteenth Amendment prohibits the states from denying "any person" due process of law and the equal protection of the laws, and the Fifteenth Amendment prohibits states from denying voting rights on account of race, color, or previous condition of servitude (that is, slavery). The Supreme Court later used the due process clause of the Fourteenth Amendment to require the states to follow most of the provisions of the Bill of Rights (see Chapter 4). Thus, states must protect the same liberties as the federal government does, resulting in a nationalizing of the country's most basic rights. Both the Supreme Court and Congress have used the Fifteenth Amendment to protect equal voting rights in the states and the equal protection clause of the Fourteenth Amendment to protect other civil rights (see Chapter 5, Civil Rights).

Groundwork for Relationships

In the U.S. federal system, where both the states and the federal governments have the final say over different matters, the Constitution specifies the powers of the national government and restrictions on the powers of both the national and the state governments. In addition, it lays the groundwork for the relationship between the national government and the state governments and for relationships among the state governments.

Image 3.2 Latina activist and DREAMer Maxima Guerrero speaking at a town-hall meeting to fellow DREAMers. Guerrero has continued her activism working with PUENTE, an Arizona-based human rights movement, and participated in BLM protests.

Public Policy and Federalism

Public Education

Despite the fact that federally elected politicians talk frequently about the importance of education, the federal government itself funds about 10 percent of all elementary and secondary education spending.[12] The primary reason for this minimal funding is the federal structure. With education among the reserved powers left to the states, state and local governments developed the responsibility for educating the populace. Originally, states set education policy that local communities then implemented through locally elected school boards.[13] Depending on the state, local school boards had differing amounts of power to establish the curriculum, support extracurricular activities, hire and fire teachers, negotiate salaries for school district employees, and set standards for graduation. Over time, funding for elementary and secondary education became based on local property taxes, with some additional assistance from state governments. Just as the overall wealth of local communities and states varies, so does the amount of funding available for education.

The federal government has intervened in public education for two main reasons: to overcome the denial of equality of educational opportunity by the states and to improve the quality of education. The Supreme Court has struck down segregated schools for black students in *Brown v. The Board of Education*[14] and for Mexican Americans in *Cisneros v. Corpus Christi*[15]; however, despite these legal restrictions on segregation, many African American and Latino students continue to attend schools that are predominantly minority, as shown in Figure 3.4.

Today the federal government has numerous programs to provide equal access to education across income level, race, and level of disability. These programs are under the jurisdiction of a variety of agencies. For example, the Department of Health and Human Services (HHS) oversees the Head Start and Early Head Start programs for low-income children, while the Department of Education has programs for homeless children, remedial education programs for disadvantaged children, and programs for children with disabilities under the Individuals with Disabilities Education Act (IDEA).

The federal government has also intervened to improve the quality of education. Congress originally played almost no role in public school (K–12) education, but its role increased after World War II. In 1958, it passed

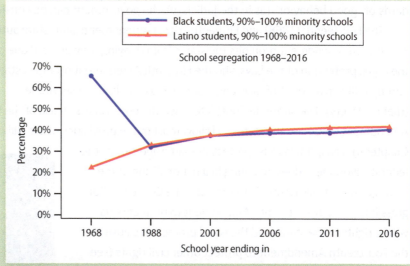

Figure 3.4 **Percent of African American and Latino Students Attending Highly Segregated Schools, 1968–2016**

The percent of African American students attending highly segregated schools (greater than 90 percent minority) dropped sharply between 1968 and 1988 but has slowly risen since then. The percent of Latino students attending highly segregated schools has been increasing as well. That number is now greater for Latino students than for African American students.

Source: Adapted from Erica Frankenberg, Jongyeon Ee, Jennifer B. Ayscue, Gary Orfield, "Harming our Common Future: America's Segregated Schools 65 Years after *Brown*," The Civil Rights Project, Proyecto Derechos Civiles, Center for Education and Civil Rights, May 10 2019, https://civilrightsproject.ucla.edu/research/k-12-education/integration-and-diversity /harming-our-common-future-americas-segregated-schools-65-years-after-brown/Brown-65-050919v4-final.pdf; U.S. Department of Education, Common Core of Data, Public Elementary/Secondary School Universe Survey Data.

the National Defense Education Act, which provided grant money for increased math and science education in elementary and secondary schools. In 1965, Congress passed the Elementary and Secondary Education Act (ESEA) and the Higher Education Act. Each of these programs widened the gateway of access to quality education by increasing federal responsibility to fund specific programs ranging from remedial reading and writing for elementary school children to subsidized loan programs for students in college and graduate school.

Presidents have also initiated educational programs. No Child Left Behind, former President George W. Bush's effort in this area, tried to impose stricter performance and accountability standards for education. Former President Barack Obama, while seeking to set higher standards for the No Child Left Behind program, in 2012 granted partial or full waivers to thirty-three states to give them more flexibility in achieving goals.[16] His administration also supported the "common core," a controversial program that ties some federal spending to states that move toward a national curriculum and greater use of student testing.

States were persuaded into adopting these common standards as part of Obama's Race to the Top initiative, which allowed states to apply for extra federal funds for education provided that they agreed to adopt these standards. Forty-six states and the District of Columbia applied to compete for the federal funds under the Race to the Top program.[17] The total budget for the program, continuing through 2016, is $4 billion established as part of the American Recovery and Reinvestment Act of 2009.[18]

Despite the stronger federal role, however, education under a federal system still permits inequality by allowing a vast disparity in how much money states and local communities choose to spend on it.

Construct Your Own Policy

1. Draft a federal law that would equalize funding for elementary and secondary education within states and across states. Be sure to state the role of the federal government in implementing this change in education funding.

2. Draft legislation that would design national universities directly funded by the federal government in order to improve access to higher education for more students.

Relationships Between the Nation and the States. The Constitution regulates the relationship between the national government and the states through three main clauses: the supremacy clause, the Tenth Amendment, and the sovereign immunity provision of the Eleventh Amendment. The **supremacy clause** (Article VI) makes the Constitution of the United States, plus all laws and treaties made under the Constitution, supreme over state law. Thus, if federal law conflicts with state law, the federal law (assuming it is within the powers of Congress) is supreme. Moreover, because state and federal courts might differ about whether state law and federal law actually conflict in a particular case, the ultimate decision rests with the U.S. Supreme Court.[19]

The supremacy clause also allows for the preemption of state laws. If Congress and the states both seek to regulate an area of concurrent authority, such as pollution control or the minimum wage, the supremacy clause requires states to meet national standards if national standards are higher than state standards. Thus, if a state sets an $8 per hour minimum wage, but Congress sets a $10 minimum wage, businesses in the state must abide by the higher national standard, as we saw in Chapter 1, Gateways to American Democracy. On the other hand, states are usually able to set higher standards than the national government does. So if Congress sets a minimum wage of $9 per hour, but a state sets a minimum wage

supremacy clause: *Makes federal law supreme over state laws (Article VI).*

of $11, businesses in the state must pay the higher state rate. There are two exceptions. First, Congress can declare that it has preempted state legislation in that area, meaning only Congress can legislate on the topic. For example, Congress preempted state regulation of warnings on cigarette packages, prohibiting the states from adding their own warnings. Second, even if Congress has not explicitly declared that it has preempted state activity, the Supreme Court can rule that Congress's regulation is so thorough that Congress must have intended to "occupy the field," thus disallowing state regulations. The Supreme Court struck down state regulations of Communist activities under this exception.

More recently, in response to illegal immigration into the United States, Arizona and various other states have passed their own laws to deal with the problems, such as the right of local police officers to request documentation of those suspected of being in the United States illegally as well as harsh punishment for employers who hire undocumented workers. In 2012, the Supreme Court declared that federal law preempted most of the provisions of the Arizona law but did allow Arizona to confirm people's immigration status while enforcing other laws.

sanctuary jurisdiction: *A state or local government that enacts laws or policies that limit its cooperation with federal immigration enforcement officials.*

There have also been attempts from states, cities, and counties to assert their authority in a different direction. Four states, California, Colorado, New Mexico, and Oregon, along with over 120 counties and cities such as Berkley, Austin, Denver, New Orleans, Philadelphia, and Houston (and thirty others) have become what are known as **sanctuary jurisdictions**. Those states, counties, and cities have laws, ordinances, or policies that limit their cooperation with the Immigration and Customs Enforcement agency of the federal government regarding undocumented immigrants. As of 2017, there were 171 such jurisdictions whose policies are at odds with current federal immigration policies.[20]

As noted earlier, the Tenth Amendment states that all powers not delegated to the national government under the Constitution are reserved to the states or to the people. The Articles of Confederation had a similar clause, but it included the word *expressly* before the word *delegated*. Because the Tenth Amendment omits the word *expressly*, the implication is that the national government retains the sort of **implied powers** granted by the necessary and proper clause.

implied powers: *Powers not expressly granted to Congress but added through the necessary and proper clause.*

If the government illegally harms an individual or seizes a person's property, that person might be inclined to sue the government. The doctrine of sovereign immunity, however, means that a government cannot be sued without its permission. For example, a state might choose to allow suits against it for racial discrimination but might choose to prohibit suits based on the hours or wages of state employees. In a federal system with both state and federal courts, however, a state can prevent suits against itself in its own courts simply by passing a law preventing such suits. It cannot necessarily prevent lawsuits against it in federal court. Thus, in 1793, the Supreme Court allowed the lawsuit of a South Carolina man against the state of Georgia.[21] Following this decision, Congress proposed and the states quickly ratified the Eleventh Amendment, which prohibits federal courts from hearing suits against a state by citizens of another state. The Eleventh Amendment is not absolute: Congress can allow suits based on provisions in constitutional amendments passed after the Eleventh, such as the due process and equal protection clauses of the Fourteenth Amendment.

commerce clause: *Gives Congress the power to regulate commerce with foreign nations, with Indian tribes, and among the various states (Article I, Section 8).*

Relationships Among the States.   One of the many problems of governance under the Articles of Confederation was that the states could establish trade barriers against one another, thus limiting economic growth. Therefore, in the **commerce clause** (Article I, Section 8), the Constitution established Congress's exclusive authority to regulate commerce among the states. Thus states may not establish trade barriers against goods from other states. For example, a state may tax goods from other states equal to the amount that it taxes goods produced in its own state, but it cannot charge extra taxes on goods that are made out of state. Congress cannot establish trade barriers in interstate commerce either because Article I, Section 9, prohibits Congress from taxing exports from any state.

The Constitution also requires agreements between two or more states to receive the approval of Congress. States that share rivers, lakes, or other natural resources frequently make agreements over the use of their shared resources so that no one state overuses or overpollutes those resources.[22]

Image 3.3 The Supreme Court ruled in *Obergefell v. Hodges* (2015) that same-sex marriages are legal. The White House was lit in rainbow lights in celebration.

Article IV of the Constitution establishes additional rules that guide relationships among the states. The full faith and credit clause generally requires states to accept court decisions made in other states. But the clause allows Congress to create exceptions. What happens in Vegas does not necessarily stay in Vegas, as couples who are married (or divorced) there are married (or divorced) throughout the United States. This seemingly simple constitutional rule was controversial, as some states had recognized same-sex marriages as valid while others did not. Under the full faith and credit clause, same-sex marriage performed in Massachusetts would presumably be valid throughout the nation. Congress passed and President William (Bill) Clinton signed one such exception into law with the Defense of Marriage Act (1996), which relieves the federal government and the states of the obligation of accepting the validity of same-sex marriages performed in other states. President Barack Obama, however, believing the law unconstitutional, in 2011 ordered the Justice Department not to defend it. In 2013, the Supreme Court declared that the provision of the act that prevented the federal government from recognizing same-sex marriages legally performed in other states was unconstitutional.[23] Moreover, the Supreme Court ruled in 2015 that states must allow same-sex couples to marry. (See Chapter 6, Supreme Court Cases: *Obergefell v. Hodges*.)

Through its privileges and immunities clause, Article IV also requires states to treat people from other states as equal to their own residents. Thus, a state may not limit the right to practice law to residents, nor may it require people to live in the state for a set amount of time to receive welfare benefits. The courts, however, have allowed certain exceptions to this constitutional guarantee, the most notable being the higher tuition that out-of-state residents pay at state universities.

Key Questions
Should out-of-state students pay higher tuition at state universities? Why or why not?

The Changing Nature of American Federalism

LO 3-3 Outline how U.S. federalism has changed over time

The ratification of the Constitution pitted the state-centered Antifederalists against the nation-centered Federalists, and pro-state and pro-nation interests have contested the relative balance between the two ever since. Because a federal system presupposes separate states with guaranteed rights, tension between the layers of government is built-in and inevitable. People who believe in relatively more national power contend that the national government does not derive its powers from the states, but from the people. They cite as evidence the statement in the Preamble that the Constitution was established by "We, the People of the United States." Others believe in greater state power, a view that considers the national government to be an agreement by thirteen independent states (the original colonies) to delegate certain limited powers that they had held to a national government. Those patriots would have preferred the Constitution begin, "We, the States . . ."[24]

From the origins of a two-party system during George Washington's presidency (1789–97) through the expansion of national authority over health care under Barack Obama, politicians and citizens have fought over the proper role of the national and state governments. Different eras show a dominance of one view over the other, but even when one side dominates, the other side pushes back. The nation began with a period of nationalization that lasted until around 1835, followed by the movement toward secession and civil war. Following the Civil War, the states and the federal government had clearly separate powers. In the era following the Great Depression and the election of Franklin Delano Roosevelt (1933–45) in 1932, national power grew enormously, only to retreat slightly following the election of Richard M. Nixon (1969–74) in 1968.

Throughout these eras, as we shall see, a recurring substantive theme in the federalism debate has involved racial equality. Americans might have sincere preferences about the relative authority of the national and the state governments, but politicians can also use federalism arguments to mask substantive concerns. For example, while Republicans in recent years have generally supported state authority more often than Democrats, Democrats will support state authority when states support liberal policies, such as medical marijuana, or now in many states, marijuana decriminalization, and Republicans will be particularly supportive of state authority when it supports policies favored by conservatives, such as tighter regulations on immigrants.[25]

Nationalization in the Founding Generation (Approximately 1789–1832)

George Washington did not run as the candidate of any political party in 1789 and 1792, and his administration had no organized opposition. Within his administration, however, divisions over the extent of the authority of the national government split Secretary of the Treasury Alexander Hamilton and his allies from Secretary of State Thomas Jefferson and his allies. Hamilton favored a nation-centered federalism. He sought expansive federal power, and in 1790 proposed that Congress establish the National Bank of the United States under a broad reading of the necessary and proper clause. Jefferson, who favored a state-centered federalism, unsuccessfully opposed the bank, which Congress created with a twenty-year charter. Jefferson's allies, however, were able to limit Hamilton's plan to promote manufacturing through subsidies to producers and taxes on imports. The split between Hamilton and Jefferson over federal authority and other issues led to the development of the first party system in the United States, with the pro-national Hamiltonians labeling themselves the Federalist Party, and the Jeffersonian supporters of **states' rights** labeling themselves the Democratic-Republicans (see Chapter 9, Political Parties).

states' rights: *View that states have strong independent authority to resist federal rules under the Constitution*

Key Questions

What do supporters of states' rights think states should have the right to do? What responsibilities do they think the federal government should have?

In 1798, when the Federalist administration of John Adams (1797–1801) passed the Sedition Act (see Chapter 4), making criticism of the government illegal, Jefferson wrote a resolution adopted by the Kentucky legislature that declared the act void, claiming that states could decide for themselves which national laws to obey. James Madison authored a similar resolution that the Virginia legislature passed. Known as the Virginia and Kentucky Resolutions, these acts argued for **nullification**, the right of states to nullify, or reject, national laws that went beyond the powers granted in the Constitution. Although the Virginia and Kentucky Resolutions met with little approval outside their home states, the doctrine of nullification has reappeared when pro-state forces have questioned national authority, with the most notable example being the run-up to the Civil War. Efforts at nullification have continued with the Arizona House of Representatives' approval of a bill reaffirming the state's ability to refuse cooperation with the federal government when it deems appropriate to do so. For example, Arizona and eight other states enacted legislation that nullifies federal gun laws in those states.[26]

nullification: *Right of states to invalidate acts of Congress they believe to be illegal.*

The debate over national authority to establish a bank resurfaced after the first National Bank charter expired, and Congress chartered a Second National Bank. The Supreme Court resolved this issue in *McCulloch v. Maryland* (1819) in an opinion written by Federalist Chief Justice John Marshall.[27] Marshall stated that Congress had the explicit authority to coin money and collect taxes and declared that the creation of a bank helped reach those goals. Thus creating a bank was an implied power that fell within the scope of authority granted by the necessary and proper clause (see Supreme Court Cases: *McCulloch v. Maryland*).

McCulloch v. Maryland: *The 1819 Supreme Court decision upholding the right of Congress to create a bank.*

Five years later, the Court, in another opinion by Marshall, established a broad construction, or interpretation, of Congress's enumerated power to regulate interstate commerce. In *Gibbons v. Ogden* (1824), the Court ruled that Congress's authority to regulate commerce among the states gave it, rather than the states, the authority to manage the licensing of steamboats traveling between New York and New Jersey. Marshall further declared that the authority of Congress to regulate commerce between the states did not begin or end at state boundaries but necessarily included commercial activities interior to each state.[28] Between the decisions in *McCulloch* and *Gibbons*, the Supreme Court under Marshall supported the Federalist Party position of a strong national government with expansive powers.

The Revolt Against National Authority: Nullification, Slavery, and the Civil War (Approximately 1832–65)

As Marshall's Supreme Court pushed the United States in a national direction, the precedent set by the Virginia and Kentucky Resolutions led some states to claim the right to disregard national laws that they believed were unconstitutional or merely unwise. Several New England states threatened to ignore the Embargo Act of 1807, and, in 1828, Vice President John C. Calhoun insisted on South Carolina's right to nullify a federal tariff. As the union was merely a compact among the states, Calhoun argued, dissenting states even had the right to **secede**. Against such claims, Senator Daniel Webster insisted that the union was not a compact of states, but a compact among the people of the United States. President Andrew Jackson (1829–37) reinforced Webster's argument in offering this toast: "Our Union. It must be preserved." Whereupon Calhoun rose to counter Jackson: "The Union, next to our liberty, most dear."[29]

secede: *To formally withdraw from a nation-state.*

Supreme Court Cases

McCulloch v. Maryland (1819)

QUESTION: May the federal government establish a bank? If so, does a state have the right to tax that bank?

ORAL ARGUMENT: February 22, 1819

DECISION: March 6, 1819 (read at http://www.law.cornell.edu/supremecourt/text/17/316)

OUTCOME: Yes, the bank is constitutional, and no, Maryland may not tax it (6–0).

Following the decision of Congress to establish the Second National Bank, the state of Maryland imposed a tax on the Maryland branch. The bank manager, James McCulloch, refused to pay the tax, and Maryland brought suit. The Maryland Supreme Court ruled that the bank was unconstitutional because the Constitution does not grant Congress the specific authority to create a bank. McCulloch appealed to the Supreme Court.

Attorney Daniel Webster, who had served in the House and would later serve in the Senate and as secretary of state, represented McCulloch before the Supreme Court. Among the most famed litigators of his day, Webster also represented the nationalist position before the Supreme Court in a District of Columbia lottery case and a New York steamboat case.*

The Supreme Court's decision, written by Chief Justice John Marshall, began by accepting the nation-centered view of the Constitution's founding: Rather than a compact of states, the government established by the Constitution "proceeds directly from the people; is 'ordained and established,' in the name of the people."

Regarding the power to establish a bank, Marshall noted that while the Constitution makes no reference to a bank, it does provide for coining and borrowing money, paying government debts, and levying taxes. It also allows Congress to pass all laws that are "necessary and proper" to any of the enumerated powers. Declaring that "necessary and proper" does

not mean "absolutely necessary," Marshall read the necessary and proper clause to mean "ordinary and appropriate."

In explaining the scope of the necessary and proper clause, Marshall declared, "Let the end be legitimate, let it be within the scope of the Constitution, and all means which are appropriate, which are plainly adapted to that end, which are not prohibited, but consist with the letter and spirit of the Constitution, are constitutional." Thus, creating a bank was an appropriate means of legitimate ends: regulating money and collecting taxes.

As for state taxation of the bank, Marshall based his response on the supremacy clause, observing that "the power to tax involves the power to destroy." Because states cannot destroy creations of the federal government, neither can they tax them.

The *McCulloch* decision created a broad scope for implied powers under the Constitution—powers that are not explicitly in the Constitution but are related to powers that are. Without this broad set of implied powers, Congress could not establish criminal laws for most offenses, investigate executive wrongdoing, provide student loans, establish administrative agencies, or conduct many of the other activities it routinely engages in today.

Thinking Critically

1. If Congress does not have the express authority to establish a national bank, by what authority may it do so?

2. What is the harm to federalism if a state can tax a national bank?

*Gibbons v. Ogden, 22 U.S. 1 (1824).

Although disagreements over federal tariff rates proved an insufficient instigation to secede, federal authority to regulate slavery eventually led to secession. Slavery concessions at the Constitutional Convention included the **fugitive slave clause** of Article IV, requiring states to return runaway slaves. Congress passed a Fugitive Slave Law in 1793 that established procedures for the return of slaves. In 1850, as part of the last compromise over slavery, Congress strengthened the national authority over runaways by actually forcing states to aid in their return.

Because nothing in the Constitution suggested that Congress had the power to limit slavery in the states, the most heated contests over congressional authority to regulate slavery involved the territories. This debate split abolitionists who wanted to ban slavery in the territories, states' rights supporters such as John C. Calhoun who thought that slave owners had the right to take their slaves into any territory, and those who favored compromises that would allow slavery in some territories but not in others. In 1857, the Supreme Court sided with the states' rights supporters, declaring in *Dred Scott v. Sandford* that Congress had no authority to regulate slavery in the territories (see Chapter 5).[30]

When Abraham Lincoln (1861–65), who favored federal efforts to prohibit slavery in the territories, won the presidential election of 1860, South Carolina seceded. Virtually every grievance listed by South Carolina involved slavery.[31] Other southern states followed, with most noting the question of slavery,[32] and they soon established their own constitution.

During the Civil War, Lincoln used his power as commander in chief to issue the Emancipation Proclamation, which prohibited slavery in states under rebellion, as slave labor was an asset to the Confederate army. Slaves in some of these states were not emancipated until ratification of the Thirteenth Amendment, which prohibited slavery throughout the nation as of December 18, 1865.

Congresses that followed the Civil War tried to exert federal power over the states to promote equality between freedmen and whites, but President Andrew Johnson (1865–69) vetoed a civil rights bill, claiming it represented a trend toward "centralization and the concentration of all legislative power in the National Government."[33] The bill granted former slaves the rights to make contracts; sue; give evidence; and inherit, purchase, lease, and convey real and personal property. In 1866, Congress passed it over Johnson's veto. But as part of the effort to ensure that all such laws would be constitutional, Congress proposed and the states ratified the Fourteenth Amendment (1868) and the Fifteenth Amendment (1870). These greatly expanded the authority of the national government over the states. The Fourteenth Amendment requires states to provide each person due process of law (see Chapter 4) and the equal protection of the laws (see Chapter 5). The Fifteenth Amendment prevents states from abridging the right to vote on account of race. Like the Thirteenth, the Fourteenth and the Fifteenth Amendments granted Congress the authority to enforce their provisions by appropriate legislation, thus adding to Congress's enumerated powers.

Cheriss May/NurPhoto/Sipa USA/Newscom

Image 3.4 The Underground Railroad provided assistance to former slaves escaping to freedom. This photo shows hidden passages that existed within houses that served as "stops" on the Underground Railroad.

fugitive slave clause:
Required states to return runaway slaves; negated by the Thirteenth Amendment (Article IV, Section 2).

Key Questions

What was the primary issue(s) that led to the Civil War—slavery, states' rights, or something else? What type of evidence would help answer this question?

Layer cake

Marble cake

Figure 3.5 **Dual Federalism and Cooperative Federalism**

Dual federalism has been likened to a layer cake (left), and cooperative federalism has been likened to a marble cake (right).

Source: LAITS, University of Texas College of Liberal Arts, © Cengage

In 1883, however, the Supreme Court decided in the *Civil Rights Cases* to keep Congress's powers within the words of the amendments: Congress could prevent states from denying people equality, but it could not prevent private businesses or individuals from doing so, for example, by refusing to hire former slaves or to serve them at inns or restaurants. The Court thus invalidated Congress's Civil Rights Act of 1875, which had prohibited this type of private discrimination. This era, covering the period before and after the Civil War, saw the defeat of the most strident (secessionist) state-centered views, but with the Supreme Court's interpretation of the Civil War amendments, state authority remained strong.

Dual Federalism (Approximately 1865–1932)

dual federalism: *Doctrine holding that state governments and the federal government have almost completely separate functions.*

Although the supporters of state-centered federalism lost the Civil War, the viewpoint of a national government with limited powers did not disappear. A new viewpoint, **dual federalism**, recognized that while the national government was supreme in some spheres, the state governments remained supreme in others, with layers of authority separate from one another; political scientists later compared this arrangement to a "layer cake"[34] (see Figure 3.5). Thus, the national government would be supreme over issues such as foreign affairs and interstate commerce, and the states would be supreme in matters concerning intrastate commerce and police powers.

The first part of this period of dual federalism left the national government and the states supreme in their respective layers but reduced Congress' range of authority. Regulations of manufacturing and mining remained under the control of the states, even if the goods later crossed state lines and entered interstate commerce. But a countertrend emerged in the latter part of this period. In 1913, Congress passed and the states ratified the Sixteenth Amendment, which granted Congress the power to tax income from whatever source derived, giving the national government access to millions (and later billions and even trillions) of dollars in revenue. The increase in federal authority over areas once left to the states was aided that same year by the ratification of the Seventeenth Amendment, which took the selection of U.S. senators out of the hands of state legislatures and required that they be directly elected by the people of each state. Before 1914, state legislatures hoped senators would be responsive to the needs of the states, but with direct elections, senators had to be responsive to the needs of the people.[35]

Cooperative Federalism: The New Deal and Civil Rights (Approximately 1932–69)

With the onset of the Great Depression following the stock market crash of 1929, the people wanted national action to aid the economy, and the nation-centered federalism signaled by the Sixteenth and Seventeenth Amendments strengthened considerably the ability of the national government to be responsive to those wishes. In 1932, voters elected Franklin Roosevelt as president. During his campaign, Roosevelt had promised a "New Deal" to Americans who had lost their jobs, their homes, and their savings. Following Roosevelt's inauguration, Congress passed a series of laws designed to lift the ailing economy.

Despite vast support from Congress and the American people for his New Deal policies, Roosevelt saw the Supreme Court strike down one law after another that were designed to lift the ailing economy, often by 5–4 or 6–3 votes. In response, Roosevelt proposed in 1937 to increase the number of justices on the Supreme Court. He would then be able to pack the Court with his own appointees. This controversial **Court-packing plan** met with fierce opposition in Congress. The Supreme Court, however, made passage of the plan unnecessary, for shortly after Roosevelt's proposal, the Court reversed itself and started accepting the broad authority of Congress to regulate the economy.

On taxing and spending, the Court accepted the view that virtually any taxing or spending plan that Congress believed supported the general welfare would be acceptable. Today, for example, although Congress has no direct authority to set drinking ages, it effectively does so by denying federal highway funds to states that set the drinking age under 21; for a variety of reasons, including low voting rates by younger Americans, no states do.

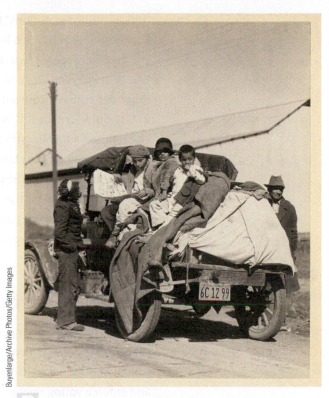

Buyenlarge/Archive Photos/Getty Images

Image 3.5 Migrant Latino farmworkers heading to California to escape the Dust Bowl during the Great Depression.

On commerce, the Court began by accepting the regulation of a giant steel company with operations throughout the United States as an appropriate regulation of interstate commerce.[36] Congress could also use the commerce clause to regulate employment conditions, said the Court, rejecting the Tenth Amendment as a limit on federal power.[37] The Court's definition of what constituted interstate commerce grew to include anything that affected interstate commerce, whether over several states or confined to one state. According to the Court, this included wheat grown on a farm that was consumed on that farm, due to the effect that such wheat and all the similarly used wheat grown by other farmers would have on the market.[38] With federal intervention in manufacturing, farming, and other areas traditionally governed by the states, Roosevelt's cooperative federalism was said by political scientists to more closely resemble a "marble cake," with specific powers under both national and state authority, than the layer-cake structure of dual federalism (see Figure 3.5).[39]

State-centered federalism gained some traction in opposition to the push toward equality and civil rights. Following President Harry S. Truman's (1945–53) expressed support for national protections of civil rights, southern segregationists formed the States' Rights Democratic Party and ran South Carolina Governor Strom Thurmond for president in 1948. Then, in *Brown v. Board of Education*, decided in 1954, the Supreme Court struck down school segregation, which had been legally mandated or permitted in twenty states plus the District of Columbia. This Supreme Court decision helped put the federal government at the forefront of the fight for equality. In response to this decision, seven states passed

Court-packing plan:
President Franklin Roosevelt's proposal to add new justices to the Supreme Court so that the Court would uphold his policies.

Key Questions
In what situations do people look the state government versus the federal government to address crisis conditions?

Key Questions

Was the Johnson administration right to use federal power to ensure equality?

"interposition resolutions" that asserted the right to nullify the Supreme Court decision. Such resolutions have no legal validity.

Nation-centered federalism continued to dominate dual federalism through World War II and beyond. President Lyndon Baines Johnson's (1963–69) Great Society program expanded national authority even further, with federal aid to public schools—traditionally a state duty—and health care coverage to the poor (Medicaid) and elderly (Medicare). The Johnson administration gave money to the states for its programs through categorical grants—money for the states to use on priorities set by the national government.

The Johnson administration also expanded national power to ensure greater equality, pushing for passage of the Civil Rights Act (1964), which prohibited job discrimination and segregation in public accommodations, and the Voting Rights Act (1965), which regulated voting rules that had largely been left to the states since the adoption of the Constitution (see Chapter 5).

The New Federalism (Approximately 1969–93)

In one of the last challenges to integration, segregationist Governor George Wallace of Alabama ran for president in 1968. His party, the American Independent Party, condemned what it considered to be the unconstitutional use of federal power to desegregate schools and enforce voting rights.[40] Wallace received more than 9 million votes and won the electoral votes of five states. Although Wallace ultimately lost the race, the strength of his campaign signaled a degree of wariness among voters about the powers of the national government. Other politicians, starting with Richard Nixon, the winner of the 1968 election, responded to these concerns.[41]

Presidents, Congress, and the New Federalism. The Nixon administration began the trend, labeled New Federalism, of shifting powers back to the states.[42] The Nixon administration began a general revenue-sharing program that gave the states greater leeway about how the funds from the national government could be spent. The main idea behind Nixon's federalism was that states could more efficiently spend governmental resources than the enormous federal bureaucracy could.

Republican President Ronald Reagan (1981–89) sought to reduce the power of government in general and, as an avid supporter of the New Federalism, of the federal government in particular. He thus cut back on categorical grants, replacing them with fewer, more flexible block grants, which set fewer restrictions on how the money could be spent. He also eliminated federal aid to state and local governments (see Figure 3.6). Nevertheless, Reagan did sign the National Minimum Drinking Age Act, which withheld a percentage of federal highway funds from states that did not increase their drinking age to 21.

The Modern Era (1993–Present). President Bill Clinton did not have strong views on federalism, but one of his early proposals was a plan for national health insurance for all Americans, traditionally an area that had been left to private parties, such as businesses and individuals, and to the states. Opposition to Clinton's plan led both to the plan's defeat and a Republican platform in the 1994 congressional elections called the Contract with America, which included limits on the powers of the federal government. Voters that year chose Republican majorities in both the House and the Senate.

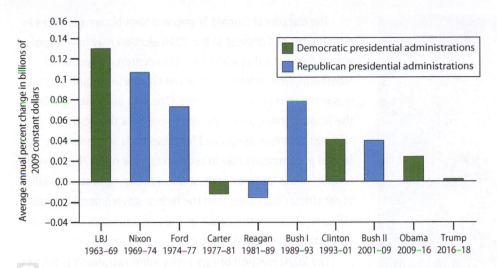

Figure 3.6 **Annual Percent Change in Federal Aid to State and Local Governments, in Constant Dollars**

The amount of federal aid to the states has varied during different presidential administrations. Since Lyndon Johnson's administration, the amount of federal aid to the states has declined dramatically.

Source: Derived by the authors from "Summary Comparison of Total Outlays for Grants to State and Local Governments: 1940–2024 (in Current Dollars, as Percentages of Total Outlays, as Percentages of GDP, and in Constant (FY 2012) Dollars)," accessed March 3, 2020, https://www.whitehouse.gov/wp-content/uploads/2019/03/hist-fy2020.pdf.

Following the Republican victories, Clinton shifted gears and worked with the Republicans on a devolution of power from the national government to the states, declaring that "The era of big government is over."[43] During the Clinton administration, Congress moved to shift the balance of power toward the states in two important ways. First, it limited unfunded mandates—legal requirements Congress imposes on the states (for example, to provide clean air, disability access, or health benefits to poor people under Medicaid) without supplying the resources to accomplish those activities. Second, Clinton and Congress overhauled the federal welfare system, ending the federal guarantee of welfare to poor families with children, leaving final say on welfare spending with the states.

Although Republicans have typically supported state authority over that of the national government since the New Deal, President George W. Bush (2001–09) oversaw an administration that strengthened national authority, sometimes at the expense of the states.[44] His most prominent actions in this regard included the No Child Left Behind Act (2002), which increased federal involvement in public education, and his prescription drug plan for Medicare, which increased federal involvement in health care.[45] The Bush administration went to court along with the auto industry in an attempt to preempt California's fuel economy and emission standards for cars, which were stricter than national standards.

Following the terrorist attacks of September 11, 2001, Congress and the Bush administration expanded national power in various ways, including the establishment of national standards for driver's licenses and new powers to monitor electronic communications.

The Obama administration endorsed state-centered federalism, in some cases: support for permitting states to set higher standards than the federal government's on fuel economy and tailpipe emissions and a reversal of the Bush administration's crackdown on state medical marijuana programs.[46] The Obama administration pushed nation-centered federalism strongly, however, with the enactment of the Affordable Care Act.

Image 3.6 When terrorists hijacked planes and crashed them into the World Trade Center Towers in New York City on September 11, 2001, most Americans said their lives changed forever. As with all national crises, following the terrorist attacks, the national government took a greater share of power because only the national government can protect against foreign adversaries. On October 26, 2001, President George W. Bush signed the USA PATRIOT Act, which granted the federal government increased powers over financial transactions, immigration, and domestic criminal activity.

AP Images/Carmen Taylor

Key Questions

Do you tend to support nation-centered federalism or state-centered federalism? Which is more responsive to citizens? Which ensures citizen equality?

Key Questions

Should policy decisions such as where victims of gender-based violence on college campuses may bring suit for damages be made by states or by the federal government? Why?

The election of Donald Trump and Republican majorities in both houses of Congress in the 2016 election may have signaled voters' dissatisfaction with the nation-centered direction of federalism. One consequence of the change in administrations was in the area of climate change. One year after taking office, the Trump administration moved to roll back the Obama administration's emission and fuel standards and assert the federal government's role in setting clean air rules. This move is a reversal of the Obama administration's relaxing of states' ability to set stricter standards than the federal government's on fuel efficiency and emissions such as the one California and thirteen other states had negotiated with car manufacturers.[47]

The 2020 election brings a new administration's priorities. The Biden administration is likely to follow the lead of the Obama years. In particular, Joe Biden has signaled a nation-centered approach with regard to the COVID-19 pandemic, creating a coronavirus advisory board to lead national efforts to address its spread.

The Supreme Court and the New Federalism.

By nominating William Rehnquist to be chief justice in 1986, Reagan hoped to move the Court toward state-centered federalism. He was not disappointed. As an associate justice (1972–86), Rehnquist had pressed, often alone on the Court, for what the Supreme Court once labeled "Our Federalism."[48] As chief justice (1986–2005), he further advanced New Federalism, now aided by a Republican bloc that grew to include seven justices. The Rehnquist Court put together pro-state majorities in decisions involving interstate commerce and sovereign immunity.

Concerning interstate commerce, for the first time since 1937, the Court rejected national laws as beyond Congress's authority to regulate under the commerce clause. In one case, the Court struck down congressional legislation banning the possession of guns near schools, declaring that the possession of a gun near a school is not an economic activity.[49] Similarly, the Court rejected a central provision of the Violence Against Women Act, which gave victims of gender-based violence the right to sue their attackers in federal court. A Virginia Tech student who had allegedly been raped by members of the football team sued her attacker and Virginia Tech, a state university, in federal court after the state chose not to bring criminal charges. The Court rejected congressional findings on the effect of such violence on commerce, and it ruled that the section of the act that allowed the lawsuits was beyond Congress's authority either under the commerce clause or under its authority to enforce the equal protection of the laws under the Fourteenth Amendment.

Although these decisions stand in contrast to the decidedly pro-national decisions of the Court since the New Deal, most questions of federal authority still are decided in favor of the national government. The Court allowed Congress to condition highway funds on states having a drinking age of 21, as the small amount of funds at risk (5 percent) made the condition a "pressure" to comply and not a "compulsion."[50] And while it did not allow Congress to take away all federal Medicaid dollars for states rejecting the growth in Medicaid under the Affordable Care Act (ACA), it did allow Congress to keep states that rejected the expansion from receiving any new Medicaid money under the act.[51] Indeed, the Supreme Court continues to uphold Congress's authority to regulate commercial activity. Like politicians, the justices' support for federalism is often dependent on the issue involved.

And while the Roberts Court (2005–present) did not uphold the health care law on commerce grounds, it did uphold the law through the taxing clause, thus allowing the further nationalization of health care policy in the United States.[52] The Supreme Court is scheduled to again take up provisions of the Affordable Care Act in late 2020 with a decision unlikely until after the presidential election. The Court will consider a federal appeals court ruling that the individual mandate of the ACA is unconstitutional "because it can no longer be read as a tax."[53]

Federal Aid to States in New Federalism. As we have seen, many state policies involve issues in which the national government does not get involved, whereas in other areas, such as welfare policies, federal mandates and incentives push the states to do what the federal government wants. Federal aid to the states is influenced by a large number of factors, including equal representation in the Senate.[54] The fact that small states have the same number of senators as large states means that small states receive a disproportionate amount of federal aid. For example, in 2018, Wyoming and Alaska received the most aid per capita.[55]

As the president is particularly responsive to the people and party who elected him, it is hardly surprising that states that heavily supported the incumbent president in the previous election, and states whose governors are of the same party as the president, get more federal aid than other states. In addition, recent research suggests that incumbent presidents may selectively direct increased spending toward electorally important swing states in an effort to improve their chances of reelection.[56]

Summing Up: Were the Antifederalists Correct?

The people of the United States ratified the Constitution over the protests of Antifederalists, who claimed that the Constitution gave virtually unlimited powers to the national government. Nevertheless, until the New Deal, either because of congressional inaction or Supreme Court reaction when Congress did act, the powers exercised by the national government were clearly limited. Today, however, due to the popular belief in the need to regulate a complex economy, the historical role that states' rights advocates have played in supporting slavery and segregation, and the Supreme Court's interpretation of the Constitution, Congress has vast powers. The fact that Congress can spend money on virtually anything as long as it is not specifically prohibited by the Constitution, and that the "necessary and proper clause" means "ordinary and appropriate" leads to the conclusion that as far as the powers of the national government are concerned, the Antifederalists were correct: The federal government's powers have few limits. But as the 1994 and perhaps the 2016 elections demonstrate, if the people believe that the national government has too much power, they can—as we have seen—vote for candidates who want to limit that power. In 2015, 60 percent of Americans reported that they thought the federal government had too much power (see Figure 3.7). In the 2016 elections, voters were asked to choose between candidates of two parties with very different views about the balance of the nation–state relationship and chose Republican majorities. In the 2018

Key Questions

Were the Antifederalists right to fear the power of the national government?

elections, voters sent a mixed message about their preferences for party control of Congress. This time, voters chose to maintain a Republican majority in the Senate but gave control of the House of Representatives to the Democrats. In the 2020 election, voters chose to keep a Democratic majority in the House of Representatives, though by a smaller margin. As election returns were completed, voters sent near equal numbers of Democrats and Republicans to the Senate with Georgia finalizing their two Senate races with runoff elections in January. Thus, in the U.S. federal system, the voters get to decide on that balance every two years.

State and Local Governments

LO 3-4 Compare and contrast national and state governments

The Constitution requires that the states maintain a republican form of government, and all have done so by patterning their structure after the national government, with separate legislative, judicial, and executive branches. With the exception of procedures that allow citizens to place proposed laws directly on the ballot, state governments look remarkably similar to the federal government. Local governments, however, use a greater range of organizational options.

State Executive Branches.   All fifty states choose the head of the executive branch by direct election. Most states have four-year gubernatorial terms, limit their governors to two consecutive terms, and provide for succession by the lieutenant governor. Figure 3.8 presents the states that use different rules.

The governors of all fifty states have the authority to veto laws subject to override by the state legislatures. Most states further grant their governors a line-item veto, the ability to veto certain parts of a spending bill without vetoing the entire bill. The president does not have this power, so when Congress passes spending bills, it usually does so by combining tens of thousands of separate spending items in an omnibus bill. The president's choice is to sign the entire bill or to veto it; he cannot veto only the appropriations he disfavors. Governors in forty-four states do have that authority, however, giving them a much stronger tool to determine spending than the president.

Of those forty-four states, twenty-six allow governors to veto not just appropriations but also language in appropriations bills.[57] Wisconsin's veto authority, known as the "Frankenstein" veto, allows the governor to create entirely new language by crossing out words and numbers throughout a bill, leaving behind new language that could radically change the meaning of the law. For example, when the state created a five-person Minority Business Development Board that gave other officials the authority to appoint three of the five members, the governor vetoed some words so that he assumed the authority to appoint all five members.

In addition to the line-item veto, some states grant governors special budgetary authority to limit spending. West Virginia's constitution does not allow the legislature to increase spending on any item over the amount proposed by the governor. New York's

Political Analytics

Antifederalism in Today's Electorate

DURING THE DEBATE OVER THE ADOPTION of the U.S. Constitution, Antifederalists expressed concerns about political power being shifted from the states to the federal government. They feared that the federal government would grow too strong at the expense of state power. This graph shows that in recent years, Americans are increasingly expressing similar concerns. Nearly two-thirds of Americans believe that the federal government has too much power, whereas very few Americans in the past decade or so have believed the federal government has too little power.

These views may be expressed in other ways. As discussed in this chapter, states' rights advocates have resurrected nullification efforts in Arizona. More extreme incidents have occurred, such as the January 2016 armed occupation of the Malheur National Wildlife Refuge in Oregon. Antigovernment activists led by Ammon Bundy occupied the facility for more than one month, and one activist died in the conflict. These are extreme examples, but the views presented in this graph may be fueling some of the anger discussed in Chapter 1.

The following graph shows answers to the question, "Do you think the federal government has too much power, has about the right amount of power, or has too little power?" Examine the graph for changes and trends in Americans' views about the power wielded by the federal government.

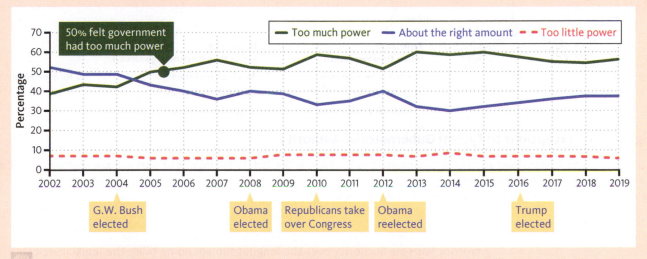

Figure 3.7 **Changing Views on the Power of the U.S. Government**

Source: Gallup News, September 3–15, 2019, accessed March 3, 2020 https://news.gallup.com/poll/27286/government.aspx.

Thinking Critically

1. Do these data support Antifederalist concerns about the growing power of the federal government? Are Americans in 2019 expressing the same concerns as the Antifederalists did in the 1780s?

2. Figure 3.7 highlights 2005 as a year when 50 percent of the public felt the government had too much power. Why is this date important to note?

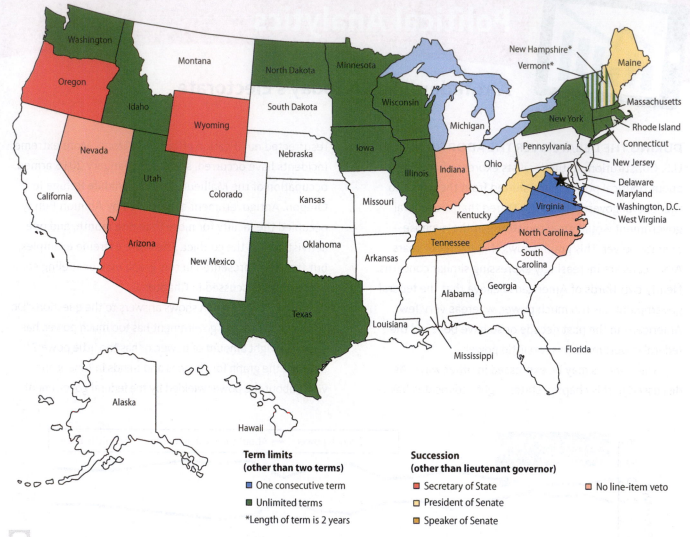

Term limits (other than two terms)
- ■ One consecutive term
- ■ Unlimited terms
- *Length of term is 2 years

Succession (other than lieutenant governor)
- ■ Secretary of State
- ■ President of Senate
- ■ Speaker of Senate
- ■ No line-item veto

Figure 3.8 **Exceptions to Typical Gubernatorial Authority**

States structure their executive branches in varying ways. Texas, for example, is different from most southern and southwestern states because it has no term limits for governors.

Source: © Cengage Learning; data from Council of State Governments, *The Book of the States*, 2019.

governor has sole authority over the language in spending bills. The legislature can increase or decrease the amounts, but it cannot add provisions excluded from the governor's budget, nor can it change formulas for distributing aid contained in spending bills.[58]

Every state except Vermont requires a balanced budget. Unlike the federal government, which can borrow money to pay for spending programs, typically popular spending increases in the states have to be matched by typically unpopular tax increases. Even states with balanced budget requirements can accumulate long-term liabilities. They may, for example, issue bonds to finance capital projects such as roads or bridges. Alternatively, they may underfund future pensions that they will have to pay to their public employees. According to one estimate, the unfunded pension liabilities of state and local governments are now over 4 trillion dollars.[59] Unlike the federal government, state and municipal governments cannot inflate their currency by printing more money. Vallejo, California; Pritchard,

Alabama; Central Falls, Rhode Island; and, most recently, Detroit, Michigan, have all gone into bankruptcy, in part due to unfunded pension obligations.[60] Some of these cities have reemerged with more solid financial standing than before but at a great cost to public workers' pensions, which were cut as a result of those bankruptcies. More broadly, some states are now trying to pass pension-reform laws, as Rhode Island has, that limit annual cost-of-living increases and raise contributions by new employees to increase the funds available to pay future pensions.

The Twenty-Second Amendment (ratified in 1947) limits the president of the United States to two terms in office. Similarly, thirty-five states limit governors to two terms, Virginia limits governors to one consecutive term, and fourteen states allow unlimited terms.

Image 3.7 Governor Michelle Lujan Grisham was elected to New Mexico's top statewide elective office in 2018. She is the second Latina elected governor in the United States.

Governors in Times of Crisis. Recall that states have reserved powers that are often exercised by governors as we saw with the COVID-19 crisis (see page 73 in this chapter). As the coronavirus began to affect state and local communities, some governors responded quicker than others and more rapidly than the federal government. The varying responses among governors and federal authorities created some friction in state–federal relations. Some of the cause for the friction stems from the shared nature of public health policy. While a health crisis such as COVID-19 is a national health and security risk and leads to an economic emergency, it is also an issue in which the states have a critical role in providing medical services to residents and preventing the spread of the disease as much as possible. Americans look to mayors, governors, and the president to solve major problems like a pandemic and, when jurisdictions overlap, coordination among all levels of our federal structure is required.

Among the governors quickest to respond to the spread of COVID-19 with more restrictive measures such as stay-at-home and shelter-in-place orders were Andrew Cuomo (D-NY), Mike DeWine (R-OH), and Andrew Beshear (D-KY). Governors in other states, such as Greg Abbott (R-TX) and Ron DeSantis (R-FL), responded more cautiously and slowly. Even governors from neighboring states took different paths to exercising police powers and securing the health of their citizens. For example, Governor Beshear declared a state of emergency on March 6 in order to flatten the curve of viral infections, an effort to slow the infection rate of the virus and prevent overwhelming hospitals and medical professionals with more cases than they are equipped to handle effectively. In contrast, Tennessee Governor Bill Lee (R-TN) waited until March 12 to declare a state of emergency. Other actions such as closing schools, making medical care readily available, and closing bars and restaurants were taken sooner by Governor Beshear as well.[61]

The COVID-19 pandemic highlights the conflict that may occur between the state executive and the president. Many governors claimed that President Trump responded too slowly to mobilize federal resources and assist states that were in need of face masks, ventilators, and other supplies. The back and forth between the president and some governors may have created confusion on the part of Americans about who is responsible for handling such a crisis.

The Changing Face of U.S. Governors.   Since the start of the republic, white males have been the primary occupants of governors' mansions. The first woman elected governor who was not a wife or widow of a former governor did not win office until 1975.[62] Since 2000, however, women have begun to seek and win the highest state-level executive political office. Since then, thirty-one women have served or are currently serving as U.S. governors.

There is a common path, or political career ladder, followed by most women who run for and win gubernatorial elections. They tend to have served in state legislatures and in other statewide offices, such as lieutenant governor or secretary of state.[63] Holding an elected office is often seen as a positive trait for candidates because it shows voters they are able to win office and understand the job of an elected official.[64] In 2020, there were nine female governors: Kim Reynolds (R-IA), Michelle Lujan Grisham (D-NM), Janet Mills (D-ME), Laura Kelly (D-KS), Kristi Noem (R-SD), Gretchen Whitmer (D-MI), Gina Raimondo (D-RI), Kay Ivey (R-AL), and Kate Brown (D-OR), who was introduced at the opening of this chapter. All served in their state legislatures or in another statewide office. As the Election 2020 section in this chapter shows, the prospects for future women governors depend somewhat on how well potential candidates fare in seeking those lower-level offices. And even when they are finished being governor, these women seek other elected offices. In New Hampshire, for example, Governor Maggie Hassan was in her final term in office and chose to run for U.S. senator in 2016. In a very tight race, Governor Hassan defeated incumbent Senator Kelly Ayotte by fewer than 700 votes, becoming New Hampshire's newest senator.

State Legislative Branches

On the legislative side, forty-nine of the fifty states have bicameral (two-chamber) legislative branches; Nebraska has only a single chamber. Nebraska also has nonpartisan elections, meaning that candidates for election are not listed under a party banner. Most states have four-year terms for their upper chambers and two-year terms for their lower chambers. Some examples of alternative structures are Arizona and Georgia, which have two-year senate terms instead of four-year ones, and North Dakota and Maryland, which have four-year lower chamber terms rather than two-year ones.

State Judicial Branches

Key Questions

What effects do judicial elections have on judges' decisions? What effects should they have?

The greatest differences between the national and the state governments appear at the judicial level. Federal judges are nominated by the president and confirmed by the Senate. States have various procedures for selecting judges: Nearly half use an appointment process for judges on their highest court, while the rest use elections (see Figure 3.9). For states that use appointments, most grant the governor the right to make appointments (usually with the consent of the state senate).

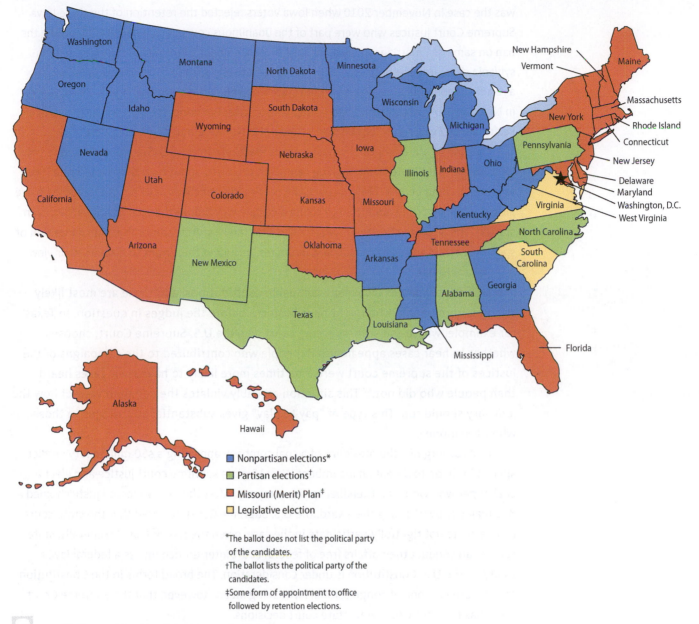

Figure 3.9 Judicial Selection to State Supreme Courts

States choose judges to serve on their Supreme Courts in a variety of ways. While most states use the Missouri Plan process, many, like Nevada, also hold nonpartisan elections to select state Supreme Court judges.

Source: National Center for State Courts, *Methods of Judicial Selection*, http://www.judicialselection.us/judicial_selection/methods/selection_of_judges.cfm?state=.

Legend within figure:
- Nonpartisan elections*
- Partisan elections†
- Missouri (Merit) Plan‡
- Legislative election

*The ballot does not list the political party of the candidates.
†The ballot lists the political party of the candidates.
‡Some form of appointment to office followed by retention elections.

While federal judges serve during good behavior, which essentially means life terms, only Rhode Island does that at the state level, with Massachusetts and New Hampshire judges serving until age 70. In the rest of the states, judges have set terms. For example, in the widely copied **Missouri Plan** for selecting judges, also known as the merit plan, a board of experts recommends candidates to the governor, who selects judges from the list. The selected judges are then subject to retention elections. When a judge's term expires, voters get to vote yes or no on retaining the judge. Although judges overwhelmingly win retention elections, being unresponsive to voter preferences on important issues can cost them their seats. Such

Missouri Plan: *Process for selecting state judges whereby the original nomination is by appointment, and subsequent retention is by a retention election.*

was the case in November 2010 when Iowa voters rejected the retention of the three Iowa Supreme Court justices who were part of the unanimous court decision in 2009 blocking the ban on same-sex marriage in Iowa. In 2013, two incumbent supreme court judges in Pennsylvania overcame a serious challenge by conservative groups to their retention in 2013 as a result of their votes to strike down the state's voter identification law. And in 2014, voters in New Mexico ousted Judge Sheri A. Raphaelson after the nonpartisan New Mexico Judicial Performance Evaluation Commission issued a "Do Not Retain" recommendation.[65]

Election of state judges obviously means election campaigns. States have tried to prohibit judicial candidates from making campaign promises about how they would rule if certain issues came before them in court; the parties in such cases have a right to come before judges who have not committed to ruling a certain way before the trial or appeal has even started. The Supreme Court, however, ruled that the First Amendment's right to freedom of speech protects the right of judicial candidates, including their right to discuss their views on relevant issues.[66]

Judicial campaigns also mean campaign contributions, and these are most likely to come from people who might have business before the judges in question. In Texas, for example, where the state supreme court, like the U.S. Supreme Court, chooses whether to hear cases appealed to it, people who contributed to the campaigns of the justices of the supreme court were nine times more likely to have their cases heard than people who did not.[67] This situation arguably violates the common view of how the judiciary should run. This type of "pay to play" gives substantial advantages to those who have money.

In West Virginia, the president of a coal company appealing a $50 million jury verdict spent $3 million to defeat an incumbent West Virginia supreme court justice and elect a challenger who would be friendlier to the company. After the newly elected justice joined a 3–2 majority overturning the award, the U.S. Supreme Court declared that the state court justice could not rightfully participate in the case, given the risk of bias.[68] Generally, state courts can conduct their affairs free of federal court interference unless a federal law, a treaty, or the U.S. Constitution is under consideration. The broad terms in the Constitution and the broad scope of congressional lawmaking mean, however, that the Supreme Court often has the ability to review state court decisions.

Local Governments

Local governments are far more diverse in function and design than state governments. First, there can be several different layers of local governments, with residents regulated by villages, cities, and towns or townships at the most local level and by counties above that. Some local governments run all local services, including police, schools, and sanitation. Many states, however, delegate specialized activities to special jurisdiction governments, such as school boards, water districts, fire districts, library districts, and sewer districts. The United States contains more than 51,000 special jurisdiction governments plus over 38,000 counties, cities, towns, and other jurisdictions. Overall, there are over 90,000 governmental units in the United States,[69] providing hundreds of thousands of citizens a ready gateway for citizen involvement in public affairs.

Key Questions
What impact does your local government have on you?

Election 2020

Beyond the Presidential Race

Most of the attention on the 2020 election was on the presidential race between Joe Biden and Donald Trump, and rightfully so. But as you have read in this chapter, there are many political offices that were on the 2020 ballot. All 435 seats in the U.S. House of Representatives were up for election. Thirty-five U.S. Senate seats were contested.[70] Across the fifty states, eleven held gubernatorial elections, and eighty-six of the ninety-nine state legislative chambers (house/assembly and senate) held elections in 2020, resulting in almost 6,000 seats being filled.[71] And numerous city councils, school boards, and other jurisdictions also held elections.

Those elections have a tremendous impact on the political landscape of the states, local communities, and national-level offices. The state legislative and gubernatorial results of those races will have an effect on the policy priorities of those states in areas such as public university funding, taxes, and social issues such as access to abortions. Moreover, the partisan makeup of state legislatures and governors' offices may affect when and how they cooperate with the Donald Trump administration. As we saw during the Obama administration, some states were hesitant to participate fully in the Affordable Care Act provisions regarding Medicaid expansion.

The Biden administration will work with a Democratic majority in the House of Representatives but will have to wait for runoff elections in Georgia to decide the two Senators from that state. If Democrats win both races, the Senate will be tied at fifty each with Vice-President Harris casting deciding votes. If Republicans prevail in one or both Senate races in Georgia, they will control the chamber. Depending on the outcomes, Biden will either face mixed majorities in the two houses of Congress or a Democratic Congress in his first two years in office. The 2020 elections brought changes for Democrats and Republicans at the state level.

Republicans maintain more governorships, picking up one governorship (Montana) in the 2020 election. Republicans increase their number of governors from twenty-seven to twenty-eight, while Democrats fell to fifteen. Control of state legislatures changed as well. Since 2018, Republicans controlled both chambers in thirty states, down from thirty-two in 2016. The 2020 election resulted in no change in control of state legislatures, with Republicans holding both chambers in thirty states and Democrats controlling eighteen. One state (Minnesota) splits control, while the remaining legislature, Nebraska, is nonpartisan.

Finally, we use another measure of how Democrats and Republicans fare at the state level called "party control." Party control is when "all three political power bases—both chambers of the legislature and the governorship—are held by the same party." Using that measure, Democrats have gained ground. Compared to 2016 when Democratic state party control was seven, after the 2018 elections, their party control doubled to fourteen. This ascendance of Democratic political power has posed challenges to the Trump administration in the past two years. As a result of the 2020 elections, Republicans control twenty-three states compared to Democrats who hold control in fifteen.

In the longer term, these races have importance for the "political career ladders" they create for upcoming elected officials. Members of Congress, governors, and presidents usually have their political start at lower-level offices such as state legislatures. These offices often are the training grounds for politicians who then may use those experiences as stepping-stones to higher office. These offices may be gateways for new generations of elected officials. The results of those elections are therefore important as they provide a glimpse into the future. There is some evidence, however, that women and candidates of color may find it difficult to break through to these lower offices, which may mean that there may be gates in their way.[72] Table 3.1 shows that the vast majority of state legislators are white men. Thus, the potential pool of candidates with experience for higher office may be more limited for women and racial and ethnic minorities because of prior barriers to entry into the political arena.

Table 3.1   Demographics of State Legislators, 2019

Group	Number	% of All State Legislators
Female	2,145	29
Male	5,238	71
African American	686	9
Asian American/Pacific Islander	125	2
Latino	330	5
White	6,328	85

Source: National Conference of State Legislatures, "NCSL State Votes," 2019, accessed February 15, 2019, http://www.ncsl.org/research/elections-and-campaigns/statevote-2018-state-legislative-races-and-ballot-measures.aspx; National Conference of State Legislatures, "Women in State Legislatures for 2020," accessed March 4, 2020, https://www.ncsl.org/legislators-staff/legislators/womens-legislative-network/women-in-state-legislatures-for-2020.aspx; National Association of Latino Elected Officials, "Latino Elections Officials in America," accessed March 4, 2020, https://naleo.org/at-a-glance/.

Second, local governments, unlike state governments, do not necessarily consist of three separate branches. One reason is that criminal and civil trials are usually handled in state courts, leaving little need for a local community to have its own judicial branch. Many local governments have elected leaders of the executive branch—mayors for villages and cities, county executives for counties, and supervisors for townships—but many use a city-manager system in which the legislative branch appoints a professional administrator to run the executive branch.

The most distinctive form of local government in the United States is the New England town meeting, in which the adult population of the town meets at least once a year to adopt the budget and vote on any legislation being considered. While this gateway to civic involvement is open to all, only about 20 percent of eligible citizens show up at such meetings; as many as 70 percent show up in the smallest towns, but as few as 10 percent attend in the larger ones.[73] This form of direct democracy eliminates concerns about whether the policies pursued by the town legislators are responsive to the wishes of the people; the legislators are the people. But it can work only in small towns.

Direct Democracy

New England town meetings are not the only direct gateways to democracy in American federalism; recall, initiative, and referendum are other examples (see Figure 3.10). Recall is allowed in eighteen states, and it enables citizens who gather enough petition signatures to force a special vote to remove state or local elected officials before their terms expire. Such was the case in Arizona when voters recalled State Senator Russell Pearce, the author of SB 1070, anti-immigration legislation.[74] Wisconsin voters in 2012 reconsidered the tenure of Governor Scott Walker, who had supported legislation that severely curtailed the collective bargaining rights of public employees. Walker won, retaining his office.

Initiative is a process that allows citizens who collect the required number of petition signatures to place proposed laws directly on the ballot for the state's citizens to vote on. Referendum allows legislatures to put certain issues on the ballot for citizen approval and requires legislatures to seek citizen approval for certain actions. Depending on the state, these actions could be proposals to borrow money, increase taxes, or approve constitutional amendments. All fifty states require referenda on some issues. Only twenty-four states allow initiatives.[75] Both procedures enable well-organized citizens to bypass the elected representatives in their state. The U.S. Constitution, in setting specific terms for senators, representatives, and presidents, prohibits recall of federal officials, and in granting all legislative powers to Congress, it similarly prohibits initiative and referendum at the national level.

Image 3.8 The New England town meeting is a fixture in some small towns in the northeastern United States. Residents come together to discuss important local issues and vote directly on resolutions. It is an example of direct democracy in action since there are no representatives who make these decision for the residents.

The number and importance of initiatives have grown in more recent years. In 2008, California voters passed Proposition 8, which banned same-sex marriages in the state. The Supreme Court later upheld a lower court decision striking down that initiative and restoring the right to same-sex marriage in California.[76] Since then and the *Obergefell v. Hodges* (2015) Supreme Court decision, all fifty states allow same-sex marriage (see Chapter 5). In 2014, voters in Alaska, Oregon, and Washington, D.C. approved initiatives legalizing recreational use of marijuana, while voters in Alaska ($9.75), Arkansas ($8.50), Illinois ($10.00), Massachusetts ($11.00), Nebraska ($9.00), and South Dakota ($8.50) approved increases in the minimum wage above the federal rate of $7.25 to the amounts in parentheses.[77] In 2015, however, Ohio voters rejected an initiative to legalize marijuana.[78]

Direct democracy is not without its critics. As are other aspects of American government, initiatives are heavily influenced by money. Although socialists and populists originally pushed for direct democracy to expand the influence of ordinary citizens, the cost of gathering enough signatures to get on the ballot means that initiatives are limited largely to those with great financial resources. For example, almost $4 million was spent in the successful fight to legalize marijuana in Colorado, with 80 percent spent by pro-legalization groups. One group supporting legalization raised almost $1.3 million, while the largest opponent raised $433,000.[79] In the past decade, total spending on state ballot measures was over $4.5 billion.[80]

Efforts to change the initiative process have begun in Arizona, where the House of Representatives recently passed legislation to require signatures from qualified voters from each of the states' thirty legislative districts. These and other efforts in Arizona increase the difficulty of initiatives to qualify for the ballot, thus curbing the effects of direct democracy.[81]

Key Questions
The last time you voted, were there any initiatives or referenda on the ballot? Did you know enough about them to make an informed choice?

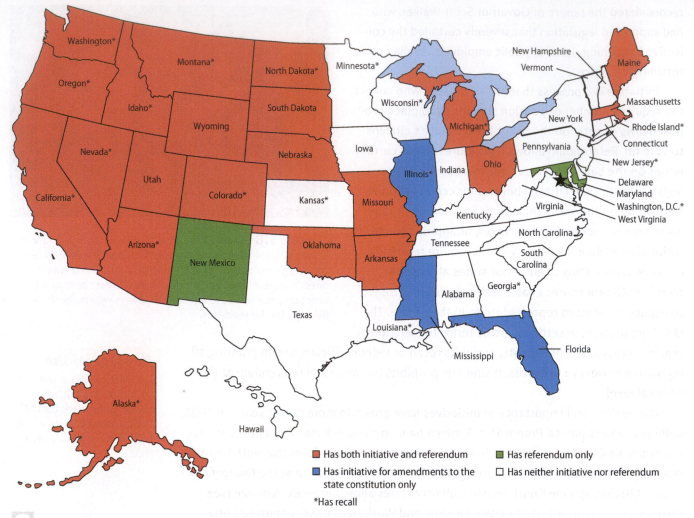

Figure 3.10 **States That Allow Recall, Initiative, and Referendum**

This map shows which states have provisions for direct democracy. Most western states allow for referendum and initiative as means of enacting laws by popular election.

Source: National Conference of State Legislatures, "Initiative, Referendum, and Recall," Accessed March 6, 2020, https://www.ncsl.org/research/elections-and-campaigns/initiative-referendum-and-recall -overview.aspx; Ballotpedia, "Laws governing the referendum process in New Mexico," Accessed March 6, 2020, https://ballotpedia.org/Laws_governing_the_referendum_process_in_New_Mexico

Federalism and Democracy

A federal system has more gateways than a confederal or unitary system. In confederal systems, citizens can influence their local governments, but there is little value in influencing the national government given its limited scope. Alternatively, in unitary systems, the national level has a lot of authority, but citizens cannot work their way through more localized structures to influence it. Federal systems create multiple gateways. However, they also make it less clear who is responsible if policies are not well run. If health care falters, for example, is that the fault of the national government or the state government?

Under a unitary system, there is little doubt about who is responsible if a policy fails. A unitary system also means that diverse state laws are replaced with one set of laws on issues such as medical marijuana, same sex marriage, divorce, and gun control. Given that Americans have different views on these issues, the strength of a federal system is that it allows people in, say, Texas, to live under laws created by other people in Texas, rather than by people throughout the United States. Citizens in states with conservative majorities can obtain conservative government by electing conservative representatives, and citizens in states with liberal majorities can elect liberal representatives.

A unitary system also increases so-called conformity costs by increasing the number of people who disagree with the policies of the government. Conformity costs are not financial; they represent the dissatisfaction that people feel when they live under laws they do not like. Consider medical marijuana, for example. Under a unitary system, the nation would have a single set of medical marijuana laws. Either medical marijuana supporters or opponents would not get their way, regardless of local public opinion. With federalism, each state gets to choose for itself whether to allow the use of medical marijuana. Federalism does not eliminate conformity costs, but it does lower them. Overall, federalism allows the people who live in the most conservative states to have local rules that favor conservative values, and those who live in the most liberal states to choose local rules that favor liberal values. These citizens can also obtain results they desire through direct governing procedures, such as the initiative and referendum. Although initiative procedures presumably provide for greater democratic responsiveness than does filtering preferences through elected representatives, initiatives may be too responsive to citizen desires. Madison, although not referring to the initiative itself, feared direct democracy, believing that citizens were prone to factions that would put self-interest over the best interests of society. Thus, Madison and the Framers preferred a large-scale republic over local democracies, fearful that local majorities would infringe upon the rights of local minorities (see *Federalist* 10 in the Appendix).

Overall, though, federalism enhances democracy by enabling more people to live under laws that are made locally, rather than forcing everyone in the nation to live under all of the same rules. State experiments with direct democracy procedures such as the initiative and referendum give citizens a gateway to influence that they do not have with the national government.

Chapter Review

Key Terms

commerce clause (p. 78). How has the Supreme Court's interpretation of the commerce clause changed over time?

concurrent powers (p. 74). Why do concurrent powers exist?

confederal system (p. 71). What are the likely problems of confederal systems?

Court-packing plan (p. 85). President Franklin Roosevelt's proposal to add new justices to the Supreme Court so that the Court would uphold his policies.

direct democracy (p. 75). What forms of direct democracy exist in the United States?

dual federalism (p. 84). Can dual federalism work in a modern nation?

enumerated powers (p. 73). Why are Congress's powers enumerated?

federalism (p. 72). What type of nation is more likely to adopt a federal system?

fugitive slave clause (p. 83). Why did fugitive slave laws cause so much friction between North and South?

implied powers (p. 78). What are some examples of implied powers?

McCulloch v. Maryland (p. 81). Does Congress need to establish a national bank?

Missouri Plan (p. 95). What are the advantages of appointing, rather than electing, judges?

necessary and proper clause (p. 73). How has the Supreme Court interpreted "necessary and proper"?

nullification (p. 81). What happens to a federal system if the subunits retain the right of nullification?

reserve powers (p. 73). What does it mean that states have reserve powers?

sanctuary jurisdictions (p. 78). Should states have the power to make and enforce policies at odds with those of the federal government in the area of immigration?

secede (p. 81). Should there ever be a right to secede from a national government?

self-government (p. 72). If you were to rank personal liberties, where would you rank self-government?

states' rights (p. 80). What are the arguments behind the states' rights position?

supremacy clause (p. 77). What would happen to the U.S. constitutional system without the supremacy clause?

unitary system (p. 71). What is the effect of unitary systems on gateways to participation?

Learning Outcomes: What You Need to...

Know	Test Yourself	Participate
LO 3-1 Explain why the Framers chose a federal system		
In writing a new Constitution in 1787, the Framers established a new system of government—federalism—in which state and national governments share power.	• Explain why the Founders chose to unify. • Compare the alternatives to federalism.	• Appreciate why you are a citizen of the nation and of a state.
LO 3-2 Summarize how the Constitution institutes the federal system		
The Constitution grants specified powers to the national government, reserving all remaining powers to the states and to the people. It also limits both federal and state powers and lays out the relationships among the states and between the states and the federal government.	• Describe the different types of powers in the Constitution. • State the limits on powers established in the Constitution. • Explain how the Constitution helps set the relationship between the state and federal governments.	• Propose additional limits that you would like to see on governmental power.
LO 3-3 Outline how U.S. federalism has changed over time		
The American system was an experiment, and its evolution has been shaped by the tensions, even conflicts, inherent in a system in which power is both divided and shared. From the beginning, nation- and state-centered interests have been pitted against each other. One recurring substantive theme in the federalism debate has involved slavery, race, and equality, with nation-centered federalism used generally to advance equality for minorities subject to discrimination. Over the years, nation-centered federalism has generally expanded through legislation and court interpretation, although there have been eras in which the Court held Congress back and elections in which the people indicated that they thought the national government had too much power.	• Compare Jefferson's and Hamilton's views on federalism. • Describe the role that federalism played in the run-up to the Civil War. • Explain the "layer cake" analogy in dual federalism. • Compare dual federalism with cooperative federalism. • Explain what led to the New Federalism. • Find Antifederalist arguments in today's political debates.	• Evaluate whether the federal government is too powerful. • Detect friction in your community between state and federal powers. • Decide whether the Antifederalists were correct.

Know	Test Yourself	Participate

LO 3-4 Compare and contrast national and state governments

All fifty states have separate legislative, executive, and judicial branches that look remarkably similar to those of the federal government, while local governments use a greater range of organizational options. The structure of the federal system has a profound effect on public policy, allowing states to learn from each other but sometimes forcing them into competition with each other. The federal system also allows for vast disparities among the states, particularly in the quality of elementary and secondary education. Benefits of federalism include multiple gateways to influence, including methods of direct democracy such as the initiative and referendum. Federalism also enhances democracy by enabling more people to live under laws that are made locally, rather than forcing nationwide conformity.

- Compare the general features of state governments to their national counterparts.
- Compare the features of local governments to their national counterparts.
- Weigh the advantages and disadvantages of direct democracy.

- Lobby a state representative on a state issue that is important to you.
- Lobby a local official on a local issue that is important to you.
- Draft a referendum on which you would like to see your state vote.

Civil Liberties

Courtesy of Stephanie Good

R. STEPHANIE GOOD
Stony Brook University, Stony Brook, New York

"*My greatest regret is that rather than believing in myself, I allowed someone else's opinion to postpone my dreams.*"

Stonybrook University, shown on the next page, is the place where Stephanie Good's passion for political activism was born.

R. Stephanie Good started her college career later in life than many people, waiting until she was in her mid-thirties before enrolling first at Nassau Community College on Long Island in New York and then at nearby Stony Brook University. She graduated from both schools with highest honors, but she was as well known for her political activism as she was for her academic excellence. During her college years, she campaigned for public officials, demonstrated on behalf of environmental issues, and got arrested at Stony Brook as part of a "tent-city" protest over housing for graduate students. Committed to the idea that justice is served only when citizens take action on their own behalf, she went on to law school, earning a law degree at Hofstra University and, ten years later, a master's degree in law.

While practicing law, Good started writing. Her first book, *Law School 101*, presents survival techniques for law school and life as an attorney. Her next two books (both coauthored) uncovered corruption in notorious criminal proceedings. *Aruba: The Tragic Untold Story of Natalee Holloway and Corruption in Paradise*, a *New York Times* best seller, recounts the disappearance and presumed murder of a high school student on a school graduation trip. *A Rush to Injustice* tells the story of the Duke University lacrosse case, in which a reelection-seeking prosecutor maliciously filed felony sexual assault charges against college students whom he knew were innocent.

Good's commitment to protection of the innocent was also personal. When she was in law school, she learned that one of her sons had been subjected to inappropriate solicitations by an instructor at their local church. After she went public about this violation, other families revealed inappropriate touching by the instructor. Yet the judicial system did not then consider the matter to be serious, and the instructor received only a fifteen-day sentence. Years later, when Good thought the instructor might be seeking out her son again, she decided to go online to try to find boys who also received unwarranted attention from the instructor, creating a fictitious 13-year-old girl with the AOL handle "teen2hot4u." That handle attracted enormous interest from adult men interested in sex with an underage girl. Good then contacted the Federal Bureau of Investigation (FBI), which asked her to continue to play out her undercover role. Agents schooled Good on how to avoid violating the rights of the people with whom she communicated

Learning Outcomes

LO 4-1 Identify what civil liberties are

LO 4-2 Explain why civil liberties are limited in times of crisis

LO 4-3 Distinguish what rights of expression the First Amendment protects

LO 4-4 Determine what religious freedoms the First Amendment protects

LO 4-5 Outline how the "right to bear arms" has been interpreted

LO 4-6 Describe what protections the Bill of Rights provides to those accused of crimes

LO 4-7 Assess what constitutes the right to privacy

because although they may have been intent on breaking laws regarding the molestation of children, their rights as citizens also had to be protected, including their right to fair legal proceedings and their right to be considered legally innocent until proven guilty. First, she could not initiate conversations with anyone. Second, she could not be the first person to mention sex. And third, she could not be the first person to suggest a meeting. Despite these restrictions, teen2hot4u attracted the attention of hundreds of men, more than twenty of whom tried to arrange a sexual meeting, got arrested, and then, with Good's testimony, were convicted and sentenced to prison. Good's efforts protected hundreds of young children. She recounted the story in her fourth book, *Exposed: The Harrowing Story of a Mother's Undercover Work with the FBI to Save Children from Internet Sex Predators*. Congressman Tim Bishop (D-NY) awarded Good a certificate of commendation for her work.

Because of her background in criminal investigations, Good taught political science at Stony Brook University, where her real-life experiences have helped make her a tremendously effective and knowledgeable instructor. In both 2012 and 2013, she won the Political Science Department's undergraduate teaching award. When asked why she did not go to college right after high school, she replied that during her teen years, she struggled with family problems, and her guidance counselor told her that she was "not college material."

In a democracy, criminal investigations must be conducted in a way that protects both the victims and society and those who are accused of crimes. Reprehensible crimes, such as sexual abuse of children, test people's willingness to recognize the rights of the accused. Yet without standard and fair criminal proceedings, citizens would be subjected to arbitrary arrest and possibly punishment, as the Duke lacrosse case shows. The tensions surrounding freedom and fair treatment in a democracy extend beyond criminal procedure. Disagreements about politics, particularly during wartime, also test people's willingness to tolerate differences in opinion. Even in peacetime, the tension between liberty, the desire to say

or do what one wants, and order, the need for rules necessary for society to function, divide society. Americans want their homes to be secure against police intrusions, but they also want the police to be able to find evidence of crimes committed by others. They want freedom to follow their personal religious beliefs, but they do not want illegal practices to be allowed just because one religion might endorse them. In this chapter, we examine the balance and tension between liberty and order, with particular attention to the liberties guaranteed in the U.S. Constitution.

What Are Civil Liberties?

LO 4-1 Identify what civil liberties are

In 1787, the most powerful argument of the Antifederalists against the proposed constitution was that it did not protect fundamental liberties. The Antifederalist declared that these liberties, including the rights of conscience and the right of accused criminals to hear the charges against them, needed to be explicitly stated.[1] As we saw in Chapter 2, the Constitution, the Federalists eventually agreed and, to secure ratification of the Constitution, promised to amend it immediately.

Civil Liberties and Civil Rights

civil liberties: *Those rights, such as freedom of speech and religion, that are so fundamental that they are outside the authority of government to regulate.*

Bill of Rights: *First ten amendments to the Constitution, which provide basic political rights.*

natural (unalienable) rights: *Rights that every individual has and that government cannot legitimately take away.*

The **civil liberties** that were then written into the Constitution as the first ten amendments, or **Bill of Rights**, were freedoms that Americans held to be so fundamental that government may not legitimately take them away. This placed into law some of the **natural (unalienable) rights** that Thomas Jefferson wrote about in the Declaration of Independence. These include, among others, freedom of speech and religious belief. Supreme Court Justice Robert Jackson wrote in a 1943 case striking down a mandatory flag salute for school children that the government has no authority whatsoever over what we say or think: "If there is any fixed star in our constitutional constellation, it is that no official, high or petty, can prescribe what shall be orthodox in politics, nationalism, religion, or other matters of opinion or force citizens to confess by word or act their faith therein."[2] Civil *liberties* are outside government's authority to regulate, whereas civil *rights* are rights that government is obliged to protect (see Figure 4.1). These are based on the expectation of equality under the law and relate to the duties of citizenship and to opportunities for full participation in civic life. Civil rights are the subject of the next chapter.

Civil liberties   Civil rights

Figure 4.1 Distinction Between Civil Liberties and Civil Rights

Civil liberties provide a gate or barrier that protects people against interference by the government in fundamental liberties, such as freedom of speech or religion. Civil rights often require active involvement of the government in opening gateways to full civic participation by all, regardless of race, gender, or religion.

Balancing Liberty and Order

The protection of civil liberties requires a governmental system designed to do so. James Madison argued in *Federalist* 10 (see the Appendix) that a representative democracy will be able to keep a minority from violating the rights of others but may not be able to hold back a majority. Thus, if a majority wishes to infringe on rights, it often falls to the judiciary, which is not designed to be responsive to public desires, to protect those rights.[3] In this way, the system of separation of powers and of checks and balances would help ensure the rights of all.

While maximizing individual liberty might seem like a great idea, complete liberty could lead to a breakdown of order. As Supreme Court Justice Oliver Wendell Holmes wrote in a World War I speech case, freedom of speech does not mean that an individual has the right to falsely shout "fire!" in a crowded theater and cause a panic.[4] Nor can liberty completely protect people from police investigations when criminal activity is suspected. Too much freedom can lead to anarchy, a state in which everyone does as he or she chooses without regard to others. Alternatively, too much order can lead to tyranny, a state in which the people are not free to make decisions about the private aspects of their lives. Protecting civil liberties thus requires a balance between individual liberty and public order.

The freedom obtained through civil liberties can conflict not only with order but also with equality. In fact, civil liberties and civil rights sometimes conflict with each other. For example, civil rights laws that forbid businesses to refuse to serve customers because of their race limit freedom of association and infringe on property rights. Efforts at colleges to create an equal environment for all students have led to speech codes that restrict what students can say on campus. Society must decide how to strike such balances, and often that decision is a difficult one. In the case of businesses serving all customers, the nation, through its elected representatives in Congress, decided that the restriction on liberty was well worth the gain in equality. In the case of campus speech codes, students have successfully pressured many universities to rescind speech codes, and where the universities have kept the codes, students have used the gateway of the judicial system to bring lawsuits against their schools. The courts have consistently ruled that speech codes at state universities violate the First Amendment.

Constitutional Rights

The main sources of civil liberties are the Constitution and the Bill of Rights. The articles of the Constitution protect the right to a **writ of *habeas corpus***, the right of individuals to be brought before a judge to have the legality of their imprisonment determined. It also prohibits *ex post facto* laws, which make an act a crime after the act is committed, and bills of attainder, legislative acts that declare individuals guilty of a crime. The Constitution also guarantees the right to a trial by jury.

The Bill of Rights, ratified in 1791, protects additional rights, such as freedom of expression, the right to keep and bear arms, and criminal procedure (see Figure 4.2). We will examine each in detail later in the chapter.

The Bill of Rights and the States

As originally written, the Bill of Rights limited the activities of the national government, not the state governments. Only at the end of the nineteenth century did the Supreme Court slowly begin to apply, or **incorporate**, the provisions of Bill of Rights to the states.

Key Questions
Why aren't civil liberties subject to majority rule?

Key Questions
Which is more important to you, liberty or order? How do you evaluate this decision?

Key Questions
Which is more important to you, liberty or equality? Why? Has this changed over time?

writ of *habeas corpus*: *Right of individuals who have been arrested and jailed to go before a judge, who determines whether their detention is legal.*

incorporate: *To apply provisions of the Bill of Rights to the states.*

Key:	Criminal Procedure	Participation	Equality	Structure	Miscellaneous

First	1791	Prohibits abridging freedoms of religion, speech, press, assembly, and petition
Second	1791	Prohibits abridging the right to bear arms
Third	1791	Prohibits the involuntary quartering of soldiers in a person's home during peacetime
Fourth	1791	Prohibits unreasonable searches and seizures
Fifth	1791	Affirms the right to indictment by a grand jury and right to due process; protects against double jeopardy, self-incrimination, and taking of property without just compensation
Sixth	1791	Affirms rights to speedy and public trial, to confront witnesses, and to counsel
Seventh	1791	Affirms right to jury trials in civil suits over $20
Eighth	1791	Prohibits excessive bail, excessive fines, and cruel and unusual punishments
Ninth	1791	Declares that the enumeration of certain rights does not limit other rights retained by the people
Tenth	1791	Reserves the powers not granted to the national government to the states or to the people
Fourteenth	1868	Makes all persons born in the United States citizens of the United States and prohibits states from denying persons within its jurisdiction the privileges or immunities of citizens, the due process of law, and equal protection of the laws; apportionment by whole persons

Figure 4.2 Constitutional Amendments that Pertain to Civil Liberties

A majority of the early amendments to the Constitution protect civil liberties.

Key Questions

Which government are citizens more likely to need a gate against—national or state?

The First Amendment is explicit about its application to the national government as it forbids certain actions by Congress. But other amendments are not explicitly tied to the national government. Thus, the Fifth Amendment prohibits taking private property without just compensation. Was this a protection of citizens only against actions by the federal government or against their state governments as well?

The original answer, given by the Supreme Court in *Barron v. Baltimore* (1833), was that the Bill of Rights applied to the national government only. Under the *Barron* decision, state governments could, without violating the Constitution, abridge freedom of speech, the press, and religion, conduct unreasonable searches and seizures, and more. State constitutions might protect such rights, but often they did not. During World War I, one citizen of Minnesota was convicted and sentenced to prison for stating that the war was a plot to protect Wall Street investments, another for stating that America needed to be made more democratic.[5] And in 1920, when a Montana farmer spoke ill of the American flag and refused to kiss it, he was sentenced to ten to twenty years of hard labor for violating a state law that prohibited bringing the flag into disrepute.[6]

Key Questions

What laws, if any, should protect the American flag?

The Fourteenth Amendment (1868), which adds several restrictions on what the states can do, became a vehicle for the applications of the Bill of Rights to the states. One section declares, "No State shall make or enforce any law which shall abridge the privileges or immunities of citizens of the United States; nor shall any State deprive any person of life, liberty, or property, without due process of law." Some of those who wrote this amendment stated that one of its purposes was to overturn the *Barron v. Baltimore* decision and make the entire Bill of Rights applicable to the states.[7]

The Supreme Court never agreed with this position, known as total incorporation. But beginning in 1897, it slowly began to use the protection of "life, liberty, or property" in the Fourteenth Amendment's due process clause to incorporate some of the provisions of the Bill of Rights as binding on the states. In the 1897 case, the Court used this clause to hold that states could not deprive a railroad of its property without just compensation, a right similarly protected by the Fifth Amendment.[8] In 1925, the Court assumed that the protection of liberty in the due process clause prevented states from restricting freedom of speech, a right similarly protected by the First Amendment.[9] By 1937, the Court had settled on a process of **selective incorporation**, using the due process clause to bind the states to those provisions of the Bill of Rights that it deems to be fundamental rights.[10] This process helps equalize the protection of rights across the United States.

Today, almost all of the provisions of the First, Second, Fourth, Fifth, Sixth, and Eighth Amendments have been incorporated, with the exception of grand jury indictment and excessive fines (see Table 4.1). Thus, states can indict people, or bring them up on charges, through the decision of judges, though charges in federal courts need the approval of a grand jury, a special jury whose sole duty is to determine whether an individual should be put on trial. The Third Amendment's protection against the quartering of soldiers in one's home during peacetime, a practice that angered the colonists, has not been incorporated but is not likely to be used today. Nor are states required, as the Seventh Amendment commands, to provide jury trials in civil suits over $20.

Once incorporated, the Court needs to determine whether that right has been violated. Generally speaking, rather than rule on each case purely on its own, the Court adopts a test to guide its decision and applies the test to the case at hand to determine whether a particular limitation of rights is acceptable. For the political rights in the Bill of Rights, such as freedom of speech, the Court most commonly uses variations of the **compelling interest test**.

selective incorporation:
Doctrine used by the Supreme Court to make those provisions of the Bill of Rights that are fundamental rights binding on the states.

compelling interest test:
Standard frequently used by the Supreme Court in civil liberties cases to determine whether a state has a compelling interest for infringing on a right and whether the law is narrowly drawn to meet that interest.

Table 4.1   Incorporated and Not Incorporated Provisions of the First Through Eighth Amendments

Amendment	Provisions Incorporated	Provisions Not Incorporated
First	Religion, speech, press, assembly, petition	
Second	Keep and bear arms	
Third		Quarter soldiers
Fourth	No unreasonable searches and seizures	
Fifth	Double jeopardy, self-incrimination, due process, taking of property without just compensation	Grand jury indictment
Sixth	Speedy and public trial, right to confront witnesses, right to counsel	
Seventh		Jury trials in civil suits over $20
Eighth	Cruel and unusual punishments, excessive bail	Excessive fines

Under the compelling interest test, the federal government or a state can limit rights only if the Supreme Court decides that (1) the government has a compelling interest in passing the law (for example, the law is necessary for the functioning of government) and (2) the law is narrowly drawn to meet that interest. For example, the government might have a compelling interest in banning speech that might incite religious wars, but such a law would have to be narrowly drawn so as not to prevent religious speech that merely calls for struggle against oppression. However, even with such a precise definition, individuals have fought over what constitutes a compelling interest throughout American history.

Civil Liberties in Times of Crisis

LO 4-2 Explain why civil liberties are limited in times of crisis

Key Questions

What civil liberties, if any, are you willing to give up to ensure more protection against terrorist attacks?

Attempts to limit civil liberties are more frequent in wartime or when other threats arise as a result of the government's increased concern for order and citizens' increased concerns about security. This pattern has existed from the earliest days of the republic. It continued during the Civil War, the two world wars, the Cold War, and following the terrorist attacks of September 11, 2001. Republican presidential nominee Donald Trump proposed excluding Muslims from the United States in 2016. Popular support for civil liberties usually rebounds after the crisis ends, though the terrorism crisis shows no signs of ending.

From Revolution to Civil War

In the aftermath of the 1789 French Revolution, while Britain and France were at war, the United States engaged in a limited and undeclared war with France over trade issues. In 1798, as part of the war effort, the Federalist-dominated Congress passed the Sedition Act, which, among other things, made it illegal to "write, print, utter, or publish" any "false, scandalous, and malicious writing" about the federal government, either house of Congress, or the president. The Federalist administration of John Adams (1797–1801) used the act to try opposition (Democratic-Republican) officeholders and newspaper owners, and lower courts upheld the act against claims that the convictions violated the freedoms of speech and press as guaranteed by the First Amendment. When Thomas Jefferson (1801–09) and the Democratic-Republicans took power following the election of 1800, they pardoned those convicted under the act, which had by then expired, and refunded the fines they had paid.

During the Civil War, President Abraham Lincoln (1861–65) suspended the writ of *habeas corpus*, thus allowing southern sympathizers in border states—slave states located between the North and South that did not secede from the Union—to be tried by military tribunals rather than by civilian courts. Military tribunals contain fewer procedural safeguards for defendants than do criminal trials, with a two-thirds vote rather than unanimity required for conviction, lesser standards of evidence, and no *habeas corpus* protections. Given the threat the Civil War posed to the United States, Lincoln thought that a restriction on *habeas corpus* was justified. He famously asked, "Are all the laws but one to go unexecuted and the government itself go to pieces lest that one be violated?"[11] Because the authority to suspend *habeas corpus* presumably rests with Congress, Congress subsequently affirmed Lincoln's order. Later, Lambdin Milligan, a civilian, was accused of aiding the Confederacy and was sentenced to hang by a military tribunal in Indiana. Because civilian courts were operating in Indiana, the Supreme Court declared in 1866 (after the war and the threat of secession ended) that the government had no authority to deprive Milligan of his right to a trial by jury.[12]

In 1868, the Supreme Court prepared to hear the appeal of journalist William McCardle, a former Confederate soldier who had been convicted of writing "incendiary and libelous articles" about the war. The pro-Union Congress, angry about the *Milligan* decision and concerned about the *McCardle* case, removed the Supreme Court's appellate jurisdiction over *habeas* petitions. As the Constitution explicitly grants Congress the authority to regulate the Court's appellate jurisdiction, the Court, backing away from a confrontation with Congress, dismissed McCardle's appeal.[13]

World War I

During World War I, Congress passed the Espionage Act of 1917, which made it a crime to obstruct military recruiting, and amendments known as the Sedition Act of 1918, which banned "disloyal, profane, scurrilous or abusive language" about the Constitution or the government of the United States, as well as speech that interfered with the war effort. Subsequently, juries convicted antiwar activist Charles Schenck, for circulating a flyer to draftees that compared the draft to the involuntary servitude prohibited by the Thirteenth Amendment, and Socialist Party presidential candidate Eugene V. Debs, for giving a speech criticizing the war. The Supreme Court upheld both convictions, noting that greater restrictions on speech could be allowed in wartime.[14] The Court also upheld the conviction of Jacob Abrams, an anarchist and immigrant from Russia who had dropped leaflets in Yiddish and English from his New York City tenement calling for a strike to protest sending American troops into Russia.[15] Russia, engulfed by the Communist revolution, had withdrawn from the war, and the United States had sent troops to aid anti-Communist forces. In a forceful dissent, Justice Oliver Wendell Holmes, who had written the opinion of the Court in the *Schenck* and *Debs* cases, voted this time to overturn the conviction, arguing that the First Amendment protected the **marketplace of ideas**. Under this concept, the government should not restrict the expression of ideas because the people are capable of accepting good ideas and rejecting bad ones.

After the war, Congress repealed the Sedition Act, and President Warren G. Harding (1921–23) pardoned Debs. The government also released Abrams from prison but deported him to Russia. Fears that Communism would spread to the United States had led to a crackdown on socialists, Communists, and other radicals. This Red Scare peaked after radicals exploded eight bombs, including one at the house of U.S. Attorney General A. Mitchell Palmer. Following the bombings, the government arrested thousands of Americans, some merely for their speech or associations.[16] Given the atmosphere of fear, the *Washington Post* declared, "There is no time to waste on hairsplitting over infringement of liberty."[17] But when Palmer's warning that radicals would attempt to overthrow the government on May 1, 1920, proved incorrect, the scare began to subside. In no subsequent wars has the government restricted speech as it did with the Sedition Acts of 1798 and 1918.

Key Questions

How free should you be to criticize the government? Should you be less free in wartime? Following a terrorist attack such as 9/11?

marketplace of ideas: *Idea that the government should not restrict the expression of ideas because the people are capable of accepting good ideas and rejecting bad ones.*

Key Questions

Can you trust the people to decide whether an idea has merit? Do good ideas survive and bad ideas fade away?

Image 4.1 Anti-Communist propaganda from the first Red Scare.

Universal History Archive/UIG/Getty Images

The Cold War and Vietnam

The fear of Communism that had led to a suppression of civil liberties following World War I recurred after World War II. As the Soviet Union forcibly installed Communist dictatorships throughout Eastern Europe, Americans worried that Communism would spread further. Though the United States never fought the Soviet Union directly during this period, frosty relations led to the so-called Cold War.

With allegations, convictions, and at least one confession that Communist spies in the United States gave the Soviets secrets about how to build atomic bombs,[18] Senator Joseph McCarthy (R-WI) began indiscriminately accusing Americans of being "card-carrying" members of Communist organizations or being sympathetic "fellow travelers" of such groups. The McCarthy era was similar to the Red Scare in its agitated suspicion that opposition to the government was Communist-inspired. Congress banned the Communist Party and membership therein and held hearings investigating the political views and personal associations of individual citizens. Hollywood studios began blacklisting screenwriters with left-wing sympathies, while state governments and school districts fired teachers and other state workers suspected of having such beliefs. The Supreme Court originally set strict limits on these investigations,[19] but, following the introduction of several bills that would have limited its authority, the Court backed down and accepted them.[20]

During the McCarthy era, the government imprisoned hundreds of individuals for their political views, and thousands more lost their jobs.[21] McCarthy himself began losing support before his movement did. During the televised 1954 hearings over alleged Communist infiltration of the Army, Americans witnessed the recklessness with which McCarthy attacked people's reputations. Edward R. Murrow, host of the TV program *See It Now*, produced a special show on McCarthy using McCarthy's own speeches to demonstrate the extent to which he had been dishonest in his charges. The public reacted overwhelmingly favorably to Murrow's broadcast. A free press—in this case, television—allowed the marketplace of ideas to flourish and led to McCarthy's downfall. In December 1954, the Senate voted 67–22 to censure McCarthy.

But suspicion of people who criticized the government rose again during the Vietnam War. In the mid-1960s COINTELPRO, the counterintelligence program of the FBI, infiltrated and disrupted groups that expressed opposition to mainline American policies, including antiwar, civil rights, left-wing, and white supremacy groups. Later, a Senate investigation by Frank Church (D-ID) into the legality of COINTELPRO revealed that the FBI's activities had included illegal wiretapping, inciting violence, and encouraging Internal Revenue Service audits of suspects. The FBI had targeted even nonviolent antiwar organizations because of a potential for violence and nonviolent citizens who opposed the war because "they gave

Key Questions

Should enemy combatants have the same procedural safeguards as American citizens? What if the enemy combatant is an American citizen?

Key Questions

Should government imprison people for their political views? Or should all views be allowed to be tested in the marketplace of ideas?

'aid and comfort' to violent demonstrators by lending respect-ability to their cause."[22] Congress reacted by putting restrictions on surveillance of political organizations, including limits on the sharing of information between the Central Intelligence Agency (CIA) and the FBI.

The War on Terror

After 9/11, Congress passed the USA PATRIOT Act, which over-turned many of the COINTELPRO reforms, blamed by some for intelligence failures prior to the attacks. The act allowed greater sharing of intelligence information and enhancement of law enforcement's ability to tap telephone and e-mail communica-tions. It also regulated financial transactions with overseas enti-ties and eased the process of deporting immigrants suspected of terrorist activities. Beyond the act, President George W. Bush (2001–2009) claimed the right, as commander in chief, to detain alleged enemy combatants indefinitely, whether U.S. citizens or foreign nationals. Thus Bush declared Jose Padilla, an American allegedly involved in a plan to detonate a radioactive bomb in the United States, an "enemy combatant" and transferred him from civilian to military authority, where he would have few, if any, procedural rights. The government kept Padilla in com-plete isolation for more than three and a half years. Unique among those declared enemy combatants, Padilla had not been captured on the field of battle but on American soil, and, having been born in Brooklyn, he was an American citizen.

When the Supreme Court ruled that noncitizens could not be held indefinitely as enemy combatants, it became clear that the government could not hold Padilla either. So, the Justice Department removed Padilla from military custody and charged him under federal criminal law with providing material support to terrorist organizations. The govern-ment did not charge him with attempting to detonate a radioactive bomb in the United States or with conspiring to commit terrorist acts in the United States, suggesting that the original claims against him might not have held up in a court of law. His trial in Miami, with the full set of constitutional rights, required that Padilla be represented by counsel, that he be allowed to cross-examine witnesses, and that the government prove its case beyond a reasonable doubt. The government proved its case, and a jury quickly determined that Padilla was guilty. The judge then sentenced him to seventeen years in prison; the sentence was increased to twenty-one years by an appeals court judge.[23]

Although fewer rights exist for enemy combatants who are not U.S. citizens,[24] the Supreme Court has ruled that Congress must authorize hearings to determine the legality of the detention of even foreign enemy combatants. Such hearings must be consistent with the 1949 Geneva Conventions, an international treaty that protects the rights of prisoners of war.[25]

Beyond the enemy combatant cases, President Bush and President Obama have ordered warrantless wiretapping of conversations and interception of e-mail between American citizens and suspected foreign terrorists; normally, wiretapping requires a warrant

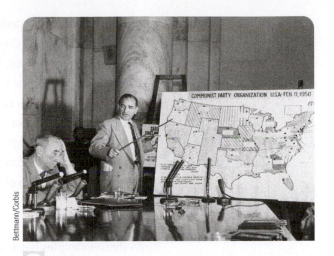

Bettmann/Corbis

Image 4.2 The name of Senator Joseph McCarthy has been attached to an era noted for fear of Communism and the use of fear tactics to suppress freedom of speech and belief. Here, during the 1954 Army-McCarthy hearings, he testifies on Communist Party organizations in the United States with the aid of a huge map. His dishonesty and abusive treatment of witnesses during these hearings turned both the Senate and the public against him.

Key Questions

Should government have access to your phone calls and e-mail messages?

Key Questions

Are alleged terrorists enemy combatants? How does one decide?

Key Questions

Why is it useful to follow the Geneva Conventions?

signed by a judge or magistrate backed by probable cause that a crime is being committed. (See Public Policy and Civil Liberties: National Security Surveillance, p. 118.)

Beyond surveillance, President Trump ordered the execution via an overseas drone airstrike of Iranian general Qasem Suleimani. Suleimani was a terrorist responsible for the killing of many Americans and Trump stated that he was planning an imminent attack on U.S. forces at the time he was assassinated. Details of that attack remain unknown, but CNN obtained a copy of the president's remarks to Republican donors at his Florida resort Mar-a-Lago. Trump told the donors that Suleimani was "saying bad things about our country" and then asked "how much of this s*&% do we have to listen to?"

Civil Liberties and American Values

As these examples have demonstrated, in times of crisis, Congress and the president limit civil liberties to secure order, often with public support. The courts, however, being less responsive to public pressure, can push back against these efforts. Thus, the courts forced the government to try Padilla in civilian courts. The courts have also blocked efforts to censor newspapers even when the government has believed that the publication of certain reports would benefit wartime enemies. Nevertheless, in wartime or other times of crisis, concerns about order are at their highest, and protections for civil liberties by national and state governments typically decline. Following the emergency, a political culture that favors freedom means that public support for civil liberties, as well as the government's protections of those liberties, generally rebounds.

The First Amendment and Freedom of Expression

LO 4-3 Distinguish what rights of expression the First Amendment protects

The civil liberties most at risk during times of crisis are those protected by the First Amendment—freedom of speech, freedom of the press, and freedom of association. In this section, we examine each of these freedoms of expression individually. Their scope has expanded over time, despite occasional ratcheting back during wartime.

Freedom of Speech

Key Questions

Given the nature of terrorist attacks, is it possible to establish a "clear and present danger" before prosecuting the advocacy of unlawful activities?

While the First Amendment declares that "Congress shall make no law . . . abridging the freedom of speech," the Court has never taken the phrase "no law" literally. Prohibitions on speech once included blasphemy (inappropriate references to God) and defamation (speaking ill of others). States have since rescinded such laws, either legislatively or judicially. Today the Court allows limits on advocacy of unlawful activities, the use of fighting words, hate speech, and symbolic speech. The Court also allows the sort of limits imposed by time, place, and manner regulations, such as prohibitions on protests near public schools when they are in session.

Advocacy of Unlawful Activities.   When Justice Holmes wrote, in the opinion in the case of Charles Schenck, that free speech does not mean that a person can falsely shout "fire!" in a theater, he went on to explain that words spoken in wartime may have a different impact than they would in peacetime. "The question in every case," he continued, "is whether the words used are used in such circumstances and are of such a nature as to create a clear and present danger that they will bring about the substantive evils that Congress has a right to prevent." From this statement, the Court adopted the **clear and present danger test**. The Court shifted standards in subsequent decades, at one point allowing states to limit speech that merely had a tendency to cause unlawful acts. But in 1969, the Court moved back toward a stricter protection of civil liberties, ruling that speech cannot be banned unless it leads to "imminent lawless action."[26]

Fighting Words and Hate Speech.   Besides speech that imminently incites unlawful activities, the Supreme Court also allows restrictions on the basis of the fighting words doctrine. "Fighting words" are phrases that might lead the individual to whom they are directed to respond with a punch. Today, hateful racial epithets are the leading examples of fighting words, but when the Supreme Court first developed the doctrine, many milder types of words offended people. Thus, in 1942, the Court used the fighting words doctrine to uphold the conviction of a defendant for calling a town marshal a "God-damned racketeer" and a "damned Fascist."[27]

Related to fighting words is hate speech, which attacks or demeans a group rather than a particular individual. Simon Shiao Tam formed a rock bad "The S*s" with several other Asian-Americans. (The group's actual name, which we do not print here, refers to a common derogatory name for East Asians.) The United States Patent and Trademark office denied the group's request for a trademark on the ground that the requested trademark disparages people of Asian ancestry. A unanimous Supreme Court decision reversed the patent office, declaring the decision to be "viewpoint discrimination."

Over the past thirty years, as we noted earlier, more than 350 public colleges and universities have attempted to provide equal, nonhostile educational environments through speech codes that tell students what they are and are not allowed to say.[28] For example, the University of Wisconsin prohibited speech that created "an intimidating, hostile, or demeaning environment for education [or] university-related work."[29] The University of Connecticut's speech code banned "inappropriately directed laughter" and purposefully excluding people from conversations.[30] Tufts University established three separate free speech zones: public areas, where speech could not be prohibited; classrooms and libraries, where derogatory and demeaning speech could be punished; and dorms, where the university placed the strictest restrictions on speech. The University of Northern Colorado hung 680 #languagematters posters on campus, urging students not to use words that "can reinforce oppression and feelings of discomfort." When someone wrote "All lives matter" and "free speech matters" on a "Black Lives Matter" poster, the school's "Bias Response Team" took down the offending poster, replacing it with one stating "This was the site of a bias-related behavior."[31]

The University of Michigan's speech code prohibited any speech that "stigmatizes or victimizes individuals or groups on the basis of race, ethnicity, religion, sex, sexual orientation, creed, national origin, ancestry, age, marital status, handicap, or Vietnam-era veteran status."

Image 4.3 California State University, Long Beach, posts a sign designating its free-speech zone, now officially renamed the "Speaker's Platform."

Image 4.4 Harvard law professor Ronald Sullivan taught criminal law classes to first year Harvard law students. Sullivan and his wife also served as the first African American house masters at Harvard, working at Winthrop House, an undergraduate dorm. Before he joined the faculty at Harvard, Sullivan won a teaching award at Yale Law School. Criminal defense attorneys often defend disreputable persons; that is part of their job in a country where the Sixth Amendment guarantees all criminal defendants the right to an attorney. When Sullivan agreed to defend accused (and subsequently convicted) serial rapist and Hollywood producer Harvey Weinstein, students protested and he lost his position at Winthrop House.

In addition to the regulations, the university created guidelines that gave examples of prohibited conduct. The examples included stating in class that women are not as good as men in a particular field, not inviting someone to a party because she is a lesbian, excluding someone from a study group because of race or sex, displaying a Confederate flag, telling jokes about gays or lesbians, laughing at jokes about people who stutter, and commenting in a derogatory way about a particular person's physical appearance.[32]

A graduate student in psychology, concerned that Michigan's code would prevent class discussions of theories that claimed the existence of biological differences between sexes and races, brought suit against the code in federal court. The court struck down the code as violating the First Amendment.[33] Two years later, a federal court struck down the University of Wisconsin's speech code.[34] Thus, the courts have made it clear that while state universities may encourage the goal of equality, they cannot do so by limiting First Amendment rights. Note that the First Amendment applies to these schools because they are state universities. The Bill of Rights limits the national government and, through the selective incorporation doctrine, also limits state governments and thus state universities. Private colleges, though subject to certain federal regulations, are not subject to the Bill of Rights.

In 2019, Harvard University relieved law professor Ronald Sullivan of his duties as Dean of Winthrop House for joining the defense team of accused, but later convicted, serial rapist Harvey Weinstein. Jones College in Ellisville, Mississippi, prevented student Mike Brown from trying to recruit fellow students to join the local chapter of Young Americans for Liberty. They also prohibited him from holding up signs supporting the legalization of marijuana. The University of Scranton refused to recognize the conservative student group Turning Point USA. These latter two cases indicate the sort of viewpoint discrimination that is completely inconsistent with freedom-of-speech principles.[35]

The movement to restrict speech on college campuses has moved from public spaces and dorms into the classroom. So-called trigger warnings originally developed among women's rights activists to alert women who may have had traumatic experiences such as physical or sexual violence in their past that an online posting might contain material that could trigger a traumatic memory. Given the rate at which undergraduate students have suffered from these assaults, it is inevitable that any moderate-sized class will have such victims. The idea of trigger warnings in class is to give students warning that readings or classroom lectures might contain such material. For example, the student senate at the University of California at Santa Barbara has resolved that trigger warnings be

Supreme Court Cases

Snyder v. Phelps (2011)

QUESTION: May antimilitary and antigay protesters be sued for the distress they caused to the father of a Marine killed in action in Iraq when they picketed at the Marine's funeral?

ORAL ARGUMENT: October 6, 2010 (listen at http://www.oyez.org/cases/2010-2019/2010/2010_09_751)

DECISION: March 2, 2011 (read at http://www.law.cornell.edu/supct/html/09-751.ZS.html)

OUTCOME: The protesters are protected by the First Amendment because they are speaking out on a question of public concern.

For more than twenty years, the congregation of the Westboro Baptist Church in Topeka, Kansas, has picketed the funerals of members of the U.S. military. The church does so to show its opposition to homosexuality and the army's toleration thereof since the establishment of the "Don't Ask, Don't Tell" policy during the Clinton administration. Their pickets infamously declare that "God hates f* [pejorative for homosexuals]" and "Thank God for Dead Soldiers." These pickets at the funeral of Matthew Snyder aggravated his father, who sued the church, the minister (Fred Phelps, now deceased), and several of Phelps's daughters for intentional infliction of emotional distress. A jury awarded Snyder nearly $11 million in damages. When the U.S. Court of Appeals overturned the verdict, Snyder appealed to the Supreme Court.

The Supreme Court ruled 8–1 in favor of the protesters, declaring that the church's views on homosexuality in the military were a matter of public concern, and as such, it did not matter how crudely those concerns were expressed. They compared this intentional infliction of emotional distress to an earlier case upholding a suit dealing with an individual's credit report, which was purely a private matter. Nor did the Court find that the Westboro protests involved "fighting words," which the Court has ruled to be beyond the protections of the First Amendment. Justice Samuel Alito, in dissent, argued that the First Amendment does not give the church the right to brutalize Matthew's father while he is burying his only son. In an earlier speech case, the Court ruled that the function of the First Amendment is to "invite dispute." The boundary between "inviting dispute," which is protected, and "fighting words," which are not, is not always clear.

Thinking Critically

1. Do you believe that the Westboro Church's position on homosexuals and the military is a question of public concern? Explain.
2. Do you believe that the Westboro Church's protests at the funeral constituted "fighting words"? Explain.

added to course syllabi to alert students to days in which classroom materials "might trigger feelings of emotional or physical distress." Oberlin College has issued official "trigger warning guidelines" that advised faculty to remove triggering materials from their courses entirely if not directly related to the course's learning goals.[36] Trigger warnings have grown substantially in recent years.[37]

Though students at Tufts fought against the university's speech codes, more typically college students have supported restrictions on campus speech. At Yale University, after a 2015 directive from the Intercultural Affairs Committee urged students to be culturally sensitive in their choices of Halloween costumes, lecturer Erika Christakis sent out an e-mail

Key Questions

How do colleges act as marketplaces of ideas? Are any kinds of speech regulation acceptable to you? If so, what?

Key Questions

Can trigger warnings lead to censorship in college classrooms? Under what conditions should they be used?

National Security Surveillance

Protection against terrorist threats requires some restrictions on liberty and privacy. Though many people think of the Central Intelligence Agency (CIA) as the main intelligence agency in the United States, it is the National Security Agency (NSA) that conducts virtually all of the security-related electronic surveillance for the government, such as listening to phone calls and reading e-mails. In 1978, Congress passed the Foreign Intelligence Surveillance Act (FISA). The act established secret FISA courts to determine whether the United States could authorize the NSA to conduct national security wiretaps within the United States. The judges on that court are all appointed by the chief justice of the United States from among the U.S. District Courts, without confirmation by the Senate. Prior to the 9/11 attacks in 2001, the FISA courts had never denied a government request for electronic surveillance (see Figure 4.3).[38]

Just six weeks after the 9/11 attacks on the United States, Congress overwhelmingly passed the USA PATRIOT Act. The act expanded the surveillance capabilities of the United States in several ways: It granted the NSA new authority to monitor e-mail, and it allowed a single warrant to cover all phones that a suspect might use.[39] President Bush ordered warrantless wiretapping (by the NSA) of conversations and interception of e-mail between American citizens and suspected foreign terrorists. Congress did endorse aspects of the president's plan after the *New York Times* published stories about the then-secret program. The program expired, but the Obama administration moved—on national security grounds—to block a lawsuit over the wiretapping brought by an Islamic charity alleged to be involved in terrorist activities.[40] In 2012, a Ninth Circuit

Court of Appeals panel overturned a district court ruling that the program was illegal and blocked damages claimed by the Al-Haramain Islamic Foundation.[41]

Then in 2013, Edward Snowden, a former employee of the NSA, stole and leaked tens of thousands of documents that he had access to. Those documents revealed that the NSA kept track of every phone call made in the United States, regardless of whether there was any evidence of suspicious activity. These records tracked who called whom and when, but they did not record conversations. The NSA believed that such records could help it uncover information to aid in preventing terrorist attacks. Snowden is under federal indictment in the United States and is currently living in Russia under a grant of asylum.

Many Americans were outraged at what they felt to be a violation of their right to privacy as detailed by Snowden. Yet the 1979 Supreme Court case *Smith v. Maryland* seemed to uphold the constitutionality of the government's warrantless use of "pen registers," devices

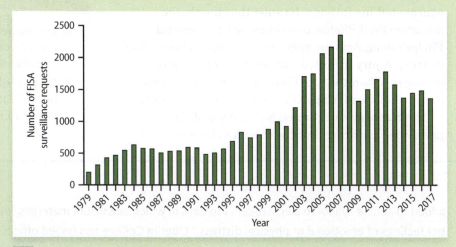

Figure 4.3 **Annual Number of FISA Surveillance Requests**

Note: There were four rejected surveillance applications in 2003, one in 2006, four in 2007, one in 2008, one in 2009, five in 2015, thirty-four in 2016, and thirty-four in 2017. In all other years, FISA courts rejected no surveillance applications.

Source: Electronic Privacy Information Center, Foreign Intelligence Surveillance Act Court Orders 1979-2017, accessed March 2, 2020, https://epic.org/privacy/surveillance/fisa/stats/default.html.

that kept track of who called whom when without recording the conversations. The fact that the Court upheld the use of pen registers suggests that the NSA program is constitutional.[42] President Obama additionally defended the program by stating, "You can't have 100% security and then have 100% privacy and zero inconvenience. You know, we're going to have to make some choices as a society."[43]

Nevertheless, a lower court judge ruled that the ability of the government to obtain these records *en masse* made the violation far more serious than the individual record keeping from the 1979 case.[44] President Obama called for an end to the NSA's bulk collection of data in March 2014.[45] Despite Obama's call to end the data collection, a lower court judge ruled that the NSA's bulk data collection program may be unconstitutional.[46]

The NSA has also filed individualized surveillance requests. Between 2002 and 2013, the court rejected only twelve of nearly twenty-one thousand surveillance applications, about 0.06 percent.[47] Part of the reason for this is that the objects of the surveillance obviously do not get to provide evidence to counter the government's position. The director of the Administrative Office of the U.S. Courts has proposed a special advocate to promote the public's privacy interests in any particular case.[48] The American Civil Liberties Union (ACLU) filed suit against the NSA, but federal courts ruled that without evidence proving they were wiretapped, they didn't have standing to sue.

Following the 9/11 attacks, public opinion shifted strongly toward governmental efforts to increase security,

Image 4.5 Facebook CEO Mark Zuckerberg testifies before Congress in 2018 about Russia's use of Facebook to try to influence the 2016 election. Zuckerberg promised to tighten Facebook's privacy policies, which allowed Russia to gain information about users' political preferences.

even at the expense of liberty and privacy. In the summer of 2016, the FBI applied for a FISA warrant to wiretap Carter Page, a foreign policy adviser to the Trump campaign after finding probable cause that Page had been illegally working as an agent of the Russian government. Early in 2018, staff of the House Intelligence Committee released a memo claiming that the probable-cause determination was based on an anti-Trump dossier prepared by former British Intelligence officer Christopher Steele for Hillary Clinton's campaign. The Clinton campaign hired Fusion GPS to conduct opposition research on candidate Trump, and Fusion GPS hired Steele to do the work.

Construct Your Own Policy

1. Design a policy that allows an advocate for privacy rights to rebut the government's case for surveillance.
2. Design a policy to investigate foreign and internal threats to the United States that distinguishes among postal mail, cell phone conversations, and e-mail activity.

supportive of the right of students to be "a little bit inappropriate or provocative or, yes, offensive." Following widespread student protests, Christakis resigned her position.[49]

Williams College in Massachusetts created an "Uncomfortable Learning" speaker series to get students to challenge their own beliefs. The students disinvited antifeminist author Suzanne Venker from this series. In the words of *The Williams Record*, "Venker's views are wrong, offensive and unacceptable. . . . The College should not allow speech that challenges fundamental human rights and devalues people."[50]

Key Questions

What is more important, freedom of speech or an equal and nonhostile educational environment? Are these ideas incompatible?

Election 2020

Filling Supreme Court Vacancies

When Supreme Court Justice Antonin Scalia died suddenly in February 2016, President Obama nominated the highly acclaimed and ideologically moderate Circuit Court Judge Merrick Garland to replace Scalia. Nevertheless, the Republican party controlled the Senate and Senate Majority Leader Mitch McConnell declared that no Supreme Court vacancy would be filled until after the November 2016 presidential election. The Senate never referred Garland's nomination to the Senate judiciary committee. There were no hearings on his nomination nor was there a vote.

When the 115th Senate took over for the 114th on January 3, 2017, all pending nominations (including of course the Garland nomination) and legislation expired with it. President Trump, who took office on January 20, 2017, nominated Neil Gorsuch to the Supreme Court on January 31, 2017. When Senate Democrats attempted to block a vote on the Gorsuch nomination through a filibuster, Senate Republicans voted to eliminate the use of filibusters on Supreme Court nominations. (During the Obama administration Senate Democrats had voted to eliminate filibusters on lower court nominations in order to stop Republicans from preventing votes on President Obama's District of Columbia, Court of Appeals nominations.)

Whatever concerns mainline Republicans may have had with President Trump did not extend to his judicial nominations. With the help of the conservative Federalist Society, President Trump named two conservatives to the Supreme Court (Gorsuch [2020] as well as Brett Kavanaugh [2018]), and dozens of conservatives to the circuit courts of appeals and federal district courts. As early as May 2019, McConnell asserted that the rule against election year appointments that had applied to President Obama would not apply in the year 2020 to a potential Trump nomination.

This was not a merely theoretical concern as 87-year-old Justice Ruth Bader Ginsburg passed away in September 2020. President Trump and the Republican party pushed through the appointment of Judge Amy Coney Barrett, who took her oath of office on October 27, 2020. In July 2020, Senator Joni Ernst (R-IA) declared that even if the Republicans lost the Senate and Donald Trump lost the presidency in November 2020, a lame-duck Senate would still confirm any Supreme Court vacancy. With Joe Biden winning the presidency but the Republican party retaining their majority in the Senate, the battle over Supreme Court appointments will continue until after the 2022 midterm elections.

Key Questions
Should Americans be required to salute the flag? Should they be prevented from burning the flag?

The Supreme Court has not reviewed any of the college speech codes, but it has heard other cases related to hate speech. In one case, the Court ruled cross burning, a terrorist tactic historically used by the white supremacist Ku Klux Klan to intimidate African Americans, to be a form of hate speech that could be banned.[51] On the other hand, the Court did not consider picketers at the funerals of U.S. soldiers to be engaged in hate speech, despite their inflammatory signs against homosexuals (see Supreme Court Cases: *Snyder v. Phelps*).

Symbolic Speech.   In the 1960s, the Des Moines school district suspended students Mary Beth Tinker, her brother John, and a third student when they wore black armbands to protest the Vietnam War. The students voiced no opinions while wearing these armbands, and no disruptions in their schools occurred. The Iowa Civil Liberties Union, an interest group that supports civil rights and liberties, brought suit against the school board, claiming that students are equal to other Americans and retain the freedom of speech rights granted by the First Amendment. The Supreme Court agreed.[52] In this instance, the armbands were considered **symbolic speech**, like other nonverbal activities that convey a political message, such as saluting the flag, burning the flag, or burning draft cards—the latter two actions also undertaken by anti–Vietnam War protesters. Alternatively, in another case, employees of a local sheriff's office "liked" the Facebook page of the person running for office against the sheriff. The sheriff fired the employees, who argued that their First Amendment rights had been violated. The court has ruled that "liking" a Facebook page is too shallow an expressive act to count as constitutionally protected speech.[53]

The Court has allowed prohibitions on the burning of draft cards because Congress has a **content-neutral** justification for requiring draft-eligible citizens to be in possession of their draft cards. That is, draft cards are essential to the smooth running of the draft,[54] and prohibiting their destruction is not intended to suppress the views of those who burn them. The Court once ruled that states also have a neutral justification for limiting protests near health care facilities that conduct abortions, even if most of the protesters are advocating pro-life positions.[55] But in 2014 the Court reached a unanimous decision striking down a Massachusetts law limiting protests at facilities where abortions are performed.[56] The Court has also overturned laws that require saluting the flag, as such laws do intend to instill a political viewpoint.[57] Similarly, the Court has overturned laws prohibiting flag burning, as such laws are not content-neutral: They are based almost entirely on opposition to the idea being delivered by flag burning.[58] (Of course, flag burners can be arrested on charges that would apply to anyone who starts a fire in public.)

On the other hand, the content-neutral rule, like most constitutional rules, is not absolute. Some messages can be regulated solely because of opposition to the message, as when the Supreme Court upheld a student's suspension for unfurling a banner at a parade that declared "Bong Hits 4 Jesus" because of the banner's promotion of drug use.[59] It is easy for the Court to formulate simple rules, such as a prohibition on content-based regulations, but harder for the Court to apply those rules consistently in the unusual cases that come before it.

Moreover, states have more authority in controlling their own speech than the speech of its residents. In 2015, the Court ruled that Texas did not have to be content-neutral when deciding which license plate designs to accept—in this case, rejecting a design featuring the Sons of Confederate Veterans that included the Confederate battle flag.[60] In North Carolina, a district court judge rejected the state's attempt to put the anti-abortion slogan "choose life" on its license plate without

Image 4.6 Mary Beth and John Tinker were teenagers in 1965 when they wore black armbands to school to protest the Vietnam War, and they were suspended. Arguing that students have free speech rights, the Iowa Civil Liberties Union sued the school district on their behalf and appealed the suspension in a series of cases that were finally appealed to the Supreme Court. In 1969, the Court ruled in the Tinkers' favor, stating: "It can hardly be argued that either students or teachers shed their constitutional rights to freedom of speech or expression at the schoolhouse gate."

symbolic speech: *Actions, such as burning the flag, that convey a political message without spoken words.*

content-neutral: *Free speech doctrine that allows certain types of regulation of speech, as long as the restriction does not favor one side or another of a controversy.*

Image 4.7 Florida license plate expressing the state's pro-life (antiabortion) position. The Supreme Court has upheld such speech by states.

Image 4.8 In 2002, high school student Joseph Frederick unfurled this banner while his class watched the Olympic Torch relay pass through Juneau, Alaska. When the principal suspended Frederick for the banner's message about drugs, Frederick sued, saying that his free speech rights had been violated. The court of appeals, relying on the *Tinker* case, reversed the suspension, but in 2007, the Supreme Court upheld it, saying a student's free speech rights did not extend to the promotion of illegal drugs.

a pro-choice alternative as an unconstitutional form of viewpoint discrimination.[61]

Time, Place, and Manner Regulations. The fact that the First Amendment protects freedom of speech does not mean there is a right to speak wherever one wants, whenever one wants. Regulations of the time, place, and manner of speech, such as when or where protests may take place, are generally valid as long as they are neutral or equal—that is, they do not favor one side or another of a controversy. Thus states can prohibit protests near school grounds that interfere with school activities as there is no indication that such bans favor one side of any controversy over any other side.[62] Alternatively, the American Nazi Party, with backing from the pro–free speech ACLU, won the right to protest in the heavily Jewish Chicago suburb of Skokie because the main reason that Skokie sought to block the march was opposition to the Nazis' views.[63] Many also feared that the march would serve as a severe psychological trigger for the many Holocaust survivors who lived in Skokie.

Key Questions
Should the American Nazi Party, the Ku Klux Klan, or the Communist Party be allowed to march in public streets? Should their ideas be suppressed, or should they be allowed to be tested in the marketplace of ideas?

prior restraint: *Government restrictions on freedom of the press that prevent material from being published.*

Freedom of the Press

Thomas Jefferson, among other Founders, thought freedom of the press crucial to a free society because the press keeps the public informed about the government's activities. When the Bill of Rights was written, "the press" meant newspapers; today the term covers not only the large companies that own television and radio stations but also individually run blogs and Internet sites that anyone can create. While freedom of the press once belonged to those who owned one, today it belongs to everyone.

Like freedom of speech, however, freedom of the press is not absolute. In extraordinarily extreme cases, the government can censor items before they are published. This practice is known as **prior restraint**. In other situations, the government can punish people after the fact for what they publish.

Prior Restraint. Following English law, freedom of the press in the colonies and in the early years of the United States meant freedom from prior censorship[64]; today, an extraordinary burden of proof of imminent harm is needed before the courts will shut down a newspaper before a story is printed. Even when the *New York Times* began publishing excerpts from a top-secret Pentagon analysis of U.S. involvement in the Vietnam War, the courts refused to stop the presses. The story of this case, *New York Times v. United States* (1971),[65] is told in more detail in Chapter 7, The News and Social Media. One case in which the courts said that the government had met the extraordinary burden standard involved the publication of instructions on how to build a hydrogen bomb,[66] but generally, court approval of censorship by prior restraint has been so difficult to achieve that the federal government has not sought it since the 1970s. Thus, even as many major newspapers published information leaked by Edward Snowden that the United States considered to be highly classified, the government did not attempt to prevent the news media from publishing it, although it did indict Edward Snowden.

First Amendment law protects the Internet and blogs from government censorship in much the same way that it protects newspapers, but the technology of the Internet makes censorship far more difficult. This was the lesson learned by a federal judge who tried to censor Julian Assange's WikiLeaks website,[67] which publishes confidential documents from government, business, and religious organizations. Though the judge ordered the Wikileaks.org domain name disabled, WikiLeaks already had mirror sites set up all over the world. Facing a barrage of criticism from bloggers and mainstream media groups, and given the ineffectiveness of his original decision, the judge reversed himself. But while many people may support the right of WikiLeaks to publish allegations of money laundering by a Swiss bank, as in this case, what happens when WikiLeaks publishes, as it has, a diagram of the first atomic bomb or secret documents about the war in Afghanistan?[68] Such cases show the difficulty of balancing freedom of the press versus censorship in a dangerous world.

Key Questions
What information on the web should the government censor?

Subsequent Punishment.   In certain instances, the government can engage in subsequent punishment, fining, and/or imprisoning writers and publishers after the fact for what they publish. Examples here include penalties for libel and for publishing obscenity, incitement to acts of violence, and secret military information.

The standards for convicting in a case of libel—the publishing of false and damaging statements about another person—vary according to whether that person is a public figure. The Supreme Court has made it harder for public figures than for ordinary individuals to sue for libel because public figures have access to the media and can more readily defend themselves without lawsuits. For public figures to sue, the materials must be false and damaging, and the writer or publisher must have acted with actual malice—that is, with knowledge that the material was false or with reckless disregard of whether it was true or false. Further, satire is largely exempt from libel laws. Such was in the case in *Hustler Magazine's* spoof on the "first time" for the Reverend Jerry Falwell, the founder of the conservative Christian group the Moral Majority.[69] For private figures to sue for libel, the material must be false and damaging, and there must be some degree of negligence, but the actual malice test does not apply.

Key Questions
How can you protect yourself from what others may say about you on social media?

Before development of the World Wide Web, only those who published printed materials could libel someone, but even then, the damage would largely be limited to those who subscribed to the publication. With the Internet, anyone can libel anyone else, and the whole world can see it. At Yale University, for example, anonymous contributors to a popular law school message board wrote derogatory comments about several female law students, including fabricated statements about their mental capacity and sexual activities. Because anyone, including potential employers, can see such statements, the potential for harm is enormous.[70] Given the anonymous nature of the posts, identifying and prosecuting the source of the statements can be difficult, if not impossible. Because freedom of speech is a fundamental right, there is no easy solution to protecting privacy in the Internet age.

The term *seditious libel* refers to the criticizing of government officials, regardless of whether the criticism is true, false, or just a matter of opinion. During the colonial era, the 1735 New York trial and acquittal of John Peter Zenger established that seditious libel is not a reason for punishment, although, as we have seen, Congress twice made sedition a crime during wartime.

Today, the government can seek subsequent punishment against individuals who publish military secrets or obscene materials. Pornographic material is not necessarily obscene, and pornography that falls short of the legal definition of obscenity receives First Amendment protection. Specifically, for materials to be obscene, they must pass all three parts of what has become known as the **Miller** test: (1) to the average person, applying contemporary community standards as established by the relevant state, the work, taken as a whole (not just isolated passages), appeals to the prurient (sexual) interest; (2) the work depicts in an offensive way sexual conduct specifically defined by the state law; and (3) the work lacks serious literary, artistic, political, or scientific value (SLAPS).[71]

Under the *Miller* test, only "hard-core" materials could be banned.[72] The government has much greater leeway to prohibit "kiddie porn" that uses actual children[73] but not "virtual child pornography," which uses computer-simulated children.[74] Nor can the government's desire to protect children from indecent materials on the Internet be used as a justification for prohibiting online pornography that does not reach the level of obscenity.[75] Similarly, the state may not ban the purchase of violent video games by minors.[76] The *Miller* test reversed a trend toward greater protection of pornography that the liberal Warren Court (1954–69) had instituted and opposed the general trend of greater rights of the press to publish without fear of prosecution by the state. According to a 2010 decision, under the *Miller* test, states may not ban fetish videos that, in the case at hand, showed women in high heels crushing the skulls of puppies.[77]

The Right of Association

The First Amendment's protections include the right of the people to peaceably assemble. This includes the right to hold public protests that meet time, place, and manner regulations, and it was crucial to the success of the civil rights and women's suffrage movements (see Chapter 5, Civil Rights).

In the United States, the right of association also includes the right to associate with whom one wants, as well as the right not to associate with those with whom one does not want to associate. As we observed earlier, here a civil liberty can conflict with a civil right, as when a restaurant owner might choose, for example, not to serve people of a certain race. This dilemma was resolved by the Civil Rights Act and subsequent court challenges in the 1960s so far as businesses that serve the public are concerned (see Chapter 5). But if a private group's expressed beliefs reject association with people of certain groups, such as Boy Scouts rejecting homosexuals and the Ku Klux Klan rejecting blacks and Jews, the group has a right of association that overrides state laws banning discrimination.

If a group discriminates for no apparent purpose, however, state laws can limit the right of association. Thus, the Court declared that Minnesota has the right to prevent the Jaycees from discriminating against women because the presence of women does not violate any of the expressive interests of the Jaycees.[78] On the other hand, New Jersey's law prohibiting private groups from discriminating against homosexuals did not override the Boy Scouts' stated belief that homosexuality is inconsistent with the group's values. The Court thus allowed the Scouts to prohibit homosexuals from being members.[79] (Due to increasing public support for the rights of homosexuals, the Scouts have since backed off this practice.[80])

Religious Freedom

LO 4-4 Determine what religious freedoms the First Amendment protects

The First Amendment sets forth two distinct protections about religion. Congress, and now the states, generally may not prevent people from practicing their religious beliefs. They also cannot pass laws that establish an official religion or even favor one religion over another.

Free Exercise

Many of the first settlers in the American colonies came because of restrictions on their religious beliefs in England, where the Anglican Church was established as the official religion. When these settlers arrived, they did not establish general freedom of religion but, rather, freedom for their religion. In 1635, for example, the Massachusetts Puritans banished Roger Williams for his disagreements with the church. Williams established a colony in what would become Rhode Island that was the first to grant religious "liberty of conscience." Other colonies followed. Maryland's Toleration Act (1649) guaranteed freedom of worship to all Christians, including Catholics, who often faced persecution in Protestant Europe. British colonists in Flushing, New Amsterdam (now Queens, New York), fought for the religious freedom of others, protesting Dutch Governor Peter Stuyvesant's persecution of Quakers. The Flushing Remonstrance (1657), a historic demand for religious freedom, called on the governor to let "every man stand or fall to his own Master."[81]

Key Questions

Should all religions get equal treatment? What about those who profess no religion at all?

Victories for religious freedom, though significant, were rare in the colonial period. In 1786, however, the Virginia General Assembly passed Thomas Jefferson's Statute for Religious Freedom, which declared freedom of religious conscience to be a natural right of mankind that governments could not restrict. Five years later, this right was affirmed in the **free exercise clause** of the Bill of Rights. Like all the provisions of the Bill of Rights, however, it originally protected individuals only against the national government, and at the time only two states—Virginia and Rhode Island—had unqualified religious freedom. Maryland demanded belief in Christianity; Delaware and North Carolina required belief in the divinity of the Bible; Pennsylvania and South Carolina required belief in the divinity of the Bible plus heaven and hell; and Connecticut, Maryland, Massachusetts, New Hampshire, and South Carolina limited civil office to Christians or Protestants.[82] So ingrained was state authority to regulate religion that when James Madison proposed an amendment that would have limited such authority, Congress rejected it.[83] Today, however, with the incorporation of the Bill of Rights, the right of individuals to the free exercise of religion is also outside of state authority to regulate.

free exercise clause: *First Amendment clause protecting the free exercise of religion.*

Under the First Amendment, the government cannot criminalize an individual's private religious beliefs. Nor can the government ban specific religious activities, including student-run publications,[84] just because they are based on religious beliefs. For example, the Supreme Court struck down a ban on religious-based animal sacrifices because killing animals for other reasons was not prohibited.[85] But not all religious-based activities are protected, and states are generally free to pass laws that restrict religious practices as long as such laws have a **valid secular (nonreligious) purpose**. For example, states can

valid secular purpose: *Supreme Court test that allows states to ban activities that infringe on religious practices as long as the state has a nonreligious rationale for prohibiting the behavior.*

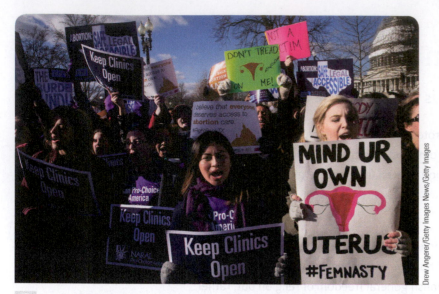

Image 4.9 Rally by pro-choice advocates against state laws that would limit the ability of clinics that provide abortions to stay open.

Drew Angerer/Getty Images News/Getty Images

ban polygamy, even though marriage with multiple wives is still a central belief in some religions.[86] The state court of Utah, however, in response to a case brought by the family featured on the television show *Sister Wives,* has recently ruled that the ban on cohabitation is an unconstitutional violation of religious freedom. Thus while the state may continue to prevent a man from having multiple marriage licenses, it cannot prevent a man from living with multiple women.[87]

Under the free exercise clause, the Supreme Court will not allow inquiries into the sincerity of someone's religious beliefs or even into what constitutes a religion. This has led Satanists, people who worship the Devil, to request Satanist prayers at the start of Phoenix city council meetings. The council has chosen to start its meetings with a moment of silence rather than include Satanic prayers at the beginning of meetings.[88]

In the 1960s, the Court ruled that states must have a compelling interest before they can abridge people's religious practices, even if the law restricting the practice has a valid secular purpose. Thus even though the government has a valid secular purpose in conducting a military draft, members of religious groups that oppose warfare, such as Quakers, may be exempt. In the case of former boxing champion Muhammad Ali, a Muslim, who argued that he could only fight wars declared by Allah or the Prophet, the Court overturned a conviction for draft evasion.[89]

One case that demonstrates the contest between the branches of government over what constitutes free exercise concerns the use of the hallucinogenic drug peyote in religious rituals. In 1990, when two Native American drug counselors who used peyote were fired from their jobs and denied unemployment compensation, the Supreme Court used the valid secular purpose test to uphold Oregon's decision to deny this compensation.[90] Members of Congress overwhelmingly disapproved, however, and passed legislation, the Religious Freedom Restoration Act (RFRA), stating that the Supreme Court must use the compelling interest test in deciding free exercise cases. The Supreme Court responded by declaring part of RFRA unconstitutional, repeating the statement from *Marbury v. Madison* that the province of the judicial branch is "to say what the law is."[91] Congress does have the authority, however, to declare the religious use of peyote to be legal, and it has done so. Moreover, Congress has decided that its own laws must have a compelling interest before they can limit religious freedom.

Generally, states need only have a valid secular purpose to pass laws that also happen to restrict religious practices. On the other hand, the Supreme Court has established a "ministerial exception" that frees religious organizations from having to abide by federal antidiscrimination laws—in this case, the Americans with Disabilities Act—when choosing their ministers. The Court here used the free exercise clause to limit the scope of an otherwise valid act of Congress.[92]

The Establishment of Religion

The **establishment clause** of the First Amendment prevents Congress from recognizing one church as the nation's official church, as Britain had done with the Anglican (Episcopal) Church. Originally, states were free to establish state religions if they chose to, and when the Constitution was adopted, nearly half the states had done so.[93] The antiestablishment movement began in Virginia, where between 1784 and 1785, James Madison fought tax assessments used to support Christian religious teachers, and Thomas Jefferson secured passage of the Disestablishment Bill in 1786, which ended Virginia's official establishment of the Anglican Church. In an 1802 letter to the Baptists of Danbury, Connecticut, Jefferson called for a "wall of separation" between church and state. The Supreme Court adopted that phrase in 1947 but declared that using taxpayer funds to provide public transportation to parochial schools did not breach the wall.[94]

The establishment clause literally prohibits not just the establishment of religion but also any law "respecting an establishment of religion." The Supreme Court has taken this phrase to mean that steps by the government favoring one religion over another, or even religion over no religion, cannot be taken, even if those steps fall far short of an official establishment of religion.

The Supreme Court's test for determining whether laws violate the establishment clause is known as the **Lemon test**, named after a litigant in a 1971 case.[95] Under this test, a challenged law must be shown to have a secular (nonreligious) legislative purpose and a primary effect that neither advances nor inhibits religion. The law must also avoid an excessive entanglement between church and state, such as a strict monitoring of church activities. Using these standards, the Supreme Court has banned organized school prayers and devotional Bible readings.[96] The Bible can be read as part of a comparative religion course, however, and students may pray silently. The Supreme Court has also used this test to strike down laws that prohibited the teaching of evolution[97] as well as laws granting equal time for creation science—the position that scientific evidence supports the biblical view of creation—if evolution is taught.[98] A district court judge in Pennsylvania ruled that "intelligent design"—a view that claims that the world is too complex to have resulted from evolution and that there must have been a purposeful designer of the universe (that is, God)—was nothing more than creation science with a new name.[99] Whether doctrines are called creation science or intelligent design, courts have ruled that they are religious doctrines that cannot constitutionally be taught as part of the science curricula in public schools. Nevertheless, state legislatures, presumably in an attempt to be responsive to their constituents, continue to approve creation science curricula. Tennessee and Louisiana explicitly allow creationist instruction, Texas and Arkansas have publicly funded charter schools that teach creationism, and ten other states fund private schools that teach creationism.[100]

It is often difficult to understand why some activities violate the establishment clause and others do not. Separationists believe, with Jefferson, that there should be a strict wall between church and state. Accommodationists, on the other hand, believe that as long as the state does not favor one religion over another, it can generally pass laws that support religion. The Supreme Court's decisions on these grounds have been mixed, with conservative justices typically supporting the accommodationist position and liberal justices typically supporting the separationist view (see Chapter 15, The Judiciary, on ideology and

establishment clause: *First Amendment clause prohibiting governmental establishment of religion.*

Lemon **test:** *Test for determining whether aid to religion violates the establishment clause.*

Key Questions

Should prayers be allowed in school? Under what circumstances? What types of prayers? Is saying a silent prayer the same as wearing an armband?

the Supreme Court). The end result has been confusion: The Court allows short religious prayers by clergy at high school graduation ceremonies as long as students are not compelled to participate,[101] but not by students at high school football games.[102] States may provide textbooks for secular subjects in parochial schools,[103] but not instructional aids such as charts and maps.[104]

The Right to Keep and Bear Arms

LO 4-5 Outline how the "right to bear arms" has been interpreted

Key Questions
What are the arguments for and against gun control? What is your position?

While many if not most Americans agree about the fundamental aims of the various First Amendment rights, no such agreement exists about the fundamental aims of the Second Amendment. The amendment declares, "A well regulated Militia, being necessary to the security of a free State, the right of the people to keep and bear Arms, shall not be infringed." Supporters of gun rights view the amendment as providing an individual right to keep and bear arms, while opponents view the "well regulated Militia" clause as limiting this right to those in organized militias.

At the time of the amendment's passage, the term *militia* meant all free, able-bodied adult males, who could be called on to protect their states or communities from external military threats. The Founders favored citizen militias, which could be called on in moments of crisis, over standing armies, which could pose a threat to liberty.

Not until the 1934 National Firearms Act did the federal government attempt to regulate gun ownership. In 1939, the Supreme Court upheld a conviction under the act for possession of a sawed-off shotgun against a Second Amendment challenge, unanimously ruling that because such weapons had never been used by any militia, they did not receive Second Amendment protection. The Court sidestepped the question about whether there was an individual right to bear arms.

The Supreme Court finally decided that issue in 2008, ruling that there is an individual right to possess a gun, at least for self-defense in one's home.[105] The case involved a law prohibiting the private possession of firearms by the District of Columbia, which is a "federal enclave" and, for constitutional purposes, thus considered part of the federal government rather than a state. The Court's 5–4 decision split along ideological lines, with the five most conservative justices, including the late Justice Antonin Scalia, supporting an individual right to keep and bear arms for self-defense, indicating that the right can be regulated

AP Images/Haraz N. Ghanbari

Image 4.10 Otis McDonald, a plaintiff in *McDonald v. Chicago*, joined the suit against Chicago's handgun law because he wanted to have a handgun at home to protect himself from gangs. On June 18, 2010, the Supreme Court ruled that the Constitution incorporated the Second Amendment, declaring that states could not ban private possession of guns for self-defense.

but not denied. The four most liberal justices dissented, arguing that the "well regulated Militia clause" limits whatever right of gun ownership exists to military purposes. Without Scalia, the Court became split 4–4 on the issue. Justice Scalia's position should prevail, though, given President Donald Trump's appointment of Neil Gorsuch to the Court.

The conclusion that the Second Amendment protects an individual right to bear arms does not answer the question of whether that amendment is also binding on the states. The Supreme Court answered that question in 2010, declaring in a 5–4 vote that the right is incorporated.[106] Again, Justice Scalia provided the crucial fifth vote for the individual-right position.

In February 2018, a crazed gunman murdered 14 students and three adults at Stoneman Douglas High School in Parkland, Florida. President Trump blamed the FBI for spending too much time "trying to prove Russian collusion."[107] Many Democrats and some Republicans called for stricter gun control in the wake of the shooting. On the other side, the National Rifle Association (NRA), a powerful pro-gun interest group (see Chapter 8, Interest Groups), used its television station, NRATV, to blame the district for security failures. Spokeswoman Dana Loesch declared in an NRA television ad "They use their media to assassinate real news. They use their schools to teach children that their president is another Hitler."[108]

Surviving students at the school organized effective anti-gun campaigns, getting Dick's Sporting Goods to stop selling assault-style rifles. Walmart raised its required age to purchase guns and ammunition to 21. Hertz rental cars as well as United and Delta airlines ended their discounts to NRA members.[109] The students also organized nationwide "March for Our Lives" rallies on March 24, 2018.[110] Conservative bloggers argued that one of the students prominently interviewed by the media was a "crisis actor" who did not attend the school, a claim that was easily debunked.[111]

Criminal Procedure

LO 4-6 Describe what protections the Bill of Rights provides to those accused of crimes

Provisions in the Fourth, Fifth, Sixth, and Eighth Amendments contain the heart of the protections afforded people against arbitrary police and law enforcement tactics. They protect the manner in which the police conduct investigations, the procedures used at trial, and the punishments that may be given following conviction. The liberal Warren Court greatly expanded the rights of accused criminals, but since then, more conservative courts have trimmed those rights.

Investigations

The major limits on investigating crimes involve the authority to search for physical evidence and the warnings that must be given before questioning a suspect. The police also cannot entrap people into committing crimes they would not otherwise commit, which is why R. Stephanie Good, in her role as "teen2hot4u," could never be the first person to bring up the subject of potential sexual activity.

Searches and Seizures.   The English practice of issuing writs of assistance, general warrants that allow searches of any person or place with no expiration until the death of the king, was among the causes that led to the American Revolution. Thus, the Fourth Amendment prohibits unreasonable searches and seizures. Although the amendment does not specify what makes a search unreasonable, it does specify that warrants must be backed by probable cause, "particularly describing the place to be searched and the persons or things to be seized."

The Supreme Court has never interpreted the amendment to require warrants for all searches or seizures. If the police see illegal goods in plain view, they may seize them without a warrant. Similarly, if they observe a crime, they do not have to get a warrant before they arrest the individual. The Supreme Court has also established a broad right to search the person and the area within his or her control following an arrest and incident to it. This right now permits the police to conduct strip searches of arrestees entering the general population of a jail, even for the most minor violations, such as driving without a seat belt.[112] The police, though, may not search the contents of a cell phone confiscated incident to a lawful arrest due to the enormous amount of private information contained on cell phones.[113]

expectation of privacy test: *Supreme Court test for whether Fourth Amendment protections apply.*

The areas over which individuals have Fourth Amendment protections are those in which there is an **expectation of privacy**. According to the Supreme Court, there are no Fourth Amendment rights in areas over which there is no expectation of privacy, such as discarded garbage, someone else's home, a hotel room once one has checked out, or an international border. The Supreme Court has not ruled on the issue, but several state supreme courts have upheld the right of schools to search lockers used by students because students have a diminished expectation of privacy over their lockers. While students at public universities do have an expectation of privacy in their college dorm rooms, many schools require them to waive their Fourth Amendment rights when they sign their dorm contracts. (Like the First Amendment, the Fourth Amendment does not limit private parties, such as private universities.) More generally, people waive their Fourth Amendment rights whenever they grant permission for the police to search, as long as the police request is not coercive.[114]

As for biological searches, police may require Breathalyzer tests of people suspected of drunk driving, but blood tests require a warrant.[115] On the other hand, the Court recently upheld Maryland's requirement that all persons charged with certain crimes submit DNA samples for the state's database.[116] The DNA samples remain with the state even if the state later drops the charges or the person is found not guilty.

For areas over which there is an expectation of privacy, the degree of Fourth Amendment protection depends on the level of that expectation, as determined by the Supreme Court. For example, the Court has ruled that individuals have the highest expectation of privacy in their homes, nearly as much in their places of business, but substantially less in their cars.[117] There is no expectation of privacy if what is exposed is in plain view, even if, like a marijuana patch on private property, it requires a low-flying plane to view it.[118] There is no expectation of privacy over smells, allowing police to use drug-sniffing dogs to establish probable cause. Drug-sniffing dogs, however, may not enter the porch outside a home in order to sniff for illegal drugs.[119] There is, however, an expectation of privacy over the thermal (heat) signals given off by homes, thus prohibiting the police from using heat monitors to establish probable cause for indoor marijuana growing.[120]

Searches of homes almost always require a warrant (and thus probable cause). Searches of businesses usually do, but the Court allows warrantless searches of businesses that are subject to health, safety, or administrative regulations, such as restaurants, construction sites, and banks. For example, a restaurant kitchen suspected of health violations may be searched without a warrant. The police may establish, without probable cause, roadblocks to stop all cars on a road to check for licenses and registration or for drunk drivers. They may, of course, pull over any car for an observed violation, and they may search the car incident to arrest if they choose to arrest the person for that violation.[121] They may also pull over a person based on an anonymous tip.[122] The Court has ruled that police require a warrant to physically place a GPS transmitter on a car to trace a person's movements, as placing the transmitter on the car requires a physical trespass.[123] In 2018, the Supreme Court ruled that a warrant is required when police use cell phone towers to track a defendant's location for 127 days. The Court also allows drug testing without probable cause in "special needs" cases, such as student athletes and people applying for jobs at the U.S. Customs Office, but not of politicians seeking elective office.[124]

Key Questions
If the police are tracking your car's movements, does it matter if they physically touched your car to do so?

If the police conduct a search that is later found to be in violation of the Fourth Amendment, the **exclusionary rule** holds that the evidence cannot be used in trial. Originally established by the Supreme Court in 1914, the doctrine was made binding on state and local governments, where most law enforcement takes place, by means of selective incorporation in *Mapp v. Ohio* (1961).[125] Defenders support the rule, which is not explicitly in the Constitution, as the only means of making sure that the police follow the Fourth Amendment. Police will have less incentive to violate the Fourth Amendment if they know that the evidence from illegal searches cannot be used in court. Critics complain that excluding such evidence allows guilty people to go free simply because the police made a mistake.[126] The Supreme Court has backtracked a bit on the rule, establishing a good faith exception, which allows evidence to be used if the police obtain a warrant but the warrant is later found to lack probable cause.[127] There is also an "inevitable discovery" exception, which allows illegally obtained evidence to be used if the court finds that the evidence would have been discovered even without the illegal search.[128]

exclusionary rule: *Supreme Court rule declaring that evidence found in violation of the Fourth Amendment cannot be used at trial.*

Key Questions
Why did the First Congress write so many protections regarding criminal procedure into the Bill of Rights?

Interrogations.   The Fifth Amendment protects the right against self-incrimination, being forced to give testimony against oneself during criminal investigations or at criminal trials. The Supreme Court originally interpreted the self-incrimination clause to prohibit coerced confessions because they are inherently unreliable. But in the famous 1966 decision *Miranda v. Arizona*, the Court declared that the right against self-incrimination would be protected regardless of whether there was any evidence of coercion.[129] Rather, prior to police interrogation of subjects who are in custody, the subjects must be told that (1) they have the right to remain silent, (2) anything they say may be used against them, and (3) they have the right to an attorney, free if they cannot afford one. Police strenuously objected to these requirements at first, fearing that they would drastically curtail legitimate confessions. But in 2000, the Court upheld the *Miranda* decision, noting that its requirements had become so embedded in routine police practice that they had become part of the national culture.[130]

Trial Procedures

The trial protections of the Bill of Rights include the right to indictment by a grand jury (Fifth Amendment), the right to counsel and an impartial jury (both Sixth Amendment),

AP Images/Matt York

Image 4.11 Booking photo of Ernesto Miranda. His case led the Warren Court to require police to give arrested suspects "Miranda warnings."

Key Questions

How do you think about "fairness" in the U.S. criminal justice system? What makes a system "fair" or "unfair"?

and the right against self-incrimination (Fifth Amendment), which, as noted, applies to trials as well as investigations. The Fifth Amendment also contains a general right to due process of law.

To prevent the government from bringing people to trial without sufficient cause, the Fifth Amendment requires indictment by a grand jury, which indicts by majority vote. This right has not been incorporated so it applies to the federal government only, which prosecutes only a small percentage of total criminal cases, as criminal law is mostly under the authority of the states.

The Sixth Amendment's right to counsel originally meant that defendants could have an attorney represent them if they could afford one. In *Powell v. Alabama* (1932), a case involving undoubtedly false allegations of rape filed against several black youths, the Supreme Court ruled that, in death penalty cases where the defendants were ignorant, illiterate, or the like, the government must provide an attorney if defendants cannot afford one.[131] In 1963, the Court recognized in the landmark *Gideon v. Wainwright* case how crucial counsel is in even simple felony cases.[132] Today, the rule applies to any case in which a defendant could receive as little as one day of jail time.[133]

The Sixth Amendment also guarantees the right to a trial by an impartial jury. Originally, a jury trial meant twelve people deciding unanimously, but the Court now allows juries as small as six people, though twelve-person juries need to decide unanimously.[134] The *impartial* part of the clause grants the defense and prosecutor unlimited rights to challenge potential jurors for cause. Examples include knowing other people in the case, having been a victim of a similar crime, and not having an open mind on the issue. These challenges must be approved by the trial judge. State rules also grant prosecutors and defense counsel a limited number of peremptory challenges, or challenges without cause. The substantive limit on peremptory challenges is that neither side may use the potential juror's race or gender as a reason for the challenge.[135]

The application of the self-incrimination clause to trials means that defendants cannot be compelled to be witnesses against themselves. That is, they have an absolute right not to testify, and the prosecution cannot even make note to the jury that the defendant chose not to testify.

Verdict, Punishment, and Appeal

At the end of a trial, the jury must decide whether to convict or acquit the defendant. Following conviction, the judge imposes a sentence, unless it is a death penalty case, in which case the jury decides. Convicted defendants may usually appeal their convictions to a higher court.

Double Jeopardy. If the jury acquits the defendant, the double jeopardy clause prevents the person from being tried again for the same offense. But if the jury cannot reach a verdict, the government can retry the defendant. Also, if the defendant is found guilty at trial but the conviction is overturned on appeal, the defendant may be tried again. The

Supreme Court does allow a defendant to be tried separately for the same offense by the state government and the federal government, even if the defendant was found not guilty at the state or federal trial that was held first. Because most crimes are either state offenses or federal offenses, this form of double jeopardy does not often occur.

The main exception concerns a trial for the federal crime of violating someone's civil rights, which is occasionally prosecuted after a state acquittal on the specific offense (such as murder or assault). For example, in 2012, George Zimmerman, an armed neighborhood watch coordinator, shot 17-year-old African American Trayvon Martin while Martin was walking through Zimmerman's gated community. Zimmerman approached Martin, a scuffle ensued in which Zimmerman suffered mild head injuries, and Zimmerman fatally shot Martin. Zimmerman was charged with murder but was acquitted based on Florida's Stand Your Ground Law, which does not require people in Florida to retreat in the face of a threat. Many people called for then-U.S. Attorney General Eric Holder to prosecute Zimmerman for violating Martin's civil rights. A federal investigation into the incident found insufficient evidence to indict Zimmerman.[136]

The federal government convicted Dylann Roof, a self-professed racist, of capital murder of nine African Americans at the Emanuel African Church in Charleston, South Carolina, in 2015 on federal "hate crime" charges. He subsequently pled guilty in state court for the murders.[137]

Sentencing. Following a guilty verdict, the judge determines the sentence, except in death penalty cases, where the jury makes the determination. Sentences must not violate the Eighth Amendment's prohibition on cruel and unusual punishment. The concern of the Framers undoubtedly grew out of English punishments that included torture.[138] The phrase itself, however, is highly ambiguous, leaving courts with a fair amount of discretion about whether punishments are unconstitutional.

As for the length of the sentence imposed, the Supreme Court grants great leeway to the states. In 1980, the Court upheld the sentencing to a life term with the possibility of parole of a defendant who had committed his third felony. The first felony was fraudulent use of a credit card for an $80 purchase, the second a forged check for $28.36, and the third accepting payment of $120.75 to fix an air conditioner that he never fixed.[139] As the defendant found out, the Supreme Court rarely finds constitutional violation in the length of a sentence.

On the death penalty, however, the Supreme Court ruled in 1972 that the complete discretion given to juries as to which people are convicted of capital crimes was so arbitrary as to constitute cruel and unusual punishment.[140] Then, in 1976, the Court ruled mandatory death sentences to be unconstitutional but allowed states to impose the death penalty provided they give jurors specific guidelines to consider, such as the brutality of the crime or whether the crime was murder for hire.[141] (See Chapter 2 for more on the death penalty.)

Joshua Sudock-Pool/Getty Images News/Getty Images

Image 4.12 Two California police officers are shown here beating a mentally ill homeless person, Kelly Thomas. After the officers were found not guilty of murder, Thomas's father filed civil charges against the officers. The suit settled for $4.9 million.

Appeals.   Convicted criminals do not have a right to appeal a trial court conviction unless a federal constitutional right has been violated. How states handle violations of state constitutional rights are largely up to the states, even if evidence is later found that the convicted criminal is factually innocent. Although the continued imprisonment or execution of a factually innocent person might appear to be a quintessential case violating due process, the Supreme Court has ruled that people convicted of crimes before DNA testing became available do not have a constitutional right to such evidence, which in many cases could definitively prove their innocence or guilt.[142] Indeed, there is no constitutional right for a factually innocent person not to be executed for a capital crime after a jury has concluded that the person is legally guilty, even if new evidence creates strong doubts as to guilt.[143]

The Right to Privacy

LO 4-7 Assess what constitutes the right to privacy

Although a number of constitutional provisions bear on privacy, such as search and seizure, self-incrimination, and First Amendment freedoms, none explicitly grants a general right to privacy. Nevertheless, the Ninth Amendment demands that the listing of certain rights, such as speech and religion, should not be understood as invalidating rights not listed. Since 1965, the Supreme Court has used the Ninth Amendment, the due process clause of the Fourteenth Amendment, and other privacy-related amendments to establish a general right to privacy. Subsequently the Court has faced decisions about whether to expand this privacy right to include abortion, homosexual behavior, and the right to die.

Birth Control and Abortion

In 1873, Anthony Comstock, a crusader for traditional morality, lobbied Congress to pass a law prohibiting the transportation in interstate commerce of both pornography and birth control. Many states, including Connecticut, passed their own Comstock Laws, which prohibited the use of birth control, even by married couples. In 1961, Estelle Griswold, executive director of the Planned Parenthood League of Connecticut, opened a birth control clinic in order to get arrested or fined so that she could challenge the constitutionality of the law. Her $100 fine, upheld by the Connecticut Supreme Court, allowed her to appeal to the U.S. Supreme Court. In *Griswold v. Connecticut* (1965), the Court voided what one justice called "an uncommonly silly law."[144] The case established a **right to privacy** (see Figure 4.4), and the Court soon expanded this decision to cover the right of unmarried people to use birth control.[145] Birth control as a political issue was then dormant until 2012, when the secretary of health and human services interpreted the Patient Protection and Affordable Care Act requirement that insurance plans cover birth control under the category of preventive medicine. The Catholic Church, which believes using birth control goes against church teachings, protested the application of these rules to cover employee health insurance at Church-affiliated schools and hospitals. The Obama administration then revised its policies to mandate that the insurance companies themselves cover the cost of birth control rather than the Church, or any other organization that objects to the use of birth control as part of its fundamental teachings.

right to privacy:
Constitutional right inferred by the Supreme Court that has been used to protect unlisted rights such as sexual privacy and reproductive rights, plus the right to end life-sustaining medical treatment.

No Soldier shall, in time of peace be quartered in any house, without the consent of the Owner . . . .

Third Amendment

Congress shall make no law . . . abridging . . . the right of the people peaceably to assemble . . . .

First Amendment

The right of the people to be secure in their persons, houses, papers, and effects, against unreasonable searches and seizures, shall not be violated . . . .

Fourth Amendment

The enumeration in the Constitution, of certain rights, shall not be construed to deny or disparage others retained by the people.

Ninth Amendment

No person . . . shall be compelled in any criminal case to be a witness against himself . . . .

Fifth Amendment

. . . nor shall any State deprive any person of life, liberty, or property, without due process of law. . . .

Fourteenth Amendment (Section 1)

In 1965, in *Griswold v. Connecticut*, the Supreme Court overturned a Connecticut law that made it a crime for any person, including married couples, to use birth control. This landmark case drew on guarantees in the First, Third, Fourth, Fifth, Ninth, and Fourteenth Amendments to establish a general right to privacy. These guarantees are the right of association, the prohibition against quartering soldiers, the protection against unreasonable searches, the protection against self-incrimination, the rights retained by the people, and the due process of law. Justice William O. Douglas, who wrote the opinion, explained the justification with reference to "penumbras," or "zones": "Specific guarantees in the Bill of Rights have penumbras formed by emanations from those guarantees that help give them life and substance." He also stated the justification more bluntly: "Would we allow the police to search the sacred precincts of marital bedrooms for the tell-tale signs of the use of contraceptives? The very idea is repulsive."

Figure 4.4 The Right to Privacy

The Supreme Court established a general right to privacy from various specific privacy-related rights in the First, Third, Fourth, Fifth, Ninth, and Fourteenth Amendments.

Far more controversial than the question of birth control is the question of abortion. Before the middle of the nineteenth century, most states followed the English practice of making abortion illegal only after "quickening"—that is, noticeable movement by the fetus, usually around the sixteenth to eighteenth week of pregnancy. By the end of the nineteenth century, most states had eliminated the quickening distinction, making abortion illegal throughout pregnancy. By the 1950s, every state but Alabama had banned abortion except to save the life of the mother; Alabama's broader exception included preserving the mother's health.

Following a substantial increase in birth defects caused by the sedative thalidomide (1957–61) and a German measles epidemic (1962–65), deaths from illegal abortion, and the resurgence of the women's rights movement, interest groups such as the National Association for the Reform of Abortion Laws (NARAL) organized for the loosening of antiabortion laws. Between 1967 and 1969, ten states passed laws allowing abortion if there were a "substantial risk" that the child would be born with a "grave physical or mental defect" or that continuing the pregnancy would "gravely impair the physical or mental health of the mother" and in cases of rape or incest.[146] In 1970, three states legalized previability abortions, those performed before the sixth month of pregnancy, when the fetus could not survive on its own.

Then, in 1973, the Supreme Court decided *Roe v. Wade*, which established a national right to abortion.[147] Using the compelling interest test, the Court declared that states had a compelling interest in preventing abortion in the third trimester, when the fetus could live on its own, and a compelling interest in regulating abortion during the second trimester to protect the health of the woman seeking the procedure. The state had no interest in regulating or preventing abortion in the first trimester. The Court's ruling took the issue out of state politics, where it had been located, and situated it in national politics, where it has become a perennial controversy, with presidential candidates regularly vowing to nominate Supreme Court justices who would either uphold or strike down *Roe v. Wade*. Since that time, states have sought to regulate and limit the procedure, and in the past twenty years, abortion rates have slowly declined.

Following years of debate about *Roe v. Wade*, the Court reconsidered the decision in 1992.[148] That decision upheld the basic right to abortion established in *Roe v. Wade* but replaced the compelling interest/trimester framework, declaring that states could regulate abortion prior to viability as long as those regulations did not constitute an undue burden on a woman's right to terminate her pregnancy. According to the Court, spousal notification constitutes an undue burden, but requiring doctors to provide the woman with information about the risks of abortion and a twenty-four-hour waiting period does not. Parental consent for minors is not an undue burden as long as the minor has an option of seeking a judge's approval if she cannot obtain a parent's consent.

Perhaps the most controversial abortion procedures are those conducted late in a pregnancy. The Supreme Court struck down Nebraska's ban of these "partial-birth" abortions in 2000 in a 5–4 decision because the state law did not contain an exception for the woman's health.[149] Congress responded with national legislation banning partial-birth abortions, and the Court upheld the statute by a 5–4 vote in 2007.[150] The difference was the replacement of Justice Sandra Day O'Connor, who voted to strike the statute in 2000, by Justice Samuel Alito, who voted to uphold the statute in 2007.

Abortion remains a salient issue in national politics, with the Supreme Court's role front and center. While the Supreme Court continues to enforce the *Roe v. Wade* decision, state legislatures have been very active in attempting to limit access to abortion. In 2020, twelve states prohibited abortion during the first trimester of pregnancy (each of these laws has been challenged in federal court). Another twenty-four states prohibit abortion during the second trimester of pregnancy but prior to viability. Many of these laws are also under court challenge.[151]

Other states have tried to limit abortions by enacting targeted regulation of abortion provider (TRAP) laws. In 2016, the Supreme Court struck down two Texas laws that set restrictions on where abortions could be obtained that, to the Court, were not necessary to protect the health of the woman.[152] Nevertheless, following the retirement of Justice Anthony Kennedy, who had provided crucial pro-choice votes, the Court decided to revisit TRAP laws and in 2020 ruled that Louisiana could not restrict doctors from performing abortions unless they had admitting rights at a nearby hospital.

Roe v. Wade: *1973 Supreme Court case extending the right to privacy to abortion.*

Key Questions

What are the arguments for and against the right of privacy in relation to abortion? What is your opinion? Are you "pro-life" or "pro-choice"?

Key Questions

When the people disagree with a Supreme Court decision, what can they do about it?

The continued importance of abortion at the national level (see Chapter 15) is evidenced at confirmation hearings for Supreme Court nominees. At these hearings senators ask more questions about *Roe v. Wade* than about any other case.[153]

Homosexual Behavior

As of 1961, every state had laws prohibiting sodomy, and these laws were broad enough to cover virtually all sexual conduct between people of the same sex. In the next decades, some states decriminalized sodomy, and by 1986, twenty-four states continued to outlaw sodomy between consenting adults. Georgia, one of the states that continued such laws, authorized twenty-four years of imprisonment for a single act of consensual sexual behavior that fell under its sodomy laws. In a case challenging this law, the Supreme Court declared that the right to privacy did not cover homosexual behavior.[154] At the time, more than 80 percent of Americans thought that homosexual behavior was "always" or "almost always" wrong.[155] But by 2003, with the percentage of Americans with this belief down more than 20 percentage points, the Supreme Court reversed itself, declaring in a 5–4 opinion by now retired justice Anthony Kennedy **Lawrence v. Texas** that "the liberty protected by the Constitution allows homosexual persons the right to choose to enter upon relationships in the confines of their homes and their own private lives"[156] (see Chapter 5, Civil Rights, for the Court's decision on same-sex marriage). In 2020, the Supreme Court declared that the Civil Rights Act prohibits employment discrimination against LGBT individuals.

The Right to Die

As part of the right to privacy, the Supreme Court has held that that people who make their wishes clearly known have a constitutional right to terminate life-sustaining care, such as artificial feeding or insertion of breathing tubes.[157] This right does not, however, include the right to assisted suicide, when physicians or family members provide ill people with pills or other means of ending life.[158]

Student Housing

The Supreme Court rejected the use of the right to privacy to strike down laws that ban more than two unrelated unmarried people from living together in the same house or apartment. Instead, it declared that states have a legitimate interest in passing land use legislation.[159]

Civil Liberties and Democracy

At the beginning of the chapter, we quoted Justice Robert Jackson's opinion from the flag salute case that no government official can declare what shall be required in terms of basic beliefs and values. But what if elected officials do so anyway? Jackson responded that it was then the courts' job to protect such rights: "The very purpose of a Bill of Rights was to withdraw certain subjects from . . . political controversy, to place them beyond the reach of majorities and officials and to establish them as legal principles to be applied by the courts. One's . . . fundamental rights may not be submitted to vote; they depend on the outcome of no elections."[160]

Lawrence v. Texas: *2003 Supreme Court case extending the right to privacy to homosexual behavior.*

Political Analytics

Tolerance of Unpopular Ideas

TOLERANCE OF THE RIGHTS of others with whom we disagree is a core value of the United States. Allowing freedom of speech contributes to lively political discussion and can, in the best of cases, elevate everyone's understanding of different points of view. Americans have a fairly high level of tolerance when it comes to allowing others to exercise freedom of speech. As Figure 4.5 shows, the willingness of Americans to allow Communists and those who are against churches and religion to give speeches has remained relatively high and slightly increased over the past decade. Tolerance toward racists has decreased slightly, but still, the majority of those surveyed thought racists should be allowed to speak publicly about their views.

A marketplace of ideas suggests that when multiple viewpoints and ideas are expressed, people will be able to consider those ideas and adopt those they support—rather than being exposed to only a narrow range of perspectives. Colleges and universities can serve as such a marketplace of ideas because students from different backgrounds and from all around the world can gather to express their views about politics and society. In the process, they may reinforce their own views or reconsider their perspectives in light of those held by others.

In Figure 4.5, examine the willingness of the Americans surveyed to allow disfavored groups to give speeches.

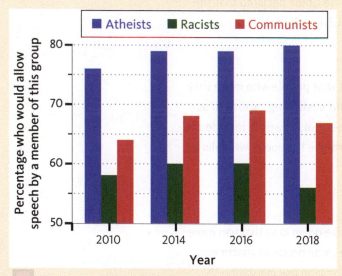

Figure 4.5 **Percentage of Americans Who Support Allowing Speeches by Members of Disfavored Groups, 2010–2018**

Sources: GSS Data Explorer, accessed May 19, 2020, https://gssdataexplorer.norc.org.

Thinking Critically

1. The y-axis that measures the Percentage Who Would Allow Speech by a Member of this Group in Figure 4.5 begins at 50 percent instead of at 0. Why do you think that is? *Hint:* What new information, if any, is gained by changing the scale of the axis?

2. The rhetoric in the 2020 presidential campaign contained what some would call racist overtones. Do you think voters should tolerate such rhetoric by political leaders?

Judicial decisions do not exist in a vacuum. Over the long run, if the Court is unresponsive to the people, new presidents will appoint new judges who better represent the people's preferences.[161] And while the Supreme Court is not accountable to the electorate in the same way that Congress and the president are, Congress and the president do have ways to try to hold the Court accountable. For example, in 1937, President Franklin Roosevelt threatened to pack the Court as a result of its decisions on economic policy. In the 1950s, Congress threatened to take away the Court's authority to hear certain types of cases in the wake of its decisions on congressional investigations of Communists. In recent years, members of Congress have threatened to impeach justices over Court decisions with which they disagreed.

These attempts failed—the older ones largely because the Court proved responsive to the threats and backed away from its original positions. This outcome suggests that one way or another, the Court cannot stand alone in protecting civil liberties if popular support is not behind it. One of the difficulties in protecting civil liberties in a democracy is that although it is easy to feel sympathy for teenagers who wear black armbands to protest war, most litigants whose cases set precedents that protect all of the nation's freedoms are not as wholesome, and the causes they espouse may be racist, sexist, or violent.[162]

Unlimited liberties can also harm social order, particularly in times of crisis. Note, however, that in the period following 9/11, Congress made no attempt to criminalize antiwar speech, as it had during World War I. There was little public demand for such restrictions, as tolerance of opposing viewpoints among Americans has increased dramatically over the years. **Political tolerance**, the willingness of people to put up with ideas with which they disagree, is essential to both the marketplace of ideas and democratic stability.[163]

Consider the willingness of Americans to allow members of disliked groups to give speeches in their community. With the exception of racists, this willingness has increased (see Figure 4.5). If the people are tolerant, elected politicians will be tolerant also.

Similarly, the appointment process furthers responsiveness. Although critics have attacked the Supreme Court for establishing a right to privacy that is not explicitly in the Constitution, this decision remains highly popular, with 98 percent of Americans considering the right essential or important.[164] In 1986, when Supreme Court nominee Robert Bork stated that he rejected the validity of this right, the Senate rejected his appointment. But if the public loses its concern over civil liberties, sooner or later, the Supreme Court will as well.

political tolerance:
Willingness of people to put up with ideas with which they disagree.

Chapter Review

Key Terms

Bill of Rights (p. 106). Why is the Bill of Rights so important?

civil liberties (p. 106). What is the difference between civil liberties and civil rights?

clear and present danger test (p. 115). How much leeway does the clear and present danger test provide to dangerous speech?

compelling interest test (p. 109). What does the compelling interest test require?

content-neutral (p. 121). Why must time, place, and manner regulations be content-neutral?

establishment clause (p. 127). What were the Framers trying to prohibit with the establishment clause?

exclusionary rule (p. 131). Is the exclusionary rule fair?

expectation of privacy test (p. 130). What problems can you foresee with the expectation of privacy test?

free exercise clause (p. 125). Can the free exercise clause protect behavior, or does it just protect beliefs?

incorporate (p. 107). Why has incorporation been so important to our liberties?

Lawrence v. Texas (p. 137). Are laws that discriminate against gays or lesbians likely to continue to survive?

***Lemon* test** (p. 127). Which prong(s) of the *Lemon* test might be violated if a state prohibits the teaching of evolution?

marketplace of ideas (p. 111). How does the marketplace of ideas relate to the First Amendment?

***Miller* test** (p. 124). Does the *Miller* test go too far in regulating pornography, or does it not go far enough?

natural (unalienable) rights (p. 106). Which rights do you believe are unalienable?

political tolerance (p. 139). Why is political tolerance so essential for democracy?

prior restraint (p. 122). How does prior restraint harm the marketplace of ideas?

right to privacy (p. 134). What rights are protected under the right to privacy?

Roe v. Wade (p. 136). What would happen if the Constitution did not protect abortion rights?

selective incorporation (p. 109). How does selective incorporation differ from total incorporation?

symbolic speech (p. 120). How might one protest inequality without speaking any words?

valid secular purpose (p. 125). Why is the valid secular purpose test necessary?

writ of *habeas corpus* (p. 107). Why was this one of the few rights originally enshrined in the Constitution?

Learning Outcomes: What You Need to...

Know	Test Yourself	Participate
LO 4-1 Identify what civil liberties are		
Civil liberties are freedoms so fundamental that they are outside the authority of government to regulate. It often falls to the judiciary to protect them. They include, among others, rights surrounding freedom of expression and criminal procedure, and they were written into the Constitution in 1791 as the first ten amendments, or the Bill of Rights. Although these protections of individual freedoms at first applied only to the federal government, Supreme Court decisions have gradually applied many of them to the states as well.	• Compare civil liberties to civil rights. • Contrast the problems of too much freedom to those of too much order. • Compare the importance of the rights in the 1787 Constitution with those in the Bill of Rights. • State the extent and the limits of the original Bill of Rights.	• Know your constitutional rights. • Decide if any constitutional rights provide too much freedom. • Consider what would happen if civil liberties were subject to majority rule.
LO 4-2 Explain why civil liberties are limited in times of crisis		
Attempts to limit civil liberties are more frequent in wartime and during other threats, given increased government need for order and increased citizen concern about security. But support for the protection of civil liberties usually rebounds after the crisis ends. The scope of First Amendment freedoms of expression has generally expanded, although during wartime they are likely to be curtailed. Even in wartime, the courts have almost always protected the press from government censorship, but the government can prosecute newspapers for publishing obscenity, secret military information, and articles that incite violence.	• State the major limits on civil liberties from the Revolution through the Civil War. • Identify the major targets of civil liberty restrictions during the world wars. • Compare the McCarthy era with the earlier Red Scare. • Describe the change and continuity in security regulations from President George W. Bush to President Obama. • Explain why wartime deprivation of rights tends to ratchet back after the crisis ends.	• Consider whether dissent in wartime is unpatriotic. • Evaluate the role of the media in times of crisis. • Evaluate the threats to freedom from responses to terrorism.
LO 4-3 Distinguish what rights of expression the First Amendment protects		
The First Amendment protects rights of speech, press, and assembly.	• State the limits on the First Amendment's right to freedom of speech. • Compare prior restraint on the press to subsequent punishment. • Explain the right of association.	• Discuss whether First Amendment rights can be absolute. • Evaluate whether the right of association or the right to equal treatment is more important.

Know	Test Yourself	Participate

LO 4-4   Determine what religious freedoms the First Amendment protects

The First Amendment also protects freedom of religious practice and prevents the government from establishing one religion over all the others.	• Explain the difference between the free exercise of religion and the establishment of religion. • State the difference between separationists and accommodationists.	• Consider what would happen if the First Amendment granted a complete exemption from secular laws that violated one's religious beliefs. • Debate the "wall of separation" between church and state.

LO 4-5   Outline how the "right to bear arms" has been interpreted

The Supreme Court has declared that the Second Amendment protects an individual right to bear arms for self-defense in one's home.	• Explain why the Second Amendment is ambiguous about an individual's right to keep and bear arms.	• Debate what limits should exist on gun rights and on what grounds.

LO 4-6   Describe what protections the Bill of Rights provides to those accused of crimes

Provisions in the Fourth, Fifth, Sixth, and Eighth Amendments protect individuals accused of crimes in police investigations and regulate trial procedures and types of punishments.	• Describe the limits on police investigations of crimes. • Explain the trial rights protected by the Constitution. • State the protections for those convicted of crimes.	• List any additional limits you might like to see on police investigations or trial rights. • Debate the death penalty.

LO 4-7   Assess what constitutes the right to privacy

Although the Constitution and its amendments do not explicitly grant a general right to privacy, the Supreme Court has used various constitutional provisions to establish this right, creating one of the most contentious areas of constitutional law and interpretation.	• Compare privacy rights in birth control and abortion. • Evaluate the role of public opinion on public laws toward homosexuality.	• Debate whether health insurance laws should require coverage for birth control. • Consider whether judicial protection of homosexual rights is necessary. • Write your own "living will" stating your preferences for medical treatment if at the time you were unable to make them known. • Find out if your housing arrangement is in violation of the law.

5 Civil Rights

ERIKA ANDIOLA
Arizona State University

> **"Yes, it's uncomfortable, but, at the end of the day, this is the reality of what the country is doing to a lot of children and a lot of people of all ages at the border and in immigration detention centers across the country."***

The gates of Erika Andiola's alma mater, Arizona State University, are shown on the next page.

Escaping domestic violence, Erika Andiola's mother came to the United States from Mexico without documentation with Erika and two of Erika's siblings when Erika was only 11. Erika originally received a scholarship to attend Arizona State University, but a new Arizona law prohibited undocumented students from receiving scholarships, so the scholarship was rescinded. Even though her undocumented status made it difficult to find employment, Erika worked to pay for tuition, studied, and graduated from Arizona State in 2009 with a B.A. in psychology. Erika then went to work for then-Congresswoman Kyrsten Sinema (see the opening vignette in Chapter 10, Elections and Campaigns). She also began lobbying to support President Barack Obama's proposed Development, Relief, and Education for Alien Minors (DREAM) Act, which would

have granted permanent residency to undocumented immigrants if they arrived in the United States before they turned 16, received an honorable discharge from the military, or completed at least two years toward a college degree. While the bill passed the House in 2010, it never received the supermajority necessary to end the filibuster against it in the Senate. In 2012, however, President Obama directed Immigration and Customs Enforcement (ICE) to stop deporting undocumented students who met DREAM Act standards.

Despite the president's order, in 2013, agents from ICE broke into the Andiola family house, arresting Erika's mother and brother. Erika organized a huge protest against the arrests, and they were released the following day. As Marielena Hincapié, executive director of the National Immigration Law Center, put it, "Not all immigrant families have the benefit of Erika to mobilize the

---

*Immigration activist Erika Andiola on putting cages up throughout Iowa on the day of the Iowa caucus to remind caucus goers of President Donald Trump's policy of caging children at the southern border.

Learning Outcomes

LO 5-1 Define civil rights

LO 5-2 Explain how the federal and state governments suppressed civil rights

LO 5-3 Assess how equal protection has expanded

LO 5-4 Identify the groups at the forefront of the civil rights movement

LO 5-5 Describe the new battles for civil rights

whole country overnight." Erika used the gateway of grassroots activism to get the government to use its discretion not to deport her family. Due to the massive support she received from around the country, her efforts succeeded.

In 2014, Andiola began a hunger strike at ICE headquarters in Phoenix, Arizona. One week later, Phoenix police arrested her, a move that could have led to her deportation but, perhaps due to her status as an activist for undocumented Americans, they did not. She launched #not1more to get President Obama, who deported more undocumented residents than any other president to date, to end deportations. She also began a hunger strike at the White House.

Andiola remains optimistic about the future. When asked by the *New York Times* where her activism is leading, the woman who originally went to college to become a psychologist replied, "I haven't been able to think that far. At this point, I just want to be able to pass immigration reform. I want to be able to keep my mom here, and we'll see where life takes me from there."[1]

In 2016, Andiola joined Bernie Sanders's presidential campaign as national press secretary for Latino outreach. In accepting the position, she declared, "For us, what matters is really again, making sure Bernie gets introduced to a lot

more Latinos. . . . Obviously, he's not as known as Secretary Clinton."[2]

In this chapter, we look at the idea of equality, how it has changed, and how the federal government's enforcement of it has changed as well. We examine how grassroots racial, ethnic, and gender-based movements pressured the courts to protect civil rights and how Congress enforced court rulings with legislation. As with civil liberties (see Chapter 4, Civil Liberties), however, finding the right balance of rights for minority groups frequently divides members of society from one another, and divides democratically responsive legislatures from lifetime-appointed judges.

SlngZamMamy/Stock Photo

What Are Civil Rights?

LO 5-1 Define civil rights

Although the Declaration of Independence proclaimed that "All men are created equal," the Constitution originally had little to say about equality, at least as the concept is understood today. Even the debate over the ratification of the Constitution had little to do with equality. It was much more about how much power to invest in the federal government. Today, however, equality is a hallowed principle of American political culture, but the notion and the reality evolved slowly over two centuries.

Civil Rights and Civil Liberties

civil rights: *Set of rights centered around the concept of equal treatment that government is obliged to protect.*

Civil rights are rights related to the duties of citizenship and the gateways for participation in civic life that the government is obliged to protect. These rights are based on the expectation of equality under the law. The most important is the right to vote. In contrast to civil liberties (see Chapter 4), Americans have struggled hard to gain civil rights.

Civil rights also differ from civil liberties in that while government is the main authority that can suppress liberties—for example, by suppressing freedom of speech or forbidding a certain religious belief—both government and private entities, such as individuals or businesses, have the capacity to engage in discrimination by treating people unequally.

The government can therefore take three different roles when it comes to civil rights. It can engage in state-sponsored or **public discrimination** by actively discriminating against people. It can treat people equally but permit **private discrimination** by allowing individuals or businesses to discriminate. Finally, it can try, as the U.S. government has since the 1960s, to treat people equally and to prevent individuals or businesses from discriminating. Thus, it falls to government to protect individuals against unequal treatment and to citizens to ensure that the government itself is not discriminating against individuals or groups. In a democracy, the majority rules, but the gateways for minorities must also be kept open.

public discrimination: *Discrimination by national, state, or local governments.*

private discrimination: *Discrimination by private individuals or businesses.*

> **Key Questions**
> Why would a government discriminate?

> **Key Questions**
> What did equality mean to the Founders?

The Constitution and Civil Rights

Despite the statement on equality in the Declaration of Independence, the role of the government regarding equality was not written into the Constitution, and the United States has a bleak history on civil rights. The Founders were not much concerned with equality as it is understood today. Many of them owned slaves, and they did not see a contradiction between doing so and the Declaration's statement that "All men are created equal." The Constitution gave the states authority over voting, and most states restricted the right to vote to free males with a certain amount of property. Slaves could not vote, and in three states, even free African Americans could not vote—neither could women (except in New Jersey) or Native Americans.[3] During the nation's first century and even thereafter, state laws and the national government actively discriminated against people on the basis of race, gender, and ethnic background.

Following the Civil War, the Thirteenth Amendment ended slavery, and the Fourteenth Amendment forbade states to deny any person "the equal protection of the laws." Nevertheless, the equality of African Americans was not thereby guaranteed. Some of the members of Congress who wrote the Fourteenth Amendment believed that equality was limited to "the right to go and come; the right to enforce contracts; the right to convey his property; the right to buy property" and little more.[4] The courts agreed, and the federal government made little effort to ensure equal treatment during the nation's second century.

Meanwhile, women won the right to vote (1920), but not the right to full participation in public life. Native Americans born on reservations became citizens (1924), but not until the civil rights and women's movements of the 1950s and 1960s did legal discrimination against African Americans, women, and ethnic minorities end. Today, the government actively aims to treat individuals and groups as equals before the law and to use its authority to prevent state and local governments, and individuals and businesses, from discriminating.

In the past half-century, the meaning of "all men are created equal" has been expanded to include women and all people subject to the jurisdiction of the United States. Yet Americans still debate the meaning of *equality*. Should, or can, the government ensure **equality of opportunity** for all people? Should, or can, it engineer **equality of outcome**? That is, is it enough for society to provide equality of opportunity by prohibiting discrimination? What if that still leaves members of groups that have historically been discriminated against, such as women and minorities, with fewer advanced degrees and lower incomes? As it has throughout the course of the nation's history, the meaning of equality continues to evolve. Lesser access of African Americans to good jobs, safe housing, and, health care are among the reasons they have been more likely to die from COVID-19. In Chicago, where African Americans are just 30 percent of the population, they have made up 72 percent of the COVID-19 fatalities. Similarly, in New Orleans African Americans constitute 32 percent of the population, but again 72 percent of the fatalities.[5]

In the next sections, we see how, as the idea of equality expanded, the federal government moved from actively treating different groups unequally under the law, to asserting equality under the law but doing little to protect it, to actively enforcing it.

Key Questions

What is your idea of equality—equality of opportunity or equality of outcome?

equality of opportunity: *Expectation that citizens may not be discriminated against on account of race, gender, or national background and that every citizen should have an equal chance to succeed in life.*

equality of outcome: *Expectation that equality is achieved if results are comparable for all citizens regardless of race, gender, or national background or that such groups are proportionally represented in measures of success in life.*

Legal Restrictions on Civil Rights

LO 5-2 Explain how the federal and state governments suppressed civil rights

Slavery split the United States from the founding of the nation through the Civil War. After the Civil War, the Constitution prohibited slavery. It also prohibited the states from denying equality, but many states continued to discriminate. Both Congress and the Supreme Court had the authority to enforce equality, but neither acted. Women, African Americans, and ethnic minorities suffered under unequal laws, with denial of the right to vote and laws that limited their full participation in labor markets, professions, and public life. Discriminatory laws also affected Asians. Such laws prohibited those who were not born in the United States from becoming citizens and later prevented them from immigrating to the United States altogether.

Image 5.1 An anti–slave trade etching from 1792.

Key Questions

Describe the role of compromise in American politics. Is it wise or foolish for politicians to compromise?

Dred Scott v. Sandford: *The 1857 Supreme Court decision declaring that blacks could not be citizens and Congress could not ban slavery in the territories.*

Slavery

Slavery came to the colonies in 1619 when a Virginian purchased Africans from a Dutch shipper. Colonial Africans originally were servants, largely indistinct from indentured servants of other races who bound themselves to service for a limited number of years in return for free passage to Britain's American colonies. But African slavery soon became established in colonial law. In 1664, Maryland passed legislation declaring that all "Negroes or other slaves hereafter imported . . . shall serve for life."[6] The law also made slaves of the children of slaves.

The compromises made at the Constitutional Convention allowed the United States to form, but they also allowed slavery to grow and spread. By 1808, when Congress banned the further importation of slaves from Africa, the slave population had reached 1 million, and it continued growing through natural increase thereafter. With neither slave nor free forces dominant politically, Congress continued to compromise. The Missouri Compromise (1820) banned slavery in the territories north of the southern border of Missouri, thus keeping most of the vast lands of the Louisiana Purchase free. The Compromise of 1850 allowed territories captured in the Mexican War to decide for themselves whether to be free or slave. The Kansas-Nebraska Act (1854) undid the Missouri Compromise by allowing each territory to vote on whether to allow slavery. The Supreme Court further extended the reach of slavery in **Dred Scott v. Sandford** (1857).[7]

Dred Scott, a slave who had moved with his master from the slave state of Missouri to the free Wisconsin Territory and then back to Missouri, sued in federal court for his freedom based on his extended stay in free territory. The Supreme Court's decision in the case, written by Chief Justice Roger Taney, a former slave owner, declared (1) that no black—slave or free—could be an American citizen, and thus that no black could sue in a federal court; (2) that blacks were "beings of an inferior order" who had "no rights which the white man was bound to respect"; (3) that the Declaration of Independence's statement that "all men are created equal" did not include men of African heritage; (4) that Congress's authority to "make all needful Rules and Regulations respecting the Territory . . . [of] the United States" did not include the right to prohibit slavery in those territories; and (5) that slaves were the property of their owners, so freeing Scott would violate his owner's Fifth Amendment right not to be deprived of his property without due process of law. With this decision, the regulation of slavery in the territories was removed from the national authority of Congress and placed in the hands of local authorities in the territories.

The 1860 election of Abraham Lincoln (1861–65), who opposed the extension of slavery, prompted southern states to secede from the union. During the ensuing Civil War, President Lincoln issued the Emancipation Proclamation, which made slavery illegal in those states in rebellion as of January 1, 1863. The Proclamation did not pertain to border states that retained slavery but remained in the Union. Needless to say, Southerners did not release their slaves based on the proclamation. When Union armies reached Galveston, Texas on June 19, 1865, the last slaves in Confederate states were freed. That date has become known as **"Juneteenth."** Slavery was finally ended in the United States following Union victory and ratification of the Thirteenth Amendment in 1865 (see Figure 5.1).

Key:	Criminal procedure	Participation	Equality	

Thirteenth	1865	Prohibits slavery in the United States
Fourteenth	1868	Makes all persons born in the United States citizens of the United States and prohibits states from denying persons within its jurisdiction the privileges or immunities of citizens, the due process of law, and equal protection of the laws; apportionment by whole persons
Fifteenth	1870	Prohibits states from denying the right to vote on account of race
Nineteenth	1920	Guarantees women the right to vote
Twenty-Fourth	1964	Prohibits poll taxes

Figure 5.1 Constitutional Amendments That Pertain to Civil Rights

Since 1865, increasing equality and participation has been an important theme in constitutional amendments.

Restrictions on Citizenship

The Constitution was not explicit on birthright citizenship, but the clause requiring that presidents be natural-born citizens seemingly implies that people born in the United States are citizens.[8] Yet on the basis of ethnic background, some groups were denied the status of **citizenship** and the privileges it entailed, such as property rights and the protection of civil liberties.

citizenship: *Full-fledged membership in a nation.*

The Constitution explicitly allows people not born in the United States to become citizens through naturalization by granting Congress the authority "to establish a uniform rule of naturalization." Congress's first such law, the Naturalization Act of 1790, restricted citizenship to "free white persons" who had lived in the United States for two years, swore allegiance to the United States, and had "good character." Though restrictive on race, the act allowed Catholics, Jews, and other "free white persons" to become naturalized citizens, rights that most European nations did not allow. The act also declared people born overseas to parents who were U.S. citizens to be natural-born citizens. Congress first allowed non-whites to become naturalized citizens in 1870, when it extended naturalization to "persons of African descent."

Native Americans.   In 1823, the Supreme Court declared that Native Americans were merely inhabitants, "an inferior race of people, without the privileges of citizens."[9] The legislative policy of the United States toward Native Americans included forcible removal from various territories under the Indian Removal Act of 1830 and the creation of land reserved for them (reservations) starting with the Indian Appropriations Act in 1851. The Fourteenth Amendment's citizenship clause did not remedy this situation: The Court ruled in 1884 that the clause did not provide citizenship to Native Americans born on reservations because reservations are not fully under the jurisdiction of the United States.[10] Not until the Indian Citizenship Act of 1924 did Congress provide natural-born citizenship to Native Americans born on reservations.

Latinos.   Latinos in the Southwestern United States arrived prior to American settlers. They lived in areas from Texas to California, and Tejanos, the term for people of Mexican descent living in Texas, fought alongside other Texans in battles against the Mexican Army. Perhaps due to the close affiliation with Mexico, many Tejanos, Californios, and other Latinos lost their properties after the Treaty of Guadalupe Hidalgo, which ended the Mexican-American War and resulted in Mexico ceding to the United States what is now California, Nevada, New Mexico, Arizona, Utah, Texas, Wyoming, and Colorado. After the United States annexed Texas, Anglos forcibly expelled many Tejanos. Those who remained, though formally granted citizenship, were often faced with "second-class" status with few recognized rights.[11]

The history of the treatment of Latinos by the U.S. government is a mixed one. In the late 1920s and early 1930s, approximately 2 million people of Mexican descent were deported to Mexico due to economic and political pressures stemming from the Great Depression. Roughly 60 percent of those expelled during what became known as the Mexican Repatriation were U.S. citizens. "Federal, state, and local governments working together involuntarily removed many U.S. citizens of Mexican ancestry, many of whom were born in the United States. These citizens cannot be said to have been 'repatriated' to their native land."[12] As a result of the Mexican "Repatriation," the nation lost roughly one-third of its Mexican population. A similar program took place in the 1950s under the offensive name "Operation Wetback,"[13] and similar "roundups" have occurred as recently as 1997.[14] In 2005, the California Assembly passed the "Apology Act for the 1930s Mexican Repatriation Program" in recognition of the coerced removal of legal residents of Mexican descent.

The Mexican Repatriation delayed for decades the full emergence of the Latino community as a political, economic, and social force in the United States.[15] Civil rights enjoyed by Latinos today were not always recognized as such, nor are they guaranteed to be so in the future. As Latinos continue to be the fastest-growing ethnic group in the United States, it is clear there have been many gates to political participation placed before them, which are discussed more in depth in Chapter 11, Voting and Participation.

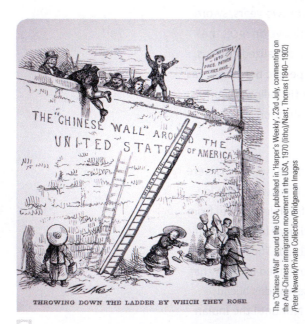

The 'Chinese Wall' around the USA, published in 'Harper's Weekly', 23rd July, commenting on the Anti-Chinese immigration movement in the USA, 1970 (litho)/Nast, Thomas (1840–1902) /Peter Newark/Private Collection/Bridgeman Images

THE "CHINESE WALL" AROUND THE UNITED STATES OF AMERICA

THROWING DOWN THE LADDER BY WHICH THEY ROSE.

Image 5.2 Drawing of a wall depicting the exclusion of Chinese immigrants from the United States.

Asian Americans. Even after Congress allowed "persons of African descent" to become naturalized citizens in 1870, Asians still could not become naturalized citizens. Often states enacted discriminatory legislation to bar Asians from benefiting from opportunities granted to other residents. California's 1879 constitution prohibited Chinese from voting and from employment in state and local government. In 1913, California prohibited Japanese immigrants from purchasing farmland.[16]

Indeed, fear of Chinese immigrants led to an 1882 prohibition on the immigration of Chinese to America. That ban was the first significant restriction on immigration to the United States. Congress extended this ban to all Asians in 1921. The ban stayed in effect until 1943, when Congress allowed an annual quota of 105 immigrants from China, a World War II ally. The 1943 act also allowed Chinese to become naturalized citizens but did not allow other Asians to do so. Congress ended this restriction on Asian naturalization in 1952 but kept strict limits on the number of Asian immigrants until 1965 (see Image 5.2).

Beyond the setbacks of the anti-Asian immigration policies, President Franklin Delano Roosevelt (1933–45), following the Japanese attack on Pearl Harbor, issued an executive order for the evacuation of all 110,000 people of Japanese ancestry who resided west of the Rocky Mountains—whether citizen (most of them) or not—and their placement in relocation camps. Congress ratified the president's order, and in 1944 the Supreme Court endorsed it in *Korematsu v. United States,* ruling that the authority for relocation was within the war power of the United States.[17]

Key Questions
Does military necessity overrule civil rights? If so, under what circumstances?

Although the government justified the program on the grounds of military necessity rather than racial animosity, it did not attempt wholesale roundups of German Americans despite the existence of the German American Bund, a pro-Nazi association with about twenty thousand members before the war. That the government even rounded up Japanese American children from orphanages suggests that racial animosity was more important than security concerns.[18] The program remained in effect through the war years, although the government filed no charges of disloyalty or subversion against any person of Japanese ancestry. Many Japanese Americans valiantly served the United States in segregated military units during the war.

Immigration Limits. Congress used immigration laws to keep out ethnic groups as well as anyone considered undesirable, including "idiots," insane people, paupers, felons, polygamists, anarchists, and people coming for "immoral purposes."[19] Immigration officials used the morality clauses to keep homosexuals from entering the country until 1979.[20] During the last several presidential elections, Democrats have consistently favored increasing immigration to the United States along with a "path to citizenship." On the Republican side nominees have taken both sides of the issue. The 2000 and 2004 Republican nominee, George W. Bush, favored increased immigration, as did 2008 Republican nominee John McCain. In 2012, Republican nominee Mitt Romney suggested that strict conditions for undocumented residents in the United States would lead to "self deportation." In 2016, Republican presidential nominee Donald Trump proposed building a wall between Mexico and the United States as well as prohibiting Muslims from entering the United States. President Trump continued his exclusionary platform in the 2020 campaign.

Key Questions
What restrictions, if any, should there be on immigration?

In the early twentieth century, immigration soared, only to drop back during World War I. After the war, the Ku Klux Klan (KKK) resurfaced, now targeting immigrants, Catholics, and Jews as well as blacks. With nearly 5 million members and chapters throughout the country, the KKK joined others with less violent supremacist beliefs to pressure Congress to limit immigration.[21] The Immigration Act of 1924 established quotas for ethnic groups based on the proportion of Americans from each nationality resident in 1890, thereby severely limiting the number of whites considered to be of "lower race"— that is, those from southern and eastern Europe,[22] who constituted a huge proportion of immigrants from the 1890s on. This also reduced the number of Jewish immigrants eligible to enter during the critical years before World War II and the Holocaust. Under the act, the quota for Italy, for example, dropped more than 90 percent[23] from the percentage allowed in the Immigration Act of 1921, which also established quotas but based them on the proportion of each nationality resident in 1910.

With the Immigration and Nationality Act of 1965, Congress rescinded the quota system and the especially severe restrictions on Asian immigration. Today, to apply for citizenship, one must have had legal permanent residence for five years, or three years if married to a U.S.

citizen. Applicants also must be of good moral character and must be able to pass a test on questions such as "who elects the president?"

Racial Segregation and Discrimination

Key Questions

After ratification of the Fifteenth Amendment, who could not vote?

The end of slavery did not make former slaves (or "freedmen") equal citizens. Immediately after the war, southern states wrote new constitutions that severely limited the civil and political rights of the freedmen. These so-called black codes prevented them from voting, owning land, and leaving their plantations. Congress responded with the Civil Rights Act of 1866, which guaranteed the right of freedmen to make contracts, sue in court if those contracts were violated, and own property. Congress also established military rule over the former Confederate states, which would end in a state when it passed a new state constitution that guaranteed black suffrage and when it ratified the Fourteenth Amendment. With former Confederates barred from voting, blacks constituted a majority of the electorate in several states, and more than six hundred freedmen served in state legislatures during **Reconstruction**, as this era was called.

Reconstruction: *The period from 1865 to 1877 in which the former Confederate states gained readmission to the Union and the federal government passed laws to help the emancipated slaves.*

The Fourteenth Amendment (1868), in addition to guaranteeing that no state shall deny any person due process of law (see Chapter 4), prohibits states from denying any person the **equal protection** of the law. It also makes all people born in the United States citizens of the United States, overturning the Supreme Court's ruling in the *Dred Scott* case that blacks could not be U.S. citizens. To prevent states from rescinding the right of black suffrage, the Fifteenth Amendment (1870) declared that the right to vote could not be abridged on account of race.

equal protection clause: *Prevents states from denying any person the equal protection of the laws (Fourteenth Amendment).*

Opponents of freedmen's rights turned to violence. In 1866, Confederate veterans formed the Ku Klux Klan (KKK), a terrorist organization aimed at restoring white supremacy. In 1873, white supremacists massacred more than a hundred blacks in Colfax, Louisiana, as part of an ongoing election dispute. The federal government brought charges against three of the perpetrators, but the Supreme Court reversed their conviction, arguing that the Fourteenth Amendment gave Congress the authority to act only against states that violated civil rights (public discrimination), not against individuals who did so (private discrimination).[24]

Reconstruction ended with a deal over the 1876 election. A close and contested race between Republican Rutherford B. Hayes and Democrat Samuel Tilden was resolved when southern Democrats in Congress agreed to allow Hayes to become president in return for the withdrawal of federal troops from the South. Freed from military rule, white supremacist groups such as the KKK embarked on a campaign of lynching and other forms of terrorism against blacks.

State governments were not responsive to the victims because, despite the Fifteenth Amendment, southern politicians established a set of rules that kept blacks from voting. **Poll taxes** limited the voting of poor blacks (as well as of poor whites). The white primary took advantage of the fact that, with the Republican Party negatively associated with Lincoln and the Civil War, the Democratic Party then completely dominated southern politics. Therefore, whoever won the local Democratic primary for an office was sure to win in the general election. Excluding blacks from voting in Democratic primaries meant that blacks had no effective vote at all. Even so, states used literacy tests to disqualify voters. These involved reading and interpreting difficult passages. To avoid disqualifying white voters as well, grandfather clauses gave exemptions to men whose grandfathers had been

poll taxes: *Tax on voting; prohibited by the Twenty-Fourth Amendment (1964).*

eligible to vote. The men who received these exemptions were, of course, always white (see Chapter 11 for further discussion of these techniques and an example of a literacy test).

These legal strategies effectively disenfranchised black men. In addition, state and local **Jim Crow laws** enforced segregation of whites and blacks in all public places. When a New Orleans civil rights organization challenged a Louisiana law requiring segregated railway cars by having Homer Plessy, who was one-eighth black, sit in the whites-only car, the Supreme Court upheld the segregation.[25] *Plessy v. Ferguson* (1896) established the **separate-but-equal doctrine**, which held that states could segregate the races without violating the equal protection clause of the Fourteenth Amendment as long as the separate facilities were equal.[26] Southern states segregated schools, libraries, and other public institutions and required the segregation of restaurants, inns, and other places of public accommodation. The facilities were almost never equal. African Americans in northern states often experienced discrimination in

Images 5.3 and 5.4 In segregated school systems, the schools for black children and the schools for white children were almost never equal. These insurance photographs show Liberty Hill Colored School and Summerton Graded School in Clarendon County, South Carolina, in 1948. They were used as evidence in *Briggs v. Elliott,* one of the school segregation cases decided with *Brown v. Board of Education* (1954).

hiring, housing, hotels, and restaurants, though segregation was not enforced by law. African Americans could serve in the military but generally in segregated units under white officers. During the late nineteenth and early twentieth centuries, discrimination was state-sponsored in the South; elsewhere in the nation, people engaged in private discrimination without challenge.

Ethnic Segregation and Discrimination

Latinos and other ethnic groups experienced many of the same discriminatory practices as did African Americans. The separate-but-equal doctrine of *Plessy v. Ferguson* (1896) applied to Latino and other minorities. White voters instituted segregation in the South and the West. Phoenix, Arizona, ran separate schools for blacks, Native Americans, and Mexicans.[27] California ran separate schools for Asians as well as Mexicans,[28] while Texas kept Mexican Americans in separate classrooms.[29] In areas of the Southwestern United States, Latinos were required to sit in the back of buses, sit in movie theater balconies, and attend separate public schools. The end of segregation practices aimed at African Americans did not necessarily end them for Latinos (see Table 5.1).

Jim Crow laws: *Southern laws that established strict segregation of the races and gave their name to the segregation era.*

separate-but-equal doctrine: *Supreme Court doctrine that upheld segregation as long as there were equivalent facilities for blacks.*

Key Questions
If some people are blocked from voting, what is the effect on government?

Table 5.1 Timeline of Civil Rights and Latinos

Year	Event
1912	New Mexico enters the union as an officially bilingual state, with voting in both Spanish and English, as well as bilingual education.
1917	The U.S. Congress passes the Jones Act, granting citizenship to Puerto Ricans.
1921	*Orden Hijos de América* (Order of the Sons of America) organizes Mexican American workers to raise awareness of civil rights issues and fight for fair wages, education, and housing.
1928	Octaviano Larrazolo (R-NM) becomes the first Latino U.S. senator.
1929	The League of United Latin American Citizens (LULAC) organizes against discrimination and segregation and promotes education among Latinos. It remains the largest and longest-lasting Latino civil rights group in the country.
1948	The American G.I. Forum forms in Texas to combat discrimination and improve the status of Latinos; branches eventually form in twenty-three states.
1954	*Hernandez v. Texas* strikes down discrimination based on class and ethnic distinctions.
1965	Congress passes the Voting Rights Act.
1965	Cesar Chavez and Dolores Huerta found the United Farm Workers association. It becomes the largest and most important farm worker union in the nation. Huerta becomes the first woman to lead such a union. The Grape Boycott becomes one of the most significant social justice movements for farm workers in the United States.
1966	*Katzenbach v. Morgan* allows Congress to prohibit English proficiency voting requirements for Puerto Ricans in New York.
1968	The Mexican American Legal Defense and Education Fund (MALDEF) is established, becoming the first legal fund to pursue protection of the civil rights of Mexican Americans. The Puerto Rican Legal Defense and Education Fund (PRLDEF) is founded in 1972.
1970	*Cisneros v. Corpus Christi Independent School District* extends the *Brown* decision to Latinos.
1973	*White v. Regester* calls for the creation of single-member election districts to prevent the dilution of Latino and African American voting strength.
1974	The first major Latino voter registration organization, the Southwest Voter Registration Education Project (SVREP) launches, registering more than 2 million Latino voters in the first twenty years.
1975	Congress votes to expand the Voting Rights Act to require language assistance at the polls and that election materials be available in multiple languages.
1982	*Plyler v. Doe* extends Fourteenth Amendment equal protection to children of undocumented workers.
1994	*Johnson v. DeGrandy* establishes the importance of proportionality as part of the totality of circumstances that must be considered in the redistricting process in this case from Florida involving Cuban Americans.
2001	The DREAM Act first introduced in Congress.
2009	Sonia Sotomayor becomes first Latino Supreme Court Justice.
2010	Susana Martinez (R-NM) becomes the first Latina governor
2013	*Shelby v. Holder* strikes down original formulas from the Voting Rights Act of 1965 that trigger requirements for states and local governments to obtain preclearance for changes to their election laws.
2016	Catherine Cortez Masto (D-NV) becomes the first Latina U.S. Senator

Source: Derived from "Latino Civil Rights Timeline, 1903 to 2006" in Teaching Tolerance, Southern Poverty Law Center, http://www.tolerance.org/latino-civil-rights-timeline and supplemented by the authors.

Women's Suffrage

By law and by custom, women were also excluded from public life from the earliest days of the nation. In 1776, Abigail Adams had urged her husband, John Adams, to "remember the ladies" in drafting the nation's founding documents. In language similar to that later used by Jefferson in the Declaration, she warned, "if particular care and attention is not paid to the ladies, we are determined to foment a rebellion, and will not hold ourselves bound by any laws in which we have no voice or representation."[30] Nevertheless, neither the Declaration nor the Constitution made any provision for women's rights. Rather, the states continued the English policy of coverture, which granted married women no rights independent of their husbands. They could not own property, keep their own wages, or sign contracts. As for voting, each state set its own rules. In 1789, only New Jersey allowed women the right to vote (provided the women met the state's property requirements), a right the people of the state rescinded via referendum in 1807.[31]

In 1848, leaders of the **women's suffrage movement** met in Seneca Falls, New York, to organize for the right to vote. They prepared a "Declaration of Sentiments" that used the language of the Declaration of Independence to assert that "all men and women are created equal," but few results came from this meeting. Then, in 1869, Susan B. Anthony and Elizabeth Cady Stanton formed the National Woman Suffrage Association (NWSA), which lobbied for the right of women to vote and unsuccessfully opposed the Fifteenth Amendment unless it was changed to include women's suffrage. With the NWSA focused on gaining national suffrage through constitutional amendment, an alternative organization, the American Woman Suffrage Association (AWSA), formed to press for state-by-state suffrage rights.

In 1872, a Missouri voting registrar prohibited suffragist Virginia Minor from registering to vote. Minor sued, arguing that the privileges of citizenship, as guaranteed by the Fourteenth Amendment, include the right to vote. The Supreme Court ruled, however, that citizenship does not imply a right to vote.[32]

That same year the Court ruled that the right to practice law was not a privilege or immunity guaranteed by the Fourteenth Amendment, allowing Illinois to keep law a male-only profession. Representing common views at the time, one justice wrote, "The paramount destiny and mission of women are to fulfill the noble and benign offices of wife and mother. This is the law of the Creator."[33] States passed various types of so-called protective legislation that limited the jobs women could work at and/or the number of hours they could work. These laws had the express purpose of protecting women because of their status as wives and mothers, but their main impact was to act as a gate that put women at a disadvantage in the employment market.[34]

Although women's rights advocates typically opposed protective legislation, they focused their attention on the right to vote. With the courts rejecting a gateway to voting through the Fourteenth Amendment, suffragists focused on the legislative arena. Anthony presented the 1887 Congress with ten thousand petition signatures demanding women's suffrage. The suffragist movement, though, was not universally admired; many people opposed voting equality for women because it threatened their notions of appropriate gender roles. In 1913, a mob attacked a suffrage parade in Washington, D.C., and suffragist protests outside the White House in 1917 led to hundreds of arrests.

While state control of voting gave southern states the power to disenfranchise blacks, it also gave western states the power to experiment with women's suffrage. The territory of

Key Questions
Should all citizens have the right to vote? Are there any citizens who should not have this right? How should this be determined?

women's suffrage movement: *Movement to grant women the right to vote.*

Key Questions
Did Anthony and Stanton right make the right choice to lobby against the Fifteenth Amendment? What might have happened if they supported it?

Key Questions
Why was there such strong resistance to women's suffrage?

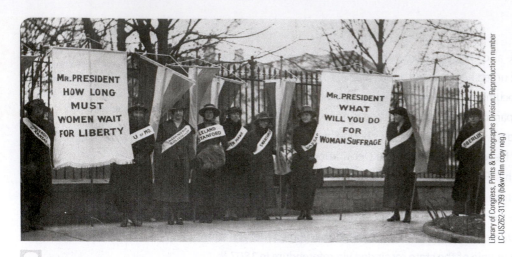

Image 5.5 During World War I, members of the National Woman's Party picketed the White House. Wearing banners announcing their colleges, they challenged President Woodrow Wilson to bring home the concern for liberty that he expressed for Europe. More than 150 women were arrested, and about 100 were sentenced to federal prisons, where some went on hunger strikes and were force-fed.

Wyoming granted women's suffrage in 1869 and continued it upon statehood in 1890. Males in Colorado voted for women's suffrage in 1893. Utah granted women the right to vote in 1895. In 1913, Illinois granted women the right to vote for president but not for other national offices. In 1916, the people of Montana elected the first woman to serve in the U.S. House of Representatives, Jeannette Rankin.

Suffragist amendments failed numerous times in Congress before receiving the necessary two-thirds vote in both chambers in 1919.[35] By August 1920, with effective lobbying by suffragist groups, three-quarters of the states ratified the Nineteenth Amendment, guaranteeing women the right to vote in the November 1920 presidential election (see Chapter 11, Voting and Participation). Even before the Amendment passed, many states, especially out west, granted women the right to vote in their state constitutions (see Figure 5.2).

Key Questions
Should the Constitution include an equal rights amendment?

Continued Gender Discrimination

Nevertheless, public law and private attitudes constituted gates that blocked women from full participation in the nation's public life. Radical feminists pushed for an equal rights amendment, which would have overturned protective legislation and other laws that treated men and women differently. Although introduced in Congress in 1923 and every year thereafter, it was not taken seriously. Even in 1945, only a minority of white males nationally thought that women should be able to take jobs outside the home.[36]

Not surprisingly, the federal and state governments were responsive to these sorts of views. As late as 1972, eleven states continued to enforce coverture laws.[37] Louisiana, for example, gave a husband, "as 'head and master' of property jointly owned with his wife," the complete right to dispose of such property without his wife's consent.[38] Teachers were commonly forced to retire if they got married.[39] Outside of coverture laws, Social Security provided survivors' benefits for children if their working fathers died but not if their working mothers died. It similarly provided unemployment benefits to children of unemployed fathers but not to children of unemployed mothers. Males in the military received benefits for their dependents that females in the military did not receive. Idaho gave preferences to men over women in determining who would administer a dead relative's estate. Utah required parents to support sons until age 21 but daughters only until age 18. A woman could not work as a bartender in Michigan unless she was the wife or daughter of the bar's owner.[40]

In more recent years, the Obama administration declared sexual harassment to be a form of sex discrimination.[41] The levels of sexual assaults on college campuses reached a point at which the Obama administration labeled it an epidemic. His administration sent a "Dear Colleague" letter to U.S. colleges and universities receiving federal aid (i.e., virtually all of them) telling them that sexual harassment was a form of sex discrimination and that institutions that did not take active steps to fight it would be in danger of losing federal funds.[42] The letter explicitly allowed complainants to remain anonymous during disciplinary hearings.[43] The Obama administration required schools to use "a preponderance of the evidence" standard for guilt (i.e., "more likely than not")—the lowest possible standard.[44] One month after President Trump's inauguration, his secretary of education, noting a lack of due process protections, withdrew the Obama "Dear Colleague" letter.[45] President Trump himself had denied numerous allegations of sexual assault during the 2016 election campaign, endorsed alleged pedophile Roy Moore in his 2017 Senate campaign, and had nothing but kind words for White House staffer Rob Porter who left his job after both of his ex-wives accused him of spousal abuse.

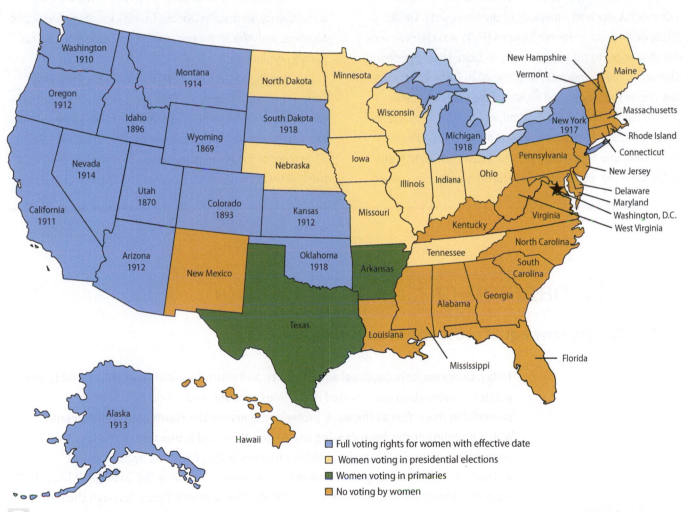

Figure 5.2 **Women's Suffrage Before 1920**

Because states control voting laws, women's suffrage advocates campaigned at the state level, and, before the Nineteenth Amendment was ratified in 1920, women could vote in some elections in most states. The Nineteenth Amendment superseded state law, stating that the right to vote could not be denied or abridged by the United States, or by any state, on account of sex.

Source: Data from Mary Beth Norton et al., *A People and a Nation: A History of the United States*, 8th ed. (Boston: Houghton Mifflin, 2008), 608.

Voting Behavior of Demographic Groups

The battle for civil rights in the United States has had many consequences, with perhaps the most important ones concerning more diverse electorates brought about by expansions of voting-rights protections. Because the Democratic Party has been at the forefront of these changes, nonwhite voters have been an ever-increasing part of the Democratic Party's constituency. Not since Lyndon Johnson in 1964 has a Democrat received a majority of the white vote. Unlike 2016, when Senator Bernie Sanders (I-VT) was the only serious challenger to former Secretary of State Hillary Rodham Clinton on the Democratic side, the 2020 Democratic race saw one of the largest and most diverse fields ever. The twenty-eight candidates who competed in the Democratic primary included five women, two Latinos, two African Americans, one East Asian, and one LGBT candidate.[46] But by the time the multistate Super-Tuesday primaries came

in early March, the only remaining candidates were Senator Bernie Sanders, former Vice President Joe Biden, and Representative Tulsi Gabbard (D-HI).

Incumbent Donald Trump saw only token competition for the Republican nomination, with both challengers being white males.

Minorities are a small proportion of the Republican constituency, so despite Donald Trump's insults to Mexicans, Muslims, and African Americans,[47] he rather easily won his party's nomination.

According to the *New York Times* exit poll, President Trump received 49 percent of the male vote, 43 percent of the female vote, 57 percent of the white vote, 12 percent of the African American vote, 32 percent of the Latino vote, and 31 percent of the Asian vote. He also received 28 percent of the LGBT vote.[48]

The Expansion of Equal Protection

LO 5-3 Assess how equal protection has expanded

Today, Congress, constitutional amendments, and court decisions have put an end to the public discrimination documented in previous sections, and no clause has been as powerful in this effort as the equal protection clause of the Fourteenth Amendment, which prohibits states from denying any person the equal protection of the law. The amendment gives Congress the authority to enforce its provisions by appropriate legislation, adding to Congress's enumerated powers by allowing the passage of laws that prevent states from discriminating. Additionally, the Supreme Court, through the power of judicial review, retains the authority to strike state laws that violate equal protection. During the first half of the twentieth century, the meaning of equality changed for many Americans, and they organized to press the federal government into playing a crucial role to fight both public and private discrimination. This section examines gradual expansion of equal protection prior to the civil rights movement.

State Action

Shortly after the passage of the Fourteenth Amendment, Congress tried to ban private discrimination at inns, public conveyances, theaters, and other public places. The Supreme Court rejected congressional authority to do so in the *Civil Rights Cases* (1883), ruling that the Fourteenth Amendment prohibited public discrimination by the states only, not private discrimination by businesses or individuals. From the 1880s until the 1940s, the federal government remained passive about discrimination, allowing states and locales to require segregation of the races and permitting public and private institutions to make their own rules regarding it.

In 1948, however, the Court ruled that private discrimination can be prohibited if it involves significant **state action**. The case involved housing. A group of homeowners signed a contract pledging never to sell their homes to blacks, but one of the homeowners did so. The neighbors sued to prevent the new owners from taking possession of the house, and the state supreme court ruled in favor of the neighbors. The U.S. Supreme Court reversed the state supreme court, ruling that judicial enforcement of the discriminatory private contract constitutes state action and thus is prohibited by the Fourteenth Amendment.[49]

Key Questions

Why is majority rule not always congruent with civil rights?

state action: *Action by a state, as opposed to a private person, that constitutes discrimination and therefore is an equal protection violation.*

Judicial Review

While the state-action doctrine allowed the Supreme Court to prohibit limited types of private discrimination, the equal protection clause of the Fourteenth Amendment is better suited to fighting public discrimination. In the next two decades, the Supreme Court actively applied the equal protection clause of the Fourteenth Amendment to do so. Congress also has the authority to enforce the equal protection clause, but democratically elected legislatures and executives are not well designed to be responsive to minority groups, for they are chosen by a majority of voters. Thus, civil rights organizations such as the National Association for the Advancement of Colored People (NAACP) and the League of United Latin American Citizens (LULAC) turned to the judiciary, whose members are not elected and so do not directly depend on majority support, for assistance in establishing legal equality.

Table 5.2 Supreme Court Scrutiny in Equal Protection Cases

Claim of Discrimination	Standard of Review	Test
Unprotected category	Lowest	Rational basis to achieve a legitimate governmental objective
Sex	Heightened	Exceedingly persuasive justification; use of sex as a governmental category must be substantially related to important governmental objectives
Race, ethnicity, religion, and legally admitted aliens	Strict	Most rigid scrutiny; use of race as a governmental category must be precisely tailored to meet a compelling governmental interest

Key Questions

Who should ensure citizen equality? State governments? The federal government? The president? Congress? The courts? Citizens?

As with civil liberties issues, for which the Court uses the standard of compelling interest (see Chapter 4), in civil rights cases, the Court has constructed tests to determine whether laws violate the equal protection clause. Depending upon the group whose right has been violated, the Court sets different standards of how closely it will scrutinize the law alleged to violate equal protection. There are at least three levels. The Court reserves the toughest standard of review, strict scrutiny, for laws alleged to discriminate on account of race, ethnicity, religion, or status as a legally admitted alien. It uses mid-level, or heightened, scrutiny for laws that discriminate on account of sex and the lowest level of scrutiny, rational basis, for general claims of discrimination (see Table 5.2).

The End of Legal Restrictions on Civil Rights

LO 5-4 Identify the groups at the forefront of the civil rights movement

The events that brought about the government's shift from enforcing discrimination to protecting against it did not begin with the government. It began with pressure from groups who were discriminated against that mobilized on their own behalf. This gateway of public pressure generally involves the use of civil liberties such as freedom of speech and of assembly to engage in protests and other activities aside from voting because minority groups, by definition, do not have the numbers to change policies through the ballot box alone.

The African American soldiers and sailors who fought for freedom in World War II often returned uneasily to their hometowns, particularly in the South, where segregation remained the law. This led to vocal demands for civil rights at home. Additionally, the difficult but ultimately successful integration of Major League Baseball by African American Jackie Robinson in 1947 showed that even the most segregated of American institutions could survive and even thrive following integration.

The three largest legal barriers African Americans faced in the post–World War II era were state-sponsored segregation of supposedly separate-but-equal public facilities, such as schools and buses; the legal right of private businesses not to serve customers or hire people on account of race; and effective prohibitions on the right to vote, such as discriminatorily enforced literacy tests. These gates blocking full civic participation existed throughout the United States but were most prevalent in the former Confederate states. After we trace the African American struggle for equal rights, we turn to the the Latino movement and then the women's movement, which likewise pressured the government to dismantle ethnic and gender-based discrimination.

Dismantling Public Discrimination Based on Race

Among the most consequential forms of segregation from the Jim Crow era was the mandatory separation of schools for whites and blacks. Beginning in 1935, the NAACP's Legal Defense Fund embarked on a legal campaign—led by Thurgood Marshall—to dismantle the system of separate-but-equal schools in southern and border states that were always separate but rarely equal. After a series of cases in which the Supreme Court struck down specific segregated schools because they were not equal,[50] the Court ruled more generally in **Brown v. Board of Education** (1954) that separate schools were inherently unequal, even if the facilities were essentially similar (see Supreme Court Cases: *Brown v. Board of Education*). Segregation in schools violated the equal protection clause of the Fourteenth Amendment. The Fourteenth Amendment only requires that states provide equal protection of the laws, but on the same day as the *Brown* decision, the Supreme Court used the due process clause of the Fifth Amendment to prohibit the national government from denying equal protection.[51]

As historic as the *Brown* decision was, the case by itself did little to desegregate southern schools. Part of the problem was that the Court allowed local circumstances to influence the rate of integration, ambiguously requiring that local districts desegregate "with all deliberate speed."[51] Further, southern segregationists launched a massive resistance to the *Brown* decision. This campaign included "The Southern Manifesto," a document signed by 101 southern members of Congress deploring the *Brown* decision; the denial of state funds to any integrated school; and tuition grants for white students to attend segregated private schools. In addition, unruly segregationist mobs threatened black students seeking to integrate previously white schools. While neither the Supreme Court nor the Dwight D. Eisenhower administration (1953–61) could prevent every school disruption by segregationist mobs, both intervened in Little Rock, Arkansas. Eisenhower federalized the Arkansas National Guard and sent in the 101st Airborne to protect the black students seeking to integrate Central High School, while the Supreme Court, declaring that it had the final say on what the Constitution means, rejected the threat of violence as a justification for delaying integration (see Chapter 13, The Presidency, and Chapter 15, The Judiciary, for more on the Little Rock case).[53]

In 1963, segregationist Governor George Wallace of Alabama famously "stood at the schoolhouse door" to prevent two black students from registering at the University of Alabama. He stepped aside only when President John F. Kennedy (1961–63) sent troops to enforce integration.

Nevertheless, with few blacks able to vote, there was little need for southern politicians or school board officials to be responsive to their concerns. Only when the federal government acted did states respond. After Congress cut off federal aid to segregated schools in 1964, many districts began to integrate.[54] The rate of integration increased further in the late 1960s when the Supreme Court ended the "all deliberate speed" era and required an immediate end to segregated schools, thus pushing open the gateways to greater equality.[55]

Outside of schools, civil rights activists fought segregation in public facilities. The first grassroots action to receive nationwide attention was a bus boycott in Montgomery, Alabama. On December 1, 1955, police arrested Rosa Parks, a 42-year-old black seamstress and an active member of the NAACP, for refusing to give her seat to a white

Brown v. Board of Education: *The 1954 Supreme Court decision striking down segregated schools.*

Carl Iwasaki/The LIFE Images Collection/Getty Images

Image 5.6 In 1950, when Linda Brown was entering third grade, her father Oliver Brown tried to enroll her in the Sumner School. The 10-year-old had been going to Monroe School, walking between train tracks and along streets without sidewalks to get there. Although it was closer, Sumner was for white students, and when Oliver Brown was told Linda could not attend, he took his case to the NAACP. Here the family stands in front of their home; Linda is on the left.

Key Questions

What are terrorists? Were the people who bombed King's house terrorists?

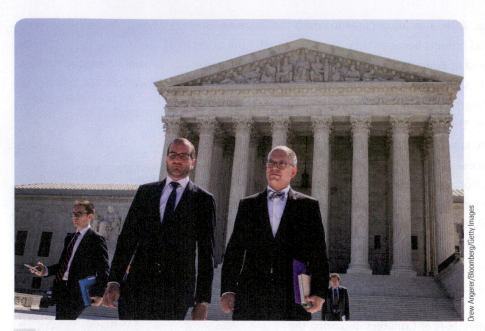

person. In response, the black community, led by a 26-year-old Baptist minister, Martin Luther King Jr., launched a boycott of city buses. Blacks walked, bicycled, and shared rides to avoid using the Montgomery bus system. Although the city arrested boycotters, and violent segregationist terrorists firebombed King's home, the boycotters held firm for more than a year. The Supreme Court then declared Montgomery's segregated bus system unconstitutional.[56] A new ordinance allowing blacks to sit anywhere on any bus ended the boycott. King became one of the national leaders of the emerging civil rights movement and Rosa Parks its first heroine.

Image 5.7 James "Jim" Obergefell, the named plaintiff in the *Obergefell v. Hodges* case, right, and Chad Griffin, president of the Human Rights Campaign, center, exit the U.S. Supreme Court in Washington, D.C., on Monday, June 22, 2015. The Supreme Court ruled 5–4 that states violate the equal protection clause when they prohibit same-sex marriages.

With the *Brown* precedent in hand, the Supreme Court struck down state-mandated segregation not only in public transportation but also in other public facilities, such as beaches and city auditoriums. Given the massive opposition to the *Brown* decision, however, the Court refused to hear the appeal by a black woman sentenced to prison for the "crime" of marrying a white man.[57] As one justice reportedly said when the Court rejected another interracial marriage case, "One bombshell at a time is enough."[58] Not until 1967 in *Loving v. Virginia* did the Court strike down laws prohibiting miscegenation, finding no compelling interest in a law that prohibited interracial marriage.[59]

Dismantling Private Discrimination Based on Race

The decisions of businesses about whether to serve customers or hire workers on account of their race (or sex) were largely beyond judicial authority because the Fourteenth Amendment's equal protection clause only prevents states from discriminating; it does not bar private discrimination. Thus, if a restaurant chose not to serve blacks or an employer chose not to hire them, there was little a court could do unless Congress passed legislation forbidding such actions. The effort to dismantle private discrimination thus took two tracks: protests to pressure businesses into serving blacks, and lobbying to pressure Congress into passing legislation that would make private discrimination in commercial matters illegal.

Supreme Court Cases

Hernandez v. Texas (1954)

Brown v. Board of Education (1954)

QUESTION: *Hernandez:* Does the equal protection clause allow Texas to exclude Mexican Americans from juries? *Brown:* Can states provide segregated schools for black and white school children?

ORAL ARGUMENT:
Hernandez: January 11, 1954 *Brown:* December 7–9, 1953

DECISION:
Hernandez: May 3, 1954 (read at https://caselaw.findlaw.com/us-supreme-court/347/475.html)*Brown:* May 17, 1954 (read at http://laws.findlaw.com/us/347/483.html)

OUTCOME:
Hernandez: No. The equal protection clause protects Mexican Americans (9–0). *Brown:* No. Separate educational facilities are inherently unequal (9–0).

As noted in Chapter 2, The Constitution, Texas systematically excluded Mexican Americans from the murder trial of Pete Hernandez. Famed attorney and activist Gus Garcia told the Supreme Court that while the intent of the equal protection clause was to prevent racial discrimination against former slaves and their descendants, Texas treated Mexican Americans as a "class apart," and they therefore should be shielded against discriminatory laws by the equal protection clause. The Court agreed.

Two weeks later, the Supreme Court decided the *Brown* case. When Linda Brown was in third grade, her father, with the help of the NAACP, brought a suit against the Topeka school board for refusing to allow her to attend the local school that white children in their neighborhood attended.

In *Plessy v. Ferguson* (1896), the Supreme Court had ruled that the equal protection clause of the Fourteenth Amendment did not prohibit the states from establishing separate-but-equal facilities for whites and blacks. The Court did not really begin to look at whether the facilities were equal or not until 1938, when it held that Missouri's paying for blacks to go to law school out of state was not the same as providing facilities within the state that were equal to its white

law school.* A pair of 1950 cases declared, first, that admitting a black to an all-white school but forcing him to sit in a separate row and dine at a separate table was unconstitutional,[†] and second, that the equality of separate schools had to be compared on both objective factors that could be measured, such as the number of faculty members, and subjective factors that could not be measured, such as the reputation of the faculty.[‡]

The *Brown* case came to the Supreme Court with similar desegregation cases from South Carolina, Virginia, Delaware, and Washington, D.C. Thurgood Marshall, who was in charge of legal strategy for the NAACP and would later become the first African American to serve on the Supreme Court, argued the *Brown* case. He readily admitted that the schools in Linda Brown's case were roughly equal in objective characteristics but argued that segregation in and of itself denied black students the equal protection of the laws by creating a feeling of inferiority among them.

The Supreme Court's preliminary vote following the arguments showed a majority favoring striking down segregation, with two or three dissenters. Chief Justice Earl Warren, however, thought that a decision that was bound to be met with resistance in the South should be unanimous if possible. Following several months of bargaining and persuasion, he eventually got every member of the Court to agree that the Court should strike down school segregation.

*Missouri ex rel. Gaines v. Canada, 305 U.S. 337 (1938).
[†] McLaurin v. Oklahoma, 339 U.S. 637 (1950).
[‡] Sweatt v. Painter, 339 U.S. 629 (1950).

Thinking Critically

1. Can separate schools ever be equal?
2. Why were the courts more likely to be responsive to the problems of segregation than the legislature would be?

The grassroots protests began when four African American freshmen at North Carolina Agricultural and Technical College in Greensboro sat down at the whites-only counter at Woolworth's, asked for coffee, and refused to leave when they were not served. Within weeks, the sit-ins spread to dozens of other cities. One protest leader, Diane Nash, along with other young participants in the sit-ins, formed the Student Nonviolent Coordinating Committee (SNCC), which along with the Congress of Racial Equality (CORE) served as the more activist "younger brothers" of the NAACP.

In 1961, CORE organized freedom rides, trips on interstate buses into the segregated South, where the integrated buses were legal under federal law even though they violated local segregation rules. Mobs attacked the buses—firebombing one of them—and beat the riders. Under pressure from the federal government, including protection of the riders by federal marshals, the states eventually agreed not to interfere with interstate travelers.[60]

In the spring of 1963, Martin Luther King Jr.'s Southern Christian Leadership Conference (SCLC) led demonstrations in Birmingham, Alabama, to bring about the integration of downtown businesses. The police met demonstrators with fire hoses, police dogs, and cattle prods. Police arrested hundreds of protesters, including King. When white clergymen questioned why King, an outsider, had come to Birmingham, King answered in his famous "Letter from Birmingham Jail": "I am in Birmingham because injustice is here."[61] Rejecting violence, King insisted that peaceful civil disobedience was the only gateway to negotiation. The negotiations took place and ended with Birmingham businesses agreeing to integrate lunch counters and hire more blacks. Nevertheless, or perhaps because of this, members of the KKK exploded a bomb at a local black church on a Sunday morning, murdering four young girls.

Key Questions

If a law is immoral, are you right or wrong to disobey it? What is the remedy?

Earlier that summer, King had led two hundred thousand protesters at the March on Washington for Jobs and Freedom. Though the march grew out of historic employment discrimination against African Americans, it is now remembered mostly as a march for civil rights. It was there that King delivered his historic "I Have a Dream" speech, in which he declared that one day the United States would live up to the national creed declared by Thomas Jefferson in the Declaration of Independence: "We hold these truths to be self-evident: that all men are created equal." He also added a line that opponents of affirmative action have frequently used (or misused) to suggest that King would have been opposed to such plans, speaking of the day when his children "will not be judged by the color of their skin but by the content of their character."[62]

Key Questions

Which branch of government has been most powerful in ensuring equality? Why?

President Kennedy proposed a civil rights bill that would have banned discrimination in public accommodations, such as restaurants and hotels. Five days after Kennedy's assassination in November 1963, President Lyndon B. Johnson (1963–69) told Congress that nothing could better honor Kennedy than passage of this bill. The next year, Congress passed the **Civil Rights Act**, which significantly strengthened Kennedy's original bill by also prohibiting employment discrimination on account of "race, color, religion, sex, or national origin."

Civil Rights Act: *Prohibits discrimination in employment, education, and places of public accommodation (1964).*

Because the Fourteenth Amendment's equal protection clause applies only to state-sponsored discrimination, the Supreme Court upheld Congress's authority to ban private discrimination under the interstate commerce clause. Given the Court's broad interpretation of interstate commerce (see Chapter 3, Federalism), the Court ruled that even small inns and restaurants had to abide by the act.[63]

In 1971, the Supreme Court interpreted the Civil Rights Act to limit job qualification requirements that had a disparate impact on whites and blacks.[64] For example, if more whites receive high school diplomas than blacks, requiring a high school diploma for a job would be more harmful to blacks than to whites. A business seeking to establish job requirements that have a disparate impact would have to prove that the requirement is necessary to the job. In the late 1970s and through the 1980s, a more conservative Supreme Court reached a series of decisions that restricted civil rights protections—for example, making disparate impact more difficult to prove and ruling that discrimination against pregnant women was not a form of sex discrimination under the Civil Rights Act.[65] Passing new laws, Congress overturned these Court decisions plus several others, thus demonstrating widespread support for the continued protection of civil rights. The new rules, for example, make it easier to find that job tests have a disparate impact but leave it to the courts to determine whether disparate impact, by taking race into account, conflicts with the equal treatment obligation of the Civil Rights Act.[66]

Key Questions
What restrictions, if any, should be placed on voting?

Dismantling Voting Barriers Based on Race

As noted previously, the end of Reconstruction left black men in the South with a constitutional right to vote but a hostile social and legal environment that made it extremely difficult for them to do so. The Supreme Court pushed things along, striking down grandfather clauses (1915) and white primaries (1944), the latter in a suit filed by the NAACP.[67] Congress and the states pushed things along further, outlawing poll taxes with the Twenty-Fourth Amendment (1964). Martin Luther King Jr. identified four gates that kept blacks from voting: white terrorist control of local governments and sheriffs' departments; arrests on trumped-up charges of those seeking to vote; the discretion given to registrars, where "the latitude for discrimination is almost endless"; and the arbitrary nature of literacy tests.[68]

During the summer of 1964, voting rights supporters from around the country, many of them college students, moved south to help with voter registration drives. Klansmen murdered three of the volunteers in Philadelphia, Mississippi, that June. In March 1965, King organized a voting rights march from Selma to Montgomery, Alabama. With national news media on hand, Alabama police, under the authority of Governor George Wallace, beat the marchers with whips, nightsticks, and cattle prods. Selma natives murdered two more voting rights activists.

A week later, President Johnson addressed a joint session of Congress, calling for passage of the strictest possible voting rights legislation. Congress responded by passing the **Voting Rights Act (VRA)** in August 1965. The act limited literacy, interpretation, and other such tests for voting. It required states with low voter registration levels, essentially seven southern states plus Alaska, to receive preclearance from the Justice Department for any changes to its voting laws. It also established new criminal penalties for those who sought to keep people from voting on account of race. The law was an enormous success. By 2008, blacks and whites voted at essentially the same rate nationwide[69] and at slightly higher rates in some southern states.[70] In 2012, blacks had a higher turnout rate than whites.[71] In 2013, however, the Supreme Court voted 5–4 in *Shelby County v. Holder* to strike down the 1965 formula that established which jurisdictions needed to obtain preclearance.[72] Until Congress passes a new formula, no jurisdictions need to obtain preclearance. This decision may depress future black turnout as states like Texas move to pass voter identification laws that were previously blocked under the VRA by the Justice Department[73] (see Figure 5.3).

While the Civil Rights Act and the VRA ended most forms of legal discrimination in the United States, much discrimination "under the color of law" (i.e., by public officials) still exists. The **Black Lives Matter** movement grew out of a series of incidents between typically

Voting Rights Act: *Gives the federal government the power to prevent discrimination in voting rights (1965).*

Black Lives Matter: *Movement that grew out of the perceived discounting of black lives by police and juries.*

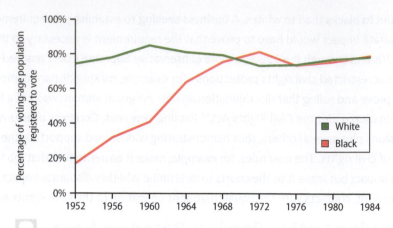

Figure 5.3 **White and Black Southern Voter Registration, 1952–1984**

Dramatic increases in black voter registration preceded passage of the Voting Rights Act in 1965, but substantial equality between whites and blacks did not occur until after its passage.

Source: Data from Harold W. Stanley, *Voter Mobilization and the Politics of Race* (New York: Praeger, 1987), Appendix A.

young male African Americans and the police officers charged with protecting them. It began after the acquittal of neighborhood watch coordinator George Zimmerman for the killing of Trayvon Martin in 2012 in Sanford, Florida.[74] The movement grew in prominence following several high-profile killings of African Americans, including the following:

- Oscar Grant by BART transit officers (2009)
- Michael Brown in Ferguson, Missouri (2014)
- Eric Garner (2014), who died from a chokehold by police in New York City after failing to refrain from selling untaxed cigarettes
- Twelve-year-old Tamir Rice (2014), shot in Cleveland, Ohio, while in possession of a toy gun that lacked the orange band that designates toy guns
- Laquan McDonald (2014), who, while in possession of a knife, was yards away from the Chicago police when they shot him sixteen times
- Freddie Gray (2015), who died from injuries suffered in the back of a police van in Baltimore, Maryland
- Sandra Bland (2015), who died in police custody following an arrest for failing to signal a lane change; she was then taken into custody following her refusal to put out her cigarette after being asked to by the arresting officer
- Walter Scott (2015), shot in the back while unarmed and running away from police
- Atatiana Jefferson (2019) shot in her home through a window by a police officer responding to a call that her nephew was not being properly cared for
- Breonna Taylor (2020), shot in her bed in the middle of the night by Louisville police officers executing a "no knock" warrant.
- Ahmaud Arbery (2020), killed by a father-son team while on a solo jog in Georgia. The Arbery-family attorney claimed that the fact that the father had been a Georgia police officer led to the long delay in the arrests.[75]
- George Floyd (2020), arrested on suspicion of passing a counterfeit $20 bill, died after police officer Derek Chauvin, kneeled on the handcuffed Floyd's neck for nearly 9 minutes while two fellow officers simply watched. Bystander videos of the killing went viral and resulted

in weeks of demonstrations against antiblack police brutality. The demonstrations turned violent in Minneapolis, Washington DC, and New York City, among other places.

- Rayshard Brooks (2020), shot in the back by Atlanta police after falling asleep in a Wendy's drive-through.

Needless to say the degree of official blame in each of these cases varies, but the Black Lives Matter movement has become a powerful force in American politics. The video of Floyd's murder led many whites to demonstrate with Black Lives Matter.

In response to these tragedies, police in Baltimore cut back on more aggressive policing, with a sharp spike in homicides.[76] Judges have acquitted each officer charged in Freddie Gray's death, finding insufficient evidence of intent to kill Mr. Gray. In Chicago, citizens have called on Mayor Rahm Emanuel to resign over the fact that the city held on to the video that showed the shooting death of Laquan McDonald for over a year. Emanuel is calling for changes in how police officers are trained.[77] All three of the officers involved in George Floyd's killing have been indicted on second or third degree murder charges.

Key Questions

How has expansion of the right to vote affected citizen participation? How has it affected public policy?

Dismantling Public Discrimination Based on Ethnicity

Like African Americans, Latinos began the struggle for civil rights in the court system through interest groups such as the American G.I. Forum, LULAC, and later the Mexican American Legal Defense and Education Fund (MALDEF). One of the first steps Latinos took toward securing civil rights was to be recognized as a protected class of people under the Fourteenth Amendment. As we have seen, the attorneys in *Hernandez v. Texas* argued that Latinos were a class of individuals entitled to the same due process guarantees as were African Americans and other racial groups.[78] The Court agreed and also ruled that Mexican Americans could not be systematically excluded from juries, a key gateway of citizenship.

In 1970, the Supreme Court extended the *Brown* ruling to apply to Latinos and other minority groups in *Cisneros v. Corpus Christi Independent School District*.[79] Because Mexican Americans were considered white, the Corpus Christi Independent School District created two sets of schools: one set for African American and Latino children and the other for

Sybille Reuter/Alamy Stock Photo

Image 5.8 An image of George Floyd who died after a Minneapolis police officer, Derek Chauvin, kneeled on Floyd's neck for over eight minutes. Floyd had allegedly passed a counterfeit $20 bill to a store clerk. The video of the homicide led to international protests, looting and rioting in several U.S. cities, and increased support for the Black Lives Matter movement.

"All-White" (non-Latino) children. In that way, they circumvented the desegregation ruling of *Brown*. Attorney James de Anda, supported by the MALDEF, argued that the separate-schools system was unconstitutional because Mexican Americans were a separate and distinct group from whites. The Supreme Court recognized Latinos as a distinct ethnic minority group that had been subject to discriminatory practices.[80] Latino American school children were no longer subject to separate but equal educational facilities. In *Plyler v. Doe* (1982), described in Chapter 1, Supreme Court cases, the Court expanded protections further, deciding that the children of undocumented workers were entitled to free public education in Texas and across the nation.[81]

Equal opportunities in education for Latinos also involved the funding systems in local school districts. In many areas, public schools are funded through property taxes. As a result, within the same metropolitan area, there may be large disparities in funding for public schools. Some districts may include geographical areas in which property values are significantly lower than others. As a result, the educational facilities and materials may be less in those areas than in affluent neighborhoods. In the early 1970s, parents of children in San Antonio claimed that such a disparity was a violation of the equal protection clause in the Fourteenth Amendment. The Supreme Court in *San Antonio Independent School District v. Rodriguez* (1973) determined that education was not a fundamental right deserving of such protections and that the funding mechanisms of the school district were constitutional.[82] Advocates for school financing reform continued their efforts in state courts with some success.[83] The Texas legislature has since made limited progress in its attempts to reform the funding disparities in public education as mandated by state courts. So, in some ways, there are now gateways to education for children of all races and ethnicities. In other ways, educational gateways are only partially open and remain unequal.

Public education is a major gateway to participation in civic life. Its denial constitutes a gate that prevents equality. Yet other gates in lesser yet still important areas also existed. Public swimming pools, buses, and water fountains, for example, were segregated. In the early 1950s, sometimes there was no "equal" facility available to Latinos. Latino elected officials helped lead the effort to break down these and other types of barriers to citizenship. Prominent among them is Henry B. Gonzalez, the first Mexican American to be elected to the San Antonio City Council. One of his first victories was opening public facilities such as swimming pools to all residents. When he served in the Texas Senate, he filibustered a series of bills aimed at circumventing the *Brown* case. He held the floor for a record twenty-two hours and defeated all but two of the bills. He later served as Congressman from the 20th District in Texas, now occupied by Joaquín Castro (see the opening vignette in Chapter 12, Congress).[84]

Dismantling Voting Barriers Based on Ethnicity

Just as segregation was not limited to African Americans, voting laws created gates blocking Latinos' ability to exercise the right to vote. Poll taxes influenced Mexican Americans in the Southwest, for whom the cost to vote was a greater burden than for white voters. And while the Jim Crow version of literacy tests often involved tests of obscure political and historical facts for first-time voters, such as African Americans in the South, literacy requirements influenced Latinos differently. New York, for example, required "new" voters (i.e., Puerto Ricans) to provide evidence of English-language proficiency as a requisite for voter registration. In 1966, however, the Supreme Court ruled in *Katzenbach v. Morgan* (see Supreme Court Cases, Chapter 11) and *Cardona v. Power* that provisions of the 1966 Voting Rights Act (VRA) prevented New York from imposing English-language requirements for voting.[85] In 1970, the VRA was amended to eliminate all literacy tests, and, in 1975, Congress further amended the VRA to protect language minorities. As a result of those and subsequent amendments to the VRA, states and other political units, such as counties or cities, must provide voting information, assistance, and ballots in the minority language if more than 5 percent of the citizens of voting age in the jurisdiction are of a language minority or their number exceeds ten thousand.[86]

Language requirements were only one type of gate. Other, less obvious gates to participation blocked Latino voters. How elections are structured may also create gates to meaningful

Shutterstock.com

Image 5.9 Jennifer Gonzalez is the nonvoting House of Representatives delegate from Puerto Rico. The Constitution limits representation in the House to "States," so while Puerto Rico and the District of Columbia have delegates in Congress, neither can vote.

participation. In Dallas County and Bexar County in Texas, for example, elections had been conducted on an at-large basis, meaning that candidates ran in multimember districts. Ethnic minorities could not garner a high enough percentage of the vote to elect Latino or other representatives who embodied their interests. This form of election is still common in many jurisdictions and was not necessarily a violation of voting rights.

In 1973, however, the Supreme Court ruled in *White v. Regester* that the VRA prohibited electoral plans that may effectively dilute the voting strength of minorities, in this case Latinos.[87] The multimember district elections in those jurisdictions were being used as a means to minimize the voting strength of Latino (in San Antonio) and African American (in Dallas) citizens. Such plans limited the effective participation of those groups to elect candidates of their choice. The Supreme Court mandated that single-member districts be used. As a result of this decision, groups such as MALDEF, Communities Organized for Public Service (COPS), and Southwest Voter Registration and Education Project (SVREP) and their leaders organized to change the way many local elections were structured (see below). Evidence shows that the impact of election practices was dramatic. After the switch to single-member districts in 1977, San Antonio elected five Mexican Americans and one African American candidate to the city council. For the first time in the city's history, a majority of the city council was composed of minorities.[88]

The effects of the increased representation of Latinos in San Antonio were not just symbolic. Most of the newly elected members came from geographical areas of the city that had previously experienced little or no representation on the council. The new city council had members from every area of the city. Policies adopted by the council changed, and new priorities in city services were devoted to previously underserved areas of the city.[89]

It was MALDEF that brought *White v. Regester* and many other cases forward. In the 1970s, MALDEF undertook ninety-three federal and state cases in Texas alone: 76 percent of the cases involved desegregation, and 14 percent were cases about voting and other political rights.[90] That is one reason why MALDEF has come to be known as the "law firm of the Latino community."

Another driving force behind the *White v. Regester* case that opened a gateway for the election of Latino from the local level to Congress is COPS. COPS exemplifies how church- and neighborhood-based organizations can open gateways for minority groups. COPS organized in San Antonio's West Side, a densely populated and poor area of the city and home to mostly Mexican American residents. Those neighborhoods were largely without sidewalks and curbs. Led by Ernesto Cortés, COPS advocated for increased services to the city's previously unrepresented areas. Streets in those areas began to be paved, homes no longer flooded when it rained due to the curbs, and school children walked to school on sidewalks. They began to hold "accountability nights" where city councilpersons were held accountable for keeping their promises. In the process, they empowered Latino residents to participate in the political process, opening a gateway.

One of many organizations aiding in the election of Latinos is SVREP, whose mission is "to empower Latinos and other minorities by increasing their participation in the American democratic process."[91] SVREP does more than register voters; it also organizes training for future Latino leaders through the Latino Academy. The motto of SVREP is "*Su Voto Es Su Voz*" ("Your Vote Is Your Voice"). The joining of that motto of the United Farm Workers (UFW), "*¡Si, Se Puede!*" ("Yes, We Can!"), which Barack Obama borrowed in his successful 2008 presidential campaign, may inspire new generations of Latinos seeking the expansion of civil rights for Latinos.

Political Analytics

State-by-State Voter Identification Requirements

ARTICLE 1, SECTION 4, OF THE U.S. CONSTITUTION permits the states to determine the time, place, and manner of elections while also reserving for Congress the power to intervene when it deems necessary. As you have read, Congress did intervene in 1965 with the Voting Rights Act (VRA). States, however, have largely been given leeway in determining the requirements their citizens must meet to vote. One requirement that some states have enacted, especially since 2010, is voter

identification. Some states require voters to provide a government-issued form of identification in order to vote.

Figure 5.4 shows how states differ in the requirements voters must satisfy. In this case, *strict photo identification requirements* mean that voters without acceptable identification, as determined by each state, may vote on a provisional ballot and may need to take additional steps after Election Day for it to be counted. *Photo Identification requested* means that at least some

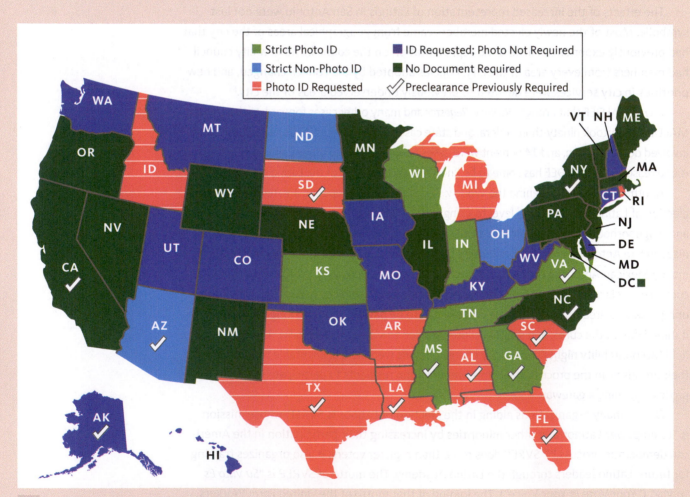

Figure 5.4 **Voter Identification Laws by State, 2020**

voters without acceptable identification have an option to cast a ballot that will be counted without further action on their part.[92] In addition, several states require no documents to vote.

Figure 5.4 also shows which states were under the VRA provision that required states to get preclearance before enacting such voter identification requirements, prior to the *Shelby County v. Holder* (2013) Supreme Court decision.

Sources: National Conference of State Legislatures. August 22, 2016. *Voter Identification Requirements, Voter Laws*. http://www.ncsl.org/research/elections-and-campaigns/voter-id.aspx; U.S. Department of Justice, Civil Rights Division, *Jurisdictions Previously Covered by Section 5*. https://www.justice.gov/crt/jurisdictions-previously-covered-section-5.

In Figure 5.4, examine the variety of voter identification requirements that exist among the states and notice which states have the strictest requirements.

Thinking Critically

1. Do requirements for voting such as photo identification place an unreasonable burden on voters?

2. In Figure 5.4, voter identification requirements by state are shown on a colored map. Would those data be easier to interpret in a table, graph, or bar chart or something else?

There have been other practices and limits to the gateways to participation for Latinos, including voter identification laws. And the Supreme Court has indicated that electoral plans such as majority-minority districts (i.e., electoral districts in which a majority of the population is composed of minorities) need not maximize the voting strength of minority communities (e.g., Cuban Americans in *Johnson v. DeGrandy*).[93] See Chapter 11 for a discussion of the impact of the VRA and Supreme Court decisions on Latino voter turnout.

Dismantling Private Discrimination Based on Ethnicity

Like women, Latinos have faced an uphill battle in the workplace. Deprived of their lands following Texas's break with Mexico, deported during the Great Depression and other periods, Latinos have long filled the demand for unskilled labor, particularly in the field of agriculture. As a result, perhaps the best known of civil rights efforts among Latinos is in the agriculture industry. Cesar Chavez and Dolores Huerta organized the United Farm Workers (UFW) union to secure safe working conditions and increased wages for laborers. Formed in 1962, the UFW continues to work to improve conditions for agriculture workers. When the UFW began, farm workers earned less than one dollar per hour. The first task of Chavez and Huerta was to organize the workers so that they could bargain collectively with growers. Once formed, they called for boycotts of fruit and vegetables as well as strikes against growers in order to gain the right to bargain collectively. The UFW counts among its successes bargaining agreements that required growers to provide rest periods for workers, toilets in fields, clean drinking water, and protections against dangerous pesticides.[94] The UFW increased the collective voice of Latinos in the agriculture industry and fought for basic human and civil rights.

The UFW also registered Latinos to vote and encouraged them to become active politically. The success of the UFW and other Latino organizations in ending segregation and discrimination continues as it does for other groups. For Latinos, efforts continue to provide adequate funding for education, expand educational opportunities to DREAMers, and prevent the efforts by some to limit political participation (see the discussion of voter identification laws in Chapter 11).[95] As with any social movement, leadership and

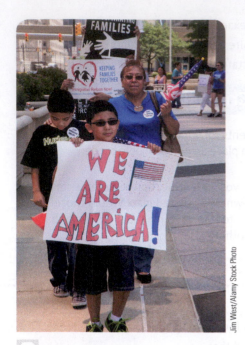

Jim West/Alamy Stock Photo

Image 5.10 Young undocumented immigrants protesting outside the Federal Building in Detroit, Michigan.

Key Questions
Why, in U.S. history, do women's rights movements follow, rather than precede, movements to remove racial barriers?

Equal Pay Act: *Prohibits different pay for males and females for the same work (1963).*

organization are vital to the success of groups seeking equal protection and due process. As noted at the beginning of this section, much of the impetus for change begins with pressure from groups. As Chavez said, "Those who attack our union often say, 'It's not really a union. It's something else: A social movement. A civil rights movement. It's something dangerous. . . .' [T]he UFW has always been something more than a union—although it's never been dangerous if you believe in the Bill of Rights."[96]

As Latinos continue to be the fastest-growing ethnic group in the United States, many gates to political participation have been placed before them. Latinos are slowly becoming a political force in the United States (see Chapter 11). Civil rights enjoyed by Latinos today were not always recognized as such, nor are they guaranteed to be so in the future. Elected officials such as Senator Marco Rubio (R-FL), Senator Ted Cruz (R-TX), Representative Alexandria Ocasio Cortez (D-NY), and Republican Governor Susana Martínez from New Mexico, as well as emerging leaders such as Julian Castro, former mayor of San Antonio, a 2020 Democratic presidential campaign contender, and former secretary of Housing and Urban Development, will have an increasing role in the nature of those rights. And emerging generations of Latinos such as Erika Andiola, leader of the Arizona DREAM Coalition, are poised to continue working to secure those rights, including volunteering to work for candidates running for office.[97]

Dismantling Discrimination Based on Gender

The success of the civil rights movement inspired other groups, most notably women, to put pressure on the political system to obtain equal rights under the law. Women active in the civil rights movement easily shifted the movement's strategies to promoting rights for women, particularly after the publication of Betty Friedan's *The Feminine Mystique* (1963), a book considered by many to have launched the modern American feminist movement. Based on a survey Friedan sent to her Smith College classmates in advance of their fifteenth reunion, the book broadcast the dissatisfaction that many American women felt in their roles as wives and mothers. About the same time, the Kennedy administration's President's Commission on the Status of Women, charged with making recommendations for overcoming sex discrimination, urged passage of the **Equal Pay Act**. Passed by Congress in 1963, the act prohibits employers from paying different wages for the same job on account of sex. Although the act did not prohibit discrimination in the hiring of male and female workers, that prohibition came with the Civil Rights Act of 1964. See Public Policy and Civil Rights: Workplace Equality.

Nevertheless, women in the United States still face substantial workplace discrimination. One obvious example of this is the fact that athletes on the men's U.S. national soccer team get paid significantly more money than athletes on the women's U.S. national soccer team. This is despite the fact that the women's team has dominated the women's World Cup since it started in 1991 (winning four of the eight tournaments to date), while in twenty-three men's tournaments, dating back to 1930, the men's team has never finished first or second. See Image 5.10.

According to the *Wall Street Journal* the women's team has even generated more revenue than the men's team in recent years.[98] In response to an equal-pay lawsuit filed by the women's team, the United States Soccer Federation (USSF) declared it to be "indisputable science" that men's soccer requires "materially higher levels of speed and strength" than women's soccer. The men players also shoulder "more responsibility" than the women players.[99]

Following passage of the Civil Rights Act, Friedan helped found the National Organization for Women (NOW), which advocated for women's rights through education and litigation. NOW protested airline policies that forced flight attendants (then known as stewardesses) to retire at marriage or age 32 and help-wanted ads that listed jobs by gender, as well as protective legislation. NOW also supported abortion rights and the proposed Equal Rights Amendment (ERA), which would have prohibited the federal government and the states from discriminating on account of sex.

In 1972, the American Civil Liberties Union (ACLU) established the Women's Rights Project, which worked to eliminate discriminatory laws. The first project director, future Supreme Court Justice Ruth Bader Ginsburg, developed a litigation strategy for ending gender-based discrimination. Prior to Ginsburg's work, the Court had rejected equal protection claims for women. Ginsburg first persuaded the Court to strike laws based on the rational-basis standard and then got the Court to approve a heightened-scrutiny standard. This is a step below the strict scrutiny used in cases discriminating on account of race, but the standard is tough enough that the Court usually strikes laws that discriminate according to sex.

Meanwhile, the ERA, passed by Congress and sent to the states for ratification in 1972, began to falter. An anti-ERA movement led by political activist Phyllis Schlafly reversed the momentum by arguing that the amendment would remove special privileges women enjoyed regarding protective legislation, Social Security benefits, and exemption from the draft. Ironically, another argument against the ERA was that it was unnecessary because the Supreme Court was striking down most laws that discriminated on account of sex. Though the proposed amendment did not receive sufficient states to ratify by a 1982 deadline, Virginia became the thirty-eighth state to ratify, in 2020 (see Figure 5.5).

By the 1980s, the civil rights era was over, and the nation had taken a conservative turn. Like African Americans, whose office-holding and participation in civic life generally increased after passage of the VRA, women were increasingly taking public roles. In 1984, two years after the ERA had seemingly failed, only 17 percent of Americans thought that the United States was ready to elect a woman president. In 2016, the presidential campaign of

Image 5.11 Megan Rapinoe, the on-field leader of the 2019 victorious U.S. World Cup team, also leads the team's battle for equal pay.

Key Questions

How should we judge if men and women are doing "the same work"?

Image 5.12 In 1960, when Columbia Law valedictorian Ruth Bader Ginsburg applied for a Supreme Court clerkship, Justice Felix Frankfurter chose not to interview her. Ginsburg went on to a distinguished career as a professor of law and chief litigator for the ACLU, eventually arguing cases before the Court, which she joined in 1993 as the second female associate justice. Ginsburg is pictured here in 1977. She passed away in September 2020.

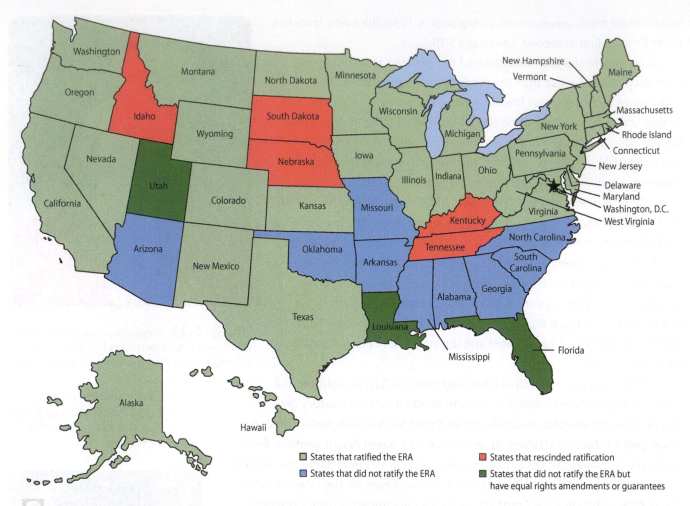

Figure 5.5 States Approving the Equal Rights Amendment

Passed by Congress in 1972 and sent to the states for ratification, the Equal Rights Amendment got a quick start and then faltered as opposition materialized and grew. In 1979, Congress extended the deadline for ratification to 1982, but in 1982, the amendment expired. Thirty-seven states (of the thirty-eight needed) had voted to ratify it, and five states had voted to rescind ratification. Illinois ratified the Amendment in 2018, Virginia in 2020

Source: ERA, Ratification Info State by State, accessed March 29, 2020, https://www.equalrightsamendment.org/era-ratification-map.

former Secretary of State Hillary Clinton demonstrated that the Democratic Party was ready to nominate a woman for the top of the ticket, and while she did not win the Electoral College, she did receive 3 million more votes than Electoral College winner, Donald J. Trump.

Public Policy and Civil Rights

Workplace Equality

Although national legislation and constitutional amendments define civil rights policy, and the Supreme Court interprets such laws—deciding whether they are constitutional and, if so, what they mean—the day-to-day protection of civil rights now falls to two separate executive branch agencies. One is the Civil Rights Division of the Department of Justice, with sections on educational opportunity, employment, housing, voting, and disability rights. The other is the Equal Employment Opportunity Commission (EEOC), which protects against sexual harassment in the workplace and promotes gender equity.

The EEOC is an independent agency with commissioners selected for five-year fixed terms. Unlike the heads of government departments, EEOC commissioners cannot be removed by the president. They are thus thought to be shielded from political pressures, but fixed terms also limit responsiveness to the president, who is the chief executive of the United States.

Congress established the EEOC as part of the Civil Rights Act of 1964. The original EEOC could receive and investigate complaints of discrimination based on race, sex, religion, and national origin (Congress later added age and disability status). As one of the compromises that allowed the act to pass, the EEOC originally had no enforcement power. Rather, it could refer to the Justice Department any case with patterns or practices of discrimination. In 1972, Congress provided the commission with the right to file lawsuits against companies that discriminate.

Although Congress passed the basic law declaring discrimination based on race or sex to be illegal, the EEOC established the guidelines that prohibited discrimination against hiring married women, pregnant women, and mothers. The commission also allowed companies that had previously engaged in discriminatory practices to establish affirmative action plans with quotas for hiring and promoting women and minorities.

From a policy standpoint, the underlying principle of equal pay is that two people who are employed in the same job and do the same quality of work should be paid the same wage. Achieving gender equality in the workplace means that there are no barriers to advancement or hiring based on gender and that gender plays no role in how employees are treated and compensated. Unfortunately, true pay equity has not been achieved in the American workplace. Though the census statistics below do not control for the type of job worked, data show that women earned only 82 percent of what men earned in 2018. For African American and Latino women, this percentage was a bit higher: African American women earned 89 percent and Latinas earned 86 percent of what African American and Latino men made.[100] Additionally, the gap moves to 87 percent for women between the ages of 25 and 34.[101]

Though the Equal Pay Act is supposed to guarantee equal pay for the same work, and the Civil Rights Act aims to protect against any form of employment discrimination on account of sex, the judicial branch has also played a pivotal role. A recent set of Supreme Court decisions has prompted changes in the laws governing discrimination, harassment, and pay equity in the workplace. In one case, the Supreme Court ruled in favor of a woman who was suspended without pay for more than a month and was reassigned to a less desirable position after she claimed sex discrimination in the workplace. The Court decided that an indefinite suspension without pay is retaliation that would reasonably deter any employee from making a discrimination complaint, and, therefore, it was illegal.[102]

But the Court's 2007 ruling in *Ledbetter v. Goodyear Tire and Rubber Co.* had the greatest impact on public policy.[103] In 1998, Lilly Ledbetter filed a complaint with the EEOC that she had consistently received poor job performance evaluations because of her gender and that over the nineteen years she had worked at the Goodyear Tire plant, her pay had fallen well below her male colleagues who did the same type of job. Her employer countered that, even if that had been true in the past, she did not file her complaint within the 180 days required by the Civil Rights Act. The Court ruled in favor of Goodyear, stating that Ledbetter's claims alleging sex discrimination were time-barred because the discriminatory decisions relating to pay had been made more than 180 days prior to the day she filed the charge with the EEOC. In her dissent, Justice Ruth Bader Ginsburg wrote that the effect of this ruling would allow "any annual pay decision not contested immediately (within 180 days) . . . [to become] grandfathered, a fait accompli beyond the province of Title VII ever to repair."[104] Basically, a company could pay a woman less on the basis of gender, and as long as she did not contest the discriminatory wage within 180 days, the discriminatory wage could not be challenged in federal court.

In 2009, Congress reversed the Court's ruling by passing the Lilly Ledbetter Fair Pay Act, which was the first act that President Obama signed into law. The act restarts the clock each time an employee receives a paycheck that has been compromised by discriminatory practices.[105] Many equal pay advocates think that this new law will be helpful but not nearly helpful enough to close the salary gap between men and women. Indeed, early reports suggest that some individual women have been able to sue who would not have been able to do so before the act but that these individual suits have done little to close the gender pay gap.[106]

In 2014, President Obama moved to increase equality through the Paycheck Fairness Act, which would revise remedies for paycheck inequality, increase enforcement activity against unequal pay, and limit exceptions to rules against sex discrimination in wages.[107] With every Republican voting against it, the Senate failed to obtain the sixty votes needed to cut off debate.[108] With this legislative stalemate, President Obama issued two executive orders to accomplish what he could on his own. First, federal contractors could not punish workers for discussing their wages among one another. He also required federal contractors to file data with the federal government showing how they pay employees by race and by sex.[109] The bill was reintroduced into the House in March 2015, but President Trump revoked Obama's orders in 2017.[110]

Construct Your Own Policy

1. Design a system of evaluation in the private sector workplace to ensure that decisions on pay raises and promotions are not made based on race, sex, or sexual orientation.
2. Develop a plan for state and local government enforcement of workplace equality, replacing federal government oversight.

Frontiers in Civil Rights

LO 5-5 Describe the new battles for civil rights

Many of the civil rights battles against legal discrimination have been won: Governments cannot discriminate on account of race or sex, and businesses cannot discriminate in hiring employees or serving customers. But the expanded notion of equality promoted by the civil rights and women's rights movements inspired other groups, such as homosexuals and the disabled, to demand full access to equality. At the same time, as the fight over the ERA made clear, the extension of rights for some may involve a loss of privileges for others, and sometimes rights clash. Congress and the courts have sought to define the meaning and limits of rights as new areas of conflict emerge over such issues as racial and religious profiling, the voting rights of felons, and the civil rights of undocumented immigrants. Whatever the new issues, however, the trend in the United States has been for a broader meaning of equality and greater support for civil rights.

Sexual Orientation, Same-Sex Marriage, and Transgender Rights

The movement to protect the rights of homosexuals first received widespread public attention in 1969 when a police raid on the Stonewall Inn, a gay bar in New York City, turned into a riot by the bar's patrons and gay rights supporters living in the area. The **Stonewall riots** became the signature event of a growing gay rights movement. Activists soon formed the Gay Liberation Front, which established branch organizations around the world. By the 1990s, the movement had expanded into a broader LGBT movement that sought to protect the rights of lesbians, gays, bisexuals, and transgendered persons. Given the historical importance of the Stonewall Inn, many supporters of the LGBT community met there following the June 2016 mass shooting at an LGBT nightclub in Orlando, Florida, to hold a vigil for the wounded survivors.

At the time of the Stonewall riots, all states banned sodomy, which would include virtually all sexual activity between same-sex couples.[111] In the following years, several states decriminalized homosexual activity, but as noted in Chapter 4, the Supreme Court ruled in 1986 that homosexual activity was not a fundamental right, so states could still keep homosexuality illegal if they so choose. Colorado went further, passing an amendment to its state constitution that prohibited the state, or any city or town in the state, from passing laws that granted civil rights protections on account of sexual orientation. The Supreme Court struck this law in 1996, claiming that it was born of dislike toward gays.[112] Then, in *Lawrence v. Texas* (2003), the Supreme Court reversed the 1986 decision and declared that states could not prohibit sexual activity between people of the same sex (see Supreme Court Cases for Chapter 6, Public Opinion).[113]

Although a current majority of Americans are accepting of homosexual partnerships,[114] issues related to homosexual rights have historically been fraught with conflict. Under President Bill Clinton (1993–2001), Congress enacted a "don't ask, don't tell" policy for the military. Prior to the implementation of this policy, simply having homosexual tendencies, without any evidence of homosexual activities, was grounds for discharge. Under the policy, sexual orientation alone was not a ground for discharge, but lesbians, gays, and bisexuals were discharged for engaging in homosexual relationships or for discussing their sexual orientation. Barack Obama opposed the "don't ask, don't tell" policy and in 2010 signed a bill repealing it. The military now directs that same-sex spouses of U.S. soldiers receive the same benefits that opposite-sex spouses receive.[115] Nevertheless, when soldiers are stationed overseas, certain spousal rights, including passports, visas, and housing allowances, may be limited, depending on the host country.[116]

When the Hawaii Supreme Court ruled in 1993 that, under the state constitution, Hawaii would have to show a compelling interest in its prohibition of same-sex marriages, opponents feared that same-sex marriages performed in Hawaii would have legal recognition throughout the United States. In 1996, Congress passed and President Clinton signed the Defense of Marriage Act (DOMA), which defines marriage, for the purpose of federal law, as between a man and a woman. The act did not prohibit same-sex marriage, but it declared that neither the individual states nor the United States must recognize same-sex marriages

Key Questions

What do future civil rights movements look like? How are they different from previous movements?

Stonewall riots: *Street protest in 1969 by gay patrons against a police raid of a gay bar in New York; the protest is credited with launching the gay rights movement.*

Key Questions

Do court decisions follow public opinion? Do they lead public opinion? What should be the relationship?

Key Questions

What government (state or federal) or branch of government (executive, legislative, or judicial) should have the power to decide whether same-sex marriage is legal?

legally performed in other states. In *United States v. Windsor*, the Supreme Court declared that the section of DOMA that limited spousal recognition under federal law to a man and a woman was unconstitutional.[117] The decision dealt only with federal recognition of same-sex marriage and said nothing about state bans on the practice.

In 2015, the Supreme Court heard a case regarding state bans on same-sex marriage. The case, *Obergefell v. Hodges*, was a consolidation of cases originating from Michigan, Kentucky, Ohio, and Tennessee. There were two primary questions the Court had to consider: Could states ban same-sex marriages, and did they have to recognize same-sex marriages performed legally out of state? In a 5–4 opinion written by the now-retired Justice Kennedy, the Court ruled that bans on same-sex marriage violated the equal-protection clause of the Fourteenth Amendment. By handing down the decision in *Obergefell*, the Supreme Court made same-sex marriages legal in all fifty states and required that they be recognized equally under the law.[118]

National public opinion remains mixed on the matter of same-sex marriage, which, despite Justice Anthony Kennedy's retirement, remains the law of the land (see Figure 5.6). While a substantial majority of Americans favor allowing same-sex marriage,[119] the major political parties are divided on the issue: Democrats are typically more supportive of same-sex marriage than Republicans are. Because support for same-sex marriage is much greater among younger Americans than among older Americans, public support for same-sex marriage will almost certainly increase over time.

As support for same-sex marriage grows, LGBT activists have started pressing for the rights of transgender individuals. In February 2016, the city of Charlotte, North Carolina, enacted a local ordinance allowing transgender people to use bathroom facilities that match their gender identities. In March 2016, the North Carolina legislature passed HB2, a law that prohibited cities from expanding on North Carolina's own antidiscrimination laws, which protect race, religion, national origin, handicap status, or biological sex. Thus, laws in cities such as Charlotte, Chapel Hill, Durham, and Raleigh that extended protections to sexual orientation or gender identity were void.[120] In response to the law, businesses General Electric and Hewlett Packard decided to boycott the state. So did musicians Ringo Starr, Bruce Springsteen, and Maroon 5.[121]

Image 5.13 Female high school athletes Chelsea Mitchel, Alanna Smith, and Selina Soule claimed that allowing athletes who were born male to compete against them placed them at an unfair competitive disadvantage.

In the spring of 2020, the Supreme Court in a 6–3 vote decided that employment discrimination against gays and transsexuals violated the prohibition against sex discrimination from the Civil Rights Act of 1964. Conservative justices Gorsuch and Roberts joined the Court's four most liberal justices in this ruling.[122]

Alternatively, in February 2020, three high school girls in Connecticut filed a federal lawsuit over the decision of the Connecticut Association of Schools, which runs interscholastic sports in Connecticut, to allow transgender high school athletes to compete with the gender of their choosing. Nineteen other states allow transgender students to do the same.[123] Under this policy, two students who were born male but identified as female could compete in female track and field events. The complainants argued that this gave those students an unfair advantage.[124]

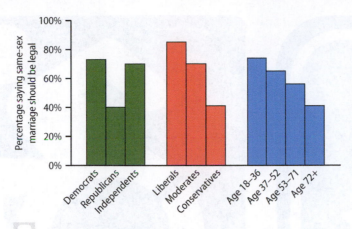

Figure 5.6 **Views on Same-Sex Marriage**

Younger voters support same-sex marriage at substantially higher rates than do older voters.

Source: Pew Research Center, Attitudes on Same-Sex Marriage, accessed May 1, 2018, https://www.pewforum.org/fact-sheet/changing-attitudes-on-gay-marriage/.

In 2016, the EEOC declared that "denying an employee equal access to a common restroom according to the employee's gender identity is sex discrimination," which is prohibited by Title VII of the Civil Rights Act.[125] Less than two weeks later, a joint directive to public schools by the Department of Justice and the Department of Education declared that such schools must allow transgender students to use the bathroom of their choice. This controversial move set off a barrage of criticism: The governor of North Carolina sued the Justice Department; Texas Lieutenant Governor Dan Patrick told school superintendents not to abide by the rules. On the other hand, House Democratic leader Nancy Pelosi tweeted support for the rules.[126] The Trump administration abandoned the Obama administration's lawsuit against the North Carolina law and proposed defining gender as an immutable condition defined at birth.[127]

Disability Rights

Advocates for the rights of the disabled, encouraged by the civil rights, women's rights, and other movements, successfully lobbied for the Rehabilitation Act of 1973, which prohibits discrimination against disabled individuals by any federal agency or by any private program or activity that receives federal funds. The landmark Americans with Disabilities Act (ADA) passed in 1990 goes further, requiring public and private employers to make "reasonable accommodations" to known physical and mental limitations of employees with disabilities and, if possible, to modify performance standards to accommodate an employee's disability.

To comply with the act, public transportation authorities have made buses and trains accessible to people in wheelchairs. Public accommodations, such as restaurants, hotels, movie theaters, and doctors' offices, must also meet ADA accessibility standards, within reason, removing barriers from existing structures. Related legislation, the Individuals with Disabilities Education Act (IDEA; 1990, updated 2004), requires states to provide free public education to all children with disabilities in the least-restrictive environment appropriate to their needs.

Congress does not provide a full list of disabilities covered under the ADA but rather covers any disability that "substantially limits a major life activity." Thus, a trucking company need not make accommodations for a driver who can see clearly out of only

Images 5.14 and 5.15 Disability-rights groups have advocated moving from the current accessibility sign (left) to the newer one (right), which is much more dynamic.

one eye because the disability does not substantially limit a major life activity. On the other hand, the ADA does protect people who have HIV or AIDS. It even protects people with severe drug and alcohol problems, provided the drug use in question is not illegal.[128]

Many organized interests support the rights of the disabled. While prejudice against people of different races, religions, sexual orientation, and country of origin might lead responsive representatives to oppose the rights of minorities, there are few if any votes to be had by lobbying against the rights of the disabled. Nevertheless, when at the end of 2011 the Department of Labor proposed new rules that would push employers toward a goal of having 7 percent of their employees be people with disabilities, business groups opposed the rules, claiming they would be costly to implement.[129]

Racial and Religious Profiling

Profiling—the use by police of racial, ethnic, or religious characteristics in determining whom to investigate for particular crimes—is controversial because it entails unequal treatment under the law. For example, along the I-95 corridor north of Baltimore, a team of observers found that about 17 percent of cars had black drivers and nearly 76 percent had white drivers and that the drivers observed traffic laws in similar proportions. Nevertheless, more than 80 percent of the cars stopped and searched by the Maryland State Police were driven by blacks and Latinos, while cars driven by whites constituted fewer than 20 percent of the searches.[130] So much more likely were blacks to be pulled over than whites that the phrase "driving while black" came to signify African American drivers' feeling that they risked being treated as criminals on the roads. State and federal courts have specifically prohibited the use of race as a factor in "drug courier profiles."[131] Many suspect that the killing of Trayvon Martin in Florida resulted from racial profiling by a neighborhood watch captain.

Following the terrorist attacks of 9/11, profiling of Arabs and Muslims increased, particularly in matters of airline security. In efforts to identify potential terrorists, mistakes are often made.[132] In 2014, for example, New York City ended its practice of having undercover police officers spy on Muslims without probable cause.[133] In January 2016, the New York Police Department agreed to two settlements resulting from cases brought by citizens regarding the department's undercover operations. The settlement prohibits investigations in which race, religion, or ethnicity is a motivating factor in the surveillance. Adopting guidelines used by the Federal Bureau of Investigation (FBI), a civilian will monitor police surveillance of religious groups.[134] Where issues of security are at stake, profiling is especially controversial.

Key Questions
Should profiling be used to protect American citizens against terrorist plots? If so, what should it look like?

Voting Rights for Felons

Since passage of the Civil Rights Act of 1964 and the Voting Rights Act of 1965, voting rights have been scrupulously protected, even as stricter requirements for voter identification have been enforced to prevent alleged fraud (see Chapter 11). But there remains a persistent inequality regarding whether felons have the right to vote, with each state making its own determinations (see Figure 5.7). At one end of the spectrum, Maine and Vermont allow prison

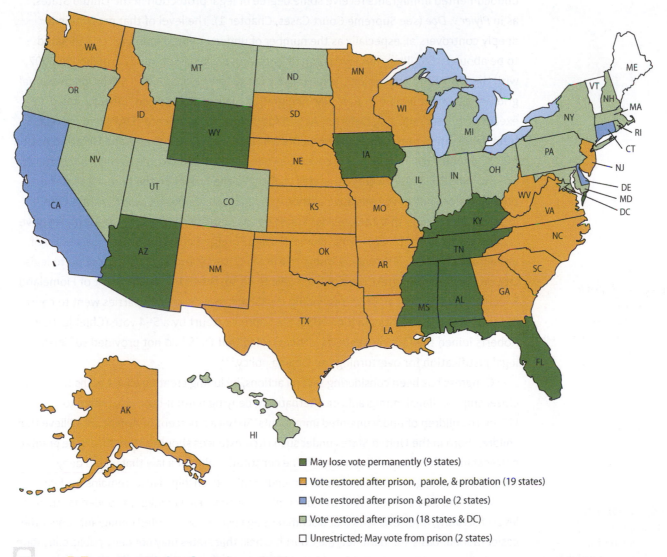

■ May lose vote permanently (9 states)
■ Vote restored after prison, parole, & probation (19 states)
■ Vote restored after prison & parole (2 states)
■ Vote restored after prison (18 states & DC)
□ Unrestricted; May vote from prison (2 states)

Figure 5.7 **Voting Rights for Felons, 2019**

Maine and Vermont allow incarcerated prisoners to vote. Many other states restore voting rights upon release from prison and after the parole period ends.

Source: ProCon.org, State Felon Voting Laws accessed March 18, 2020, http://felonvoting.procon.org.

inmates to vote. Eighteen states and the District of Columbia allow felons to vote upon release from prison, and nineteen more allow them to vote upon completion of probation or parole.[135] Nine states do not automatically restore voting rights, with the specifics of restoration varying among them. Recent estimates have placed the number of disenfranchised felons in the United States at approximately 6.1 million; this represents 2.5 percent of the voting-age population in the United States, or one in every forty adults.[136] Such laws markedly influence close elections given the racial disparities in the American political justice system. Nationwide, 7.44 percent of African Americans have been disenfranchised by felony-voter laws. That percentage reaches a nationwide high of 26.2 percent in Kentucky.

Key Questions

Should being convicted of a felony mean forfeiting the right to vote? Forever? While in prison? Until completion of probation or parole?

Undocumented Immigrants

The Fourteenth Amendment's equal protection clause prohibits states from denying to *any* person—in other words, not just citizens—equal protection under the law. Thus even undocumented immigrants receive some degree of legal protection in the United States, as in *Plyler v. Doe* (see Supreme Court Cases, Chapter 1). The level of that protection is deeply controversial, especially as the number of undocumented immigrants, estimated to be about 10.5 million, has leveled off after having peaked at about 12.2 million in 2007, with the 2007–2009 recession the most likely cause for the drop-off.[137] With Congressional gridlock leaving it unable to pass any immigration measures, President Obama issued executive orders requiring Deferred Action for Parents of Americans (DAPA), to protect from deportation undocumented residents whose children are citizens, and Deferred Action for Childhood Arrivals (DACA), to cover the young children who came to the United States prior to June 15, 2012. Twenty-six states challenged the orders on the grounds that the president does not have legislative authority. In 2016, the Supreme Court affirmed the lower court decision that the president does not have the authority to issue such executive orders (see Chapter 16, Economic, Domestic, and Foreign Policy, for further discussion of immigration policy).[138] President Trump rescinded Obama's order, asking Congress to legislate on the issue. Congress has not been able to do so. When the Department of Homeland Security (DHS) issued an order rescinding the Obama policy, several parties went to court to block the DHS decision. In June 2020, the Supreme Court by a 5–4 vote (Chief Justice Roberts joined the four most liberal justices) ruled that DHS had not provided sufficient legal justification for overturning the Obama policy.[139]

Key Questions

Should children of undocumented persons who are born on American soil be U.S. citizens?

Congress has been considering several actions, including creating easier paths to citizenship for illegal immigrants or, alternatively, denying natural-born citizenship to U.S.-born children of undocumented immigrants. Sixty-two percent of Americans believe that children born in the United States under such circumstances should automatically be granted citizenship, with 31 percent opposed.[140] The constitutionality of a law that would deny them citizenship, given the Fourteenth Amendment's citizenship clause, remains unclear.[141]

While the Court reviews laws that discriminate against legal immigrants under its strictest level of scrutiny, it reviews laws that discriminate against undocumented immigrants under the easier rational-basis standard. Yet, the Court has held that states may not deny public education to undocumented immigrants,[142] and federal law requires hospitals to provide emergency care to undocumented immigrants through Medicaid, the federal program that supports health care to poor people. The growth of civil rights to cover undocumented immigrants is surely one of the most controversial of the frontiers we have examined.

Key Questions

Why do women still earn less than men do for performing the same job? What tools are available to change this?

Civil Rights and Democracy

The core demand of civil rights is equal opportunity under the law. When laws discriminate or allow discrimination, people are effectively excluded from civic life. The demands for equal opportunity are often made to government, which alone has the authority to prohibit discrimination.

While a democratic system of government works to be responsive to its citizens, responsiveness to minorities is harder to obtain when majorities seek to limit minority rights. As noted in Chapter 2, The Constitution, James Madison saw a large republic with varied interests as a cure for the mischiefs of faction. But when factions form on the basis of majority group versus minority group, such as white versus black, heterosexual versus gay and lesbian, or native-born versus immigrant, responsiveness to minority preferences has been achieved through the gateways of lawsuits, protests, and other forms of civic engagement by the minority group. In response, the government has struck down laws that discriminated and passed laws that prevented other people from discriminating.

Out of all the activities by groups seeking equal rights, voting might be key. With the ballot, declared Martin Luther King Jr. in 1965, comes accountability. Blacks could "vote out of office public officials who bar the doorway to decent housing, public safety, jobs, and decent integrated education. It is now obvious that the basic elements so vital to Negro advancement can only be achieved by seeking redress from government. . . . To do this, the vote is essential."[143]

While voting rights provide accountability by allowing citizens to "throw the bums out," they also provide responsiveness. A minority group's elected opponents are not as forceful once a group has the right to vote. Former Texas Governor Rick Perry, who twice unsuccessfully sought the Republican nomination for president, was never known as a supporter of civil rights. Indeed, one of the controversies from his 2012 campaign was a piece of family property Perry inherited that included a landmark rock at the entrance that included the "n-word." The parcel of property where the rock is located was officially known by that name. While Perry decried the name on the rock when first running for president, he took no steps to change the name when he originally became its owner, whether as a private citizen, when elected a Texas state official, or even when elected governor. With less than 12 percent of the Texas population being African American, he was not offending a very large group. He did, however, support in-state tuition for children of undocumented Texas residents. Latinos made up nearly 40 percent of Texas's population when Perry was governor.[144] More generally, the voting patterns of southern House and Senate members on issues related to civil rights have moderated over the past forty years, proving that King was certainly correct about the value of the ballot.[144] While members of Congress representing southern states once voted in lockstep opposition to civil rights issues, their votes on such issues now differ only slightly from those of representatives of other states.[146]

These changes are part of a larger evolution in the idea of equality that has proceeded over the course of the nation's more than two centuries. Americans once believed that slaveholding was not inconsistent with demands for equality; today African Americans, women, and others once discriminated against have achieved full participation in the nation's civic life. But the frontiers of civil rights will continue to evolve. Some Americans believe that equal opportunity is not enough, that the government must take stronger measures to ensure greater equality of outcome. Because there is no constitutional right to equal results, the battle over this meaning of equality will be fought not in the courts, but in democratically elected legislatures.

Martin Luther King Jr. once declared that the "arc of the moral universe is long, but it bends toward justice." Two recent examples from the world of sports show how far we have come. When light middleweight boxing champion Manny Pacquiao declared that gay people are "worse than animals," he lost his $1 million annual endorsement deal with Nike.[147] When Donald Sterling, the owner of the Los Angeles Clippers basketball team, scolded his girlfriend for bringing African American superstar Magic Johnson to Clippers games, he was roundly condemned by nearly everyone, north and south, Republican and Democrat, and was forced to give up his interest in the team. Considering that segregation in public facilities was legal in much of the United States until 1965, and that until the *Lawrence v. Texas* (2003) case states were free to make homosexual relations illegal, the arc of the moral universe appears to be opening more gateways for Americans than ever before.

Chapter Review

Key Terms

Black Lives Matter (p. 163). Why do you think Black Lives Matter limits the name of the group to "black lives"?

Brown v. Board of Education (p. 159). What was the reasoning behind the *Brown* decision?

citizenship (p. 147). What are the different paths to citizenship?

civil rights (p. 144). What is the government's role with regards to civil rights?

Civil Rights Act (p. 162). What did the Civil Rights Act prohibit?

Dred Scott v. Sandford (p. 146). What seems wrong about the *Dred Scott* decision?

equality of opportunity (p. 145). How would you measure equality of opportunity?

equality of outcome (p. 145). How would you measure equality of outcome?

Equal Pay Act (p. 170). How effective has the Equal Pay Act been?

equal protection clause (p. 150). What does the equal protection clause command?

Jim Crow laws (p. 151). What were Jim Crow laws?

poll taxes (p. 150. What were the various types of poll taxes?

private discrimination (p. 144). What constitutes private discrimination?

public discrimination (p. 144). What constitutes public discrimination?

Reconstruction (p. 150). What happened when Reconstruction ended?

separate-but-equal doctrine (p. 151). Can separate schools ever be equal?

state action (p. 157). What makes state action so important to government efforts to protect civil rights?

Stonewall riots (p. 175). What movement did the Stonewall riots spark?

Voting Rights Act (p. 163). What did the Voting Rights Act prohibit?

women's suffrage movement (p. 153). What gateways did the women's suffrage movement use to gain the right to vote?

Learning Outcomes: What You Need to...

Know	Test Yourself	Participate
LO 5-1 Define civil rights		
Civil rights relate to the duties of citizenship and opportunities for civic participation that the government is obliged to protect. They are based on the expectation of equality under the law. The most important is the right to vote.	• Compare civil rights to civil liberties. • Track changes in civil rights from the Constitution as originally ratified to today.	• Know your civil rights. • Understand the debt you owe to the actions of citizens for the civil rights you enjoy today.
LO 5-2 Explain how the federal and state governments suppressed civil rights		
Regarding civil rights, the government can engage in state-sponsored or public discrimination; treat people equally but permit private discrimination; or try, as it has since the 1960s, both to treat people equally and to prevent individuals or businesses from discriminating. It falls to government to protect individuals against unequal treatment and to citizens to ensure that government does not discriminate against individuals or groups. During the nation's first century, and even thereafter, state laws and the national government actively discriminated against people on the basis of race, gender, and ethnic background.	• Describe the role of the Supreme Court in the expansion of slavery. • Enumerate ways that racial discrimination persisted after emancipation. • Track the steps in the achievement of women's suffrage. • Survey the laws that discriminated against women. • Identify the groups that have been denied rights to U.S. citizenship. • Discuss restraints on civil rights during wartime.	• Read excerpts from the *Dred Scott* decision (http://web.utk.edu/~scheb/decisions/dredscott.htm) and from the Mississippi black codes established after the Civil War (http://web.mit.edu/21h.102/www/Primary%20source%20collections/Reconstruction/Black%20codes.htm) and comment on them. • Consider how disenfranchisement of women affected U.S. politics before 1920. • Speculate on why the United States limited citizenship. • Evaluate what these mean for living in a time of prolonged terrorism.
LO 5-3 Assess how equal protection has expanded		
During the nation's second century, discrimination was state-sponsored in the South; elsewhere private discrimination was practiced without challenge.	• Track the changing meaning of equality. • Explain why "state action" is so important to the equal protection clause. • Demonstrate that the judicial branch might be a better protector of civil rights than the legislative branch.	• Decide whether we are all equal now. • Weigh your respect for the legislative branch versus the judicial branch.

Know	Test Yourself	Participate

LO 5-4 Identify the groups at the forefront of the civil rights movement

Today public discrimination has been ended by constitutional amendments and the courts, largely through the Fourteenth Amendment's equal protection clause. Beginning in the 1950s, litigation and grassroots protests led the federal government to end segregation and secure voting rights for African Americans and to end limits to women's full participation in public life.

- Explain why the *Brown* decision by itself had only a minimal effect on school desegregation.
- Identify the grassroots protests that opened the gateways to ending private discrimination.
- Describe how Congress and the courts have pushed along voting rights.
- Draw parallels between the civil rights movement for African Americans, Latinos, and women.

- Weigh the impact on social policy of the legislative branch against that of the judicial branch.
- Appreciate the impact active citizens can have on government.
- Appreciate the impact law can have on politics and society.

LO 5-5 Describe the new battles for civil rights

The expanded notion of equality promoted by the civil rights and women's rights movements inspired other groups, such as homosexuals and the disabled, to demand full access to equality. The extension of rights for some may involve a loss of privileges for others, and sometimes rights clash. Congress and the courts seek to define the meaning and limits of rights in new areas of contention. The trend has always been for a broader meaning of equality and greater support for civil rights.

- Explain why support for same-sex marriage is likely to increase over time.
- Recall why legislatures have been so responsive to people with disabilities.
- Define racial, ethnic, and religious profiling.
- Describe different state regulations on voting rights for felons.
- State why the U.S.-born children of illegal immigrants are automatically U.S. citizens.

- Determine whether you think all of the civil rights battles have been won.
- Find disability rights organizations in your community.
- Find instances of profiling in the news or in your community.
- Analyze the racial and ethnic composition of the prison population, and determine if prohibiting voting rights for felons is discriminatory.
- Debate whether the Constitution should be amended with regard to citizenship.

6 Public Opinion

Courtesy of J. Ann Selzer

J. ANN SELZER
University of Kansas

> "*We let the voters speak to us.*"

Shown on the next page, the University of Kansas where J. Ann Selzer earned her undergraduate degree.

J. **Ann Selzer's** gateway to American politics has been her ability to accurately measure public opinion in the state of Iowa—the home of the nation's first presidential caucus. Iowa, being the first contest, shapes the presidential race in important ways. Candidates spend huge amounts of time and money courting Iowans. Selzer understood the importance of this battle and realized that good estimates of what Iowans thought about the candidates prior to voting would be invaluable to the democratic process. She has been involved with the *Des Moines Register* Iowa Caucus Poll for over three decades. In 2008, she stunned the political world by predicting Barack Obama's easy victory over Hillary Clinton.

Selzer's curiosity about people's attitudes and how best to capture those opinions began when she was 5 years old. Unhappy with a nickname her parents had given her, she asked neighborhood mothers about their opinions on it.[1] Her question was, "Do you think it is a good name for a witch?" Her results showed maternal support for making her parents abandon her nickname, cementing her interest in public opinion.

Selzer grew up in an upper-middle-class setting in Topeka, Kansas. She was a competitive and driven child who wanted to stand out among her four siblings.[2] After graduating from the University of Kansas, she earned her PhD in Communication Theory and Research from the University of Iowa. She started her career in Des Moines,[3] briefly working as director of research for Starr and Associates, a research institute and law office, before moving to Washington, D.C., to work for a public opinion research firm.[4]

In 1987, she moved back to Des Moines and took a job running the Iowa Poll for the *Des Moines Register*.[5] She understood that this position offered a chance to influence politics through the ability to assess accurately the thinking of Iowans. When she took over, the poll was a unit within the paper's operation and included surveys of people who had participated in previous polls, who were likely to be repeat caucus-goers. But Selzer wondered if the opinions of newly found caucus-goers matched those of people the Iowa Poll had surveyed before. She looked at the data and determined that they did not. She urged the editors to end the practice of interviewing previous poll participants. This approach helped to establish her credibility as a trusted pollster.[6] With this methodology,

Selzer predicted that Bob Dole would win the 1988 Republican caucus over George H. W. Bush, the favorite in almost every other poll the newspaper had conducted. From this point on, her innovative methodologies and attention to detail helped her gain a reputation of pursuing the truth with new techniques.

She worked for the *Register* until 1992, when she left to develop her own polling firm, Selzer & Company.[7] In 1997, her company won the bid to conduct the *Des Moines Register* Iowa Poll when the newspaper decided to outsource the operation, and from there she has solidified her reputation as a preeminent pollster.[8] Some of the races that have helped cement her prowess are the 2004 last-minute victory of John Kerry in the Democratic caucus and Joni Ernst's 8.5-point victory over Bruce Braley in the 2014 Iowa senate race.[9] In the 2008 Democratic caucus polls, her firm's research indicated that caucus attendees would include a high proportion of first-time caucus-goers and independents—enabling them to reach a voice underrepresented in campaign projections and other polls. Her controversial projection that Obama would easily win led the Hillary Clinton and John Edwards campaigns to question her credibility.[10] But her accurate prediction proved that this methodology enabled her firm to out-predict other leading polls.

It is this stellar reputation that Selzer and the *Des Moines Register* wanted to protect when they made the difficult decision to cancel the release of the results from the 2020 Iowa Poll—just two days before the voting began. There were apparent irregularities in the methodology raised first by Pete Buttigieg's campaign, including the possibility that his name was left off some of the questionnaires.[11] Out of an abundance of caution, the final 2020 caucus poll was kept under wraps. The decision speaks to the importance of accurate polling that CNN, the *Des Moines Register*, and Selzer & Co. seek when predicting Iowa caucus winners.[12] It is worth noting that her last poll in 2020 showed Trump winning the state by about 7 points, which is nearly exactly what he did win the state by.

Selzer's gateway to participation in the American political system—measuring public opinion with accuracy—highlights its importance in a democracy. The expression of the public will is the bedrock of democracy. For politicians, knowing which way the public leans is a gateway to power. For citizens, expressing an opinion and knowing it is being heard is a gateway to influence. But reading public opinion correctly is not easy. Polls can be a great help, but they can easily be flawed. It is also worth noting that even if well measured, public opinion does not always point toward the best path for the country; the public can make the wrong call. To guard against such outcomes, it is critical the public be informed so they can make wise choices. In this chapter, we investigate the contours, sources, and impact of public opinion.

B.O'Kane/Alamy Stock Photo

The Power of Public Opinion

LO 6-1 Decide why public opinion is powerful

"Our government rests on public opinion," claimed Abraham Lincoln. "Public sentiment is everything. With public sentiment, nothing can fail. Without it, nothing can succeed."[13] The nation's sixteenth president (1861–65) was the great champion of "government of the people, by the people, and for the people," as he expressed it in his Gettysburg Address. He understood that democratic government must be responsive to the will of the people. The hope in a democracy is that each citizen has an equal voice and that those voices, collectively, will be heard by government officials and will guide their actions. Knowing what the public is thinking and having public support are a powerful combination. Writing more than one hundred years ago, James Bryce, a famous observer of U.S. politics, contended that public opinion is "the greatest source of power" in the United States, more important than the power of presidents, Congress, and political parties.[14]

The Power of Presidential Approval

Perhaps no one appreciates the power of public opinion more keenly than former President George W. Bush (2001–2009). He came to office in 2001, following a contested election in which more than half the electorate had voted against him. However, following the terrorist attacks on September 11 of that year, the country rallied to his side.[15] President Bush then enjoyed the approval of 90 percent of the public. No president had ever scored higher—not Ronald Reagan (1981–89), not John F. Kennedy (1961–63), and not Franklin Delano Roosevelt (1933–45). With this unprecedented level of public support, Bush was able to get Congress to agree to nearly everything he wanted. It passed the PATRIOT Act, which expanded the powers of the federal government in the area of national security, and it approved his call for a new cabinet-level Department of Homeland Security. But such popularity is always short-lived. Bush, for example, tumbled in popularity during his remaining years in office. By the time he left office, Bush's approval stood in the mid-20s, and one CBS/*New York Times* poll indicated only 20 percent of Americans approved of his job—the lowest rating for any president since the start of scientific polling in the 1930s.

approval rating: *Job performance evaluation for the president, Congress, or other public official or institution that is generated by public opinion polls and is typically reported as a percentage.*

President Obama's **approval rating**, by contrast, was much more stable than President Bush's. Obama's popularity was pretty steady during his presidency, usually hovering in the mid-40-percent range. He did enjoy a brief surge immediately following the assassination of Osama bin Laden on May 2, 2011, and his successful reelection in 2012. Over the last year of his presidency, his approval moved above 50 percent. That gain likely reflects improvement in the economy and inevitable comparisons to Hillary Clinton and Donald Trump, who were both very unpopular candidates.

Pete Souza/White House Photo/Getty Images

Image 6.1 Standing in the Control Room, President Obama watches the unfolding of events after ordering the assassination of Osama bin Laden in May 2011.

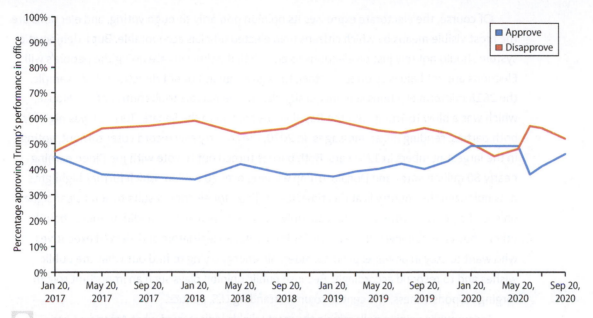

Figure 6.1 **Approval Ratings of President Donald Trump, 2017–2020**

President Trump's approval rating never was very high, reflecting his controversial path to the White House. He has consistently been the least popular president in the modern era. These low ratings are even more surprising in light of a growing economy.

Source: Gallup, Presidential Approval Ratings – Donald Trump, accessed November 17, 2020, https://news.gallup.com/poll/203198/presidential-approval-ratings-donald-trump.aspx.

As Figure 6.1 shows, Trump has never enjoyed much popularity. His approval ratings in January 2017 started in the mid-40s and then descended to the mid-30s by 2018. However, his popularity ticked up in 2018 as the economy improved, but his ratings remained low–hovering in the low 40s. He did have a brief surge in popularity immediately following the COVID-19 crisis, getting close to 50 percent. But as questions arose about his handling of the crisis and his tendency to share controversial ideas (e.g., injecting Lysol into humans might kill the virus), his numbers started to decline again. There are two clear patterns in Trump's popularity. First, he has never been very popular among Americans. His average rating sits at 40 percent, whereas, the average rating for a sitting U.S. president is 53 percent.[16] Second, he maintained strong support among Republicans and almost no support among Democrats during this time in office. The only group that changed their ratings of the president much was independents.

By the 2020 election, President Trump's approval sat at 46 percent. He lost the 2020 presidential election to former Vice President Joe Biden. However, he still earned over 70 million votes and is projected to win 232 electoral votes.

Presidents, for the most part, start off with public support during the so-called honeymoon period. But as time unfolds and governing continues, the public becomes more dissatisfied. It seems as if staying in office is costly for presidents. We certainly saw that with Obama, and this pattern is a common one for presidents. President Trump faces this same basic fate during this term. It is an enduring feature of American politics.

What Is Public Opinion?

Public opinion is recognized for its power, but it is ever-changing, hard to measure, harder to predict, and nearly impossible to control. **Public opinion** is the aggregate of individual attitudes or beliefs about certain issues or officials, and it is the foundation of any democracy.

Key Questions

Why didn't President Trump ever enjoy a honeymoon as his predecessors did?

public opinion: *Aggregate of individual attitudes or beliefs about certain issues or officials.*

Of course, the electorate expresses its opinion primarily through voting, and elections are the most visible means by which citizens hold elected officials accountable. But a democratic system should not rely just on elections to ensure that politicians are doing the people's will. Elections are not held very often. Further, they give signals but not directions. For example, the 2018 midterm elections sent mixed signals. The Democrats took control of the House, which was a blow to Trump. But the Republicans held on to the Senate. Turnout was high for both parties, sending mixed messages. In 2020, the country saw record voter turnout, voting in the largest numbers in 120 years. Both parties turned out to vote with Joe Biden earning nearly 80 million votes and Donald Trump winning over 70 million, which further highlights how polarized the country is at this time. It is difficult for election results to send clear signals on specific policies. Voters can indicate only whether they like one candidate more than the other; they cannot convey the reasons for their vote. So legislators and elected executives who want to stay in power expend considerable energy trying to find out what the public wishes and to respond accordingly. Because public opinion plays such an important role in forging responsiveness, it is central to understanding U.S. politics.

Today, public opinion polls remain the most reliable indicators of what Americans are thinking, and a whole industry and science have grown up around measuring people's opinions on everything from presidents to toothpaste. Polls are not the only sources of public opinion; others are the size of rallies and protests, the tone of letters sent to elected officials or newspapers, the amount of money given to particular causes or candidates, the content of newspaper editorials, and information gleaned from day-to-day conversations with average Americans. Shifts in public opinion can also be detected in Supreme Court decisions, as cases pertaining to birth control, abortion, and marriage equality indicate (see Chapter 4, Civil Liberties, for specific cases).

The Public's Support of Government

The health and stability of a democracy rest with the public. Just as government must respond to what the people want, so citizens must view the system as legitimate and want to be part of it. If the public withdraws its support, the government collapses. For these reasons, political scientists have sought to measure the public's faith in the political system. Two of the most common efforts involve assessing whether the people trust their government and whether they believe their participation in government matters. Political scientists call the latter **efficacy**— the extent to which people believe their actions affect the course of government. **Political trust** is the extent to which people believe the government acts in their best interests. It has generally declined over the past fifty years, with steeper declines following the beginning of the Iraq War in 2003 and the financial collapse that began in 2008. In January 2018, only 14 percent of Americans say they can trust the government in Washington to do what is right "almost all of the time" (2 percent) or "most of the time" (12 percent).[17] By April 2020, Americans were more trusting of local government (55 percent) to handle the COVID-19 crisis than the federal government (38 percent). This pattern continued into the summer as Americans gave governors and mayors higher marks for handling the pandemic than President Trump.[18]

Efficacy has also declined. It stood at more than 70 percent in 1960; by 1994, it had fallen by half. In other words, only one-third of Americans felt that their opinions mattered to government. The figure rebounded to 60 percent by 2002 but then declined again during the Iraq War and financial crisis. It has fallen well below 40 percent in the current

efficacy: *Extent to which people believe their actions can affect public affairs and the actions of government.*

political trust: *Extent to which people believe the government acts in their best interests.*

Key Questions

What does a decline in efficacy and public trust mean for American democracy?

Supreme Court Cases

Bowers v. Hardwick (1986)
Obergefell v. Hodges (2015)

QUESTION: *Bowers:* May states prosecute consensual sexual activity by members of the same sex? *Obergefell:* May states prohibit same-sex marriage?

ORAL ARGUMENT: *Bowers*: March 31, 1986 (listen at http://www.oyez.org/cases/1980-1989/1985/1985_85_140) *Obergefell*: April 28, 2015 (listen at http://www.oyez.org/cases/2014/14-556)

DECISION: *Bowers*: June 30, 1986 (read at http://caselaw.findlaw.com/us-supreme-court/478/186.html). *Obergefell*: June 26, 2015 (read at http://caselaw.findlaw.com/us-supreme-court/14-556.html).

OUTCOME: *Bowers*: There is no right to homosexual sodomy (5–4) (1986). *Obergefell*: States may not prohibit same-sex marriage (5–4) (2015).

When the police came to Michael Hardwick's home looking for him, his roommate let them in. When the police got to Hardwick's room, they observed him engaged in sexual behavior with another male. They arrested him under Georgia's anti-sodomy statute, which prohibits "any sexual contact involving the genitals of one person and the mouth or anus of another." Hardwick argued that the statute violated the right to privacy that the Court established in the *Griswold* birth control case (1965), which the Court later held to protect rights that were "deeply rooted in this Nation's history and tradition."* Noting that prohibitions on sodomy had "ancient roots," the Court voted 5–4 against the claim, calling the argument that homosexual sodomy is among those traditions "facetious." Chief Justice Warren Burger concurred, approvingly citing medieval English sources that declared sodomy as an offense of "deeper malignity" than rape. At the time, only about 32 percent of the American public agreed with the opinion that homosexual relations should be legal.

The Supreme Court reversed that decision nearly twenty years later in *Lawrence v. Texas* (2003). With seven new members on the Court, the justices voted 6–3 that the Texas law prohibiting sodomy was unconstitutional, with the majority opinion resting the decision on the liberty protected by the due process clause of the Fourteenth Amendment.

In the *Obergefell* case (2015), the Supreme Court struck down state laws that prohibited same-sex marriage. Citing the Supreme Court's 1967 *Loving v. Virginia* decision striking bans on interracial marriage, as well as the Supreme Court's 2003 *Lawrence v. Texas* decision overturning *Bowers v. Hardwick*, the Supreme Court ruled that the liberty protected by the Fourteenth Amendment includes the right to marry a partner of the same sex.

In fewer than thirty years, the Supreme Court had gone from holding that states could criminalize homosexual activity to determining that states may not prohibit same-sex marriage. These changes coincide with a more than quadrupling of support for marriage equality in the United States during that time. Whether this new result was directly due to the change in public opinion or due to new justices from a different generation who reflected that changed opinion, the Court's decision aligned with changes in public opinion.§

*Griswold v. Connecticut, 381 U.S. 479 (1965); Washington v. Glucksberg, 521 U.S. 702, 721 (1997).
§Marriages with members of the same sex should be legalized, September 1985, 11 percent agree. Do you favor or oppose allowing gay and lesbian couples to marry legally? December 2015, 52 percent favor. Both polls accessed on February 2, 2016, from Roper Opinion index, ropercenter.cornell.edu/ipoll-database.

Thinking Critically

1. Should the justices of the Supreme Court be influenced by public opinion?
2. How should the Court decide which rights, among those not specifically listed in the Constitution, should be protected as fundamental rights?

environment.[19] There is little doubt, as President Obama said in his first inaugural address, that there has been a "sapping of confidence across our land."[20]

Public trust and efficacy react to changes in government and whether the nation is experiencing good or bad times. Yet, through it all, Americans' commitment to the country and its core institutions has remained relatively strong. Patriotism, for example, showed little decline until very recently. Only 14 percent of Americans in 2017 thought there were other countries better than the United States.[21] In that same year, 91 percent of Americans had pride in being American.[22] However, in 2019, just 70 percent of Americans say they are proud to be Americans. It is the second year that less than a majority, 45 percent, has been "extremely" proud of being American. It seems that highly polarized politics is harming patriotism.[23] That being said, almost no one in the country favors overthrowing the government.[24]

Public Opinion Polls

LO 6-2 Describe how well polls measure public opinion

Polls make it possible to gauge the public's thinking on a variety of issues or officials, but they have been scientifically conducted only since the 1930s. One needs to be careful, since a poorly designed or executed poll can produce misleading results. It is, therefore, important to know which findings warrant attention and which warrant caution. Poll results can be biased, contradictory, and confusing (see, for example, many of the statewide polls along the so-called rust belt that wrongly predicted that Clinton would defeat Trump in 2016), which is why Selzer's accurate assessment of Iowans' political views has been so valued during presidential elections.

Key Questions

How do public officials learn what citizens think?

Gauging Public Opinion in the Past

In the eighteenth and nineteenth centuries, the contents of letters, the sizes of crowds at rallies, and people's willingness to sign petitions were used to gauge public opinion. They were crude indicators. Politicians had to go to great lengths to secure information about the public mood. George Washington (1789–97) was so frustrated with not being able to sense what voters thought about his policies as president that he literally mounted his horse and rode into the countryside to talk to the people. Abraham Lincoln held public meetings at the White House "to renew in me a clearer and more vivid image of that great popular assemblage out of which I sprung," he said, and he called these receptions his "public opinion baths."[25] President William McKinley (1897–1901) had his staff clip newspaper articles and put the clippings in a folder at night so he could read them to gauge the public's thinking.[26] Franklin Roosevelt also paid close attention to newspapers. And both Lincoln and Roosevelt, presidents in times of crisis, learned what the people thought through the many letters that citizens wrote to them. Even in the twenty-first century, citizens still write to the president. President Obama received thousands of letters a day, and his staff selected ten a day for him to read.[27]

Arizona Republic and Phoenix Gazette, September 27, 1941

Image 6.2 Presidents—such as Franklin D. Roosevelt, depicted here—often got their information on public opinion by reading the newspaper.

Yet none of these sources of "public sentiment," as President Lincoln called it, gave very precise indicators. Lincoln once said that he wanted to "get done . . . what the people desire to have done," but the problem was that he did not know what they desired.[28] Given that public opinion was so difficult to determine, there were many disagreements about its shape and direction. Moreover, because it was based on the content of newspapers and letters, on petitions, and on conversations with political observers, it was really elite opinion.[29] In other words, the most activist and literate elements of society were defining public opinion. Those who could write letters, for example, and would take the time to do so were the ones whose voices were heard. Thus, politicians had biased readings of public opinion because the views they heard tended not to represent the people equally.

Scientific Polling and the Growth of Survey Research

In the 1800s, newspapers and other organizations polled the people to assess public opinion, but these polls were of limited help because it was unclear who was being surveyed. So-called straw polls, for example, sought to predict the outcome of elections. During the presidential campaign of 1824, the *Harrisburg Pennsylvanian* canvassed the opinion of newspaper readers and concluded that Andrew Jackson would get 63 percent of the vote and win easily.[30] As it turned out, Jackson received only about 40 percent of the popular vote.

Though straw polls were often inaccurate, newspapers and magazines continued to poll readers' opinions well into the twentieth century. During the 1936 presidential campaign, the *Literary Digest* conducted a poll that predicted Republican Alf Landon would win the election by 57 percent over President Franklin Roosevelt. The reverse happened: Roosevelt won with a landslide 61 percent of the vote. Why did the *Literary Digest* get it so wrong? It had sent out 10 million ballots. But it had sent them to names drawn from automobile registration lists and telephone books and asked recipients to mail the ballots back. The sample, as a result, was biased. First, in 1936 those who owned automobiles and had telephones were wealthier than average Americans and were more likely to be Republicans. Less wealthy Americans, responding favorably to Roosevelt's actions to end the Great Depression, were increasingly aligning themselves with the Democrats. Second, the poll asked respondents to mail in their ballots, introducing additional bias. Those who would take the time to do so would likely be better off, further increasing the Republican bias of the sample. Even though 2 million ballots were returned, the poll did not offer a very sound basis on which to make a prediction.

George Gallup, who had founded the American Institute of Public Opinion in 1935, correctly predicted the outcome of the 1936 election by using a **random sample** to generate a way to select people to participate in surveys. He made his sample representative of the American public by giving, in effect, every American an equal chance to be part of it. The end product was a sample of 5,000, which was far smaller than the *Literary Digest's* sample but far more representative of average Americans. As a result of his innovative approach, Gallup is often considered the father of modern polling, and the best-known name in polling

random sample: *Method of selection that gives everyone who might be selected to participate in a poll an equal chance to be included.*

W. Eugene Smith/The LIFE Picture Collection/Getty Images

Image 6.3 In the 1930s, George Gallup developed a scientific approach to polling, greatly increasing its accuracy and authority.

today remains the Gallup Poll. His scientific polling and survey research techniques have been refined over the years.

The advent of scientific polling made it possible to assess the opinions of the public with some degree of ease and accuracy. V. O. Key, a leading scholar of public opinion in the 1950s and 1960s, described its impact this way:

> In an earlier day public opinion seemed to be pictured as a mysterious vapor that emanated from the undifferentiated citizenry and in some ways or another enveloped the apparatus of government to bring it into conformity with the public will. These weird conceptions . . . passed out of style as the technique of the sample survey permitted the determination, with some accuracy, of the opinions within the population.[31]

Scientific polling also permitted greater equality in assessing public opinion because the polls had the ability to tap the opinions of all Americans. George Gallup understood this aspect of polling—that scientific polls democratized the measurement of public opinion.[32]

By the early 1940s, the federal government began to see the value of survey research, too, and in October 1941, the U.S. Army conducted a survey to understand the opinions of enlisted men and officers. Today, the federal government continues to undertake a wide variety of polls, ranging from surveys about health issues to tapping the public's thinking on the economy. Polls are undertaken by other organizations as well. After the end of World War II, the University of Michigan founded the Survey Research Center, now the academic center for all sorts of polling.[33] By the 1960s, John Kennedy was making use of pollsters, and both Lyndon B. Johnson (1963–69) and Richard M. Nixon (1969–74) followed his lead.[34] The news media also saw the value of information about the public's thinking. By the 1980s, all the major television networks had polling operations in conjunction with major newspapers or news services.

Today Americans are regularly surveyed on a wide range of things other than politics. Polls ask about sexual practices, television viewing preferences, car purchases, and how often people go bowling. Extensive polling has revealed what proportion of the nation believes in UFOs, what kind of soap people buy, and at what age children stop believing in Santa Claus. With the COVID-19 crisis, polling firms across the country started to ask questions about social distancing, wearing masks, going to restaurants, willingness to fly on planes, etc. The information provided offers important insights in the impact of COVID-19 on the daily lives of people around the world.

Types of Polls

In a nation of more than 200 million adults, gathering opinions from everyone is not practical. Even the U.S. Census, a count of the population required by the Constitution every ten years, has trouble reaching every adult.[35] So polls draw a sample from a larger population. But first the population must be defined. It might be all adults over age 18, or only voters, or only citizens who contributed to Republican candidates in 2018.

The typical size of a sample survey is 1,000 people, though it can vary between 500 and about 1,500. Size does not matter as much as whether the sample is representative of the population being assessed. Having a **representative sample** means, in effect, that everyone in that population has an equal chance of being asked to participate in the poll. If a random 1,000 people are asked to be part of the survey, they should be representative of

Key Questions

Are polls the best way to find out what the public thinks? What are other methods of learning about public opinion?

representative sample:
Method of selection that allows a sample to be representative of the entire population, ensuring that key groups are accurately reflected in the sample.

the population generally—in, say, wealth, ethnicity, or educational attainment. The key to a representative sample is the randomness. It should be much like drawing numbered balls for a lottery: Each ball has the same chance of being chosen.

There are various ways to collect the information being sought. For in-person interviews, survey researchers send interviewers into neighborhoods and communities to ask questions in person. This was long the favored method, but it became increasingly expensive. With the near-universal presence of telephones by the 1970s, calling people became a more viable and much less expensive option. Telephone polls have dominated survey research over the past thirty years and continue to be used much of the time. Automated telephone polls, the so-called robo-polls, are on the rise. They are cheaper but tend not to be very accurate.[36] Phone-based surveys are increasingly hard to do, as the response rate continues to drop. These problems can be overcome, but the solutions are costly and often make the automated polls more appealing with their higher rate of error. An increasingly important platform for polling is the Internet. Internet polls have much potential, but there are hurdles. Consider that older and poorer Americans may lack access to the internet, which introduces bias. Additionally, surveyors cannot yet draw random samples of the population on the internet, which poses some additional obstacles.[37] As with telephones in the past century, however, more and more people are using computers and have access to the web. So in the future, internet polling will likely become the dominant platform for survey research.

Call-in polls or write-in polls are other means of securing a sample. For the former, a telephone number is posted on the television screen, for example, and people are asked to call to register their views. In the latter, a newspaper publishes an appeal for subscribers to write letters offering their opinions. Such approaches can yield a large number of participants, but the size of the sample can be misleading, for those who are willing to call or write are different from those who are not. The samples yielded in these polls are not representative and, thus, are highly suspect.

The COVID-19 crisis threw an unexpected wrench into telephone surveys. Prior to the start of the crisis, it was getting harder and harder to get people to answer their phones. But with the stay at home orders across the country, Americans were more willing to answer the phone. It was a kind of lifeline in a time of self-isolation. No one expects responses rates to stay at this elevated level once the crisis eases, but the shift speaks to one of many implications of the pandemic.[38]

Presidential elections are awash in polls. In the heat of the fall campaign, nightly polls gauge changes in voters' preferences for the major contenders. These surveys are called **tracking polls**. Another type of survey involving elections is the **exit poll**, conducted as voters leave the polling booth. The goal here is to learn about the reasoning behind the votes citizens just cast but, more important, to predict the outcome of the election before all the ballots are formally counted.

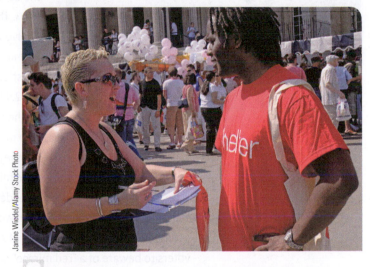

Janine Wiedel/Alamy Stock Photo

Image 6.4 In-person interviews were long considered the best method for polling the people; despite the expense, they are still used occasionally.

tracking polls: *Polls that seek to gauge changes of opinion of the same sample size over a period of time; they are common during the closing months of presidential elections.*

exit polls: *Polls that survey a sample of voters immediately after exiting the voting booth to predict the outcome of the election before the ballots are officially counted.*

The most famous and consequential exit poll took place in Florida during the 2000 presidential elections, fueling one of the most controversial electoral struggles of all time. The major networks used an exit poll to predict that the Sunshine State would go to Vice President Albert Gore Jr. (1993–2001). Florida's electoral votes would put Gore over the 270 needed, making him the apparent winner of the presidency. These predictions started to roll in at 8 P.M. on election night. The campaign of Republican George W. Bush protested, saying it was too early to call the state and that the race was still too close to know who won. By 10 P.M., the earlier forecast was withdrawn, and the outcome of the presidential election was again unclear. By 2 A.M. the next morning, Fox News called the election for Bush, with the other major networks soon following. Just two hours later, however, the call was retracted. There followed a thirty-six-day legal battle over which candidate actually won in Florida. It was not settled until the U.S. Supreme Court halted the Florida recount in mid-December, giving Bush the presidency (see Supreme Court Cases: *Bush v. Gore*, in Chapter 10, Elections and Campaigns).

Key Questions

Have you ever looked at a poll and questioned its validity? How might you gauge a poll's validity?

Key Questions

Do polls make sure the people's voices are heard?

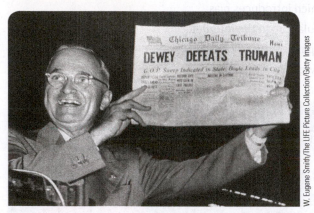

Image 6.5 President Harry Truman holding up a newspaper proclaiming that he lost the 1948 presidential election to Thomas Dewey. The *Tribune's* polls were wrong, and Truman had actually won.

Many have wanted to blame exit polls for the confusion that election night, but the polls were not as big a problem as the news media's use of them. The networks feel real pressure to make early calls, and that pressure sometimes leads them to go beyond what the data support. So while CBS was making that first call around 8 P.M., its polling experts behind the scene were urging caution.[39] Twelve years later, the tables were turned. It was Karl Rove, the well-known Republican consultant from the 2000 campaign, who questioned Fox News when it called Ohio for President Obama in 2012. He did so on live TV and Megyn Kelly, the Fox News anchor on the air at the time, challenged Rove, going directly to the experts who made the prediction. The exit polls proved Rove wrong: Romney did, in fact, lose that crucial state. In 2016, early exit polls were misleading as well, showing Trump down in key states that he ended up winning. Journalists being briefed on the first wave of exit polling felt confident Clinton would win race.[40] In 2020, the coronavirus impacted early exit polling because record numbers of Americans voted by mail and early. Pollsters were warning voters to beware of a "red mirage" or "blue mirage" that would show one candidate up by a significant amount before absentee ballots started being counted. For example, there was a blue mirage in Texas based on early voting, which ended up being called for Trump. Conversely, Americans saw a red mirage in Pennsylvania, which ended up giving 20 electoral votes to Biden.

push polls: *Polls that are designed to manipulate the opinions of those being polled.*

A final kind of election poll is actually a campaign strategy. **Push polls** are conducted by interest groups or candidates who try to affect the opinions of respondents by priming them with biased information. During the 2016 presidential primary in South Carolina, for example, Donald Trump claimed that Ted Cruz (R-TX) ran a push poll against him, trying to undermine his candidacy.[41] For these reasons and others, Trump started to call Cruz "lyin' Ted" on the campaign trail. Such polls seek to shift public opinion, not to measure it.

Error in Polls

Pollsters like J. Ann Selzer do everything they can to ensure that their samples are representative. Even if the sample is drawn properly, however, there is still a chance of error, like in Selzer's 2020 Iowa Poll mentioned at the start of the chapter. To capture this uncertainty, all poll numbers come with a **confidence interval** that captures the likely range 95 percent of the time. The poll produces a single estimate of the public's thinking, but the best way to think of that estimate is as a range of possible estimates. For a sample of 600 respondents, the sampling error is 4 percent. That 4 percent generates the confidence interval. Assume, for example, that 65 percent of those sampled support the efforts of Congress to reform the campaign finance laws. With a sampling error of 4 percent, the best way to think of the proportion is that, with 95 percent certainty, the actual amount of public support is somewhere between 61 percent and 69 percent. This range is the confidence interval. Note, however, that there is still a one in twenty chance (5 percent) that the true proportion is above or below that eight-point confidence interval. Hence, caution is always required when interpreting poll data.

In addition to sampling error, the wording of the question can introduce bias. The controversial issue of abortion offers a vivid example. What the public thinks about this issue depends a great deal on the way the question is asked. An NBC News/*Wall Street Journal* poll asked a representative sample of Americans the following question: "Which of the following best represents your views about abortion—the choice on abortion should be left up to the woman and her doctor, abortion should be legal only in cases in which pregnancy results from rape or incest or when the life of the woman is at risk, or abortion should be illegal in all circumstances?"

The answers show that 53 percent of the public felt that abortion was a decision best left to the woman and her doctor. Only 15 percent of Americans felt it should be illegal in all circumstances, with 29 percent wanting to have exceptions. In short, a majority of the public appeared to support abortion rights for women. That is an important finding.

But is it true? Consider the following question asked at about the same time by Fox News/Opinion Dynamics: "Once a woman is pregnant, do you believe the unborn baby or fetus should have all the same rights as a newborn baby?" The answers tell a different story. Nearly 60 percent of the public said yes, the unborn fetus should have the same rights as a newborn baby. Only 26 percent said no. According to this poll, a strong majority wants to protect the rights of the unborn and, therefore, to limit abortion rights for women.[42]

So what is American public opinion on abortion? Clearly, the answer depends on the wording of the question, specifically on whether respondents are asked to focus on the rights of women or the rights of the unborn. This same dynamic applies to other controversial issues, such as attitudes on race. Because of America's long and tortured history of race relations, people often try to give socially acceptable responses so as to suggest they are tolerant and not bigoted or racist. Although interviewers are trained to be neutral in their questioning, respondents sometimes try to give responses that they think the questioner wants to hear.

Another source of error in polls involves what political scientists call **nonattitudes**.[43] When asked, many people feel compelled to answer, even if they do not have opinions or know much about the question. They do not want to seem uninformed, but their responses create error in the survey.

The Future of Polls.   Donald Trump's upset win cast doubt on the accuracy of polls. It is, however, a mixed story. The national polls were correct: Clinton had a 2-percentage-point lead, and she ended up winning the popular vote by 2 percentage points. But many state polls were off, especially in the rust belt. Those errors tended to be in the highly competitive states, giving Trump unexpected wins in states like Michigan, Pennsylvania, and Wisconsin,

confidence interval:
Statistical range with a given probability that takes random error into account.

Key Questions
Should public officials be influenced by polls?

nonattitudes: *Sources of error in public opinion polls in which individuals feel obliged to give opinions when they are unaware of the issue or have no opinions about it.*

which won him the White House. It is hard to know the exact cause of the problem, but two possible issues have arisen. Some key states had little to no public polling right before the 2016 election and missed undecided voters swinging to Trump. Another issue was that many state pollsters did not change their polls to reflect that college graduates were more likely to take surveys than adults with less formal education, which was important because these groups had more partisan differences in 2016.[44] With the overall confusion between national and state polls, polls suffered a black eye in 2016.

Key Questions
Do all Americans have an equal chance of being included in polls?

Polling was in transition even before 2016. Representative sampling in telephone surveys is increasingly affected by the growing number of cell phones, especially for young people who usually do not have landlines. Telephone polls are increasingly moving toward cell phones and away from landlines. Even for those who continue to have landlines, the widespread use of caller ID and answering machines allows more and more Americans to screen their calls and refuse to participate in surveys. In fact, save for the brief increase in willingness to answer polls tied to the stay at home orders during COVID-19 crisis, there is a general "polling fatigue" among the public. People are asked to participate not only in political polls but also in surveys for insurance companies, health care providers, and an endless array of commercial products. Automobile service centers call customers to see if they are satisfied with their most recent visit; banks make similar calls. The result is that fewer people are willing to participate in telephone surveys. The declining response rate is lessening the ability of pollsters to capture public opinion accurately.[45] In 1997, the rate of response to telephone polls was 37 percent; however, in 2019 response rates dropped to just 6 percent, harming polling results.[46]

Traditional pollsters must find better ways to ensure accurate results. Internet-based polls represent the future. Through the internet, polls can be done quickly and cheaply, but respondents may not be representative of the population. Statisticians have developed reliable ways to correct for bias, making the web a powerful tool to measure the public's thinking. As more people gain access to the web, the amount of bias will decline and this method will gain even wider favor. But the lessons from 2016 need to be kept in mind.

What Drives Public Opinion?

LO 6-3 Identify who drives public opinion—citizens or elites

Where does public opinion come from? If it is the aggregate of citizen attitudes and beliefs, it starts with individuals. In this section, we examine the major forces that shape political thinking on a personal level, including the social and political environment in which one grows up and the generation and family into which one is born. Self-interest also affects political attitudes, as do the ideas of opinion leaders such as journalists, political observers, policy makers, and experts.

Social and Political Environment

Political attitudes are shaped by environment—the kind of place in which one grows up and lives. Someone who grew up in a small town in Alabama centered around the local Baptist church would be influenced by that setting and would be different from someone who grew up in, say, Seattle, Washington, in a family that was not religious. Attendance at a suburban private high school would yield differing influences than attendance at an urban public school. Each of us is a product of our family, friends, and community. We call the process by which our attitudes are shaped **socialization**.

The way we live our lives, the kinds of foods we eat, the types of vacations we enjoy, and the houses of worship we attend—they all shape how we are socialized. Our political attitudes are no different. The clearest embodiment of political socialization is partisanship, and evidence shows that parents pass their partisan views along to their children. If parents are Democrats, there is a two-thirds chance that their children will identify themselves as Democrats. They might identify as **Independents**, but there is just a 10 percent chance they will be Republicans. The impact of socialization depends, of course, on whether both parents identify with the same party. If the parents are split on partisanship, the chance of the children being Independents rises considerably.[47]

High divorce rates have changed family structure in recent years, but there is no evidence that they have interfered with the passing along of political values, even when children are exposed to many more potential influences. Recent research concludes that "despite [the] transformation in the political environment and the character of family life over the last thirty years, our findings about youth coming of age in the 1990s strongly parallel those based on youth socialization in the 1960s."[48]

It may be that political values are passed on in families by genes as well as by socialization. Recent research offers some tantalizing hints that genetics may shape political views.[49] John Hibbing, a political scientist at the University of Nebraska–Lincoln, has been studying how political views can be influenced by genetics for years. He has found that, on average, 30 to 40 percent of our political attitudes come from genetics.[50] Other political scientists have been slow to embrace the possibility, but it should not be dismissed. That some people are more outgoing and more willing to build social networks appears to have a basis in one's genes.[51] If so, such a tendency could explain a willingness to become involved in politics, and it may even shape political views. Data show that identical twins, who share their entire genetic code, expressed more similar political attitudes than did fraternal twins, who are no more similar than any set of siblings. Such data are far from conclusive but still worth thinking about.[52] The bottom line is that this new area of research offers fascinating possibilities for understanding the sources of public opinion.[53]

Whether through family socialization or genes, parents have the biggest impact during a child's early life, but, starting in the teenage years, friends also influence attitudes and behavior, as do schools and communities. Communities that are homogeneous, in which most people share many of the same views and opinions, are likely to reinforce the attitudes of parents. Colleges, too, influence attitudes, and college attendance often offers students a chance to break out of the homogeneous settings of their early years. Students meet people from different states or communities, as well as people with different backgrounds and attitudes. College classes and experiences can also shape political leanings (see Chapter 4, Political Analytics on page 138).

socialization: *Impact and influence of one's social environment on the views and attitudes one carries in life, a primary source of political attitudes.*

Independents: *Individuals who do not affiliate with either of the major political parties.*

Key Questions

How do individuals form their political opinions?

Ryan Anson/AFP/Getty Images

Image 6.6 Parents generally pass political attitudes, including party identification, on to their children.

Key Questions

Have your political opinions ever changed? If so, what led to the change?

Socialization does not end at college graduation, however. It continues as young people pursue careers and choose where and how they will live. Consider people who live in San Francisco versus those who live in Dallas. Those different environments will surely have different effects on residents. Of course, those who choose to live in San Francisco may have different attitudes from those who move to Texas. But for the most part, it is between the ages of 18 and 24 when people's worldviews begin to crystallize and shape how they view work, family, and politics.

Generational Effects

Major events can change an entire generation's thinking about politics. The Great Depression, for example, which started in 1929 with the crash of the stock market, shaped the attitudes of millions of Americans. It was an economic calamity that even the severe economic downturn of 2008–2009 did not match. Millions lost their savings and their homes. In 1932, one of every four Americans was out of work, and incomes had declined by 50 percent. One consequence was that the public blamed the party in power, the Republicans, and switched party allegiance. The Democrats, as a result, became the majority party for the first time in generations.

The public's thinking on same-sex marriage has changed greatly over the past decade, as Figure 6.2 suggests. The public support for same-sex marriage has surged across the board, but opinions vary greatly by age. Millennials have long been supportive of same-sex marriage. Even in 2003, about 50 percent of the youth favored same-sex marriage. That proportion is now about 75 percent. Among the oldest Americans, support for same-sex marriage has been much more limited. In 2003, fewer than one in five of the "silent generation" favored it. But within a decade, this support more than doubled. The speed with which this issue has changed is impressive, especially with the Supreme Court making same-sex marriage legal nationwide. However, in the last two years, since 2017, the percentage of both Generation X and Baby Boomers who favor same-sex marriage has decreased slightly, which could potentially be tied to the current administration and its views.

Generational effects are also tied to the era in which one is young and first active as a citizen. Those who were young during the presidency of Republican Ronald Reagan are likely to think of politics differently from those who came of age during the presidency of Democrat Barack Obama. The former will be more likely to hold favorable views about Republicans; the latter will likely be favorable to Democrats. Exit polls from 2008 indicated that 66 percent of all 18- to 29-year-old voters supported Obama.[54] By historical standards, this level of support was quite high. Four years later, Obama won 60 percent of the youth vote, which is still a substantial chunk.[55] In 2016, Hillary Clinton secured 55 percent of the youth favor, compared to 37 percent for Donald Trump.[56] In the 2020 election, Biden won 62 percent of voters aged 18 to 29—a striking 27 point advantage over Trump with youth voters.

Although it remains to be seen whether being a member of what may be called the "Obama generation" will have an enduring effect on partisan identification and politics, America's **Millennial** generation does seem distinctive. There is evidence that suggests this group is less patient

Millennials: *Generation born between 1981 and 1996.*

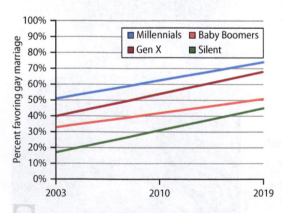

Figure 6.2 Shift in Public Opinion on Same-Sex Marriage, 2003–2019

Respondents were asked, "Do you strongly favor, favor, oppose, or strongly oppose allowing gays and lesbians to marry legally?"

Source: Pew Research Center, "Attitudes on Same-Sex Marriage," accessed February 20, 2019, https://www.pewforum.org/fact-sheet/changing-attitudes-on-gay-marriage/.

than previous generations and has "a thirst for instant gratification."[57] Perhaps having a world of information at one's fingertips has altered the expectations held by this new generation of Americans. The impact of information would have even more applicability for the new **Generation Z**.

Self-Interest and Rationality

Forming political opinion is much more than just a psychological process tied to socialization, however. People also respond to the context in which they find themselves. That is, to a certain extent people are "rational" in that they act in a way that is consistent with their **self-interest**. For example, as income rises, the chance of someone being a Republican increases. Why? The Republicans have pursued tax policies that protect individual wealth, while the Democrats pursue tax policies that tax the wealthy at higher rates to pay for social programs that benefit the less wealthy. In fact, one could argue that although the transmission of partisanship reflects socialization, the reason it sticks is that it is in one's self-interest.

Examples of **rationality** and self-interest abound. Couples with school-age children get interested in education policy. Homeowners become more focused on issues tied to property taxes than do individuals who rent. As citizens approach retirement age, they become protective of Social Security and Medicare benefits. Recently, young people, too, have been concerned about these benefits, but in ways that reflect their self-interest. They wonder if the entitlement programs will be bankrupt before they are of age to receive the benefits. Gay Americans are more interested in debates over whether same-sex couples can get married than straight Americans are. Similarly, Latinos show greater concern for reforms in immigration laws than do Americans who are not recent immigrants.[58]

Self-interest clearly shapes political attitudes, but that does not mean that people are selfish. It means that they are trying to advance and protect their own interests, and that in itself is encouraging. Because a democracy rests on the sound judgments of the electorate, it is good to know that there is some evidence that citizens act rationally.

Elites

One of the big questions in the field of public opinion is what role elites—leaders of opinion—play in shaping citizens' thinking. A democracy is supposed to be a system in which the average person has a say in government, and the people's preferences drive public policy. Yet some people worry that experts, policy makers, political observers, journalists, and others in the news media have an undue influence in shaping public opinion. If elites shape public opinion, can the United States be a democratic nation? One way to approach the question of what political scientists call "elite theory" is to recognize, first, that it is not so simple a matter as elites offering an opinion and the public swallowing it. That assumption attributes far too much influence to elites and far too little credit to the people. Instead, it appears that elites can influence citizens if two conditions are met: first, citizens must be exposed to the message, and, second, they must be open to it.[59]

Let's assume that scientists find clear evidence that being gay is completely genetic. Such evidence does not exist, but if it did, that would mean that sexual orientation is fixed, just as eye color is fixed. If true, the public's attitudes toward homosexuality would surely change, as it is harder to justify discrimination against homosexuals if sexual orientation is an inborn characteristic. Yet some citizens, when learning this new information, would

Political Analytics

Generational Views of Political Issues

Most college students today are part of what is known as Generation Z (born after 1996). Comparisons of that generation to Millennials and Baby Boomers are widespread in the media. Figure 6.3 shows how multiple generations of Americans view the role of government. One notable observation of the data is how similar Generation Z respondents and Millennials (born between 1981 and 1996) are in support of government doing more to solve problems. The similarities continue when survey respondents were asked about climate change, American exceptionalism, and NFL protests.

In all three cases, Generation Z and Millennials share very similar views compared to other, older generations of respondents. These two generations believe climate change is due mostly to human activity, are less likely to believe the United States is superior to other countries, and support NFL players taking a knee as a form of protest.

The patterns of respondents become more complicated when we consider the partisan leanings of the generations. The second figure shows respondents' views on whether blacks are treated less fairly than whites. Here, most Democrats overwhelmingly agree.

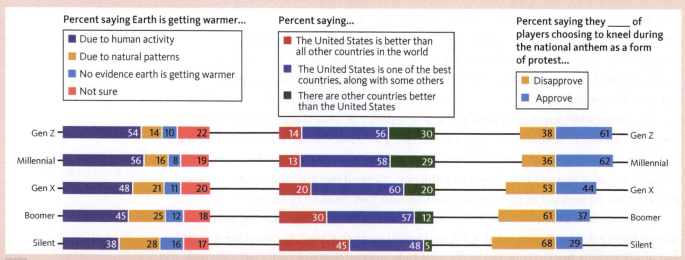

Figure 6.3A Generational Views of Political Issues

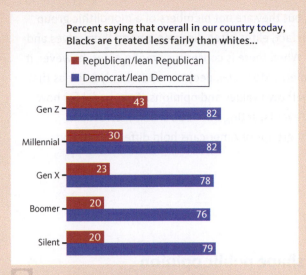

Percent saying that overall in our country today, Blacks are treated less fairly than whites...

- Republican/lean Republican
- Democrat/lean Democrat

Generation	Republican/lean Republican	Democrat/lean Democrat
Gen Z	43	82
Millennial	30	82
Gen X	23	78
Boomer	20	76
Silent	20	79

Figure 6.3B **Treatment of Blacks by Generation and Party**

Source: Kim Parker, Nikki Graf, and Ruth Igielnik, "Generation Z Looks a Lot Like Millennials on Key Social and Political Issues," Pew Research Center, January 17, 2019, https://www.pewsocialtrends.org/2019/01/17/generation-z-looks-a-lot-like-millennials-on-key-social-and-political-issues/.

Among Republicans, though, Generation Z stands out as more in support of that belief than older Republicans.

Examine the graphs and notice the comparisons among other generations on these issues.

Thinking Critically

1. What do you think the first set of graphs would reveal if we accounted for partisan leanings?
2. Do you think other considerations, such as gender or race and ethnicity, would show similar or different patterns than the ones in these graphs?

be resistant to the idea due to their moral beliefs. Social conservatives, for example, would on average be far less likely to accept this information than social liberals would. The prior beliefs of social conservatives would serve as a check on accepting it. By comparison, social liberals would have preexisting views that would fit better with the new information. They would be open to it.

This theory of who changes opinions and who does not has a number of implications. First, massive change in public opinion is not likely because the public is not made up of puppets. There is stability to opinion, although a major event such as 9/11 can and will shift the public's thinking on a number of important topics. Second, elites' ability to change public opinion is a product of the intensity and consistency of the message. Disagreement among elites on a new issue will decrease the potential for change. The public, for example, remained divided on global warming in the 1990s. Liberals were more willing to believe that climate change was caused by human activity. Conservatives had more doubts. As the scientific evidence mounted and more elites embraced the notion, the public collectively began to shift its thinking. In 1997, 60 percent of Americans felt that more research about global warming was needed to be sure of its effects, and only 28 percent felt that it was a serious problem. Ten years later, only 25 percent felt that more research was needed, and 64 percent felt that action needed to be taken to address climate change.[60] With the spate of bad weather in 2014 and 2015, the public views climate change as an increasingly serious problem. In June 2015, 51 percent of Americans were extremely or very concerned about climate change. Two years later, after additional natural disasters, the number jumped to 62 percent.[61] As of early 2020, 58 percent of Americans were either "alarmed" or "concerned" about climate change. The percentage of "alarmed" individuals, those with the highest belief in and most concern about climate change warming, tripled from 2014 to 2019 in the wake of multiple "once-in-a-century" natural disasters and record high and low temperatures across the world.[62]

Elites do influence public opinion, but they are not members of a monolithic group seeking to advance its own interests; in fact, elites often disagree among themselves and that disagreement can change as well. When there is consensus among elites, however, it probably means that the position has merit. Moreover, people respond only to ideas that they find appealing and that fit with their own values and opinions. As a model for how people change opinions in response to events, acting out of both self-interest and rationality, we can look at how different groups of Americans hold different opinions.

The Shape of Public Opinion

LO 6-4 Discover how ideology and partisanship shape public opinion

To understand public opinion, it is essential to appreciate the ways it is shaped by partisanship and ideology. These two variables can, to a large extent, explain the opinions of citizens. Although not everyone is partisan or ideological, these forces provide useful frameworks for understanding the public's thinking on issues. With a firm understanding of partisanship and ideology in place, we can address two major questions about public opinion: How informed is the public? And is the public polarized?

Key Questions
Does party loyalty shape public opinion?

Partisanship

party identification:
Psychological attachment to a political party; partisanship.

Party identification, or partisanship, is central to understanding how people think politically. Party identification represents an individual's allegiance to a political party. This psychological attachment usually forms when an individual is young. The attachment, through what is called the perceptual lens, shapes the way partisans view the political world and process information. The perceptual lenses of partisans act like prisms that bend light. Democrats have prisms that bend light in one direction; Republicans' prisms bend it in another direction. The result, for example, is that Republicans are far less sympathetic to Obamacare than are Democrats.[63]

By knowing party identification, political scientists can predict—with considerable accuracy—attitudes on a range of issues. Republicans, for example, are less likely than Democrats to support government spending to help the poor and elderly. Republicans are not opposed to helping such people, but they want to do so through private charities and individual initiative. More generally, Republicans are less supportive of an activist federal government, while Democrats are more open to giving government an active role in the lives of citizens.

An easy indicator of the power of partisanship is the public's approval of President Trump. In April 2020, 43 percent of Americans approved of the job he was doing as president. He had a brief surge to the high 40s in approval right after the COVID-19 crisis hit, but he was down to his typical low 40s within a few weeks. These numbers hide a powerful finding about partisanship. Among Republicans, 93 percent approved of Trump's performance. By contrast, only 7 percent of Democrats supported the president.[64] This gap of 86 percentage points speaks to the polarization in the country. The general pattern is not new—both President Obama and President Bush had similar partisan gaps in support.

Because party identification is central to understanding public opinion, pollsters have been asking about partisanship since the 1940s. The American National Election Studies, a premier academic survey organization, has been asking the same question since 1952: "Generally speaking, do you usually think of yourself as a Republican, a Democrat, an Independent, or what?"[65] This question asks respondents how they think about themselves in order to capture political identification and the general tendency, or the perceptual lens, of their thinking. The theoretical underpinnings are psychological. Partisanship can also be likened to loyalty, like the loyalty to sports teams or to friends that lasts through ups and downs. Partisanship can change over a person's life, but it tends to be stable, especially when compared to other political attitudes.

In the past few years, there has been much discussion in the press about Independents, with claims that they are the "largest group in the electorate."[66] With the rise of the Tea Party movement, their numbers are increasing. The idea that Americans are mostly Independents has largely been viewed as a myth, however. Most citizens who claim to be Independents actually behave like partisans; that is, most of them lean toward one party or the other.[67] In 2019, only 7 percent of the 38 percent of American adults who identified as politically independent did not express any partisan leaning.[68]

Figure 6.4 suggests that Millennials are tilting toward the Democrats. At the start of the century, there was a relatively even split between the two parties. Now the Democrats enjoy about a 20 percentage point lead, and very few people identify as "pure" Independents—just 7 percent in 2016.

Ideology

Political ideology has a complex relationship with partisanship. **Liberals** tend to be Democrats, and **conservatives** tend to be Republicans, but ideology speaks to both political and social values. Conservatives view a good society as one that allows individuals to

political ideology: *Set of coherent political beliefs that offers a philosophy for thinking about the scope of government.*

liberals: *Individuals who have faith in government to improve people's lives, believing that private efforts are insufficient. In the social sphere, liberals usually support diverse lifestyles and tend to oppose any government action that seeks to shape personal choices.*

conservatives: *Individuals who distrust government, believing that free markets offer better ways than government involvement to improve people's livelihood. In the social sphere, conservatives have more faith in government's ability to enforce traditional values.*

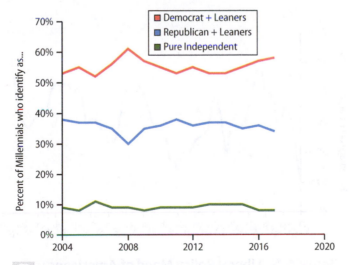

Figure 6.4 Trends in Partisanship Among Millennials

Among Millennials, Democrats have held a steady lead over Republicans during the past decade.

Source: Pew Research Center, "Party Affiliation Among Voters: 1992–2017," accessed March 2, 2020, https://www.people-press.org/2016/09/13/2-party-affiliation-among-voters-1992-2017/.

pursue their economic interests in an unfettered fashion. Liberals worry that, without some governmental regulation to curb abuse and moderate economic cycles, the rich will get very rich and the poor will get very poor. This concern leads liberals to believe that government can improve people's lives and prevent inequalities that harm society and the economy as a whole. Conservatives are much more leery of government and view it as a problem in and of itself. They contend that less government interference will give the poor the opportunity to improve their lives by themselves. On social issues, the tables are turned. That is, liberals tend to believe that people should be able to make personal choices free from government interference. Conservatives, by contrast, value more traditional lifestyles and want government, at times, to enforce such choices.

Not all citizens think of themselves as liberals or conservatives. In 2019, about 35 percent of Americans viewed themselves as ideological **moderates**, 24 percent as liberals and 37 percent as conservatives.[69]

There is an important debate among political scientists about whether citizens think ideologically at all. That is, do people have coherent views about politics? One famous effort to measure the ideological foundations, or **levels of conceptualization**, of the public's thinking found little evidence of such organized opinions. Data from the 1950s indicated that only about 12 percent of the public viewed the political parties in ideological terms, whereas more than 40 percent judged the parties by the groups (such as social classes or racial and ethnic groups) they were thought to represent rather than the policies they pursued.[70] This general pattern has remained much the same over the ensuing sixty years.

It is hard to argue that a majority of the public has a coherent, ideologically driven view of politics. Nevertheless, it is still worth looking at the public's overall policy mood. Is the public, collectively, becoming more liberal or more conservative? Such changes should aid understanding of the general direction of the country. Figure 6.5 maps changes in the public's ideological mood between 1952 and 2018.

moderates: *Individuals who are in the middle of the ideological spectrum and do not hold consistently strong views about whether government should be involved in people's lives.*

levels of conceptualization: *Measure of how ideologically coherent individuals are in their political evaluations.*

Figure 6.5 **Liberal Policy Mood of Americans, 1952–2018**

The policy mood of Americans is rarely fixed. It moved toward liberalism following George W. Bush's election in 2000 and then toward conservatism following Barack Obama's election in 2008.

Source: K. Elizabeth Coggins, "Policy Mood," accessed February 22, 2020, http://kelizabethcoggins.com/mood-policy-agendas/.

This sixty-four-year time period reveals some interesting trends. The increasingly liberal nature of public opinion was apparent between 1952 and 1964—an era dominated by the Democrats. In the mid-1960s, with the unpopularity of the Vietnam War and growing concerns about civil rights, crime, and excessive government involvement in the economy, conservatism grew—and grew quickly. The pattern between 1980 and the early 1990s was a move back toward liberalism, culminating in the election of Bill Clinton in 1992. During the Clinton years, the public veered toward conservatism again. Following the election of George W. Bush in 2000, the public shifted more toward liberalism. And following Barack Obama's election in 2008, the pendulum swung back toward conservatism, which continues to the present. The rise of the Tea Party and Donald Trump certainly gives credibility to this recent shift. It is an interesting pattern, underscoring the different moods of the public. These different moods do not, however, last long, leading to frequent changes in the party that controls the White House.

Is the Public Informed?

A democracy depends on having an engaged and well-informed electorate. Otherwise, how can the public make good choices? If the power is to rest with the people, the people need to be knowledgeable about the issues of the day and the candidates who compete for public office.

The Framers were definitely concerned about the public's capacity to be informed and make good choices, especially because only 10 percent of Americans at the time were literate.[71] These concerns were one of the driving forces behind the gates and gateways in the Constitution, a document that sought to represent the public's views but also to establish institutions that would, according to James Madison, "refine and enlarge" them (see *Federalist* 10 in the Appendix). By that Madison meant that elected officials would react to public sentiment but not be a slave to it. Instead, they would debate it in a way that would improve it and allow for better government. Over time, the amount of input by citizens has increased; senators, for example, are now voted into office by direct election, not by state legislatures. Education levels have also greatly increased. The literacy rate has stood at about 99 percent since 2014,[72] suggesting that citizens are better able today than in the eighteenth century to meet the demands of being "informed."

But are they really "informed"? When survey research began in the 1940s, it became possible to gather systematic information on the public's knowledge about politics. The early evidence was not encouraging. In a detailed study of the 1940 presidential campaign, scholars from Columbia University assumed that voters would act like consumers and would look for the best deal and that the campaign would be an important source of information as they made their choices. But the data told a different tale. Instead, most voters made up their minds before the campaign, and their choices were driven by where they lived and whom they knew.[73] In a subsequent study, the Columbia researchers went so far as to argue that low turnout in elections might actually be a good thing because the uninformed would not be involved in choosing the nation's leaders.[74] This argument has strong elitist overtones and certainly strays far from the assumptions about government responsiveness and citizen equality on which American democracy rests. Together with previous findings about levels of conceptualization,[75] the argument suggested that the public may not be capable of meeting its democratic responsibilities. What ensued was a debate over the accuracy and interpretation of these core findings.

Key Questions
How does party identification relate to ideology?

Key Questions
How coherent is public opinion?

Key Questions
Is the public becoming more liberal or more conservative? How can you tell?

Key Questions
Is public opinion worth listening to? Should elected officials care about public opinion?

Political scientists went, in effect, in search of the "informed voter." It is clear that citizens do not know many details about politics. Only 10 percent of the public knows the name of the Speaker of the House. Only about a third can name one U.S. Supreme Court justice. Only about half of Americans know which party controls Congress, and fewer than half know the name of their own congressional representative.[76]

Should these data be taken as evidence that the public is not able to meet its democratic responsibilities? Let us consider some findings that give reason for optimism.

First, the public, *collectively*, seems to make reasonable choices. For example, when the economy is doing poorly, the party in power suffers. Voters hold presidents and legislators accountable; failures are punished, and successes are rewarded. Further, Americans do not favor costly wars, and they tend to reward candidates who pursue peace.[77]

Second, although individuals do not know all the details about candidates' views on all the issues, they do tend to know candidates' views on the issues that are salient to them. Hunters are much more likely to know candidates' views on gun control; college students are much more likely to know candidates' views on student loans. One study estimates that when an issue is salient to an individual, that individual knows candidates' views on that issue correctly more than 90 percent of the time.[78]

Third, the public can learn quickly about important issues, especially given the attention they receive from the news media. The public quickly learned about AIDS when it started to become a public health crisis in the 1980s. Following 9/11, the public understood the need to consider some curtailment of civil liberties to ensure security (see Public Policy and Public Opinion: Antiterrorism).

Fourth, public opinion is more stable than is suggested by the shifting answers individuals give to the same question asked just a few months apart. Such instability in an individual's answers does not mean that the public is fickle or poorly informed; instead, it appears that polls themselves may be at fault.[79] That is, survey questions and the normal error associated with asking questions make people's attitudes appear more unstable than they really are. Further, most issues are complex and leave many people genuinely conflicted. Being conflicted is not a sign of lack of information, but perhaps a realization that some problems are thorny and not easily answered. The following is one example:

> Vincent Sartori cannot decide whether or not the government should guarantee incomes because he cannot decide how much weight to give the value of productivity. He believes that the rich are mostly undeserving and . . . yet he is angry at "welfare cheats" who refuse to work. . . . Caught between his desire for equality and his knowledge of existing injustice, on the one hand, and his fear that a guaranteed income will benefit even shirkers, on the other, he remains ambivalent about policies toward the poor.[80]

So Sartori could easily give different answers to the same survey question, depending on what he is thinking about at the time. But different answers say more about the issue's complexity than about his lack of information.

Last, decisions we make on personal matters are rarely based on complete information, so why should political decision making be expected to conform to such high standards? Individuals often rely on cues and instincts to make decisions, rather than on analyses of detailed information. Scholars have termed such thinking "low information rationality."[81] There are two famous examples from presidential campaigns. In 1976, President Gerald R. Ford (1974–77), campaigning in Texas, bit into a tamale with the husk still on, a gaffe suggesting that he knew little about the foods and habits of the Latino community he was hoping to court. In 2016, Hillary Clinton claimed that many of Donald Trump's supporters were a "basket of deplorables." Her comment suggested she was out of touch with ordinary Americans and was quick to label people unfairly. Simple things like not knowing how to eat a tamale or off-handed comments can turn voters against political candidates. The public concludes that these contenders are not like them and, thus, are not likely to understand their problems. Small bits of information can be informative.

It is easy to make any member of the public—even a president—look uninformed, and of course it would be better if the public knew more about politics. But individuals do appear to learn about the issues that matter to them. Gaining information is a gateway to influence because, individually, people learn what they need to know to advance their interests, and collectively voters do hold government officials accountable.

Image 6.7 Senator and 2020 presidential candidate Elizabeth Warren poses for a selfie. She did well over 100,000 during the campaign.

Is the Public Polarized?

The engaged and informed citizens of a democracy cannot be expected to agree on everything. They will naturally have different views on issues. When the differences become stark, however, the danger is that **polarization** will fuel controversy and personal attacks to the point that compromise and consensus become impossible. Congress has clearly become more polarized over the past thirty years. Figure 6.6 tries to capture the idea of polarization on a simple left–right continuum. In the 1970s, the parties adopted positions that were closer to the middle; forty years later, their positions are more at the extremes. And these differences continue to grow. In fact, Democrats and Republicans disagree on more issues now than at any time since the end of the Civil War.[82]

polarization: *Condition in which differences between parties and/or the public are so stark that disagreement breaks out, fueling attacks and controversy.*

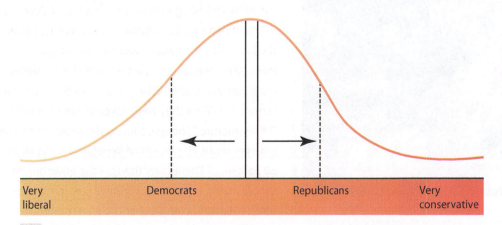

| Very liberal | Democrats | Republicans | Very conservative |

Figure 6.6 How Polarization Works

When the parties are polarized, they move toward the tail of these distributions. When parties are depolarized, they adopt positions near each other. Currently the parties are polarized, but that was not the case in the 1970s.

Source: John G. Geer, © Cengage Learning.

Figure 6.7 **Party Polarization, 1879–2019**

Since 1975, polarization in the U.S. Congress has been on the rise.

Source: Voteview: Congressional Roll-Call Votes Database, accessed March 2, 2020, https://voteview.com/data.

In the 1970s, there were numerous liberal Republicans and conservative Democrats. By 2008, these two groups were nearly extinct. In 2009, for example, Pennsylvania Senator Arlen Specter, one of the few moderate Republicans in Congress at the time, bolted from the Republican Party and became a Democrat. He switched parties because of what he saw as a swing to the right by the Republicans. The differences between the parties have continued to grow (see Figure 6.7),[83] evidenced by victories by candidates from the Tea Party movement in the 2010 and 2014 congressional elections.[84] There is little doubt that the parties have polarized since the 1970s, along the lines described in Figure 6.7.

Key Questions

Do political parties influence public opinion, or is it the other way around?

Image 6.8 At town hall meetings held on police shootings in Cincinnati, community leaders protested the death of Nathaniel Jones. Such meetings have only become more contentious after the recent spate of shootings, such as in Parkland, El Paso, and Las Vegas.

What is less clear is whether the public is also polarized. Some scholars have argued that the public has polarized along with parties, but the evidence is mixed. It depends very much on the issue. Consider the long-standing debate over the role of government. Members of both parties very much believed the government should keep the "country safe from terrorism." When they were asked about maintaining "infrastructure," though, some differences started to emerge: about 70 percent of Republicans and about 80 percent of Democrats thought the government should maintain roads and bridges (i.e., infrastructure). Polarization arose over the government's role in "ensuring access to health care:" 83 percent of Democrats but just 34 percent of Republicans thought it should play a role.[85] Given how different issues have different patterns, it is no surprise that scholars disagree about the extent of differences among the electorate, with some suggesting that the political center has collapsed.[86]

Public Policy and Public Opinion

Antiterrorism

To see how public opinion affects the policies pursued by government, we examine foreign policy—in particular, antiterrorism. With continuing terrorist attacks around the world, it is important to consider the public's support for policies that advance our security and how public opinion impacts policy making in this area. This issue came even more into focus following the domestic terrorist attack in San Bernardino, California, in December 2015.

The September 11, 2001, terrorist attacks prompted a huge increase in government's efforts to secure U.S. citizens at home and abroad. In general, public opinion was highly supportive of the steps that President George W. Bush took to fight terrorism. These steps were taken with advice from Defense Department agencies, the Federal Bureau of Investigation, and the Department of Justice. The Bush administration authorized the detention of suspects, whether U.S. citizens or not, without charges or trials, and wiretapping (eavesdropping) without a warrant. With the onset of the 2003 war in Iraq, the measures employed in the name of antiterror security increased. Then, in 2004, CBS News and the *New Yorker* magazine broke the story about the Abu Ghraib facility in Iraq, where Iraqi prisoners were subject to activities that violated international norms of treatment and might be considered torture.[87] Subsequently, it was revealed that the U.S. interrogators used waterboarding, a near-drowning technique, as a means of getting information from prisoners about potential terrorist plots. The international community considers waterboarding to be torture, and many Americans were shocked by the news and demanded an end to the practice. The Bush administration also argued that suspected terrorists detained at the Guantánamo Bay facility located in Cuba, outside the United States, were not entitled to protections guaranteed to all prisoners of war by the Geneva Convention. In the 2006 *Hamdan v. Rumsfeld* case, the Supreme Court

ruled that the detainees were protected by Article 3 of the Geneva Convention. Yet allegations of torture continued.

The issue of the treatment of detainees has become a major issue in recent presidential campaigns, such as when the Republican nominee, Donald Trump, said he would support reforming laws to allow more extreme use of torture against ISIS. After he took office, President Obama declared that the United States would no longer engage in any practice that violated international norms. The president also announced that the Guantánamo Bay facility would be closed. Despite an early consensus in the White House to close this controversial facility, deciding what to do with existing detainees and how best to handle others who may be engaged in terrorism has proven difficult.[88]

One of the reasons that these policies are hard to pursue is that Americans remain conflicted about the type of force necessary to preserve national security. In 2017, a Pew Research Poll reported that Americans were evenly divided on the use of harsh interrogation techniques on suspected terrorists.[89] Americans also held varying opinions regarding the Trump administration's killing of Iranian military leader, General Soleimani, in January 2020 and whether that would make America safer from or more vulnerable to terrorist attacks from Iran.[90] The core dilemma is that antiterrorism policies must remain secret to be effective, and the only opportunity the public has to register an opinion about government action is after that action has been taken. If harsh interrogation techniques save American lives by uncovering and then preventing a terrorist attack, the public will support the use of these techniques. But how can we be sure that such efforts are really effective? Does the government go too far sometimes? These are tough questions. How much liberty should we sacrifice to be safe?

Public uncertainty can also be seen in regards to the public's reaction to Edward Snowden's release of intelligence information. In January 2014, 46 percent of Americans thought what he had done was "bad for the country" and 40 percent thought it was good.[91] These are not easy issues, and the public's thinking reflects this kind of division. The public wants society to be open but realizes that security demands some secrecy. It is easy to see, therefore, why people can have different opinions about how to approach such a tough topic. The tragic events in San Bernardino are only the latest reminder about the importance of this long-standing debate and how the public changes in reaction to such events. Americans, for example, were more likely to feel we need to go farther to protect the country even at the expense of undermining people's liberties.[92]

The debate over secrecy is now taking place in a very different context than it was just a decade ago. The public is generally less inclined these days to get involved in international affairs. In 2013, more than 50 percent of the public wanted the United States to mind its own business. That proportion dropped to 43 percent in 2016. Following the 9/11 terrorist attacks in 2001, for example, the proportion of citizens who held such views stood at just 30 percent.[93] This broader context has important implications for U.S. foreign policy and how we approach antiterrorism measures.

Construct Your Own Policy

1. Using modern technology, devise a way of accurately measuring public opinion so that the president and Congress consider it before deciding how best to fight terrorism.
2. Design a comprehensive antiterrorist policy that can effectively protect the United States from attack and safeguard individual liberty at the same time.

Even some who think that the public is not as polarized as the parties are worried that polarization will yield more personal attacks and greater incivility. Others offer a more optimistic view, arguing that increasing polarization will activate people's interest in elections, which in turn will spur more interest in politics. In fact, the share of the public that cares about which party wins the presidential election has increased since 1988. Interest in elections, generally, also seems to be on the rise. In 1988, 44 percent of the public paid "a lot" of attention to the presidential campaign. In 2000, the proportion stood at 53 percent, a notable gain.[94] In 2016, the proportion jumped, with two-thirds of Americans paying "a lot" of attention to the Clinton–Trump battle.[95] However, despite a rise in those interested in presidential elections, voter turnout is surprisingly low, especially compared to other developed countries. In 2016, around 56 percent of the voting-age population cast a ballot, even though close to 70 percent said they were interested in who won.[96] In record-breaking turnout, over 150 million Americans voted in the 2020 presidential election. This constitutes the highest voter turnout since 1900 with about two-thirds of eligible voters casting a ballot. However, a record-breaking 77 percent of voters said this election is more important to them than any previous election—there are still discrepancies in interest and voter turnout.

Key Questions

How would you explain the fact that political trust has declined in recent decades, yet interest in elections has increased?

Having a clear choice engages people and gives them a stake in an election outcome. If the system became depolarized, as in the 1950s, the public would no longer face a stark choice. It would matter far less whether Democrats or Republicans won because they would do similar things once in office. For these reasons, many scholars in the 1950s called for parties that would offer the public a real choice (see Chapter 9, Political Parties). Citizens, under such conditions, can more effectively hold officials accountable for misdeeds and reward successes.

Group Differences

LO 6-5 Describe how demographic characteristics influence public opinion

Public opinion is shaped by more than partisanship and ideology. Demographics also matter—that is, the tendency for certain groups within the American population to hold similar views. In this section, we look at the ways socioeconomic status, religion, gender, race and ethnicity, and education tend to organize public opinion.

Socioeconomic Status

Socioeconomic status is a combined measure of occupation, education, income, wealth, and relative social standing or lifestyle. It influences where one lives, what kind of work one does, whom one knows, the kinds of schools one attends, and the kind of opportunities one can take advantage of. These matters inevitably mold political attitudes. Working-class people are more likely than wealthier people to favor more government programs to help the poor and provide child care, more funding for public education, and more protection for Social Security. Around 70 percent of Americans earning between $15,000 and $35,000 support increased spending by government on such social services. Among those earning between $75,000 and $105,000, the proportion drops to about 55 percent.[97]

Part of the reason for the strong differences in opinion among different income groups is that political parties have a class bias. Republicans draw far more support from those who come from higher socioeconomic strata than do Democrats. Starting in the 1980s, however, Republicans also began to draw support from working-class people who supported a conservative social agenda and a decreased role for government welfare-based programs. These so-called Reagan Democrats were central to Republican success in the ensuing decades. The candidacy and election of Donald Trump have in many ways reinvigorated the Reagan Democrats, as he draws support from lower-middle-class segments of the electorate who have been unhappy with stagnant wages and the way Washington works.

Age

Age also influences opinions on issues because the stage of one's life affects how one thinks about issues. For instance, 70 percent of people under 30 years of age favor increased spending on student loans. That drops to 42 percent among those over 55. This gap makes sense because younger people are more likely to need student loans. Younger people are much more likely to favor making marijuana legal than are older people. According to a CBS News poll, as of 2019, around 72 percent of Americans 18 to 34 years old, favor making marijuana legal. For those 65 and older, the percentage drops to 49 percent.[98] In general, older citizens are more socially conservative than are younger citizens,[99] and there is evidence that people tend to become more conservative as they age.

Religion

Religious affiliation is another indicator of opinion. Overall, for example, Protestants are more conservative than Catholics or Jews. Only 12 percent of Jews describe themselves as conservative, compared to 36 percent of Protestants. It is worth noting, however, that views differ between the sects of Judaism, with more religious Jews tending to be more conservative.[100] On some issues, Muslims have been found to be more liberal than the general population and significantly more liberal than Protestants and Catholics. For

Key Questions
Does being a member of
a certain demographic group
shape a person's opinion?

example, 70 percent of Muslims favor an activist government, whereas just 43 percent of the public as a whole subscribes to that view. On social issues, however, Muslims show a much more conservative tendency. When asked "Which comes closer to your view? Homosexuality is a way of life that should be accepted by society, or homosexuality is a way of life that should be discouraged by society," 61 percent of Muslims said that homosexual lifestyles should be discouraged, but only 38 percent of all Americans gave that response.[101]

Recent studies of religion and public opinion have focused on differences within denominations, particularly with the rise of evangelical Christianity among Protestants. Starting in the 1970s, and especially after the *Roe v. Wade* Supreme Court decision made abortion legal under some conditions in 1973, evangelicals became more active in politics. They strongly oppose abortion and gay rights, and they support school prayer. On the issue of same-sex marriage, evangelical Protestants in the early part of this century were six times more likely to oppose same-sex marriage than were non-evangelical—or "mainline"— Protestants.[102] Table 6.1 explores differences among Protestants, Catholics, and those not affiliated with a religious group on the issue of abortion. There are big differences, with evangelical Protestants very much more opposed to abortion than non-evangelicals.

Gender

Starting in 1980, a **gender gap** emerged in U.S. politics. Before 1980, the differences in political attitudes among men and women were not large and did not draw much attention. However, in elections since Ronald Reagan's 1980 victory over Jimmy Carter (1977–81), women have been generally more supportive of Democrats than of Republicans. In 1980, the gap was 8 percentage points: 54 percent of men backed Reagan, and only 46 percent of women backed him. The gap has varied from 4 percent in 1992 to 11 percent in 1996. In 2008, Barack Obama secured 56 percent of the female vote and just 49 percent of the male vote. There was a 13-point gap in 2016, with 54 percent of women supporting Clinton and just 41 percent of men supporting her.[103] This gender gap has been enduring: If only women were allowed to vote, the Democrats would have won every presidential election since 1980 save for Reagan's landslide against Walter Mondale in 1984.[104] The gender gap was central to the Democrats taking back the House of Representatives in the 2018 midterm elections. Nearly 60 percent of women cast ballots for their district's Democratic congressional candidate. This was more than 10 percentage points higher than men in 2018.[105] The gender gap continued in 2020, with more women voting for Joe Biden; however, not in as large of numbers as polling suggested. Overall, 56 percent of women voted for Biden. the reason the gap was not much larger is because over half of white women voted for Trump. Women broke for Biden because of the overwhelming support from women of color. That being said, there is no doubt that the gender gap continues to shape American policies.

In general, women are more liberal than men, and gender gaps are also evident on specific issues. Women tend to favor more spending on social programs than men. In December 2017, 50 percent of men favored Obamacare, while 61 percent of women did.[106] Men are much less supportive of gun control than women. In 2019, about 55 percent of men backed stricter gun control compared to nearly 64 percent of women.[107]

Race and Ethnicity

Another divide in public opinion involves race and ethnicity. The issue of slavery tore the nation apart, and more than one hundred years after the Civil War, Americans remained divided about

Table 6.1 Differences of Opinion on Abortion Among Religious Groups

Abortion Should Be . . .	Legal in (most) All Cases	Illegal in (most) All Cases
Mainline Protestant	60%	35%
Evangelical Protestant	33%	63%
Historically Black Protestant	52%	42%
Catholic	48%	47%
Jewish	83%	15%
Muslim	55%	37%
Unaffiliated	73%	23%
Total	53%	43%

Source: Pew Research Center, "Views about Abortion," accessed March 7, 2020, http://www.pewforum.org/religious-landscape-study/views-about-abortion/.

issues involving race. In 1964, African Americans overwhelmingly endorsed desegregation, whereas white Americans were split on the issue. In 1974, only 23 percent of white Americans felt "government should help blacks," whereas 69 percent of African Americans believed that government should take that role.[108] Similar gaps exist today in regard to support for affirmative action policies that grant preferences to people (not only African Americans but also women) who have suffered discrimination in the past in job hiring, school admissions, and contracting. In 2017, 66 percent of whites, 82 percent of blacks, and 83 percent of Latinos said "affirmative action programs designed to increase the number of black and minority students on college campuses were a good thing."[109]

The term *Latino* is used to describe a broad array of groups that do not necessarily share common experiences, so opinion among Latinos tends to be divided. There is a push from many to start disaggregating data, or collecting and analyzing data on race and ethnicity at a more detailed level. This method could help the country better understand different Latino experiences and views.[110] Some Latino families have lived in the Southwest for centuries, since before the area became part of the United States in 1848. Others have come to the United States within the past few years from homelands throughout Central and South America. Cuban immigrants, who left their homeland following the rise of Fidel Castro and the Communists in the late 1950s, tend to be much more conservative than Puerto Ricans and Mexican Americans. According to one study, about 47 percent of Cuban Americans are Republican identifiers, compared to only about 27 percent of Mexican Americans.[111] Latinos are divided in other ways as well. According to one group of prominent scholars:

> On many key domestic issues, significant majorities of each [Latino] group take the liberal position. On other issues, there is no consensus and, depending on the issue, Mexicans may be on the right, while Cubans and many Puerto Ricans are on the left of the nation's current political spectrum. Thus, labels such as liberal or conservative do not adequately describe the complexity of any one group's political views.[112]

Geopix/Alamy Stock Photo

Image 6.9 On November 7, 2020, Senator Kamala Harris made history when she became Vice President-Elect. She is the first woman to ever be elected Vice President. She is also the first Black woman, woman of Indian descent, and daughter of immigrants to be elected VPOTUS.

Key Questions

Is your political opinion shaped by your social class, age, religion, gender, race and ethnicity, and/or education level? If so, how?

Thus, both parties compete for the support of the Latino community. In 2004, Latino support for President George W. Bush helped him defeat John Kerry. In 2008, however, Barack Obama gained two-thirds of the Latino vote, a shift partly owing to actions by Republicans in Congress to block immigration reform. The importance of this group will only grow, as suggested by Figure 6.8. In the key battleground states of Pennsylvania and Florida, the share of the Latino vote jumped, as it did nationally and across all states. As Latinos make up more and more of the electorate, issues salient to them will also become increasingly important. For example, Latinos support bilingual education and policies that favor immigration more than do Anglos. Donald Trump's controversial rhetoric on Mexican immigration and his desire to build a wall further complicated Republican efforts to make inroads in the Latino community. Trump secured only 28 percent of the Latino vote and his actions since being in office may only lower that proportion in 2020.[113] Thirty-two million Latinos, or 13.3 percent of the overall voting population, are projected to be eligible to vote in 2020. Additionally, about half of all Latino voters cast a ballot or caucused on or before March 3, 2020—Super Tuesday. That Nevada voted so early in the presidential nomination process underscored the growing importance of Latinos, given their sizable population in the Silver State.[114] Both parties must win Latino votes to forge a path to the White House this coming general election.

Asian American public opinion has not drawn the same level of attention as that of other groups. Asian Americans are, however, a growing segment of the population and constitute a sizable part of the population of some states, especially California. In 2018, Asian immigrants accounted for 31 percent of the foreign-born electorate. This number is even higher going into the 2020 election.[115] Like Latinos, the Asian American population is diverse, including people from the many nations in Asia. In general, however, Asian Americans are a bit more liberal than white Americans. In 2012, for example, about 73 percent of Asian Americans supported President Obama, whereas only 39 percent of white Americans did so. This support of Democrats by Asian Americans is on the rise as well. Hillary Clinton continued this pattern, attracting about two-thirds of the support of Asian Americans.[116]

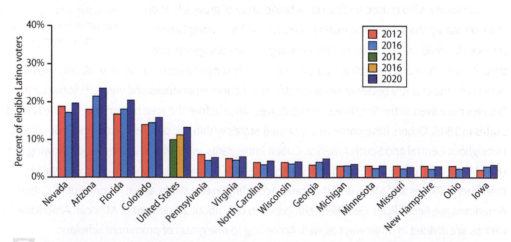

Figure 6.8 **Latino Electorate Projected to Grow in Key States**

Both parties need to find ways to reach out to Latino voters if they want to win elections in the coming years.

Source: Pew Research Center, "Mapping the 2020 Latino Electorate," accessed March 2, 2020, https://www.pewresearch.org/hispanic/interactives/mapping-the-latino-electorate/.

Election 2020

The "Latino" Identity

Democrats and Republicans are in a long-standing battle to attract Latino voters, especially as this group continues to become a bigger part of the electorate. The 2016 presidential election saw a huge amount of attention paid to these voters, especially given the harsh anti-immigrant rhetoric of Donald Trump. Political observers use the terms *Hispanic* and *Latino* (which we treat interchangeably) to refer to this increasingly powerful set of voters. But does this label provide an accurate indication of the thinking of this "group"? This question becomes even more important to ask when we realize that some members of this group think of themselves as Mexican American or Cuban American. What political effects arise from these different identities?

As we saw in Chapter 1, the use of Hispanic and Latino labels began more than forty years ago when Congress added "Americans of Spanish origin" to the types of social statistics that would be collected by the federal government. When asked about their identity, however, most Latinos prefer to use their family's country of origin rather than terms like Latino or Hispanic. Moreover, large majorities of Latinos (69 percent) see differences within those catchall labels. That is, Mexican Americans do not believe they share a common identity with, say, Cuban Americans.

These distinctions do yield some political differences. Surveys in 2020 revealed overwhelming identification with the Democratic Party among Latinos, close to 60 percent among registered Hispanic voters[117] (see Table 6.2). However, unpacking these data to see how Latinos of different national origin view the parties reveals a slightly different story. While most groups of Latinos identify with the Democratic Party, Cuban Americans more closely identify with the Republican Party.

Of the generational groupings we identified in this chapter, members of the Latino Baby Boomer and Silent Generations are most likely to identify with the Democratic Party (70 percent) while the Millennial generation shows the lowest, though still strong, level of attachment (61 percent). Ten percent of this youngest generation of Latino voters chooses neither party, perhaps providing a glimmer of hope to Republican Party efforts to woo them into their camp.[118] Dampening that glimmer, possibly, is the trend that as noncitizen Latinos move toward citizenship, roughly half identify or lean toward the Democrats—a trend that will likely continue in light of the 2016 presidential election. In 2018, 69 percent of all eligible Hispanics voted for Democrats, while only 29 percent voted for Republicans.[119] In 2020, a record 32 million Latinos are projected to be eligible to vote and, currently, 68 percent of those Latinos disapprove of the job Trump is doing as president.[120]

As we think about different groups in American politics, we need to be sensitive to key differences within the group as we offer general claims. The case of Latinos is an example: Key subgroup differences yield a more nuanced story, especially as we think about Cuban Americans. But 2016 may prove to be a watershed election for Latinos in light of the views on immigration of Donald Trump. There is recent evidence that this harsh rhetoric activates the Latino community.[121] This can be seen in the results of the 2018 midterm elections. One fourth of Latino voters cast a ballot for the first time in 2018, Latino voter registration reached an all-time high in Florida, and nine U.S. House districts where Latinos make up at least 10 percent of eligible voters changed parties.[122] These votes led to a record number of Latinos serving in the 116th Congress with thirty-eight Latinos in the House (thirty-three Democrats and three Republicans) and four Latinos in the Senate (two from each party).[123] This activation of Latino voters has the potential to significantly impact future elections similarly to 2018.

Table 6.2 Partisan Identification Among Hispanics

Partisan Identification Among Hispanics			
	Democrat	Republican	Independent
Percent Identifying	58	19	22

Source: Univision Noticias/Latino Community Foundation Poll, National Latino registered voter survey, N=1000, field dates, February 9–14, 2020.

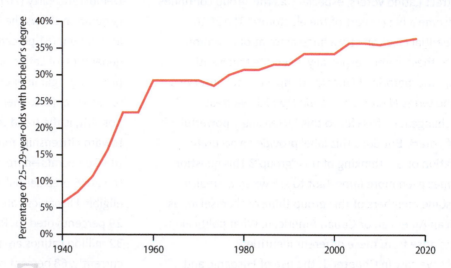

Figure 6.9 **Percentage of Population with Bachelor's Degree, 1940–2020**

Since the end of World War II, education levels have steadily increased. Level of education is a factor affecting public opinion on a range of specific issues.

Source: National Center for Education Statistics, "Percentage of Persons 25 to 29 Years Old with Selected Levels of Educational Attainment, by Race/Ethnicity and Sex: Selected Years, 1920 through 2018," accessed March 2, 2020, https://nces.ed.gov/programs/digest/d18/tables/dt18_104.20.asp.

Education

One important change in the American population is the increasing level of education. Figure 6.9 charts the share of Americans who had graduated college over the last seventy-five years. The pattern is striking. In 1940, about one in fifteen Americans had college degrees. By 2016, more than one in three Americans had graduated college. And more than seven of ten Americans had attended college—another vast increase from the 1940s. The upward trend has been continuous since the end of World War II in 1945 for two key reasons. The first is that more young people have access to a college education. The second is what is called "generational replacement"—that is, older, less-educated citizens have passed on, and the average level of education of the American public has thus increased.

It matters that people in the United States are more educated. In broad strokes, there is a long-standing belief that a democracy is best able to endure when its citizens are engaged and informed. With more education, the public should be more aware of politics and better able to find ways to ensure that government responds to them. In the language of this book, a better-educated public should be in better position to travel through the gateways of influence and find ways around the many gates in the American political system.

Education level is also connected to public opinion. Views on the controversial issue of immigration reform offer an instructive example. Among college graduates, three-quarters favored making it possible for those here illegally to become citizens (providing they pass background checks, pay relevant fines, and have jobs). Among those with a high school education or less, the proportion falls to just over half.[124] The 20-percentage-point gap is significant. Individuals with a higher level of education generally take a more liberal position on a variety of social and economic issues, ranging from government spending to defense policy to gay marriage.[125]

Public Opinion and Democracy

For a country to be considered democratic, the views of the public must affect the course of government. For this reason, the public must be sufficiently well informed to be able to make good decisions and to ensure that politicians act in a way consistent with public preferences. Average Americans do not know a lot of details about politics, but the nation's many successes indicate that the public is equal to the task of self-government. As V. O. Key observed fifty years ago, "Voters are not fools."[126] In 2008, when most people thought the country was on the wrong track, they voted for change and put Barack Obama in office. By supporting Obama, the public signaled a desire for a clear break from the policies of the Bush administration. In 2016, most Americans still thought the country was on the wrong track, and that judgment fueled Donald Trump's rise to the presidency as he called for a real shakeup in Washington.

Elections are one means by which the public expresses its will, but on a year-to-year, even day-to-day, basis, public officials can stay in touch with what the public thinks through public opinion polls. Scientific polling permits researchers to measure people's thinking with considerable accuracy and gives average Americans a chance to speak out on policy and contribute to policy making. Scientific polling, introduced eighty years ago, not only created greater equality but also provided the gateways through which the public could affect the course of government. Polls are not perfect, but they do open up the democratic process.

Although it is clear that public officials are generally responsive to public opinion,[127] there are legitimate questions about the responsiveness of American government. Some observers suggest that the connection between opinion and policy is weak. Others point out that the public has mixed feelings on many issues and does not have concrete opinions about some of the toughest questions and can thus offer little guidance. Still others argue that politicians use policy to manipulate public opinion. That interaction is troubling and not the way a democratic system in which the government is accountable to the people should work. These concerns are why it is so instructive to look at the general patterns and the nation's general successes.

It is also important to recognize that, in a democracy, politicians know the kinds of issues the public will respond to and rebel against, and so they adopt views that will not arouse the electorate's anger. They are aware, in other words, of what political scientists call latent public opinion,[128] and this awareness makes them responsive and accountable. The ability to anticipate public opinion is an invaluable skill, helping officials avoid quagmires and stress issues that hit a responsive chord with the public. Thus the power of public opinion in a democracy is both direct and indirect. It is also imperfect in that there are both gates and gateways that shape how citizens direct the course of government.

Chapter Review

Key Terms

approval rating (p. 188). Why do presidential approval ratings tend to fall?

confidence interval (p. 197). Why do you need to know the confidence interval for any poll?

conservatives (p. 205). What party do conservatives usually support?

efficacy (p. 190). Why is the efficacy of citizens important in a democracy?

exit polls (p. 195). Describe problems with exit polls.

gender gap (p. 214). Which party do women tend to support?

Generation Z (p. 201). How will easier access to information impact Generation Z's public opinion and involvement in politics?

Independents (p. 199). What has happened to Independents over the past thirty years?

levels of conceptualization (p. 206). How sophisticated is the public's ideological thinking?

liberals (p. 205). Why did the ideological direction of public mood move away from liberalism following Barack Obama's inauguration as president in 2008?

Millennials (p. 200). How are the Millennials' political opinions generally different from previous generations?

moderates (p. 206). Are most Americans moderates?

nonattitudes (p. 197). Give an example of a nonattitude that might arise from a poll.

party identification (p. 204). What is the main way people develop a party identification?

polarization (p. 209). Describe trends in party polarization over the past twenty years.

political ideology (p. 205). What is the relationship between ideology and partisanship?

political trust (p. 190). What are the trends in public trust in recent years?

public opinion (p. 189). Why is public opinion so important to a democracy?

push polls (p. 196). Why are push polls less accurate than random telephone surveys?

random sample (p. 193). Why is it important to have a random sample?

rationality (p. 201). What is an example of a shift in public opinion that speaks to the rationality of citizens?

representative sample (p. 194). Why is it crucial to have a representative sample?

self-interest (p. 201). Why can self-interest be a good thing in a democracy?

socialization (p. 199). How does socialization help to shape people's partisan leanings?

tracking polls (p. 195). How do tracking polls work?

Learning Outcomes: What You Need to...

Know	Test Yourself	Participate
LO 6-1 Decide why public opinion is powerful		
Public opinion—the aggregate of citizen attitudes—is essential to the workings of a democracy.	• State the reasons public opinion has a powerful impact on the presidency. • Define public opinion. • Track efficacy and public trust in government.	• Express your opinion of the presidency. • Grasp the connection between public opinion and democracy. • Evaluate why public trust in government is low.
LO 6-2 Describe how well polls measure public opinion		
Scientific polling enables public officials to gauge public opinion with some degree of confidence, though polls can be in error.	• Describe how politicians measured public opinion before there were polls. • Define scientific polling. • Identify three types of polls. • Explain potential errors in polls. • State why the internet is important to the future of polling.	• Evaluate whether polling is more or less accurate. • Participate in a political poll. • Improve your reading of polls. • Evaluate internet polling.

Know	Test Yourself	Participate

LO 6-3   Identify who drives public opinion—citizens or elites

Know	Test Yourself	Participate
Citizens' opinions and attitudes are shaped by environment, political socialization, generational effects, and self-interest. Elites do drive public opinion, but only to the extent that citizens are exposed and open to their message.	• State why socialization is so important to public opinion. • Track the influence of generational effects on political attitudes. • Explain both self-interest and rationality as shapers of public opinion. • Describe the influence of elites on public opinion.	• Examine the sources of your political socialization. • Evaluate how your views differ from those who are older or younger than you. • Determine whether your views on issues arise from self-interest or rationality. • Evaluate whether elites have the power to dictate public opinion on issues.

LO 6-4   Discover how ideology and partisanship shape public opinion

Know	Test Yourself	Participate
Party identification can help predict individual attitudes, and liberal or conservative leanings shape people's views on political and social issues. Generally, the public has been becoming less liberal, although there has been a recent uptick. People generally know what advances their interests and hold government accountable. Although parties have grown more polarized in recent years, the electorate is more moderate than party choices allow. In recent years, efficacy and public trust in government have fallen.	• Explain how partisanship relates to public opinion. • Explain the importance of political ideology. • Assess how well informed the American public is and whether it matters. • Describe polarization and its effects.	• Examine your partisanship in the context of public opinion. • Examine your political ideology in the context of public opinion. • Determine whether the American public is worth listening to. • Evaluate the impact of partisanship on democracy.

LO 6-5   Describe how demographic characteristics influence public opinion

Know	Test Yourself	Participate
Socioeconomic status, age, religion, gender, race, ethnicity, and educational background can all impact political values, ideology, and partisanship. Even within an ethnic group, such as Hispanic, the country of origin of one's parents or grandparents shapes one's political values.	• State the relationship between socioeconomic status on the one hand and partisanship and ideology on the other. • Describe how age affects political thinking. • Distinguish differences in political views between evangelical and non-evangelical Protestants. • Characterize the impact of the gender gap. • Survey the impact of race and ethnicity on political thinking. • Track the effect of increasing educational levels on political views.	• Examine your socioeconomic status in light of your partisanship and political ideology. • Speculate whether your position on issues will change as you age. • Evaluate the effect of religion on politics. • Evaluate the effect of race and ethnicity on politics. • Speculate whether your college education and experience will change your political views.

7 The News and Social Media

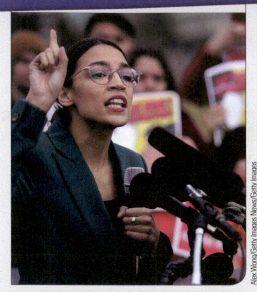

ALEXANDRIA OCASIO-CORTEZ
Boston University

Alex Wong/Getty Images News/Getty Images

> **"***The fundamental question, in the beginning, is, 'Why you?' The reason 'why' was 'cause, nobody else would. So literally anybody could, right? Because the alternative is no one.***"**

Shown on the next page, Boston University where Alexandria Ocasio-Cortez earned her undergraduate degree.

Congresswoman Alexandria Ocasio-Cortez (D-NY), better known today as AOC, was born in 1989 to Puerto Rican parents in the Bronx, New York. As a child, her entire extended family worked together to help her parents buy a small house in Westchester County to have access to better public schools. Her family saw education as a gateway to later influence and success. While AOC lived in an affluent county, she spent a good deal of time in the Bronx with family and friends. Ocasio-Cortez could see firsthand the difference in opportunity based on one's zip code. The decision to move to Westchester paid off. She attended Boston University, graduating with a degree in Economics and International Relations in 2011. While a student at BU, she interned for the late Senator Ted Kennedy and worked as an organizer in the Bronx. She later organized her home for Bernie Sanders' 2016 presidential race.[1] She was starting to make the most of her opportunities.

In 2016, Ocasio-Cortez received a call from an organization called Brand New Congress, a group with the mission of recruiting outsider candidates to run against established politicians and congressional corruption. The leaders asked her to consider running in 2018 for the House of Representatives to represent NY-14, a district that covers parts of the Bronx and Queens—her home. She was going to have to challenge Joe Crowley, a ten-term incumbent who, as the fourth most powerful Democrat, was in line to become Speaker of the House.[2] Thus began her journey to unseat this Queens political boss and become a politician who everyday Americans felt represented them. She was not supposed to win. She was a 29-year-old woman of color with no legislative experience and no ties to the party establishment. She grew up in a working class family, speaking fluent Spanish. She was an unabashed liberal. However, through a true grassroots campaign, AOC defeated Crowley by 15 points, about 4,000 votes, in the New York Democratic primary. On November 6, 2018, she became the youngest person ever elected to Congress.[3]

Ocasio-Cortez credits her quick rise to fame and increasing popularity to social media. For her, it has served as gateway to influence. She uses Instagram and Twitter to get her message out, share her ideas, and communicate with supporters. Thousands tune in to watch her Instagram Live videos of her doing everyday activities, and she is amassing a huge following of people from across the nation with her clever use of social media. The summer before she

Learning Outcomes

LO 7-1 Determine why the media are important in a democracy

LO 7-2 Analyze how the law protects the press

LO 7-3 Define trends in the history of the press

LO 7-4 Explain how changes in the mass media have changed the information environment

LO 7-5 Assess how the news media affect public opinion

LO 7-6 Evaluate the news media

was elected to Congress, Ocasio-Cortez had 49,000 Twitter followers. That number has now risen to over 8 million and keeps climbing. She is skilled at creating viral moments, from her primary campaign video to her campaign finance reform speech that made dark money easier for the average American to understand.[4] She also uses these platforms to combat political adversaries, ridiculing Fox News' coverage of her and turning attacks on her clothes and past jobs into memes. AOC also writes all of her tweets and replies—she's in total control of her Twitter account, which is rare for a politician.[5] This ability has greatly aided her steep rise in popularity and allows her to control the media narrative surrounding her.

Using both social media and other types of news media, AOC has been able to spread her ideas and open a direct line of communication with the electorate. This can be seen in her tweets and replies on Twitter, her Instagram Live videos, her guest appearances on popular shows like RuPaul's Drag Race, and her many interviews. After she won her primary, over 1,000 media outlets called her requesting interviews. She has already appeared on the cover of *Time Magazine* and made Time's 100 Most Influential People 2019 list before age 30. AOC tends to use social media more like an influencer than a politician. She talks like a normal person, details her challenges, gives advice, and answers questions from constituents from her district and the entire country.[6] Using these platforms to her advantage also allows AOC to speak directly to young people, people of color, and immigrants—constituencies that the Democratic Party needs to be successful, but who are often ignored in politics. But with this visibility comes challenges, because every word she utters is scrutinized and almost always criticized by her many opponents. In July 2020, she won her primary easily and then in November she won nearly 70 percent of the vote to keep her seat.

Regardless of one's own political views or opinions of Congresswoman Ocasio-Cortez, her background and rise to influence is a strong example of the "American dream" at work. Born into a working-class family, she used her education to learn and teach others about injustice and get involved in making progress toward equality. By nature of AOC's experience organizing and being a Millennial, she had the ideas and

skills to reach voters through social media. This expert use of social media will be touched on throughout the chapter, as it is increasingly being employed by candidates and those in office to connect with constituents, voice their opinions, and share information. Media can be both a gateway and gate to influence and power, depending on its usage. AOC made it a gateway.

To discuss "the media," we analyze the functions and impact of the press, survey its history, and describe and evaluate new forms of communication. By so doing, we can better understand the workings of the media and whether and under what conditions it can offer gateways to influence.

Political News

LO 7-1 Determine why the media are important in a democracy

In a democracy such as the United States, citizens are supposed to be the ultimate source of power. The decisions made by the public shape the course of government. The public, therefore, needs information about politics to make good choices. Most people cannot directly observe political events, so they rely on the mass media for information about politics and government.

What Are the Mass Media?

mass media: *News sources, including newspapers, television, radio, and the Internet, whose purpose is to provide a large audience with information about the nation and the world.*

The **mass media** represent the vast array of sources of information that are available to the public, including newspapers, television, radio, podcasts, various online sources, text messages, and social media such as Facebook, Twitter, or TikTok. The **news media** (also called the press) are a subset of the mass media that have traditionally provided the news of the day, gathered and reported by journalists. With all the new technologies of the twenty-first century, however, the news media are changing; now the average citizen is able to participate in politics through Instagram, Twitter, Facebook, Snapchat, TikTok, or Reddit. These types of social media have recast journalism by providing a proliferation of news outlets without a monolithic entity that shapes and defines political reporting. In this chapter, we use the term *mass media* to describe the many ways citizens learn about government and politics.

news media: *Subset of the mass media that provides the news of the day, gathered and reported by journalists.*

One aspect of the mass media today is speedy communication. What used to take days, weeks, and sometimes months, now takes seconds. For example, it took up to four days for some Americans to learn about the assassination of President Abraham Lincoln (1861–65) in April 1865. But no longer: Twitter feeds, for instance, bring information nearly as quickly as it happens. There is no need to wait for the evening news on TV. Most young people today (Millennials born between 1981 and 1996 and Generation Z born from 1997, onward) grew up with the 24-7 news cycle, an information world that is very different from that of their parents (and their professors). This chapter takes those changes into account.

Key Questions
How do you get your news?

Key Questions
How often do you pay attention to the news?

Access to information is important because an enduring and effective democracy demands a knowledgeable public.[7] For the people to be informed, the press needs to be able to do its job free from government interference, and journalists must feel free to be critical of the government. This **watchdog** role of the press lies at the very heart of a democracy. In 1787, Thomas Jefferson observed, "Were it left to me to decide whether we should have a government without newspapers, or newspapers without a government, I should not hesitate a moment to prefer the latter."[8] What Jefferson meant is that only a well-informed public is capable of self-governing. Freedom of the press is intertwined with the very idea of democratic government, and the First Amendment to the Constitution protects it.

watchdog: *Role of the press in monitoring government actions.*

Functions of the News

The mass media help ensure government accountability and responsiveness by performing three important tasks: informing, investigating, and interpreting the news.

Informing. Journalists, simply put, inform. Coverage of COVID-19 in 2020, for example, might include stories on number of cases, deaths, impact on the health care system, the effects on the economy, closing of schools, or whether people were following safe practices when out in public. Coverage of a political campaign, on the other hand, might include information about candidates' previous experience, their personal temperaments, or their views on important issues. If there is a crisis in the economy, journalists provide information about the problem, explain the solutions being proposed, and indicate what can be expected in the future. In August 2008—just a month before a financial crisis rocked the nation— about 5 percent of news stories dealt with the economy. In September 2008 that proportion soared to nearly

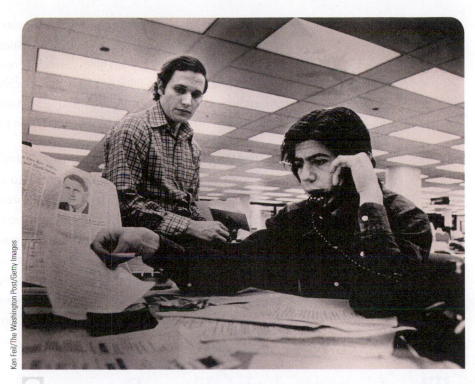

Ken Feil/The Washington Post/Getty Images

Image 7.1 *Washington Post* reporters Bob Woodward and Carl Bernstein became legends for their work in following up on a news story about what seemed to be a routine break-in. But it was the Democratic campaign headquarters that was broken into on June 17, 1972, and the trail they picked up led to the White House. Certain to be impeached, President Richard M. Nixon resigned on August 9, 1974.

30 percent.[9] Gun violence was also suddenly given much more attention by journalists following the tragic mass shootings in Las Vegas, NV; Sutherland Springs, TX; and Parkland, FL. And starting in March 2020, the news covered the COVID-19 crisis nearly nonstop. In more normal times, a quick scan of any newspaper or news website can inform readers about a wide range of topics.

Investigating. The media can also *make* news by researching and revealing information about events. The Watergate scandal, uncovered by two reporters from the *Washington Post*, revealed questionable activities in the Richard M. Nixon administration (1969–74; see also Chapter 13, The Presidency). Bob Woodward and Carl Bernstein played the ultimate role of watchdog, creating a news story that gripped the country for more than a year. The episode ended with Nixon's resignation on August 9, 1974, the only time a U.S. president has resigned. This scandal would never have been uncovered without the tireless efforts of the *Post's* investigative reporters.[10] More recently, the rise of the #MeToo was originally sparked by investigative reporting about allegations of sexual misconduct by Harvey Weinstein. These revelations gave rise to an outpouring of additional reports about other prominent people who had engaged in sexual harassment and violence.

Because of the importance of the press, politicians often court journalists, as they seek favorable coverage. They want reporters to share their accomplishments with voters. Yet journalists and politicians are usually in an adversarial relationship because journalists want to report new stories on topics of interest to the public. Those topics often include information

Key Questions

How well does the news inform you about American government and politics?

Key Questions

Why is the relationship between the press and politicians adversarial?

unfriendly to candidates, which they want to downplay or ignore. In addition, reporters love to unearth scandals—something that politicians desperately want to avoid. Scandals are fresh and exciting, and uncovering them gives journalists real influence. The investigative function not only allows the press to fulfill its role as the watchdog of democracy, but it also makes reporters' jobs interesting and important. Also, scandals attract an audience, increasing profits. As you can see, the interests of politicians and the press often do not align.

Interpreting. When the media inform, they also interpret the news. Just giving one story front-page coverage and relegating another to an inside page involves interpreting what is more and less important. The role of interpretation has taken on even greater significance in the past few decades. In 1960, for example, journalists covered presidential campaigns in a very descriptive fashion: About 90 percent of campaign stories focused on describing what happened in the campaign that day. But in the following decades, journalists started to interpret events more frequently, assessing *why* something happened.[11] Much of the press is now about commentary than hard news. We need both, as suggested by the slogan of *The Washington Post*: "Democracy Dies in Darkness."

Key Questions

Which function do you think the press uses the most? Informing, investigating, or interpreting?

The Law and the Free Press

LO 7-2 Analyze how the law protects the press

The First Amendment to the Constitution states that "Congress shall make no law . . . abridging the freedom . . . of the press." This protection is not unlimited, however. During times of war (or threat of war), national security concerns may require that the press not publish a story. The government, however, is often too eager to stop publication of controversial stories, whereas the press may be too willing to report on controversial stories that will boost sales. This conflict plays out in debates over prior restraint—government's ability to restrict the publication of sensitive material (see Chapter 4, Civil Liberties). When can government invoke prior restraint? At what point does prior restraint become censorship and thus undermine the ability of the press to be a watchdog?

Answers to these difficult questions have been shaped by Supreme Court decisions. In the early 1930s, for example, the state of Minnesota stopped a small newspaper from publishing controversial claims about the mayor of Minneapolis and convicted the publisher, Jay Near, under state libel laws. Near appealed the conviction all the way to the Supreme Court. In *Near v. Minnesota* (1931), the Court ruled that only in exceptionally rare cases could the government stop the printing of a story, overturning Near's conviction and invalidating the Minnesota law that led to his conviction.[12] The Court has reinforced the protections of press freedom in a **libel** case, *New York Times v. Sullivan* (1964), which also set a very high standard—proof of **actual malice**—to convict in a libel suit. Justice William J. Brennan wrote, "We consider this case against the background of a profound national commitment to the principle that debate on public issues should be uninhibited, robust, and wide open, and that it may well include vehement, caustic, and sometimes unpleasantly sharp attacks on government and public officials" (see Supreme Court Cases: *New York Times v. Sullivan*).

The modern landmark case on the freedom of the press was the *Pentagon Papers* case (1971).[13] During the Vietnam War, the *New York Times* secured a copy of

libel: *Publishing false and damaging statements about another person.*

actual malice: *Supreme Court test for libel of a public figure, in which the plaintiff must prove that the publisher knew the material was false or acted with reckless disregard of whether it was true or false.*

Supreme Court Cases

New York Times v. Sullivan (1964)

QUESTION: What level of negligence must be found when public officials sue newspapers for libel?

ORAL ARGUMENT: January 6–7, 1964 (listen at http://www.oyez.org/cases/1960-1969/1963/1963_39)

DECISION: March 9, 1964 (read at http://caselaw.lp.findlaw.com/scripts/getcase.pl?navby=case&court=us&vol=376&page=254)

OUTCOME: Actual malice must be found to convict for libel, thus overturning the libel conviction of the *New York Times* (9–0).

Libel is the publication of false and damaging information about someone. Prior to libel laws, the defamed person often responded to libel by challenging the libeler to a duel, as when Vice President Aaron Burr challenged *Federalist* author and former Treasury Secretary Alexander Hamilton to a duel and killed him. To prevent such acts, various states made libel a criminal act. Today libel is almost exclusively a question for a civil suit, in which one person sues another for monetary damages.

The *Sullivan* case derived from an advertisement placed in the March 29, 1960, *New York Times* by an ad hoc group of civil rights supporters called the Committee to Defend Martin Luther King. The ad condemned the "wave of terror" against nonviolent civil rights activists by unnamed "southern violators." Because some of the actions against King included arresting him, the chief of the Montgomery, Alabama, police department claimed that all of the allegations were about him and that he had been libeled.

Under Alabama law, once damaging statements were found, the only defense was for the publication to prove that all the particulars were true. The ad in this case was not true in all the particulars. For example, it claimed that protesting students sang "My Country 'Tis of Thee" when they actually sang "The Star-Spangled Banner." The jury thus found against the *Times*, awarding the police chief $500,000 in damages.

The Supreme Court reversed the verdict, declaring that a law holding a newspaper liable for criticism of a public official only if the paper could prove that every statement in the article was true would lead to massive self-censorship by the press. Instead, the Court declared that libel against a public official required a finding of actual malice—that is, knowledge that the statement was false or reckless disregard of whether it was true or false. Under this standard, the Court found that the ad was substantially true, but even if it had not been substantially true, there was no evidence that the *Times* acted with malice.

This decision has made it much easier for newspapers to criticize public officials. The Court has expanded the ruling to cover public figures as well. When a supermarket tabloid trashes a popular actor or singer, the individual thus harmed has to prove actual malice to win a suit for libel.

Thinking Critically

1. What would happen if the media were held legally responsible for any false statement they made?
2. Should the burden of proof for proving libel of public officials be treated equally to the burden of proof for libel of private people?

a top-secret Department of Defense analysis detailing U.S. involvement in Vietnam and began publishing it, believing that the information, some of which contradicted official statements, was essential to public understanding of government policy. Citing national security, the Nixon Administration secured a court injunction forcing the *Times* to cease publication, but the newspaper appealed, and the case quickly went to the

Key Questions

Should the standard for press freedom be the same in cases of terrorism as in wartime?

Supreme Court. While not denying the possibility that censorship can be warranted, the Court in this instance rejected the government's argument that national security took precedence over the right to publish documents embarrassing to the government. The government, said the Court, had not met the extraordinary burden of proof needed for prior restraint.

While journalists are protected by the *Pentagon Papers* decision, a new brand of "journalists" has arisen in social media. For example, a federal case about six years ago held that bloggers are afforded the same protections as journalists working for established news outlets. This case expanded First Amendment protections beyond those in previous rulings to include persons other than "institutional media defendants."[14]

In general, the courts have tended to give the edge to the press in the belief that, in the long run, it is better to protect press freedoms so that the press can, in turn, help inform the public, which can then hold elected officials accountable. Consistent with this general predisposition, there are very few laws that constrain the print media, such as newspapers and magazines. The electronic media, however, are more heavily regulated by government. As early as the 1920s, Congress sought to regulate radio to ensure it would serve the public interest. It was a new medium, and Congress wanted to guard against it being used in a way that might undermine equality and fairness. In 1934, Congress created the Federal Communications Commission (FCC), now a powerful independent agency that regulates all forms of electronic media, including radio, broadcast television, cable television, cell phones, and even wireless networks. Anyone can start a newspaper, but starting a radio station requires a license from the FCC.

The FCC monitors media ownership as well. For a long time, the FCC worked to ensure that ownership of the news media was not concentrated in just a few hands; it was concerned that a monopoly would undermine the ability of the media to be fair and able to perform its watchdog function. The Telecommunications Act of 1996 eased the rules concerning multiple ownership, and the FCC has started to relax this standard. As a result, there has been a trend toward greater concentration of media ownership in the past decade. In 1995, major companies generally owned around ten television stations each; ten years later, each owned nearly forty. The ownership of radio has also changed. Clear Channel Communications owned 520 radio stations in 1999; two decades later, Clear Channel Communications is now iHeartCommunications. It owns 850 AM and FM radio stations worldwide and several satellite radio stations, and it has a substantial online streaming presence.[15]

Key Questions

What are the newspapers in your city or town? Who owns them?

This recent concentration of media ownership is not unique. Concerns about the consequences of control of the news by just a few people date to the late nineteenth century, when individuals such as William Randolph Hearst controlled major news organizations. Without genuine competition, the press, some fear, will become lapdogs, not watchdogs. But even the changes of the past few years have not eliminated competition. It is true that newspapers are now dominated by seven major chains; Gannett alone has a presence in over 100 media markets across the country.[16] But with so many outlets for news in the twenty-first century, one person or company is not able to control information. The public has access to a wide range of information from a variety of sources and mediums.

Any effort to monopolize the press or curtail its freedom will be met by strong protests from citizens fearing a trend toward authoritarian rule (see Public Policy, the News, and Social Media: Censorship). A government that limits press freedom seeks to insulate itself from criticism, thereby decreasing the chance for the public to hold leaders accountable. The absence of a robust press means that government will no longer be responsive, but that it will instead pursue policies that advance the interests of the few rather than the many. In this situation, greater inequality arises between those in power and those out of power. It is for all these reasons that an evaluation of how democratic a nation is rests on how much freedom, including protection from **censorship**, its press enjoys.

censorship: *The suppression of words, images, or ideas that are considered "offensive" or "dangerous" by a government or private group. Protection from being censored is guaranteed by the First Amendment.*

The History of the Press in America

LO 7-3 Define trends in the history of the press

The press in America has always been dynamic. Newspapers have developed from occasional pamphlets in the early 1700s, to comprehensive daily publications that aimed for objective reporting of political news, to today's online enterprises filled with a mix of news and entertainment. By the 1900s, journalism emerged as a profession with a commitment to objectivity. In the twentieth century, radio and then television changed how Americans received the news and how they reacted to it. Throughout, the press has at times supported government and elected officials and at times assumed an adversarial role as it has given citizens the information they need to make government accountable and responsive.

The Colonial Era, 1620 to 1750

In the early colonial period, newspapers were not widely available, and there were few printing presses. *Public Occurrences,* which began publication in Boston in 1690, had only a few pages and was more a pamphlet than a newspaper. Circulation was small, usually fewer than two thousand copies.[17] Newspaper publication was more of a hobby for publishers than anything else, and the notion that the press had the right to criticize government was not widely accepted. In fact, colonial governments feared that harsh criticism would incite the public and create instability, so publishers who attacked those in power could be thrown into jail and have their printing presses confiscated.

In 1734, John Peter Zenger was jailed for criticizing the colonial governor of New York in his *New York Weekly Journal.* When his case came to trial the next year, his lawyer, Andrew Hamilton of Philadelphia, decided on a bold strategy. Zenger would admit guilt—he had published the critical statements—and then argue that the jury should find him not guilty because the statements were true. In other words, the press had a fundamental right to criticize government, and a free press was more important than the law against

Key Questions

Why was freedom of the press so important to the colonists and members of the Founding generation?

Public Policy, the News, and Social Media

Censorship

Any effort by government to control the media or to curtail the freedom of the press faces an immediate debate and often strong protest. The advent of radio and television and the recent proliferation of electronic media have brought new challenges to determining what kinds of content should be restrained and what kinds should be allowed to flow freely. No government agency regulates the print media, but the FCC has the authority to regulate the content and ownership of radio, television, the Internet, and all electronic media. One area of special concern has been what might be considered obscene, offensive, or harmful material.

The landmark Supreme Court decision in *FCC v. Pacifica Foundation* (1978) established the precedent that the FCC has the legal authority to fine any media outlet that knowingly allows the expression of obscene content, under certain circumstances. The background of the case was that in 1973 a New York radio station aired George Carlin's monologue "Filthy Words," which included seven words that could not be said on the public airwaves. The station had prefaced the monologue with a warning to listeners that it included "sensitive language which might be regarded as offensive to some." A listener who was in the car with his young son when he heard the broadcast filed a complaint with the FCC.

The underlying question in this case was whether the First Amendment inhibits the power of the government to restrict the public broadcast of indecent language under any circumstances. The Supreme Court ruled in a 5–4 decision that the government could invoke limited civil sanctions against the radio broadcast of patently offensive words dealing with sex and excretion without violating the First Amendment. The Court also said that the words did not have to be obscene to warrant sanction and that, in decisions on whether sanctions on media content are fair and justified, other factors such as audience type, the time that the broadcast was aired, and how it was transmitted are relevant.[18]

In today's television, music, and video climate, the boundaries for socially acceptable visual and verbal content are constantly evolving. In *FCC v. Fox Television Stations (2009)*, Fox Broadcasting Company appealed fines that the FCC imposed for its broadcasts of the Billboard Music Awards, during which participants uttered expletives. Fox claimed that participants on previous broadcasts had used similar language and that the FCC had ruled that the use was "fleeting" and was not seriously harmful. The Supreme Court ruled that the FCC needed to prove only that its new policy was justifiable and reasonable.[19] In response, network television and radio stations have taken to "bleeping" or "buzzing" over words that might be viewed as harmful by the FCC. In live broadcasts, networks typically use a five-second delay in sending their signals over the airways to make sure they have time to bleep out offensive language. Cable television outlets are not under this same type of restriction because they broadcast to paid subscribers who thus have more control over the content they choose to view.

Social networking and the Internet present new challenges, particularly in the area of child safety. The Internet is not exactly a broadcast medium, but given its wide availability to the general public, Congress has sought to restrict its content. In 1996, Congress passed the Communications Decency Act (CDA), which established broadcast-style content regulations for the Internet. The act banned the posting of "indecent" or "patently offensive" materials in a public forum on the Internet, including in newsgroups, chat rooms, web pages, and online discussion lists. The American Civil Liberties Union (ACLU) challenged the law, and in 1997, the Supreme Court ruled unanimously that many portions of the law were unconstitutional because they imposed sweeping restrictions that violated the free speech protections of the First Amendment.[20] However, Section 230 of the CDA still stands today. It serves as a valuable tool for protecting freedom of expression and innovation on the Internet by protecting sites from laws that could hold them responsible for things that users post. This has allowed free speech online to flourish because since these user-generated sites like Facebook and YouTube are not liable for users' actions, they can host content without needing to censor it. So although much of the law was struck down by the Supreme Court, Section 230 is currently still the most influential law to protect Internet innovation.[21]

In 1998, Congress tried for a second time to limit content on the Internet when it passed the Child Online Protection Act (COPA).[22] The act made it a crime for anyone using an Internet site or e-mail over the Internet to make any communication for commercial reasons considered "harmful to minors" unless the person had prohibited access by minors by requiring a credit card number to access the material. Again, the legislation was ultimately struck down, this time by the Court of Appeals for the Third Circuit. Further, in 2009, the U.S. Supreme Court refused to hear the government's appeal of this decision.

Congress subsequently responded by passing the Children's Online Privacy Protection Act (COPPA), which requires sites directed to children under the age of 13 to gain parental consent before collecting, maintaining, or using children's information. Parents can review their children's online activity under COPPA. The act also requires such a site to post a privacy policy on its home page and a link to the privacy policy on every page where personal information is collected.[23] In addition, Congress passed a law designed to prevent the exploitation of children by prohibiting pornographic websites from showing sexually explicit material involving children on their home pages.[24]

Given the vastness of the Internet and the speed at which technology evolves, it becomes fundamentally harder to keep the Internet "safe" for users of all ages as well as to preserve the security of information that is passed over it. Because the Internet is an engine of commerce as well as a media outlet, it is also regulated by the Federal Trade Commission (FTC).[25] The FTC offers detailed information to consumers about what information they should never release on the Internet, what websites are not secure, how to determine secure websites, and how to report wrongdoing. Citizens who fail to read privacy policies or are not careful about the information they release are vulnerable, and the FTC is the government agency responsible for helping to prevent Internet abuse and fraud.

Construct Your Own Policy

1. Establish a set of definitions for what constitutes indecent language or indecent exposure in public communication that is consistent with Supreme Court rulings.
2. Describe how social media companies such as YouTube and Google can take steps to prohibit individuals from using the Internet to commit crimes against children but also maintain freedom of speech.

seditious libel that had put Zenger behind bars. Much to the surprise of the governor and his supporters, the jury agreed and freed Zenger. The case is a landmark in advancing the idea of a free press.

In the same decade, in Philadelphia, Benjamin Franklin was laying the groundwork for the press as a viable institution in America with his *Philadelphia Gazette*. The paper would set the standard for American news with its ability to present news accounts in an interesting and enlightening manner. Franklin had a gift for writing and a flair for satire

seditious libel: *Conduct or language that incites rebellion against the authority of a state.*

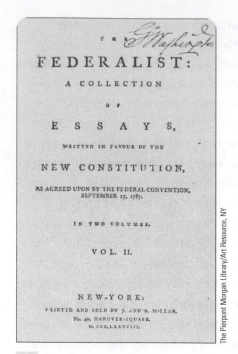

Image 7.2 *The Federalist Papers* are an early example of the power of the press in America. Writing as "Publius," James Madison, Alexander Hamilton, and John Jay published seventy-seven essays in New York newspapers arguing for the ratification of the Constitution. In 1788, these and eight other essays were republished in two volumes. They are still read today for insights into the interpretation of the Constitution and the Framers' vision for a republic.

Federalist Papers: *Series of essays written by James Madison, Alexander Hamilton, and John Jay arguing for the ratification of the Constitution; today a leading source for understanding the Constitution.*

and parody. His accounts of government and stories of personal interest, including crime, sex, violence, and mysteries, became the foundation for modern American news coverage. He is considered by many to be one of America's first sensationalist journalists. But Franklin was trying to do much more than simply pique the interest of readers: He also believed that the news was critical to educating the public. His "An Apology for Printers" (1731) defended objectivity in journalism. Though it contradicted the prevailing view at the time, it helped set the standard for the future of American journalism.[26]

The Founding Era, 1750 to 1790

As tensions between the colonies and Britain increased, interest in politics grew as well, and the press responded. The circulation of newspapers grew twice as fast as the population between 1760 and 1776.[27] That year, when Thomas Paine published *Common Sense*, a pamphlet attacking King George, it sold 150,000 copies, far more than the 2,000 copies political documents normally sold.[28] Given that there were only 2.5 million people in the colonies, that is the equivalent of 18 million copies today.

The press helped spread the idea of independence because newspapers served as networks for sharing information. They reached not only subscribers but also many people who could not read, for the papers were read aloud in taverns and town squares. During the Revolution, some papers backed independence; others supported the British Crown.[29]

Partisanship in the press carried over to the battle for ratification of the Constitution, and newspapers provided a vital forum for debate. The Antifederalists waged a fierce campaign against the Constitution,[30] and those supporting the Constitution responded, most famously in a series of essays published in New York newspapers, which are today known as the *Federalist Papers*.

The Partisan Era, 1790 to 1900

Following the adoption of the Constitution, most newspapers allied themselves with the Federalists or with the newly emerging Jeffersonian party. In this era of the partisan press, writers made no effort to adjudicate between the claims and ideas of competing parties. Consequently, rhetoric was often harsh. During George Washington's time in office (1789–97), he was attacked constantly by the Jeffersonian press.

Even worse criticism was leveled at the second president, John Adams (1797–1801), who was not as universally admired as Washington. Adams was called a liar and feeble-minded, among other things.[31] His administration's Sedition Act (1798) made it illegal to print or publish any "false, scandalous, and malicious writing" about the federal government, either house of Congress, or the president.[32] At the time, the United States was engaged in a limited and undeclared war with France over trade issues, and the Federalists believed that attacks on Adams and the government were ripping apart the new nation, which was barely a decade old. The Articles of Confederation had not even lasted ten years; might not the same fate await the Constitution? But the Jeffersonians were equally adamant that laws suppressing criticism of the government violated the Constitution. Jeffersonian publishers did not cease their attacks, and some went to jail and paid fines. After he and his party won the 1800 presidential election, Thomas Jefferson (1801–09) pardoned all publishers convicted under the act, and Congress refunded their fines.

Now it was Jefferson and his party's turn to be attacked. The Federalist opposition was very critical of Jefferson, calling him the "anti-Christ."[33] While Jefferson had long been a proponent of a free press and had severely criticized the Sedition Act, the attacks he endured were so vicious that he began to question the merits of this partisan press. In 1807 he conceded, "The man who never looks into a newspaper is better informed than he who reads them."[34] This was quite a change for a man who, twenty years earlier, had argued that newspapers were more important than the institutions of republican government itself. Jefferson's dilemma reveals a core issue about the press. The media do inform, playing a vital function. But informing almost always carries some bias, and when informing is deliberately intended to manipulate public opinion, the public responds with distrust.

Newspapers continued to have close alliances with political parties in the next decades of the nineteenth century. They not only served to attack the opposition but also provided a way for presidents and party leaders to express their opinions on the issues of the day. Some presidents, such as James K. Polk (1845–49), even started their own newspapers to get out their message.[35]

During the 1830s and 1840s, new steam presses reduced the cost of publishing newspapers. In 1833, Benjamin Day sold his *New York Sun* for a penny per issue, initiating the era of the **penny press**. At the same time, literacy throughout the nation was growing, and newspaper owners began to realize that they could make higher profits through circulation and advertising than as arms of political parties.[36] They also saw that partisanship drove away customers who did not share their political views. So to increase circulation, newspapers began to move toward sensationalism, printing news of crimes and scandals and stories about personalities, much as tabloids do today and as Ben Franklin did in the 1700s. In 1870, for example, only about 13 percent of all newspapers were independent of a political party. By 1900, that proportion had swelled to nearly 50 percent.[37]

The circulation of newspapers rose from about 1.4 million in 1870 to more than 8 million within the next thirty years. The quest for market share led to competition over which newspaper could grab the most attention with sensational headlines and stories. Known as **yellow journalism**, this form of news reporting distorted the presentation of events and could mislead the public, all in the interest of boosting sales. Joseph Pulitzer and William Randolph Hearst, the most famous newspaper publishers at the time, used large type, provocative head-lines, pictures, and color to attract readers. Hearst introduced comics as a way to sell more papers. The competition became particularly fierce over American relations with Spain, as stories of Spanish atrocities in Cuba inflamed the public. When the USS *Maine* sank in Havana Harbor on February 15, 1898, the newspapers quickly blamed Spain. The U.S. Navy launched a four-week investigation, finding that the *Maine* had been destroyed by an underwater mine but placing no blame. However, the American public, fed by the press, continued to blame Spain, and on April 25, the U.S. Congress declared war on Spain. Many observers credit these sensational newspaper stories with fueling the start of the Spanish-American War.[38]

The Professional Era, 1900 to 1950

The development of mass circulation newspapers also led journalism to develop into a serious profession with an ethic of objective reporting. Pulitzer, despite his role in

Key Questions
What are the advantages and disadvantages of partisan control of the press?

Key Questions
In the standoff between Adams and Jefferson over the Sedition Act, who do you think was right?

penny press: *Newspapers sold for a penny, initiating an era in which the press began to rely on circulation and advertising for income and not on political parties.*

yellow journalism: *Style of journalism in the late-nineteenth century characterized by sensationalism intended to capture readers' attention and increase circulation.*

863,956 **The** 🦅 **World.** 863,956

MAINE EXPLOSION CAUSED BY BOMB OR TORPEDO?

Capt. Sigsbee and Consul-General Lee Are in Doubt—The World Has Sent a Special Tug, With Submarine Divers, to Havana to Find Out—Lee Asks for an Immediate Court of Inquiry—Capt. Sigsbee's Suspicions.

The New York World a day after

who had been Populists and those who became Progressives — clamored for the United States to rescue the Cuban people from the Spanish malefactors.

President William McKinley and the conservative Republican leaders in Congress reluctantly gave way before this pressure. Senator Henry Cabot Lodge warned McKinley, "If the war in Cuba drags on through the summer with nothing done we [the Republican party] shall go down in the greatest defeat ever known."

Already, in November 1897, Spain, at the urging of President McKinley, had granted

Image 7.3 William Randolph Hearst's *New York Journal* and Joseph Pulitzer's *New York World* competed for circulation with sensational news and screaming headlines. The frenzy they stirred up over the sinking of the USS *Maine* in Havana Harbor in February 1898 helped lead to war with Spain. It is now generally believed that the explosion on the *Maine* was not caused by a Spanish bomb or torpedo but was accidental, a spontaneous combustion in inadequately vented coal bunkers.

muckraking: *Journalistic practice of investigative reporting that seeks to uncover corruption and wrongdoing.*

Key Questions

What are examples of sensationalized news stories today?

Key Questions

Give other examples of investigative journalism that have made government responsive. What effect did they have?

Key Questions

Should the press expose the personal lives of politicians? Why or why not?

advancing yellow journalism, was a key figure in this transition, believing that a vibrant independent press was essential for a democracy to endure. In 1904, he observed that "our Republic and its press will rise or fall together. An able, disinterested, public-spirited press ... can preserve that public virtue without which popular government is a sham and a mockery."[39]

The idea of a public-spirited press was increasingly realized in efforts to investigate wrongdoing in government, business, and industry. Adolph Ochs purchased the *New York Times* in 1896 with the goal of pursuing objective reporting. Such commitments led journalists, with the backing of people such as Ochs and Pulitzer, to expose corruption and encourage genuine reform. Although President Theodore Roosevelt (1901–09) labeled such efforts as **muckraking**—after a character in *Pilgrim's Progress* who rakes "muck," looking for the worst rather than the best—he came to appreciate the service these investigative journalists provided. Perhaps the most famous example was Upton Sinclair's *The Jungle* (1906), a novel that exposed the horrors of the meatpacking industry. Roosevelt, who had read an advance copy of the book, called for government regulation of the food industry.[40] In response, Congress passed the Pure Food and Drug Act and the Meat Inspection Act to help ensure food safety.

The rise of professional journalism is also tied to an ethic of objectivity. The goal of being impartial and unbiased in reporting became part of the journalist's creed, especially as taught in new schools of journalism. The American Society of Newspaper Editors adopted a set of principles declaring that "news reports should be free from opinion or bias of any kind."[41] Reporters were trained to present facts, not personal opinions, and to describe, not judge.

With the rise of investigative journalism, a key goal became to "get the scoop"—to write a story that presented the public with new and important information that was well researched and carefully documented. Journalists sought to cultivate politicians for access to news and stories, and this cultivation led to a different dynamic between politicians and the press. It remained adversarial, but both sides knew they needed each other. As the press and politicians formed closer relationships, the potential for conflicts of interest increased. To retain the relationship, politicians made certain statements "off the record," with the understanding that journalists would not use them in a story except as background information that could help set the context and provide a broader understanding for the story. As a result, journalists have a strong ethic about not revealing confidential sources.

The press took some topics off the table, including the personal lives of politicians. For example, few Americans realized that President Franklin Delano Roosevelt (1933–45) was paralyzed from polio; the press chose not to cover his physical challenge and rarely photographed him being carried from his car. Journalists did not deem Roosevelt's condition relevant to governing, and his paralysis did not interfere with his performance as president, seemingly justifying the press's decision.

This practice did have costs, however. Using the same example, one could argue that the press relinquished its role of watchdog in not covering Roosevelt's health, especially as it declined. Roosevelt died in April 1945, three months after taking the oath of office for his fourth term. There were clear signs that he was ill, but the press chose not to report them.[42]

The Television Era, 1950 to 2000

The rise of television recast the news media and the information available to the public. At mid-century, the *New York Times* was the most influential newspaper and clearly the leader in American journalism. News magazines such as *Time* and *Life* had nationwide circulations, but they were not daily sources of information. Most people got their daily news from local newspapers and radio stations that broadcast news summaries—usually five minutes of news, weather, and sports on the hour. Then television began to nationalize the news. That is, the evening broadcasts from the three major networks—ABC, CBS, and NBC—gave Americans across the country access to the same news, and by the 1960s, they relied on television for political information.[43]

TV news was shaped by a handful of "anchormen." In fact, there were no women on the national networks, nor were there any anchors of color, in the first few decades of television. In 1976, Barbara Walters became the first woman to anchor the evening news (ABC). It was not until 2015 that an African American, Lester Holt, solo-anchored an evening news program.[44]

When TV news anchors are discussed, Walter Cronkite's name is soon to follow. Walter Cronkite, anchor of the *CBS Evening News*, was an icon. Not only was he famous, but he was also widely admired and trusted. In 1973, Americans rated him "the most trusted man in America."[45] Can you imagine that happening today? Cronkite represented both the height of what might be called "objective" journalism and the dominance of TV network news. Most Americans assumed that Cronkite provided the facts and did not let partisanship shape his reporting. He closed his evening news show by saying "and that's the way it is," and viewers agreed.

Image 7.4 In 2015, Lester Holt became the first African American solo news anchor in the United States.

Television's visuals also redefined the news and even political events. Politicians now aimed to look good on television because viewers could detect nervousness and judge body language. The 1960 presidential campaign is a well-known example of the new emphasis on the visual side of politics. Most viewers of the televised presidential debates between Senator John Kennedy and Vice President Richard Nixon thought that Kennedy performed better.[46] He looked tanned and rested; in fact, he had spent a few days before the debate resting on a beach. Nixon, by contrast, had continued to campaign and had spent time in the hospital for a very sore leg. He was tired and in pain. He also refused to wear makeup. Nixon was not at his best, while Kennedy looked presidential. People who listened to the debate on the radio, however, thought that Nixon had won, further suggesting the power of visuals. Many commentators attribute Kennedy's razor-thin victory in the election to his performance in the debates.[47]

The general rule is that visuals in debates (and other campaign events) remain central to campaigns. It is important to look presidential. Some may now, however, question that rule in

image 7.5 Television proved its importance as a source for political information when the NBC board chair invited the 1960 presidential candidates to debate the issues on television. John F. Kennedy accepted first, saying, "I believe you are performing a notable public service in giving the American people a chance to see the candidates of the two major parties face to face." More than 70 million Americans watched the Kennedy–Nixon debates, and today presidential debates are fixtures of the fall campaign.

light of Donald Trump's weak performance during the 2016 presidential debates. He was widely criticized for his lack of policy knowledge and his often harsh rhetoric and disrespect toward moderators and Hillary Clinton in those debates. Yet, he won the presidency despite his "disastrous debate performances."[48] The 2020 presidential debates were heavily influenced by COVID-19. The first was marked by President Trump consistently interrupting. The second debate was canceled because of Trump's COVID-19 diagnosis—instead each candidate held a virtual town hall. The last debate was calmer because the moderator was able to "mute" both candidates if they went over time.

Mass Media in the Twenty-First Century

LO 7-4 Explain how changes in the mass media have changed the information environment

The media have always been a dynamic institution, but the speed of changes in the past few decades is truly staggering. The impact of television, for example, changed further with the rise of cable television from the 1970s to the 1990s. It was now possible to bring news to the public any time of day, reshaping the American news environment. Recent advances in technology have opened up additional avenues of communication—nearly all at the same time. The pace and the depth of these changes make the information environment of the twenty-first century different from those that preceded it.

The Changing Media Environment

The options open to Americans for gathering information about politics have constantly expanded. Figure 7.1 displays the changing media environment and suggests two main lessons. First, Americans adopt new media quickly. In the early 1920s, there were only five radio stations, and few households owned radios. By 1927, there were seven hundred stations, and ownership was rapidly increasing.[49] By the end of the 1930s, almost everyone in the United States had access to a radio. Television caught on even more quickly. Only 10 percent of Americans had TV sets in their homes in the early 1950s; by 1960, the figure was 90 percent. Today, nearly all American households have not one TV but often two or three. Internet access also shows a steep upward trend, from few households in the mid-1990s to currently around 90 percent of Americans.[50]

The speed by which these new media have entered the marketplace itself increases. It took television thirteen years to reach 50 million users. In just three years on the market, more than 50 million iPods were sold, and when the iPad was released in 2010, about 3 million were sold in eighty days.[51] The number of Twitter users has jumped tenfold, from about 30 million in March 2010 to about 330 million in January 2020.[52] Of course, among the younger generation, Twitter is a much more common feature of daily lives: estimates are that about one-third of Millennials use Twitter and three in five have accounts.[53] Overall, 22 percent of all Americans have a Twitter account.[54]

Second, there are more options for gathering news than ever before. In the 1930s, newspapers and radio were the main sources. In the 1950s, television was a new option, but there were only three networks, and they broadcast the news only in the evening. Now cable TV, satellite TV, and the Internet make news available night and day.

Key Questions
What newspapers do you read? Print or online?

The Decline of Newspapers

Traditional printed newspapers are in decline. The number of daily papers has been dropping since 1990.[55] Newspaper readership is also declining. Figure 7.2 shows the drop in readership since the turn of the century. This decline has been going on for forty years. In the mid-1970s, about 70 percent of the public read newspapers. This decrease in the last decade and a half is true for all generations, but there are notable differences by age in regard to newspaper readership. Currently, about 25 percent of the Millennial generation are newspaper readers as compared to about 55 percent of those over 65 years of age.[56]

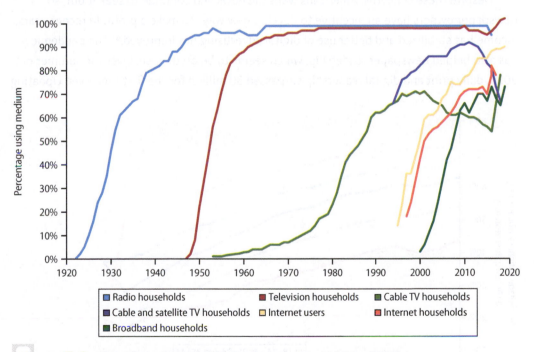

Legend:
- Radio households
- Cable and satellite TV households
- Broadband households
- Television households
- Internet users
- Cable TV households
- Internet households

Figure 7.1 **The Changing Media Environment, 1920 to 2020**

When a new medium arises, the public quickly adopts it.

Source: http://www.nytimes.com/2011/05/03/business/media/03television.html?_r=0, http://www.nielsen.com/us/en/insights/article/2016/nielsen -estimates-118-4-million-tv-homes-in-the-us-for-the-2016-17-tv-season.html, http://tvbythenumbers.zap2it.com/2007/08/28/us-television-households -by-season/273,http://www.tvb.org/media_comparisons/4729/72512, http://www.nielsen.com/content/damcorporate/us/en/newswire/uploads /2009/07/tva_2008_071709.pdf, http://www.tvhistory.tv/Cable_Households_77-99.JPG, http://www.ibtimes.com/forget-cable-cord-cutting-83-percent -american-households-still-pay-tv-2081570, http://www.pewinternet.org/2015/06/26/americans-internet-access-2000-2015, http://www.pewinternet .org/three-technology-revolutions, http://www.pewinternet.org/2015/12/21/home-broadband-2015, https://www.pewresearch.org/internet/fact-sheet /internet-broadband/.

This gap suggests a grim future for the print version of the news as generational replacement unfolds. The decline of newspapers and newspaper readership raises concerns because newspapers tend to contain more **hard news**—fact-based stories, as opposed to interpretive narratives. Alex Jones, who is one of the leading observers of the press, in his book *Losing the News* indicated that 85 percent of hard news comes from newspapers rather than from TV.[57] Will the decline of newspapers deprive Americans of hard news, of the facts they need to hold government accountable?

Some observers counter that readers are simply migrating from printed newspapers to online versions. In January 2004, online newspapers had about 41 million visitors; within the next decade the number had jumped to well over 100 million.[58] Although the move from the printed to online versions may offer some hope about the continued significance of the newspaper industry, it has not solved the industry's financial difficulties. With revenue plummeting, newspapers survive only by cutting staff. The *Boston Globe* no longer sends journalists overseas to report on international events. The *Los Angeles Times* has seen its newsroom decline from 1,200 to 850 reporters.[59] Over the past decade, the number of people who worked as reporters or editors has dropped 37 percent, from 65,440 in 2004 to 41,400 in 2015.[60] Fewer reporters, editors, and other journalists mean that newspapers have less ability to inform and investigate. In 2020, the *Cleveland Plain Dealer* laid off additional reporters, leaving the once highly respected newspaper with just a handful of journalists to cover the region.[61] If the press cannot perform its watchdog role, the people stand to lose the means by which they hold government accountable.[62]

Despite these concerns, Americans want the news and continue to seek it out, so newspaper owners have an incentive to develop new ways to make a profit. In recent years, income has stabilized and better use of digital advertising has improved.[63] The pandemic has also helped newspaper readership, which seems to be on the rise. Over the summer of 2020, daily print and digital readership surpassed 30 million for the first time ever. Updating

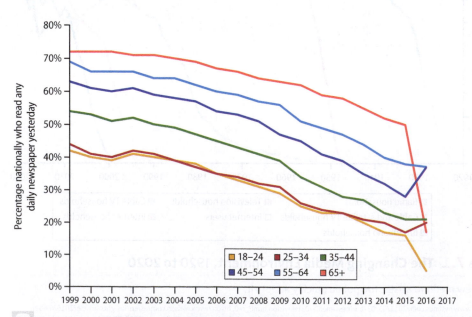

Figure 7.2 Newspaper Readership by Age

Newspaper readership is declining across all ages.

Source: Pew Research Center, *State of the News Media,* accessed May 1, 2018, http://www.journalism.org/media-indicators/newspaper-readership-by-age.

the format of digital newspapers and charging for online subscriptions has been crucial for the industry. The bleeding, in other words, has stopped, and that may be a hopeful sign. But even for those who see a grim future for newspapers (as we currently think of them), it is important to remember that today's leading newspapers, such as the *New York Times,* have been powerful for only about seventy-five years, whereas American democracy has survived for 230 years. The press, in other words, will endure, regardless of form.

The Durability of Radio

In many ways, radio is underappreciated as a medium of communication; current debates center on newspapers, television, and the Internet. But radio remains important, especially considering how often Americans listen to the radio in their cars. The percentage of Americans who listen to the radio has remained unchanged in the past decade. In 1998, 95 percent of the American public tuned into an AM or FM station at least once a week; thirteen years later, 93 percent had listened to the radio in the previous seven days. Radio is expanding its reach by means of satellite radio and streaming audio on desktop and laptop computers. In fact, it is possible that "radio" is becoming "audio," reflecting advances in digital technology (see Figure 7.3).[64] These data underscore the growth in this area, and this trend should continue.

Political talk radio, a medium dominated largely by conservatives, is increasingly popular.[65] In recent years, around 60 million Americans listened to talk radio,[66] most to conservative programs. In fact, as Table 7.1 shows, conservatives dominate the airwaves of talk radio. No "liberal" shows are even close to the popularity of the top-rated conservative commentators. Rush Limbaugh is by far the best known and the most controversial. Liberals at one time tried to make inroads into talk radio with the Air America radio network, but it did not last long. The reasons for this lack of success are unclear. Perhaps it is because there are more conservatives than liberals in the United States. In addition, conservatives tend to live in the suburbs and rural areas and therefore spend more time in their cars than do city dwellers. Their greater opportunities for listening may be another reason for the dominance of conservative programming.[67]

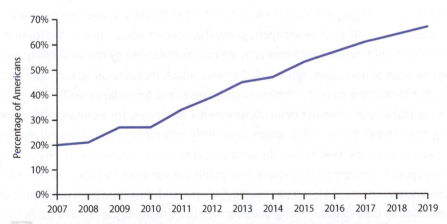

Figure 7.3 Monthly Online Radio Listeners, 2007–2019

The use of online radio is on the rise.

Source: Pew Research Center, "Online Radio Listenership," accessed March 2, 2020, http://www.journalism.org/chart/sotnm-radio-online-radio-listenership/.

Table 7.1 Top Talk Radio Hosts, 2009–2020 (in millions of listeners)

Host	Political Leaning/ General Topic	2009	2012	2016	2020
Rush Limbaugh	Conservative	15.00	14.75	13.25	15.50
Sean Hannity	Conservative	14.00	14.00	12.50	15.00
Dave Ramsey	Financial Advice	8.00	8.25	8.25	14.00
Mark Levin	Conservative	8.50	8.25	7.00	11.00
Michael Savage	Conservative	9.00	8.75	5.25	7.50
Glenn Beck	Conservative	9.00	8.25	7.00	10.50
Jim Bohannon	Ind./Moderate	3.75	3.75	2.75	6.50
Neal Boortz	Libertarian	6.00	5.75	—	—
Laura Ingraham	Conservative	6.00	5.75	2.00	—
Jerry Doyle	Conservative	3.50	3.75	1.25	—

Source: Pew Research Center, *State of the News Media*, accessed May 1, 2018, https://www.pewresearch.org/topics/state-of-the -news-media/; Takers, "Top Talk Audiences," accessed March 2, 2020, http://www.talkers.com/top-talk-audiences/.

The Transformation of TV News

Key Questions

Do you watch cable news? If so, which cable news station do you watch? Do you think the presentation of the news is fair?

Newspapers are not the only news outlets facing a decline in customers; the audience for the TV network evening news is also shrinking (see Figure 7.4). Nearly 25 percent of Americans watched the evening news in 1980; by 2017, only 6 percent watched the major networks' evening news.[68] The downward trend is likely to continue because older Americans make up the current audience for TV news. Young people, who represent the future audience, are not big consumers of network news. In 2018, just 8 percent of Americans aged 18 to 29 consumed network news, while 35 percent of those aged 50 to 64 did and 49 percent of those over 65 got news from network TV.[69] Young people's habits are not likely to change, painting a bleak picture for the industry in the coming years.

This decline, like that of newspapers, generates concern about how well informed the public is about politics. But these concerns are counterbalanced by the availability and uses of other sources of news (see Figure 7.4). TV news, which includes cable, has been on the decline, but look at the trend for "online/mobile" news and for radio as well.

The availability of news has been transformed. Cable news, for example, is not like the evening news shows of the 1970s, which were thirty-minute broadcasts around dinnertime. Cable news is available twenty-four hours a day. Events are covered live, transforming the news cycle. No longer do politicians time public appearances to appear on the evening news. News now comes at viewers at a rapid-fire rate, and cable news networks include interpretation in their constant programming. MSNBC's *Morning Joe* and *The Rachel Maddow Show* are examples. Cable news has taken the interpretive function of the news media to a whole new level in response to the demands of 24-7 news programming. All these kinds of news, and others, can be gathered from handheld devices.

Key Questions

Would you describe the news you seek as hard or soft?

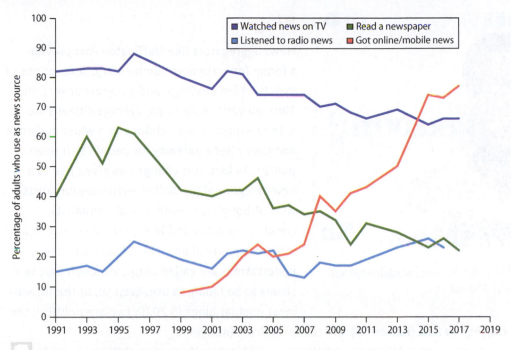

Figure 7.4 Different Sources of News

Americans are getting their news increasingly from digital and online sources.

Source: Reuters Institute for the Study of Journalism, *Overview and Key Findings of the 2019 Report,* accessed February 26, 2020, http://www .digitalnewsreport.org/survey/2019/united-states-2019/.

Infotainment

Television viewers also get political news through talk shows, such as *The Tonight Show starring Jimmy Fallon* and *Jimmy Kimmel Live.* These sources offer what is called "infotainment" or **soft news,** which is news with fewer hard facts of the kind newspapers generally report and more emphasis on personal stories that engage (or shock) the public and often appeal to the emotions rather than the intellect.

For example, about 3 million people, mostly younger Americans, watch the *Late Show with Stephen Colbert,* which delivers the news with humor and satire in the evening.[70] These kinds of shows often ask some tough questions, however, so it is an overstatement to claim that the news such shows provide is "soft." The guests who appear, for example, on *Real Time with Bill Maher* cover the full ideological spectrum, and Maher subjects those in power—regardless of party—to his rapier wit. In 2016, his popularity was challenged by *Last Week Tonight with John Oliver,* which has as many as 4 million viewers.[71]

Though some might look to NBC's *Saturday Night Live* (*SNL*) as a way to learn about political events, this type of parody does not qualify as infotainment. The political sketches performed on SNL are much less focused on portraying fact than they are about poking fun at various politicians or situations. However, the show often touches on actual events in American politics using sketches that mimic debate performances, press conferences, speeches, Senate hearings, and more. Although it is not objective fact, the knowledge that the event took place reaches the average 6 million Americans who view the show each week.[72] This is another way that the American people can absorb news with more attention to humor than factual evidence even if it does not quite qualify as infotainment.

soft news: *News stories focused less on facts and policies than on sensationalizing secondary issues or on less serious subjects of the entertainment world.*

Image 7.6 In the summer of 2020, MSNBC announced that Joy Reid would host a nightly show at 7 PM EST, The ReidOut.

Blogs

News aggregators like *Huffington Post* provide a forum for bottom-up commentary, descriptions of events, video postings, and general conversation. Through various postings, average citizens are able to express their opinions to a wider audience, and they offer a gateway for people to influence politics. In fact, this change has given rise to a new category of journalists—citizen-journalists—who, although not professional journalists, circulate opinions and interpretations that clearly influence political debates. Often times these undertakings are called blogs, although that term seems to be fading in use. Even so, of the fifteen most popular blogs in 2020, two are political: the *Huffington Post* (number 1) and the *Daily Beast* (number 8).[73]

In many ways, blogging symbolizes the modern transformation of the mass media. Blogs capture the interest of people of all ages, and some observers hope that they will provide a forum for more participation and deliberation. While there is some evidence that blogs do foster participation, they do not seem to foster deliberation. Liberals read liberal blogs, and conservatives read conservative blogs—in fact, 94 percent of people read blogs that share their ideological viewpoint. These data suggest that blogs reinforce existing preferences and do not provide opportunities to hear the other side.[74] In addition, blogs usually have clear ideological leanings. Conservative blogs include those of Matt Drudge and Rush Limbaugh.[75] *Daily Kos* and *Huffington Post* are liberal blogs.

Blogs have the potential to spread false information. Because no one checks the accuracy of a posting, individuals—some call them trolls—can say outrageous things merely to get attention without penalty.[76] In contrast, the traditional press has a well-established set of norms for vetting the accuracy of information; when false statements do get through, the journalists are likely to pay a heavy penalty. Trolls, on the other hand, often gain notoriety for lying.

Nevertheless, the importance of blogs continues to increase. Bloggers write about business news, iTechnology, political news, trends in Hollywood, and so on. News that is not picked up in the mainstream media often gets play in the blogosphere and can force the mainstream media to cover the story. Politicians understand the powerful effects blogs can have on the news. In modern presidential campaigns, candidates established blogs on their websites (e.g., tedcruz.org) with commentary on topics ranging from the cost of college tuition to how best to achieve peace in the Middle East.[77] The Trump White House has invited popular conservative blogs to join the daily White House press briefings.

Podcasts

Podcasts, which have some overlap with blogs, are also an increasingly important piece of a changing media landscape. As can be seen in Table 7.2, the percentage of Americans who listen to podcasts has grown incredibly quickly in the last few years. The amount of time spent listening to podcasts has increased 122 percent since 2014. Approximately 144 million

Key Questions
How could you be a citizen-journalist?

Key Questions
Have you ever written a blog post? What inspired you?

Table 7.2   Podcast Listenership, 2013–2019 (in percentage of listeners)

Year	Listened Ever	Listened in Last Month	Listened in Last Week
2013	27%	12%	7%
2015	33%	17%	10%
2017	40%	24%	15%
2019	51%	32%	22%

Source: Pew Research Center, "Audio and Podcasting Fact Sheet," accessed March 10, 2020, https://www.journalism.org/fact-sheet/audio-and-podcasting/.

Americans listened to podcasts in 2019 with many of these listeners in the age range of 12 to 24 years old. Seventy-four percent of listeners said they listen to podcasts to "learn new things" and 60 percent said they use them to "stay up to date with the latest topics." Out of all podcast topics, a great deal focus on politics and news. In 2019, 36 percent of podcast consumers were interested in listening to news on podcasts.[78] Part of this trend of listening to podcasts for news comes from a rise in daily news podcasts. Pods like *The Daily*, *The New York Time*'s daily twenty minute podcast, and NPR's *Up First* are listened to every morning. *The Daily* had around 2 million listeners per day in late 2019.   In April 2020, at the start of the COVID-19 pandemic, podcast listeners decreased. This was most likely due to the change to so many Americans' schedules and lack of commute time to listen. Despite this dip, which rebounded by May, time spent listening to podcasts is steadily growing. By 2022, the average consumer will listen about 36 minutes per day. Podcasts, especially as news sources, attract a younger audience and become part of people's daily routine because of the quick "front page" type format.[79] By delivering news stories in succinct audio, the daily news podcasts give more people the ability to add news into their daily lives.

Social Networking

The Internet has also enabled new social networks for sharing information. Just as personal conversations are important sources of information, social networking websites are increasingly important ways to spread political news. In 2018, approximately two-thirds of American adults got their news from social media.[80] Facebook is, of course, the leading platform for social networking. Its website announces that its mission is "to give people the power to share and make the world more open and connected."[81] And for Millennials, Facebook remains an important source of information.[82] As Figure 7.5 shows, Facebook increased in importance from 2013 to 2020. But as the figure also shows, Twitter has made real inroads, becoming a more common way to stay abreast of breaking news than Facebook. With the recent revelations about Facebook's handling of people's private data, this social media giant may lose additional ground.[83]

Mark Zuckerberg started Facebook from his Harvard dorm room in February 2004 as a social networking service limited to the Harvard campus. By the end of the year, the network had more than 1 million users, and it reached 5.5 million by the end of 2005 when it was extended to all universities and high schools in the United States and Canada. In December 2019, Facebook had more than 2.5 billion users.[84] Facebook is a worldwide phenomenon with launches in more than fifteen different languages.

Key Questions

How important is Facebook as a source of political news or action for you, and is it changing?

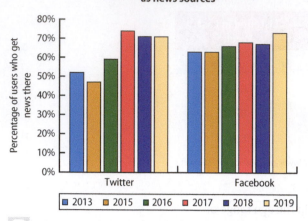

Rising use of Facebook and Twitter as news sources

Figure 7.5 Use of Facebook and Twitter as News Sources

Facebook and Twitter matter in today's political climate, with Twitter showing very steep user gains recently, but perhaps plateauing in 2018.

Source: Pew Research Center, *News Use Across Social Media Platforms 2018*, accessed March 10, 2020, http://www.journalism.org/2018/09/10/news-use-across-social-media-platforms-2018/.

Zuckerberg predicted that Facebook would have 5 billion users by 2030. With worldwide population estimated to be 8.5 billion by then, the Harvard graduate is anticipating usage by 60 percent of all humans.[85] But all these platforms are dynamic and undergoing constant change. Consider the growing use of TikTok, especially among Millennials and Generation Z. Just a few years ago it did not even exist. By the start of 2020, it had more than 800 million users.[86]

Politicians are making increased use of social media to communicate with the public (see also Chapter 12, Congress, for additional examples). Donald Trump took this to a new level during his quest for the presidency in 2016. Nearly all presidential candidates use Twitter, but Trump made it an art form: His tweets often drove the coverage of the campaign and forced candidates to respond to his claims and ideas. In November 2016, Trump enjoyed nearly 13 million followers on Twitter.[87] Every attack or self-promotion claim he made through Twitter drew comment from journalists, activists, competing candidates, and the average voters. In March 2020, President Trump had over 73 million followers on Twitter. Donald Trump's use of Twitter transformed the campaign and the news media's coverage of it. In previous elections, political ads shaped the narrative of the campaign, but Trump drove the narrative during the 2016 presidential election by sending multiple tweets on any given day.

As aforementioned in the vignette on Representative Alexandria Ocasio-Cortez, many politicians, apart from Trump, use Twitter to reach supporters, share ideas, and build their brand. In 2018, Twitter was the most popular social media platform for lawmakers of both parties, followed by Facebook and Instagram. Members of the 115th Congress posted over 500,000 times on their official Twitter, Facebook, Instagram, and YouTube accounts. However, the amount Twitter is used varies by party. In 2018, Democratic lawmakers sent 42 percent more tweets than Republican lawmakers.[88] Politicians in both parties have significant Twitter influence, though some have more than others. For example, Speaker of the House Nancy Pelosi had 4 million followers in early 2020. Senate Majority Leader Mitch McConnell had 1.4 million followers at the same time, which enforces the research that Democratic lawmakers have larger followings and use Twitter more frequently than their Republican counterparts.[89] Instagram is a platform used by lawmakers and candidates as well. They use it to show snapshots of life in Congress or on the campaign trail. It serves as a visual way to reach constituents and supporters whether through videos explaining a position or a photo from a major event or scenes from daily life. Representative Ocasio-Cortez employed Instagram Live in a way that allowed her to connect with Americans very easily and answer their questions. Social media is being used by certain politicians to make what goes on in the lives of lawmakers more transparent to the American public. It has enhanced the ability of Members of Congress to fulfil their representational duties by opening a direct line of communication (see also Chapter 12).[90] That being said, Twitter—like all social media—is susceptible to becoming an echo chamber. Users are much more likely to follow other people with the same political views and politicians from the party they identify with as well. Additionally, political tweeters tend to have more extreme views about their party and the opposing one than the average American.[91] Research has shown that Americans are drawing from smaller and smaller pools of news within their homogenous newsfeeds. Social media algorithms and networks limit exposure to views and information that do not align with someone's already held beliefs, which increases polarization.[92] It is important to recognize these trends when thinking about the use of social media in connection to American politics.

In addition to the increasing significance of Facebook and Twitter in American politics, various other social media platforms are gaining popularity as sources of news, ways for politicians to reach supporters, and ways for engaged citizens to share their own opinions. In 2018, 73 percent of users on Reddit got their news using the site, a higher percentage than got their news from Twitter or Facebook. YouTube, Instagram, LinkedIn, and Snapchat also had a fair percentage of users using the social media site to get news. Interestingly, over half of all social media news users expect the news they consume there to be inaccurate. Despite this, 68 percent of adults still got news from social media sites in 2018.[93]

An aspect of increased use of social media for political purposes is the phenomenon of "slacktivism" or "armchair activism," phrases that describe engaging in activism on social media with little personal effort involved. One example of this is the practice of adding a filter to one's Facebook profile photo declaring support for a cause or candidate.[94] Sharing petitions like 2018's Clemency for Cyntoia Brown or 2020's call not to replace Justice Ginsburg's seat before the election are further examples.[95] Social media users constantly share articles, viral videos, hashtags, and their own opinions. Previously, the majority of Americans stopped there; however, there is a new movement of using social media as a way to organize, which goes beyond posting or retweeting. Movements are beginning to start online and be carried out in real life like the March For Our Lives, which sought to empower young people to curtail senseless gun violence in the country. Throughout the COVID-19 pandemic, protests for racial justice, and the election, many took to social media platforms to share information and concrete ways to get involved in their communities.

Social media has an impact on civic engagement in a variety of ways. Consider that with public reaction to the death of George Floyd, the #BlackLivesMatter hashtag was used nearly 48 million times on Twitter—an average of just under 3.7 million times per day—from May 26 to June 7, 2020.[96] Or consider that in 2019, Greta Thunberg, a teen activist, documented her journey sailing across the Atlantic Ocean on an emission-free boat to help promote global school climate strikes.[97] It seems as if these social media movements are somewhat important for accomplishing political and civic goals. Sixty-nine percent of Americans said using social media sites for activism is important for getting politicians to pay attention to issues, and 67 percent said it was important for creating sustained social change movements in 2018. Notably, black and Hispanic social media users felt these platforms were extremely important tools for their own political engagement and making their voices heard. On the flip side, many Americans feel that social media distracts people from more important issues, and 71 percent agree that social media makes people think they are making a difference when they are not doing so.[98] There are obviously costs and benefits to social media activism; however, it is strong in 2020 and does not seem to be dying down any time soon.

It is crucial to examine social media's role in political campaigns as well. Aside from politicians growing their support base and popularity with a skillful use of social media, the sites serve as another space for advertisements to be disseminated. Social media started playing a larger role in campaigning in 2016 and has increased greatly from there. Many Americans started turning to social media for election news and information. In July 2016, 34 percent of American adults said they went to Clinton and Trump's social media posts for updates, while only 15 percent went to the candidates' websites or e-mails. A significant 44 percent of U.S. adults reported learning about the 2016 presidential election from social media.[99] In 2016, Clinton and Trump spent over $81 million on Facebook advertisements alone. However, in addition to paid ads from the candidates on Facebook, the lack of policy regarding social media ads led to mysterious ads popping up on American newsfeeds. Because social media is exempt from FEC disclosure laws requiring political ads to state who is paying for them, Facebook served as the perfect platform for Russia to anonymously place ads that influenced the outcome of the 2016 presidential election.[100]

As a response to what took place in 2016, a bipartisan bill, the Honest Ads Act, was proposed in October 2017 to help solve the issue of unclaimed social media ads and outdated laws. This purpose of this act is to "enhance transparency and accountability for online political advertisements by requiring those who purchase and publish such ads to disclose information about the advertisements to the public."[101] Despite being supported by a broad coalition of government reform organizations, experts, and elected officials in both parties, the Honest Ads Act had still not been passed in March 2020.[102] However, since the bill was first introduced, some tech companies have started to self-regulate. Facebook, Twitter, and Google have all introduced political ad archives and created their own policies for dealing with political ads overall.[103]

microtargeting: *A marketing technique that employs user data to identify interests of specific individuals or groups and inform advertisers what message is most effective for those users. Used by politicians in campaigning to target ads to certain groups.*

Twitter made the decision to ban all political advertising, including **microtargeting**, in late 2019. It drew criticism for this choice because many say it infringes on freedom of expression and favors incumbents and candidates with more money. Microtargeted digital advertisements help candidates with less money communicate their message to specific audiences, allowing them to make the most of limited financial resources with effective social media advertising. For example, microtargeted digital ads helped Obama earn recognition and support in 2008 and helped "The Squad," Alexandria Ocasio-Cortez, Rashida Tlaib (D-MI), Ayanna Pressley (D-MA), and Ilhan Omar (D-MN), win seats in the House in 2018.[104] Less extremely, Google made the decision to limit microtargeting in political ads instead of outrightly banning political ads as Twitter did. Facebook has approached political ads very differently. The site supported the Honest Ads Act; however, it said it would not fact-check content posted by politicians.[105] The platform cited its "fundamental belief in free expression" and "respect for the democratic process" in explaining why it will not fact-check political ads.[106] Each of these major sites have faced backlash for their policies in response to foreign influences using social media to impact the 2016 election. It seems as if uniform regulation for social media sites would be helpful in preventing individualized policies that can be hard to enforce and potentially harmful to the democratic process in the United States.

The use of social media in the 2020 Democratic primary was a complete escalation of the trend of candidates using social media daily. While Facebook and Twitter continued to be popular platforms for political ads and interaction, the 2020 candidates used many more sites. Senator Bernie Sanders held "Ask Me Anything" question and answer sessions on Reddit. Senator Elizabeth Warren shared videos on Instagram of her calls to donors to inspire more contributions. Mayor Pete Buttigieg and his husband used social media accounts to shape his image and spread his name because he was relatively unknown before his campaign. Political outsider Andrew Yang built a strong social media base that called themselves the "Yang Gang" and Senator Kamala Harris' supporters named themselves the "KHive." Social media provides a forum for supporters from across the nation to come together and share information and ideas about campaigns. It allowed Democratic candidates to reach those who may not otherwise be involved and to reach out to the ever-growing base of young Democrats.[107] Two candidates, in specific, tapped into this base in a different way than the rest of the candidates. Billionaires Tom Steyer and Michael Bloomberg spent hundreds of millions of dollars on digital advertisements for their campaigns. By mid-January, Tom Steyer had spent approximately $23.2 million on digital ads all over social media. He spent $1.8 million on digital ads in Iowa ahead of the caucuses and $1.5 million in New Hampshire. Although he spent greatly, Steyer suspended his campaign after the New Hampshire primary because he did not have enough support.[108] There was a point in early February, leading up to Super Tuesday, when Bloomberg was spending about $1 million per day on Facebook ads alone. Bloomberg's social media campaign was unlike any other candidate's strategy. In his short three-month campaign, he outspent every other Democratic nominee using different strategies for each platform that were proven to be effective in going viral. This included paying popular meme accounts and influencers on Instagram to post promoting Bloomberg and tweeting strange things that made users wonder if he had been hacked. This very specific social media usage met Millennials and Gen Z where they were and attracted a lot of attention.[109] That being said, despite spending a total of over $500 million on his campaign, Bloomberg still dropped out of the Democratic primary after Super Tuesday when former Vice President Joe Biden won a majority of the states.[110] The huge ad buys from both Steyer and Bloomberg increased their name recognition and won them some support, proving the influence money can have in politics. However, neither candidate got the support necessary to keep running a presidential campaign by spending far more money on ads than the other candidates. This begs the question of analyzing money and advertisements versus experience and party support in campaigns.

Key Questions

Do you think that social media political advertisement policy should be regulated by the government or by each site or application?

Key Questions

Do you think money and ads can buy an election? If so, what are the negatives of this? If not, why?

Political Analytics

Media Bias

There are obstacles for Americans who want to be informed about politics. The rise of news and information that is fabricated (i.e., fake news) and circulated on social media and other outlets has made the task of

Overall Quality	Most Extreme Liberal	Hyper-Partisan Liberal	Skews Liberal	Neutral Minimal partisan bias OR Balance of biases	Skews Conservative	Hyper-Partisan Conservative	Most Extreme Conservative
Original Fact Reporting				AP, Reuters, Bloomberg, ABC News, CBS News			
Fact Reporting			Politico	Washington Post, New York Times / PBS, NPR, USA Today	The Wall Street Journal, TIME / THE HILL		
Complex Analysis			The New Yorker, The Nation		National Review, The Fiscal Times		
Analysis		Daily Beast	Vanity Fair		Weekly Standard	reason.com	
Opinion; Fair Persuasion		MSNBC, Mother Jones				The American Conservative, The Washington Times	
Selective or Incomplete Story; Unfair Persuasion		Daily Kos, New Republic, and Huffington Post				The Federalist, OAN	
Propaganda/ Contains Misleading Info		Forward Progressives				Daily Caller	
Contains Inaccurate/ Fabricated Info	Occupy Democrats						INFOWARS

Liberal ← Partisan Bias → Conservative

Figure 7.6 Media Bias Chart

Source: ad fontes media, The Media Bias Chart, https://www.adfontesmedia.com/wp-content/uploads/2018/01/Media-Bias-Chart_Version-3.1_Watermark-min.jpg.

obtaining accurate information daunting. Moreover, as the discussion about trust in the media in Figure 7.8 shows, many Americans do not trust the news, and some of that mistrust is due to concerns of media bias.

Figure 7.6 arrays a variety of news organizations along two dimensions: ideology and overall quality. The graphic shows well-known and more obscure news outlets. At the bottom of the graph are conservative and liberal news outlets that are evaluated to contain fabricated and/or inaccurate information. The top of the figure shows outlets deemed to produce higher quality news. Along the right side of the figure are news organization considered to be conservative in their leanings with liberal sources on the left side of the graphic.

One of the takeaways from the graphic is that ideological leanings are not incompatible with fact reporting and complex analysis. *The Wall Street Journal* and the *New York Times* both receive high marks for the quality of their news. Examine the graphic for the variety of news sources presented and evaluated.

Thinking Critically

1. There are a handful of sources that are both politically balanced and present high-quality news. What do you think contributes to their ability to satisfy what many Americans are looking for in their news? Do you think there are consumers of information who are not concerned with accuracy and unbiased information?

2. How would you check the accuracy of the graphic and the evaluation of the news sources?

The News Media and Latinos

Latinos, as the fastest-growing ethnic group in the United States, are also prompting change in the media environment. One recent trend in the dissemination and consumption of news is the increase in viewership for the two major Spanish language networks, Univision and Telemundo.[111] The two networks reach over 5 million Spanish-speaking viewers in more than forty markets in the United States. To compete, other outlets are reaching out to Latino audiences. The growth in Spanish-language television now includes, for example, MundoFox, CNN Latino, and Fusion, a twenty-four-hour cable news channel that broadcasts content in English that is directed at English-speaking Latino Millennials.

Fusion, a joint venture between ABC News and Noticias Univision, reflects that many Latinos continue to rely on both English and Spanish sources of news. Public broadcasting also has responded to the growing number of Latino viewers who consume news in English and Spanish. In Arizona, for example, PBS produces the public affairs program *Horizonte,* an English-language public affairs program about political issues of interest to Latinos.

Of course, the news media's attention to politics is heightened during presidential campaigns. During the 2016 presidential campaign, Donald Trump and Jorge Ramos, the most influential Latino anchorman (Univision), had a heated exchange during a 2015 news conference. Trump had Ramos escorted out of the room, only to be let back in ten minutes later. This incident drew wide attention and underscored not only Trump's testy relationship with the press but also the reach of Univision. Presidential candidates cannot ignore that network or the audience it reaches.

In 2016, Univision announced an effort to register more Latino voters, which reflects its commitment to empowering this voting bloc. In the Romney–Obama battle in 2012, 11 million Latinos voted, and Univision was hoping to register many new voters for the 2016 election. Those efforts paid off in that over 13 million Latinos voted in 2016, with two of three voting for Hillary Clinton.[112] In 2018, Latinos made up 11 percent of all voters nationwide. One fourth cast a midterm ballot for the first time in 2018 with 69 percent voting for Democrats. Latino voter registration reached a new high in Florida—over 2.2 million Latinos registered between the 2016 and 2018 elections. Nine U.S. House districts where Latinos made up at least 10 percent of the voting population switched parties from Republican and Democratic in the midterms as well.[113] This led to a record number of Latinos being elected to the 116th Congress with thirty-eight Latinos in the House and four in the Senate.[114] These numbers have kept rising and can further stimulate participation. A record 32 million Latinos are projected to be eligible to vote in the 2020 general election, and as of March 2020, 68 percent of registered Latino voters disapproved of President Trump.[115] These changing demographics will continue to shape American politics in 2020 and beyond.

The News Media and Millennials

The changes in the media environment do not affect all citizens equally, as suggested by Figure 7.7. The Millennial generation, for example, is more than three times more likely to get its news from BuzzFeed than are Baby Boomers. Google News is much more heavily used by Millennials than either Generation Xers or baby boomers. By contrast, PBS's audience draws far more heavily from baby boomers than Millennials.

When younger Americans read a newspaper or listen to a radio program, they do so for a much shorter period of time than do those who are older than 50. The youth seem to do more channel surfing, while older Americans are more likely to sit down and watch an entire news program. These habits may reflect differences in lifestyles between, for example, college students and adults with full-time jobs and families.[116] It could also reveal enduring differences between the generations.

Conventional wisdom has always said that young people are less interested in politics than older Americans are, but Millennials appear to be more interested in politics at this point in their lives than were previous generations. This interest is not gauged by whether they watch the evening news or read newspapers, but by the ways they use new media to share information and learn about and express interest in politics.[117] Young adults tend to reject the top-down approach to learning about politics in which the news is filtered by professional journalists and trusted news anchors such as Cronkite. Instead, they seem much more interested in the bottom-up approach made possible by the wide-open availability of new media for citizen participation.

These changes are going to become more important over time as more Millennials become eligible to vote and older

Consumption of News Sources

YouTube, Yahoo News, Washington Post, Wall Street Journal, USA Today, Twitter, Think Progress, The Blaze, Slate, Sean Hannity Show, Rush Limbaugh Show, Politico, PBS, New Yorker, New York Times, NPR, NBC News, Mother Jones, MSNBC, Local TV News, LinkedIn, Huffington Post, Guardian, Google Plus, Google News, Glenn Beck Program, Fox News, Facebook, Ed Schultz Show, Economist, Drudge Report, Daily Show, Daily Kos, Colbert Report, CNN, CBS News, BuzzFeed, Breitbart, Bloomberg, BBC, Al Jazeera America, ABC News

X-axis: Percentage who use as news sources (0, 0.5, 1, 1.5, 2)

Legend: Millennial, Generation X, Baby boomer

Figure 7.7 Main Sources of News by Age

Millennials tend to get their news from different sources than do older citizens.

Source: Pew Research Center, "Political Media Habits Across Millennials, Gen Xers and Baby Boomers," accessed May 1, 2018, https://www.journalism.org/interactives/generational-media-habits/.

generations pass on. Technological change continues to spread, making the Internet and all of its information increasingly available to more Americans. The United States is in the midst of a major transformation in the media environment, and observers are only beginning to understand the changes in how Americans transmit and consume the news.

One of the new ways that Millennials and other voters become aware of political information is through viral videos. In Texas, for example, Mary Jennings Hegar released an ad that went viral for its raw honesty, talking about her family, military service, and abusive father. It was called "Doors." She gained much notoriety but lost in a close congressional election. In fact, she ran again, this time for Senate, in 2020, Hegar lost to incumbent John Cornyn by 10 points; however, Texas Democrats turned out in record numbers.

Image 7.7 Senator Joni Ernst faced a tough reelection battle in 2020. She defended her seat against Democrat Theresa Greenfield, winning 51.8 percent of the vote.

Key Questions
Which do you trust more—bottom-up or top-down journalism?

The Impact of the News Media on the Public

LO 7-5 Assess how the news media affect public opinion

The press provides information, investigation, and interpretation of the news. The news media, both old and new, make decisions about what to cover, what not to cover, and how to cover it. How does the public respond to this information? This section looks at several models ranging between two extremes: that the mass media have no effect on the public and that the mass media dominate the public's thinking.

The Propaganda Model

Few people believe that the media have no influence on citizens. To hold such a view, one must either believe that the public ignores the media or that citizens learn about politics by observing the events themselves. Neither is true, so we can confidently label this the "naïve model" and dismiss it.

The polar opposite has been called the **propaganda model**. This approach is exemplified by the Nazi dictatorship in Germany in the 1930s and 1940s. The Nazi Party controlled the content of newspapers and radio. It dictated the information available to citizens, affecting the direction and shape of public opinion. Through controlled programming, the German people often heard about the greatness of Adolf Hitler and the dangers of racial impurity.

Key Questions
What is the future of political communication?

propaganda model:
Extreme view of the media's role in society, arguing that the press serves the interest of the government only, driving what the public thinks about important issues.

By holding a monopoly on information, the government could easily marshal public support. This is a dangerous model, and it is also inconsistent with how the press works in open societies. In the United States, media sources control programming, and they compete for audience share; the government does not control the flow of information. In fact, since the Freedom of Information Act (FOIA) was passed in 1967, the federal agency has provided the American public with the right to request access to federal records. Federal agencies are required to disclose any information requested unless it falls under an exemption, like classified documents or trade secrets or privileged communications. That being said, the government often denies FOIA requests in the name of national security.[118] In 2008, the government withheld or gave censored information in 58 percent of FOIA requests, while in 2017, the government did this with 78 percent.[119] So although the United States does not control the news media, it is still able to decide if specific federal agency information is released to the public.

The Minimal Effects Model

minimal effects model:
View of the media's impact as marginal because most people seek news reports to reinforce beliefs already held rather than to develop new ones.

Toward the end of World War II, having seen the powerful effects of propaganda in Nazi Germany, scholars in the United States began to study public opinion and the influence of the media on it. Paul Lazarsfeld and others examined the media's influence on voting in the 1940 presidential election. The results were surprising: The researchers discovered that people had made up their minds before the campaign, and new information altered only a handful of people's choices.[120] Lazarsfeld's study gave rise to what has been called the **minimal effects model**. Lazarsfeld and his colleagues contended that the news media had only marginal influence on the public's thinking about politics. The public did not have much information about politics, and attitudes were shaped by long-standing forces such as partisanship or the neighborhood in which people lived.

selective exposure:
Process whereby people secure information from sources that agree with them, thus reinforcing their beliefs.

selective perception:
Process whereby partisans interpret the same information differently.

According to this model, in a process described as **selective exposure**, people secured information from sources that agreed with them, leading to the reinforcement of beliefs, not to a change of beliefs. The minimal effects model was also based on a complementary process called **selective perception**—a concept developed in a study of the American voter published by Angus Campbell and three coauthors in 1960.[121] Selective perception describes partisans as interpreting the same information differently. In other words, partisanship involves a perceptual lens (see Chapter 6, Public Opinion) that shapes how outside events are viewed. So, for example, in May 2014, 79 percent of Democrats supported President Obama's health care reform legislation, passed in 2010, whereas only 8 percent of Republicans did.[122]

Key Questions

What are your sources for the news? Do you select sources that agree with your views or that challenge your views?

The Not-So-Minimal Effects Model

not-so-minimal effects model: *View of the media's impact as substantial, occurring by agenda setting, framing, and priming.*

In the 1970s, scholars started to gather better data that could more effectively test for the impact of the news media. This next generation of research produced the **not-so-minimal effects model**. While not overstating the power of the news media, the model acknowledges that the coverage of politics by the press matters in subtle and important ways. In particular, there are three kinds of media effects: agenda setting, priming, and framing.

Agenda Setting. By stressing certain issues, the media influence what the American public views as the most pressing concerns. This effect is called **agenda setting**. Given that on any particular day there are literally hundreds of stories that could be reported, journalists' decisions about which stories to cover (and which story to lead with, and which to bury inside the paper or at the end of a newscast) matter considerably. Politicians and their advisers make a huge effort to convince the media to cover some stories and ignore others. Should the news lead with a story about the protests that continued after the Parkland shootings or perhaps the scandals that faced the former EPA head, Scott Pruitt? As one scholar explains, the media "may not be successful most of the time telling people what to think, but it is stunningly successful in telling its readers what to think about."[123] The evidence is compelling. If the media talk about crime, the public starts to care about it. If the press starts paying additional attention to the federal budget deficit, the issue becomes more salient to citizens. Since only about 1 percent of news coverage is dedicated to the topic of education, it is not surprising that education policy rarely rises to the top of politicians' agendas.[124]

agenda setting: *Ability of the media to affect the way people view issues, people, or events by controlling which stories are shown and which are not.*

Priming. An extension of agenda setting is **priming**. Emphasis by the media can alter the criteria that citizens use when evaluating political leaders. Following 9/11, for instance, the news media's coverage of terrorism was the most powerful force shaping President Bush's popularity.[125] The public gave Bush credit for dealing effectively with these tragic events. So when terrorism was the focus of the media, Bush's approval rating was high. But late in Bush's second term, when the primary topic covered by the media shifted to the economy, the public was less supportive of the president.

priming: *Process whereby the media influence the criteria the public uses to make decisions.*

© Randy Glasbergen
www.glasbergen.com

"Today in school we learned about the three main branches of government: lobbyists, fund-raisers and media."

Image 7.8 Many think the media have more power than the president or Congress.

Priming can also affect how people vote. In the 2016 campaign, Republicans wanted the public to focus on stagnant wages and terrorism, while the Democrats sought to focus on gains in the economy and Donald Trump's harsh rhetoric. The election was decided by a razor-thin margin, with Trump effectively tapping into the anger the public had with politics as usual.

Key Questions

Have the news media changed your mind about a political issue or figure? If so, how?

Framing. **Framing** is the ability of the media to alter the public's view on an issue by presenting it in a particular way. If the battles waged in Afghanistan are framed as an issue of fighting terrorism, the public thinks about the war in a much more favorable light than

framing: *Ability of the media to influence public perception of issues by constructing the issue or discussion of a subject in a certain way.*

if these conflicts are framed by the casualties incurred. Framing can have a very powerful effect, actually changing public opinion on an issue.

Perhaps the most famous example of framing comes from the work of Amos Tversky and Daniel Kahneman.[126] These scholars showed in a powerful way that one could produce very different policy solutions based solely on how the options were presented. In other words, "spin" or "framing" matters. Tversky and Kahneman told research subjects that the United States was preparing for the outbreak of an unusual disease, which was expected to kill six hundred people. The research subjects were asked how to combat it. Two comparable groups of research subjects were given different policy options to compare.

The first group was told that if program A were adopted, two hundred people would be saved; if program B were adopted, there was a one-third probability that six hundred people would be saved and a two-thirds probability that no one would be saved. Of those surveyed, 72 percent favored program A and 28 percent favored program B. It appears that citizens favor the sure thing of saving two hundred people and not taking the chances represented by program B. Such a strong result suggests that the government, if responsive to public opinion, should adopt program A.

The second group of research subjects were also given a choice between two policy options. If program C were adopted, four hundred people would die. If program D were adopted, there was a one-third probability that nobody would die and a two-thirds probability that six hundred people would die. Here, 22 percent of the subjects favored program C and 78 percent favored program D. These results suggest that the public does not respond favorably to the idea that four hundred people will die, leading them to favor option D.

Yet compare closely program C to A. While there is a 50-percentage-point difference in the number of people willing to support program A versus program C, the programs actually yield the exact same policy outcome: Two hundred people live, and four hundred people die. The *only* difference is that the description of program A stressed saving people, while the description of program C stressed the deaths of people. This experiment underscores the power of framing—that the public reacts to a news event or a policy depending on how it is presented. These data offer a powerful statement about the potential impact of the press, and how they cover events can shape our thinking about them.

Key Questions

What issues are the media putting on the political agenda right now? What issues do you think should be on the political agenda?

Evaluating the News Media

LO 7-6 Evaluate the news media

Key Questions

Do you trust the news media? What source, if any, gets it right?

"The American Press is in crisis," wrote Lance Bennett and his colleagues in their book *When the Press Fails*.[127] Concerns about the modern news media are widespread.[128]

Worries about the news media often center on two general concerns. One is that the media are biased and do not present objective information. The second, which is related, focuses on the general quality of information available to the public. The emphasis on soft news, for example, worries observers who do not think the public has enough exposure to more substantive hard news. Without enough hard news, these observers fear, the public will not be well enough informed to hold elected officials accountable.

Whether these concerns are valid or not (we examine them later), it is clear that the public's faith in the press has declined (see Figure 7.8). Just in the last twenty-five years the share of Americans who had confidence in the press has dropped by half. As of 2017, only about one in five Americans had faith in journalists.[129] In September 2019, when asked how much trust and confidence Americans had in mass media reporting the news fully, accurately, and fairly, 30 percent said they did not have much trust and 28 percent had none at all. This means the majority of Americans do not have confidence in the press at this point in time.[130] The COVID-19 crisis did little to solve this problem. According to data from May 2020, Americans trusted journalists (42 percent) less than in Vietnam (89 percent) and China (55 percent).[131]

Are there reasons to worry about the media? Are the mass media of the twenty-first century less able to fulfill their watchdog role? This section looks at media bias, the quality of information, and the implications of the Internet and media choice.

Are the Media Biased?

The press claims to be objective, and professional journalists subscribe to an ethic of neutrality. Yet, given that even the selection of stories covered influences public opinion, bias may be inevitable. Nevertheless, it need not be evil or ideological. David Broder, one of the leading journalists of his time, attributed bias to the speed with which journalists have to act. "The process of selecting what the reader reads involves not just objective facts but subjective judgments, personal values, and, yes, prejudices," he confesses. Broder points out that:

> the newspaper that drops on your doorstep is a partial, hasty, incomplete, inevitably somewhat flawed and inaccurate rendering of some of the things we have heard about in the past 24 hours—distorted, despite our best efforts to eliminate bias, by the very process of compression that makes it possible for you to lift it from the doorstep and read it in about an hour.[132]

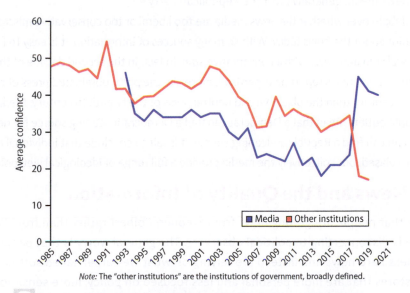

Note: The "other institutions" are the institutions of government, broadly defined.

Figure 7.8 Public Confidence in the Press, 1985–2020

The public's confidence in the press continues to decline.

Sources: Jonathan M. Ladd, *Why Americans Hate the Media and Why It Matters* (Princeton, N.J.: Princeton University Press, 2012). Reprinted by permission of Princeton University Press; updated data provided by Johnathan M. Ladd. https://news.gallup.com/poll/321116/americans-remain-distrustful-mass-media.aspx.

With the rise of the 24-7 news cycle, bias in selecting what to cover becomes even more evident. A common claim of "media bias" comes from politicians themselves. A good example comes from the feud between Fox News's Megyn Kelly and then Republican nominee Donald Trump. Trump claimed in 2015 that Kelly was biased and unfair in her treatment of him, asking him, for example, about his statements about women as "fat pigs." She pressed him on this matter, and Trump fought back. Yet she stood her ground, leading him to ramp up the rhetoric through Twitter and other platforms and to skip a Fox News–sponsored debate prior to the Iowa caucuses. Kelly tried to calm things down, telling ABC's George Stephanopoulos, "It was bizarre because I became the story. He was so very focused on me that I became the story and, you know, you never want to be the story when you're a news person."[133] This battle underscores the power of the media and how politicians often react negatively to criticism. Even so, the Trump–Kelly feud is unusual, but we may be entering a new era of relations between the press and politicians with President Trump now in office.

Key Questions

Do you think the media have an ideological slant? If so, what does it look like?

A broader point is that, for many years, conservative commentators have claimed that the news media are liberal. Accuracy in Media (www.aim.org), a conservative watchdog organization, contends that more than 80 percent of mainstream journalists support the Democratic Party. Such partisan loyalties, according to critics, drive the liberal bias.[134] Yet the people who own the most major media outlets—such as Rupert Murdoch, whose media properties include the *Wall Street Journal* and Fox News—are conservative. Should one assume that because most news outlets are owned by conservatives, the media are really conservative? It is far from clear whether the media are liberal or conservative.

Key Questions

Does the potential bias of a news source affect the chances of you listening or viewing it? How can you evaluate it?

Yet complaints about a liberal press seem to resonate with the public. Gallup Poll data measuring the public's belief about ideological bias in the news media indicate that about half the public believes the news media have a liberal bias and perceive a liberal tilt to the press's coverage of politics. The proportion has been quite stable. About 64 percent of the public thinks that the news media generally favor the Democratic Party, while only 22 percent think that the news media generally favor the Republican Party.[135]

The debate over whether the news media are too liberal or too conservative misses the central point about the news today. With so many sources of information, it is easy to find news with a liberal spin and news with a conservative spin. In fact, in the second decade of the twenty-first century, much news reporting is partisan, more like the party-dominated press of the nineteenth century than the objective and neutral press of the twentieth century. Media choice and multiple outlets mean that a Democrat can find a Democratic-leaning source for news and a Republican can find a Republican-leaning source. It is fair to conclude that individual news outlets are biased, but collectively the media provide a full range of ideological viewpoints.

Fake News and the Quality of Information

The idea that people are getting news from Stephen Colbert rather than from Walter Cronkite is disconcerting to political observers. The general worry is that people are getting less hard news and instead are relying on what we earlier called soft news—feature stores that are more personal and less focused on policy, more sensationalized and less objective, than the political facts of hard news.[136] News about crime or natural disasters can fit the soft news category when the focus is about the drama surrounding the event (such as loss of life or homes) rather than a discussion of public policy that could reduce crime or perhaps provide a quicker government response to disasters.[137]

Part of this underlying concern is the emphasis on image as opposed to substance. The assumption here is that visuals (television and Internet news, in contrast to print news) appeal to the emotions more than to the intellect, so visual news formats are in themselves less "hard" and more superficial. It is true that visual images convey impressions that go beyond the facts, but that does not mean that such information is not valuable. In the 1950s, for example, televised congressional hearings gave the public a chance to see Senator Joseph McCarthy in action and undid his credibility (see Chapter 4). While newspapers had covered the excesses of his charges about Communist infiltration of the government, his actions on camera were much more harmful to his reputation.[138] There is a great deal to be learned from images.

All forms of communication shape how information is shared and digested. Radio, for example, puts a premium on the quality of people's voices. Franklin D. Roosevelt probably made the most famous use of radio with his compelling and reassuring voice. He was the first president to use radio to communicate directly with the people, broadcasting what he called "fireside chats" from the White House in which he explained what he was doing to end the Great Depression.[139] Other politicians with less appealing voices would not have been able to put radio to such good use. Consider politics before the invention of the microphone. Who were the most effective politicians? Perhaps it was individuals with deep voices that could project to a large audience. A soft-spoken politician would have been at a real disadvantage.

It is also important to realize that images did not begin with the advent of television. Although it may be easier to engage in "image" politics in an era of video, politicians have always wanted to convey a favorable image and have done so using the media of their time. Abraham Lincoln sought to project himself as the self-made man that he was, so his 1860 campaign distributed pictures depicting him working with his hands as a rail-splitter.[140] Andrew Jackson (1829–37) built a successful run to the White House in part on his reputation as a tough military leader. Image has always been important to politicians.

In the same way, so-called sound bites—very brief snippets of information—did not begin with the advent of television. Many observers fear that by stressing short catchy statements rather than more detailed substantive statements, sound bites undermine the quality of information. Campaigns, however, have always made effective use of simple slogans. In 1900, for example, President William McKinley (1897–1901) sought reelection with the slogan "A full dinner pail," reminding voters about the economic prosperity they enjoyed during his first term.[141]

Bettmann/Corbis

Image 7.9 During the Great Depression, President Franklin D. Roosevelt used radio to speak directly to the American people. His first fireside chat was broadcast on March 12, 1933, a week after he took office. Addressing the banking crisis, he explained government's response in clear terms: "We have provided the machinery to restore our financial system," he said, "and it is up to you to support and make it work.... Together we cannot fail."

The Granger Collection, NYC

Image 7.10 During the presidential campaign of 1860, Republican candidate Abraham Lincoln sought to portray himself as a common man with a humble background who understood the needs of the people. To develop this image, Lincoln's campaign stressed that as a young man he split rails to build a fence around his home. The image became part of campaign lore.

fake news: *Fabricated news that has no basis in evidence and is often designed to mimic traditional news sources, but is not factually accurate.*

The purpose of this discussion is to urge caution in making hasty judgments about differences in the kinds of information available via the news media over the past two centuries. Soft news may be more informative than hard news because people find it easier to understand and more enjoyable. It is important, therefore, not to let the definition of what counts as news shape judgment of the press. Despite recent changes in the mass media, evidence suggests that Americans have as much information about politics as they did before the arrival of the Internet and the 24-7 news cycle. According the Pew Research Center for the People & the Press, "the coaxial and digital revolutions and attendant changes in the news audience behaviors have had *little* impact on how much Americans know about national and international affairs."[142] Americans do not appear less informed; they simply secure information in new ways.

The rise of **fake news** is another important development. President Trump's frequent references to fake news has fueled its rise. Journalistic misinformation, however, is not new. It has existed in some form since news began to circulate widely, nearly 600 years ago. What is new, though, is the emergence and growth of social media, which has allowed for fake news sources and stories to be disseminated quickly and efficiently to a significant number of individuals. On Twitter, false news stories are 70 percent more likely to be retweeted than true stories. Some spread fake news on purpose, while others unknowingly share unverified stories. Regardless of the motive, true stories take six times as long to reach 1,500 people as false stories take to reach that number.[143] The statistics for false political news are even more staggering. In 2017, fake political news traveled more broadly and deeper than any other category of false information. It reached 20,000 people three times faster than all other types of fake news reached 10,000 people.[144] Unfortunately, fake news travels extremely quickly and widely on all forms of social media and, despite efforts by social media sites, is continuing.

Americans' deeply entrenched partisan bias against the opposing party has also fueled the rise of fake news, as partisans are more and more inclined to believe stories, real or fake, that reinforce their partisan beliefs. Rather than figuring out whether stories are real, Americans rely on these partisan cues and trust stories that denigrate the opposing candidate and support their candidate regardless of the actual validity of the content. For example, Trump's tensions with the national news media from his constant attacks and criticism have led Trump supporters to trust the media less. There is a strong link between the public's approval of Trump and views of the news media. Thirty percent of Republicans and Republican-leaning Independents believe journalists have "very low ethical standards." However, only 5 percent of Democrats and Democratic-leaners agree.[145] This shows that Americans truly look to partisan cues when examining media and news stories.

The rise of social media has also provided foreign governments an easy and efficient channel to try to influence elections through the promulgation of fake news. There was much discussion about possible Russian influence on the 2018 midterm elections, but no tangible evidence of such interference. That stands in contrast to continuing speculation about Russia's role in 2016 when it used tactics such as social media bots and placing advertisements to spread false and inaccurate news. Leading up to the 2016 general election, Russia bought over 3,500 political ads on Facebook that reached over 126 million Americans.[146]

What makes fake news in the age of social media particularly worrisome is that people often believe the content of fake news stories. Studies have shown that people have a hard time determining whether news is fake or not. In a postelection survey of American adults, respondents believed fake news stories to be true about 75 percent of the time and a significant portion of the surveyed population remembered these stories and found them to be credible. In another study, about half of those surveyed believed fake news stories to be true.

The regulation of fake news, however, walks a fine line and can lead to general media censorship. Furthermore, the regulation of news sources and social media platforms can limit freedom of speech and of the press. Despite this, the news industry and tech companies can play an active role in calling out and delegitimizing fake news. Namely, these institutions can rely on fact-checkers to decide whether stories are fake news and label them as such. One of the best ways to decrease the effect of fake news is to increase the availability of news literacy programs to the population so the public can more easily discern for themselves what is fake and what is not. Various tech companies have created information literacy programs in an attempt to combat the spread of fake news. Facebook created a "Digital Literacy Library" with a range of resources from the Berkman Klein Center for Internet and Society at Harvard in 2018. The library includes lessons and activities for numerous aspects of digital literacy.[147] In 2019, Twitter partnered with UNESCO to launch a handbook called "Teaching and Learning with Twitter" to help educators teach students media literacy skills.[148]

Implications of the Internet

There is evidence that the Internet and social media have not changed the overall amount of information the public possesses, but it is important to acknowledge that new media are not equally available to all Americans. In 2016, 64 percent of low-income Americans had a smart phone versus 84 percent of high-income Americans. Age is an even bigger divide: Ninety-two percent of those younger than 35 had a smart phone versus 65 percent of those older than 35, and this divide only grows for the 65-and-up group.[149] A similar pattern exists in regard to Internet access. In 2015, 84 percent of Americans overall used the web versus 60 percent of senior citizens. Income differences exist as well.[150] But these patterns are changing as access to smart phones and the Internet spreads, which will help bridge the digital divide.[151]

These data suggest a further inequality—that those with Internet access may be much better informed than the public generally just twenty years ago, whereas those without access may be even less informed. Variations among groups buried in discussions of the public as a whole are significant, but these variations will likely decrease as more people secure access to the Internet. Figure 7.1, which shows the many options people have for information, suggests that Americans will move toward universal access. There will always be a gap between the well informed and the poorly informed, but in time, the Internet will give older and less wealthy Americans a better chance to become more informed about politics than they currently are.

Key Questions
What kinds of news do you seek? What should the American people seek?

The Era of Media Choice

Perhaps the best word to describe today's media environment is *choice*.[152] The spread of cable television, the Internet, and satellite radio means that people have many possible sources for political information, as well as a huge array of entertainment programming that may lead them to opt out of political news altogether. In the mid-twentieth century, when the network evening news was the source of information, viewers had fewer choices and less opportunity to opt out. They might change channels at dinnertime, but they would get similar news from a different network. The evening news was the only show available during the dinner hour. The lack of choice may have given people more exposure to politics than they wanted.[153]

Key Questions
What are the consequences of media choice?

The Role of the Media

The 2016 presidential election was historic and path breaking. The upset that denied Hillary Clinton the presidency and gave Donald Trump the keys to the White House will be discussed for decades to come. The rise of President Trump is a story about the changing news media, the role of social media, and his unconventional approach to campaigning.

Trump challenged conventional wisdom about the role of the media. The typical presidential campaign since the 1950s had been focused on staying on message and avoiding gaffes. Television and then the Internet put a magnifying glass on mistakes, and candidates were advised to avoid them at any cost. But Donald Trump ignored that advice. He waged a war against the establishment using very harsh rhetoric. He comments about immigration at the launch of his campaign were seen by members of the news media as evidence that he was out of touch and that his campaign was destined to fail. Instead, he hit a chord with many Americans, especially those who were alienated and angry with the inability of the national government to improve the lives of those struggling with stagnant wages and the changing structure of the economy.

Trump continued to make controversial statements, including attacks against war heroes such as John McCain, gold-star families, former Miss Universes, prominent journalists, and his presidential adversaries (e.g., "Little Marco," "Lying Ted," and "Crooked Hillary"). He often made statements that were not consistent with evidence. But again, that did little to derail his candidacy. It was as if the news media were focused on the small stuff, while he kept his eye on the big picture—that the country wanted an end to politics as usual.

The 2018 midterm elections underscored the continued polarization of American politics. Trump nationalized the congressional races in many ways

by getting the news media to cover him nonstop as he sought to make these elections about him and his controversial views on immigration and nationalism. Few Democratic newcomers employed social media as masterfully as Trump. "The Squad"—four freshman Congresswomen—Ocasio-Cortez, Rashida Tlaib, Ilhan Omar, and Ayanna Pressley, used their social media savvy to make their names and positions known throughout the nation. Each made history in being elected to the House of Representatives in 2018 and continue to use social media in a way that reaches Americans.[154] The results on Election Day were significant gains by the Democrats in the House and governor's races while Republicans retained control of the Senate.

The 2020 election promised to be highly competitive, nasty, and perhaps as important as any election since 1864—when the North back continuing the Civil War to keep the country united. But then just as the general election was shaping up between Joe Biden and Donald Trump, the COVID-19 crisis hit and turned the country upside down again. As predicted, the race was nasty between the former vice president and president. Trump continued his attacks on the process and on Biden himself. The personal attacks did not work very well. Biden became slightly more popular over the course of the campaign and was certainly more favorably viewed than Hillary Clinton four years earlier. Even Trump testing positive for COVID-19 did not alter the dynamics of the race. The country voted him out of office in a convincing fashion, with Biden winning more than 300 Electoral College votes and nearly 80 million popular votes. Even after losing, Trump continued his attacks. The then president-elect sought to project calm and competence. The turbulence of 2020 will likely continue in the coming years.

The TV network news standardized the information that many Americans had access to. With the wide array of choices now available, information is more polarized today. Viewers who choose a conservative TV network such as Fox and listen to Rush Limbaugh on the radio will have different information from those who watch MSNBC and tune in to National Public Radio. Those who lack interest in politics can avoid political news altogether. In other words, media choice cuts two ways: polarizing the type of information available, and making it possible to receive no political information at all.

The consequences of media choice are complex and are only beginning to be understood. New technologies in the future could further fragment what Americans as a people know. Efforts to make political news more interesting may mean a further "softening" of the news. The main point is that Americans have access to a vast amount of information, but the availability of more information does not necessarily mean that the public as a whole is better informed. Moreover, people follow news outlets that conform to their existing ideological preferences. This self-selection can fuel further polarization because many people are not getting information from the other side.

The News, Social Media, and Democracy

The news media, as watchdogs, are a central player in democratic politics. In the twenty-first century, the mass media are far more open than they were just a few decades ago, providing additional chances to forge accountability, responsiveness, and equality. But these are only chances because the media are in the midst of a transformation whose repercussions are not yet known.

For example, nearly all public appearances and statements of political figures can now be caught on video or audiotape. As a result, politicians have a tougher time ducking responsibility; they are more easily held accountable for their actions and words.[155] However, the threat of being caught on tape in an embarrassing moment may encourage politicians to stay in "the bubble," sheltered from public scrutiny and shielded from assertive journalists or potentially harmful situations. Politicians build staffs and organizations designed to keep them from making mistakes and from interacting with journalists and citizens. They want to appear at staged events where they can control the message. Of course, President Trump has put a hole in this bubble, avoiding efforts to "handle" him. Trump seems to make mistakes and offer misstatements on a nearly daily basis, and his supporters seem unphased by them.

The more open and more democratic new media thus have the potential to let citizens know more about the politicians who lead them; they also give people more opportunities to express opinions for politicians to consider as they develop and enact laws. Thus blogs and other new media may help forge responsiveness. But these gateways have potential costs: The opinions may come from people who are not representative of the American mainstream. Information offered as fact in these settings has not been checked and is potentially filled with errors.

The many changes in the news media have also led to a decline in the number of professional journalists who are covering politics. With fewer professional journalists, the press may be less able to investigate stories that might unearth corruption or provide a more complete account of some politicians' backgrounds.

The decline in investigative reporting could, in short, undermine accountability. But there is reason for optimism. While it is true that the days of Woodward and Bernstein are gone, the Internet offers new ways to forge accountability. For example, politifact.com tracks whether presidents keep their promises and also assesses the accuracy of claims by candidates during campaigns. When candidates are not telling the truth, the website labels the statement as "pants on fire." In 2018, politfact.com evaluated statements from President Trump. As of February 2018, only 4 percent were deemed as truthful, with nearly 15 percent earning the label "pants on fire."[156]

Such use of information and the Internet should ease some worries about democratic accountability. It is also worth noting that current doubts about the media's ability to advance democratic government comes mostly from people who favor a top-down approach for providing political information. For those who see the merit and appeal in a bottom-up approach that can be advanced by the Internet, the changes seem far less worrisome. On average, the Millennial generation will not be so worried; these young people have grown up with the transformed mass media. They see the potential that the Internet and other media have for promoting equality—and for providing more chances to be part of the process. But until access to the Internet becomes universal, these changes offer more hope than reality.

Chapter Review

Key Terms

actual malice (p. 226). Why should actual malice be hard to prove in a nation with a free press?

agenda setting (p. 253). How can the news media influence political agendas?

censorship (p. 229). How can a democracy justify censorship?

fake news (p. 258). What is driving the rise of the claims of fake news in recent years?

Federalist Papers (p. 232). Why were the *Federalist Papers* so important in the ratification of the Constitution?

framing (p. 253). Describe the health care debate as an example of framing.

hard news (p. 238). What is a good source of hard news today?

libel (p. 226). Why is libel not protected by the First Amendment's freedom of speech clause?

mass media (p. 224). How are the mass media different than the news media?

microtargeting (p. 246). How do politicians use microtargeting in advertisements?

minimal effects model (p. 252). Why did scholars think the media only had "minimal effects"?

muckraking (p. 234). Why is muckraking protected by the First Amendment's freedom of the press clause?

news media (p. 224). What is the role of the news media in a democracy?

not-so-minimal effects model (p. 252). What do scholars mean when they contend the media's effects are "not so minimal"?

penny press (p. 233). What was the effect of the penny press?

priming (p. 253). How do the news media prime the American public to hold certain opinions?

propaganda model (p. 251). Could the propaganda model ever be applicable to the United States?

seditious libel (p. 231). What is seditious libel?

selective exposure (p. 252). Why does selective exposure lead to reinforcement of beliefs?

selective perception (p. 252). How did selective perception help support the minimal effects model?

soft news (p. 241). What are sources for soft news today?

watchdog (p. 224). How do the news media serve as watchdogs in the twenty-first century?

yellow journalism (p. 233). How does yellow journalism undermine accountability?

Learning Outcomes: What You Need to...

Know	Test Yourself	Participate

LO 7-1   Determine why the media are important in a democracy

In a democracy, the people rely on the mass media for the information they need in order to hold government accountable and make it responsive. The press plays the role of watchdog, and the First Amendment protects the freedom of the press. The mass media perform three important tasks: informing, investigating, and interpreting the news.

- Describe the role of the press as watchdog.
- State the functions of the news media.

- Evaluate whether the media are fulfilling this role today.

LO 7-2   Analyze how the law protects the press

When the government attempts to constrain the press, the Supreme Court generally sides with the press, believing that it is better to protect press freedoms than to permit government censorship.

- Name the laws, government agencies, and court rulings that regulate press freedom.

- Consider whether the government should protect or regulate the news media.

LO 7-3   Define trends in the history of the press

Unlike the press, radio, television, and electronic media are heavily regulated by the Federal Communications Commission. The history of the press in America is dynamic, developing from occasional pamphlets to comprehensive daily publications and online enterprises with a mix of news and entertainment. The profession of journalism has developed over time as well, with a commitment to objectivity. In the 1950s, television began to replace newspapers as the source of news.

- State the Zenger case's importance.
- Describe the role of the press in the Revolution and ratification of the Constitution.
- Track the evolution from partisan press to yellow journalism.
- Elaborate on the ethics of professional journalism.
- State the effect of television on news reporting.

- Analyze the importance of a free press to American democracy.
- Decide if the profit motive for the mass media is a gateway to democracy or a gate.
- Weigh the value of professional journalists against the value of citizen-journalists.
- Weigh the value of nationalized news against the value of media choice.

LO 7-4   Explain how changes in the mass media have changed the information environment

In the twenty-first century, technological advances are changing the media environment once again. Cable TV, satellite TV, and the Internet make news available day and night. Soft news, with personal stories and emotional content, is replacing hard news. The decline of newspapers is a real concern. The decreasing number of journalists means that newspapers have less ability to inform and investigate. If the press cannot perform its watchdog role, the public loses a means by which it holds government accountable. Technology has changed the media and the way Americans receive the news since before the nation was founded. Tools such as blogs and podcasts have changed how people access and interact with news and information. Americans quickly adopt new technologies, and they have always sought the news. Increasing Internet access will eventually even out inequalities, giving all Americans a chance to be informed about politics.

- Describe the changing media environment.
- Survey the impact of the decline of newspapers.
- Survey the impact of developments in radio.
- Survey the impact of the transformation of TV news.
- Survey the impact of the rise of infotainment.
- Survey the impact of blogs.
- Survey the impact of social networking.
- Survey the impact of the changing media environment on young people.

- Assess the twenty-first-century mass media as democratic and in service to democracy.
- Speculate on how the role of the news media will continue to change as the Millennial generation matures.

Know	Test Yourself	Participate

LO 7-5   Assess how the news media affect public opinion

Political scientists describe the impact of the news media on the public as agenda setting, priming, and framing.

- Define the propaganda model.
- Distinguish selective exposure from selective perception.
- State three ways media coverage of the news affects politics.

- Understand how your partisanship shapes your understanding of political news.
- Understand how the mass media can alter your political views.

LO 7-6   Evaluate the news media

Although the public has lost faith in the media and generally think the media are too liberal, media choice and multiple outlets ensure a full range of ideological viewpoints. The sources of information are changing, but the public has as much information about politics as ever.

- State the concerns over media bias.
- Track changes in the quality of news and information over time.
- Survey the implications of the Internet.
- Connect media choice to polarization.

- Assess media bias.
- Decide which source for news you trust.
- Debate whether the Internet increases citizen equality or impedes it.
- Assess the connections between media choice and polarization.

Ida Mae Astute/Walt Disney Television Group/Getty images

GABRIELLE GIFFORDS AND MARK KELLY
Americans for Responsible Solutions and the
Giffords Law Center to Prevent Gun Violence

"*America, you have the power to change our Congress. ...This year, voters will demand that our leaders imagine and act to create a world where gun violence is not a daily problem.*"
Gabby Giffords, February 28, 2018

Pictured on the next page, Scripps College, where Gabby Giffords earned her undergraduate degree.

In January 2011, Gabrielle "Gabby" Giffords was a rising star in the Democratic Party. She attended Scripps College in California, where she studied Latin American history and sociology; won a Fulbright scholarship after college; and received her master's in planning from Cornell University. After working in the private sector, she returned to her hometown of Tucson, Arizona, to work in her family's business. She ran and won a seat in the Arizona House in 2000 and then ran for state senate and won in 2002. In 2006, she ran for Congress in an open seat district and won, becoming the third woman from Arizona to be elected to the U.S. House. She won reelections in 2008 and 2010. In 2011, she was shot in the head by a deranged gunman at a public appearance near a supermarket in Tucson. Six other people were killed in that shooting. Today, she still bears the injuries from that shooting with a paralyzed right arm and leg, limited speech, and limited sight. Her husband, Mark Kelly, gave up his career as an astronaut and retired to help her recover from her injuries.

Prior to being shot, Gabby Giffords was known as a supporter of gun rights and moderate gun-control measures. But after the shooting, Giffords and her husband Mark Kelly decided they could not sit by and do nothing to try to prevent future gun violence. They founded Americans for Responsible Solutions in 2013, which donates money to candidates who support their policies—mostly Democratic candidates, but the group has also supported Republicans who work on gun-control measures. The organization is also able to make independent expenditures in elections without directly contributing to a candidate's campaign. In subsequent years, it distributed those funds more widely across candidates for federal office.

In 2016, Giffords and Kelly decided to merge their organization with a longstanding public interest group

Learning Outcomes

LO 8-1   Outline how interest groups have developed over time

LO 8-2   Identify the types of interest groups that have evolved

LO 8-3   Describe activities interest groups engage in

LO 8-4   Analyze what balances out power among interest groups

LO 8-5   Assess what makes an interest group successful

called the Legal Community Against Violence. Together, they created what is now known as the Giffords Law Center, which focuses on proposing workable solutions to gun violence in America and supports political candidates who support those types of measures (http://lawcenter. giffords.org/). The Giffords Law Center issues a scorecard on state gun laws, tracks trends in gun violence, analyzes court cases involving gun rights and restrictions, and issues policy briefs on solutions that appear to work to limit gun deaths in America. Having run for elected office and won, Giffords herself participates in political ads designed to oppose candidates who stand in the way of measures aimed to reduce gun violence and to support candidates who promise to act on legislation that her group supports.

Gabby Giffords has remained an inspiration to all those who seek to reduce gun violence while still respecting the guarantees of the Second Amendment. In the wake of tragic mass shootings at Sandy Hook Elementary School, Las Vegas, Parkland, and El Paso, Giffords and her husband Mark Kelly have persisted in their commitment to educating voters and elected official about policies that can reduce gun violence and to using their full participatory powers in the American democracy to advance their cause. The Giffords Law Center is an example of how interest groups serve as a mechanism of representation in a democracy in that they translate individual opinions and interests to outcomes in the political system. In 2020, Mark Kelly took up the mantle of activism in politics by running for U.S. Senate in Arizona against Republican incumbent Martha McSally. He won the Democratic Party nomination in August, and subsequently

defeated McSally in the general election to become a U.S. Senator from Arizona.

Interest groups form for many reasons: to advance economic status, express an ideological viewpoint, influence public policy, or promote activism in international affairs. In this chapter, we examine the history of interest groups, why they form, what they do, and their impact on democratic processes. We also identify how and why some groups are more influential than others. We focus on interest groups as gateways to citizen participation and, at the same time, point out how they can erect gates when they pursue narrow policy interests.[1]

Interest Groups and Politics

LO 8-1 Outline how interest groups have developed over time

Key Questions

Why do you think Americans like to join organizations? How does this tendency relate to American political culture?

In 1831, the French political theorist Alexis de Tocqueville came to the United States to observe American social and political behavior. He stayed for more than nine months and later published his study as *Democracy in America,* a classic of political literature. He wrote, "The most natural right of man, after that of acting on his own, is that of combining his efforts with those of his fellows and acting together. Therefore the right of association seems to me by nature almost as inalienable as individual liberty."[2] Tocqueville noticed that Americans in particular liked to form groups and join associations as a way of participating in community and political life. To Tocqueville, the formation of group life was an important element of the success of the American democracy.

What Are Interest Groups?

interest groups: *Groups of citizens who share a common interest—a political opinion, religious or ideological belief, a social goal, or an economic characteristic—and try to influence public policy to benefit themselves.*

Tocqueville used the term *association* to describe the groups he observed throughout his travels in America; today we call them interest groups. An **interest group** is a group of citizens who share a common interest—whether a political opinion, religious affiliation, ideological belief, social goal, or economic objective—and try to influence public policy to benefit its members. Other types of groups form for purely social or community reasons, but this chapter focuses on the groups that form to exert political influence.

Most interest groups arise from conditions in public life. A proactive group arises when an enterprising individual sees an opening or opportunity to create the group for social, political, or economic purposes. A reactive group forms to protect the interests of members in response to a perceived threat from another group, to fight a government policy that the members believe will adversely affect them, or to respond to an unexpected external event. Groups whose members share a number of common characteristics are described as homogeneous, whereas groups whose members come from varied backgrounds are described as heterogeneous. All interest groups are based on the idea that members joining together in a group can secure a shared benefit that would not be available to them if they acted alone.

Citizens most often join groups to advance their personal economic well-being, to get their voices heard as part of a larger group's efforts on an issue, or to meet like-minded citizens who share their views. There is no legal restriction on the number of groups that people can join, and citizens are frequently members of a number of organizations. On the large scale, citizens join groups as a gateway toward participating in democratic society.

The Right to Assemble and to Petition

right of association: *Right to freely associate with others and form groups, as protected by the First Amendment.*

faction: *Defined by Madison as any group that places its own interests above the aggregate interests of society.*

The First Amendment states that Congress cannot prohibit "the right of the people peaceably to assemble, and to petition the government for a redress of grievances." This right to assemble is the **right of association**. The Framers believed that the opportunity to form groups was a fundamental right that government may not legitimately take away. At the same time, however, they were fearful that such groups, which Madison called **factions**, might divide the young nation. Although Madison recognized that such groups could not be suppressed without abolishing liberty, he also argued in *Federalist* 51 that, in a large and diverse republic, narrow interests would balance out each other and be checked by majority rule. (See *Federalist* 10 and *Federalist* 51 in the Appendix.) Madison feared that factions could have the same divisive or polarizing effect in a democracy. Nevertheless, the Bill of Rights contains protections for the rights of association and petition because these rights are essential for citizens to be able to hold their government accountable, ensure the responsiveness of elected officials, and participate equally in self-government.

The **right of petition** gives individuals with a claim against the government the right to ask for compensation, and it also includes the right to petition to ask for a policy change or to express opposition to a policy. It was the earliest and most basic gateway for citizens seeking to make government respond to them, and it has been used from the beginning of government under the Constitution. For example, in the First Congress, cotton growers asked the government for direct payment of subsidies to allow them to keep their farms in years with low crop yields. Owners of shipping companies petitioned Congress to limit the amount of goods that foreign ships could deliver to the United States so they could maximize their share of the carrying trade. Even the makers of molasses got together to ask the government to impose higher taxes on imported molasses so they would face less competition.[3] In the nineteenth century, petitions were used for broader and more sweeping issues, such as appeals to end slavery, to ban alcoholic beverages, and to secure the right to vote for women. In the twenty-first century, groups such as change.org use the Internet to make it possible for individuals to directly "ask" Congress for a benefit via e-mail or to sign a virtual petition that can be presented to Congress. Interest groups also use their high membership numbers as a proxy for the direct expression of support that once came from petitioners' personal visits to lawmakers.

Today the rights of association and petition most often take the form of **lobbying**, or trying to persuade elected officials to adopt or reject a specific policy change. Lobbying is a legitimate form of petitioning, and interest groups of all sizes and purposes engage in it, from Americans for Responsible Solutions, to big companies such as Uber and Google, to large-scale grassroots groups such as the Sierra Club. The term *lobbying* was coined more than three hundred years ago when individuals seeking favors from the British government would pace the halls, or lobbies, of the Parliament building, waiting for a chance to speak with members. The practice was immediately adopted in the new United States.

Interest groups lobby the legislative, executive, and even judicial branches of government at the state and federal levels. For example, when groups lobby Congress or state legislatures, they typically meet with members' staff aides to make the case for their policy

The Granger Collection, NYC

Image 8.1 Citizens have been using their right to petition to influence government since the earliest days of the democracy. Here female lobbyists in the late nineteenth century are trying to persuade members of Congress in the Marble Room of the U.S. Capitol. Although women did not yet have the right to vote, they still went to Washington, D.C. to make their voices heard on issues that were important to them.

Image 8.2 Abolitionists used stark imagery and words to rally citizens against slavery. In 1843, Lydia Maria Child compiled *The American Anti-Slavery Almanac*. Its cover alone makes the case for abolition. Child was a writer and editor who was also active in the women's suffrage movement.

Key Questions

How did interest groups work to end slavery? How long did it take women's suffrage groups to accomplish their goal?

Key Questions

Are groups representing manufacturers and corporations more or less powerful than citizens' interest groups? Do groups balance out each other?

unions: *Interest groups of individuals who share a common type of employment and seek better wages and working conditions through collective bargaining with employers.*

goals. Lobbyists may also try to influence the executive branch by meeting personally with key bureaucrats and policy makers. Lobbying of the judicial branch takes the form of lawsuits against government policies that interest groups see as fundamentally unconstitutional or that go against the original intent of the law. Such lawsuits can be high profile and are initiated by groups of all political ideologies. For example, cases orchestrated by the National Association for the Advancement of Colored People (NAACP), the Mexican-American Legal Defense and Education Fund, and other progressive interest groups ended school segregation (see Chapter 5, Civil Rights). For other cases, interest groups can also submit *amicus curiae* briefs ("friend of the court") that record their opinions even if they are not the primary legal participants in a case. Interest groups also lobby for and against judicial nominees, especially Supreme Court appointments. Lobbying strategies and tactics differ according to the branch of government at the federal and state levels, but no government entity is outside the scope of lobbyists' efforts.[4]

The History of Interest Groups

As the nation expanded its geographic borders, its population, and its economic base, government took on more responsibilities that affected individual lives. Issues that were once considered local became nationally important, and improvements in travel and communications enabled citizens with a national concern to band together. Slavery was the most divisive of these national issues, and citizens who opposed slavery formed the American Anti-Slavery Society in 1833. Soon many other groups were urging the abolition of slavery, creating the abolitionist movement. Abolitionists held rallies, distributed pamphlets, and collected signatures on petitions to persuade Americans, specifically members of Congress, to abolish slavery.

Advocates for women's suffrage (the right to vote) paid close attention to antislavery efforts, seeing in them an example of the power of organization. In 1848, the women's suffrage movement was officially launched at Seneca Falls, New York.[5] To the members of this group, the refusal to allow women to vote was a gate that stood in the way of true political equality among all citizens. The abolitionist and the women's movements paralleled each other in relying on the principle of equality as a rationale for supporting their policy goals.

Later in the nineteenth century, as America industrialized, the business community began to strengthen its efforts to influence policy. Large trade associations formed, both regional and national, with members that included sugar manufacturers, mining companies, and railroad owners. These businesses combined to form interest groups based on their common economic interests, and these groups gave wealthy owners of corporations a disproportionate influence over public policy.

To counteract the power of wealthy business corporations, workers organized **unions** to protect their interests, which were different from the interests of the people who owned industries but at the same time were interconnected with them.

The International Ladies' Garment Workers' Union (ILGWU) is an instructive example. It was formed in 1900 by workers (mostly women) who assembled women's clothing. By 1910, workers in this industry had staged several strikes against employers to secure better working conditions. The turning point for the union came in 1911, when 141 workers died in a fire at the Triangle Shirtwaist Factory in New York City because they were trapped on the factory's upper floors. The fire escapes were inadequate, and the elevator was broken. Most of the victims were young, immigrant women who needed this kind of work because it did not require English reading or writing skills.[6] Leaders

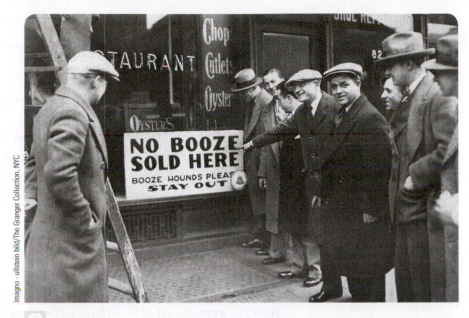

Imagno - ullstein bild/The Granger Collection, NYC

Image 8.3 Prohibition was enacted by the Eighteenth Amendment to the Constitution in 1919. Here a restaurant owner in New York City makes it clear that no alcohol is sold on the premises. Prohibition was hard to enforce and was ultimately repealed by the Twenty-First Amendment to the Constitution in 1933.

of the union saw a chance to turn tragedy into accomplishment by expanding its membership and lobbying the government to force manufacturers to improve worker safety. In part due to the efforts of the ILGWU, the Department of Labor was created as a separate cabinet-level department in 1913. It enforces mandatory standards for worker safety and oversees bargaining agreements between management and labor unions.[7] In 1935, unions were successful at getting more protections for workers through the National Labor Relations Act (NLRA), which allowed unions to engage in collective bargaining. The act also provides that only one union can be selected to represent workers in a specific location, so that after a union successfully organizes a work location, those workers have to abide by that union's decisions.[8]

Today business and trade associations, unions, citizens' organizations, and **grassroots movements** are a familiar part of the landscape of interest group politics. With the growth in the economy and in the size and scope of government in the American democracy, citizens have responded by forming more groups. The Chamber of Commerce, the National Rifle Association (NRA), AARP (formerly known as the American Association of Retired Persons), the League of United Latin American Citizens (LULAC), and the Sierra Club have existed for more than fifty years. Each claims to have millions of members, and each has different policy goals. However, not all modern interest groups are national in scope, and some are newly formed, so it is difficult to know how many groups are in existence at any one time. One study by political scientists estimated that there are approximately seven thousand groups operating in the American political system.[9] Their methods of communication and persuasion may differ from those of the very first petitioners of Congress, but they share the common role of serving as a gateway through which the opinions of ordinary citizens are expressed to their elected officials.

grassroots movement: *Group that forms in response to an economic or political event but does not focus on only one issue.*

Types of Interest Groups

LO 8-2 Identify the types of interest groups that have evolved

Because the universe of interest groups is so large and diverse, it can be helpful to categorize groups by their core organizing purposes and the arenas in which they seek to influence public policy. In this section, we survey three types of interest groups—economic, ideological, and foreign policy–focused—to illustrate and explain differences in interest group policy goals and strategies.

Economic Interest Groups

economic interest group:
Group formed to advance the economic status of its members.

Key Questions

What are the professional associations in the career field you are thinking of now? Are they worth joining?

Economic interest groups form to advance the economic status of their members and are defined by a specific set of financial or business concerns. Their membership bases tend to be exclusive because their purpose is to secure tangible economic benefits for themselves; if they grow too large or too inclusive, members' benefits are necessarily diluted. However, if the underlying industries represented by these groups disappear or merge with others, the groups have to adapt in order to attract new members.

Trade and Professional Associations.   Trade associations focus on particular businesses or industries and make up a subcategory of economic interest groups. Examples include the National Association of Manufacturers, the Chamber of Commerce, the National Retail Federation, and the Semiconductor Industry Association. Trade associations form because business owners believe that they will have more influence on the policy process collectively than they would individually.

Professional associations are formed by individuals who share similar jobs. Examples include the American Bar Association (lawyers), the American Medical Association (doctors), and the American International Automobile Dealers Association (car dealers). These associations are frequently responsible for setting guidelines for professional conduct—from business practices to personal ethics—and for collectively representing the members in the policy process.

Corporations.   Large corporations are a type of economic interest group in that they try to influence policy on their own as well as by joining trade associations comprising businesses with similar goals. Corporations such as Walmart, Comcast, and Boeing have thousands of employees, and that fact alone encourages politicians to listen to their concerns. In the past decade, corporations have aggressively contributed to political campaigns to influence policy, as will be discussed in detail later in this chapter. (For more on campaigns, see Chapter 10, Elections and Campaigns.)

Unions.   Unions are a type of economic interest group that aims to protect workers through safer working conditions and better wages. They are traditionally organized as local chapters that are part of a national organization representing workers in specific fields and industries. For example, autoworkers might join the United Auto Workers (UAW), truck drivers might join the International Brotherhood of Teamsters, health care workers might join the Service Employees International Union, and high school teachers might join the National Education Association. Unions typically require dues from all the people employed in a workplace that they represent in collective bargaining whether or not they voted in support of unionization. Typically collective bargaining can yield better wages and benefits for workers than when they are not represented as a collective. In June 2018, the Supreme Court ruled that public sector unions violate their members' First Amendment rights by requiring them to pay union dues. Nonpaying members can now receive all the benefits that dues-paying members receive. Private sector unions are not bound by the First Amendment.

Unions' strength comes from their ability to call or threaten strikes and to bargain collectively with employers over wages and working conditions. Starting in February 2018, education workers represented by unions such as the American Federation of Teachers, the Democratic Socialists of America, and the National Education Association went on strike throughout the country in response to budget cuts, low salaries, and decreased employee benefits. The unionized strikes began in West Virginia when the state's branches of the American Federation of Teachers and National Education Association held a strike vote, which then inspired related strikes in Oklahoma, Arizona, California, North Carolina, and Colorado. In general, the unions gained considerable concessions; education workers received a 5 percent pay raise in West Virginia, a 20 percent pay raise in Arizona, a 6 percent pay raise in Los Angeles, and a 2 percent pay raise and increased school spending in Colorado. In Oklahoma, workers saw increased school funding, teacher salaries were raised by $6,000, and the salaries of support staff were raised by $1,250.[10]

Unions such as National Nurses United, which has 150,000 members nationwide, also played a key role in advocating for worker safety protections for nurses, medical assistants, lab technicians, and first responders, among others, during the COVID-19 pandemic (see Chapters 14, Bureaucracy and 16, Domestic, Economic, and Foreign Policy for more on COVID-19).[11] Many hospitals and clinics were overwhelmed with patients seeking help, and there was a critical shortage of protective equipment such as outerwear and N95 masks for protect workers. Amnesty International estimates that as of July 2020, 3000 health care workers have died from COVID-19 in the United States and internationally.[12]

The biggest threat to unions, however, is the loss of jobs in the industries they represent. For example, the UAW was formed to represent the growing auto industry in the United States in 1935.[13] Over time, automation, foreign competition, and periodic economic downturns have resulted in the loss of thousands of jobs in this industry, which has in turn reduced the membership in the UAW. Just in the past decade, the union has lost nearly 250,000 members. From

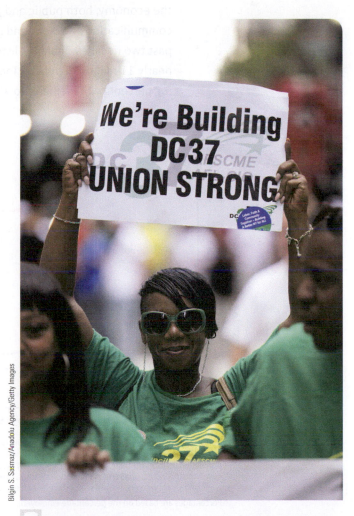

Bilgin S. Sasmaz//Anadolu Agency/Getty Images

Image 8.4 Unions organize to provide collective benefits to workers in specific industries and professions. Here a union member expresses support for her union by marching in a Labor Day parade.

2017 to 2018, UAW membership decreased from 430,871 to 395,703. This loss of more than 35,000 members reflects a nearly 10 percent decrease in membership in just one year.[14] To combat their general membership loss, the UAW has branched out to other industries ranging from dining service employees at colleges to workers in gambling venues. This strategy is showing some signs of progress as the 2020 UAW membership increased by 3,125 members.[15]

Overall, private sector union membership has been declining (see Figure 8.1). Part of the reason for this decline is that government regulations now require the protections that unions long sought in terms of safe working conditions, overtime compensation, and nondiscrimination. In a sense, unions have been victims of their success in pushing for government regulations, and workers do not have to join a union to receive these protections. Consequently, over time the incentive for union membership has decreased.

Additionally, as of 2019 twenty-eight states have right-to-work laws that allow individuals to choose not to join a union even if their workplace has a designated union in place.[16] As in the case of the UAW, unions have responded to this downturn in membership by seeking to represent workers in a wider range of industries. Despite the downturn in membership in large industrial and manufacturing unions, unions in other sectors of the economy, both public and private, representing teachers, health service workers, communications workers, and government employees have all made large gains over the past two decades. Table 8.1 lists the top six unions in the country, which together have nearly 11 million members. Today unions represent 10.8 percent of the male workforce and 9.7 percent of the female workforce in the United States.[17]

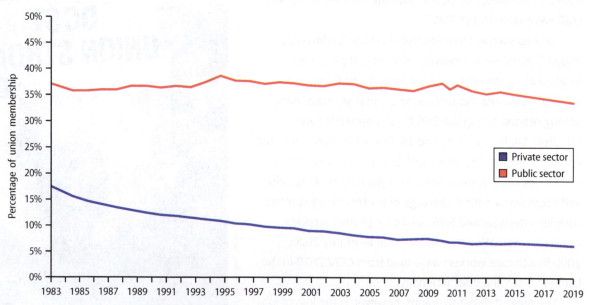

Notes: Data refer to the sole or principal job of full- and part-time workers. All self-employed workers are excluded, regardless of whether or not their businesses are incorporated. Data for 1990–93 have been revised to reflect population controls from the 1990 census. Beginning in 2000 data reflect population controls from census 2000 and new industry and occupational classification systems. Beginning in 2000 private sector data refer to private sector wage and salary workers; private sector data for earlier years refer to private nonagricultural wage and salary workers.

Percentages are based on the percentage employed.

Figure 8.1   **Percentage of Wage and Salary Workers with Union Membership, 1983–2019**

Private-sector union membership has been declining over time, while public-sector union membership has increased.

Source: Bureau of Labor Statistics, "Economic News Release: Union Members Summary," accessed January 22, 2020, https://www.bls.gov/news.release/union2.nr0.htm.

Table 8.1 Unions with the Largest Membership, 2020

Union	Number of Members (in millions)
National Education Association (NEA)	2.9
Service Employees International Union (SEIU)	2.0
American Federation of State, County and Municipal Employees (AFSCME)	1.3
American Federation of Teachers (AFT)	1.7
International Brotherhood of Teamsters (IBT)	1.4
United Food and Commercial Works International Union (UFCW)	1.3

Sources: Union Facts, National Education Association, https://www.unionfacts.com/union/National_Education_Association; Service Employees International Union, http://www.seiu.org/about; American Federation of State, County and Municipal Employees, http://www.afscme.org/union; Union Facts, American Federation of Teachers, https://www.unionfacts.com/union/American_Federation_of_State_County_%26_Municipal_Employe; International Brotherhood of Teamsters, https://teamster.org/about/teamsters-structure; United Food and Commercial Workers International Union, http://www.ufcw.org/about_ufcw/.

American unions are both economically and politically powerful because they can mobilize their members to vote for candidates they see as favorable on issues such as higher minimum wages, standards for overtime pay, better access to health care insurance, worker safety, and international trade agreements. Today, public employee unions are coming under increasing challenge over issues related to wages and pensions with efforts to reduce their bargaining power with state and local governments. Unions have countered these challenges with a combination of legal challenges and grassroots mobilization.

Ideological and Issue-Oriented Groups

Ideological interest groups form among citizens with the same beliefs about specific issues. We describe these groups as ideological rather than economic because economic benefits are not the primary basis for their existence. This category can include **citizens' groups** (Common Cause, Public Citizen), **single-issue groups** (NRA, National Right to Life), and grassroots movement groups (MoveOn.org, National Organization for Women). Citizens' groups, sometimes called public interest groups, are typically formed to draw attention to public issues that affect all citizens equally, such as environmental protection, transparency in government, consumer product safety, ethics reform, and campaign finance reform. Single-issue groups form to present one view about a highly salient issue that is intensely important to its members, such as the national debt and the federal deficit to members of the American Family Association (AFA). In contrast, broader organizations typically emerge in response to an economic or political event but do not focus solely on one issue. For example, MoveOn.org was founded by two wealthy men who were angry that President William Jefferson (Bill) Clinton (1993–2001) was impeached even though most people opposed the proceedings. MoveOn.org called for an end to the Iraq War during the George W. Bush administration (2001–09). During the Obama administration (2009–17), the group worked hard to promote the health care exchanges and Medicaid expansion set forth under the Affordable Care Act.[18] During the years 2017–20 of the Trump administration, MoveOn.org has continued its efforts to protect the ACA from further cuts and opposed policies that separated migrant families and cut taxes for the wealthy. They increased their digital activism in combination with more traditional mobilization methods through encouraging e-mails and phone calls to Congress.[19]

ideological interest groups: *Groups that form among citizens with the same beliefs about a specific issue.*

citizens' groups: *Groups that form to draw attention to purely public issues that affect all citizens equally.*

single-issue groups: *Groups that form to present one view on a highly salient issue that is intensely important to members, such as gun control or abortion.*

Key Questions

How do ideological interest groups contribute to polarization?

Ideological groups provide a way for individual members to express their opinions on issues more forcefully than would be possible for any one person alone. Members of ideological groups benefit from knowing that others share their views and from feeling empowered. In this way, ideological groups can encourage political participation in a democratic society. At the same time, these groups contribute to the polarization of the American public. Because a group of this type gets its power from agreement within its ranks on a highly salient issue, it discourages debate and disagreement within the group and any type of compromise on that issue.

For example, NARAL (formerly known as the National Abortion Rights Action League) takes the position that a woman has the right to terminate a pregnancy without limitations, whereas the Right to Life organization holds that all abortions should be forbidden except when the life of the mother is endangered by the continuation of the pregnancy. Individual members in each group may hold more moderate views, but the leadership believes that any public compromise will alienate core members and diminish the group's status on the issue within the media and government. In this case, ideological groups not only balance out each other but also block the way forward. The intensity with which each side holds its position discourages cross-group dialogue and makes it harder for elected officials to achieve a reasonable and widely acceptable resolution of the issue. Because an interest group seeks a favorable government response on a narrowly defined issue important to that group, the group can also create imbalances that verge on inequalities.

Foreign Policy and International Groups

Some interest groups address cross-border concerns. Foreign policy groups form to generate support for favorable U.S. policies toward one or several foreign countries. International aid groups encourage citizens to provide voluntary assistance to people in need all over the world. International groups concerned with human rights work to call attention to violations in the hopes of ending oppression.

Groups That Influence Foreign Policy.   One of the best-known organizations that seek to influence foreign policy is the American Israel Public Affairs Committee (AIPAC). This group aims to ensure a strongly pro-Israel American foreign policy and uses public advocacy, member mobilization, and campaign contributions to influence members of Congress to support its goals. AIPAC first formed in the early 1950s, and it claims credit for getting the first aid package to Israel—$65 million to help relocate Holocaust refugees—passed by Congress in 1951.[20] Today, AIPAC has more than one hundred thousand active members and is widely considered to be one of the most influential groups of its kind in Washington.

Groups That Advocate International Aid and Support for Human Rights.   Religious organizations often encourage members to provide international assistance. For example, Catholic Relief Services sponsors the Global Solidarity Network, which allows college students to communicate with people living in small villages or towns in developing countries. The National Council of the Churches of Christ in the United States provides funding and coordinates religious and humanitarian missions to foreign countries.[21]

Other interest groups, such as Amnesty International and Human Rights Watch, focus attention on human rights violations or starvation in certain areas of the world. Many are **nongovernmental organizations (NGOs)**, which are not affiliated with any government and work hard to preserve their neutrality so that they can operate in as many parts of the world as possible. These groups monitor human rights abuses and wartime violence around the world.[22] Other groups focus their efforts more specifically. The International Rescue Committee has worked to help relocate refugees who are fleeing violence in their countries, with a considerable emphasis on the violence in Syria in recent years.[23] They illustrate the power of interest groups to draw attention to a situation occurring in a foreign land and to solicit a powerful response from both average citizens and elected officials.

Image 8.5 Humanitarian groups are often essential to providing services to civilians in war-torn areas. Here members of the International Organization for Migration (IOM) work with the United Nations to help refugees caught in the Syrian conflict.

STR/European Pressphoto Agency/HOMS/SYR/Syrian Arab Republic/Newscom

nongovernmental organizations (NGOs):
Organizations independent of governments that monitor and improve political, economic, and social conditions throughout the world.

What Interest Groups Do

LO 8-3 Describe activities interest groups engage in

Interest groups perform a number of functions in the political process. They collect information about the implications of policy changes and convey that information to lawmakers and other policy makers. Their lobbying efforts aim to construct policies in ways that will most benefit their members. This section examines the tactics of lobbying, from providing information, to contributing to campaigns, to orchestrating grassroots movements that increase political participation on an issue. Lobbying is one of the fundamental gateways for expressing views and securing a favorable response from government officials.

Inform

All interest groups provide information about the issues they care about to their members, the media, government officials, and the general public. The type of interest group dictates the kind of information it disseminates. Before the Internet, groups provided members with information about government policies and new developments in their issue areas through newsletters and sessions at annual conventions. Today they disseminate such information on their websites and try to limit access by requiring members to register and sign into the websites. Social media, such as Facebook, Snapchat, Twitter, and Instagram, also enable groups to keep members informed and to rally them to take action on the group's behalf.

Interest groups do more than merely report on current policy developments; they also provide members with interpretations of how the developments will affect their mission and goals. For example, in the area of environmental and energy policy, interest groups are very active in keeping their members up to date on policy developments. For example, in November 2015, when then President Obama denied the application to build the Keystone Pipeline XL, which was considered a strong stance against climate change, the Sierra Club issued a press release claiming credit for its efforts to help defeat the pipeline and informing its members that their support of the Sierra Club made a difference.[24] In March 2020, the Sierra Club reached an agreement with the main power supplier in Detroit, Michigan, on an energy efficiency pilot program aimed at minimizing utility shutoffs. Even though it took multiple years of activism, the Sierra Club helped create a program that will offer a subsidy to community members who fall behind on their utility bills or encounter shut-offs of their power services, or to improve their energy efficiency and lower their energy consumption.[25] (For more on climate change, see Chapter 16, Economic, Domestic, and Foreign Policy.)

Interest groups also work hard to inform government officials about the impact of specific public policies. Most of the time, lobbyists have pro or con positions on a policy proposal, and their goal is to persuade government officials to agree with their perspective. Legislators and government officials are generally knowledgeable in their areas of expertise, but the vast size of the federal and state governments makes it hard to know the impact of policies on every citizen. Economic and ideological groups constantly monitor policies that might affect their members in a positive or negative way and strive to make legislators and government officials aware of the impact of policy proposals (see Public Policy and Interest Groups: Fracking).

Groups convey information via e-mail; telephone; personal meetings with staff, elected officials, and bureaucrats; and testifying before Congress and state legislatures. Groups also use the bureaucratic regulatory process to respond to regulations with comments to influence how laws are carried out by the executive branch (see Chapter 14). For example, the National Education Association (NEA) sent a letter to the Obama administration commenting on its proposed rules for implementing the Race to the Top program, which was designed to provide funds to local communities to improve education. In this letter, the NEA supported some of the provisions but was critical of others, in this way conveying the views of its members to bureaucrats.[26] The NEA then posted the letter on its website to inform teachers across the country about the specific ways that the program might impact their schools and school systems.

Key Questions

When interest groups gather and disseminate information, are they performing a public service? Or do they do it just to advance their own causes? If so, is there anything wrong with that?

Groups also can engage in several of these types of activities at once. For example, LULAC (mentioned above) has a long history of engaging and informing its Latino membership on numerous political issues. They were active in bringing the court case *Hernandez v. State of Texas* (featured in Chapter 5) to the Supreme Court to secure the right of Mexican Americans to participate on juries. LULAC has also worked to mobilize Latino voters by informing them of registration and voting procedures in their communities. And they were very supportive of President Obama's successful nomination of Sonia Sotomayor to the Supreme Court.[27] Furthermore, in February 2020, LULAC was victorious in bringing a lawsuit against Conteva, a company that makes Chlorpyrifos, a poisonous pesticide with a chronicled history of causing below normal birth weights and subsequent developmental deficits in children. They estimated that "millions of Latino farmworkers and their families" were continuously exposed to this agricultural pesticide.[28] When the COVID-19 crisis emerged in 2020, LULAC established a website called LULAC@Home, which was specifically aimed at providing information to Latinos about the epidemic.[29]

Lobby

Almost every kind of group with every kind of economic interest or political opinion—including business firms, trade and professional organizations, citizens' groups, labor unions, and universities and colleges—engages in one form of lobbying or another.[30] State, county, and city government officials maintain lobbying offices in Washington, D.C., both separately and as part of larger national groups such as the National Governors Association or the United States Conference of Mayors. Lobbyists for these government entities frequently visit with the state's congressional delegation to keep the representatives informed about how federal programs are operating back home and to ask for legislation that will benefit their states. Mayors and county executives do the same thing, trying to influence their state legislators and governor by keeping them informed about how policies affect their constituents.

The Lobbyists. Groups can use their own employees as lobbyists or contract with firms that specialize in lobbying. In 2019, there were 11,862 individuals registered as active lobbyists in Washington. That amounts to more than twenty-two lobbyists for each member of the House and Senate.[31] The offices of many of these lobbyists are concentrated in an area of northwest Washington known as the K Street corridor; when people say they work on K Street, it is safe to assume that they are lobbyists.

AP Images/Rich Pedroncelli

Image 8.6 At the end of a legislative session, lobbyists gather in a hallway outside the state capitol in California to see how their proposals fared.

Although lobbyists are frequently stereotyped as representing only the narrow interests of their clients, they are typically individuals who have held public service jobs at some point in their careers. There are three common pathways to becoming a Washington lobbyist: working on Capitol Hill, working in the executive branch, or working on a political campaign. Lobbyists may start out on a political campaign for a congressional candidate or work in a congressional office, and then leave to join a corporation, lobbying firm, or a law firm with a branch that lobbies on specific legal matters. Or lobbyists may start out as practicing attorneys, then go to work in Congress or the executive branch, and subsequently join a company or lobbying firm.

In 2019, interest groups and lobbying firms spent nearly $3.5 billion on a wide range of expenses associated with lobbying, including salaries for in-house lobbyists, consulting fees charged by lobbying firms, overhead for office space, and travel costs of staff (see Table 8.2).[32] In the past, the costs of lobbying also included paid trips for members of Congress and their staffs (known as junkets), as well as expensive meals. Lobbyists justified these expenses as a way of getting to know members of Congress in a smaller and more relaxed setting, which they claimed would enable them to enhance their or their client's influence in the policy process.

Key Questions

Why is the public perception of lobbyists so negative? Do they have a useful role to play in the political process?

Table 8.2 **Top Spenders on Lobbying, 2019**

Lobbying Clients	Issues	Dollars Spent
U.S. Chamber of Commerce	Product liability, finance, copyright, patent and trademark	$77,245,000
National Association of Realtors	Taxes, finance, housing	$41,241,006
Business Roundtable	Manufacturing, regulation, corporate tax policy	$19,990,000
Pharmaceutical Research & Manufacturers of America	Prescription drug regulation and pricing controls, tax policy for research	$29,291,000
Blue Cross/Blue Shield	Health issues, taxes, Medicare and Medicaid	$25,146,590
American Hospital Association	Health issues, Medicare and Medicaid, federal budget and appropriations	$26,222,680
American Medical Association	Health issues, taxes, Medicare and Medicaid	$20,910,000
Alphabet Inc. (Parent company of Google)	Net neutrality, telecommunications, regulation of privacy	$12,660,000
AT&T	Telecommunications	$12,820,000

Source: Adapted from Center for Responsive Politics, "Top Spenders, 2019," accessed February 23, 2020, https://www.opensecrets.org/federal-lobbying/summary?inflate=Y.

Public Policy and Interest Groups

Fracking

The struggle for power over policy decisions is ongoing, and interest groups are always moving forward to accomplish their agendas within the larger policy-making arena. The issues within the energy and environmental arena are vast, and in this section, we focus on the interest group activity surrounding the use of hydraulic fracturing, otherwise known as fracking, which is a technique that extracts oil and natural gas. Since 1997, the use of fracking has expanded greatly, bringing with it increases in jobs and overall production of oil and gas nationwide, which has contributed to economic growth in some areas.[33] At the same time, there have been serious allegations that fracking poses a threat to the environment, particularly safe drinking water. In response to concerns expressed by residents in areas with fracking, in 2010 Congress requested that the Environmental Protection Agency (EPA) conduct a study of the effects of fracking on drinking water. The EPA then launched a study and focused on locations in four states (North Dakota, Pennsylvania, Texas, and Colorado) where fracking had already been occurring for some time.[34] In June 2015, the EPA released its draft report of the study's findings and concluded that although hydraulic fracking does interact and rely on water systems that also provide drinking water, they did not identify any serious negative effects from the process to date.[35] In this way, the issue of fracking presents a clear case study of the trade-offs between jobs, energy production, and environmental protection and how interest groups try to influence public policy in these areas.

Both America's Natural Gas Alliance (ANGA), a group that promotes the use of natural gas, and the Natural Resources Defense Council (NRDC), an environmental advocacy group that opposes fracking,

responded to this investigation in ways that advance their own perspective. ANGA is an example of a corporate interest group designed to advance the policies preferred by its industry members. NRDC is typical of a public interest nonprofit group that addresses issues of public policy that affect a wide group of citizens.

Each group is committed to representing the views of its members. For ANGA that consists of oil and gas companies, and for NRDC, that consists of individual and group donors, as well as foundations that support NRDC's environmental protection stances.[36]

In response to the EPA study, ANGA issued an extensive report on the question of water pollution and its ties to fracking. The report focused on one community, Washington County, Pennsylvania, an area that engaged in coal mining before turning to fracking. In this report, which was shared with other major oil and gas interest groups, ANGA argued that any existing water contamination could be a result of a number of industrial

Mark Ovaska/Redux

Image 8.7 Fracking is becoming more widespread across previously undeveloped lands. Here a fracking site known as the Marcellus Shale Well sits among farmland in Pennsylvania.

activities, not solely tied to fracking, and that if this were true for Washington County, it could be true for other such affected areas.[37] In June 2019, a report dated August 31, 2018, was made public, revealing that a $3 million settlement had been reached between Range Resources, a gas drilling company, and families in Washington County who had claimed that fracking had not only contaminated their properties but had also made them sick. There is an ongoing investigation into possible fracking-related "environmental crimes" in Washington County.[38]

In contrast, NRDC created the Community Fracking Defense Campaign (CFDC), which raises money and awareness of the issue and focuses on the impacts on residents of Pennsylvania as well as other states, including New York, Ohio, California, Illinois, and Texas.[39] CFDC posts videos on its website featuring residents of areas with fracking talking about the degraded quality of the water and air in their communities. These videos are human interest stories designed to gain sympathy for these residents and persuade viewers to support NRDC's efforts to oppose fracking.[40] In addition to trying to generate grassroots opposition to fracking, the group also responds to government action on this issue. CFDC severely criticized the EPA study and pointed to dissenting voices in the scientific community to support their ongoing efforts to limit fracking.[41]

Each group's strategy reflects its core organization. As an industry-based organization, ANGA issued a comprehensive study that relies heavily on technical evidence designed to be used to oppose EPA restrictions on fracking. As a public issue group, NRDC works to build grassroots support for its position and inform its members, which the group hopes in turn will influence regulators and lawmakers. Overall, the struggle to sway public opinion on the issue of fracking is just one illustration of how interest groups try to influence public policy on key issues.

Construct Your Own Policy

1. Develop policy criteria for deciding whether to grant permits for fracking in local communities.
2. Evaluate which set of interest groups should weigh more heavily in this decision from a public policy perspective and explain why.

A decade has passed since congressional ethics reforms prohibited paid trips and meals for members and staff.[42] Still, lobbyists can use money to maintain their influence in other ways. For example, their salaries typically include allocations to make strategic campaign contributions to members of Congress who preside over issues that are important to their companies or clients.

During a typical day, lobbyists phone, e-mail, or meet with congressional staffers, their clients, and possibly members of the media to gather information about relevant issues for their clients or to promote their clients' policy positions. Lobbyists also attend congressional hearings, executive branch briefings, and even committee markups in which members of Congress write legislation. Interest groups, businesses, and industries do not survive by lobbying only, but lobbying is a natural outgrowth of their purpose because members expect their leaders to advocate for them when necessary.

Lobbying Strategies.　Lobbying frequently involves a multipronged strategy. Groups usually try an inside lobbying strategy first, in which they deal directly with legislators and their staff to ask for a specific policy benefit or to try to stop a policy that they oppose.

These insider meetings require access to policy makers, which typically comes about as a result of longtime interactions that build mutual trust. The key aspect of the **inside strategy** is to keep the policy request narrowly tailored to the group's needs because the broader the policy request, the more likely other groups will become involved in the negotiations, and complications can ensue. Either the policy request has to expand, so that each group gets a high level of benefits, or each group has to be satisfied with less, and few groups are ever satisfied with less. Nevertheless, if several groups share the same policy goals, they may form a temporary coalition, working together to improve their chances of success.

When an inside strategy does not work, groups adopt a more public or outside lobbying strategy by getting the press and their members more directly involved. A group may go straight to the press to provide details about the adverse effects of the proposal, hoping that the journalists will inform the general public. In this way, interest groups try to make use of the press's watchdog role over the government. For example, a nonprofit group called Citizens for Responsibility and Ethics in Washington (CREW) consistently tries to get the press to focus on whether government officials are obeying ethics and campaign finance laws.[43] They monitor the use of campaign funds by members of Congress and frequently call for investigations into what they see as misuse of funds. Through publicity and coordinated activities, groups also try to promote grassroots lobbying by encouraging action by their own members and the larger public. Energizing constituents in congressional districts used to be the work of regional offices. Today interest groups can generate citizen involvement through the Internet, asking that a message be sent by e-mail, text messaging, or cell phone, or show their members how to start their own Internet petitions. MoveOn.org, for example, gets grassroots support by asking members to e-mail, call, or send letters to their local legislator as well as to others who might be sympathetic to their cause. In addition, marches and rallies show strength in numbers to elected officials and also generate publicity that can attract new people to join advocacy efforts. In these ways, groups directly give their membership a stronger voice in the policy-making process.

The core organizational purpose also helps shape a group's lobbying strategy. For example, economic groups typically adopt an insider lobbying strategy and limit their activity to key actors in Congress and the executive branch. In contrast, citizens' groups typically adopt the outsider strategy to take advantage of the strength that comes from their large memberships. If they can mobilize their members to communicate with elected officials and simultaneously use the media to spread their message, they believe they will be successful.

inside strategy: *A strategy employed by interest groups to pursue a narrow policy change and influence legislators directly rather than using a wider grassroots approach.*

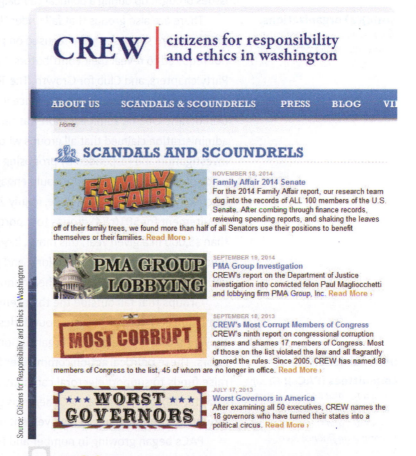

Source: Citizens for Responsibility and Ethics in Washington

Image 8.8 Watchdog groups hold public officials accountable for their behavior. Citizens for Responsibility and Ethics in Washington (CREW) publishes a website listing major scandals committed by public officials.

Image 8.9 Peaceful protests are frequently an effective way of voicing opinion on an issue. This gathering was organized to show opposition to fracking.

501(c)(3) organizations:
Tax-exempt groups that are prohibited from lobbying or campaigning for a party or candidate.

501(c)(4) organizations:
Tax-exempt groups that exist to promote social welfare and can advocate for specific policy issues.

political action committees (PACs): *Groups formed to raise and contribute funds to support electoral candidates and that are subject to campaign finance laws.*

Campaign Activities

Interest groups also promote their views by engaging in campaign activities, although federal law regulates their participation through the Federal Election Commission (FEC). Candidates and their campaign organizations must comply with reporting and disclosure requirements, which are monitored by the FEC. Groups with tax-exempt status are prohibited from engaging in any activity on behalf of a candidate or party in an election campaign. These groups, commonly referred to as **501(c)(3) organizations** after the section of the Internal Revenue Code that governs their activities, are likely to be charities, religious organizations, public service organizations, employee benefit groups, and fraternal societies, which are exempt from paying federal tax. Although they cannot engage in lobbying in any significant way, they can produce voter education guides or other nonpartisan educational materials that explain issues brought up during a political campaign and keep the public informed.[44]

There are also groups that fall under the **501(c)(4) organization** category, which are non-profit and are supposed to be focused on public policy issues, not politics. These groups are not required to reveal their contributors. Such groups include the Sierra Club, the NRA, Tea Party chapters, and Club for Growth. The Tea Party's status as "apolitical" came under close scrutiny by the Internal Revenue Service in 2012 and 2013, leading some to allege that the Democratic Obama administration was targeting conservative groups. However, the Obama administration claimed that all groups who were seeking this status were subject to intense investigation and responded by proposing new regulations that more closely restricted what kinds of activities these groups could engage in so that it would be clear they could not be overtly political.[45] Furthermore, in July 2018, the Trump administration eliminated the requirement for 501(c)(4) groups to report to the IRS names of donors who contributed more than $5,000 in a given year; this move, largely favored by Republicans, allows thousands of nonprofit organizations, labor unions, and political groups such as the NRA and the AARP to withhold information related to their donors from the government and the public at large.[46]

Groups that fall outside the tax-exempt category are free to engage in lobbying and campaign activities. But to set boundaries between the group's core mission and politics, they generally create parallel organizations that make campaign contributions to legislators. These **political action committees (PACs)** and their larger versions, Super PACs, raise funds to support electoral candidates and are subject to campaign finance laws (see Chapter 10). In one sense, PACs serve as gateways for expanding interest groups' political influence through financial involvement in campaigns.

PACs began growing in number and force after the Supreme Court's landmark decision *Buckley v. Valeo* (1976) upheld limits on donations to congressional campaigns.[47] As the costs of campaign spending rose over time, groups realized that creating or expanding an affiliated PAC to make campaign contributions could increase their influence over elected officials. Unaffiliated PACs, groups that make campaign contributions but are not associated with specific interest groups, also grew in size as a means of coordinating campaign contributions from individual citizens who wanted to express their campaign support as part of a larger group. All PACs make campaign contributions to the candidates they believe will be supportive of their policy goals (see Table 8.3). Thus PACs expand the reach of interest groups well beyond lobbying to include active engagement in the electoral arena.

Given the amount of money that PACs spend on campaign support, many observers have expressed concern that PACs exert a disproportionate influence over legislators, which creates an imbalance in government responsiveness toward some groups. In the age of so-called Super PACs and 501(c)(4) groups that can spend nearly unlimited money on issue ads directed at persuading the public to support their policy position, interest group interaction can get captured by big money battles among these groups. Supporters of open and equal democratic participation fear that such money battles could simply favor the richest and loudest groups and slant policy making to benefit specific groups rather than the majority of the people.

For example, the Club for Growth is a PAC that collects funds and makes campaign contributions to members who support its platform of lower taxes and federal deficits, and they issue a Congressional Scorecard to track how members vote on legislation. Under President Obama, the Club for Growth supported members of Congress who shut the

Key Questions

Should there be limits on how much money interest groups can contribute to campaigns? Why or why not?

Table 8.3A **Top 5 PAC Contributors to Republican Candidates, 2019–2020**

PAC Name	Total Amount Given to Republicans
Majority Committee PAC	$1,035,000
American Bankers Association	$954,000
House Freedom Fund	$905,819
Comcast Corp	$788,700
Koch Industries	$781,000

Table 8.3B **Top 5 PAC Contributors to Democratic Candidates, 2019–2020**

PAC Name	Total Amount Given to Democrats
Sheet Metal, Air, Rail, & Transportation Union	$1,356,850
American Association for Justice	$1,220,500
Operating Engineers Union	$1,146,000
American Federation of Teachers	$999,750
American Federation of State/County/Municipal Employees	$945,000

Source: Center for Responsive Politics, www.opensecrets.org, adapted from data released by the Federal Election Commission, accessed February 23, 2020, https://www.opensecrets.org/pacs/toppacs.php?Type=C&pac=A&cycle=2020&Pty=A.

Supreme Court Cases

Citizens United v. Federal Election Commission (2010)

QUESTION: Can the government limit campaign spending by corporations and unions without violating First Amendment rights?

ORAL ARGUMENT: March 24, 2009, reargued September 9, 2009 (listen at http://www.oyez.org/cases/2000-2009/2008/2008_08_205)

DECISION: January 21, 2010 (read at http://caselaw.lp.findlaw.com/scripts/getcase.pl?court=US&vol=000&invol=08-205)

OUTCOME: No, governmental restrictions on corporate speech violate First Amendment rights (5–4).

In an attempt to equalize finances in political campaigns, Congress passed the Bipartisan Campaign Reform Act of 2002, also called the McCain-Feingold Act after its two leading sponsors. In 1976, the Supreme Court upheld limits on contributions to congressional campaigns but struck down limits on what independent groups unaffiliated with the campaign could spend. In response, McCain-Feingold restricted corporations and unions from using television or radio ads for "electioneering communications"—commercials that refer to a candidate by name—within thirty days of a primary or sixty days of a general election.

While corporations are often for-profit operations, such as General Motors or Microsoft, nonprofit and political entities such as the NAACP also organize as corporations under the tax code. One such political organization is Citizens United, a conservative interest group "dedicated to restoring our government to citizen control." During the 2008 Democratic primary campaign, it released a documentary called *Hillary: The Movie,* which was severely critical of Senator Clinton (D-NY). Citizens United planned to show the documentary on pay-per-view television and to market it in advertisements on broadcast television. Concerned about violating McCain-Feingold, Citizens United sued the FEC, seeking an injunction prohibiting enforcement of the act as a violation of the First Amendment rights of corporations.

In a break with past decisions, the Supreme Court declared that corporations and unions had the same First Amendment rights as U.S. citizens. Using the compelling interest test (see Chapter 4, Civil Liberties), the Court ruled that Congress cannot disfavor certain subjects or different speakers. While recognizing that corporations may have more money to spend than individual citizens do, the Court ruled that First Amendment protections do not depend on the speaker's "financial ability to engage in public discussion." Such limitations violate the marketplace of ideas that the First Amendment is designed to protect. The ruling left open the question of whether Congress could limit the speech rights of foreign corporations operating within the United States.

The dissenters claimed that money is not equivalent to speech and that the law was a reasonable attempt to level the playing field in campaigns.

Thinking Critically

1. Why is campaign spending a form of speech?
2. Should corporations receive the same free speech protections as ordinary citizens?

government down over increased federal deficits. Under President Trump, this PAC supported members who voted for a tax bill that lowered taxes but was projected to significantly raise the federal deficit. The fact that Club for Growth opposed deficits under Obama but supported them under Trump shows that interest groups can prioritize one policy over another, such as tax cuts over reducing the federal deficit.

The Libre Initiative

One newer example of a 501(c)(4) organization that was founded to mobilize voters is the Libre Initiative (www.thelibreinitiative.com). According to its website, this group was founded with the purpose of "informing the U.S. Hispanic community about the benefits of . . . limited government . . . and free enterprise"; their slogan is #BeLibre.[48] Typically Latinos have been viewed as more progressive, and approximately 66 percent of Latino voters voted for Hillary Clinton in the 2016 election.[49] This organization exists to encourage community networks of economic and political support among Latinos and to build support for conservative policy positions such as school choice and less regulation of small business. At the same time, it supports a moderate immigration reform policy that opposes mass deportations while calling for stronger enforcement of the legal immigration laws. Located in nine states, it also provides information about a range of issues, including where to finish high school and how to get a driver's license.[50]

The Libre Initiative was founded by Daniel Garza, who serves as its executive director. He previously served in the George W. Bush administration and worked in Spanish-language television before taking on the job of heading an organization that was geared up to play a significant role in the 2016 election cycle. With two Latino presidential candidates, Ted Cruz (R-TX) and Marco Rubio (R-FL), contesting for the GOP nomination, 2016 presented a major opportunity for a Latino conservative organization to gain attention and potential supporters in the Latino community. As with any interest group, that requires informing and persuading individuals that the group best represents their opinions and policy goals. Some of their efforts include rallying their members around immigration reform and the more fiscally conservative policies that they support, and they include a direct appeal to women with their #MsLibre campaign designed to attract Latina women supporters. The Libre Initiative also works with other conservative groups and has received funding from the Koch brothers, who have been very public about wanting to expand the reach of their conservative fiscal message to the Latino community.

In terms of outcomes, the Libre Initiative was poised to exert continued influence in the 2018 midterm elections with its location in several key swing states, such as Florida, Colorado, Nevada, and Virginia. It ultimately proved to be successful in 2016 in a broad sense in that Latino turnout increased in the general election, and 28 percent of Latinos voted for Donald Trump for president.[51] The 2018 midterm elections resulted in an overall increased number of Latinos throughout state legislatures in the United States: an analysis by the National Association of Latino Elected and Appointed Officials recorded a rise from 307 to 321 seats held by Latinos.[52] During the 2018 midterm elections, five House of Representative members who identify as Latino were elected from the Democratic Party, whereas the House Republicans lost two Latino House members.[53] In 2020, 32 percent of Latinos voted for Donald Trump's failed reelection bid.[54] The Libre Initiative is one example of how interest group participation has expanded significantly among Latino groups along the range of ideological viewpoints in American politics.

More generally, however, scholars have had difficulty establishing exactly what PACs are getting for their money. Although campaign contributions can make it easier for groups to get access to legislators, they generally do not buy results in terms of policy outcomes—at least not directly. For example, an auto maker and a union might team up to lobby for a policy that benefits their industry and their affiliated PACs may also contribute money to elected officials. The combination of lobbying and campaign money may get lawmakers' attentions, but it is also the case that those lawmakers want to secure benefits for any employees in their districts who work in the auto industry. Interest groups tend to lobby and contribute to members of Congress who are leaning in their direction, and have constituents who may be employed in the areas represented by the interest groups, so it is difficult to prove the impact of a campaign contribution.[55]

Campaign finance laws impose limits on what interest groups can do in terms of issue advocacy, the practice of running advertisements or distributing literature on a policy issue rather than for a specific candidate. In general, the Supreme Court ruled that campaign spending is a form of speech and that, as with other forms of speech, Congress must show a compelling interest before it can pass laws to regulate it. The McCain-Feingold Bipartisan Campaign Reform Act (2002) restricted corporations and unions from using television and radio ads for "electioneering communications"—commercials that refer to a candidate by name—within thirty days of a primary and sixty days of a general election. Since 2002, many groups have run ads that could be interpreted as issue advocacy or as outright campaigning. In 2007, in *Federal Election Commission v. Wisconsin Right to Life, Inc.*, the Supreme Court ruled that if a campaign advertisement could be reasonably viewed as issue-based, it was protected under the guarantee of free speech and could not be prohibited under the McCain-Feingold Act.[56]

Running issue ads has become a regular feature of interest group activity, even in nonelection years. Before 2010, interest groups could run issue ads on specific issues within a certain time frame prior to an election according to federal election laws; many interest groups used these ads to generate support or opposition to then President Obama's health care plan before it became law. Although they served the purposes of interest groups, they also encouraged elected officials to be more responsive to constituents' needs because they focused attention on issues of importance to constituents. In 2010, the Supreme Court removed virtually all limits on issue ads, and individuals, corporations, and unions can spend as much money as they want on issue ads. (See this chapter's Supreme Court Cases: *Citizens United v. Federal Election Commission*, as well as the discussion of issue ads in Chapter 10.) In 2014, the Supreme Court went even further, in their ruling in *McCutcheon et al. v. Federal Election Commission*, by removing the overall limits on the amount of money one individual can contribute to all federal elections; there are still limits on how much money can be given to one candidate, but an individual can now contribute to every single candidate running for federal office, as well as political parties.[57] In 2016, 2018, and 2020, this ruling enabled very wealthy individuals to use larger campaign contributions to seek more influence in elections for Congress and the presidency.

The Impact of Interest Groups on Democratic Processes

LO 8-4 Analyze what balances out power among interest groups

"I have often admired the extreme skill," wrote Tocqueville, "with which the inhabitants of the United States succeed in proposing a common object to the exertions of a great many men, and in inducing them voluntarily to pursue it."[58] Both Tocqueville and James Madison assumed that voluntary association or the forming of factions was a natural process of citizens interacting in a free society. Scholars have been interested in the same process, examining why interest groups form and what effects they have in a democratic society. In this section, we survey various perspectives on interest groups that relate to government responsiveness and citizen equality.

Natural Balance or Disproportionate Power

Over the past seven decades, scholarly debate has centered on the process of interest group formation and its consequences. In the 1950s, David Truman agreed with Tocqueville and Madison, describing interest group formation as natural. Truman observed that when individuals have interests in common, they naturally gravitate toward each other and form a group. As long as those individuals share a characteristic, opinion, or interest, the group continues to exist, but if the commonality disappears, the group disappears.[59]

Writing in the mid-1960s, however, Mancur Olson argued that merely having something in common with other people was not enough to give a group life and keep it going as an effective organization.[60] Olson focused on the costs of organizing and maintaining a group, noting that costs increase as a group grows in size and reach. The people who pay membership dues expect benefits in return. Since the governmental decisions that interest groups obtain are "public goods" that apply whether one has joined the group or not, Olson argues that the cost–benefit structure that underlies group formation contradicts Truman's claim that all groups naturally form and sustain themselves.

The debate between Truman and Olson raises the fundamental issue of whether interest groups are natural and can compete on an equal basis or artificial because they distort public policy in favor of some citizens over others. Other scholars have addressed this question in different ways. Robert Dahl argued that in a **pluralist** society, the battles over public policy by the varied interest groups that emerge to represent their members will produce a consensus that serves the public's common interest.[61] Scholars such as C. Wright Mills worried that a power elite controlled power in the American democracy.[62] His concerns were echoed by Theodore Lowi, who argued that in a democracy, some voices are louder than others and that government is more responsive to louder voices and will consistently serve such groups at the expense of those who cannot make their voices heard.

According to Lowi, this kind of policy making is elitist and fundamentally antidemocratic.[63] Political scientists Larry Bartels and Martin Gilens have each written extensively about the disproportionate impact of the wealthy on public policy making and demonstrated that ideas put forth by groups that represent the interests of the wealthy, especially in the issue areas of tax policy and social welfare, receive more attention from lawmakers than other groups.[64]

Traditionally, the narrow focus of interest groups has engendered a sense of illegitimacy. Interest groups form and survive by appealing to a particular segment of society (economic, ideological, or social), so they are inherently exclusive. Exclusive groups act only in the best interests of their members, even if nonmembers thereby lose out. E. E. Schattschneider described this aspect of interest groups as an actual threat to democracy. He argued that if interest groups are given legitimacy because they claim to represent citizens' interests, but in fact they seek narrow benefits for their members at the expense of nonmembers, there is an inherent unfairness to them. Moreover, citizens will be lulled into a false sense of security about living in an "interest group society" because they believe that every interest group has an equal opportunity to be influential.[65]

Key Questions

Do you think interest groups form from the bottom up or from the top down? Which type of group would you find more trustworthy?

Key Questions

Do interest groups bring people into the democratic process, or do they strengthen some voices at the expense of others

Key Questions

What distinguishes a legitimate interest from an illegitimate interest?

Key Questions

Do modern-day interest groups balance out each other the way that Madison thought they would?

pluralist: *View of democratic society in which interest groups compete over policy goals, and elected officials are mediators of group conflict.*

Image 8.10 As the website indicates, MoveOn.org is a nonprofit grassroots organization that is geared toward increasing political participation on a wide range of issues.

special interests: *Set of groups seeking a particular benefit for themselves in the policy process.*

There is a middle ground between these contrasting views. Given the approximately seven thousand registered groups in America today, it is clear that group formation is a natural outgrowth of the freedom to associate and of community life in which human beings share social, economic, and political goals. But if Olson is right, and successful cost–benefit strategies determine whether a group can survive or grow, groups led by individuals with sufficient time and money stand a greater chance of winning a policy fight than do groups without such resources. In this view, interests become **special interests**, a term with negative connotations that is more frequently used during campaign season to suggest that some groups exert a disproportionate amount of power in the American democracy. To the extent that a well-funded interest group can more easily pressure the government to produce policies that are beneficial to its members, government responds unequally across all citizens. In this view, financial advantage creates an artificial imbalance of influence that acts as a gate against equality.

When a group is founded explicitly to represent one group of people or set of interests, does that mean that its activities will not benefit the society as a whole? Take, for example, Black Lives Matter, a group formed out of a mass social movement protesting the deaths of Michael Brown in Ferguson, Missouri, Eric Garner in New York City, and George Floyd in Minneapolis, among others. Although the group's core focus is the deaths of unarmed African Americans during interactions with law enforcement, its message has spread further and wider into discussions of racism more generally, from schools to the workplace to the judicial arena. In moving from a broad social movement to an interest group that changes policy, Black Lives Matter may experience the challenges of all interest groups in voicing the concerns of those it represents while maintaining its effectiveness in gaining the support of a broad enough coalition to secure policy change in these arenas.

Similarly, the #MeToo movement, which started in 2006 and was later reinvigorated in 2017, is a social movement against sexual assault that has influenced public and social attitudes about gendered harassment. It was initially started by activist Tarana Burke, geared toward raising awareness of the reality and impact of sexual violence for African American women and other young women of color from low-income communities. It has since expanded to involve notions regarding the general treatment of all women, whether it be in the workplace, on athletic teams, or in the political sphere. #MeToo has successfully influenced policy on what constitutes acceptable and legal behavior in the workplace. States such as New York expanded their sexual harassment laws to cover more types of working relationships and introduced greater protections for female workers, and Congress has taken steps to improve its procedures that enable staffers to report sexual harassment. A parallel movement, #TimesUp was inspired by #MeToo and targeted powerful men in the entertainment industry for reported behavior ranging from inappropriate touching to allegations of rape. Harvey Weinstein, once a very successful movie producer, was one of the more prominent men accused of such behavior. He was convicted of multiple counts of sexual assault in February 2020, and in March of that year, he was sentenced to twenty-three years in prison.[66]

Self-Service or Public Service

In assessing the relative power of interest groups in a democratic political system, it is essential to remember that interest groups do not pass or implement laws; they try to influence state and federal governments to enact their policy goals. To do so, they constantly interact with political parties, members of Congress, executive branch bureaucratic agencies, and even the judicial system. The question of legitimacy of an interest group's activities comes when a victory for one group means a loss for another, or more broadly a loss for the general public.

Key Questions

Name two or three interest groups that you think have a lot of power in American politics. Do you agree or disagree with their positions?

For example, during most of the 1990s and 2000s, car manufacturers—acting alone and as part of their larger trade association, the American Association of Automobile Manufacturers—successfully lobbied to block efforts by environmental groups to secure an increase in government-mandated fuel efficiency standards. These standards, known by the general term *corporate average fuel economy* (CAFE), are designed to ensure that automobiles use as little fuel as possible to run efficiently. The government has an interest in requiring such efficiency in order to promote energy conservation more generally. However, automobile manufacturers argued that increased fuel efficiency is more expensive to produce and that CAFE standards would cut into their profits and might even decrease sales. In other words, the auto manufacturers would pay the price for accomplishing the public goal of promoting energy conservation. When auto companies violate these standards, they have to pay monetary fines to the federal government; between 1991 and 2012, those fines added up to more than $873 million.[67] But to automobile manufacturers, the total sum of these fines was viewed to be much less expensive than modifying car designs to increase efficiency. On this issue, the self-interest of the auto manufacturers conflicted with that of the general public.

In 2007, with high increases in fuel prices and a general increased awareness of climate change, then President George W. Bush agreed to a modest increase in fuel efficiency standards to 33.6 miles per gallon by 2012. When President Obama took office in 2009, he reiterated support for those standards. At the same time, an economic crisis hit the American automobile industry, undermining its financial and organizational ability to fight the increases. As the economic health of the domestic automobile industry slowly improved, the Obama administration felt freer to speed up the timetable for implementing those standards. As a result, the EPA issued regulations, first in 2010 and again in 2012, that require automobile manufacturers to produce vehicles that get 54.5 miles per gallon by 2025 (see Figure 8.2).

Trump promised to address the issue of fuel economy standards and their impact on the auto industry when he ran for president in 2016. His administration proposed lowering anti-pollution and fuel efficiency standards for automobiles in 2018, but there have been differing opinions as to whether doing so would save consumers money. Such a policy would lower the short-term costs of trucks and SUVs but increase the longer term costs of gasoline consumption.[68] In late March 2020, the Trump administration issued final regulations that would require an improvement of 1.5 percent in fuel economy standards each year until 2026 to reach 40 miles per gallon (see Chapter 14 for a description of the regulatory process).[69] To help understand and evaluate CAFE standards for automobiles, the National Highway Traffic Safety Administration (NHTSA) developed a website to inform consumers called CAFE PIC; this website not only helps aid consumers but also keeps a public record of which automobile manufacturers are complying with the standards.

The regulatory process is one gateway for interest groups to offer comments directly to the federal government on public policy proposals. The case of CAFE standards is one example of how time and circumstances almost always shift the playing field and the balance of power in the interest group arena.

The frustrating aspect of the role that interest groups play in a democracy is that groups contesting a single issue frequently talk over each other, not with each other. It is often left to members of Congress and the executive branch to balance their own responses to interest group requests and still maintain responsiveness to constituents and the nation at large. Over time, most interest groups experience wins and losses in the policy system; the necessary condition for a democracy is that every group has a chance to make its case.

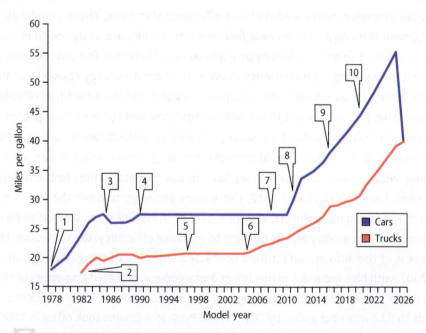

Figure 8.2 Fuel Economy Standards

Over time, the government has steadily increased the standards for fuel economy for cars and trucks. The numbered boxes indicate times when the federal government has taken action to regulate fuel economy.

Source: Center for Climate and Energy Solutions, "Federal Vehicle Standards," accessed March 1, 2018, https://www.c2es.org/content/regulating-transportation-sector-carbon-emissions/.

Open or Closed Routes of Influence

Although interests may ultimately balance each other, and changing conditions may ultimately level the playing field, the fact that a tightly knit group of specialists often controls policy areas raises concern about fairness both inside and outside interest group organizations. For example, lobbyists work to build good relationships with legislators and officials in the bureaucracy. Given their knowledge of particular policy areas, many of them move in and out of government. Are lobbyists always thinking of their groups' members when they engage in their activities, or are they thinking about their next jobs? Do they constitute an insider group that is ultimately self-serving rather than serving the public?

Scholars have long used the phrase **iron triangle** to describe the relationship among interest groups, members of Congress, and federal agencies. In essence, an iron triangle is a network forged by members in three categories that works to seal off access to public policy making. Lobbyists and interest groups want to maximize their benefits from federal programs; members of Congress want to maximize their power to shape the programs; and federal bureaucrats want to maximize their longevity as administrators of these programs.

Critics of the influence of interest groups in a democracy often describe iron triangles as unbreakable and argue that they contribute to the inefficiency of the federal government because they sustain programs that should be eliminated or enlarge programs beyond what is necessary to meet their intended purposes. The criticism is not limited to scholars. In his farewell address in 1961, President Dwight D. Eisenhower (1953–61) warned of what he called the military–industrial complex, a self-serving interconnection among branches of the U.S. military, the defense manufacturing industry, and federal agencies overseeing scientific research. Eisenhower was greatly concerned that the defense industry had undue influence that would be used to unnecessarily increase spending on defense programs. "This conjunction of an immense military establishment and a large arms industry is new in the American experience," he said. "The total influence—economic, political, even spiritual—is felt in every city, every State house, every office of the Federal government. We recognize the imperative need for this development. Yet we must not fail to comprehend its grave implications. Our toil, resources, and livelihood are all involved; so is the very structure of our society."[70] President Eisenhower's stature as a decorated general who commanded U.S. and Allied forces in World War II gave him credibility on the issue of defense spending, and his depiction of the military–industrial complex as a type of iron triangle drew a great deal of notice. Even today, efforts by the Secretary of Defense to reduce the size of the armed forces and eliminate military equipment are met with stiff resistance by the members of the iron triangle that Eisenhower identified more than fifty years ago.[71] Moreover, today the term *iron triangle* is applied to a wide range of issue areas, including health care and prescription drugs (see Figure 8.3).

Yet the well-known interest group scholar Hugh Heclo claims that the interconnection of interest groups and the government is more benign, suggesting that the term **issue networks** is better than *iron triangle* to describe the relationship.[72] Heclo argues that interest groups, members of Congress, and bureaucrats all share information constantly, and that their interactions are open and transparent, not closed. Heclo wrote thirty years ago, before the advent of the 24-7 news cycle, Twitter messaging, and other telecommunications innovations, so it stands to reason that it is harder than ever for self-serving

Key Questions

Is government responsive to interest groups? Are interest groups responsive to the people as a whole, or only their memberships?

iron triangle: *Insular and closed relationship among interest groups, members of Congress, and federal agencies.*

Key Questions

Do you think the military–industrial complex exists today? What evidence do you have for your position?

issue network: *View of the relationship among interest groups, members of Congress, and federal agencies as more fluid, open, and transparent than that described by the term iron triangle.*

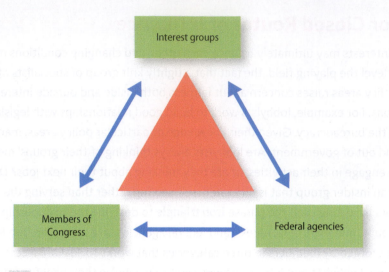

Figure 8.3 **Iron Triangle**

The *iron triangle* is a policy-making structure that includes congressional committees, federal agencies, and interest groups.

Key Questions

How does government prevent corruption among government officials?

revolving door: *Movement of members of Congress, lobbyists, and executive branch employees into paid positions in each other's organizations.*

interconnections to go unnoticed. In addition, citizens' watchdog groups, such as Common Cause, and policy institutes, such as the Center for Responsive Politics, monitor interest group influence on government activities and policies. When these groups find evidence of wrongdoing in government, they loudly blow a whistle by issuing reports and holding press conferences to inform the media and the general public.

What remains true is that lobbyists, members of Congress and their staffs, and members of the executive branch do pass through what scholars describe as a revolving door of paid positions in one another's organizations, with knowledge and experience on a specific issue as the valued commodity. The term **revolving door** has a negative connotation, suggesting that an iron triangle of influence consists of the same set of people moving from one branch of government to another and then to the private sector. The image of a revolving door also suggests that the system does not stop to include outsiders with new perspectives; in other words, it can act as a gate against wider political participation.

Take, for example, Jim DeMint, a Republican from South Carolina who resigned in January 2013, early in his second term as a U.S. senator, to become head of the Heritage Foundation, a conservative think tank. DeMint had been a leader among the conservative Republicans in the Senate, especially those affiliated with the Tea Party, and political observers were surprised to see him leave that position of power. However, in his new position DeMint's salary was about $1 million per year, compared to his previous salary of $174,000. DeMint used his position at the Heritage Foundation to more actively promote conservative policies on two fronts. First, he focused the efforts of the Heritage Foundation on opposing the Affordable Care Act. Second, he increased the role of the political arm, known as Heritage Action, by raising money for it and using it to support political candidates who oppose the Affordable Care Act. DeMint represented a new version of the revolving door where elected officials who are closely tied to ideological agendas leave their office to head organizations that seek to influence public policy at the grassroots level as well as inside the Beltway—and earn a much higher salary in the process.

Political Analytics

Top National Associations in the United States

THOUSANDS OF INTEREST GROUPS in the United States try to influence public policy at all levels of government. Interest groups amplify the voices of like-minded citizens to policy makers in Congress, in state legislatures, and at local levels. There is a wide variety of interest groups, each representing the views of citizens and groups in the electoral, legislative, judicial, and executive arenas of government.

Figure 8.4 shows two ways of looking at important resources interest groups have in their attempts to affect

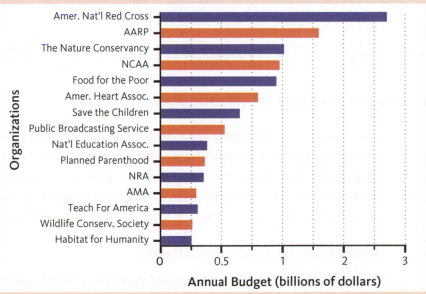

Figure 8.4 **Selected Top Interest Groups by Membership and Budget**

Sources: Encyclopedia of Associations, National Organizations of the U.S. 54th edition, 2015, Gale Publishing; Open Secrets: Influence and Lobbying, The Center for Responsive Politics, http://www.opensecrets.org/influence/, accessed March 10, 2016.

The Impact of Interest Groups on Democratic Processes   **295** public policy to benefit their members: their membership size and their budget. Interest groups provide information to their members about the activities of their elected officials. They may also call on their membership to contact their representatives to express their views. The larger the membership, the more influence the group may enjoy. Likewise, associations with large budgets may be able to direct large-scale efforts to keep up with government activity and support candidates more effectively than those with fewer resources. Notice the variety of associations and the interests they represent, as well as the overlap between the two categories of associations shown.

Thinking Critically

1. The two bar graphs in Figure 8.4 list amounts only for the organizations with the highest and lowest values. Is this sufficient? Or should the values be listed for each organization? How might you point out which organizations appear in both charts?

2. The associations in the graphic are the largest by membership and by budget. What other characteristics might be important for associations?

Sometimes that can be very successful for the organization that hires former members of Congress; however, in the case of DeMint, it also produced conflict. In 2015, Republican members of Congress complained about Heritage Action's "scorecard," which assigns ratings to members based on a series of roll call votes that they take to advance the group's ideas, saying that it was not realistic and could damage their electoral prospects. DeMint continued to push a political rather than policy agenda for Heritage and because of that, he left the Heritage Foundation in May 2017.[73]

It is also essential to remember that not all relationships among lobbyists, members of Congress, and federal officials are tainted or suspicious. Congress and the federal bureaucracy each have elaborate rules governing their behavior with respect to interest groups and lobbyists, and most members and bureaucrats follow them closely.

Characteristics of Successful Interest Groups

LO 8-5 Assess what makes an interest group successful

Key Questions

Identify two interest groups with an enduring voice in American democracy. What characteristics do they have in common? How are they different?

The measure of a successful interest group is how well it accomplishes its goals. Some groups want to stay in existence forever, but other groups form temporarily for a specific purpose and disband after they accomplish their goal. For the groups that want to establish an enduring voice in a democracy, success can be measured in four ways: leadership accountability, membership outreach, financial stability, and public influence.

Leadership Accountability

As anyone who has tried to get a group of students together to perform a task, lodge a protest, or plan an event knows, coordination can be difficult. It typically takes an individual who acts as an interest group entrepreneur to organize citizens into a formal group that agrees on a united purpose. In return for organizing the group, the interest group entrepreneur typically takes a leadership role in directing the group's activities.

For example, in 1985 Grover Norquist founded the group Americans for Tax Reform, which is dedicated to lowering taxes, and he has remained its leader and public voice ever since.[74]

Benefits that come from being a group leader range from salary as a paid staff member to prestige and influence over the group's goals and strategies. The interest group scholar Robert Salisbury calls the trade-off between the work and the benefits of being a leader the "exchange theory of interest groups," and he argues that no one would rationally expend the energy and time to start a group if he or she could not take a prominent role in directing it.[75] Members are willing to pay their group leaders and give them power in the group in return for accomplishing the group's collective goals.

Transparency about the group's political and financial activities in pursuit of its goals is an important democratic element of an interest group; without it, there is a risk that the leaders could act in ways that do not properly serve the members. However, leaders do sometimes act in their own self-interest (by misusing group finances, for example), or they may take the group in an ideological direction that does not mirror the majority opinion in the group. More than a hundred years ago, Robert Michels coined the phrase **iron law of oligarchy** to describe this behavior. When leaders take such actions at the expense of rank-and-file members, the internal governance of the interest group breaks down. Flaws in interest group management can be a major problem for a democracy if citizens join a group with the expectation that the group will accurately represent their opinions and interests, and it does not.

Members must be able to register satisfaction or dissatisfaction with the group's leadership. The simplest way to do that is to leave the group, but in doing so, the individual may lose the benefits that the group provides. Using the group's website, members can convey their opinions to the leadership, but members cannot really control the group's actions, especially if the group is large. Citizens have a right to expect accountability from interest group leaders, and interest groups that want to sustain themselves understand that their membership needs to remain satisfied over time.

Membership Stability

Whether a group is small or large, attracting members and keeping them over time are essential to its survival. People join groups because they share similar interests or political viewpoints or because they want to protect their economic livelihoods. For the leaders of groups, the challenge is to find the right balance between membership size and the organization's purpose. Having too many members may create internal disagreements about policy goals, but having too few may weaken the group's ability to exert influence in the policy system.

Selective Benefits.   One way to attract and keep members is to provide **selective benefits** exclusive for members.[76] These can include *material benefits*, such as direct monetary benefits from policies that the group advocates, discounts on travel or prescriptions, and even monthly magazines. *Solidary benefits* are less tangible. They range from the simple pleasure of being surrounded by people with similar interests and perspectives to the networking benefits of interacting with people who share professional or personal concerns. *Expressive benefits* are the least tangible in that they consist of having a specific opinion expressed in the larger social or political sphere. When individuals join a group, they know that their viewpoint is being actively represented in the policy system, and that knowledge can be gratifying all by itself.

iron law of oligarchy: *Theory that leaders in any organization eventually behave in their own self-interest, even at the expense of rank-and-file members; the larger the organization, the greater the likelihood that the leader will behave this way.*

Key Questions
How do groups perpetuate themselves at the expense of their mission? Can you give an example?

selective benefits: *Benefits offered exclusively to members of an interest group.*

Key Questions

Would you join an interest group for its material benefits? Its solidary benefits? Its expressive benefits? What would make you decide to join?

public goods: *Goods or benefits provided by government from which everyone benefits and from which no one can be excluded.*

free rider problem: *Problem faced by interest groups when a collective benefit they provide is so widespread and diffuse that members and nonmembers alike receive it, reducing the incentive for joining the group.*

The Free Rider Problem. Many of the benefits that large interest groups seek on behalf of their members—clean air by the Sierra Club or gun rights by the NRA—are **public goods**. In other words, they are available to all people, whether they have contributed toward the provision of that good or not. Public goods are typically the spillover effects of public policies that affect all citizens. If a group lobbies for public goods or collective benefits that are so widespread that members and nonmembers alike receive them, incentives to join the group disappear. Olson addressed this collective action dilemma, calling it the **free rider problem**.[77] Why pay to join a group if one can get the benefits for free? Why join if the group is so large that it does not actually need an additional member?

The Economic and Political Change Problem. Changes in the economy and the political environment can also have a negative impact on a group's membership stability. The decline of membership size of the UAW discussed earlier is an example of what can happen to union membership when an industry experiences job losses. From a political standpoint, groups can "succeed" their way out of existence but then reemerge when policies turn against their cause. For example, after the passage of McCain-Feingold campaign finance reform (noted earlier), Common Cause lost some influence because it had succeeded in lobbying Congress to address its core issue of the role of money in campaigns. However, within a decade, the Supreme Court drastically weakened the regulation of money in campaigns with its rulings against core provisions of the legislation. In response, Common Cause increased its visibility in leading the fights to reverse the Supreme Court decisions and to reinstate limitations on the donation and use of money in campaigns.

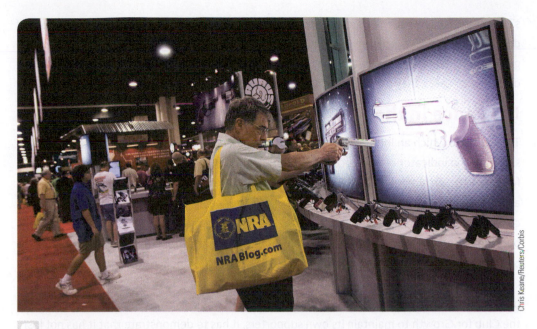

Chris Keane/Reuters/Corbis

Images 8.11 and 8.12 Interest groups offer tangible benefits to individuals to encourage them to join. Messenger bags and totes with the organization's name also provide free advertising.

Concern for survival in an increasingly crowded interest group society can sometimes bring an interest group into conflict with its core principles. Groups can try to counteract declining membership by creating new issues to rally members around or by portraying serious threats to the issues most important to members, although such actions can be criticized as "disinformation campaigns."

Financial Stability

Together with keeping a membership base, a group must also maintain financial stability. Groups of all types require money to sustain their staffing, lobbying, and information distribution. The Internet has made fundraising easier because it allows groups to solicit money without incurring costs for printed advertising, mailers, and postage. Most organizations also rely on dues. Grassroots groups that seek to attract as many members as possible keep their dues relatively modest. For example, in 2018 the NRA raised its annual dues from $40 to $45 but in 2020 was facing financial challenges due to overspending in some areas, legal investigations, and the inability to convene in-person gatherings due to COVID-19.[78]

Interest groups also achieve financial stability by creating nonprofit businesses within the organization. AARP is a classic example of a large interest group that wears two hats: a politically powerful lobby on policies that affect senior citizens and a multimillion-dollar business that provides health insurance, life insurance, and discounts on movies, travel, and prescriptions to members, who must be at least 50 years old to join. A basic AARP membership costs only $16 a year, and it provides the opportunity to purchase the other services at discounted rates. In turn, AARP receives payments from businesses that it contracts with to provide services to its members. AARP is among the most successful large-scale interest groups in American history; in 2017, it claimed a membership of nearly 38 million.[79]

The financial challenge for many groups is to keep their operating costs in line with their expected income. For the very largest interest groups, such as AARP, a single year's operating budget can be more than one billion dollars; in 2018 the group took in $1.65 billion and spent

$1.66 billion.[80] For most other groups, the operating budget ranges from thousands to millions of dollars per year. Groups can experience financial difficulty as a result of financial mismanagement by group leaders, or, in some cases, they may simply outlive their usefulness and members cease paying dues. In such cases, they may be forced to scale back their activities and close local chapter offices.

Influence in the Public Sphere

The extent to which an interest group appears to influence public debate is a sign of its success. One indicator of influence is being quoted in the press. Earlier we discussed Club for Growth, a group devoted to lowering taxes. Their current president is Dave McIntosh, a former Congressman from Indiana, who was known for being an outspoken champion of fiscal conservatism. The group has sought to increase their direct influence over supporting incumbents in Congress who agreed with their positions rather than trying to punish, or threatening to withdraw support from, members who did not support their policy positions. The Club for Growth is responding to competition from other conservatives, namely the billionaire Koch brothers, who have become very strong financial backers of fiscal conservatism as well.[81] For the Club for Growth to maintain its own supporters, it has to demonstrate that it has not lost influence to the Koch brothers and others who advocate for similar policy positions. This competition from other groups may be why they chose to overlook how the 2017 tax bill raises federal deficits in light of other conservative groups' support for it. Groups face constant pressure to signal to members, as well as to the public at large, that they have a significant role in policy formation on the issues about which members are most concerned.

Interest Groups and Democracy

Interest groups are a powerful instrument of democracy because they crystallize the opinions and interests of average citizens and present those views to elected officials during the policy-making process. It was precisely this power to influence policy that Madison feared so much and why he hoped that in a large republic, competition among interest groups would prevent any one of them from gaining too much influence. Interest groups contribute to a democracy by holding the government accountable for its actions, pressuring elected officials to be responsive to their constituents, and serving as a vehicle to equalize the influence of different groups of citizens in the policy process.

A group can channel the power of separate individuals into a single collective voice that is more likely to be heard throughout the policy system. In addition, the very existence of an interest group can keep citizens informed about the direct impact of policy on their lives; with that information, constituents can better hold their elected officials accountable for those policies.

Interest groups engage in several methods to influence economic, social, and foreign policy, including direct lobbying, media campaigns, legal challenges, and grassroots organizing. When interests clash, as in the case of education reform or energy policy, elected officials, bureaucrats, and even the judiciary often act as intermediaries. In Congress, political parties adopt positions that are favored or opposed by specific interest groups and thus create alliances between parties and interest groups. Although there are more interest groups today than ever before, political parties serve as a counterweight to the influence of interest groups. As partisanship has grown stronger in the House, the Senate, and even the White House, members who are asked to choose between an interest group and a political party choose the party. However, given that political parties tend to align very closely with supportive interest groups, members do not have to make that choice very often. To the extent that interest groups can influence politicians to address narrow or exclusive interests to the detriment of what is best for all citizens, they can be viewed as a negative aspect of the U.S. democracy.

Yet interest groups also represent a positive aspect of democracy when they serve to express wide-ranging viewpoints, and they continue to be an effective way of giving voice to citizens' needs and concerns. Interest groups continuously win and lose within the American policy-making system, and they reinvent their lobbying strategies in response to changing political and economic conditions. However, sole reliance on interest groups as a means of citizen participation is dangerous because some groups have more resources—time, money, and membership—than others and consequently win more often. In this way, interest groups can be both gateways and gates to citizen equality and the securing of policy benefits. Ultimately, citizens must hold both their interest group leaders and their elected officials accountable for public policy outcomes.

Chapter Review

Key Terms

citizens' groups (p. 275). How are citizens' groups different from single-interest groups?

economic interest groups (p. 272). What are the concerns of economic interest groups?

faction (p. 268). When is an interest group the same as a faction, and when is it different?

501(c)(3) organizations (p. 284). Why are 501(c)(3) organizations prohibited from lobbying?

501(c)(4) organizations (p. 284) Do 501(c)(4) organizations slant public policy toward particular interests?

free rider problem (p. 298). Why are free riders a problem for interest groups?

grassroots movement (p. 271). How is a grassroots movement different from an interest group?

ideological interest groups (p. 275). How do ideological interest groups differ from economic interest groups?

inside strategy (p. 283). How do interest groups lobby staff and members of Congress to advance their policy goals through direct contact?

interest groups (p. 268). How are interest groups a gateway to democracy?

iron law of oligarchy (p. 297). How is the iron law of oligarchy a problem for democracy?

iron triangle (p. 293). Describe the iron triangle as a gate against democracy.

issue network (p. 293). How is an issue network different from an iron triangle?

lobbying (p. 269). How is lobbying a form of an individual's rights of association and petition?

nongovernmental organizations (NGOs) (p. 277). What role do NGOs play in shaping U.S. foreign policy?

pluralist (p. 289). What is the role of interest groups in a pluralist society?

political action committees (PACs) (p. 284). How are PACs gateways for expanding interest groups' political influence?

public goods (p. 298). How should a public good be defined in a democracy?

revolving door (p. 294). What steps should Congress take to dismantle the revolving door?

right of association (p. 268). Why is the right of association a constitutional guarantee?

right of petition (p. 269). Why is the right of petition a constitutional guarantee?

selective benefits (p. 297). How do selective benefits attract and keep interest group members?

single-issue groups (p. 275). What is the impact of single-issue groups on campaigns and elections?

special interests (p. 290). What is a negative aspect of special interests?

unions (p. 270). What techniques do unions use to gain better wages and working conditions?

Learning Outcomes: What You Need to...

Know	Test Yourself	Participate
LO 8-1 Outline how interest groups have developed over time		
Interest groups are groups of citizens who share a common interest—political opinions, religious affiliations, ideological beliefs, social goals, or economic objectives—that try to influence public policy to benefit their members. The constitutional basis for interest groups lies in the First Amendment, which guarantees both the right to assemble and the right to petition the government for redress of grievances. Individuals and interest groups have lobbied legislators from the nation's earliest days, and their numbers have vastly increased. Today groups also lobby executive branch officials and attempt to influence judicial appointments and the courts through lawsuits and *amicus curiae* briefs.	• Describe what an interest group is. • Explain why Madison and the Framers feared factions. • Track the history of interest groups.	• Explain how you think interest groups influence the economic and social policies that affect your life.
LO 8-2 Identify the types of interest groups that have evolved		
Interest groups can be categorized as economic, ideological, and foreign policy and international, and each has different policy goals and strategies.	• Describe the different types of economic interest groups. • Explain how ideological and issue-oriented groups can lead to polarization. • Compare and contrast the missions of foreign policy and international interest groups.	• Create a set of interest groups that would represent different characteristics of voters such as gender, income, age, race, ethnicity, and ideology.
LO 8-3 Describe activities interest groups engage in		
Generally, interest groups gather and disseminate information in their issue areas, lobby using various strategies such as meeting with staff and legislators as well as workers in the executive branch, and contribute to political campaigns and advertising to the extent that federal law allows.	• Explain how interest groups keep members informed. • Describe how interest groups lobby. • Define *political action committee*.	• Take the position as head of an interest group, and describe your policy goal and what strategy you would use to influence legislators, voters, and other groups to support your policy goals.

Know	Test Yourself	Participate

LO 8-4   Analyze what balances out power among interest groups

Scholars who study why interest groups form and their effects in a democratic society debate whether the wealthy have disproportionate power to use interest groups to their advantage, and so to the disadvantage of others. Scholars also debate whether interest groups balance out each other. Lobbyists, federal regulators, and members of Congress form networks that some describe as "iron" and closed to citizen influence and some describe as transparent and open to citizen influence. In today's democracy, elected officials, bureaucrats, and even the judiciary often act as intermediaries in interest group conflict.

- Compare the pluralist and elitist views of democratic society.
- Explain why interest groups may be detrimental to the general public.
- Recall the routes of influence that interest groups can use.

- Propose ways of balancing power across interest groups to make sure that government is equally responsive to as many people as possible on a given issue.

LO 8-5   Assess what makes an interest group successful

The success of interest groups can be measured in four ways: leadership accountability, membership stability, financial stability, and public influence. The longer an interest group exists, the more powerful it is. When a policy is debated, some interest groups will win by maintaining the status quo, and others might win by changing current policy.

- Explain the importance of leadership accountability in interest group success.
- Describe issues in membership stability.
- Name sources of financial stability.
- Identify indicators of interest group influence.

- Consider how internally democratic interest groups really are.
- Evaluate whether the free rider is a problem for democracy.
- Debate whether an interest group can be too powerful.

PETE BUTTIGIEG
Harvard University, MA

> " *The case here is simple, it is time for a new generation of leadership in our country.* "

Harvard Gate, shown on the next page, is a prominent feature of Harvard campus, where Pete Buttigieg completed his undergraduate studies.

Pete Buttigieg (pronounced boot-edge-edge) burst onto the national political scene with a short-lived, but surprisingly successful campaign for the 2020 Democratic party nomination for president. Pete Buttigieg's unlikely foray into national politics began from a position as an obscure former mayor of South Bend, Indiana, a city of just over 100,000 people. At 38 years old, Pete Buttigieg ran as the youngest candidate in the Democratic field, the only openly gay candidate, and the first millennial to run for the presidency.

Peter Paul Montgomery Buttigieg grew up in South Bend, Indiana, with his parents, who both taught at the nearby University of Notre Dame. Active in high school, he was class president. He enrolled at Harvard University in 2000, where he majored in history and literature, graduating in 2004. He subsequently was awarded a Rhodes Scholarship from Oxford. Along the way, Buttigieg found that politics was his passion. As an 18-year-old, he volunteered for Al Gore's 2000 presidential campaign and four years later worked on John Kerry's presidential campaign. While still in college and between presidential campaigns, Buttigieg interned for Senator Ted Kennedy. He also worked as an intern on the campaign for Congresswoman Jill Long Thompson (D-IN) and later on her gubernatorial campaign.

Buttigieg was hired by the prestigious McKinsey and Company management strategy organization as a consultant following his time at Oxford, working there for three years. While employed at McKinsey, he joined the Navy Reserves in 2009 before the repeal of the "don't ask, don't tell" policy and became a lieutenant working as an intelligence officer. He deployed to Afghanistan for seven months in 2014. During this time he also learned to communicate in eight languages. Buttigieg is married to Chasten Glezman, a middle school teacher in South Bend.

After leaving McKinsey in 2010, Buttigieg returned to politics in earnest. At 27 years old, with no previous experience as an elected official, he nonetheless aimed high with a run for Indiana state treasurer. He lost that race by 27 points, but not the desire to serve in government. He learned from that experience and turned his sights back home to run for mayor of South Bend. Though only 28 years old, he became "Mayor Pete" in 2012 and served until January of 2020. He even ventured into national politics, unsuccessfully running for the chairmanship of the Democratic National Committee in 2017.

Mayor Pete's tenure in office was not without its challenges and controversies. His urban redevelopment programs are considered by some a model for the revitalization efforts of depressed urban areas. Known as the Vacant and Abandoned Properties Initiative, Buttigieg's plans included demolishing or repairing 1,000 properties in 1,000 days. The plan was successful and completed ahead of schedule. Over 1,100 properties were affected, and nearly 40 percent of the properties were repaired.

While his urban redevelopment programs are impressive, Mayor Pete also faced challenges, particularly in the black community of South Bend. Upon taking office in 2012, controversy over South Bend's first African American police chief Darryl Boykins' taping of alleged racist phone calls by white police officers came to Buttigieg's attention. Mayor Pete ended up demoting Chief Boykins, who retired soon after. Lawsuits and other legal disputes followed, and Buttigieg's judgment came into question with some charging that he was "tone deaf" to the African American community.

Mayor Pete decided to make his unlikely run for the presidency in 2019 at the age of 37 with a simple question that he asked during his deployment, "Why not me?" and became the youngest in the crowded field of candidates. With the slogan "Freedom, Security, and Democracy," Buttigieg began raising campaign funds and speaking to growing crowds. As the quote at the top of the page suggests, Pete Buttigieg, represents a new generation of leadership. Though he seemed to come out of nowhere, his ability to articulate his vision for America resonated with many Democrats. His impressive ability to connect with voters and communicate his centrist approach to politics propelled him to the national spotlight. His message of steady governance, leadership, and judgment led him to a surprising first place finish in the Iowa caucuses and a strong second place finish in New Hampshire. From that quick start, however, Buttigieg's performance waned, coming in third in Nevada and a disappointing distant fourth in South Carolina, receiving only 8 percent of the vote. It was at this point, on March 1, 2020, that Mayor Pete ended his candidacy and endorsed Joe Biden for the nomination.

Though his run for the Democratic nomination was brief, Pete Buttigieg figures to remain active in national politics and is forming a nonprofit political action committee named "Win the Era." The mission of the organization is to endorse and support young candidates in lower level races with the aim of creating a "pipeline" of future Democratic Party leaders. And, the chants of "2024!" have already begun.

Pete Buttigieg's gateways into politics began at an early age with a strong appetite for the political world. He found entry into that world through internships and active participation in all things political. His trajectory in politics is a testament to the opportunities for younger generations to voice their views, be part of the national political conversation about the future of government and politics in America, and ask themselves, "Why not me?"

The Role of Political Parties in American Democracy

LO 9-1 Outline how political parties evolved in American politics

A democratic government must be responsive to its citizens, and for government to be equally responsive, every citizen must have an equal opportunity to influence it. But mobilizing the more than 325 million people in the United States to take an active role in monitoring their government is a truly momentous challenge. In the United States, political parties fill an essential need by shaping the choices that voters face in elections, which serve as the key mechanism by which voters hold their government accountable. With so many public offices to fill, voters need some sort of road map to compare candidates and make the choices that will serve their best interests. The potential danger of relying on parties to shape these choices is that parties become interested only in winning office, not in serving the interests of the people. It takes action and vigilance on the part of voters to ensure that parties do not go in this direction.

In this section, we look at the role that parties play in the American democratic system. Specifically at the way they organize the electorate, shape the elections that determine whether their candidates win office, and guide the actions of elected officials.

What Are Political Parties?

A **political party** is a group of individuals who join together to choose candidates for elected office—whether by informal group voting or a formal nominating process. These candidates agree to abide by the **party platform**, a document that lays out the party's core beliefs and policy proposals. Parties operate through national, state, and county committees; members include party activists, citizen volunteers, and elected officials. A party's main purpose is to win elections in order to control governmental power and implement its policies; this fundamental goal distinguishes parties from interest groups, which also seek to influence electoral outcomes but do not formally run candidates for office.

At the national level, the party issues its platform during presidential election years. In their 2020 platforms, for example, the Republican Party (www.gop.org) and the Democratic Party (www.dnc.org) stated their positions on national security, health care, energy policy, the environment, and taxes. These platforms not only define the positions of the presidential and vice presidential candidates but also serve as a general guide to the policy positions of all the candidates running under the party label. From time to time, individual candidates may disagree with elements of the party's platform, but, in general, candidates who choose to run under a party label are defined by it. Using party labels as a shortcut for the party platform, when parties hold majorities in Congress, for example, voters can hold the elected officials accountable for their policy successes and blame them for policy failures.

Citizens tend to vote for one party over the other in somewhat predictable patterns. Classic political scientists, such as V. O. Key Jr., use the term *party in the electorate* to describe the general patterns of voters' party identification and their behavior on Election Day. A main goal of any political party is to maximize party affiliation among voters so that it translates

Key Questions

In what ways are parties gateways for citizen participation? As you read this chapter, look for evidence.

political parties: *Broad coalitions of interests organized to win elections in order to enact a commonly supported set of public policies.*

party platform: *Document that lays out a party's core beliefs and policy proposals for each presidential election.*

into a solid majority of the party in the electorate, which can in turn translate to a solid majority of the *party in government*. To accomplish this goal, the *party as an organization* is created, with internal structures that guide how the party functions.[1] The modern American political party is multilevel, with committees at the federal, state, and local levels.

What Political Parties Do

Key Questions
Which political party, if any, do you identify with?

In this section, we move from theoretical ideas about political parties to what they actually do in the American political system.

Parties in the Electorate.   Parties offer several layers of opportunity for political participation. Most simply, a person can claim to be a member of a party by stating that he or she identifies with it, for example, by saying "I am a Republican." That statement is an acknowledgment of party identification—an attachment or allegiance to a political party. Voters identify with parties for several reasons. The simplest is the belief that the policies put forth by one party will serve their interests better than the policies proposed by other parties in the political arena. Another reason to join a party stems from family or social environment, in which being a member of a party is similar to other personal characteristics. As Chapter 6, Public Opinion, explains, many young people adopt the party identification of their parents. Although parties always ask for contributions, there are no membership fees. For this reason, parties provide the broadest and most open gateway to participation in American politics.

Key Questions
Have you formally affiliated with a political party? What are the advantages and the disadvantages of doing so?

A more formal step of party identification is stating party affiliation when registering to vote. Voter registration rules vary by state, but they typically require a citizen to show proof of identity and address to an official government office. In some places, voters can register by mail or when they get their driver's licenses, but in others, they must fill out the forms in person at a local board of elections.

At the next level of participation, voters can become active in the party at the town, county, state, and federal level. Parties encourage people to volunteer on campaigns at every level—making phone calls to prospective voters, passing out bumper stickers, or maintaining e-mail contact through the campaign website. Of course, political parties expect their members to vote on Election Day and to bring their friends, coworkers, and family members to the polls with them. Parties also rely on supporters to build up the organization and candidates by making financial contributions.

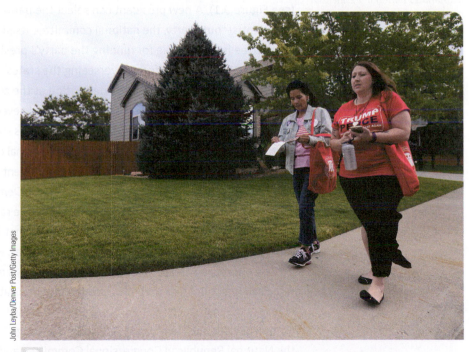

John Leyba/Denver Post/Getty Images

Image 9.1 Get-out-the-vote efforts are a crucial part of local party organization work. Campaigns with organized "ground games" are essential in ensuring their candidates' voters vote in early balloting and on election day. These supporters of the Trump-Pence campaign are canvassing a neighborhood in Thornton, Colorado, a battleground state.

Political parties also serve as a gateway to elected office. Pete Buttigieg, for example, got his start in politics while in college, working on a congressional campaign, and later working on John Kerry's 2004 presidential campaign. Many candidates who seek public office start out by affiliating with a party in college and rise through the ranks of party organizations. Parties also actively recruit individuals in their county, district, or state to run for elected office. Candidate recruitment involves party leaders at all levels trying to identify people who would make good candidates for elected office because they are well known in the community, have personal wealth, or have a professional record that speaks to current issues and would appeal to voters.

Parties in Government.

party caucus: *Group of party members in a legislature.*

Parties also serve to organize members of Congress and state legislatures into cohesive groups, known as **party caucuses**, which consistently vote, year after year, for the policies that the parties promise in their platforms. The party in government is made up of the elected officials who share the same party affiliation and work together to accomplish the party's electoral and policy goals. Elected officials often hold positions in party organizations as well. For example, Terry McAuliffe, who served as the chair of the national Democratic Party from 2001 to 2005, was elected governor of Virginia, serving from 2014 to 2018. Even the president, whose primary responsibility is to govern, is expected to serve as leader of his political party by setting the agenda according to party policy goals. The president is also increasingly expected to engage in political support for party candidates, from campaign appearances to party fundraisers.

Party Organization.

national committee: *Top level of national political parties; coordinates national presidential campaigns.*

The modern political party is structured as a multilevel organization with units at the federal, state, and local levels. **National committees** are at the top of the party organization, and their members are chosen by each state party organization (see Figure 9.1). A new president can select the national committee chair; in the case of the presidential "out" party, the national committee itself elects the party chair. The national committee is responsible for running the party's presidential nominating convention every four years. Key to that effort is overseeing the states' primary delegate selection process and officially recognizing a state's delegation at the convention.

The main job of the national committee is to do everything possible to elect the party's presidential nominee every four years, which requires strengthening all party organizations from the national down to the local levels. The national committee runs training workshops on party-centered activities, such as candidate recruitment and fundraising. It has to raise money; for example, in the 2020 presidential campaign, the Democratic National Committee raised $986 million, and the Republican National Committee raised $756 million.[2] The national party can spend its money on coordinated expenditures (that is, in cooperation with the presidential campaign), and it can make independent expenditures, which are funds spent separately on general efforts to increase voter turnout for the party's nominee.

Each major political party has a committee dedicated to raising money for incumbent House and Senate members. For the Democrats, it is the Democratic Congressional Campaign Committee and the Democratic Senatorial Campaign Committee; for the Republicans, it is the National Republican Congressional Committee and the National Republican Senatorial Committee. These congressional party committees are also responsible for recruiting qualified challengers to run for seats held by the opposing party and helping to fund their campaigns. Through November 2020, the four congressional party organizations raised approximately $592 million in the 2019–20 cycle.[3]

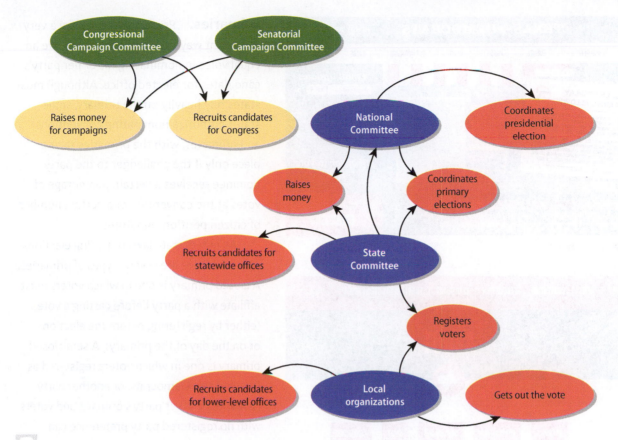

Figure 9.1 Party Organization at the National, State, and Local Levels

This figure shows the three levels of political party organizations and their primary functions. American political parties are interconnected and work to elect their candidates to office.

State political parties are the next level of party organization, and they are regulated by state law, so their responsibilities can vary by state. Typically a political party has a state central committee that tries to elect candidates to statewide office and also works with local organizations to recruit new voters and raise money. As you can see from the websites of the Texas Republican and Democratic parties in Images 9.2 and 9.3, each state party organization displays the structure of the state party organization, gives information about how to become involved with the party, and provides information about the key issues. Each state party organization has its own website, which displays the structure of the state party organization and provides information about how to become involved with the party.

Local party organizations exist at the county, town, and precinct or ward levels. The essential functions of local party organizations are to recruit candidates for lower-level elected offices, register voters, and, most important, ensure that voters get to the polls on Election Day.[4]

The Party Nomination Process

One of the most important functions of parties is to nominate candidates for office and then elect them, a process accomplished in two stages. In elections with more than one candidate seeking the party's nomination, states hold **primary elections**, in which voters determine the party's choice to run in the next stage—the **general election**.

primary election: *Election in which voters select the candidates who will run on the party label in the general election; also called direct primary.*

general election: *Election in which voters choose their elected officials.*

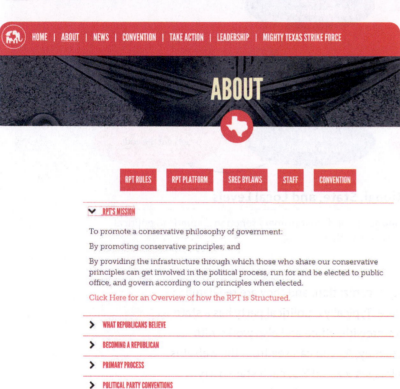

Images 9.2 and 9.3 State political parties can be powerful in shaping state politics. They help recruit candidates for the state legislatures; after the primaries, they work hard to elect their party's nominees to statewide office. Here the websites of the Texas Democratic Party and the Texas Republican Party announce news, activities, and opinions on issues.

ballot: *List of candidates who are running for elected office; used by voters to make their choice.*

Primaries. Primary elections are a very important way that each voter can have an equal voice in nominating his or her party's candidates for elected office. Although most states rely heavily on the primary, some states authorize nominating conventions and primaries, with the primaries taking place only if the challenger to the party nominee receives a certain percentage of votes at the convention or a certain number of citizen petition signatures.[5]

As noted, state laws regarding elections vary, and there are several types of primaries. A closed primary is one in which voters must affiliate with a party before casting a vote (either by registering before the election or on the day of the primary). A semiclosed primary is one in which voters registered as Republicans, Democrats, or another party cast votes in their party's primary, and voters with no registered party preference can choose a party's primary ballot at the polls. In an open primary, voters do not have to affiliate with a party before voting. Instead, they are given **ballots** with each party's list of candidates, and they can choose which ballot to use but are restricted to voting for only one party's nominees. In a blanket primary, voters are given the ballots from all parties and allowed to cast votes for any party's candidates as long as they cast only one vote per elective office. But, in 2000, the Supreme Court ruled that blanket primaries were unconstitutional if the parties themselves wished to keep their nominations to actual party members (see Supreme Court Cases: *California Democratic Party v. Jones*). Currently some states use a modified version of a blanket primary, known as the nonpartisan blanket primary, in which all the candidates, from all parties, who are running for office are listed without identifying their party affiliation, and if no majority winner emerges, the top two vote-getters face each other in a runoff election.

Primary elections are a fact of political life, but insofar as they create competition within a political party and encourage candidates to reveal negative aspects of each other's professional or personal lives, they can weaken the party's eventual nominee when he or

Supreme Court Cases

California Democratic Party v. Jones (2000)

QUESTION: Do blanket primaries, in which voters can vote for any party's candidate regardless of their own party affiliation, violate the right of association of political parties that want to limit their primaries to those who belong to the party?

ORAL ARGUMENT: April 24, 2000 (listen at http://www.oyez.org/cases/1990-1999/1999/1999_99_401)

DECISION: June 26, 2000 (read at http://caselaw.lp.findlaw.com/cgi-bin/getcase.pl?court=US&navby=case&vol=000&invol=99-401)

OUTCOME: Yes, the right of association means that states cannot force parties to open their primaries to voters who are not party members (7–2).

In 1996, voters in California approved Proposition 198 (see Chapter 3, Federalism, on citizen initiatives), which established a blanket primary in which each voter can vote in any primary election, regardless of party affiliation. In 2000, to prevent Republicans from voting in its primary, the California Democratic Party went to court, claiming that California's blanket primary law violated the state Democratic Party's right to freedom of association as guaranteed by the First Amendment.

Ultimately, the case reached the Supreme Court, where Justice Antonin Scalia wrote the majority opinion in favor of the California Democratic Party.

The Court ruled blanket primaries to be unconstitutional because they violated the First Amendment. The majority argued that a blanket primary violated a political party's right to associate exclusively with its members, which can be extended to mean that political parties have the right to allow only registered party members to choose their party's nominees in a primary. Scalia wrote that "Proposition 198 forces political parties to associate with—to have their nominees, and hence their positions, determined by—those who, at best, have refused to affiliate with the party, and, at worst, have expressly affiliated with a rival."

Thinking Critically

1. Should a political party be forced to give voters who are not members the same privileges that party members have?
2. Why might a political party want to be responsive to voters who are not members?

she faces opponents in the general election. Because party organizations want the candidate who is most likely to win the election nominated under the party banner, they try to exert control over the primary election process in several ways. First, state laws govern party ballot access—literally, who can actually get on the primary election ballot. The relationship between elite state party members and state legislators is very close, so the party controls the gate by determining how open or restrictive ballot access is for candidates seeking to run for office on the party label. Second, although party organizations remain technically neutral during the primary election season, they can steer donors toward their preferred candidates and away from candidates who do not agree with their goals. As a consequence, individuals who are perceived as weak or as not loyal to the party may run into major roadblocks set up by the party organization. Later in this chapter, we discuss a examples of intraparty conflict.

Key Questions

Have you voted in a primary election? What kind of primary was it? Did you have to identify your party affiliation?

The Presidential Nomination. The process by which each party nominates its presidential candidate has evolved from one that was concentrated in the hands of a small group of elites to the modern process that allows millions of voters to participate directly in choosing the party's presidential nominee (see Figure 9.2).

In a presidential primary, voters cast a vote for a particular candidate, but what they are really doing is choosing delegates who will support that nominee at the party's national nominating convention. In a presidential **caucus**, which serves the same nominating purpose, the process is less formal and more personal in that party members meet in town halls, schools, and even private homes to choose a nominee. Each state is awarded a number of delegates to the convention by the national party organization based largely on the number of Electoral College votes the state has but also on the size of party support in that state. The candidate who wins a majority of the delegates from the primary and caucus elections is selected at the national convention as the party's nominee for president.

The Democratic Party and Republican Party allocate their delegates within the primaries and caucuses differently. The Democratic Party has had a more tumultuous nominating process due in large part to some key rule changes in the 1970s and 1980s. In the 1960s, members of underrepresented groups, such as women and African Americans, began calling for a change in the presidential nominating procedures for the Democratic Party. Specifically, they objected to the use of the unit rule, or **winner-take-all system**, which meant that whoever won the majority of primary or state nominating convention votes would win the entire state's delegates. Activists believed that the unit rule allowed conservative white men to dominate the nominating process. In response to this grassroots movement, the Democrats formed the McGovern-Fraser Commission in 1972, which recommended changes in the way that delegates were chosen and awarded to candidates during the primary season. One result of the commission's work was seen in the 1976 election when the Democrats formally instituted **proportional representation**; that is, the number of delegates that

caucus: *Meeting of party members in town halls, schools, and private homes to select a presidential nominee.*

winner-take-all system: *Electoral system in which whoever wins the most votes in an election wins the election.*

proportional representation: *An electoral system that assigns party delegates according to vote share in a presidential primary election or that assigns seats in the legislature according to vote share in a general election.*

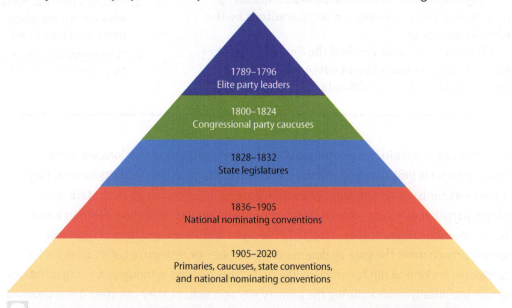

Figure 9.2 **The Evolution of the Presidential Nominating Process, 1789–2020**

This figure depicts the changing nature of the way American political parties nominate candidates for president. The decision-making process in American parties has evolved from small groups of elites, called cadres, to large, mass-based decision making in caucuses and primaries.

a candidate receives is based on the percentage of the vote received in the primary or caucus, either at the state level or in each congressional district. In most states, delegates are committed to a candidate before the primary election takes place.

To further address the activists' concern that the nominating process was dominated by white men, the 1972 reforms required a certain percentage of each state's delegates to be women, African Americans, young people (defined as eligible voters under 30), and other underrepresented groups based on their proportion in each state's population.[6] If states did not comply with this requirement, the national party reserved the right not to "seat" or count their delegates in the final nominating vote held at the party's national convention. Although the party stated the goal of increasing delegates from underrepresented groups, it did not really increase African American convention participation until 1984, when Jesse Jackson, an African American, ran for the Democratic presidential nomination. Although the nomination went to former Vice President Walter Mondale, Jackson was successful enough to insist that more people of color be delegates to the convention. The cumulative effect of these reforms created a gateway for members of underrepresented groups to exert influence in determining the Democratic Party presidential nominee.

In 1981, the Democratic Party made several other changes, including requiring that each state's delegation comprise an equal number of men and women, and creating a category of delegates known as superdelegates. The superdelegates are not chosen through the primary voting process but rather are active members of the party who will be instrumental in turning out party voters in the general election. Most superdelegates are elected officials in the party, such as governors and members of Congress from each state, as well as state party committee chairs and key activists in interest groups that are loyal to the Democrats. They are uncommitted and free to choose whomever they wish to support at the convention.[7] Their role changed in the 2020 nomination process. In contrast to the Democratic Party, the Republican Party had rarely faced an internal demand for more diverse representation, so it had not significantly changed its nominating system. But in 2010, the Republican Party adopted proportional representation in its nominating system in the hopes of generating more competition and a lengthier campaign season, both of which would increase turnout and enthusiasm among

Logan Cyrus/AFP/Getty Images

Image 9.4 In 2020, the number of Democrats vying for the party's nomination reached twenty-seven at one point. As the primary season progressed, the number of contenders qualifying for the debates by demonstrating sufficient support in polls, narrowed to seven (seen here) with former Vice President Joe Biden ultimately winning the nomination.

Key Questions

How does proportional representation affect the dynamics of primaries?

Key Questions

How do primaries allow voters to register their opinions with party leaders about candidates and about party policy positions?

The Role of Political Parties in American Democracy **313**

Stefani Reynolds/Bloomberg/Getty Images

Image 9.5 In 2020, former Vice President Joe Biden was nominated for president of the United States by Democrats. Biden chose Senator Kamala Harris (D-CA) as his vice-presidential running mate. The Biden and Harris Democratic Party ticket was celebrated at their national party convention in Milwaukee.

Republican voters.[8] States that did not abide by this system, including Florida and Arizona, were penalized by losing some of their delegates to the national convention. Republicans have no requirements as to the racial or gender composition of a state's delegates, and they have no superdelegates. However, they did add a category of bonus delegates to the 2012 nominating process, awarding these to states based on the percentage of votes cast for the Republican presidential candidate in past elections; in general, bonus delegates are often elected officials and loyal party activists.

However, the 2012 GOP nomination process proved to be too drawn out and conflictual, and turnout among Republicans did not increase appreciably in the general election. Proportional representation, combined with the role of Super PACs, allowed candidates who did not have a strong majority to stay in the nomination contest and collect delegates longer than under a winner-take-all system (see Chapter 10, Elections and Campaigns, for a discussion of Super PACs).

For the 2016 nomination process, the Republicans made more changes to their rules, including scheduling the New Hampshire and South Carolina primaries and Iowa and Nevada caucuses all in February and barring all other states from holding their nominating contests earlier than those four states. States holding their contests between March 1 and March 14 awarded all their delegates proportionate to the vote received by the candidates; states holding contests from March 15 onward could choose either a proportional or a winner-take-all system. Due to concerns that the twenty-seven debates damaged the eventual 2012 nominee, Mitt Romney, the Republican Party chose to hold twelve debates in 2016.[9]

The 2020 nomination contests saw the Democrats change their rules as a result of the Clinton-Sanders battle for the nomination four years earlier. Prior to 2020, superdelegates were allowed to vote on the first nomination ballot at the party's national convention. Hillary Clinton had overwhelming support from superdelegates and was able to secure the party's nomination, in large part, due to that support. Sanders, while popular among primary and caucus participants, lost the nomination to Clinton in a contentious process. Amid calls for changes in the process to rely more heavily on party rank and file voters, the rules were changed to only allow superdelegates to vote if no candidate received the required number of votes necessary on the first ballot (1,991 out of 3,979 delegates in 2020) and require a candidate to receive at least 15 percent of support in the primary or caucus to secure any delegates from a state. Senator Sanders started the 2020 season strong, accumulating more delegates than any candidate in the first three contests in Iowa, New Hampshire, and Nevada. His lead in delegates stopped in South Carolina when former Vice President Joe Biden won by a large margin and continued to build on his lead through Super Tuesday and until there was a pause in the primaries due to the COVID-19 pandemic. With other candidates dropping out of the nomination race, the only viable candidates remaining were Biden and Sanders.

As the country attempted to slow the spread of the coronavirus in spring 2020, Americans were encouraged to stay at home. Large gatherings such as political rallies and candidate events were not allowed. Some states postponed primaries. Though campaigns and rallies paused, the nomination process nonetheless continued until Bernie Sanders conceded and ended his campaign. Biden went on to secure the required number of delegates in succeeding primaries.

Invisible Primary.   Recent theories about the role of political parties in managing the presidential nomination process note that three factors have a strong predictive effect on which candidates emerge as the party's nominee: (1) party support as measured by endorsements by party activists, (2) support among party voters as indicated by polls, and (3) financial support as candidates enter the nomination phase known as the "**invisible primary**."[10] The invisible primary phase of the process is that period of time between when candidates announce their run for the nomination and the first party caucuses and primary elections. It is so named because it takes place before a single vote is taken. The invisible primary is when networks of party activists, donors, and elected officials from the respective parties begin the informal sorting of potential candidates and winnowing of the field of viable nominees. Likewise, it is when the candidates actively seek donor support, name recognition, and early endorsements from elected officials. Although the "winner" of the invisible primary is not a guaranteed winner of the nomination, endorsements, money, and popular support are seen as essential to a viable candidacy. (See the full description of the invisible primary in Chapter 10, Elections and Campaigns, pp. 353–355.)

invisible primary: *Period just before the primaries begin during which candidates attempt to capture party support and media coverage.*

The 2016 nomination process was a good test of the invisible primary thesis and offered mixed results. On the Democratic Party side, Hillary Clinton led in all three categories. She had a large "war chest" of money, most of the possible endorsements from members of Congress and Democratic governors, and was leading in most polls of party supporters heading into the Iowa caucuses and New Hampshire primaries. She maintained her lead in all of those areas and emerged as the winner of the party's nomination, despite substantial support for the candidacy of Senator Bernie Sanders. The Republican nomination process unfolded much differently, with Governor Jeb Bush leading the GOP candidates in money raised, early endorsements from party leaders, and support among party voters. That support quickly eroded with

Saul Loeb/AFP/Getty Images

Image 9.6 As the incumbent president, Donald J. Trump was the 2020 Republican Party presidential nominee after facing only token and short-lived opposition. Here he is seen with his running mate, Mike Pence, as they are formally recognized at the Republican National Party convention in Charlotte, North Carolina.

the Donald Trump campaign. Though then-candidate Trump had few endorsements, he presented himself as capable of self-funding his campaign, and he maintained a steady level of support relative to the other candidates. Once the caucus and primary season began, his level of support remained steady while other candidates dropped out of the race for lack of support at the polls. Republican elected officials switched their endorsements from Jeb Bush, to Senator Marco Rubio, and then to Senator Ted Cruz as each ended their campaigns before Donald Trump secured the nomination. The role of endorsements among Republican party elected officials was not enough to stem the tide of Donald Trump's campaign.

Questions remain about whether Donald Trump's successful campaign for the nomination over objections from the GOP in government reaches beyond his candidacy. Was his success due solely to his message and charisma, or is his approach a new recipe for earning a political party's nomination? Is the Republican Party particularly vulnerable to candidates winning without approval from establishment party officials? One election year provides too little evidence to know for sure, though in 2020, there were no Republican debates and what primaries did have other candidates on the ballots were won overwhelmingly by President Trump. The strongest challenger to Trump, former Massachusetts governor William Weld, dropped out of the race on March 18, having secured only one delegate to the national convention.

The Dynamics of Early Party Development

LO 9-2 Identify which issues divided the first political parties

Political parties in 2020 seem well established, as if they have existed as long as the nation itself. But parties were not intended to be part of the original fabric of the political system. They emerged from disagreements among the Framers. Today, two large parties include a broad swath of the electorate and must make internal compromises to stay unified. In this section, we trace the background to these developments.

Political Factions: Federalist Versus Antifederalist

Key Questions

Given the Framers' views on factions and political parties, do you think the development of parties has been good or bad for American democracy?

James Madison, writing in *Federalist Papers* 10 and 51 (see the Appendix), predicted the rise of factions, groups of individuals who share a common political goal and ally with each other on a temporary basis to accomplish that goal. Although factions were not considered the same thing as political parties of the kind that had emerged in Britain, the Framers feared that both factions and parties might encourage divisions in the young democracy that could threaten its existence.

Yet factions emerged even before the Constitution was adopted. In the debate over ratification (see Chapter 2, The Constitution), those who argued for the Constitution called themselves Federalists. They believed that a stable federal government that could collect tax revenue, raise and maintain an army and navy, regulate foreign and domestic trade, and stabilize currency would make the American democratic experiment a success. Opponents of a strong national government, however, viewed the future of the United States in terms of loosely affiliated but sovereign states that governed themselves, managing their own tax policies and internal security. These were the Antifederalists. In their view, the United States had just fought a war to overturn a strong monarch, and they did not want to put themselves under the rule of an oppressive new centralized government that would govern from the top down (see Table 9.1).

Ultimately, the Federalist viewpoint triumphed, and the Constitution was ratified. But the debate did not end there. The nation's first president, George Washington (1789–97), formed a government that included proponents of a strong national government (led by Alexander Hamilton and John Adams) and strong state governments (led by Thomas Jefferson). Washington worried that opposing views could lead to organized political parties that would cause conflict in the new nation.[11]

Key Questions

Try to relate the modern Democratic and Republican Parties to the viewpoints of the Federalists and the Antifederalists. Which party comes closest to which viewpoint?

Thomas Jefferson, Andrew Jackson, and the Emergence of the Democratic Party

After winning the election of 1800, Thomas Jefferson used his victory to transform his fledgling political party into a viable long-term organization known as the Democratic-Republicans (most candidates shortened the name to Republican), while the supporters of Adams and Hamilton united around the Federalist Party.[12] The Democratic-Republicans occupied the White House for the next twenty-eight years with the terms of Jefferson (1801–09), James Madison (1809–17), James Monroe (1817–25), and John Quincy Adams (1825–29). The Federalist Party slowly faded away as a force in politics.

The Democratic-Republicans soon split over the nomination process for president. Specifically Andrew Jackson, an ambitious politician, wanted to take the party to a new level of inclusiveness and use that wider reach to become president. Jackson, from Tennessee, had served in both the House and the Senate, but he made his national reputation during the War of 1812, especially as the hero of the Battle of New Orleans. After his military service ended, Jackson returned to Congress and attempted to win the presidential nomination of the Democratic-Republicans in 1824.[13] At that time, presidential nominations were decided by party caucuses in Congress. Only about a fourth of the members of the party showed up to cast their votes, and no one won a majority. As a result there were four Democratic-Republican "nominees": Andrew Jackson, John Quincy Adams, William Crawford, and Henry Clay.[14] None of the candidates received a majority of electoral votes, and the House of Representatives chose John Quincy Adams as president in what Jackson charged was the result of a "corrupt bargain" between Adams and Clay. (See Chapter 11, Voting and Participation, for a discussion of that election.)

Key Questions

How did Jackson open gateways to citizen participation? What were the consequences?

Table 9.1   Federalist and Antifederalist Policies

Federalist	Antifederalist
Ratify the Constitution	Oppose ratification of the Constitution
Establish central bank	Oppose central bank
Protect commercial interests	Support agricultural interests
Assert federal supremacy	Preserve state power
See no need for Bill of Rights	Pass Bill of Rights

Source: Adapted from John H. Aldrich and Ruth Grant, "The Antifederalists, the First Congress, and the First Parties," *Journal of Politics* 55 (1993): 295–326.

Image 9.7 Andrew Jackson originated the modern political party by encouraging grassroots participation by voters and party organizations in his election campaigns and by building the Democratic Party while he served as president from 1829 to 1837.

Universal History Archive/Universal Images Group/Getty Images

By 1828, the nomination process had begun to change, with nominations by parties located at the state level, in legislatures and state conventions, rather than the national Congress. By locating the nomination process in the states instead of in Congress, parties enlarged the number of people involved in making the decision about who could run for president. In 1828, using a grassroots state-level strategy to attract both the support of state legislators and the voters themselves, Jackson worked closely with Martin Van Buren, a powerful New York politician, to challenge Adams for the nomination of the Democratic-Republicans; this time, Jackson won the nomination and the presidential election. Then, as now, it is rare for a challenger to defeat the incumbent president in American politics.

As president, Jackson worked closely with Van Buren to knock down the gates that stood in the way of public access to party decisions, to make their political party more accessible to the general public, and to attract the votes of an ever-expanding nation. They recognized that parties could be more than mere coalitions of politicians who agreed on policy; they could be full-fledged grassroots organizations.[15] To accomplish that goal, they had to offer incentives to individuals to join the party organization, including the patronage system discussed later in this chapter. They even shortened the name of the party to the Democratic Party to signal that they were building a new kind of political party organization.

By 1832, the end of Jackson's first term in office, politics had changed in fundamental ways because of the nation's rapid geographic and population growth.[16] The Jackson-led Democrats emerged as a large grassroots majority political party, and Jackson used all the powers of the presidency to strengthen his political party around the country. In the meantime, the anti-Jackson wing of the old Democratic-Republicans had taken the name National Republicans. In the presidential election of 1832, the National Republicans nominated Henry Clay, a U.S. senator from Kentucky, to run against Jackson.

Although Henry Clay lost that election to Jackson, he returned to the Senate and started laying the groundwork for a new political party that would oppose Jackson's policies. He encouraged members of the National Republicans to join forces with others who opposed Jackson and to form the Whig Party, which objected to what they viewed as Jackson's abuse of presidential power for partisan gains. From 1832 to 1856, the Democrats and the Whigs dominated American politics and presidential elections. However, the issue of slavery soon emerged to shake up the party balance.

The Antislavery Movement and the Formation of the Republican Party

The Democratic Party's general strategy for opening a larger gateway for citizen participation in politics inadvertently encouraged alternate groups and political parties to emerge on the political scene. In 1833, William Lloyd Garrison, a white journalist, formed the American Anti-Slavery Society to press for the abolition of slavery. Former slave Frederick Douglass and other African Americans in the North also led efforts to end slavery, and the abolitionist movement grew large and vocal enough to pressure the Democrats and Whigs to take a formal position on slavery, especially the extension of slavery into western territories.

Northern and southern Democrats were united against the abolitionist movement, but for different reasons. Northern Democrats recognized that if the slavery question came to the forefront of politics, the nationally dominant Democratic Party would be split between the North and the South. Southern Democrats opposed abolishing slavery outright or limiting its expansion because the plantation economy of the South was heavily dependent on slave labor.

Further complicating party politics were smaller **third parties** that arose in the North, some explicitly antislavery. Third parties are minor political parties that present an alternative to the two dominant political parties in the American political system. They have been a part of the political system since the early nineteenth century. Typically, third parties focus on a single issue; the Liberty Party, for example, was explicitly antislavery, while the Green Party, active today, focuses on environmental protection (we discuss third parties in greater depth later in this chapter). As frequently happens in American politics, however, third parties are absorbed into larger parties; the Liberty Party was absorbed into a larger coalition of groups, led by the Free Soilers, which opposed the expansion of slavery in the territories. Meeting in Ripon, Wisconsin, in 1854, these groups were also joined by some antislavery northern Democrats, and the modern Republican Party was born. In the words of one activist, Alvan E. Bovay, "We went into the little meeting held in a schoolhouse Whigs, Free Soilers, and Democrats. We came out of it Republicans."[17] Six years later, the Republican Party had consolidated its support and elected Abraham Lincoln (1861–65) to the presidency.

Shortly after Lincoln's election, seven southern states seceded from the union, and the Civil War erupted. The Confederacy dissolved after the war ended in 1865, but southerners resented northerners and the Republican Party because of both the South's physical and economic losses and the continued occupation of the South by northern troops. Since that time, the Democrats and the Republicans have been the nation's two major political parties.

Party Loyalty and Patronage

Andrew Jackson set an example of how to build a political party organization using government resources. Just as Jackson worked to expand the electorate, he sought to expand the size of the federal government in order to increase the number of federally funded jobs his party could control. The Jacksonian era provided many opportunities to bring the federal government into the state and local arena by establishing programs to build forts, post roads (for mail delivery), customhouses, and lighthouses. Whoever

third parties: *Minor political parties that present a third alternative to the two dominant political parties in the American political system.*

Provided courtesy HarpWeek

"THAT'S WHAT'S THE MATTER."
Boss Tweed. "As long as I count the Votes, what are you going to do about it? say?"

Image 9.8 William Marcy "Boss" Tweed was the head of the Democratic Party machine in New York City in the 1850s and 1860s. He was notorious for using political office to hand out favors and benefits to loyal party members and to accumulate personal wealth. The editorial cartoons of Thomas Nast helped expose the graft and corruption of the "Tweed Ring."

patronage system: *Political system in which government programs and benefits are awarded based on political loyalty to a party or politician.*

controlled the jobs associated with these federal programs could also demand political allegiance from those who filled them. By the late nineteenth century, a system emerged whereby the politician became the "patron" of the businessmen and workers who were on the payrolls of the federal or the state governments. Jobs built party loyalty, and those hired often had to declare their political allegiance to the politician who arranged for the job and promise to vote for him. Such a system is commonly referred to as a **patronage system**.

As the government expanded, so did the party organization. At each level—federal, state, and local—there were parallel party committees. Parties became the organizations they are today, with a national committee, state committees, and local chapters at the county, ward, town, or precinct level. At each level, leaders who had power within the party acted as party bosses, controlling the distribution of public funds and making sure to reward supporters and withhold funds from opponents. The key element in this system was the loyalty of supporters who voted for the boss's preferred set of candidates on Election Day. Voter support in this kind of system was so reliable and predictable that it became known as machine politics; it ran like a well-oiled machine.

The expansion of party machines was fueled by a huge influx of new immigrants in the late nineteenth century who mostly settled in large cities of the North and Midwest. Democratic bosses in these cities recognized that immigrants, once naturalized, would be a major source of new voters and courted their loyalty through patronage. In turn, parties served as a type of gateway for immigrants to become integrated into American political life. As city populations increased at a much faster rate than rural populations, Democrats gained political power in cities, while Republican power in the North and Midwest tended to be concentrated in rural areas.

Key Questions

Do you see the patronage system still at work today in American politics? Explain.

Reform and the Erosion of Party Control

A critical factor in the success of machine politics was party control of voting. In contrast to today's system—in which states manage most aspects of elections, including ballot design and ballot counting—local parties in the late nineteenth century printed their own ballots, called party strip ballots, which listed only their candidates, and gave them to voters on their way into the polling places. In many places, party officials counted the votes as well, further manipulating the voting process to their advantage.

However, three developments eroded party organizations' control over government jobs and elections: the creation of a merit-based system of government employment, the introduction of ballot reforms, and a change in the way nominees for elected office were selected. All three reforms were led by Progressives, coalitions of Democrats and Republicans who believed that government had been captured by corrupt elites who were using government resources to enrich themselves rather than to serve citizens.

Since Andrew Jackson's day, bosses in the old patronage system had taken for granted the right to distribute government jobs to their supporters. But in 1883, the Pendleton Act reformed the civil service by requiring that government jobs be filled based on merit, not on political connections (see Chapter 14, The Bureaucracy, for more on the civil service). This was the first of several laws that slowly transformed the federal bureaucracy from a corrupt insider organization to a neutral, policy-based organization.[18]

Voting procedures were also reformed between 1888 and 1911 as states adopted the so-called **Australian ballot** system, which originated in Australia in 1858, to replace the party strip ballots[19] (see Figure 9.3). When parties had printed the ballots and had given them to

Australian ballot: *Voting system in which state governments run elections and provide voters the option of choosing candidates from multiple parties; also called the secret ballot.*

Figure 9.3 **Ballot Reform**

On the left are examples of party strip ballots used in Rhode Island in 1888. These types of ballots were printed by political parties and handed to voters on Election Day. They gave voters no opportunity to split their vote among different parties. On the right is an example of the so-called Australian ballot. Like this ballot used in Rhode Island in 1892, Australian ballots were printed by state governments rather than by political parties. They listed all candidates for elected office, not just candidates from a single party, and therefore allowed voters to split their vote among different parties.

Source: Russell J. DeSimone and Daniel C. Schofield, "Rhode Island Election Tickets: A Survey," Technical Services Department Faculty Publications (Kingston: University of Rhode Island, 2007), Private collection, Russell J. DeSimone and Daniel C. Schofield.

voters, who then put them in the ballot box, there was no privacy, and party officials monitored citizens' votes. The Australian ballot system introduced the secret ballot; each ballot listed all of the candidates from all of the parties who were running for office, and voters marked their choices in private. This reform greatly reduced party boss control over election outcomes.[20]

Last, Progressives launched grassroots campaigns for direct primaries run by the state for nominating party candidates. These primaries aimed to replace the nomination of candidates in local and state party conventions, which were typically dominated by party bosses. Although states were relatively slow to adopt direct primaries, eventually this system became the dominant means of choosing party candidates. The effect of direct primaries was to greatly reduce the control that party bosses and machines had over the choices offered in elections.

The Effects of a Two-Party System

LO 9-3 Explain why two parties dominate the U.S. political system

Following the Civil War, party divisions ran largely along geographic lines, with Republicans dominant in the Northeast and West and Democrats dominant in the South and increasingly in the nation's largest cities. Today, the Democratic and Republican Parties have reversed their geographic strongholds, but the two-party system remains intact. In this section, we examine the effects of a two-party system not only on citizens' choices but also on the ways that government can respond. We also examine the reasons why the United States, even before the Civil War, never had more than two major parties, and we explore the role of the third parties that have occasionally arisen to challenge two-party dominance.

Limited Political Choice

Surely, there are more than two views on how to solve important policy problems. If a group of students has a conversation about a political issue, whether it is war, civil liberties, education, crime, or same-sex marriage, there will likely be more than two opinions expressed. It might seem logical, therefore, that a large democracy such as the United States should have many parties that vie with each other to capture political offices. But the United States has only two major parties.

In 1957, the scholar Anthony Downs argued that voters whose views fall between the two parties were actually represented in a two-party system. His **median voter theorem** proposed that, in a two-party race, if voters select candidates on the basis of ideology and everyone participates equally, the party closer to the middle will win. As candidates from each party seek to attract a majority of votes, and because most voters fall in the middle of the ideological spectrum, both parties move toward a compromise, or middle position. In this way, moderates have a great deal of potential political influence in a two-party system.[21]

Nevertheless, the impact of ideologically extreme campaign activists and interest groups that align with a party can pressure parties and candidates to move away from the center.[22] In today's highly partisan atmosphere, it seems as though the political center has almost entirely disappeared. Each party appears to be so dominated by its more extreme wing that there is little opportunity within each to make moderate views known or to compromise. The current polarization in the two-party system increasingly appears to contradict Downs's expectations about convergence to the middle. In regions where one party is very dominant, elected officials may not be responsive to voters from the other party.

The Structural Limits

The two-party system is built into the American electoral system. As the political scientist Maurice Duverger explains, the American electoral system is a **single-member plurality system**, in which one legislative seat (on a city council, in a state assembly, in the House of Representatives) represents citizens who live in a geographically defined district.[23] To win that seat, a candidate usually needs only a **plurality of votes**, not a pure **majority**—that is, more votes than any other candidate, but not necessarily 50 percent plus 1. Because there is only one seat to be won in a district, only the party or parties with the strongest support have a chance to win a seat. In the United States, many districts are noncompetitive—that is, one of the two major parties dominates. Other districts are competitive; the two major parties vie for electoral support. As a result, voters have become accustomed to choosing between candidates from the two major parties.

Other electoral systems work differently. Many democracies assign the number of seats a party wins according to proportional representation, based on the percentage of votes it receives in a particular election. This type of electoral system encourages smaller parties to form around specific issues and to field candidates for office. Voters are likewise encouraged to support smaller parties. With so many parties fielding candidates, no single party is likely to receive a majority, and parties govern by forming coalitions.

median voter theorem: *Theory that, in a two-party race, if voters select candidates on the basis of ideology and everyone participates equally, the party closer to the middle will win.*

Key Questions

Do you think the major political parties reflect the views of citizens? If not, what can be done to change that?

single-member plurality system: *Electoral system that assigns one seat in a legislative body to represent citizens who live in a defined area (a district) based on which candidate wins the most votes.*

plurality vote: *Vote in which the winner needs to win more votes than any other candidate.*

majority vote: *Vote in which the winner needs to win 50 percent plus 1 of the votes cast.*

In the United States, however, the single-member plurality system encourages a two-party system, and the two-party system in turn encourages political debates that ask Americans to take a "for" or an "against" position on an issue. During an election, there is little effort to arrive at the middle ground, although there is often debate within a party as to what its position will be. In fact, the two-party system works to transfer the battleground from between parties to within parties. Each party—rather than government itself—is a coalition.

Key Questions

Do the political parties provide citizens with opportunities for debate on the issues? Do the political parties drive citizens' views?

The Role of Third Parties

Scholars have debated whether this two-party system adequately reflects the range of views among citizens. In one sense, a two-party system stands as a gate that blocks the emergence of alternative viewpoints and reduces the choices available to voters in terms of perspectives on how to govern. On the other hand, when the two parties together do not offer policy proposals that a significant number of voters want to see enacted, third parties form. These third parties can mount challenges so significant that the major parties are compelled to act, often by incorporating the third party's policy proposal into their platforms.

We have already seen how the antislavery ideas of the Liberty Party and the Free Soil Party were absorbed into the Republican Party when it was founded in 1854. A second example occurred in the late nineteenth century, when farmers were in an uproar about declining crop prices, the lack of available credit, and the constricting use of gold rather than silver as the collateral for U.S. currency. Splinter parties rose up around these issues. Of these, the Populist Party was the largest and most viable; its presidential candidate in the 1892 presidential election, James Weaver, won four states outright and split the vote in two other states.[24] In the 1896 election, the Democrats thought they saw an opportunity to win votes by incorporating into their party platform the Populist demand for free and unlimited coinage of silver, which would drive up prices, thus helping those who were in debt. They even nominated the Populist candidate, William Jennings Bryan, as their own. Bryan lost the election, and with that defeat, the "free silver" movement, which had been strong in the West, rapidly declined.

Image 9.9 Protesters assemble at the Capitol building in Washington, D.C., to rally against what they deem an intrusive federal government.

A little over a decade later, Theodore "Teddy" Roosevelt ran for president as the Progressive Party candidate. Roosevelt, a Republican, had served as president from 1901 to 1909. He decided to run for president again in 1912 to mobilize voters around a host of progressive reforms that would weaken party machines, most notably the idea of popular elections for U.S. senators. At that time, U.S. senators were elected in state legislatures rather than directly by the voters. Although Roosevelt lost, the Progressives were successful in getting Congress to pass and the states to ratify the Seventeenth Amendment on April 8, 1913, which allowed for the direct election of U.S. senators.

Since Teddy Roosevelt's run, five contenders representing significant third parties have entered presidential elections, but none has been able to build a sustained organization over time. Two of these candidates, Strom Thurmond (Dixiecrats) and George Wallace (American Independent Party), ran on segregationist platforms of parties that were splinter groups of the Democratic Party. John Anderson (National Unity Party) and Ross Perot (United We Stand) each ran on a platform that favored moderate social policy and strict fiscal discipline. Ross Perot was given credit for using his United We Stand Party to force the two major party candidates in 1992, President George H. W. Bush (1989–93) and William Jefferson (Bill) Clinton (1993–2001), to address the federal deficit, the amount by which annual government spending exceeds incoming revenue. Ralph Nader ran for president on the Green Party ticket in 2000, 2004, and 2008, promoting a platform that called for stronger environmental and consumer protections. Although Nader did not win, his messages of change and open government were clearly echoed by the mainstream Democratic candidate, Barack Obama, in his successful first campaign for president. For a compact list of significant parties in American politics, see Figure 9.4.

Figure 9.4 **American Political Parties, 1789–2020**

Note that the Democratic Party is the nation's oldest political party. The graph shows it beginning under President Andrew Jackson, but some argue that it actually began with President Thomas Jefferson's Democratic-Republicans.

Though third parties have not fared well in national electoral contests, they sometimes find success in lower-level elections. The Libertarian Party, for example, claimed more than 232 elected officials as of early 2020.[25] Most are members of school boards and town councils, with mayors holding the highest offices. Another example of a third party that found success in local elections was the La Raza Unida Party (LRUP) in the 1970s.[26] The LRUP organized in 1970 in the south Texas counties of Zavala, Dimmitt, and La Salle, all near the U.S.–Mexico border. Its founders' goals were to advance the economic, social, and political interests of Mexican Americans. Their mobilizing efforts led to electoral victories in the Crystal City, Cotulla, and Carrizo Springs school boards and town councils, all areas heavily populated by Latinos yet whose local offices Anglos had historically held. The LRUP spread throughout the Southwest into rural and urban areas from Texas to California, electing members to various local offices. Part of its legacy is the activation of Latinos into the political process and providing a gateway for Latinas; one notable veteran of the party is Rosie Castro, former Bexar County LRUP chairwoman and mother of Secretary of Housing and Urban Development Julián Castro and his twin brother, Congressman Joaquín Castro (D-TX, who is featured in Chapter 12, Congress).

Key Questions
What are the benefits and the risks of voting for a third-party candidate?

The Tea Party

Third parties do not have to stand by themselves to have an impact on party politics; they can also be an influential force within one or more parties. For example, in 2010 and 2012, the Tea Party movement was very effective at supporting challengers to incumbents in primary elections in the Republican Party or supporting a third candidate in the general election. By one count, 129 candidates running for the House of Representatives and nine candidates running for the U.S. Senate in the 2010 congressional elections affiliated themselves with the Tea Party.[27] Its message was fiscal responsibility, lower taxes, and paying down the national debt, and the Tea Party was successful in electing members of Congress, such as Senator Rand Paul (R-KY), who share its concern that the federal budget ought to be at the top of the American political agenda.[28] The results from the 2014 midterm elections, however, may have revealed some cracks in the Tea Party movement as many Republican incumbent U.S. senators successfully fought back against Tea Party–backed challengers.[29]

At the presidential level, members of the Tea Party movement were also active in the Republican nominating process and were vocal in demanding that the Republicans commit to their concerns. In the 2016 Republican nomination process, multiple candidates courted and claimed to be supported by the Tea Party, including Ted Cruz (R-TX), Rand Paul (R-KY), Marco Rubio (R-FL), and Donald Trump. Though Donald Trump's nomination by the Republican Party and subsequent election as president may be seen as evidence of the Tea Party movement's continued influence, there are also signs that the Tea Party's influence may be waning.

As mentioned, the establishment wing of the Republican Party started to fight back against efforts to undermine incumbent Republicans or candidates who did not subscribe entirely to the Tea Party's agenda. In March 2014, Senator Mitch McConnell (R-KY), who was facing a Tea Party challenger in his primary, was quoted as saying, "I think we will crush them everywhere." The first test of that came in Texas, where a Tea Party challenger, Representative Steve Stockman, was in fact overwhelmingly defeated by the incumbent Republican candidate, John Cornyn, in the Senate primary. In the face of the enormous resources of the mainstream Republican Party, the Tea Party had more difficulty in 2014 recruiting and funding strong challengers to Republican incumbents in the House and Senate.[30]

image 9.10 As an outsider candidate for president in 2016, Donald Trump campaigned untraditionally, relying heavily on social media and his status as a nonpolitician. Trump drew on the frustration some voters felt in 2016. Here he is pictured speaking to a crowd in New Hampshire.

The success of the establishment Republican party continued in the 2016 elections. For example, candidates supported by the Tea Party failed to unseat any establishment candidates in Republican primary elections. In addition, about 25 percent of the Republicans elected in the 2010 Tea Party wave mentioned earlier have lost reelection bids or chosen to retire from office.[31] The Tea Party movement, although not officially a political party, illustrates how third parties can force the two major political parties to be more responsive. In this case, the Tea Party has given voice to more conservative voters. When they are large enough, these groups have the potential to move the party platforms in new directions and, in turn, to change federal laws.[32]

Party Control of Presidential Nominations

Trump's candidacy in 2016 proved problematic for the Republican Party's ability to steer the nomination process. Though not the preferred candidate of the so-called Republican Party establishment, Trump was nevertheless able to earn primary and caucus victories. Though the parties set the rules of the nomination process, such as the number of debates held and how states allocate delegates (proportional versus winner-take-all), no apparatus has ultimate control over Republican voters' choice of nominee.

In 2020, some Democrats saw the candidacy of Senator Bernie Sanders in a similar way. Though he has caucused with Democrats since he entered the Senate in 2007, ran for the nomination in 2016, and signed a loyalty pledge to govern as a Democrat if elected, Senator Sanders was still seen by some Democrats as an outsider. This outsider status was due in part to his identification as a Democratic Socialist and his past criticism of the party. Candidates for the Democratic nomination in 2020 complained of Sanders' supporters trolling his competitors and his lack of support for the Democratic party beyond the nomination. He received few endorsements from members of Congress or governors. On April 8, 2020, after the Wisconsin primary election carried by Biden, Senator Sanders dropped out of the race for the nomination and less than a week later he endorsed Joe Biden for the nomination.

Obstacles to Third Parties and Independents

Because third-party candidates can act as spoilers, the two major parties do everything they can to discourage them, from challenging signatures for ballot access in court to preventing them from participating in presidential debates. The Democrats and Republicans have

Public Policy and Political Parties

Assault Weapons Ban

In Chapter 4, Civil Liberties, we explained how the Supreme Court has interpreted the provisions of the Second Amendment to allow individuals to own firearms. As we noted, gun control is a highly contested public policy area, especially between the Democrats and the Republicans. However, tragic events such as the shooting of former Congresswoman Gabby Giffords and six other people in Arizona; the Newtown school shootings; Las Vegas shootings; and the Sutherland Springs, Texas, church shootings have precipitated a national discussion over whether assault weapons should be banned.

Although not all party members agree, a majority of self-described Democrats favor most stricter gun laws. Among Republicans, attitudes vary depending on the type of policy proposal. In a 2019 Pew Research Center Poll, majorities of both party identifiers agreed on requiring background checks at gun shows: 93 percent of Democrats and 82 percent of Republicans.[33] On the question of an assault weapon ban, though, the margin was much wider, with 88 percent of Democrats favoring such a ban, compared with 50 percent of Republicans in favor.[34] Compared to 2017, support for both policies has increased for both Republicans and Democrats.[35]

During the 2016 presidential election, the Democratic Party made gun control part of its party platform, stating that "To build on the success of the lifesaving Brady Handgun Violence Prevention Act, we will expand and strengthen background checks and close dangerous loopholes in our current laws; repeal the Protection of Lawful Commerce in Arms Act (PLCAA) to revoke the dangerous legal immunity protections gun makers and sellers now enjoy; and keep weapons of war—such as assault weapons and large capacity ammunition magazines (LCAM's)—off our streets."[36] The Republican Party had a contrasting statement in their platform about the assault weapons ban, stating that "We oppose ill-conceived laws that would restrict magazine capacity or ban the sale of the most popular and common modern rifle. We also oppose

any effort to deprive individuals of their right to keep and bear arms without due process of law."[37] By including these statements in their party's platforms during a presidential candidate, each party was staking out a distinct policy position designed to attract support from its base.

In Congress, these party differences are also strongly visible. For example, in the 113th Congress, Senator Dianne Feinstein (D-CA) introduced a bill to reinstate the assault weapons ban that would outlaw a number of types of firearms capable of holding large amounts of ammunition. Her bill, the Assault Weapons Ban of 2013, had twenty-four Senate cosponsors, all of them Democrats. In the House of Representatives, Representative Carolyn McCarthy (D-NY) introduced a bill with the same language, and there were eighty-one House cosponsors, all of them Democrats. However, because the House of Representatives was controlled by the Republicans, and Republicans in the Senate could filibuster the legislation, there was little to no chance that it would have passed. Despite the odds against passage, the assault weapons ban was an important focal point for Democrats to mobilize supporters of gun control. Since the attempt in 2013, only one similar piece of legislation was introduced to curb assault weapons. Congressman David N. Cicilline (D-RI) introduced the Assault Weapons Ban of 2015. One hundred twenty-five Democrats signed as cosponsors, while no Republicans did so. There was no companion legislation introduced in the Senate.

Interest groups influence gun policy as well. The National Rifle Association (NRA), which is a large grassroots group and one of the most effective in the nation, figures prominently in the national discussion on a ban on assault weapons. Like many interest groups, the NRA has formed a PAC to contribute to campaigns. Most PACs contribute to incumbents, current members of Congress who are much more likely to win than challengers. Most PACs support incumbents from both parties. Unlike many groups, however, the NRA's PAC contributes overwhelmingly to candidates from one party: the Republican Party. In the 2018 congressional election cycle, the NRA's affiliated PAC contributed a total of $699,800 to congressional campaigns, with 97 percent going to Republicans and 3 percent going to Democrats. Safari Club International, a group that promotes wildlife conservation and protects the rights of hunters, also throws its support primarily behind Republican candidates. Its Arizona-based PAC contributed $454,000 with 95 percent going to Republicans and 5 percent going to Democrats. There was only one group, the Brady Campaign to prevent gun violence, that overwhelmingly supported Democrats, contributing a total of $140,411 to pro–gun-control Democrats in 2018 and no funds to Republicans. Everytown for Gun Safety emerged in 2018 as another group supporting efforts to curb gun violence.[38] Campaign contributions are important and so is the potential to bring voters out the door to vote for candidates who support their policy positions. Political parties depend on interest groups who agree with their policy stances to help mobilize voters; without them, that job becomes much more difficult. The issue of thwarting gun violence through gun control, with specific measures such as the assault weapons ban, will likely remain a strong source of division in parties at the top levels of the organizations, among party identifiers, and among members of Congress.

Construct Your Own Policy

1. Write a version of an assault weapons ban that you believe might attract more support from Republicans who are currently opposed to it.
2. Construct a strategy of cooperation between parties on the issue of gun violence that does not involve any new restrictions on gun ownership.

Key Questions

Should laws that discourage third parties be changed? What would be the effects in terms of government responsiveness?

Key Questions

What are the advantages and disadvantages of being an Independent?

Key Questions

What are the advantages and disadvantages of being registered as a Democrat or Republican? Is it better to be an Independent?

controlled state legislatures and Congress for so long that they have successfully established gates within state electoral laws that favor a two-party system over a multiple-party system. In addition, without the backing of a major party to get out the vote, collect campaign contributions, and arrange for media coverage, most third-party and Independent candidates do not stand much chance of being elected. Consequently, voters who consider themselves Independents do not have the opportunity to vote for candidates who might be closest to them in terms of policy preferences.

Candidates who are elected from third parties have little influence in legislatures because parties shape the internal power structure there. The party that wins the majority of seats in the legislature becomes the majority party and consequently controls the legislative process. After the legislative session begins, members are asked to express their opinions in subcommittees, in committees, and on the floor by voting with or against their party's proposed legislation, and it is rare that an alternative to the major party proposal is considered (see Chapter 12, Congress). Those who are elected as Independents, such as Senator Bernie Sanders (I-VT), have no party organization to join in the legislature. Independents must pledge to support one of the two major parties in order to sit on committees and perform their other responsibilities as legislators. Since being elected to the Senate in 2006, Sanders has chosen to caucus with the Democrats.

In 2016 and 2020, Sanders even sought the nomination of the Democratic Party, though not officially a Democrat. Sanders appealed to Democrats by claiming to be the "authentic" progressive in the race. His campaign resonated with the progressive wing of the party. That segment of the Democratic Party, many of whom are younger voters, supported his candidacy. Though he was unsuccessful in both attempts in winning the party's nomination, Sanders campaigned for Hillary Clinton and Joe Biden, urging his supporters to elect the Democratic nominee and prevent Donald Trump from becoming and then retaining the presidency.

Key Questions

How do interest groups encourage citizen participation in political parties? How do they limit it?

Challenges to Party Power from Interest Groups

In addition to challenges from third parties, the two major parties face challenges from established interest groups and from broader social groups formed at the grassroots of American politics (see Chapter 8, Interest Groups). These groups and movements draw attention to each party's failings in specific issue areas and engage in activities from staging protest rallies to nominating alternative candidates to run in primaries in order to get parties to move closer to the policy positions the group or movement advocates.

Over the past two decades, interest and social movement groups have become more tightly aligned with specific political parties, and that alignment has undermined their capacity to serve as independent checks on—or competitors with—political parties. For example, unions such as the Service Employees International Union (SEIU) and environmental groups such as the Sierra Club are generally supportive of the Democratic Party, whereas business groups such as the Chamber of Commerce and the NRA are supportive of the Republican Party.

For interest groups, the risk in continuously supporting one party is that the party will take their support for granted. In fact, parties are most responsive to interest groups when they threaten to withdraw their support or start their own party organizations. Consequently, interest groups maintain their influence with political parties by constantly expressing their preferences on policies to party leaders and providing support only when the party is responsive to their concerns. For example, on the issue of gun control, interest groups on both sides of the issue have been very active in lobbying elected officials and trying to persuade the public to support their preferred policy position.

Party Alignment and Ideology

LO 9-4 Define partisan affiliation and ideology

Throughout U.S. history, there have been long stretches of time during which the party affiliations of voters remained stable, but there have also been key elections in which parties lost or gained significant blocs of voters. Scholars have tried to identify the factors that explain why voters make large, permanent shifts from one party to another. Shifts in party allegiance can occur when there is an external shock to the nation, such as an economic depression or a foreign military attack. Shifts can also occur when public attitudes change considerably and one party appears to respond more quickly to those changes than another.

The Parties After the Civil War

party alignment: *Voter identification with a political party in repeated elections.*

Following the Civil War, as we have seen, the Republicans were dominant in the Northeast and West and the Democrats were dominant in the South and increasingly in large cities with big immigrant populations. This **party alignment**—voters identifying with a party in repeated elections—was relatively stable until 1896, when a number of smaller parties challenged the Republican and Democratic Parties. The Republican Party emerged from that election with a victory, and the smaller parties faded from the national political scene.

From 1896 to 1932, the basic geographic pattern of party alignment stayed the same, but the combination of the stock market crash of October 24, 1929, the global depression that followed, and a drop in worldwide agricultural prices brought political trouble to the Republican Party. By 1932, voters in every part of the country were ready for a change, not only in political leadership but also in the entire approach to government.

The New Deal and the Role of Ideology in Party Politics

During the election of 1932, voters were exposed to a new political ideology, or set of consistent political views, about the way that the federal government could work. Today's voters might describe themselves as liberal or conservative, but voters before 1932 typically identified themselves with a political party. In that election year, Franklin Delano Roosevelt (1933–45), governor of New York, ran for president on a platform designed to reverse the effects of the Great Depression. The idea that the federal government would help individuals to help themselves was transformative in American politics. The Democratic Party platform resonated with voters, and Roosevelt won the election.

Key Questions

Should the federal government help individuals to help themselves? If you think so, in what ways? If not, why not?

After he took office, Roosevelt championed a vast array of new government programs that are commonly referred to as the New Deal. These programs were designed to help individuals who were jobless, homeless, or otherwise in financial need. Essentially the New Deal was a promise by the federal government to provide a safety net for workers and their families who fell on hard times. Following his electoral victory in 1932, Roosevelt built a coalition of white southerners, working-class ethnic northerners, advocates for liberal social policies, and northern African Americans who had previously been Republicans. This was a radical shift for African Americans, who since the Civil War had followed the party of Abraham Lincoln and shunned the Democrats, whom they associated with racism and slavery. This electoral coalition was large but fragile, and Roosevelt engaged in a great deal of political balancing and a wide distribution of government benefits to maintain it.

In supporting the New Deal, voters came to accept the ideological viewpoint that government involvement in the economic aspects of individuals' lives was legitimate and, on balance, a good thing. As we noted in Chapter 1, Gateways to American Democracy, this perspective on government serves as a foundation for the modern definition of a liberal. Today the liberal viewpoint builds on the

Image 9.11 In his campaign for president in 1932, Franklin Delano Roosevelt introduced an innovative campaign platform. "I pledge you," he said, "I pledge myself, to a new deal for the American people." The term "New Deal" came to describe federal programs that took an active role in helping individual citizens find jobs, save for retirement, and benefit from fair working conditions.

AP Images

New Deal perspective by favoring government redistribution of income through higher taxes on the wealthy to provide social benefits, such as health care, unemployment insurance, and welfare payments to the poor. Those who opposed the New Deal are the forefathers of the modern conservatives, who believe in lower taxes and less government involvement in economic life.

In response to Roosevelt's big government approach, the Republicans seized what they saw as the main weakness of the New Deal, which was the high cost of all these newly created programs. To pay for them, the federal and state governments would have to raise taxes on businesses and workers alike. The Republicans recognized that they had an opportunity to reshape their party platform to exploit the Democrats' weakness.

In the aftermath of 1932, the two parties transformed; it was almost as if they had switched places. The Democrats changed from a party that believed in states' rights, low taxes, and little government intervention in individuals' lives to the party that created a large social safety net that relied on the federal government to ensure personal economic stability. The Republicans changed from a party that believed in a strong central federal government and in intervention in the economy when necessary to the party of a strictly limited federal government and fiscal responsibility.

Voters responded to these partisan and ideological changes by changing their own party allegiances over time, essentially producing a **realignment** of the electorate. In the broadest sense, today's Democrats generally support expanding the size of government to accomplish specific policy goals, even if it means raising taxes, and support liberal social values. In contrast, Republicans generally support limiting the size of government by keeping taxation and regulation of the economy to a minimum and support preserving conservative social values.

Civil Rights, the Great Society, and Nixon's Southern Strategy

The Democratic and Republican Parties remained divided mainly along this economic dimension until the early 1960s, when the Democratic Party established itself as the party of civil rights for African Americans. During the presidency of Lyndon Baines Johnson (1963–69), the Civil Rights Act of 1964, the Voting Rights Act of 1965, the Department of Housing and Urban Development Act of 1965, and the Fair Housing Act of 1966 were all signed into law. These acts gave the federal government strong enforcement powers to guarantee African Americans the fullest extent of the civil rights afforded to every American and served as a key gateway for full political participation by African Americans. Johnson's policies brought a second dimension to liberal ideology: now the federal government was granted the power not only to help individuals in need economically but also to take affirmative steps to overrule state and local governments to prevent discrimination on all levels. As noted in Chapter 5, Civil Rights, the government's role evolved from preventing unequal treatment under the law to ensuring equality in all walks of life, from education to employment to housing.

By putting the stamp of the Democratic Party on the pledge to preserve civil rights, Johnson appealed to those who opposed segregation. Today African Americans remain the most loyal of any demographic constituency in the Democratic Party. In 2008 and 2012, over 93 percent of African American voters chose the Democratic candidate, Obama, the nation's first African American president.[39] In 2014, a nonpresidential election year, 90 percent of African American voters cast their ballots for Democratic candidates for Congress.[40] In the 2016 presidential election, 88 percent of African Americans supported Hillary Clinton.[41] And, exit polls in the recent 2020 election, indicated that 87 percent of African Americans voted for Joe Biden.[42]

Key Questions

How does the realignment that followed the election of 1932 echo the divisions between the Federalists and the Antifederalists? Or is the political ideology of the modern era entirely different?

Key Questions

Which perspective comes closest to your own views—liberal or conservative? Do you think this aligns with your political party preference?

realignment: *Long-term shift in voter allegiance from one party to another.*

Political Analytics

Latinos and the Political Parties: Votes and Issues

LATINOS ARE AN IMPORTANT AND GROWING group of voters in the United States. Both major U.S. political parties have a large stake in attracting their affinity and votes. Democrats have enjoyed strong support from Latinos in presidential elections, and Latinos most often identify with them. Latinos also see Democrats as the party best able to handle important political issues.

Figure 9.5 shows three ways in which to gauge Latinos' preference for the two major political parties. Though Democrats have an edge in Latino support, the data on party identification among Latinos suggest that a growing number of Latinos may be choosing the Republican Party. In the 2018 midterm elections, Democrats received almost 70 percent of the Latino vote. This underscores the extent to which Latino voters may be a group for which both parties will actively compete. Joe Biden and Donald Trump will both vie for the Latino vote with Biden hoping to come near the midterm figures and Trump hoping to improve on his support among Latinos in 2016.

Consider the data on voting patterns as well as the trend and magnitude of difference in Latino party identification and beliefs.

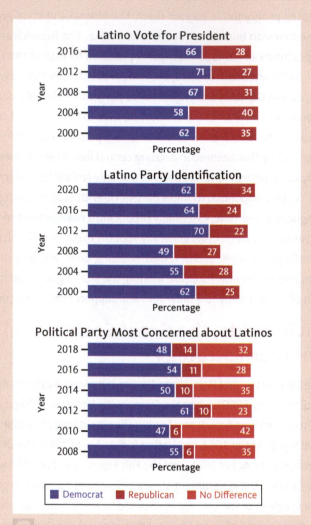

Figure 9.5 Democrats, Republicans, and Latinos

Sources: Pew Hispanic Center analysis of national exit poll data, 1980–2012; Pew Research Center, 2002–2014 National Survey of Latinos; Pew Research Center, 2002–2014, National Survey of Latinos, September 11–October 9, 2014, "The Latino Vote in Presidential Elections, 2008–2016," November 8, 2016, http://www.pewresearch.org/fact-tank/2016/11/29/hillary-clinton-wins-latino-vote-but-falls-below-2012-support-for-obama/ft_16-11-09_latinovoteyears/; Mark Hugo Lopez, Ana Gonzalez-Barrera, Jens Manuel Krogstad, and Gustavo Lopez, "Democrats Maintain Edge as Party 'More Concerned' for Latinos, but Views Similar to 2012," October 11, 2016, http://www.pewhispanic.org/2016/10/11/democrats-maintain-edge-as-party-more-concerned-for-latinos-but-views-similar-to-2012/.

*Alec Tyson and Shiva Maniam, "Behind Trump's Victory: Divisions by Race, Gender, Education," Pew Research Center, November 9, 2016, http://www.pewresearch.org/fact-tank/2016/11/09/behind-trumps-victory-divisions-by-race-gender-education/; Jon Huang, Samuel Jacoby, K. K., Rebecca Lai, and Michael Strickland, "Election 2016: Exit Polls," *New York Times*, November 8, 2016, http://www.nytimes.com/interactive/2016/11/08/us/politics/election-exit-polls.html; Luis Noe-Bustamante, Abby Budiman, and Mark Hugo Lopez, "Where Latinos Have the Most Eligible Voters in 2020," Pew Hispanic Center, January 31, 2020, accessed March 10, 2020, https://www.pewresearch.org/fact-tank/2020/01/31/where-latinos-have-the-most-eligible-voters-in-the-2020-election/; National Survey of Latinos conducted July 26–July 19, 2018, Pew Hispanic Center, https://www.pewresearch.org/hispanic/dataset/2018-national-survey-of-latinos/; Jens Manuel Krogstad, Ana Gonzalez-Barrera, and Christine Tamir, "Latino Democratic Voters Place High Importance on 2020 Presidential Election," Pew Research Center, January 27, 2020, accessed May 19, 2020, https://www.pewresearch.org/fact-tank/2020/01/17/latino-democratic-voters-place-high-importance-on-2020-presidential-election/.

Thinking Critically

1. How do you think the 2020 presidential election campaign represented Latinos' views about the way in which the Democratic and Republican Parties handle key issues?

2. Figure 9.5 presents data on support for Democrats and Republicans in the same bar. Why do you think this was done? In what other ways might these data be presented?

Election 2020

The Partisan Inclinations of Latinos

Democrats and Republicans would, of course, like to have support from voters of all ages, races, ethnicities, sexual orientations, and so forth. At least since the 1960s, most African Americans have supported Democrats. The same is true of Latinos, who, according to exit polls, supported Joe Biden over Donald Trump by 34 percent in 2020.[43] Like African Americans, Latinos have become a vital part of the Democratic Party's coalition of voters. Since 2000, the Democratic presidential candidate has received at least 58 percent of the Latino vote, and much more in recent elections (see Figure 9.5). Moreover, Latinos tend to self-identify as Democrats and have for some time and by large margins: 62 percent in 2020 (see Figure 9.5). Because Latinos are also the fastest-growing group of eligible voters (see Chapter 1), they are considered an important part of both major parties' electoral fortunes.

The influence of the Latino vote is a function of party preference and turnout. Latinos generally see Democrats as "better" for them in some key areas, such as immigration policy (see Figure 9.5). Heading into the 2020 election, Republicans needed to make significant inroads into the Latino vote. Donald Trump received 32 percent of the Latino vote. Some estimates of the Latino vote share that Republicans needed to be competitive in 2020 were as high as 47 percent, a figure higher than any Republican presidential candidate has ever received.[44]

Did Latinos' affinity for Democrats translate into support for Joe Biden? Probably. While exit polls showed that 66 percent of Latinos voted for the Democratic candidate, the same as for Hillary Clinton, it was insufficient to result in victory for the Democratic candidate. Republican candidates, as Donald Trump demonstrated, can win the presidency with less than 30 percent support from Latinos (see Figure 9.5).[45] But past support does not guarantee continued votes. Some signs, although slight, suggest that there is room for Republican inroads. Figure 9.5 indicates that Latinos are self-identifying less as Democrats since a high point in 2012. The trend toward identifying with the Republican Party shows an upward trajectory since around 2011. As new generations of Latinos become eligible to vote—the estimate is around 800,000 per year become eligible[46]—they become potential Republican identifiers. Complicating this scenario, however, was Donald Trump's presidential campaign, which many Latinos viewed as hostile. His comments that Mexicans entering the United States illegally were rapists and murderers did not encourage Latinos to support him or the Republican Party, and some polls indicated that upwards of 80 percent of Latinos viewed Trump unfavorably.[47]

The partisan inclinations of Latinos may not be as clearcut as they seemed at first glance. Add to that the other factor that affects the extent of the Latino influence: voter turnout. Even with a large influx of Latinos eligible to vote, if they do not go to the polls, their influence is muted. The data show an apparent ceiling to voter turnout among Latinos in the high 40 percent range.[48] In the long term, the numbers of potential new Latino voters who become eligible to vote will only increase, and Latinos will continue to be sought after by both parties.

In addition to advancing civil rights and earning the enduring loyalty of African American voters, the Johnson administration also expanded federal programs that granted aid to individuals and to state and local governments in the areas of health care, education, housing, job training, and welfare to families with children (see Chapter 13, The Presidency, for an extensive discussion of Johnson's programs). This set of policies was called the Great Society and was founded on the idea that federal expansion would strengthen American

Key Questions
What would the Federalists think of the federal government today? What would the Antifederalists think?

society by helping all citizens reach their potential. By expanding the reach of the federal government this way, Johnson reinforced the liberal ideological underpinnings of the Democratic Party.

As this shift in Democratic policies occurred, Republicans saw a new opportunity to attract support from voters who opposed the expansion of the federal government into race relations or the regulation of the economy. Beginning with the campaign of Barry Goldwater in 1964 and continuing with the campaigns of Richard M. Nixon (1969–74) in 1968 and Ronald Reagan (1981–89) in 1980, the Republicans employed a so-called southern strategy, presenting themselves to southern white voters as holding views on civil rights and race that were opposite those of the Democrats.

Although Republicans did not sanction racism and discrimination, they made it clear that they would not take the same strong steps as the Democrats to impose federal law on states to remedy these problems. Republicans extended their philosophy of limited government intervention by asserting that each state was responsible for enforcing civil rights and that the federal government was overstepping its bounds by interfering at the state and local levels. At the same time, Republicans opposed the Great Society policies as too expensive, and they were philosophically opposed to the federal government giving so much aid directly to individuals without asking for something in return. In this way, the Republican Party continued to move toward a more conservative ideology that sought to limit the powers and programs of the federal government.

The Reagan Revolution and Conservative Party Politics

In 1980, Ronald Reagan, former Republican governor of California, defeated the incumbent President Jimmy Carter (1977–81), a Democrat, partly by appealing to those who opposed the Supreme Court's legalization of abortion in *Roe v. Wade* (1973). Following the ruling, the national stance of the parties diverged, with the Democratic Party publicly supporting the decision and the Republican Party split on the issue. When Reagan won the Republican Party's presidential nomination, he moved the Republicans more firmly into the antiabortion camp. In the general election, Reagan's campaign offered a consistent conservative ideology that focused on limiting the size of the federal government, opposing abortion, and allowing prayer in public schools, which had been prohibited by the Supreme Court ruling in *Engel v. Vitale* in 1962 (see Chapter 4, Civil Liberties, for further discussion of prayer in school).[49] Reagan's campaign strategy was designed to attract conservative Democrats who were alienated by their party's official position on abortion and to attract the growing numbers of active evangelical Christian voters, especially in the South.

Reagan also took advantage of the instability in foreign relations that marked Jimmy Carter's four years in office. Although Carter had increased defense spending for the military while in office, he focused on protecting human rights. For Reagan, protecting individual political freedom was a moral obligation for the United States. Reagan campaigned on a strong defense and tough foreign policy that actively promoted freedom, and he made it clear that, under his administration, the United States would work to undermine the Communist political and economic system that was dominant in the then-Soviet Union, eastern Europe, and Cuba.

The combination of these issues brought Reagan the support of many working-class ethnic northers and southern white voters. These voters were subsequently referred to as Reagan Democrats, and it was in large part due to them that he won the presidential election of 1980.

Although the Republicans held the presidency for the next twelve years, many of the voters who supported Republicans at the national level stayed loyal to the Democrats in congressional, state, and local elections, especially in the South. This split-ticket voting made it hard for parties to sustain complete voter allegiance at all levels of elected office.

Bill Clinton was governor of Arkansas when he successfully ran for president in 1992. As had Reagan, Clinton changed his party's direction with a campaign platform that advocated dropping opposition to the death penalty, facilitating free trade, and promising a middle-class tax cut. These policies moved the Democrats away from liberal policies, but Clinton still ran under the established Democratic Party label. Clinton thus appealed to a wider range of voters, and he was able to recapture some electoral territory the Democrats had lost in the southern states.

Image 9.12 During his two terms as president from 2009 to 2017, Barack Obama pursued a policy agenda that included the Affordable Care Act, the promotion of marriage equality, and the negotiation of a nuclear treaty with Iran. The extent to which these policy initiatives remain, however, was limited with the election of Donald Trump who, as a presidential candidate, vowed to overturn many of the Obama administration's defining achievements.

In office, however, Clinton lost popularity by veering away from core issues such as the middle-class tax cut and economic growth to address socially liberal policies on abortion and gays in the military, to which he had given far less emphasis on the campaign trail. This political misstep set the stage for a Republican Party resurgence.

In the 1994 midterm congressional elections, Republicans took control of both the House and the Senate for the first time since 1954. Led by Newt Gingrich, a Republican House member from Georgia, the Republicans put forth a party platform called the Contract with America, which promised ten major policy initiatives, such as a balanced federal budget and less federal regulation. Every Republican candidate for the House signed it, and by coordinating candidates this way, the Republican Party presented a single national message to voters about what it would do if it won control of Congress. At the presidential level, George W. Bush, the son of former President George H. W. Bush and a conservative Republican governor of Texas, built on the momentum of the Republicans to launch a successful bid for the presidency in 1999.

The Modern Partisan Landscape

In 2006, the Democrats began to regain electoral momentum with voters who self-identified as Democrats but had not been voting that way in recent elections, as well as with Independent voters. That year, powerful short-term forces, such as corruption scandals and the Iraq War, put voters in a particularly sour mood toward incumbent Republicans.

The results of the 2008 elections, however, were a sign that the party landscape was shifting again.[50] Clearly the election of an African American president was a significant turning point in race relations; Barack Obama received 43 percent of the white vote in 2008,

> **Key Questions**
> Is realignment a generational change of the social contract?

> **Key Questions**
> Do political parties help voters hold government responsible? Why?

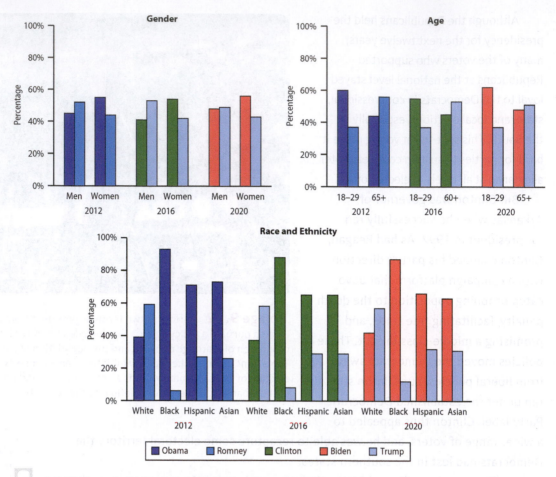

Figure 9.6 **Votes for President by Demographic Group**

Patterns of support among voters can change over time but have remained relatively consistent for the last three election cycles.

Source: New York Times, https://www.nytimes.com/elections/2012/results/president/exit-polls.html;https://www.nytimes.com/elections/2016/results/president; https://www.nytimes.com/interactive/2020/11/03/us/elections/exit-polls-president.html.

2 percentage points higher than John Kerry, a white Democrat, received in 2004. Obama won five states that had been considered solidly Republican in previous presidential elections: Florida, Indiana, North Carolina, Ohio, and Virginia.

However, when voters give one party majority party control of the White House and Congress, they have high expectations for a strong governing track record. In one way, that is what political scientists mean by **responsible parties**; if the parties offer voters clear choices, voters can hold the party in charge responsible for policy outcomes. When President Obama and the Democrats took charge of government in 2009, they faced some of the greatest economic challenges since the Great Depression, as well as ongoing wars in Iraq and Afghanistan. Additionally, Obama and the Democrats in Congress set out to build on the Great Society legacy of government social policy by passing the Affordable Care Act to make health insurance available to all Americans. The 2010 congressional midterm elections were the first opportunity that voters had to register their satisfaction or dissatisfaction with the president and his party, and they did so by giving Republicans control of the House of Representatives and electing more Republicans to the Senate. The Democratic losses and Republican gains showed the responsible party system in action because voters held the incumbent majority party accountable for its performance on the economy, health care, and the ongoing wars.

responsible parties: *Parties that take responsibility for offering the electorate a distinct range of policies and programs, thus providing a clear choice.*

Key Questions

What are the advantages and disadvantages of responsible parties?

However, in 2012, Barack Obama won reelection by a margin of 51 to 47 percent and a margin of 5 million votes, although his share of the white vote declined to 39 percent[51] (See Figure 9.6). From the president's perspective, winning reelection as an incumbent was a reaffirmation of his—and by extension the Democratic Party's—policy agenda. At the same time, Republicans held on to their majority control of the House of Representatives and the Democrats held on to the U.S. Senate, which made responsible party government difficult to achieve.

The 2014 midterm elections saw the continuance of divided government, with Republicans in the majority in both houses of Congress and Obama holding the executive branch. The continued divided government led to little bipartisanship and culminated in the decision of the Republican-held U.S. Senate not to act on President Obama's nomination of Merrick Garland to replace Justice Antonin Scalia, who died on February 13, 2016. In the fall of 2016, voters were faced with an open seat in the White House because Barack Obama could not run for president a third time. America again faced a choice between the two parties' candidates with differing visions of the role of government in American society.

The 2016 election results significantly changed party control of government. With Donald Trump winning the presidency and Republicans retaining control of both the House of Representatives and the U.S. Senate, the country had a united party government for the first time since 2009. The results of a Republican-controlled White House and Congress were mixed. In December 2017, President Trump and the majority-Republican Congress passed an overhaul of the tax system—with no Democrats in the House of Representatives or in the Senate voting in favor. On the other hand, Republican attempts to repeal the Affordable Care Act failed when three Republican senators (John McCain [R-AZ], Lisa Murkowski [R-AK], and Susan Collins [R-ME]) voted no in July 2017. In addition, Democrats and Republicans were unable to avert a short government shutdown over the call by Democrats for the inclusion of protections for persons affected by the phasing out of DACA (Deferred Action for Childhood Arrivals) beneficiaries, known as "DREAMers," as part of the deal to raise the federal debt ceiling. In all these cases, it is difficult to determine which party will be held responsible for the legislation. Polls indicate that Americans generally favor protections for DREAMers, oppose the changes to the tax system, and have mixed views regarding the Affordable Care Act.[52]

Since the 2018 midterm elections, Democrats have controlled the House of Representatives. With control of the Senate still in in the hands of Republicans, President Trump was successful in some areas such as judicial nominations. The parties have had to compromise on tax and other policy legislation. The COVID-19 pandemic began sweeping the nation in early spring 2020 and was marked by severe disruptions in government and politics. On the legislative front, the pandemic brought the parties together in both houses of Congress to pass historic legislation to combat the spread of the virus and address the potential catastrophic economic effects. Congress and the president worked together to pass three bills to provide relief to individual Americans and businesses, the third of which provided for $2 trillion of spending, the largest in American history. Bipartisan cooperation on coronavirus-related legislation broke down as the presidential election approached. After the election, negotiations between Democrats and Republicans in Congress stalled over disagreements about how to address funding for coronavirus programs and mitigate the negative effects on the economy.

Key Questions
Do you think partisanship is taking precedence over policy making? What can be done about that?

Key Questions
Are consensus and compromise good or bad for American democracy? Give examples.

There is a trade-off between responsible party government and bipartisan cooperation; where there is one, there is almost never the other. Members of Congress from opposite parties rarely communicate directly with each other anymore; instead, they take to the airwaves on cable TV and Twitter to criticize each other. Despite the wide divide between the two major parties, within each party, members do not always agree on issues, and party leaders are not always able to forge internal cooperation. Elected officials are constantly exposed to a wide range of opinions, and they face pressures to respond both to the voters and to party elites. Politicians and party activists can communicate directly with voters, and citizens have many ways to register their opinions on most issues. In addition, party activists are able to track elected officials and monitor how well they adhere to the party's policies. Although increased participation in the deliberation of important issues is a welcome development in a democracy, it makes it hard to represent constituents, toe the party line, and still be able to compromise when necessary to enact good public policy. National emergencies such as the COVID-19 pandemic do require both parties to work in concert to address the scope and severity they bring to the nation.

Political Parties and Democracy

Political parties, which emerged in the nation's first decade, now play a major role in American democracy. The Democrats and the Republicans together claim the allegiance of over 80 percent of voters when one includes strong identifiers and voters who consistently lean toward one party.[53] Political parties determine the choices voters have at the polls by crafting the laws that allow candidates to be on the ballot and overseeing the primaries that allow voters to choose candidates. Parties also recruit candidates for elected office, raise funds for campaigns, register voters, and organize get-out-the-vote drives. In sum, parties shape the selection of candidates who seek, run for, and win elected office.

Do political parties make it easier for voters to hold elected officials accountable? Party platforms tell voters what candidates intend to do if elected, and voters can compare their actions against their campaign pledges. If pledges and policies match up, voters typically reelect the officials; if they do not, voters can vote for the opponents in the next election. One advantage of clear dividing lines between the parties is that it makes the job of monitoring the government easier for the average voter. However, such clear divisions also bring the disadvantages of conflict and stalemate that make bipartisan policy making difficult.

Parties do a mixed job of promoting equal political participation among all citizens. On the one hand, they are a gateway to participation because membership in a political party is free, and citizens can work a little or a lot on behalf of the party. Primaries and caucuses give every party member a say in determining who will represent the party in elected office, and they force candidates who seek the party's endorsement to shape their campaign platforms according to party voters' preferences. Because voters are free to join and leave political parties as frequently as they wish, parties are always seeking to represent their members' viewpoints.

On the other hand, parties can discourage political participation by acting as gatekeepers in the way of third-party formation. The U.S. party system is structured around two major parties, and even though third parties have arisen at various times, they are quickly subsumed or defeated by one of the two major parties. The two-party system reduces major policy issues to two-sided questions, when, in fact, the complexity of these issues warrants multiple perspectives. The problem for democracy is that there is no formal venue for presenting multiple perspectives in elections or in the governing institutions.

The larger question is whether the twenty-first-century U.S. party system fulfills the role of enabling widespread participation in the governing process. In terms of responding to changes in public opinion, political parties fall short of meeting their responsibilities as agents of democratic government. They are large, entrenched organizations with multiple layers—federal, state, and local—that can differ in their viewpoints on specific issues. The breadth of the national parties makes it difficult to reach internal consensus on issues at every level of government.

The combination of intraparty divisions with interparty polarization and conflict has produced a party-dominated democracy that is not consistently responsive to voters' interests and opinions. However, in a democracy, power rests on winning elections, and for that, parties will always depend on voters like you, who hold the power to change them by staying loyal or switching your allegiance.

Chapter Review

Key Terms

Australian ballot (p. 320). How did the Australian ballot reduce the party bosses' control over election outcomes?

ballot (p. 310). What types of ballots were used before electronic voting?

caucus (p. 312). How is a caucus different from a primary?

general election (p. 309). What is the role of parties in general elections?

invisible primary (p. 315). How is the invisible primary different from the New Hampshire and other state primaries?

majority vote (p. 322). What is the difference between plurality and majority vote?

median voter theorem (p. 322). Why does the median voter theorem contribute to limited political choice?

national committee (p. 308). What are the responsibilities of the national committees?

party alignment (p. 330). Is party alignment stable today?

party caucus (p. 308). Which form of the party—party in the electorate, party in government, party as an organization—are party caucuses affiliated with and why?

party platform (p. 306). What role do party platforms play in electoral politics?

patronage system (p. 320). How did the patronage system strengthen political parties?

plurality vote (p. 322). How does plurality voting encourage third parties?

political parties (p. 306). How are political parties a gateway to democracy?

primary election (p. 309). When did primaries first emerge in U.S. politics?

proportional representation (p. 312). How does proportional representation work?

realignment (p. 331). What precipitates a realignment?

responsible parties (p. 336). How does a responsible party system produce accountability?

single-member plurality system (p. 322). Why does a single-member plurality system promote a two-party system?

third parties (p. 319). Are third parties viable options in the United States?

winner-take-all system (p. 312). What are the advantages and disadvantages of a winner-take-all system?

Learning Outcomes: What You Need to...

Know	Test Yourself	Participate

LO 9-1   Outline how political parties evolved in American politics

They have one primary purpose: to win elections in order to control government power and implement their policies. Parties organize the electorate by giving them choices of policies and candidates, and they also organize Congress and state legislatures into cohesive groups that consistently vote for the policies that they promise in their platforms. Parties nominate candidates for office in primary elections, which are open to all voters, although in some states voters must affiliate with a party before voting.

- Define political party.
- Identify the three arenas in which parties operate.
- Track the party nomination process.

- Design a system that allows the greatest number of voters to participate in choosing the party nominee.

LO 9-2   Identify which issues divided the first political parties

The basic division between the Federalists and the Antifederalists over the ratification of the Constitution survived into the Washington administration to become factions; by the time of Jefferson's election in 1800, the factions had become political parties. Between 1800 and the Civil War, various parties rose and fell, but since the end of the war, the two major parties—the Democratic Party and the Republican Party—have dominated the American political system.

- Explain the differences between the Federalists and the Antifederalists.
- Describe the events that opened up the presidential nomination process.
- Explain how the Republican Party formed.
- Connect patronage and party power.
- Describe reforms that reduced party power.

- Design your own political party, identify which issues to focus on, and explain how you would attract members; explain why your party would be more accountable than the existing two major parties.

LO 9-3   Explain why two parties dominate the U.S. political system

The effects of the two-party system are to limit voter choices to "for" and "against" and to discourage third parties, although the issues third parties arise to address are frequently adopted by one of the major political parties.

- Explain the median voter theorem.
- Describe how a single-member plurality system encourages two parties.
- Summarize the role third parties have played in American politics.
- Survey the obstacles to third parties and independent candidates.
- Explain how interest groups and political parties have become more closely aligned.

- Imagine yourself as head of the Tea Party, and devise a strategy that would enable this third party to win the presidency.

LO 9-4   Define partisan affiliation and ideology

Voter realignments occur when the parties readjust the focus of their policies, typically as a result of a major event such as an economic depression or a military conflict. Since Franklin D. Roosevelt's New Deal of the 1930s, liberals have generally aligned with the Democratic Party and conservatives with the Republican Party. The modern political landscape is marked by a partisan divide, with the parties taking on starker opposing positions and ramping up the rhetoric to the point that voters sometimes wonder if partisanship is taking precedence over policy making.

- Explain how voters align and realign with political parties.
- Describe the impact of the New Deal on political ideology.
- Explain how the Democratic Party came to be seen by African Americans as the party that supported civil rights.
- Recall how Ronald Reagan's campaign strategy appealed to conservative Democrats.
- Describe the general shift in the ideological core of the Democratic and Republican Parties since 1994.

- Identify three issues that you believe cut across ideological dividing lines. How would you encourage lawmakers to use these issues as examples of how to work together?

Elections and Campaigns

> **"**It's my hope I'll be reelected to serve this community. . . . There's a lot of work we still have to do to fight for the middle class and make sure every Arizonan has a shot at the American dream.**"**

The campus of Brigham Young University where Kyrsten Sinema received her undergraduate degree is shown on the next page.

KYRSTEN SINEMA
Brigham Young University

Senator Kyrsten Sinema (D-AZ) is unconventional. Just consider her educational background. She graduated high school at the age of 16 in Arizona as valedictorian and graduated Brigham Young University (BYU) in 1995 at the age of 18. She earned a master's degree in social work in 1999, a JD in 2004, and her PhD in Justice Studies in 2012—all from Arizona State University. Sinema also has a strong bipartisan streak—again something unconventional these days. She first ran for state legislature in 2002 as an Independent, but after losing the race, ran as a Democrat in 2004 and won. In the Arizona state legislature, she worked closely with Republicans on legislation tied to human trafficking. In her first race for Congress, the *Arizona Republic*, the local Phoenix newspaper, endorsed her for her nonpartisan style, arguing that for "Sinema, it's always about the issue, not the personalities."[1] Finally, Sinema's personal choices make her unique: Although raised in a conservative Mormon family, she is the first openly bisexual person elected to Congress. In an era when the country has become quite used to openly gay politicians, her sexuality drew quite a bit of attention. She was not fond of the attention either, explaining that "I'm not a pioneer. I'm just a regular person who works hard."[2]

Yet Sinema is a pioneer. She uses the political process as a gateway to make a difference. During her childhood, she faced some hard times, living for a while in an abandoned gas station without electricity or running water.[3] Those early experiences shaped her life and convinced her to get involved and make the lives of people better. She supported the DREAM Act as a member of the Arizona state legislature. She also fought to rein in Maricopa County Sheriff Joe Arpaio's hardline immigration stances, which often drew attention across the entire country.[4] She hired undocumented DREAM activist Erika Andiola (featured in Chapter 5, Civil Rights) on her staff—a strong signal about her position on that issue. Since being in the U.S. Congress, she has focused a good deal of attention on issues tied to veterans.[5] She argues that "our country has a moral responsibility to do right by the men and women who serve in our military."[6]

Learning Outcomes

LO 10-1	Describe the ideas that molded the Framers' thinking about elections
LO 10-2	Outline the steps in presidential campaigns
LO 10-3	Identify the issues that shape presidential campaigns
LO 10-4	Outline the steps in congressional campaigns
LO 10-5	Determine which issues shape congressional campaigns

Her congressional career started in 2012 when she won in a new district that arose from the redistricting following the 2010 census. In this fairly competitive district, she won the election with about 49 percent of the vote. Her Republican opponent, Vernon Parker, garnered 45 percent, and a Libertarian candidate secured about 6 percent of the vote. As a first-term member of Congress from a competitive district, she knew she would face a tough battle for reelection. Having tackled the difficult issues in Congress and being openly bisexual, she faced harsh attacks. But knowing that her reelection would not be easy, she raised a good deal of money not only to respond to any attacks but also to scare off potential challengers.

In 2018, Sinema ran for Senate. She faced, as she always has, a tough battle. Her bitter race against Martha McSally (R) was too close to call even a week after the election. But as the final votes were counted, she pulled ahead and became Arizona's first elected female senator. As senator, she has continued to carve out a moderate path on policy, which should play well in an increasingly competitive state. McSally was later appointed by the governor of Arizona to be her Senate colleague following the death of Senator John McCain in 2017. McSally narrowly lost her bid for a full term to Mark Kelly in 2020. Kelly will join Sinema in the Senate to become the first team of two Democrats from Arizona since 1952.

Elections and campaigns, as Kyrsten Sinema knows, offer an important gateway into the American political system. They provide many opportunities for participation, not only running for office but also volunteering and working at the polls. During campaigns, candidates offer competing visions of the role of government and promise to enact specific policies. The people then decide which candidate to support. Elections provide the most common (and easiest) gateway for the people to express their opinions and to hold elected officials accountable, shaping the course of government. In this chapter, we examine how elections and campaigns work, asking whether, and how, these institutions both promote government responsiveness and foster accountability.

The Constitutional Requirements for Elections

LO 10-1 Describe the ideas that molded the Framers' thinking about elections

Key Questions

Why did the Framers set up gates against popular participation in elections?

Key Questions

Why did the Framers give so much authority over presidential elections to the states?

Given the importance of elections to the democratic process, it is surprising that the Constitution says so little about them. The requirements that the Constitution lays out for elections indicate that the Framers wanted to set up barriers against direct democracy. Only the House of Representatives was to be elected directly by the people. In elections for the president and for the Senate, the public's role was indirect and complex. Today, senators are elected directly by the people. Presidential elections also give citizens more say in the process, but these contests continue to be shaped by constitutional requirements that serve as a gate between the people and the presidency. In this section, we explain the constitutional requirements for American elections as background for understanding the ways in which presidential and congressional campaigns are run.

Presidential Elections

The constitutional rules governing the selection of the president reflect three fundamental themes that guided the Framers' thinking. First, the states were given broad discretion on key matters regarding presidential elections to ensure their importance and to counterbalance the power of the national government. Second, the Framers designed the presidency with George Washington in mind and did not spell out all aspects in great detail, including elections. Over time, the details were filled in. Third, the presidency was intended to stand above party politics, doing what was right for the nation rather than supporting one faction over another. That assumption went awry early on, and political parties formed almost from the start.

The Electoral College.   The means by which the president of the United States is selected was born of compromise between the interests of the states and the interests of the people, yielding a system that even today is indirect and confusing. Like the Connecticut Compromise that produced a legislature with an upper chamber to represent the states and a lower chamber to represent the people, the system for electing the president was intended to be similarly balanced. The formal selection of the president is in the hands of electors, who collectively constitute the **Electoral College**.

Electoral College: *The presidential electors, selected every four years to represent the votes of their respective states, who meet to cast the electoral votes for president and vice president.*

The Constitution gave state legislatures the responsibility of deciding how best to choose electors, either by choosing the electors themselves or granting the people the right to choose the electors. Because state legislators were, for the most part, elected by the people, this arrangement gave the public an indirect say in the choice. The idea was that the Electoral College would serve as a gatekeeper against rash or ignorant voters. There was little support among the Framers for letting the people choose the president directly. In fact, during the debates at the Constitutional Convention, George Mason said that allowing the people to select the president would be like referring "a trial of colors to a blind man."[7] Today the people of each state, not the members of state legislatures, choose the electors in an arrangement that has given citizens a new gateway for influence (see Figure 10.1).

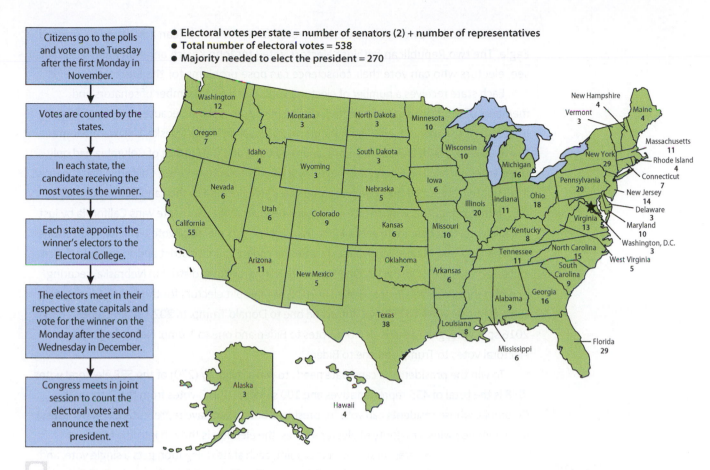

Citizens go to the polls and vote on the Tuesday after the first Monday in November.

↓

Votes are counted by the states.

↓

In each state, the candidate receiving the most votes is the winner.

↓

Each state appoints the winner's electors to the Electoral College.

↓

The electors meet in their respective state capitals and vote for the winner on the Monday after the second Wednesday in December.

↓

Congress meets in joint session to count the electoral votes and announce the next president.

- Electoral votes per state = number of senators (2) + number of representatives
- Total number of electoral votes = 538
- Majority needed to elect the president = 270

Washington 12
Oregon 7
Montana 3
North Dakota 3
Minnesota 10
New Hampshire 4
Vermont 3
Maine 4
Idaho 4
South Dakota 3
Wisconsin 10
Massachusetts 11
New York 29
Rhode Island 4
Connecticut 7
Nevada 6
Wyoming 3
Iowa 6
Michigan 16
Pennsylvania 20
New Jersey 14
California 55
Utah 6
Colorado 9
Nebraska 5
Illinois 20
Indiana 11
Ohio 18
Delaware 3
Maryland 10
Washington, D.C. 3
Kansas 6
Missouri 10
Kentucky 8
Virginia 13
West Virginia 5
Arizona 11
New Mexico 5
Oklahoma 7
Arkansas 6
Tennessee 11
North Carolina 15
South Carolina 9
Texas 38
Louisiana 8
Alabama 9
Georgia 16
Mississippi 6
Florida 29
Alaska 3
Hawaii 4

Figure 10.1 How the Electoral College Works

This map shows each state's number of electors for the 2020 election, allocated on the basis of the 2010 census. In every state but two, the winner of the popular vote takes all of the electoral votes. Maine and Nebraska allocate votes by congressional district and so can split their electoral votes. The flowchart on the left shows the process by which popular votes are transferred to Electoral College votes.

The electors, however, remain the formal decision makers for choosing the president. In fact, they meet in December to vote formally for the president—five or so weeks after Election Day in November. These electors are selected in a variety of ways in the fifty states. It is very much a state-centered process. Before the election, each party lines up electors for its nominee. In the 2016 presidential election, when Hillary Clinton won the most votes in the state of California, her electors were then eligible to vote in December's meeting of the Electoral College. Republican candidate Donald Trump had different electors ready to serve if he had won. Presidential nominees seek to identify people who will be loyal to them. This is important because thirty-two states allow electors to vote their conscience, meaning they are not legally bound by the results of the election in their state. These electors are often referred to as **faithless electors** and states handle electors deviating in various ways. Some states, like Virginia and California, have no penalties in place for deviant votes. As of 2020, only eleven states cancel the vote and replace the elector if he or she is a faithless one.[8] Electors rarely deviate from supporting the candidate to whom they are pledged—there have only been 168 faithless electors in the history of the Electoral College; however, the possibility for defection remains as seen in the 2016 election when an unprecedented ten electors deviated. Three Democratic electors cast rogue votes for Bernie Sanders, one chose Republican primary candidate John Kasich, three chose former national security advisor and

Key Questions

Is a winner-take-all system fair? If not, what system would be fair?

Republican Colin Powell. A lone deviator voted for Native American activist Faith Spotted Eagle. The two Republican faithless electors voted for John Kasich and Ron Paul.[9] As one can see, electors who can vote their conscience can pose problems for the Electoral College.

Each state receives a number of electoral votes equal to its number of senators and members of the House of Representatives. The minimum is three because every state has at least one House member and two senators. In 2016, seven states (Alaska, Delaware, Montana, North Dakota, South Dakota, Vermont, and Wyoming) and the District of Columbia had only three votes each in the Electoral College. With fifty-five electoral votes, California had the most. In all but two states, all the state's electoral votes are allocated to the candidate who finishes first in the voting. This winner-take-all system means that if a candidate wins California by just a single vote, that candidate gets all fifty-five of the state's electoral votes. The two exceptions are Nebraska and Maine, which allocate votes by congressional district and so can split their electoral votes. In 2008, Barack Obama won one congressional district in Nebraska, securing one of Nebraska's five electoral votes. In 2016, Maine split electors for the first time, awarding three electoral votes to Hillary Clinton and one to Donald Trump. In 2020, Maine repeated its 2016 split vote, giving three electoral votes to Biden and one to Trump. Nebraska gave four electoral votes to Trump and one to Biden.

To win the presidency, a candidate needs to win a majority (270) of the 538 electoral votes (538 is the total of 435 representatives and 100 senators plus 3 votes from the District of Columbia, whose residents can vote for president but do not have representation in Congress). If no nominee wins a majority of electoral votes, the election is thrown into the House of Representatives. At this point, each state delegation gets a single vote, and the candidate who wins a majority of the states becomes the next president. That last happened in 1824.

Image 10.1 Following passage of the Twelfth Amendment, presidential and vice presidential candidates campaigned on the same ticket. This campaign poster from the 1872 election shows President Ulysses S. Grant and his vice presidential candidate using their humble beginnings to appeal to workingmen.

The Granger Collection, NYC

Problems with the Electoral College.
The Electoral College has never worked as the Framers envisioned, as an institution that would allow a group of independent decision makers to get together in the many states and deliberate over who would make the best president. The Framers viewed the presidency as a contest between individuals, not between political parties, and in the first four presidential elections (1789, 1792, 1796, and 1800), electors cast ballots for their top two choices; the winner became president, and the second-place finisher became vice president. The process ignored the parties of the candidates; the goal was to select the most qualified person. In 1796, the process yielded John Adams (1797–1801) as president and his chief rival, Thomas Jefferson, as vice president. Just imagine Hillary Clinton serving as Donald Trump's vice president!

Serious problems arose in 1800, when political parties had fully emerged. Thomas Jefferson and Aaron Burr, both running as Democratic-Republicans, received the same number of Electoral College votes, even though everyone knew that Jefferson was seeking the presidency and Burr the vice presidency. To achieve that outcome, one of the Democratic-Republican electors needed to withhold a vote from Burr, giving Jefferson the most votes and Burr the second most. That did not happen. Adams, who was also running again as a Federalist, finished third. Because no candidate had an outright majority in the Electoral College, Burr decided to try to become president. The election, as a result, was sent to the House of Representatives, since there was no majority winner. A lengthy battle in the House ensued, lasting thirty-seven ballots before Thomas Jefferson (1801–1809) finally won the presidency. The Twelfth Amendment, adopted in 1804, fixed this problem by combining the vote for president and vice president into one ballot, with the person running for each office named.

Another source of problems in the system was that states were free to set their own rules for selecting electors. In the first presidential election in 1789, four states (Delaware, Maryland, Pennsylvania, and Virginia) held direct popular elections to choose electors.[10] Other states used their legislatures to select electors. Further, there was no agreed-upon time for holding these elections. In 1800, voting took place any time between April and November. New York selected its electors in April, and Pennsylvania and South Carolina did not even have rules for selecting theirs until November. States also frequently changed their methods of selecting electors. Only Maryland used a **popular vote** for selecting electors in the first four presidential contests.

Because of this odd hodgepodge of frequently changing rules, the presidential contest in the early nineteenth century was very different from the campaigns of today. Now states hold elections all on the same day—the first Tuesday after the first Monday in November— and electors meet in December to choose the next president. The Electoral College is an historical artifact of the Framers' constitutional design. But the mishmash of state rules, as noted earlier, always makes it possible for some new twist to unfold that would fuel controversy surrounding the formal selection of the president.

Electoral College Reform.
The biggest problem with the Electoral College occurs when winning the nation's popular vote does not automatically translate into a win in the Electoral College, meaning that the individual who received fewer votes could become the president. This happened in the 1824, 1876, 1888, 2000, and 2016 presidential elections. Such outcomes raise questions about equality. If a democracy rests on the idea of majority rule—that is, the candidate with the most support in the public wins the election— then about 10 percent of our presidential elections have been "undemocratic."

Some may wonder why the country does not just change the rules to select the president through the popular vote. This method would appear more

Key Questions

How did the emergence of political parties change the way the Framers hoped elections would work?

popular vote: *Tally of total votes from individual citizens, as opposed to the electoral vote.*

Key Questions

Should the Electoral College be eliminated? What would be the consequences?

Library of Congress Prints and Photographs Division [LC-DIG-ggbain-03136]

Image 10.2 The 1876 election was contested, and its outcome was determined by an electoral commission. Some feared public disturbances at the inauguration, so Rutherford B. Hayes, who had won the Electoral College but not the popular vote, took the oath of office privately in the White House. The formal ceremony at the Capitol, two days later, was peaceful.

Supreme Court Cases

Bush v. Gore (2000)

QUESTION: Does Florida's subjective recount mechanism violate equal protection of the law? If so, should there be a recount using more objective standards?

ORAL ARGUMENT: December 11, 2000 (listen at http://www.oyez.org/cases/2000-2009/2000/2000_00_949/)

DECISION: December 12, 2000 (read at https://caselaw.findlaw.com/us-supreme-court/531/98.html)

OUTCOME: Yes, Florida's recount procedures violate the equal protection clause (7–2), and no, there is insufficient time to conduct a recount (5–4).

The presidential election of 2000 came down to Florida's electoral votes. The candidate who won the state—Republican Governor George W. Bush of Texas or Democratic Vice President Al Gore—would win the election. The early counts were excruciatingly close, with the news networks first calling the election for Gore, then declaring it undecided, then declaring Bush the winner, and then putting it back in the undecided column.

Due to the closeness of the race, an automatic machine recount took place. Bush led Gore by 537 votes out of nearly 6 million cast. Because elections, even for federal office, are administered under state law, Gore went to state court in Florida, asking for a hand recount in four counties that would require election officials in those counties to determine, from each ballot, the intent of the voter. In punch card ballots, the machine will not read a ballot unless the chad—the area that is to be punched out by the voter—is completely removed. But a hand count might be able to determine the voter's intent from a "hanging" or "dimpled" or "pregnant" chad—indented but not sufficiently punched out so as to break off or even break the corners.

The Florida Supreme Court ruled for Gore by a 4–3 vote on December 8. Bush then filed suit in federal court, claiming that the standard of the intent of the voter that Florida used, which could mean different

standards by different officials, was so arbitrary as to violate the equal protection clause. The Bush legal team asked for an injunction, an order blocking further recount. Both the U.S. District Court and the U.S. Court of Appeals rejected Bush's request. Bush then appealed to the Supreme Court.

The Supreme Court agreed to hear the case, and on December 9, it decided, by a 5–4 vote, to halt the recount before the Court's decision. The Court heard oral arguments on December 11 and announced its decision at 10 p.m. on December 12.

The Supreme Court ruled by a 7–2 vote that the absence of specific standards for gauging the intent of the voter was so arbitrary as to violate the equal protection clause. The Court also declared by a 5–4 vote that Florida's legislature intended all recounts to be completed by December 12, thus making a recount impossible.

The dissenters declared that the machinery of running elections is a state question that should not involve the federal courts; that the Court's prior interpretation of the equal protection clause has allowed differential treatment as long as there is no intent to discriminate against certain groups; and that the Court's December 12 deadline was never stated in Florida law.

Vice President Gore conceded the election the next day.

Thinking Critically

1. Why was the Supreme Court so rushed in its decision?
2. In what way did Florida's recount plan violate equality?

democratic because all votes would be treated equally. But the current system has some advantages. For example, the Electoral College system encourages candidates to secure support in all corners of the country, not just in areas with dense populations. A system of popular votes would privilege Los Angeles over Oklahoma. In America's federal system, the states do matter. Eliminating the Electoral College would decrease the role of the states, dampening the significance of state interests. There are also practical problems. Doing away with the Electoral College through a constitutional amendment would be difficult because it is unlikely that three-quarters of the states, needed to ratify an amendment, would support such a reform. Small states see merit in the system, since it forces presidential candidates to consider their needs and gives them a chance for influence.

The 2000 and 2016 Presidential Elections.   Because elections are a centerpiece of democracy, it is important for them to be viewed as fair. The events surrounding the 2000 presidential election tested the credibility of the American electoral process. The margin between Vice President Albert Gore Jr. and George W. Bush (2001–09) was razor thin. In the popular vote, Gore received nearly 600,000 more votes than Bush—just a 0.5 percentage point difference (48.4 percent to 47.9 percent). The number of electoral votes did not identify a winner on election night because the state of Florida was too close to call, and without that state's electoral votes, neither candidate had the necessary 270 votes. Bush led in Florida by 537 votes out of 5.8 million votes cast—a 0.0001 percent difference. Demands for a recount ensued, and the Florida recount revealed how difficult it is to produce an accurate vote count. A series of court cases resulted in a Supreme Court decision that determined the outcome of the election (see Supreme Court Cases: *Bush v. Gore*).

Many votes had not been counted in Florida, and some had been counted for the wrong candidate. Citizens across the country lost faith in American elections. Since that time, the public's confidence had been restored. But the 2016 presidential election raised the issue again. Hillary Clinton won almost 3 million more votes than Trump, but lost the Electoral College by a substantial margin. This election had the largest discrepancy in popular votes versus Electoral College votes in American history. Many see this outcome as unfair, but both sides understood the rules of the game. The results of the 2016 contest continue to be questioned as we learn more about the extent of Russian interference in the election. Since 2016, the public has learned that Russia engaged in a variety of tactics to influence the outcome of the election, including hacking the DCCC and Clinton campaign, spreading fake information on the internet, staging rallies, and more. Although there is no evidence that Russia changed individual votes, scholars have not ruled out the possibility that Russia was able to sway the outcome of the 2016 election.[11]

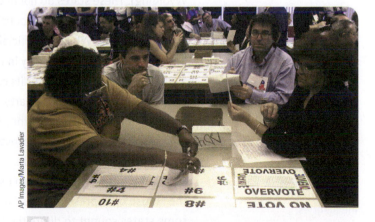

Image 10.3 Election workers in Miami manually recount votes while representatives of both parties observe. The 2000 Florida recount was fraught with difficulty, and a series of court cases regarding the election culminated in a Supreme Court decision on December 12 that halted the recount and essentially made George W. Bush the winner of the election.

Congressional Elections

The constitutional guidelines for congressional elections also reflect the compromise between the interests of the states and the interests of the people. The Framers

Key Questions

How do differences in term lengths and constituencies affect how senators and House members behave?

intended that the Senate would bring state interests to bear on the legislative process, while they intended that the House would represent "the people." Each state, regardless of size, has two senators, while representatives are elected from congressional districts within states whose boundaries are adjusted to accommodate changes in population. Senators serve staggered six-year terms, while House members serve two-year terms.

Senate Elections.

The Constitution originally gave the choice of senators to state legislatures. Again the Framers inserted a gate between the people and those who were to serve their interests in the Senate. In the late nineteenth century, however, Progressive reformers called for elimination of this gate, arguing that the people ought to have a direct say in the election of senators. This reform became a reality with the adoption of the Seventeenth Amendment in 1913. Even with this change, however, there are barriers against overwhelming change in the composition of the Senate because elections are staggered; only one-third of senators are up for election at any one time. This arrangement ensures that the Senate is insulated from large shifts in public sentiment.

House Elections and Redistricting.

In contrast to the Senate, the entire House of Representatives is up for election every two years. Also in contrast to the Senate, House members have always been elected directly by the people.[12]

The Constitution requires that states apportion representatives by population, which is counted every ten years in the **U.S. Census**. Originally, each member was to represent no more than thirty thousand people. As the population grew, the House of Representatives grew as well, from 65 members in 1789 to 237 members in 1857. The House continued to grow until 1911, and in 1929, the number was capped at 435. A member now represents, on average, more than seven hundred thousand people, as set by the 2010 census. Every ten years, states draw new district lines following a census. Depending on patterns of population growth or decline, states win or lose congressional seats with each new census. Currently seven states have populations so small that they qualify for only one member of the House of Representatives (Alaska, Delaware, Montana, North Dakota, South Dakota, Vermont, and Wyoming). These states do not need to worry about drawing new congressional districts.

State legislatures are responsible for drawing the district lines in a process known as **redistricting**. While the official aim of redistricting is to try to keep districts equal in population, the majority party in the state legislature tries to construct each district in such a way as to make it easier for its candidates to win congressional seats. Although citizens are not required to disclose party affiliation in the census, past voting patterns give parties a strong indication of where they have the advantage. In addition to equal population in districts, another important constraint facing the redistricting is that the boundaries must be contiguous (uninterrupted).

Redistricting has also been used as a tool to achieve greater minority representation in the House of Representatives. Following passage of the Voting Rights Act (VRA) in 1965, some states sought to dilute the effect of minority voters by drawing district lines so as to split their voting strength. In 1982, amendments to the VRA forbade this practice, and in response, state legislatures created majority-minority districts, in which African Americans or Latinos would constitute a majority of the voters in the district, thereby increasing the possibility of their electing African American or Latino candidates. In 2012, for example, Joaquín Castro won election to the House from the 20th Congressional District in Texas,

U.S. Census: *Article 1, Section 2 of the Constitution mandates that the United States population be counted every 10 years to determine the number of seats each state gets in the House of Representatives and how to distribute federal funds.*

redistricting: *Process whereby state legislatures redraw the boundaries of congressional districts in the state to make them equal in population size.*

Key Questions

Do majority-minority districts help advance equality or introduce inequalities?

Greensboro
Winston-Salem
Durham
High Point
Charlotte

North Wind Picture Archives/Alamy Stock Photo

Election Data Services, Inc.

Images 10.4 and 10.5 The term *gerrymander* comes from the salamander-shaped district in Massachusetts (above left), which Governor Elbridge Gerry approved following the census of 1810. Political rivals denounced the blatant seeking of political advantage that had produced such an oddly shaped congressional district, and the taunt stuck, passing into common usage in politics. Nevertheless, gerrymandered districts remain. In 1991, a North Carolina redistricting was designed to create a district with African Americans in the majority (above right). Federal courts later ruled that North Carolina had to revise these district lines so that the congressional district was more compact.

which is a Latino majority-minority district (see Chapter 12, Congress). In the past decade, however, the federal courts have ruled that state legislatures overemphasized the racial composition of these districts to the point that the districts made no geographic sense. As a result, current guidelines on redistricting call for the consideration of race in drawing district lines, but not to the extreme that it had been employed in the past.[13]

Any change to the size and shape of a district can have political implications because shifts in its partisan makeup alter which party might be able to capture the seat. For these reasons, there are major battles over the composition of districts. The politicization of drawing districts is called **gerrymandering**. Chapter 12 provides more details about this process and explains how different compositions of districts can alter the kind of gateway congressional elections offer.

The battle over redistricting and gerrymandering has recently reemerged, as state and federal courts have started to weigh in on the validity of many states' congressional district maps. Since 2016, federal courts in Wisconsin, North Carolina, Michigan, Maryland, and Pennsylvania all ruled that their states' congressional maps are unconstitutionally tilted toward one party. As of February 2018, the Supreme Court has upheld the Pennsylvania State Supreme Court's ruling but has temporarily blocked the North Carolina lower court's order to redraw their map.[14] In an August 2018 rehearing of the North Carolina case, a three-judge panel ruled the Republican state legislature explicitly and unconstitutionally drew the district lines to favor Republicans. This decision was appealed to the United States Supreme Court along with another similar case from Maryland. In June 2019, the Court ruled on the consolidated cases of *Rucho v. Common Cause* and *Lamone v. Benisek*. The decision allowed for state legislatures to continue to redistrict in ways that benefit the party in charge and weakened the federal courts' power when hearing challenges to partisan gerrymandering.[15]

gerrymandering:
Redistricting that blatantly benefits one political party over the other or concentrates (or dilutes) the voting impact of racial and ethnic groups.

Key Questions
Do you think more elections mean more democracy? How many elections are too many?

Other Elections

The only type of election mentioned in the Constitution in which the people could directly participate is the election of members of the U.S. House of Representatives. Today, however, U.S. citizens elect the president (through electors), members of Congress, governors, state legislators, and a range of local officials, including at the city, town, or village level. In some states, voters can cast ballots on specific policies through initiatives and referenda[16] (see Chapter 3, Federalism). In addition, we have primary elections in which parties ask citizens to vote for the nominee for the general election (see Chapter 9, Political Parties). Further, in thirty-eight of the fifty states, some sort of election is involved in the selection or the retention of judges for the state's highest court.[17] No other developed country has as many elections as the United States.[18]

Key Questions

What are the consequences of electing judges?

There are three reasons for this heavy reliance on the ballot. First, the public views elections as legitimate devices for making political choices.[19] Second, the Constitution was vague about rules surrounding the choice of presidents and members of Congress, allowing states to make greater use of elections, and many have done so. Third, the federal system created layers of government and multiple political offices to fill them, most of which are elected. At the local level, the people generally elect school board members and commissions that deal with various public tasks, such as water and road construction.

Presidential Campaigns

LO 10-2 Outline the steps in presidential campaigns

Presidential campaigns capture the interest of the vast majority of Americans. In September 2016, two months before the presidential election, 85 percent of the electorate paid at least some attention to the contest between Donald Trump and Hillary Clinton.[20] Every move a presidential candidate makes is watched and assessed. This focus on the presidency would have surprised the Framers, who expected the legislative branch to be the center of attention. But as the executive branch has gained power, so has the importance of the contest to fill the office of president.

Key Questions

Do presidential campaigns ensure that the best person for the office wins?

The course of the modern presidential campaign is long and difficult. From the decision to run to the final victory and concession speeches, the road to the White House is shaped by constitutional requirements, interparty struggles, and strategies for attracting votes that highlight the many gates and gateways along the way.

Evolution of the Modern Campaign

As in so many matters of custom and protocol, George Washington shaped the way future presidential aspirants would campaign for president. Like others at the Constitutional Convention, he worried that a chief executive could morph into a monarch, so he deliberately avoided doing anything to advance his candidacy. He took these steps even though he and all the Framers knew that they created the office of president with him in mind. Washington stayed at Mount Vernon, his estate on the Potomac River, and let others work on his behalf. The electors met on February 4, 1789, and the vote for Washington was unanimous. Only then did

Washington proceed to New York City, then the new nation's capital, where he took the oath of office on April 30.

Washington's conduct continued to influence presidential campaigns until the start of the twentieth century. Candidates allowed their political parties to campaign on their behalf but avoided looking too ambitious. In 1896, William McKinley (1897–1901) stayed home in Canton, Ohio, speaking to well-wishers from his front porch. This so-called front porch campaign proved successful, but only because his campaign manager, Mark Hanna, and the Republican Party were raising funds and securing votes behind the scenes.

Although candidates in the early nineteenth century sought to appear aloof and above the fray, their supporters took every opportunity to advance their candidacies. Buttons and slogans promoted favorites, and parades and barbeques sought to convince the undecided. Participation had much more of a social component than it does now. Many observers argue that the high rate of voting in the late nineteenth century reflected the fact that campaigns were often fun.[21]

By the early twentieth century, presidential contenders began to campaign actively, too, and campaigning started earlier and earlier. The 2016 presidential campaign officially began in March 2015, when Senator Ted Cruz (R-TX) formally announced his intention to seek the presidency. He was hoping an early start would help him win.[22] Throughout 2015, seventeen candidates announced their decision to seek the White House, including Jeb Bush, Ben Carson, Rand Paul, Mike Huckabee, Donald Trump, John Kasich, Carly Fiorina, and Marco Rubio. Starting the day after the 2016 election, speculation began about who might run in 2020. Would Senator Kirsten Gillibrand, Senator Cory Booker, or Vice President Joe Biden try for the Democratic nomination? As it turns out, all three of them did run, along with about 25 other Democratic hopefuls; ultimately Joe Biden prevailed. It is no wonder that many observers have expressed concern over what has been called the **permanent campaign**,[23] a worry that politicians, especially presidents, spend too much time working toward reelection and not enough time governing. Some argue that if politicians spent more time governing and less time running for elections, the nation would be better off. Nevertheless, politicians must win elections to be able to govern, and constant campaigning may be an indication of responsiveness.

The Granger Collection, NYC

Image 10.6 In 1896, William McKinley, former House member and governor of Ohio, ran for president from his front porch in Canton, Ohio. Visitors arrived by train, and he spoke to groups of them, sometimes several times a day. In contrast, his opponent, William Jennings Bryan, traveled all over the country by train, speaking to crowds from the back of train cars. McKinley won.

permanent campaign:
Charge that presidents and members of Congress focus more on winning the next election than on governing.

The Decision to Run and the Invisible Primary

The decision to seek the presidency is a serious one. The presidency is the highest elective office in the land and a position that offers a chance both to influence the course of the nation and to leave a legacy as the leader of the free world. It is perhaps for these reasons that so many of the nation's political leaders consider running for this great office. The decision is not, however, an easy one to make, and potential candidates must ask themselves many difficult questions:

- How will a presidential campaign affect my family?
- Will my indiscretions in college come back to haunt me?
- Can I build a team of advisers that will allow me to win the presidency?
- Can I raise enough money to be competitive?
- Who else might run for the office?
- What do I want to accomplish if elected?

Key Questions
Were you satisfied with the options you were offered in 2020, a choice between Joe Biden and Donald Trump? Why or why not?

- Am I prepared to campaign eighteen hours a day for nearly two years straight?
- Am I capable of handling the pressure that comes with being in the Oval Office?
- Can I win?
- What happens if I lose? Will I still have influence in my party? Can I run again? Or maybe run for a different office?

These are some of the questions that swirl in a potential candidate's mind when he or she thinks about throwing "my hat in the ring," a phrase from the sport of boxing that Theodore Roosevelt used to announce his candidacy in 1912. The campaign for president is unlike that for any other office. The demands are intense. Every move a major candidate makes is discussed and analyzed by journalists and political pundits. Presidential campaigns are pressure cookers—perhaps appropriately because the office is so demanding. The American public wants to know whether a candidate has the toughness to serve as commander in chief and the wisdom to identify the best policies. Candidates often describe the process as being put through a meat grinder. For an overview of the two- to three-year-long ordeal, see Table 10.1.

invisible primary: *Period just before the primaries begin during which candidates attempt to capture party support and media coverage.*

After a candidate decides to run for president, he or she enters what is called the **invisible primary**. No votes are cast, but candidates are jockeying for position so they can be ready to do well in the initial primaries and caucuses. Usually, candidates must line up party support, financial backing, and credibility with journalists in the news media. Candidates who can get attention from the news media can raise more money and secure more endorsements from party leaders. Over the last fifty years, the invisible primary has been very much an insider's game, but that was not the case for Donald Trump. He stormed the Republican Party from the outside, with few endorsements (at first), limited fundraising, and doubts from journalists about the viability of his campaign. Yet he took his case to the broader public and hit a chord with

Table 10.1 The Road to the White House

Time Frame	Event
Beginning two to three years prior to the election year	Decision to run, in which candidates weigh their options and make formal announcements
	Invisible primary, in which candidates jockey for position and try to build momentum
Beginning in the election year	Caucuses and primaries, in which the people vote, and one candidate in each party emerges as the front-runner
Summer of election year	National party conventions, in which the front-runner in each party is formally nominated and gives an acceptance speech that kicks off the fall campaign
Fall of election year	National campaign, during which televised presidential debates are a highlight
November of election year	Election Day, in which the people vote
December of election year	Electoral College, in which electors meet in their state capitals and formally choose the president
January after election year	Inauguration Day

many voters that sparked his campaign during the invisible primary. By contrast, Hillary Clinton in 2016 was very traditional in her approach to the nomination. She raised money, collected numerous endorsements, and built an organization designed to turn out the vote. What is not clear is whether Trump's unique approach can be duplicated in future campaigns.

Incumbent presidents usually win their party's nomination for a second term. If that part of the contest is a struggle, as it was in 1980 for President Jimmy Carter (1977–81), it is a sign that the incumbent is in trouble, and he usually goes on to lose the general election. But when the seat is open—when an incumbent is in his second term or decides not to run again, as Lyndon Baines Johnson (1963–69) did in 1968—a battle unfolds. These struggles tend to be multicandidate affairs, often with numerous serious contenders seeking the nomination. In 2016, both parties' nominations were open, meaning that neither the sitting president nor the sitting vice president was seeking the nomination—a situation that has occurred only two times since 1928 (1952 and 2008). As noted above, seventeen Republicans sought the 2016 nomination. In 2020, twenty-nine credible candidates officially sought the Democratic nomination for president. This was a record number of candidates, reflecting the lack of a clear front-runner and the strong desire to defeat President Trump. For a time near the end of 2019, it looked like no candidate would emerge as the nominee until the summer of 2020. But that all changed very quickly. Although former Vice President Biden got off to a slow start, he won the all-important South Carolina primary and used that victory to vault into first place, as the competition folded and threw their support to Biden. The importance of South Carolina for Democrats is tied to two main factors. First, it is a very early contest, following on the heels of Iowa, New Hampshire, and Nevada. Second, South Carolina has a large African American vote and that constituency is vital to the Democrats. With Biden's unrivaled support among the black community, he recast the race immediately and became the presumptive Democratic nominee for president by early March. Bernie Sanders had hoped to do better, but he officially suspended his 2020 campaign on April 8, 2020.

Caucuses and Primaries

To win a party's nomination, a candidate must secure a majority of delegates to the National Party Convention. The national party allocates delegates to each of the fifty states (plus the District of Columbia, Guam, and Puerto Rico) and sets guidelines on how the states may choose their delegates. (See Chapter 9, Political Parties, for more details about the delegate distribution process.)

In 2020, we saw the Democrats move toward primaries and away from caucuses. In the past for Democrats, about 70 percent of states used primaries. Nearly 90 percent of the states use some form of primary election in which citizens go to the polling booths and vote for their favorite party candidates. The other 10 percent use caucuses, which are something like town meetings. The Republicans went in a different direction. Trump sought to close the process to candidates who might challenge him for the nomination, so the number of primaries and caucuses dropped. It became a much more closed process. It will be interesting to see if the rules for 2024 shift back to more openness and more primaries for the GOP.

Al Diaz/Miami Herald/TNS/Alamy Live News/Alamy Stock Photo

Image 10.7 In 2020 the Democrats had 27 candidates—so many that one debate stage could not hold them all.

Image 10.8 Republicans meet to discuss who should be their party's nominee for president. A caucus allows people to talk about their views, which is one of its advantages.

The most famous caucus happens in Iowa. It is usually the nation's first test of the appeal of the various presidential contenders. Caucuses require people to attend a lengthy meeting in which they indicate their preferences. Because caucuses demand more time and investment from voters, the rate of participation is much lower than in primaries. In 2016, for example, turnout in presidential primaries about was 36 percent and just around 11 percent for caucuses.[24]

Caucuses and primaries take place over six months, from January through June of the election year. The first states to hold these events wield a good deal of influence, since the early contests provide momentum for those who do well and force those who do poorly to drop out. After the 2020 New Hampshire primary, for example, Senator Michael Bennet (D-CO) ended his bid for the presidency. Senator Rand Paul (R-KY) quit following a disappointing showing in Iowa in 2016. Iowa and New Hampshire are critical states in the process, since the former is the first state to hold a caucus and the latter holds the first primary (for more on this process, see Chapter 9). However, Iowa could be at risk of losing its position as first in the nation to vote for president after a tumultuous 2020 Iowa caucus night. With the most crowded Democratic primary field in history, the results of the Iowa Caucus were supposed to shed some light on who might be the nominee; however, there were massive flaws in the reporting system and it took over twenty-four hours to release results. Instead of making things more clear, the meltdown caused confusion and frustration for both campaigns and Democrats across the country.[25] There is a chance that in 2024, Iowa will play a very different role in the selection of presidential nominees.

Another incredibly important event is Super Tuesday. The phrase first emerged in 1984 when states started to hold their primaries on the same day. The modern-day Super Tuesday was born in 1988 when nine southern states voted on the same day.[26] Because so many delegates are available on one single day, Super Tuesday can shed a lot of light on who will be the eventual nominee.

In 2020, Super Tuesday, March 3, saw fourteen states vote, including the most delegate-heavy ones, California and Texas. Approximately one third of all delegates for the Democratic nominating convention were at stake.[27] By the time all the votes were counted and the delegates allocated, former Vice President Biden was the likely nominee, winning ten of the fourteen states and Senator Sanders winning the other four. Both Michael Bloomberg and Elizabeth Warren dropped out of the race soon thereafter.[28] Super Tuesday narrowed the largest Democratic primary field in history to two viable candidates—Joe Biden and Bernie Sanders. Representative Tulsi Gabbard stayed in the race despite having only two pledged delegates and very little funding. Immediately before Super Tuesday, both Senator Amy Klobuchar and Mayor Pete Buttigieg dropped out of the race and endorsed Joe Biden, which gave him even more momentum. Biden ended the day with a total of 610 pledged delegates and Sanders ended with 541 pledged delegates going into the nominating convention.[29] Biden's unexpected and incredible comeback continued as former contenders for the nomination threw their support to him, including Kamala Harris, Cory Booker, Beto O'Rourke, Mike Bloomberg, John Delaney, and Deval Patrick. At that point, Biden's nomination was a foregone conclusion; Super Tuesday made this transformation possible.

Key Questions
What are the gates imposed by the primary system?

Election 2016 and 2020

Insiders Versus Outsiders as Presidential Candidates

Presidential nominations are often a battle between "insiders" and "outsiders." The insiders are candidates with ties to the party establishment. The outsiders are seeking to force change in the party by challenging the existing leadership. Over the last half-century, party insiders have been more successful than the outsiders, having won over 80 percent of presidential nominations (see Table 10.2). Some outsiders have, however, had notable successes. Both Ronald Reagan (1980) and Barack Obama (2008) challenged the party establishment, went on to win the nomination and the general election, and forged change in the party. The 2016 election saw both an insider (Hillary Clinton) and an outsider (Donald Trump). Trump captured the party with his successful bid to be president, and he will now be able to transform the party. In 2020, the Democrats nominated an insider, Joe Biden. Biden won the presidency with a wide coalition of support from both sides of the aisle. In this case, being an experienced insider was helpful to his campaign amid COVID-19 chaos and unknowns.

It should come as no surprise that party insiders, on average, do better than party outsiders. To win the nomination, it is important to have the support of the existing party organization. The "party organization" includes current officeholders, party officials, and interest groups attached to the parties like unions or business organizations. These stakeholders can provide access to important resources. Candidates need volunteers to organize rallies, knock on doors, and call prospective voters. These activists may also have fundraising networks that candidates can tap into to finance their campaigns.[30]

One way to evaluate the influence of the party establishment is to catalog the number of endorsements a candidate receives. Endorsements not only indicate public support for a candidate and a willingness to help this person win, they also signal to other party insiders that this is the endorser's preferred candidate, helping to generate

Table 10.2 Outsider Candidates (shown in boldface) in Presidential Elections, 1968–2020

Year	Republican	Democrat
1968	Richard Nixon	Hubert Humphrey
1972	Richard Nixon	**George McGovern**
1976	Gerald Ford	**Jimmy Carter**
1980	**Ronald Reagan**	Jimmy Carter
1984	Ronald Reagan	Walter Mondale
1988	George H. W. Bush	Michael Dukakis
1992	George H. W. Bush	Bill Clinton
1996	Robert Dole	Bill Clinton
2000	George W. Bush	Al Gore
2004	George W. Bush	John Kerry
2008	John McCain	**Barack Obama**
2012	Mitt Romney	Barack Obama
2016	**Donald Trump**	Hillary Clinton
2020	Donald Trump	Joe Biden

additional support for the candidate within the party. The general rule is simple: the more endorsements, the better.

Hillary Clinton had more than five hundred elected officials endorse her in 2016. Bernie Sanders had fewer than twenty.[31] Donald Trump—a true outsider—had only a handful of endorsements from GOP insiders when the campaign began. When New Jersey Governor Chris Christie endorsed Trump in late February 2016, it was big news because he was the first prominent Republican insider to support the real-estate mogul. In 2020, Biden had far more endorsements than Sanders. But Sanders was not the only outsider in the race, as he was in 2016. Tom Steyer, Andrew Yang, and Marianne Williamson all threw their hats in the ring with no previous political experience or party ties. Michael

Bloomberg was a different kind of outsider, having access to nearly unlimited resources, and actually had been a Republican most of his life. He entered late in the race only to be beaten by Biden on Super Tuesday.

While party insiders have real advantages over candidates who challenge the establishment, outsiders can, however, succeed if the public wants change. Trump's success in 2016 was tied in large part to his ability to tap into the public's unhappiness with Washington insiders. In fact, the GOP establishment spent much of the first four months in 2016 looking for ways to stop Trump. But those efforts failed: The Republican primary voters were angry and wanted change. Trump understood that and parlayed that sentiment into a successful campaign. Outsiders who became president, such as Reagan and Trump, become insiders given their power in government. Reagan embraced this role far more than Trump. Trump was trying to run as an outsider from the inside until the COVID-19 crisis upended his game plan to win reelection. He now faced a very different landscape. He no longer could claim a strong economy and how America was great again. Vast unemployment and more than 225,000 deaths due to COVID made that impossible.

The National Convention

Following the primary season, each party meets in a national convention. Before the 1960s, conventions were often exciting because it was uncertain who the nominee would be. Conventions often started with numerous contenders, which meant no candidate had enough delegates to win the nomination on the first round of voting at the convention. In 1924, for example, it took the Democrats 124 ballots to select their nominee (John W. Davis from West Virginia). Over the last six decades, however, the likely nominee was known except for a handful of cases. In 1976, there was a big battle between then Governor Ronald Reagan and President Gerald Ford. Ford ended up prevailing in a very close contest. During the early part of 2016, there was much speculation about a so-called open convention for Republicans. Trump did manage to secure enough delegates to win the nomination, but that was not clear until early May. The same dynamic unfolded on the Democratic side in January and February of 2020, but Biden defied the expectations of many pundits and effectively sealed the nomination by March 2020.

National conventions do more than select the presidential nominee. They provide a chance for activists and party leaders to get together to discuss strategy and policy behind the scenes. They approve the party platform and also approve the vice presidential nominee. A highlight of these four days is the acceptance speech, in which the party's nominee speaks directly to the nation, laying out a vision for the country. There is much excitement surrounding these events. Because the party dominates the news for these four days, the convention is both an advertisement for the party and its candidate and an important springboard for the fall campaign.

Starting in the 1960s, conventions began to be televised. Party leaders, therefore, wanted to ensure that they were orderly. To avoid projecting an unruly image that might cost votes in the upcoming general election, parties work to forge consensus and avoid public disagreements. Convention planners do not want to impress television viewers but instead want to use this gathering of party electors to jumpstart the general election campaign.

Both the Democratic and Republican conventions in 2016 posed challenges to having orderly gatherings of delegates. Donald Trump had detractors from the more mainstream Republicans, while Hillary Clinton faced real unhappiness from her left from Bernie Sanders' supporters. But for the most part, these differences were papered over during the conventions.

The 2020 Democratic National Convention took place from August 17–20—a full month later than planned due to COVID-19. The health constraints posed by the pandemic required the entire convention to be a virtual event. A different celebrity hosted each of the four nights and the program was filled with activists, party leaders, former primary candidates, and videos from

Democrats across the nation. Both President Obama and First Lady Obama spoke, as well as Dr. Jill Biden. Kamala Harris made history when she became the first Black and South Asian woman to accept the Vice Presidential nomination of a major party. Joe Biden accepted the official nomination with a speech that drew widespread praise in the press.

The Republican National Convention took place from August 24–27. It was a mixture of in-person events in Charlotte, NC and virtual events. Members of the Trump family spoke along with prominent Republicans and average Americans. One segment included a couple who had pointed loaded guns at Black Lives Matter protesters in St. Louis. Trump accepted the nomination from the White House, which marked an unprecedented use of federal property that some observers viewed as illegal.

Presidential Debates

With both party nominees chosen, campaigning for the general election formally starts and the election battle ensues on many fronts. One significant event in the fall is the series of televised presidential debates. In 2016, more than 220 million people watched Hillary Clinton and Donald Trump address the issues in a debate format.[32] In 2020, there were only two presidential debates because one was canceled due to Trump's COVID-19 diagnosis. The debates that took place followed social distance guidelines and were watched by millions. That being said, the second debate had 10 million fewer viewers than the first. Today these events, as well as a vice presidential debate, are managed by the nonpartisan, nonprofit Commission on Presidential Debates, which was established in 1987. The commission chooses the locations and sets the rules.

The first presidential debate was between John Kennedy and Richard Nixon in 1960, and many felt that Kennedy's performance was critical to his narrow win.[33] Thereafter, incumbent candidates were reluctant to participate in televised debates, fearing that they might have more to lose than to win. But in 1976, President Gerald R. Ford (1974–77), behind in the polls, viewed the debates as a chance to narrow Jimmy Carter's lead. Since that time, the presidential debates have been a regular feature of the fall campaign.

The debates draw tremendous amounts of attention from the news media. Any mistake by a candidate generates scrutiny. In 1992, President George H. W. Bush (1989–93) was caught looking at his watch during one of the debates, giving the impression that he was bored. That perception fueled the belief that Bush was out of touch, causing him problems in his reelection bid against Arkansas Governor Bill Clinton. In 2012, Mitt Romney turned in a very good performance against President Obama in their first debate in Denver. Obama seemed disengaged. The debate made Romney look presidential and gave his campaign a short-term boost. Hillary Clinton scored well in her debates with Donald Trump, but there were no long-term effects. Debates usually have much more risk than reward, and campaign insiders usually hope for no more than an error-free performance by their candidate.

Key Questions
Do you recall any 2020 presidential debates? If so, what do you remember?

Kevin Dietsch/UPI/Alamy Stock Photo

Image 10.9 President Trump and Former VP Biden debate during the 2020 general election while following social distance guidelines.

Issues in Presidential Campaigns

LO 10-3 Identify the issues that shape presidential campaigns

Citizen participation in American politics peaks during presidential campaigns. Supporters and people who are undecided have the chance to attend rallies, hear speeches, read commentary, and watch the never-ending advertisements on television. There seems to be almost no way for the public not to be involved. Because the campaigns are important gateways for public participation, we look in particular at fundraising and campaign strategies that make public engagement possible but may also introduce inequalities.

Fundraising and Money

Of course, no one could run for president without funding. How candidates raise money, how much money they raise, and the influence of money in presidential elections have been concerns of Congress and voters for decades, especially as the amount of spending on campaigns has risen sharply. Some believe these huge sums inject inequalities into presidential campaigns, as it seems candidates who lack personal fortunes and established fundraising operations are less likely to be able to compete.

In 1971, Congress tried to put candidates on an equal financial footing and make them less beholden to special interests by passing the Federal Election Campaign Act (FECA). This law transformed campaigns, since it requires candidates and political parties to disclose their campaign financial records. In 1974, Congress amended the law to set strict limits on how much money could be contributed by individuals and parties to campaigns, and created the Federal Election Commission (FEC) as an independent agency to monitor campaign finance.[34] Under the rules, candidates seeking their party's nomination are given public funds for the campaign in the form of matching funds: a dollar amount equal to the amount the candidates raise from private contributors, with a limit per individual contributor and an overall cap. As of 2020, the limit per contributor was $2,800 in the primary and $2,800 in the general campaign.[35] After the Supreme Court's ruling in *McCutcheon, et al. v. FEC*, individuals have no limit on the number of campaigns to which they may contribute.[36]

There are complicated rules for the public financing of presidential nomination campaigns, but they have not really mattered over the last few presidential elections. Candidates now tend to raise huge amounts of money outside of the public system, spending as they see fit in the primaries and caucuses. This change has introduced a lot more money into the political system. Bernie Sanders raised over $215 million in 2020.[37] in his quest to win the Democratic nomination in 2020. By October 22, 2020, Biden and the DNC had raised about $1.5 billion, while Trump and the RNC raised over $1.57 billion for his reelection bid.[38] In the first half of October alone, Biden raised $167 million. Trump raised $82 million in the first half of October, which highlighted the passion of the Democrats nearing Election Day. There are reasons to worry about the amount of money now in the election process, but raising these amounts of money does open some gates to influence. Consider Bernie Sanders. In January 2020, he raised $25 million from 648,000 individuals, an average of $18 per donation.[39] This level of engagement is impressive. The internet makes it efficient to raise small amounts of money, and presidential candidates welcome that kind of broad-based support.

Key Questions

What are the pros and cons of laws that regulate campaign finance?

John McCain in 2008 was the last major party nominee to use public funds, receiving about $80 million from the government. Barack Obama that year opted out of general election funding for the first time since the system began in 1976. By so doing, he spent far more money than did McCain. In the 2012 presidential election, both nominees raised their own money for the general election. That pattern has continued and appears very likely to continue for the foreseeable future, unless some new law arises to check the spending.

Figure 10.2 documents the huge surge in spending that began about a decade ago and shows little sign of abating. Just consider that in 1992 about $190 million was spent by presidential candidates. In 2016, it was about $1.8 billion—nearly ten times the amount spent in 1992.[40] And the 2020 election is even higher. By January 2020, the Democratic primary candidates had already spent over

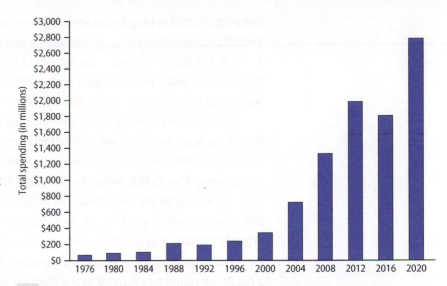

Figure 10.2 **Total Spending by Presidential Candidates, 1976–2020**

Spending in presidential campaigns has been increasing greatly in the past four decades, with particularly large increases in the past decade.

Sources: From "Presidential Fundraising and Spending 1976–2008." Center for Responsive Politics, 2008. Copyright © 2008 by Center for Responsive Politics. www.opensecrets.org and http://elections.nytimes.com/2012/campaign-finance, accessed January 25, 2014; https://www.bloomberg.com/politics/graphics/2016-presidential-campaign-fundraising/https://www.npr.org/2020/05/20/858347477/money-tracker-how-much-trump-and-biden-have-raised-in-the-2020-election.

$859.6 million.[41] Former New York City mayor, Michael Bloomberg, spent over $500 million during his three-month, self-funded campaign. This is another example of the huge increase in political spending, especially for presidential elections. By the end of the nomination process, the 27 Democratic candidates had spent more than $2.2 billions dollars.[42]

Much of this surge in money can be tied to the Supreme Court ruling in *Citizens United v. Federal Election Commission* (2010; see Supreme Court Cases in Chapter 8, Interest Groups). This landmark case allowed for increased campaign fundraising (and spending) as it undid many of the restrictions formerly placed on corporations and unions. One critical consequence was the rise of **Super PACs**, which—unlike PACs—can raise funds from corporations, unions, interest groups, and individuals without legal limits.[43] These organizations are not allowed to coordinate directly with the candidates they support, but often those who run a Super PAC are friends and former aides to the candidates, making the distinction questionable. This has given the wealthy a chance to influence the electoral process in dramatic ways, since a single individual can fund a Super PAC. In April 2016 more than 40 percent of all campaign contributions had been made by just fifty donors.[44] This concentration of funding in a handful of mega-donors poses a problem for the election process and stands in sharp contrast to the breadth of participation that Sanders' campaign represented. The 2020 Democratic primary saw two self-funded campaigns. Billionaires Tom Steyer and Mike Bloomberg spent almost $400 million (mostly on advertisements) between them before any primary votes were even cast.[45] This amount of money coming directly from the candidate is a different type of mega-donor campaign funding. However, Super PACs continue to matter. After dropping out of the 2020 Democratic primary, Bloomberg started his own Super PAC to help defeat Trump. He spent $100 million to support Joe Biden in Florida alone.

In the 2016 Republican presidential primary alone, Trump's Super PACs spent $45 million, and in the Democratic primary, Clinton's Super PACs spent $133 million.[46] Trump did run a leaner

Super PACs: *Independent groups that can raise unlimited amounts of money from individuals, labor unions, and corporations and can spend it to support or oppose political candidates but cannot coordinate directly with candidates or political parties.*

Key Questions

Are presidential campaigns too expensive? How much should a presidential campaign cost?

campaign in 2016, relying on less spending than his opponents.[47] Trump depended a lot on the media's coverage of his campaign. He was focused heavily on ratings for news programs, especially for cable. For 2020, he raised a huge amount of money to fund his reelection effort. By Election Day, over $6.6 billion had been spent on the presidential race alone. In 2016, a total of $2.4 billion was spent on the presidential race. Money seems even more important with each cycle.

Many observers worry about the influence of money on the election process, believing that these huge amounts undermine the fairness of the process by giving the wealthy more gateways to influence politicians and policy. But it is far from clear that candidates are being "bought" with this influx of money. Big donors often give money to the candidate they agree with on the largest number of issues. It is worth remembering that most of this money is being spent on getting candidates' messages out to the public and building organizations to get out the vote—so one could argue that additional money in the electoral system informs people and activates them to participate.[48] Campaign spending, as a result, can stimulate interest in the election, which is also a benefit. It is also not clear that money drives the outcomes of elections. Trump was vastly outspent by Clinton in 2016 and won. Or consider Bloomberg's and Sanders' fund raising edge over Biden. It did not keep the former vice president from winning the nomination. The bottom line is that money buys advertisements, but not always votes. Like most of American politics, campaign fundraising and spending offer a mixed story of gates and gateways.

The real problem with Super PACs and the issue ads they sponsor is that voters do not always know where the money is coming from. Under the new campaign rules, there is less transparency. Thus, as noted above, it is possible for one or two wealthy donors to fund a Super PAC, and to the extent that the Super PAC's issue ads impact an election outcome, some observers contend that these results distort the electoral process. It should be noted that despite all the Super PAC spending against Donald Trump during the 2016 primaries and caucuses ($381,776,844[49]), he continued to do well. The same was true for Barack Obama in 2012. In 2020, 197 Super PACs spent over $1.8 billion on the election. Both sides used Super PACs to attack Donald Trump and Joe Biden. For example, the conservative Senate Leadership Fund spent over $308 million and the liberal Senate Majority PAC spent over $254 million in support of their respective candidate.

Swing Voters and States

Although partisanship remains high, **swing voters** still exist—people who do not fall into either the Republican or Democratic camp—and so do **swing states** that might vote either Democratic or Republican in a presidential election. Parties and candidates avidly pursue swing voters during an election, as they can swing the results one way or the other. In the past, swing voters have constituted about 20 percent of the electorate, but that share has been falling. Two weeks before the November 2020 election, less than 3 percent of likely voters in the electorate was undecided between Donald Trump and Joe Biden.[50] Partisanship remains an anchor driving the preferences of most Americans, leaving only a handful of "persuadable" or swing voters.

Regardless of the percentage of swing voters, perhaps the more critical strategic feature of presidential campaigns are swing states. These states can mean the difference between victory and defeat. Because of the Electoral College's winner-take-all system, presidential candidates invest time and effort only in states that they can win. In 2020, for example, it

swing voters: *Voters who are neither reliably Republican nor reliably Democratic and who are pursued by each party during an election, as they can determine which candidate wins.*

swing states: *States that are not clearly pro-Republican or pro-Democrat and therefore are of vital interest to presidential candidates, as they can determine election outcomes.*

made no sense for Joe Biden to campaign in Tennessee, a reliably Republican state that he could not win. At the same time, he did not spend much time in Massachusetts—a state that he was able to win easily. But both Biden and Trump campaigned hard in Pennsylvania—a **battleground state** that each thought they had a chance to win; winning Pennsylvania was critical to securing 270 votes in the Electoral College.[51]

Citizens in these close states got lots of attention. Nearly 90 percent of campaign visits by presidential candidates are to battleground close states.[52] TV viewers are deluged with campaign ads, and party-based get-out-the-vote organizations are active in even the smallest towns. This flurry of activity filters down to the public. Citizens in these close states are well informed and increasingly interested in the campaign. But the strategy of pursuing votes in swing close states yields an important inequality, for citizens in close states other than swing close states do not get such attention, and interest in the campaign lags, especially among the poor. In 2016, eleven close states were considered to be battleground close states: Colorado, Florida, Iowa, Michigan, Nevada, New Hampshire, North Carolina, Ohio, Pennsylvania, Virginia, and Wisconsin. Only 28 percent of the nation's population resides in these close states.[53] Going into the 2020 election, the battleground states were Arizona, Colorado, Florida, Georgia, Maine, Michigan, Minnesota, New Hampshire, North Carolina, Pennsylvania, Texas, and Wisconsin. Michigan, Pennsylvania, and Wisconsin all flipped and went for Biden, which secured him the necessary 270 electoral votes to win. Following Election Day, many mail-in ballots had to be counted, which took some states multiple days. By the Sunday following Election Day, Biden was ahead in Arizona and Georgia. Those long time "red" states flipped as well, giving Biden a comfortable lead in the Electoral College.[54] It is a problem that voters in different close states are treated differently by the campaigns. Theoretically, all voters should receive equal treatment, yet about one in five Americans is the focus of attention of presidential candidates.

Microtargeting

Since the 1960s, when consumer behavior became a popular field of study, direct marketers have refined the practice of gathering detailed information about different cross sections of consumers to sell their products.[55] Today, the technique of **microtargeting** has become a boon to political parties and electoral campaigns. By identifying and tracking potential supporters, campaign strategists can design specific political messages tailored for each of the voting profiles developed from the data. In 1996, for example, President Bill Clinton's reelection campaign sought to reach so-called soccer moms—"busy suburban women devoted to their jobs and kids, who had real concerns about real presidential politics."[56] Polls and other information suggested that these voters could be moved into the Clinton camp, although men, for the most part, seemed to have already made up their minds. In 2004, the focus was on "NASCAR dads"—working-class white males who lived mostly in the South. Many thought the Democrats had to win this group to capture the presidency. In the 2012 campaign, both Mitt Romney and Barack Obama microtargeted Latino voters, believing that this growing bloc of voters was critical to the election outcome.[57] In the 2016 campaign, Latino voters were important "targets," as were women and Millennials.[58] The Clinton campaign pursued more microtargeting than did Trump's team, which relied more on free media to get their message out. In 2020, the efforts continued, although most voters seemed set on who they would support.

As a campaign strategy, microtargeting has begun to replace traditional polling techniques and precinct-by-precinct get-out-the-vote drives (see Chapter 6, Public Opinion).

battleground state: *State in which the outcome of the presidential election is uncertain and in which candidates invest much time and money, especially if its votes are vital for a victory in the Electoral College.*

> **Key Questions**
>
> Do you live or attend school in a swing or a battleground state? What is the impact on you?

microtargeting: *Gathering detailed information on cross sections of the electorate to track potential supporters and tailor political messages for them; also called narrowcasting.*

> **Key Questions**
>
> What is your microtargeting profile? Can the category predict how you will vote?

Justin Sullivan/Getty Images News/Getty Images

Image 10.10 In Julian Castro's bid to become president in 2020, he focused on social issues and championed health care, immigration, and housing reforms to combat inequality.

By combining information from polling surveys with political participation and consumer information obtained from data-gathering companies such as Acxiom and InfoUSA, political parties and campaigns can establish profiles of the many different types of voters and the issues they support. The resulting database can then be "mapped" to get a geographic depiction of the trends in voting habits and political interests of different voters. Each party builds its own database that it can share with candidates: The Democratic National Committee's database is called VoteBuilder, and the Republican National Committee's database is called GOP Data Center.[59]

Rather than a general political message sent through a specific medium, campaigns are now able to send dozens of versions of the message using various methods—mail, phone calls, e-mail, text messages, social media, home visits—to reach targeted audiences. This strategy takes a person-by-person view of the electorate rather than a view of the electorate en masse. So, instead of targeting a broad category such as women, campaigns can now focus on narrow subgroups such as undecided iPhone owners in their 30s who follow the news and hence are open to a message from a campaign.

Twitter has become a mainstay in campaigns, since politicians can target potential supporters directly, quickly, and cheaply. The messages must be short—originally it was only 140 characters, but that has now been doubled to 280. But a lot of information can be communicated in short messages. Other social media platforms, like Instagram and Facebook, are used in campaigns as well. Campaigns can pay for ads to be put directly into a user's newsfeed. In the 2020 Democratic primary, it is likely a voter saw ads for candidates all over the internet—from Instagram to Hulu to YouTube. Mike Bloomberg and Tom Steyer utilized social media in unprecedented ways by spending a great deal of their funds on these types of ads.

Unlike political ads aired on TV, radio, or the internet, Twitter and Instagram allow the audience to participate. Through retweets and stories, politicians can reach a broader audience, with their followers disseminating the politicians' message to their own followers, potentially even to people willing to donate to a candidate whom they may not otherwise have heard of. This can provide a signal boost, amplifying visibility in ways that allow politicians to circumvent traditional gatekeepers like the Sunday morning talk shows or newspapers.

But social media's ability to reach millions of people, of course, carries risk, since bad news often moves faster than good news. Even so, candidate Donald Trump has used Twitter to set the agenda and move the national conversation. Much of what he tweeted was controversial, but it got attention, and that trend has only continued since he became president. He now has more than 86 million followers.

Trump will continue to use Twitter, even after he leaves the White House. It is a cheap way to message millions of people. Joe Biden seems far less interested in using Twitter for such purposes. It will be interesting to watch how the White House works with Trump no longer in the Oval Office.

Campaign Issues

Issues shape campaigns. Many observers think that the personalities of the candidates frame elections, but that view is not consistent with the evidence. In general, about half of the content of advertising in presidential campaigns involved policy, with a quarter concerning the personal traits of the candidates, and the remaining quarter focusing on general values such as freedom, hard work, and patriotism.[60] In 2008, the economy dominated the discussion between John McCain and Barack Obama. According to one estimate, more than 50 percent of the appeals made by these contenders dealt with the economy alone.[61] That should be no surprise with the crash of the stock market in September 2008. The ensuing "Great Recession" made the economy the main issue in 2012. In 2016, the economy remained front and center, but the two nominees gave substantial attention to other issues such as terrorism, immigration, and trade.[62] In 2020, the economy continued to matter, but the COVID-19 crisis recast the entire campaign. Containing and defeating the pandemic became central to all Americans. Biden was able to use Trump's poor job handling COVID-19 to help provide an image of a future America that has beat the coronavirus and has "built back better."

To understand how issues influence campaigns, political scientists have drawn a distinction between **valence issues** and **position issues**.[63] A valence issue is a vague claim to a goal, such as "a strong economy," "improved education," or "greater national security." These are goals all candidates talk about and voters seek: No candidate has ever opposed a strong economy or called for less national security. Valence issues provide limited insight into the policies a candidate might pursue once in office. A position issue is different. Here candidates adopt views that allow voters to understand specific plans for government. Two examples from the 2016 campaign are Hillary Clinton's support for making college debt free for students and Donald Trump's opposition to the Affordable Care Act. Because taking clear positions on issues may drive some votes away, presidential candidates rely more heavily on valence issues. According to one study, about three-quarters of their TV ads highlight valence issues.[64]

Candidates can use issues strategically to win votes. But candidates rarely agree on the issues that should define the campaign. Imagine if an incumbent is running for reelection and the economy is growing at a brisk pace. That nominee will want to talk about the economy at every stop and use his or her political ads to remind voters about this economic growth. The challenger will not share that view: He or she will duck that issue in favor of other issues that the campaign thinks will work for him or her. Therefore, campaigns are often about not just the positions candidates adopt on issues but also which issues define the campaign. Trump sought to tar Clinton with terrorism, while Clinton pushed questions about temperament against the then Republican nominee. In 2020, Biden pointed to Trump's lack of leadership in domestic and foreign politics, racial strife, and a tanking economy. Trump spent the bulk of the election spreading misinformation about COVID-19 and the legitimacy of vote-by-mail.

Because campaigns are competitive struggles for votes, candidates look for ways to secure extra votes while maintaining existing support. This dynamic is especially true for candidates who trail because they need to find some way to break up the support for the candidate in the lead. One strategy is to use a **wedge issue** that has the potential to break up the opposition's coalition.[65] Wedges usually involve controversial policy concerns, such as affirmative action, that divide people rather than build consensus. In recent years, the Democrats also sought to use various gender issues as wedges against the Republicans, including debates over contraception

Key Questions

What should shape a presidential campaign—issues or character? Which is more important to you?

valence issues: *Noncontroversial or widely supported campaign issues that are unlikely to differ among candidates.*

position issues: *Political issues that offer specific policy choices and often differentiate candidates' views and plans of action.*

Key Questions

Identify three wedge issues that are important to you. Do they determine your vote?

wedge issue: *Divisive issue focused on a particular group of the electorate that candidates use to gain more support by taking votes away from their opponents.*

negativity: *Campaign strategy of telling voters why they should not vote for the opponent and of highlighting information that raises doubts about the opponent.*

and equal pay. Race, too, has served as common wedge issue.[66] In the initial phases of the Democratic battle for the 2020 presidential nomination, candidates spoke about such things as health care, jobs, gun control, and climate change. In addition, electability was a central theme, since the desire to beat Trump was so strong. With the COVID-19 crisis, the game changed in many ways and the stakes became even higher. Joe Biden's message of caring and unity struck a chord and gave him a platform to fend off Bernie Sander's so-called revolution. Biden was able to shift the focus to uniting a deeply divided country that was in pain from COVID-19, racial injustice, a struggling economy, and intense polarization. This message beat President Trump's message that everything was great while he was in the Oval Office.

UNION AND LIBERTY! AND UNION AND SLAVERY!

The Granger Collection, NYC

Image 10.11 Negative campaigning is not new. This poster from the 1864 election shows Abraham Lincoln defining his opponent, General George McClellan, as the ally of Confederate President Jefferson Davis and perpetuator of the slave system. Lincoln, on the other hand, is for the workingman and freedom. Notice the integrated school with happy children.

Negativity

Candidates are very good at telling voters why they should vote for them. They are also pretty good at telling the public why they should not vote for their opponents. Candidates' use of claims against the opposition is labeled **negativity**.

One of the most famous examples of negativity is the so-called Daisy spot. This was a television commercial aired only once by President Lyndon B. Johnson in his 1964 campaign against the Republican nominee, Arizona Senator Barry Goldwater. The implication in the ad was that if Goldwater were elected president, he would start a nuclear war. It was a very hard-hitting claim that many thought unfair.[67] But was it? Goldwater had called for the tactical use of nuclear weapons and made some loose statements about attacking the Soviet Union with nuclear weapons. This issue was among the most important facing the nation—much like terrorism is now. The public needed to know Goldwater's views, and this negative ad helped generate a debate.

National Archives and Records Founation/
Democratic National Convention

Image 10.12 The "Daisy spot" is perhaps the most famous negative ad in American history. It was aired only once by President Lyndon Johnson in the 1964 campaign, and it never explicitly mentioned his opponent, Senator Barry Goldwater. But Goldwater had made statements about the possible use of nuclear weapons, and those statements made the meaning of this ad clear and emotionally resonant.

In recent years, the amount of negativity in presidential campaigns has been on the rise (see Figure 10.3). In the 2008 election, less than 30 percent of campaign ads were positive, and another 20 percent were a mix of negative and positive appeals (so-called contrast ads). That means half the ads were negative. Over 60 percent of the ads in the 2012 presidential campaign were negative, with just 14 percent of spots being purely positive.[68] In 2016, only 60 percent of ads were negative, which is largely a result of Trump running primarily positive ads. Of the Trump campaign's ads, only 37 percent were negative, versus more than half of the Clinton campaign's ads.[69] Many observers worry about negativity, viewing attacks on the opposition as weakening the fabric of democracy, especially since about 80 percent of the public say they dislike negative ads.[70] Both 2020 campaigns aired negative ads throughout the cycle on all types of media. When President Trump tested positive

Key Questions

What is your response to negative ads?

for COVID-19, the Biden campaign paused all attack adds until it was clear that he was doing alright. That being said, both sides used negative ads.

Negative ads, however, serve a purpose. To ensure accountability, candidates need to be able to criticize the other side. In 2016, Donald Trump reminded the public of the job losses in some areas of the economy that were associated with the trade deals cut under Democratic administrations working with Republican Congresses and argued that Hillary Clinton would just bring more of the same (see Chapter 16, Economic, Domestic, and Foreign Policy for more on trade policy). This was potentially important information that forced Clinton to respond. At the same time, Clinton questioned whether Trump could be trusted with the presidency given his inflammatory statements about women, Muslims, and Mexicans. Such attacks demand a response and can thus increase accountability. Trump's 2020 attack ads focused more on the economy and less on divisive issues of race and policing. Whereas Biden focused heavily on his plan to tackle COVID-19 and handle it better than the sitting president had in 2020.

In other words, negative appeals contain information about the candidates that voters need to know. After hearing each side attack the other during a campaign, voters are better able to make informed decisions. It is also important to know that although negativity is on the rise, it is not new. In 1948, President Harry S. Truman (1945–53) equated the Republicans with the Nazi leadership in Germany during World War II.[71] In 1800, the Federalist Party claimed that Thomas Jefferson was the Antichrist.[72] These attacks make Trump's claims about Clinton's flip-flops look tame.

Note: Data from 2000, 2004 and 2008 come from the Wisconsin Advertising Project. Data from 2012, 2016, and 2020 come from the Wesleyan Media Project.

Figure 10.3 **Share of Positive, Contrast, and Negative Ads in Presidential Campaigns, 2000–2020**

Negativity in presidential campaigns is generally on the rise. In 2020, 38 percent of all ads were negative. The Trump campaign and Super PACs supporting him aired more negative ads about Biden than positive ads about Trump. The Biden campaign and Super PACS promoting Biden aired more positive ads and contrast ads comparing Biden and Trump.

Sources: Erika Franklin Fowler and Travis N. Ridout, "Negative, Angry, and Ubiquitous: Political Advertising in 2012," DOI 10.1515/forum-2013-0004, *The Forum 2012*, 10(4): 51–61; https://mediaproject.wesleyan.edu/releases-101520/.

Polls and Prediction Models

Given Donald Trump's victory in 2016, it is easy to overestimate his skill and Hillary Clinton's lack of skill. The winners always look brilliant and the losers misguided. Such simplistic judgments are not, however, very useful, since we are letting the outcome shape the evaluation of the process. To take a more systematic look at how campaigns work, political scientists have developed prediction models that yield specific estimates of the vote share in presidential elections. The goal is to provide a general understanding of who wins and why. In 2008, nearly all models predicted an Obama win. The economy was bad and the public was ready for a change. In 2016, the fundamentals of these prediction models sent more mixed signals. The economy was growing, which helped the Democrats. But Obama had been in office for eight years and that helped the Republicans—the country was ready for a change in the party that controlled the presidency. Five of the seven models predicted a Clinton win, but it was narrow.[73] It is important to remember that these models predict the national popular vote.[74] So in that regard, these models actually did pretty well. In 2020, these models had to be thrown out, since most rely on economic indicators from the second quarter of the election year. The COVID-19 crisis shut down the economy, leading to a huge surge in unemployment and a steep drop in gross domestic product (GDP).

That would normally spell a disaster for the incumbent, losing by a landslide. Trump did not lose by a landslide. He managed to maintain an edge on which candidate was best able to handle the economy. But that edge was not enough to win re-election. Concerns about the pandemic carried the day and carried Biden into the White House. In fact, Biden secured a bigger share of the popular vote than any presidential candidate since George H. W. Bush in 1988, except for Obama's win in 2008 (he won 53 percent of the popular vote).

The best prediction models use some combination of the following key structural factors:

1. **The economy.** What is the condition of the economy? A strong economy leads voters to support the incumbent party. A struggling economy gives an edge to the challenger.

2. **Presidential popularity.** How popular is the sitting president? An unpopular president will hurt the chances for his party's candidate.

3. **The incumbent party's time in office.** How long has the incumbent party controlled the presidency? The American public has shown a consistent preference for change. A party that has been in power for a long time usually has made enough mistakes to lead citizens to vote for the other side. Over the course of American history, parties have tended to control the White House for about two terms before turning power over to the other side. Harry Truman's win in 1948 was the fifth straight win by the Democrats. This winning streak is unprecedented. Since 1948, there has been only one time a party won three presidential contests in a row (1980, 1984, and 1988).

Normally, the 2020 election would have been an easy win for Trump. The economy appeared on a good track, and he was in his first term. Change tends to happen only after two terms. But Trump's popularity has been consistently below 50 percent, and then the global pandemic hit. The Trump Administration's lack of belief in science and hesitation in creating policies to slow the pandemic made the losses much worse. By the end of October 2020, Trump had an approval rating in the mid 40s, which is a problem for an incumbent seeking re-election.

Congressional Campaigns

LO 10-4 Outline the steps in congressional campaigns

Nearly all congressional campaigns start with a primary election in which the party's official candidate is selected. The general election follows. These campaigns occur every two years. In the Senate, one-third of all seats are contested every two years. For the House of Representatives, every member faces reelection every two years.

The Decision to Run and the Primaries

People who choose to run for Congress are usually visible residents of their district or state. Often they already hold local or state-level elected offices (see the Political Analytics sections in Chapter 3, Federalism, and in this chapter). They might—like Kyrsten Sinema—be school board members, city council members, or state legislators. Many grew up in the district or state and can claim long-standing ties to it; this was certainly true of Sinema. Contenders with strong local roots can organize core supporters who volunteer time, and often money, to advance their candidacies.

Political Analytics

Latina Elected Officials in the United States

AS DISCUSSED IN CHAPTER 1, Gateways to American Democracy, a primary reason for identifying gateways to participation is to provide the citizenry a voice in the governing process. This chapter and the following one discuss voting as a means for citizens to register their preferences about whom they wish to make policy decisions on their behalf. As the saying goes, "Elections have consequences," and one of them is how well the policy preferences of voters are translated into actual policies. For some (as discussed in Chapter 12, Congress), demographic representation of the citizenry is crucial to the link between those who govern and those who are governed. Many people believe that representatives should look like a cross section of the American public.

Figure 10.4 showcases the status of one particular American demographic group, Latinas, and how successful

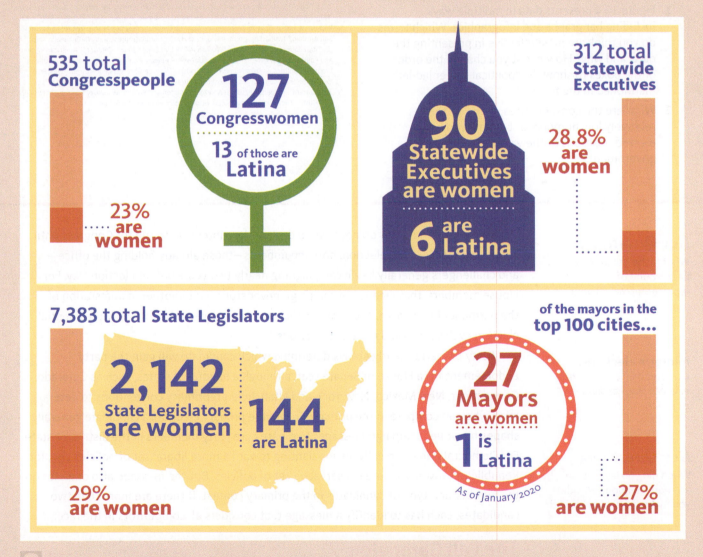

535 total **Congresspeople**

127 Congresswomen

13 of those are **Latina**

23% are women

312 total **Statewide Executives**

90 Statewide Executives are women

6 are **Latina**

28.8% are women

7,383 total **State Legislators**

2,142 State Legislators are women

144 are Latina

29% are women

of the mayors in the **top 100 cities...**

27 Mayors are women

1 is **Latina**

As of January 2020

27% are women

Figure 10.4 **Latina Elected Officials at National, State, and Local Levels of Government**

Source: National Association of Latino Elected Officials, "National Directory of Latino Elected Officials, 2019," https://naleo.org/wp-content/uploads/2019/12/2019 _National_Directory_of_Latino_Elected_Offcials.pdf. Accessed May 12, 2020.

they have been in gaining elected office at different levels of government. As the graphic demonstrates, Latinas hold very few elected offices. Only twelve Latinas serve in the House of Representatives. In 2016, Nevada elected Catherine Cortez Masto to the Senate, making her the first ever Latina senator. Given that Latinos make up about 17 percent of the U.S. population (and Latinas about half of that), Latinas are underrepresented demographically. To the extent that descriptive representation is a good indicator of policy representation, Latinas appear to be lacking a political voice commensurate with their numbers in the population.

One encouraging sign is that close to two thousand Latinas serve on city councils and in other local political offices, and they might run for higher office in the near future. Further, no less than four national organizations—LatinasRepresent, Political Parity, the National Hispanic Leadership Agenda, and Emily's List—have launched efforts to increase the number of Latinas elected to office in 2020.

Examine Figure 10.4 to see the proportion of female and Latina elected officials compared with the total number of available elected seats at each level of office.

Thinking Critically

1. Figure 10.4 presents data in multiple ways, including bar graphs and infographics. Which forms do you think are most effective in presenting the data, and why? How might you change the order of the boxes to show the "political career ladder" mentioned in the text?

2. What are the consequences, if any, of the relatively low numbers of Latinas who hold elected positions at the various levels of government?

Sources: Nia-Malika Henderson, "Report: Latinas Vastly Underrepresented in Elected Offices," *Washington Post,* February 6, 2014, https://www.washingtonpost.com/blogs/she-the-people/wp/2014/02/06/report-latinas-vastly-underrepresented-in-elected-offices; "Emily's List Announces New Initiative to Get More Latinas Elected to Office," Fox News Latino, March 2, 2016, http://latino.foxnews.com/latino/politics/2016/03/02/emily-list-announces-new-initiative-to-get-more-latinas-elected-to-office; "Latina Representation in National Elected Office," Latinas Represent, https://latinasrepresent.org; Brianna Dimas, "Latina Leadership Institute Launches in San Antonio," LatinasRepresent, July 6, 2015, https://latinasrepresent.org/latina-leadership-institute-launches-san-antonio; "Women in Elective Office 2016," Center for American Women and Politics, http://www.cawp.rutgers.edu/women-elective-office-2016; Center for American Women in Politics, *Current Numbers 2018,* http://www.cawp.rutgers.edu/current-numbers; Center for American Women and Politics, *Current Numbers 2020,* https://www.cawp.rutgers.edu/current-numbers; Center for American Women and Politics, *Women of Color in Elective Office 2020,* https://www.cawp.rutgers.edu/women-color-elective-office-2020.

Key Questions

What is the personal background of your representative? Of your senators?

midterm elections:
Congressional elections held between the presidential elections.

Key Questions

When did you last vote in a Senate election? Why did you make the choice you did?

Although candidates do not have to declare their intention to run for Congress until about a year before the election, both incumbents—those already holding the office—and challengers generally begin campaigning nearly two years before Election Day. For House members, that means the campaign never stops—yet another manifestation of the permanent campaign. The contests that occur in between the four-year presidential election cycles are called **midterm elections**.

Party primaries nearly always determine which candidate will gain the party endorsement for a House or Senate seat, although a handful of states, such as Colorado, Connecticut, New Mexico, New York, and Utah, hold preprimary conventions to determine who can compete in the primary. To win the primary election, a candidate generally shapes his or her campaign messages to please core party members in the district or state. For Democrats, that typically means slanting toward a more liberal set of policies and, for Republicans, toward a more conservative set of policies. But the message also depends on the number and type of candidates in the primary contest. If there are more than two candidates, each has to identify a message that considers all competitors in the race.

The Fall Campaign

Following the primaries, the two winning candidates often revise their campaign messages to attract more moderate voters. Anthony Downs explained this shift in message with the median voter theorem, which argues that candidates in their quest for votes should adopt moderate positions on issues. If one candidate fails to do so, the other candidate can move to the center, winning a majority of votes and the election.[75] To win the general election, candidates usually need votes from party members as well as from Independents and members of the opposing party. It is for these reasons that elections are often battles over the so-called middle.

Running for Congress requires attending local gatherings such as town meetings, parades, festivals, and high school sporting events. Candidates meet with as many key businesspeople, members of the press, and local interest groups as possible. They give speeches, and their campaigns develop slogans and TV ads. Elections to the House of Representatives typically focus more on local issues intrinsic to the district and less on national programs and issues. Senate elections pay more attention to national issues because the Senate is viewed as more nationally focused and usually faces larger and more diverse electorates. The differences in running for the House versus the Senate can be seen in the campaigning strategies and styles of Cori Bush who ran in 2020 to represent Missouri's First Congressional District versus Mark Kelly who ran to represent Arizona as a whole that same year.

The geographic size of a congressional district or state can affect campaign strategy. Some urban districts are small, such as in New York City, but often very expensive to campaign in due to costs of television. Other districts involve much more territory to cover: Crisscrossing Wyoming to meet voters is a much larger task than driving across Rhode Island. Because it is so difficult to establish a personal relationship with constituents in large districts and states, congressional campaigns in these areas are typically less about the personal characteristics of the candidates and more about issues and party policies.[76]

Issues in Congressional Campaigns

LO 10-5 Determine which issues shape congressional campaigns

Congressional elections do not draw as much attention as presidential elections, but they involve many of the same issues. Money and fundraising are concerns, and again the FEC sets limits. Political parties attempt to work within—or get around—these limits to help their candidates. Voters usually reelect House and Senate members, so whether congressional elections actually serve to hold Congress accountable is a question for American democracy. Voters know less about these candidates than about the candidates in presidential elections, suggesting perhaps that there is not much accountability. Nevertheless, the composition of Congress changes in response to conditions in the country. If times are good, voters reward the party that controls the presidency. In general, the pattern of Republican and Democratic gains and losses indicates that voters hold members of Congress accountable and that Congress is, therefore, a responsive institution.

Fundraising and Money

A key element in launching and running a congressional campaign is fundraising. Every campaign needs an office, staff members, computers, posters and pamphlets, a website, and money for television and radio ads. Senate campaigns generally cost more than House campaigns because they seek to reach voters across an entire state rather than just a district.

Federal campaign finance laws set the same limits on congressional elections as on presidential elections: An individual could contribute up to $2,700 to a candidate for the primary election in 2018, and the same amount for the general election for as many campaigns as he or she wishes. Candidates also raise money from PACs, which are limited to donating $5,000 for a primary election, and $5,000 for a general election, to a single candidate.[77] These limits did not keep the 2018 midterm elections from being the most costly in history, according to the Center for Responsive Politics. Democrats spent over $2.9 billion and Republicans approximately $2.4 billion. In Texas alone, the Senate race spent an unprecedented $125 million. The $5.7 billion spent in 2018 far outpaced the 2014 midterm election spending record of $3.8 billion.

The amount of money required to wage a competitive contest for a seat in Congress is formidable, and it gives an advantage to people who are personally wealthy and able to make good use of personal or business connections. Name recognition also helps in fundraising. For example, a local sports hero or decorated war veteran who chooses to run for office gets enough free publicity to attract interest. In 2020, Mark Kelly—famous astronaut married to Gabby Giffords—ran for Senate in Arizona. He won the nomination and narrowly defeated Martha McSally for the seat.

The Role of Political Parties

Of the other sources of financial support available to candidates, the most important is the political party. Parties are forbidden by campaign finance laws from actively coordinating a specific individual's congressional or senatorial campaign, but local parties can engage in general activities, such as voter registration drives, partisan rallies, and get-out-the-vote efforts on Election Day that help party-endorsed candidates at every level.

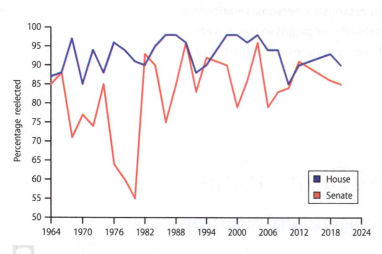

Figure 10.5 **Reelection Rates of Incumbents in Congress, 1996–2020***

Once elected, U.S. senators and representatives often are reelected to office as many times as they choose to run again.

Note: *An approximate percent pending results from undecided elections.
Sources: Center for Responsive Politics, "Reelection Rates Over the Years," accessed May 1, 2018, https://www.opensecrets.org/overview/reelect.php; https://www.270towin.com/2020-election-results-live/senate/.

Incumbency Advantage

vanishing marginals:
Trend marking the decline of competitive congressional elections.

Incumbents almost always win,[78] and in the past two decades, more than 70 percent of House incumbents won by 60 percent or more of the vote[79] (see Figure 10.5). Since the 1960s, the number of competitive races has been in decline, a trend called **vanishing marginals**. Fewer and fewer congressional elections are competitive. Noncompetitive districts are often referred to as **safe seats**. The high rates of incumbent reelection may indicate that incumbents are doing a good job, especially with constituent services that build support with voters (see also Chapter 12).

Concerns about incumbency advantage have led some observers to fear a lack of accountability and to call for **term limits**, which would force members to retire after serving a maximum number of terms. Presidents, for example, can serve only two terms, and most governors are similarly constrained. But chief executives have more concentrated power than do legislators, so ensuring turnover in the executive branch does keep gateways to responsive government open. That said, term limits would keep senators and representatives from holding seats for decades, which would allow for more people to hold office. Some legislators elected in the 1970s are still in office in 2020. This is true for both parties; for example, Senator Patrick Leahy (D-VT) has held the position for forty-five years and Representative Don Young (R-AK) has been his district's representative in the House for forty-six years.[80] Turnover is important, but building experience also matters and legislators like Young and Leahy are highly skilled.

Further, more turnover actually occurs in the House than the 90 percent reelection rate suggests. Members often engage in strategic retirement, deciding not to run for reelection when the outcome is likely to be unfavorable. It is also unclear what reelection rates exactly mean. For example, the lower reelection rates of senators do not imply that the Senate is less responsive than the House. Instead, the gap may be a function of differences between the two chambers. A seat in the Senate, the upper house, is a more coveted position than a seat in the House, and Senate races generally attract higher-quality challengers than do House races. Better challengers yield more competitive elections and more defeats for incumbents. The ability of challengers to do better in Senate races than in House races is also related to the additional media attention these races receive; quite simply, voters learn more about the challengers. Finally, the difference in terms—six years as opposed to two—may indicate that House members stay in closer touch with constituents than do senators, and their constituents reelect them.[81]

Incumbents also win reelection at high rates because their constituents know them. Name recognition for House and Senate incumbents is often higher than 80 percent. Senate challengers do better than House challengers, but still about a quarter of the electorate does not recognize their names.[82] Compare these percentages to those of the 2020 presidential in which nearly every American knew the names Joe Biden and Donald Trump.

Additional explanations have been advanced to explain incumbency advantage. For example, with the bureaucracy growing in size and reach, people expect more from their government. As a result, citizens need a mediator to handle issues that arise with the bureaucracy. Members of Congress serve as a conduit to help connect people with government services. Thus a citizen who fails to receive a Social Security check or has trouble with a passport calls his or her member of Congress for help. The result is constituent loyalty and an increased willingness to support that official's reelection. Other scholars have offered a more sinister interpretation: In this view, members of Congress deliberately design bureaucratic agencies and programs in ways that ensure they will be unable to carry out the tasks that constituents demand. In a sense,

safe seat: *Seat in Congress considered to be reliably held by one party or the other.*

term limits: *Rule restricting the number of terms an elected official can serve in a given office.*

Key Questions

Are term limits for Congress a good idea? What are the pros and the cons?

---

the bureaucracy is built to fail, so constituents have to contact their representative or senator to make it work; when help arrives, loyalty to the incumbent is built.[83] There is also a simple explanation for why reelection rates of incumbents are so high: Candidates who win once obviously have the skills to be elected, and these serve them well in reelection campaigns.[84]

In addition, recent evidence suggests that members of Congress may be the beneficiaries of the migration of Americans. That is, incumbency advantage appears to be increasing because districts are becoming "deep red" (Republican) and "deep blue" (Democratic) due to people's decisions about where to live. The assumption is that a Republican who has a choice to live, for example, in San Francisco or Dallas will tend to choose Dallas because it offers a political culture more in line with his or her preferences. In this sense, because of the redrawing of district lines and the desire of individuals to live near people with similar values and political leanings, congressional districts are becoming heavily Democratic or heavily Republican. The result is that fewer races are competitive and incumbents are more successful.[85]

Relative Lack of Interest

Key Questions

If Congress is supposed to be the branch closest to the people, why do congressional campaigns generate less interest than presidential campaigns?

presidential coattails:
Effect of a popular president or presidential candidate on congressional elections, boosting votes for members of his or her party.

Voting rates in congressional elections, particularly in midterm elections, are always lower than in presidential elections. In recent elections, midterm elections have had a voter turnout of around 40 percent while presidential elections have had closer to 60 percent participation.[86] Presidential elections are high-stimulus elections, whereas congressional elections are low-stimulus ones. The attention and excitement of a presidential election means that voters are bombarded with information about the contest. Congressional elections generate far less attention. A major consequence of these differences is that voters in congressional elections often do not know much about the candidates.

As a result, voting is driven largely by two major forces: partisanship and incumbency. Voters follow party identification and vote for their party's candidates. And, as we have seen, voters also tend to vote for incumbents. There is also the effect of **presidential coattails**—that is, a popular president running for reelection brings additional party candidates into office. Voters going to the polls in high-stimulus elections to vote for president cast ballots for other members of the party for lower-level offices. While scholars debate this effect, it is clear that the partisan makeup of Congress reflects the popularity of the president or presidential candidate.[87] In 2016, Donald Trump was able to keep the Republicans in control of both houses of Congress despite a good deal of speculation that the Democrats would capture the Senate. However, in 2018, the Republicans lost control of the House of Representatives, which was viewed as a repudiation of Trump's actions as president. Of course, the Republicans did hold the Senate in 2018, but that reflected the fact Democrats were defending more seats than Republicans were, and some of them were in red states that were very favorable to the GOP. In 2020, Republicans were defending twenty-three seats to twelve for Democrats, but again, most of the GOP seats were in states won handily by Trump in 2016.

Public Policy, Elections, and Campaigns

Party Platforms

Elections and campaigns are the key instruments of American democracy because they allow voters to judge their elected officials and replace them if enough voters disapprove of their job performance. One key part of this electoral process is the **party platform**. The platform lays out the party's thinking on key issues and can be usefully thought of as a set of promises the party makes about their plans for governing (see Chapter 9, Political Parties). Those issues, as a result, can be used to attract the support of voters and activists and also serve as a basis to judge performance once in office. Further, the creation of the platform provides an opportunity for participation, especially among the more politically active segments of the public. In this section, we will analyze how the platforms are formed and whether candidates, once elected, do follow through on their own and their party's promises.

The party platform is officially adopted at the party's national convention every four years (which nominates a presidential and vice presidential candidate). The platform is a document that tends to be driven by party activists. These actors care about policy and work hard to ensure their views are reflected in the platform. The writing of the platform takes place months prior to the convention in an array of meetings among activists.

Since party platforms are one indicator of promises made by parties and their candidates, do candidates fulfill these promises once elected to office? According to one study, about 66 percent of campaign promises in congressional campaigns have been enacted, only about 10 percent were ignored, and the remaining 20 percent or

so were blocked in Congress.[88] Another study comparing campaign appeals in House elections to subsequent introduction and cosponsorship of legislation finds that House members also keep their promises.[89] It appears that even images in television advertisements aired in congressional elections, which are usually thought of as vague and empty, serve to guide the policies House members support.[90] In short, platforms matter.

Is this also true for presidents? This question is a bit more challenging to answer, since presidential candidates make so many visible public speeches and statements. The data in Figure 10.6 suggest that President Trump is trying

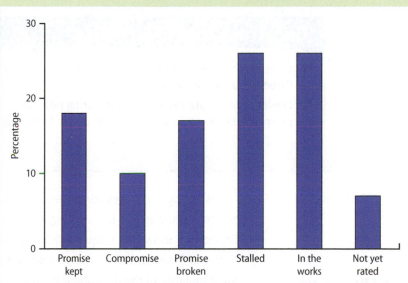

Figure 10.6 **President Trump's Campaign Promises Kept and Broken**

There is a common perception that politicians do not keep their campaign promises, and this data suggest that President Trump has struggled to keep many of his promises from his 2016 campaign when compared to presidents Clinton, Bush, and Obama.

Note: PolitiFact compiled more than five hundred promises that Donald Trump made during the campaign and has tracked their progress, rating those that are completed as "promise kept," "compromise," or "promise broken," and the others as "not yet rated," "in the works," or "stalled."

Source: PolitiFact, "Tracking Trump's Campaign Promises," accessed April 7, 2020, https://www.politifact.com/truth-o-meter/promises/trumpometer/.

to deliver on his promises. As we near the end of his first term, it seems that he broke more campaign promises than he kept or compromised.

The larger takeaway from the preceding data is that politicians do try to keep their promises. They are not perfect, but these data offer a bit of optimism about the connection between campaigns and public policy. Even Trump explicitly broke only one of five promises as of 2020.

When the president or other elected officials do stray too far from their party platform or campaign promises, the public can vote them out of office in the next election. Perhaps the most famous example of breaking a promise occurred in 1991, when President George H. W. Bush agreed to a tax increase as part of a budget deal with congressional Democrats. In his acceptance speech at the 1988 Republican National Convention, Bush had pledged he would not raise taxes, saying, "Read my lips, no new taxes." This emphatic statement was his best-known line, and it came back to haunt him. In his bid for reelection, Democratic ads played video recordings of his promise over and over to discredit him. Although he regretted breaking his promise, it is not clear that his actions were wrong: Political, economic, and social situations change, and elected officials need to change with them. In response to external events, such as a foreign policy crisis or a downturn in the economy, responsive and responsible politicians act accordingly.

Every democratic government rests on fair and open elections. Elections serve an important public policy purpose because they allow voters to change the course of government. Politicians recognize that they have to offer voters some blueprints for their future actions in office, and they do so during the campaign. Voters then choose the candidate they think will do the best job. This linkage is one of the fundamental gateways of democracy. It is important that each citizen make the most of this gateway to ensure that elected officials are responsive to the needs of the public. It is also important that the rules governing elections make it possible for this gateway to function well.

Construct Your Own Policy

1. Construct your ideal party platform for the next presidential election that addresses three important issue areas.
2. Devise an accurate system for measuring how well presidents keep their campaign promises. How would you invite the public to participate in such a system?

party platform: *Document that lays out a party's core beliefs and policy proposals for each presidential election.*

Key Questions

What were the factors that went into your vote in the 2020 presidential election?

Is voting in congressional elections a means by which citizens in a democracy hold government responsible? Does voting in congressional elections yield the will of the majority? Figure 10.7 shows the frequent shifts in the share of seats the president's party has in the House of Representatives. These shifts are often attributed to the state of the economy and the popularity of the incumbent president. According to estimates from political scientists, a party can lose up to forty-six seats when its president is highly unpopular. At the same time, a gain of 2 percent in people's income can produce eleven more seats in Congress for the incumbent party.[91]

Because of these aggregate shifts in midterm congressional elections, many scholars have viewed midterm elections as referenda on the sitting president. But given the fact that the president's party has just come off a victory in the previous election, winning seats that might often go to the other party, the normal occurrence is that the president's party loses seats in the midterm election. The 2018 midterm elections continued this pattern, with the Republicans losing nearly 40 congressional seats to the Democrats. The extent of these losses, or whether they can even be turned into gains, depends on the approval rating of the president. So in 1994, the sweep by Republicans was interpreted as a repudiation

Figure 10.7 **Loss of Seats in the House of Representatives by the President's Party in Midterm Elections, 1938–2018**

The president's party usually loses seats in midterm elections, sometimes with the consequence that the majority in the House of Representatives or the Senate changes hands.

Source: Gerhard Peters, "Seats in Congress Gained/Lost by the President's Party in Mid-Term Elections," *The American Presidency Project*, ed. John T. Woolley and Gerhard Peters, Santa Barbara: University of California, 1999–2012, http://www.presidency.ucsb.edu/data/mid-term_elections .php. © 1999–2012, Gerhard Peters, *The American Presidency Project*. Reproduced by permission. Data for 2018, https://www.realclearpolitics.com /elections/live_results/2018/house/.

of President Bill Clinton's policies, and the Republican success in the midterm elections in 2002 was viewed as a vindication of President George W. Bush. In 2010, voters were unhappy with President Obama, whose approval ratings had slipped throughout the year. To signal their discontent, voters handed the Republicans control of the House of Representatives. The tables were turned in 2018, with the Democrats taking control of the House. President Trump's unpopularity helps to explain this change in power.

Economic conditions and presidential popularity indirectly influence voters in another way. Because politicians are ambitious and want to run for office when the prospects for success are high, they survey conditions when deciding whether to run. In December 2001, with President George W. Bush's sky-high popularity, conditions looked good for Republicans in the 2002 midterm elections, and many high-quality Republican candidates decided to run. In contrast, during 2017 and 2018, many Republicans decided not to run in 2018 for fear of a tidal wave against President Trump. The aggregate effect of these decisions produces an outcome for congressional elections that correlates with economic conditions and presidential popularity. Political scientists call this influence the **strategic politician hypothesis**.[92]

Much has been written on the exact mechanisms that drive voters and congressional elections. While there is disagreement over the specifics, it is clear that the composition of Congress changes in response to economic conditions. When there are good times, the president's party benefits. When times are bad, the president's party suffers. It is also true that big issues can matter. In 2018, the controversy over immigration and tariffs shaped a lot of congressional campaigns and outcomes in those elections as well.

strategic politician hypothesis: *Effect that the strength of the economy and the popularity of the sitting president have on the decision to run for Congress.*

Elections, Campaigns, and Democracy

American elections and the campaigns that precede them are the means by which citizens participate in selecting those who will govern them. It is inevitable that they are at the center of concerns about American democracy. Many observers worry that campaigns are too long, that candidates spend too much money, and that the voters are not very well informed. These concerns often focus on the fairness of the process and of the outcome. In the long term, the process has worked reasonably well. In the short term, those who lose see the process as unfair.

In any assessment of the American political system, your own partisanship needs to be set aside. In 1980, for example, many Americans were unhappy with the state of the economy and foreign affairs. More than 70 percent of the electorate felt that the nation was on the wrong track.[93] The 1980 campaign offered the public a chance to correct course by changing presidents, and the public did so by electing Ronald Reagan. Reagan promised to end the era of big government by slashing taxes and domestic spending. Four years later, only 26 percent of the electorate felt that America was on the wrong track,[94] and President Reagan won the 1984 election in a landslide, losing only one state. In 2008, the public again was very dissatisfied with the direction of the country—only 14 percent felt the nation was on the right track.[95] The Republicans lost control of the White House, giving Barack Obama a chance to correct course. In 2016, the discontent in the country gave rise to Trump's presidency. More than 60 percent of Americans thought the country was on the wrong track, and around 30 percent felt we were on the right track.[96] In September of 2020, about 67 percent of Americans felt that country was on the wrong track and just 28 percent felt we were on the right track—an even larger gap than in 2016.[97] Candidates seek the support of the public through speeches, ads, press releases, and other methods of campaigning. The public digests that information and chooses a candidate. People's votes are a blunt instrument, but they help forge accountability. If elected officials want to stay in office, they need to act in a way that will increase the chances of continued support. Of course, the party out of office would like to get back in, and it, too, seeks the support of the public. It is through this competitive struggle that American democracy works. Critics worry that the public does not know many of the details of candidates and their platforms, and that is clearly true. But the American public should not be underestimated. That the country has not only survived for more than two centuries but thrived suggests just the opposite. The fact that the public collectively seems to act in reasonably coherent ways is testimony to political scientist V. O. Key's classic observation that "voters are not fools."[98]

Chapter Review

Key Terms

battleground state (p. 363). Why do presidential candidates focus on battleground states?

Electoral College (p. 344). Is the Electoral College a gate or a gateway to democracy?

faithless electors (p. 345). Do states without penalties for faithless electors risk not having voices heard during a presidential election?

gerrymandering (p. 351). Does gerrymandering weaken responsiveness?

invisible primary (p. 354). What is the importance of the invisible primary?

microtargeting (p. 363). Why do politicians engage in microtargeting?

midterm elections (p. 370). What is the relationship between the outcome of midterm elections and sitting presidents?

negativity (p. 366). What are the benefits of negativity for voters?

party platform (p. 375). What role do party platforms play in electoral politics?

permanent campaign (p. 353). Why is the permanent campaign a problem for Congress?

popular vote (p. 347). Why does the presidential candidate with the most popular votes not always win?

position issues (p. 365). Why are position issues uncommon in campaigns?

presidential coattails (p. 374). Do presidential coattails enhance government responsiveness?

redistricting (p. 350). What is the difference between redistricting and gerrymandering?

safe seat (p. 373). Are safe seats a sign of government responsiveness or unresponsiveness?

strategic politician hypothesis (p. 377). How does this hypothesis explain why parties sometimes lose (or gain) seats in Congress?

Super PACs (p. 361). What was the effect of Super PACs on the 2020 presidential election?

swing states (p. 362). Is your state a swing state?

swing voters (p. 362). Why are swing voters less common today?

term limits (p. 373). What are the advantages and disadvantages of term limits?

U.S. Census (p. 350). Did you fill out the 2020 Census? Why or why not?

valence issues (p. 365). Why are valence issues common in campaigns?

vanishing marginals (p. 372). Why do vanishing marginals mean elections are less competitive?

wedge issue (p. 365). Why do politicians like to use wedge issues?

Learning Outcomes: What You Need to...

Know	Test Yourself	Participate
LO 10-1 Describe the ideas that molded the Framers' thinking about elections		
The constitutional requirements for elections set up gates against direct democracy by allowing only the House of Representatives to be elected by the people. State legislatures chose both senators and the electors who would elect the president. Today senators are elected directly by the people, and presidential elections give the people more influence, but the Electoral College enhances the influence of small states over states with large populations and affects the strategy of presidential campaigns. Because of the structure of the Electoral College, the candidate with the highest number of popular votes sometimes does not win the presidency. Each state has two senators. House members represent state congressional districts whose lines are redrawn every ten years following the census to make the population represented roughly equal.	• Summarize the constitutional requirements for presidential elections. • Summarize the constitutional requirements for congressional elections. • Explain why there are so many elections in the United States.	• Argue that the constitutional requirements for elections create citizen inequality. • Vote in a local or state election this year.

Know	Test Yourself	Participate

LO 10-2 Outline the steps in presidential campaigns

Know	Test Yourself	Participate
Presidential campaigns are demanding on the candidates and are shaped by constitutional requirements, interparty struggles, and strategies for attracting votes.	• Compare and contrast nineteenth-century and twenty-first-century presidential campaigns. • State the importance of the invisible primary to candidate momentum. • Explain how caucuses and primaries work. • Tell what happens at national conventions. • Describe the significance of presidential debates.	• Debate whether the permanent campaign increases government responsiveness or impairs government performance. • Attend a caucus or vote in a primary. • Watch the national conventions, and decide if they are informative or propaganda. • Watch presidential debates, and decide if they are a valid means for evaluating the candidates.

LO 10-3 Identify the issues that shape presidential campaigns

Know	Test Yourself	Participate
Campaigns make public engagement possible but are very expensive. Strategies for winning states crucial to winning the electoral vote introduce inequalities, as does the shaping of appeals to voters.	• Track trends in fundraising for presidential campaigns. • Describe the impact of the Electoral College on presidential campaigns. • Explain microtargeting as a campaign strategy. • Compare and contrast valence issues and position issues. • Describe the role of negativity in campaign strategies. • Name the key factors in predicting who wins the presidential election.	• Evaluate the role of money in presidential elections. • Assess whether the Electoral College creates citizen inequality. • Determine if American voters pay attention to issues that matter. • Evaluate the pros and cons of negative advertising. • Critique the applicability of prediction models for the 2016 presidential election.

LO 10-4 Outline the steps in congressional campaigns

Know	Test Yourself	Participate
Congressional elections take place every two years, when terms end for one-third of senators and all members of the House. Congressional incumbents almost always win. Congressional campaigns do not draw as much attention as presidential elections.	• Describe midterm elections. • Relate how candidates try to win election.	• Know why it is important to vote in midterm elections. • Critique the applicability of the median voter theorem to the 2018 congressional elections.

LO 10-5 Determine which issues shape congressional campaigns

Know	Test Yourself	Participate
Campaign promises, including those in party platforms, are the measure against which citizens can evaluate the performance of the president and Congress. The presidency and the composition of Congress change in response to economic conditions and foreign relations, and the pattern of party gains and losses indicates that voters use elections to hold officials accountable and that the presidency and Congress are responsive institutions.	• Explain how fundraising needs restrain candidates. • Describe the role of political parties in congressional campaigns. • Give reasons for incumbency advantage. • Explain the relationship between the outcome of midterm elections and public opinion of the president.	• Decide if campaigns are too expensive. • Decide if incumbents are too entrenched.

11 Voting and Participation

> " . . . *we should seek not a world where the black race and the white race live in harmony, but a world in which the terms black and white have no real political meaning.*"[1]

The photo on the opposite page shows the entrance to Howard University, where Ta-Nehisi Coates began his training as a writer and where he was mentored by his professors.

TA-NEHISI COATES
Howard University

Ta-Nehisi Coates was born in 1975 and grew up in segregated northwest Baltimore. While he did not grow up poor, he was surrounded by urban violence. His sense of racial consciousness developed at an early age, and he listened to a recording of Malcolm X's "The Ballot or the Bullet" speech. Though not a campaign organizer or political operative, Coates has emerged as a prominent social and political voice of a generation of African Americans.[2] His primary and most visible means of participating in politics is through writing.

Coates arrived at Howard University in 1993, pursuing his interest in poetry and writing. He reached out to several older black writers connected with the university who helped to mentor and shape his writing. His in-depth research and his willingness to immerse himself in the material grew out of this period of mentorship at Howard. Inspired by the faculty he met at Howard, Coates went to the library each morning and immersed himself in books about nationalism, integration, and the American experience. He often recalls this time as painful, but an extremely necessary pain that was integral to writing and

the development of his writing process: "The process of getting conscious for me was a very, very uncomfortable, disturbing and sometimes physically painful process. And so that's the standard to which I write, because it was what I've experienced over my time."[3] Coates left Howard to begin a career in journalism. Though he did not graduate from Howard, the school afforded him to the ability to read, to learn, and to develop a clear ideological position on critical issues of importance to him. He credits his time spent at Howard as the key juncture in his development as a writer.

After working as a freelance writer for about seven years, Coates began working at *The Atlantic* in 2008 and was a national correspondent when he departed that publication in 2018. His influential piece "The Case for Reparations" sparked a new national conversation about the lasting effects of slavery on the African American community. Coates was described as being adept at "digest[ing] the central paradox of the time: how, within an increasingly progressive era, a country led by a black president could still act with such racial brutality."[4] For Coates, writing became his gateway to political participation.

Learning Outcomes

LO 11-1 Explain why there are battles over ballot access

LO 11-2 Outline how the right to vote has expanded

LO 11-3 Identify who tends to turn out in American elections

LO 11-4 Articulate the main theoretical approaches that explain voting

LO 11-5 Evaluate how low turnout is in American elections

LO 11-6 Analyze how changes in voting laws have affected participation rates

LO 11-7 Describe other important forms of participation

Coates's 2015 book *Between the World and Me* propelled him further into the spotlight, offering a powerful perspective on race relations in the United States. In this extended message to his 14-year-old son, Coates writes about his fears of what his son will have to experience as an African American. He notes that the history of the African American experience is one of a tradition of destroying the black body. He reminds his son, "you must always remember . . . that the sociology, the history, the economics, the graphs, the charts, the regressions all land, with great violence, upon the body." This powerful imagery led observers to note that Coates "speaks unpopular, unconventional and sometimes even radical truths in his own voice, unfiltered."[5]

Coates continued to voice opinions on issues such as race and politics, and the 2016 presidential election. He credits his influence to his growing audience and the community that is forming around him. "There is some group of Americans who are really, really curious to understand how we ended up at this point," he said, explaining that these are the people who have contributed to his recent popularity. While he does not believe they will immediately "go forth and create some sort of long-lasting policy,"[6] there does seem to be some hope in the way that he addresses his readers, hope that maybe his ability to reach this broader audience is helping to educate and bring conscious awareness to at least some of the nation. His goal, in short, is to encourage Americans to participate in this important conversation.

This chapter describes the many gateways to political participation, ranging from voting to campaigning to protest. Coates's story highlights an additional means of participating in the political process: His writing has opened new conversations about race in the United States. His voice is an important one, and he found his gateway through his investment at Howard University to understand his place in the American experience and in communicating his thoughts as a writer.

The Practice and Theory of Voting

LO 11-1 Explain why there are battles over ballot access

Americans enjoy near-universal opportunities to vote. Even so, no one should assume that such opportunities have always existed or that they are permanent. Despite the widespread belief in the importance of elections for democratic institutions, some Americans have argued that voting rights should not be universal. Who votes shapes the outcome of elections and the conduct of government. Voting, in short, is a central gateway to power, so there are always battles over who gets access to the ballot.

The Constitution and Voting

The Constitution is nearly silent on the rules about voting in elections, leaving such choices to the states. As Article I, Section 4, of the Constitution states, "The Times, Places and Manner of holding Elections for Senators and Representatives, shall be prescribed in each State by the Legislature thereof." The Constitution does spell out in some detail the workings of the Electoral College, which chooses the president (see Chapter 10, Elections and Campaigns). But state legislatures were given nearly complete latitude about how to select their members for the Electoral College. Similarly, the Constitution makes the states the prime players in setting voting requirements.

The consequence of this delegation of authority is a system of voting that is very complicated because state rules vary considerably. The differing rules also lead to inequalities among the states. It is, for example, easier to vote in some states than in others. We explore some of these issues in this chapter and in Chapter 10.

Competing Views of Participation

Debates about voting and the removal of obstacles to voting have often centered on whether potential voters would be qualified to cast ballots. For example, in the nineteenth century, many lawmakers did not think women would make wise political choices and were therefore reluctant to consider granting them **suffrage**.[7] Others worried that too much participation yields too many demands on government, making government less able to respond. It seems that those opposed to removing obstacles to voting feared that too much democracy could be bad for democracy.[8]

We label these ideas the Hamiltonian model of participation. Alexander Hamilton represents a perspective that sees risks in greater participation and, thus, favors a larger role for elites. In this model, not only would the quality of the decision be diluted by more participation, but government would also be less able to advance the national interest because it would be responding to uninformed voters. The Hamiltonian model stands in stark contrast to the Jeffersonian model, which holds that more participation yields a more involved and engaged public and that, in turn, produces better outcomes.[9] In other words, democracy thrives with more democracy. Thomas Jefferson had more faith than Hamilton did in the people's ability and worried that excessive reliance on elites would make government less responsive to its citizens.

Key Questions

Why does the Constitution say so little about voting? Should it say more?

suffrage: *Right to vote; also called* franchise.

Figure 11.1 offers a summary of these competing views. Proponents of the Hamiltonian model do seek accountability, but they place much more faith in the ability of elites than in the ability of the general public to make the right decisions. The people, they contend, are often uninformed and cannot make the best choices. In contrast, proponents of the Jeffersonian model want to see more participation, believing that the people can be trusted and that getting more people involved will push government to be more responsive to the people's interests. They contend that if certain groups of people are disenfranchised, government will be less responsive. People may not be well informed about politics, but if they have a chance to be involved, they will become better informed. An informed citizenry that actively participates in politics will ensure that government is both accountable and responsive.

Figure 11.1 **Hamiltonian and Jeffersonian Models of Participation**

This figure shows two ways of thinking about how citizens' participation in government affects various aspects of politics and governance. The two models offer contrasting viewpoints about the value and consequences of political participation.

The Jeffersonian model holds equality as an important political value, whereas the Hamiltonian model places more emphasis on efficient and effective outcomes. These competing visions of citizen involvement have played out in nearly all debates about expanding the opportunity for more citizens to cast ballots. In the course of the nation's history, proponents and opponents of expanding the right to vote have each achieved victories. Although the overall trend has been constant expansion, the contest has been fraught with conflict—not only debate in Congress and the courts but also violence in the streets, as the following section will attest.

Key Questions

Can you think of any reason why a citizen should not be allowed to vote?

Key Questions

Do you lean toward the Hamiltonian or the Jeffersonian model of participation?

The History of Voting in America

LO 11-2 Outline how the right to vote has expanded

The history of voting in America falls into three general eras.[10] First, from the 1790s to 1870, voting rights expanded, and by 1860 universal white male suffrage had been achieved. After the Civil War, voting rights were extended to African American males by means of the Fifteenth Amendment. But states, localities, and political parties sought by various means to block African Americans, Asian immigrants, and others from voting. From the 1870s until 1920, the barriers to voting often increased. Reforms were under way as well, and beginning with the Nineteenth Amendment in 1920, which granted women the right to vote, voting rights began to expand again. The civil rights movement of the 1950s and 1960s culminated in the passage of laws protecting voting rights for African Americans, Latinos, and others, and a Constitutional amendment in 1971 extended the right to vote to 18-year-olds. In 1961, citizens of the District of Columbia were given the opportunity to vote in presidential elections (see Figure 11.2). Thus, in the twentieth century, there was a second wave of expansion of voting rights.

These three eras suggest that voting and the electorate have expanded in the long run, though not consistently and with contractions that have violated civil rights (see Chapter 5, Civil Rights). In this section, we survey these developments by looking at the first era of expanding voting rights, women's suffrage, the denial and then protection of voting rights for African Americans and Latinos, and voting restrictions and opportunities for other groups.

Expansion of Voting, 1790s to 1870

George Washington (1789–97) was elected to the presidency twice, unanimously both times.[11] By all accounts, he was a popular president and the overwhelming choice of the public. Yet a close look at the first presidential elections shows that very few citizens actually voted for Washington. In fact, for the first nine presidential elections (1789–1820), popular votes were not even recorded across all the states. Most states did not allow the public to cast ballots for president; state legislators chose the electors who voted in the Electoral College. State legislators also chose U.S. senators. The people could vote for representatives to the House of Representatives, but eligibility to vote was largely limited to white males who owned a certain amount of property or paid a certain amount of taxes. Slaves could not vote, and free black males often did not have the right to vote. South Carolina, Georgia, and Virginia blocked free blacks from voting when the Constitution was first adopted. In New Jersey, women who owned property could vote from 1776 until 1807, when the right was rescinded.[12]

franchise: *Right to vote; also called* suffrage.

Not until the rise of Jacksonian democracy in the 1820s did the **franchise** (the right to vote) begin to expand significantly. In the 1824 presidential election, only about 366,000 votes were cast, representing just over 25 percent of eligible voters.[13] None of the four candidates won a majority in the Electoral College, though Andrew Jackson won the most popular votes (41 percent), so the election was decided by the House of Representatives. In one of the most controversial deals in American politics, Henry Clay, who had come in third, threw his support to John Quincy Adams, who had come in second, thereby enabling Adams to win the presidency. Once in office, President Adams (1825–29) named Clay secretary of state.

Color Code:	Participation	Equality

Fifteenth	1870	Prohibits states from denying the right to vote on account of race
Seventeenth	1913	Gives the people (instead of state legislatures) the right to choose U.S. senators
Nineteenth	1920	Guarantees women the right to vote
Twenty-Third	1961	Grants residents of the District of Columbia votes in the Electoral College
Twenty-Fourth	1964	Prohibits poll taxes
Twenty-Sixth	1971	Guarantees 18-year-olds the right to vote

Figure 11.2 Constitutional Amendments That Pertain to the Right to Vote

These six amendments to the Constitution were designed to increase the role of citizens in governance. They removed obstacles from voting and expanded suffrage, and the Seventeenth Amendment provided for direct election of U.S. senators.

Jackson's supporters charged that Adams and Clay had made a "corrupt bargain," generating widespread outrage over the "deal."[14] Determined to get Jackson elected to office the next time, they pursued a number of strategies (see also Chapter 9, Political Parties). One was to press states to remove property requirements for voting and to allow citizens, instead of state legislatures, to vote for president. This effort paid off. In the presidential election of 1828, turnout tripled to more than 1.1 million votes cast and produced a landslide for Jackson (1829–37), who won 56 percent of the popular vote and two-thirds of the Electoral College vote. By the time of the Civil War, property and tax

Library of Congress, Prints & Photographs Division, Reproduction number: LC-DIG-ppmsca-50970 (digital file from original) LC-USZ62-1805 (b&w film copy neg.) LC-USZC4-970 (color film copy transparency)

Image 11.1 When the 1824 presidential election produced no majority in the Electoral College, the House of Representatives selected John Quincy Adams, who had received fewer votes than Andrew Jackson. Jackson's supporters, angered at this outcome, worked to expand the right to vote before the next election. In 1828, Jackson beat Adams in the popular vote and in the Electoral College. Following Jackson's inauguration on March 4, 1829, crowds of supporters celebrated at the White House.

qualifications had been largely eliminated, but the franchise was still limited mainly to white males. Women could not vote, nor could many free blacks.

Following the Civil War, the Fifteenth Amendment, ratified in 1870, gave African American males the right to vote. Efforts by southern states to deny that right (covered later in this chapter) have shaped American politics into the present.

The Road to Women's Suffrage, 1848 to 1920

In 1848 in Seneca Falls, New York, the first women's rights meeting initiated a movement for women's suffrage. The movement gained energy after the Civil War, as women individually and through suffrage organizations pressured state legislatures to change state laws to allow women to vote. Susan B. Anthony, a leader in the National Woman Suffrage Association, worked tirelessly for most of her life to secure women the right to vote. In 1872, for example, she went to the polls in her hometown of Rochester, New York, and cast a ballot, claiming that the Fourteenth Amendment's statement that "all persons [not just men] born or naturalized in the United States . . . are citizens" gave women the right to vote. Later, she was arrested (as she hoped she would be), and her trial gave the issue of suffrage for women much attention. She was found guilty of breaking the law, but not before she had used the trial as a platform for her cause.[15]

The efforts of the suffrage movement were gradually successful. In 1869, the territory of Wyoming granted the right to vote to women, and that right was retained when Wyoming became a state in 1890. By 1916, eleven states, all in the West, allowed women to vote (see Figure 5.2, Women's Suffrage Before 1920, in Chapter 5). The piecemeal approach of statewide campaigns came to an end on August 26, 1920, when the Tennessee legislature

Key Questions

Why has Jackson been called "the people's president"?

Key Questions

Describe theories of representation that could have been used to justify denying women the right to vote.

ratified the Nineteenth Amendment by a single vote. With Tennessee, three-quarters of the states had ratified the amendment, giving constitutional protection to women's suffrage. The amendment states, "The right of citizens of the United States to vote shall not be denied or abridged by the United States or by any State on account of sex." Some southern states used the late date of the Tennessee ratification, only ten weeks before the presidential election, to deny women's access to the ballot until the next election cycle.[16]

The effect of the women's vote was debated and even feared at the time. There was speculation that women were not well-suited to be active participants in the political process and that allowing them to vote would provide "an unpredictable or volatile addition to the electorate."[17] Others were concerned about nearly doubling the voting electorate and the additional demands that would place on government. Such views are closely associated with the Hamiltonian model of voting. But evidence gathered by political scientists suggests that these worries were unfounded. Women in the 1920s voted in ways that reflected their interests just as much as men's did.[18] The adoption of the Nineteenth Amendment did not, in other words, undermine the basic stability of electoral politics—a finding supportive of those who favor the Jeffersonian approach to participation.

With women able to vote, overall **turnout** did drop in the short term. From 1904 to 1916, the average rate of turnout in presidential elections was about 63 percent.[19] With the inclusion of women as eligible voters, turnout fell to 49 percent in both 1920 and 1924. But then it started to climb as women increasingly exercised their right to vote, reaching 57 percent in both 1928 and 1932. By 1940, the turnout rate was 62 percent—essentially at the pre-1920 level. These data strongly suggest that women quickly became involved in the political process. By 1984, women voted at a slightly higher rate than men—a trend that continues today. Turnout for women was 4 points higher than for men in the 2018 midterm election.[20]

turnout: *Share of all eligible voters who actually cast ballots.*

Image 11.2 In the early 1870s, suffragists such as Susan B. Anthony tried to exercise the right to vote. When Virginia Minor was blocked from registering to vote in Missouri, she sued. Her case, decided by the Supreme Court in 1875, determined that women were citizens but that the Constitution does not confer a right to vote. In this drawing, Victoria Claflin Woodhull points to the Constitution as she tries to vote in a local New York City election; her sister, Tennessee Claflin, stands behind her.

The Granger Collection, NYC

Denial of African American Suffrage, 1870 to 1965

The story of gates against African American participation is long and agonizing. Five years after the Civil War ended, Congress and the states ratified the Fifteenth Amendment, which reads, "The right of citizens of the United States to vote shall not be denied or abridged by the United States or by any State on account of race, color, or previous condition of servitude." With such constitutional protection, African Americans should have been able to exercise their right to vote. During Reconstruction (1865–77), the period when the federal government effectively controlled the state governments in the South, southern blacks were able to vote. Their votes made it possible for South Carolina—the first state to secede and the first to fire on federal troops—to elect the first African American member of the House of Representatives, Joseph Rainey, in 1870.

The presidential election of 1876 ended any hope of integrating blacks into American political life. Neither the Democrat Samuel Tilden nor the Republican Rutherford B. Hayes won a majority in the Electoral College. Contested votes in three southern states and Oregon, with charges of fraud, led Congress to appoint an Electoral Commission to resolve the matter of who should count the votes of the electors (the Constitution does not say who should resolve disputed votes). In an unofficial bargain between Southern Democrats and Republicans, all the disputed votes went to Hayes (1877–81) in return for his promise that federal troops would be removed from the South and the region would return to self-governance. With this agreement, Reconstruction was effectively over, and so was African American participation in the political process.

In an era known as **Jim Crow**, southern state legislatures, no longer under federal authority, started to pass laws that denied African Americans basic political rights. State and local laws systematically undermined the political, economic, and social standing of African Americans by requiring segregation of the races in public schools, parks, accommodations, and transportation. Those who disobeyed segregation laws were subject not only to fines and jailing but also to lynching and other acts of brutal violence. Between 1889 and 1930, more than 3,700 lynchings were reported, most of them of southern blacks, and many other lynchings and mob actions were not reported in the press.[21] The law-based means of denying African Americans the right to vote included the following strategies.

Literacy Tests.   **Literacy tests**, which required potential voters to prove they could read, were applied differently to whites and blacks. African Americans were often given harder tests to ensure they would not pass. In some cases, the tests were set up to guarantee failure, as there were no correct answers. Figure 11.3 reproduces some questions from the Louisiana literacy test, a test that is impossible to pass.

epa european pressphoto agency b.v./Alamy Stock Photo

Image 11.3 Segregation was a harsh reality throughout the United States, but in the South, states passed laws formally separating the races. These examples are reminders of those laws, and that era is referred to as "Jim Crow."

Jim Crow laws: *Southern laws that established strict segregation of the races and gave their name to the segregation era.*

literacy tests: *Tests requiring reading and interpretation skills in order to vote.*

poll taxes: *Tax on voting; prohibited by the Twenty-Fourth Amendment (1964).*

Poll Taxes. **Poll taxes** were another means of discouraging blacks from voting. In the 1890s, an individual had to pay $1 in Mississippi and $2 in South Carolina to vote, an amount that may seem small today but was huge in the poverty-stricken postwar South, where the average annual income was equivalent to $86 in today's dollars; the South Carolina poll tax would be equivalent to about $1,000 today.[22] For most blacks, almost all poor farmers, this tax made voting impossible.[23]

The State of Louisiana

Literacy Test (This test is to be given to anyone who cannot prove a fifth grade education.)

Do what you are told to do in each statement, nothing more, nothing less. Be careful as one wrong answer denotes failure of the test. You have 10 minutes to complete the test.

1. Draw a line around the number or letter of this sentence.

2. Draw a line under the last word in this line.

3. Cross out the longest word in this line.

4. Draw a line around the shortest word in this line.

5. Circle the first, first letter of the alphabet in this line.

6. In the space below draw three circles, one inside (engulfed by) the other.

7. Above the letter X make a small cross.

8. Draw a line through the letter below that comes earliest in the alphabet.

ZVSBDMKITPHC

9. Draw a line through the two letters below that come last in the alphabet.

ZVBDMKTPHSYC

10. In the first circle below write the last letter of the first word beginning with "L".

11. Cross out the number necessary, when making the number below one million.

10000000000

12. Draw a line from circle 2 to circle 5 that will pass below circle 2 and above circle 4.

13. In the line below cross out each number that is more than 20 but less than 30.

31 16 48 29 53 47 22 37 98 26 20 25

Figure 11.3 **Louisiana Literacy Test**

These questions, excerpted from a three-page test, make it clear that the test was not intended to test literacy but to deny African Americans the right to vote.

Source: Rethinking Schools, "The Louisiana Voter Test," accessed May 1, 2018, https://www.rethinkingschools.org/articles/the-louisiana-voter-test.

Grandfather Clauses.   To help keep literacy tests and poll taxes from discouraging white voters, exemptions were allowed for those whose grandfathers had voted. Because the grandfathers of most African Americans had been slaves with no voting rights, these **grandfather clauses** never benefited them.

The White Primary.   Following the Civil War, the Democratic Party dominated in the South. By restricting its primary to white voters, it kept black voters—even if they could exercise the right to vote—from having any influence because whoever won the Democratic primary always won the general election. In 1944, the U.S. Supreme Court, in *Smith v. Allwright*, ruled the **white primary** unconstitutional.[24]

The Civil Rights Movement and African American Voting, 1950s and 1960s

The era of Jim Crow lasted for decades because, despite the guarantee of the Fifteenth Amendment, states retained authority over voting laws, and these laws were not challenged. In addition, Democratic Party dominance ensured the continuation of the so-called Solid South, a voting bloc critical to all Democratic presidential candidates from Woodrow Wilson (1913–21) to Franklin Delano Roosevelt (1933–45) to John F. Kennedy (1961–63), who therefore did not push for civil rights. Southern senators had the power to block efforts to end Jim Crow laws, given their seniority and the option (or threat) of using the filibuster (see Chapter 12, Congress).[25]

Beginning in the 1950s the civil rights movement challenged the denial of basic political rights. Boycotts, sit-ins, and marches called attention to the lack of equal treatment for African Americans in the South (see Chapter 5), and public support for ending the legal barriers grew. For instance, in October 1963, 86 percent of the American public approved of "a federal law that requires negroes be given equal rights in voting."[26] In 1964, support by the public helped give Congress the impetus to pass the Civil Rights Act, which protected voting rights and put severe restrictions on the administration of literacy tests. To strengthen protections of voting rights, Congress passed the Voting Rights Act in 1965, which effectively ended literacy tests and other strategies that had discriminated against African Americans at the polls and gave the Justice Department the authority to supervise **voter registration** in locales that had discriminated (see also Chapter 5). The Twenty-Fourth Amendment, ratified in 1964, banned poll taxes.

One consequence of these measures was a huge upswing of voter participation in the South. From 1920 to 1960, the turnout rate in southern states averaged 23 percent in presidential elections, whereas in the rest of the country it was 65 percent. The low turnout in the South was due not only to the exclusion of blacks; the South was also poorer than much of the rest of the country, and poverty generally depresses turnout. In addition, Democratic Party dominance meant that elections were not competitive and generated little public interest. But **voter apathy** in the South has declined as wealth has risen, and Democratic Party dominance has ended as well. Voter participation of southerners in elections is much the same as for the rest of the nation now.[27]

Those with the Hamiltonian model mind-set worried that African Americans would not have the necessary education and skills to recognize how their interests could be best served at the polls. But, as in the case of women, the worries were unfounded. The political revival of African Americans gave them reason to become more attentive, more informed, and better citizens overall. As one study reports, African Americans developed the attitudes and skills necessary to 'learn the trade' of politics in a remarkably short period of time."[28] In 2012, black turnout was

grandfather clauses: *Election rules that exempted people from difficult literacy and interpretation tests for voting if their grandfathers had been eligible to vote.*

white primary: *Election rules that prohibited blacks from voting in Democratic primaries.*

voter registration: *Enrollment required prior to voting to establish eligibility.*

voter apathy: *Lack of interest in voting and in politics generally.*

Supreme Court Cases

Katzenbach v. Morgan (1966)

QUESTION: May Congress prohibit states from enforcing English-language literacy tests?

ORAL ARGUMENT: April 18, 1966 (listen at http://www.oyez.org/cases/1960-1969/1965/1965_847)

DECISION: June 13, 1966 (read at https://caselaw.findlaw.com/us-supreme-court/384/641.html)

OUTCOME: Yes, Congress has the authority (7–2).

Section 4(e) of the Voting Rights Act of 1965 prevented states from establishing English-language literacy tests for voting if the resident had finished the sixth grade in an accredited school in the U.S. Commonwealth of Puerto Rico in which the language of instruction was "other than English" (this almost always meant Spanish). Although voting qualifications were traditionally left to states, the Fourteenth Amendment, which, among other things, prohibited states from denying to any person the equal protection of the laws, also gave Congress the authority to enforce its provisions through "appropriate legislation." As many people of Puerto Rican heritage had been denied the right to vote in New York due to an inability to read and write English, Congress added the above-noted protection.

Morgan and other registered voters in New York City brought the lawsuit to challenge Congress's authority to prohibit English-language voting requirements. A special three-judge district court struck down the congressional requirement. U.S. Attorney General Nicholas Katzenbach appealed that decision directly to the Supreme Court, as the Voting Rights Act allows.

The Supreme Court ruled that the enforcement provision of the Fourteenth Amendment gave Congress the same broad powers to enact legislation to protect voting rights that the necessary and proper clause did for the enumerated powers in the Constitution (see Supreme Court Cases: *McCulloch v. Maryland* in Chapter 3, Federalism). The Court declared that legislation prohibiting discrimination in voting on account of language fell within the constitutional authority of Congress.

Thinking Critically

1. What reasons, valid and invalid, might New York have had for restricting the right to vote to those who can read or write in English?

2. Why might the Voting Rights Act have protected Americans educated in Spanish in Puerto Rico but not Americans educated in Spanish in Mexico?

Key Questions

In what ways did African Americans and Latinos face similar barriers to political participation?

higher than white turnout for the first time in a presidential election, 66 percent to 64 percent. In the 2016 election, turnout among blacks dropped slightly yet remained relatively high.[29] The fact that blacks overcame the informational and educational disadvantages imposed on them in the Jim Crow era casts doubts on the Hamiltonian theory of participation, giving advocates of the Jeffersonian school reason for optimism.

The Latino Vote

The Jim Crow laws designed to limit the franchise of blacks had the same effects on Latinos. Poll taxes placed an additional, and relatively high, cost on Latinos wanting to vote. One of the major gates to Latino voter participation involved language. After Reconstruction and well into the twenty-first century, many Latinos speak Spanish as their first language.[30] Literacy tests, as applied to Latinos, were English-language tests. These tests constructed a real gate to participation. As we saw in Chapter 5, in the 1960s, New York's English requirements prevented Puerto Rican Americans from registering to vote prior to 1955 (see Supreme Court Cases: *Katzenbach v. Morgan*).[31] That decision, while important, did not break down all the gates because it did not require that voter registration, ballots, and other voting materials be made available to non-English-speaking voters in their native language.

In 1975, Congress extended the Voting Rights Act to include "Language Assistance Amendments." Those laws ensured that in areas in which more than 5 percent of the citizens of voting age are members of a single language minority and have limited English proficiency, governments must provide election materials and assistance in their native language (as well as in English).[32] This change opened a significant gateway for Latinos and other non-English speakers to participate in elections. In comments before the Senate Judiciary Committee, Senator Orrin Hatch (R-UT) explained his support for the provisions this way:

> *The right to vote is one of the fundamental human rights. Unless government assures access to the ballot box, citizenship is just an empty promise. Section 203 of the Voting Rights Act, containing bilingual election requirements, is an integral part of our government's assurance that Americans do have such access.*[33]

Considering the many gates facing Latino voters, their socialization into the electoral arena has been stilted. Gates such as Jim Crow laws, Mexican Repatriation (see Chapter 5, page 148 for a discussion of this policy), and language requirements, for example, discouraged Latinos from voting and inevitably passed this uneven and constrained sense of citizenship to succeeding generations. Even so, the Voting Rights Act proved a boon to the participation of Latinos. Together with voter mobilization, Latinos are overcoming these early gates and now voting in much larger numbers. Although it seems that there are now more gateways to participation, new efforts in the form of voter identification laws have been enacted by some states, constructing new gates that will hinder many Latinos (and others) from exercising the right to vote. (See Public Policy and Voting: Voter ID Laws.)

Figure 11.5 provides some clear data on Latino voting by comparing the rates of participation to other relevant groups. As the figure shows, Latino voting in presidential elections continues to lag behind the rates of both white and African American voters. Over the past four election cycles, whites have voted at rates between 60 and 70 percent, while African American turnout has increased from 52 percent to an historic 66 percent in the 2012 election. In the same time period, voting rates for Latinos have hovered in the mid 40 percent range. The gap between black and Latino turnout has increased in recent years, surely reflecting the mobilization of the African American community with the Obama candidacy.

However, this lower turnout masks the fact that Latinos represent an ever-growing segment of the total voting population. While turnout rates have been pretty flat, the number of eligible Latino voters has grown from 13.2 million to 32 million since the year 2000. While the 2000 Latino turnout rate of 45 percent brought around 6 million people to the polls, the 2016 turnout rate of 47 percent resulted in almost 12 million Latino voters. Latinos now constitute about 13 percent of the electorate,[34] and the percentage will only grow in the coming years.[35]

Key Questions

How did the votes of 18-year-olds affect the responsiveness of government?

Public Policy and Voting

Voter ID Laws

To avoid voter fraud, many states have instituted voter identification requirements. As of 2018 thirty-four states have voter identification laws in force.[36] Of these, seventeen states require voters to show a photo ID, and sixteen states require a nonphoto ID, such as a bank statement with the voter's address. Other states ask voters to show ID with or without a photo but do not prevent individuals from voting if they do not present a ballot ID at the polling stations. (See the Political Analytics section in Chapter 5.) Voter ID laws, however, are controversial as some argue that they create a gate to participation. The poor and less educated, for example, may find it harder to meet these new standards and, if so, may be disenfranchised. Even for those who are better educated and have ID, 2016 showed that these requirements greatly lengthened the time it takes to vote, creating very long lines at polling places across America.

Opponents of Indiana's 2005 photo identification law sought to block its implementation through a lawsuit. The fundamental issue in this case was whether state laws that were intending to prevent voter fraud had the result of preventing citizens who were legally entitled to vote from doing so. Indiana argued that the requirement of a photo ID was not unduly burdensome because the state provided voter identification cards to citizens who had no other photo IDs. But opponents argued that the process of getting such a card was too complicated and that the overall effect of the law would be to disenfranchise thousands of citizens. In 2008, the Supreme Court upheld the Indiana law by a 6–3 vote. Justice John Paul Stevens wrote on behalf of the majority, "The state interests identified as justifications for [the law] are both neutral and sufficiently strong to require us to reject" the lawsuit. However, Justice David Souter wrote in dissent that the law "threatens to impose nontrivial burdens on the voting right of tens of thousands of the state's citizens."[37]

The issue is still not settled. Starting in 2012, the American Civil Liberties Union filed suit against Pennsylvania's strict new voter ID law, and the State Supreme Court struck down the law.[38] In addition to not "[assuring] fair and free elections," as the Pennsylvania judge wrote, these laws may have a disproportionate effect on some groups of voters.

For example, elderly, poorer citizens, and even women whose surnames may change as they marry, divorce, or simply maintain their maiden names[39] may not have acceptable forms of photo identification. Latinos may also be less likely than other voters to have valid photo identification. In Texas, for example, scholars showed that not only were Latinos less likely to have such IDs, but they were also less likely to have the documents necessary to obtain them (see Figure 11.4).[40] In a federal court case brought by the Texas State Conference of the NAACP and the Mexican American Legislative Caucus of the Texas House of Representatives, the courts used such evidence to strike down a Texas law requiring citizens to present photo identification to vote. At issue was whether the Texas law violated Section 2 of the Voting Rights Act (VRA) that prohibits voting practices or procedures that discriminate on the basis of race, color, or membership in one

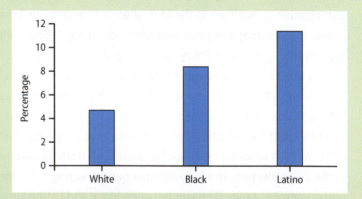

Figure 11.4 Percent of Eligible Voters in Texas Who Lack an Accepted Photo ID

This figure shows recent data from Texas about who is affected by voter identification laws. It is clear from the data that blacks and Latinos are least likely to hold an acceptable form of photo identification that would allow them to vote.

Source: Matt A. Barreto and Gabriel R. Sanchez, "Accepted Photo Identification and Different Subgroups in the Eligible Voter Population, State of Texas," Expert Report Submitted on Behalf of Plaintiffs in *Veasey v. Perry*, Case 2:13-cv-00193, June 27, 2014, http://www.latinodecisions.com/blog/wp-content/uploads/2014/10/Texas-Voter-ID-Expert-Report_Barreto_Sanchez.pdf.

of the language groups identified in the VRA.[41] The Texas law was temporarily stayed for the November 2014 election and was since reinstated following the *Shelby County v. Holder* (2013) decision. (See the discussion of the *Shelby* case and the Political Analytics feature in Chapter 5.)

These are all complicated issues and as such must be thoughtfully assessed, especially as they affect differentially the ability of certain groups to influence the political process. One consideration is access to and interpretation of the necessary data to assess the effects of voter identification laws.[42] Political considerations also come into play. The two political parties may see their electoral fortunes tied to either increased or decreased voter participation and thus have different incentives to cooperate with each other on voting requirements. Latinos, for instance, are substantially more likely to vote Democratic than Republican.

With the Hamiltonian and Jeffersonian views of voting in mind, it is important to decide what standards should be imposed for citizens to vote. Clearly, the federal government has taken steps to make the voting process easier and more convenient. But ultimately states and localities administer and oversee elections, and states have responded inconsistently to the federal efforts. Some appear to have made it easier to vote, but others, such as Indiana, have made it harder by requiring photo identification at the polling place. It would seem that, in a democracy, all citizens should have an equal opportunity to cast their votes because voting is the fundamental mechanism by which we hold government accountable. As states introduce more laws regarding identification, disparities in the opportunity to vote may be growing.

Construct Your Own Policy

1. Write a set of requirements that you think citizens should meet in order to vote and that balances concerns for voter fraud with easing access to voting.
2. Construct a strategy for cooperation regarding voting requirements that addresses voter fraud concerns mostly voiced by Republicans as well as easy access for voters that Democrats embrace.

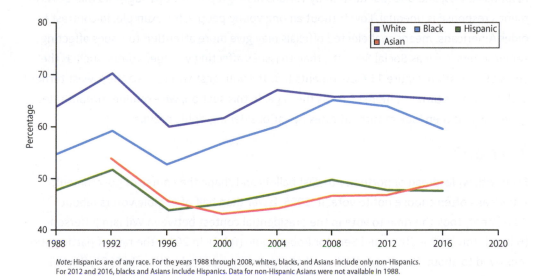

Note: Hispanics are of any race. For the years 1988 through 2008, whites, blacks, and Asians include only non-Hispanics. For 2012 and 2016, blacks and Asians include Hispanics. Data for non-Hispanic Asians were not available in 1988.

Figure 11.5 **Voter Turnout Rates in Presidential Elections, by Race and Ethnicity**

This figure demonstrates the disparities in turnout rates among four racial and ethnic groups. Latinos and Asian Americans have continued to exert less of an effect on elections than their growing populations might suggest.

Source: Pew Research Center, May 11, 2017, http://www.pewresearch.org/fact-tank/2017/05/12/black-voter-turnout-fell-in-2016-even-as-a-record -number-of-americans-cast-ballots/ft_17-05-10_voter-turnout/.

The Vote for 18-Year-Olds, 1971

Until 1971, nearly all states set the minimum age for voting at 21,[43] but with the adoption of the Twenty-Sixth Amendment that year, the Constitution mandated that states could not deny the right to vote to anyone age 18 or over. The impetus for this extension of the franchise was the Vietnam War, which heightened awareness of the fact that young men were being sent off to fight at age 18 but could not participate in elections. The call for the 18-year-old vote also took place in the context of campus antiwar protests and student demands for greater rights and in the wake of African American achievements in civil and voting rights—protests that had achieved protection of the right to vote. At that moment in the country's history, people were receptive to arguments in favor of greater participation. Unlike the extension of the franchise to women and African Americans, the amendment was not controversial. President Richard M. Nixon (1969–74) supported it even though he knew from polling data that the young voters were not likely to support him in the upcoming 1972 presidential election.

Who Votes?

LO 11-3 Identify who tends to turn out in American elections

Voting is an important gateway to influence, but not everyone has the inclination or the desire to participate. Failure to vote has real implications for the political process; it affects which representatives govern and make laws, and who governs has policy consequences that affect everyone in the United States. Low turnout raises questions about government's responsiveness, and unequal turnout by various demographic groups suggests that government's response is unequal. Low turnout among young people, for example, in contrast to older Americans, means that elected officials may give more attention to issues affecting senior voters, such as Social Security, than to issues affecting younger voters, such as the costs of education. Figure 11.6 documents that the youngest voters have the lowest turnout and that voters turn out more often as they age. In this section, we examine turnout rates generally and then look at turnout rates by various demographic groups.

Turnout

Even with widespread opportunity to cast ballots and shape the course of government, Americans often choose not to vote. In 1996, fewer than half of eligible voters (about 48 percent) took the time to vote in the presidential contest between William Jefferson (Bill) Clinton (1993–2001) and Senator Robert Dole (R-KS). In 2016, the rate of participation improved to about 61 percent.[44] While that proportion was higher than in 1996, it was less than in 2008. Presidential elections are high-stimulus events (see Chapter 10) that generate more interest and voting than any other American election. In midterm congressional elections, which are low-stimulus elections, turnout is usually less than 40 percent. For primary elections during presidential nominations, turnout is even lower. In 2020, in the all-important New Hampshire presidential primary, turnout was 42 percent, an all-time high perhaps due to the high stimulus created by the closeness of the Democratic candidates in the polls

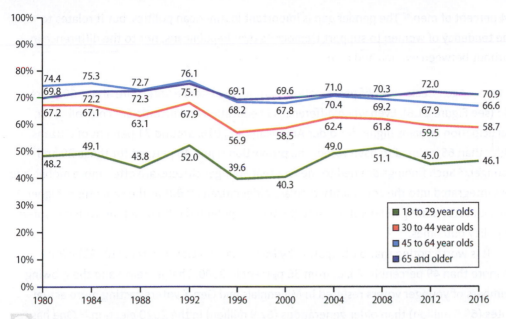

Figure 11.6 Turnout by Age in Presidential Elections

Young voters have turned out in greater numbers in the past three presidential elections, but their rate of turnout is still considerably lower than that of people over 30, decreasing the likelihood that government will be responsive to their interests.

Source: United States Census Bureau, "Voting in America: A Look at the 2016 Presidential Election," accessed May 10, 2017, https://www.census .gov/newsroom/blogs/random-samplings/2017/05/voting_in_america.html.

after the Iowa caucuses. Still, in other states, turnout remained low, rarely reaching 40 percent. Texas had a turnout of less than 25 percent, and Florida had only 19 percent.[45] However, many of the March primary contests took place at the beginnings of the widespread stay-at-home orders due to the COVID-19 pandemic, which may account for the significant drop in turnout. The 2020 primary election season was disrupted by the coronavirus pandemic when governors worked to limit social interactions among their states' residents (see Chapter 3). For local school board elections, the electorate is even smaller: Often fewer than 10 percent of eligible citizens vote in such contests. A general assessment of turnout in the United States is offered later in the chapter. Here, we turn to the demographics of turnout.

The Demographics of Turnout

Given the important power that voting brings in a democracy, the following becomes a central question: Who votes? Do various demographic groups vote in equal proportions? If not, what are the consequences for government responsiveness?

The data suggest that people who are most likely to vote tend to be better educated, better paid, and older than those who are unlikely to vote. There are some modest race, ethnicity, and gender differences, but when scholars control for differences in education and income, differences in race pretty much disappear.[46] The key lesson is that the driving force of participation is the development in young people of the kinds of skills and habits that prepare an individual for active citizenship.

Sex. Women turn out at a higher rate than men, by perhaps 3 to 5 percentage points. According to one estimate, 58 percent of women reported voting in 2016 compared to

54 percent of men.[47] The gender gap is important in American politics, but it relates to the tendency of women to support Democrats over Republicans, not to the difference in turnout between women and men.

Key Questions

What can you do to get young people in your community to vote? Why is it important?

Age.   Age affects rates of participation. Turnout peaks once voters are about 60 years old (see Figure 11.6). Even when differences in education and income are controlled for, participation remains higher for older Americans. In 2016, around 71 percent of citizens older than 65 claimed to have voted. The proportion is just 46 percent for those 29 and younger.[48] Such findings are tied to the fact that younger citizens are often more mobile and less integrated into the community than are older citizens.[49] But at the same time, higher turnout rates among older voters gives them more potential influence than younger voters in policy outcomes.

It is worth noting that participation by Millennial and Gen X voters (18–35) climbed to more than 49 percent in 2020, from 36 percent in 2000. That increase and the growing numbers of younger voters resulted in Millennials and Gen X voters casting more actual votes (69.6 million) than older generations (67.9 million) in the 2020 election.[50] One has to be cautious in making too much of these changes, but it does suggest that younger people can, under some conditions, become more active in politics. The general shift from the mid-1990s, where turnout was about 35 percent, to now being above 40 percent is in line with some of the early patterns of greater participation that have been found among the Millennials.

Race and Ethnicity.   Patterns of turnout vary by the race and ethnicity of voters. Figure 11.5 shows the turnout rates for four racial/ethnic groups. There is a clear increase in the turnout of African American voters, most notably since 1996, but with a noticeable drop since the high of 2008. Latinos and Asian Americans continue to lag behind whites and African Americans in their propensity to vote. It is also important to remember that once we take into account the education levels of all of these groups, the variation in turnout diminishes. For example, Latino and white voters who both hold college degrees have about the same likelihood of voting.

A closer look at a pattern regarding white voters is shown in Figure 11.7. Because of changing demographics in the U.S. population, the percentage of the total vote composed of white voters has declined dramatically from 1980 to 2020. This trend is significant because the two political parties' coalitions are, to some extent, composed of the different racial and ethnic groups. The Republican Party, for example, has found more support among white voters. In contrast, the Latino vote in 2016 reached 11 percent of the total vote, respectively, and Latinos supported and Hillary Clinton by substantial margins.[51] As the share of the white vote declines and the share of nonwhite voters rises, political parties will be forced to be more responsive to the needs of nonwhite voters.

Income.   The higher one's income, the more likely one is to vote. More income generally means that people believe they have more at stake and thus more reason to vote. Individuals with higher incomes are also likely to be in environments in which politics is frequently discussed and that provide greater opportunities for learning about the political process. Political knowledge is strongly correlated with the propensity to vote. Further, individuals with higher incomes are more likely to be able to arrange to vote than are those with low-paying jobs, who may be less able to take time off from work to go to the polls.

Data from the U.S. Census Bureau in Table 11.1 strongly confirm this relationship. In 2016, about 76 percent of people with total family incomes between $100,000 and $150,000 reported that they went to the polls. For people whose incomes fell in the range that represents the annual median family income in America—$40,000 to $50,000—turnout was 62 percent. For the least well off (those earning less than $15,000), 48 percent said they voted.

Education. Although race and ethnicity, sex, age, and income have some effects on the propensity of people to vote, the number of years of formal education seems to be the most important influence. Social science research has documented the connection between education and voting.[52] The youngest voting-eligible citizens (18- to 24-year-olds) who have college degrees have turnout rates 20 percentage points higher than the rates of older citizens (65–74) who do not have a high school education.[53] Table 11.2 shows the propensity to vote by educational level. The gap between people with the least education and those with the most is over 50 percentage points—a huge difference. Nearly three-fourths of college-educated people vote, whereas less than a quarter of those with just a grade-school education do so.

The relationship between education and voting may not be as simple as these data suggest, however. New evidence indicates that going to college does not matter as much as childhood socialization, which imbues the values of citizenship and similarly affects the

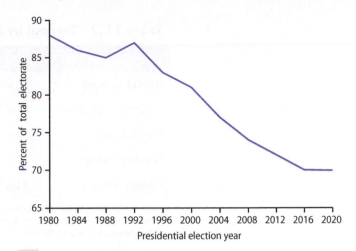

Figure 11.7 White Share of the Vote in Presidential Elections

Between 1980 and 2020, the percentage of voters in U.S. presidential elections who were white dropped from 88 percent to 69 percent. The way proposed policies affect African American, Latino, and Asian American voters will be an important factor in determining which candidates win future elections.

Source: Roper Center for Public Opinion Research, "How Groups Voted," Cornell University, http://ropercenter.cornell.edu/polls/us-elections/how-groups-voted/; https://ropercenter.cornell.edu/polls/us-elections/how-groups-voted/groups-voted-2016/. Pew Research Center, "What the 2020 electorate looks like by party, race and ethnicity, age, education and religion," https://www.pewresearch.org/fact-tank/2020/10/26/what-the-2020-electorate-looks-like-by-party-race-and-ethnicity-age-education-and-religion/.

Table 11.1 Turnout by Income in the 2016 Presidential Election

	Turnout
Less than $15,000	48%
$15,000–$19,999	49%
$20,000–$29,999	52%
$30,000–$39,999	59%
$40,000–$49,999	62%
$50,000–$74,999	68%
$75,000–$99,999	71%
$100,000–$150,000	76%
More than $150,000	80%

Source: U.S. Census Bureau, Voting and Registration in the Election of 2020, accessed May 1, 2018, https://www.census.gov/hhes/www/socdemo/voting/publications/p20/2012/tables.html; https://www.census.gov/data/tables/time-series/demo/voting-and-registration/p20-580.html.

Table 11.2 Turnout by Education in Recent Presidential Elections

Years of Education	1992	1996	2000	2004	2008	2012	2016
8 years or fewer	35%	30%	27%	24%	23%	22%	18%
Less than high school	41%	34%	34%	34%	27%	32%	29%
High school	58%	49%	49%	50%	50%	49%	47%
Less than college	69%	61%	60%	66%	65%	61%	61%
College or more	81%	73%	72%	74%	73%	72%	72%

Source: Harold Stanley and Richard Niemi, *Vital Statistics on American Politics* (Washington, D.C.: CQ Press, 2013) and Voting and Registration in the Election of November 2016, United States Census, https://www.census.gov/data/tables/time-series/demo /voting-and-registration/p20-580.html.

decision to attend college. It is not, therefore, spending four years in college that makes college graduates more likely to vote; rather, it is having been raised in an environment that stresses the importance of education that shapes willingness to vote.[54]

The gap in turnout between people who are more educated and those with little education has increased over the past forty or so years. The increase can be explained by expanded access to education. Individuals who lack a high-school education are at a much larger disadvantage than in the past. These patterns suggest that inequalities may result as government responds more effectively to those who vote than to those who do not.

Why Citizens Vote

LO 11-4 Articulate the main theoretical approaches that explain voting

With the right to vote guaranteed and widely available, why do some people choose not to vote? Perhaps we can start to answer that question by reversing it—that is, by looking at why people *do* vote. Political scientists have developed three approaches to explain why eligible voters choose to cast ballots. One model draws from the field of economics, the second draws from psychology, and the third focuses on the rules and context of the election. In this section, we present these explanations as well as some new ideas about the relationship of genetics and voting. Last, we briefly discuss the impact of weather on voting.

Economic Model of Voting

self-interest: *Concern for one's own advantage and well-being.*

The economic model of voting starts with the assumption that all choices involve calculations about **self-interest** that balance costs and benefits. In choosing a college, students consider the price of tuition, the location of the school and its reputation, the quality of the education, and the potential social life. The decision to vote is no different. According to the economic model, citizens consider the costs and benefits of voting; when the benefits exceed the costs, they turn out to vote. So, according to this model, if voting becomes less costly to all citizens, there should be an increase in participation. If it becomes more costly, fewer people will turn out. Under this model, voters act in a rational, self-interested fashion.

However, economic voting is not straightforward. In *An Economic Theory of Democracy* (1957), Anthony Downs describes **rational voting** as a puzzle. He points out that there are some costs tied to voting, such as the time it takes to become informed, to register to vote, and to go to the polls.[55] Costs could also involve lost work time and the cost of gas to drive to the local polling place. These costs are not huge, but they are real.

The benefits of voting are less clear. If benefits are defined in a narrow, self-interested fashion, there are no tangible benefits to be had from voting. A voter may favor a candidate (or party) because of a specific policy, such as the promise of a tax cut that would provide a big financial benefit. But a tax cut is a public good that is shared by all in society, including those who do not vote. In addition, and perhaps most important, the chance that one vote will alter the outcome of the election is very small—so small, in fact, that there is a greater chance of being killed in an accident on the way to the polls than of changing the outcome of the election. Even in the razor-thin contest in Florida in the 2000 presidential election, the margin was 537 votes.[56] One vote did not make the difference. Thus, given that there are some financial costs to voting, why should a self-interested person participate?

In short, the conclusion of the economic model is that voting is not in one's self-interest and in fact is irrational. If the decision to vote is driven by a self-interested assessment of costs and benefits, people should not take the time to vote. That is a troubling conclusion for the workings of democratic government. Obviously, if citizens do not bother to vote, government cannot be responsive, and public officials will not be held accountable.

Downs understood the troubling implications of his model and claimed that people voted because they knew that the system would collapse if no one voted. To save the system from collapse, it was rational to vote. This observation has appeal at first glance, but the logic is flawed: One vote will not save the system from collapsing. So even if the system is about to crumble, it remains rational to abstain from voting.

The prediction from Downs's model has drawn much attention from scholars. William Riker and Peter Ordeshook sought to save the model by introducing the idea of **civic duty** as a benefit of voting. The notion of civic duty is important, but the argument describes a psychological attitude voters might have.[57] Thus Riker and Ordeshook's argument does not solve the problem in Downs's model.[58] Narrow self-interest does not explain why people vote. As a consequence, political scientists tend to view voting as more of a psychological process than as a narrow economic or self-interested process.

Psychological Model of Voting

The psychological model views participation in elections as a product of citizens' attitudes about the political system. These attitudes are often a product of socialization and early political experiences. People who are raised in households in which voting is important are likely to think that participation matters. Those who have a strong sense of trust in government or believe that their votes matter are more likely to participate. The focus here is on what we called **civic interest** in Chapter 1, Gateways to American Democracy.

Riker and Ordeshook's concept of civic duty fits well in this psychological model of voting. Many people who vote recognize that being a citizen in a democracy carries the obligation to vote. In 2018, for example, 91 percent of the public believed that "it is very or somewhat important to vote in elections in order to be a good citizen."[59] The act of voting

rational voting: *Economic model of voting wherein citizens weigh the benefits of voting against the costs in order to take the most personally beneficial course of action.*

Key Questions

Should the government adopt laws that advance the Jeffersonian or Hamiltonian approach to participation? What would these laws look like?

Key Questions

Do you feel like you have a civic duty to vote? If so, where did you get that sense of duty?

civic duty: *Social force that binds a person to actively participate in public and political life.*

civic interest: *Concern for the well-being of society and the nation as a whole.*

makes citizens feel good and feel that they are part of the political system. Surveys have found a strong correlation between civic-mindedness and the propensity to vote. In fact, there is often guilt associated with not voting, so much so that people tend to over-report the frequency with which they go to the polls.[60]

Another psychological component tied to the act of voting is partisanship. Citizens who align themselves with the Democratic Party or the Republican Party are more likely to vote. Being a partisan implies an engagement in politics, and partisans see importance in the outcomes of elections. Partisanship increases the prospects that an individual will vote.

Both civic duty and partisanship are attitudes formed in childhood. One survey found that a person's attitude about citizenship expressed in 1965 was a powerful predictor of his or her voting in the 1980 presidential election.[61] The relationship between socialization and voting holds even after education and other important variables that drive participation are taken into account. In addition, parents' electoral activism in 1965 also explains their children's willingness to vote in 1980. Much has changed since 1980, but socialization continues to have a long and powerful reach.

It is also clear that citizens who express greater trust in government are more willing to participate. In addition, people who think they have a voice in government are more likely to vote. Political scientists call this attitude **efficacy**—the belief that one's involvement influences the course of government.

efficacy: *Extent to which people believe their actions can affect public affairs and the actions of government.*

institutional model: *Model of voting that focuses on the context of the election, including whether it is close and whether the rules encourage or discourage participation.*

Key Questions

Have you participated in or been contacted by a get-out-the-vote program? How did it affect you?

Institutional Model of Voting

A third explanation of voting looks at political context. In the **institutional model**, voting is understood to be shaped by the rules of the system, by political party behavior, by the ways candidates run their campaigns, and by the context of the election.[62] This model does not ignore individuals' personal resources or psychological attitudes; it simply points out that the political environment is a factor that shapes participation.

It is clear, for example, that the popularity and appeal of the candidates affect turnout.[63] Contenders who are viewed as unexciting, even boring, offer voters few reasons to participate. But both very popular and very unpopular candidates might spur turnout. A highly controversial candidate might lead people who are strongly opposed to show up in great numbers on Election Day. A highly popular candidate likewise brings out supporters.

The competitiveness of an election also influences motivation. Elections that look to be close draw voters' interest and attention, especially if they think their votes might influence the outcome. A close race is exciting, and people like to be part of it. But elections often are not competitive, lessening citizens' incentive to make time to cast their ballots.

Because voting takes time, the efforts by parties, interest groups, and civic organizations to bring people to the polls can make a difference. Get-out-the-vote drives seem to pay big dividends, especially at the local level. For example, direct personal contact, such as going door to door, may increase the rate of voting by 7 to 10 percentage points in local elections.[64] Even text messaging seems to increase turnout by about 3 percentage points, according to a recent study.[65] The size of these effects is not likely to apply to presidential elections because many people are already inclined to vote in these high-stimulus elections. Parties, too, can increase turnout by mobilizing their base to participate.[66] Canvassing by telephone or in person not only may lower information costs but also may activate citizens' sense of civic duty. In some cases, parties or other organizations pick up people and bring them to the polls, lowering the costs of voting. College students are encouraged through social media to register and vote—through organizations such as Campus Vote Project whose website is shown in Image 11.4—as well as find information about why their participation can make a difference.

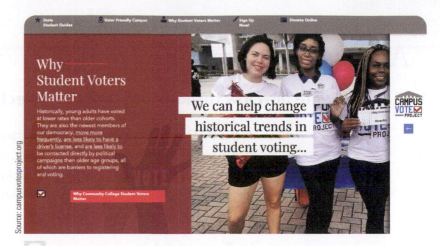

Image 11.4 Campaigns try many methods to encourage younger citizens to participate. College students are encouraged to register and vote by organizations such as Campus Vote Project, whose website is pictured here.

Source: campusvotesproject.org

Is Voting in Your Genes?

It makes sense that voting is a product of psychological forces or perhaps of the costs and benefit of participating. But might the choice to be active in politics have a deeper cause? Might it be in your genes? More than two thousand years ago, Aristotle contended that "man is by nature a political animal." Political scientists have tended to believe that citizens are "blank slates," nurtured by socialization, education, and environment. Recent evidence, however, has suggested a genetic component to participation. James Fowler and his colleagues found a strong relationship between genes and turnout.[67] Another study reported "that two extensively studied genes are significant predictors of voter turnout."[68] These data are important because they suggest that scholars may need to move beyond looking at the nurture side of the equation and start to consider the role nature plays in shaping individuals politically. Even so, much more evidence is needed before a genetic model of participation is accepted. In fact, a recent study called into question this relationship between genes and voting.[69] Nevertheless, the idea is intriguing and worth considering as an alternative way of thinking about voting.

Weather

There has been a long-standing view that weather affects why some people vote and others do not. With bad weather, potential voters may ask: Why bother voting? Is it worth dealing with the unpleasant weather? People who would have to travel through an ice storm in Oklahoma may have less incentive to turn out than those in Arizona on a day with sunny skies and pleasant temperatures.

The impact of weather has produced much speculation. People deal with varying weather conditions all the time, and perhaps bad weather has little effect on them. Political scientists have undertaken a comprehensive examination of this question using data "from over 22,000 weather stations to provide election day estimates of rain and snow for each U.S. County." The results are clear: Rain significantly reduces voter participation by a rate of just less than 1 percent per inch, and an inch of snowfall decreases turnout by almost 0.5 percent. These scholars go on to show that bad weather benefits Republicans slightly by discouraging less-well-off voters from participating, giving weather a potential partisan bias. However, some recent scholarship shows that, in general, weather negatively affects turnout, but has no effect in competitive elections.[70]

Assessing Turnout

LO 11-5 Evaluate how low turnout is in American elections

As this chapter has established, most Americans do not vote in most elections. Even in presidential elections, for which turnout is highest, only slightly more than half of eligible voters go to the polls. In this section, we assess turnout in the United States. Is it too low for responsive and responsible government? Even more important, does turnout increase the prospects of governmental action that ensures equality?

Is Turnout Low?

There is a widespread belief among political scientists, political observers, and journalists that turnout in American elections is low. Consider the titles of the following books on the topic of voting in the United States: *Why Americans Still Don't Vote, Where Have All the Voters Gone?*, and *The Vanishing Voter*.[71] When just 37 percent of the American public took the time to vote in the 2014 congressional elections, the concern about low turnout expressed in these books seems justified. The 2018 midterm elections gave some reason to believe the trend was reversing with turnout reaching a new high of 50 percent voter turnout.[72] With all the attention and interest surrounding the 2020 presidential elections, turnout of the voting-age population was about 61 percent.[73] Such data strike many as disappointing. But further investigation of turnout can offer a different way to interpret the situation.

The United States Compared to Other Democracies. Compared to other democracies, turnout in the United States is low. Between 1948 and 2020, the average rate of turnout in U.S. presidential elections was about 58 percent,[74] while in other democracies it was 90 percent or more. These numbers compel an assessment of why U.S. turnout is so low.

One reason has to do with the rules for voting. Australia has **compulsory voting**—citizens are required by law to vote. Those who do not vote must pay a $20 fine, and the fine increases to $50 if the nonvoter does not answer the Australian Election Commission's inquiry about why he or she did not vote. New Zealand requires all citizens to register to vote. In most of the countries of Western Europe, the government is responsible for registering citizens to vote. In the United States, by contrast, both voting and registering are voluntary, and only about 70 percent of the public is registered. That means that nearly one-third of potentially eligible voters cannot cast votes on Election Day even if they want to do so.

Another reason has to do with the convenience of voting. Most European countries lessen the costs of voting by allowing it to take place on Sunday. In the United States, voting takes place on Tuesday, a workday for most people. Federal law stipulates that the first Tuesday after the first Monday in November is the day on which voting for president and members of Congress will take place, and most states have also selected Tuesdays as the day for voting in primaries and in state and local elections. The costs of voting are increased because people may be at work and may have difficulty finding the time to vote. With more costs to voting, turnout is lower in the United States than in many European democracies. This discussion highlights the importance of considering the context of each election, which is the theoretical focus of the institutional model of voting.

Key Questions

What does it mean for democracy when only 37 percent of Americans vote in midterm elections?

compulsory voting:
Practice that requires citizens to vote in elections or face punitive measures such as community service, fines, or imprisonment.

Key Questions

Should the United States adopt compulsory voting?

Key Questions

Should the United States vote on Saturday or Sunday instead of a weekday? What effect do you think this might have?

According to one estimate, turnout in the United States would be 27 percentage points higher (or more than 80 percent) if the nation had laws and rules that foster voting.[75] At the least, this figure suggests that comparisons of turnout in various democracies require a careful accounting of the rules and institutions that shape the willingness of citizens to go to the polls. (See the discussion of same-day voter registration on page 411 of this chapter.)

Trends in Turnout.   A second way turnout in American elections looks problematic is the trend over the past fifty years. One of the lines in Figure 11.8 represents the percentage of turnout in presidential elections measured against the **voting-age population (VAP)**, an estimate of those old enough to vote. In the United States, all persons 18 or older constitute the VAP. The graph shows a lot of change—a decline in the 1970s, a surge in 2004 and 2008, a drop-off in 2012 and another increase in 2016. In the 2020 election, though, despite the COVID-19 pandemic, Americans voted early, by mail, and in person to set record highs in voter turnout over the last century. This pattern is much the same for midterm elections. In 1962, turnout for congressional elections was 48 percent. It fell to a low of 38 percent in 1986, with a slight rebound to about 41 percent in 2010. But regardless of how you want to interpret these shifts, one thing is clear: Turnout today is volatile and subject to changes in political candidates and situations. Still, overall, voter turnout in the United States lags behind other democracies.

This pattern becomes more worrisome in light of rising levels of education since 1960, as education is one of the strongest predictors of turnout. Even though education levels have increased over the past fifty years (see Table 11.2), the rate of participation in elections has not increased.

voting-age population (VAP): *Used to calculate the rate of participation by dividing the number of voters by the number of people in the country who are 18 and over.*

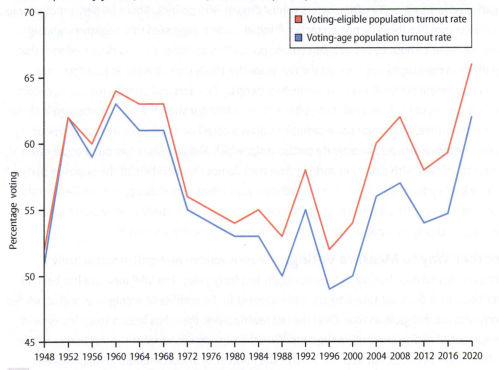

Figure 11.8 Presidential Turnout Rates

The VAP measure is the traditional approach to assessing turnout, dividing the number of voters by the voting-age population. The VEP seeks to correct for overcounting in the voting-age population by removing noncitizens and people in jail who are not eligible to vote. Until 1972, this correction made only a modest difference. But given the surge of immigration and the growth in the number of convicted felons since then, the VEP measure is more accurate. Turnout in the 2004 and 2008 elections was actually comparable to turnout in the 1950s and 1960s, but turnout dropped in 2012. Turnout increased in 2016 but set new records in 2020 despite the COVID-19 pandemic.

Source: "Presidential Turnout Rates, 1948–2016," United States Elections Project, accessed February 17, 2018, http://www.electproject.org/2016g.

These kinds of data have led political scientists to study why fewer Americans seem to be voting.[76] Explanations have varied. One explanation looks at the difference between those who enter the electorate and those who leave. The concept of **generational replacement** describes a trend in which older voters who pass away are replaced in the electorate by less reliable young voters.[77] It is difficult, however, to sort out generational differences from changes in self-interest. That is, do older voters turn out to vote because of the generation they were part of, because they are older and have more experience in dealing with politics, or because they want to protect their interests or expand the benefits that directly affect them, such as Medicare and low payments for prescription drugs?

A second explanation has been the decline of party organizations.[78] Local parties have been less able to turn out the vote on Election Day than they were in the late nineteenth and early twentieth centuries, and therefore the voting rate has declined. Some scholars have estimated that half of the decline in turnout can be attributed to the drop in mobilization efforts.[79] This explanation has appeal, but parties in many ways are stronger today than they were in the past, although the days of big-city bosses and urban political machines are gone (see Chapter 9). Obama and the Democratic Party were successful in turning out the vote in 2012, especially in key states such as Ohio, and citizens are voting along party lines more than any time since scientific surveys began in the 1950s. So a decline in party strength (perceived or real) is not an adequate explanation for low turnout.

A third explanation for declining turnout is the increasingly harsh tone of political campaigns. Some argue that negative campaigns have fueled voter apathy. It is clear that negative advertising on TV often fosters voters' disgust with politics. About 80 percent of people say they do not like these campaign tactics.[80] Initial studies suggested that negative campaigns could decrease turnout by about 5 percentage points.[81] In addition, there is clear evidence that negativity in campaigns has been on the rise since the 1960s (see Chapter 10), so there has been an apparent correlation between the two trends.[82] Scholars and pundits rushed to endorse this hypothesis, but subsequent studies have called it into question.[83] A harsh campaign is likely to be competitive, and competitive campaigns draw interest and therefore increase turnout. Further, negative attacks can activate partisanship, which also increases turnout. People often choose to affiliate with a party in part because they do not like members of the opposite party. An attack ad by the Republicans can remind their supporters why they oppose the Democrats, giving them more reason to participate. A recent comprehensive study of all research on this topic shows clearly that negativity is not responsible for lowering turnout.[84]

Another Way to Measure Voting.   There is another explanation that actually contends that turnout has *not* declined over the last forty years: The VAP measure has been in error because it does not take into account increases in the number of immigrants and convicted felons who are ineligible to vote. Over the last few decades, there has been a steep increase in the number of undocumented immigrants. With the sagging economy of the last few years, the numbers have declined, but even so, in 2017 the number of undocumented immigrants was estimated to be about 10.5 million (or about 3.2 percent of the population).[85] Though there have been some recent declines, there are still over to 700,000 people in prison in the United States.[86]

A new measure called the **voting-eligible population (VEP)** corrects for these trends. The top line in Figure 11.8 presents the VEP estimates for turnout. It indicates that aggregate turnout in the 2008 presidential election was actually about 62 percent. By this measure, turnout has not declined over the last thirty years. In fact, turnout is now a full 14 percentage points higher than in the presidential election of 1948, when it was 52 percent. These revised estimates put a new spin on what has been perceived as a problem with U.S. elections, suggesting that Americans are not less willing to vote than in the past or than citizens in other democracies.[87]

In 2016, the Supreme Court rejected a challenge to Texas's voting law that would have required states to apportion districts based on VEPs. The Supreme Court unanimously declared that state legislatures may include all residents in determining legislative districts (including children, felons, whether incarcerated or free, and noncitizens) and not just residents who are eligible to vote.[88]

Do Turnout Rates Create Inequality?

Voting is a hallmark of democratic politics and is certainly a cherished American value. The idea is simple. Each person has one vote, and each vote should be equal. The fact that those who are better educated or better off participate at a greater rate is a potential source of concern (see Tables 11.1 and 11.2). That the wealthy are more likely to vote than the poor is an especially troubling trend because the income gap between the rich and the poor is increasing.[89] As the rich become richer, they become better able to contribute more money to parties and candidates.[90] Such donations only further advance their potential influence.

That individuals with more resources participate more is not a new idea. Its implications have fueled much speculation but were supported by little evidence until Larry Bartels provided a systematic account of the impact of these differences. Focusing on the behavior of U.S. senators, Bartels shows that they respond more to the rich, less to people of middle income, and not at all to the poor.[91] Others have gone even further, showing that rich Americans have much more influence on public policy than those less well off.[92] It makes sense that politicians respond to people who participate and do not respond to those who do not. That is why it is so important for people to get involved in politics and also why the increasing rate of participation in the past decade or so is such good news.

Key Questions

Do Americans have equality in voting? Explain.

Voting Laws and Regulations

LO 11-6 Analyze how changes in voting laws have affected participation rates

The rules surrounding voting affect participation rates. Voting policies are made at both the federal and state levels. State governments continue to manage most voting laws and procedures, although the federal government steps in to prevent discrimination at the polls. The federal government is committed to increasing participation by making voting as easy as possible. At the same time, both state and federal governments work to prevent voter fraud, as we saw when we examined voter ID laws. Thus, voting policies have the effect of both expanding and potentially contracting turnout. This section reviews policies that have altered the way voting works in the United States.

Reforms to Voting Laws in the 1890s

Rules matter, as the institutional model of voting suggests. Any change in the laws governing voting (or any process related to voting) will alter how that process works. A classic example of the power of rules can be found in the late nineteenth century, when the Progressives called for a series of reforms to the voting process to end corrupt practices. The reforms affected who was eligible to vote and the way people actually voted. In other words, they altered who participated in elections.

Corrupt voting practices needed to end. Big-city political machines routinely "stuffed" the ballot box,[93] and party members manipulated the results to ensure victory. (See Chapter 9, pages 319–320 for a full description of party machine politics.) Party members often rounded up people and brought them, in sequence, to various polling precincts around the city, making sure they voted in each one. Someone who had died would remain on the rolls, and the party machine would "allow" that person to vote. This corrupt practice has been referred to as **graveyard voting**.[94]

graveyard voting: *Corrupt practice of using a dead person's name to cast a ballot in an election.*

In response to these excesses, Progressives called for voter registration.[95] The idea was that voters would have to preregister with a government official to be placed on an official list of voters. The list would be updated when someone died, and it would be used at the polls on Election Day to ensure that a potential voter had the right to vote and had not already voted. This reform spread rapidly. Today, all states except North Dakota require voter registration. The specific rules of registration vary a great deal among the states. For example, in only eleven states can a person register and vote on Election Day.[96] All other states require earlier registration.

Key Questions

If you are a registered voter, what was your experience with registration? Was it a gate or a gateway?

Voter registration laws prevented outright fraud at the polls. An additional consequence was that they prevented immigrants from voting. Party machines had benefited greatly from the support of immigrants in city elections, and many of the newcomers to America who came in great numbers in the late nineteenth and early twentieth centuries were among those whom parties encouraged to vote multiple times. Some states, such as Wisconsin, allowed white immigrants to vote, providing they declared their intention to become citizens.[97] But the new registration laws made voting a two-step process, requiring potential voters to document, before the election, that they met the conditions for voting. Voter registration added a new gate to the system. While it reduced fraud, decreased the strength of the party machines, and pleased Americans who were worried about the impact of immigrants, it caused an overall decline in turnout. In 1888, turnout in presidential elections stood at 81 percent. By 1912, it had fallen to 59 percent. It is surely true that the 81 percent turnout was inflated due to corrupt voting practices, but the introduction of voter registration had negative effects on participation as well.[98]

Key Questions

How can the government prevent fraud and still encourage citizens to vote?

An important change in voting rules was the adoption in 1888 of the Australian ballot, also known as the secret ballot (see Figure 9.3, Ballot Reform, in Chapter 9). Those who operated the polling precincts would know how voters planned to vote by observing which party strip they requested. The introduction of the secret ballot meant that voters faced less intimidation, but voting also became more complicated. Voters now could choose candidates for each office separately; they no longer had automatic access to party-line voting as they did with the strip ballot. With a more complicated process, once again turnout declined. Despite decreasing turnout, the secret ballot has become a cornerstone of American democracy.

The National Voter Registration Act

In 1993, Congress sought to streamline voter registration procedures so that more Americans would exercise their right to vote, at least in federal elections. The National

Voter Registration Act, commonly known as the "Motor Voter" law, requires states to allow citizens to register to vote at the same time they apply for or renew their driver's licenses. This law also requires states to inform citizens who are removed from the approved voter rolls and limits removal to a change of address, conviction for a felony, and, of course, death. These requirements were in response to charges that local governments, controlled by political parties, improperly removed voters from the voter rolls without their knowledge; under the guise of updating voter registration lists, officials of one party were disqualifying voters who would tend to vote for the other party's candidates. The 1993 law imposes criminal penalties on anyone who tries to coerce or intimidate voters on their way to the polling place or tries to prevent registered voters from casting their ballots.[99]

The Help America Vote Act

In 2002, the Help American Vote Act (HAVA) was passed by Congress and signed by President George W. Bush. The impetus for the law was the 2000 presidential election which, in addition to being one in which the winner (George Bush) won the electoral vote but lost the popular vote (to Al Gore), saw many ballots disqualified due to irregularities in voting procedures. This law was designed to provide federal guidelines and minimum standards of voting procedures as well as resources to the states. These included the creation of the Election Assistance Commission (EAC) and funding for states to update their voting systems. Among other provisions, the law authorizes the EAC to certify voting software and hardware, serve as a clearinghouse of election information, and provide standards for provisional voting. The law also required states to maintain statewide voter registration databases.[100]

Key Questions

Should the government take steps to increase voting? Why?

New Forms of Voting

As indicated earlier, some states are experimenting with laws that make voting easier. Some have instituted early voting, allowing voters to cast ballots before the Tuesday on which a general election is held. This flexibility helps working people, who might find it hard to find time to vote on a Tuesday. It also provides more than a single day for voting, so that schedule conflicts (such as a dental appointment or a sick child) do not interfere. In Texas, for example, citizens can vote any time between seventeen and four days before election day, "to make the voting process more convenient and accessible"[101] Other states, such as Oregon, have started to make use of a **vote-by-mail (VBM) system**. Voters get ballots in the mail two weeks before the election, giving them a chance to research the candidates and cast their ballots. They can make their choices at home and avoid the often long lines at the polling booth. This innovation, proponents argue, lowers the cost of voting, and there is some evidence it has increased participation. Oregon has had a very high rate of voting, reaching a high of about 70 percent in 2008 to about 68 percent in 2016 and 61 percent in the 2018 midterm election.[102] California has had less success with voting by mail. Some now worry that, under the rules of VBM systems, less-educated people are less likely to vote.[103]

vote-by-mail (VBM) system: *Method of voting in an election whereby ballots are distributed to voters by mail, and voters complete and return the ballots by mail.*

Over the past three decades, nearly two-thirds of states passed "early voting" provisions that allow citizens to cast ballots prior to election day (see Figure 11.9).[104]

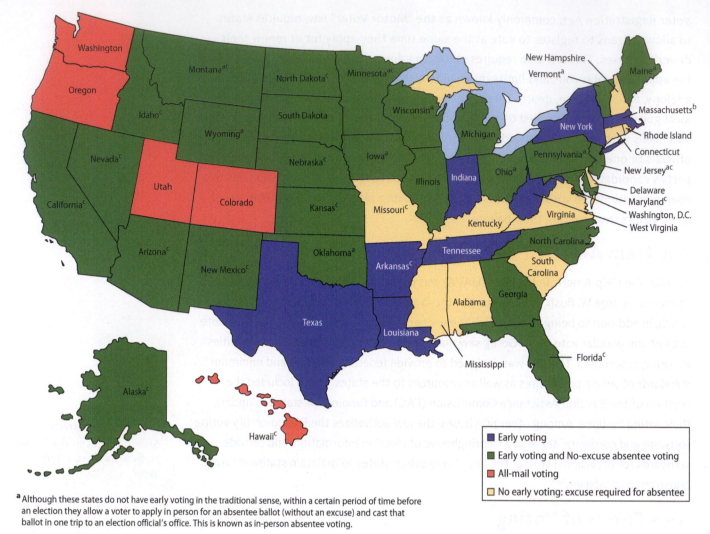

Early voting

Early voting and No-excuse absentee voting

All-mail voting

No early voting: excuse required for absentee

^a Although these states do not have early voting in the traditional sense, within a certain period of time before an election they allow a voter to apply in person for an absentee ballot (without an excuse) and cast that ballot in one trip to an election official's office. This is known as in-person absentee voting.

^b Massachusetts has early voting only during even-year November elections, beginning in 2016. It does not permit early voting in primaries or municipal elections.

^c Certain elections may be held entirely by mail. The circumstances under which all-mail elections are permitted vary from state to state.

Figure 11.9 Absentee and Early Voting by State

States determine most of the rules about forms of voting. This map shows which states have embraced new forms of voting such as early voting, no-excuse absentee voting, and vote by mail—all of which are designed to ease the voting process.

© Cengage 2018 *Source:* National Conference of State Legislatures, Absentee and Early Voting, accessed April 10, 2020, https://www.ncsl.org/research/elections-and-campaigns/absentee-and-early-voting.aspx.

The idea was that limiting participation to a single day kept many people from participating. The idea seemed sensible, and a lot of states followed suit. Although there is little evidence that early voting increases turnout, the provisions clearly lower the costs of voting.[105] Recently, however, some states have begun to reverse those laws and reduce the availability of early voting, and enacted new strict photo identification requirements.[106] Opponents say these new laws increase the cost of voting, making it more difficult for some citizens to vote. Others say the laws are necessary to protect the integrity of the ballot box.

The COVID-19 pandemic brought the method of vote-by-mail to the nation's attention. In the spring of 2020, in the midst of primary election postponements and social distancing requirements, some called for changes to the November general election process to allow for widespread use of VBM to avoid the spread of COVID-19 and allay voters' fears of contracting the virus. Over 35 states made some modifications to their rules for vote by mail for the November 2020 election. Changes ranged from ballots automatically mailed to voters (California, Nevada, and Montana for example), to extending deadlines for receipt of mail-in ballots (Minnesota, New York, and North Carolina). The issue took on a partisan flavor with President Trump and many Republicans resisting the adoption of VBM due to vote fraud concerns. Democrats, on the other hand, viewed VBM as a way to prevent low voter turnout and provide an alternative way to exercise the franchise. Other observers claimed that VBM did not result in widespread fraud nor provide an advantage to either political party.[107]

Key Questions

What are the risks and benefits of early voting? Of voting by mail?

Though not a new form of voting, some states have changed the registration process for voters. All voters, except those in North Dakota, which does not require voters to register, must register to vote in order to receive a ballot. States determine the length of time prior to an election in which voters in must register. Heading into the 2020 election, twenty-one states adopted **same-day voter registration**. This practice allows voters to register and cast a vote on the same day. Six of those states—Maine (79 percent), Minnesota (79 percent), Iowa (78 percent), Colorado (77 percent), New Hampshire (76 percent), and Wisconsin (76 percent)—use same-day voter registration. In contrast, states with the lowest voter turnout required registration up to four weeks prior to the election.[108]

Same-day voter registration: *Practice allows voters to register and cast a vote on the same day.*

Nevertheless, new technologies could make it easier for some people to vote (elderly and disabled people, for example), thus increasing turnout. However, opponents of using these technologies argue that they would be too susceptible to voter fraud for two reasons. First, there would be no way to identify the person who is casting the vote, unless citizens are given individual PIN codes or use their Social Security numbers. Given the number of internet security breaches, opponents argue that such a system would not guard personal privacy. Second, votes at polling places are counted by election officials, but internet and cell phone voting data would likely be collected and counted by computer servers, which are vulnerable to hacking and other security breaches.

Key Questions

Aside from voting, how have you participated in politics and civic life?

In evaluating the effects of voting by new technologies, the beneficial effects on community and civic life of having everyone vote on a single day should also be considered. The act of standing in line and talking with fellow voters, or discussing the act of voting with friends and family at the end of the day, can reinforce the sense of political efficacy and provide a foundation for the democratic process. Voting by mail, cell phone, or Twitter may detract from this shared experience, and that cost must be weighed against the added benefits of increased voter participation.

Participation Beyond Voting

LO 11-7 Describe other important forms of participation

Voting is by far the most common form of participation, but in a democracy, citizens have opportunities to express their views in other ways. In fact, voting is a very constrained form of participation: Voters select one person from a limited set of candidates. There is no way to tell from a single vote whether the citizen agrees or disagrees with the candidate on the key issues of the day. But the American political system gives individuals the opportunity to express their preferences and the intensity of those preferences in other ways. Although far fewer Americans join political campaigns or protest movements, both are important gateways for the expression of political views.

Involvement in Political Campaigns

Campaigns give citizens a chance to talk about politics, volunteer, promote issues they care about, and make financial donations to candidates and causes. The weeks leading up to an election allow candidates and interest groups to connect with the public. The campaign is an important gateway that allows the public to influence politics and politicians to influence the public.

As a result, political scientists try to understand the motivations for people's involvement in campaigns and the nature of their involvement. Do Americans try to influence other citizens? According to a survey done in 2014, about 70 percent of Americans indicate that they discuss politics at least a few times a month.[109] Table 11.3 reports that 28 percent of Americans claimed in 1996 that they tried to influence others to vote a certain way. This was the lowest rate over the last seven presidential elections and probably reflects the fact that few doubted that President Bill Clinton would beat the Republican nominee, Bob Dole. In 2008, 45 percent of Americans said they tried to influence others' votes, a greater than 50 percent jump from 1996. The 2008 contest between Democrat Barack Obama and Republican John McCain captured the public's interest. Four years later, the numbers declined

Table 11.3 Nonvoting Measures of Political Participation

Year	Tried to Influence Others' Votes	Attended a Political Meeting	Worked for a Party or a Candidate	Wore a Button or Displayed a Bumper Sticker	Gave Money to a Campaign
1980	36%	8%	4%	7%	8%
1984	32%	8%	4%	9%	8%
1988	29%	7%	3%	9%	9%
1992	37%	8%	3%	11%	7%
1996	28%	5%	2%	10%	8%
2000	34%	5%	3%	10%	9%
2004	48%	7%	3%	21%	13%
2008	45%	9%	4%	18%	14%
2012	37%	5%	3%	14%	10%
2016	49%	7%	3%	13%	11%

Source: American National Election Studies, ANES 1948–2016, accessed May 1, 2018, https://electionstudies.org/data-center/anes-time-series-cumulative-data-file/.

to 37 percent, which is much more typical for presidential elections. However, the 2016 election between Hillary Clinton and Donald Trump saw the highest rate yet, with 49 percent of people reporting that they tried to influence someone's vote.

By contrast, as shown in Table 11.3, the proportion of people who work in a campaign has been small and very stable over the past three decades, hovering around 3 percent. A little more than one in twenty Americans attended a political meeting during the course of the 2016 campaign. Willingness to give money to a campaign was higher, hitting 11 percent in 2016.

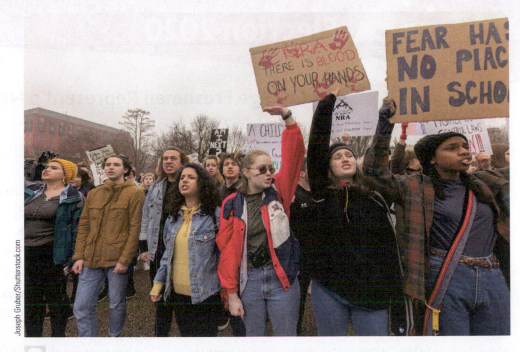

Image 11.5 High school students protest gun violence after shootings in Marjory Stoneman Douglas High School in Parkland, Florida, in 2018.

This evidence about political participation suggests that Americans do get involved in elections in a number of different ways. If active citizens are defined as individuals who vote and engage in at least one of the activities reported in Table 11.3, about 40 percent have met the standard over this twenty-eight-year period. More than 15 percent of the public voted and engaged in two of the activities. One may want to debate whether these numbers are high or low, but regardless of interpretation, Americans do more than just vote come election time.

Key Questions
Have you ever contributed time or money to a political campaign? Why or why not?

Protest Politics

Political protests are an important means of expressing opinions and bringing about change. The Boston Tea Party, in which protesters dumped tea into Boston Harbor rather than support the British government-backed monopoly, is perhaps the first and most famous American protest. This protest was not about taxes, but rather about the fact that the British were undermining local merchants. Throughout American history, abolitionists seeking an end to slavery, women seeking the vote, working people seeking the right to strike and organize unions, civil rights activists calling for an end to segregation and discrimination, antiwar activists seeking to end the wars in Vietnam and Iraq, and many others have called attention to their causes though marches, street demonstrations, petitions, and advertising campaigns.

Key Questions
Why is the right to protest important for democracy?

Do College Freshmen Represent a New Protest Generation?

Though voting is the most common form of political participation, there are other forms beyond voting in which some Americans also choose to engage. Ta-Nehisi Coates, for example, participates through his books and other writings. Table 11.3 shows the rate of participation in a variety of forms of participation beyond voting. Protest politics is, as the text indicates, also an important, and nontraditional, means of political expression with a long history in the United States, dating back at least to the original Tea Party protest of 1773.

At various times in history, the American people chose to use this form of participation to raise awareness and demand change from policy makers. Martin Luther King Jr. encouraged the "March on Washington" in 1963, rallying more than 200,000 Americans to the nation's capital in the name of jobs, freedom, and civil rights. (See Chapter 5 for a description of King's famous "I Have a Dream" speech at that event.) Young Americans protested American involvement in the Vietnam War in the 1960s led, in part, by Students for a Democratic Society.[110] That generation of Americans was dubbed by some as a "protest generation."[111] What about your generation? How do you and your peers feel about protest behavior?

For the past fifty years, incoming college freshmen have been surveyed about a variety of topics ranging from financial concerns to political engagement. In fall 2018, close to 140,000 students were surveyed by the Higher Education Research Institute at UCLA. The 2018 Freshman Survey revealed that 11 percent of college freshmen expected to engage in student protest and demonstrations.[112] Compared to their fall 2015 freshman counterparts, that is an increase of 3 percent who believe

there was a "very good chance" they will participate in student protests and demonstrations and 6 percent higher than in 2014.[113] Though a relatively small increase, combining those figures with those who believe there is a "good chance" of protesting raises the percentage to over 30 percent. These responses represent the highest level recorded since the questions were first asked of freshmen in 1967.

Are today's college students poised to be the new protest generation? There are already signs that college students are willing to raise their voices in campus demonstrations. As the student protest at the University of Missouri in September 2015 showed, students are responding positively to calls from fellow students to take action to protest what they see as disturbing incidents of racial intolerance.[114] Students at the Columbia, Missouri, campus claimed that university officials were not doing enough to stop incidents of racism on campus. Other students joined the protests, including the football team, supported by their coach. Their protests led to the resignation of the president of the university. Some protesters indicated that they have been inspired by other demonstrations, including the Black Lives Matter movement.[115]

There are signs of increased political engagement by younger voters. Senator Bernie Sanders' presidential nomination campaign, for example, engaged many younger voters. As the text notes, younger voters have tended to be less engaged politically than older Americans. Perhaps the newest generation of college students will be distinguished by their increased propensity to engage in politics.

Protest movements do not always result in electoral shifts and the creation of major party factions within political parties. Protests may also occur as a result of critical events. For example, in the aftermath of the mass shooting at Marjory Stoneman Douglas High School in Parkland, Florida, on February 14, 2018, many high school students in Parkland organized protests against gun violence. Students staged walkouts from classes and held rallies to gather support for new measures that would curtail the use of assault weapons. The efforts that began among high school students at Marjory Stoneman Douglas spurred similar walkouts and protests as far away as Arizona. The Never Again MSD movement was created by the students and called for a national "March for Our Lives" on March 24, 2018.[116]

Image 11.6 Sometimes incidents prompt concerned Americans to attend rallies and demonstrations. Here protesters hold a rally in Baltimore after charges were announced against the officers involved in the April 2015 arrest of Freddie Gray, a 25-year-old African American man who died due to injuries he sustained while being taken to the police station.

Protests can become so controversial and stir up such strong emotions that the government takes steps to limit them. Such action, one could argue, constrains First Amendment rights of speech and assembly (see Chapter 4, Civil Liberties). But do protesters have the right to undermine the freedoms of others? This is not an easy question to answer. The courts have weighed in on such debates, seeking to balance competing rights. One of the most controversial cases concerns the right of anti-abortion protesters to protest outside abortion clinics and in particular to try to convince women coming to the clinics for services to change their minds. For instance, in *Hill v. Colorado* (2000), the Supreme Court upheld the right of states to limit protests near sites that conduct abortions.[117] But in 2014, the Supreme Court's *McCullen v. Coakley* decision cut back on *Hill* by unanimously striking a Massachusetts law that had kept antiabortion protestors at least 35 feet from health facilities that perform abortions.[118] (See also *Snyder v. Phelps* (2011) discussion in Chapter 4.)

In general, very few Americans participate in protests. Overall, only about 10 percent of Americans claim to have ever participated in a protest.[119] However, the propensity of Americans to engage in nontraditional forms of political participation may be changing. The Occupy Movement that took place in 2011, the protests in Ferguson, Missouri, and the subsequent Black Lives Matter movement suggest a willingness to protest policies and practices Americans deem unfair. The death of George Floyd on May 25, 2020 in Minneapolis while in police custody spurred nationwide BLM protests. Thousands of people marched in protest in multiple cities across the United States calling for reform of police practices and an end to systemic racism. Recent student protests on the campuses of the University of Missouri, Harvard University, Princeton University, and other campuses suggest that younger Americans, in particular, may be poised to become more engaged in traditional and nontraditional forms of participation.[120]

Political Analytics

Discussing Politics

DISCUSSING POLITICS IS AN IMPORTANT political activity. In the classroom, college students are often encouraged to express their attitudes and beliefs as a means of exposing a variety of viewpoints for students to consider. In that situation, it is common for opposing views to be discussed and, perhaps, argued as part of a learning experience. Americans also discuss politics through social media outlets. It is estimated that over half of Americans often or sometimes receive their political news through social media and that Facebook is the site most used. Figure 11.10 shows how Americans view their social media experience when it comes to discussing politics with people with whom they disagree.

When given a choice between the experience of talking politics with someone whose views they do not share being "interesting and informative" or "stressful and frustrating," majorities of social media users opt for the latter. In both 2016 and 2019, nearly two-thirds of respondents reported the negative effects of online interactions. In 2019, less than a third of people reported the experience as positive.

Social media users were also asked whether the experience of discussing politics through social media revealed that they had more or less in common with those with whom they disagreed. The results were not encouraging. Little common ground was discovered in the online interactions. Perhaps that is why, while over half of Americans receive their news from social media sources, many are also worn out by political discussions and posts.

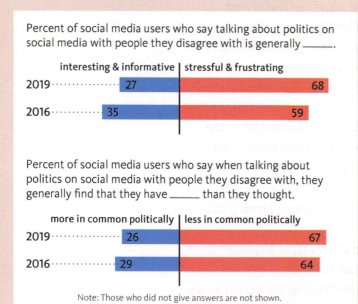

Percent of social media users who say talking about politics on social media with people they disagree with is generally _____.

interesting & informative | stressful & frustrating

2019 · · · · · · · · 27 | 68
2016 · · · · · · · · 35 | 59

Percent of social media users who say when talking about politics on social media with people they disagree with, they generally find that they have _____ than they thought.

more in common politically | less in common politically

2019 · · · · · · · · 26 | 67
2016 · · · · · · · · 29 | 64

Note: Those who did not give answers are not shown.

Figure 11.10 **Discussing Politics on Social Media**

Thinking Critically

1. The data in the graphics suggest that many social media users are dissatisfied with their experience when it comes to political discussions. What are some reasons why people nonetheless engage in online political discussions? What are some differences between online political discussions and face-to-face ones?

2. The graphics present two alternative ways of expressing social media users' experiences discussing politics online. What are some alternatives that could have been presented to respondents that would elicit other useful information?

Sources: Elisa Shearer and Elizabeth Grieco, "Americans Are Wary of the Role Social Media Sites Play in Delivering the News," Pew Research Center, October 2, 2019, https://www.journalism.org/2019/10/02/americans-are-wary-of-the-role-social-media-sites-play-in-delivering-the-news/; Monica Anderson and Dennis Quinn, "Forty-six Percent of U.S. Social Media Users Say They Are 'Worn Out' by Political Posts and Discussions," Pew Research, FactTank, August 8, 2019, https://www.pewresearch.org/fact-tank/2019/08/08/46-of-u-s-social-media-users-say-they-are-worn-out-by-political-posts-and-discussions/.

In 2020, governments' responses to the COVID-19 pandemic became the focus of protests by Americans. People wanting their states to ease stay-at-home restrictions imposed by some governors protested outside state capitols calling for government to open up businesses and allow workers to return to work. Nurses protested that the federal government was not providing adequate supplies of personal protective equipment (PPE) such as masks and gowns for health care workers. In Arizona, protesters against the statewide closure of nonessential businesses and stay-at-home orders protested alongside nurses and health care workers who counter protested in opposition. The protests included Americans concerned about preventing the spread of the virus by adhering to medical experts and those who believed that governments were going too far in imposing stay-at-home and business closures for extended periods, threatening their economic and personal freedoms.[121]

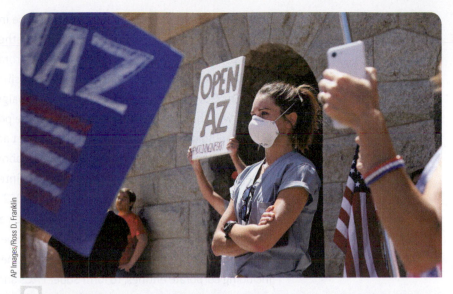

Image 11.7 A nurse in Phoenix stands defiantly in front of local protesters opposed to restrictions imposed during the COVID-19 pandemic.

The death of George Floyd in Minnesota by a police officer that was recorded and viewed worldwide resulted in weeks long protests led by Black Lives Matter. Those protests took place in most major U.S. cities including Washington, D.C. Protesters numbered in the thousands and called for substantial reform of police actions, including the ban on choke holds, and an end to protections of police when using force. Congress convened hearings and members of both political parties offered legislation to address police use of force, particularly in communities of color.

Digital Participation

In the past decade, many Americans have engaged in politics through e-mail and the internet. It is easier and cheaper to send an e-mail message to a member of Congress than to write a letter, and Americans do so with increasing frequency. In 1998, members of Congress received more than 23 million e-mails; two years later that number had doubled to 48 million.[122] Some estimates put the figures at well over 100 million, demonstrating that the use of e-mail to contact members of Congress has exploded over the past decade, underscoring the ease and convenience of e-mail and transforming the way voters communicate with politicians.[123] Members of Congress facilitate this gateway by encouraging citizens through their websites to contact them via e-mail.[124]

Beyond e-mail, people express their opinions through blogs. As mentioned in Chapter 7, The News and Social Media, demonstrates, blogs have become an important way to share information and to influence the political process. Candidates now hire their own bloggers in an effort to influence the direction of these exchanges. Most recently, politicians now use Twitter to share information with the public. President Trump is perhaps the most highly visible and prolific user of Twitter. Despite the attention to the president's tweets, Facebook remains the social media platform of choice for most Americans. Participating in politics by writing a blog, tweeting, or using other electronic

Key Questions
What is the effect of new technology on voting and participation?

communications will continue to rise.[125] Those involved in social media do participate in politics more than those who do not, but whether that difference is due to social media or just a preexisting desire to participate is far from clear.

The internet has also transformed fundraising and campaign involvement. Former Vermont Governor Howard Dean's 2004 campaign for the Democratic presidential nomination was the first to tap successfully into the power of this new technology. Since then, other candidates have made use of the internet and social media to raise money. Obama in 2008 broke all records for fundraising with about $500 million. Just four years later, he raised nearly $700 million through e-mail, the internet, and social media.[126]

Fundraising for presidential campaigns in 2012 was different due to a change in regulations following the Supreme Court's 2010 decision in *Citizens United v. Federal Election Commission* (see Chapter 8, Interest Groups). While 2008 can be thought of as the year of the small internet donor, 2012 can be thought of as the year of the mega-donor. New regulations permit the rich, including corporate entities, to form Super PACs and contribute unlimited amounts to support or oppose political candidates as long as they do not coordinate directly with candidates or parties. It is not yet clear what will be the impact of all this money. Certainly the millions of dollars spent to defeat President Obama in 2012 did not work. In 2014, over $600 million was spent by Super PACs and other independent groups. It is unclear whether those funds made a difference in the congressional elections since the groups spent money on behalf of Republicans and Democrats.[127]

In 2016, large expenditures by Super PACs across all elections continued, reaching nearly $1 billion. Hillary Clinton was the beneficiary of close to $200 million in Super PAC money, three times as much as was spent to support Donald Trump. Overall, more than $2 billion were spent in the 2016 presidential election by the political parties, Super PACs, and the candidates' campaigns. Though the Clinton campaign saw almost twice as much money spent on her behalf, Donald Trump nonetheless won the election.[128]

In the 2020 presidential election, nearly $7 billion were spent, doubling the 2016 figures. Joe Biden's campaign received $1 billion in individual donations of $200 or less, while Donald Trump raised over $500 million. These so-called small donors accounted for 22 percent of money raised in the election, exceeding their contributions in 2016 by 5 percent. Super PACS and other outside groups provided approximately $1.2 billion to the presidential campaigns in October alone, with Biden receiving close to $700 million. Overall campaign spending in all elections in the 2020 election was, by far, the highest ever in the United States at nearly $14 billion.[129]

Voting, Participation, and Democracy

The U.S. government has lasted more than two centuries. This longevity is not an accident. It is attributable in large part to the fact that Americans have, collectively, taken the time to participate. There have been many barriers, from limited suffrage to rules that discourage voting. But the long-term trend has been increased participation, and that speaks to the health of American democracy. Now suffrage—the right to vote—is available to all citizens except, in some states, those convicted of a felony (see Chapter 5).[130] The rate of voting in the United States is not as low as many observers tend to assert. Further, looking at participation more broadly, Americans do more than just vote in elections: They are engaged in political campaigns and in making their communities better at the local level. The internet offers a world of possibilities for increased participation in different forms.

There is a danger to a democracy from a distortion in turnout; the rich participate more than the poor, and this gap seems to be growing. With nonvoters being poorer and less educated, their failure to participate may help explain why government is not as responsive to their needs. Put another way, the government may be overly responsive to the needs of the well-off. This disparity in responsiveness threatens the underpinnings of a democratic and egalitarian society. If the political system responds to one segment of the population and systematically ignores other segments, general support for democracy, based on principles of fairness, could drop significantly.

With the internet's growing influence, there may be other dangers to democracy. Wealthier citizens have more access to the information and resources on the internet and therefore may become even more informed and better able to make government responsive to their needs. The rich have always had advantages, but their advantages may be growing. At the same time, the internet might be used to extend participation. As recent presidential campaigns have demonstrated, this technology can be used to expand the number of contributors to include people who have only a few dollars to contribute or who might want to show up at a local meeting to learn about an issue of relevance to them.

Let us return to Figure 11.1, which offered two models of participation. The Hamiltonian model argued that more participation is not always a good thing and that government works best with limited involvement from the public. The Jeffersonian model contended that greater participation improves both the quality of the input and the lives of citizens. Within our book's gateway approach, the participatory model of voting has more appeal than the elite model. Democracy becomes more responsive, more accountable, and more equal if more people participate. The cycle is reinforcing. Citizens themselves need to do all they can to encourage participation; doing so is in their self-interest and their civic interest. Democracy rests on the active and healthy participation of the citizenry. In other words, as the number of gateways increases, so does the quality of American civic life.

Chapter Review

Key Terms

civic duty (p. 401). What is the importance of civic duty in the decision to vote?

civic interest (p. 401). Why is civic interest essential to advancing good public policy?

compulsory voting (p. 404). Should the United States make voting compulsory?

efficacy (p. 402). How should democracy increase people's sense of efficacy?

franchise (p. 386). Why is the extension of the franchise so essential to democracy?

generational replacement (p. 406). What changes in turnout can be expected as young people become eligible to vote and older citizens no longer can?

grandfather clauses (p. 391). How were grandfather clauses used to deny African Americans the right to participate?

graveyard voting (p. 408). How was graveyard voting curtailed?

institutional model (p. 402). What are the weaknesses of the institutional model of participation?

Jim Crow laws (p. 389). Why are Jim Crow laws a great example of a gate, not a gateway, to democracy?

literacy tests (p. 389). What was the real purpose of literary tests?

poll taxes (p. 390). On what basis were poll taxes declared unconstitutional?

rational voting (p. 401). Why might rational voting be bad for democracy?

same-day voter registration (p. 411). How might same-day voter registration affect turnout?

self-interest (p. 400). Why might someone vote out of self-interest?

suffrage (p. 384). When were women first extended the right of suffrage?

turnout (p. 388). Evaluate the trends in turnout over the past thirty years.

vote-by-mail (VBM) system (p. 409). Why might VBM increase turnout?

voter apathy (p. 391). Explain why a voter might be apathetic.

voter registration (p. 391). Why was voter registration adopted in this country?

voting-age population (VAP) (p. 405). How is VAP different from VEP?

voting-eligible population (VEP) (p. 406). Explain the merits of this measure.

white primary (p. 391). How did the white primary serve as a gate against democracy?

Learning Outcomes: What You Need to...

Know	Test Yourself	Participate
LO 11-1 Explain why there are battles over ballot access		
Participation is essential to the functioning of democracy, and voting is the most common means by which people get involved. The Constitution gives states authority over the "Times, Places and Manner of holding Elections." State rules vary, introducing some inequalities in access. Because voting shapes the outcome of elections and the conduct of government, there have always been debates over who gets access to the ballot. The Hamiltonian model of participation sees risks in the extension of the franchise to groups that may be uninformed and favors a larger role for elites. The Jeffersonian model of participation maintains that greater participation produces better outcomes and encourages citizens to get more involved in self-government.	• Explain why it matters that the Constitution delegated authority over voting to the states. • Compare and contrast the Hamiltonian and Jeffersonian models of participation.	• Debate the relationship between citizen voting and democratic government.
LO 11-2 Outline how the right to vote has expanded		
Today Americans enjoy almost universal opportunities to vote, but in the past, the vote was denied to African Americans, women, Native Americans, and immigrant groups denied citizenship.	• Survey the expansion of suffrage between 1790 and 1860. • Trace the steps by which women achieved the right to vote. • List the ways in which African Americans were denied the right to vote between 1870 and 1965. • Explain how the civil rights movement achieved the right to vote for African Americans. • Put the right to vote for 18-year-olds in historical context. • Describe how minorities and immigrants have at times been prohibited from voting.	• Appreciate your right to vote. • Evaluate whether the United States was a democracy at its founding and identify when it became a democracy. • Investigate the status and causes of disfranchisement today.

Know	Test Yourself	Participate

LO 11-3 Identify who tends to turn out in American elections

Unequal turnout by various demographic groups suggests that government's response is unequal. Most troubling for democracy is the tendency for people with higher incomes to vote at higher rates than the poor. Older people and those with more education also tend to vote at higher rates than younger people and those with less education.

- Generalize about turnout in the United States.
- Identify the characteristics of individuals who are more likely to vote.

- Critique citizen equality in light of turnout.

LO 11-4 Articulate the main theoretical approaches that explain voting

Political scientists explain why people vote (and choose not to vote) using theoretical models. The economic model examines the costs and benefits of voting. The psychological model examines attitudes, including the idea of civic duty and the influence of partisanship. The institutional model examines the rules and regulations surrounding voting, including political party behavior, campaign strategy, and the context of the election. Genetic factors are a new consideration, and the weather is often considered a factor as well.

- Describe the economic model of voting.
- Describe the psychological model of voting.
- Describe the institutional model of voting.
- Address the genetic model of voting.
- Explain the effect of weather on voting.

- Analyze your own reasons for voting.
- Assess the impact of civic duty, partisanship, and the competitiveness of elections in turning out the vote.

LO 11-5 Evaluate how low turnout is in American elections

Turnout in the United States is lower than in many other democracies, but it can be explained by the institutional model.

- Explain why turnout is lower in the United States than in some other democracies.
- Address the issue of turnout and inequality.

- Evaluate whether low turnout invalidates the idea of self-government.
- Assess whether higher turnout among the wealthy than among the poor has an impact on public policy.

LO 11-6 Analyze how changes in voting laws have affected participation rates

From the 1790s to the 1870s, voting rights expanded. From the 1870s to 1920, barriers to voting, especially for African Americans, increased. After 1920, voting rights expanded again and were increasingly protected by the federal government. The overall trend has been toward constant expansion of the right to vote. Voter registration helps prevent fraud in elections but also poses a gate that decreases turnout. Early voting and mail-in ballots help decrease the cost of voting.

- Identify the goals of the Progressive voting reforms.
- Assess how the Motor Voter law, vote-by-mail, and early voting have affected voter turnout.

- Propose ways to increase turnout in the United States.

LO 11-7 Describe other important forms of participation

Americans participate in the political system in other ways, including being involved in political campaigns, participating in protests that call attention to causes, and, with the rise of the internet and other new technologies, engaging in political debates, fundraising, and political campaigns on the web.

- Discuss how many Americans are involved in political campaigns and in what ways they participate.
- Survey the effectiveness of protest politics.
- Describe new trends in participation made possible by the internet.

- Recognize small ways you can make your community better.
- Participate in a protest or an internet movement, or interview someone who has to assess the role of citizen participation in a democracy.

12 Congress

JOAQUÍN CASTRO
Stanford University

> "Just as there are streets and highways that help us get to where we want to go on the road, there is an infrastructure of opportunity in America that allows us to get to where we want to go in life."

Joaquín Castro developed his passion for politics while an undergraduate at Stanford University and alongside his brother Julian, served in the student government.

Very few people can claim that their sibling was the Secretary of Housing and Urban Development and a candidate for the 2020 Democratic nomination for president, but even fewer can say this while they are already a sitting member of the U.S. House of Representatives. Joaquín Castro (D-TX) from Texas's 20th District was born in 1974 to a community activist mother and a schoolteacher father. As a second-generation Mexican American, Representative Castro and his identical twin brother Julián were well aware of the sacrifices their grandparents had to make to give their children a better life in America. His family history has deeply affected how he serves his congressional district.

Public service did not come naturally for one of the Castro brothers: Joaquín Castro was uninterested in politics despite growing up in a political household. Only after they left Texas and went to school at Stanford did both the Castro brothers recognize the importance of public service. After earning law degrees from Harvard Law School, they returned home and joined a private law firm. Representative Castro ran for the state legislature in District 125, while Julián Castro entered city politics, running for the city council seat his mother lost three decades before. Julián went on to be elected the mayor of San Antonio and then served in President Obama's cabinet as Secretary of Housing and Urban Development. During his five terms in the state legislature, Joaquín Castro took a deep interest in education and health care, and he served as the vice chairman of the Higher Education Committee.

During his 2012 campaign for the U.S. House, Representative Castro promised to pursue his "infrastructure of opportunity," a program that he believes "allows each of us to pursue our American dreams." Castro wants to see the United States build an infrastructure of exemplary public schools and universities, a strong health care system, and an economy that pays people well so they can support their families.

As Representative Castro passionately declared from the House floor after he won election to Congress with nearly 64 percent of the vote, the infrastructure of opportunity is just as important for the future of America as

Learning Outcomes

LO 12-1   Describe how Congress has developed

LO 12-2   Define the powers of Congress

LO 12-3   Outline how Congress is structured

LO 12-4   Explain how a law is made in Congress

LO 12-5   Assess what a member of Congress does

is a sound transportation infrastructure. Representative Castro put his support behind bills that will help improve the infrastructure of opportunity, such as his sponsorship of the Rebuild America's Schools Act, the Child Care for Working Families Act, and the Paycheck Fairness Act. He even spends a large portion of his free time improving education opportunities in his home district, which includes parts of San Antonio. He has raised money for underprivileged youths to go to college through the Trailblazers College Tour, and he created SAReads, which has provided more than 200,000 books to more than 150 schools and shelters in San Antonio.

Beyond education and health care, Representative Castro also cares deeply about the nation's defense and military needs. Through his assignments on the House Armed Services Committee and the House Foreign Affairs Committee, Representative Castro was able to visit Afghanistan as it was holding elections in March 2014. While he no longer serves on the House Armed Services Committee, his prior service is particularly important for his constituents, as the city of San Antonio has three military bases, and the state of Texas has more than 120,000 active military personnel and 1.7 million veterans.

Representative Castro was reelected in 2014 with 76 percent of the vote, in 2016 with 80 percent of the vote, in 2018 with 80.9 percent of the vote, and again in 2020 with 64.7 percent of the vote. In 2019, he introduced a bipartisan bill with three Republican congressmen, the Feeding Hungry Students in Schools Act. The bill allows schools to set up food pantries with extra food they do not use for school lunch programs, and would address food insecurity by letting schools receive and store food donations from charitable organizations. Castro's committee service as well as his prior service in the state legislature have distinctly positioned him as a trusted leader willing to give voice to the needs of his constituents and act as an advocate for the many servicemen and women whom he represents.[1]

In this chapter, we explain how members of congress navigate the gates and gateways embedded in the legislative branch to best serve the interests of their constituents. The fact that members of Congress must repeatedly return home to ask voters to reelect them helps keep them responsive to their constituents, who hold them accountable for the policies they enact into law. But the process of congressional representation—that is, of putting good ideas into practice as law—is difficult and complex. Structural gates are embedded in a separation of powers system of government and in a democratic legislative process that encourages competition among groups with conflicting interests. Navigating this terrain is not easy, but Joaquín Castro's efforts to represent his district show how an individual member of Congress seeks to be an advocate as well as a legislator.

Congress as the Legislative Branch

LO 12-1 Describe how Congress has developed

Key Questions

Is Congress a gateway to democracy, or a gate?

Key Questions

What did the Framers do to control Congress's power?

In Chapter 2, The Constitution, we discussed the ideas of representation that shaped the Framers' thinking. They believed that a democratic government had to be responsive and accountable to the people. In such a government, leaders would not inherit power; rather, they would be chosen by the people at regular intervals, and these elections would be the key way that voters would hold government officials accountable for their actions. The Framers of the Constitution designed Congress to be the legislative branch of the federal government, and they gave it broad powers to enact laws. At the same time, they wanted the process of lawmaking to be complex and deliberative so that members of Congress would not succumb to impulsive actions that might harm constituents or violate fundamental constitutional rights. Over time, Congress has increased the scope and range of its powers, but the new responsibilities have added a layer of complexity that makes it harder than ever to pass laws.

Representation and Bicameralism

Essential to understanding how Congress facilitates representation in the American democracy is to recognize that it is bicameral; that is, it is divided into two separate chambers: the House of Representatives and the Senate. This structure reflects the Framers' fear that the power of the legislative branch might grow to the point where it could not be controlled by the other two branches. Because the legislative branch is closest to the people—its members represent specific population groups, by region, and can be removed by election—the Framers believed that Congress would have a democratic legitimacy that neither the executive nor the judicial branches would possess.

The solution, according to James Madison, was to divide the legislature into two parts that would check each other. In *Federalist* 51 he explained that this would "render them . . . as little connected with each other, as the nature of their common functions, and their common dependence on the society, will admit." The House of Representatives would be a large body that reflected population size within states and was directly elected at frequent intervals (every two years). The Senate would be an elite chamber, with two senators for every state regardless of population size elected by state legislatures for six-year terms. In that way, both the popular opinions of average voters and the elite opinions of the well-educated and the wealthy would be represented in Congress. This arrangement also guaranteed that large states could not overwhelm smaller states in determining the content of laws. The specific differences between the two parts of Congress are discussed in the next section.

Constitutional Differences Between the House and Senate

To accomplish Madison's goal, the Constitution establishes four key differences between the two chambers of Congress: qualifications for office, mode of election, terms of office, and constituencies (see Table 12.1).

Qualifications for Office. To serve as a member of the House of Representatives, an individual must be at least 25 years old, reside in the state that he or she represents, and have been a U.S. citizen for seven years before running for office. The qualifications for the Senate are that an individual must be at least 30 years old, reside in the state he or she represents, and have been a U.S. citizen for nine years before taking office. Senators are expected to be older and to have lived in the United States for a longer period of time than House members because the Framers believed those characteristics would make the Senate the more stable partner in the legislative process.

Although the members of the First Congress (1789–91) were all white men, no provision in the Constitution delineates a specific race, gender, income level, or religion as a prerequisite for serving in Congress. Twenty-first-century Congresses have been much more diverse, with female, African American, Hispanic, Pacific Islander, and Native American members in the House (see Figure 12.1). Nevertheless, note that women held only 20 percent of the seats in the 115th Congress (House and Senate combined), although they constituted 51 percent of the nation's population. African Americans held forty-six House seats and two Senate seats, while Latinos held thirty-two House seats and four Senate seats. Despite the advancements made by underrepresented groups in electing members to Congress, it was still predominantly white and male.[2] The average age of a House and Senate member is nearly sixty. House members tend to serve an average of four terms (ten years) and Senators an average of close to two terms (ten years).[3] The twenty-first-century House has included members from the Protestant, Catholic, Hindu, Jewish, Greek Orthodox, Mormon, Buddhist, Quaker, and Muslim faiths. The religious background of senators has been slightly less varied but has also included members from the Protestant, Roman Catholic, Mormon, Buddhist, and Jewish faiths.[4]

House members have more varied prior experience than their Senate colleagues. A majority of House members served in their state legislatures before coming to Congress; others were mayors, law enforcement officers, teachers, doctors, ministers, radio talk show hosts, accountants, Peace Corps volunteers, software business executives, and ranchers. Just as House members use state legislatures as stepping-stones, senators use the House of Representatives to launch their bids for the Senate. In the 115th Congress, fifty senators had previously served in the House of Representatives, and others had been mayors, governors, and attorneys general.

Table 12.1 Comparison of House and Senate Service

Characteristic	House	Senate
Minimum age	25 years old	30 years old
Citizenship	7 years	9 years
Term of office	2 years	6 years
Geographic constituency	District	State
Redistricting	Every 10 years	—
Mode of election until 1914	Direct	Indirect through state legislatures
Mode of election after 1914	Direct	Direct

Political Analytics

Who Are Your Representatives?

WHEN THE U.S. CONSTITUTION WAS BEING DEBATED, Antifederalists complained that the Congress would comprise people who were unrepresentative of the American population. They worried that only a select few would be chosen to represent the views of the electorate.[5] One way to judge whether the legislative branch is equipped to reflect the American people's views on public policy is to examine who represents us.

Figure 12.1 shows the demographic compositions of the 116th Congress and of the U.S. population. Some disparities exist when we compare the demographic profile of the American population with those who represent us in Congress. For example, while women are a majority of population, they make up only 24 percent of the representatives in Congress. Of course, demographic representation is only one

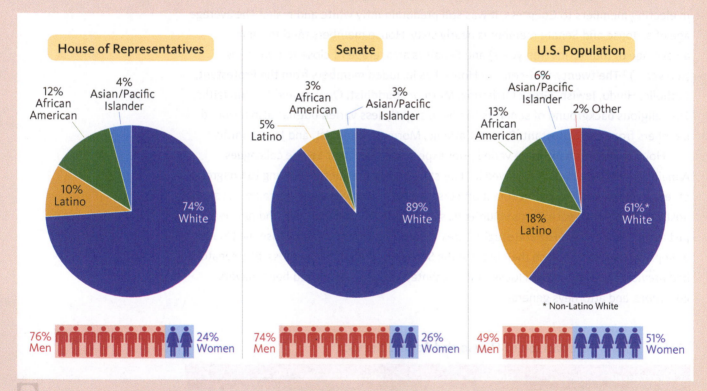

Figure 12.1 Profile of Members of the 116th House and Senate

Sources: Jennifer E. Manning. Membership in the 116th Congress: A Profile, Congressional Research Service, January 14, 2020, https://fas.org/sgp/crs/misc/R45583.pdf; U.S. Census, https://www.census.gov/quickfacts/fact/table/US/SEX255216#viewtop; Kristen Bialik, "For the Fifth Time in a Row, the new Congress Is the Most Racially and Ethnically Diverse Ever," Pew Research Center, February 8, 2019, https://www.pewresearch.org/fact-tank/2019/02/08/for-the-fifth-time-in-a-row-the-new-congress-is-the-most-racially-and-ethnically-diverse-ever/.

426 Chapter 12: Congress

form of representation, albeit an important one. How House members and Senators represent the public policy views of Americans is the key to our representative democracy.

Examine the demographic composition of the U.S. House of Representatives and the U.S. Senate. Notice how the profile of Congress compares with the population characteristics of the United States.

Thinking Critically

1. Would public policy be "better" if the Congress looked more like the demographic profile of the U.S. population? Who would you prefer to have represent your views on public policy?

2. Do the pie charts in Figure 12.1 make it easy to compare the demographics of these three groups? What other way would you propose to present these data to make comparisons easier? What other groups would be important to include?

iStock.com/VisualField

Image 12.1 The Framers created the House of Representatives and the Senate as separate chambers of Congress, but both are located in the U.S. Capitol. In this view from the National Mall, the Senate chamber is on the left and the House chamber is on the right. There are six office buildings for members of Congress and their staff members, three on each side of the Capitol.

Mode of Election.   House members are elected directly by citizens. Senators are elected directly as well, but that is a more recent development. From 1789 to 1914, the mode of election for the Senate was indirect: Citizens voted for members of their state legislatures, who then selected the U.S. senators. The mode of election for the House and Senate was different on purpose. The House was supposed to be more immediately responsive to the opinions of the people, but the Framers designed the Senate to insulate senators from the direct voice of the people—in other words, to make them less directly responsive to the people.

The mode of election for the Senate changed from indirect to direct with the ratification of the Seventeenth Amendment in 1913. At the end of the nineteenth century, in response to charges of deadlock and corruption during the election of U.S.

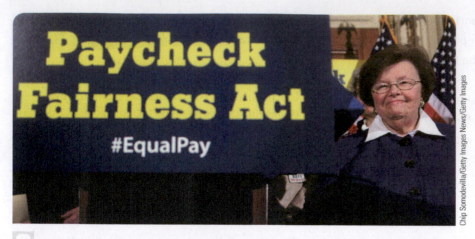

Image 12.2 Barbara Mikulski (D-MD) was the longest-serving woman in Congress. She served in the House of Representatives from 1977 to 1986, when she was elected to the Senate and she chose to retire in 2016. Throughout her career, she championed women's health and labor issues. She was also a strong advocate for her home state of Maryland. Her Senate seat was won by Chris Van Hollen (D).

senators in state legislatures, Progressives led a movement to allow voters to directly elect their senators.[6] The amendment opened up a much more direct gateway of influence for constituents over their U.S. senators.

Terms of Office. A term of office is the length of time that an elected official serves before facing the voters again in an election. The term of office for House members is two years, and the term of office for U.S. senators is six years. The difference in term of office leads to key differences in how each chamber operates. House members have a shorter amount of time to demonstrate their effectiveness before they face reelection, so the House of Representatives as a whole is usually in a greater hurry to pass legislation than is the Senate. Senators know they have six years before they have to face their voters, so they have a bit more flexibility in working out disagreements among their constituents and balancing constituents' interests against the interests of the nation as a whole. Because senators know they have a longer time in which to establish a good reputation among their home state voters, the Senate takes more time to deliberate over legislation.

In any given election year, the entire membership of the House of Representatives must face the voters, but only one-third of senators stand for reelection. To guarantee that the whole Senate would never stand for reelection all at once, the Constitution divided the first Senate, which met in 1789, into three classes of senators who would be elected at different six-year intervals.[7] To this day, the maximum number of senators who stand for regularly scheduled reelection in the same year is 34 (out of a possible 100), thereby ensuring that a majority of the Senate is never up for reelection at the same time as the entire House of Representatives.[8] This electoral condition reinforces the stability of the Senate's membership; it also limits the electoral incentives for House and Senate members to cooperate with one another to pass legislation.

Constituencies. A constituency is the set of people that officially elects the House or Senate member; in the United States, constituency is defined geographically. Each member of the House of Representatives represents a congressional district with established geographic boundaries within the state (except for seven states with populations so small that they have just one congressional district; see Figure 12.2). Each U.S. senator represents an entire state, and two U.S. senators are elected from each state.

In 1789, the average size of a congressional district was about 30,000 people and the average size of a state was about 300,000 people; in 2018, a congressional district had about 711,000 people and the nation's largest state, California, had approximately

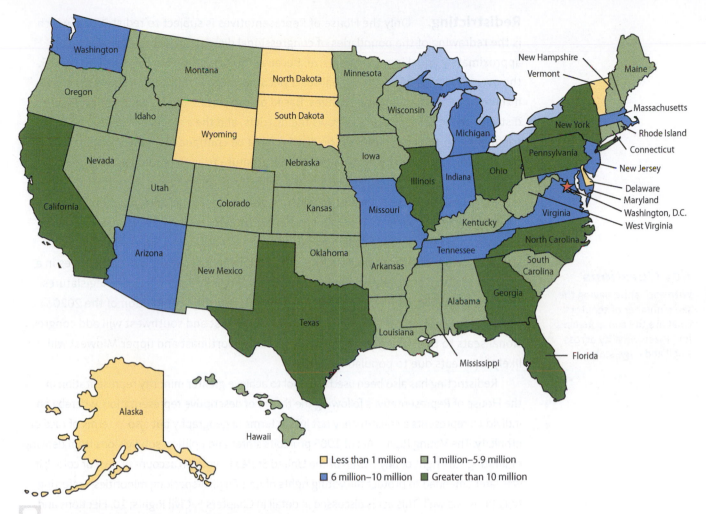

Figure 12.2 States by Population, 2019

Less than 1 million □ 1 million–5.9 million
6 million–10 million ■ Greater than 10 million

The U.S. Senate has two senators for every state, regardless of population. This arrangement makes states equal in Senate votes: Wyoming has the same number of votes as California. But it also means that the approximately 578.8 thousand residents of Wyoming have the same voice in the Senate as the more than 39.5 million citizens of California. Equal representation in the Senate did not seem as imbalanced when states had more similar population sizes, but today, with such huge differences, some observers think representation in the Senate is inherently unfair.

Source: © Cengage Learning; data from U.S. Census Bureau, see Table nst-est2019-alldata.

39 million residents.[9] In 2021, the average congressional district size is expected to increase by anywhere between 30,000 and 60,000 residents.[10] Because the Framers knew that the country's population would change, they required a count, or census, of the population every ten years. Following the census, the number of congressional districts in each state would be adjusted to reflect population changes. The House started with 65 members and, when capped by Congress at 435 in 1929, had increased by 670 percent.[11] Congress was concerned that if the House grew any larger it would not be possible to conduct legislative business.[12] Today, because there is an absolute limit on the total number of House members, population growth or decline has a direct bearing on a state's representation, increasing or decreasing the state's number of representatives and thus its relative influence in the House.

Redistricting. Only the House of Representatives is subject to redistricting, which is the redrawing of the boundaries of congressional districts in a state to make them approximately equal in population size. Because the size of the House is limited to 435, the overall number of congressional seats per state must be adjusted following a census if there have been population changes. Based on the state's allocation of congressional districts, the state legislature redraws the districts, and the only real limitation on redistricting is that the boundaries of the district must be contiguous (uninterrupted). During redistricting, the majority party in the state legislature tries to influence the process to construct each district in such a way that a majority of voters favors its party, thereby making it easier for its candidates to win, in a process known as gerrymandering. Sometimes the majority party will combine two existing districts that have House members from the other party, forcing them to run against each other. In a limited number of states there are bipartisan redistricting commissions that seek to draw district lines in a nonpartisan way, but the vast majority of redistricting is still done by state legislatures. Redistricting will occur in state legislatures in 2021 after the completion of the 2020 census; it is widely expected that states in the southeast and southwest will add congressional seats to their delegations, while states in the northeast and upper Midwest will likely lose seats due to population shifts.[13]

Key Questions

With each state having the same number of senators, what are the consequences for citizen equality across small and large states?

Redistricting has also been used as a tool to achieve greater minority representation in the House of Representatives following the theory of descriptive representation, whereby an individual represents a constituency not just in terms of geography but also in terms of race or ethnicity. The Voting Rights Act of 1965 prohibits states and political subdivisions from denying or limiting "the right of any citizen of the United States to vote on account of race or color"; it was later amended to protect the voting rights of non-English-speaking minorities—referring to Latinos—as well. This act is discussed in detail in Chapters 5, Civil Rights; 10, Elections and Campaigns; and 11, Voting and Participation; here we focus on the fact that many states initially responded to the law by redrawing congressional districts to group minority voters in a way that would deny them the voting strength to elect a minority member of Congress. In 1982, Congress amended the Voting Rights Act to prevent this kind of manipulation. In response, some state legislatures created so-called majority-minority districts in which African Americans or Latinos would constitute a majority of the voters and would have enough votes to elect an African American or Latino candidate.[14] The Texas district that Congressman Castro represents is considered a majority-minority district, with 70 percent of the population there identifying as Latino.[15] Since then, the federal courts have ruled that state legislatures overemphasized the racial composition of these districts to the point that the districts made no geographic sense. Current guidelines on redistricting call for the consideration of race in drawing district lines but not to the extent that it was employed in the past.[16]

Key Questions

How do majority-minority districts provide a gateway for better representation of minority interests? Do they create any gates?

Because representation in the Senate is related to state boundaries, not to population size, some scholars have argued that the Senate is less responsive than the House. It is true that there are vast differences in population size among the states[17] (see Figure 12.2). As we explore later in this chapter, the rules of the Senate amplify this imbalance of influence by granting each senator equal power to delay, or block, legislation. As a result, a senator who represents a state such as Wyoming, with fewer than six hundred thousand people, can delay, or in the final day of a session actually prevent, the passage of a policy that might benefit a state such as California, with 39 million people.

The Powers of Congress

LO 12-2 Define the powers of Congress

As Chapter 2 describes, the Framers granted Congress powers that were necessary to construct a coherent and forceful federal government. Some of these, such as the power to tax and to regulate commerce among the states, had been denied to Congress under the Articles of Confederation, and their absence had weakened the new republic. At the same time, the Framers worried that the legislative branch would grow too powerful, so they limited the powers of Congress to a list in Article I, Section 8, of the Constitution, together with a few stated responsibilities in other sections. The following discussion highlights the most important powers of Congress. It also examines the ways that Congress has used its constitutional powers to expand its role in the policy-making system and ways that Congress is balanced and checked by the executive and judicial branches.

Key Questions

How have the powers of Congress changed over time? Why did they change?

Taxation and Appropriation

Congress has the power "To lay and Collect Taxes." In a division of this important power, the Constitution states that all bills for raising revenue should originate in the House of Representatives, but the Senate "may propose or concur with Amendments, as on other Bills." Initially, the Framers thought that tax revenue would come primarily from levies placed on imported goods. As the industrial economy grew, so did the need for government services and programs that cost money. With the Sixteenth Amendment, ratified in 1913, Congress gained the power "to lay and collect taxes on incomes," whatever the source. This amendment overturned prohibitions on certain types of income taxes.

Key Questions

Why do you think the Framers gave the House, rather than the Senate, the authority to originate revenue bills?

Paralleling the power to tax, Congress also has the power to spend—"to pay the Debts and to provide for the common Defence and general Welfare." The general welfare clause has proven to be a major means by which Congress's power has expanded. Congress **appropriates** (or allocates) federal monies on programs it **authorizes** (or creates) through its lawmaking power. This "power of the purse" has been instrumental in the expansion of Congress's relative strength among the branches of government.[18] The Constitution also gives Congress the authority to borrow money, to coin money, and to regulate its value, and it requires a regular accounting of revenue and expenditures of public money.

appropriate: *Congress's power to allocate a set amount of federal dollars for a specific program or agency.*

authorize: *Congress's power to create a federal program or agency and set levels of federal funds to support that program or agency.*

War Powers

The Constitution gives Congress authority to "provide for the common Defence." In reality, the war powers are shared with the president. For example, Congress has the sole power to declare war, but this power is typically used only after the president has requested a declaration of war. In many cases, the president may ask Congress for specific authorization to take military action; under its power of taxation and appropriation, Congress has the authority to fund or refuse to fund military operations. Generally, Congress also has the power "to raise and support Armies," "to provide and maintain a Navy," "to provide for calling forth the Militia," and to make rules and regulations regarding the armed forces and their organizations. Relations between Congress and the president over war powers have

Key Questions

What is meant by the term "general welfare" with respect to Congressional power? How would you define it today?

Regulation of Commerce

The Constitution gave Congress an important power that it did not have under the Articles of Confederation: the power "to regulate Commerce with foreign Nations, and among the several States, and with the Indian Tribes." Using the power in this commerce clause, Congress established a national set of laws regulating commerce that are applicable to all states equally.[19] In time, the authority to regulate interstate commerce has allowed Congress to expand its power to the point that almost no economic activity is beyond its reach. For example, in 1942 the Supreme Court upheld Congress's power to regulate wheat production even when that wheat is not sold or transported in interstate commerce but is consumed on the farm where it was planted and harvested.[20] In the name of regulating interstate commerce, Congress has passed laws that permit the federal government to break up monopolies, protect labor unions, set a minimum wage, and outlaw racial discrimination by businesses and commercial enterprises. In 2012, the Court ruled that Congress's requirement, set forth in the Patient Protection and Affordable Care Act, that individuals purchase health insurance went beyond Congress's commerce clause authority but upheld most of the act as within Congress's taxing authority (see Supreme Court Cases: *National Federation of Independent Business et al. v. Sebelius*). The Supreme Court agreed to hear a severability challenge to this law with arguments in fall 2020, with a ruling expected in 2021.

Appointments and Treaties

In recognition of the Senate's perceived wisdom and stability, the Framers gave the Senate, and not the House, the power of advice and consent. In the appointment of high-level executive branch appointees, such as cabinet secretaries and ambassadors, this power allows the Senate to evaluate the qualifications of a presidential nominee and, by majority vote, to approve or reject the nominee. Similarly, the appointment of all federal judges, from district courts to the Supreme Court, is subject to the approval of the Senate (see Chapter 15, The Judiciary, for more details on this process). Additionally, the Senate acts as a check on the president's power to make treaties with foreign nations: Treaties must be approved by a two-thirds vote, or they fail to take effect (see Chapter 13 for more on treaty negotiation and ratification). The advice and consent role of the Senate acts as a gateway for citizen influence over presidential appointments and treaties because senators are more likely to block appointments and treaties that they believe are unpopular with their constituents.

Key Questions

Why did the Framers give the Senate the power of advice and consent?

Impeachment and Removal from Office

Congress's ultimate check on the executive and judicial branches is its power to remove officials and judges from office by impeachment. The president, vice president, and high-level officials are subject to impeachment for "Treason, Bribery, or other high Crimes and Misdemeanors." This power is rarely used. In Chapter 13, we examine the three presidents who have been impeached but not removed from office: Andrew Johnson, Bill Clinton, and Donald Trump. In the case of President Richard Nixon (1969–74), the threat of impeachment was credible enough that he resigned from office.

Supreme Court Cases

National Federation of Independent Business et al. v. Sebelius (2012)

QUESTION: May Congress impose a mandate to purchase health insurance on those who do not wish to carry it? Did Congress exceed its spending authority with the Medicaid expansions?

ORAL ARGUMENT: March 26–28, 2012 (listen at https://www.oyez.org/cases/2011/11-393)

DECISION: June 28, 2012 (read at http://www.oyez.org/cases/2010-2019/2011/2011_11_400)

OUTCOME: Yes, the authority is within Congress's taxing power (5–4). Yes, Congress exceeded its spending authority (7–2). Overall, however, the law is constitutional.

The Obama administration argued that because the decisions of individuals not to purchase health insurance have a substantial effect on hospitals and insurance companies involved in interstate commerce, Congress has the right to mandate the purchase of such insurance. Those opposed to the act argued that if Congress could make people purchase health insurance because of the substantial effect it has on interstate commerce, why couldn't it, under the same reasoning, make people buy broccoli? As a fallback, the administration argued that even if the act was not itself a regulation of commerce, it was necessary and proper to the regulation of commerce (see Supreme Court Cases: *McCulloch v. Maryland* in Chapter 3, Federalism). As a second fallback, the administration argued that the mandate was a valid exercise of Congress's authority to tax to provide for the general welfare. Opponents pointed out that when Congress was debating the bill, the Obama administration insisted that the payments for not purchasing health insurance were a penalty and not a tax, so that members of Congress could not be accused of passing unpopular tax increases. Additionally, opponents claimed that the threat states faced of losing all Medicaid funding if they did not voluntarily expand their Medicaid coverage was coercive, in violation of the Tenth Amendment (see Chapter 3).

In a complicated decision, Chief Justice John Roberts, joined by the Court's four more conservative justices (Samuel Alito, Anthony Kennedy, Antonin Scalia, and Clarence Thomas), declared that Congress did not have the authority under the commerce clause or the necessary and proper clause to mandate that individuals enter the insurance market. This part of the opinion weakens Congress's commerce clause powers. Crucially, however, Chief Justice Roberts, joined by the Court's four more liberal justices (Stephen Breyer, Ruth Bader Ginsburg, Elena Kagan, and Sonia Sotomayor), ruled that the penalty for not purchasing insurance could be considered a tax, and that as a tax, it was well within Congress's authority.

Finally, by a 7–2 vote, all justices except Ginsburg and Sotomayor argued that Congress cannot rescind previously committed funds to states that refuse to accept the new Medicaid requirements, imposing the first limits on Congress's spending power in seventy-five years. But by a 5–4 vote, with Roberts joining the liberal bloc, the Court upheld the withholding of new funds from states that did not accept the new Medicaid expansion, as well as the rest of the law.

In 2015, in *King v. Burwell*, the Supreme Court ruled that citizens in the thirty-four states that did not establish statewide exchanges for the purchase of insurance could receive insurance subsidies even though the law stated that the subsidies would be granted through "state-run exchanges."

Thinking Critically

1. Why does it matter whether the payment for not having health insurance is a "penalty" or a "tax"?

2. What was unusual about the Court's decision involving Congress's spending authority?

The process of impeachment and removal from office takes place in two steps. First, a majority of the House of Representatives votes to bring formal charges against the president or other federal official, an action called impeachment. Then the Senate conducts the trial, with the chief justice of the United States presiding in the case of the president's impeachment, and votes to convict or acquit. If two-thirds of the senators present vote to convict, the president or the federal official will be removed from office.

Image 12.3 The Senate exercises its advice and consent powers when it holds hearings on presidential nominees and then votes to approve or reject them. In the winter of 2017, senators questioned President Donald Trump's first Supreme Court nominee, Neil Gorsuch, an appeals court judge from the Tenth Circuit. He was confirmed on April 7, 2017, by a vote of 54 to 45.

Stephen Crowley-Pool/Getty Images News/Getty Images

Lawmaking

Congress, as the legislative branch, is responsible for lawmaking. Unlike the enumerated powers listed at the beginning of Article I, Section 8, and explained previously, the final paragraph of Section 8 gives Congress broad authority "to make all Laws which shall be necessary and proper for carrying into Execution the foregoing Powers." In combination with the general welfare clause and the commerce clause, this necessary and proper clause allows Congress a great deal of leeway to carry out its responsibilities under the assumption that additional powers are implied in these clauses, although not explicitly stated in the Constitution. Over time, Congress has made full use of this flexibility to expand its authority in a wide range of areas, such as regulating interstate railroads, establishing civil rights protections, funding school lunch programs, limiting greenhouse gases, and providing student loans. Essentially, if an argument can be made that a service or program is reasonably tied to an enumerated power, Congress has used its powers to create that service or program.

Authorization of Courts

In Article I, the Constitution also gives Congress the power to "constitute Tribunals inferior to the Supreme Court." Article III, the section on the judiciary, reiterates congressional control by saying that Congress may "ordain and establish" courts at levels lower than the Supreme Court. In 1789, Congress used this power to pass the Judiciary Act, which established federal district courts and circuit courts of appeal. Today, there are ninety-four district courts and thirteen appellate circuits.[21]

The federal judicial branch asserted more authority over the other two branches in the Supreme Court case of *Marbury v. Madison* (see Chapter 2). This case established judicial review, which is the federal judiciary's power to declare laws passed by Congress as unconstitutional. The *Marbury* decision gave the courts the power to interpret the Constitution and determine how congressional laws (and even executive branch actions) conform to its explicit language and its intent (see Chapter 15 for further explanation of this decision).

In recent years the Senate has tried to reassert its influence over the federal courts through the nomination process.[22] As we discuss later in the chapter, individual senators can try to defeat presidential nominees for federal judgeships with whom they disagree on key constitutional questions. More broadly, senators in the opposite party from the president can refuse to hold hearings or vote on a presidential nominee, even to the Supreme Court.

Oversight

After a bill becomes a law, the executive branch, headed by the president, is supposed to carry out the law according to Congress's wishes. But the executive branch is a bureaucracy with many departments and agencies that have authority to implement laws. The sheer size and complexity of the federal bureaucracy make it difficult for Congress to determine whether laws are being administered according to the intent behind them (see Chapter 14, The Bureaucracy, for more details). These executive departments and agencies each have inspectors general (IGs) who are supposed to monitor the implementation of laws and the administration of executive responsibilities, but these individuals ultimately serve at the pleasure of cabinet secretaries or agency heads, and even the president. As we saw in 2020, several of these IGs were fired without clear reasons provided for their dismissal. Both Democratic and Republican members of Congress objected to what appeared to be political interference with internal oversight within the executive branch.

In order to avoid being dependent on internal oversight within the executive branch, Congress has asserted its oversight authority to monitor the ways in which the executive branch implements law. This authority stems from Congress's responsibility to appropriate money to provide for the general welfare of the nation. Congress constantly exercises this authority, but less so under unified government, when the same party controls Congress and the White House, than under **divided government**, when the party that controls Congress is not the party of the president. Under unified government, members of Congress assume that because they share the same partisan affiliation as the president, his administration is more likely to implement laws according to congressional intent.

In contrast, legislatures in countries that have parliamentary systems typically choose their executives from among the members of the majority party, so that the executive and legislative branches always share the same policy goals. Consequently, legislative oversight is not a fundamental element of those political systems.

Members of Congress engage in oversight activities in several ways. They hold hearings with cabinet officials and bureaucrats to analyze how well programs are working, and they frequently invite members of the public to describe how federal programs operate in their communities. Members of Congress regularly write letters to executive branch agency heads to inquire about specific programs, and they keep careful track of the responses they receive. In cases of oversight hearings, special investigations, or suspected wrongdoing by members of the executive branch, Congress can legally require members of the administration to testify. For example, in 2019, the House Ways and Means Committee issued subpoenas to Mazars LLP, President Trump's accounting firm, requesting his tax returns. The president has spent years avoiding giving out that information, and Democrats believe that the country has a right to know how the president made his money. The Supreme Court heard arguments on two related cases on this issue, *Trump v. Mazars* and *Trump v. Deutche Bank AG* on May 12, 2020, and ruled that

divided government:
Situation in which one party controls the executive branch and the other party controls one or both parts of the legislative branch.

Key Questions

Think about the power to investigate. Which branch should have this power? Should it always be the same branch?

presidents do not have absolute immunity from subpoenas for personal records that are part of a criminal investigation, but Congress's subpoena must be "no broader than reasonably necessary" to achieve its legitimate legislative functions.[23] Nearly three decades earlier, the Democrats in the House and Senate created a special committee, known as the Iran-Contra Committee (see Chapter 13 for more details), to investigate actions involving President Reagan and his staff in the sale of military weapons to support an insurgency in Nicaragua. These congressional oversight investigatory committees have the power to subpoena key government personnel whom they believe might provide information about the conduct of the executive branch. In these ways, Congress provides a gateway for the people to constantly monitor and hold the federal government accountable for how it implements policy or reacts to foreign affairs.

The Organization of Congress

LO 12-3 Outline how Congress is structured

The House and the Senate have evolved into very different institutions by virtue of their differences in size, rules, structure, and responsibilities. The Constitution establishes few guidelines for how the House and Senate should operate, so it was left to the members to determine how to choose their leaders and how much power to give them. Some aspects of leadership are shared by the House and Senate, but there are important differences in the amount of power each grants to its leaders. Notably, the power of political parties to shape policy is vastly different in each chamber.

The Role of Political Parties

In today's political world, political parties seem natural and intrinsic to the organization of Congress. Indeed, members of Congress align more closely with their political parties in the House and Senate than in any time in the past 100 years (see Chapter 6, Figure 6.7). But this degree of difference between the political parties did not always exist in Congress. The House did not organize itself along strict partisan lines until well into the nineteenth century. As Congress scholars Sarah Binder and Eric Schickler each show, not until after the Civil War did the House change its internal rules to give the majority party the ability to get its preferred policies passed over the objections of the minority party.[24] Since then, party affiliation and party loyalty have become the defining features of how policy is made in the House of Representatives.

Key Questions

Are political parties in the House too powerful? Are they a gate or a gateway to passing legislation?

The reason parties could become so powerful inside the House chamber was that they were important outside Washington, back home in local districts. Being identified with a political party became an essential stepping-stone to political office. Political parties controlled the nomination process for Congress, and anyone who wanted to run on a party ticket had to pledge support for the party's policies. Consequently, each individual member had a strong incentive to align with a political party both at home in the district and in Washington (see Chapter 9, Political Parties, for more on party affiliations).

With the rise in party strength at the district level, House members were increasingly judged on the performance of their party in office, and elections became centered on gaining majority control of the chamber. If the majority party could pass policies that it favored and prevent those who disagreed with them (the minority party) from gaining any power, majority party members could return to their districts and claim credit for being effective legislators.

Although the Senate also became more party-oriented at the end of the nineteenth century, its members never changed the rules of the chamber to give the majority party complete dominance. Because the number of senators has remained small, it is still possible to conduct legislative business in a personal manner, and each senator exerts individual influence over policy outcomes. Senators also have the chance to make individual impressions on voters over a longer time (six years) and from a more visible vantage point, as they represent entire states rather than just one district. In this age of increased polarization, voters weigh a senator's ideology and party affiliation more heavily than they used to, but it is still not as important as in House elections. Consequently, senators have had fewer incentives to hand over their individual powers to a single party leader to accomplish party goals.

As a result, members of the minority party in the Senate have far more power in the policy-making process than do their counterparts in the House.[25] In essence, getting any legislation passed in the Senate usually requires compromise and cooperation among all senators—majority and minority party members—in one way or another.

The House of Representatives

As is the case with any large organization, success requires leadership. To maximize party cohesion, members of the House meet in a party caucus ("to caucus" literally means "to gather") of the members of their political party. Each party's caucus chooses its party leaders: For the majority party, the top party leader is the Speaker of the House, and for the minority party, it is the minority leader.

The Speaker of the House.   **Speaker of the House** is the only formal leadership position written into the Constitution. Article I, Section 2, states that "the House of Representatives shall chuse their Speaker and other Officers," but there the official description ends. The Speaker is elected by a majority of House members every two years, on the first day of the first session of each new Congress. The position first became organizationally powerful under the tenure of Thomas Brackett Reed (R-ME), who served as Speaker from 1889 to 1891 and again from 1895 to 1899.[26] Reed was elected to the House in 1876, and by the early 1880s he was already displaying political ambition.

As Speaker, Reed implemented a set of procedural changes known as Reed's Rules that strengthened the power of the majority party over the minority party. Because the House ran on majority rule, the party that had the most votes could pass a bill outright. Reed's party granted him the power to appoint all committee chairmen, approve all members' committee assignments, refer bills to committee, bring bills that reflect the majority party's ideas to the House floor, and refuse to allow the minority party to delay legislation.[27] Both Nancy Pelosi (D-CA) and Paul Ryan (R-WI) used many of the same powers to run the House when Speaker, although they each presided over a more complex decision-making environment than did Reed.

Key Questions
What evidence of compromise and cooperation do you see in the Senate today?

Key Questions
Why is the Speaker of the House so powerful? Why is the person who holds this position third in line in presidential succession, after the vice president?

Speaker of the House: *Constitutional and political leader of the House.*

Library of Congress Prints and Photographs Division [LC-USZ62-132187]

Image 12.4   Thomas Brackett Reed (R-ME) served as Speaker of the House from 1889 to 1891 and again from 1895 to 1899. He changed the rules of the House to give the majority party the advantage in setting the policy agenda and passing bills that accomplished its goals.

In the century following Reed, the leadership styles of Speakers varied according to how much power the rank-and-file party members wanted to give to their leaders. The scholar David Rohde and others argue that the variation in leadership style can be explained by the underlying coherence of the majority party during these years. When the rank-and-file membership of the majority party is unified in its policy goals, it hands power to party leaders, especially the Speaker, to accomplish those goals under what Rohde called conditional party government.[28] The leadership of Speaker Newt Gingrich (1995–98) represents this model of party leadership because he came to power with a large class of newly elected Republicans on a party platform called the Contract with America. They captured control of the House from Democrats after forty years in the minority and produced a cohesive ideological party that was willing to give Gingrich strong powers to accomplish policy goals. However, just three years later, Gingrich resigned the Speakership after the 1998 midterm elections; the Republicans lost seats as a result of an unpopular attempt to impeach President Bill Clinton (see Chapter 13).

After Gingrich, the Republicans chose a less powerful Speaker, Dennis Hastert (R-IL), and moved from a conditional party government system to what scholars call a party cartel system. According to Gary Cox and Mathew McCubbins, in this system, the power of party leaders rests on their ability to set the legislative agenda and provide services, such as campaign finance funds, and organizational positions, such as committee positions, to party members in exchange for their loyalty.[29] This type of cartel system worked better for the Republicans after 2001, when a Republican was elected to the White House and set the policy agenda for members of the party. Typically under unified government, members of the majority party in the House use the president's agenda as a starting point. As a result, the Speaker can lose independence in setting the policy direction for the House. A case in point is the Hastert Rule, named after former Speaker Dennis Hastert. The Hastert Rule states that when the Republicans are in majority control of the House, they will not bring a bill to the House floor without a majority of Republicans (i.e., a majority of the majority) agreeing to do so. In adopting that rule, the House Republican Party as a whole was ensuring that the Speaker would only bring bills to the House floor that followed their preferences.

After the Democrats won control of the House in the 2006 elections, Nancy Pelosi was elected the first female Speaker of the House. She lost that post after the Republicans gained a House majority in 2010 and elected John Boehner as Speaker. The ability of the Speaker to make the most of party power depends a great deal on how unified the party is on any given issue, or a whole range of issues, and on whether he or she represents the same party as the president. In the 112th and 113th Congresses, Speaker Boehner, with an opposite-party president, had the most difficulty holding his majority party together on votes related to federal spending and deficit reduction. On these issues, he faced both an internal party division and a small wing of the Republican majority, led by

Kevin Dietsch/United Press International (UPI)/Washington DC, United States/Newscom

Image 12.5 Nancy Pelosi (D-CA) was elected the first female Speaker of the House of Representatives in 2007 and served as Speaker until 2011; from 2011 to 2018 she served as minority leader. When the Democrats regained control of the House in the 2018 midterm elections, she was elected Speaker again after having promised to serve only two terms in that role; in 2020, as the Democrats retained majority control of the House, Nancy Pelosi was reelected Speaker.

Tea Party-affiliated members, that did not want to cooperate with President Barack Obama under any circumstances. In fact, cooperation broke down so severely over the federal budget and national debt in late 2013 that the government shut down for sixteen days (see Chapter 16, Economic, Domestic, and Foreign Policy, for a full discussion). To resolve this impasse, Speaker Boehner had to violate the Hastert Rule in order to make sure the government was funded and the debt ceiling was increased. These problems persisted throughout the 114th Congress until finally the pressure on Speaker Boehner grew so great that he resigned his office (and his seat in Congress) in October 2015. He was replaced as Speaker by Paul Ryan (R-WI), who had run

Image 12.6 Paul Ryan (R-WI) was elected Speaker of the House in October 2015 after John Boehner (R-OH) stepped down due to internal party divisions over his leadership. Ryan was viewed as being able to bridge differences in the Republican majority. But in April 2018, he announced he would not seek reelection. In 2019, Kevin McCarthy (R-CA) replaced Ryan as leader of the House Republican Party but not as Speaker; he was minority leader of the House because the Republicans were no longer in the majority.

for vice president with Mitt Romney on the Republican ticket in 2012 and subsequently served as chair of the House Ways and Means Committee before being elected Speaker.[30]

Whether he or she works with a same- or an opposite-party president, the Speaker's most important responsibility is to maintain power in the House for the majority party, and that means getting the members of the majority party reelected. To do so, the Speaker supports a set of policies that he or she believes are popular with voters, and he or she tries to get those policies enacted into law. For example, during the consideration of health care reform in the House, the Democrats shared the goal of passing a health care reform bill, so they allowed the Speaker to use all the tools at her disposal to get the bill passed. The Democrats suffered big losses in the 2010 elections in part due to voter backlash on this issue. For Speaker Boehner, the 2012 elections represented his first test of holding on to power in the House, and he focused his efforts on bringing bills to the House floor on issues such as federal aviation, transportation, and insider trading in Congress, all of which he knew had support within Congress and were popular with voters. By the time the 2014 elections came around, Boehner and the Republicans were more secure in holding the majority. Still, Pelosi and Boehner shared the dubious distinction of presiding over Congresses with some of the lowest approval ratings ever recorded; in early 2014, only 12 percent of Americans approved of the job that Congress was doing.[31] The numbers in 2018 were not much improved; only 15 percent of voters approved of the job Congress was doing, and 81 percent disapproved.[32] By April 2020, however, the numbers had improved somewhat to 30 percent approval; it is possible that the rise in approval was a direct result of the passage of the first federal COVID-19 stimulus package. By September of 2020, the approval ratings for Congress had declined again. [33]

House Party Leaders.

The **House majority leader**, as second in command, works with the Speaker to decide which issues the party will consider. He or she also coordinates with committee leaders on holding hearings and reporting bills to the House floor for a vote. The House majority leader must strike a compromise among many competing forces, including committee chairs and external interest groups. He or she is also expected to raise a significant amount of campaign contributions for party members, and that role produces more pressure to appease as many interest groups as possible. The majority leader also has nine majority whips to help "whip up" support for the party's preferred policies and keep lines of communication open between the party leadership and the rank-and-file membership. The majority leader and whips work hard to track members' intended votes—in a process called the whip count—because they want to bring to the floor only those bills that will pass; any defeat on the floor could weaken voter confidence in the majority party.[34]

The minority party in the House is the party that has the largest number of House members who are not in the majority party. The highest-ranking member of the minority party is the **House minority leader**, and his or her main responsibility is crafting the minority party's position on an issue and serving as the public spokesperson for the party. If the minority party is the same as the president's party, the House minority leader is also expected to garner support for the president's policies among minority-party members. The House minority leader works with minority whips, who are responsible for keeping all the minority members in line with the party's public positions.

The challenge for the minority party in the House of Representatives is that it has very little institutional power; the majority party uses its numerical advantage to control committee and floor actions. Because of its institutional disadvantages, the minority party in the modern House of Representatives rarely has the power to stop majority party proposals from passing. Minority party members can vote no, but their real power lies in making speeches, issuing press releases, and stirring up grassroots opposition to majority party proposals.

House minority leader:
Leader of the minority party in the House.

Key Questions

Does the institutional structure of the Senate promote party dominance? Responsible lawmaking? Individual careers?

Other Types of Influencers in Congress

More ideological members of both parties have been gaining greater influence recently. On the left, the 2018 midterm elections ushered in four young progressive congresswomen, Alexandria Ocasio-Cortez (D-NY), Ayanna Pressley (D-MA), Ilhan Omar (D-MN), and Rashida Tlaib (D-MI), who were known collectively as "The Squad" (see Chapter 7 for more on Alexandria Ocasio-Cortez). They had frequent conflicts with Speaker Pelosi and more moderate Democrats, as they attempted to push the party leftward and support primary challenges of establishment Democrats. But Pelosi and other Democratic Party leaders in the House responded by emphasizing the importance of party loyalty, especially in terms of gaining influence as policymakers inside the House. These women's electoral success encouraged other young women progressives, often people of color, to run for office, like Jessica Cisneros, who waged an intra-party challenge and almost beat Texas Congressman Henry Cuellar (D-TX), and Morgan Harper, who waged an unsuccessful challenge in Ohio against long-time Congresswoman Joyce Beatty. Supporters praise their use of social media to better reach and excite more young voters, while critics claim they are sowing division within the party in a time when unity is key.

On the Republican side, the Freedom Caucus, considered the furthest-right bloc of the congressional Republicans, was formed by Republican members who were originally affiliated with the grassroots Tea Party movement outside of Congress. They brought many of the Tea Party's ideas inside the halls of Congress, and pressed for a more conservative agenda within the Republican Party when it controlled the House majority from 2011 to 2019 by trying to block spending increases and reduce the federal deficit through government shutdowns. After President Trump was elected, its focus shifted to vociferously defending Trump and his policy agenda. Mick Mulvaney, who was a founding member of the Freedom Caucus, was named the director of the Office of Management and Budget, which oversees the implementation of the federal budget, and then the acting chief of staff to President Trump. In late March 2020, he was replaced as chief of staff by Mark Meadows, the former chair of the Freedom Caucus. Other prominent members of the Freedom Caucus include Jim Jordan, Matt Gaetz, and Louis Gohmert, all of whom have been among Trump's staunchest defenders. One other former member of the Freedom Caucus has played in important role in the impeaching the president: Justin Amash, who left the Republican Party and voted in favor of impeachment.

The Senate

The Senate has always been a smaller chamber than the House because it is based on the number of states in the union and does not adjust according to population growth. Since 1959, when Hawaii and Alaska joined the union, the Senate has had 100 members, and the magic number to secure majority control in the Senate has been 51 senators. Not until the 1910s did senators formally appoint individual senators to speak for them as majority and minority party leaders. However, the Senate majority leader has fewer formal powers to advance the party's agenda compared to the Speaker of the House. Because the Senate never grew to be as large and unwieldy as the House, the individual members have rarely seen the benefit of giving up power to party leaders to make the Senate run efficiently or enact the party's agenda.

President Pro Tempore.   Article I, Section 3, of the Constitution states that the vice president shall be the president of the Senate, but that in his absence the Senate may appoint a president pro tempore (temporary president) to preside over the Senate. For most of the Senate's history, the vice president presided over the Senate, and his main functions were to recognize individual senators who wished to speak and to rule on which procedural motions were in order on the Senate floor. The vice president can also break a tie vote in the Senate, a power that can give the president's party control of the outcome on the floor. But in the 1950s, the vice president became more active in executive branch business and less active in the Senate. Subsequently, the Senate began appointing the longest serving member from the majority party as the president pro tempore. The president pro tempore is closely advised by the Senate parliamentarian, who is responsible for administering the rules of the Senate.

Senate Party Leaders.   The majority party elects the **Senate majority leader**, but unlike the Speaker of the House, this position is not written into the Constitution. The job of the Senate majority leader is to make sure the Senate functions well enough to pass legislation. To accomplish that goal, the Senate majority leader tries to craft legislation as close to the preferred policies of his or her party as possible, necessitating a great deal of compromise and the "power of persuasion."[35]

Senate majority leader: *Leader of the majority party in the Senate.*

Key Questions

Does the institutional structure of the Senate promote party dominance? Responsible lawmaking? Individual careers? What can be done about the structure of Congress?

Senate minority leader:
Leader of the minority party in the Senate.

Still, the Senate majority leader does have several formal powers. For instance, he or she is the official scheduler of Senate business and is always recognized first to speak on the Senate floor. Every senator has the right to speak on the Senate floor, but senators must speak one at a time. Being recognized first, before any other senator, gives the majority leader the power to control the floor and prevent any other senator from speaking. But because the Senate majority leader relies on the senators' voluntary cooperation to conduct the business of the Senate, there are limits on how tough he or she can be on Senate colleagues. If a Senate majority leader tries to bully senators, they might retaliate by constantly using their individual floor powers to try to delay or block key legislation.

The **Senate minority leader** is the leader of the minority party in the Senate and is expected to represent minority-party senators in negotiations with the majority leader on which bills are brought to the Senate floor and under what circumstances. Similar to the House counterpart, the Senate minority leader's job is to organize minority-party senators into a coherent group that can present viable alternatives to the majority party's proposals.

The extended leadership structure of the Senate looks similar to that of the House (see Figure 12.3). It consists of an assistant majority leader, majority and minority whips, and conference chairs, all of whom are responsible for uniting the senators in their respective parties and crafting legislative proposals that can garner enough support to pass the Senate.

The Committee System

Almost all legislation that passes the House or Senate goes through a committee. The House and Senate are organized into separate committees to deal with the different issues, such as agriculture, energy, and education. The party that has the majority in the entire House or Senate also has the majority of seats on each committee, and the committee chair is chosen from the majority party, with the approval of the party caucus. Typically, each House member or senator gives the party leadership a list of desired committee assignments, and the leadership assigns committee seats according to seniority and the availability of seats on specific committees.

The House and Senate each have several types of committees. A standing committee is a permanent committee with the power to write legislation and report it to the full chamber. Select committees, joint committees, and special committees are usually focused on a more narrow set of issues, such as aging or tax policy, but none has the same legislative clout and authority as a standing committee. In the House, there are twenty standing committees, and the average House committee has forty-three members. In the Senate, there are sixteen standing committees, and the average Senate committee has twenty members. The committee system is the central hub of legislative activity in Congress.[36] Committees hold hearings to consider members' bills, to conduct oversight of the executive branch, or to draw attention to a pressing issue. Committees also write the legislation that is eventually considered on the House and Senate floors. Table 12.2 lists the standing committees in each chamber.

During committee hearings, committee members hear testimony on the content and impact of a bill from other members of Congress, executive branch officials, interest groups, businesses, state and local government officials, and citizens' groups. For the public, hearings are a direct gateway for influence on members of Congress because important information is conveyed in a public setting. Committee hearings serve five basic functions for members of Congress: They draw attention to a current problem or issue that needs public attention, inform committee members about the consequences of passing a specific bill, convey constituents' questions and

House of Representatives

Majority Party

- Speaker of the House
- Majority Leader → Congressional Campaign Committee Chair
- Majority Whip
- Caucus Chair
- Caucus Vice Chair

Minority Party

- Minority Leader → Congressional Campaign Committee Chair
- Minority Whip
- Conference Chair
- Policy Committee Chair

Senate

Majority Party

- President Pro Tempore
- Majority Leader → Senatorial Campaign Committee Chair
- Assistant Majority Leader
- Conference Vice Chair
- Policy Committee Chair
- Conference Secretary

Minority Party

- Minority Leader → Senatorial Campaign Committee Chair
- Minority Whip
- Conference Chair
- Policy Committee Chair
- Conference Secretary

Figure 12.3 The Structure of Party Leadership in Congress

Because members of the House and Senate have different kinds of districts and electoral incentives, uniting them to support party policy can be challenging, even when the same party controls both chambers. Consequently, each chamber of Congress has its own separate party leadership structure designed to help party leaders keep rank-and-file members united and accomplish the party's policy goals.

concerns about an issue, exert oversight of the executive branch to determine whether congressional intent is being honored, and provide an arena in which individual members make speeches to attract media attention that is often used later in a campaign as evidence that the member is doing his or her job. Committee chairs decide which bills receive hearings and which go on to **markup**, a meeting in which committee members write the version of the bill that they may send to the entire chamber for a vote. In both the hearing and markup process, the committee chair gives preference to the views of the majority-party members of the committee.

markup: *Process by which bills are literally marked up, or written, by the members of the committee.*

Table 12.2 Standing Committees in Congress

House of Representatives (20 committees)	Senate (16 committees)
Agriculture	Agriculture, Nutrition, and Forestry
Appropriations	Appropriations
Armed Services	Armed Services
Financial Services	Banking, Housing, and Urban Affairs
Budget	Budget
Education and the Workforce	Health, Education, Labor, and Pensions
Energy and Commerce	Commerce, Science, and Transportation Energy and Natural Resources Environment and Public Works
Foreign Affairs	Foreign Relations
Homeland Security	Homeland Security and Governmental Affairs
Oversight and Government Reform	
House Administration	Rules and Administration
Judiciary	Judiciary
Natural Resources	
Transportation and Infrastructure	
Rules	
Science, Space, and Technology	
Small Business	Small Business and Entrepreneurship
Ethics	
Veterans' Affairs	Veterans' Affairs
Ways and Means	Finance

Source: U.S. House of Representatives, http://www.house.gov/committees/; U.S. Senate, http://www.senate.gov/pagelayout /committees/d_three_sections_with_teasers/committees_home.htm. See the committee membership lists.

Committee chairs have powerful roles. The chair is typically the majority-party member who has the most seniority (longest time) on the committee. However, the Speaker or the Senate majority leader reserves the right to suggest a less senior member as chair if he or she believes that person will better serve the party's interests. One of the most dramatic uses of this power came in 2010, when the Republicans selected Fred Upton (R-MI) as chair of the Energy and Commerce Committee, passing over Joe Barton (R-TX), who had served as **ranking member**—the member of the committee from the minority party with the greatest seniority—since 2006. The party leadership believed that Congressman Barton's views were out of sync with the party majority, especially after his public apology to the BP oil company for the federal government's demand for a monetary settlement to pay for the cleanup of the Gulf oil spill. In 2017, Representative Barton announced his retirement and in 2018, his district stayed in Republican control with the election of his former aide Ron Wright, who

ranking member: *Leader of the minority-party members of a committee.*

was reelected in 2020.[37] This case illustrates the steps that party leaders will take to maintain control over committee agendas through the selection of committee chairs. Additionally, the Republicans have a three-term limit on committee chairmanships; the Democrats do not. These term limits sustain the party's power to make a change in leadership of committees on a regular basis; in fact, Fred Upton ended his term as chair of the Energy and Commerce Committee in 2017 because his three terms were up.

In general, when a bill is referred to a committee, it is assigned to a subcommittee, a smaller group of committee members who focus on a specific subset of the committee's issues. Subcommittees can consider legislation, but only the full committee can report a bill to the chamber floor for consideration. In 1973, the House expanded the number of subcommittees and subcommittee chairs, largely as a result of the efforts of young representatives who wanted to enact policies that older committee chairs opposed. By creating more subcommittees, the House created smaller centers of power in which individual members could exert influence over the content of legislation.[38] The Senate did not make similar changes; each senator already had individual power and did not see the need to make changes in the committee structure.

Chip Somodevilla/Getty Images News/Getty Images

Image 12.7 Representative Maxine Waters (D-CA) presiding over a House Financial Services Committee hearing where Steven Mnuchin, the secretary of the Treasury, testified about the international financial system and Congress's requests for President Trump's tax returns. Congress and President Trump frequently fought during his first term in office over congressional requests for information and executive branch personnel testifying in hearings. Representative Waters lost her own sister to the COVID-19 pandemic in 2020.

Advocacy Caucuses

In addition to committees in the House and Senate, there are also advocacy caucuses, groups whose members have a common interest and work together to promote it. Members might have similar industries located in their districts and states, such as coal mining; share a background, such as the Hispanic Caucus, of which Representative Castro is a member; or hold similar opinions on issues, such as abortion or land conservation. Members join an advocacy caucus because it gives them an opportunity to work closely with colleagues to represent specific interests and to draw attention to issues of concern to them and to their constituents. Many advocacy caucuses are bipartisan—that is, both Democrats and Republicans join as members. Advocacy caucuses are important to the interactions of Congress because they bring together members from different parties and regions that might not otherwise work closely with each other.[39]

Nearly three hundred advocacy caucuses are registered with the Committee on House Administration. In contrast, the Senate has only one official caucus, on international narcotics control. However, the Senate has a number of informal caucuses, such as the Senate Air Force Caucus and the Senate Steel Caucus, with members from both parties.

Advocacy caucuses have no formal legislative power, but they can be influential on a bill, especially in the House, because they represent a bloc of members who could vote

Key Questions

How do advocacy caucuses counteract the role of parties in Congress? How can they be a gateway for citizen influence?

together in support or opposition. As an alternative to joining a caucus, senators can join together in a temporary coalition and call a press conference to draw attention to the group, industry, or issue that unites them. Senators can also join a congressional caucus even though it is lodged in the House.

The Lawmaking Process

LO 12-4 Explain how a law is made in Congress

In this section, we examine the lawmaking process. The process by which a policy proposal becomes a bill and then a law is long and winding, and the Framers designed it deliberately to ensure that laws were reasonable and well thought out. The gates against passage are almost too successful. In the 115th Congress (2017–18), members introduced 8,876 public bills in the House of Representatives and 4,680 public bills and resolutions in the Senate. Of the total 13,556 bills and resolutions, Congress enacted only 429 or 3.2 percent into law.[40] Passing a law requires compromise and cooperation; for an overview of the process, see Figure 12.4.

The Procedural Rules of the House and Senate

Just as the roles of political parties and leaders differ in the House and Senate, so do the internal rules of these chambers. Over time, House and Senate members have adopted different procedures for considering legislation, and these procedures can make compromise between the two chambers more difficult.

The House Committee on Rules.   To proceed from committee to the House floor, all bills must pass through the House Rules Committee. Because the House is so large, bills cannot proceed to the floor from committee unprotected; otherwise, the number of legislative amendments that could be offered by the 435 members of the House would overwhelm lawmaking.

The Rules Committee maintains control before the bill goes to the floor by issuing a **rule** dictating how many amendments may be considered. A closed rule means that no amendments may be offered; a modified closed rule allows a few amendments; and an open rule, as its name suggests, allows any number of amendments. The most typical rule is a modified closed rule, which allows the minority party to offer at least one alternative to the bill supported by the majority party. The rule is voted on by all members of the House; if it is approved, debate on the bill begins. If the rule is defeated, the bill is returned to the House Rules Committee or the originating committee for further consideration.

The majority party has learned over time how to use the Rules Committee to maintain policy advantages over the minority party. The majority party uses its numerical advantage on the Rules Committee (9–4 in the 116th) to structure floor debate to limit the minority party's opportunity to amend or change a bill. The Speaker appoints all the majority-party members to the Rules Committee, and they are expected to use their powers to advance the party's preferred version of a bill.

Key Questions

Do the procedural rules of the House and Senate serve as gates or gateways to legislation? Why would there be gates that prevent Congress from fulfilling its fundamental responsibility to pass laws?

rule: *Guidelines issued by the House Rules Committee that determine how many amendments may be considered for each bill.*

Figure 12.4 How a Bill Becomes a Law

The path by which a bill becomes a law is a long and winding one with lots of obstacles in the way to final enactment. Members of the House and Senate introduce thousands of bills in each Congress, but a very small percentage of them are ever signed into law.

Agenda-Setting Tools in the Senate.

The Senate does not have a gatekeeper committee like the Committee on Rules in the House, and all senators have the power to try to amend legislation on the floor. The tool that they use is Rule XIX of the Standing Rules of the Senate, which grants senators the right to speak on the Senate floor. Over time, senators have used this right to make speeches, offer amendments to bills, object to consideration of a bill on the floor, or engage in a **filibuster**, an extended debate that members start with the purpose of delaying or even preventing the passage of a bill.[41] All senators in the majority and the minority parties can use the filibuster. Throughout Senate history, a wide range of bills, from civil rights legislation to product liability legislation, have been delayed or defeated by filibusters.[42]

filibuster: *Tactic of extended speech designed to delay or block passage of a bill in the Senate.*

cloture: *Vote that can stop a filibuster and bring debate on a bill to end.*

The only way to stop a filibuster is by invoking **cloture**, a motion to end debate that requires a supermajority of sixty votes to pass. In November 2013, the Democratic majority, led by Senator Harry Reid (D-NV), changed the threshold for cloture on presidential nominations and judicial nominations for district and appeals court judges to fifty-one rather than sixty. This made it easier for President Obama to get his nominees confirmed because the Democrats had a working majority of fifty-five members, which meant that approval for these nominees was virtually guaranteed and could not be blocked by the Republicans. This was an historic change; the Senate had not changed the cloture threshold since 1975, when it lowered it from two-thirds of the Senate (sixty-seven) to three-fifths (sixty).

However, this cloture change was not without significant controversy. Typically major rules changes in the Senate require two-thirds of senators to agree, but in this case, the majority party used procedural tools to get around this requirement. When the Republicans blocked an Obama judicial nominee for the Court of Appeals, Senator Reid made a motion to reduce the threshold for cloture for judicial nominations other than for the Supreme Court to fifty-one votes rather than sixty votes. The presiding officer of the Senate, who chairs the proceedings, ruled that Reid's motion was out of order. Reid in turn asked for a roll call vote; it takes only a majority of the Senate to accept or reject the ruling of the chair. The Democrats had fifty-five votes, and fifty-two of them voted to reject the ruling of the chair, which allowed Reid's motion to replace existing rules and effectively eliminate the filibuster on presidential executive branch nominees and federal judges (except for the Supreme Court).[43]

However, it is important to note that the Democrats did not seek to eliminate the sixty-vote threshold for filibustering legislation. Given that the majority control of the Senate and the White House can change hands, it was deemed too risky to shut off the option in case the Democrats became the minority party in the Senate and lost the White House in 2016. After the GOP gained control of the Senate in 2014, and Trump won the presidency in 2016, the GOP controlled Senate did exactly what the Democrats would not do: they eliminated the filibuster altogether on judicial nominations, including the Supreme Court, in order to secure confirmation of Neil Gorsuch, to the Supreme Court. The Senate Republicans also succeeded in confirming Brett Kavanaugh to the Supreme Court as well as nearly 200 hundred district and appeals court judges (see Chapter 15, The Judiciary for more details about the federal judicial confirmation process under Trump).[44] After cloture has been invoked on a bill, no more than thirty additional hours of debate are permitted. All amendments must be germane to the bill's issues, and a time for a final vote is set. Figure 12.5 illustrates the variation in the number of cloture motions in the Senate over time.

In addition, Senate rules no longer require those seeking to block a bill to speak continuously on the floor. Senators who oppose a bill can merely state their intention to filibuster, and that will be sufficient to block the bill from consideration on the floor. Filibusters of this type are an expression of partisanship or ideology, and they can disrupt the operation of the federal courts.[45] To counteract the filibuster in recent years, the Senate has resorted to a two-track system in which a bill that is being filibustered can be set aside to allow the Senate to proceed to other bills. But even with this two-track system, the filibuster has imposed substantial costs on the Senate, both in terms of the legislation that has failed to pass and the legislation that could not be brought to the floor.

Key Questions

Is the filibuster a legitimate means of protecting minority rights?

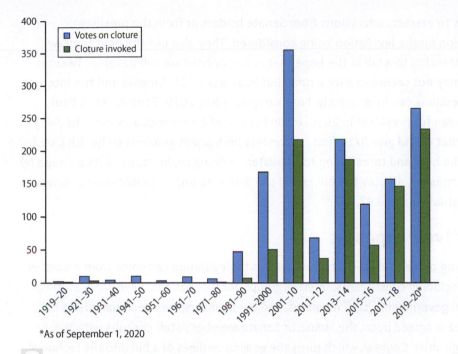

*As of September 1, 2020

Figure 12.5 **Senate Action on Cloture Motions, 1919–2020**

In November 2013, the number of votes required to invoke cloture on executive nominations and federal judicial nominations lower than the Supreme Court was lowered from sixty votes to fifty-one votes. In 2017, that was extended to Supreme Court nominations as well. In the 116th Congress, there have been 265 motions filed, with cloture being invoked 223 times.

Source: United States Senate, Cloture Motions, accessed September 1, 2020, https://www.senate.gov/legislative/cloture /clotureCounts.htm.

Some scholars have argued that the filibuster has been used too frequently as a way of blocking action on important public policies and is not a legitimate democratic instrument of power. Others argue that filibustering is a responsive and effective means of representation in Congress; if there is intense opposition to a bill in a senator's state, or from a minority of voters nationwide, the senator may consider it a responsibility to block the bill's passage.[46]

Without a gatekeeper like the House Committee on Rules and with the constant threat of a filibuster, there are few restrictions on a bill when it comes to the Senate floor. When the Senate majority leader wishes to bring a bill up for consideration, he or she must ask for unanimous consent. Consequently, the Senate typically operates under **unanimous consent agreements** to establish guidelines for debating a bill. Senators strike a deal about how a bill will be debated on the Senate floor, how and when amendments will be offered, how much time will be allocated to debate and vote on amendments, and at what time on what date the final vote on the complete bill will take place. Senators have accepted this form of limitation on their rights to amend or block a bill because it requires their consent and enables the Senate to move forward and pass key legislation.

Nevertheless, a senator can object to a unanimous consent request to bring a bill to the Senate floor in a practice known as a **hold**. A hold is a less drastic measure than a filibuster, but it can be used by any senator to delay a bill for a minimum of twenty-four hours. The majority leader can circumvent a hold by requesting a vote on cloture; if sixty senators agree, the Senate proceeds to consider the bill. Typically, senators

unanimous consent agreement: *Agreement among all 100 senators on how a bill or presidential nomination will be debated, changed, and voted on in the Senate.*

hold: *Power available to a senator to prevent the unanimous consent that allows a bill or presidential nomination to come to the Senate floor, which can be broken by invoking cloture (currently sixty votes on most items).*

hold up bills to extract concessions from Senate leaders or from the president's administration on the legislation being considered. They also use the hold to draw increased attention to a bill in the hope that public opposition will develop. Twenty-four hours may not seem like a long time, but in an age of 24-7 media and the internet, public impressions can form quickly. For example, in July 2019, Senator Rand Paul (R-KY), who ran for president in 2016, made full use of his individual powers to delay legislation that would give 9/11 first responders permanent guaranteed health care by exercising the hold and threatening to filibuster. In doing so, he stopped its passage by unanimous consent, arguing the bill raised the deficit to unacceptable levels. However, the bill eventually passed 97 to 2.[47]

Legislative Proposals

The lawmaking process starts with an idea. Ideas for legislation can come from a number of sources, including constituents, interest groups, local or national newspaper stories, state or local governments, staff members, and the members' own personal interests.[48] When an idea is agreed upon, the House or Senate member's staff consults with the Office of Legislative Counsel, which turns the general outlines of a bill into the technical language that will alter the U.S. Code, the set of federal laws that governs the United States. After approving the final legal language of a bill, the member introduces the bill into the respective chamber (House or Senate), an action known as bill sponsorship. After a bill is introduced, other members can sign on to be cosponsors (sponsorship of legislation is discussed in more detail later in this chapter). In reality, many freestanding bills that are introduced separately are later incorporated into larger omnibus bills that are passed by Congress. Combining bills into omnibus legislation can be useful, especially in periods of divided government. These big bills allow Congress to pass numerous provisions that might not pass if each were presented separately.[49]

Committee Action

After a member introduces a bill, it is referred to one or more committees or subcommittees that have jurisdiction over its subject matter. The first step in getting the bill enacted into law is to secure a hearing on a bill in subcommittee or full committee. In general, a committee tends to act first on bills that are sponsored by the chair of the committee, then on those sponsored by the subcommittee chairs, and last on bills sponsored by regular members of the committee. If the sponsor is not on the committee to which the bill is assigned, it is much harder to get action on the bill. This arrangement also makes sense because committee members are more likely to have expertise on the issues covered by the committee than are other legislators, so their bills are taken more seriously by their fellow committee members.[50] In rare cases, however, as a result of intense interest group lobbying or media pressure, a committee might hold a hearing on a bill sponsored by someone who is not a committee member, but the committee typically drafts its own bill to address the same issue.

After the hearings, the committee may move to the markup. At this point, the stakes intensify in terms of what the bill will ultimately look like, so the stakeholders in the policy process try to exert influence. In this era of increased partisanship and party leadership

Key Questions

How can you as a citizen influence legislation in Congress? Have you ever tried to influence legislation?

Key Questions

How do omnibus bills make accountability more difficult?

control, committees have less freedom to craft legislation that differs from the leadership's goals. After the full committee approves a bill, it and an accompanying committee report are sent to the full House or Senate for consideration by all members.

Floor Action and the Vote

When a bill is sent to the full House or Senate—commonly known as "going to the floor"—all the members of the chamber gather to debate and vote on it. Debate takes different forms in each chamber. In the House, it is heavily structured, and most members are allowed no more than five minutes to speak on a measure, leaving almost no time for actual deliberation among members. In contrast, the Senate has few limits on the time allowed for members to speak on an issue on the floor. If the Senate is operating under a unanimous consent agreement or cloture, time is limited; otherwise, senators can make speeches and even engage in active debate on an issue for much longer than their House counterparts. Unfortunately for the current political system, real debate rarely occurs on the floor; instead, representatives and senators use their opportunity to speak to make partisan speeches or to direct their remarks to their constituents back home, knowing that the proceedings are televised by C-SPAN and C-SPAN2.

During a roll call vote, the clerks of the House or Senate call the name of each member, who registers his or her vote in person in the chamber; in the House it is done electronically, but in the Senate, each individual Senator states their vote. However, during the COVID-19 pandemic, the House changed its rules temporarily to allow roll call votes to be cast remotely, but the Senate did not adjust its voting rules. Members cast up or down votes to pass or reject legislation, to table (set aside) legislation, or to approve a motion to recommit (send it back to committee with instructions to rewrite it). In addition to individually recorded votes, general voice votes can be taken when a consensus exists and there is no perceived need to record each member's vote.

A roll call vote is the most fundamental way that a member of Congress represents his or her constituents. When members of Congress cast their votes, they can act as trustees who exercise independent judgment about what they believe is best for the people or as delegates who do exactly as the people wish. Over time, congressional representation has evolved into a hybrid of both types of representation; thus, members of Congress act as both trustees and delegates. Roll call voting is therefore a key gateway for citizen influence in the legislative process.

Scholars have long characterized roll call voting by partisan dimension and by ideological or spatial dimension because in the past both the Democratic and Republican Parties contained both liberals and conservatives.[51] Currently, the vast majority of Democratic members are liberal and the vast majority of Republican members are conservative. Consequently, scholars now can examine roll call voting through both the partisan and ideological lens simultaneously. They confirm that most members of the House and Senate vote along party lines; in the 115th Congress, in the House, 91.5 percent of Republicans and 91 percent of Democrats voted with their party; in the Senate, 94.5 percent of Republicans and 89.5 percent of Democrats voted with their party. Overall, 67.5 percent of all votes taken in the House and 59.2 percent of all votes in the Senate divided along party lines.[52] Party leaders in Congress frame

Key Questions

What is the purpose of floor debate? Does it change minds and votes?

Key Questions

Who are your representatives and senators? Do you want them to be trustees or delegates?

the content of bills and the choices for roll call votes along the lines of party platforms and ideology. Essentially, they are engaging in what is called message politics, designing legislation to push members into casting votes that may later be used in campaigns against them.[53] This framework reflects a responsible parties system (see Chapter 9) in which voters can clearly distinguish Democratic and Republican legislative policy goals. Although the increased emphasis on partisanship makes it easier for citizens to more clearly hold Congress accountable, it decreases the likelihood of bipartisan cooperation and makes passing legislation more difficult.

Conference Committee

For a bill to become law, the House and Senate have to pass an identically worded version of it to send to the president for his or her signature. The last stage in the congressional legislative process takes place when the House and Senate meet in conference committee to resolve any differences in the versions that passed each chamber. The Speaker of the House and the Senate majority leader typically appoint the chairs and ranking members from the committees that originated the bills, plus other members who have been active on the bill. If the bill is very important to the party leaders, they also have the power to appoint themselves to the committee. If the conferees can reach agreement, the conference committee issues a conference report that must be voted on by the entire House and Senate. Because the conference report represents the end of the negotiation process between the two chambers, members cannot offer amendments to change it. However, if a majority of members of the House or Senate are displeased with the final results of the conference, they can defeat the report outright or vote to instruct the conference committee to revise the agreement.

In the past twenty years, Congress has decreased its use of conference committees. Instead, party leaders take on the responsibility of producing a final bill themselves. In choosing this path, they concentrate power in the hands of fewer members of Congress than in the traditional conference committee system.[54] Although this alternative provides a more streamlined way of legislating, it also acts as a gate against input from committee members who wish to represent their constituents' views on the final version of the bill.

The Budget Process and Reconciliation

federal budget deficit: *Difference between the amount of money the federal government spends in outlays and the amount of money it receives from revenues.*

Although the federal government tries to spend about as much money as it takes in from revenues, it does not typically succeed. Instead, it usually runs a **federal budget deficit**, which requires it to borrow money to meet all its obligations (see Chapter 16 for more detail on the impact of COVID-19 on the federal deficit and national debt). Although the process is complex, essentially this means that the federal government pays interest on outstanding loans, and the loans and interest that accumulate over time constitute the **national debt**.

national debt: *Sum of loans and interest that the federal government has accrued over time to pay for the federal deficit.*

Public Policy and Congress

Unemployment Insurance Policy Over Time

In times of economic difficulty, Congress is often asked to act quickly to help individuals in need of income support. During the Great Depression, President Franklin Delano Roosevelt (1933–45) proposed a number of programs that would try to help workers get back on their feet and provide a safety net for their retirement years. In 2020, the COVID-19 crisis brought about unemployment levels that approached those of the Great Depression; as of May 2020, the unemployment rate was estimated at close to 15 percent, which is equivalent to about 30 million people, and just three months earlier, it stood at 3.5 percent.[55] Congress and the president responded to the explosion of unemployment by expanding eligibility and increasing the amount of unemployment payments by $600 a week through July 2020. As part of the Social Security Act of 1935, Congress enacted a program designed to provide temporary cash payments to unemployed workers who have lost their jobs due to downsizing or layoffs, known as unemployment insurance. Workers who quit their jobs or are fired from their jobs are not eligible for unemployment insurance. In nearly all states, unemployment insurance is funded by a tax on employers, which is collected by the federal government and placed in the Unemployment Trust Fund, but the program is administered by state governments. Although the federal government gives states the power to run the program, it sets basic rules for its administration. For example, to address the COVID-19 crisis, Congress allowed individuals who were self-employed to collect unemployment benefits and provided funds to states to cover these costs.

Since its creation, the unemployment insurance program has grown from covering businesses that employ eight or more workers to any business that employs one or more workers, essentially covering the entire workforce. Typically, unemployment benefits are available for twenty-six weeks before an individual exhausts his or her benefits. However, during economic crisis periods, as with COVID-19, Congress has agreed to extend unemployment insurance for longer periods of time and provide federal funding to states to pay for the extra weeks of benefits for unemployed workers. In late July 2020, President Trump bypassed Congress to issue a presidential memorandum to extend the additional COVID-19 unemployment subsidy by $400. However, the order required that states contribute $100 and many states could not afford to do that so they offered unemployed workers only the federal subsidy of $300.

As a guide to what federal policy could be in short and longer term aftermath of COVID-19, it is useful to revisit the federal government response to the Great Recession which began in 2008. In that year, President George W. Bush worked with a Democratic-controlled House and Senate to pass a federally funded extension program, called Emergency Unemployment Compensation (EUC), that allowed workers to collect unemployment insurance for up to seventy-three weeks on top of the twenty-six weeks normally allowed, for a total of ninety-nine weeks of eligible benefits. In summer 2020, the Congress and the President agreed to expand and extend unemployment benefits due to the impact of COVID-19. In February 2009, shortly after President Obama took office, the unemployment rate stood at 8.3 percent, and he requested that Congress extend EUC as part of the American Recovery and Reinvestment Act of 2009, otherwise known as the stimulus package.[56] The Democratic-controlled Congress passed that bill, and the extended time frame for benefits lasted until June 1, 2010. However, the unemployment rate had increased in the intervening year, and after several short-term renewals, in December 2010, President Obama worked with Congress to renew EUC through June 2012.

After the House Republicans took control of the House of Representatives in 2011, it was unclear whether future renewals of extended unemployment would be possible because of their general opposition to longer-term government relief programs. Proponents of extended unemployment benefits argue that by giving cash benefits to individuals who are out of work, the government is helping to keep the economy afloat; this is an argument made most frequently by Democrats. By some estimates every dollar paid out in unemployment benefits generates $1.60 in return.[57] However, opponents argue that extending unemployment benefits beyond twenty-six weeks discourages individuals from taking jobs that might pay less than the value of their unemployment benefits. In turn, individuals who stay out of the workforce for longer periods of time have a more difficult time finding jobs, thereby creating an entrenched cycle of long-term unemployment. This is an argument made most frequently by Republicans. However, despite these objections, the Republicans in the House did agree to renew EUC through January 2, 2013, because unemployment continued to be very high, but they insisted on reducing the total number of weeks a recipient could receive benefits.[58] As it was set to expire at the end of 2012, Congress and President Obama agreed to renew the program for one more year as part of a larger bill that also extended tax cuts that were enacted in the Bush administration.

However, in December 2013, as EUC was again set to expire, the unemployment rate stood at 6.7 percent, and Republicans in the House and Senate argued that it was no longer necessary to extend unemployment benefits past the traditional twenty-six weeks. Because the Republicans controlled the House of Representatives, it was not possible to renew the program without their support. In the months that followed in 2014, President Obama negotiated with the U.S. Senate, which was controlled by the Democrats, and asked for bipartisan support from Republican Senators to put pressure on the House Republicans to support a limited extension of EUC. The Senate did pass a temporary extension in April 2014, but the Republican controlled House did not take up the measure; with unemployment rates falling steadily through September 2014, the Congress adjourned without passing the extension.

The extension of unemployment insurance was an effective tool in helping individuals who lost their jobs during the Great Recession and the COVID-19 crisis, but in times of job growth, the political incentive to extend these benefits is reduced.

Construct Your Own Policy

1. Construct an unemployment safety net that would help those who lose their jobs but not discourage people from seeking employment.
2. Create a government work program that would employ individuals who have no other job and who have run out of unemployment benefits. How long could people stay employed by such a program?

The modern Congress operates under a budget process created in the Congressional Budget and Impoundment Control Act of 1974, which was enacted to give Congress more power over the federal budget.[59] It was passed at a time of relatively low deficits, but many new government programs were being implemented and government financial obligations were steadily rising. The act created the House and Senate Budget Committees and the Congressional Budget Office so that Congress could construct its own budget blueprint as an alternative to the president's annual budget.

concurrent budget resolution: *Congressional blueprint outlining general amounts of funds that can be spent on federal programs.*

The federal government's fiscal year begins on October 1 and ends on September 30, and the key aspect of the budget process is that the congressional budget, known as the **concurrent budget resolution**, is supposed to be approved by both chambers by April 15. Because the budget resolution does not have the force of law, it is not sent to the president for his or her signature; rather, it serves as general instructions to congressional committees about how much money can be allocated for federal programs in the fiscal year. The authorizing committees take this blueprint into account when they reauthorize existing programs or create new ones, and the appropriations committees in the House and Senate use it to allocate funds in twelve separate bills. They typically begin their work in May in the hope of enacting all appropriations bills by September 30. If Congress and the president fail to agree on any one of the twelve appropriations bills, Congress enacts a **continuing resolution** that funds the government temporarily while disagreements about spending are worked out.

From 2009 to 2012, the House of Representatives passed a budget resolution, but the Senate did not. This failure to produce a concurrent budget resolution left the appropriations process less structured. As a result, Congress relies more heavily on continuing resolutions than on passing separate appropriations bills. Congress's failure to produce a budget resolution makes it more difficult for voters to hold it accountable for federal budget policy. In December 2013, Congress broke the trend and passed a two-year budget bill that essentially lasted until October 1, 2015. In November 2015, after the new Speaker of the House had taken office, Congress passed a new budget bill that President Obama signed, which funded the government until October 1, 2016. Ultimately Congess and the president agreed on a bill that funded the government through March 2018; President Trump and the Congress agreed on another bill then that funded the government through March 2019. For more details on the conflicts surrounding budget bills, see Chapter 16, Economic, Domestic, and Foreign Policy.

The new Speaker also secured several big legislative victories by passing a multiyear infrastructure bill that had been stuck in Congress for several years and passing a revised multiyear reauthorization of the Elementary and Secondary Education Act. For a Congress that had been virtually at a standstill in working with a Democratic president, these were significant legislative accomplishments.

The 1974 Budget Act created a parallel budget bill, known as **reconciliation**, which does require the president's signature. Reconciliation was specifically designed as umbrella legislation to bring all bills that contain changes in the tax code or entitlement programs in line with the congressional budget. Entitlement programs, such as Social Security, Medicare, and Medicaid, are considered mandatory because they pay out benefits to individuals based on a specified set of eligibility criteria. When Congress wants to make a change to one of these programs, it must pass a reconciliation bill. The reconciliation bill has special procedural protections in the Senate: It cannot be filibustered, and it can be debated for no more than twenty hours. A bill that cannot be filibustered was a tempting target for those who wanted to add nonbudget-related provisions. Consequently, in 1985, the budget process was modified to include the Byrd Rule, which required that reconciliation be used only to reduce the federal deficit, which at the time was $212.3 billion.[60] In subsequent years, the Byrd Rule has been interpreted to mean that all provisions of reconciliation must be directly related to the budget.[61]

Despite the Byrd Rule, Congress has found ways to use the reconciliation process to pass controversial legislation. In 2017, the Republican majority in Congress used it to pass a major tax cut bill. Both Democrats and Republicans have used the reconciliation process to go beyond changes in the tax code, or to balance the budget, on issues ranging from welfare reform to children's health insurance.[62]

continuing resolution: *Measure passed to fund federal programs when the appropriations process has not been completed by September 30, the end of the fiscal year.*

Key Questions
Does the congressional budget process help or hurt deficit reduction efforts?

reconciliation: *A measure used to bring all bills that contain changes in the tax code or entitlement programs in line with the congressional budget.*

Key Questions
Why did the Framers give Congress the final say in whether a bill should become a law?

Presidential Signature or Veto, and the Veto Override

In the last step in the legislative process, the bill is sent to the president for his approval or rejection. A president can actively reject, or veto, a bill. If Congress will be going out of session within ten days, the president can wait for the session to end and simply not sign the bill, a practice known as a pocket veto. If Congress remains in session and the president neither vetoes the bill nor signs it, the bill becomes law.

The veto is a powerful balancing tool for the president against the overreach of Congress; however, the Framers also gave Congress the **override**, which is the power to overturn a presidential veto with a two-thirds vote in each chamber. When the president vetoes a bill, it is returned to the chamber from which it originated; if two-thirds of the members of that chamber vote to override the veto, it is sent to the other chamber for a vote. A two-thirds vote by each chamber, rather than just a majority vote, is required for an override because the Framers wanted to enable the president to block a bill passed by Congress if he does not believe that it is in the best interest of the nation as a whole. The president can use the veto either to prevent a bill from becoming law or to pressure Congress into making changes that are closer to his policies.[63]

The Member of Congress at Work

LO 12-5 Assess what a member of Congress does

The cardinal rule of succeeding in the House or Senate is simple: Never forget where you came from. Representative Joaquín Castro has shown how a member tries to balance the competing demands of legislating with the core responsibility of serving constituents. The following sections describe exactly what the job of a House or Senate member entails.

Offices and Staff

For all newly elected members in the House and Senate, the first steps are to set up an office and hire staff members. In the House, each representative receives about the same amount of money for office operations. In the Senate, the office budget is determined by the population of the senator's state, based on the reasoning that senators from larger states have more constituents and more issues to deal with than their smaller-state colleagues. Most members bring some of their campaign workers to Washington to work on their staffs and try to hire people from their districts or states. New members of Congress also seek out individuals with prior Capitol Hill experience to help orient them to their new surroundings and provide specific issue expertise.

Generally, a member of Congress's Washington office has a chief of staff who oversees the entire office, a scheduler who makes the member's appointments, a press secretary who handles all interactions with the media, and a legislative director who supervises the member's legislative work. In addition, legislative assistants handle specific issues, and legislative correspondents are responsible for answering constituent letters, phone calls, and e-mails.

House and Senate members aim to be responsive to constituents, and that means providing prompt and extensive constituent services. To do so, they establish district offices in the congressional district for representatives and around the state for senators. These offices help constituents navigate federal agencies if they have difficulty—for example, getting a Social Security check or a passport—and advise constituents on how to win federal contracts. Specific requests for help are assigned to caseworkers. These local offices serve as direct and important links between voters and members of Congress and affect both accountability and responsiveness.[64]

Legislative Responsibilities

A successful legislator typically fulfills four responsibilities: securing desired committee assignments and performing committee work, sponsoring and cosponsoring bills, casting votes, and obtaining federal funds for the district or state.

Committee Work. Just before the start of each new Congress, members are asked which committees they would like to join, and party leaders try to accommodate their wishes, although freshman members rarely get their most favored committees immediately. Freshman members choose committee assignments based on the needs of their district or state, their professional background, their personal experience, and their desire to increase chances for reelection. A House member from Oregon might seek a seat on the House Natural Resources Committee because that committee oversees logging and other land use issues that are important to constituents. A senator from Iowa might seek membership on the Senate Agriculture, Nutrition, and Forestry Committee because farming is a key economic interest in that state. However, a new senator has to accommodate his or her committee assignment wish list to the reality of the existing committee assignments of the senior senator from the state. All members of the House and Senate try to put themselves in the best possible institutional position to address issues that matter to their constituents.

Committee work consists of attending hearings and participating in markups as well as initiating ideas for legislation for consideration by the committee. Committee members also meet with interest groups, businesses, and citizens' groups that are specifically concerned about bills to be considered in the committee. The extent to which members participate actively in committee business varies according to the local concerns of their constituents, their personal interests, and whether the committee might provide an opportunity for political advancement.[65]

Committees themselves provide different gateways for members to serve their constituents and advance their careers. For example, the Appropriations Committee and the Environment and Public Works Committee distribute federal funds for a wide range of programs and projects and thereby provide an opportunity for members to influence how these funds are spent. Serving on other committees, such as the Armed Services Committee, can provide members with credentials in the area of defense policy, which can be useful if they represent areas with high military employment or envision themselves running for president one day.

Bill Sponsorship.   Members can sponsor a bill by themselves, or they can ask colleagues to cosponsor bills with them; the more cosponsors, the greater the show of support for the bill. Members sponsor and cosponsor bills for three important reasons. First, bill sponsorship is an effective tool for giving voters in a district or state a voice in the federal policy-making system. Second, it is a means of staking out specific territory that members can claim as their area of expertise and can be a means of fulfilling campaign promises.[66] Third, it attracts the attention of the media, relevant interest groups, and the press and thereby can help House and Senate members build their reputations as legislators.

Roll Call Votes.   Each representative and senator is expected to cast a roll call vote on the bills and amendments that reach the floor of the House and Senate. In the House alone, members cast 680 roll call votes during the 115th Congress, and senators cast 599 roll call cast votes.[67] Given the large number of roll call votes, voters have difficulty identifying how their members of Congress voted on bills that affect them directly. Because most members of Congress vote the party line, party identification can be helpful in holding members accountable for their roll call votes. If members do not vote the party line, they risk losing the support of party voters in their district or state. However, most members will not vote for a measure that goes against their constituents' opinions or interests. For this reason, majority party leaders try to construct bills that will benefit the constituents of the members of their party.

Federal Funds.   Most members of Congress try to secure federal funds for their districts and states. The effort to carve out some piece of the federal financial pie is typically referred to as "bringing home the bacon" or pork barrel spending, and it can work through funding formulas for federal programs. Federal funds can be used to rebuild a highway, build a fairground, fund a local orchestra, construct a research center on the effects of pig odor, and even support a water taxi service in Connecticut. Up until 2011, there was also the opportunity to secure dedicated projects, or **earmarks**, which were narrowly defined federally funded projects.[68] However, after the Republicans won back control of the House of Representatives in the 2010 elections, they proposed a total ban on earmarks, which the Senate also adopted. It is not clear that this ban actually eliminates the kind of localized spending that earmarks directed toward constituents because now legislators find ways to hide their efforts to direct federal dollars back home. For this reason, it may be that the ban on earmarks actually makes it harder for voters to hold Congress accountable for federal spending.

Despite the conflict over the earmark and federal funding process generally, one could argue that obtaining federal dollars for the district is a form of

Key Questions

Federal funds for local projects are often denounced as "pork." How does pork figure into your decision to vote for or against an incumbent?

earmark: *Federal dollars devoted specifically to a local project in a congressional district or state.*

Tom Williams/CQ Roll Call/Getty Images

Image 12.8   All members of Congress try to build a good reputation among their constituents. Part of that effort includes going back to the district and meeting with voters to hear their concerns. Here Joaquín Castro is shown meeting with residents of his district.

responsiveness to the local needs of voters. Voters are taxpayers, and members of Congress are simply seeking to bring some of that tax money back home in a directed fashion. On the other hand, many of the projects are not necessary to most voters, and they create waste and inefficiency that can make the federal government less effective. As we saw in the COVID-19 crisis, Congress responded by making funds available to individuals through the expansion of unemployment and offering temporary loans to small businesses. Congress also included funding that went to state governments to address the unanticipated costs associated with COVID-19, from testing to purchasing protective equipment for front line health care workers.

Communication with Constituents

Congressional representation depends on good communication between constituents and their representatives and senators. It is important to remember that members of Congress have two distinct places of work: Washington, D.C., and their home district or state.

In Washington, members take advantage of technological innovations, such as e-mail and the internet, to stay in touch with their constituents. Before e-mail and the rise of social media, members used the franking privilege, which is free mail service, to respond to constituent letters and to send quarterly newsletters as updates on their activities. Today the vast majority of members of Congress use social media such as Twitter, Instagram, and Facebook to transmit information about their activities to constituents, in addition to hard-copy mailings. To help members stay in touch with their constituents, the federal government pays for House and Senate members to return home to their districts or states approximately thirty-three times a year. These trips home are crucial for building bonds with voters, and members make sure to meet with individuals, speak to local interest groups, attend local parades and business openings, and attract local media coverage. During the COVID-19 pandemic, the House of Representatives conducted business remotely, which allowed members to stay in their districts for longer than usual during a typical Congressional session.

Cultivating direct links with constituents and making a good impression on them is what the political scientist Richard Fenno called **home style**, or the way members portray themselves to constituents.[69] Members can choose to emphasize their local work for constituents, or they can emphasize their influence on national policy; some try to do both. Members can be very good at giving charismatic speeches, or they can be quiet, unassuming workers; successful members adapt their home style to the expectations and customs of constituents. As we mention above, social media platforms have greatly expanded the avenues that members of Congress can reach their constituents. Shaping home style no longer depends nearly as much on in-person meetings or town halls in the district; building a coherent social media presence is increasingly as important. Members of Congress also multitask their platform use; they may use Facebook Live to communicate with constituents directly but use Twitter to state their policy preferences and interact with journalists. With the rise of social media, the job of managing communications has become a far more essential part of congressional home style than ever before.

home style: *The way in which incumbents portray themselves to constituents.*

The Next Election

As political scientist David Mayhew explains, members of Congress are always looking ahead to the next election.[70] Elections are the means by which constituents express approval or disapproval of the job members of Congress are doing, and they are the fundamental tool that voters use to hold their members accountable for individual legislative work and the collective performance of their party in office. House members have only two years to show that they can manage to gain influence in the House and be responsive to local concerns at the same time. Senators have six years, but a senator has to share the job with another senator from the same state and compete for voter support, media attention, committee assignments, and the chance to be the "go-to" senator on key issues affecting the state. Because Senate elections are staggered, voters in a state elect each senator separately, at different times. A newly elected senator almost always finds that the senior colleague is established on key committees and well positioned on issues that are important to the state. Junior senators, therefore, are left to scramble for the leftovers and to establish good reputations among constituents in the shadows of their senior colleagues.[71]

There is frequently a large difference in the relatively low approval rating that constituents give to Congress as a whole, and the generally high approval ratings that they give to their own senators or House member. Members of Congress enjoy a significant advantage as incumbents because challengers are usually less well known to voters. For example, in 2016, 98 percent of House incumbents, and 93 percent of Senate incumbents won reelection, and in 2018, 93.5 percent of House incumbents and 84 percent of Senate incumbents won reelection.[72] Considering that the House flipped from Republican to Democratic control in 2018, one may wonder what happened to the incumbency advantage in the House? In fact, many Republican members of the House decided to retire that year because they believed that they might be defeated if they tried to run for reelection. Incumbent House members who did choose to seek reelection in 2018 were relatively confident they could prevail. In 2020, the freshman Democrats who were integral to gaining majority control of the House in 2018 faced competitive challenges from Republicans and lost a number of seats but kept control of the chamber. In the Senate, Republicans defended twenty-three seats, with nineteen incumbents running for reelection; Republicans lost 3 of those seats but managed to keep slim control of the chamber with a 51-49 margin.

Congressional campaigns are typically divided into two categories: those with an incumbent seeking reelection and those with open seats, where no incumbent is seeking reelection. In elections in which an incumbent is running, the contest becomes an evaluation of the job he or she has done in office compared to what the challenger promises to do if elected. Incumbents have major advantages because they have already won at least one election in the district, they are likely to have moderate name recognition, and they have the power to use their congressional offices to provide services to constituents. However, incumbents can also suffer if the reputation of

The Presidential Effect on Congressional Elections 2016–2020

Election year 2020 was a very competitive year at both the congressional and presidential levels. Four years earlier, in 2016, President Trump had won a narrow victory, winning the Electoral College but losing the popular vote. In that year, the Republicans retained majority control of both the House and Senate. In the 2018 midterm elections, however, the Republicans did not fare nearly as well. Typically in midterm elections, when only members of Congress are seeking reelection, the party of the president loses seats in the House or Senate, or both. The entire House of Representatives is up for reelection during a midterm election, but Senate elections are staggered so that typically no more than one-third of the Senate is up for reelection in any federal election year. The partisan balance of Senators seeking reelection will therefore vary in every midterm election. In 2014, the Democrats had to defend more Senate seats. In 2016, the situation was reversed in that the Republicans had many more incumbent senators seeking reelection. In 2018, the Democrats had more incumbent seats to defend, but in 2020 the situation was again reversed with the Republicans defending nearly twice as many incumbent seats as the Democrats.

Sometimes, midterm election losses are large enough to flip partisan control of one or both of the chambers, as occurred in 1994 under Bill Clinton (D), 2006 under George W. Bush (R), 2010 under Barack Obama (D), and in 2014, also under Obama. The explanation most frequently offered by scholars for these losses is that voters use the congressional midterm elections to send a clear message to the president about whether they like or dislike the policies that are adopted during his administration.

The complicated aspect of predicting congressional elections is the impact of the presidential election on these contests. With strong competitive presidential candidates at the top of the party ticket on the ballot, both parties can expect high voter turnout among their bases, which produces greater competition at both the presidential and congressional levels. But if one party nominates a candidate who is popular with the party base but not with independents or swing voters, then that party can risk negative effects in congressional elections as well.

As we interpret the outcome of congressional midterm elections, it is also important to examine the role of key groups of voters, especially in light of the changing demographics of the American electorate. In comparing the 2014 midterm elections to the 2018 midterm elections, overall voter turnout rose from 41.9 percent to 53.4 percent. Among women, turnout rose from 43.0 percent to 55.0 percent. There were similar increases in voting turnout among other demographic groups; Latino turnout rose from 27.0 percent to 40.4 percent and among African Americans, turnout rose from 40.6 percent to 51.4 percent. Younger voters, between the ages of 18and 29 also increased their voter turnout from 19.9 percent to 35.6 percent.[73] Turnout among these demographic groups can affect both the presidential electoral outcome and the election outcome in congressional races. For example, in 2016, Latinos in Nevada were thought to play a large role in electing Catherine Cortez Masto to the U.S. Senate; she is the first Latina U.S. senator ever elected. In 2020, she was among several women considered by Democratic Presidential candidate Joe Biden to be the vice presidential nominee but subsequently dropped out of consideration.[74] Biden ultimately chose U.S. Senator Kamala Harris (D-CA) as his vice presidential running mate in 2020.

Congressional reelection rates are the product of many forces—some of which are outside of candidates' control. Part of the incumbent advantage rests on incumbents' efforts to use all their resources to serve their constituents responsively. Members' concern for their local districts or states can be one of the biggest gates standing in the way of a productive Congress. Parties provide a collective set of policy goals that will benefit or appeal to party members at the local level. For a member of Congress, however, tying his or her electoral fortunes to the political party can be risky if the majority party falls out of favor with voters who hold it accountable for policy outcomes. In 2018, voters apparently punished incumbent Republican members of the House of Representatives by electing enough Democratic challengers to regain the majority in the House. In the Senate however, voters elected Republican challengers over Democratic incumbents in states where President Trump was popular. In that sense, 2018 sent mixed messages on the performance of President Trump. Although these types of election upsets are infrequent, they are powerful reminders that incumbents must constantly balance the needs of their constituents with their party and stay responsive, or risk losing the next election.

In 2020, there was record voter turnout and voters appeared to offer a split decision. Joe Biden won the presidential election with over 50 percent of the vote, but Democrats lost seats in the House and gained fewer than expected in the Senate. Overall, the election was more a referendum on Donald Trump than anything else.

Key Questions

If an election were held today, would you vote for the incumbent in the House? In the Senate? What would you base your decision on?

Congress suffers (see Figure 12.6), and so they work to stake out individual reputations that contrast to the institution as a whole.

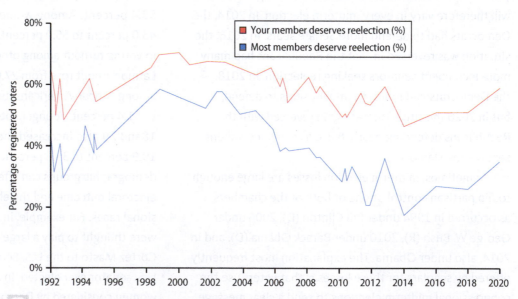

Figure 12.6 **Voter Opinion of Congressional Incumbents, 1992–2020**

Although congressional incumbents typically enjoy high reelection rates, negative impressions of Congress as an institution can present obstacles to gaining voter support and give challengers material to use to criticize incumbents on the campaign trail. For example, if African American or Latino voters do not see Congress as a whole as responsive to the needs of their communities as a whole, individual members running for reelection may have less support among those voters in their districts.

Source: Gallup poll, https://news.gallup.com/poll/286316/support-congressional-incumbents-highest-2012.aspx.

Congress and Democracy

The composition of Congress has changed considerably over the nation's history. The lawmaking body is five times larger and now includes men and women from a wide range of ethnic, racial, and religious backgrounds. From the standpoint of equality of opportunity in a democracy, the increased diversity in Congress is a positive step.

Is Congress a responsive decision-making body? Individual members clearly work hard to address the concerns of their constituents, both at home in the district or state and in their Washington offices. But Congress as a whole is not always capable of addressing the immediate needs of the nation in a timely fashion. The bicameral nature of the institution, with each chamber's separate rules of operation, makes the legislative process time-consuming and complex. In the House, the majority party almost always succeeds in passing legislation that reflects the party's policy goals. In the Senate, the minority has much greater power to block the majority through the threat of a filibuster, so minority-party views are typically incorporated into legislation. These differences offer advantages and disadvantages; if Congress acts too hastily, it can pass harmful legislation, but if it acts too slowly, it can fail to meet its fundamental responsibilities to address issues that citizens care about.

Are individual members of Congress accountable for the collective output of Congress as a whole? Not always. The fundamental difficulty with the representative structure of Congress is that each member is elected separately, so that voters may reelect their own representative or senator but still be unhappy with Congress as a whole. It is too easy for one member of Congress to say to constituents, "I am working hard to help you; it is all those other men and women who are not doing their jobs." Only in the rarest of election years do voters actually hold all the members of Congress accountable for their collective performance. This lack of collective accountability can be a significant obstacle or gate to Congress's productivity and responsiveness to important policy needs.

Is Congress equal in its treatment of each citizen relative to all others? Because each state has the same number of senators regardless of population size, are the citizens of small states more powerful in the Senate than citizens who live in large states? Are the laws that Congress passes fair and balanced, or do they benefit one group more consistently than another? There are no simple answers to these questions. Some voices in society are louder and more prominent than others are, and members of Congress tend to respond to citizens whom they perceive to be supportive, who donate more money, and who vote regularly. In some issue areas, the more prominent members of society win out over citizens who are less active and less visible. It is not clear that Congress sets out to give some people greater advantages but the process of balancing the different individual and regional interests in national policy making produces winners and losers. The fundamental challenge to Congress is to make sure that there are no permanent winners or losers, and the challenge to all citizens is to monitor their members of Congress to be sure they are performing their legislative responsibilities.

Chapter Review

Key Terms

appropriate (p. 431). What is the difference between appropriation and authorization?

authorize (p. 431). How is authorization a part of Congress's "power of the purse"?

cloture (p. 448). How is cloture invoked?

concurrent budget resolution (p. 454). How is a concurrent budget resolution used by congressional committees?

continuing resolution (p. 455). When is a continuing resolution used?

divided government (p. 435). How does divided government make it harder to compromise?

earmark (p. 458). Why did Congress ban earmarks?

federal budget deficit (p. 452). What causes the federal government to run a budget deficit?

filibuster (p. 447). How does the filibuster give power to individual senators?

hold (p. 449). How is a hold used in relation to unanimous consent agreements?

home style (p. 459). How does a member of Congress use home style to help get reelected?

House majority leader (p. 440). What is the House majority leader's role within the House?

House minority leader (p. 440). What is the role of the House minority leader in policy making when he or she shares the president's party?

markup (p. 443). What is the committee chair's role in relation to markup?

national debt (p. 452). How is the national debt related to the federal budget deficit?

override (p. 456). How does the override strengthen Congress's power over the president?

ranking member (p. 444). Who gets to serve as ranking member on a committee?

reconciliation (p. 455). Why was the reconciliation process created?

rule (p. 446). What are the different types of rules and their implications?

Senate majority leader (p. 441). What is the primary means through which the Senate majority leader wields power?

Senate minority leader (p. 442). How does the Senate minority leader represent his or her party members?

Speaker of the House (p. 437). How did Thomas Brackett Reed increase the power of the Speaker of the House and the majority party in the House of Representatives?

unanimous consent agreement (p. 449). What does a unanimous consent agreement do?

Learning Outcomes: What You Need to...

Know	Test Yourself	Participate
LO 12-1 Describe how Congress has developed		
The Framers designed Congress as a bicameral legislature so that the House of Representatives and the Senate—with different qualifications for office, modes of election, terms of office, and constituencies—would check and balance each other. Although its enumerated powers are limited, Congress has built on its implied powers to become the powerful legislative branch it is today. Differences in size, rules, structure, and responsibility have molded the House and the Senate into very different institutions.	• Explain the reasons for and consequences of bicameralism. • Explain the constitutional differences between the House and Senate.	• Weigh the gridlock caused by bicameralism against the checks and balances it provides.

Know	Test Yourself	Participate

LO 12-2   Define the powers of Congress

The Framers structured Congress to give it the powers necessary to govern the newly formed union, especially the powers to tax and spend and declare war. Over time, the powers of Congress have evolved under the separation of powers system. In some ways, congressional powers have expanded, especially in the area of advice and consent, but at the same time congressional productivity has declined.

- State what the general welfare clause allows Congress to do.
- Recall why war powers are shared with the president.
- Define the commerce clause and explain its power.
- Explain the power of advice and consent.
- Describe the process of impeachment.
- Compare and contrast the enumerated and implied powers.
- Explain Congress's role in the authorization of courts.
- Characterize how Congress uses its powers of oversight on the other two branches.

- Debate whether Congress's power over interstate commerce should be limited but its power over going to war should be strengthened.
- Consider whether Congress's power over the executive and judicial branches should be expanded, and, if so, how.

LO 12-3   Outline how Congress is structured

Political parties play a stronger role in the organization and operation of the House than of the Senate. In the Senate, each member has relatively equal power, and passing legislation requires compromise and cooperation. In recent years, intense partisanship, including party-line voting and message politics, has decreased the likelihood of bipartisan cooperation and made it more difficult for Congress to pass legislation.

- Describe the role parties play in Congress.
- Explain the role of party leaders in the House of Representatives.
- Compare and contrast the functioning of the Senate and House.
- State how the committee system works.
- Identify the role of advocacy caucuses in Congress.

- Is Congress too partisan? If so, how would you change the structure of the House and the Senate to encourage bipartisan cooperation? Would you have to change our electoral structure?

LO 12-4   Explain how a law is made in Congress

The procedures through which a bill becomes a law are different in the House and Senate, but each chamber engages in committee work, hearings, floor debate, and voting. Following passage by each chamber individually, a formal conference committee or an informal group of party leaders resolves differences between the two bills to produce a single bill that is presented to the president for signature. If the president vetoes a bill, Congress can override the veto with a two-thirds majority in each house.

- Compare the procedural rules in the House and Senate.
- State how a bill is proposed.
- Describe what happens to a bill in committee.
- Characterize floor action and voting.
- Explain what happens in conference committees.
- Identify the key components of the congressional budget process.
- Define the president's role in the lawmaking process.

- Map out ways you could influence the content of legislation as it is being considered in Congress.
- Design a federal budget that does not create a deficit.

LO 12-5   Assess what a member of Congress does

Members of Congress try to balance the competing demands of legislation and constituent service, and they are always anticipating the next election. A successful legislator seeks to be responsive to constituents by engaging in committee work, sponsoring and voting on bills, and securing federal funds for his or her district or state.

- Explain the importance of constituent services.
- Recall the four legislative responsibilities of congressional members.
- Describe the key ways in which members of Congress communicate with constituents.
- State how elections shape the work of members of Congress.

- Identify three policies you believe your representative and senators should address, and devise a plan to communicate to them about your interests.

The Presidency

> *"As a second-generation Greek immigrant, I was raised to be thankful for the gifts that this great nation gave to me and to my parents before me."*[1]

Sylvia Mathews Burwell found her love of politics and policy while studying at Harvard University as an undergraduate.

SYLVIA MATHEWS BURWELL
Harvard University

From a very young age, Sylvia Mathews Burwell showed a keen interest in politics. In elementary school, she helped campaign for a friend's father, and at age 11, she volunteered for Jay Rockefeller's bid for governor. Later her mother ran for mayor of her hometown, Hinton, West Virginia, at age 65, and won, without ever having run for public office before. Sylvia graduated from Harvard with a degree in government and became a Rhodes Scholar at Oxford University, which introduced her to the world of professional politics. In 1992, she worked on Bill Clinton's presidential campaign. She led Clinton's economic transition team, and after he won the election, became a staff director on the National Economic Council (NEC).

Burwell was promoted to the chief of staff for the Treasury Secretary and then served as Clinton's deputy chief of staff. In 1998, she assumed the position of deputy director in the Office of Management and Budget (OMB). When Republican candidate George W. Bush won the 2000 presidential election, she turned her focus to the world of nonprofit foundations, initially working for the Bill and Melinda Gates Foundation. As president of the Walmart Foundation, she tackled global health issues. Her past experience with the OMB put her on the top of a short list of candidates to head the agency after Democratic President Barack Obama was reelected in 2012. In 2013, Obama nominated her for the position. Burwell's appointment as OMB director was impressively smooth, and she was confirmed by the Senate in a 96–0 vote on April 24, 2013. On April 11, 2014, President Obama nominated Burwell as the next Secretary of Health and Human Services (HHS). The president put one of his most important policy legacies—the Affordable Care Act—in her hands. The Senate Finance Committee approved her nomination by a vote of 21–3 on May 21, 2014, and the full Senate confirmed her on June 5, 2014, by a vote of 78–17. Burwell served until President Trump appointed a new Secretary of HHS. Burwell was appointed President of American University in June 2017; she was the first woman to serve in that position.

Burwell's career exemplifies the gateways that open when you get involved in politics: the political networks that talented and hardworking volunteers establish on campaigns. Her experience demonstrates how campaign work can be the beginning of a lifetime of public service. Burwell's appointment is also the perfect example of how the gates of Congress can get in the way of executive branch policy implementation, even for laws that have already passed through their chambers.[2]

In this chapter, we examine how the president governs and how responsive he can be to the people. We look at his constitutional powers and the way he uses the executive

power to achieve his policy goals, from nominating appointees to issuing executive orders to accomplish policy goals. We also look at the limits on presidential power. Successful presidents work within a separation-of-powers system and alongside the legislative and judicial branches, compromising, persuading, and overcoming opposition. The most successful presidents are strong leaders with clear policy visions and excellent communication and negotiation skills. In the twenty-first century, the American president has to implement existing law and lead the effort to turn his policy goals into law and achieve his visions for the nation.

Presidential Qualifications

LO 13-1 Outline the requirements to serve as president

The American presidency was invented at the Constitutional Convention in 1787. The Framers had no definitive models to help them determine what sort of person should serve as a democratically elected head of state because nations were still run by monarchs whose power to rule was hereditary. But the Framers had George Washington, the hero of the Revolutionary War, in mind for the office, and he helped shape the idea of what a president should be. Still, they left the qualifications as open as possible, and men with diverse experiences have served as president.

Constitutional Eligibility and Presidential Succession

Article II, Section 1, of the Constitution states that the president must be a natural-born citizen (or a citizen at the time the Constitution was adopted), at least 35 years old, and a resident of the United States for at least 14 years. The original Constitution did not specify eligibility for the vice presidency, as the person who came in second in the vote for president would be vice president. But in 1800, Thomas Jefferson (1801–09) and Aaron Burr ended up in a tie in the Electoral College when in fact supporters wanted to elect them as a team, with Jefferson as president and Burr as vice president. The Twelfth Amendment, ratified in 1804, changed the process so that candidates are elected for president and vice president separately. The amendment also directs that the vice president must meet the same eligibility requirements as the president and that electors cannot vote for both a president and a vice president from the elector's home state. This requirement makes it difficult for parties to nominate presidents and vice presidents from the same state.

The Constitution also states that when the president is removed from office by death, resignation, or inability to perform the duties of the office, the vice president becomes president. It stipulates that if neither the president nor the vice president is able to complete the elected term, Congress should designate a successor by law. In 1792, Congress passed the Presidential Succession Act, which designated the president pro tempore of the Senate as next in line, and then the Speaker of the House. In 1841, John Tyler (1841–45) became the first elected vice president to succeed a president when President William Henry Harrison insisted on giving a two-hour inaugural speech in the freezing rain while wearing no hat or coat, and consequently came down with a cold. Besieged by candidates hoping that he would appoint them to public office, he had little time to rest. Only one month after assuming office, the new president died after his cold developed into pneumonia. The order of succession today is illustrated in Table 13.1.

There was no constitutional provision for replacement of the vice president, and in the course of the nation's history, the office has occasionally been vacant. Eventually, the Twenty-Fifth Amendment, ratified in 1967, required the president to nominate a replacement vice president, who must be approved by a majority vote of the House and the Senate.

The first vice president to assume office in this manner was Gerald R. Ford, nominated by President Richard M. Nixon (1969–74) in 1973, following the indictment and subsequent resignation of Vice President Spiro T. Agnew on charges of tax fraud.

The amendment also allows for a temporary transfer of power from the president to the vice president in cases of incapacity when invoked by either the president or vice president and a majority of the cabinet. To date, only the president has invoked this clause and then only when he has had to have surgery that would require sedation. For example, in 1985, when President Ronald Reagan (1981–89) had a colonoscopy, Vice President George H. W. Bush was acting president for eight hours.[3] In contrast, no one invoked the clause when President Reagan was shot in a failed assassination attempt in 1981; Vice President Bush stood in for him at official functions and meetings for approximately two weeks but did not serve as the official acting president during this time.

Today another constitutional amendment, the Twenty-Second (1951), limits the president to two elected terms. For a century and a half, presidents followed the precedent established by George Washington (1789–97) when he stepped down after two terms. But in 1940, President Franklin Delano Roosevelt (1933–45) chose to run for a third term and won, and also won election to a fourth term in 1944. Though the dangers of World War II were a factor in his staying in office, many Americans, especially Republicans, worried that a long-standing president could expand executive branch power too much, so they sought a way to limit presidential terms of service. In 1946, Republicans captured a majority in the House and Senate, and on the very first day the new Congress met, they proposed a constitutional amendment limiting the president to two full terms in office.[4] For a list of constitutional amendments that pertain to the presidency, see Figure 13.1.

Presidential term limits enforce turnover and open opportunity for new leadership, but they also act as a gate that prevents voters from reelecting a popular president whom they want to keep in office. Because a president in his second term cannot seek reelection, he is commonly referred to as a **lame duck**. Lawmakers know that the president's time in office is limited, so they are less likely to cooperate or compromise with him. On the other hand, a president who wants to chart a policy course that is unpopular may be more likely to do so when he does not have to face the voters. Lame-duck status therefore has the advantage of giving the president more political freedom, but the disadvantage of making him less directly responsive to public opinion. Barack Obama (2009–2017) provides an example. During his second term, public opinion was unfavorable toward continuing troop involvement in Afghanistan, but President Obama maintained U.S. commitments in that area even after declaring the end of U.S. combat there. Some critics believe he should have heeded the public and withdrawn troops, but others argue that he was taking the unpopular but correct course of action for the nation. Absent the pressure of seeking reelection to

Table 13.1 Presidential Order of Succession

1. Vice president
2. Speaker of the House
3. President pro tempore of the Senate
Cabinet Secretaries
4. State
5. Treasury
6. Defense
7. Attorney General
8. Interior
9. Agriculture
10. Commerce
11. Labor
12. Health and Human Services
13. Housing and Urban Development
14. Transportation
15. Energy
16. Education
17. Veterans' Affairs
18. Homeland Security

Key Questions

How do term limits make the president less responsive to public opinion?

lame duck: *Term-limited official in his or her last term of office.*

The Granger Collection, NYC

Image 13.1 George Washington was a successful military general who led American troops in the Revolutionary War. He was widely admired and was chosen to be the first president of the United States because it was believed that his experience and personal characteristics would be a model for the future. He took the oath of office on April 30, 1789, on the balcony of Federal Hall in New York City, then the nation's capital.

Key Questions

Unlike members of Congress, presidents represent all the people of the United States. How can a president represent all the people?

a third term, Obama had the flexibility to pursue a policy on what he perceived to be its merits. But being a lame duck comes with costs, as was the case with Obama's nomination of Merrick Garland to serve on the Supreme Court. The Republican-controlled Senate refused to hold hearings on the nomination for all of 2016, effectively killing it.

Background and Experience

In keeping with the democratic spirit of the founding of the United States, the Framers did not specify qualifications for the presidency beyond age and citizenship, and in the ensuing two centuries, men of varying backgrounds have served in the office. Presidents have come from all walks of life and from almost all regions of the country. Harry S. Truman (1945–53), born in Missouri, was a farmer and owner of a men's clothing store. Ronald Reagan, born in Illinois, was a radio sports announcer and actor. Barack Obama, born in Hawaii, was a community organizer and constitutional law professor. Until John F. Kennedy (1961–63), a Catholic, was elected in 1960, all presidents were from Protestant backgrounds. Until Barack Obama, an African American, was elected in 2008, all presidents were white and male. In 1984, Walter Mondale made history by selecting Geraldine Ferraro as the first woman to run for vice president. In 2008, Hillary Clinton ran for the Democratic Party presidential nomination but lost to Obama. In 2016, she ran again for the Democratic Party nomination and was successful; in November 2016, she and her male vice presidential running mate, Senator Tim Kaine (D-VA), lost the presidential election to Donald Trump. In 2020, Democratic nominee

Twelfth	1804	Requires that electors cast separate votes for president and vice president and specifies requirements for vice presidential candidates
Twentieth	1933	Declares that presidential term begins on January 20 (instead of March 4)
Twenty-Second	1951	Limits presidents to two terms
Twenty-Fifth	1967	Specifies replacement of the vice president and establishes the position of acting president during a president's disability
		Of the twenty-seven Amendments to the Constitution, four pertain directly to the presidency: the Twelfth, Twentieth, Twenty-Second, and Twenty-Fifth.

Figure 13.1 **Constitutional Amendments Pertaining to the Presidency**

Joseph Biden chose an African American and South Asian woman, Senator Kamala Harris (D-CA) as his vice presidential running mate. Overall, it has taken more than two centuries, but women and minorities have joined white men as viable candidates for the presidency and vice presidency.

The clearest path to the White House is through the office of the vice president, but most presidents have some combination of service in the military, in a state legislature, or as governor; in the U.S. House of Representatives and Senate; or in a prior presidential administration. For example, James Monroe (1817–25) was a soldier in the Revolutionary War, a U.S. senator, Minister to France, Secretary of State, and Secretary of War. Herbert Hoover (1929–33) was an international food relief worker and Secretary of Commerce.[5]

Image 13.2 Being born in a log cabin was an asset for presidential hopefuls in the nineteenth century, and candidates liked to portray their humble origins and demonstrate that they were men of the people. In 1840, William Henry Harrison cultivated the connection with campaign images such as this one, although he was born in an elegant plantation manor house. But the claims of other presidents, such as Abraham Lincoln, were legitimate. The log cabin birthplace of James Buchanan still stands.

There are advantages and disadvantages for presidents, depending on their prior experience. Lyndon Baines Johnson (1963–69) was very successful in passing his domestic policy agenda, in large part due to his experience as a House member, U.S. senator, and Senate majority leader. His prior experience taught him crucial negotiating skills with members of Congress, and he used his skills to their fullest extent. In contrast, Jimmy Carter (1977–81) was generally considered to have failed in getting his domestic policy agenda enacted because of his lack of experience in Washington. He came to the White House from the governor's mansion in Georgia, where he exercised executive power with little challenge from the legislature. When he faced a Congress that did not embrace his agenda, he lacked the negotiating skills to be successful. Of course, no single set of qualifications or experiences can guarantee success as a president. When voters cast their ballots for president, they take a leap of faith that the person who wins will be trustworthy, accountable, and responsive to their needs and will implement the laws equally for every citizen. For a list of the presidents of the United States, see Table 13.2.

Expansion of the Presidency

President George Washington had the enormous responsibility of setting the standard for how a president should govern in a democracy, and he was very careful not to infuse the office with airs of royalty or privilege. The Framers anticipated that the executive

Key Questions
What defines an imperial presidency?

Table 13.2 Presidents of the United States, 1789–2021

President	Term Dates	Party	Prior Experience
1. George Washington	1789–97		General, delegate to First Continental Congress
2. John Adams	1797–1801	Federalist	Vice president
3. Thomas Jefferson	1801–09	Democratic-Republican	Vice president, Secretary of State
4. James Madison	1809–17	Democratic-Republican	Secretary of State, U.S. House, state legislator
5. James Monroe	1817–25	Democratic-Republican	Secretary of War, Secretary of State, U.S. Senate
6. John Quincy Adams	1825–29	Democratic-Republican	Secretary of State, U.S. Senate
7. Andrew Jackson	1829–37	Democrat	U.S. Senate, general, U.S. House
8. Martin Van Buren	1837–41	Democrat	Vice president, U.S. Senate
9. William Henry Harrison	1841 (died in office)	Whig	U.S. Senate, general, territorial governor
10. John Tyler	1841–45	Whig	Vice president, U.S. Senate, governor, U.S. House
11. James K. Polk	1845–49	Democrat	Governor, U.S. House
12. Zachary Taylor	1849–50 (died in office)	Whig	General
13. Millard Fillmore	1850–53	Whig	Vice president, U.S. House
14. Franklin Pierce	1853–57	Democrat	U.S. Senate, U.S. House, state legislator
15. James Buchanan	1857–61	Democrat	Secretary of State, U.S. Senate, U.S. House
16. Abraham Lincoln	1861–65 (died in office)	Republican; National Union	U.S. House
17. Andrew Johnson	1865–69	Democrat; National Union	Vice president, U.S. Senate, U.S. House
18. Ulysses S. Grant	1869–77	Republican	General
19. Rutherford B. Hayes	1877–81	Republican	Governor, U.S. House, general
20. James A. Garfield	1881 (died in office)	Republican	U.S. Senate, general, U.S. House, state legislator
21. Chester A. Arthur	1881–85	Republican	Vice president, collector of the port of New York
22. Grover Cleveland	1885–89	Democrat	Governor, mayor
23. Benjamin Harrison	1889–93	Republican	U.S. Senate
24. Grover Cleveland	1893–97	Democrat	U.S. president, governor, mayor
25. William McKinley	1897–1901 (died in office)	Republican	Governor, U.S. House
26. Theodore Roosevelt	1901–1909	Republican	Vice president, governor
27. William Howard Taft	1909–13	Republican	Secretary of War, governor general of the Philippines, federal judge
28. Woodrow Wilson	1913–21	Democrat	Governor, university president

Table 13.2 Continued

President	Term Dates	Party	Prior Experience
29. Warren G. Harding	1921–23 (died in office)	Republican	U.S. Senate, lieutenant governor, state legislator
30. Calvin Coolidge	1923–29	Republican	Vice president, governor
31. Herbert Hoover	1929–33	Republican	Secretary of Commerce
32. Franklin Delano Roosevelt	1933–45 (died in office)	Democrat	Governor, Assistant Secretary of the Navy, state legislator
33. Harry S. Truman	1945–53	Democrat	Vice president, U.S. Senate
34. Dwight D. Eisenhower	1953–61	Republican	University president, general
35. John F. Kennedy	1961–63 (died in office)	Democrat	U.S. Senate, U.S. House
36. Lyndon Baines Johnson	1963–69	Democrat	Vice president, U.S. Senate, U.S. House
37. Richard M. Nixon	1969–74 (resigned)	Republican	Vice president, U.S. Senate, U.S. House
38. Gerald R. Ford	1974–77	Republican	Vice president, U.S. House
39. Jimmy Carter	1977–81	Democrat	Governor, state legislator
40. Ronald Reagan	1981–89	Republican	Governor, actor, union president
41. George H. W. Bush	1989–93	Republican	Vice president, CIA director, U.S. House
42. William J. Clinton	1993–2001	Democrat	Governor, state attorney general
43. George W. Bush	2001–2009	Republican	Governor
44. Barack Obama	2009–2017	Democrat	U.S. Senate, state legislator
45. Donald Trump	2017–2021	Republican	Businessman/television personality
46. Joseph Biden	2021–	Democrat	U.S. Senator, vice president

branch would be led by one person whose primary responsibility would be the defense of the United States. As commander of the Continental Army during the Revolutionary War, Washington had military experience, but he was also a cautious and thoughtful statesman who wanted to establish a precedent for how the chief executive should operate.

In the course of the nineteenth century, from the presidencies of Thomas Jefferson, to Andrew Jackson (1829–37), to Abraham Lincoln, and finally to William McKinley (1897–1901), the nation grew in size, population, and economic power. The job of the chief executive grew accordingly, but, though increasingly demanding and complex, it remained essentially focused on national defense and economic growth. In the twentieth century, however, the United States became a leading international military and economic power. Its role in World War II and the subsequent Cold War against the Soviet Union expanded the authority of the presidency. Historian and presidential adviser Arthur Schlesinger Jr. used the term **imperial presidency** to describe the power of the president to speak for the nation on the world stage and to set the policy agenda at home.[6] Schlesinger's view suggests that as long as the United States is engaged in military conflicts all over the world to promote and protect its interests, the president will be considered the most important figure in American politics. However, after two very long wars, public opinion has shifted against intervening in foreign conflicts (see Chapter 6, Public Opinion), which leaves less support for presidential military action on foreign soil. As the public looks more inward and focuses on domestic policy, Congress and the president stand on more balanced scales.

Presidential Power: Constitutional Grants and Limits

LO 13-2 Identify the powers of the president and explain how they are limited

As we saw in Chapter 12, Congress, the Framers enumerated Congress's powers, both to assert powers that were missing under the Articles of Confederation, such as the powers to collect taxes and to regulate commerce, and to constrain the branch they anticipated would be the most powerful. The Framers expected the executive branch to be smaller and less powerful and did not believe it necessary to enumerate the executive powers as they did the legislative powers (see Table 13.3). Instead, in the very first sentence of Article II, they "vested" the president with a general grant of "executive Power" and then, later in the article, stated certain additional powers and responsibilities. The general grant of executive power has allowed the presidency to become the powerful office it is today. In this section, we look at the constitutional sources of the president's powers, the ways in which presidents have sought to expand their constitutional powers, and the ways in which the other branches, especially Congress, act to check and balance the president.

Commander in Chief

commander in chief: *Head of the armed forces of the United States.*

The president is the **commander in chief** of the armed forces of the United States, which includes the Army, Navy, Air Force, Marine Corps, and Coast Guard, plus their Reserve and National Guard units. An elected commander in chief, rather than an appointed military officer, is a distinctly important element of American democracy. The president directs all war efforts and military conflict. Congress, however, has the power to officially declare war and to authorize funding for the war effort. Because the war powers that are divided between the president and Congress are so contentious, we examine them later in the chapter.

Key Questions

Why is it important that the commander in chief of the U.S. military is a civilian?

Table 13.3 A Comparison of Legislative and Executive Authority Under the Constitution

While the Constitution grants specific legislative authority to Congress, it provides a general grant of authority to the president that does not require specific enumerated grants of power, nor is there an executive equivalent of Article I, Section 9, which specifically limits congressional authority.

	Legislative	Executive
Authority	"All legislative Powers herein granted shall be vested in a Congress of the United States"	"The executive Power shall be vested in a President of the United States"
Specific Powers	Article I, Section 8, including: • lay and collect taxes • provide for the common defense • regulate interstate and foreign commerce • authorize courts • set uniform rules for naturalization and bankruptcy • establish post offices • make all laws that are "necessary and proper" for carrying out the listed powers	Article II, Section 2, including: • act as commander in chief of armed forces • grant pardons • make treaties • receive foreign ministers • appoint ambassadors, judges, cabinet-level officials Article II, Section 3: • ensure that the laws are faithfully executed Article I, Section 7: • veto legislation
Limits on Power	Explicit limits on powers: Article I, Section 9, including: • no bills of attainder • no ex post facto laws • no titles of nobility Bill of Rights: • substantive limits of the First through Eighth Amendments Ninth Amendment: • enumeration of rights does not grant general authority Tenth Amendment: • people and states retain reserved powers not granted to Congress	Mostly through checks and balances: • veto override • Senate confirmation on appointments • Senate treaty ratification • removal by impeachment

Power to Pardon

The president has the power to grant clemency, or mercy, for crimes against the United States, except in the case of impeachment from federal office. Clemency is a broad designation that includes a **pardon**, which is forgiving an offense altogether, and a commutation, which is shortening a federal prison sentence; in general, pardoning someone is considered a more sweeping act of clemency than commuting a sentence. Election considerations can also come into play because presidents who are in their first term may want to appear tougher on crime than in their second term, when they will not be seeking reelection. For example, in his first term in office, President George W. Bush issued 19 pardons and commuted 2 sentences, but in his second term, Bush granted 170 pardons and commuted 7 sentences. In comparison, President Obama issued 22 pardons and commuted 1 sentence in his first term, but by the end of his second term, he had issued 212 pardons and commuted 1,715 sentences. In his first term, President Trump issued 25 pardons and commuted 11 sentences.[7]

pardon: *Full forgiveness for a crime.*

Key Questions

Should the president have the power to pardon? What impact does this power have on citizen equality?

The crimes for which people are pardoned also differ across presidencies. Under George H. W. Bush, many of the pardon recipients had been part of the Iran-Contra scandal under President Reagan. In contrast, his son, President George W. Bush, refused to pardon a former White House staff member, I. Lewis Libby, who had been convicted of lying and obstruction of justice in a federal investigation about a leak of confidential information (although he did commute his prison sentence).[8] President Bill Clinton's most famous pardon was to a wealthy campaign contributor, Marc Rich, who had been indicted for tax evasion and fraud. President Obama focused most of his pardons on less prominent individuals who were convicted of crimes and served their sentences but who petitioned to have their full citizenship rights reinstated. President Trump has focused his pardons and clemency on more well-known individuals who tended to share his conservative beliefs, including Sheriff Joe Arpario and Dinesh D'Souza but he also pardoned an African American woman named Mary Alice Johnson who served 21 years for a conviction on a nonviolent drug offense.[9]

Treaties and Recognition of Foreign Nations

The president or his designated representative has the power to negotiate and sign treaties with foreign nations, but he must do so with the "Advice and Consent of the Senate," as specified by the Constitution. For a treaty to be valid, two-thirds "of the Senators present" must approve. Historically, the Senate has refused to approve some notable treaties, ranging from the Treaty of Versailles ending World War I signed by President Woodrow Wilson (1913–21), to the Kyoto Protocol on climate change signed by Vice President Albert Gore Jr., who was representing President William Jefferson (Bill) Clinton (1993–2001).

These examples illustrate how the requirement that the Senate approve treaties serves as a gateway for public input into presidential actions, and how it can be a gate that blocks a president's attempt to reach agreements with foreign nations. Today, with the expansion of globalization, the president's representatives negotiate treaties over a wide range of areas, such as military alliances, human rights accords, environmental regulations, and trade policies. For example, President Obama spent considerable time and energy negotiating the Trans-Pacific Partnership trade agreement with twelve nations, foremost Japan, while in office, but Congress did not ratify it and President Trump withdrew from negotiations on it. President Trump also withdrew the United States from the Iran Nuclear Deal, the Paris Climate Accord (see Chapter 16, Economic, Domestic, and Foreign Policy), and the Open Skies Treaty, which allowed nations to conduct unarmed surveillance over each other's territories, The president also enters into executive agreements, which do not require Senate approval and tend to be less expansive in scope than treaties.

The president's authority in foreign affairs includes the power to "receive Ambassadors and other public Ministers," which allows the president to recognize the legitimacy of foreign regimes. Such decisions are frequently based on the internal political system of the foreign nation. For example, revolutionaries overthrew Russia's czarist regime in 1917, but the new Soviet Union, a Communist nation, was not recognized by the United States until 1933, through the action of President Franklin

Political Analytics

A Day in the Life of the President

MOST AMERICANS KNOW THAT THE PRESIDENT of the United States resides and works in the White House in Washington, D.C. Many people probably assume that the president spends his day immersed in international and domestic policy discussions and decisions. But what does a president's daily schedule actually look like? Do all presidents follow the same schedule? Is every minute of the day filled with an activity?

Figure 13.2 shows a day in the life of former President Barack Obama and President Donald J. Trump. President Obama's schedule began early in the morning and extended into the early evening. President Trump's day appears to begin later in the morning for official business

and extends into the afternoon. In March of 2020, President Trump was dealing with the COVID-19 crisis and he held daily press conferences for a time. Much of the president's whereabouts are closely guarded. Still, we can see similarities in the schedules. For example, both include an intelligence briefing, which usually is in the form of a report from the Central Intelligence Agency (CIA) and the State Department regarding national security.

Notice the length of the president's daily routine and the variety of events and duties of the president. Find the similarities and differences between the schedules of Presidents Obama and Trump.

President Trump, March 27, 2020

10:00	In-House Pool Call Time
Noon	The President receives his intelligence briefing, Oval Office
4:00	The President participates in a signing ceremony for H.R. 748, the CARES Act
5:00	Members of the Coronavirus Task Force hold a press briefing

Figure 13.2 **What Is the President Doing Today?**

Sources: Schedules were condensed adapted from https://www.whitehouse.gov/blog and https://www.georgewbushlibrary.smu.edu/~/media/GWBL/Files/Digitized%20Content/2014-0098-F/2008/t003-026-080307-2014-0098-f.ashx; FACTBASE, *Donald Trump - President's Public Schedule*, https://factbase.se/topic/calendar; BBC News, *Trump's daily schedule v Obama and Bush*, http://www.bbc.com/news/world-us-canada-42610275.

President Barack Obama, March 31, 2016

Early am	With the vice president, began the day with the Presidential Daily Briefing, White House, Oval Office
10:35	Held a trilateral meeting with President Park Geun-Hye of the Republic of Korea and Prime Minister Shinzo Abe of Japan; the vice president also attended Walter E. Washington Convention Center, Washington, D.C.
2:10	Held a bilateral meeting with President Xi Jinping of the People's Republic of China; the vice president also attended Walter E. Washington Convention Center, Washington, D.C.
4:15	Held a brief bilateral meeting with President Francois Hollande of France, Walter E. Washington Convention Center, Washington, D.C.
7:15	Held a working dinner with heads of delegations at the Nuclear Security Summit; the vice president also attended White House, East Room

Thinking Critically

1. What do you think are the most important parts of the president's day?

2. These presidents' daily schedules show what a typical day for the president at the White House looks like. What information about presidential activities is not shown and would be interesting to know?

Figure 13.2 **What Is the President Doing Today?** **(Continued)**

Roosevelt. In contrast, in 2008, when the young democracy of Kosovo declared its independence from Serbia, President George W. Bush immediately recognized it as an independent nation.[10] However, the president also reserves the power not to recognize self-declared independent nations, as in the case of Russian separatists who took over control of the Crimean peninsula and eastern parts of Ukraine.

Executive and Judicial Nominations

The president has the power to appoint all federal officers, including cabinet secretaries, heads of independent agencies, and ambassadors. The presidential appointment process has two steps: (1) nomination and (2) subsequent approval by a majority of the Senate. The appointed officers are typically referred to as political appointees, and they are expected to carry out the president's political and policy agenda (in contrast to civil servants, who are hired through a merit-based system and are politically neutral; see Chapter 14, The Bureaucracy). During Senate recesses, the president can make appointments that will expire when the Senate officially adjourns at the close of a Congress (adjourns *sine die*), unless the appointee is subsequently confirmed. Presidents have sometimes used recess appointments to bypass the Senate, as President Obama did in appointing Richard Cordray director of the Consumer Financial Protection Bureau in 2012. Obama used the recess appointment power to get around strong Republican opposition to Cordray's appointment and the creation of the bureau he was nominated to lead (for more on this bureau, see Chapter 14).

In order to prevent the president from making recess appointments when the Senate is on short breaks, the Senate has taken to officially staying in session but not conducting any business. In response, President Obama acted as if the Senate were in recess and made a set of appointments to several agencies, including the National Labor Relations Board. In the 2014 case *National Labor Relations Board v. Noel Canning*, the Supreme Court ruled that only the Senate can decide when it is in recess, thus striking down three of Obama's appointments.

President Trump has used his appointment powers to bypass the Senate in a different way than Obama did. In his first term, two cabinet secretaries resigned by choice, seven resigned under pressure from Trump to leave their jobs, and one, Secretary of Defense James Mattis, resigned in protest of Trump's decision to withdraw U.S. forces from Syria. In some cases, Trump kept these positions open for extended periods of time, relying on acting (temporary) secretaries, but subsequently nominated replacements who were confirmed by the Senate.[11]

The president also nominates judges in the federal judicial system, from the district court level to the Supreme Court, and they too must receive majority approval in the Senate (see Chapter 15, The Judiciary, for more details on the judicial nomination process). In recent years, this process has become more ideological and contentious; rather than considering only qualifications for the job, presidents and members of the Senate also consider a nominee's ideological views on key issues. As we discussed in Chapter 12, the Senate changed its rules in 2013 to make it easier to confirm district and appeals court nominees but did not change the process for Supreme Court nominations until 2017; since then, President Trump has nominated two Supreme Court justices who were confirmed by the Republican controlled Senate by narrow margins. As with the treaty process, the Senate's advice and consent role in appointments and nominations is a gateway for citizen influence but the elimination of the filibuster has reduced the power of individual Senators to block federal court nominations.

The president has the power to fire federal officers but not to remove judges, who can be removed only by impeachment. Most presidents are reluctant to remove cabinet members except in the case of corruption or severe incompetence. However, more recently, President Trump asked his first Secretary of HHS, Tom Price, to resign after a scandal, he fired his first Secretary of State because of disagreements on the direction of U.S. foreign policy, and he asked his EPA administrator to resign after a series of financial scandals involving misuse of federal dollars.

Veto and the Veto Override

The president has an important role in the enactment of legislation. He has the power to **veto** bills passed by Congress before they become law by refusing to sign them and sending them back to the chamber in which they originated with his objections. If Congress will be going out of session within ten days, he can simply not sign the bill, a practice known as a **pocket veto**. If the president refuses to sign the bill and Congress remains in session, the bill is enacted into law.

To counter the power of the veto, the Framers gave Congress the veto override, the power to overturn a presidential veto with a two-thirds vote in each chamber. Because the

Key Questions

Consider the Senate's power to check the president in making treaties and appointments. What are the costs and benefits of this power sharing in terms of government efficiency and responsiveness?

veto: *Authority of the president to block legislation passed by Congress. Congress can override a veto by a two-thirds majority in each chamber.*

pocket veto: *Automatic veto that occurs when Congress goes out of session within ten days of submitting a bill to the president and the president has not signed it.*

two-thirds threshold is higher than the majority vote needed to pass a bill in the first place, it is difficult for Congress to overcome presidential opposition to a bill. The high threshold reinforces the power of the president in blocking congressional action and so serves as a gateway for presidential influence in the legislative process. One could also see the veto as a gate that legislation must pass through to become law, which can be unlocked only with a congressional supermajority.

The veto is the most direct way that the president checks the power of Congress. Presidents use the veto power either to prevent a bill from becoming law or to pressure Congress into making changes to bring the bill closer to his policies and his view of the national interest[12] (see Table 13.4). For most of the twentieth century, Congress sent the president a large number of single-issue or narrowly drawn bills each year. In recent decades, however, Congress has learned to get around the threat of a presidential veto by passing **omnibus bills** that include provisions affecting a number of issue areas. These bills are costly to veto because they affect a wide range of voters and generate a lot of public support, so they give Congress an advantage in negotiating with the president.[13]

omnibus bill: *One very large bill that encompasses many separate bills.*

Presidents naturally tend to veto more bills when Congress is controlled by the opposite party, a condition known as divided government. One of the most dramatic veto battles occurred in the fall of 1995 and early winter of 1996 between Democratic President Bill Clinton and the Republican-controlled Congress led by then-Speaker Newt Gingrich (see Chapter 3, Federalism). President Clinton and Congress differed

Table 13.4 Presidential Vetoes, 1945–2019

President	Congresses	Regular Vetoes	Pocket Vetoes	Total Vetoes	Vetoes Overridden
Harry S. Truman	79th–82nd	180	70	250	12
Dwight D. Eisenhower	83rd–86th	73	108	181	2
John F. Kennedy	87th–88th	12	9	21	0
Lyndon Baines Johnson	88th–90th	16	14	30	0
Richard M. Nixon	91st–93rd	26	17	43	7
Gerald R. Ford	93rd–94th	48	18	66	12
Jimmy Carter	95th–96th	13	18	31	2
Ronald Reagan	97th–100th	39	39	78	9
George H. W. Bush	101st–102nd	29	15*	44	1
William Jefferson Clinton	103rd–106th	36	1	37	2
George W. Bush	107th–110th	11	1	12	4
Barack Obama	111th–114th	12	0	12	1
Donald Trump	115th–116th	6	0	6	0
Total		495	310	805	52

*President George H. W. Bush attempted to pocket veto two bills during intrasession recesses. Congress considered the two bills enacted into law because the president had not returned the legislation. These two disputed vetoes are not included in Table 13.4.

Source: Kevin R. Kosar, *Regular Vetoes and Pocket Vetoes: An Overview*, CRS Report for Congress, RS22188 (Washington, D.C.: Congressional Research Service, November 18, 2010), 2–4, https://www.hsdl.org/?view&did=740060; source for veto information is John T. Woolley and Gerhard Peters, "Presidential Vetoes: Washington–Obama," The American Presidency Project, accessed September 1, 2020, http://www.presidency.ucsb.edu/data /vetoes.php.

over the size of cuts in **entitlement programs** such as Medicare, the health care program for the elderly (see Chapter 16, Economic, Domestic, and Foreign Policy, for a longer discussion of entitlement programs). Clinton vetoed two omnibus funding bills that Congress sent him, resulting in the shutdown of the entire government both times. The second shutdown lasted several weeks and affected veterans' hospitals, all national parks and monuments, and other government-run services. The public blamed the Republican Congress, not the president, for the impasse, and many of the voters who generally supported the Republicans lived in areas that were hard hit by the shutdown. In January 1996, Congress compromised by agreeing to a funding bill that was closer to President Clinton's position. For the rest of 1996, President Clinton and the Republican majority in Congress worked to produce key legislation on welfare reform, health insurance portability, and the minimum wage. In this case, the president used the threat of more vetoes to get members of Congress to produce legislation closer to his policy positions.[14] Flash forward more than twenty years, and it is clear that presidents still hope to use the veto power to extract concessions from Congress. President Trump did just that when he threatened to veto a bill to fund the government over appropriations to build a southern border wall, which was a major part of his 2016 campaign platform. After shutting down the government briefly, the Congress agreed to authorize funding for the wall. Trump, however, believed it to be insufficient so he diverted additional funds from the Department of Defense for it, even though these funds were originally appropriated for a different purpose.[15]

Other Powers

The president works within this framework of formal powers and constraints to lead the nation, and in doing so becomes the chief agenda setter for domestic and foreign policy. In a later section of this chapter, we discuss agenda setting in more detail; here it is important to note that, over time, smaller tasks assigned to the president in the Constitution have evolved into powerful tools for influencing legislation. One tool is the **State of the Union address**, which is authorized in Article II, Section 3: The president "shall from time to time give to the Congress Information of the State of the Union, and recommend to their Consideration such Measures as he shall judge necessary and expedient." Nothing in this passage requires the president to inform Congress on a yearly basis or to do so in person. Presidents George Washington and John Adams (1797–1801) delivered the State of the Union address in person, but subsequent presidents began sending a written message instead, a tradition that lasted until 1913, when President Wilson went to Congress once again to give the report as an address.[16] Over the past century, presidents have turned this obligation into an opportunity to outline a broad policy agenda for the nation. That same passage also says that the president "may, on extraordinary Occasions convene both Houses, or either of them." Thus the president can call Congress into a special session to consider legislation or to hear him deliver an important speech.[17]

Congress's Ultimate Check on the Executive: Impeachment

Congress has general oversight of the executive branch (a power discussed in Chapters 12 and 14), but its ultimate check on the president is its power to remove him from office.

entitlement programs: *Federal programs, such as Social Security, Medicare, or Medicaid, that pay out benefits to individuals based on a specified set of eligibility criteria.*

Key Questions
How does the veto power give the president influence in the legislative process?

State of the Union address: *Speech on the condition of the country given by the president to Congress every January.*

Key Questions
Have you watched a State of the Union address? What do you think its purpose was? What did you learn from it?

As discussed in Chapter 2, The Constitution, Article II, Section 4, of the Constitution stipulates that the president, vice president, and all civil officers (including cabinet secretaries and federal judges) are subject to removal for "Treason, Bribery, or other high Crimes and Misdemeanors." Should these officers be removed from office, they may be subject to normal criminal charges and proceedings, where applicable.

The process of removal begins with **impeachment** in the House of Representatives. Typically, the House Judiciary Committee investigates charges and recommends to the full House whether to impeach or not. If the House votes to impeach a federal officer, the Senate holds a trial, and if the president is impeached, the chief justice of the Supreme Court presides. If two-thirds of the senators vote to convict, the official is removed from office.

At the highest level of federal office, three presidents—Andrew Johnson, Bill Clinton, and Donald Trump—have been impeached, but none of them was convicted by the Senate, and all remained in office. Impeachment resolutions have been introduced by individual members of the House of Representatives against other presidents, but they were not acted on. (For discussion of the 2019–2020 impeachment proceedings against Donald Trump, see Chapter 2, The Constitution; Chapter 12, Congress; and Chapter 15, The Judiciary.) The greatest impact stemming from the power to impeach came in the case of Richard M. Nixon, which shows how the threat of impeachment can be enough to remove a president from office. Knowing he was about to be impeached, Nixon resigned instead. As we saw in the cases of Clinton and Trump, partisanship can influence some members of Congress in their votes to move forward with impeachment proceedings.

As the following discussion of Richard Nixon will show, impeachment is a rarely used but powerful instrument that makes it possible for Congress to hold the president accountable for his actions. In a democratic nation guided by the rule of law, all citizens are equally obligated to obey the laws of the land, including the president.

Richard M. Nixon. President Richard Nixon was embroiled in a serious scandal known as Watergate, after the name of a complex in Washington where the Democratic National Committee had its headquarters. It was there that the scandal began with a break-in on June 17, 1972. In August, the *Washington Post* reported that the bank account of one of the five men caught in the act and arrested had $25,000 in funds originally given to the Nixon 1972 reelection campaign.[18]

Nixon denied any connection and was reelected in the fall, but all the while he and his aides were working to cover up the fact that his reelection committee had ordered the break-in to install listening devices on Democratic Party phones. Two *Washington Post* reporters, Bob Woodward and Carl Bernstein, continued to investigate the story (see Chapter 7, The News and Social Media). As connections between Nixon and the break-in were revealed, several of his aides were convicted of conspiracy, burglary, and wiretapping, and others resigned. In May 1973, the Senate's newly formed Watergate Committee began televised hearings on the Watergate break-in and cover-up, and the Justice Department appointed Archibald Cox as the special prosecutor in charge of the Watergate investigation.

In the months that followed, a Nixon staffer revealed that the president had tape-recorded all of his White House conversations, and both the Senate Watergate

impeachment: *Process whereby the House brings charges against the president or another federal official that will, upon conviction by the Senate, remove him or her from office.*

Key Questions
Think about the impeachments and the near-impeachment described here. What was the basis for impeachment in each case?

Key Questions
As you read the story of Richard Nixon, contrast it to the impeachment proceedings against Clinton and Trump, respectively.

Key Questions
In a democracy, should the president have executive privilege?

Committee and the House Judiciary Committee formally issued subpoenas demanding that Nixon turn over the recordings. The turning point in the Watergate scandal came on Saturday, October 20, 1973, when President Nixon asked his attorney general, Elliot Richardson, to fire Archibald Cox and abolish the office of special prosecutor entirely. Richardson refused, as did the deputy attorney general. Both resigned. Solicitor General Robert Bork, next in command, then carried out the president's wishes. What had been a struggle for information became a question of obstruction of justice by the president.

Bettmann/Corbis

Image 13.3 When Richard Nixon resigned the presidency in August 1974, it was the first time in U.S. history that a president had relinquished his office. President Nixon left office under charges of abuse of power arising from a cover-up of the Watergate scandal, which forever changed the nation's faith in the presidency as a trustworthy institution.

President Nixon turned over a limited number of tapes, but there was an eighteen-and-a-half-minute gap on one tape, and Congress wanted to know what was discussed during that time and why it was erased. The administration claimed that the tape was erased by mistake. During the next months, Nixon released only partial transcripts and said that others were protected by **executive privilege**—the president's right to engage in communications with his advisers that he does not have to reveal. The justification for this privilege is that the president must make difficult choices and, without the guarantee of privilege, may not receive or deliver the fullest information in the course of his deliberations.

The Supreme Court created an exception to this privilege in *United States v. Nixon* when on July 24, 1974, it unanimously ruled that executive privilege is not absolute and must give way when the government needs the information for a trial. The tapes showed that Nixon and his aides had conspired to cover up the Watergate break-in. Three days later, the House Judiciary Committee approved three articles of impeachment against Nixon.[19] With the full House of Representatives ready to vote on the articles, President Nixon resigned on August 9, 1974.

In 1975, Nixon's successor, former Vice President Gerald R. Ford (1974–77), pardoned Nixon of all federal offenses he might have committed. The Watergate scandal had a negative impact on the American presidency, raising public mistrust of the office and of the federal government more generally. However, the process leading up to Nixon's resignation also revealed the ways in which members of both parties can work together in Congress to exercise congressional oversight of the executive.

Impeachment is not a power to be used lightly. However, it does serve as a gateway for the public, through its elected officials in Congress, to try to hold the president, cabinet officials, and federal judges accountable for abuses of power.

executive privilege:
President's right to engage in confidential communications with his advisers.

The Growth of Executive Influence

LO 13-3 Describe the growth of executive influence

Key Questions

Should the president be subjected to civil lawsuits while he is in office? State the reasons for your answer.

Key Questions

What should be done about the growth of executive power? Is it a problem for checks and balances among the separate branches?

presidential directive: *Official instructions from the president regarding federal policy.*

executive order: *Presidential directive that usually involves implementing a specific law.*

With all the formal constitutional restrictions on the president, one has to wonder how the modern presidency became so powerful. The answer lies in the general grant of executive power and the constitutional provision that the president "take Care that the Laws be faithfully executed," which he promises to do when he takes the oath of office. Presidents have found ways to unlock the enormous powers inherent in these constitutional provisions to expand their informal powers over policy making and implementation. The president's veto power and Congress's power to override and to impeach the president counteract each other and help ensure that each branch remains responsive to its governing responsibilities. However, Congress has no formal means to balance and check the president's growing executive power, though at times the judicial branch has been able to do so.

Presidential Directives and Signing Statements

Presidents use the executive power to issue **presidential directives** that give specific instructions on a federal policy and do not require congressional approval. Recent presidents have used this unilateral power much more frequently than previous presidents, especially under conditions of divided government or interbranch policy conflict.[20] Presidential directives might take the form of executive orders, proclamations, or military orders. They are the primary way that presidents shape policy implementation, and they are the instruments presidents use to act quickly in national emergencies.[21]

The best-known type of directive is the **executive order**, which can be used for a wide range of purposes. Typically, executive orders instruct federal employees to take a specific action or implement a policy in a particular way. Some scholars argue that executive orders are an important source of "independent authority" that is used solely at the discretion of the president.[22] Even though presidents since Washington have issued executive orders, the orders were not officially numbered until 1862 and not published in the *Federal Register* until 1935.[23] In 1948, President Truman integrated the armed forces with Executive Order 9981, stating "there shall be equality of treatment and opportunity for all persons in the armed forces, without regard to race, color, religion, or national origin."[24] Truman used the power of executive order to bypass congressional and some military opposition to integration of the armed forces because he believed it was the right thing for the country.

Similarly, in 1957, President Dwight D. Eisenhower (1953–61) used a combination of executive orders, proclamations, and military orders to enforce school integration in Little Rock, Arkansas. Following the 1954 and 1955 *Brown v. Board of Education* Supreme Court rulings that struck down the practice of segregation in public schools, the governor of Arkansas, Orval Faubus, called up the Arkansas National Guard to block nine African Americans from attending Central High School in Little Rock. President Eisenhower responded by issuing a proclamation calling on the governor to cease and desist, and when the governor ignored the proclamation, Eisenhower issued Executive Order 10730 to send the 101st Airborne Division to Little Rock to ensure that the students would be allowed into the school (see also the Supreme Court Case *Cooper v. Aaron* in Chapter 15). He also used his authority as commander in chief to take command of the Arkansas National Guard and order it to assist in the school's integration. Eisenhower intervened because he believed it was his obligation as president to enforce the laws of the land as set forth by the rulings of the Supreme Court.[25]

Still, a presidential directive is not completely immune from scrutiny or accountability. In 1952, during the Korean War, the United Steelworkers union threatened to stop work at steel mills. In response, President Truman used his execu-

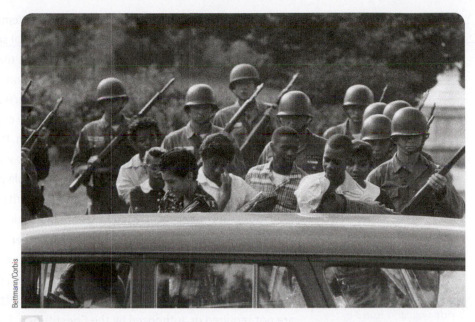

Bettmann/Corbis

Image 13.4 In September 1957, in a move that demonstrated federal power over state power as well as the authority of the commander in chief, President Dwight D. Eisenhower sent the 101st Airborne Division to Little Rock, Arkansas, to protect nine African American students attempting to attend previously all-white Central High School. He also federalized the Arkansas National Guard for the same purpose.

tive powers to order the seizure of steel mills and put them under the control of the U.S. government. Although the steel workers were willing to put off the strike and work in the newly government-controlled mills, the steel mill owners sued to challenge the legality of the seizure. In *Youngstown Sheet and Tube Co. v. Sawyer,* better known as the Steel Seizure case, the Supreme Court ruled against the president, claiming he had no statutory authority from Congress to seize the mills and that his commander in chief status did not allow him to seize domestic property when the United States was at war in a foreign land (see Supreme Court Cases: *Youngstown Sheet and Tube Co. v. Sawyer*).

In foreign and military affairs, presidents can issue presidential directives on national security; these have a similar purpose to executive orders but are not published in the *Federal Register,* which is the official record of government regulations (see Chapter 14). These directives can announce specific sanctions against individuals who are considered enemies of the United States or make larger statements about U.S. policy toward a foreign country. President George W. Bush used this power frequently in what he described as a war on terror and in the conduct of the wars in Afghanistan and Iraq. For example, he issued an order in 2001 to create military tribunals that would try suspected enemy combatants and terrorists, rather than allowing them to be tried in a regular military court. These tribunals were later struck down by the Supreme Court, which ruled that while Congress could establish these tribunals, the president did not have the authority to create a separate judicial system outside the military court system. He also created a special subcategory called homeland security presidential directives, which are not as widely publicized as other directives and deal only with homeland security policy.

Donald Trump has also used his power to issue executive orders under the national security justification. Shortly after taking office, he issued a travel ban against individuals coming from Iraq, Iran, Libya, Somalia, Syria, and Yemen, which were all predominantly Muslim countries, saying that they posed a national security risk due to terrorism. After that ban was challenged in lower federal courts on the grounds of discrimination based on religion, the Trump administration dropped Iraq from the list and reissued the ban that was again blocked by lower federal courts. The third version of the ban included Chad, North Korea, and Venezuelan government officials, these changes also meant that all the countries subject to the ban were not predominantly Muslim. It was this version of the ban that made it to the Supreme Court for a full hearing; in *Trump v. Hawaii*, the Supreme Court upheld the ban in a 5-4 ruling. The Court accepted the rationale put forth by the Trump administration that the travel ban was within the statutory authority of the executive and that it was based on national security concerns, and was not discriminatory against Muslims from these countries based on their religion.[26] As of September 2020, after just over three years in office, Trump had issued 181 executive orders as compared to Obama, who issued a total of 147 by the end of his first term in office.[27] When a president signs a bill into law, he can issue **signing statements**, written remarks that reflect his interpretation of the law that are not required or authorized by the Constitution. Signing statements can be classified as nonconstitutional and constitutional. Nonconstitutional statements are typically symbolic, celebrating the passage of the law or providing technical instructions for implementing a new law. Constitutional statements are more serious in that the president uses them to indicate a disagreement with Congress on specific provisions in the law. In constitutional signing statements, the president may go so far as to refuse to implement specific provisions of laws. This kind of statement is a challenge to Congress's constitutional authority to legislate.[28] Even when the presidency and the Congress are controlled by the same party, signing statements can be used to shift the implementation of policy toward presidential preferences. President Obama recognized the controversy over signing statements, and he issued a memorandum early in his first term stating that he would use signing statements "to address constitutional concerns only when it is appropriate to do so as a means of discharging my constitutional responsibilities."[29] In issuing this memorandum, President Obama was trying to alleviate concerns about abusing executive power but at the same time preserving the presidential power to interpret legislation that is inherent in signing statements. In his first term, Trump issued fifty-seven signing statements, compared to President Obama, who issued twenty-one by the end of his first term.[30]

Presidential directives and signing statements create tension between the president and Congress and between the president and the judiciary because they are an expansion of presidential power. At times they have been deemed illegal.[31] Many presidents, from Lincoln to Franklin D. Roosevelt to George W. Bush, have taken temporary actions that have violated constitutional rights in the name of national security, from suspending *habeas corpus* to interning Japanese Americans and repatriating Latinos to eavesdropping on U.S. citizens (see Chapter 4, Civil Liberties, and Chapter 5, Civil Rights, for expanded discussions of these actions). Judging the merit of such actions is difficult because citizens have to decide whether the president is acting in good faith on behalf of the country or seeking to expand his own power and agenda.

Power to Persuade

Presidents understand that communicating well with the public is essential to building support for their policies. They also face the challenge of using their personal reputations

signing statements:
Written remarks issued by the president when signing a bill into law that often reflect his interpretation of how the law should be implemented.

Key Questions
What limits can Congress, the courts, and/or the American people place on the president?

and negotiating skills to generate support among members of Congress. President Theodore Roosevelt (1901–09) described the office of the president as a **bully pulpit**, where presidents could use the attention associated with the office to make a public argument in favor of or against a policy.[32] The key to using the bully pulpit effectively is to explain a policy in simple and accessible terms, to get the public's attention, and to frame an issue in a way that is favorable to the president's policy position. Using the bully pulpit can accomplish the president's goals only if he already has a receptive audience. In today's highly partisan and divided political climate, there is no guarantee that the president's detractors will listen to his message.[33]

A president's relationship with the members of the news media is a crucial factor in successful communication, and it has evolved dramatically over time. Samuel Kernell, a presidential media scholar, argues that over the past seventy years, presidents have increased the extent to which they control their interactions with the press. Press conferences are one important way of sustaining a relationship with the news media, and presidents have tried to use them to their advantage. Some presidents are more comfortable with the press than others. Franklin D. Roosevelt held an average of eighteen solo press conferences per year, Lyndon Johnson held twenty-five, Ronald Reagan held six, Bill Clinton held six, and George W. Bush held five. President Obama averaged five press conferences per year, and through the first three years of his presidency, Trump held four press conferences per year.[34] Press conferences are somewhat risky because, unlike speeches, presidents do not control the content of the questions that are asked, and they can sometimes make unrehearsed statements that have political consequences.

President Trump always understood that press conferences presented unpredictable environments to convey his messages, and that was never more true than during the height of the COVID-19 pandemic. Trump appeared almost daily at press briefings held specifically on that topic for a few weeks, but after being criticized for imprecise and conflicting statements about the trajectory of the virus, testing for it, and when lockdowns should be lifted, he returned to his usual posture of limiting his exposure to the press in traditional press conference settings. In contrast, President Trump did not hold a press conference on the protests and unrest that unfolded after the death of George Floyd at the hands of a Minneapolis police officer. In addition to press conferences and televised speeches, Presidents Obama and Trump also used new technologies to bypass the media and speak directly to the people. Recognizing that many voters get their news and political information from sources such as Facebook and Twitter instead of from traditional network television, Obama created a blog on the White House website, posted videos of his speeches, and sent mass e-mails to citizens who inquired about specific proposals.[35]

Donald Trump relied mostly on Twitter as his social medium of choice with a significant amount of in-person rallies held across the country to shore up his electoral base. During 2020, the COVID-19 pandemic limited Trump's ability

bully pulpit: *Nickname for the power of the president to use the attention associated with the office to persuade the media, Congress, and the public to support his policy positions.*

Bettmann/Corbis

Image 13.5 President Theodore Roosevelt was a larger-than-life figure who challenged corporate monopolies, sought to strengthen U.S. international power, and increased federal efforts at land conservation. He was known for using the office of the president as a bully pulpit to persuade the public to support his policies.

Supreme Court Cases

Youngstown Sheet and Tube Co. v. Sawyer (1952)

QUESTION: Can the president seize steel mills to prevent a strike during wartime?

ORAL ARGUMENT: May 12, 1952

DECISION: June 2, 1952 (read at http://caselaw.lp.findlaw.com/scripts/getcase.pl?court=US&vol=343&invol=579)

OUTCOME: No, the seizure was overturned (6–3).

After North Korea's invasion of South Korea in June 1950, President Harry Truman sought and received a United Nations resolution permitting intervention on behalf of South Korea. In 1952, with the Korean War still raging, the United Steelworkers announced plans for an April strike. President Truman feared that the strike would severely harm America's war effort. One alternative for putting off the strike was to seek a temporary court order prohibiting a strike when national security is at stake, a provision allowed under the Taft-Hartley Labor Act.

Uncomfortable with what was perceived to be an anti-labor policy, Truman instead ordered Secretary of Commerce Charles Sawyer to seize the steel mills and run them under the flag of the United States. Because the steelworkers preferred working at the steel mills under the government to the Taft-Hartley alternatives, they agreed to come back to work after the seizure.

The steel mill owners then brought suit challenging the seizure. Truman claimed the authority to do this under his power to make sure that the laws were faithfully executed and under his power as commander in chief of the armed forces. The Court's decision rejected the president's authority to seize the steel mills, noting that Congress had not passed a law allowing the seizure, so there were no laws involving the seizure to be faithfully executed. The

Court also ruled that the president's authority to rule as commander in chief did not extend to domestic seizures during foreign wars. Without congressional authorization, the president could not seize the steel mills. A separate concurring opinion, since treated as the heart of the case, noted that the president's authority is at its peak when he acts under the express authority of Congress, is in a middle category when Congress has not acted, and is at its lowest when the president acts contrary to congressional will. As Congress had rejected granting the president the authority to seize property in labor disputes, Truman was acting under the lowest level of authority. Without congressional authorization, the president could not seize the steel mills.

The Steel Seizure case still stands as the leading decision on presidential authority. The Supreme Court relied heavily on it in deciding that President George W. Bush did not have the authority to hold enemy combatants from the war in Afghanistan at the U.S. naval base at Guantánamo Bay, Cuba, without a hearing, since Congress had not authorized the action.*

Thinking Critically

1. Why did the Court block President Truman's seizure of the steel mills?
2. Did the decision place the president above Congress, below Congress, or equal to Congress in terms of making policy?

*Hamdi v. Rumsfeld, 548 U.S. 557 (2006).

---

to travel and to reach thousands of supporters in event style arenas, so he ramped up his other communication outlets, notably Twitter, as well as used digital advertising on Facebook and other platforms, turning them into his own version of the bully pulpit. It was not until May 2020 that Twitter put a fact checking modifier on tweets sent by President Trump. In one case, Trump tweeted about supposed widespread fraud associated with mail in balloting but was fact checked by Twitter to show this was false. Trump then tweeted about the protests of George Floyd's death and threatened to retaliate by shooting the protesters; in that case Trump violated Twitter's policy of not encouraging violence. Trump subsequently used his power as president to issue an executive order ordering the Federal Trade Commission (FTC) to investigate whether social media companies had an anti-conservative bias and to look into whether these companies should be protected from liability for what their users post. (See Chapter 7, The News and Social Media, for more on these communication outlets.)

In conjunction with public outreach, the president also tries to personally persuade members of Congress and other policy makers to support his policies. Political scientist Richard Neustadt has argued that this personal persuasion is the root of presidential power. Several factors affect a president's power to persuade, notably his professional reputation and his approval ratings.[36] A presidential approval rating is usually expressed as the percentage of the American people who say the president is doing a good job. A president's professional reputation is a combination of his prior experience and the steps he takes throughout his term. When a president comes to the Oval Office with executive experience or a strong reputation as a productive legislator, he is likely to have a reservoir of respect from members of Congress, the public, and the media. That reservoir can become depleted if the president makes missteps and is not successful with his legislative agenda.

Lawmakers are more likely to pass a president's policy proposals when his approval rating is high, and they are less cooperative when the president is unpopular. Members of Congress pay attention to presidential approval ratings because national polls are a barometer of public opinion. Members of Congress from districts or states in which a majority of voters chose the incumbent president generally want to support him. It follows, then, that a large presidential electoral victory will yield a greater number of supportive members of Congress. Even members of Congress from districts that did not support the incumbent president want to be careful in the way that they oppose a popular president for fear of looking unpatriotic or unresponsive to majority public opinion. Public approval can be essential to presidential policy success, which is why the president tries to maintain public support throughout his years in the White House[37] (see Chapter 6 for more on presidential approval ratings and presidential effectiveness). More recently, the increase in partisan polarization has made national approval ratings somewhat less important in relation to the approval ratings among a president's own partisan supporters. Despite President Trump's inability to cross the 50 percent approval threshold on a consistent basis in his first term, he maintained an approval rating above 85 percent among Republican voters (see Chapter 6, Public Opinion). Given that strong level of approval among Republicans voters, members of Congress who are Republicans feel significant pressure to support President Trump even when they may disagree with his policies or political tactics.

To be persuasive, a president typically has to balance his own policy preferences with those of members of Congress and convince the American public that he is leading the country in the right direction.[38] The stakes can be very high for presidents as they navigate the legislative process (see Chapter 12). The president's need to be responsive to public opinion serves as a gateway for influence by the public on his decision making.

Agenda Setting

As the chief executive officer of the entire federal government, the president has an obligation and an opportunity to work with Congress to set the foreign and domestic policy

Key Questions
Does the bully pulpit serve as a communication gateway between the president and citizens? How has it changed over time?

Key Questions
How does the current president use the bully pulpit to generate public support for his ideas?

Key Questions
Has the increased emphasis on job approval ratings strengthened the power of the public to hold the president accountable?

agenda for the nation, from determining how to configure military strength, to overseeing economic growth, to ensuring the health and safety of individual citizens. The president is the sole occupant of his elected office, as compared with 535 members of the House and Senate. Consequently, the president has the power to focus the nation's attention on his or her ideas and policy proposals.

In dealing with foreign powers, the president is **head of state** and commander in chief of the military. As head of state, the president oversees a vast organization of employees in the State Department and the office of the U.S. Trade Representative who lay the groundwork for negotiations with foreign leaders on issues ranging from nuclear weapons control to trade policy. Upon their recommendation, the president proposes new treaties or revisions to existing agreements as needed.

As we have seen in the Trump administration, presidents can take existing agreements that were negotiated by their predecessors and either abandon them completely or push to renegotiate them. In Chapter 16 (Economic, Domestic, and Foreign Policy), we discuss the ways in which President Trump reshaped U.S. trade relations with China through the use of tariffs, and successfully negotiated a new trade agreement with Canada and Mexico, the USMCA, to replace NAFTA. Ultimately, the president is the public face of and the authority behind U.S. foreign policy decisions. He establishes the tone and type of working relationships with foreign leaders, which can be highly cooperative as in the case of George H. W. Bush and Barack Obama, or more contentious as it has been during the Trump administration. Every U.S. president operates under more constraints than their foreign counterparts, especially the extent to which the executive power is placed in one person or shared, as it is in parliamentary systems (see Chapter 12).

Because the president is presumed to serve the best interest of the entire nation, the American public frequently supports most of his foreign policies—at least initially. The main congressional counterweights to the president's powers in these areas are the power of the Senate to ratify treaties and the power of

Bettmann/Getty Images

Image 13.6 President John F. Kennedy was completely at ease with the press and held sixty-four press conferences during his time in office. They were televised, and not only White House reporters but also the American public looked forward to the lively exchanges between the press and the president, who was known for his sense of humor and ready wit.

AP Images/Andrew Harnik

Image 13.7 The president, as head of state, engages in direct diplomacy with foreign leaders in a number of different settings. Such formal functions expose world leaders to elite members of the American political and economic arenas. These events can serve to enhance diplomatic relations between the United States and its allies. At this state dinner in April 2018, President and Mrs. Trump welcomed Emmanuel Macron, the president of France, and his wife Brigitte.

Congress to appropriate money for federal programs, including foreign aid and diplomatic programs. These congressional powers come in the form of responses to the president's proposals. Congress can have some influence on the president's foreign policy agenda through hearings and press statements, but if the president is able to persuade the public to support his or her positions, he or she is typically able to forge their own path on foreign policy.

In the area of domestic policy, the president uses the State of the Union address, the federal budget, the power to make executive appointments, the bully pulpit, the executive power to implement laws, and the veto power as his agenda-setting tools. He issues his federal budget in early February, shortly after he delivers the State of the Union address. The budget is a blueprint that indicates his spending priorities for all areas of the federal government. Congress does not have to abide by this budget, and Congress frequently ignores it and constructs its own federal budget (see Chapter 12 for a discussion of the budget). All measures that raise taxes and spend federal money can be vetoed by the president, and, as we have seen, the veto or the threat of a veto gives the president a means of exerting pressure on Congress to follow his budget priorities.

The president engages in domestic policy agenda setting in other ways as well. For example, as in the case of President Obama and health care and President Trump and tax cuts, presidents can propose legislation that changes existing programs or creates new ones and ask Congress to consider his suggestions. He can also be even more proactive by issuing presidential directives that direct the bureaucracy to implement laws as he sees fit, as Trump has done to reduce the regulation of the environment (see Chapter 16, Economic, Domestic, and Foreign Policy). The president's major speeches, press conferences, interviews, social media communication, and travels always command media attention, so he has a constantly open forum to try to persuade voters to support his proposals.[39]

Key Questions
How effective are the president's agenda-setting tools? Are any tools more useful than others?

The President in Wartime

LO 13-4 Analyze why the president is so powerful during wartime

As executive branch powers have grown, presidents have increasingly come into conflict with the judicial branch and Congress, especially in times of national crisis and war (see also Chapter 4). In this section, we examine the power struggle between the president and Congress over war powers, which the Constitution divides between the two branches, and the power struggle between the president and the judiciary on the scope of presidential powers and civil liberties. It is crucial to understand that the balance of power among the three branches of the federal government is constantly evolving in response to changing internal and external conditions.

Key Questions
What powers should the president have during wartime?

Power Struggles Between the President and Congress

The Constitution gives Congress the power to declare war, but it has been the practice for presidents to first formally ask Congress for a declaration of war. After Congress declares war, the president as commander in chief has the authority to direct the conflict. Through its constitutional powers in Article I, Section 8, "to raise and support Armies" and "to provide and maintain a Navy," Congress retains the power to cut off the flow of money for the war effort. Generally, the president and Congress have worked together in times of military conflict, but in the late 1960s, opposition to the Vietnam War brought about significant divisions between the executive and legislative branches over war powers.

Vietnam and the War Powers Act.

Vietnam had been a divided nation since 1954, with Communist forces controlling North Vietnam and anti-Communists controlling South Vietnam, and a civil war had erupted between them. President Eisenhower and then Presidents Kennedy and Johnson believed that containing Communism and keeping the North Vietnamese Communists from taking over South Vietnam were important, but the U.S. troop buildup was slow at first. In 1964, however, President Johnson presented evidence to Congress that the North Vietnamese were attacking U.S. ships on patrol duty in international waters in the Gulf of Tonkin off the shore of North Vietnam. Johnson asked Congress for the authority to fight back, and Congress responded with the Tonkin Gulf Resolution, stating that "The Congress approves and supports the determination of the President, as Commander in Chief, to take all necessary measures to repel any armed attack against the forces of the United States and to prevent further aggression."[40] Congress passed the resolution with only two dissenting votes, few restrictions, and no time limit on how long the United States would stay involved in the conflict.[41]

By 1968, the United States had more than five hundred thousand troops in Vietnam, and the conflict was commonly referred to as the Vietnam War, although there was never a formal declaration of war by Congress. The conflict had become highly unpopular, and President Johnson was forced to give up his bid for reelection. That year, Richard Nixon was elected president and promised to end the Vietnam War; however, he actually broadened the conflict to the neighboring countries of Cambodia and Laos in his efforts to win the war.

By 1971, Congress had repealed the Tonkin Gulf Resolution, and, following the Paris Peace Accords signed in January 1973, U.S. troops were withdrawn from Vietnam. In October 1973, Congress passed a more formal proposal to limit presidential authority to engage in military conflict. This **War Powers Act** states that the president cannot send troops into military conflict for more than a total of ninety days without seeking a formal declaration of war, or authorization for continued military action, from Congress. President Nixon vetoed the act, but Congress overrode the veto.

The War Powers Act was ostensibly a gate that would stand in the way of a president's decision to launch a war without first gauging congressional support. Although the act tried to clarify presidential authority and limits, the scholar Louis Fisher argues that it is flawed because the ninety-day limit does not begin until the president has officially reported the troop engagement to Congress. A president could send troops into a conflict and not report it to Congress, thereby avoiding a trigger of the War Powers Act.[42] In addition, the act did not really give Congress the power to end a military conflict except by denying all funding for it, as it ultimately did with Vietnam. However, if there is considerable public support for an ongoing military engagement, the president can make the case that it is too dangerous to cut off all funding, and Congress would be reluctant to cut off funding when troops were still in the field and could be harmed. The irony of the War Powers Act is that it gives presidents an incentive to seek a declaration of war or authorization to use military

War Powers Act: *The 1973 act that provides that the president cannot send troops into military conflict for more than a total of ninety days without seeking a formal declaration of war, or authorization for continued military action, from Congress.*

force, after which time Congress loses much of its control of the operation of the conflict.[43] In other words, once Congress gives the president permission to go to war, it is next to impossible for Congress to stop the war.[44]

The Iraq War.   The United States was involved in major military conflicts in Iraq and Afghanistan for the first two decades of the twenty-first century. The two wars ran parallel to each other, but their origins are quite different. The Iraq War began in 2003, but its origins date back to August 1990, when Iraq, led by Saddam Hussein, invaded Kuwait. This act of aggression prompted multilateral military action known as the Gulf War, which aimed to push Iraq out of Kuwait. The Gulf War was short-lived; as part of the peace settlement, Iraq was prohibited from developing weapons of mass destruction and was required to submit to constant United Nations (UN) monitoring.

By 2002, it had become increasingly difficult for UN inspectors to accurately assess Iraq's capabilities for producing weapons of mass destruction. Although there had been no concrete evidence of such weapons, President George W. Bush argued that a preemptive strike against Iraq was necessary to preserve the security of the United States. In accordance with the War Powers Act, President Bush asked Congress for a resolution authorizing military action. On October 10, 2002, the House of Representatives approved a joint resolution that gave the president the authority to use all military force to "defend the national security of the United States."[45] The Senate approved the resolution the next day by a vote of 77–23.

The Iraq War was launched on March 19, 2003; Saddam Hussein was captured in December 2003 and was tried and hanged for war crimes. Nevertheless, instability in Iraq continued. By 2006, with violence in Iraq at a high level, the Democrats in Congress—many of whom had initially supported the war—withdrew their support and called for the return of all U.S. troops and an end to the war. During the midterm congressional elections that year, Democrats made ending the war a campaign issue, and they won majority control of the House and the Senate. However, in January 2007, President Bush increased the number of troops in Iraq in an effort known as the "surge," which was intended to reduce violence there.

As of January 2009, the three dominant groups in Iraq—the Sunnis, the Shiites, and the Kurds—were operating under a parliamentary system of government, and the U.S. government worked with the Iraqis to end the war and transfer full governmental control to them. On August 31, 2010, President Obama announced the end of the nation's formal combat involvement, and by the end of December 2011, the last official combat personnel departed from Iraq, although some U.S. soldiers are there in an advisory role. Since then, the Iraqi government has struggled to maintain security among the different factions vying for power, in addition to the incursions by the extremist group ISIS, which has led to violence and casualties. Iraq today represents a nation forever changed by U.S. involvement; what remains uncertain is whether that change will enable or prevent democratic government there.

The Afghanistan War.   The war in Afghanistan began after the September 11, 2001, terrorist attacks were traced back to al-Qaeda operatives harbored by the Afghan Taliban regime. President George W. Bush addressed Congress on September 20, 2001, indicating that the Taliban would be held responsible for the attacks, and, in October, the United States and its allies launched a military action on Afghanistan designed to find those responsible for the 9/11 attacks and bring down the Taliban regime. However, Bush did not

Key Questions

Think about the conduct of war. Who should be in charge? The president? Congress? The military?

Key Questions

How much responsibility should Presidents Bush and Obama assume for the Iraq and Afghanistan wars, respectively? Does Congress have shared responsibility for those conflicts? Will President Trump bear any responsibility for these conflicts?

ask for a declaration of war against the nation of Afghanistan. Although the Taliban regime was subsequently toppled and a new leader, Hamid Karzai, was elected and later reelected, the Taliban mounted a resurgence in Afghanistan. In 2009, President Obama, as commander in chief, responded to resurgent Taliban-sponsored attacks on U.S. troops and civilian Afghans by ordering a surge of thirty thousand additional troops to Afghanistan, bringing the total there to nearly a hundred thousand.[46] In the next two years, as the number of American and Afghan casualties increased, public support for the war decreased, and it was hard for President Obama to maintain U.S. involvement there. The Republicans' takeover of the House of Representatives in the 2010 election complicated his decision making because they publicly resisted efforts to reduce the U.S. presence in Afghanistan until the government could demonstrate it had defeated the Taliban and al-Qaeda.

On May 1, 2011, President Obama announced that Osama bin Laden, who had claimed to be the head of al-Qaeda and the coordinator of the 9/11 attacks, had been killed in a military operation in Pakistan. With the death of bin Laden, public support for the war diminished further. In 2012, President Obama and Secretary of Defense Leon Panetta announced their intention to work with the Afghanistan government to reduce the number of U.S. troops in Afghanistan at a faster rate. But that goal was not accomplished, and as of spring 2018, the number of U.S. troops stationed in Afghanistan was approximately 15,000.[47]

When Trump campaigned for president, he promised to bring U.S. troops home from Afghanistan and end the nation's involvement in that country's civil conflicts. However, extricating the United States from the Afghanistan War proved as complicated for him as it was for Obama. Still, Trump was adamant that it would be under his presidency that American troops would return home from that conflict, and he appointed a special envoy to negotiate a peace agreement between the Afghan government and the Taliban which were the two main forces competing for control of that nation. In February 2020, a peace agreement was signed; at that time, there were about 12,000 troops in Afghanistan. By July 2020, there were 8,600 troops remaining in that country.[48]

Uprisings in Foreign Lands.   Ongoing military conflicts such as those in Iraq and Afghanistan have spillover effects that can limit the president's flexibility in responding to conflicts in other foreign nations. Protests in 2011 known as the Arab Spring that threatened to topple authoritarian regimes offer an example. Seeking UN approval and international cooperation, the U.S. military became involved only in Libya. When in March 2011 President Obama authorized the use of air strikes and drones in Libya, he was acting in conjunction with NATO forces to enforce a UN Security Council resolution that authorized international military action to enforce a no-fly zone to stop the Libyan leader, Muammar al-Qaddafi, from committing violence against his own people. The decision to intervene in Libya was controversial given ongoing involvement in Afghanistan, so Obama gave a national address to explain his decision and inform the American people that U.S. ground troops would not be deployed. Nevertheless, some members of Congress argued that the air strikes violated the War Powers Act because the president had not formally notified Congress of military involvement there. The president moved forward anyway, and by October 2011, the rebel forces had prevailed, and Qaddafi was killed as he resisted capture.[49] Without a strong leader, the country fell into chaos. The power vacuum enabled ISIS to control substantial amounts of Libyan territory.

Unlike Libya, President Obama did not propose intervening in the Syrian conflict, although the United States did support a UN resolution condemning the violence committed by President Bashar al-Assad's regime against opposition forces. That resolution was vetoed by Russia and China, and without multilateral or congressional support for intervention, Obama lacked the same justification for entering that conflict that he did in the case of Libya.[50] However, Obama worked with the United Nations and Russia to broker a deal whereby Syria agreed not to use chemical weapons and to turn over all chemical weapons to the United Nations for safe destruction. Although that turnover has been completed, the

Image 13.8 The conflict in Syria was a major issue in President Obama's second term in office and continued to be an issue for President Trump. While the United States focused its efforts on ISIS in Syria, Russian forces aided the Assad regime by engaging in air strikes across Syria. Here we see the aftermath of a Russian strike in the town of Aleppo, which had been the site of strong resistance to Assad.

civil war rages on in Syria. Meanwhile, the Obama administration has supplied Syrian rebels with light arms and humanitarian aid, while Russia has sold advanced aircraft and missile systems to the Syrian government. With the rise of ISIS, the United States has played a much larger role in the Syrian conflict. The United States led a coalition of nations in air strikes against ISIS and provided weapons to groups fighting against ISIS.

Tensions with Russia intensified when Ukrainian rebels ousted their pro-Russian president. Ukraine, Russia's neighbor to the West, is home to many individuals of Russian heritage. Subsequently, Russian separatists staged takeovers of Ukrainian government buildings in southern and eastern Ukraine, essentially declaring them part of Russia. The Ukrainian government was not well prepared to stop these takeovers, which Russia actively supported. In response, President Obama and leaders of European nations imposed economic sanctions on Russia in an effort to pressure them to withdraw their support of these separatists. After Russian interference in the U.S. elections of 2016, President Obama and Congress agreed on additional sanctions on Russia, which President Trump has also enforced, although at times he has suggested that the sanctions could be made less severe. President Obama and Congress understood that the United States is expected to take the lead in responding to international crises of the type that occurred in Ukraine as well as Syria. At the same time, Americans view global instability as a threat to their safety. In recent years, it became increasingly clear to Obama, Trump, and members of Congress that public opinion among the American people leans more strongly against intervention in foreign conflicts and against starting a foreign war. For example, in 2019, when tensions between the United States and Iran were building after Iran shot down an unmanned U.S. drone, President Trump responded by ordering the killing of Iranian General Qasem Solameini while he was on a visit to Iraq. But he did not go beyond that action and start a direct war with Iran; in one poll, 78 percent of respondents supported Trump's decision and 57 percent of respondents more generally opposed a military confrontation with Iran.[51] This broader context has important implications for U.S. foreign policy because presidents and members of Congress recognize the difficulty of waging a military intervention without public support.

These examples demonstrate that tension between the presidency and Congress over war powers compels the president to make the case to Congress that military action is necessary. Moreover, as in the cases of Ukraine, Syria, and Iran, presidents face challenges in persuading a war-weary nation to intervene with military force.

Power Struggles Between the President and the Judiciary

Key Questions

What limits should the judiciary impose on presidential actions in wartime? Give examples.

Power struggles between the president and the judiciary in wartime generally focus on civil liberties. In Chapter 4, we examined the Court's rejection of Abraham Lincoln's argument about the suspension of *habeas corpus*, and in Chapter 5, we discussed the Court's acquiescence in President Roosevelt's executive order on the internment of Japanese Americans. In this chapter, we have already noted the limits on presidential actions imposed by the Steel Seizure case during the Truman administration.

The most significant recent clash between the president and the judiciary over wartime powers arose during President George W. Bush's declared war on terror. Following 9/11, President Bush greatly expanded the powers of the executive branch. As we have seen in previous chapters, he created separate military tribunals to try captured terrorists, claimed exemption from the Geneva Convention rules on the treatment and detainment of prisoners, and authorized the National Security Agency to monitor conversations of suspected terrorists with residents of the United States without obtaining warrants. President Bush's justification was that, as commander in chief, he had the foremost responsibility to protect American citizens and actions taken for that purpose should not be subject to the approval of Congress or the courts.

Key Questions

How are acts of terrorism different from or the same as acts of war? How should the president, Congress, and the judiciary respond to terrorist attacks?

A combination of congressional action and Supreme Court decisions following the guidelines of the Steel Seizure case constrained most of these presidential actions. In 2004, the Supreme Court's *Hamdi v. Rumsfeld* decision rejected Bush administration attempts to deny *habeas corpus* protections to an enemy combatant who was a U.S. citizen because federal law prohibits such denial to U.S. citizens.[52] That same day, the Court also rejected the administration's authority to deny *habeas corpus* to an enemy combatant who was not a U.S. citizen.[53] The Bush administration then established special military tribunals to review the detention of enemy combatants at Guantánamo Bay, but the Court rejected the authority of the tribunals because Congress had not authorized them.[54] The Court rejected congressional and presidential efforts to limit the Court's jurisdiction to hear such appeals, claiming that those limits did not apply to cases that had been filed before Congress passed the law.

Even when Congress and the president authorized tribunals, the Supreme Court declared that neither Congress nor the president has the authority to suspend the writ of *habeas corpus*, which the Constitution allows only during "Cases of Rebellion or Invasion."[59] Thus, in cases involving terrorism, the Court has put gates in the way of Congress and the

Public Policy and the Presidency

Use of Drones

Since the terrorist attacks of 9/11 and subsequent terror attacks in the United States, such as the Boston Marathon bombings, and others around the world, the United States has sent ground forces into Iraq and Afghanistan, and also used alternative means of warfare such as drones. Drones are unmanned aircraft that are guided remotely and can be used to target individuals who are viewed to be engaged in terrorist activities directly against the United States and its allies. However, these aircraft are not 100 percent accurate and have resulted in the deaths of innocent civilians.

As commander in chief, the president has the authority to order a drone strike. President Obama starkly increased the number of these attacks in Pakistan, Yemen, and Somalia, where known terrorist groups, such as al-Qaeda, have set up bases of operations. In 2014, President Obama began targeting drone strikes against ISIS, which was then a new and ultraviolent terrorist group operating in Syria and Iraq. A British organization, the Bureau of Investigative Journalism, has reported that more than three thousand people have been killed by drone attacks, including civilian men, women, and children.

Drone strikes became controversial as the media began to report on civilian casualties (see Table 13.5). In 2011, a drone strike in Yemen killed two American citizens, Anwar Al-Awlaki, a known leader of al-Qaeda, and his associate, Samir Kahn.[55] That same year, a U.S. drone strike also killed Al-Awlaki's 16-year-old son, also a U.S. citizen, in Yemen.[56] Some people claim that as American citizens, these individuals should have been captured and tried in an American court of law, and these drone attacks deprived them of their rights under the U.S. Constitution. Others argue that by engaging in activities designed to harm U.S. security, they relinquished those rights.

President Obama defended the use of drones as a more effective way of combating individuals and groups that are intent on killing Americans and that as commander in chief, his first obligation was to take any and all steps that he believed would protect Americans. After signing a type of presidential directive known as a Presidential Policy Guidance statement on the use of drones in May 2013, President Obama said this:

Nevertheless, it is a hard fact that U.S. strikes have resulted in civilian casualties, a risk that exists in every war. . . . But as commander in chief, I must weigh these heartbreaking tragedies against the alternatives. To do nothing in the face of terrorist networks would invite far more civilian casualties—not just in our cities at home and our facilities abroad, but also in the very places like Sana'a and

Table 13.5 U.S. Drone Strikes and Related Casualties in Selected Countries, 2004–2020

	Pakistan (June 2004 to January 2018)	Yemen (Nov. 2002 to June 2019)	Somalia (Jan. 2007 to February 2020)	Afghanistan (Jan. 2015 March 2020)
U.S. drone strikes	430	336	202	13,072
Total reported killed	2,515–4,026	1,020–1,389	1,197–1,410	4,126–10,076
Civilians reported killed	424–969	174–225	12–97	300–909
Children reported killed	172–207	44–50	13	66–184
Reported injured	1,162–1,749	155–303	55–101	658–1,769

Source: Author constructed from data provided by The Bureau of Investigative Journalism, at Drone Warfare, https://www.thebureauinvestigates.com/projects/drone-war.

Kabul and Mogadishu where terrorists seek a foothold. Remember that the terrorists we are after target civilians, and the death toll from their acts of terrorism against Muslims dwarfs any estimate of civilian casualties from drone strikes. So doing nothing is not an option.[57]

Presidents weigh the costs of ensuring the safety of American citizens, both in terms of dollars and the lives of American soldiers, against the costs of using tactics that may result in civilian deaths.

The American Civil Liberties Union (ACLU) and the Center for Constitutional Rights filed lawsuits on behalf of Al-Awlaki both before and after his death in an attempt to block the president and the executive branch from targeting American citizens. However, federal courts have dismissed these suits. Moreover, American public opinion indicates strong bipartisan support for drone strikes, with 74 percent of Republicans and 52 percent of Democrats approving Obama's decision.[58] In such an atmosphere, it is no surprise that President Trump continued to use this advanced technology; however, if public opinion shifts dramatically, support for such policies may be harder to find.

Construct Your Own Policy

1. Devise a more transparent policy on reporting the use of drones and the number of casualties associated with this type of weapon.
2. Create a set of guidelines for the executive branch to follow in determining who will be the subject of a drone attack.

---

president in their efforts to restrict civil liberties in the name of national security. (For a broader discussion of the balance between laws against terrorism and civil liberties, see Chapter 4.)

Organization of the Modern White House

LO 13-5 Summarize how the White House is organized

Key Questions

How does the Executive Office of the President reflect individual management styles? What are the consequences of these different management styles?

The way that a president organizes the Executive Office and the cabinet reveals a great deal about his management style as well as his policy preferences. The president relies on his White House advisers for policy recommendations. The modern president has the challenge of encouraging cooperation between political appointees and members of the civil service and making sure that employees in each category are held accountable for their decisions.

The Executive Office of the President

The president runs a large organization known as the Executive Office of the President (EOP), a loosely knit unit of several key organizations that report directly to him. These include the White House Office; the Office of Management and Budget (OMB), which Sylvia Mathews Burwell led until she became Secretary of HHS; the National Security Council (NSC); and the Council of Economic Advisers. Each office has influence over budgetary, military, and economic policies.

The growth of the president's staff in the past seventy-five years is stunning. President Franklin Roosevelt established the EOP, and his decision in 1939 to move the Bureau of the Budget from the Treasury Department to the EOP gave him more direct control over the federal budget. At that time, there were about sixty people working in the EOP; under President Obama, there were nearly eighteen hundred.[60] A key change in the structure of the EOP occurred when President Eisenhower, a highly decorated army general who was accustomed to a formal chain of command, appointed the first **chief of staff**, Sherman Adams. Eisenhower also raised the status of the NSC and the Bureau of the Budget to full advisory roles reporting directly to his office.

Staff organizations can have a real impact on the success of a presidential administration. For many presidents, the choice of how to organize their staffs rests with their own personalities and operating styles. These personal characteristics can make a president more or less likely to take advice from one adviser, or balance the advice from several advisers and come to a final decision on his own; how much presidents rely on their advisers often depends on how much they trust their own judgment.[61] In the case of President Trump, he has chosen to rely most heavily on his own family members, including his son-in-law Jared Kushner and his daughter Ivanka, more consistently than he has relied on White House staff.

In general, a tightly organized White House staff organization yields a productive presidency, and the chief of staff is central to that effort in several ways. He serves as a gatekeeper by controlling the flow of staff and paperwork, and focuses the president's attention on key issues. The chief of staff also monitors the coherence of presidential policies across cabinet departments and can serve as a referee for disagreements among members of the president's senior staff. Last, he can be important in forming bridges between the president and Congress. By the fourth year of his first term, Trump was working with his fourth chief of staff, Mark Meadows, a former member of Congress from North Carolina who chose not to run for reelection in 2020 and left Congress in the middle of his term to work for Trump. Throughout his presidency, Trump projected a persona of an executive at the helm who relied most of all on his own judgement and did not rely on any particular staff members. President Jimmy Carter had a similar management style where he relied on his own experience, as a former naval officer and governor of Georgia, in making many of his executive decisions. It is hard to conclude that this style of leadership contributed to electoral success or not but Jimmy Carter lost his reelection bid to Ronald Reagan in 1980 and Trump lost his reelection bid in 2020.

Another important element in presidential productivity is staff continuity, and new presidents often bring former executive branch personnel into their administrations. These staff members bring personal experience to a new president's organization. They also bring policy expertise that will help bolster the president in dealing with members of Congress who specialize in specific policy areas. When President Trump took office, he selected Cabinet members with varying levels of experience, including generals who served in the military under Obama, as well as members of Congress and a former governor. Trump also brought in individuals from the private sector in the areas of commerce and education. Some of these individuals ended up leaving their jobs earlier than expected but others, particularly those from the private sector such as Betsy DeVos, Secretary of Education, and Wilbur Ross, Secretary of Commerce, stayed for the entire first term of the Trump presidency.

chief of staff: *Person who coordinates and oversees interactions among the president, his personal staff, and his cabinet secretaries.*

Key Questions
President Harry S. Truman had a sign on his desk that read "The Buck Stops Here." What did it mean?

The Office of the Vice President

Traditionally, the office of the vice president has not had many important responsibilities. It was not until the twentieth century that vice presidents were chosen by presidential candidates to enhance their electoral prospects, and even then, once they were in office, they were given little more than ceremonial tasks. However, with the increasing complexity and international significance of the presidential role following World War II, President Eisenhower assigned his vice president, Richard Nixon, the task of traveling around the world to meet with foreign leaders. Twenty years later, Walter Mondale, President Jimmy Carter's vice president, expanded the role of the office by serving as a close adviser to the president on issues ranging from national security to domestic policy.[62]

Twenty years after the Carter presidency, George W. Bush allowed his vice president, Richard (Dick) Cheney, to play a prominent role in the nation's military and foreign policy. Cheney had been secretary of defense under Bush's father, George H. W. Bush (1989–93), and oversaw the Gulf War; he was widely perceived to be highly influential on such issues as the Iraq War, antiterrorism policies, and energy development. The fact that George W. Bush relied so heavily on Cheney to make key decisions elevated the power, visibility, and even controversy of the role of the vice president.[63] Joseph Biden, who was the Democratic nominee for president in 2020, served as vice president under President Obama and was also given considerable responsibility for foreign affairs. Vice presidents can push policies forward even when the president is reluctant to do so. Mike Pence, who serves as vice president under President Trump, has pushed the president to stay conservative on social issues such as abortion rights and was put in charge of the president's efforts on the COVID-19 pandemic. Ultimately, however, even if a vice president exerts influence, it is the president who bears the responsibility for the outcomes.

Key Questions

What constitutional responsibilities does the vice president have? What authority should he or she have?

Key Questions

What do Americans expect from the first lady? Does her office serve as a gateway for the expression of views on women's issues?

Alex Wong/Getty Images News/Getty Images

Image 13.9 Michelle Obama, the first African American first lady, came to the White House from a career as a practicing attorney. She is also the mother of two daughters. The first lady has a wide range of duties as the wife of the president, including hosting dignitaries, overseeing White House events, and advancing social causes. As first lady, Michelle Obama emphasized healthy eating habits. After she left the White House in January 2017, Michelle Obama went on to write a best-selling memoir and was among the most popular women in the world. Here she is shown working with young people in the vegetable gardens she planted on the White House grounds.

The Office of the First Lady

The role of the first lady has evolved over the history of the presidency, paralleling in some ways the increasing public roles available to women over the past century. Although the wife of the president has always been seen as an important partner in the president's social and diplomatic activities and as caregiver in the event of a health crisis, her role as a public advocate on policy issues emerged in the twentieth century. Eleanor Roosevelt, the wife of Franklin Roosevelt, was widely believed to hold considerable sway over her husband's views, but her most public moment as first lady came in 1939 when she came to the defense of Marian Anderson, a famous African American opera singer. When the Daughters of the American Revolution canceled a performance by Anderson at Constitution Hall on account of her race, Eleanor Roosevelt arranged for Anderson to perform on the steps of the Lincoln Memorial in front of thousands of cheering listeners.[64] Eleanor Roosevelt's action was interpreted as a strong stand for civil rights, despite the fact that her husband's administration was not actively pursuing civil rights as part of the domestic agenda.

The modern office of the first lady has no formally stated responsibilities, but the first lady has a staff that includes a press secretary, a scheduler, and speechwriters. Since Eleanor Roosevelt, first ladies have often taken on single issues to champion, such as Lady Bird Johnson on nature conservation; Betty Ford on alcoholism; Rosalynn Carter on mental health; Nancy Reagan on drug addiction; Barbara Bush on literacy; Hillary Clinton on health care, women's rights, and child welfare; and Laura Bush on reading and education. Michelle Obama took a broad approach to her role by emphasizing the contribution each individual can make in his or her community on a range of issues from homelessness, to education, to childhood nutrition. As first lady to Donald Trump, Melania Trump led a campaign against bullying in schools and on social media.

Presidential Greatness

LO 13-6 Assess presidential greatness

President Joseph Biden is the forty-sixth president of the United States. The preceding presidents served with varying degrees of success as leaders in foreign and domestic policy. Presidential leadership is judged by whether a president is able to get his or her preferred policies passed by Congress and enacted into law and by how well he or she oversees the bureaucracy to make the government run effectively and efficiently (for more on the bureaucracy, see Chapter 14).

Scholars typically judge presidential greatness by looking at the clarity of a president's vision for policy, his communication and negotiation skills, and the effectiveness of his use of presidential powers, especially the general grant of executive power. Good presidents do not have to excel in every one of these categories, but they have to compensate for a weakness in one area with greater strength in another. Stephen Skowronek argues that presidents have opportunities to continue the policies of their predecessors or forge new paths, but that a president's success is often determined by external events, such as a terrorist attack, a pandemic, or a global economic downturn.[65] The scholar Aaron Wildavsky suggested that there are actually "two presidencies": a foreign policy presidency and a domestic policy presidency.[66] On foreign policy, the president often must work quickly and in private, as negotiations must be conducted discreetly. Domestic politics rarely require immediate action and usually entail open debate, with many citizens and interest groups vested in the outcome.[67]

The following discussion focuses on three presidents who are frequently singled out for their impact on domestic and foreign policy: Franklin D. Roosevelt, a Democrat from a wealthy, elite New York family; Lyndon Johnson, a Democrat from a very poor Texas family; and Ronald Reagan, a Republican from a middle-class family in Illinois.[68] Each had strengths and weaknesses, and each knew how to maximize his greatest asset—intellect, negotiating skills, public communications—to try to accomplish his goals.

Key Questions

Who are two presidents you think should be called great? What makes them great?

Roosevelt: The New Deal and World War II

When Franklin D. Roosevelt took office in 1933, the nation was experiencing the Great Depression. Unemployment had reached 25 percent, and Americans, many of them homeless and hungry, were suffering. To combat the effects of the depression, FDR had a clear policy vision, which he called the **New Deal**. In the first three years of his presidency, he succeeded in getting Congress to pass legislation that radically altered the size and shape of the federal government. His immediate need was to find a way to get cash into the hands of individual citizens, but he opposed handouts. Instead, he created job programs, including the Conservation Corps, the Works Progress Administration, and the Tennessee Valley Authority, all of which both employed and trained workers.

FDR also expanded the government's role in regulating the economy. The creation of the Securities and Exchange Commission and other laws relating to banking and finance helped restore confidence in banks and the stock market. The National Labor Relations Act established federal oversight of working conditions, labor standards, and labor disputes. This legislation brought the government and the business and labor sectors closer together. The Social Security program, a pension program to which workers contributed through a payroll tax that was also paid by employers, further entwined business and government.

FDR used the bully pulpit and advanced the use of communication technology in the office of the president. He invented the fireside chat, a radio address to voters explaining the reasoning behind his governing decisions. Because fewer than half of all Americans owned radios at this time, FDR also turned the chats into newsreels that were shown in movie theaters. Ever since, presidents have found direct communications with voters to be an effective governing device.[69] President Roosevelt was also open and available to the Washington press corps, and his very first press conference in 1933 was a success. As a media-savvy president, FDR created the formal position of White House press secretary.[70]

Roosevelt took a personal role in negotiating legislative deals with members of the House and Senate, which were controlled by the Democrats. He allowed his staff to lay out the conditions for a compromise, but Roosevelt would finish the negotiations himself.[71] During his first five years in office, Roosevelt had great success in getting legislation through Congress, but in 1937, he overstepped by proposing to expand the size of the

New Deal: *Franklin Delano Roosevelt's program for ending the Great Depression through government intervention in the economy and development of a set of safety-net programs for individuals.*

Key Questions

What was one of Franklin Roosevelt's successes and one of his failures?

PhotoQuest/Archive Photos/Getty Images

Image 13.10 Franklin Delano Roosevelt faced the worst economic crisis in the nation's history during the Great Depression. He proposed a series of policies known as the New Deal to provide economic opportunity and financial security in old age for America's workers. Here people lined up for food provided for the unemployed by private organizations.

Supreme Court. The Court had struck down several of Roosevelt's favored policies, often by closely divided votes, and his so-called Court-packing plan would have allowed him to appoint additional justices and secure a majority favorable to him. Congress rejected Roosevelt's attempt to circumvent the checks and balances, and after that, his relationship with Congress began to falter.

On December 7, 1941, Japan attacked the United States at Pearl Harbor in Hawaii, drawing the United States into World War II. From that point on, foreign affairs dominated Roosevelt's presidency, but the New Deal legislation of the previous decade laid the groundwork for the modern structure of domestic programs in the United States. On April 12, 1945, President Roosevelt died in office and was succeeded by Vice President Harry Truman.

Image 13.11 Lyndon Baines Johnson proposed sweeping changes to the nation's civil rights laws, as well as domestic health and welfare programs. Here he is signing the Civil Rights Act on July 2, 1964; Dr. Martin Luther King is standing behind him.

Johnson: The Great Society and Vietnam

As president, Lyndon B. Johnson focused his mission on improving race relations and ending poverty because he believed they stood in the way of social, political, and economic progress. Most of his programs, which he called the **Great Society**, built on the infrastructure of FDR's New Deal, but they went much further in connecting the individual to the federal government. Johnson believed that as president he had an obligation to try to guarantee civil rights to all Americans.[72] In the area of race relations, he persuaded Congress to pass the Civil Rights Act of 1964, the Voting Rights Act of 1965, and the Fair Housing Act of 1968, which together formed a powerful set of laws protecting the rights of African Americans and subsequently the rights of other minority groups as well (see Chapter 5).

As 2020 marked the fifty-sixth anniversary of the passage of the Civil Rights Act (see Chapter 5), it is worthwhile to revisit President Johnson's legacy, especially on current issues such as income inequality and fair pay. LBJ believed that it was possible for people to work very hard but still remain poor and that poor people were severely disadvantaged in terms of education, access to jobs, and affordable housing. He transformed the relationship between the individual and the federal government into one that included pure need, rather than merit based on work. He created two major federal health insurance programs: Medicaid, a health insurance program for the poor, and Medicare, a health insurance program for the elderly. He was also responsible for creating the Food Stamp Program, the School Lunch Program, Head Start, the Job Corps, and the Elementary and Secondary Education Act.

Great Society: *Lyndon Johnson's program for expanding the federal social welfare programs in health care, education, and housing and for ending poverty.*

Key Questions

What is one of Lyndon Johnson's successes, and what is one of his failures?

Johnson was not a skilled communicator or comfortable giving speeches, and he did not come across well on television, which by this time had succeeded radio as the dominant form of political communication. He compensated for his lack of communication skills by relying more heavily on his very strong negotiation skills. From his prior experience as a member of Congress and Senate majority leader, Johnson understood how to convince members of Congress that it was in their best interests to pass legislation. Johnson made sure that his programs would benefit all poor people, white and black, rural and urban. By creating wide eligibility criteria, Johnson almost guaranteed that every congressional district in the country would receive some benefit from the programs. For example, both Medicaid and Medicare legislation included subsidies to rural hospitals and to big inner-city hospitals for services and capital expenditures such as improving facilities and building new ones. School lunch programs benefited school children as well as farmers, who sold the federal government their meat, milk, cheese, and grains at a guaranteed price, so they always had a market.

Johnson also used his presidential powers to distribute and award federal contracts and federal funds to key members of Congress and key state officials in return for their support of his programs. He understood that if a member of Congress needed to explain his vote in support of a liberal bill, he could do so more easily if he could point to some other federal benefit he had secured, such as a bridge, a Navy or Army base, or a new hospital wing.

Key Questions
What is one of Ronald Reagan's successes, and what is one of his failures?

Although Johnson's personal relationship with the press and the public started out reasonably well, as U.S. involvement in the Vietnam War escalated, the press began to distrust him, and many journalists believed he was not being candid with them and the American people about the war. By the end of his presidency, Johnson's relationship with the press was downright hostile. In fact, negative reporting on the progress of the Vietnam War, combined with significant health concerns, was among the reasons that Johnson ultimately chose not to seek reelection, a decision he announced on March 31, 1968. He died five years later, on January 22, 1973.

Reagan: The Reagan Revolution and the End of the Cold War

Ronald Reagan's vision of the relationship between the individual and the federal government was different from the views of Roosevelt and Johnson, and it is still invoked to this day by conservative Republicans seeking to limit the size and scope of the federal government. President Reagan believed that the New Deal and the Great Society had combined to weaken individual initiative and responsibility. When he took office, he mounted an aggressive campaign to scale back federal programs that provided benefits to individuals without asking for anything in return. He believed that big government and high taxes were crushing personal initiative, creativity, and innovation. "Government is not the solution to the problem. It is the problem," Reagan announced in his first inaugural address.

Tax cuts were the first thing on Reagan's agenda for two reasons. First, he believed that if taxes went down, the economy would flourish. Second, he knew that if tax revenue went down and spending increased,

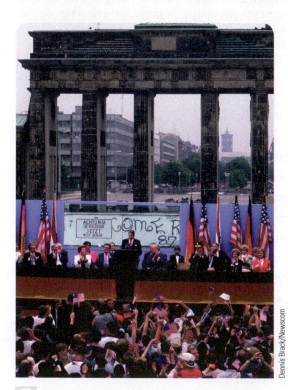

Image 13.12 Ronald Reagan was known for his tough foreign policy and pressuring the Soviet Union to withdraw from nations that it had controlled since World War II. Here he is at the Brandenburg Gate at the Berlin Wall, which separated free West Germany from Communist East Germany. It is at this spot that he uttered the famous words, "Mr. Gorbachev, open this gate; Mr. Gorbachev, tear down this wall."

Dennis Brack/Newscom

A Referendum on Donald Trump

An incumbent president's reelection chances always depend, in some part, on the voters' perceptions of that president's job performance over the previous four years. The presidential election of 2020 was no different, with Donald Trump running on a record of economic success and foreign policy victories especially in the area of trade negotiations. His opponent, Joe Biden, ran against Trump by emphasizing the mishandling of the COVID-19 virus and the loss of life that resulted, as well as the economic downturn that came afterwards. He also emphasized the demeanor of President Trump, his statements containing factual errors, and his fractious relationship with leaders of foreign nations around the world. Ultimately, voters may have accepted Joe Biden's depiction of Trump because they chose not to reelect him.

Every presidency is subject to differences of opinion, and as we have noted in this chapter, presidents have some policy authority when they issue regulations and executive orders to implement laws. But in general all presidents must work with Congress to enact laws to meet the basic responsibilities of the federal government such as taxes and spending, and maintaining a national defense.

Trump inherited policies from his predecessor Barack Obama: Iran Nuclear Deal, the Paris Climate Accord, the Afghanistan war, and the ending of a major recession. President Trump withdrew from the Iran Nuclear Deal, the Paris Climate Accord, and negotiated a peace agreement in Afghanistan designed to withdraw U.S. troops. For most

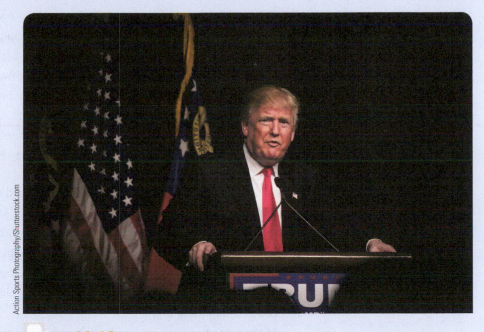

Image 13.13 Donald Trump was elected president of the United States in November 2016. Here we see him making one of many speeches on the campaign trail during the presidential election in 2016.

of his time in office, the economy grew at a steady pace and unemployment at the beginning of 2020 was around 3.7 percent. Trump also nominated two Supreme Court justices, both confirmed, and succeed in nominating and getting confirmation for dozens of federal judges to the district and appeals courts.

Throughout the Trump administration, the United States was still actively engaged in fighting terrorism in several countries. In addition, there were a number of mass shootings, including one that killed fifty-eight people and injured hundreds in Las Vegas, and a racially motivated mass shooting in El Paso, Texas. Still, up until the COVID-19 pandemic hit, with the accompanying economic damage, Trump looked quite strong going into the 2020 campaign.

Joe Biden shaped his presidential campaign relying on his experience as a U.S. senator and then vice president under President Obama to persuade voters that he could

Presidential Greatness **505**

lead the country back from the devastation of the COVID-19 pandemic and the civil unrest associated with racism and structural injustice. He also positioned as a more stable international leader who could rebuild partnerships with foreign nations that had traditionally been allies to the U.S. before Trump took office. A large part of his campaign strategy was to use President Trump's words, actions, and overall record against him and persuade voters in particular that the country could not risk another four years with Trump as president in terms of the economy and national security (see Chapter 10, Elections and Campaigns). Given that Biden believed he was a "known commodity" to most voters due to his past experience in office, he did not face the pressure of defining himself to the voters. However, as Hillary Clinton discovered, being associated with past presidential administrations, even successful and popular ones, does not guarantee victory.

Ultimately, voters chose to elect Joe Biden and deny Donald Trump a second term by a margin of 306 to 232 in the Electoral College. As we discussed in Chapter 10, Elections and Campaigns, every presidential candidate also runs on his or her own platform, and Trump was held accountable for his own decisions, successes, and failures as the president of the United States.

federal deficits would be created. These deficits would serve as justification for proposing cuts in entitlement programs, such as Social Security, Medicaid, and Aid to Families with Dependent Children (replaced in 1996 by the Temporary Aid to Needy Families program). Entitlement programs put a strain on the federal budget, especially as the number of people living in poverty grew and the elderly lived longer. Reagan managed to make cuts in the programs for the poor and elderly by restricting eligibility for benefits, but he did not succeed in dismantling them.

At the same time Reagan was implementing his domestic policy vision, he was also implementing his foreign policy vision. He took a firm stand against the Soviet Union, which he perceived as a direct threat to the United States and as a major promoter of Communism throughout the world. The defense buildup he ordered set off a military spending race that strained the Soviets' state-controlled economy to the breaking point. By the end of Reagan's second term, it was clear that the Soviet Union was moving toward collapse and could no longer control its satellite nations in Eastern Europe. Reagan's foreign policy was arguably an important factor in the end of Communism and the Cold War.

Reagan was referred to as the "Great Communicator" because he came across very well on television; as a former actor, he was able to give engaging, persuasive, and even comforting speeches. He won American hearts in 1981 during a failed assassination tempt, when he turned to his wife, Nancy, and quipped, "Honey, I forgot to duck."[73] In January 1986, when the space shuttle *Challenger* blew up shortly after takeoff as millions of Americans watched their TVs in horror, Reagan's words eased the national pain: "The crew of the space shuttle *Challenger* honored us by the manner in which they lived their lives. We will never forget them, nor the last time we saw them, this morning, as they prepared for their journey and waved goodbye and slipped the surly bonds of earth to touch the face of God."[74] The power of speech cannot be overestimated in an analysis of presidential success because it is the most basic way that the president tries to connect with the people.

Reagan did not hesitate to use his formal presidential powers to their fullest. Early in his presidency, when the air traffic controllers' union went on strike in 1981, he ordered the controllers back to work. When they refused, he fired all of them and replaced them with Air Force and civilian (private) air traffic controllers. Eventually, the union relented, and most of the air traffic controllers were hired back, but with fewer benefits and at lower salaries. This action sent a clear signal to members of Congress and to interest groups that Reagan was not afraid to take a potentially unpopular stand to accomplish his goals.

President Reagan delegated much of the actual negotiating over policy to staff members. He also enhanced the power of the OMB director to negotiate with Congress on budgetary matters. Reagan and his staff were frequently successful in these negotiations, but on issues on which they were at a public disadvantage, Reagan knew when to compromise. During his last two years in office, he worked with a Democratic-controlled Congress to pass trade legislation, welfare reform, and the first comprehensive AIDS funding and treatment bill.

Reagan's presidency was not without controversy, however. In late 1986, the Iran-contra scandal erupted when it was revealed that NSC members were selling U.S. weapons to Iran for cash, which was then given to the contra resistance movement in Nicaragua that was fighting the Communist-leaning Sandinista regime. Congress had passed a law expressly prohibiting aid to the contras and held hearings to investigate the administration's actions. President Reagan himself was never directly implicated, but the scandal raised questions about the accountability of the president for his staff's actions, and it tarnished the last two years of his presidency. Although Reagan enjoyed relatively consistent popularity and was perceived as highly responsive to his base of supporters, his record came under greater scrutiny after he left office because his policies produced higher federal budget deficits and reduced funding for programs for the disadvantaged.

The example of Reagan, in the context of Roosevelt and Johnson, shows how the office of the presidency can shape domestic and foreign policy for future generations. Thirty-five years after Roosevelt died and eleven years after Johnson left office, Reagan ran for president on a campaign platform of scaling back the New Deal and the Great Society. In turn, Reagan left a conservative political legacy about the limited role of the federal government that remains a powerful rallying cry for Republicans today. Ronald Reagan died on June 5, 2004.

The Presidency and Democracy

From George Washington to Donald Trump, the presidency has evolved from an institution with strictly limited responsibilities to the large and powerful institution it is today. Donald Trump's presidency has had to address an ever-changing and increasingly complicated policy landscape. Certainly the Framers would be surprised by the growth of the presidency, and they might wonder whether the executive branch is too focused on serving the president individually and not focused enough on the needs of citizens more generally.

Nevertheless, the president operates in a separation-of-powers system, and laws must be passed with the cooperation of Congress, so the president cannot be rewarded or blamed entirely for the federal government's policies.[75] Moreover, individuals have gateways of influence on the presidency. Voters can render their direct verdict on the president's job performance when they choose whether to reelect him, provided he runs for a second term. Voters also indirectly register their opinions in congressional midterm elections, which focus on members of the House and Senate but are also interpreted as judgments on the president's record. Because high presidential approval ratings help presidents sway Congress, presidents are frequently responsive to public opinion. Because there is no possibility of a third term in office, presidents in their second term are typically freer from public accountability. In cases of very serious wrongdoing, Congress has the power to impeach and convict the president, but the threshold for impeachment is extremely high, it happens very rarely, and there has never been a Senate conviction of an impeached president, which would be necessary to remove a sitting president from office.

In the course of the nation's history, presidents have grown less accessible to the average voter. However, technological innovations as simple as fast airplane travel and, more recently, e-mail, texting, and social networking websites, provide many more modes of communication between voters and the president or the president's staff. Although the president will not meet most of the people he represents, each public speech he gives is an opportunity for an exchange of views, and social media platforms such as Twitter give voters the chance to reply "directly" to the president. Presidents also have access to constant public approval ratings and other polling data, in the public sphere and through their campaign operation, which allows them to gauge how popular their proposals are to potential voters. In the modern age, presidents are considered their political party's leaders, and they want their records to reflect well on other elected officials from their party. All presidents see it as their responsibility to do what they believe to be best for the country, even in the face of opposition from the media, the public, and Congress. At times, this opposition can result in a less effective president than some might want, but the operation of checks and balances on presidential power accords with the Framers' vision of presidential leadership.

Overall, the modern presidency acts as both a gate and a gateway to democracy at the same time. It is a gate in that the president oversees a very large federal government that can be complex and difficult to change in response to public needs. It is a gateway in that any natural-born citizen can run for the most powerful office in the land, and although wealth, education, and connections are extremely helpful in winning, they are not prerequisites for victory. To date, the men who have been elected president have come from a wide range of economic, educational, and professional backgrounds. With the election of an African American president, and most recently, a man with no prior political experience, major entry barriers to the presidency have been broken; one might argue that the path to the White House is more open than ever before.

Chapter Review

Key Terms

bully pulpit (p. 487). Give examples of presidents using the bully pulpit.

chief of staff (p. 499). What is the role of the chief of staff?

commander in chief (p. 474). What are the responsibilities of the commander in chief?

entitlement programs (p. 481). Should entitlements be considered rights?

executive order (p. 484). Give an example of when the president used an executive order to exercise his independent authority.

executive privilege (p. 483). What is the basis for executive privilege?

Great Society (p. 503). How did Johnson's Great Society expand the role of government in society?

head of state (p. 490). How does the president function as head of state?

impeachment (p. 482). Is impeachment an effective check on executive power?

imperial presidency (p. 474). What defines an imperial presidency?

lame duck (p. 469). Why are legislators less likely to cooperate with a lame-duck president?

New Deal (p. 502). How did Roosevelt's New Deal expand the role of the government in the economy?

omnibus bill (p. 480). Why are omnibus bills harder to veto?

pardon (p. 475). What does a presidential pardon mean?

pocket veto (p. 479). How is a pocket veto different from a regular veto?

presidential directive (p. 484). What are the forms a presidential directive can take?

signing statements (p. 486). How has the use of signing statements increased the powers of the presidency?

State of the Union address (p. 481). How has the use of the State of the Union address evolved from its creation in the Constitution?

veto (p. 479). How can Congress counteract the president's veto power?

War Powers Act (p. 492). How did the events of the Vietnam War lead to the passage of the War Powers Act?

Learning Outcomes: What You Need to...

Know	Test Yourself	Participate
LO 13-1 Outline the requirements to serve as president		
The American presidency was an innovation in governance. As the nation grew, the presidency grew accordingly. Today the president speaks for the nation on the world stage and sets the policy agenda at home. Presidents have come from a wide range of backgrounds.	• State the constitutional qualifications and succession requirements for the presidency. • Summarize the background and experience of U.S. presidents. • Explain what is meant by "imperial presidency."	• Discuss ways to open the pathways to the presidency.
LO 13-2 Identify the powers of the president and explain how they are limited		
Among the president's constitutional powers are those associated with being commander in chief. The president also has the power to pardon, to negotiate and sign treaties and recognize foreign nations, to veto bills passed by Congress, and to appoint federal officers.	• Characterize the presidential power of commander in chief. • Compare pardon and commutation. • Describe the role of the Senate in the president's power to negotiate and sign treaties. • Recall the steps to presidential appointments. • Survey the power of the veto. • Explain how the State of the Union address has evolved as a tool for the president. • Compare and contrast examples of impeachment (or impending impeachment).	• Evaluate the president's power over the military. • Design a way to make appointments and judicial selection less partisan. • Evaluate the role of partisanship in impeachment.

Know	Test Yourself	Participate

LO 13-3   Describe the growth of executive influence

The Constitution vests the president with a general grant of executive power and requires that he "take Care that the Laws be faithfully executed." These responsibilities have been used by presidents to vastly increase presidential power. The president uses his executive power to issue presidential directives. He also uses the office to persuade the people and Congress and to set the agenda for domestic and foreign policy.

- Recall the different types of presidential directives.
- List the tools available to a president as he uses his power to persuade.
- Describe how the president can set the public agenda.

- Determine whether you think the presidency has become too powerful.

LO 13-4   Analyze why the president is so powerful during wartime

As presidential power has grown, the president has come into increasing conflict with the other two branches of government, particularly during wartime. The War Powers Act has proven to be weak because when Congress authorizes military action, the president has sole powers as commander in chief.

- Track trends in the struggle between the president and Congress over war powers.
- Describe issues in the struggle between the president and the judiciary in wartime.

- Design a way to broaden Congress's power to limit intervention in foreign conflicts.
- Evaluate the importance of civil liberties in wartime.

LO 13-5   Summarize how the White House is organized

The Executive Office of the President has great influence over budgetary, military, and economic policies. The roles of vice president and first lady have grown in recent years.

- Track the growth of the executive staff.
- Explain how the role of the vice president has evolved over time.
- Discuss the role of the first lady in the presidency.

- Evaluate whether the vice president should be given an expanded set of formal powers.

LO 13-6   Assess presidential greatness

Presidential leadership is generally judged on how successful a president is in getting his preferred policies passed into law and in getting the bureaucracy to be effective and efficient. Americans also judge their presidents on their communication and negotiation skills.

- Explain how Franklin D. Roosevelt had such a large impact on public policy.
- Recall the programs of Lyndon B. Johnson's Great Society and how they were passed.
- Describe the impact of Ronald Reagan on the economy with his support of tax cuts.

- Develop criteria for judging presidents.
- Describe the ideal president for the twenty-first century.

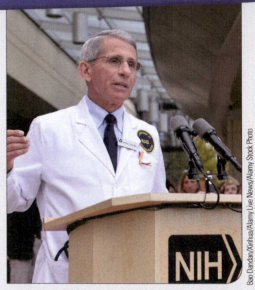

DR. ANTHONY FAUCI
Director, National Institute of Allergy and Infectious Diseases

> "*It's almost like the fog of war. After the war is over, you then look back and say, 'Wow, this plan, as great as it was, didn't quite work once they started throwing hand grenades at us.*"[1]

Anthony Fauci earned his BA from College of the Holy Cross, shown on the following page.

By mid-March 2020, it was hard to hear the term coronavirus or COVID-19 without hearing about Dr. Anthony Fauci, who at the time was serving as the director of the National Institute of Allergy and Infectious Diseases, a branch of the U.S. National Institutes of Health (NIH), which had a nearly $6 billion budget for fiscal year 2020. As he stood side by side with President Trump answering questions about the COVID-19 pandemic, he walked the fine line of many who work for government. These individuals are not partisan employees, but rather civil servants who typically have an expertise related to a government responsibility or function. As such, they are not held accountable in elections per se, but can be removed from leadership positions in the bureaucracy by the president, and are frequently held accountable by the public and press when disaster strikes.

We frequently refer to people like Dr. Fauci as "bureaucrats," and even though these government workers can have a lot of influence over the conduct and quality of our daily lives, we rarely associate a name with a face when it comes to the bureaucracy. National disasters or shocking events can change that, from hurricanes, to tornadoes, to airplane disasters, to pandemics like COVID-19. COVID-19 was not Dr. Fauci's first encounter with a deadly disease that had the potential to rob thousands of Americans of their lives. He has been at the front lines of fighting infectious disease since he was appointed in 1984, serving under President Ronald Reagan and every president since, Republican and Democrat. When he took his job, he was immediately confronted by a new virus that was killing gay men and for which there was no working treatment widely available to the public. This new disease was AIDS, caused by HIV infection. Because of a combination of small numbers of cases and widespread homophobia and discrimination, it was difficult to generate political and public support for prevention efforts. As it spread to heterosexual men and women drug users through shared needles, and then infants born to drug addicted or infected women, the public remained unsympathetic.

Despite all that, Dr. Fauci kept his focus on the importance of science and medical research in an effort to find a treatment, and on educational efforts to avoid the spread of AIDS. Much like the coronavirus epidemic, he was confronted with the difficult task of persuading Americans to change their interactions and habits, and to fight against prejudice based on the supposed source of the disease. By 1994, ten years after he had taken the position, approximately 210,000 people in the United States had died of AIDS, and the available drugs had proven less successful than most people, including him, had hoped.[2] Over the next decade, nearly 550,149 people in the United States died. However, in 2003, Fauci helped formulate President George W. Bush's PEPFAR plan (see Chapter 16, Economic, Domestic, and Foreign Policy), a campaign to treat AIDS patients around the world and limit the spread of the disease. Since 2005, the rate of infection and the death rate have both declined in the United States due to the combination of testing and effective treatments. Dr. Fauci has also applied the lessons he learned, and the expertise he accumulated over time, to help stem the tide of other infectious diseases, such as SARS, H1N1, and Ebola.

If someone had asked Anthony Fauci when he was a student at the College of the Holy Cross whether he would go on to medical school at Cornell University, work his way up from the position of clinical associate at NIAID to director, and keep that job for 36 years, he probably would not have predicted this lifelong devotion to medical service in the federal bureaucracy. It takes a combination of expertise and political skills to serve so long in a top bureaucratic position that has the responsibility for pleasing presidents and saving lives.

Individuals like Dr. Fauci comprise the organizations that form the foundation of the executive branch of government; sometimes they are efficient and successful, and sometimes they make mistakes and fail to be responsive. In this chapter, we examine the cabinet-level departments, agencies, and other organizations and delve deeply into their structure, characteristics, rationale, procedures, accountability, and responsiveness to citizens' concerns. A fundamental question for students of American government is whether the sprawling nature of the bureaucracy makes it a gate or a gateway to serving the people effectively.

The American Bureaucracy

LO 14-1 Explain what the bureaucracy does

Just mention the word *bureaucracy* and most people roll their eyes and utter phrases like "red tape" or "slow as molasses." Of all the components of American government, the bureaucracy is most likely to be perceived as annoying and daunting, as a gate against getting things done. Yet the bureaucracy is also the most likely to have a direct impact on citizens' lives. Most Americans have never met a president or a member of Congress or a federal judge, but every American has likely interacted with an employee of the government. Whether the interaction involves showing identification to a TSA agent in the airport or waiting in line at the post office, the rules and regulations of the federal bureaucracy present numerous opportunities for frustration.

Bureaucracies generally are not afforded much respect because they seem so complicated and impenetrable, and bureaucrats are often portrayed as faceless robots who merely enforce the rules. Yet enforcing the rules is the bureaucracy's job; as an extension of the presidency, bureaucratic implementation is how the president executes the law. Rules must be enforced equally across all citizens. In the most obvious example, a first-class stamp costs the same in every state and will take a letter to any place in the nation, just across town or from Houston to Honolulu.

Despite the well-known problems associated with bureaucracies, organization is essential to modern government. In the late nineteenth century, the German sociologist Max Weber described bureaucracies as highly rational organizations that enabled large numbers of people to get difficult jobs done efficiently.[3] If the federal bureaucracy does not seem efficient today, that may be because of the enormous responsibilities it bears, not only to implement complex policy and law established by the president and Congress, but also to do so in a way that is orderly, predictable, fair, equal for all citizens, and transparent. The formal aspects of bureaucratic structure promote accountability, while the informal operations—the bureaucratic culture—determine how well the organization carries out its own mission and how well it interacts with other organizations. We discuss these elements in detail to draw a practical road map not only to understand the federal government but also to actually make it work better for ordinary citizens.

What Is the Bureaucracy?

The **bureaucracy** is the large collection of executive branch departments, agencies, boards, commissions, and other government organizations that carry out the responsibilities of the federal government. At first, the nation did not require many employees to fulfill the

Key Questions

What federal employees have you come in contact with? What was the most recent experience like?

Key Questions

What is your impression of the federal bureaucracy? Which branch of government do you think works best? Which works least well?

bureaucracy: *Executive branch departments, agencies, boards, and commissions that carry out the responsibilities of the federal government.*

Chip East/Reuters/Corbis

Image 14.1 The federal bureaucracy has a direct impact on your life. Most Americans are familiar with waiting in line at the post office, but not many people think about the fact that the quality of the grains in their breakfast cereal, the safety of the highways they drive on, and the purity of the water they drink are also regulated by government agencies.

government's duties, which were limited to large national issues such as defense, tariffs on imported goods, and settling western lands. As the nation's lands and economy grew, so did the need for a more complex structure at the federal level to oversee government activities. These responsibilities are established by laws passed by Congress and signed by the president; however, for execution, they often entail expertise, so the legislature relies on specialists—the bureaucrats—to write the **regulations** that implement the law.

In 2019, the number of federal employees, including the armed services, totaled about 4.1 million people.[4] Federal employees do a wide variety of jobs. A national park ranger is a federal employee, as is a TSA officer, a border patrol officer, a bridge designer with the Army Corps of Engineers, an accountant with the Securities and Exchange Commission, and a lawyer with the Department of Justice. For every federal job classified as "professional," there are also staff jobs, including clerks, office managers, janitors, mechanics, and delivery personnel, who keep the bureaucracy running. Skills and specialties in almost any type of work can be a gateway to employment in the federal government, which we discuss in more detail later in the chapter.

One simple way to understand the basic structure of the bureaucracy is to imagine a piece of furniture called a cabinet that stores different types of items in different drawers. It is no accident that the term *bureaucracy* has *bureau* at its base, an old-fashioned term for a cabinet. President Thomas Jefferson (1801–09) had a separate room in the White House that he called his cabinet, and the centerpiece of the room was a long table with drawers on each side that served as his desk, in which he stored all important federal papers according to issue area.[5] A modern president could not fit all the paperwork of the federal bureaucracy in a single desk, but the idea of compartmentalizing federal responsibilities has endured over time.

Today, a president builds a **cabinet**—his set of key advisers who are responsible for the areas under their jurisdiction. As noted in Chapter 13, The Presidency, the cabinet is distinct from the president's White House staff, which works directly for the president, because cabinet members oversee entire departments constructed to implement federal policy. Most cabinet members are **cabinet secretaries** and head executive departments, but presidents may select additional advisers for cabinet-rank status. In the Trump administration, these included the vice president, the chief of staff, the heads of the Environmental Protection Agency (EPA) and of the Office of Management and Budget, the U.S. trade representative, the U.S. ambassador to the United Nations, and the chair of the Council of Economic Advisers.[6] When a new president is elected, he or she typically selects new membership for the cabinet, although there have been cases where a president has asked a cabinet member to stay on. Notably, President Barack Obama asked Robert Gates, who was Secretary of Defense under George W. Bush, to stay on in that position to ensure that the leadership of U.S. military involvement in Iraq and Afghanistan remained consistent despite the transition to a new commander in chief.

Constitutional Foundations

The word *bureaucracy* does not appear in the U.S. Constitution, but the foundations of the federal bureaucracy can be traced to a few key sentences in Article II that relate to the powers of the president.

regulations: *Guidelines issued by federal agencies for administering federal programs and implementing federal law.*

cabinet: *Set of executive departments responsible for carrying out federal policy in specific issue areas.*

cabinet secretaries: *Heads of cabinet departments and chief advisers to the president on the issues under their jurisdiction.*

Key Questions

Why do you think the Constitution provides so little direction for the bureaucracy?

Appointments.   Article II, Section 2, gives the president the power to "nominate, and by and with the Advice and Consent of the Senate, . . . appoint . . . all other Officers of the United States, whose Appointments are not herein otherwise provided for, and which shall be established by Law." This section goes on to state that Congress can "by Law vest the Appointment of such inferior Officers, as they think proper, in the President alone, in the Courts of Law, or in the Heads of Departments." Thus the discussion of the president's appointment power implies the existence of executive departments.

Opinions on Federal Policies.   Article II, Section 2, references the executive branch more directly when it authorizes the president to "require the Opinion, in writing, of the principal Officer in each of the executive Departments, upon any subject relating to the Duties of their respective Offices." The Framers envisioned that the president would manage a staff of federal officers who would oversee executive departments managing the operations of government, although it is doubtful that they expected the president's staff to be as large as it is today.

Execution of the Laws.   Article II, Section 3, gives the president broad powers to "take Care that the Laws be faithfully executed." At the same time that the Framers wanted to make sure that the president would follow the intent of Congress, they also gave him wide discretion in how he carried out the laws. This broad executive power is the foundation for the growth of the federal bureaucracy as well as for the growth of the presidency, as discussed in Chapter 13.

Structure of the Bureaucracy

For more than two centuries, the federal bureaucracy has been changing, growing, and developing into today's interlinked set of organizations that implement federal policy. Some organizations are vast, such as the executive departments, and some are small advisory boards and commissions. Coordinating the authority and operations of these different types of organizations is a significant challenge for the executive branch as it carries out its constitutional duties. The structure of the U.S. bureaucracy and the challenges it faces are not unique. Bureaucratic organization is essential for the operation of modern governments and organizations.

Executive Departments.   Today there are fifteen executive, or cabinet-level, departments in the federal bureaucracy. A cabinet department is an executive branch organization led by a cabinet secretary appointed by the president. Cabinet departments are responsible for implementing laws and policies in specific areas through the regulatory and enforcement process. Regulations are the guidelines that detail how a law will be carried out, and what has to be done to comply with the law (see Chapter 16 for a full description). Regulations go through several versions, and after a lengthy review process, the final regulations are printed in the **Federal Register**, which is the federal government's official publication for implementation of laws.

Federal Register: *Official published record of all executive branch rules, regulations, and orders.*

The job of the secretary is to oversee implementation, provide advice to the president about the issues under the department's control, and develop an annual budget for the department. Congress has the authority to create a cabinet department, but once it is created, it is under the control and supervision of the president as head of the executive branch. Table 14.1 lists each department, the year it was created, its website, and its number of employees.

Each cabinet department consists of subdivisions arranged in a hierarchical form to divide up its tasks and theoretically maximize efficiency and responsiveness. Figure 14.1 shows how the Department of Health and Human Services (HHS) is organized. This organizational chart makes it clear that each department has many subdivisions, or layers, with each assigned a specific federal policy to implement. HHS oversees more than 100 programs, with more than 73,000 employees and a budget of almost $1.3 trillion.[7] This massive and complex organization is necessary to respond to the needs of all the individuals affected by the programs that HHS manages.

The responsibilities of HHS grew even broader when President Obama signed the Patient Protection and Affordable Care Act into law on March 23, 2010. Because HHS oversees Medicaid, Medicare, and other federal health-related programs, it bears the bulk of the responsibility to implement programs associated with this legislation. For example, HHS tries to remedy deficiencies in the Medicare prescription drug program for senior citizens and inform citizens about expanded eligibility for health insurance through Medicaid. It also coordinates health insurance exchanges, works with states to enhance existing state-based insurance programs, and joins with other federal agencies to encourage wellness and disease-prevention programs.[8] Health care reform is just one example of federal policy that is implemented by a cabinet department, in conjunction with state governments. For an in-depth discussion of the Affordable Care Act, see Chapter 16.

Table 14.1   Cabinet Departments, 2019

Department	Year Established	Website	Employees (in thousands)
State	1789	http://www.state.gov	25.3
Treasury	1789	http://www.treasury.gov	88
Defense (originally War)	1789	http://www.dod.gov	741.5
Interior	1849	http://www.interior.gov	61.6
Agriculture	1862	http://www.usda.gov	81.4
Justice	1870	http://www.justice.gov	111.9
Commerce	1903	http://www.commerce.gov	45
Labor	1913	http://www.dol.gov	14.8
Housing and Urban Development	1965	http://www.hud.gov	7.4
Transportation	1966	http://www.transportation.gov	53.1
Energy	1977	http://www.energy.gov	14
Education	1979	http://www.education.gov	3.6
Health and Human Services	1980	http://www.hhs.gov	73
Veterans Affairs	1989	http://www.va.gov	375.8
Homeland Security	2003	http://www.dhs.gov	192.4

Source: The White House, http://www.whitehouse.gov; FY2021 Budget, Table 5-1: Federal Civilian Employment in the Executive Branch, https://www.whitehouse.gov/wp-content/uploads/2020/02/ap_5_strengthening_fy21.pdf P 52. For the history of each department, see the websites listed.

Figure 14.1 Organizational Chart of the Department of Health and Human Services

Cabinet departments are complex hierarchical organizations with layers of authority and sublevel agencies that have jurisdiction over specific federal programs and policies. This organizational chart of the Department of Health and Human Services shows sublevel agencies with lines of responsibility.

Source: U.S. Department of Health and Human Services, Organizational Chart, http://www.hhs.gov/about/orgchart/index.html.

Other Types of Federal Organizations.

In addition to cabinet-level departments, there are numerous independent organizations that constitute the federal government, including agencies, commissions, administrations, boards, corporations, and endowments (see Table 14.2). These organizations vary by structure, mission, and degree of independence from the president. For example, the **Office of Management and Budget (OMB)** has final authority over the entire federal budget, and each agency and department must submit its proposed budget to OMB for approval before it is included in the president's official proposed budget. The OMB's director is part of the president's cabinet, although OMB is not a cabinet department. Additionally, all regulations must go through OMB before they take effect.

Office of Management and Budget (OMB): *Federal agency that oversees the federal budget and all federal regulations.*

Table 14.2 Selected Independent Agencies and Commissions, 2019

Department	Year Established	Website	Employees (in thousands)
Environmental Protection Agency (EPA)	1970	http://www.epa.gov	13.6
Equal Employment Opportunity Commission (EEOC)	1965	http://www.eeoc.gov	2.1
Federal Communications Commission	1934	https://www.fcc.gov	1.4
Food and Drug Administration (FDA)	1906	https://www.fda.gov/home	16.8
General Services Administration (GSA)	1949	http://www.gsa.gov	11
National Aeronautics and Space Administration (NASA)	1958	http://www.nasa.gov	17.2
National Labor Relations Board (NLRB)	1935	http://www.nlrb.gov	1.3
Securities and Exchange Commission (SEC)	1935	http://www.sec.gov	4.4
Small Business Administration (SBA)	1953	http://www.sba.gov	4.2
Social Security Administration (SSA)	1935	http://www.socialsecurity.gov	61.2

Source: The White House, http://www.whitehouse.gov; FY2021 Budget, Table 5-1: Federal Civilian Employment in the Executive Branch, https://www.whitehouse.gov/wp-content/uploads/2020/02/ap_5_strengthening_fy21.pdf, P 52; Department of Health and Human Services Fiscal Year 2021, Food and Drug Administration, https://www.fda.gov/media/135078/download, P.343.

The EPA is an **independent agency**, a type of federal organization established by Congress with authority to regulate an aspect of the economy or a sector of the federal government. Independent agencies do not operate within a cabinet department. Congress designs such agencies to operate with their own authority. The EPA bears the responsibility for preserving the quality of the air, water, and land. It can issue regulations and create policy in a wide range of areas, including limiting emissions from coal-fired plants and auto fuel emissions. Its regulations are subject to OMB approval, just like regulations from any cabinet department.

independent agency: *Federal organization that has independent authority and does not operate within a cabinet department.*

A **federal regulatory commission** is an agency typically run by a small number of officials, known as commissioners, who are appointed by the president for fixed terms and are responsible for overseeing a sector of the economic or political arena. One example is the Securities and Exchange Commission (SEC), which is responsible for monitoring all business practices involving the stock market. The SEC has five commissioners who serve staggered five-year terms and together manage 4,400 employees.[9] The SEC oversees the work of accountants, stockbrokers, hedge fund managers, financial advisers, and small business owners. It has legal authority to demand information from these professionals, impose fines for bypassing investment rules, and even bring formal charges for serious violations of the law.

federal regulatory commission: *Federal agency typically run by a small number of officials, known as commissioners, who are appointed by the president for fixed terms and oversee economic or political issues.*

A federal administration is responsible for running a federal program or overseeing specific areas of federal responsibility. The Transportation Security Administration (TSA), is a type of federal administration that was created after the attacks of 9/11 and later placed under the Department of Homeland Security (discussed later in this chapter).

A federal board typically has a more narrow scope of authority but can possess the power to require changes in operating procedures and to suggest fines. It usually consists of individuals who are appointed for a specific term and who, ideally, have expertise in

Image 14.2 The National Transportation Safety Board investigates the causes of accidents, such as the crash of the Silkorsky S-76 helicopter that killed Kobe Bryant and eight others. Many of these accidents have similarly fatal outcomes, and the NTSB makes recommendations for preventing similar accidents in the future.

NTSB/Reuters

the area of the board's jurisdiction. For example, the National Transportation Safety Board (NTSB) is responsible for investigating transportation-related accidents, such as the helicopter crash in Calabasas, California, that resulted in the death of former basketball star Kobe Bryant and eight others, or car accidents like the crash on the Pennsylvania Turnpike in Mount Pleasant Township, Pennsylvania, which resulted in five deaths and numerous injuries. Whenever an accident involves any form of transportation, one of the NTSB's five board members is appointed to oversee an investigation of the event. The NTSB also goes abroad to foreign destinations when U.S. citizens are killed in major transportation accidents. When the investigation is completed, the agency issues a report that includes findings about the accident's cause and recommendations for avoiding a similar event. Despite its authority in these investigations and its members' knowledge of safe transportation practices, the NTSB does not have the power to issue federal regulations.

A federal corporation is a type of federal organization similar to a private business in that it provides a service or commodity for a price to the public, but it also receives federal funding. For example, the National Railroad Passenger Corporation, better known as Amtrak, is essentially a for-profit railroad, but it receives federal funding and is subject to federal restrictions and controls.

A national endowment is also a type of federal organization that uses funds specifically allocated to promote a public good or service. The National Endowment for the Arts, for example, was created to support scholarship and art that would be available to the general public, but it does not have any formal responsibility to monitor private- and public-sector activities in a specific set of issue areas. Because endowments are funded by the federal government, they are expected to serve as gateways for the expression of a wide range of viewpoints and perspectives in the work that they support.

Key Questions

Why would the government fund a for-profit railroad? Are there any other industries where a similar arrangement would work?

Core Components of the Bureaucracy

LO 14-2 Outline the essential elements of a bureaucracy

All these bureaucratic organizations share four core components that determine how government implements policy and, more immediately, how government responds to the individual needs of citizens. These components are mission, hierarchical decision-making process, expertise, and bureaucratic culture.

Mission

Each federal agency has a stated mission that defines its role and responsibilities within the federal bureaucracy. For example, the mission of the Department of Health and Human Services is stated on its website:

> The Department of Health and Human Services (HHS) is the United States government's principal agency for protecting the health of all Americans and providing essential human services, especially for those who are least able to help themselves.[10]

A mission statement is important as the public face of the department, and it is the measure by which members of Congress and the general public can hold the department accountable for the success or failure of its efforts.

Hierarchical Decision-Making Process

To carry out its mission, every federal organization has a hierarchical decision-making process that structures the way policy is implemented. The hierarchy of authority in a bureaucracy means that an employee's decision on the implementation of policy is reviewed at each higher level in the organization. For example, HHS contains the following levels of authority, in ascending order: bureau chief, assistant secretary, deputy secretary, secretary. Each of these officials puts his or her expert input into policy implementation and then sends the decision up to the next level for approval. Not every department uses these levels of authority in the same way, but each leads up to the secretary, who is responsible for all of the policy decisions that come out of a department, and, ultimately, to the president.

The hierarchical decision-making process has advantages and disadvantages. It ensures that the unit responds consistently and predictably. The process also requires careful consideration of a policy before it is implemented. These two structural characteristics, taken together, are designed to ensure that policies are administered equally across citizens. However, this same hierarchical structure can present an obstacle to speedy decision making. Despite efforts to streamline the process, the step-by-step review of decision making inevitably slows down the implementation of federal laws.

Expertise

Fundamental to the core of the federal bureaucracy is the presumption that the people who hold bureaucratic positions have expertise in the issue areas they oversee and implement. This expertise can come from a number of sources. Individuals can enter the bureaucracy at the lowest possible levels and stay in their jobs long enough to acquire knowledge about federal programs. An employee might have worked in a particular industry, such as nuclear energy, and then have brought his or her preexisting knowledge to the bureaucracy—in this case, the Nuclear Regulatory Commission—as a mid-level employee. Other bureaucrats may have studied a federal policy area in academia or at policy think tanks and then may have been offered government positions. Congress, with members who chaired or served on relevant congressional committees, is a major source of cabinet secretary appointments.

Key Questions

How has the Internet made it easier to interact with, and influence, the bureaucracy? Are there cases where it has gotten more difficult?

Key Questions

How important is a hierarchical decision-making process to government responsiveness and citizen equality?

Bureaucratic Culture

Key Questions

What are the causes of bureaucratic failure? Can they be avoided? How?

The fourth core component of a bureaucracy is the bureaucratic culture. As one political scientist explained, "Every organization has a culture, that is, a persistent, patterned way of thinking about the central tasks of and human relationships within an organization. Culture is to an organization what personality is to an individual. Like human culture, it is passed on from one generation to the next."[11]

Fundamental to bureaucratic culture is the constant drive to self-perpetuate; employees in a bureaucratic organization want to preserve their jobs and their influence in the policy-making system. For this reason, bureaucratic culture can act as a gate that prevents efficiency and responsiveness in government because it can create situations in which employees in different organizations duplicate tasks, counterbalance one another's efforts, and ultimately fail to accomplish their agency's or department's mission.

At its worst, bureaucratic failure can result in a terrible loss of life, as in the case of the 9/11 terrorist attacks. Many politicians, members of the media, and citizens blamed the federal agencies that oversee intelligence gathering—the Federal Bureau of Investigation (FBI), the Central Intelligence Agency (CIA), and the National Security Agency (NSA)—for failing to uncover and prevent the attacks. Each agency detected warning signs of such an attack, but the agencies did not work together. The bureaucratic culture of each agency was insular and distrustful, and lack of coordination among them resulted in an intelligence failure.[12]

To remedy the lack of coordination among the nation's national security and disaster relief agencies, Congress created the cabinet-level Department of Homeland Security in 2003. The hope was that a single large federal organization, presumably with one culture and one overarching mission, would be more effective. The new department consolidated several key units that had been operating independently, including the Coast Guard, U.S. Citizenship and Immigration Services, Customs Service, Secret Service, and Federal Emergency Management Agency, and also created new intelligence offices that would try to serve as bridges between the FBI and the CIA.

In addition to addressing natural and man-made disasters, the federal government also oversees a wide range of safety compliance for everyday activities such as driving. The National Highway Transportation Safety Administration (NHTSA) is responsible for regulating car and truck safety, including mechanical issues, airbags, seat belts, and child restraints, as well as promoting road safety by trying to limit drunk driving. Between 2015 and 2020, Takata, a now bankrupt automotive parts company, issued the recall of more than 70 million front airbags after a settlement with NHTSA. Takata used ammonium nitrate, causing a small explosion to deploy airbags, which led to hurled shrapnel or burning when the airbags were deployed. Over twenty-five people were killed with hundreds more injured because of these faulty airbags. Vehicles made by some of the biggest brands in the world, including Honda, General Motors, Subaru, Toyota, and Volkswagen were affected. The NHTSA still must decide whether to recall numerous other inflators that used ammonium nitrate with a moisture absorbing chemical. It also must deal with several companies, like General Motors, that are seeking exceptions from the recall.[13]

In addition to safety, the federal government also regulates automobile emissions. In 2015, the EPA found that Volkswagen rigged the engines on their diesel cars to perform differently when being tested on emission standards. The scandal forced a recall of at least

500,000 cars in the United States and millions more around the world. The EPA had the legal power to impose fines on Volkswagen of $37,500 per car, which would have amounted to $18 billion. Rather than imposing the fines outright, the EPA joined with the Department of Justice to sue Volkswagen over their violations of emissions standards; in addition, the Federal Trade Commission sued Volkswagen for false advertising of their diesel cars as "clean diesel." All parties were trying to work out a settlement and in June 2016, Volkswagen agreed to pay approximately $14.7 billion in fines and payments to consumers.[14]

Image 14.3 In 2020, the COVID-19 global pandemic reached the United States and nearly every facet of American life was negatively affected. By November of that year, more than 10 million were infected with the virus, and nearly 243,000 died. Among other precautions taken, many colleges and universities moved from on-campus classes to online teaching, and students were asked to leave the university and return home for the remainder of the academic year. The following Fall, many colleges and universities were still offering their classes online.

Source: Data is taken from Johns Hopkins University, accessed September 17, 2020, https://coronavirus.jhu.edu/map.html.

Most recently, the global pandemic of COVID-19 tested the federal bureaucracy in ways unseen since in modern times. Indeed, governments all over the world were challenged by how quickly this particular virus spread, how lethal it was, and how unprepared government agencies and public health organizations were to cope with it. The virus began in Wuhan, in the Hubei province of China and was first brought to public attention in December 2019. By early March 2020, China had nearly 81,000 cases with more than 3,000 deaths; the United States had 1,323 cases with 38 deaths; and the global total at that time reached nearly 128,000 cases with 4,718 deaths.[15]

In the United States, the initial response to the epidemic by the Trump administration was relatively casual; President Trump expressed the view that the illness was thought to be confined to China and not especially contagious or lethal. In fact, President Trump's budgets called for cutting funding for the unit within the Centers for Disease Control and Prevention that dealt with global pandemics, saying that it was not needed, but Congress did not approve those budget cuts.[16] While no president can predict future global health crises, the absence of trained experts in containing epidemics cost the administration valuable time in testing for the presence of the COVID-19 and educating the public about ways to deal with and combat the spread of the virus.

The bureaucratic difficulties in handling COVID-19 stemmed from a failure to coordinate early enough with the Centers for Disease Control, the Department of Health and Human Services, and the White House. President Trump put Vice President Mike Pence in charge of coordinating the team. Starting in mid-March, President Trump made repeated press appearances to acknowledge the severity of the epidemic. He committed to a unified and coordinated public health response by the federal government and to provide assistance to state governments that had already taken steps to contain the virus. He also imposed restrictions on air travel to the United States for anyone who had been in any of twenty-six European countries that comprise what is known as the Schengen Area and closed the borders with Canada to all but essential travel. The Trump administration described these measures as necessary; however, the bans did not apply to U.S. citizens or permanent legal residents.[17]

Despite these security related measures, members of Congress complained that the primary aim of containing the virus was severely hampered by the difficulty in getting a test, and that the American government was falling behind many other countries around the globe in testing.[18] By the end of March 2020, much of America was under restricted movement or self-quarantine to stem the spread of the corona virus.

Although each of the disasters just discussed was brought about by entirely different circumstances, a common lack of communication and expert direction exposed the inherent dangers of a flawed bureaucratic culture. If such failings are serious enough, and they are accompanied by a significant downturn in the economy, the president may ultimately be held accountable for them, as President Trump appeared to be in his bid for reelection. Federal agencies may continue to resist change, not wanting to give up any authority. Change in any long-standing organization is difficult to achieve and generally happens only when the people at the top of the chain of command tear down the barriers to cooperation.

Bureaucratic culture can be shaped by the type of person drawn to work in a government bureaucracy. Bureaucrats are often depicted as narrow-minded and resistant to innovation, but many different types of people seek jobs in the bureaucracy.[19] A person who works in a long-standing government division may seek job security and stability, but someone who joins a newly formed department or agency might seek opportunities for creativity. In addition, policies evolve over time in response to changing external conditions. For example, twenty years ago, the Department of Energy might have focused on more efficient ways of drilling for oil and subsequently hired geologists; today, with the emphasis on reducing national dependence on fossil fuels, the Department of Energy seeks to hire individuals with expertise in new energy technologies. There is no single personality type in the bureaucracy. The bureaucracy is so complex and diverse that individuals with a wide range of skills and interests choose to work within it.

One counteracting force to the drawbacks of bureaucratic culture and its tendency to block cooperation among agencies is bureaucratic reputation. Federal agencies want to develop good reputations for their effective implementation of federal policy. Most people take pride in the jobs they do, and bureaucrats are no different.[20]

Key Questions
What are the advantages of a government job? What are the disadvantages?

Historical Evolution of the Bureaucracy

LO 14-3 Describe the growth of the bureaucracy over time

Key Questions
What made the bureaucracy grow? Is it too big?

The federal bureaucracy is as old as the nation itself, but it has evolved in ways that some of the Framers would barely recognize. Although they understood that the population would increase and the country's borders would expand, they could never have imagined that the federal government would have so many responsibilities and be so integral to citizens' daily lives. Over time, in tandem with economic, social, and technological developments, Congress passed laws creating new executive departments and other bureaucratic organizations. Here we trace the growth of the federal bureaucracy and the development of professional staff positions to implement federal policy.

Expansion of Executive Branch Departments

The first departments created by Congress in 1789 were State, Treasury, and War. The attorney general also sat on the president's cabinet, though he did not yet head a department. In addition, the Postal Service first created in 1775 by the Continental Congress to serve the vital function of establishing communication routes among the colonies, became a permanent government organization in 1794.[21] Through these organizations, Congress intended to fulfill the constitutional responsibilities set forth in Article I, Section 8—to regulate commerce among the states and with foreign nations, to provide for defense, to collect taxes and borrow money, and to establish post offices and post roads.

In 1849, Congress created the Department of the Interior to deal with the demands of western expansion, such as sale of federal lands and management of the federal government's interactions with Native Americans. The Department of Agriculture was created in 1862 to mitigate the hardships caused by crop and price fluctuations through crop subsidies that remain in place today. In 1870, the Office of the Attorney General, first set up in 1793, was transformed into the Department of Justice to handle the legal business of the nation.

The next two departments, Commerce and Labor, represented economic concerns. Congress addressed them by creating a single department in 1903, but within a decade, the issues of child safety and workers' standards became so important that Congress divided the department, giving Labor its own cabinet status. This sequence was paralleled later in the twentieth century by the creation of the Department of Health, Education, and Welfare in 1953 and its subsequent division into two departments—the Department of Education, created in 1979, and the Department of Health and Human Services in 1980 to oversee health care and welfare programs. In 1949, the War Department was transformed into the Department of Defense, coordinating the Army, Navy, and Air Force. In 1965, Congress created the Department of Housing and Urban Development to oversee federal programs designed to build more affordable housing for people with low incomes and to help restore inner cities that were losing residents. The Department of Transportation was created in 1966, following a decade of interstate highway building authorized by the Highway Act of 1956. Increases in trucking also put pressure on the federal government to maintain highways and regulate business and labor practices in trucking and the air travel industry. As a direct response to the energy crisis of the early 1970s, the Department of Energy was created in 1977 to promote fuel conservation as well as the development of alternatives to fossil fuels, including nuclear, ethanol, and solar power.

In 1989, the Department of Veterans Affairs was created with the support of President George H. W. Bush (1989–93). Finally, as noted earlier, Congress created the Department of Homeland Security in 2003 in a direct response to the widely perceived intelligence failures associated with the terrorist attacks of 9/11.

Growth of Regulatory Agencies and Other Organizations

In addition to the formal cabinet departments, the executive branch contains numerous regulatory agencies and other organizations that are responsible for administering the details of laws in specific areas, as well as for overseeing the practices of businesses and individuals involved in all facets of economic and political life. These agencies serve as

Key Questions
Why was the Postal Service so important in the early days of the United States?

Key Questions
In his 2020 campaign for president, Andrew Yang proposed a new executive department, the Department of Technology, so our government can better deal with technological innovation. What do you think will be the next executive department created?

Key Questions
How did the government go from monitoring railroads to funding them? How does this change illustrate the increased role of government in private industry?

Public Policy and the Bureaucracy

Net Neutrality

The federal bureaucracy has grown, in part, because Congress has continually responded to changes in the economy and society that have required government action. However, at times, industries that are regulated by the government create new technologies or business practices that become widely adopted so quickly that the government cannot keep up with them in terms of regulation. Or use of a technology becomes so widespread that the companies that sell it, use it, or otherwise engage with it find themselves unable to keep up with demand or sustain profitability. One example of this kind of innovation has been the advent of social media and streaming services that enable users to communicate, engage with social media platforms, make purchases, and watch entertainment and sports content on the Internet.

The Federal Communications Commission (FCC) is the agency in charge of regulating the Internet. There are five FCC commissioners, each appointed by the president and confirmed by the U.S. Senate; the typical term of service is five years, unless a commissioner is appointed to fill an unexpired term. Not more than three commissioners can be from the same political party.[22]

In 2015, under President Obama, the FCC issued regulations that required Internet service providers to practice Net Neutrality. In doing so, the FCC determined that broadband Internet service is a utility and as such can be regulated by the federal government. In brief, Net Neutrality meant that Internet service providers could not charge more money to users who watched specific content or used some websites or apps more frequently than others and could not block access to certain programs. The policy also meant that Internet and app providers could not provide faster service to customers—ranging from individual consumers to small businesses to larger e-commerce companies—who agreed to pay more for it.[23]

When President Trump came into office in 2017, he elevated a member of the FCC, Ajit Pai, to chair the commission. Pai, who had worked in the communications industry, was originally appointed to the FCC by President Obama. Pai had been an outspoken critic of Net Neutrality and voted against issuing the 2015 regulations, so it was not surprising that one of his early initiatives as FCC chair was to work to repeal those regulations. In addition, President Trump was able to nominate a commissioner to the FCC in 2017 so the balance of Republicans to Democrats flipped in favor of those seeking to repeal Net Neutrality. Consequently, in late 2017, the FCC finalized regulations that repealed Net Neutrality and prohibited state governments from instituting net neutrality policies at the state level. As with all regulations, there was a public comment period, during which a reported 23 million comments pro and con were received. However, seventeen attorneys general wrote a letter to the FCC commissioner asking to delay the issuing of the Net Neutrality repeal because it was alleged that a significant number of those comments, nearly 1 million, were submitted by individuals who used other people's identities.[24] They argued that no matter what side of the policy these commentators were on, using false identities to submit comments was a threat to the open comment power of Americans to react to government regulations.[25] The FCC did not agree to their request for a delay in implementing the regulations, and the Federal Circuit Court of Appeals upheld the repeal of Net Neutrality, although it ruled that the FCC could not prohibit state governments from instituting net neutrality policies at the state level.

It remains to be seen what the ultimate impact of the repeal of Net Neutrality is on consumers and businesses; it may or may not raise the cost of using a wide range of services or create a tiered system in which some consumers and businesses have access to much faster Internet services than others. In the meantime, advocates of Net Neutrality have been attempting to mitigate the potential damage from its repeal. California passed a bill in 2018 that is considered even stronger than Obama era measures. Internet providers are prohibited from blocking or slowing down the transmission of web traffic to the state's broadband customers, and websites are not allowed to promote free streaming for apps, a practice that can stifle the businesses of other websites that do not have the resources to offer such promotions.[26] Net Neutrality is just one example of how federal regulations can generate strong support and opposition and how those regulations can be greatly affected when the power in the White House changes party hands.

Construct Your Own Policy

1. Design three reforms that would provide consumer protections for Internet use.
2. Develop a system of governmental regulation for the Internet that would address consumer and business protection for use of Internet services.

gateways for the federal government to respond to citizens in targeted ways on a localized level, and they are especially important in ensuring safety and economic fairness for citizens in daily life. Among the concerns these agencies address are highway and air travel, food inspection and product labeling, and bank and stock market practices.

One of the most familiar regulatory agencies is the Food and Drug Administration (FDA), which monitors food safety and handling practices as well as pharmaceutical development and approval procedures for medical testing, including tests for the coronavirus. The motto of the FDA summarizes its mission, "Protecting and Promoting *Your* Health." The agency fulfills its mission by issuing guidelines and standards for companies to follow. Well-publicized cases of *E. coli* contamination in ground beef and salmonella in raw tuna, which resulted in illness and even death, illustrate just how difficult it is for the FDA to monitor food safety.[27] As the initially slow pace of coronavirus testing illustrated, the FDA also faces an ongoing balance between strictly regulating medical testing equipment and having the ability to respond quickly to a pandemic; the same is true of the vaccine approval process.

As the nation's economy has grown, so has the number of industries, products, and services that may warrant government regulation. This growth has expanded the workload of existing agencies and may require the creation of new ones. For example, Congress established the Federal Trade Commission to protect consumers from unfair financial and marketplace practices and the Consumer Product Safety Commission to ensure that basic goods purchased by consumers are safe.[28] In 2010, President Barack Obama and Congress worked together to create a new regulatory agency—the Consumer Financial Protection Bureau—that would help consumers navigate credit card interest rates and late fees, mortgage and other housing loans, as well as real estate investments.[29] Under President Trump, a new director, Kathy Kraninger, was appointed and confirmed with a mission to reduce the scope of the bureau and limit enforcement of judgments against companies who are found to have defrauded consumers.[30]

There are limits to the effectiveness of regulatory agencies. They have government authority to monitor practices, issue fines, and even shut down businesses, but the

Key Questions

Is protecting people from ineffective medical treatment the government's job? Why? What are the tradeoffs?

OFFICE-SEEKERS AT WASHINGTON DURING THE INAUGURATION.

These Gentlemen, who are ready, like good Patriots, to serve their Country, are all ORIGINAL LINCOLN-MEN. 'Tis true, they voted for PIERCE and BUCHANAN; but this was a deep game to insure the Election of LINCOLN in 1860.

Provided courtesy HarpWeek

Image 14.4 Nineteenth-century presidents complained of being besieged by office seekers, men who hoped their connections with members of Congress or the president could help them land lucrative or powerful positions in the executive departments. In this engraving, office seekers wait to see Abraham Lincoln.

government must rely on voluntary cooperation by the vast majority of private businesses in following agency guidelines. The distinct separation between the government and private businesses that is the hallmark of the American economy can also stand as a gate against effective government regulation and **oversight**. Nevertheless, regulatory agencies are gateways through which citizens can ask government to protect them from fraudulent and unsafe products sold in the marketplace.

From Patronage to the Civil Service

oversight: *Powers of Congress to monitor how the executive branch implements the laws.*

For the nation's first forty years, jobs in the executive branch were filled by wealthy elites who had personal political and social connections to members of Congress and the president.[31] But President Andrew Jackson (1829–37) used the executive powers of the president to appoint people from wider social and economic backgrounds to federal positions. He also demanded political loyalty from federal employees; to get a job in the Jackson administration, one had to be an active political supporter of Jackson and the Democratic Party. This arrangement, in which the politician appoints employees who pledge loyalty to him, is generally referred to as the patronage system. Jackson's political enemies called it the spoils system, charging Jackson with awarding jobs to political friends in the manner of the saying, "To the victor belong the spoils."

For most of the nineteenth century, Congress and the president shared the patronage power; the president allowed members of Congress to recommend individuals for government posts. With each election in which a different party assumed office, there was a large turnover in staff. The federal patronage system allowed politicians to manipulate federal programs and positions for political and private gain.[32] For example, the Republican-controlled Congress created programs to provide pensions for Civil War veterans who had fought for the North, which was heavily Republican.

As the nation grew larger and the economy more complex, the federal bureaucracy needed more expertise and stability. The assassination of President James A. Garfield in 1881 by an individual who had sought, but had not received, a federal job caused a public outcry against patronage in government employment. Although the assassin had had no direct contact with Garfield, he evidently held the president responsible for his failure to secure a federal job. In response, Congress passed the **Pendleton Act**, which was signed into law by President Chester A. Arthur (1881–85) on January 16, 1883. It was the first of the reforms that slowly changed the federal bureaucracy from a corrupt and partisan insider organization to a neutral, policy-based organization.[33]

Pendleton Act: *1883 act that established a merit- and performance-based system for federal employment.*

However, there are examples of federal agencies being accused of overstepping their authority for political purposes. At one time, the Internal Revenue Service (IRS) was under scrutiny for targeting groups that claim to be nonprofit but might also be engaged in political activity; in the past decades, the IRS was accused of giving extra scrutiny to groups ranging from the NAACP to Tea Party–affiliated nonprofit organizations. It could be argued that these actions stem from a deeply ingrained culture at the IRS of auditing individuals, businesses, and groups to make sure they comply with tax laws, but to the public, it looked as if the bureaucracy failed to maintain its mission of neutrality in implementing the law.

The Pendleton Act created the **Civil Service Commission** to administer entrance exams for the federal civil service and set job requirements and promotion standards based on a **merit system** and performance, not political affiliation. At first the civil service covered only a small fraction of federal jobs; the rest were controlled primarily by powerful members of Congress who used their influence to direct federal jobs to loyal supporters. But over time, successive presidents wrested more control over the federal bureaucracy from Congress by issuing executive orders to classify a greater percentage of jobs as merit-based and as part of the **civil service**. By 1897, 50 percent of federal jobs were covered by the civil service, and by 1951, 88 percent of federal jobs were civil service jobs.[34] The remaining federal employees are **political appointees** appointed by the president to carry out his political and partisan agenda within the federal policy-making system.

Career Civil Service

Career civil servants are nonpolitical personnel who must pass an exam to secure their jobs and compete on an equal playing field with anyone else who has the same credentials. For the number of executive branch employees, and other members of the federal workforce, see Figure 14.2. The largest percentage of executive branch employees are located in the metropolitan Washington, D.C., area.[35] In general, federal civil service employees fall into three categories: blue-collar, white-collar, and senior executive positions. Blue-collar jobs consist of "craft, repair, operator, and laborer jobs," and employees in this category are under the Federal Wage System, which sets pay levels associated with specific jobs. Executive-level management employees are governed by the Senior Executive Service guidelines, which generally follow the General Schedule (GS) pay scale. All federal employees are subject to performance evaluations and may receive gradual raises, promotions up the career ladder, and incentive and merit bonuses for outstanding job performance.[36]

Some departments and agencies are staffed by career employees who are not in the civil service but nonetheless operate under similar structures. For example, the State Department oversees a corps of diplomats known as Foreign Service Officers who are sent all over the world to manage U.S. embassies and consulates. To join the Foreign Service, one must meet certain qualifications and pass an

Civil Service Commission: *Created by the Pendleton Act to administer entrance exams for the federal civil service and set standards for promotion based on merit.*

merit system: *System of employment under which employees are chosen and promoted based on merit.*

civil service: *The nonpartisan federal workforce employed to carry out government programs and policies.*

political appointees: *Federal employees appointed by the president with the explicit task of carrying out his political and partisan agenda.*

career civil servants: *Federal employees who are hired through a merit-based system to implement federal programs and who are expected to be neutral in their political affiliations.*

Key Questions
How did the merit-based civil service change the job performance of federal employees?

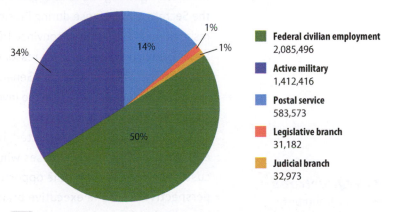

Figure 14.2 Distribution of Federal Government Workforce, 2019

Federal employment is divided into several categories: executive branch, active military forces, and the U.S. Postal Service.

Source: The White House, http://www.whitehouse.gov; FY2021 Budget, Table 5-2: Federal Civilian Employment in the Executive Branch, p. 53, https://www.whitehouse.gov/wp-content/uploads/2020/02/ap_5_strengthening_fy21.pdf.

Legend:
- **Federal civilian employment** 2,085,496
- **Active military** 1,412,416
- **Postal service** 583,573
- **Legislative branch** 31,182
- **Judicial branch** 32,973

entrance exam, similar to the procedure for entering the civil service generally. However, the Foreign Service has its own pay scale and promotion criteria.

Although politics may permeate any workplace, the civil service is designed to protect employees from partisanship, and employees are expected to be objective as they carry out their job responsibilities. Civil servants remain in their positions from one administration to the next, and they cannot be asked to resign for partisan reasons. In his role as director of NIAID, Dr. Fauci falls under the category of civil service employee and cannot be fired for partisan reasons; however, he can be removed from his position for other reasons by the director of the National Institutes of Health, who oversees Fauci's institute.

Political Appointees

Key Questions

What are two gateways to becoming a presidential appointee?

Political appointees, unlike civil servants, get their jobs because they are members of the same party that controls the executive branch, they have connections to politically powerful people, or they have served in a prior presidential administration. Political appointees can occupy a wide range of positions, from cabinet secretary to commissioner to administrator. Although it is uncommon, political appointees can also come from the opposition party, especially when they have particular expertise in a policy area or a president wants continuity in department leadership early in his administration. Regardless of their personal views, political appointees are expected to carry out the president's policy agenda.[37]

Political appointees can come from a variety of backgrounds. Typically they are members of the president's inner circle or campaign team, served as congressional committee chairs, or served in former presidential administrations. In some cases, they come from the private sector. There are advantages and disadvantages to the president in choosing people from any of these backgrounds. Sometimes a president's trusted campaign advisers are not talented administrators; sometimes members of the private sector find government work too frustrating. Presidents try to make the best choices possible, but occasionally a cabinet secretary is replaced during a presidential term, especially if he or she has become a lightning rod for a broader controversy or an unpopular position. James Mattis, the Secretary of Defense during President Trump's first two years in office, announced his resignation after failing to convince the president to halt the withdrawal of all troops from Syria. Trump, unhappy with his reasoning, accelerated his resignation by over a month. Jeff Sessions, the first Attorney General for Trump also left office early, after months of conflict about his recusal from the investigation relating to Russian interference in the 2016 elections.

When a president is reelected, he customarily requests the resignations of his entire cabinet and then chooses which resignations to accept and which to reject. This custom gives presidents the opportunity to change policy direction and bring fresh perspectives into the executive branch at the start of a second term. When a president loses his bid for reelection, members of his cabinet may be fired or choose to resign before the next president takes office. For example, President Trump fired Mark Esper, his Secretary of Defense, after the November 2020 election.

Key Questions

How much authority should the president have over executive branch employees?

Top-level political appointees require Senate confirmation, a process made slightly easier when the Senate is controlled by the president's party and by the Senate rules changes that reduced the cloture threshold to fifty-one votes for presidential nominees and judicial appointments (see Chapter 12, Congress, for more details). Under Franklin Delano Roosevelt (1933–45), the number of such employees was 73, but it rose to 499 under President Obama. But there are hundreds of other jobs that are considered political appointments. For example, President Dwight D. Eisenhower (1953–61) appointed a layer of federal employees, known as **Schedule C appointees**, to oversee civil service employees. By some accounts, in creating this category Eisenhower was able to add approximately one thousand politically appointed positions to the bureaucracy over the course of his administration.[38] Subsequently, Presidents John F. Kennedy (1961–63), Lyndon Baines Johnson (1963–69), and Richard M. Nixon (1969–74) added more political appointees.

In 1978, President Jimmy Carter (1977–81) created the **Senior Executive Service (SES)**, experienced personnel who can be assigned by the president to senior management positions throughout the federal bureaucracy. For SES positions, the president generally chooses career civil service employees who have shown expertise in their jobs, but the president also has the authority to bring in individuals from the private sector. The SES provides a layer of administration over federal programs that is directed by the president, infusing the federal bureaucracy with political perspectives that can clash with the goal of objective implementation of federal policy. Since 1980, the total number of political appointees has averaged about three thousand.[39] Although that may not seem like a high number compared to the total federal workforce, the category of political appointee has been used successfully by many presidents to expand their direct influence within the bureaucracy.

Schedule C appointees: *Federal employees appointed by the president to oversee civil service employees.*

Senior Executive Service (SES): *Senior management personnel in the federal government appointed by the president.*

Diversity in the Federal Bureaucracy

As we noted above, as far back as President Andrew Jackson, the government was an employer in the U.S. workforce, from the post office to the Army Corps of Engineers. Over time, workforce opportunities in the federal government have expanded in different ways, from the 1883 Pendleton Act, which created the civil service, to the New Deal, which put people to work with federal dollars during the Great Depression, to Lyndon Johnson's Great Society, which created the need for thousands of new federal employees and opened doors for previously excluded groups, such as African Americans and women, to hold well-paying and stable jobs.

In the late twentieth and early twenty-first centuries, Presidents Clinton, George W. Bush, and Obama explicitly aimed to better diversify the federal workforce. Figure 14.3 and its caption show the percentage of ethnic, racial, gender, and LGBT groups that make up the federal bureaucracy.[40]

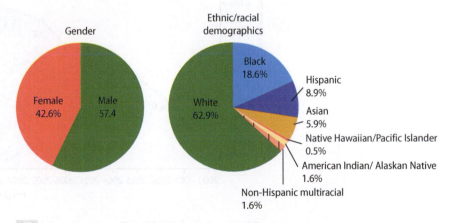

Figure 14.3 Composition of the Federal Workforce

These charts show the demographics of the federal workforce. For the first time, statistics on lesbian, gay, bisexual, and transgender (LGBT) workers are available, with 2.8 percent of the federal workforce identifying in this category. Additionally, 9.0 percent of all federal workers have a designated disability.

Source: U.S. Office of Personnel Management, Diversity & Inclusion. *Federal Equal Opportunity Recruitment Program (FEORP) Report, October 2019,* accessed February 17, 2020, https://www.opm.gov/policy-data-oversight/diversity-and-inclusion/reports /feorp-2017.pdf.

In addition to high-ranking appointments, the Obama administration also tried to recruit members of underrepresented groups to lower-level federal jobs, both political and in the civil service, to ensure that future administrations will have as diverse a talent pool to hire from as possible.

Building a diverse federal workforce serves as a gateway to the advancement of women and minorities within the public and private sectors, as these employees can later obtain political appointments to the president's cabinet. At this highest level of cabinet appointees, former President Obama can lay claim to having had the largest number of women to date. However, he was criticized by advocates for failing to attract other underrepresented groups such as Latinos and African Americans. The head of the National Council of La Raza (now UNIDOS US), Janet Murguia, pointed out that these groups heavily supported Obama in 2008 and 2012 and should have been rewarded with a greater number of prominent appointments in the administration.[41] In Figure 14.4, we show the percent of Latino employment in the federal bureaucracy from 2000 to 2017. Under Obama, it started at around 8.0 percent, and when he left office in early 2017, it stood at 8.6 percent. At the end of Donald Trump's first year in office, it stood at 8.9 percent. The highest number of Latinos work in the Department of Homeland Security and at the Department of the Treasury. No matter the gains over the past decade, the percent of Latino employment in the federal government is far less than the percent of Latinos in the general population, which is approximately 18.1 percent.

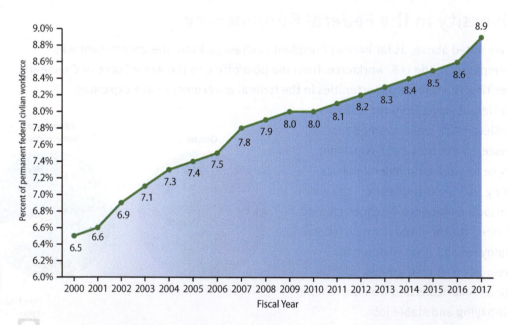

Figure 14.4 Latino Employment in the Federal Bureaucracy, 2000-2017

This chart shows the rate of change in Latino employment in the federal bureaucracy over the tenures of President Bush, President Obama, and President Trump. Although the percentage has slowly increased, the overall percent of Latino employment in the federal government is less than half of the proportion of Latinos in the general population.

Source: United States Office of Personnel Management Annual Report to the President, Hispanic Employment in the Federal Government Fiscal Year 2017, https://www.opm.gov/policy-data-oversight/diversity-and-inclusion/reports/hispanic-2017.pdf.

Political Analytics

Younger Americans in the Federal Workforce

JUST AS THE FEDERAL WORKFORCE CAN BE A gateway for the advancement of women and minorities, it can also serve that purpose for Millennials and others preparing to enter the workforce. Diversity in the federal bureaucracy serves the goal of representing the population in public service and may present

opportunities for those employed. A broad workforce may also be important as a mechanism for the input of new ideas and personnel into the bureaucracy.

Figure 14.5 features data about Millennials, defined as born between 1981 to 1996, and Generation Xers, defined as born between 1965 to 1980, in the federal workforce. Taken

68% ····· of the ····· **federal workforce are** ✦ ★ ✦ ★ ✦ **Millennials & Gen Xers**

66% report positive **job satisfaction**

88% feel the work I do is ❗ **important** ❗

86% see how their **work relates** ····· to their ····· **agency's goals & priorities**

Millennial & Gen Xer minorities =

22% of the **total** workforce

35% of the **federal** workforce

35% earned **bachelor's degrees** or higher

Figure 14.5 **Millennials and Generation Xers in the Federal Bureaucracy**

Source: Bureau of Labor Statistics, Labor Force Statistics from the Current Population Survey, accessed February 17, 2020, https://www.bls.gov/cps/.

from an annual survey of federal workers, the data show that these two groups make up almost 20 percent of the federal bureaucracy. Those who found employment with the federal government report high levels of satisfaction with their jobs and believe that the work they do is important. Millennials and Generation Xers who are also racial or ethnic minorities are also well represented in the federal bureaucracy as compared to the overall U.S. workforce.

Thinking Critically

1. Figure 14.5 uses infographics to present statistics on the federal workforce. Do you think infographics is a more effective way to present these statistics than graphs or charts; why or why not?
2. What do you think Millennials and Gen Xers bring to the federal bureaucracy?

Private-Sector Contract Workers

In addition to civil service employees and political appointees, the federal government hires thousands of individuals and companies from the private sector to administer programs and carry out tasks associated with specific policies. These companies can range from nonprofit community organizations, to midsize security firms, to large health care conglomerates. They are not under the direct control of the federal bureaucracy, but they carry out crucial tasks for it. President Bill Clinton was the first Democrat since the 1930s to suggest that some of the services provided by the federal government could be more efficiently done by the private sector. In addition, incentive programs were put in place to reward federal civil servants for efficiency, in the same way that employees in the private sector receive bonuses.

Image 14.5 The federal bureaucracy often employs private-sector workers and organizations to administer federal programs or help support military operations. Here private security personnel help government officials in Afghanistan. Although there is a need for more personnel to supplement U.S. efforts, controversies can arise in terms of oversight of private workers, as well as the dangers they encounter on the job.

Umit Bektas/Reuters

President George W. Bush continued this trend of contracting out the performance of government tasks to private companies. For example, during the Iraq War, the federal government contracted with major construction companies to work with the Army Corps of Engineers to rebuild war-torn areas of Iraq. It also contracted with private security firms to provide additional security for U.S. diplomatic and civilian personnel in both Iraq and Afghanistan. At home, much of the actual administration and provision of benefits under the Medicare and Medicaid programs is carried out by large private health maintenance organizations (HMOs) and other private service providers. When such large programs are run by private-sector organizations, it is sometimes more difficult to conduct proper oversight to prevent cost overruns or unnecessary billing charges.[42]

There are costs and benefits to the privatization of federal services. One concern is that the federal government does not have close oversight over the quality, experience, or job performance of the employees who work in the private companies. Although company employees have an incentive to do their jobs well, fraud, waste, and abuse can go undetected for years because of the lack of direct federal oversight. Sometimes the federal government ends up paying more for the provision of services through private contractors than it would if federal employees administered the program directly. The benefit of using private firms is that they do not technically count as additional federal employees, so when they are used, the overall size of the federal workforce appears smaller, and costs associated with job-related benefits are reduced. In some cases, it is more efficient to use a private firm that has expertise in an area to provide a service at a lower cost than to use permanent employees and achieve the same outcome. That allows the government to increase or decrease employment for specific projects; it is much more difficult to eliminate federal positions.

Bureaucrats and Politics

The civil service was created to protect federal employees from partisan politics, but by 1939 it had become clear that political influence was still rampant throughout the bureaucracy, not only at the federal level but at state and local levels as well. In response, Congress passed the Hatch Act, which prohibited government employees from working on political campaigns, using their positions to solicit campaign donations, or promoting candidates for elected office. This mandated separation of politics from the bureaucracy was designed to eliminate the last vestiges of patronage. It took pressure off bureaucrats, who could tell campaigning politicians that they were prohibited from engaging in certain political activities. In 1993, the Hatch Act Reform Amendments significantly loosened restrictions on political activities by government employees as long as the activities occurred while they were off duty. Now political appointees are explicitly allowed to engage in political activities on behalf of the president so long as the costs for these activities are not paid with tax dollars. Bans on political activities remain in force for employees in law enforcement and intelligence agencies as well as for employees of the Federal Election Commission (FEC), which monitors federal campaign activities.[43] However, as of January 2020, the FEC had only three sitting members and could not function; the FEC requires four members to achieve a quorum, which is necessary to have any kind of oversight power. In March 2020, President Trump nominated a fourth member to the FEC supported by the Republicans in the Senate and by April, the FEC was once again able to meet as a governing commission.

Conflict between civil servants, who take a programmatic approach and aim to make programs work efficiently over the long term, and political appointees, who want to carry out the president's partisan agenda while the president is in office, was addressed by the Civil Service Reform Act of 1978. President Jimmy Carter proposed the act to encourage cooperation between political appointees and civil servants and to make sure that each was held accountable for decision making. The act created the Office of Personnel Management to oversee both categories of federal employees. The Office of Personnel Management, under the direct control of the Executive Office of the President, can expand the number of political appointees and reduce the number of career civil servants.

Key Questions
Are there government services that should not be contracted out to the private sector?

Key Questions
Should there be a gate that blocks government employees from engaging in certain kinds of political activities? Would such a gate compromise citizen equality?

Key Questions

Why was the civil service designed so that employees remain in place despite turnover in the presidency and in Congress?

With more politically appointed personnel in the bureaucracy, presidents assert greater control over how federal policy is formulated and implemented. To preserve the essential political neutrality of the career civil service, the act also created the Merit Systems Protection Board, which ensures that the protections afforded to career civil servants through the merit system remain in place.

Nevertheless, bureaucrats do face conflicting pressures when Congress is controlled by one political party and the executive branch is controlled by the other political party, a condition known as divided government. Under divided government, federal bureaucrats are frequently caught in the middle because they are pressured by Congress to implement policy one way and by political appointees in their agencies to implement policy in a different way. Objectively, policy is supposed to be implemented in a manner that will produce the most efficient and responsive results, but trying to please two powerful bosses can result in inefficient and ineffective policy. Fortunately, the career nature of the civil service, with its built-in protections against political pressure, helps mitigate the negative consequences of divided government. In addition, because career civil servants frequently outlast presidents and some members of Congress, they have a longer-term perspective on the impact of their decisions.

At the same time, bureaucrats tend to form long-term working relationships with members of Congress and even with interest group lobbyists in the policy areas in which they specialize. In Chapter 8, Interest Groups, we explored the concepts of iron triangles (see Figure 8.3) and issue networks, both of which are used to describe these relationships. Bureaucrats want to maximize their longevity as administrators of federal programs, so they try to be as responsive as possible to the other members of the network, and each member constantly shares information with the others.[44] Critics of iron triangles and issue networks argue that they contribute to the inefficiency of the federal government because they sustain programs that may be duplicative or outdated, and they may encourage corruption within the government. However, given the 24-7 news cycle and the amount of government information available on the Internet, the public, the media, and watchdog groups are able to monitor such relationships, and they are now more transparent than ever before. Nevertheless, iron triangles are another indication that, despite the protections of a merit-based civil service, politics will always influence, to some degree, the bureaucrats who implement federal policy.

Accountability and Responsiveness in the Bureaucracy

LO 14-4 **Assess how the bureaucracy is both accountable and responsive, and how it can fail**

Typically, the power of the vote in regularly scheduled elections is used to monitor elected officials, but there are no ways for the average voter to register an opinion about the collective job performance of employees of the federal bureaucracy. Because the bureaucracy varies by type of agency, size of agency, and type of employee, it is difficult for citizens to evaluate job performance and hold bureaucrats collectively accountable for their actions. At the individual level, the job performance of civil servants is reviewed by supervisors at regular intervals, and political appointees can be removed by the president if the president is unhappy with their work. But democracy requires that citizens be able to hold their entire government accountable for the policies it implements, and there is no readily available mechanism for the public to hold civil servants accountable for their job performance. There are, however, certain standards and procedures that Congress has put in place to hold the bureaucracy accountable and encourage responsiveness. Legal challenges to regulations are another means by which the bureaucracy can be held accountable.

Key Questions

Is it easy or hard for citizens to hold the bureaucracy accountable for its actions? Why?

Roles of the Legislative and Judicial Branches

Congress contributes to the accountability and responsiveness of the bureaucracy through its oversight of implementation and its so-called power of the purse. Congressional committees with jurisdiction in a set of issue areas can request that agency and cabinet officials testify before them to explain the way they implement programs under their jurisdiction.[45] In the age of the 24-7 news cycle, on-demand internet viewing, and YouTube, the audience that can watch congressional oversight and investigation hearings has expanded enormously. Members of Congress understand that they are playing to the vast and unseen audience when they make statements or ask questions in hearings. That can work in their favor to build a reputation among constituents, party activists, and interest groups (which we discuss further in Chapter 12). But it can also work against them because they are competing against all of their colleagues for the attention of viewers, and more frequently than not, their remarks are reduced to small sound bites. In this way, congressional oversight has weakened considerably because it is harder to mobilize the public to hold the executive branch accountable for the issues that are considered in these hearings.

As noted in the discussion of constitutional powers of impeachment in Chapter 2, The Constitution, President Donald Trump was investigated by Congress after allegations surfaced in August 2019 that he withheld military aid from an ally, Ukraine, in order to force them to investigate 2020 Democratic presidential candidate Joe Biden and his son Hunter Biden, who served on the board of a Ukrainian gas company while his father was a sitting vice president. Speaker Nancy Pelosi initiated an impeachment inquiry, and after months of hearings, the Democrat-controlled House impeached Trump on two charges: abuse of power and obstruction of Congress. In the Senate, however,

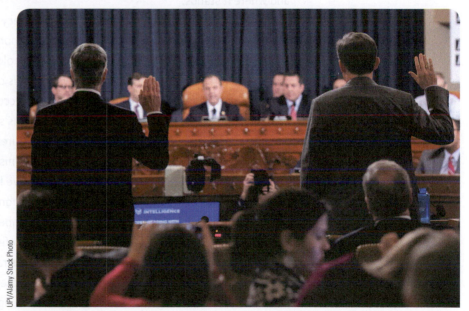

UPI/Alamy Stock Photo

Image 14.6 Impeachment trials are very rare in American history and have only happened three times, for Andrew Johnson, Bill Clinton, and Donald Trump. The House of Representatives considers bringing charges against the president for high crimes and misdemeanors and conducts investigatory hearings. If the House votes to impeach the president, the Senate then takes up the case in a trial format where evidence is presented by the House and the president, and Senators vote to either acquit or convict. If a president is convicted in an impeachment trial, he or she is removed from office. Here we see the House of Representatives holding hearings on charges that President Trump used his powers to pressure a foreign nation into investigating his opponent.

Source: John F. Harris, "Trump Exposed: A Brutal Day for the President," Politico.com, November 13, 2019, https://www.politico.com /news/magazine/2019/11/13/impeachment-trump-nixon-clinton-070837.

Republicans voted against allowing witnesses to testify on the matter, and speedily acquitted Trump, with only one Republican, Mitt Romney, voting to convict on the abuse of power charge. Overall, congressional actions in Trump's presidency demonstrate the complexities and limits of congressional oversight.

One of Trump's biggest campaign proposals was to build a massive wall at the southern border with the purpose of lowering undocumented immigration. As president, Trump continued and surpassed President Obama's policy of holding migrants in detention centers, but with the additional action of separating families and holding children in cages in what human rights advocates and lawyers called a human rights crisis. Trump also required that individuals requesting asylum be held in Mexico before crossing the border to request a processing of their status, and his policy was upheld by the U.S. Supreme Court. Members of Congress journeyed to the border to see these detention centers and tried to focus public attention through traditional and social media on the conditions in these holding centers. Their efforts paid off to a limited extent when the negative publicity became so great, both domestically and internationally, that the Trump administration had to change its policy. Trump's policies were ultimately successful in reducing border crossings by undocumented individuals, but members of Congress from both parties recognized that the moral cost of the policy might have been too high a price to pay for reducing undocumented immigration. Another very important issue to the Latino community is the status of the DREAM Act and extension of status for DACA designees. In Chapter 16, we discuss the history of this policy and where it stands.

Another way Congress can hold the bureaucracy accountable is through its powers to authorize and appropriate. Authorization and appropriation hearings give Congress a chance to evaluate federal agencies and to withhold or reduce funds if there is dissatisfaction. Agency heads are fully aware of this congressional power, and it is a key reason why they take congressional opinion into account when they implement federal programs. Congressional influence of this type thus serves as a gateway for the public—which elects members of Congress—to hold the bureaucracy accountable for its actions. However, in recent years even this power has diminished as in the case of President Trump's border wall funding. When Congress refused to give him the amount he asked for, he used his executive implementation authority to move money from the Pentagon to fund the building of the wall. There was very little that members of Congress could do to stop him from using funds that were appropriated for the Defense Department in this way.

The judicial branch, too, helps hold the bureaucracy accountable. The courts can serve as effective monitors of implementation because they are a gateway for groups adversely affected by a federal regulation to argue their case against it. Typically, the courts intervene when there is a dispute between Congress and the executive branch on the interpretation of a law, and not when the two branches agree (see Supreme Court Cases: *Chevron U.S.A. v. Natural Resources Defense Council*).

Efficiency and Transparency

One of the biggest challenges a bureaucratic organization faces is carrying out its mission efficiently while maintaining transparency to the American public. A chronic complaint about the bureaucracy is that it is slow. Yet issuing rules and regulations takes so long because the process solicits input from all sectors, including members of Congress, businesses and

Supreme Court Cases

Chevron U.S.A. v. Natural Resources Defense Council (1984)

QUESTION: Can the Environmental Protection Agency (EPA) allow pollution-producing plants to update equipment at some sources of pollution at a plant without requiring that it update all equipment at the plant?

ORAL ARGUMENT: February 29, 1984 (listen at http://www.oyez.org/cases/1980-1989/1983/1983_82_1005)

DECISION: June 25, 1984 (read at http://www.law.cornell.edu/supremecourt/text/467/837)

OUTCOME: Yes, the EPA can adjust regulations because courts recognize a responsibility to defer to agency decisions in the absence of specific congressional instructions to administer the law differently (6–0; three justices did not participate).

Congress establishes agencies to handle both routine administrative chores and highly technical decisions. Because Congress cannot foresee all questions that may arise, it delegates rule-making authority to agencies. These rules are subject to review by the federal judiciary to ensure that they are consistent with the intent of Congress.

Under the Carter administration, the EPA made rules governing the emission of air pollution from sources such as plants and factories. Under those rules, replacing any equipment at a source would mean that all equipment at the source would have to meet the stringent standards of the 1977 amendments to the Clean Air Act. During the Reagan administration, the EPA loosened the rules so that plants with multiple sources of pollution could update some of the sources as long as total pollution from the plant did not increase.

The National Resources Defense Council sued Chevron U.S.A., claiming that the EPA's decision to loosen the rules violated congressional intent. The Court of Appeals for the District of Columbia agreed,

striking the new EPA rule and restoring the older rule. Chevron appealed the court of appeals decision to the Supreme Court.

The Supreme Court reversed the decision of the court of appeals. Although the decision allowed looser regulations of pollution control, it also stated that federal courts should grant a great deal of deference to the decisions and rules made by federal agencies. Specifically, the Court declared that if Congress has explicitly expressed a preference on an issue, the agency must follow that intent. If, however, as is often the case, Congress has not explicitly expressed a preference on the issue, courts must accept the agency's rule as long as the rule is reasonable. In the *Chevron* suit, the Supreme Court declared that it was reasonable for the EPA to allow plants to replace equipment at some sources without having to replace equipment at all sources. Otherwise, plants might simply put off any improvements in equipment. Reasonableness is a very broad standard, so this decision grants federal agencies a great deal of flexibility in how to implement federal law.

Thinking Critically

1. Why would the Supreme Court generally want to defer to the judgment of bureaucracies on a rule?
2. How might responsiveness suffer when Congress and the Court delegate authority to the bureaucracy?

industries that are being regulated, and average citizens with a stake in the issue. For example, it took President Obama six years into his administration to issue sweeping regulations to reduce emissions from coal-fired power plants by 20 percent as part of his policies on climate change. As he approached the end of his first term, several of President Trump's efforts to reverse Obama's policies through regulations were not implemented fully due to court challenges to them. The government can justify the slowness of the decision-making process on the grounds that it considers many points of view in implementing policy. Unfortunately, inclusiveness comes at the expense of efficiency.

Key Questions

Why is transparency important in a democracy?

In addition, the issues related to food and drug safety, transportation safety, working conditions, and antiterrorism measures can be matters of life and death. Citizens expect the federal government to act in their best interests, but such issues require caution, and caution can lead to delay. On the other hand, if the government fails to make its practices transparent and does not consider all the implications of its decisions, citizens may lose trust in government.

These concerns were part of the rationale behind a series of bills designed to open up the workings of the federal bureaucracy to the general public. In 1966, the Freedom of Information Act established a procedure by which ordinary citizens can directly request documents and reports from the federal government by paying a nominal fee, as long as the documents are not classified. Access to a classified document or report is automatically restricted to federal employees who hold security clearances and have a legitimate need to see the document. In times of military conflict, such as during the Vietnam and Iraq wars, presidents typically restrict access to public documents relating to war efforts. In response to the mistrust of the federal government that grew out of the Vietnam War and the Watergate scandal, in 1976 Congress enacted the Government in the Sunshine Act, which tried to increase transparency by requiring government agencies to hold open forums to allow the public to comment on their decisions, regulations, and performance.

To highlight the tension between efficiency and transparency, let us return to the FDA, discussed earlier in the chapter. One of the agency's most important responsibilities is monitoring pharmaceutical development from the initial testing of drugs to final approval for widespread use. Even before a drug is submitted to the FDA for approval, pharmaceutical companies have conducted three phases of clinical trials, which are experiments and applications on human subjects that measure the efficacy and safety of the drug. If the drug shows promise, the company submits a New Drug Application to the FDA. If agency employees agree that the clinical trial results are reliable, the FDA forms a review panel whose members have different types of expertise about the potential effects of the drug. The panel serves as a gateway for nonemployees of the agency to participate in the drug approval process. Members of the panel consider all the results of the trials and offer opinions as to whether the drug can be approved for sale. Ultimately, the FDA makes the final decision.

This process illustrates the trade-off between efficiency and transparency.[46] When a new drug is effective against disease, the public wants access to that drug as soon as possible. This cry for new drugs and vaccines was certainly heard worldwide during the COVID-19 pandemic, and it was up to medical experts such as Anthony Fauci to explain that every new drug has unforeseen side effects, some of which may not be visible in the short term, so the more information the FDA has, the more likely the drugs it approves for the market will be safe. Forming review committees with members from outside the agency is one way of collecting a wide range of information about the possible impacts of the drug. Yet this process is time-consuming; the more participants, the more slowly it moves. Like many federal agencies, then, the FDA must weigh the cost of efficient decision making against the cost of approving a drug before it has been thoroughly tested. The FDA is constantly updating consumer advisories about a wide range of food and medical products. For example, the FDA issued a warning to diabetics using a specific type of glucose test strip because it was found to be inaccurate.[47] In most, if not all, instances when the FDA issues such an advisory to the public, the manufacturer withdraws the product from the market.

Whistleblowing

Most federal employees are careful, dedicated, and hardworking. However, as in all organizations run by human beings, there can be inefficiency, error, abuse of power, and corruption. Each federal agency has an Office of Inspector General that monitors the activities of the agency's employees. But unless a wrongdoing is identified and brought to the inspector general's attention, it frequently goes unpunished.

To encourage more candid disclosure of wrongdoing in federal agencies, Congress passed the Whistleblower Protection Act in 1989 to protect **whistleblowers**, government employees who report mismanagement, corruption, or illegal activity within their agencies.[48] Before the passage of this act, whistleblowers had no real protection against reprisals from their colleagues, especially from those at higher levels of authority. The act established grievance and appeal procedures for employees who believe they have been retaliated against for reporting wrongdoing in their agencies. In 2010, Congress extended protections to employees in the financial services industry who act as whistleblowers. In 2019, this law was invoked to protect the identity of the individual who first brought up the issue of presidential interference against President Trump for holding up the delivery of military aid to Ukraine in return for investigating his potential political opponent, Joe Biden.[49]

Bureaucratic Failure

Whether whistleblowers come from inside or outside the federal government, it is up to the federal government to respond to them in an effective fashion. As we saw in the Trump impeachment case, when members of Congress supporting Trump called for the release of the whistleblower's name, the principles underlying confidentiality in the whistleblower act can be sorely challenged when a charge is made against powerful people or interests. Unfortunately, there are serious cases in which a government agency has failed to respond. What happens when an entire agency fails to accomplish its mission?

One of the realities of federal management and oversight is that a federal agency or a congressional committee needs to be aware of a problem in order to address it. The dual responsibilities of accountability and responsiveness in the federal

Key Questions

What is more important, transparency or efficiency? Under what conditions might your answer differ?

Key Questions

Are private contractors working for the government likely to be whistleblowers? Why or why not?

whistleblowers: *Employees who report mismanagement, corruption, or illegal activity within their agencies.*

Key Questions

What can be done about lack of responsiveness by the bureaucracy?

FDA/Michael J. Ermarth/Science Source

Image 14.7 The Food and Drug Administration conducts onsite inspections of food products both domestically produced and imported. Here two FDA field employees are inspecting fish shipments at Los Angeles International Airport.

Ensuring the Integrity of the Voting Process

The vast size and reach of the federal bureaucracy and its impact on the daily lives of voters make elections about more than just choosing a new president; they are a verdict on how well the federal government does. Similarly, state-level governments also have bureaucracies that are overseen by elected officials who are also judged on Election Day by voters. No matter what priorities voters hold up as important, one common concern dominated them all: protecting the integrity of the voting process itself.

The 2016 elections brought with them new and public concerns voiced by both the Democratic and Republican presidential campaigns that the voting process was tampered with to give one side the edge over the other. Specifically, allegations were made that the Russian government worked together with members of Donald Trump's presidential campaign, spent money on Facebook trying to steer users to specific news stories, and created thousands of fake Twitter users in an effort to sway the election in favor of Trump. It is key to remember here that the actual election process (where you vote, how you vote, and what it takes to register to vote) is controlled by state governments, not the federal government.

But the bureaucratic response to these allegations on both sides of the political aisle occurred primarily at the federal level, and they appeared disjointed and generally confusing to the average voter. The Federal Bureau of Investigation had been looking into these allegations under the Obama administration although that information was not released to the public; the head of the FBI at that time, James Comey, was subsequently fired by President Trump early in his first year as president. After that, the Justice Department authorized the appointment of a Special Counsel, Robert Mueller, to investigate whether the Trump campaign colluded with a foreign power, namely Russia, to win the presidential campaign and whether the firing of James Comey constituted an attempt to obstruct justice on

Alex Wong/Getty Images News/Getty Images

Image 14.8 Robert Mueller, who served as FBI Director under President George W. Bush and President Barack Obama, returned to government to serve as Special Counsel to investigate Russian involvement in the 2016 presidential election. He concluded the investigation and left federal service on May 29, 2019.

the part of the president. In addition to the Special Counsel, the U.S. House of Representatives Intelligence Committee, and the U.S. Senate Intelligence Committee each conducted their own investigations into these allegations. Mueller's report found no hard evidence of direct collusion between President Trump and Russia, although many of Trump's closest allies were found guilty for campaign-related crimes.

In the 2018 midterm elections, the Democrats won control of the House of Representatives, picking up forty-one seats in the process. In the Senate, the Democrats actually lost seats, and the Republicans won two additional seats to give them a 53-47 majority. At the time, there were strong concerns that the Russians would try to intervene in the midterm elections on behalf of the Republican Party as a way of boosting President Trump similar to how they were alleged to have done in the 2016 elections. But there was no evidence that they did intervene, or that they were effective in doing so in any extensive way.

Despite the results of the 2018 elections, a range of voices subsequently raised concern about the possibility of Russian interference in the 2020 presidential election. In February 2020, intelligence officials warned House lawmakers that Russia was once again working to interfere in the United States presidential election. Most newsworthy was the information that Russia was trying to affect the Democratic primary, in addition to the general election.[50] With the selection of Joe Biden as the Democratic Party nominee, it appears that any alleged Russian electoral interference on behalf of Bernie Sanders was not effective.

In the 2020 elections, the elections were complicated by the COVID-19 pandemic, which pushed many states into offering vote by mail to their voters. States, and the Postal Service, which is federally run, worked hard to make sure all the ballots arrived on time and were counted.

Securing the integrity of the election process is a vital component of holding elected officials accountable, and is equally important in enabling voters to hold the bureaucracy accountable through those elected officials. It may be that leaving elected officials to investigate corruption in the voting process is ineffective because it is asking those who stand to benefit from a slanted election process to make sure it does not happen. While House Democrats passed a number of bills to reform our electoral process and make them more secure, Republicans in the Senate refused to hold votes on these bills. As it turns out, there was record high voter turnout in the 2020 elections and historically large numbers of votes were cast by mail. Election officials from both political parties stated that they did not find any significant voting issues or examples of fraud.

bureaucracy require the bureaucracy to do its job well enough to protect citizens from physical and financial harm. Unfortunately, the American people are so familiar with the failures of the federal bureaucracy that its successes are overlooked. The fact that 330 million people live in relative peace and security; experience safe and reasonable working conditions; trust that the medications they take are well tested; travel on trains, buses, and planes without incident; drink clean water; and receive their mail every day is a testament to the ways in which the federal bureaucracy meets its obligations. It is up to the voters to hold their elected officials—in Congress as well as the president—accountable for the performance of the federal bureaucracy.

The Bureaucracy and Democracy

The federal government that started with three cabinet departments has grown to include fifteen cabinet departments and many powerful independent agencies. The federal bureaucracy, including the armed services, employs about 4.1 million people. Their jobs affect the lives of all citizens, from the quality of the food they eat, to the safety of the highways they drive, to the purity of the water they drink.

In some important ways, the federal bureaucracy has become far more responsive to the needs of average individuals in the course of the nation's history, especially in the areas of social benefits, health care, environmental protection, and civil rights enforcement. The federal bureaucracy has tried to be more transparent in its operations by placing comprehensive information on the Internet for the public to access at any time. However, the responses to the COVID-19 pandemic and the Takata airbag case show that there have been notable and serious failures in the government's action to secure the safety of citizens.

The structure of the bureaucracy includes many gates against speedy implementation of federal policy. That there are so many layers of authority even within one agency, much less an entire cabinet department, adds considerable delay to the process of policy implementation. Multiple agencies can have jurisdiction over the same federal program or share responsibility for responding to natural disasters such as hurricanes. Such overlap can lead to miscommunication and to competition over authority and power. The hierarchy and procedural barriers that come with a large federal bureaucracy can stand in the way of efficient government.

At the same time, the rules and guidelines governing decision making in the bureaucracy are designed to ensure equal implementation of the law, which is a crucial element of a democracy. Americans expect federal laws to be applied in a consistent manner, with openness and vigilant congressional and public oversight. Understanding how laws are implemented, especially the gateways through which federal regulations are issued and enforced, gives citizens the power to hold the government accountable.

Citizens have the opportunity, in a democracy, to pressure the government to be responsible and implement the laws with vigor in all areas. But one might also argue that advocates should not be needed to ensure that the bureaucracy works with efficiency and transparency, and that the average citizen should not experience frustration in trying to navigate the gateways of the bureaucracy. Fortunately, it is possible to overcome these gateways—with enough persistence.

Chapter Review

Key Terms

bureaucracy (p. 514). Is the bureaucracy a gate or a gateway to democracy?

cabinet (p. 515). What departments make up the cabinet?

cabinet secretaries (p. 515). What do cabinet secretaries do?

career civil servants (p. 529). How do career civil servants move up the career ladder?

civil service (p. 529). Why is the civil service important to implementing federal law fairly and equitably?

Civil Service Commission (p. 529). What role does the Civil Service Commission play in overseeing federal employment practices?

Federal Register (p. 516). What is the role of the Federal Register in executive implementation of the law?

federal regulatory commission (p. 519). What does a federal regulatory commission do?

independent agency (p. 519). How is an independent agency different from a cabinet department?

merit system (p. 529). Compare the merit system with the patronage system.

Office of Management and Budget (p. 518). What is the OMB's role in the regulatory process?

oversight (p. 528). How does congressional oversight serve as a check on the bureaucracy?

Pendleton Act (p. 528). What is the significance of the Pendleton Act?

political appointees (p. 529). How do political appointees implement the president's policies?

regulations (p. 515). What are regulations, and how do they facilitate implementation of federal law?

Schedule C appointees (p. 531). Explain this category of presidential appointees.

Senior Executive Service (SES) (p. 531). How can the SES be used to expand a president's influence in the bureaucracy?

whistleblowers (p. 541). Does the government provide enough incentives and protections to whistleblowers?

Learning Outcomes: What You Need to...

Know	Test Yourself	Participate

LO 14-1 Explain what the bureaucracy does

Know	Test Yourself	Participate
The bureaucracy is the collection of executive branch departments, regulatory agencies, and other organizations that carry out the responsibilities of the federal government. Today nearly 4.1 million people, including those in the armed services, work for the federal government. The constitutional foundations for the bureaucracy include the president's power to nominate and appoint officers of executive departments, from whom he may request advice. The bureaucracy is also based in the president's broad grant of executive power.	• Define bureaucracy. • Explain how the Constitution provides a basis for bureaucratic power. • Describe the structure of the federal bureaucracy.	• Recognize how the federal government affects your daily life. • Evaluate how well bureaucrats serve the people. • Consider whether the bureaucracy is too large to be responsive.

LO 14-2 Outline the essential elements of a bureaucracy

Know	Test Yourself	Participate
Each bureaucratic organization has a clear mission, a hierarchical decision-making process, an area of expertise, and a bureaucratic culture. Aside from cabinet departments, there are various types of organizations within the bureaucracy, some designed to be more or less independent of the president.	• Explain how the mission of a bureaucracy shapes its goals. • State the advantages and disadvantages of the hierarchical decision-making process. • Characterize bureaucratic expertise. • Describe bureaucratic culture.	• Evaluate the degree of accountability associated with a bureaucratic mission. • Design a bureaucracy that is more efficient and responsive.

LO 14-3 Describe the growth of the bureaucracy over time

Know	Test Yourself	Participate
Since 1789, the bureaucracy has grown from three to fifteen executive departments as government's responsibilities have grown, primarily in the area of the economy. The first regulatory agency was established in 1887 to regulate railroad practices. Federal employment has developed from a corps of wealthy elites with political connections to members of the Congress and the president into a merit- and performance-based civil service designed to be protected from political influence. The president appoints cabinet secretaries and other high-level political appointees who are expected to carry out the president's agenda.	• Equate the establishment of cabinet departments with developments in the U.S. economy and society. • Describe what regulatory agencies do. • Explain how and why the civil service evolved. • Survey the types of jobs career civil servants perform. • Recall why political appointees have increased in number over time. • Explain the growth of the use of private-sector contract workers.	• Evaluate the bureaucracy in terms of government responsiveness. • Assess why merit-based employment is better than patronage in a democracy. • Consider whether you would like to work for the government. • Evaluate the accountability of private-sector contract workers.

Know	Test Yourself	Participate

LO 14-4   Assess how the bureaucracy is both accountable and responsive, and how it can fail

Following a consistent regulatory process, agencies draft regulations, which are open to comment by citizens, members of Congress, interest groups, and relevant businesses and industries before they are finalized. Congress exercises influence over policy through its oversight responsibilities and power to authorize and allocate funds. Lawsuits can involve the judicial branch in the interpretation of public policy. The bureaucracy is subject to criticism for acting slowly, but in a democracy, the need for efficiency is counterbalanced by the need for transparency. Reform efforts have improved transparency by providing protections for whistleblowers. The policy-making process and regulatory process together exemplify government responsiveness and accountability to citizens even as they reflect the concerns of competing interests.

- Explain ways the legislative and judicial branches can check the bureaucracy.
- Examine how the need for bureaucratic efficiency and transparency can counteract each other.
- Describe what it means to be a whistleblower.
- Relate the consequences of bureaucratic failure.

- Describe how you can influence the bureaucracy.
- Evaluate the importance of offering protection to whistleblowers.

The Judiciary

WDC Photos/Alamy Stock Photo

> "*Theresa, I think this fish has found her pond.*"

The gates of Princeton University, where Sonia Sotomayor attended undergraduate school, are shown on the following page.

SONIA SOTOMAYOR, TO A PROFESSIONAL FRIEND AFTER OVERCOMING HER FEARS ABOUT BEING A JUDGE
Princeton University

Many gates blocked Sonia Sotomayor's path to the Supreme Court. She was female (no female had served on the Court until Sandra O'Connor in 1981), she was Puerto Rican (no Latino had ever served on the Court until Sotomayor), she had juvenile diabetes (which, at the time, substantially lowered life expectancy), and she had an alcoholic father who died when she was 9. Sotomayor used her intelligence and diligence to overcome what for others would have been disadvantages. As she noted in her memoir, despite these setbacks, "I did have sources of deep happiness, and these bred in me an optimism that proved stronger than any adversity." That inner strength led her to become high school valedictorian; attend Princeton University, where she won the prestigious Pyne Prize, the highest general distinction Princeton confers on an undergraduate; and then attend Yale Law School. She has readily admitted that she probably got admitted to Princeton due to its affirmative action program.

In 2014, affirmative action faced one of its more recent challenges at the Supreme Court. In 2006, the voters of Michigan passed an amendment to their state constitution banning race- and gender-based affirmative action in public education, public employment, and public contracting. The Coalition to Defend Affirmative Action filed suit against the amendment, and, in 2012, a federal district court ruled that the ban was unconstitutional. Michigan's attorney general, Bill Schuette, appealed the ruling, and the U.S. Court of Appeals declared the amendment unconstitutional. Schuette then appealed the court of appeals decision to the Supreme Court, which agreed to hear the case. On April 22, 2012, the day that the case came before the U.S. Supreme Court, Sonia Sotomayor found herself sitting in judgment over the constitutionality of efforts to block racial- and gender-based affirmative action.

The 2014 case, *Schuette v. Coalition to Defend Affirmative Action*, culminated from two prior cases involving the University of Michigan. In 2003, the Supreme Court struck down the affirmative action plan at Michigan's undergraduate college (*Gratz v. Bollinger*) but upheld the constitutionality of the affirmative action plan at the University of Michigan Law School (*Grutter v. Bolinger*). One of the litigants, or parties to the suit, Jennifer Gratz helped organize the initiative for the 2006 statewide constitutional amendment that banned the state of Michigan or any of its public universities from taking race or gender into account in hiring or admissions.

On April 22, Sonia Sotomayor was in the minority as she argued that the Michigan amendment banning affirmative action was unconstitutional. The Supreme Court upheld that amendment in a 6–2 vote in 2014. Justice Clarence Thomas joined the concurring opinion of Justice Scalia, which cited an earlier opinion of Justice Thomas that disputed whether affirmative action plans *ever* helped minority students (emphasis in original). Justice Sotomayor, on the other hand, read her dissent from the bench, a rare occurrence for any justice and the first time Justice Sotomayor had ever done so. She took issue with Chief Justice Roberts' statement that "the way to stop discriminating on the basis of race is to stop discrimination on the basis of race," declaring it to be "out of touch with reality." Sotomayor insisted that it is the role of the judicial system to protect minorities from the tyranny of the majority. She wrote, "The Court abdicates that role, permitting the majority to use its numerical advantage to change the rules mid-contest and forever stack the deck against racial minorities in Michigan."

For a Puerto Rican girl raised in the poverty-stricken South Bronx, affirmative action was a gateway to an Ivy League education. That gateway eventually led to Sonia Sotomayor being the first Latino to sit on the U.S. Supreme Court.[1]

As the Court's **affirmative action** cases show, the judicial system of the United States, because of its authority to rule on the constitutionality of federal and state laws and policies, has an extraordinary amount of power in the American political system. As the highest court in the land, the Supreme Court not only decides whether affirmative action may be allowed but also decides other issues, such as whether health insurance can be mandated (yes), same-sex marriage can be prohibited (no), or the death penalty inflicted (yes, with restrictions). The justices on the Court make important decisions that affect the lives of individuals and the policies of the nation at large even though they are not elected by the people and cannot be removed from office if the people disagree with the decisions they make. In this chapter, we investigate the structure and procedures of the judicial system; the factors that influence judicial decisions; how judges are selected; how representative of American society the Court is; the role that race, ethnicity, and gender might have in judicial decision making; and the role the Supreme Court has played in determining public policy and federal authority. Thus, we examine, too, the controversial role and power of the judiciary in a democracy.

The Role and Powers of the Judiciary

LO 15-1 Describe what the judicial branch does

affirmative action: *Policies that support greater equality, often by granting racial or gender preferences in hiring, education, or contracting.*

adversary process: *Confrontational legal process under which each party presents its version of events.*

Key Questions

Do courts produce the fairest decision possible? Can you give examples?

appeal: *Legal proceeding whereby the decision of a lower court on a question of law can be challenged and reviewed by a higher court.*

courts of appeals: *Intermediate federal courts that are above the district courts and below the Supreme Court.*

criminal case: *Government prosecution of an individual for breaking the law.*

civil suit: *Lawsuit by a person, organization, or government against another person, organization, or government.*

common law: *Judge-made law in England and the United States that results from gaps in statutory law.*

precedent: *Practice of reaching decisions based on the previous decisions of other judges.*

The job of courts is to resolve legal disputes. The American legal system is based largely on the English system, which is the system that the colonists were familiar with. The legal system under the Constitution kept many of the same practices but added some innovations.

English Legal Traditions

Resolution of legal disputes follows an **adversary process**. In an adversarial system, each party, usually represented by an attorney, presents its version of events, with virtually all attempts to slant information short of lying under oath deemed acceptable.

Although in some cases a judge decides which side is correct, a group of ordinary citizens usually determines the outcome. The right to trial by jury dates back in England to the Magna Carta (1215), where it replaced trial by ordeal, the practice of subjecting people to drowning or burning to see if they were innocent. Trial by jury is crucial to liberty because it inserts a gate of citizen judgment between the accused person and the government that protects the accused from arbitrary detention and unjust punishment. It also provides a gateway of citizen involvement through juror participation.

Trials involve questions of fact (for example, did the University of Michigan set different standards for white and minority students?) and questions of law (for example, do such differing standards violate the Fourteenth Amendment?). Trial court decisions about questions of fact are presumed to be valid because the trial judge or the jury directly hear the evidence in the case. But because trial courts sometimes make mistakes about questions of law, the American legal system has followed the British practice by allowing **appeals** from trial court rulings. In the U.S. federal system, the **courts of appeals** and the Supreme Court hear appeals, which involve issues of law. These courts do not retry the facts as established by the trial court.

Trials resolve two distinct types of disputes. In a **criminal case**, the government prosecutes an individual for breaking the law. Criminal cases are based almost exclusively on prohibitions on behavior written into statutes (laws) passed by federal, state, or local legislatures. In a **civil suit**, a plaintiff, such as Jennifer Gratz, sues a defendant, such as the University of Michigan, to enforce a right or to win monetary damages.

Criminal law is based on statutory authority, but statutory authority cannot cover all possible civil disputes between individuals. Many disputes involve actions that no legislative authority could have ever imagined. When there are gaps in statutory law, courts rely on judge-made law known as **common law**. Common law requires judges to accept and rely on previous decisions (if each judge makes his or her own decisions on each case, there can be no common law). Thus, British royal judges developed the practice of reaching decisions based on **precedents**, the previous decisions of other royal judges. Deciding cases based on precedents means that similar cases are decided similarly. Precedent is perhaps the most fundamental feature of British and American law. Because similar cases get decided similarly, following precedent promotes greater equality, predictability, and stability in law.

Constitutional Grants of Power

Article III of the Constitution establishes the judicial branch of government. It briefly refers to a Supreme Court of the United States and grants Congress the authority to create lower courts at its discretion. The Constitution grants the federal courts the authority to hear "cases" or "controversies." The Supreme Court has interpreted this provision to require that people who initiate lawsuits have standing. That is, they must establish that they have suffered a harm that the law protects them against. Standing is a gate that limits access to the judicial system.

Because the Constitution says so little about the judicial branch, one of the early acts of the First Congress, the Judiciary Act of 1789, established thirteen **district (trial) courts** and three circuit courts with both trial and appellate authority that serve at an intermediate level between the district courts and the Supreme Court. Today, there are 673 district court judges serving in 94 separate district courts and 179 court of appeals judges serving in thirteen intermediate appellate circuits.[2] The thirteen intermediate appellate courts include eleven numbered courts, a court of appeals for the District of Columbia, which handles most litigation involving federal agencies, and the Court of Appeals for the Federal Circuit, which handles customs and patent claims. In addition, Congress established the Foreign Intelligence Surveillance Court in 1978 (see Chapter 4, Civil Liberties) and the Court of International Trade in 1980. Separately, Congress has established six so-called Article I or legislative courts whose purpose is to help Congress perform its Article I duties. Unlike Article III judges, Article I judges do not serve for life. These courts are listed in Table 15.1.

The lawful authority of a court to hear a case is its **jurisdiction**. In general, jurisdiction for any federal court requires either that the case involves federal law (including the Constitution and treaties); or that the parties include the United States, ambassadors, or other public ministers; or that the parties are residents of different states. The Constitution further divides the Supreme Court's jurisdiction into original jurisdiction, the authority to hear a case

Key Questions

If you recognize an injustice but have not been harmed by it, what role do you have in getting government to respond?

district courts: *Federal trial courts at the bottom of the federal judicial hierarchy.*

jurisdiction: *Lawful authority of a court to hear a case.*

Table 15.1 Article I Courts

Name	Jurisdiction	Location
Bankruptcy Court	All bankruptcy cases	Each federal district
Military Appeals	Appeals of court-martial trials	Washington, D.C.
Veteran Appeals	Appeals of veterans and survivors' benefits	Washington, D.C.*
Federal Claims	Suits against the United States for more than $10,000	Washington, D.C.
Tax Court	Taxpayer lawsuits	Washington, D.C.*
Territorial Courts**	U.S. trial courts for Guam, U.S. Virgin Islands, and Northern Mariana Islands	In their respective territories
Foreign Intelligence Surveillance Courts	Their jurisdiction consists of surveillance requests of foreign intelligence agents within the United States	Washington, D.C.

*Can hear cases outside Washington, D.C.

**Established under Congress's Article IV authority to regulate territories.

Source: http://www.lectlaw.com/def/a148.htm; http://www.uscourts.gov/FederalCourts/Bankruptcy.aspx.

directly from a petitioning party (as in a trial), and appellate jurisdiction, authority to hear cases on appeals from lower courts. The Supreme Court has original jurisdiction in "all Cases affecting Ambassadors, other public Ministers and Consuls, and those in which a State shall be Party" (Article III, Section 2). The Constitution then declares that "in all the other Cases" properly before the Court, it would have appellate jurisdiction subject to such exceptions and regulations that Congress shall make.

The Constitution grants the federal courts the authority to hear cases of law and equity. Cases of law and equity can involve (1) the common law when there are gaps in legislative authority; (2) statutory interpretation, where the courts have to determine what Congress meant by a statute (for example, is discrimination against transgender people included in the prohibition on sex discrimination in the Civil Rights Act of 1964?); and (3) constitutional interpretation, where the courts must decide whether a law or practice violates a provision of the Constitution.

Constitutional interpretation brings forth the greatest power of the federal judiciary, **judicial review**. Judicial review, established by *Marbury v. Madison* (1803), is the power of courts to declare actions of Congress, the president, or state officials unconstitutional and therefore void (see Chapter 2, The Constitution). The Supreme Court, for example, has exercised the power of judicial review on laws pertaining to affirmative action (see Public Policy and the Judiciary: Affirmative Action).

judicial review: *Authority of courts to declare laws passed by Congress and acts of the executive branch to be unconstitutional.*

Marbury v. Madison: *An 1803 Supreme Court decision that established the Supreme Court's power of judicial review.*

State and Lower Federal Courts

LO 15-2 Explain how state and lower federal courts operate

While the Supreme Court is the highest court in the United States, it hears only a small percentage of the cases filed in federal court. The overwhelming majority of federal cases are resolved in the district courts, which conduct civil and criminal trials. Cases appealed from the district courts go to one of the U.S. Courts of Appeals, in which three-judge panels usually decide cases. From those panels, losing parties can appeal cases to the entire circuit for an *en banc* ("by the full court") hearing, or they can appeal directly to the U.S. Supreme Court (see Figure 15.1).

en banc: *Decision by an entire court of appeals circuit, typically following an original judgment by a three-judge panel of the circuit.*

State Courts in the Federal Judicial System

Each state has its own judicial system, and unless a case involves federal law or the type of parties that create federal jurisdiction, cases get resolved in state courts, each of which has its own hierarchy of trial and appellate courts. Cases that involve federal issues that begin in one of the fifty separate state court systems can be appealed to the federal court system in one of two ways. First, criminal defendants who have exhausted their state appeals (that is, have gone through their last appeal at the state level) can file a writ of *habeas corpus* with a U.S. District Court, which then allows the court to determine whether one or more of the defendant's federal legal rights have been violated. Second, any parties who have exhausted their state appeals can file a request for review, known as a **petition for a writ of *certiorari***, directly with the Supreme Court.

petition for a writ of certiorari: *Request to the Supreme Court that it review a lower court case.*

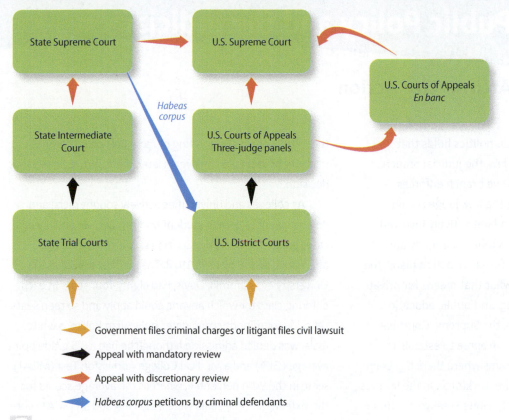

Government files criminal charges or litigant files civil lawsuit

Appeal with mandatory review

Appeal with discretionary review

Habeas corpus petitions by criminal defendants

Figure 15.1 Judicial Organization in the United States

Cases can reach the U.S. Supreme Court from both the federal and state judicial systems.

Source: Adapted from Lee Epstein, Jeffrey A. Segal, Harold J. Spaeth, and Thomas G. Walker, *The Supreme Court Compendium*, 5th ed. (Washington, D.C.: CQ Press, 2010), Figure 7-3.

District Courts

The Judiciary Act of 1789 established thirteen district courts for the thirteen states. Today, there are ninety-four districts. Many states have more than one district, but no district covers more than one state. Districts that cover only part of a state receive geographic names, such as the Northern District of Illinois. Altogether there are 673 district judgeships. Many districts have only one judge, but the Southern District of New York has twenty-eight, and the Central District of California has twenty-seven. Nevertheless, with rare exceptions, district judges oversee trials alone, not in panels.

Trials in the district courts are either criminal or civil. In civil suits, plaintiffs (the parties bringing the suit) often request monetary damages to compensate for harm done to them, such as by a broken contract or a defective product. When rights are alleged to have been violated, they may ask that the practice be stopped. Litigants filed more than 292,000 civil suits in the district courts in 2017, and the federal government initiated approximately 76,000 criminal prosecutions.[3]

When Gratz and Grutter sued the University of Michigan over its admissions policies, the first stop for each was the U.S. District Court. Both had standing to sue, as their rejections by the university were real injuries, and because they claimed that their rights to equal protection under the Fourteenth Amendment had been violated, their cases raised a constitutional issue

Public Policy and the Judiciary

Affirmative Action

An overly simple view of American politics holds that the legislative branch makes the law, the judicial branch interprets the law, and the executive branch enforces the law. However, in interpreting the law, judges often go beyond mere interpretation and get actively involved in policy making. While Presidents John F. Kennedy and Lyndon Johnson first proposed affirmative action plans, the Supreme Court has interpreted what that means for private business, government contracting, and public education.

Regarding private businesses, the Supreme Court has ruled that businesses and unions can agree to establish voluntary affirmative action programs where there has been a substantial racial imbalance in the workforce. In the famous case of *Steelworkers v. Weber* (1979), white steelworker Brian Weber was turned down for a promotion to craft worker. In a workforce that was 39 percent black, fewer than 2 percent of the skilled craft workers were black. Kaiser Aluminum and the United Steelworkers had agreed that 50 percent of future promotions would go to black employees, even if that bypassed white employees with higher seniority. Weber sued, but the Supreme Court upheld the affirmative action plan.[4] On the other hand, the Court ruled that seniority cannot be overridden when it comes to layoffs: Whites with higher seniority cannot be laid off ahead of minorities with lower seniority, even if seniority-based layoffs will harm racial balance and even if minorities had less seniority because original hiring practices discriminated against them.[5]

National and state governments have established preferences for minority-owned businesses when they grant contracts and licenses, although the Court has wobbled. In 1987, the Court upheld a plan, similar to the one in the *Steelworkers* case, that granted preferences to women.[6] A 1980 decision allowed the federal government to require 10 percent of its grants to state and local governments for public works projects to go to minority-owned businesses.[7] Nine years later, however, a more conservative Court prohibited the city of Richmond, Virginia, from doing the same thing.[8] In 1990,

the Court upheld the granting of radio license preferences to minority broadcasters; six years later, the Court reversed that decision.[9]

As colleges and universities actively sought racial and gender balances in their student bodies, several controversial cases arose. The Supreme Court first confronted college affirmative action plans in 1978. The medical school at the University of California, Davis, had eighty-four seats in each entering class for which anyone could apply and sixteen seats set aside for minority candidates only. Allan Bakke, a white male, was denied admission although he had a 3.5 grade point average (GPA) and a Medical College Admission Test (MCAT) score in the 90th percentile, whereas the average scores for the sixteen minority seats were a 2.6 GPA and an MCAT score in the 20th percentile. Bakke sued, and a split Court decreed in *Regents v. Bakke* that this sort of quota system violated the Civil Rights Act. Nevertheless, the Court held that affirmative action plans in which race is a "plus" in an applicant's overall file did meet the state's compelling interest in establishing a diverse student body.[10]

In 1996, a court of appeals panel in Texas declared affirmative action unconstitutional within the Fourth Circuit.[11] The University of Texas responded by implementing a program that guarantees admission to the University of Texas to anyone who graduates in the top 10 percent of his or her high school class. Because public schools are highly segregated in Texas, the university believed this would be an effective means of obtaining a diverse student body.

In the meantime, the Supreme Court revisited the *Bakke* decision in a pair of 2003 cases (*Gratz* and *Grutter*), discussed in this chapter. Despite surpassing the average qualifications required by the University of Michigan to gain entrance, Jennifer Gratz and Barbara Grutter were both rejected—Gratz from the undergraduate program and Grutter from the law school. With the legal assistance from the Center for Individual Rights, a conservative legal group that actively sought students looking to fight affirmative action, both women sued the university. As we saw earlier, the Supreme Court struck down the undergraduate, but upheld the law school's admissions policy.

In the case of the law school, then sitting Justice Sandra Day O'Connor, the first woman appointed to the Supreme Court (1981), expressed the belief that the Constitution required affirmative action programs to be temporary solutions only and the hope that by 2028 they would no longer be necessary. Opponents of affirmative action, such as Ward Connerly, chair of the American Civil Rights Institute, hope that such plans will not last that long. Connerly has launched state-level initiatives in Arizona, California, Colorado, Michigan, Nebraska, and Washington to let voters decide whether such programs should be allowed. Voters rejected affirmative action in all those states except Colorado.

California voters passed their amendment in 1996. Since that time, and despite fears that the initiative would reduce the number of underrepresented minorities in colleges and universities, Latino students have become the largest ethnic group at the University of California.[12]

In 2014, the Michigan case reached the Supreme Court, which declared in *Schuette v. Coalition to Defend Affirmative Action* that the people of Michigan had the right to pass a constitutional amendment via initiative that prohibits the state's public universities from using race as a factor in admissions or public employment.[13]

While the University of Texas largely replaced its affirmative action program with guaranteed admission to anyone who finished in the top 10 percent of his or her high school class, it was unable to fill all entering spots with this plan. To fill the remaining spots, the university used an admissions plan that gave preferences based on race and ethnicity. Abigail Fisher, a white female whom the university rejected for admission despite scores that were higher than many of the nontraditional admittees, filed

suit claiming that the continuing use of race violated her rights under the equal protection clause of the Fourteenth Amendment. Both the district court and the court of appeals upheld the university's admission plan under the precedent established in *Grutter v. Bollinger*. Because the lower courts did not use the strict-scrutiny standard that the Supreme Court had required in cases involving racial or ethnic classifications, the Supreme Court sent the case back (remanded) to the lower courts for reconsideration using the appropriate standard.[14]

The Fifth Circuit reheard the case and again ruled in favor of the University of Texas. Fisher appealed to the Supreme Court and once again the Court granted review. Only seven justices participated. Justice Antonin Scalia passed away after the oral arguments. Justice Kagan also did not participate due to her prior involvement in the case while serving in President Obama's Justice Department. Justice Kennedy wrote the majority opinion in the case, but with his retirement, the constitutionality of affirmative action plans is in doubt. The Supreme Court's 2016 decision upheld the university's program.[15]

More recently, several prospective Asian American students sued Harvard University claiming that its admissions policy discriminated against Asian Americans. Harvard, as a private institution, is not bound by the equal protection clause of the Fourteenth Amendment. However, it does accept federal money for research and student aid thus making it bound to the Civil Rights Act of 1964, which declares in relevant part "No person in the United States shall, on the ground of race, color, or national origin, be excluded from participation in, be denied the benefits of, or be subjected to discrimination under any program or activity receiving Federal financial assistance."[16] Resolution of the dispute will ultimately fall to the Supreme Court, which has lost most of its liberal backers of affirmative action (including Marshall, Brennan, and Blackmun).

Construct Your Own Policy

1. Construct an admissions policy that maintains equal opportunity but does not explicitly consider race, ethnicity, or gender.
2. Revise the judicial nomination and confirmation process to reduce the emphasis on ideology as a legitimate consideration.

class action lawsuit: *Lawsuit filed by one person on behalf of that person plus all similarly situated people.*

and entered the federal court system. Gratz and Grutter sought not only their own admission to the University of Michigan but also an end to the university's use of race in admissions decisions. The district courts allowed both suits to move forward as **class action lawsuits**, meaning that Gratz and Grutter were suing not only on behalf of themselves but also on behalf of all people denied admission at Michigan on account of their race. Class action lawsuits can open the gateways of access to groups of citizens in the same circumstances, thus broadening the impact over the possible result of an individual lawsuit.

Civil Procedure.   The overwhelming majority of lawsuits filed in federal court settle out of court with a negotiated agreement between the plaintiff and the defendant. In 2017, the district courts terminated over 287,000 civil cases.[17] Litigants settled nearly 99 percent of these cases before going to trial. Of the few cases that went to trial, nearly two-thirds were decided by juries. The other third were bench (nonjury) trials, as the *Gratz* and *Grutter* cases were.

After a case is assigned to a judge, the next step in a civil suit is discovery. Discovery grants each side access to information relevant to its suit held by the other side. Crucial to the *Gratz* and *Grutter* suits were University of Michigan documents showing differential admission rates for whites and minorities who had similar grades and standardized test scores. During discovery, the attorneys for each side can also question witnesses for the other side in a process known as deposition. Following discovery, litigants file briefs with the court, laying out their arguments.

amicus curiae: *Latin term meaning "friend of the court" that is used to describe individuals or interest groups who have an interest in a lawsuit but are not themselves direct parties to the suit.*

Outside interests can file **amicus curiae** ("friend of the court") briefs, stating their concerns in a case.[18] The most influential *amicus* briefs are those filed in the name of the United States, as represented by the Office of the **Solicitor General** in the Justice Department.[19] In the *Gratz* and *Grutter* cases, the Clinton administration filed briefs in favor of the University of Michigan, which argued that affirmative action was necessary to obtain a diverse student body. General Motors also filed a brief in favor of the university's affirmative action program, stating that it needed a diverse pool of highly qualified attorneys, managers, and the like. Eventually, Microsoft and nineteen other Fortune 500 companies signed briefs supporting the university.[20]

solicitor general: *Official in the Justice Department who represents the president in federal court.*

Kevin Lamarque/Reuters

Image 15.1 Abigail Fisher sued the University of Texas over its affirmative action policy, which she claimed denied her equal protection under the law.

Civil trials begin with opening statements by the plaintiff and respondent. The plaintiff then calls its witnesses, who can be cross-examined by the respondent's attorney. Once the plaintiff rests the case, the respondent calls its witnesses, who can be cross-examined by the plaintiff's attorney.

Trial courts make determinations as to fact and as to law, whereas appellate courts generally make determinations only as to law, applying the facts as determined by the trial court. That would normally mean that it would be up to the district court to determine factually whether race played a role in admissions at Michigan and how much of a role it played. Then it would decide as a matter of law whether that role was allowable or not. The parties in the *Gratz* and *Grutter* cases made the decision a bit easier for the judges, for the University of Michigan readily admitted—indeed, strongly defended—its use of race in admissions. Therefore, the question for the trial judge was not a question of fact, but a question of law: Does the equal protection clause of the Fourteenth Amendment prohibit the use of race as a factor in university admissions?

While trial judges or juries have nearly complete discretion in deciding questions of fact, they are constrained by the courts above them on questions of law. In affirmative action, the key precedent was the 1978 Supreme Court decision in *Regents of the University of California v. Bakke*.[21] A divided Court ruled in *Bakke* that the University of California's quota system of reserving a certain number of seats for minorities was unconstitutional, but that a system in which race was a "plus" in admissions could be justified due to the benefits that a diverse student body provides all the students.

In December 2000, Judge Duggan ruled in the *Gratz* case that the point system used by the university—in which each applicant could receive up to 150 points, including 20 for being from an underrepresented minority group—was a valid and necessary means of obtaining a diverse student body. On the other hand, Judge Friedman ruled in March 2001 that the law school's use of race in admissions violated the Constitution, finding that it was an "enormously important factor" in admissions and not the mere plus approved by the Supreme Court in *Bakke*. The University of Michigan appealed Friedman's decision to the Sixth Circuit Court of Appeals, while the Center for Individual Rights backed Gratz's appeal to the same circuit.

Criminal Procedure.

Beyond civil cases such as the Michigan affirmative action suits, trial courts also conduct criminal trials. A federal criminal prosecution begins with an alleged violation of federal criminal law. In the U.S. federal system, states have primary authority over law enforcement, but the federal government frequently prosecutes drug, weapons, terrorism, and immigration cases, plus other crimes that involve interstate commerce or the instrumentalities of the federal government, such as the post office and government buildings.

The clearance rate for state and federal crimes—that is, the percentage of reported crimes in which someone is arrested, charged, and turned over for prosecution—is highest for violent crimes (45.6 percent in 2016) but much lower for property crimes such as burglary (13.6 percent).[22] Under the Constitution, an accused criminal in a federal court has a right to indictment by a grand jury, a specially empaneled jury consisting of between sixteen and twenty-three citizens who determine whether the government has sufficient evidence to charge the suspect with a crime. In the rare occasions in which a grand jury chooses not to indict, the suspect is freed.

Following indictment, the accused is arraigned, or informed of the charges against him or her, and asked to enter an initial plea of guilty or not guilty. About 90 percent of federal criminal cases are resolved through **plea bargains**, in which the accused person pleads guilty, usually in exchange for reduced charges or lesser sentences.[23] This arrangement greatly enhances the ability of trial courts to deal with large criminal caseloads.

In the small number of cases that proceed to trial, the accused person has the right to a trial by jury but is free to request a bench trial, in which the judge decides guilt or innocence. A jury in a federal felony case consists of twelve individuals who must reach a verdict unanimously. (Neither twelve people nor unanimity is required in a state court.)

Key Questions

How important is a diverse student body on your campus? How important is a diverse workforce? What is your experience?

Key Questions

Should race be a factor in university admissions? What role should it play?

plea bargain: *Agreement by a criminal defendant to plead guilty in return for a reduced sentence.*

The defendant can appeal a guilty verdict, but the double jeopardy clause of the Constitution prohibits the government from appealing a verdict of not guilty. If the defendant is found guilty, the judge determines the sentence based on guidelines that depend on the nature of the offense, the number of prior convictions, and other factors as recommended by the U.S. Sentencing Commission. In death penalty cases, the decision on the punishment is left to the jury. That is, following a guilty verdict, the jury hears new testimony by the prosecutor and defense attorney about whether death is the appropriate punishment.

Courts of Appeals

Sitting hierarchically above the ninety-four district courts are the U.S. Courts of Appeals. Congress has divided the Courts of Appeals into eleven numbered circuits plus a circuit for the District of Columbia and a "federal circuit" that hears appeals from specialized lower courts that deal with patents and customs (see Figure 15.2). Each of the numbered courts of appeals has

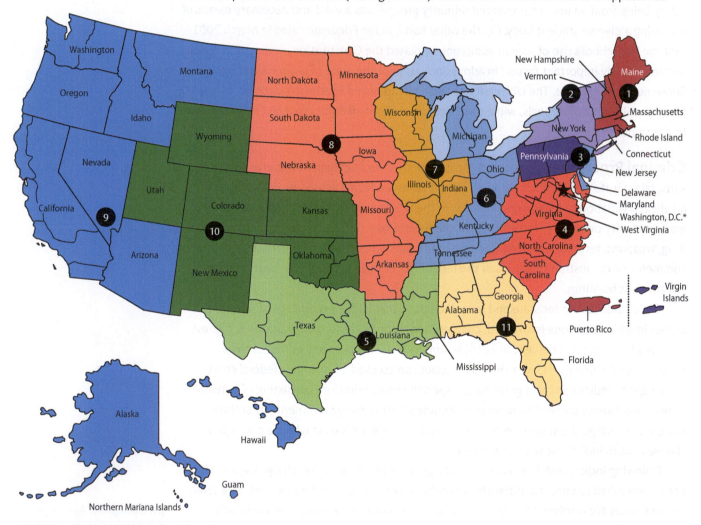

*U.S. Court of Appeals for the District of Columbia
The Federal Circuit Court, in Washington, D.C., hears appeals in trade and patent cases.

Figure 15.2 U.S. Courts of Appeals and U.S. District Courts

Every state has one (Colorado, Wyoming, Kansas) or more (Texas, California, Florida, New York) district courts. Every court of appeals circuit covers several states.

Source: Data from U.S. Courts, Court Locator, http://www.uscourts.gov/court_locator.aspx.

jurisdiction over several states. For example, the Sixth Circuit Court of Appeals, which sits in Cincinnati, hears appeals from district courts in Kentucky, Michigan, Ohio, and Tennessee.

The number of judgeships in each circuit ranges from six in the First Circuit, which covers some of the New England states, to twenty-nine in the Ninth Circuit, which covers California and six other western states, plus Alaska and Hawaii. Regardless of the number of judgeships, randomly assigned three-judge panels usually hear appeals from the district courts.

The courts have mandatory jurisdiction over cases appealed to them. That is, if a losing party from the district court appeals to the appropriate court of appeals, the court must hear the case. Because the circuit courts are in the middle of the federal judicial hierarchy, cases can be both appealed to the court of appeals and appealed from the court of appeals (refer to Figure 15.1). Appeals from a court of appeals can happen in two ways. First, losing litigants at the court of appeals who believe that the three-judge panel that heard their case did not represent the judgment of the entire circuit can request an *en banc* review. Alternatively, losing litigants can request review by the Supreme Court. In both cases, further review is at the discretion of the court that is being petitioned.

Given the importance of the *Grutter* and *Gratz* cases, the cases made it through the U.S. Court of Appeals in anything but a normal manner. Rather than a hearing with a three-judge panel, possibly followed by *en banc* and/or Supreme Court review, the Center for Individual Rights, which represented Gratz and Grutter, requested and was granted an immediate *en banc* review. On May 14, 2002, the Sixth Circuit ruled in favor of the university in the law school case by a 5–4 vote. The **majority opinion** argued that the law school's approach resembled the plus system approved by the Supreme Court in the *Bakke* case. All three Republicans on the circuit sided with Grutter; five of the six Democrats sided with the university, consistent both with generally greater support among Democrats than Republicans for equality of outcome over equality of opportunity and with evidence that such attitudes often influence judicial decisions. Not surprisingly, Barbara Grutter appealed the decision to the Supreme Court.

majority opinion: *Opinion of a court laying out the official position of the court in the case.*

On October 1, 2002, ten months after oral arguments, the court of appeals still had not issued its ruling in the undergraduate case. In an unusual step, Gratz's attorneys asked the Supreme Court to bypass the court of appeals and rule directly on their appeal. On December 1, the Supreme Court accepted review in both cases.

The Supreme Court

LO 15-3 Review the procedures the Supreme Court uses

The Supreme Court's procedure in handling cases consists of deciding whether to grant review and, if review is granted, of receiving briefs, hearing oral arguments, deciding who wins, and writing the majority opinion. If desired, justices who do not agree with the decision of the Court majority (that is, the decision about who wins the case) can write dissenting opinions. Those who agree with the majority opinion on who should win but differ as to the reasoning can write concurring opinions. The majority opinion, however, stands as the precedent for lower-court judges to apply in similar cases dealing with the same issue.

The Supreme Court   **559**

Granting Review

Each year, about eight thousand losing litigants ask the Supreme Court to review their cases. Most have lost in one of the U.S. Courts of Appeals or one of the fifty state supreme courts. The vast majority of appeals to the Supreme Court come in the form of petitions for writs of *certiorari*, often shortened to petitions for "cert." The Supreme Court's decision to grant cert is purely discretionary, but its rules suggest that a grant of cert is more likely when a lower court resolves issues of law differently from the way other lower courts have or issues a decision that conflicts with decisions of the Supreme Court. The Supreme Court is also more likely to grant review when the U.S. government, represented by the solicitor general's office, requests it, either as a petitioning party or as *amicus curiae*. The filing of *amicus* briefs by other parties can also be important to the Court, as it signals that the case involves important questions of public policy.[24]

The large number of petitions for cert prevents the justices from fully reviewing each one. Instead, they rely on their clerks, who are usually recent law school graduates, to write summaries. One recent study finds that law clerks exert a mild persuasive ideological influence on their justices[25] Most of the justices' chambers have joined the "cert pool," which splits the cert petitions among the clerks of the justices in the pool.

The large number of petitions also prevents the justices from fully discussing each one. Rather, the chief justice passes around a "discuss list," a set of cases he thinks worthy of discussion. Any justice can add any other case to the list if he or she wishes. Cases not on the discuss list are automatically denied cert, leaving the lower court's decision as final. The justices then meet in conference to consider each of the cases on the discuss list. The

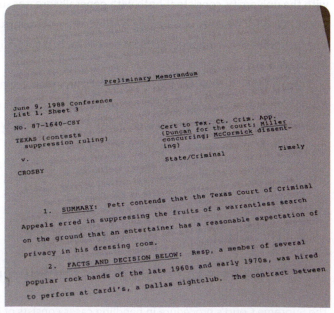

Images 15.2 and 15.3 At left is a mug shot of 1960s rock star David Crosby; at right is a Pool Memo regarding the cert petition by the State of Texas appealing the Texas Supreme Court decision excluding evidence of crack cocaine smoking and possession by Crosby, who was smoking the crack in his dressing room before a show. The Texas Supreme Court ruled that a dressing room was akin to a hotel room and as such Crosby had a legitimate expectation of privacy there. As no justice thought the appeal even worthy of consideration, the case did not make the Court's "discuss list," leaving the Texas Supreme Court decision in favor of Crosby standing. The full pool memo is available at http://epstein .wustl.edu/research/blackmunMemos/1987/Denied-pdf/87-1640.pdf.

Court grants cert through a **rule of four**. That is, although five votes constitute a majority, the Court will agree to hear a case if any four justices vote to grant cert. Overall, the Court grants only about 1 percent of cert petitions, leaving the lower court decision as final in the remaining 99 percent of the cases.

The justices' votes on petitions for *certiorari* remain secret unless a justice leaves his or her papers to the public, as justices sometimes do after they retire. To date, the justices' votes in the *Gratz* and *Grutter* cases are unavailable, but the importance of the issue plus a split between the Sixth Circuit Court upholding affirmative action and an earlier Fifth Circuit decision striking it down at the University of Texas made a grant highly likely.[26] On December 2, 2002, the Court granted review to both cases.

Oral Arguments

Following a grant of cert, the justices receive written briefs from the litigants explaining why their position should win. Other parties may file *amicus curiae* briefs urging the Court to affirm or reverse the lower-court decision. Again, the most influential of these briefs come from the solicitor general's office, which represents the current presidential administration at the Supreme Court. Thus, while the Clinton administration sided with the university at the district-court level in the *Gratz* and *Grutter* cases, the George W. Bush administration switched sides and asked the Supreme Court to strike down the law school and undergraduate admissions programs. On the other hand, seventy-four organizations filed *amicus* briefs supporting the university, which, until the 2015 same-sex marriage case, *Obergefell v. Hodges*,[27] was the most ever in a Supreme Court case.[28] One of the briefs in the affirmative action case came from a group of high-ranking military officers, who wrote about the need for a diversified officer corps and thus the need for diversified service academies. Critically, they argued that without affirmative action, the service academies would be overwhelmingly white.

Parties normally receive thirty minutes each for oral argument, although the justices frequently interrupt with questions. The quality of oral argument varies enormously, and not surprisingly, can influence which party wins.[29]

The Supreme Court broke with long-standing oral argument traditions during the COVID-19 pandemic of 2020. Several cases scheduled to be heard in April were postponed until May, with two of the cases being postponed until the fall 2020 term. The Supreme Court heard arguments in the cases that were postponed until May over the telephone. One of those cases was the "faithless-elector" controversy we discussed in the Election 2020 section in Chapter 2. Additionally, the Court allowed live streaming of the oral arguments, something it had never previously allowed.

The Supreme Court heard oral arguments in the *Gratz* and *Grutter* cases on April 1, 2003, hearing the *Grutter* case first. Grutter's attorney, Kirk Kolbo from the Center for Individual Rights, spoke first, arguing that the Constitution prohibits distinctions based on race. Justice O'Connor immediately interrupted, asking the attorney about Court precedents holding that race could be used if the government had a compelling interest in doing so. Kolbo responded that the school could legally achieve a diverse student body without using racial preferences by using factors that are not explicitly racial, such as economic status. U.S. Solicitor General Theodore Olson spoke next, opposing the University of Michigan's (hereafter just "Michigan") use of affirmative action but, under President

rule of four: *Supreme Court rule that grants review to a case if as few as four of the justices support review.*

Key Questions

Should the federal government be allowed to try to influence a court decision?

Key Questions

Why did the Office of the Solicitor General switch positions in the Michigan affirmative action cases between 2000 and 2001?

Bush's directive, not calling for a complete ban on the use of race. Olson chose not to answer questions about the military's use of affirmative action, stating that he had not examined military policies. Michigan's attorney, Maureen Mahoney, a former law clerk for Chief Justice Rehnquist, tried to distinguish between the university's attempt to obtain a diverse student body and the type of quota system declared unconstitutional in the *Bakke* case. "She's very good," Justice Ginsburg whispered to Justice David Souter after the arguments ended. "She's fabulous," replied Souter.[30] Her ability, of course, would help Michigan's chances; political science studies have demonstrated that the attorneys' abilities at oral argument significantly influence the justices' decisions.[31]

Kolbo represented Gratz as well as Grutter, arguing in Gratz's case that the use of race as a factor must be extraordinary and rare, and that diversity does not meet that extraordinary standard. Michigan's attorney in the undergraduate case defended the need for a "critical mass" of minority students so that those students would not feel like tokens.

The Decision

Within a few days of oral argument, the justices meet in conference to vote on the merits of the case (that is, to decide which side wins) and to assign a justice to write the Opinion of the Court in the case. If the chief justice is in the majority, he determines who will write the opinion. If the chief justice is not in the majority, the assignment is made by the most senior justice who is in the majority.

The opinion is the heart of the Court's legal and policy-making power. It explains the Court's justification for its decision and sets guidelines for other courts to follow in subsequent cases. To have this authority, it must become a majority opinion by gaining the assent of a majority of the justices.

Assigning the writing of the Opinion of the Court to a justice does not mean that a majority opinion will result. If a justice writes an opinion siding with one side, and other justices agree with the result (that is, agree on who wins) but not with the reasoning, they can concur in the judgment. That means that they are not joining the Opinion of the Court. Such justices will typically write a **concurring opinion** that explains their reasoning or join the concurring opinion of another justice. Justices who disagree with the result reached by the majority can write a **dissenting opinion** explaining why they believe the Court's decision was in error. If, due to a combination of concurring and dissenting justices, fewer than five justices join the Opinion of the Court, that opinion becomes a plurality judgment rather than a majority opinion. Plurality judgments have less value as precedents than majority opinions.[32]

The vote in the affirmative action cases revealed a split in the justices' preferences: 5–4 in favor of the law school program, but 6–3 against the undergraduate program. As Figure 15.3 shows, four conservative justices thought that both the undergraduate and the law school affirmative programs violated the Fourteenth Amendment and were unconstitutional, whereas the three most liberal justices thought that both programs were acceptable because of the university's compelling interest in creating a diverse student body and the narrow tailoring of the affirmative action programs to meet that interest. Justices Sandra Day O'Connor and Stephen Breyer were the swing justices. They agreed that diversity constituted a compelling interest but did not believe that the undergraduate program, which automatically gave a set number of points to minority

concurring opinion: *Opinion that agrees with the results of the majority opinion (that is, which party wins) but sets out a separate rationale.*

dissenting opinion: *Opinion that disagrees with the majority opinion as to which party wins.*

Ruth Bader Ginsburg   Stephen Breyer   Anthony Kennedy   Antonin Scalia

John Paul Stevens   David Souter   Sandra Day O'Connor   William Rehnquist   Clarence Thomas

Most liberal   **Most conservative**

Figure 15.3 **Ideology and Votes of Supreme Court Justices in the *Gratz* and *Grutter* Cases**

The justices are aligned from most liberal to most conservative. The six justices to the right of the blue vertical line voted with Gratz to strike the undergraduate affirmative action program at the University of Michigan. The five justices to the left of the orange vertical line voted with the University of Michigan in upholding the law school's affirmative action program.

Source for justices' ideology: Martin-Quinn scores, http://mqscores.berkeley.edu. Jeffrey A. Segal. *Photos:* Ginsburg, Breyer, Kennedy, Scalia, Stevens, and Thomas by Steve Petteway, Collection of the Supreme Court of the United States; Souter by Joseph Bailey, National Geographic Society, Collection of the Supreme Court of the United States; O'Connor and Rehnquist by Dane Pennland, Smithsonian Institution, Collection of the Supreme Court of the United States.

applicants, was narrowly tailored to meet that interest. They thus voted with the more conservative justices to strike the undergraduate program. But O'Connor and Breyer voted with the liberals to uphold the law school program, which overall gave strong preferences to underrepresented minorities but was more careful in considering the importance of race in everyone's application.

Because the conservative former Chief Justice William Rehnquist dissented in the law school case, Justice Stevens, then the senior justice in the majority, assigned the opinion. Given former Justice O'Connor's role as the swing justice in the case, he assigned the opinion to her. O'Connor declared that while racial categorizations could be used only if the state had a compelling interest in doing so, the need for diversity was such an interest. She quoted from *amicus* briefs by businesses, which cited the need for a diverse workforce in the global economy, and she cited extensively from the military brief's stated need for a diverse officer corps.

Chief Justice Rehnquist was in the majority in the undergraduate case, and he assigned the majority opinion to himself. His opinion accepted the notion that diversity was a compelling interest—he did not have the votes to declare otherwise—but wrote that the automatic granting of twenty points toward admission to every minority student did not meet the precedent required in *Bakke* of considering each particular applicant as an individual.

Though Gratz won her case, she had by this point graduated from a different Michigan campus, the University of Michigan–Dearborn. The University of Michigan changed its admissions procedures to be more like the law school's procedures: Race would still be used as an admissions factor, but there would be no automatic point total added just because of an applicant's race.

Judicial Decision Making

LO 15-4 Identify factors that influence judicial rulings and the impact those decisions have

Key Questions

Is judicial review a problem for democracy?

countermajoritarian difficulty: *Alexander Bickel's phrase for the tension that exists for representative government when unelected judges have the power to strike laws passed by elected representatives.*

We have now discussed the structure of the court system and the procedures it follows in both civil and criminal cases. In this section, we will examine how judges make decisions about a case and the impact those decisions have on public policy. Because federal judges are not elected, and serve for life, they are not accountable to the people in the same way that presidents and members of Congress are. Nevertheless, they have an extraordinary power—the power of judicial review. Judicial review allows an unelected branch of government to strike the laws and actions of the elected branches of government—Congress and the president. This authority by the judicial branch is questionable in a democracy, where the people are supposed to have the final say. Therefore, along with judicial review comes what the late law professor Alexander Bickel has labeled the **countermajoritarian difficulty**.[33] We expect the judiciary to enforce limits on governmental power, but when it does so, it acts in a countermajoritarian manner because unelected judges are using this power to strike the actions of democratically elected executives and legislatures.

The Supreme Court first held an act of Congress unconstitutional in 1803, and then did not hold another one unconstitutional until 1857. Since that time, however, the Court has struck down 191 congressional laws, slightly more than one per year, with 7 laws struck down in 1935 during the height of the Court's battle with the New Deal (see Figure 15.4). Since

Figure 15.4 Number of Federal Laws Declared Unconstitutional, 1790–2019

The Supreme Court declared two federal laws unconstitutional in the 2010 term, three in the 2011 term, three in the 2012 term, one in the 2013 term, two in the 2014 term, none in the 2015 term, two in the 2016 term, two in the 2017 term, two in the 2018 term, and three in the 2019 term.

Sources: Harold W. Stanley and Richard G. Niemi, Eds., *Vital Statistics on American Politics*, 3rd ed. (Washington, D.C.: CQ Press, 1992); Lawrence Baum, *The Supreme Court*, 8th ed. (Washington, D.C.: CQ Press, 2004), 170, 173; Harold J. Spaeth, Lee Epstein, Andrew D. Martin, Jeffrey A. Segal, and Thomas W. Walker, U.S. Supreme Court Database, scdb.wustl.edu. Jeffrey A. Segal, © Cengage Learning.

the 1986 term, the Court has struck down more than twice as many state and municipal laws (147) as federal laws (60).[34]

Given the undemocratic nature of judicial review, politicians frequently decry **judicial activism**, judges who go beyond what the law requires and seek to impose their own policy preferences on society through their decisions. These critics insist that judges should act with **judicial restraint**—that is, judges should respect the decisions of other branches or, through the concept of precedent, the decisions of earlier judges.

We will explore two broad approaches to understanding judicial policy making: a legal approach, which suggests that courts rely on legally relevant factors, and an extralegal approach, which suggests that courts rely on legally irrelevant factors. We then examine the consequences for a democracy of the reliance on extralegal factors by an unelected judiciary.

Judicial Restraint: The Legal Approach

According to the legal approach, justices base their decisions on legally relevant materials, such as prior court precedents, the plain meaning of the text of the law under consideration, and the intent of the framers of the law, rather than on their own preferences. This viewpoint is known as judicial restraint.

As we explained earlier in the chapter, precedent means a reliance on the prior decisions of the Court. In the *Grutter* case, the Court accepted the arguments from the *Bakke* case that the government had a compelling interest in achieving a diverse student body but concluded that systems that establish racial quotas go too far. Reliance on precedent creates stability in law: Decisions change gradually rather than abruptly. Reliance on precedent also generates a degree of equality and fairness. If you slip on your neighbor's walkway, it is not necessarily clear whether your neighbor is at fault for a slippery surface or you are at fault for not being careful. It is hard to say in advance that ruling one way is just and ruling the other way is unjust. But if the judge rules that the owner is not liable and the next week under similar conditions the neighbor slips on your walkway, fairness demands that the judge should again rule that the owner is not liable. That is what ruling based on precedent accomplishes. Lower courts are bound by Supreme Court precedents, but the Supreme Court does not necessarily consider itself strictly bound to its own precedents. Otherwise, there would be no growth in the law, and, for example, the United States might still have the separate-but-equal school systems that were declared unconstitutional in *Brown v. Board of Education*.

Beyond precedent, legal-based approaches consider the plain meaning of the law being interpreted. In recent history, the late Justice Antonin Scalia was the Court's foremost proponent of this approach. If there is no right to privacy written in the Constitution, he claimed, then the Supreme Court should not be creating privacy rights. As Scalia argued, if such rights are to be protected, they should be granted by democratically elected legislatures, not by life-appointed judges. However, while a textual approach makes some issues perfectly clear—for example, that a 34-year-old cannot be president—it does not necessarily answer whether affirmative action plans designed to increase diversity or fair representation in an unequal society violate equal protection of the law.

Similarly, Justice Clarence Thomas often argues for decision making based on the intent of the Framers. This approach places the meaning of the Framers ahead of the literal meaning of the words that they wrote. Thus, while dissenting in a case that upheld federal prohibitions

judicial activism: *Decisions that go beyond what the law requires, made by judges who seek to impose their own policy preferences on society through their judicial decisions.*

judicial restraint: *Decisions by judges respecting the decisions of other branches or, through the concept of precedent, the decisions of earlier judges.*

Key Questions
On what should judges and justices base their decisions? Should they always use the same decision making criteria?

on medicinal marijuana under Congress's authority to regulate interstate commerce, Thomas ignored more than seventy years of precedent that had expanded the scope of the commerce clause. He argued that local activities such as the medical use of homegrown marijuana were not what the Framers meant by commerce.[35] This may well be true, but in many circumstances, it is difficult to know what the Framers meant or what they would have thought if they could have envisioned modern American society. For example, does the Fourth Amendment's protection of one's person, houses, papers, and effects against unreasonable searches and seizures include telephone wires, cell phones, and wireless e-mail?

Judicial Activism: The Extralegal Approach

Legal approaches often fail to provide a good indicator of what the Supreme Court will do. While some precedents, notably the 1978 *Bakke* decision, supported affirmative action, more recent cases prior to *Grutter* had pushed in the opposite direction. The text of the Fourteenth Amendment guarantees equality, but there is no evidence that the Framers of the amendment intended it to prohibit policies that tried to help disadvantaged groups.

Alternatively, we can consider extralegal approaches to Supreme Court decision making. Extralegal factors go beyond the legal factors that courts are supposed to consider. The most important sets of extralegal considerations include the justices' own preferences and strategic considerations based on the preferences of others. Many, if not most, justices may be labeled activists, justices who decide cases based on their own policy preferences.[36]

Key Questions

What role should ideology play in judicial decisions? What role does it play?

The Justices' Preferences. In the affirmative action cases, the four most conservative justices voted to strike both the undergraduate and the law school plans, the three most liberal justices voted to uphold both, and the two justices in the middle voted to uphold the law school program but to strike the undergraduate program. (For the ideology of the justices currently on the Court, see Figure 15.5.)

This sort of relationship between the justices' ideology and their votes is common. But because Supreme Court scholars cannot obtain information from the justices themselves about their ideology, they use indirect measures. As Figure 15.6 shows, there exists a very strong relationship between the justices' ideology and their votes once on

Figure 15.5 **Estimated Ideology of the Supreme Court Justices, 2018 Term**

Statistical analysis of Supreme Court justices by Andrew Martin and Kevin Quinn place Justices Ginsburg and Sotomayor at the left (liberal) end of the scale while Justice Thomas anchors the right (conservative) end of the scale.

Source: Justices' ideology: Martin-Quinn scores, http://mqscores.lsa.umich.edu/Jeffrey A. Segal, © Cengage Learning. Photos: Steve Petteway, Collection of the Supreme Court of the United States.

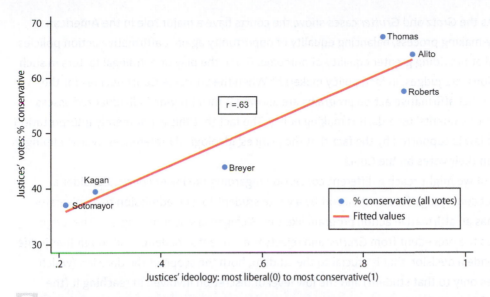

Figure 15.6   Justices' Votes by Justices' Ideology

The graph shows that, as the justices' ideologies line up from the left (most liberal) to the right (most conservative), the percentage of the time they vote conservatively increases substantially. Generally speaking, the most liberal justices, those farthest to the left on the graph (Sotomayor and Kagan), vote in the liberal direction (toward the bottom of the graph), whereas the most conservative justices (Alito, Roberts, and Thomas) vote conservatively most of the time (toward the top of the graph). The correlation coefficient, r, ranges from −1.0 to +1.0. A score of −1.0 signifies a perfect negative relationship, that is, that the most liberal justices vote the most conservatively. A score of +1.0 0 signifies a perfect positive relationship, that is, that the most conservative justices vote the most conservatively. While human behavior is never perfectly predicted by political variables, the correlation coefficient of .63 indicates a very strong relationship between the justices' political ideology and how they vote once on the Court.

Source: Justices' ideology: Data updated by Jeffrey Segal from Jeffrey Segal and Albert Cover, "Ideological Values and the Votes of Supreme Court Justices," *American Political Science Review* 83 (1989): 557–65. Justices' votes: Harold J. Spaeth, Lee Epstein, Andrew D. Martin, Jeffrey A. Segal, Theodore J. Ruger, and Sara C. Benesh, 2018 Supreme Court Database, Version 2018, Release 01, http://Supremecourtdatabase .org. Jeffrey A. Segal, © Cengage Learning.

the Court.[37] Note, however, that this strong relationship does not necessarily apply to state courts or lower federal courts, both of which must follow precedents established by the Supreme Court, at least on matters of federal law.

Strategic Considerations.   Justices cannot behave solely based on their ideological preferences. Justice Rehnquist (1972–2005), while writing the *Gratz* opinion, may have preferred to declare that virtually all affirmative action plans are unconstitutional, but if he had done so, he might have lost the support of Justices O'Connor (1981–2006) and Breyer (1994–). So he compromised and accepted diversity as a rationale, but nevertheless was able to strike down the undergraduate program. Negotiations over the content of the majority opinion are a routine part of Supreme Court decision making.[38]

A justice may need to consider not only the preferences of other justices but also the preferences of other actors in the political environment. The efforts of President Franklin Delano Roosevelt (1933–45) to pack the Court in the face of the Court's rejection of his New Deal programs assuredly played a role in the Court's about-face and subsequent approval of such programs, as we will see later in the chapter. Similarly, the Court backed down from efforts to limit congressional investigations into Communism in the 1950s when Congress threatened to remove the Court's jurisdiction from such cases. Considerations about the legitimacy of its decisions may have led to Chief Justice John Roberts's purported switch from striking the Affordable Care Act to upholding it.[39]

As the *Gratz* and *Grutter* cases show, the courts have a major role in the American policy-making process, balancing equality of opportunity against affirmative action policies aimed at providing greater equality of outcome. Given the play of extralegal factors in such decisions, are judges, in fact, policy makers?[40] When the Supreme Court decides for the nation that affirmative action programs are allowed if they provide individualized assessments of students' records, it is making policy. The fact that this is not merely interpretation of the law is supported by the fact that the justices' ideological preferences overwhelmingly explain their votes on the Court.

But we might reach a different conclusion regarding the lower courts. Consider a district court judge faced with a suit by a white student to gain admission to a university that has an affirmative action program like the Michigan law school program. The judge applies the precedent from *Grutter* and rejects the student's challenge. Although that judge has made a decision that is crucial to the student, both the scope of the decision (which applies only to that student) and the low level of discretion involved in reaching it (the judge felt bound by the Supreme Court precedent in *Grutter*) make this sort of behavior distinct from policy making.

Restraint and Activism in Judicial Decision Making

Contemporary research suggests that justices respect the decisions of legislatures and earlier judges when those decisions are consistent with the justices' ideology. Thus, for example, liberal justices such as Ginsburg and Breyer overwhelmingly vote to uphold liberal precedents[41] or federal laws favored by liberals.[42] But when conservative precedents or laws favored by conservatives are under consideration, liberal justices are more than willing to strike them. Similarly, conservative justices such as Alito and Thomas overwhelmingly vote to uphold conservative precedents or the constitutionality of federal laws favored by conservatives. But when precedents are liberal in direction or when liberals favor the laws under review, conservative justices are more than willing to strike them.

Most justices are restrained toward laws and precedents that they agree with ideologically but are quite willing to overturn laws and precedents that they are distant from ideologically. Does this bode poorly for a democratic society that expects its judicial system to exhibit impartiality? Perhaps, though as we shall see later, our elected representatives appoint judges and so indirectly the people help choose which judges will make judicial policy in the United States.

The Impact of Court Rulings

Now that we understand how judges make decisions, we will examine what impact those decisions have for our democratic system. The fact that the federal court issues a decision does not necessarily mean that government officials charged with implementing it will comply. The courts have no power of enforcement. The Supreme Court's school desegregation decision in *Brown*, for example, met with massive resistance from supporters of segregation: Elected officials urged disobedience, local boards of education ignored the decision, and lower courts complied with the decision halfheartedly at best. All the while, citizens rallied in the streets in opposition (see Supreme Court Cases: *Cooper v. Aaron*; see also Chapter 13, The Presidency). In part because of these reactions, very few schools desegregated in the ten years following *Brown*.[43] And the fact that a decision might be complied with does not necessarily mean that it will have the impact that the Court intended. The advances in school desegregation over time have not meant that educational equality has been achieved in the United States.

Additionally, many types of court decisions can be overturned by Congress, state legislatures, or other legislative mechanisms such as state-level referenda. When a court's decision is based on the meaning of a statute (for example, is carbon dioxide considered a pollutant under the Clean Air Act?), Congress can simply overturn the court's decision if it disagrees with the court's conclusion.

In the constitutional realm, if the Court declares that a practice is not unconstitutional, as in the law school affirmative action case, that practice can still be prohibited through the legislature or, if the state allows, through a referendum. So, when the Supreme Court rules that affirmative action is not prohibited by the Constitution, that does not mean that the university is required to implement an affirmative action program or that the state is required to allow such a program. As we saw earlier, following the Supreme Court decision in her case, Jennifer Gratz used the gateway provided by Michigan's initiative procedure, organizing a statewide proposal in Michigan that banned the use of race, gender, or ethnicity for admissions or hiring in higher education.

On the other hand, when the Supreme Court declares that the Constitution prohibits an activity, legislatures find that prohibition difficult to overturn. For example, when the Court declared that Congress did not have the authority to set the voting age at 18 for state elections, the only recourse was for Congress and the states to pass a constitutional amendment overturning that decision. Only five of the Supreme Court's constitutional decisions have ever been overturned via amendment (see Table 15.2). While relatively more of the Court's statutory decisions get overturned by Congress, such instances are still rare.

In addition, most Supreme Court decisions are complied with, even when the consequences for the losing litigants are serious. Following the Supreme Court's Watergate decision, President Richard M. Nixon (1969–74) turned over the Watergate tapes, even though doing so meant the end of his presidency.[44] Following the Supreme Court's decision

Key Questions
How are court decisions enforced? Would government work better if the courts had the power of enforcement?

Key Questions
Did the Michigan ballot initiative undermine justice or help ensure it?

Table 15.2 Constitutional Amendments Overturning Supreme Court Decisions

Supreme Court Decision	Amendment
Chisolm v. Georgia (1793) allowed citizens to sue other states in federal court.	Eleventh Amendment (1795) establishes sovereign immunity for states.
Dred Scott v. Sandford (1857) denied citizenship to African Americans.	Fourteenth Amendment (1868) makes all people born in the United States citizens of the United States.
Minor v. Happersett (1874) denied voting rights to women.	Nineteenth Amendment (1920) guarantees women the right to vote.
Pollock v. Farmers' Loan and Trust (1895) limited Congress's authority to tax income.	Sixteenth Amendment (1913) grants Congress the authority to tax income from whatever source derived.
Oregon v. Mitchell (1970) prompted Congress to set the voting age at 18 for all elections. The case struck the law as applied to state elections.	Twenty-Sixth Amendment (1971) sets the voting age at 18 for all elections.

Supreme Court Cases

Cooper v. Aaron (1958)

QUESTION: Does the threat of violence negate a school district's obligation to desegregate?

ORAL ARGUMENT: September 11, 1958 (listen at https://www.oyez.org/cases/1957/1_misc)

DECISION: September 12, 1958 (read at https://caselaw.findlaw.com/us-supreme-court/358/1.html)

OUTCOME: No, desegregation is required, even when mobs threaten violence (9–0).

Despite substantial opposition in the South to the 1954 *Brown* desegregation decision, the Little Rock school board approved a plan in May 1955 that would begin to integrate its schools as of September 1957. In response, the state legislature declared that no student could be required to attend an integrated school. Nevertheless, the National Association for the Advancement of Colored People (NAACP), a civil rights interest group, selected John Aaron, his sister Thelma, and seven other exceptional African American students to attempt to integrate Central High School.

As September 1957 approached, Governor Orval Faubus called out the Arkansas National Guard to physically prevent the students from entering the school. For three weeks, the Guard kept the school off limits to the nine students. This action encouraged segregationists, who took to the streets around the school to protest integration.

On September 20, 1957, a federal district court issued an order prohibiting the Arkansas Guard from interfering with desegregation efforts. In response, Faubus withdrew the Guard, leaving the streets under the control of a dangerous and angry mob.

On September 23, the African American students entered school under police protection, but the police were unable to control the mob and quickly removed the students. Two days later, President Dwight D. Eisenhower sent the 101st Airborne Division to Little Rock to disperse the mobs and protect the students. Eight of the nine black students remained at the school for the remainder of the school year. Given the unrest, William Cooper and other members of the Arkansas Board of Education filed suit to thwart the board's own desegregation plan. In June 1958, the district court upheld its request. In August, the court of appeals reversed the district court. The Supreme Court granted the board's petition for a writ of *certiorari*.

In an unusual opinion signed the day after oral argument by all nine justices, the Supreme Court refused to allow the board to back out of its desegregation plan due to the threat of violence. The Court declared that the U.S. Constitution and the Supreme Court's interpretation of the Constitution are the supreme law of the land. In response, Governor Faubus closed the school for the year, but it reopened as an integrated school in 1959. The Court's expansion of its authority—adding its interpretation of the Constitution to those items that are the "supreme law of the land"—has drawn criticism of judicial overreaching from people on the right and the left.

Thinking Critically

1. Why is the judiciary the branch of government best able to make decisions that most citizens strongly oppose?
2. Can the Supreme Court be effective in guaranteeing equality when most citizens actively oppose equality?

in reapportionment cases, state legislatures reapportioned their states, even though it meant that many of the legislators would be reapportioned out of their seats.[45] Similarly, states stopped prosecuting doctors for providing abortions following *Roe v. Wade*.[46]

Thus, the federal court system and the Supreme Court in particular play an important role in determining public policy. Yet, as we have seen, the people play an indirect role in choosing federal judges. We will now take a closer look at how the selection process occurs.

Jonathan Ernst/POOL/AFP/Getty Images

Image 15.4 Due to the COVID-19 pandemic, Congress conducted hearings virtually in 2020. Here, Senator Amy Klobuchar (D-MN) of the Senate judiciary committee interviews Justin Walker for a U.S. Court of Appeals nomination.

The Appointment Process for Federal Judges and Justices

LO 15-5 Discuss how federal judges get selected

The Constitution grants the president the authority to nominate judges, but these nominations are subject to the advice and consent of the Senate. Judges confirmed by the Senate serve during "good behavior," which, short of impeachment, essentially means a life term. The House has impeached only one Supreme Court justice, Samuel Chase (1805), in an attempt by the Democratic-Republicans to remove an ardent Federalist from the bench. The Senate rejected every charge against Chase (just three votes short of the required two-thirds majority on one of the counts),[47] establishing a custom crucial to **judicial independence** that judges would not be removed due to partisan disagreements with their decisions.

As procedures have evolved, the president and the Senate accommodate each other on district court appointments, but they sometimes clash at the appeals court level. At the Supreme Court level, presidential nominees face intense scrutiny by the Senate, which often reflects concerns by citizens and interest groups.

judicial independence: *Ability of judges to reach decisions without fear of political retribution.*

Key Questions

Describe the lasting impact of Supreme Court appointments.

District Courts

When a vacancy occurs in a district court, the president consults the senators from the state in which the court is located. If one of them is opposed to the nomination, he or she can invoke the norm of senatorial courtesy and receive the support of other members of the Senate in blocking that nominee. When the two senators are from different parties, the senator from the president's party sometimes offers the other senator a percentage of the appointments, hoping the favor will be returned if the other party wins the presidency.

Image 15.5 Senator Daniel Patrick Moynihan (D-NY) signed a blue slip approving the appointment of Robert Katzmann to the Second Circuit Court of Appeals. The photocopy that Judge Katzmann gave us was white.

Courtesy of Robert A. Katzmann

This norm is enhanced by the chair of the Judiciary Committee sending "blue slips," so called because of the color of the paper, to the senators of the president's party of a nominee's home state, asking whether they approve of the choice. Without a positive response, the Judiciary Committee generally will not hold a hearing on the nominee; with no hearing, there is no vote. Even with a positive response to the blue slip, the Judiciary chair may choose not to hold a hearing, particularly if he or she is of the opposite party of the president.

Sonia Sotomayor, who would go on to become President Barack Obama's first Supreme Court nominee, received her district court nomination during the presidency of Republican George H. W. Bush (1989–93) due to an appointment-sharing deal between New York's two senators at the time, Republican Alfonse D'Amato and Democrat Daniel Patrick Moynihan. Like the president, senators use a variety of criteria in naming district court judges, including ideology, qualifications, and the rewarding of party loyalty.[48]

Confirmation of district court judges is generally routine, with nearly 90 percent of nominees between the administration of Jimmy Carter (1977–81) and Barack Obama approved.[49] With an increasingly partisan confirmation environment following the 2010 elections, and a Republican majority in the Senate following the 2014 election, the confirmation rate during the Obama administration was closer to 80 percent.[50] Following the nomination, the Senate Judiciary Committee conducts hearings on nominees. At the hearings, the American Bar Association (ABA), an organized interest group representing the nation's attorneys, evaluates the merits of nominees. District court nominees may also be requested to testify. If the Judiciary Committee approves the nomination, it moves to the Senate floor for a vote. Under recent rules changes that prohibit filibusters on lower-court nominees, a majority is all that is needed for approval. One result of this is that Donald Trump has been able to seat virtually all of his judicial nominees given that the Republican Party has held a majority in the Senate throughout his first term of office.

Courts of Appeals

The formal process of appointment for court of appeals judges is the same as that of district court judges, but the greater authority of court of appeals judges means that the Senate and outside interest groups pay much closer attention to the president's nominees. While court of appeals judges formally represent multiple states, seats are informally considered to belong to particular states. Thus, senatorial courtesy still applies.

Key Questions

Is the judicial appointment process fair? How would you change it, if at all?

Senate Democrats twice blocked the nomination of current Chief Justice John Roberts, a conservative Republican, to the U.S. Court of Appeals. Only after a third nomination in 2003, at which point Republicans controlled the Senate (and thus the Judiciary Committee), did Roberts receive a hearing and a vote. Overall, the Senate has failed to confirm more than 20 percent of court of appeals nominees since Clinton's administration (1993–2001), with the overwhelming majority being blocked in the Judiciary Committee.[52] In 2010, Senate Republicans began extensive use of holds, a process by which a single senator can block the unanimous consent agreements by which the Senate operates, to delay votes on many of President Obama's nominees. The Democrats responded by changing Senate rules to prohibit filibusters on all executive or judicial nominations except those for the Supreme Court. Republicans eliminated filibusters for Supreme Court nominees in 2017.

The federal courts were for many years the exclusive province of white men. Not until President Franklin Roosevelt nominated Florence Allen to the U.S. Court of Appeals in 1934 did a female serve as either a district or circuit court judge.[53] No African American served on the federal courts until President Harry Truman nominated William Hastie to the U.S. Court of Appeals in 1949.[54] President John F. Kennedy made Reynoldo Garza the first Latino federal judge to serve on the U.S. District Court. In 1978, President Jimmy Carter made Garza the first Latino to serve on the U.S. Court of Appeals.[55]

Today, the federal courts increasingly reflect the diversity of the United States. Women make up 32 percent of district and court of appeals judges, and African Americans make up 19 percent of district and circuit court judges. Latinos make up 9 percent of court of appeals judges and 10 percent of district court judges.[56] Table 15.3 presents the female and minority appointment records of Presidents Donald J. Trump and Barack Obama (2009–17).

Does such diversity matter? While it is not the case that judges' votes are generally caused by their gender, race, or ethnicity, on certain issues there are substantial effects. Women are substantially more likely than men to support sex-discrimination claimants[57]—in fact, judges who have daughters are more likely to support pro-female positions than judges who only have sons.[58] African American judges are more likely to rule "liberally on cases

Image 15.6 Born in Honduras, Miguel Estrada immigrated to the United States at age 17. Despite a limited command of English, he graduated with honors from Columbia University in 1983 and Harvard Law School in 1986. After Estrada clerked for Justice Kennedy and worked in the Justice Department, President George W. Bush nominated him to the U.S. Court of Appeals in 2001. Democrats in the Senate blocked a vote on his nomination. Among the reasons, according to a leaked memo from the office of then Senate majority whip Richard Durbin (D-IL), was that "he has a minimal paper trail, he is Latino, and the White House seems to be grooming him for a Supreme Court appointment."[51]

Key Questions

Should judicial appointments be subject to partisanship?

Table 15.3 Federal Court Appointments of Presidents Obama and Trump

Demographic	Trump (Total: 194)	Obama (Total: 324)
Gender		
Male	146 (75%)	191 (58.1%)
Female	48 (25%)	138 (41.9%)
Race or Ethnicity		
African American	8 (4.1%)	62 (18.8%)
Native American	0 (0%)	1 (0.3%)
Asian American	12 (6.2%)	21 (6.4%)
Latino	8 (4.1%)	36 (10.9%)
White	165 (85%)	211 (64.1%)

Source: Pew Research. Accessed October 18, 2020, https://www.pewresearch.org/fact-tank /2020/07/15/how-trump-compares-with-other-recent-presidents-in-appointing-federal-judges/.

Political Analytics

Diversity on the Federal Courts

FOR THE FIRST 178 YEARS OF THE REPUBLIC, the U.S. Supreme Court was composed of all white men. Thurgood Marshall became the first African American when he was named to the court in 1967. The Supreme Court was all male until 1981, when Justice Sandra Day O'Connor was appointed. You read about political career ladders for women in Chapter 3, Federalism (see Election 2020: Beyond the Presidential Race). There is also a pool of persons who are prepared to serve on the Supreme Court. Though no particular judicial experience is required, nominees are vetted by the American Bar Association, and their judicial experience is usually relevant to the confirmation process. Like members of Congress who gain political experience in local offices and state legislatures, Supreme Court nominees have usually served on lower federal courts. To the extent that those courts contain a diverse pool of judges, presidents have a greater pool from which to draw when choosing nominees for the Supreme Court.

Figure 15.7 shows how the past three presidents' appointments have affected the diversity of the pool of lower-court judges. The demographic profiles of G. W. Bush, Obama, and Trump show how the pool of judges in the federal courts is changing. In addition to these changes, the

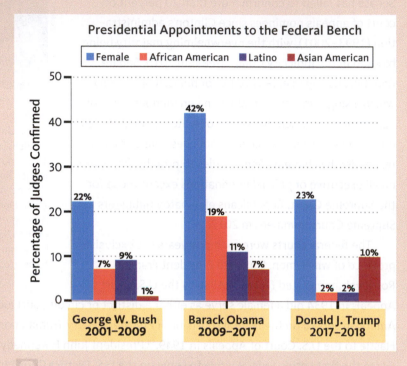

Figure 15.7 The Changing Face of the Judiciary

Senate confirmed eleven judges nominated by President Obama who are openly gay or lesbian, compared to one prior to his presidency. The face of the U.S. federal courts is always changing, increasing and decreasing in diversity.

Examine the demographic profiles of judges nominated by Presidents Bush, Obama, and Trump.

Sources: "Infographic: President Obama's Judicial Nominees," The White House, September 24, 2013, https://www.whitehouse.gov/share/judicial-nominees; "This Is the First Time Our Judicial Pool Has Been this Diverse," The White House, December 17, 2015, https://www.whitehouse.gov/share/judicial-nominations; "Women in the Federal Judiciary: Still a Long Way to Go," National Women's Law Center, http://nwlc.org/resources/women-federal-judiciary-still-long-way-go/; Barry J. McMillion, "U.S. Circuit and District Court Judges: Profile of Select Characteristics," Congressional Research Service, March 19, 2014, https://www.fas.org/sgp/crs/misc/R43426.pdf; Barry J. McMillion, "Judicial Nomination Statistics and Analysis: U.S. District and Circuit Courts, 1977–2018," Congressional Research Service, March 21, 2019, https://crsreports.congress.gov/product/pdf/R/R45622.

Thinking Critically

1. How important is it for the federal courts to include judges who resemble the general population of the United States?

2. The bar graph in Figure 15.7 includes the categories Female, African American, Latino, and Asian American. Are the data mutually exclusive? Does this matter in your interpretation of the data? What other categories might be important to include?

having a substantive racial dimension."[59] Latino and white judges do not decide similarly to each other, with Latino judges often granting more conservative decisions in criminal justice and civil liberties cases.[60] Latino judges also decide differently than African American judges, voting more conservatively in criminal cases, race discrimination cases, and cases involving economically disadvantaged litigants.[61] The fact that both African Americans and Latinos are members of discriminated-against minorities in the United States is not enough to result in similar decision making.

The Supreme Court

Given the Supreme Court's authority, the appointment of a Supreme Court justice is a high-stakes affair with extensive media coverage, interest group mobilization, public opinion polls, and the occasional scandal. As President Nixon correctly noted, "The most important appointments a President makes are those to the Supreme Court of the United States."[62] While Nixon was no doubt referring to the ideological and policy implications of such appointments, presidents also use Supreme Court appointments for electoral advantage.

Key Questions

Should judges be appointed without regard to race, ethnic background, gender, or religion, or should a diverse bench be a goal?

This was undoubtedly the case in October 1956, a month before the presidential election, when Republican President Dwight D. Eisenhower (1953–61), burnishing his above-politics credentials, nominated Democrat William Brennan to the Court. Brennan was a Catholic, and Cardinal Spellman of New York had been lobbying hard for a Catholic nominee.[63] Presidential candidate Ronald Reagan promised to nominate the first woman to the Court and did so with his 1981 appointment of Sandra Day O'Connor. Fear that George W. Bush would get credit for nominating the first Latino to the Supreme Court was one of the factors that led Democrats to oppose Miguel Estrada's court of appeals nomination,[64] and he was thus denied the judicial experience that would be important for a Supreme Court nomination. President Obama received credit for nominating the first Latino to the Supreme Court with Sonia Sotomayor's appointment in 2009.

Although electoral advantage certainly influences presidential decisions, presidents also try to choose nominees who are close to them ideologically, hoping to shape the direction of the Court for years to come. Donald Trump had this in mind when he nominated the conservatives Neil Gorsuch (whom a Republican-controlled Senate confirmed) and Brett Kavanaugh (whom a Republican-controlled Senate also confirmed). Considerations of ideology are not new. George Washington named eleven consecutive Federalists to the first Supreme Court, and Franklin Roosevelt appointed only supporters of his New Deal programs, most of whom were Democrats.

In recent times, nominees for the Supreme Court always receive hearings before the Senate Judiciary Committee, though Merrick Garland, nominated to replace the late Justice Scalia, did not. These hearings include testimony by the ABA on the qualifications of the nominee, comments by organized interests for and against the nominee, and testimony by the nominee. Every nominee since 1986 has received a unanimous vote of "well qualified" from the ABA except Robert Bork (of the fifteen members of the ABA Standing Committee on Federal Judiciary, ten voted that he was well qualified, one voted not opposed, and four voted that he was not qualified), Clarence Thomas (twelve voted qualified, two not qualified, and there was one recusal), and Harriet Miers, who withdrew her nomination in the face of substantial opposition to her ties to the president and her lack of qualifications.

Other interest groups mobilize for and against nominees, too. When President Obama nominated Sonia Sotomayor to the Court in 2009, various interest groups spoke against her, including Americans United for Life, the libertarian Independence Institute, the conservative Cato Institute, and the New Haven Fire Department due to a vote she cast against a white plaintiff in an affirmative action case. On the other hand, she received support from representatives of the ABA, the Leadership Conference on Civil Rights, the Federal Bureau of Investigation, the Fraternal Order of Police, and the National Association of Women Lawyers. Overall, representatives from 210 groups supported her confirmation whereas representatives from only 8 groups opposed it. Having 210 groups in favor is substantially more than any other nominee has ever received.[65]

Once the nomination is on the floor, senators debate the pros and cons of the nominee until the vote is set. Floor votes can no longer be blocked by filibusters, a technique that had frequently been used against court of appeals nominees.

The confirmation process has also become a much more partisan process over the years. While Chief Justice John Roberts received unanimous support from Republicans, then-Senator Barack Obama (D-IL) and seventeen other Democrats opposed him. Similarly, while Sonia Sotomayor, nominated by Democratic President Obama, received unanimous support from Democrats (57 of 57), only 9 out of 40 Republicans supported her.

This partisanship as to Supreme Court nominations continued into 2016. Just hours after Justice Antonin Scalia passed away, Republican Senate majority leader Mitch McConnell (R-KY) declared that the Senate would not consider any nomination made by President Obama.

Among opposition-party senators, ideology can sometimes be decisive. In the Roberts vote, only 25 percent of liberal Democrats supported him whereas more than 80 percent of more moderate Democrats did so. With Sotomayor, however, support was below 40 percent for both moderate Republicans (33 percent) and more conservative Republicans (10 percent; see Figure 15.8). Constituent preferences matter too[66] only three of the Republicans who voted for Sotomayor came from a state that Obama lost in 2008.

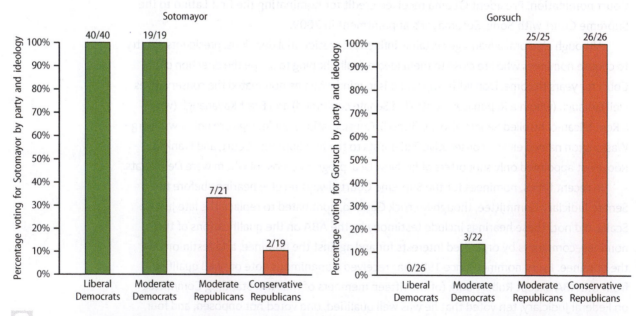

Figure 15.8 Ideology and Partisanship in the Sotomayor and Gorsuch Confirmation Votes

Every Republican voted to confirm Neil Gorsuch for associate justice, while his three votes from Democrats all came from moderates. Every liberal Democrat opposed him. Similarly, all Democrats voted to confirm Sonia Sotomayor for associate justice, while moderate Republicans were more likely to support her than conservative Republicans.

Source: Data collected by Lee Epstein, Jeffrey A. Segal, and Chad Westerland, http://epstein.wustl.edu/research/ApptIdeology.html. Democrats for the Gorsuch vote includes two independents who caucus with the Democrats.

The Supreme Court and the 2020 Election

Despite the enormous role the Supreme Court plays in American life, barely a word was mentioned about it in early in the 2016 presidential campaign. Then, in February, eight months before the election, Justice Antonin Scalia, the great conservative icon, passed away unexpectedly. The Court quickly rose to be one of the leading issues in the campaign. Within twenty-four hours of Justice Scalia's passing, Republican senators declared that no replacement should be named until after the 2016 election. Nevertheless, on March 16, President Obama nominated Merrick Garland, chief judge on the U.S. Court of Appeals for the District of Columbia, to fill Scalia's seat.

Despite stellar credentials (Harvard College valedictorian, Harvard Law School, Supreme Court clerkship, experience on the D.C. Court of Appeals, as well as a moderate image burnished by several years of prosecutorial experience), the Republicans would not even consider his nomination. They never requested the traditional FBI investigation that is conducted on all judicial nominees and, with minor exceptions, they did not grant him the courtesy meetings in their offices that all nominees get in the days following their nomination.

Similarly, the Supreme Court was not a huge issue early in the 2020 campaign, especially given the COVID-19 crisis and the civil rights demonstrations that followed the killing of George Floyd in Minneapolis. Then, in September 2020, liberal icon Ruth Bader Ginsburg passed away following a long battle with cancer. Even though early voting had begun in a few states, Senate majority leader Mitch McConnell declared that the Senate would vote on a Trump nominee prior to the November election.

Shortly before coming down with COVID-19 himself, President Trump nominated Judge Amy Coney Barrett, a court of appeals judge from the Seventh Circuit, to fill Justice Ginsburg's seat.

Decisions at risk given President Trump's replacement of Justice Ginsburg with Judge Barrett include:

- *Obergefell v. Hodges* (2015) and *Lawrence v. Texas* (2003). The *Obergefell* case declared by a 5–4 vote that states may not deny marriage certificates to same-sex couples. Justice Ginsburg was one of the justices in the majority. The *Lawrence* case was 6–3 to strike down a Texas law that made all sodomy (but in this case, homosexual sodomy) a crime. Given Justice Ginsburg's departure, five of the six justices in the *Lawrence* majority would be gone.

- *Grutter v. Bolinger* (2003). The Supreme Court upheld the affirmative action plan of the University of Michigan Law School by a 5–4 vote. With Ginsburg's departure, four of those five justices would be off the Court.

- *Roe v. Wade* (1973). With Ginsburg's departure, the number of justices likely to support *Roe*'s right to abortion would be down to Breyer, Kagan, and Sotomayor. It is always possible that Chief Justice Roberts would back away from such a momentous decision, much as he did in the Obamacare case (see Supreme Court Cases: *National Federation of Independent Business et al. v. Sebelius* in Chapter 12, Congress).

Even though Donald Trump lost the 2020 election, his appointment of three justices onto the Supreme Court changed that branch of government for the next few decades.

Given the highly partisan nature of Supreme Court nominations over hot-button issues such as affirmative action, many Republicans reacted negatively to an earlier statement expressing her hope that "a wise Latina with the richness of her experiences would more often than not reach a better conclusion than a white male who hasn't lived that life."[67]

The nominees' perceived qualifications are no less important than ideology. While the high-quality nominees of recent years—Kagan, Sotomayor, Alito, and Roberts—all received substantial opposition, the Senate confirmed all of them. Alternatively, Merrick Garland never received a Judiciary Committee hearing, much less a vote. Lower-qualified nominees have long faced decisive trouble; a case in point was G. Harrold Carswell, a little-known, frequently reversed, federal judge whom Richard Nixon nominated to the Supreme Court in 1970.

The question of qualifications includes not just ability, but also ethics. The Reagan administration withdrew the nomination of Douglas Ginsburg in 1987 following media reports that he had smoked marijuana while a professor at Harvard Law School. Much larger ethical questions surrounded the nomination of Brett Kavanaugh in 2018. During the televised hearings for Kavanaugh, Professor Christine Blasey Ford, who knew him when they were both in high school, charged Kavanaugh with sexual assault. Kavanaugh vociferously denied the charges and accused Democrats in the Senate of engaging in a "search and destroy" mission against the court of appeals judge. Retiring Republican Senator Jeff Flake of Arizona broke partisan lines when he threatened to oppose the nomination unless the FBI were given a week to investigate the new charges. With no direct corroboration of the allegation, senators acted the way elected officials of both parties normally do in such circumstances: Those who were ideologically close to the nominee—in this case, Republicans—believed him, whereas those who were ideologically distant (that is, Democrats) did not.[68] The end result was that the Senate approved Kavanaugh by a 50–48 vote.

ZUMA Press, Inc./Alamy Live News/Alamy Stock Photo

Image 15.7 In 2018, President Donald J. Trump nominated Brett Kavanaugh to the Supreme Court to replace the retiring Anthony Kennedy, the swing justice on many social issues such as same-sex marriage. Kavanaugh was a staunch conservative and most liberal interest groups opposed his confirmation. Then Dr. Christine Blasey Ford, who knew Kavanaugh from her high school years, accused him of having sexually assaulted her thirty-five years earlier. Despite her testimony, the Senate confirmed Kavanaugh by a narrow 50–48 margin.

Demographic Diversity on the Court

In a Court long dominated by white males, Clarence Thomas was only the second African American to serve; the first was Thurgood Marshall (1967), a distinguished lawyer for the National Association for the Advancement of Colored People (NAACP) who argued *Brown v. Board of Education* (1954) before the Court. The Senate has confirmed 115 justices to seats on the Supreme Court. Of those 115, only 4—Sandra Day O'Connor (1981), Ruth Bader Ginsburg (1993), Sonia Sotomayor (2009), and Elena Kagan (2010)—have been female. Sotomayor is the first and only Latino. By some measures, the current Supreme Court, with three women, one African American, and one Hispanic, is the most diverse ever.

The first thirty-two Supreme Court nominations went to Protestants, long the dominant religious group in American politics. The first Roman Catholic was Roger Taney in 1836; the first Jew was Louis Brandeis in 1916. Today, in a sign that the gateways to prominent positions have opened dramatically, the Court has five Roman Catholic justices, three Jewish justices, and one Protestant.

This diversity matters in a number of ways, both on lower courts and at the Supreme Court.[69] As Justice Sotomayor's "wise Latina" comment suggests, judges' backgrounds and experiences can influence their views on the proper outcome of a case. Given that the Court has tremendous discretion about which cases to hear, greater diversity means that the Court may be more responsive to the issues that matter most to an increasingly diverse national population. Historic appointments such as O'Connor's or Sotomayor's can also have an influence on how their colleagues vote.[70] As more women serve on the U.S. Supreme Court, the bias found against female attorneys might lessen.[71]

On the other hand, for the first time in history, not one member of the Supreme Court held elective office prior to service on the Court. This lack of experience in electoral politics might play into their decisions striking down campaign finance laws (see *Citizens United v. Federal Election Commission* in Chapter 8, Interest Groups). The educational background of the current justices also is narrow. Every one of the attended either Harvard or Yale Law School, though Justice Ginsburg transferred to and graduated from Columbia Law School. Professionally, only Sotomayor served as a trial judge, and all the justices except Kagan came to the Supreme Court from federal appeals courts. This narrowness of background has not always been the case. In the past, many Supreme Court nominees graduated from modestly ranked law schools, and the justices often came to the Court from governorships, cabinet positions, the Senate, and private practice. To people who believe that the justices simply make decisions that are commanded by the Constitution, this narrowness does not matter. But to those who believe that experience does matter, the lack of this form of diversity hurts both the Court and the nation.

Key Questions
Does diversity on the Court matter? Should the Supreme Court be diverse in terms of age?

Historical Trends in Supreme Court Rulings

LO 15-6 Outline how the Supreme Court has expanded and contracted national powers

In *Federalist* 78, Alexander Hamilton described the judiciary as "the least dangerous branch" because it has no power over the sword or the purse. But, as we have seen, due to the power of judicial review, the Supreme Court has actually played a major role in policy making: dividing authority between the nation and state, between Congress and the president, and between all levels of government and the people. Through the Court's history, its interpretations have expanded, then contracted, and once again expanded national powers. After a long and slow start, it has also moved consistently toward greater protections of equality. In this section, we will examine the policies issued by this least dangerous but also least democratic branch of American government.

Expansion of National Power Under the Marshall Court

During George Washington's administration (1789–97), the Supreme Court had so little power or status that its first chief justice, John Jay, resigned to become governor of New York. Not until the fourth chief justice, John Marshall, did the Court begin to establish itself as a major player in national politics. The Marshall Court (1801–35; Courts are often named after the sitting chief justice) did so not only by affirming its power of judicial review in the *Marbury* case (see Supreme Court Cases: *Marbury v. Madison* in Chapter 2) but also by setting forth a broad interpretation to the scope of national power in the cases of *McCulloch v. Maryland* (1819) and *Gibbons v. Ogden* (1824) and by limiting the authority of state judiciaries in a series of decisions culminating in *Cohens v. Virginia* (1821; see Supreme Court Cases: *McCulloch v. Maryland* in Chapter 3).[72]

Key Questions

In *Marbury*, the Court established its power over laws made by Congress. Why, then, did the Marshall Court also expand Congress's power?

The decision in *McCulloch v. Maryland* expanded national power in two ways: by granting the national government the right to create a bank through the necessary and proper clause, and by limiting state power by denying the states the authority to tax activities of the national government. Similarly, in *Gibbons v. Ogden*, the Court took an expansive view of national power, declaring that the commerce clause, which granted the national government the authority to regulate commerce "among the several States," would be broadly defined to include not just the shipping of goods across state lines but also the economic activities within a state that concern other states. As in *McCulloch*, what the Constitution grants as a legitimate object of national authority (here, interstate commerce) could not be regulated by a state. By establishing judicial review, expanding national power, and ensuring the uniformity of federal law, the Marshall Court set the United States on the path to a strong and unified nation.

Limits on National Power, 1830s to 1930s

Starting in the 1830s, the Supreme Court began limiting national power over slavery and, later, civil rights, as well as governmental efforts to regulate the economy. Although the Constitution permitted slavery, the justices did not address the issue directly until the case of *Dred Scott v. Sandford* (1857).[73] As noted in Chapter 5, Civil Rights, the Supreme Court declared that no black person could be an American citizen and that Congress did not have the authority to regulate slavery in the territories.

Following the Civil War, Congress proposed and the states ratified the Fourteenth Amendment, which prevented states from denying any person due process of law or the equal protection of the laws and from abridging the privileges or immunities of citizens of the United States. The Supreme Court interpreted the Fourteenth Amendment narrowly, thus limiting national power. For example, the *Slaughterhouse Cases* restricted the privileges or immunities clause that states could not abridge to the right of access to the seat of government, the right to pass freely from state to state, and the right to demand the protection of the federal government on the high seas or abroad, but little more.[74] Through precedent, the limited reading of the clause largely remains in effect today.

In *United States v. Cruikshank*, the Supreme Court reversed federal charges against the perpetrators of the Colfax massacre (see Chapter 5), arguing that the right to enforce the Fourteenth Amendment's due process clause gave Congress the authority to act only against states, not against individuals.[75] Similarly, in the *Civil Rights Cases,* the Court refused to grant Congress the authority to prohibit discrimination by private individuals under the equal protection clause, declaring that state-sponsored inequality was all that the amendment prohibited.[76]

The Supreme Court limited national authority in the economy, too. Following the Civil War, as the American economy shifted from agriculture to industry, powerful business and industrial interests sought to limit attempts by Congress and the states to regulate economic activity and labor. The Supreme Court generally backed business and industrial interests by setting up barriers to regulation. It promoted *laissez-faire*, the belief that the government should not intervene in the economy.

Strengthened National Power, 1930s to the Present

Following the onset of the Great Depression in 1929, citizens called on the states and the national government to try to regulate the economy and to assist workers, but the Supreme Court held firm in creating a constitutional gate that declared much of the economic legislation passed in the early years (1933–36) of Franklin Roosevelt's administration unconstitutional. Under pressure from Congress and Roosevelt, the Court eventually reversed itself, opening a gateway by allowing government greater leeway in regulating the economy. During this same period, the Court began restricting state government limits on civil rights and liberties, while strengthening national power to protect civil rights.

Economic Regulation.   Elected president in 1932 on a platform of economic recovery and reform, Franklin Roosevelt saw several pieces of his New Deal legislation—which aimed to alleviate the nation's economic hardships—struck down by the Court, often by closely divided votes. After his 1936 reelection, Roosevelt struck back at the Court, proposing a so-called Court-packing plan that would have allowed him to appoint a new justice for every justice older than 70 who failed to resign. This scheme would have increased the Court's size to fifteen and guaranteed judicial support for his economic plans.

In the historic "switch in time that saved nine," two of the moderate backers of the Court's *laissez-faire* policies, Owen Roberts and Chief Justice Charles Evans Hughes, proved themselves responsive to the hostile political environment facing the Court. They began to change their votes, providing majorities for both national and state plans to regulate the economy, thereby removing the need for the Court-packing plan. In a series of cases decided in 1937, the Court upheld state-level minimum wage laws. Nationally, the Court recognized the right of unions to organize and bargain collectively as within the powers of Congress to regulate under the commerce clause.

Increased Protections for Civil Liberties and Civil Rights.   With the government's authority over the economy established, cases before the Court dealt increasingly with questions of civil rights and civil liberties, topics discussed more fully in Chapters 4 and 5. The Court incorporated various provisions of the Bill of Rights, making them binding on the states. This selective incorporation doctrine began slowly, with First Amendment rights among the few incorporated before the 1950s. The doctrine expanded during the

Key Questions

Do you think justices over the age of 70 should be allowed to stay on the Supreme Court? Is appointment for life a good or a bad idea?

liberal Warren Court (1953–69), which made most of the criminal procedure guarantees of the Bill of Rights binding on the states.

Outside of incorporation, the Warren Court greatly expanded the interpretation of liberties involving the First Amendment, equal protection, the right to privacy, and criminal procedure. In First Amendment cases, the Court protected the speech rights of those advocating violence against religious and racial minorities, the press rights of newspapers against libel suits by public figures, and the right to publish allegedly obscene materials as long as they had even the slightest amount of redeeming social value. It also limited prayer and Bible readings in the schools.[77] Regarding equal protection, beyond the momentous *Hernandez v. Texas* and *Brown v. Board of Education* decisions, the Court launched a reapportionment revolution, setting forth a "one person, one vote" requirement.[78] The Warren Court also created a right to privacy that is not explicitly in the Constitution.[79] Finally, regarding criminal justice, the Warren Court demanded that evidence obtained by police in violation of the Fourth Amendment's protection against unreasonable searches or seizures should be excluded at trial (the exclusionary rule) and that subjects in custody not be interrogated without being informed of their rights to remain silent and to have an attorney (the so-called *Miranda* warnings, after the plaintiff in the case).[80]

The more conservative Burger (1969–86), Rehnquist (1986–2005), and Roberts (2006–) Courts have not reversed what the liberal Warren Court had done. For a summary of the Supreme Court's leading decisions, see Table 15.4. The Burger Court allowed children to be bused away from their neighborhood schools to increase integration. The Burger Court also established abortion rights, limited the death penalty, protected women's rights under the equal protection clause of the Fourteenth Amendment, and, in a precursor to the *Gratz* and *Grutter* lawsuits, first allowed affirmative action at colleges and universities.[81] On the other hand, the Burger Court chose not to extend equal protection rights to the unequal funding of school districts and, in the criminal justice area, limited the reach of the exclusionary rule and the *Miranda* warnings.[82]

Although conservative, the Rehnquist Court, over Chief Justice William Rehnquist's dissent, first extended privacy rights to homosexual conduct.[83] On the other hand, the Rehnquist Court limited, however slightly, the scope of abortion rights and cut back, again only slightly, the scope of congressional authority under the commerce clause and sovereign immunity.[84] And perhaps most important, as noted in Chapter 10, Elections and Campaigns, it ended the dispute over the 2000 presidential election with its decision in *Bush v. Gore*.[85]

The Roberts Court has been decidedly pro-business, hearing more such cases than previous courts and ruling on them in a decidedly pro-business direction.[86] It protected Walmart against a large discrimination lawsuit.[87] Even more important, it ruled that corporations have the same speech rights as citizens, enabling corporations to spend unlimited amounts of money on political campaigns[88] (see Chapters 8 and 10). On the liberal side, the Court upheld Obama's health care plan in 2012.[89] It also ruled that state denial of marriage licenses to same-sex couples was a violation of the equal protection clause of the Fourteenth Amendment.[90] In 2014, it upheld the Michigan initiative that banned affirmative action in that state.[91]

Table 15.4 Leading Decisions of the Marshall, Taney, Warren, Burger, Rehnquist, and Roberts Courts

Court	Case (Year)	Description
Marshall (1801–35)	Marbury v. Madison (1803)	Established judicial review
	McCulloch v. Maryland (1819)	Used implied powers to allow Congress to establish a national bank
	Cohens v. Virginia (1821)	Declared that federal courts have final say on meaning of federal law
	Gibbons v. Ogden (1824)	Established expansive interpretation of commerce clause
Taney (1836–64)	Dred Scott v. Sandford (1857)	Stated that "negroes of the African race" cannot be citizens and that Congress cannot prohibit slavery in the territories
Warren (1953–69)	Hernandez v. Texas (1954)	Recognized Latinos as a separate class for equal protection purposes
	Brown v. Board of Education (1954)	Prohibited segregation of public schools
	Wesberry v. Sanders (1964)	Required equality in the size of legislative districts
	New York Times v. Sullivan (1964)	Made it very difficult for public officials to sue newspapers for libel
	Griswold v. Connecticut (1965)	Established the right to privacy
	Miranda v. Arizona (1966)	Required that criminal defendants be told of their rights
Burger (1969–86)	Reed v. Reed (1971)	Granted women rights under the equal protection clause
	New York Times v. United States (1971)	Set extremely high bar for government censorship of newspapers
	Roe v. Wade (1973)	Extended privacy rights to cover abortion rights
	United States v. Nixon (1974)	Required President Richard M. Nixon to hand over incriminating evidence in Watergate case
	Regents v. Bakke (1978)	Allowed universities to use race-based affirmative action admissions
	Plyler v. Doe (1982)	Guaranteed right of undocumented children to attend public schools
Rehnquist (1986–2005)	Planned Parenthood v. Casey (1992)	Cut back but did not eliminate abortion rights established in Roe v. Wade
	Bush v. Gore (2000)	Ended the Florida presidential recount with George W. Bush holding a small lead, leading to Al Gore's concession
	Lawrence v. Texas (2003)	Extended privacy rights to homosexual conduct
	Gratz/Grutter v. Bollinger (2003)	Upheld race-based affirmative action if racial considerations are made on a case-by-case basis
Roberts (2005–present)	District of Columbia v. Heller (2008)	Upheld the right to bear arms as an individual right
	Citizens United v. FEC (2010)	Declared that corporations and unions have the same First Amendment rights to contribute to political campaigns as individuals
	National Federation of Independent Business v. Sebelius (2012)	Upheld the constitutionality of the Affordable Care Act
	Obergefell v. Hodges (2015)	Struck down state bans on same-sex marriage, legalizing same-sex marriage throughout the United States

Source: Compiled by authors.

The Judiciary and Democracy

The judicial system of the United States promotes the equal right of participation by allowing a single individual who has been harmed by a law to challenge its constitutionality. People who have financial resources or who can find support from organized interests may fare better than those who must act on their own. The action may not be successful. Nevertheless, the judiciary provides a separate gateway to the political system, one that is different in kind from the gateway to the legislative or executive branch. By filing a suit through the judiciary, a single individual—such as Oliver Brown (in the *Brown v. Board* school desegregation case) or the anonymous "Jane Roe" (in the *Roe v. Wade* abortion decision)—can have an enormous influence on the American political system.

Representative democracy requires government to be accountable and responsive to the public. Yet the judicial branch is not accountable in any meaningful way: Even if the public is dissatisfied with justices' decisions, Congress has not successfully used the impeachment process to remove justices for those decisions. Yet this does not mean that the Court is not responsive to the public or to the public's representatives. Responsiveness can happen through four different gateways.

The first gateway is through the electoral process.[92] During the 1960s, the Warren Court made a series of decisions on contentious issues such as criminal procedure and religious freedom that were significantly more liberal than many Americans might have preferred. Richard Nixon campaigned for president in 1968 with promises to appoint justices who were significantly more pro-police and significantly less pro-defendant. Nixon won the election and, in his first term, appointed four justices, all of whom were considerably more conservative on criminal procedure than the rest of the Court. The result was a conservative shift in Supreme Court decisions in criminal cases that mirrored public preferences as expressed in the 1968 election.

Second, in cases in which the Court is unresponsive to congressional preferences, Congress can threaten the Court's institutional authority. During the Civil War, Congress took away the Court's appellate jurisdiction over *habeas corpus* appeals. In the 1930s, Franklin Roosevelt threatened to dilute the Court by adding six new members. In both cases, the Court backed down and responded favorably to congressional (and thus, presumably, public) preferences.

The third gateway is through current events, which can move public opinion and judges' behavior in the same direction. During the Vietnam War, as events in Southeast Asia led American citizens to oppose the war in greater numbers, those events also led federal judges to impose shorter sentences on draft dodgers.[93] As society became more progressive on women's rights and same-sex marriage, judges, who themselves are members of society, presumably became more progressive on those issues, too. Immediately after the attacks of September 11, 2001, Americans were increasingly willing to allow the government to examine personal mail and internet activity (see Chapter 6, Public Opinion), and judges moved in the same direction.

Fourth, judges might believe that they have an obligation to rule consistently with public opinion, even if they are not subject to electoral sanctions. It is probably no accident that the Supreme Court's split decision in the Michigan affirmative action cases reflected America's ambivalence about whether equality meant treating everybody the same or whether, to promote equality of outcomes, underrepresented groups should be given advantages in admissions. Justice O'Connor, who split the difference over what can be done in the name of equal protection in the *Gratz* and *Grutter* cases, has spoken often about the need of the Supreme Court not to vary too far from public preferences.

That argument cuts both ways. As Justice Robert Jackson declared in a 1943 case striking down mandatory flag salutes, "The very purpose of a Bill of Rights was to withdraw certain subjects from . . . political controversy, to place them beyond the reach of majorities and officials and to establish them as legal principles to be applied by the courts. One's right to life, liberty, and property, to free speech, a free press, freedom of worship and assembly, and other fundamental rights may not be submitted to vote; they depend on the outcome of no elections."[94] If justices are responsive, it is not because the Constitution's framework requires it; it is because they choose to be.

Chapter Review

Key Terms

adversary process (p. 550). How does the adversary process seek to discover truth?

affirmative action (p. 549). Why might Justice Sotomayor view affirmative action differently from other justices?

amicus curiae (p. 556). Why might courts care about the position in a case taken by an *amicus curiae*?

appeal (p. 550). What sort of questions can generally be appealed to a higher court?

civil suit (p. 550). Why do civil suits exist?

class action lawsuit (p. 556). How do class action lawsuits promote equality in the legal system?

common law (p. 550). What led to the development of common law?

concurring opinion (p. 562). Why might a justice concur in an opinion rather than dissent?

countermajoritarian difficulty (p. 564). Why is the countermajoritarian difficulty a bigger problem for the federal courts than for most state courts?

courts of appeals (p. 550). What is the role of the U.S. courts of appeals?

criminal case (p. 550). What is the most likely outcome when a criminal case is filed?

dissenting opinion (p. 562). How might dissenting opinions influence the public's view of the Supreme Court?

district courts (p. 551). What is the role of the U.S. district courts?

en banc (p. 552). Why might losing litigants prefer to appeal *en banc* rather than to the Supreme Court?

judicial activism (p. 565). How do judges who are judicial activists behave?

judicial independence (p. 571). Why does the United States need judicial independence?

judicial restraint (p. 565). What is the evidence for the practice of judicial restraint at the Supreme Court level?

judicial review (p. 552). How does judicial review create the countermajoritarian difficulty at the federal level?

jurisdiction (p. 551). What generally happens if a court does not have jurisdiction to hear a case?

majority opinion (p. 559). Why is the majority opinion so important for the Supreme Court?

Marbury v. Madison (p. 552). What doctrine did the *Marbury* case establish?

petition for a writ of *certiorari* (p. 552). How often are petitions for writs of *certiorari* granted?

plea bargain (p. 557). Why is plea bargaining so prevalent?

precedent (p. 550). Why is a general rule for the following of precedent essential to justice?

rule of four (p. 561). How does the rule of four work?

solicitor general (p. 556). What is the role of the solicitor general?

Learning Outcomes: What You Need to...

Know	Test Yourself	Participate
LO 15-1 Describe what the judicial branch does		
The American legal system is based on the English system, following an adversary process, guaranteeing a right to trial by jury, and depending on common law in the absence of statuary authority. The Constitution established the Supreme Court. Congress has created federal district courts and courts of appeals. The Supreme Court has both original jurisdiction and appellate jurisdiction. Through the power of judicial review established in *Marbury v. Madison*, the Supreme Court has the authority to declare laws and executive actions unconstitutional and thus void.	• Summarize the U.S. legal traditions that derive from English legal traditions. • Restate what the Constitution says about the organization and powers of the federal judiciary. • Explain *Marbury v. Madison* and its importance.	• Assess whether courts are gateways to citizen influence and to justice. • Determine the extent to which judicial review is consistent with democratic government.
LO 15-2 Explain how state and lower federal courts operate		
State cases that contain issues of federal law or that contain particular types of parties can be appealed from state courts to the federal courts. District courts conduct civil and criminal trials, while courts of appeals hear appeals from district courts. Cases from the courts of appeals can be appealed to the Supreme Court.	• Explain how state court cases can end up in federal court. • Give an overview of the responsibilities and procedures in district courts. • Give an overview of the responsibilities and procedures in courts of appeals.	• Understand what would happen if federal courts could not review state court decisions on questions of federal law. • Evaluate whether average citizens are able to use the gateway of filing lawsuits.
LO 15-3 Review the procedures the Supreme Court uses		
Supreme Court decisions are made by a majority, though the justices sometimes write concurring opinions that agree with the majority but give a different rationale. The minority who disagree may write dissents.	• Explain how cases reach the Supreme Court. • Describe the process of oral argument.	• Read and critique a recent majority opinion (http://supreme.lp.findlaw.com).
LO 15-4 Identify factors that influence judicial rulings and the impact those decisions have		
Judicial policy making can be explained by both legal and extralegal approaches, with legal approaches having more sway at lower levels and extralegal approaches at higher levels, where judicial activism can be problematic for a democracy. Although the Supreme Court is not directly accountable to the public, it is to some degree responsive to public opinion.	• Survey how the Court reaches and issues decisions. • Discuss the impact Court decisions do and do not have.	• Evaluate why and whether Supreme Court decisions might have limited impacts. • Identify the gateways that create responsiveness of Supreme Court decisions to public opinion.

Know	Test Yourself	Participate

LO 15-5   Discuss how federal judges get selected

The president appoints federal judges with the advice and consent of the Senate. The higher the court, the more likely the Senate is to scrutinize nominees and refuse consent on the basis of nominees' ideology and/or qualifications. The Supreme Court, which once contained only white male Protestants, has increasingly diversified with respect to religion, race, and gender. This more equal access to the Supreme Court may also make the Court more responsive to an increasingly diverse nation.

- Explain senatorial courtesy.
- Describe issues in nominations to courts of appeals.
- Discuss the ways in which partisanship and ideology influence Supreme Court nominations.

- Consider the merits of diversity in the courts.

LO 15-6   Outline how the Supreme Court has expanded and contracted national powers

Through the Court's history, its interpretations have expanded, then contracted, and once again expanded national powers, especially with regard to economic regulation. After a long and slow start, the Court has also moved, fairly consistently, toward greater protections of equality.

- Describe the ways in which the Marshall Court expanded national power.
- Explain how the Supreme Court acted to limit equality between the 1830s and 1930s.
- Discuss what might have led the Supreme Court to accept greater national authority starting in 1937.

- Understand why it is important for courts to protect minority rights.

16 Economic, Domestic, and Foreign Policy

"First, in order to tackle the violence, we must address it as a public health crisis. Framing the challenges in this way will compel the city to address the root causes of the violence and meet those challenges head on with a toolkit that extends beyond law enforcement."

LORI LIGHTFOOT
University of Michigan

Lori Lightfoot grew motivated to forge a career of politics and policy during her studies at the University of Michigan.

In 2019, Lori Lightfoot was elected the first African-American female mayor and first LGBTQ mayor of Chicago, as well as the first openly gay African-American woman to be elected mayor of a major city in the United States. She grew up in a small city in Ohio and graduated from the University of Michigan with a degree in Political Science. In order to pay for college, she worked multiple jobs throughout her university career. After college, Lightfoot worked for Congressman Ralph Regula (R-OH) and Congresswoman and future Senator Barbara Mikulski (D-MD), before choosing to attend the University of Chicago Law School on a full scholarship. Lightfoot viewed law school as a means to achieving her goals and gaining potential financial stability. While there, she was selected to be president of the law school student body, and she led a successful movement to ban a law firm from campus that had sent a recruiter who made racist and sexist remarks.

After graduation from law school, she joined a large law firm in Chicago, Mayer Brown, and after six years, she left to become a prosecutor with the U.S. Attorney's office in Chicago. Lightfoot served there for six years before joining the Chicago Police Department to oversee professional standards. She rejoined her law firm in 2005 in the position of partner and stayed there until she began her campaign for Mayor of Chicago in 2018.

Lori Lightfoot's belief in police accountability is a big reason why she decided to run for Mayor. Over the course of her legal career, she devoted a significant amount of attention to police accountability, most recently as president of the Chicago Police Board and Police Accountability Task Force. In her last year in that position, she publicly clashed with then Mayor Rahm Emanuel over his support for reaching a police reform deal with the Trump administration's Department of Justice. Lightfoot believed that the deal did not incorporate enough reform proposals to investigate and prosecute police misconduct and to prevent it in the first place.

The city of Chicago holds a two-round mayoral election every four years with all the candidates running in February and, if no candidate achieves a majority of the vote, the top two candidates face each other in a runoff election in April of the same year. In 2019, Lori Lightfoot ran for Mayor of Chicago with thirteen other candidates, and advanced to a runoff with Toni Preckwinkle, who served as a local alderman and then president of the Cook County Board of Commissioners, as well as Chair of the Cook County Democratic Party (Chicago is located in Cook County). It was historic that two women ran against each other in this mayoral race in Chicago, and even more so because they were both African American. Before the runoff, her opponent Preckwinkle had gathered a number of key endorsements from local elected politicians and key unions but when the runoff part of the campaign began, Lightfoot demonstrated that she was the more popular of the two candidates with voters.

She was elected with 73.7% of the vote, which was considered a resounding victory for her.

Lightfoot has displayed a passion for changing public policy nearly all her life, and her chosen career path allows her to work to achieve her policy goals. Since she has been mayor, she has worked to reduce violence, provide better affordable housing in Chicago, increase the minimum wage, and perhaps most pressingly, has dealt with the twin issues of police misconduct and the COVID-19 pandemic. As of June 2020, Lightfoot remained a highly popular mayor, with nearly 80% of Chicagoans supporting her. Overall, her career path has taken her from a concentrated focus on the law to a broader range of social justice policy, including access to safer communities, better housing, quality education, and economic opportunity.[2]

Quantum Images/Alamy Stock Photo

Public Policy Under a Constitutional System

LO 16-1 Outline the steps in the policy-making process

public policy: *Intentional actions of government designed to achieve a goal.*

Public policy can be described as the set of laws and regulations that govern American political and social life to meet a specific need and accomplish a goal. It is in the arena of public policy—in determining who gets what, when, and how, and with what result—that we can see whether the constitutional system created by Madison and the Framers really works. Can the people pursue policies that advance their own interests? Can the people's representatives, while pursuing policies that advance their constituents' interests, produce a nation that looks out for the welfare of all the people?

With a government deliberately designed to represent competing interests, public policy has tended to cycle. One argument gains favor, driving policy in one direction. But new problems arise, calling for a redirection of policy. In the early years of the American republic, for example, Congress raised tariffs (taxes on imports) to help support new manufacturing enterprises, which could then undersell foreign competitors. But when agricultural interests complained about having to pay high prices for foreign goods, Congress lowered tariffs. Banking policies were similarly adjusted, sometimes to favor debtors and other times to favor creditors.

The Process of Policy Making

The development of good public policy is always difficult and complex. A policy, for example, of providing tax benefits to homeowners to spur home ownership sounds like a good thing, as would policies that make it easier for people to obtain mortgages. It would help homeowners, support the home construction industry, and create jobs, building more stable communities. But what sounds simple rarely is that simple because there are usually unintended consequences. A policy of tax benefits for homeowners can also encourage sprawl that turns agricultural land into suburbs, thus decreasing crop yields and altering food production, while leaving cities with vacant housing and declining tax bases. Making it easier for people to obtain mortgages means more people default on their loans when the economy goes into a downturn, as happened during the 2007–2009 recession. Government officials and members of the private sector are often forced to respond to new crises quickly. During the COVID-19 crisis, private banks suspended mortgage payments for several months and the federal government suspended student loan payments, and interest accrual on those loans, largely because of the lessons learned from the previous recession. Policy making at the federal, state, and local levels is always evolving in response to the combination of past experiences and current circumstances.

With so many competing interests and the potential for unintended negative consequences, government seeks to pursue policies that maximize benefits and minimize costs. This is not easy and often does not happen. Political scientists—scholars who study politics and the processes of government—have categorized the steps in policy making to make the process more understandable.

The main stakeholders in the policy-making process include members of Congress, the president, the executive branch agency that deals with the issue, the courts, political parties, interest groups, and interested citizens. These stakeholders attempt to formulate a policy that will address the problem (see Figure 16.1).

Although presidents and members of Congress formally appear to be in command of the federal policy-making process, they face a complex set of gates standing in the way of implementing policy. In Chapter 3, Federalism, we explained how governmental powers are shared among the federal, state, and local governments. Frequently, policy changes at the federal level require cooperation from these other governmental units, and that can be a complicated task across all fifty states. Encouraging all the states to adopt the same policy is not always possible; from the adoption of health care exchanges under Obamacare to the response to the COVID-19 crisis, states have wide latitude to adopt different policies in the same issue domain. In this chapter, we discuss economic, domestic, and foreign policy and show how public policy is an outcome of all the actions taken by a wide array of stakeholders at the federal, state, and local levels.

The first step is **problem identification**. For example, constituents might complain to members of Congress that the cost of college is too high. The second step is for the issue of the cost of higher education to make it to the **policy agenda** of policy makers.[3] Of all the problems that government might be able to solve, only a small fraction can receive attention at any one time. Those that make it onto the policy agenda get the attention of Congress, the president, the executive branch agency that deals with the issue, the courts, political parties, interest groups, and interested citizens. These stakeholders attempt **policy formulation** that will solve the problem. In the example of the high cost of college, the stakeholder network considered three proposals: direct federal loans to college students; promoting private loans by paying banks the interest on student loans while the student is in college; and guaranteeing the loans if students are unable to repay them.

In a fourth step, **policy enactment**, the legislative branch passes a law that enacts one or more of those proposals Congress did with student loans in 2010. Following passage of a law, the legislature grants the executive branch **policy implementation** authority over the program. In this case, the Department of Education was given the authority to direct the student loan program. After a few years, Congress or the Department of Education may engage in **policy evaluation** of the program. Following this policy evaluation, the cycle of policy making might begin again with new legislation to adjust the program to make it work better (see Figure 16.2).

In this chapter, we will focus on domestic, economic, and foreign policies. In each of these domains, the stakeholders mentioned earlier wield influence in different ways, depending on the characteristics of the issue being considered. In most cases, the origins of an implemented policy start with Congress when it passes a law and the president approves it (discussed in more depth in Chapter 12, Congress). But in other cases, the president can use his executive regulatory power to effect change without a new congressional law, or Congress can decide to change funding allocations for specific programs in order to slow

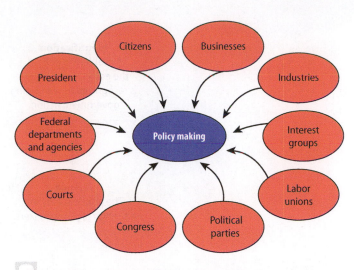

Figure 16.1 **Stakeholders in the Policy-Making Process**

The U.S. policy-making process includes people and groups with a wide range of different interests, ranging from the president to average citizens.

problem identification: *The first step in the policy-making process, in which a problem in politics, the economy, or society is recognized as warranting government action.*

policy agenda: *The second step in the policy-making process, in which a problem that has been identified gets the attention of policy makers.*

policy formulation: *The third step in the policy-making process, in which those with a stake in the policy area propose and develop solutions to the problem.*

policy enactment: *The fourth step in the policy-making process, in which Congress passes a law that authorizes a specific governmental response to the problem.*

policy implementation: *The fifth step in the policy-making process, in which the executive branch develops the rules that will put the policy into action.*

policy evaluation: *The final step in the policy-making process, in which the policy is evaluated for its effectiveness and efficiency; if changes are needed, the issue is placed back on the policy agenda, and the cycle starts again.*

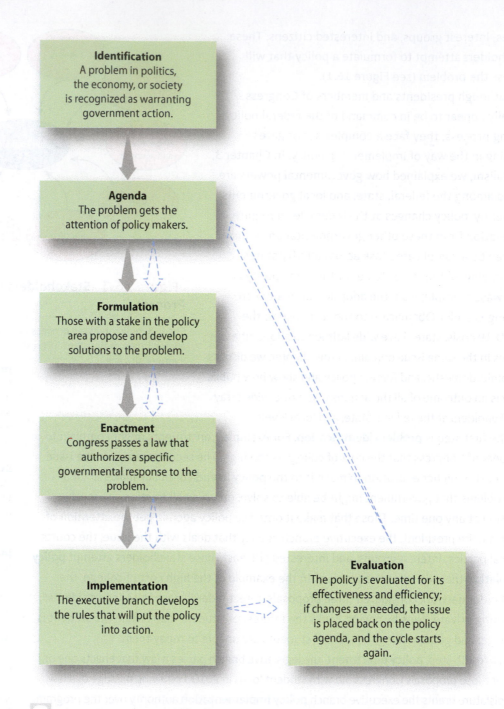

Identification
A problem in politics, the economy, or society is recognized as warranting government action.

Agenda
The problem gets the attention of policy makers.

Formulation
Those with a stake in the policy area propose and develop solutions to the problem.

Enactment
Congress passes a law that authorizes a specific governmental response to the problem.

Implementation
The executive branch develops the rules that will put the policy into action.

Evaluation
The policy is evaluated for its effectiveness and efficiency; if changes are needed, the issue is placed back on the policy agenda, and the cycle starts again.

Figure 16.2 The Public Policy-Making Process

The process by which policy is made has six major steps: identification, agenda, formulation, enactment, implementation, and evaluation.

down or prevent their implementation. In the next section, we will examine more closely this second method of policy implementation.

The Regulatory Process

For laws to be implemented, there must be rules to instruct policy makers, government officials, organizations, and businesses. The formal responsibility for policy implementation falls to the bureaucracy in what is commonly called the **regulatory process** (see Figure 16.3).

The current framework for the regulatory process has its foundation in the Administrative Procedure Act that Congress passed in 1946 to provide a consistent blueprint for all federal agencies in the issuing of regulations.

The federal government typically issues regulations when a law is first enacted and when a new circumstance or policy need arises that requires updates to the way the law is implemented. One such circumstance might be a change in the political control of the White House. Frequently, an incoming president of a different party issues new regulations to reverse the previous administration's policies. More commonly, a new president instructs federal agencies and the Office of Management and Budget (OMB), which oversees budgetary and regulatory issues, to revise existing regulations to better reflect his policy preferences. For example, in May 2017, President Trump issued an executive order that reversed protections against discrimination by federal contractors based on sexual identity or orientation.[4]

The bureaucracy produces these regulations by working within a process that begins with identifying the agency that has jurisdiction. The agency in charge will then offer preliminary **regulations**, and the political appointees of the agency will determine whether they are in line with the president's policy views. Although the bureaucracy is theoretically supposed to be insulated from direct political pressure, the reality is that the president's policy preferences are considered during this process.

When there is some agreement on the content of the preliminary regulations, they are submitted to the Office of Information and Regulatory Affairs within the OMB for approval to be published in the *Federal Register*, the official record of all executive branch rules, regulations, and orders. As noted previously, the OMB must review all regulations before they take effect. When preliminary regulations appear in the *Federal Register*, a period for public comment is defined (typically outlined in the originating legislation) ranging from thirty to ninety days. During this period, ordinary citizens, interest groups, and relevant industries and businesses can submit their opinions to the agency about the regulations. In addition, the agency or its local affiliate can hold public hearings in locations across the country to solicit opinions on the regulations.

Based on all the responses it receives, the responsible agency revises the preliminary draft regulations and issues final regulations. These are once again sent to the OMB and then are published in the *Federal Register* thirty days in advance of taking formal effect. Once the final regulations are issued, the program is officially ready to be implemented. A vivid example of this process concerned the disposal of coal ash from coal-burning power plants. After a major coal ash spill into local rivers and streams in Tennessee, environmental groups pushed the Environmental Protection Agency (EPA) to issue new regulations outlining the requirements for safe coal ash disposal. The preliminary regulations were issued in October 2009, but after the public comment period was up, the EPA still had not issued final regulations. In response, environmental groups, led by Earthjustice, sued the EPA, and a judge forced the agency to agree to issue the final regulations by December 19, 2014, which it did. Only a few days later, a second major coal ash spill occurred in North Carolina, adding more pressure for the EPA to act in a timely manner.[5] It was not until October 19, 2015, nearly 6 years after the preliminary regulations were first issued, that the EPA regulations on safe coal ash disposal took effect. Such extreme delays in issuing and implementing final regulations are not typical, but this example shows how the regulatory

Implementation

Identify agency that has jurisdiction

Write preliminary regulations

Review by OMB

Print preliminary regulations in *Federal Register*

Period for public comment

Revise regulations

Review by OMB

Print final regulations in *Federal Register*

Figure 16.3 **The Regulatory Process**

After policies are enacted, they need to be implemented and regulated under a structure that is overseen by the Office of Management and Budget (OMB). This figure outlines the regulatory process from start to finish.

regulations: *Guidelines issued by federal agencies for administering federal programs and implementing federal law.*

Federal Register: *Official published record of all executive branch rules, regulations, and orders.*

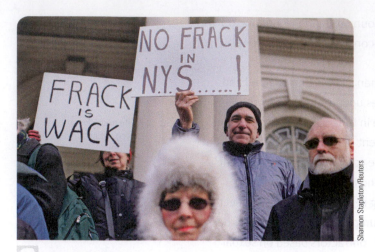

Image 16.1 There are multiple ways that citizens can offer feedback into the regulatory process. They can write or email their comments, they can testify at public hearings, and they can hold rallies and protests. Here residents of communities affected by fracking make their views known through protest.

process itself can act as a gate to effective oversight of industry and environmental protection.

Blocking Implementation

Even after final regulations are issued, groups can challenge the legality of them in the federal court system. For example, in 2016, the Supreme Court considered a challenge to regulations issued requiring the inclusion of contraception in employer-sponsored health insurance plans under the Affordable Care Act (ACA). The case, *Zubik v. Burwell*, involved the Little Sisters of the Poor; this religious group refused the ACA's accommodation, which only required it to notify the government that the ACA violated its religious views. In April 2016, in the wake of a likely 4–4 split, the Court asked for more briefs so that a compromise could be reached. In addition to court action, the House or Senate can pass appropriations bills with language that prevents an agency or department from using federal money to implement the regulations. However, the president typically threatens to veto the bill if this type of language is included because it undermines his policy priorities and, more broadly, his executive power to implement laws. As a result, legislative leaders usually remove such language in the final version of appropriations bill sent to the president (see Chapter 12 for more on the appropriations process).

State Governments and Public Policy

As we noted in Chapter 3, it is important to understand how the federal government interacts with state governments in implementing policy and, at the same time, how states interact with each other. In this section, we will take a closer look at how states can influence each other through processes referred to as policy diffusion and the race to the bottom.

Policy Diffusion. In a 1932 opinion, Supreme Court Justice Louis Brandeis wrote, "It is one of the happy incidents of the federal system that a single courageous State may, if its citizens choose, serve as a laboratory; and try novel social and economic experiments without risk to the rest of the country."[6] As far back as the Revolutionary era, New Jersey experimented with women's suffrage, as did several western states at the end of the nineteenth century. Nebraska has a unicameral legislature, and Wisconsin experimented with an unemployment insurance program in the 1920s. A little more than a decade later, the federal government created a national unemployment insurance program. As of 2021, fifteen states and the District of Columbia have legalized the use of recreational marijuana, and at least another thirty-six states have legal medical marijuana.[7] When one state adopts a policy and then other states follow, such policy adoption at the state level often encourages the federal government to see the benefits of such policies as well.

policy diffusion: *Process by which policy ideas and programs initiated by one state spread to other states.*

The main benefit of states serving as laboratories of change is that other states can learn about successful programs and copy them or learn what not to do if an experimental program fails. This takes place through a process known as **policy diffusion**, and it typically starts with states that border one another. Examples are numerous, including the Children's Health Insurance Program,[8] regulation of air pollution,[9] school choice plans (allowing students to choose which school in a district to attend),[10] health care reform,[11] and Native American casinos.[12] States learn not only from neighboring states but also from their local governments. Such was the case with antismoking ordinances, which cities and towns successfully adopted before states did, and currently, localities are adopting higher minimum wage laws before entire states are doing so.[13]

Source: National Governors Association

Image 16.2 The federal system of government requires cooperation between the national and state governments, and federal policy is frequently implemented by state governments. Here Governor Andrew Cuomo (D-NY), vice-chair of the National Governors Association, leads a discussion with Speaker of the House Nancy Pelosi (D-CA) during the association's February 2020 meeting.

The Race to the Bottom.

If diffusion is the good side of policy making in a federal system, the race to the bottom can, depending on one's point of view, potentially involve negative consequences. A race to the bottom exists when states compete against each other to reduce taxes, environmental protections, or welfare benefits in order to create incentives for businesses to come to the state or disincentives for poor people to come. For example, lower tax rates draw people to a state, yet to keep people there, the state cannot raise taxes even when the public might desire more spending.[14] When states compete economically with one another, if one state decreases environmental enforcement, a neighboring state may be forced to do so as well.[15] In terms of welfare benefits, individuals seeking benefits move to the most generous states. This situation led states to establish residency requirements for welfare until the Supreme Court prohibited them.[16] Consequently, states that want to increase welfare benefits for their own citizens hesitate to do so unless neighboring states also do so, lest they attract an overload of recipients from those other states.[17]

Key Questions

How does policy diffusion serve as an example of policy making in a federal system?

Domestic Policy

LO 16-2 Identify the key federal programs that make up domestic policy

The term "domestic policy" covers a wide range of policy areas in which the government plays a role, at the federal, state, and local levels, in the lives of average citizens. Table 16.1 lists the major federal programs generally considered under the category of domestic policy, when they were enacted into law at the federal level, and a brief description of what they do.

Table 16.1 Major Federal Programs

Names	Year	Description
Social Security	1935	Old-age retirement insurance program that pays a monthly amount to retired workers
Unemployment Insurance	1935	Temporary replacement income for job loss
Social Security Disability Insurance	1935	Payments to individuals who can no longer work due to disability
Temporary Aid to Needy Families	1935	Subsidy for low-income individuals with children; originally known as Aid to Families with Dependent Children but replaced in 1996 by TANF
Public Housing Assistance	1937	Subsidy for low-income individuals for housing
Immigration and Nationality Act	1952	Laws governing documented entry and citizenship into the United States
Food Stamps	1964	Subsidy for low-income individuals for food purchase
Medicare	1965	Health care insurance for the elderly and disabled
Medicaid	1965	Health care insurance for low-income individuals
Clean Air Act	1963/ 1970	Laws requiring minimum standards for air quality; amended in 1970 to create the Environmental Protection Agency
Clean Water Act	1972	Regulations for the discharge of potential contaminants into water sources
Supplemental Security Income	1972	Subsidy for low-income individuals who are over 65, blind, or disabled
Medicare Prescription Drug Act	2003	Expanded Medicare to provide insurance coverage for prescription drugs for the elderly and disabled
Affordable Care Act	2010	Mandate that requires every individual to have health insurance coverage and provides access and subsidies through exchanges and expanded Medicaid

Throughout the book, we have covered major issues in domestic policy, including public education (see Chapter 3), affirmative action (Chapter 15, The Judiciary), and workplace equality (Chapter 5, Civil Rights). In this chapter, we explore three major areas of domestic policy that are sparking intense debate today: entitlement programs, income security, and health care; immigration; and energy and environmental policy. In each of these issue areas, we will provide an overview of public policy and analyze an example of how a specific policy has been crafted and implemented (see the Public Policy features).

Entitlement Programs, Income Security, and Health Care

Social Security: *Federal pension program that makes a monthly payment to retired elderly workers and disabled persons.*

During the twentieth century, the federal government enacted laws to create a social safety net to provide income stability for the elderly and disabled, and assistance with food, health care, and housing for the poor. **Social Security** is one of the largest and likely best-known federal domestic policy programs; it is essentially a federally guaranteed pension program funded by taxes imposed by employers and workers. Social Security was created in 1935 as part of the set of policy programs known as the New Deal proposed by President Franklin Delano Roosevelt (1933–45; see Chapter 13, The Presidency). The New Deal represented a major change in the relationship between the federal government and individuals by establishing a set of programs that would guarantee payment to an individual if he or she met certain criteria (for example, age, children, low income, or disability). This type of program is commonly known as an **entitlement program**, which means that individuals are "entitled" to receive the benefit as long as they qualify under these criteria. The passage of the Social Security Act marked the beginning of the transformation of the role of the federal and state governments in providing a social safety net for individuals in need of financial assistance as well as aid to secure food, housing, and health care.

Social Security itself is a mandatory retirement account for all workers that is funded by taxes paid by both employers and workers. The amount of Social Security retired workers receive is calculated based on the amount of time they worked while paying into the program; when they retire, they receive a monthly payment directly from the federal government. The drive to provide this kind of income security for individuals was in large part a response to the dire effects of the Great Depression, which left millions of people without jobs and income. At the same time, the federal government created Unemployment Insurance, which is run by state governments according to federal guidelines; it provides short-term payments to workers who lose their jobs and is funded by taxes imposed on employers.

In addition to these programs, which are targeted at the working population, the Social Security Act of 1935 and its subsequent legislative expansions have created several other programs that are designed to help individuals who need assistance supporting themselves or their families. Two of these, Social Security Disability Insurance and Supplemental Security Income, are designed to help those who are no longer able to work or who have a disability that prevents them from working full time. Another major program is Temporary Aid to Needy Families (TANF), which is a program to provide payments to women in poverty with children (it was originally called Aid to Families with Dependent Children). The majority of this program's costs are funded by the federal government through a single amount of funding per year, known as a block grant, although states are expected to contribute a minimum amount of money to help administer the program.

In addition to income security, as part of the New Deal, the federal government also put in place sets of programs to help individuals get mortgages to buy houses through the Fannie Mae Corporation and to build affordable housing by offering subsidies to developers. These programs were aimed at helping people buy houses because that was believed to help ensure financial stability and help the economy through new housing construction.[18]

In the 1960s, under President Johnson's Great Society initiative (see Chapter 13), these types of income security programs were expanded to include health care, food security, and expanded housing assistance. In terms of health care, **Medicare** was created as a federal program, funded through a payroll tax that provided health insurance to people over the age of 65. **Medicaid** was created as a shared program between the federal and state governments, funded through general taxation, to provide health care coverage for low-income people.[19] The Food Stamp Program, today known as the Supplemental Nutrition Assistance Program, was designed to provide money to low-income families to purchase

entitlement programs: *Federal programs, such as Social Security, Medicare, or Medicaid, that pay out benefits for individuals based on a specified set of eligibility criteria.*

Key Questions
What policy goals do entitlement programs address?

Medicare: *Federal health insurance program for the elderly and disabled.*

Medicaid: *Shared federal and state health insurance program for low-income persons.*

Key Questions

Why has the implementation of the Affordable Care Act been so complicated?

food and household items and is fully funded through general taxation. Lastly, federal housing assistance was expanded under the Section 8 program to provide payments to housing developers to cover the rental costs of housing for low-income individuals, who typically must pay a minimum of $25 or 30 percent of their income toward rent under the program.[20]

The Social Security Act passed more than eighty-five years ago, and the federal government has expanded many of the programs the act first established, but not without controversy and opposition. When the act was passed, opponents claimed it was an overreach of federal power to take money from individuals only to give it back to them in their later years. Moreover, establishing other anti-poverty subsidies that would be paid directly to lower-income individuals might create a dependency on that payment that would discourage them from securing independent financial security. Lastly, opponents of expanding the role of the federally guaranteed safety net have argued that as the population expands and lives longer, the cost of these programs is unsustainable; for example, the Social Security old age pension program by itself accounted for 20 percent ($939 billion) of the FY 2020 federal budget.[21] The federal bureaucracy, specifically the Department of Health and Human Services (HHS), is largely responsible for administering these programs in conjunction with state and local government. We provide a brief overview of HHS in Chapter 14, The Bureaucracy, but here we embed it in the larger context of the expansion of the federal role in health care over the past decade. The expansion of federal programs that came with the ACA, enacted in 2010, required all individuals to purchase health insurance, either on their own or, if they are low income, with subsidies from the federal government. It was the last major expansion of federal social programs.

When the ACA was enacted, there were approximately 44 million Americans without access to health insurance coverage.[22] In 2019, 23 million of those formerly uninsured people had access to health insurance through the ACA either through purchasing it on the exchanges or through Medicaid.[23] Moreover, some of the largest gains in health insurance coverage from the ACA are among Latinos and African Americans.[24]

Most Americans receive health insurance through their employment or purchase it independently from private insurance companies; as noted previously, federal programs are available to help cover the costs of health insurance. At the federal level, HHS is responsible for overseeing these programs, as well as implementing new ones. Each state also has a department of health, as do many cities and counties; importantly, states also have the power to regulate insurance providers who provide coverage there.

The process by which the ACA (otherwise known as Obamacare) moved from proposal to bill to law was long and winding, as lawmaking always is, and it was especially complicated because of the fragmented nature of America's health care system, party politics and partisanship, and the heightened political rhetoric that surrounded the effort (see Chapter 12). Ultimately, the Democrats used their majority party power in the House and Senate to pass the law, with no Republican support.

The primary impetus of the law was to provide access to health insurance to the nearly 10 percent of Americans who did not have it. They did not have health insurance for a range of reasons: their employer did not offer it; they

Image 16.3 Senior citizens who are recipients of Social Security and Medicare are very vocal in seeking to protect their benefits. This group of elderly activists traveled to Capitol Hill in Washington, D.C., to oppose proposed cuts to those programs.

AP Images/J. Scott Applewhite

were self-employed and could not afford to purchase it; they were unemployed but not poor or old enough to qualify for a government program; or they were deemed ineligible by private insurance companies because they had health conditions that made them high risk and expensive to cover.[25]

The Affordable Care Act (ACA)

The Affordable Care Act (ACA) established a number of new programs, the most notable of which extended access to health insurance coverage to uninsured citizens and legal immigrants through an expansion of Medicaid eligibility and the provision of federal subsidies to workers to purchase private health insurance through health insurance exchanges that would be set up by states or, if the states refused, by the federal government directly.[26] The act provided for increased regulation of the medical services covered by private health insurance companies, mandated that individuals carry health insurance, required that young adults under the age of 26 be able to stay on a parent's insurance policy, and banned the denial of health insurance or an increase in premiums based on a preexisting condition. The act also increased payment levels to doctors who participate in the Medicaid program and helped senior citizens by closing a loophole in Medicare coverage for prescription drugs. From 2017 to 2018, President Trump and the members of the Republican Party in Congress tried to repeal and replace the ACA, but they succeeded in repealing only the individual mandate. When the GOP lost control of the House of Representatives to the Democrats, the Republicans tried to use the regulatory process as well as the federal courts to challenge the law. They secured a victory when a federal district court judge ruled the individual mandate unconstitutional, and a federal appeals court upheld that ruling in December 2019. The Supreme Court consolidated the cases *California v. Texas* and *Texas v. California* into one case that was scheduled to be heard after Election Day in 2020.[27] At the time the COVID-19 crisis erupted in 2020, states with their own health care exchanges reopened them to allow more people to enroll, but the Trump administration refused to open up the federal exchange, which serves individuals in states that did not form their own exchanges. Relying on the ACA to provide much needed health care insurance primarily for individuals who lost their job-related health insurance slowed the legislative momentum to undermine the program.

The implementation of the act came in stages, with some of the regulations issued very soon after the bill passed and others taking much longer to finalize. Part of the delay was attributable to a key lawsuit filed against the bill claiming that some of its provisions were unconstitutional. Twenty-six state attorneys general signed on to a lawsuit challenging the constitutionality of the federal health insurance mandate included in the law. The lawsuit made its way to the Supreme Court, which upheld the mandate in 2012 (see Chapter 12).

The *Sebelius* Court case cleared the way for implementation of the insurance provision through health care exchanges under ACA. However, only fourteen states set up their own health insurance exchanges; the federal government established exchanges in the remaining thirty-six states. The ACA also encouraged states to expand Medicaid to cover individuals at or below 138 percent of the poverty level because the federal government paid the extra costs of the expansion for up to three years. As of September 2020, thirty-eight states and the District of Columbia agreed to the Medicaid expansion and twelve states refused it. Additionally, individuals at 100 to 400 percent of the poverty level are eligible for subsidies (the federal government will pay part of their premiums).[28] Traditionally underserved communities, such as Latinos, are estimated to comprise nearly 25 percent of those eligible for coverage under ACA; the Obama administration made it a point to engage in targeted outreach to encourage them to enroll, but the Trump administration did not continue those outreach efforts.[29] As we noted above, the ACA has enabled significant expansion of health care coverage in these communities.

The dynamics surrounding the ACA reflect the complexity of implementing health care policy for millions of Americans across states. The ACA brings up the larger question of whether major policy overhauls can be accomplished without bipartisan support in the American federalism structure because states are so vital in the implementation process. Without their full cooperation, it becomes much more difficult for a federal program to succeed.

Immigration Policy

Another very important and often contentious issue in the public policy sphere is immigration policy—for both legal and unauthorized immigration. The Department of Homeland Security, the Department of Justice, and the Department of State share jurisdiction over immigration policy. Immigration has fueled U.S. population growth since the nation's founding, and the United States now comprises citizens with ancestries from many different foreign lands. The most recent data available indicate that there are 13.2 million legal permanent residents (LPR) in the United States—people born outside of the United States who have been granted legal status and reside in the United States.[30] The largest percentage of foreign-born people come from Latin America (mostly Mexico), followed by Asia and then Europe. Immigration laws serve simultaneously as gates regulating entry into the United States and as gateways to eventual citizenship. For those individuals who entered the United States without authorization and have put down roots, there is no current pathway to legal citizenship available. However, children who are born to unauthorized immigrants living in the United States are legal citizens because of the Fourteenth Amendment to the Constitution.

The Legal Immigration Process. The legal immigration process is jointly administered by the Department of State and the U.S. Citizenship and Immigration Services (USCIS), an agency of the Department of Homeland Security. Immigrants seeking to come to the United States apply for visas, which are granted by the Department of State; once they arrive, their journey toward citizenship is overseen by USCIS.[31]

To come to the United States with the intention of staying on a permanent basis, individuals can apply for a general immigration visa, a family relations visa, or an employment visa. In addition, individuals fleeing violence or persecution in their home countries can petition to enter the country under refugee or asylum status. The Immigration and Nationality Act of 1990 sets an annual limit of between 416,000 and 675,000 on these types of visas; in addition, 50,000 visas are set aside for people born in countries that have recently had the lowest numbers of immigrants to the United States.[32] In 2019, 459,000 individuals entered the United States as legal permanent residents.[33]

However, the Trump administration changed policies limiting immigration; in fiscal year 2019, there was a 13 percent drop in the overall number of immigrants admitted to the United States. Trump began his presidency with a travel ban on citizens of countries

Key Questions
How do immigrants become naturalized citizens?

he deemed to be a national security threat, but in reality targeted predominantly Muslim countries. The ban was challenged in federal court, upheld by the Supreme Court, and then expanded to additional countries in January 2020.[34]

The number of refugees and asylum seekers granted legal permanent status has also dropped under the Trump presidency as compared to the Obama administration in large part due to a tightening of the eligibility to be considered a refugee. In addition, the Trump administration has required that individuals seeking asylum file for that status in their home country, or a third country, as opposed to crossing into the United States and then asking for asylum. In fiscal year 2016 there were 120,216 refugees granted legal permanent status, as compared to 81,061 in fiscal year 2019. However, the overall number of asylum seekers granted legal permanent residence remained about the same across the two presidential administrations.[35]

To become a naturalized citizen, an immigrant must first apply to be a legal permanent resident of the United States, a step known as getting a green card, which is the permanent resident card issued to those who are eligible. (The green card is no longer green, but the name has remained.) To get a green card, an individual must secure a sponsor who will attest that the individual has some means of financial support. The individual must also take a medical exam and secure proof of employment if he or she intends to hold a job in the United States. This criterion can present a significant barrier to permanent residency: The federal government requires an individual seeking permanent residence to have talents or skills for a particular job that a current U.S. citizen could not provide. Marriage to an American citizen can also serve as a gateway to a green card, although the federal government has imposed stricter oversight on such marriages to counteract fraud. In 2013, the federal government also extended this gateway to apply to same-sex marriages, in response to a Supreme Court ruling that struck down discrimination against same-sex partners under federal law.[36] To become a fully naturalized U.S. citizen, a green card holder must reside in the United States continuously for at least five years; be able to read, write, and speak English; pass a citizenship test on the history and government of the United States (see Chapter 5); and pledge support for the United States.[37] In 2020, President Trump took the extraordinary step of issuing an executive order to temporarily suspend some immigration visas that would have allowed entry into to the United States, as a result of the COVID-19 pandemic.

The Debate over Unauthorized Immigration.   In recent years, pressure to reform immigration laws to address the issue of unauthorized immigration has mounted because of the millions of individuals who have entered the United States outside the legal immigration process.[38] Proponents of reform argue that individuals who arrived illegally but have since established productive lives should be legally incorporated into society and have the opportunity to be full and active citizens, a position that opponents refer to as "amnesty." Opponents tend to counter-argue that individuals who broke the law to enter the United States must be forced to return to their country of origin and apply for legal immigration status, and that without stronger border security, the hope of amnesty will just drive greater unauthorized immigration. The Republican and Democratic Parties are split along these lines as well; Democrats are stronger supporters of immigration reform that includes a gateway to amnesty and citizenship, while Republicans typically support a stronger border enforcement program with no amnesty and no gateway to citizenship. When he ran for president

Image 16.4 "Green card" is a commonly used term for the legal document that authorizes an immigrant to live in the United States as a permanent resident and makes him or her eligible to become a naturalized citizen.

Image 16.5 An immigrant goes through a long and complex process to become a naturalized U.S. citizen. In this photo, immigrants who have come from many different nations are sworn in as U.S. citizens.

Key Questions

Why is immigration the responsibility of the federal government? Should that change—why or why not?

in 2016, Trump promised to expand the existing barrier on the southern border of the United States by building a larger and longer wall. He managed to secure approval from Congress to fund construction of the wall by taking money from the Department of Defense military construction budget. As of September 2020, 371 miles of new wall had been built out of a 2,000 mile long southern border.[39]

The last law that was enacted to specifically address unauthorized immigration was the 1986 Immigration Reform and Control Act, which passed with bipartisan support and was signed into law by President Ronald Reagan (1981–89). The act granted amnesty, or forgiveness, to almost 2.8 million individuals who had entered the country without authorization and wished to stay as legal residents.[40] The 1986 reform bill did not stem the flow of unauthorized immigrants to the United States. In 2007, President George W. Bush (2001–2009), a Republican, and the Democratic-controlled Congress tried to produce a new immigration reform bill that would give unauthorized immigrants who were already in the United States an opportunity to become citizens but would, at the same time, discourage future unauthorized immigration. They failed to reach agreement.

One reform bill that gained traction was the Development, Relief, and Education for Alien Minors proposal, known as the DREAM Act, which would allow children who entered the country illegally with their parents to get on a path to legal citizenship at age 16 if they have been in the country for five years, have graduated from high school, and have no criminal record.[41] In his first term, President Obama announced his support for the DREAM Act. By June 2012, Congress had not passed it, so, using his authority over border control and national security, President Obama ordered the Department of Homeland Security to stop deporting young people who met the criteria of the DREAM Act and to allow them to apply for temporary work permits. Although it did not create a full path to citizenship, President Obama's action did partially implement the policy goals of the DREAM Act by putting in place what is now known as the DACA program.[42]

In 2014, President Obama went further when he announced a program that would allow parents of individuals who were citizens by birth or legal permanent residents to apply to avoid deportation and be allowed to submit applications for work permits in the United States. The plan was called Deferred Action for Parents of Americans and Lawful Permanent Residents. Before the plan could be fully implemented, Texas sued in federal court to stop the program, arguing that President Obama had exerted authority that was constitutionally held by Congress; twenty-five other states joined in the lawsuit.[43] The case, *United States v. Texas*, made it all the way to the Supreme Court, which in June 2016 upheld the lower court decision stating that President Obama's orders went beyond his executive authority. In 2017, President Trump effectively rolled back Obama's DACA program for new registrants and required a short window for current DACA designees to apply for an extension of their status. His decision was challenged in federal court in three separate cases, *Trump v. NAACP*, *Department of Homeland Security v. Regents of California*, and *McAleenan v. Vidal*, that were combined into one set of arguments before the Supreme Court. In June 2020, the Court ruled by a 5–4 vote that the Department of Homeland Security did have the authority to "rescind DACA" but that the way that it did so violated the Administrative Procedure Act (APA). If the Trump administration wishes to try to end the DACA program again, it will have to revise its procedures in doing so.[44]

In 2018, Trump also tightened border security resulting in parents being separated from their children and placing children in camps along the southern border and in some cases in areas far away from their parents. As of 2020, some of these children still had not been reunited with their families. This policy came under heavy criticism and was rolled back primarily through the insistence that families seeking refugee or asylum status stay in Mexico while their applications were processed. In both 2018 and 2019, Trump proposed sweeping immigration reform bills, but they were rejected first by a Republican controlled House, and again by the Democrats when they took control of the House in 2019.[45]

Local and Federal Action on Unauthorized Immigration.   States and localities, especially those along the border with Mexico, have tried to address unauthorized immigration in their own ways and in opposite policy directions. States with Republican-dominated legislatures have taken more punitive action than those controlled by Democrats. The most publicized effort took place in Arizona, where in April 2010 then-Governor Jan Brewer signed a law, S.B. 1070, that allowed police officers to ask about immigration status when they stopped individuals for any other police inquiry. Under the law, it was a crime to fail to show documentation establishing legal residence in the United States, and police officers could hold someone until their immigration status was verified.[46] Later that year, the U.S. Justice Department sued to get the law struck down in federal court on the basis that the state was infringing on the proper role of the federal government on immigration. The case made its way to the Supreme Court in 2012, and in *Arizona v. United States*, the court struck down the law because it assumed state powers over immigration that are granted to the federal government.

However, more recently, the state of Kansas enacted a law that applied its identity theft laws to non-citizens. The application of that law was challenged in a series of three different cases combined into one, *Kansas v. Garcia*, which was decided by the Supreme Court in March 2020.

Supreme Court Cases

Arizona v. United States (2012)

QUESTION: Does the supremacy clause prevent the state of Arizona from supplementing federal immigration law?

ORAL ARGUMENT: April 25, 2012 (listen at http://www.oyez.org/cases/2010-2019/2011/2011_11_182)

DECISION: Decided June 25, 2012 (read at http://caselaw.lp.findlaw.com/scripts/getcase.pl?court=US&vol=000&invol=11-182)

OUTCOME: 5–3. The Supreme Court struck down three restrictions in the law.

As noted in Chapter 3, the national government has only those powers granted to it in the Constitution. While the remaining powers remain with the states, the supremacy clause declares that where federal and state laws conflict, federal law is supreme.

In response to a large influx of undocumented persons across the border with Mexico into Arizona, the Arizona state legislature passed S.B. 1070. The United States believed that the law encroached on federal power to regulate immigration and sought to prohibit enforcement of its provisions. A federal district court found four provisions to be beyond the constitutional authority of Arizona to regulate: (1) creating a state-law crime for being unlawfully present in the United States, (2) creating a state-law crime for working or seeking work while not authorized to do so, (3) requiring state and local officers to verify the citizenship or alien status of anyone who was lawfully arrested or detained, and (4) authorizing warrantless arrests of aliens believed to be removable from the United States.

All eight of the justices hearing the case (Justice Kagan did not participate due to her prior work on issues related to the case while in the Justice Department) agreed that the provision requiring local police officers to check the immigration status of anyone lawfully arrested was constitutional. With Justices Scalia, Thomas, and Alito dissenting in part, a majority of the justices held that the rest of the provisions violated the supremacy clause given Congress's regulation of the subject.

The Court, in an opinion by Justice Kennedy, held that the Constitution's grant to Congress to "establish an uniform Rule of Naturalization," combined with Congress's extensive regulation of immigration, deprives states of the authority to: (1) make it illegal under state law for people to enter the United States without legal documentation, (2) make it illegal under state law for people without proper documentation to find employment, or (3) allow warrantless arrests of people believed to be in the United States without proper documentation. In all three provisions, the Court ruled that Congress's regulation of those facets of immigration was so extensive that states were "preempted" from adding to those regulations.

Thinking Critically

1. Why do you think the Arizona legislature might have passed the law in question?
2. Do you think any of the Arizona provisions were in fact unconstitutional (that is, they would be invalid even if Congress had not extensively regulated the areas in question)?

In that 5–4 ruling, written by Justice Samuel Alito, the Court ruled that the state of Kansas had the right to use information filed on federal tax forms to prosecute state charges of stealing and illegally using Social Security numbers. The Kansas Supreme Court had earlier ruled that because the forms were federal in nature and were immigration related, which is a federal function, the state could not use that information to prosecute violations of state law. The case has repercussions in that it expands the capacity of states to use information gathered on federal forms to prosecute noncitizens for other violations of state law.[47]

Not all state responses to unauthorized immigration have been punitive. For example, California, Texas, and New Mexico each adopted policies that allow unauthorized immigrants to receive private and public aid to attend state colleges and universities. Additionally, states and cities across the nation also declared themselves sanctuary cities and would not actively cooperate with federal authorities to seek out and deport undocumented residents.[48] The Trump administration threatened to withhold federal funds for these states and cities, and has challenged their authority over immigration related policy in federal court.

Ultimately it will be a major challenge for policy makers in both major political parties to construct a holistic immigration policy that is both fair and practical. Although there is general agreement within the core membership of each party, there are enough dissenting voices on how best to cope with illegal immigration that a clear policy position may not emerge. One factor that might affect the future of immigration reform is the growing number of Latinos in the United States, who typically express strong opposition to punitive measures on unauthorized immigration. As the number of Latino voters grows, the United States may see more convergence on a single policy position by the parties in an effort to win this increasingly important voting bloc (see the Political Analytics feature in Chapter 1).

Energy, Environmental Policy, and Climate Change

The public policy sphere of energy and environmental issues is ever expanding, from the domestic production of energy in the coal, oil, and natural gas sectors, to the protection of clean air and water, to the cleanups of toxic waste, to the global concern over climate change. Over the course of the twentieth century, these issues became ever more important with the expansion of manufacturing, population growth, geographic mobility, technology, and consumer consumption of natural resources. In the early part of our nation's history, Americans chiefly relied on wood as a source of energy to heat their homes and businesses until coal helped power the second industrial revolution during the late nineteenth century. During the twentieth century, the discovery of oil and natural gas as well as the construction of hydroelectric dams through New Deal projects, such as the Tennessee Valley Authority, helped satisfy the growing demands for energy. Following the Manhattan Project and the first explosions of the atomic bomb, the United States spearheaded research into nuclear power and built nuclear power plants to supplement fossil fuel (coal, oil, and natural gas) production.

In the 1960s, however, Americans became increasingly concerned about the impact of new energy and other technologies on the environment. Rachel Carson's epic study of the effects of pesticides on the bird population, called *Silent Spring*, provoked an intense debate between large chemical companies and the scientific community and created national concern that gave rise to the environmental movement. The United States took sweeping steps to regulate the effects of energy use on the environment in 1963, when Congress passed the **Clean Air Act** to reduce pollution in response to growing public concerns and calls for stricter government controls.[49] However, in order to effectively

Clean Air Act: *Broad federal legislation that expanded the federal government's ability to monitor and protect the environment against pollution.*

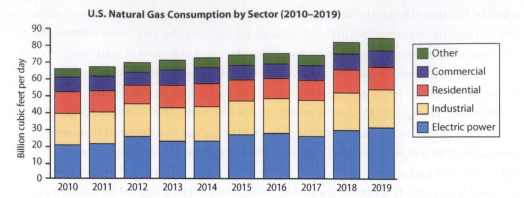

Figure 16.4 **Energy Production in the United States, 2010–2019**

Energy sources have evolved over the course of American history, starting with wood and coal and moving toward oil, natural gas, and nuclear energy. Here we show the energy production in different sectors from 2010 to 2019.

Source: U.S. Energy Information Administration, Today in Energy, accessed April 13, 2020, https://www.eia.gov/todayinenergy/detail.php?id=43035.

Clean Water Act: *Broad federal legislation that expanded the federal government's ability to monitor and protect the safety and quality of water.*

oversee the government's role in regulating the environment, it became necessary to create an agency with jurisdiction specifically designed to protect the environment. Consequently, Congress revisited the Clean Air Act in 1970 and created the Environmental Protection Agency (EPA) to implement the act. In 1972, the **Clean Water Act** was passed; it was based on a 1948 act that gave the government the authority to regulate the quality of both drinking water and navigational waters. Together, the Clean Air and Water acts provide a significant amount of power to the federal government to regulate pollution in our air and water.

Since that time, the federal government has grappled with balancing the need to protect the environment and the nation's need for energy sources to fuel the economy and everyday living. Over the past forty years, the nation has experienced several energy crises where the demand for and cost of energy (for example, gasoline prices) rose so high that businesses and consumers suffered. In response, the government has encouraged alternative sources of energy as well as the expanded development of fossil fuels in the United States. Today, the nation is almost to the point where it is entirely energy self-sufficient, which somewhat reduces the reliance on foreign nations for energy and at the same time decreases the chances of getting involved in international conflicts waged over energy.[50]

Just as the United States depends on energy to drive its economy, developing nations around the world also require energy as their economies grow. As nations around the world expand their economies and increase the standard of living for their residents, pressure builds on both the supply of energy that is required to fuel that economic growth and the environmental impact of that growth. Fears regarding global climate change are fueled not only by the continued reliance of developed countries on fossil fuels but also by the increased consumption of fossil fuels by nations such as India and China in their efforts to develop industrialized economies.[51] There is an inherent tension between industrialized nations that have used the world's energy resources freely for more than a 100 years and more recently developed nations that are seeking to industrialize their economies. Unexpected economic shocks, like the lockdowns of 2020 in response to COVID-19 outbreak, reduce the amount of energy consumption across countries. The effect of a sharp decrease in the world's energy consumption on air quality was apparent for all to see as levels of global air pollution decreased from Los Angeles to New Delhi to Beijing.

Image 16.6 In this photo, we see the difference in air pollution in the Los Angeles, California area before and during the COVID-19 pandemic. With millions of residents unable to access their workplaces, either from work from home policies, or because they lost their jobs, the number of cars on the road diminished greatly. The additional slowdowns in manufacturing and heavy industry, and reduced air travel, reduced overall air pollution in California, around the country, and throughout the world, during the height of the COVID-19 pandemic.

Now that more advanced nations are concerned about the environment—and climate change in particular—they want to encourage, even require, all nations to use energy-efficient technology. However, this type of technology can be expensive and add to the costs of production, which developing nations fear would slow their economic growth. Although the international community has tried to forge agreements, such as the Paris Climate Agreement, with developing nations to limit pollution and other damage to the environment, those efforts have not been widely successful. There is also inconsistent commitment to international climate change goals, which was illustrated by President Trump's withdrawal of the United States from the Paris Agreement in June 2017.

The United States has had more success pursuing domestic energy policies. Within the federal government, the EPA shares jurisdiction with the Department of Energy and the Department of Interior over federal energy and environmental policy, from regulating carbon emissions and auto fuel efficiency to granting leases to drill for oil and natural gas both on- and offshore of the continental United States. In rare instances, the Department of State might also be involved in environmental policy if it will have an international impact. We discuss one such case in this chapter (see Public Policy and the Environment: Keystone XL Pipeline). Once an agency has been created, it is responsible for policy implementation within its jurisdiction. When the federal government proposes a policy change in an issue area, whether independently or as a response to a new law passed by Congress, the agency with jurisdiction in that issue area issues regulations to guide implementation.

Domestic policy, such as health care, immigration, and environmental protection, has several important layers. Congress and the president enact laws, which are then implemented by the executive branch through the regulatory process. At the same time, state and local governments are also helping to implement federal policies, as well as put in place policies that fall under their own set of powers (see Chapter 3). There are advantages and disadvantages to this layering; on the one hand, layering acts as a gateway for a wide range of voices to be heard in the policy process, but on the other hand, layering can serve as a gate that stands in the way of quickly and efficiently addressing important policy issues.

Political Analytics

COVID-19 Pandemic in the United States

IN EARLY SPRING 2020, the United States saw its first cases of the coronavirus in Washington state. Cases rapidly extended to other communities in California and became widespread in New York City. As the White House, the Centers for Disease Control, and state-level agencies moved quickly to provide information to the public about the spread of the virus, precautions to take, and updates on treatments, Americans were provided with a lot of information, some of it difficult to comprehend. State and local governments and the media began updating the numbers of cases and deaths daily. Figure 16.5A shows a typical way a map of the United States was used to show the variation of reported cases across the states.

Although such maps are useful, there are considerations to make when using these types of data. First, the map shows the compilation number of reported cases by states and local communities. Not all of the fifty states used the same metrics when reporting cases or deaths. Such data

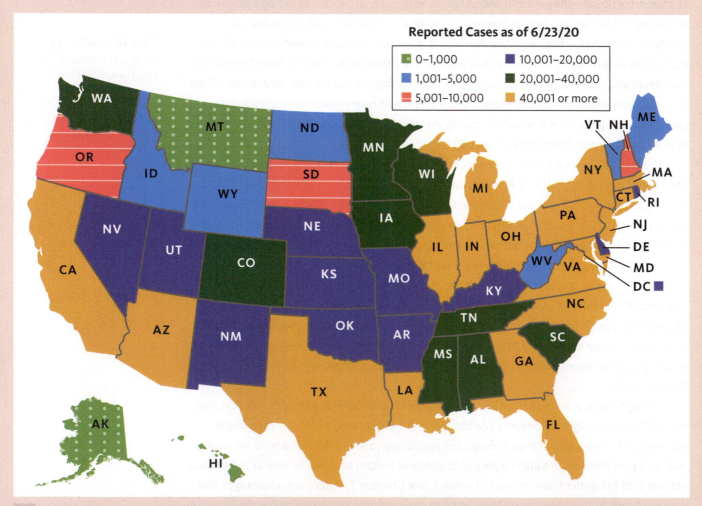

Figure 16.5A Cases by State

require also knowing the number of COVID-19 tests administered to the states' populations. Some states had robust testing while others had limited testing. So the number of cases was probably always underreported, but it is difficult to know by how much. Moreover, not all states are of equal population, which led some outlets to report the number of cases per 100,000 people in a state to allow for cross-state comparisons adjusted for population size.

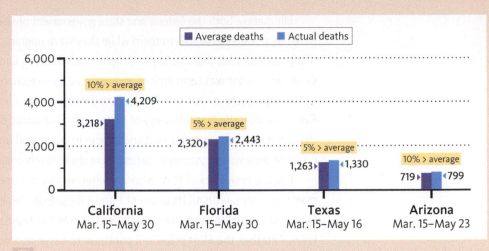

Figure 16.5B **Cases by State**

An alternative method of assessing the spread and mortality rate of the virus is to use the number of deaths in a particular time frame, such as March, and compare it to a state's average number of deaths over previous months of March. The result is an estimate of the number of deaths that may reasonably be attributed to the coronavirus (see Figure 16.5B).

Examine the figures and note the different information being provided by both.

Thinking Critically

1. There are many ways to assess the spread and death rate of COVID-19 in the United States. Which of the two graphics presented here provides information you find useful and why?

2. The graphics present data from the overall population. What types of demographic characteristics about populations would be important to examine?

A glaring example of this type of gate occurred in Flint, Michigan, where bureaucratic decision making and cost-cutting measures has posed a real danger to the residents in terms of the quality of their drinking and bathing water for nearly a decade. Flint is a city of approximately 99,000 residents, 42 percent of whom live in poverty.[52] In April 2014 city officials in Flint decided to use the Flint River as the main water source for the city, even though the water from the river would flow through potentially corrosive pipes.[53] City officials decided not to put corrosion control technology in place unless evidence emerged of contaminants in the water. Over the next two years, that is exactly what happened: Tests first showed bacteria, then corrosive elements, then toxic chemicals, and finally lead. In fact, samples of water taken from Flint showed nearly three times the limit recommended by the EPA, and the percentage of children found to have higher amounts of lead in their blood doubled.

The reaction among local and public officials to the revelations about the drinking and bathing water in Flint were mixed: Some officials denied they knew about the problem, others said the problem was not widespread or severe, and still others claimed that they had warned city officials but did not get a response. By October 2015, the city of Flint switched its water supply and officials stated that the proper corrosion controls were in place, but many of the old pipes in Flint were not replaced. In January 2016, then-governor Rick Snyder (R-MI) and President Obama declared a state of emergency at the state and federal levels.

Ultimately, both the federal and state government provided millions of dollars to Flint to make clean water available to them while they were upgrading their entire water system. Still, many residents felt that the improvements took too long and that public officials were negligent. Governor Snyder was term limited and replaced by Gretchen Whitmer (D-MI), who promised to keep the pressure on to hold officials accountable for the Flint water disaster. In October 2019, five years after the first discovery of issues with Flint water, the EPA issued regulations raising the standards for testing for lead and copper in water, and requiring states and localities to upgrade their water systems in cases where these levels are unacceptably high.[54]

For the residents of Flint who were harmed by pollutants in their water, the policy-making system, with all its oversight and safeguards, clearly failed them. And the case of Flint shows the limits of the government's power to regulate the environment at the local level. Whether the Flint crisis will continue to serve as a wakeup call to communities and the elected officials who govern them remains to be seen.

Economic Policy

LO 16-3 Explain how the federal government intervenes in the economy

Ever since the founding, Americans have debated whether and how the federal government should intervene in the economy. For the first 100 years of the nation's existence, the major source of government intervention in the economy was to impose taxes (known as tariffs) on goods imported from outside the country. Tariffs served as a way both to protect domestic industries and to raise revenues. But as the economy grew in the late 1800s, pressure mounted to regulate the growth of big business and to improve working conditions, which resulted in a series of laws dealing with antitrust (against big monopolies) to safety in the workplace. In the twentieth century, the federal income tax replaced tariffs as the key financing mechanism for federal government spending. The reality in today's world is that the government is heavily involved in the economy and that U.S. fiscal and monetary policy has a major impact in the national and international arena. The federal government intervenes in the economy to support economic development, regulate business practices, oversee banking and finance, and maintain a safety net of retirement, unemployment, and disability benefits.

Intervention in the Economy

Beginning with Theodore Roosevelt (1901–09), presidents have overseen the federal role in the nation's economy; some have wanted more intervention and some have wanted less. Republican presidents typically want to lower all taxes, a policy that provides less revenue to the federal government and subsequently decreases federal spending. Democratic presidents have typically wanted to cut taxes for individuals with lower incomes and to raise taxes on wealthier citizens to support federal programs. The key advisors to the president on economic policy are the Secretary of the Treasury, the National Economic Council, and the Council of Economic Advisers. The president also appoints the chairman of the Federal Reserve (discussed later in this section), which has a major role in monetary policy. The set of stakeholders in federal economic policy includes the president, Congress, business interests, and consumers (see Figure 16.6).

When the economy is weak, there is pressure on the president to take extraordinary steps to strengthen it. This is what President Franklin Roosevelt did during the Great Depression, what

President Obama did a little more a decade ago in response to the 2007–2009 recession, and what President Trump did in response to the COVID-19 economic crisis. Whether the economic impact of COVID-19 is termed a **recession**, typically defined as a downturn in economic activity, with declines in employment levels, income, retail spending, and industrial production, or a full blown depression, the power of the federal government to respond to these crises with stimulus packages has grown over time. When people lose jobs, consumer spending declines, forcing business and industry to cut back production and lay off workers, potentially leading to a vicious circle in which consumer spending declines even further, forcing businesses and industry to cut back production even more and lay off even more workers. From March 2020 to May 2020, the U.S. unemployment rate went from 4.4 percent to 13.3. percent, which meant that millions of workers lost their jobs.[55] As the effects of a lockdowns and social distancing began to be felt across the country, President Trump worked with Congress to pass a $2.2 trillion dollar stimulus package that provided extended unemployment, some paid sick leave, and sent $1,200 to millions of Americans whose household income was less than a total of $99,000.[56] It also provided billions of dollars to small business owners and larger companies that agreed to keep at least 80 percent of their employees on their payrolls. As of November 2020, President Trump and Congress had not enacted another stimulus and economic relief bills designed to aid individuals and businesses.

President Obama responded to the economic crisis by adopting a mixed strategy on taxes and spending. He continued President George W. Bush's program, which effectively bailed out banks, and he instituted a bailout program for the auto industry; the majority of those funds were paid back to the government with interest. Additionally, he worked with Congress to enact a nearly $800 billion stimulus bill that was a combination of spending increases favored by Democrats and tax credits (which amount to tax cuts) favored by Republicans to boost the economy. Because raising taxes during a recession is widely believed to have a negative impact on consumer spending and job growth, Obama and Congress extended tax cuts in 2010 and 2012. When President Trump took office in 2017, he made it a priority to pass a tax cut bill that provided large tax cuts to the wealthy and corporations with some modest tax relief for middle class income earners. At that time, the Republican Party controlled the House, Senate, and the White House. The Republicans lost control of the House in the 2018 midterm elections, although the tax cuts remained relatively popular. Although the bill promised to fuel additional job growth, which it did primarily in low tax states, it added $1 trillion dollar deficit for FY 2020.[57]

Just as there are specific stakeholders that often participate in the formation and implementation of economic policy, there are also specific tools that have been developed over time to achieve specific economic goals.

Fiscal Policy

Government can use fiscal policy to intervene in the economy through taxing and spending. Fiscal policy can also be used to manipulate the money supply to avoid recession.

Figure 16.6 Stakeholders in Federal Economic Policy

A diverse set of public and private organizations and individuals impact economic policy.

recession: *A period of time marked by successive quarters of lower economic output.*

Key Questions
How can the federal government intervene in the economy during periods of economic recession?

Public Policy and the Environment

Keystone XL Pipeline

Against the backdrop of higher energy costs, projects such as the Keystone XL oil pipeline, a Canadian-funded oil pipeline that would have run from Canada to the Texas coast, underscore the way in which federal policy has to balance the nation's demand for energy and employment against competing demands to live in a clean and safe environment. Energy projects such as the Keystone XL can act as a gateway for Americans today in terms of jobs, but it can be a gate against a future that ensures a clean environment in which to live and work. It served as an important example of the dynamics of domestic policy making because it involves the executive branch, Congress, interest groups, private industry, and even a foreign nation.

In 2008, the energy company TransCanada submitted an application to the State Department to build a 1,700-mile oil pipeline from Alberta, Canada, to Nederland, Texas[58] (see Figure 16.7). Because the project crossed over the border from a foreign nation, it fell under the jurisdiction of the U.S. State Department, which does not normally have a role in this policy area; the State Department required TransCanada to submit an application for a presidential permit.[59] The State Department also conducted a study for an environmental impact statement (EIS) to see if the pipeline would have any adverse environmental effects on the regions through which it would run. Although the State Department was designated as the lead agency for the review of the project, the EPA was also involved and reviewed the environmental impact of the project.[60]

Almost two years later, the State Department released a draft of its EIS, which stated that the construction and operation of the pipeline would have minimal environmental impacts. The State Department then solicited public comment on the

draft. By the time the opportunity for public comment closed, it had received thousands of public comments from interest groups and industry members on the proposal. In 2011, the State Department released its final EIS, which concluded that the project was in line with President Obama's environmental policies.[61]

Although the State Department gave the go-ahead for the project, the EPA and numerous environmental interest groups were not persuaded by the State Department's findings. Congress also reflected the division over

Figure 16.7 Keystone Pipeline Map

This map illustrates the proposed route of the Keystone XL Pipeline.

© Cengage 2018 Source: Laris Karklis/*The Washington Post*, http://www.washingtonpost.com/national/health-science/canadian-firm-to-push-ahead-with-part-of-keystone-pipeline/2012/02/27/gIQavJftdr_story.html/; for the state of Nebraska, http://www.montrealgazette.com/technology/route+Keystone+pipeline+proposed+through+Nebraska/6486974/story.html.

the pipeline, where representatives from both sides of the aisle struggled over the project and its merits. Proponents of the project saw it as key to economic growth in the United States, while opponents had serious concerns about the potential for environmental damage from a pipeline leak. The Republican majority in the House of Representatives wanted to push President Obama into making a final decision on the project, so, as part of a bill to extend the payroll tax cut (see Chapter 13), they attached a provision requiring that the president issue a decision within sixty days. Obama responded by denying TransCanada the permit to build the pipeline, citing inadequate information to gauge its full environmental impact. One major concern was the pipeline's proximity to the Sand Hills region that covers the Ogallala Aquifer, which provides most of the drinking and irrigation water for the Midwest. In response, TransCanada reapplied for the permit, proposing a route that avoided the Sand Hills region in Nebraska.[62]

Throughout the presidential permit process, numerous interest groups, including labor unions, environmental activists, Native American activists, and energy producers, stated their positions on the pipeline. In an interesting twist, labor and energy interest groups were allies, as both supported the construction of the pipeline. Environmental groups vigorously voiced their objections. In contrast, both the House and Senate passed resolutions calling for the approval of the pipeline. In fact, the amount of public response was so great that Obama announced in 2014 that he had to delay his final decision on the pipeline because the public comments on the project numbered in the millions, and the administration needed more time to consider all the views expressed.

Ultimately, on November 6, 2015, President Obama accepted the recommendation by the State Department to reject the application to build the Keystone XL pipeline. In March 2017, President Trump reversed President Obama and approved the application to build the pipeline, which was a significant step for proponents of it.[63] Initial construction began in March 2020 but less than a month later, a coalition of environmentalists and Native American activists sued to stop it due to threats to the water supply on tribal lands as well as violations of the Endangered Species Act; a federal court ruled in their favor and construction was temporarily halted.[64] In July 2020, the U.S. Supreme Court upheld a lower court ruling that blocked use of a federal drilling permit that was to be used by the Keystone Pipeline project, adding to existing delays.[64] The Keystone XL pipeline case illustrates many of the major components of policy making, from the private sector to the federal bureaucracy, Congress, interest groups, and finally the office of the president.

Construct Your Own Policy

1. Propose a policy review process for energy-related proposals that you believe is more efficient than current practice.
2. Suggest alternative routes for the delivery of oil from Canada that might have addressed environmentalists' concerns.

More spending or lower taxes increases the money supply, while lower spending or more taxes decreases the money supply. In times of severe economic crises, the president may support a policy of increasing the money supply to ward off a recession. Alternatively, an increase in prices can cause workers to demand raises. Higher wages will lead to even larger increases in prices, setting off inflation. In this case, the president may support a decrease in the money supply to ward off or reduce the extent of inflation. It also remains true in the American economic system that there is a business cycle, based on innovation, production, and consumer demand, that operates independently but simultaneous to the implementation of government economic policy. In other words, both the private and public sectors shape the direction of the economy.

Monetary Policy

Federal Reserve Board:
Independent regulatory commission that affects the money supply by setting the reserve requirements of member banks, establishing a discount rate for loans to member banks, and buying or selling government securities.

Key Questions

What roles do fiscal and monetary policy play in the economy?

The president is limited in his or her power to directly influence the nation's economic conditions because monetary policy is under the control of the **Federal Reserve Board**, an independent agency that serves as the nation's central bank, increasing or decreasing the money supply by changing the reserve requirements—the amount of cash reserves that banks must keep on hand. To control the flow of money in the economy, Congress created the Federal Reserve in 1913 as a system of twelve regional banks in one national banking system. The Federal Reserve System is led by a seven-member board of governors, each nominated by the president and confirmed by the Senate. Members serve fourteen-year terms, and the president selects the board chair, who serves a four-year term, with the option of reappointment. Janet Yellen was the first female chair of the Federal Reserve. President Trump did not reappoint her and instead replaced her with Jerome Powell.

When the Federal Reserve increases reserve requirements, banks have less money to lend, and the money supply decreases. This action tends to raise interest rates. When the Federal Reserve decreases reserve requirements, banks have more money to lend, and thus the money supply increases (see Table 16.2). This move tends to lower interest rates. The Federal Reserve Board also controls the money supply through the discount rate, which is the interest rate that the Federal Reserve charges other banks on loans. When the discount rate is lower, banks are not able to charge high interest rates on the money they lend to consumers and businesses.

Although the president can name people to the Federal Reserve, he or she cannot fire them if they promote monetary policy that differs from his policy preferences. His or her only power over them comes from the nomination process.

The power of the federal government to steer the economy has been debated since our nation's founding. In times of crisis, the president and Congress can enact programs that target specific problems, as in the case of the auto industry bailout and COVID-19 stimulus package. But more generally, it is the Federal Reserve that has a strong role in setting monetary policy by setting interest rates, which in turn controls the flow of money to businesses and individuals seeking to take out loans. In 2019 and 2020, the Federal Reserve lowered interest rates in response to fears of slowing economic growth. In 2020, the Federal Reserve made strategic purchases of U.S. Treasury bonds and mortgage securities to shore up financial markets. They also took the extraordinary

Table 16.2 Comparison of Fiscal and Monetary Policy

Type of Policy	Policy Maker	Action	Direct Effect	Effect on Money Supply
Fiscal	Congress, president	Increase spending or cut taxes	Consumers have more money to spend.	Increases
	Congress, president	Decrease spending or increase taxes	Consumers have less money to spend.	Decreases
Monetary	Federal Reserve Board	Increase reserve requirement	Banks have less money to loan.	Decreases
	Federal Reserve Board	Decrease reserve requirement	Banks have more money to loan.	Increases
	Federal Reserve Board	Increase the discount rate	Loans are more expensive.	Decreases
	Federal Reserve Board	Decrease the discount rate	Loans are less expensive.	Increases

step, with the permission of the Secretary of Treasury, of making nearly $2 trillion dollars available to banks and other financial institutions to make loans during the COVID-19 crisis.[66]

Trade Policy

International trade—the exchange of commerce with other nations—is also an integral component of our nation's economic policy. President Washington's Farewell Address in 1796 acknowledged the importance of international commerce to the new nation, and the Framers knew that trade with foreign nations was integral to its economic success and stability. Over time, the United States grew economically strong through innovation, exploitation of its vast natural resources, and an increasing population that expanded both its workforce and its consumer base. In the twentieth century, the United States built on its economic strength by becoming an innovator in intellectual and technical services. In the twenty-first century, trade remains an important gateway to economic, political, and cultural relationships with other nations, though in recent years the nation has begun to import more goods than it exports.

Protectionism Versus Free Trade.   Trade policy has long been aligned with foreign policy and has been used by the United States to export both capitalism and democracy. International trade policy is complex because each nation wants to negotiate deals that give its industries the greatest advantages either to sell their goods abroad or to be protected from cheaper imports from foreign nations. A policy that protects against foreign imported goods more than it promotes exports is known as **protectionist**, and a policy that strikes down barriers on imported foreign goods is known as **free trade**. A third and relatively recent policy, **fair trade**, encourages foreign trade as long as there are comparable working conditions and wages within the industries in the trading nations. Environmental regulation has also become increasingly important in trade negotiations. If one nation exploits its workers with long hours, unsafe conditions, environmental pollution, and low pay to produce and sell goods more cheaply than another, it violates fair trade practices. When a nation violates fair trade practices, individuals may boycott its products, or, more significantly, other nations may refuse to trade with it.

The president takes the lead in negotiating international trade agreements, either bilaterally (with one other country) or multilaterally through the office of the U.S. Trade Representative (USTR), an office created within the Executive Office of the President by President John F. Kennedy (1961–63) in 1963. The USTR is responsible for negotiating the terms of international trade agreements. To present a balanced position on behalf of the U.S. government, the USTR solicits information and feedback about the potential impact of the trade agreement from import- and export-related industries, cabinet departments, and members of Congress. Gathering such information is helpful not only in crafting an agreement that benefits U.S. industries but also in building the necessary support to get the trade agreement ratified by Congress.

During the late nineteenth and twentieth century, protectionist trade policies enabled U.S. industries to corner the consumer market and make

protectionist: *Policy designed to raise import barriers for goods that are domestically produced.*

free trade: *Policy designed to lower import barriers to encourage trade across nations.*

fair trade: *Policy designed to make sure that the working conditions are relatively equal in nations that trade with each other.*

Alex Wong/Getty Images News/Getty Images

Image 16.7   A number of Federal Reserve chairs have served multiple terms and under different presidents. Jerome Powell was appointed chair of the Federal Reserve in February 2018 by President Trump. He replaced Janet Yellen, who was the first female chair of the Federal Reserve. Although he clashed at times with President Trump's economic policies, he was widely considered a successful steward for the economy during the COVID-19 crisis.

Public Policy and the Economy

Federal Deficit and the Debt Ceiling

As we noted in Chapter 12, the federal deficit is the difference between the amount of money that the government takes in and the amount of money that it spends. When the federal government runs a deficit, it must borrow money to make up the shortfall. Consequently, the federal government pays interest on this borrowed money, and the combined amount of the borrowed money and the interest that accumulates over time constitutes the national debt.

There are two components to the federal debt: (1) public debt, which is the money that comes from issuing debt instruments, such as U.S. Treasury bonds, that investors buy with a promise of getting a set amount of interest on the bonds at a later date; and (2) intragovernment held debt, which is the amount of money that the federal government borrows from itself when it transfers money from one program to another or uses built-up reserves in one program as collateral for borrowing. The **debt ceiling** is a cap on the amount of money that Congress authorizes the president to borrow to pay the federal government's bills. Before 1917, there was no legal limit on the government's ability to issue such debt. However, to fund operations for World War I, Congress passed the Second Liberty Bond Act, which allows the federal government to issue longer-term debt as long as Congress issues its approval for doing so.[67] Today the president must ask to raise the debt ceiling and cannot do so without congressional approval.

Under President Obama, the issue of the debt ceiling became a major source of contention between the president and Congress. When President Obama first took office, he inherited a federal deficit of $1.4 trillion and a total national debt of $11.9 trillion dollars (see Figure 16.8); both were the cumulative effect of past presidential policy making, including the Bush tax cuts and the Iraq and Afghanistan wars. But during the first two years of the Obama administration, the national debt climbed to $13.5 trillion.[68] In the 2010 midterm congressional elections, the Tea Party movement became active within the Republican Party in order to strengthen the GOP's existing commitment to reduce taxes and federal spending. When the Republicans won control of the House of Representatives, those members who were elected with Tea Party support stayed adamant in their position against raising the debt ceiling. As noted in Chapter 12, the majority of those members were reelected in 2012, and again in 2014, and President Obama was reelected as well, which maintained divided party control between Congress and the presidency.

During Obama's two terms in office, the issue of the federal debt ceiling caused standoffs with Congress on two separate occasions. In 2011, President Obama proposed a "grand bargain" that would have cut the debt by $4 trillion over ten years with a combination of spending reductions and increased taxes. Republicans in the House rejected any plan that included tax increases. Eventually, the president, Senate leaders, and then-Speaker John Boehner agreed to raise the debt ceiling in exchange for cutting $900 billion over ten years from the federal budget.

In October 2013, a similar scenario occurred, but this time, the Republicans in the House tied all government spending to the debt ceiling and refused to act unless implementation of the ACA was delayed or repealed. The Senate was then controlled by the Democrats and supported the president's position to raise the debt ceiling with no strings attached. Still, the House GOP action resulted in a government shutdown that lasted sixteen days, and the United States came close to the brink of defaulting on its debt obligations.

When President Trump took office, the federal deficit had already started to increase slightly, but the economy was strong and unemployment was low. Under those conditions, governments usually do not cut taxes or engage in other stimulus activity. But Trump had campaigned on tax reform and worked with the GOP-controlled Congress to pass significant tax cuts at the end of 2017. Despite the

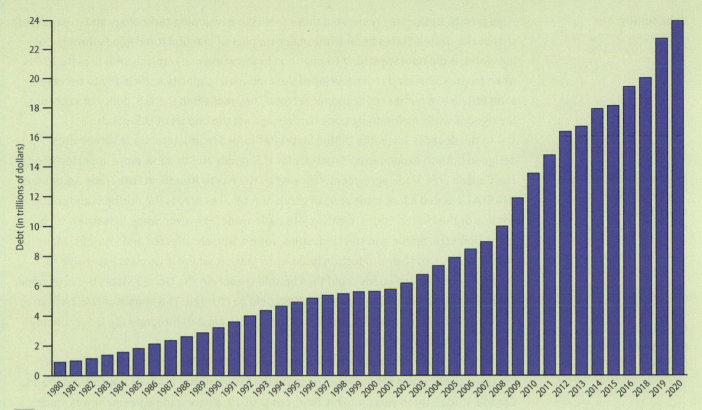

Figure 16.8 **U.S. National Debt, 1980–2020**

Over the past four decades, the national debt has grown much larger. In 1980 it was less than $2 trillion, but by 2020 it had risen to more than $23 trillion.

Source: The White House, Office of Management and Budget, Table 7.1, Federal Debt at the End of Year: 1940–2025, U.S. budget for FY 2022, https://www.whitehouse.gov/omb/historical-tables/.

fact that the bill was projected to raise annual deficits, it passed with overwhelming Republican support. At the end of 2018 and into 2019, Congress and the president once again fought over the budget and produced another government shutdown that lasted 35 days, which was the longest in history.[69] The Republicans had lost control of the House to the Democrats in the 2018 midterm elections, and they clashed with Trump over spending, especially for his southern border wall. The president relented and the government opened up, but the issue emerged again in the summer of 2019. This time, Congress and the president

were successful in striking a longer term deal which authorized some increased spending and eliminated the debt ceiling cap until 2021; as important, it did not include any provisions preventing the president from using Defense Department funds to build the southern border wall.[70]

Combined, these actions increased the deficit to nearly $1 trillion a year, which, until the COVID-19 crisis, had been the largest federal yearly deficit in modern history. With the COVID-19 stimulus spending, and much lower revenues coming into the federal government, the fiscal year 2020 deficit was projected to exceed $3 trillion.

Construct Your Own Policy

1. Devise a set of tax increases and budget cuts that you believe are fair and would reduce the federal deficit.
2. Create a mechanism for raising the federal debt ceiling that does not create conflict between Congress and the president.

huge profits. Businesses reinvested those profits in developing technology and in expanding so that the United States became the major supplier of manufactured goods throughout the world. It did not face strong competition in the world marketplace until the late 1980s, when Japan, China, and India developed their industrial capacity sufficiently to become competitive in a number of economic sectors. They replicated the U.S. policy of exporting their goods while maintaining trade barriers against the import of U.S. goods.

In the decades since, the United States has forged multilateral trade agreements designed both to expand export markets for U.S. goods and to allow more imported goods. The Canada Free Trade agreement, followed by the **North American Free Trade Agreement (NAFTA)**, created a free trade zone of goods and services across the northern and southern borders of the United States, creating jobs nationwide. However, some industries, such as the domestic textile and steel industries, were adversely affected and lost jobs. Many businesses moved their production facilities to Mexico, where it was less expensive to produce goods. These goods could then be sold cheaply in the United States because, under the free trade agreement, no import duties could be charged. The impact of NAFTA is an example of the consequences of policies that are designed to integrate the U.S. economy into the global world of trade.

When President Trump took office, he argued that NAFTA had negative effects on the U.S. economy and set out to renegotiate the terms of that trade deal with Mexico and Canada. It took three years into his term, but in 2019, a new trade agreement was stuck called the **United States-Mexico-Canada Agreement (USMCA)**, which updated the terms of the deal to address intellectual property rights, digital information flows, labor rights, and environmental protections.[71] Mexico ratified it in 2019, the United States ratified it in January 2020, and it was ratified by the Canadian government in March 2020.

In 2000, the United States normalized trade status with China, which reduced trade barriers and opened up Chinese markets to U.S. goods. In doing so, it also encouraged American producers of goods such as textiles, apparel, steel, and electronics to relocate their production facilities to China. More than two decades later, the United States has a very large trade imbalance with China: at the end of 2019, U.S. imports exceeded exports to China by $345.6 billion.[72] A large trade imbalance means that American consumers are buying far more goods made in China than Chinese consumers are buying goods made in the United States. During his presidency, Trump has stated that he believes the United States needs to take a more protectionist position in world trade. In 2018, Trump began imposing tariffs on imported goods from several major trade partners, including China, in an effort to reduce the trade imbalance by forcing China to reduce its tariffs and restrictions on imported U.S. goods, among other measures. By 2020, there had been some breakthroughs, but not all outstanding issues had been resolved.

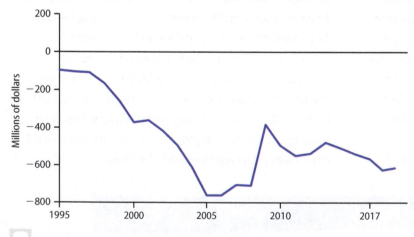

Figure 16.9 **U.S. Balance of Trade, 1995–2019**

The balance of trade is the difference between how much the United States imports from other countries and how much it exports to other countries. This graph shows the dollar value of all goods and services that the United States trades; negative numbers indicate that the country imports more than it exports.

Source: United States Census Bureau, Foreign Trade, accessed April 18, 2020, https://www.census.gov/foreign-trade/statistics/historical/gands.pdf.

Trade and International Economic Organizations.   In addition to the unilateral trade agreements that it has struck with other nations, the United States also participated in the General Agreement on Tariffs and Trade (GATT), which governed multinational trade agreements between 1948 and 1994. In 1994, during the eighth round of GATT, the **World Trade Organization (WTO)** was created to deal with the explosive expansion of the global trade community and to establish a single international organization with the authority to resolve trade disputes.[73] If one country claims that another country is engaged in unfair trading practices, it can bring its case to the WTO; each party to the dispute must abide by the WTO's ruling or face monetary fines and trade limitations. For example, in 2009, China imposed a ban on broiler products, which covers chicken, from the United States, and the United States lodged a formal complaint with the WTO citing unfair trade practices. The WTO formed a panel to resolve the issue.

It took nearly four years for the WTO to return a decision, and it ruled that China had violated fair trade practices and had to remove the barriers to imported chicken from the United States.[74] The slow pace of the WTO deliberation illustrates how an international organization can serve as a gate to efficient resolution of economic disputes. Entering the WTO was a major change in U.S. trade policy because it required the United States to relinquish its right to act unilaterally in trade disputes. At the same time, by agreeing to abide by WTO rulings, the United States gave assurance to foreign nations that it would respect international rules and would be a fair and reliable trading partner while expecting other nations to do the same.

Another significant development in international trade relations was the creation of the **European Union (EU)**, a major expansion of a preexisting European economic organization known as the European Community.[75] In June 2016, Great Britain held a referendum, known as Brexit, on whether to exit the EU, a decision that would have global trade and economic implications. It was narrowly approved by a vote of 52 percent to 48 percent. Because the sitting Prime Minister had opposed Brexit, he stepped down and was replaced by another member of his party. Great Britain officially left the EU on January 31, 2020, but is still negotiating many of the details of how it will conduct trade and employment practices with the countries that remain in the EU.[76]

Economic policy is an enormously complicated arena in which the U.S. government tries to implement policies that will encourage stability and growth. In the past two decades especially, continuous deficit spending and severe swings in the economy have created a large national debt and pressure to reduce the government's spending and its overall role in the economy. Moreover, the expansion of U.S. businesses around the world has created a highly interdependent global economy, where another nation's trade and monetary policies may have direct effects on the U.S. economy. Navigating this ever-changing economic arena continues to be one of the great challenges facing U.S. policy makers.

World Trade Organization (WTO): *International organization that considers and resolves trade disputes among member nations.*

European Union (EU): *Association of European nations formed to facilitate economic and political interactions across their borders.*

Foreign Policy

LO 16-4 Evaluate the effectiveness of U.S. foreign policy

The international arena in which the United States is positioned today is nothing like the world in which the Framers wrote the Constitution. Travel to Europe is now a matter of hours instead of months; communication with all parts of the world is instantaneous.

Key Questions

How has globalization changed the types of political challenges the United States must overcome?

Conflict, terrorism, disease and pandemics, as well as poverty are not just localized problems but are international in scope. In this section, we examine how the United States came to its position as global leader and discuss the constitutional gates and international conditions that constrain its actions. As we noted in Chapter 13, the conduct of foreign policy is the purview of the executive branch led by the president as commander in chief but with significant input from Congress; the Department of Defense, the Department of State, the Department of Homeland Security, and the National Security Agency all play vital roles in our foreign and military policy.

International Relations and U.S. Foreign Policy Goals

When the Framers wrote the Constitution, the United States, as a democracy, stood virtually alone in a world ruled by monarchs. Though independent and isolated by geography, the new nation was still vulnerable, and in its first years, it was caught up in European rivalries. In 1796, when he was leaving the presidency, George Washington (1789–97) warned against foreign entanglements: "The great rule of conduct for us in regard to foreign nations," he wrote in his Farewell Address, "is in extending our commercial relations, to have with them as little political connection as possible."[77] More than 200 years later, Washington's isolationist tendencies have been swamped by the evolution of **globalization**, which intertwines the fate of the United States with hostilities, health crises and epidemics such as the Ebola and COVID-19 viruses, and natural disasters and environmental degradation wherever they occur.

globalization: *The interconnectedness of nations around the world on economic, political, cultural, social, and military dimensions.*

With globalization, regional economies, societies, and cultures have become increasingly integrated through trade, capital investment, labor flows, migration, travel, and, most strikingly, the Internet and instantaneous communication (for example, Twitter). In one sense, these changes opened the economic and political gates that long kept nations apart. People are today interconnected on multiple levels. Citizens of China drink Coke and eat McDonald's hamburgers, and Americans wear clothing with "Made in China" on the label. Over the course of the late twentieth century and through today, developed nations have found it cheaper to manufacture goods in developing countries, and the proponents of free trade believe that it can be a gateway to more open and democratic societies in nations previously closed to outside influences. However, China has been in the global free trade community for two decades, and their society has not opened up politically to the extent that supporters of free trade would have desired or predicted.

The interdependence of the new globalized world might sound like a formula for peace, but in fact the connections are complex. Being connected does not mean sharing political systems and religions, or even cultures below the level of popular culture. The differences that do exist have intensified in the new global age and have produced political, social, and military conflict. America has objective strategic interests that it must protect, such as maintaining its energy supplies from abroad. But it also has a strong commitment to human rights and democratic principles of government, and sometimes these guiding principles clash. As a leading military, diplomatic, and economic power, the United States has to balance the need to preserve its own interests against the benefits that arise from working with other nations under an international framework of laws and policies. To recognize the challenges the United States faces in achieving its goals today, we must first understand the nature of the international system and how it evolved.

The Origins of U.S. Foreign Policy. The dawn of the twentieth century witnessed the first large-scale U.S. involvement in international conflicts on foreign soil with World War I (WWI). Prior to that, the United States had fought conflicts mostly within its contiguous geographic borders; in the late nineteenth century, the United States ventured into the Southern Hemisphere with the Spanish-American War, and annexed the Philippines. But full international involvement by the United States did not commence until WWI. In 1914, when WWI began in Europe, President Woodrow Wilson (1913–21) proclaimed neutrality, but German attacks on U.S. commercial shipping in international waters convinced him to change course. In asking for a declaration of war from Congress on April 2, 1917, Wilson argued, "The world must be made safe for democracy. Its peace must be planted upon the tested foundations of political liberty."[78]

Wilson had a vision for peace that inspired Americans and Europeans alike, and he took a leading role in writing the treaty that ended the war. One provision of the treaty created an international organization—called the League of Nations—that would help preserve the political independence of its members against aggressor nations. But in 1920, the Senate rejected the treaty and, with it, Wilson's vision of a role for America in the world. Politicians and voters alike feared that membership in the League of Nations would compromise the nation's sovereignty. WWI overturned old empires and established new nations. Despite President Wilson's efforts to engage the United States in international democracy building, the United States turned inward and adopted a policy of isolationism.

In Russia, a **Communist** revolution installed a political and economic system that used government management of the economy to prevent large concentrations of private wealth. A long-term goal of this system was economic security and equality for all citizens. The Communist Party was the only political party in the new Soviet Union, stifling virtually all dissent. In Germany, a new democracy struggled such that voters elected Adolf Hitler and the Nazi Party, who promised to restore Germany's economic and military power. Under Hitler's dictatorship, Germany became an aggressor once again, and in 1939, its invasion of Poland triggered World War II (WWII). In Asia, Japan had launched a similar course of aggression, and its air assault on Pearl Harbor on December 7, 1941, led President Franklin Delano Roosevelt (1933–45) to ask Congress for a declaration of war against Japan the next day (and against Germany and Italy on December 11, 1941, after those nations, in alliance with Japan, had declared war on the United States).

When WWII ended in 1945, Europe was on the brink of collapse. The United States emerged as a leading world power and could no longer sustain its isolationist policies. New weapons technologies, especially airpower, expanded the reach and level of destruction that one nation could impose on another. Like Wilson, Roosevelt envisioned a peace in which an international organization, stronger than the League of Nations, could prevent aggression and meet humanitarian needs. The **United Nations (UN)** was founded in April 1945, and Congress ratified U.S. membership in December. Its headquarters was built along the East River in New York City, and it became a gateway for nations to interact with each other and try to resolve disputes in a neutral environment.

Hopes for a peaceful world were shortly shattered, however, as rivalry between the United States with its Western democratic allies and the Soviet Union and Eastern

Image 16.8 Frequently residents of foreign nations complain about the "Americanization" of their food and culture, but at the same time, American businesses are very successful internationally. Here we see customers at a McDonald's in Beijing, China.

Communist: *Government management and ownership of key elements of a nation's economy.*

United Nations (UN): *Organization formed after World War II to mediate disputes among nations around the world.*

European states provoked a **Cold War**. As new nations emerged from the aftermath of the war, they were forced to align themselves with the forces of democracy or Communism. On March 12, 1947, President Harry Truman (1945–53) spoke to a joint session of Congress convened to consider a growing economic crisis in Greece. He clearly stated his belief that the economic stability of Greece was essential to keeping it from falling to the Communists. During this speech, Truman set forth the policy that the United States would take active steps to preserve democracy and contain Communism throughout the world, a policy that became known as the Truman Doctrine or the policy of containment.

For the next decades, U.S. efforts to contain Communism involved the nation in military interventions, most notably in Korea and Vietnam but also in the Middle East and Latin America. As we saw in Chapter 13, these military interventions were undertaken by the president in his role as commander in chief. Presidential power grew in accord with America's commitment to world leadership. In an age when atomic bomb capabilities called for split-second decisions, the president's authority to command military response went mostly unchallenged.

Beginning in 1989, facing enormous economic difficulties and organized political dissent, the Communist regimes of Eastern Europe began to fall, which was symbolically represented by the collapse of the Berlin Wall that separated East (Communist) and West (democratic) Germany. In 1991, the Soviet Union itself disintegrated into separate states, with the most powerful being Russia. The United States declared victory in the Cold War but subsequently faced the challenge of winning and keeping the peace.

The context for international relations at the end of the Cold War was vastly different from earlier eras. After that struggle ended, the old bipolar world of the two superpowers quickly became **multipolar**, with numerous centers of power competing for regional dominance and with numerous regional conflicts. Since the end of WWII, many nations in addition to Vietnam and Iran had gained independence from such former colonial powers as France and the United Kingdom. Some of these nations—India and Indonesia, for example—had risen to prominence by attempting to remain neutral in the superpower struggle, forming the nonaligned movement. Modernization in China gave that huge nation new international stature. In the Middle East, tensions between Israel and the Arab states went unresolved. In Africa, decolonization had created a patchwork of new states across tribal lines struggling against corruption, poverty, and disease. And in the old Soviet bloc, especially in Central Asia, new states struggled to suppress regional, religious, and ethnic hostilities and to resist Russian dominance. Cold War tensions still resonate when issues of sovereignty emerge, as they did with the Russian takeover of the Crimean peninsula, which was part of the country of Ukraine. In that case, the majority of residents in Crimea were of Russian descent and welcomed the aggressive takeover by the Putin-led government. Western nations responded by imposing economic sanctions on Russia, but tensions only escalated when Russian sympathizers in eastern Ukraine waged war against the government. Russia kept control of Crimea, but as of 2020, simmering tensions still existed in eastern Ukraine. In 2020, President Zelensky of Ukraine declared February 26 as a memorial day to mark Russia's annexation of Crimea.[79] Tensions between Russia and the United States worsened with accusations of Russian interference in the 2016 presidential race at the center of the first years of the Trump presidency. In Trump's third and fourth years of his presidency, he was impeached but not convicted of charges of abusing power and obstructing Congress for withholding U.S. military aid to Ukraine unless they initiated an investigation Joe Biden, who was at the time viewed as one of Trump's possible 2020 presidential opponents.

Foreign Policy Tools

Nations have a wide array of policy tools available to them. Some involve cooperation through bilateral or multilateral treaties, diplomatic relations, and aid; others entail conflict through the use of force or the threat of military action. In this section, we will examine how the United States uses these tools.

Military Action.   The president, as commander in chief, has always made the decision to engage in military action. Although Congress has formally declared war only five times, U.S. troops have been sent into conflicts and potential conflicts more than 280 times since the beginning of the nation.[80] Today, in making the decision to engage in military action, the president is heavily influenced by the recommendations of the secretary of defense, the national security adviser, and the director of the Central Intelligence Agency (CIA).

For military missions that are publicized, not secret, a president usually enjoys widespread support if the mission can be clearly tied to preserving national security. In cases in which the United States is attacked on its own soil, support for a military response is even higher. This so-called **rally-around-the-flag effect** is a surge in patriotic sentiment that translates into presidential popularity.[81] For example, when President George H. W. Bush commenced the first Gulf War, his approval ratings shot up to 89 percent.[82] His son, President George W. Bush, experienced a similar spike in popularity after 9/11; his job approval ratings went from 52 percent to 90 percent, and they remained above 70 percent for almost an entire year.[83]

The public's influence on the president's decision to engage in military action is always limited because the amount of information available to the public is purposely restricted, both to ensure the safety of the troops involved and to preserve military advantages in conflict. Simply put, the president and his military advisers have access to far greater amounts of information than does the average citizen, and in turn, the average citizen expects the president to act on this information in a way that preserves national security. Even when Congress debates sending troops or funding military action, most classified information is held in secret and not revealed to the public (but see Chapter 4, Civil Liberties, on the Snowden National Security Agency revelations). The fundamental imbalance of information held by the government and what the general public understands poses a major problem for the assumptions of a democracy because the people cannot hold the government fully accountable if they are not fully informed. Nevertheless, when a president decides to send troops, he or she has to anticipate public reaction and hope that the public maintains its trust and confidence in his decision to take such action.

The twenty-first century has ushered in new weaponry and new levels of violence committed by nations and **nonstate actors**, such as terrorist groups who take up violence against civilians as a means of attacking the United States and other Western nations.

The Bush administration used this new reality to justify military action against the Taliban regime in Afghanistan. President George W. Bush went one step further to launch a preemptive attack—that is, an attack prior to an act of aggression by another—against Iraq in 2003 to remove Saddam Hussein from power and dismantle alleged weapons of mass destruction that might be used against the United States and its allies (see Chapter 13 for more on the Iraq and Afghanistan wars). In invading Afghanistan and Iraq, Bush was trying to leverage the full strength of the U.S. military to combat terrorism.

However, many critics argue that in conflicts between a state and nonstate actors, traditional military weapons and strategies are ineffective, and new tools, such as

rally-around-the-flag effect: *Surge of public support for the president in times of international crisis.*

> ## Key Questions
> How does the emergence of nonstate actors change the nature of how war is defined?

nonstate actors: *Individuals or groups that do not represent any specific national government and may take action across borders.*

surveillance, intelligence gathering and analysis, and the use of unmanned drones, are the only way to prevent future attacks. This is perceived to be particularly true of efforts to combat terrorist groups such as ISIS and Boko Haram. As such, the policy infrastructure dedicated to addressing terrorism has grown dramatically over the past decade, with a greater reliance on cooperation among the Department of Homeland Security (see Chapter 14), Department of Defense, Department of Justice, and the president's National Security Council. Coordinating across such a vast portion of the federal government can produce both gates and gateways to effective antiterrorism policies, both at home and abroad (see Chapter 4 and Chapter 6, Public Opinion, for more on U.S. antiterrorism policy).

Anti-Nuclear Proliferation Measures. Compounding the challenges of fighting terrorism is the fear of nuclear proliferation among established nations and nonstate terrorist groups. In addition to the United States and Russia, the United Kingdom, France, China, India, North Korea, Pakistan, and Israel have nuclear capabilities. Because India and Pakistan have experienced border clashes and are generally unfriendly toward each other, their possession of nuclear weapons poses a threat to the stability of Southeast Asia. Most recently, the United States has focused intense concern on nuclear weapons development in Iran and North Korea (see Figure 16.10).

As the preeminent international peacekeeping organization, the United Nations has long led efforts to curb nuclear proliferation through treaties that would ban the testing of nuclear weapons and set up an official verification system whereby countries would be regularly inspected to make sure they were not developing nuclear capabilities. The Nuclear Non-Proliferation Treaty that went into effect in 1970 was designed to discourage nations from developing nuclear weapons technology; currently, 191 nations are signatories.[84] The key element of this treaty is the use of the International Atomic Energy Agency (IAEA) to monitor and inspect nations' weapons capability. The United States and the rest of the international community rely on this organization and its powers to monitor nuclear facility development in countries that do not currently have nuclear weapons, such as Iran.

To that end, President Obama instructed his Secretary of State, John Kerry, to participate in multilateral negotiations (which included China, France, Germany, the Russian Federation, and Great Britain) with Iran to limit that country's progress toward acquiring a nuclear weapon. In July 2015, the United States and these other nations agreed to a Joint Comprehensive Plan of Action that required Iran to stop its progress toward developing a nuclear bomb for at least ten years and agree to regular inspections by the IAEA. Contingent on Iran's compliance and

Figure 16.10 Monitoring Nuclear Facilities in North Korea

North Korea has been developing the capability to produce nuclear weapons and is believed to have conducted active tests of long range missiles to carry such weapons. This figure shows the estimated North Korean capability as of 2018, although international inspectors are not able to inspect any facilities in North Korea so an accurate assessment of their nuclear capability is hard to confirm.

Source: James Martin Center for Nonproliferation Studies; Nuclear Threat Initiatives. Created by CNS; Funded by NTI cooperation, the United Nations agreed to lift existing sanctions on Iran, which enabled it to participate in the world economic arena and gain access to funds that had been frozen by other nations.[85] In 2016, the IAEA certified that Iran had taken the necessary first steps to limit its progress toward a nuclear bomb, and as a result, some sanctions were lifted. However, in his comments on the Iran deal at that time, President Obama reiterated that any violation of the agreement on Iran's part would result on an immediate reimposition of the sanctions.[86] Supporters of the Iran deal argued that keeping nuclear weapons out of Iran would make the Middle East more stable, but opponents warned that allowing Iran access to its previously frozen money, and allowing it to sell oil, would only make it more powerful in the region. In 2018, President Trump withdrew from the Iran deal, decertifying Iran's compliance and reimposing the sanctions that were lifted under Obama. By November 2020, it appeared that Iran had amassed enough uranium to achieve active nuclear capability but had allowed IAEA inspectors to visit several sites associated with their nuclear program.[87]

Image 16.9 A number of U.S.-based organizations provide aid to individuals in need all around the world. Here workers with the U.S. Agency for International Development (USAID) help administer assistance to Sudanese refugees.

Diplomacy and Humanitarian Assistance.

In addition to military actions, another cornerstone of U.S. foreign policy is diplomacy. The Department of State is responsible for formulating foreign policy using nonmilitary methods; these efforts are conducted by diplomatic personnel in U.S. missions, consulates, and embassies around the world. There are also agencies within the Department of State that oversee a key component of our foreign policy—the provision of humanitarian assistance. The interdependence of nations today provides an opportunity for Americans, from the average citizen to the president, to participate on a wider level and improve living conditions everywhere. A world with more stable nations that treat their citizens equally and with dignity benefits the United States because it means that fewer internal conflicts will emerge that warrant military intervention. Governmental and nongovernmental organizations that provide funds for economic, health, and educational development provide an avenue for the U.S. government, groups, and individual citizens to take an active role in international life.

For example, within the U.S. federal government, the U.S. Agency for International Development (USAID) is an independent agency with the mission of providing training, education, and materials to developing nations and of promoting democracy.[88] It is led by an administrator appointed by the president who works closely with other federal departments, including the Department of State, on international aid issues. USAID was created by President John F. Kennedy in 1961 as part of the Foreign Assistance Act. Today its activities include disaster relief, child health and nutrition, and disease treatment and prevention. For example, USAID disaster assistance response teams were very involved in fighting the Ebola virus in West Africa. In fiscal year 2020, USAID had an operating budget of $1.66 billion.[89]

In addition to unilaterally promoting economic development, the United States is also a member of the World Bank and the International Monetary Fund, two global economic organizations. The **World Bank** was founded in 1944 as an international aid and reconstruction organization to help rebuild nations that had been badly damaged during WWII.[90] Today it has 189 members, known as shareholders, and five divisions that work together to provide low-interest loans, grants, and investment capital to build and improve infrastructure and alleviate poverty.

> ### Key Questions
> What goals can the United States accomplish through humanitarian aid?

> **World Bank:** *International organization that distributes grants and low-income loans in developing countries.*

Public Policy and International Relations

Promotion of Democracy

President Woodrow Wilson's idea was that the United States should make the world "safe for democracy," and President Truman's view was that the United States should intervene militarily to promote and defend against Communist takeovers. Truman's approach drew strength from the theory of "democratic peace," which holds that the world is a safer place if nations are democratic. The core contention is that democracies, reflecting the will of the people, have almost never gone to war against other each other.[91] The public's desire for peace simply makes that outcome rare.

The federal government attempts to export democratic values through diplomatic and cultural programs. The Voice of America broadcasts news and programming in more than forty different languages across the world and cooperates with private organizations, such as Radio Free Asia, that provide a forum for democratic activists in Myanmar, China, and other nondemocratic states. American interest groups and nonprofit organizations also promote democracy abroad. Freedom House supports nonviolent civil initiatives in societies where freedom is denied or threatened. Since 1972, the organization has issued reports on every country around the world, classifying countries as free, partially free, or not free based on a freedom index that takes into account the electoral process, civil liberties, and human rights (see Figure 16.11).

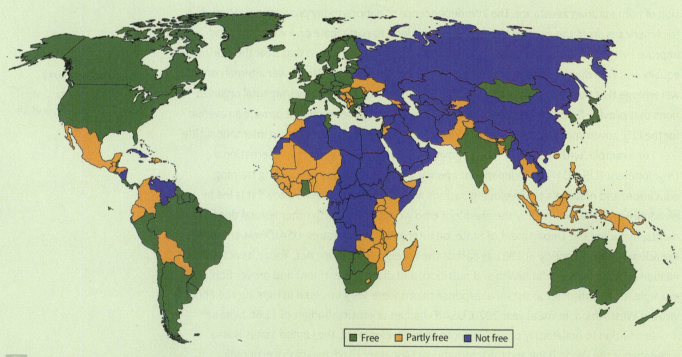

Free   Partly free   Not free

Figure 16.11   Freedom House Map

Freedom House is an organization that monitors freedom around the world. It produced this map to illustrate which countries were free, partly free, and not free as of 2020.

Source: Freedom House, Global Freedom Status, accessed April 21, 2020, https://freedomhouse.org/explore-the-map?type=fiw&year=2020.

Today, the question of what is justified in the name of preserving and promoting the American form of democracy remains unresolved, especially in the face of old and new conflicts in nations such as Iraq and Syria where internal forces are battling for control of their governments. President Trump argued that it is hard to make the case to the American people that direct U.S. intervention is necessary in distant regions with long histories of conflict, such as the Middle East. He pulled back the U.S. role in international conflicts and institutions based on the belief that many countries around the world no longer needed U.S. assistance and that they had to take more of a role in their own safety and protection. This was a controversial position and proved to be an obstacle to international cooperation in fighting the COVID-19 pandemic in 2020. For example, President Trump suspended U.S. payments and promised to withdraw the U.S. from the World Health Organization (WHO) amid complaints that it did not adequately assess the crisis and give countries sufficient warning about it.

Construct Your Own Policy

1. Outline guidelines for active U.S. engagement in foreign conflicts.
2. Devise a policy that only allows peaceful or nonmilitary U.S. involvement in promoting democracy.

The United States is the largest shareholder in the World Bank and consequently has leadership responsibilities; the president nominates the head of the bank, who serves a five-year renewable term.[92] The World Bank funds specific projects to improve transportation, provide clean water, build energy utilities, modernize medical care, initiate crop development programs, and provide start-up money for new businesses in poor and developing countries. In fiscal year 2019, the World Bank provided $49.39 billion in grants, loans, and investment capital to nations around the world.[93]

The **International Monetary Fund (IMF)** was created alongside the World Bank in 1945 with a different mission. The IMF focuses on preserving economic stability, including currency values, among nations and makes short-term loans to nations that cannot balance their budgets or need immediate funds.[94] The IMF also works with nations to try to reduce their government debt by renegotiating loans or by providing loans on better terms. The IMF has the same set of members as the World Bank, and each member makes a financial contribution to the fund based on its share of the global economy. The IMF has a board of governors, which includes a governor from each member nation, but the daily operations of the fund are overseen by a managing director and a twenty-four-member executive board. In contrast to its role in the World Bank, the United States does not play a prominent role in directing IMF operations and does not nominate the managing director.

International Monetary Fund (IMF): *International organization that works to stabilize currency values and government debt for nations in economic difficulty.*

However, the United States pays the largest single share (17.5 percent) of the IMF's fund, so it wields significant influence over lending decisions. In 2020, the IMF had the capacity to make nearly $1 trillion available to countries and businesses all over the world in various forms of lending arrangements.[95]

Holding Steady or Changing Course?

Presidential elections can be thought of as referendums on the incumbent president's party policies. In 2016, Democratic nominee Hillary Clinton promised to continue the policies of Barack Obama's presidency in both the economic and foreign spheres as well as to preserve Obamacare. Republican nominee Donald Trump promised to change many of Obama's policies, including reforming or repealing Obamacare, changing U.S. positions on military interventions, reworking the NATO alliance, altering trade policies to protect U.S. manufacturing industries, and strengthening border security. Voters had a stark contrast between the two candidates in terms of how they would each have upheld or reversed the White House policies of the previous eight years. Although Clinton won the popular vote by several million votes, Trump won the Electoral College.

Trump crafted his campaign around the idea that he was a businessman who knew how to bring back jobs across many sectors of the economy. Despite the fact that Trump did not provide specific proposals or policy suggestions to show how he would strengthen the U.S. economy, voters responded to his personal style as a leader who would produce better policies for them. It was not surprising that his message resonated with a significant portion of the electorate who believe that the policy-making process has gotten too big and inefficient to serve the average American. Revelations such as lead poisoning in Flint, Michigan, also provided examples of government failure of the type that Trump promised to fix if elected.

Since taking office, President Trump has used his executive powers to reverse a number of Obama-era regulations. He has also passed a large tax cut and signed a spending bill that increased the deficit and the debt limit. On the military and diplomatic front, he has not dramatically changed the U.S. positions from those of the Obama era. He has used tougher language in his tweets and speeches, but as of 2018, policies in these areas remained much the same as under his predecessor. Voters typically use the midterm elections to register approval or disapproval of the incumbent president and majority party in Congress. In 2018, voters sent Trump a mixed message by electing a majority of Democrats to the House and keeping the Senate under Republican control.

In 2020, the electoral setting was quite different for Trump in that he was a sitting incumbent president who was judged based on his record while in office, as well as the promises he made for his second term. The economy, which Trump had promised to improve in 2016, and had largely been credited with strong improvements until the COVID-19 pandemic, was once again in need of repair. In that way, Trump was judged on both his handling of the pandemic itself, and his efforts at building a strong economic recovery.

His challenger in 2020 was Joe Biden, who had served as U.S. senator and vice president of the United States with President Obama. Biden centered his campaign around his economic experience dealing with the 2008–2010 recession and his leadership in international affairs as vice president. He emphasized the fact that he could deal effectively with public health crises and international affairs, and improve the economy. Biden chose Senator Kamala Harris (D-CA) who is Black and South Asian, and who was the third female vice presidential nominee after Geraldine Ferraro (D) in 1984 and Sarah Palin (R) in 2008. Ultimately, Biden's campaign strategy paid off in a victory over Donald Trump in both the popular vote and the Electoral College vote. Senator Harris became the first female, and person of color, to be elected vice president.

The United States supports organizations that send individuals to foreign nations for peacekeeping, educational, and cultural purposes. The **Peace Corps** is perhaps the best known of these organizations. The Peace Corps was established in 1961; since then, more than 240,000 U.S. citizen volunteers have lived and worked in seventy-six countries all over the world.[96] The mission of the Peace Corps is to help train citizens of other nations in essential skills, establish communication about Americans with other nations, and bring more knowledge about foreign peoples back to America through the volunteers. Today the Peace Corps operates on a budget of $410.5 million, and it still attracts recent college graduates and others who work in wide-ranging fields, including teaching, agriculture, HIV/AIDS prevention, medicine, engineering, communications, environmental conservation, and construction.[97] The model of the Peace Corps has spurred the creation of domestic volunteer organizations such as AmeriCorps and Teach for America, which operate within the United States but pursue similar goals of education and economic development in underserved areas. During the COVID-19 pandemic in 2020, the U.S. Peace Corps was forced to take the unprecedented step of recalling all of its volunteers back to their home bases.

However, the fact that nations are more connected to each other in our global world does not mean that they share political systems, religions, or cultures. The differences that do exist have come into the forefront through regime change in recent years, which has resulted in political, social, and military conflict. The scope of U.S. involvement in international relations is decided by each presidential administration, in consultation with Congress; in that way, every presidential election is a gateway through which the American voters have the opportunity to render their opinions on whether to reset the boundaries of engagement.

Peace Corps: *U.S. government-funded organization that sends individuals on educational and cultural missions around the world.*

Public Policy and Democracy

Public policy covers a lot of territory in the language of American politics. It is essentially the set of outputs by federal, state, and local governments that address the interests and opinions of citizens. In this chapter, we have presented an overview of the federal regulatory system that serves as the main vehicle to implement the laws that Congress and the president enact. Once a law is passed, the executive branch produces a set of guidelines for how the law will work, and the public has a chance to comment on those regulations before they are finally put into place.

The three broad policy areas discussed in this chapter—domestic, economic, and foreign—all differ in the ways that policy outcomes can be directly controlled by policy makers. In domestic policy, our federal system of government has expanded over the past century to provide direct and indirect assistance to individuals in the area of income security, food security, housing, and health care. Our system of federalism allows states some leeway in how they implement federal law, especially when the policy overlaps with areas that are solely controlled by the states. As we have seen during the COVID-19 pandemic, states have significant leeway to diverge from the federal government in times of crisis.

In the economic sphere, the president, Congress, and the Federal Reserve all have a role to play in how much money the government spends and how cheaply consumers can borrow money. But the independent business cycle also has a strong impact on whether those policies succeed in contributing to economic growth and stability.

In the area of foreign policy, the United States has always had to balance its own principles regarding human rights and freedoms with its military and economic self-interest around the world. Also, military and humanitarian crises emerge frequently and fall out of direct U.S. control; however, the United States is still faced with the choice of whether to intervene and to what extent. As events in Ukraine, Syria, and North Korea, have shown, choosing the right policy is no easy task.

At times, it seems that there are more gates to influencing public policy in our system of government than there are gateways. Policy makers can be well-intentioned and sincerely interested in reflecting the interests and concerns of the majority of the people, but the process itself can be slower and less efficient than most of us would like. The policy-making process is complicated because it involves elected officials in multiple branches of government at all levels (federal, state, and local), the business community, interest groups, and private citizens who choose to make their opinions heard. Our system has about as much participation as James Madison would have expected; the question remains as to whether it is enough to address the pressing needs of the twenty-first century.

Chapter Review

Key Terms

Clean Air Act (p. 606). What role does the Clean Air Act play in U.S. environmental policy history?

Clean Water Act (p. 606). What role does the Clean Water Act play in keeping our drinking water safe?

Cold War (1946–91) (p. 622). What were the causes of the beginning and end of the Cold War?

Communist (p. 621). What is a Communist regime?

debt ceiling (p. 616) What is the relationship between the debt ceiling and the federal deficit?

entitlement programs (p. 597). What is the definition of an entitlement program?

European Union (p. 619). What is the European Union, and what role does it play in international economics?

fair trade (p. 615). How does fair trade try to promote economic equality around the world?

Federal Register (p. 593). Where are all official federal government regulations published?

Federal Reserve Board (p. 614). When was the Federal Reserve created, and what does it do?

free trade (p. 615). What is the definition of free trade?

globalization (p. 620). How has globalization emerged as an international process over time?

International Monetary Fund (IMF) (p. 627). How does the IMF help stabilize nations that are in economic difficulty?

Medicaid (p. 597). Who is eligible for Medicaid, and what does it do?

Medicare (p. 597). Who is typically served through the Medicare program?

multipolar (p. 622). What does it mean to have a multipolar world?

NAFTA (p. 618). How did NAFTA affect trade among Canada, the United States, and Mexico?

nonstate actors (p. 623). How do nonstate actors complicate international peacemaking efforts?

Peace Corps (p. 629). When and why was the Peace Corps created?

policy agenda (p. 591). How do issues get on the policy agenda?

policy diffusion (p. 594). How do policy ideas spread across states?

policy enactment (p. 591). What does it mean when a policy is enacted?

policy evaluation (p. 591). What is the role of evaluation in the policy process?

policy formulation (p. 591). How does formulation work as the third step in the policy-making process?

policy implementation (p. 591). How does the executive branch implement public policy?

problem identification (p. 591). How does identification work as the first step in the policy-making process?

protectionist (p. 615). Who benefits from protectionist trade policy?

public policy (p. 590). Define public policy.

rally-around-the-flag effect (p. 623). Why do citizens tend to increase their support for government when facing a military threat?

recession (p. 611). How did the government react when the economy went into a recession in 2007–2008?

regulations (p. 593). How do regulations help government officials and individuals follow federal law?

regulatory process (p. 592). How would you describe the role of the regulatory process in our public policy system?

Social Security (p. 596). How is Social Security funded?

United Nations (p. 621). When and why was the United Nations created?

USMCA (p. 618). Why did President Trump replace NAFTA with a new trade agreement between the United States, Canada, and Mexico?

World Bank (p. 625). What function does the World Bank serve in international economic development?

World Trade Organization (WTO) (p. 619). When was the WTO created and why?

Learning Outcomes: What You Need to...

Know	Test Yourself	Participate
LO 16-1 Outline the steps in the policy-making process		
The path from idea to a policy involves six key steps. First a problem has to be identified, then it has to be on the congressional and executive agenda, then it has to be formulated into a policy according to federal guidelines, then it has to be enacted into law, then it has to be implemented (put into practice), and finally it has to be evaluated to see if it is accomplishing its stated goals.	• Describe how an idea becomes a policy proposal. • Identify the three key parts of the regulatory process. • Explain how the judiciary can be used to block implementation of policy. • Outline the role of state governments in implementing federal policies.	• Evaluate how the average citizen can get an idea on the policy agenda. • Design a way to streamline policy implementation.
LO 16-2 Identify the key federal programs that make up domestic policy		
The federal government oversees a wide range of programs designed to address the income, health, and environmental safety of its citizens. These programs include Social Security, Medicaid, Medicare, Temporary Aid to Needy Families, Unemployment Compensation, and the Affordable Care Act. The federal government also takes responsibility for ensuring that citizens have clean air and clean water. Immigration is also a responsibility of the federal government, both to regulate the documented process and to address the situations of longtime undocumented residents.	• Describe what an entitlement program is, and identify two key programs that meet this description. • Explain the costs and benefits of the Affordable Care Act in terms of domestic policy. • Evaluate federal immigration policy. • Identify the key agency designated to oversee environmental protection.	• Devise a way of controlling the costs of entitlement programs. • Explain how you would improve the Affordable Care Act. • Create a new system of immigration, and state whether you would include remedies for undocumented residents. • Propose two steps that individual citizens could take to reduce carbon emissions.

Know	Test Yourself	Participate

LO 16-3   Explain how the federal government intervenes in the economy

The federal government intervenes in the economy through its fiscal, monetary, and trade policy. The federal government has the constitutional power to impose taxes to raise revenues, and the power to spend those revenues for the general welfare. The balancing of taxing and spending is known as fiscal policy. Monetary policy is not directly controlled by the federal government but rather by the Federal Reserve, which is a private/public banking institution that controls the flow of money by raising or lowering interest rates. The president appoints the chairman of the Federal Reserve. Trade policy uses a combination of tariffs and trade agreements with individual nations and trading blocs to sell U.S. goods abroad and maintain fair competition between U.S. domestically produced and imported goods.

- Explain the relationship between federal taxes and the federal deficit.
- Describe the level of control that the federal government has over the Federal Reserve.
- Explain why trade agreements are so important for the U.S. economy.

- Propose a strategy for reducing the federal deficit.
- Devise a means of giving the average citizen more control over the Federal Reserve.
- Write a trade agreement with China that opens up new markets for U.S. goods but also protects existing U.S. industries.

LO 16-4   Evaluate the effectiveness of U.S. foreign policy

U.S. foreign policy has undergone tremendous change since the beginning of the twentieth century. The United States first became engaged in global military conflict in World War I, and then became involved in World War II, the Korean War, the Vietnam War, the Gulf War, and at the start of the twenty-first century, wars in Iraq and Afghanistan. Given the financial and human costs of the wars in Iraq and Afghanistan, Americans have begun to question the effectiveness of military intervention, and U.S. foreign policy has shifted toward relying more on economic sanctions, international agencies, and when necessary the use of unmanned drones to engage in targeted actions against perceived enemies.

- Describe the evolution of U.S. foreign policy over the past 100 years.
- Explain the limitations of military action as a foreign policy tool.
- Evaluate the effectiveness of U.S. efforts to limit the spread of nuclear weapons.
- Identify two key international agencies that the United States works with to engage in diplomacy and address humanitarian concerns.

- Which nation do you believe is more important strategically, China or Russia?
- Devise a way of reducing the U.S. military role in conflict around the world while at the same time fighting human rights abuses.
- State whether and why you would increase U.S. reliance on the United Nations as an international peace-keeping organization in order to reduce military engagement in foreign conflicts.

APPENDIX A

The Declaration of Independence

In Congress, July 4, 1776

The Unanimous Declaration of the Thirteen United States of America

When, in the course of human events, it becomes necessary for one people to dissolve the political bands which have connected them with another, and to assume, among the powers of the earth, the separate and equal station to which the laws of nature and of nature's God entitle them, a decent respect to the opinions of mankind requires that they should declare the causes which impel them to the separation.

We hold these truths to be self-evident: That all men are created equal; that they are endowed by their Creator with certain unalienable rights; that among these are life, liberty, and the pursuit of happiness; that, to secure these rights, governments are instituted among men, deriving their just powers from the consent of the governed; that whenever any form of government becomes destructive of these ends, it is the right of the people to alter or to abolish it, and to institute new government, laying its foundation on such principles, and organizing its powers in such form, as to them shall seem most likely to effect their safety and happiness. Prudence, indeed, will dictate that governments long established should not be changed for light and transient causes; and accordingly all experience hath shown that mankind are more disposed to suffer, while evils are sufferable, than to right themselves by abolishing the forms to which they are accustomed. But when a long train of abuses and usurpations, pursuing invariably the same object, evinces a design to reduce them under absolute despotism, it is their right, it is their duty, to throw off such government, and to provide new guards for their future security. Such has been the patient sufferance of these colonies; and such is now the necessity which constrains them to alter their former systems of government. The history of the present King of Great Britain is a history of repeated injuries and usurpations, all having in direct object the establishment of an absolute tyranny over these states. To prove this, let facts be submitted to a candid world.

He has refused to assent to laws, the most wholesome and necessary for the public good.

He has forbidden his governors to pass laws of immediate and pressing importance, unless suspended in their operation till his assent should be obtained; and, when so suspended, he has utterly neglected to attend to them.

He has refused to pass other laws for the accommodation of large districts of people, unless those people would relinquish the right of representation in the legislature, a right inestimable to them, and formidable to tyrants only.

He has called together legislative bodies at places unusual, uncomfortable, and distant from the depository of their public records, for the sole purpose of fatiguing them into compliance with his measures.

He has dissolved representative houses repeatedly, for opposing, with manly firmness, his invasions on the rights of the people.

He has refused for a long time, after such dissolutions, to cause others to be elected; whereby the legislative powers, incapable of annihilation, have returned to the people at large for their exercise; the state remaining, in the mean time, exposed to all dangers of invasions from without and convulsions within.

He has endeavored to prevent the population of these states; for that purpose obstructing the laws for naturalization of foreigners; refusing to pass others to encourage their migration hither, and raising the conditions of new appropriations of lands.

He has obstructed the administration of justice, by refusing his assent to laws for establishing judiciary powers.

He has made judges dependent on his will alone, for the tenure of their offices, and the amount and payment of their salaries.

He has erected a multitude of new offices, and sent hither swarms of officers to harass our people and eat out their substance.

He has kept among us, in times of peace, standing armies, without the consent of our legislatures.

He has affected to render the military independent of, and superior to, the civil power.

He has combined with others to subject us to a jurisdiction foreign to our constitution, and unacknowledged by our laws, giving his assent to their acts of pretended legislation;

For quartering large bodies of armed troops among us;

For protecting them, by a mock trial, from punishment for any murders which they should commit on the inhabitants of these states;

For cutting off our trade with all parts of the world;

For imposing taxes on us without our consent;

For depriving us, in many cases, of the benefits of trial by jury;

For transporting us beyond seas, to be tried for pretended offenses;

For abolishing the free system of English laws in a neighboring province, establishing therein an arbitrary government, and enlarging its boundaries, so as to render it at once an example and fit instrument for introducing the same absolute rule into these colonies;

For taking away our charters, abolishing our more valuable laws, and altering fundamentally the forms of our governments;

For suspending our own legislatures, and declaring themselves invested with power to legislate for us in all cases whatsoever.

He has abdicated government here, by declaring us out of his protection and waging war against us.

He has plundered our seas, ravaged our coasts, burned our towns, and destroyed the lives of our people.

He is at this time transporting large armies of foreign mercenaries to complete the works of death, desolation, and tyranny already begun with circumstances of cruelty and perfidy scarcely paralleled in the most barbarous ages, and totally unworthy the head of a civilized nation.

He has constrained our fellow-citizens, taken captive on the high seas, to bear arms against their country, to become the executioners of their friends and brethren, or to fall themselves by their hands.

He has excited domestic insurrections among us, and has endeavored to bring on the inhabitants of our frontiers the merciless Indian savages, whose known rule of warfare is an undistinguished destruction of all ages, sexes, and conditions.

In every stage of these oppressions we have petitioned for redress in the most humble terms; our repeated petitions have been answered only by repeated injury. A prince, whose character is thus marked by every act which may define a tyrant, is unfit to be the ruler of a free people.

Nor have we been wanting in our attentions to our British brethren. We have warned them, from time to time, of attempts by their legislature to extend an unwarrantable jurisdiction over us. We have reminded them of the circumstances of our emigration and settlement here. We have appealed to their native justice and magnanimity; and we have conjured them, by the ties of our common kindred, to disavow these usurpations, which would inevitably interrupt our connections and correspondence. They, too, have been deaf to the voice of justice and of consanguinity. We must, therefore, acquiesce in the necessity which denounces our separation, and hold them, as we hold the rest of mankind, enemies in war, in peace friends.

We, therefore, the representatives of the United States of America, in General Congress assembled, appealing to the Supreme Judge of the world for the rectitude of our intentions, do, in the name and by the authority of the good people of these colonies, solemnly publish and declare, that these United Colonies are, and of right ought to be, FREE AND INDEPENDENT STATES; that they are absolved from all allegiance to the British crown, and that all political connection between them and the state of Great Britain is, and ought to be, totally dissolved; and that, as free and independent states, they have full power to levy war, conclude peace, contract alliances, establish commerce, and do all other acts and things which independent states may of right do. And for the support of this declaration, with a firm reliance on the protection of Divine Providence, we mutually pledge to each other our lives, our fortunes, and our sacred honor.

John Hancock, *President and delegate from Massachusetts*

Georgia

Button Gwinnett

Lyman Hall

George Walton

North Carolina

William Hooper

Joseph Hewes

John Penn

South Carolina

Edward Rutledge

Thomas Heyward Jr.

Thomas Lynch Jr.

Arthur Middleton

Maryland

Samuel Chase

William Paca

Thomas Stone

Charles Carroll of Carrollton

Virginia

George Wythe

Richard Henry Lee

Thomas Jefferson

Benjamin Harrison

Thomas Nelson Jr.

Francis Lightfoot Lee

Carter Braxton

Pennsylvania

Robert Morris

Benjamin Rush

Benjamin Franklin

John Morton

George Clymer

James Smith

George Taylor

James Wilson

George Ross

Delaware

Caesar Rodney

George Read

Thomas McKean

New York

William Floyd

Philip Livingston

Francis Lewis

Lewis Morris

New Jersey

Richard Stockton

John Witherspoon

Francis Hopkinson

John Hart

Abraham Clark

New Hampshire

Josiah Bartlett

William Whipple

Matthew Thornton

Massachusetts

Samuel Adams

John Adams

Robert Treat Paine

Elbridge Gerry

Rhode Island

Stephen Hopkins

William Ellery

Connecticut

Roger Sherman

Samuel Huntington

William Williams

Oliver Wolcott

The Constitution of the United States

We the People of the United States, in Order to form a more perfect Union, establish Justice, insure domestic Tranquility, provide for the common defence, promote the general Welfare, and secure the Blessings of Liberty to ourselves and our Posterity, do ordain and establish this Constitution for the United States of America.

Article I.

Section 1.   All legislative Powers herein granted shall be vested in a Congress of the United States, which shall consist of a Senate and House of Representatives.

Section 2.   The House of Representatives shall be composed of Members chosen every second Year by the People of the several States, and the Electors in each State shall have the Qualifications requisite for Electors of the most numerous Branch of the State Legislature.

No Person shall be a Representative who shall not have attained to the age of twenty five Years, and been seven Years a Citizen of the United States, and who shall not, when elected, be an Inhabitant of that State in which he shall be chosen.

Changed by the Fourteenth Amendment, Section 2.

Representatives and direct Taxes shall be apportioned among the several States which may be included within this Union, according to their respective Numbers, which shall be determined by adding to the whole Number of free Persons, including those bound to Service for a Term of Years, and excluding Indians not taxed, three fifths of all other Persons. The actual Enumeration shall be made within three Years after the first Meeting of the Congress of the United States, and within every subsequent Term of ten Years, in such Manner as they shall by Law direct. The Number of Representatives shall not exceed one for every thirty Thousand, but each State shall have at Least one Representative; and until such enumeration shall be made, the State of New Hampshire shall be entitled to chuse three, Massachusetts eight, Rhode-Island and Providence Plantations one, Connecticut five, New-York six, New Jersey four, Pennsylvania eight, Delaware one, Maryland six, Virginia ten, North Carolina five, South Carolina five, and Georgia three.

When vacancies happen in the Representation from any State, the Executive Authority thereof shall issue Writs of Election to fill such Vacancies.

The House of Representatives shall chuse their Speaker and other Officers; and shall have the sole Power of Impeachment.

Section 3.   The Senate of the United States shall be composed of two Senators from each State, chosen by the Legislature thereof, for six Years; and each Senator shall have one Vote.

Changed by the Seventeenth Amendment.

Immediately after they shall be assembled in Consequence of the first Election, they shall be divided as equally as may be into three Classes. The Seats of the Senators of the first class shall be vacated at the Expiration of the second Year, of the second Class at the Expiration of the fourth Year, and of the third Class at the Expiration of the sixth Year, so that one third may be chosen every second Year; and if Vacancies happen by Resignation, or otherwise, during the Recess of the Legislature of any State, the Executive thereof may make temporary Appointments until the next Meeting of the Legislature, which shall then fill such Vacancies.

Changed by the Seventeenth Amendment.

No Person shall be a Senator who shall not have attained to the Age of thirty Years, and been nine Years a Citizen of the United States, and who shall not, when elected, be an Inhabitant of that State for which he shall be chosen.

The Vice President of the United States shall be President of the Senate, but shall have no Vote, unless they be equally divided.

The Senate shall chuse their other Officers, and also a President pro tempore, in the Absence of the Vice President, or when he shall exercise the Office of President of the United States.

The Senate shall have the sole Power to try all Impeachments. When sitting for that Purpose, they shall be on Oath or Affirmation. When the President of the United States is tried the Chief Justice shall preside: And no Person shall be convicted without the Concurrence of two thirds of the Members present.

Judgment in Cases of Impeachment shall not exceed further than to removal from Office, and disqualification to hold and enjoy any Office of honor, Trust or Profit under the United States: but the Party convicted shall nevertheless be liable and subject to Indictment, Trial, Judgment and Punishment, according to Law.

Section 4. The Times, Places and Manner of holding Elections for Senators and Representatives, shall be prescribed in each State by the Legislature thereof; but the Congress may at any time by Law make or alter such Regulations, except as to the Places of chusing Senators.

The Congress shall assemble at least once in every Year, and such Meeting shall be on the first Monday in December, unless they shall by Law appoint a different Day.

Changed by the Twentieth Amendment, Section 2.

Section 5. Each House shall be the Judge of the Elections, Returns and Qualifications of its own Members, and a Majority of each shall constitute a Quorum to do Business; but a smaller number may adjourn from day to day, and may be authorized to compel the Attendance of absent Members, in such Manner, and under such Penalties as each House may provide.

Each House may determine the Rules of its Proceedings, punish its Members for disorderly Behaviour, and, with the Concurrence of two thirds, expel a Member.

Each House shall keep a Journal of its Proceedings, and from time to time publish the same, excepting such Parts as may in their Judgment require Secrecy; and the Yeas and Nays of the Members of either House on any question shall, at the Desire of one fifth of those Present, be entered on the Journal.

Neither House, during the Session of Congress, shall, without the Consent of the other, adjourn for more than three days, nor to any other Place than that in which the two Houses shall be sitting.

Section 6. The Senators and Representatives shall receive a Compensation for their Services, to be ascertained by Law, and paid out of the Treasury of the United States. They shall in all Cases, except Treason, Felony and Breach of the Peace, be privileged from Arrest during their Attendance at the Session of their respective Houses, and in going to and returning from the same; and for any Speech or Debate in either House, they shall not be questioned in any other Place.

Amplified by the Twenty-Seventh Amendment.

No Senator or Representative shall, during the Time for which he was elected, be appointed to any civil Office under the Authority of the United States, which shall have been created, or the Emoluments whereof shall have been encreased during such time; and no Person holding any Office under the United States, shall be a Member of either House during his Continuance in Office.

Section 7. All Bills for raising Revenue shall originate in the House of Representatives; but the Senate may propose or concur with Amendments as on other Bills.

Every Bill which shall have passed the House of Representatives and the Senate, shall, before it become a Law, be presented to the President of the United States; If he approve he shall assign it, but if not he shall return it, with his Objections to that House in which it shall have originated, who shall enter the Objections at large on their Journal, and proceed to reconsider it. If after such Reconsideration two thirds of that House shall agree to pass the Bill, it shall be sent, together with the Objections, to the other House, by which it shall likewise be reconsidered, and if approved by two thirds of that House, it shall become a Law. But in all such Cases the Votes of both Houses shall be determined by yeas and Nays, and the Names of the Persons voting for and against the Bill shall be entered on the Journal of each House respectively. If any Bill shall not be returned by the President within ten Days (Sundays excepted) after it shall have been presented to him, the Same shall be a Law, in like Manner, as if he had signed it, unless the Congress by their Adjournment prevent its Return, in which Case it shall not be a Law.

Every Order, Resolution, or Vote to which the Concurrence of the Senate and House of Representatives may be necessary (except on a question of Adjournment) shall be presented to the President of the United States; and before the Same shall take Effect, shall be approved by him, or being disapproved by him, shall be repassed by two thirds of the Senate and House of Representatives, according to the Rules and Limitations prescribed in the Case of a Bill.

Section 8. The Congress shall have Power To lay and Collect Taxes, Duties, Imposts and Excises, to pay the Debts and provide for the common Defence and general Welfare of the United States; but all Duties, Imposts and Excises shall be uniform throughout the United States.

To borrow Money on the credit of the United States;

To regulate Commerce with foreign Nations, and among the several States, and with the Indian Tribes;

To establish an uniform Rule of Naturalization, and uniform Laws on the subject of Bankruptcies throughout the United States;

To coin Money, regulate the Value thereof, and of foreign Coin, and fix the Standard of Weights and Measures;

To provide for the Punishment of counterfeiting the Securities and current Coin of the United States;

To establish Post Offices and post Roads;

To promote the Progress of Science and useful Arts, by securing for limited Times to Authors and Inventors the exclusive Right to their respective Writings and Discoveries;

To constitute Tribunals inferior to the Supreme Court;

To define and punish Piracies and Felonies committed on the high Seas, and Offences against the Law of Nations;

General welfare clause gives Congress the power to tax to provide for the general welfare.

Commerce clause gives Congress the power to regulate commerce with foreign nations, with Indian tribes, and among the various states.

To declare War, grant Letters of Marque and Reprisal, and make Rules concerning Captures on Land and Water;

To raise and support Armies, but no Appropriation of Money to that Use shall be for a longer Term than two Years;

To provide and maintain a Navy;

To make Rules for the Government and Regulation of the land and naval Forces;

To provide for calling forth the Militia to execute the Laws of the Union, suppress Insurrections and repel Invasions;

To provide for organizing, arming, and disciplining, the Militia, and for governing such Part of them as may be employed in the Service of the United States, reserving to the States respectively, the Appointment of the Officers, and the Authority of training the Militia according to the discipline prescribed by Congress;

To exercise exclusive Legislation in all Cases whatsoever, over such District (not exceeding ten Miles square) as may, by Cession of Particular States, and the Acceptance of Congress, become the Seat of the Government of the United States, and to exercise like Authority over all Places purchased by the Consent of the Legislature of the State in which the Same shall be, for the Erection of Forts, Magazines, Arsenals, dock-Yards and other needful Buildings;—And

To make all Laws which shall be necessary and proper for carrying into Execution the foregoing Powers, and all other Powers vested by this Constitution in the Government of the United States, or in any Department or Officer thereof.

Necessary and proper clause gives Congress the power to pass all laws necessary and proper to the powers enumerated in Section 8.

Section 9. The Migration or Importation of such Persons as any of the States now existing shall think proper to admit, shall not be prohibited by the Congress prior to the Year one thousand eight hundred and eight, but a Tax or duty may be imposed on such Importation, not exceeding ten dollars for each Person.

The Privilege of the Writ of Habeas Corpus shall not be suspended, unless when in Cases of Rebellion or Invasion the public Safety may require it.

No bill of Attainder or ex post facto Law shall be passed.

No Capitation, or other direct, Tax shall be laid, unless in Proportion to the Census or Enumeration herein before directed to be taken.

Changed by the Sixteenth Amendment.

No Tax or Duty shall be laid on Articles exported from any State.

No Preference shall be given by any Regulation of Commerce or Revenue to the Ports of one State over those of another; nor shall Vessels bound to, or from, one State, be obliged to enter, clear or pay Duties in another.

No Money shall be drawn from the Treasury, but in Consequence of Appropriations made by Law; and a regular Statement and Account of the Receipts and Expenditures of all public Money shall be published from time to time.

No Title of Nobility shall be granted by the United States: And no Person holding any Office of Profit or Trust under them, shall, without the Consent of the Congress, accept of any present, Emolument, Office, or Title, of any kind whatever, from any King, Prince, or foreign State.

Section 10. No State shall enter into any Treaty, Alliance, or Confederation; grant Letters of Marque and Reprisal; coin Money; emit Bills of Credit; make any Thing but gold and silver Coin a Tender in Payment of Debts; pass any Bill of Attainder, ex post facto Law, or Law impairing the Obligation of Contracts, or grant any Title of Nobility.

No State shall, without the Consent of the Congress, lay any Imposts or Duties on Imports or Exports, except what may be absolutely necessary for executing its inspection Laws; and the net Produce of all Duties and Imposts, laid by any State on Imports or Exports, shall be for the Use of the Treasury of the United States; and all such Laws shall be subject to the Revision and Control of the Congress.

No State shall, without the Consent of Congress, lay any Duty of Tonnage, keep Troops, or Ships of War in time of Peace, enter into any Agreement or Compact with another State, or with a foreign Power, or engage in War, unless actually invaded, or in such imminent Danger as will not admit of delay.

Article II.

Section 1. The executive Power shall be vested in a President of the United States of America. He shall hold his Office during the term of four Years, and, together with the Vice President, chosen for the same Term, be elected, as follows

Each State shall appoint, in such Manner as the Legislature thereof may direct, a Number of Electors, equal to the whole Number of Senators and Representatives to which the State may be entitled in the Congress: but no Senator or Representative, or Person holding an Office of Trust or Profit under the United States, shall be appointed an Elector.

The Electors shall meet in their respective States, and vote by Ballot for two Persons, of whom one at least shall not be an Inhabitant of the same State with them-selves. And they shall make a List of all the Persons voted for, and of the Number of Votes for each; which List they shall sign and certify, and transmit sealed to the Seat of the Government of the United States, directed to the President of the Senate. The President of the Senate shall, in the Presence of the Senate and House of Representatives, open all the Certificates, and the Votes shall then be counted. The Person having the greatest Number of Votes shall be the President, if such Number be a Majority of the whole Number of Electors appointed; and if there be more than one who have such Majority, and have an equal Number of Votes, then the House of Representatives shall immediately chuse by Ballot one of them for President; and if no Person have a Majority, then from the five highest on the List the said House shall in like Manner chuse the President. But in chusing the President, the Votes shall be taken by States, the Representation from each State having one Vote; a quorum for this Purpose shall consist of a Member or Members from two thirds of the States, and a Majority of all the States shall be necessary to a Choice. In every Case, after the Choice of the President, the Person having the greatest Number of Votes of the Electors shall be the Vice President. But if there should remain two or more who have equal Votes, the Senate shall chuse from them by Ballot the Vice President.

The Congress may determine the Time of chusing the Electors, and the Day on which they shall give their Votes, which Day shall be the same throughout the United States.

No Person except a natural born Citizen, or a Citizen of the United States, at the time of the Adoption of this Constitution, shall be eligible to the Office of President; neither shall any person be eligible to that Office who shall not have attained to the Age of thirty five Years, and been fourteen Years a Resident within the United States.

In Case of the Removal of the President from Office, or of his Death, Resignation, or Inability to discharge the Powers and Duties of the said Office, the Same shall devolve on

Vesting clause gives the president the executive power.

Changed by the Twelfth Amendment.

Changed by the Twenty-Fifth Amendment.

the Vice President, and the Congress may by Law provide for the Case of Removal, Death, Resignation or Inability, both of the President and Vice President, declaring what Officer shall then act as President, and such Officer shall act accordingly, until the Disability be removed, or a President shall be elected.

The President shall, at stated Times, receive for his Services, a Compensation, which shall neither be encreased nor diminished during the Period for which he shall have been elected, and he shall not receive within that Period any other Emolument from the United States, or any of them.

Before he enter on the Execution of his Office, he shall take the following Oath or Affirmation:—"I do solemnly swear (or affirm) that I will faithfully execute the Office of President of the United States, and will to the best of my Ability, preserve, protect and defend the Constitution of the United States."

Section 2.   The President shall be Commander in Chief of the Army and Navy of the United States, and of the Militia of the several States, when called into the actual Service of the United States; he may require the Opinion, in writing, of the principal Officer in each of the executive Departments, upon any Subject relating to the Duties of their respective Offices, and he shall have Power to grant Reprieves and Pardons for Offences against the United States, except in Cases of Impeachment.

He shall have Power, by and with the Advice and Consent of the Senate, to make Treaties, provided two thirds of the Senators present concur; and he shall nominate, and by and with the Advice and Consent of the Senate, shall appoint Ambassadors, other public Ministers and Consuls, Judges of the supreme Court, and all other Officers of the United States, whose Appointments are not herein otherwise provided for, and which shall be established by Law: but the Congress may by Law vest the Appointment of such inferior Officers, as they think proper, in the President alone, in the Courts of Law, or in the Heads of Departments.

The President shall have Power to fill up all Vacancies that may happen during the Recess of the Senate, by granting Commissions which shall expire at the End of their next Session.

Section 3.   He shall from time to time give to the Congress Information of the State of the Union, and recommend to their Consideration such Measures as he shall judge necessary and expedient; he may, on extraordinary Occasions, convene both Houses, or either of them, and in Case of Disagreement between them, with Respect to the Time of Adjournment, he may adjourn them to such Time as he shall think proper; he shall receive Ambassadors and other public Ministers; he shall take Care that the Laws be faithfully executed, and shall Commission all the Officers of the United States.

Take care clause requires the president to make sure that the laws are "faithfully executed."

Section 4.   The President, Vice President and all civil Officers of the United States, shall be removed from Office on Impeachment for, and Conviction of, Treason, Bribery, or other high Crimes and Misdemeanors.

Article III.

Section 1.   The judicial Power of the United States, shall be vested in one supreme Court, and in such inferior Courts as the Congress may from time to time ordain and establish. The Judges, both of the supreme and inferior Courts, shall hold their Offices during good

Behaviour, and shall, at stated Times, receive for their Services, a Compensation, which shall not be diminished during their Continuance in Office.

Section 2.   The judicial Power shall extend to all Cases, in Law and Equity, arising under this Constitution, the Laws of the United States, and Treaties made, or which shall be made, under their Authority;—to all Cases affecting Ambassadors, other public Ministers and Consuls;—to all Cases of admiralty and maritime Jurisdiction;—to Controversies to which the United States shall be a Party;—to Controversies between two or more States;—between a State and Citizens of another State;—between Citizens of different States;—between Citizens of the same State claiming Lands under Grants of different States, and between a State, or the Citizens thereof, and foreign States, Citizens or Subjects.

In all Cases affecting Ambassadors, other public Ministers and Consuls, and those in which a State shall be Party, the supreme Court shall have original Jurisdiction. In all the other Cases before mentioned, the supreme Court shall have appellate Jurisdiction, both as to Law and Fact, with such Exceptions, and under such Regulations as the Congress shall make.

The Trial of all Crimes, except in Cases of Impeachment, shall be by Jury; and such Trial shall be held in the State where the said Crimes shall have been committed; but when not committed within any State, the Trial shall be at such Place or Places as the Congress may by Law have directed.

Section 3.   Treason against the United States, shall consist only in levying War against them, or in adhering to their Enemies, giving them Aid and Comfort. No Person shall be convicted of Treason unless on the Testimony of two Witnesses to the same overt Act, or on Confession in open Court.

The Congress shall have Power to declare the Punishment of Treason, but no Attainder of Treason shall work Corruption of Blood, or Forfeiture except during the Life of the Person attainted.

Article IV.

Section 1.   Full Faith and Credit shall be given in each State to the public Acts, Records, and judicial Proceedings of every other State. And the Congress may by general Laws prescribe the Manner in which such Acts, Records and Proceedings shall be proved, and the Effect thereof.

Section 2.   The Citizens of each State shall be entitled to all Privileges and Immunities of Citizens in the several States.

A person charged in any State with Treason, Felony, or other Crime, who shall flee from Justice, and be found in another State, shall on Demand of the executive Authority of the State from which he fled, be delivered up, to be removed to the State having Jurisdiction of the Crime.

No Person held to Service or Labour in one State, under the Laws thereof, escaping into another, shall, in Consequence of any Law or Regulation therein, be discharged from such Service or Labour, but shall be delivered up on Claim of the Party to whom such Service or Labour may be due.

Section 3.   New States may be admitted by the Congress into this Union; but no new State shall be formed or erected within the Jurisdiction of any other State; nor any State be formed

Changed by the Eleventh Amendment.

Full faith and credit clause requires states to accept civil proceedings from other states.

Privileges and immunities clause requires states to treat nonresidents equally to residents.

Fugitive slave clause required states to return runaway slaves; negated by the Thirteenth Amendment.

by the Junction of two or more States, or Parts of States, without the Consent of the Legislatures of the States concerned as well as of the Congress.

The Congress shall have Power to dispose of and make all needful Rules and Regulations respecting the Territory or other Property belonging to the United States; and nothing in this Constitution shall be so construed as to Prejudice any Claims of the United States, or of any particular State.

Section 4. The United States shall guarantee to every State in this Union a Republican Form of Government, and shall protect each of them against Invasion; and on Application of the Legislature, or of the Executive (when the Legislature cannot be convened) against domestic Violence.

Guarantee clause provides a federal government guarantee that the states will have a republican form of government.

Article V.

The Congress, whenever two thirds of both Houses shall deem it necessary, shall propose Amendments to this Constitution, or, on the Application of the Legislatures of two thirds of the several States, shall call a Convention for proposing Amendments, which, in either Case, shall be valid to all Intents and Purposes, as Part of this Constitution, when ratified by the Legislatures of three fourths of the several States, or by Conventions in three fourths thereof, as the one or the other Mode of Ratification may be proposed by the Congress; Provided that no Amendment which may be made prior to the Year One thousand eight hundred and eight shall in any Manner after the first and fourth Clauses in the Ninth Section of the first Article; and that no State, without its Consent, shall be deprived of its equal Suffrage in the Senate.

Article VI.

All Debts contracted and Engagements entered into, before the Adoption of this Constitution, shall be as valid against the United States under this Constitution, as under the Confederation.

This Constitution, and the Laws of the United States which shall be made in Pursuance thereof; and all Treaties made, or which shall be made, under the Authority of the United States, shall be the Supreme Law of the Land; and the Judges in every State shall be bound thereby, any Thing in the Constitution or Laws of any State to the Contrary notwithstanding.

Supremacy clause makes federal law supreme over state laws.

The Senators and Representatives before mentioned, and the Members of the several State Legislatures, and all executive and judicial Officers, both of the United States and of the several States, shall be bound by Oath or Affirmation, to support this Constitution; but no religious Test shall ever be required as a Qualification to any Office or public Trust under the United States.

Article VII.

The Ratification of the Conventions of nine States, shall be sufficient for the Establishment of this Constitution between the States so ratifying the Same.

Done in Convention by the Unanimous Consent of the States present the Seventeenth Day of September in the Year of our Lord one thousand seven hundred and Eighty seven and of the Independence of the United States of America the Twelfth In witness whereof We have hereunto subscribed our Names,

George Washington, *President and deputy from Virginia*

Delaware

George Read
Gunning Bedford Jr.
John Dickinson
Richard Bassett
Jacob Broom

Maryland

James McHenry
Daniel of St. Thomas Jennifer
Daniel Carroll

Virginia

John Blair
James Madison Jr.

North Carolina

William Blount
Richard Dobbs Spaight
Hugh Williamson

South Carolina

John Rutledge
Charles Cotesworth Pinckney
Charles Pinckney
Pierce Butler

Georgia

William Few
Abraham Baldwin

New Hampshire

John Langdon
Nicholas Gilman

Massachusetts

Nathaniel Gorham
Rufus King

Connecticut

William Samuel Johnson
Roger Sherman

New York

Alexander Hamilton

New Jersey

William Livingston
David Brearley
William Paterson
Jonathan Dayton

Pennsylvania

Benjamin Franklin
Thomas Mifflin
Robert Morris
George Clymer
Thomas FitzSimons
Jared Ingersoll
James Wilson
Gouverneur Morris

[The first ten amendments, known as the Bill of Rights, were ratified in 1791.]

First Amendment

Establishment clause prohibits governmental establishment of religion.

Free exercise clause protects the free exercise of religion.

Congress shall make no law respecting an establishment of religion, or prohibiting the free exercise thereof; or abridging the freedom of speech, or of the press; or the right of the people peaceably to assemble, and to petition the Government for a redress of grievances.

Second Amendment

A well regulated Militia, being necessary to the security of a free State, the right of the people to keep and bear Arms, shall not be infringed.

Third Amendment

No Soldier shall, in time of peace be quartered in any house, without the consent of the Owner, nor in time of war, but in a manner prescribed by law.

Fourth Amendment

The right of the people to be secure in their persons, houses, papers, and effects, against unreasonable searches and seizures, shall not be violated, and no Warrants shall issue, but upon probable cause, supported by Oath or affirmation, and particularly describing the place to be searched, and the persons or things to be seized.

Fifth Amendment

No person shall be held to answer for a capital, or otherwise infamous crime, unless on a presentment or indictment of a Grand Jury, except in cases arising in the land or naval forces, or in the Militia, when in actual service in time of War or public danger; nor shall any person be subject for the same offence to be twice put in jeopardy of life or limb; nor shall be compelled in any criminal case to be a witness against himself, nor be deprived of life, liberty, or property, without due process of law, nor shall private property be taken for public use, without just compensation.

Double jeopardy clause prevents the government from retrying someone for a crime after an initial acquittal.

Self-incrimination clause protects people from having to testify against themselves at trial.

Due process clause prevents the federal government from denying any person due process of law.

Takings clause requires just compensation when the government seizes private property for a public purpose.

Sixth Amendment

In all criminal prosecutions, the accused shall enjoy the right to a speedy and public trial, by an impartial jury of the State and district wherein the crime shall have been committed, which district shall have been previously ascertained by law, and to be informed of the nature and cause of the accusation; to be confronted with the witnesses against him; to have compulsory process for obtaining witnesses in his favor, and to have Assistance of Counsel for his defence.

Seventh Amendment

In Suits at common law, where the value in controversy shall exceed twenty dollars, the right of trial by jury shall be preserved, and no fact tried by a jury, shall be otherwise reexamined in any Court of the United States, than according to the rules of the common law.

Eighth Amendment

Excessive bail shall not be required, nor excessive fines imposed, nor cruel and unusual punishments inflicted.

Cruel and unusual punishment clause prohibits cruel and unusual punishments.

Ninth Amendment

The enumeration in the Constitution, of certain rights, shall not be construed to deny or disparage others retained by the people.

Tenth Amendment

The powers not delegated to the United States by the Constitution, nor prohibited by it to the States, are reserved to the States respectively, or to the people.

Reserve powers clause reserves to the states or to the people those powers not delegated to the United States.

Eleventh Amendment (1798)

The Judicial power of the United States shall not be construed to extend to any suit in law or equity, commenced or prosecuted against one of the United States by Citizens of another State, or by Citizens or Subjects of any Foreign State.

Twelfth Amendment (1804)

The Electors shall meet in their respective states and vote by ballot for President and Vice President, one of whom, at least, shall not be an inhabitant of the same state with themselves; they shall name in their ballots the person voted for as President, and in distinct ballots the person voted for as Vice President, and they shall make distinct lists of all persons voted for as President, and of all persons voted for as Vice President, and of the number of votes for each, which lists they shall sign and certify, and transmit sealed to the seat of the government of the United States, directed to the President of the Senate;—The President of the Senate shall, in the presence of the Senate and House of Representatives, open all the certificates and the votes shall then be counted;—The person having the greatest number of votes for President, shall be the President, if such number be a majority of the whole number of Electors appointed; and if no person have such majority, then from the persons having the highest numbers not exceeding three on the list of those voted for as President, the House of Representatives shall choose immediately, by ballot, the President. But in choosing the President, the votes shall be taken by states, the representation from each state having one vote; a quorum for this purpose shall consist of a member or members from two-thirds of the states, and a majority of all the states shall be necessary to a choice. And if the House of Representatives shall not choose a President whenever the right of choice shall devolve upon them, before the fourth day of March next following, then the Vice President shall act as President, as in the case of the death or other constitutional disability of the President.—The person having the greatest number of votes as Vice President, shall be the Vice President, if such number be a majority of the whole number of Electors appointed, and if no person have a majority, then from the two highest numbers on the list, the Senate shall choose the Vice President; a quorum for the purpose shall consist of two-thirds of the whole number of Senators, and a majority of the whole number shall be necessary to a choice. But no person constitutionally ineligible to the office of President shall be eligible to that of Vice President of the United States.

Changed by the Twentieth Amendment, Section 3.

Thirteenth Amendment (1865)

Section 1. Neither slavery nor involuntary servitude, except as a punishment for crime whereof the party shall have been duly convicted, shall exist within the United States, or any place subject to their jurisdiction.

Section 2. Congress shall have power to enforce this article by appropriate legislation.

Fourteenth Amendment (1868)

Citizenship clause makes all persons born in the United States citizens of the United States and of the state in which they reside.

Privileges or immunities clause prohibits states from abridging certain fundamental rights.

Due process clause prevents state governments from denying any person due process of law.

Equal protection clause prevents states from denying any person the equal protection of the laws.

Section 1. All persons born or naturalized in the United States and subject to the jurisdiction thereof, are citizens of the United States and of the State wherein they reside. No State shall make or enforce any law which shall abridge the privileges or immunities of citizens of the United States; nor shall any State deprive any person of life, liberty, or property, without due process of law; nor deny to any person within its jurisdiction the equal protection of the laws.

Section 2. Representatives shall be apportioned among the several States according to their respective numbers, counting the whole number of persons in each State, excluding Indians not taxed. But when the right to vote at any election for the choice of electors for President and Vice President of the United States, Representatives in Congress, the Executive and Judicial officers of a State, or the members of the Legislature thereof, is denied to any of the male inhabitants of such State, being twenty-one years of age, and citizens of the United States, or in any way abridged, except for participation in rebellion, or other crime, the basis of representation therein shall be reduced in the proportion which the number of such male citizens shall bear to the whole number of male citizens twenty-one years of age in such State.

Changed by the Nineteenth and Twenty-Sixth Amendments.

Section 3. No person shall be a Senator or Representative in Congress, or elector of President and Vice President, or hold any office, civil or military, under the United States, or under any State, who, having previously taken an oath, as a member of Congress, or as an officer of the United States, or as a member of any State legislature, or as an executive or judicial officer of any State, to support the Constitution of the United States, shall have engaged in insurrection or rebellion against the same, or given aid or comfort to the enemies thereof. But Congress may by a vote of two-thirds of each House, remove such disability.

Section 4. The validity of the public debt of the United States, authorized by law, including debts incurred for payment of pensions and bounties for services in suppressing insurrection or rebellion, shall not be questioned. But neither the United States nor any State shall assume or pay any debt or obligation incurred in aid of insurrection or rebellion against the United States, or any claim for the loss or emancipation of any slave; but all such debts, obligations and claims shall be held illegal and void.

Section 5. The Congress shall have power to enforce, by appropriate legislation, the provisions of this article.

Fifteenth Amendment (1870)

Section 1. The right of citizens of the United States to vote shall not be denied or abridged by the United States or by any State on account of race, color, or previous condition of servitude.

Section 2. The Congress shall have power to enforce this article by appropriate legislation.

Sixteenth Amendment (1913)

The Congress shall have power to lay and collect taxes on incomes, from whatever source derived, without apportionment among the several States, and without regard to any census or enumeration.

Seventeenth Amendment (1913)

The Senate of the United States shall be composed of two Senators from each State, elected by the people thereof, for six years; and each Senator shall have one vote. The electors in each State shall have the qualifications requisite for electors of the most numerous branch of the State legislatures.

When vacancies happen in the representation of any State in the Senate, the executive authority of such State shall issue writs of election to fill such vacancies: *Provided,* That the legislature of any State may empower the executive thereof to make temporary appointments until the people fill the vacancies by election as the legislature may direct.

This amendment shall not be so construed as to affect the election or term of any Senator chosen before it becomes valid as part of the Constitution.

Eighteenth Amendment (1919)

Section 1. After one year from the ratification of this article the manufacture, sale, or transportation of intoxicating liquors within, the importation thereof into, or the exportation thereof from the United States and all territory subject to the jurisdiction thereof for beverage purposes is hereby prohibited.

Repealed by the Twenty-First Amendment.

Section 2. The Congress and the several States shall have concurrent power to enforce this article by appropriate legislation.

Section 3. This article shall be inoperative unless it shall have been ratified as an amendment to the Constitution by the legislatures of the several States, as provided in the Constitution, within seven years from the date of the submission hereof to the States by the Congress.

Nineteenth Amendment (1920)

The right of citizens of the United States to vote shall not be denied or abridged by the United States or by any State on account of sex.

Congress shall have power to enforce this article by appropriate legislation.

Twentieth Amendment (1933)

Section 1. The terms of the President and Vice President shall end at noon on the 20th day of January, and the terms of Senators and Representatives at noon on the 3rd day of January, of the years in which such terms would have ended if this article had not been ratified; and the terms of their successors shall then begin.

Section 2. The Congress shall assemble at least once in every year, and such meeting shall begin at noon on the 3d day of January, unless they shall by law appoint a different day.

Section 3. If, at the time fixed for the beginning of the term of the President, the President elect shall have died, the Vice President elect shall become President. If a President shall not have been chosen before the time fixed for the beginning of his term, or if the President elect shall have failed to qualify, then the Vice President elect shall act as President until a President shall have qualified; and the Congress may by law provide for the case wherein neither a President elect nor a Vice President elect shall have qualified, declaring who shall then act as President, or the manner in which one who is to act shall be selected, and such person shall act accordingly until a President or Vice President shall have qualified.

Section 4. The Congress may by law provide for the case of the death of any of the persons from whom the House of Representatives may choose a President whenever the right of choice shall have devolved upon them, and for the case of the death of any of the persons from whom the Senate may choose a Vice President whenever the right of choice shall have devolved upon them.

Section 5. Sections 1 and 2 shall take effect on the 15th day of October following the ratification of this article.

Section 6. This article shall be inoperative unless it shall have been ratified as an amendment to the Constitution by the legislatures of three-fourths of the several States within seven years from the date of its submission.

Twenty-First Amendment (1933)

Section 1. The eighteenth article of amendment to the Constitution of the United States is hereby repealed.

Section 2. The transportation or importation into any State, Territory, or possession of the United States for delivery or use therein of intoxicating liquors, in violation of the laws thereof, is hereby prohibited.

Section 3. This article shall be inoperative unless it shall have been ratified as an amendment to the Constitution by conventions in the several States, as provided in the Constitution, within seven years from the date of the submission hereof to the States by the Congress.

Twenty-Second Amendment (1951)

Section 1. No person shall be elected to the office of the President more than twice, and no person who has held the office of President, or acted as President, for more than two years of a term to which some other person was elected President shall be elected to the office of the President more than once. But this Article shall not apply to any person holding the office of President when this Article was proposed by the Congress, and shall not prevent any person who may be holding the office of President, or acting as President, during the term within which this Article becomes operative from holding the office of President or acting as President during the remainder of such term.

Section 2. This Article shall be inoperative unless it shall have been ratified as an amendment to the Constitution by the legislatures of three-fourths of the several States within seven years from the date of its submission to the States by the Congress.

Twenty-Third Amendment (1961)

Section 1. The District constituting the seat of Government of the United States shall appoint in such manner as the Congress may direct:

A number of electors of President and Vice President equal to the whole number of Senators and Representatives in Congress to which the District would be entitled if it were a State, but in no event more than the least populous State; they shall be in addition to those appointed by the States, but they shall be considered, for the purposes of the election of President and Vice President, to be electors appointed by a State; and they shall meet in the District and perform such duties as provided by the twelfth article of amendment.

Section 2. The Congress shall have power to enforce this article by appropriate legislation.

Twenty-Fourth Amendment (1964)

Section 1. The right of citizens of the United States to vote in any primary or other election for President or Vice President, for electors for President or Vice President, or for Senator or Representative in Congress, shall not be denied or abridged by the United States or any State by reason of failure to pay any poll tax or other tax.

Section 2. Congress shall have power to enforce this article by appropriate legislation.

Twenty-Fifth Amendment (1967)

Section 1. In case of the removal of the President from office or of his death or resignation, the Vice President shall become President.

Section 2. Whenever there is a vacancy in the office of the Vice President, the President shall nominate a Vice President who shall take office upon confirmation by a majority vote of both Houses of Congress.

Section 3. Whenever the President transmits to the President pro tempore of the Senate and the Speaker of the House of Representatives his written declaration that he is unable to discharge the powers and duties of his office, and until he transmits to them a written declaration to the contrary, such powers and duties shall be discharged by the Vice President as Acting President.

Section 4. Whenever the Vice President and a majority of either the principal officers of the executive departments or of such other body as Congress may by law provide, transmit to the President pro tempore of the Senate and the Speaker of the House of Representatives their written declaration that the President is unable to discharge the powers and duties of his office, the Vice President shall immediately assume the powers and duties of the office as Acting President.

Thereafter, when the President transmits to the President pro tempore of the Senate and the Speaker of the House of Representatives his written declaration that no inability exists, he shall resume the powers and duties of his office unless the Vice President and a majority of either the principal officers of the executive department[s] or of such other body as Congress may by law provide, transmit within four days to the President pro tempore of the Senate and the Speaker of the House of Representatives their written declaration that the President is unable to discharge the powers and duties of his office. Thereupon Congress shall decide the issue, assembling within forty-eight hours for that purpose if not in session. If the Congress, within twenty-one days after receipt of the latter written declaration, or, if Congress is not in session, within twenty-one days after Congress is required to assemble, determines by two-thirds vote of both Houses that the President is unable to discharge the powers and duties of his office, the Vice President shall continue to discharge the same as Acting President; otherwise, the President shall resume the powers and duties of his office.

Twenty-Sixth Amendment (1971)

Section 1. The right of citizens of the United States, who are eighteen years of age or older, to vote shall not be denied or abridged by the United States or by any State on account of age.

Section 2. The Congress shall have power to enforce this article by appropriate legislation.

Twenty-Seventh Amendment (1992)

No law varying the compensation for the services of the Senators and Representatives shall take effect, until an election of Representatives shall have intervened.

Federalist Papers 10 and 51

10

James Madison
November 22, 1787

To the People of the State of New York

Among the numerous advantages promised by a well constructed Union, none deserves to be more accurately developed than its tendency to break and control the violence of faction. The friend of popular governments, never finds himself so much alarmed for their character and fate, as when he contemplates their propensity to this dangerous vice. He will not fail therefore to set a due value on any plan which, without violating the principles to which he is attached, provides a proper cure for it. The instability, injustice and confusion introduced into the public councils, have in truth been the mortal diseases under which popular governments have every where perished; as they continue to be the favorite and fruitful topics from which the adversaries to liberty derive their most specious declamations. The valuable improvements made by the American Constitutions on the popular models, both ancient and modern, cannot certainly be too much admired; but it would be an unwarrantable partiality, to contend that they have as effectually obviated the danger on this side as was wished and expected. Complaints are everywhere heard from our most considerate and virtuous citizens, equally the friends of public and private faith, and of public and personal liberty; that our governments are too unstable; that the public good is disregarded in the conflicts of rival parties; and that measures are too often decided, not according to the rules of justice, and the rights of the minor party; but by the superior force of an interested and over-bearing majority. However anxiously we may wish that these complaints had no foundation, the evidence of known facts will not permit us to deny that they are in some degree true. It will be found indeed, on a candid review of our situation, that some of the distresses under which we labor, have been erroneously charged on the operation of our governments; but it will be found, at the same time, that other causes will not alone account for many of our heaviest misfortunes; and particularly, for that prevailing and increasing distrust of public engagements, and alarm for private rights, which are echoed from one end of the continent to the other. These must be chiefly, if not wholly, effects of the unsteadiness and injustice, with which a factious spirit has tainted our public administrations.

By a faction I understand a number of citizens, whether amounting to a majority or minority of the whole, who are united and actuated by some common impulse of passion, or of interest, adverse to the rights of other citizens, or to the permanent and aggregate interests of the community.

There are two methods of curing the mischiefs of faction: the one, by removing its causes; the other, by controlling its effects.

There are again two methods of removing the causes of faction: the one by destroying the liberty which is essential to its existence; the other, by giving to every citizen the same opinions, the same passions, and the same interests.

It could never be more truly said than of the first remedy, that it is worse than the disease. Liberty is to faction, what air is to fire, an aliment without which it instantly expires. But it could not be a less folly to abolish liberty, which is essential to political life, because it nourishes faction, than it would be to wish the annihilation of air, which is essential to animal life, because it imparts to fire its destructive agency.

The second expedient is as impracticable, as the first would be unwise. As long as the reason of man continues fallible, and he is at liberty to exercise it, different opinions will be formed. As long as the connection subsists between his reason and his self-love, his opinions and his passions will have a reciprocal influence on each other; and the former will be objects to which the latter will attach themselves. The diversity in the faculties of men from which the rights of property originate, is not less an insuperable obstacle to a uniformity of interests. The protection of these faculties is the first object of Government. From the protection of different and unequal faculties of acquiring property, the possession of different degrees and kinds of property immediately results: and from the influence of these on the sentiments and views of the respective proprietors, ensues a division of the society into different interests and parties.

The latent causes of faction are thus sown in the nature of man; and we see them every where brought into different degrees of activity, according to the different circumstances of civil society. A zeal for different opinions concerning religion, concerning Government and many other points, as well of speculation as of practice; an attachment to different leaders ambitiously contending for pre-eminence and power; or to persons of other descriptions whose fortunes have been interesting to the human passions, have in turn divided mankind into parties, inflamed them with mutual animosity, and rendered them much more disposed to vex and oppress each other, than to co-operate for their common good. So strong is this propensity of mankind to fall into mutual animosities, that where no substantial occasion presents itself, the most frivolous and fanciful distinctions have been sufficient to kindle their unfriendly passions, and excite their most violent conflicts. But the most common and durable source of factions, has been the various and unequal distribution of property. Those who hold, and those who are without property, have ever formed distinct interests in society. Those who are creditors, and those who are debtors, fall under a like discrimination. A landed interest, a manufacturing interest, a mercantile interest, a monied interest, with many lesser interests, grow up of necessity in civilized nations, and divide them into different classes, actuated by different sentiments and views. The regulation of these various and interfering interests forms the principal task of modern Legislation, and involves the spirit of party and faction in the necessary and ordinary operations of Government.

No man is allowed to be a judge in his own cause; because his interest would certainly bias his judgment, and, not improbably, corrupt his integrity. With equal, nay with greater reason, a body of men, are unfit to be both judges and parties, at the same time; yet, what are many of the most important acts of legislation, but so many judicial determinations, not indeed concerning the rights of single persons, but concerning the rights of large bodies of citizens; and what are the different classes of legislators, but advocates and parties to the causes which they determine? Is a law proposed concerning private debts? It is a question to which the creditors are parties on one side, and the debtors on the other. Justice ought to hold the balance between them. Yet the parties are and must be themselves the judges; and the most numerous party, or, in other words, the most powerful faction must be expected to prevail. Shall domestic manufactures be encouraged, and in what degree, by restrictions on foreign manufactures? are questions which would be differently decided by the landed and the manufacturing classes; and probably by neither, with a sole regard to justice and the public good. The apportionment of taxes on the various descriptions of property, is an act which seems to require the most exact impartiality; yet, there is perhaps no legislative act in which greater opportunity and temptation are given to a predominant party, to trample on the rules of justice. Every shilling with which they over-burden the inferior number, is a shilling saved to their own pockets.

It is in vain to say, that enlightened statesmen will be able to adjust these clashing interests, and render them all subservient to the public good. Enlightened statesmen will not always be at the helm: Nor, in many cases, can such an adjustment be made at all, without taking into view indirect and remote considerations, which will rarely prevail over the immediate interest which one party may find in disregarding the rights of another, or the good of the whole.

The inference to which we are brought, is, that the *causes* of faction cannot be removed; and that relief is only to be sought in the means of controlling its *effects*.

If a faction consists of less than a majority, relief is supplied by the republican principle, which enables the majority to defeat its sinister views by regular vote: It may clog the administration, it may convulse the society; but it will be unable to execute and mask its violence under the forms of the Constitution. When a majority is included in a faction, the form of popular government on the other hand enables it to sacrifice to its ruling passion or interest, both the public good and the rights of other citizens. To secure the public good, and private rights, against the danger of such a faction, and at the same time to preserve the spirit and the form of popular government, is then the great object to which our enquiries are directed: Let me add that it is the great desideratum, by which alone this form of government can be rescued from the opprobrium under which it has so long labored, and be recommended to the esteem and adoption of mankind.

By what means is this object attainable? Evidently by one of two only. Either the existence of the same passion or interest in a majority at the same time, must be prevented; or the majority, having such co-existent passion or interest, must be rendered, by their number and local situation, unable to concert and carry into effect schemes of oppression. If the impulse and the opportunity be suffered to coincide, we well know that neither moral nor religious motives can be relied on as an adequate control. They are not found to be such on the injustice and violence of individuals, and lose their efficacy in proportion to the number combined together; that is, in proportion as their efficacy becomes needful.

From this view of the subject, it may be concluded, that a pure Democracy, by which I mean, a Society, consisting of a small number of citizens, who assemble and administer the Government in person, can admit of no cure for the mischiefs of faction. A common passion or interest will, in almost every case, be felt by a majority of the whole; a communication and concert results from the form of Government itself; and there is nothing to check the inducements to sacrifice the weaker party, or an obnoxious individual. Hence it is, that such Democracies have ever been spectacles of turbulence and contention; have ever been found incompatible with personal security, or the rights of property; and have in general been as short in their lives, as they have been violent in their deaths. Theoretic politicians, who have patronized this species of Government, have erroneously supposed, that by reducing mankind to a perfect equality in their political rights, they would, at the same time, be perfectly equalized and assimilated in their possessions, their opinions, and their passions.

A republic, by which I mean a government in which the scheme of representation takes place, opens a different prospect, and promises the cure for which we are seeking. Let us examine the points in which it varies from pure democracy, and we shall comprehend both the nature of the cure and the efficacy which it must derive from the union.

The two great points of difference, between a democracy and a republic, are, first, the delegation of the government, in the latter, to a small number of citizens, elected by the rest; secondly, the greater number of citizens, and greater sphere of country, over which the latter may be extended.

The effect of the first difference is, on the one hand, to refine and enlarge the public views, by passing them through the medium of a chosen body of citizens, whose wisdom may best discern the true interest of their country, and whose patriotism and love of justice, will be least likely to sacrifice it to temporary or partial considerations. Under such a regulation, it may well happen, that the public voice, pronounced by the representatives of the people, will be more consonant to the public good, than if pronounced by the people themselves, convened for the purpose. On the other hand the effect may be inverted. Men of factious tempers, of local prejudices, or of sinister designs, may by intrigue, by corruption, or by other means, first obtain the suffrages, and then betray the interest of the people. The question resulting is, whether small or extensive republics are most favorable to the election of proper guardians of the public weal, and it is clearly decided in favor of the latter by two obvious considerations.

In the first place, it is to be remarked that, however small the republic may be, the representatives must be raised to a certain number, in order to guard against the cabals of a few; and that however large it may be, they must be limited to a certain number, in order to guard against the confusion of a multitude. Hence, the number of representatives in the two cases not being in proportion to that of the constituents, and being proportionally greatest in the small republic, it follows, that if the proportion of fit characters be not less in the large than in the small republic, the former will present a greater option, and consequently a greater probability of a fit choice.

In the next place, as each Representative will be chosen by a greater number of citizens in the large than in the small Republic, it will be more difficult for unworthy candidates to practise with success the vicious arts, by which elections are too often carried; and the suffrages of the people being more free, will be more likely to center on men who possess the most attractive merit, and the most diffusive and established characters.

It must be confessed, that in this, as in most other cases, there is a mean, on both sides of which inconveniences will be found to lie. By enlarging too much the number of electors, you render the representatives too little acquainted with all their local circumstances and lesser interests; as by reducing it too much, you render him unduly attached to these, and too little fit to comprehend and pursue great and national objects. The Federal Constitution forms a happy combination in this respect; the great and aggregate interests being referred to the national, the local and particular, to the state legislatures.

The other point of difference is, the greater number of citizens and extent of territory which may be brought within the compass of Republican, than of Democratic Government; and it is this circumstance principally which renders factious combinations less to be dreaded in the former, than in the latter. The smaller the society, the fewer probably will be the distinct parties and interests composing it; the fewer the distinct parties and interests, the more frequently will a majority be found of the same party; and the smaller the number of individuals composing a majority, and the smaller the compass within which they are placed, the more easily will they concert and execute their plans of oppression. Extend the sphere, and you take in a greater variety of parties and interests; you make it less probable that a majority of the whole will have a common motive to invade the rights of other citizens; or if such a common motive exists, it will be more difficult for all who feel it to discover their own strength, and to act in unison with each other. Besides other impediments, it may be remarked, that where there is a consciousness of unjust or dishonorable purposes, communication is always checked by distrust, in proportion to the number whose concurrence is necessary.

Hence it clearly appears, that the same advantage, which a Republic has over a Democracy, in controlling the effects of factions, is enjoyed by a large over a small Republic—is enjoyed by the Union over the States composing it. Does this advantage consist in the substitution of Representatives, whose enlightened views and virtuous sentiments render them superior to local prejudices, and to schemes of injustice? It will not be denied, that the Representation of the Union will be most likely to possess these requisite endowments. Does it consist in the greater security afforded by a greater variety of parties, against the event of any one party being able to outnumber and oppress the rest? In an equal degree does the increased variety of parties, comprised within the Union, increase this security? Does it, in fine, consist in the greater obstacles opposed to the concert and accomplishment of the secret wishes of an unjust and interested majority? Here, again, the extent of the Union gives it the most palpable advantage.

The influence of factious leaders may kindle a flame within their particular States, but will be unable to spread a general conflagration through the other States: a religious sect, may degenerate into a political faction in a part of the Confederacy but the variety of sects dispersed over the entire face of it, must secure the national Councils against any danger from that source: a rage for paper money, for an abolition of debts, for an equal division of property, or for any other improper or wicked project, will be less apt to pervade the whole body of the Union, than a particular member of it; in the same proportion as such a malady is more likely to taint a particular county or district, than an entire State.

In the extent and proper structure of the Union, therefore, we behold a Republican remedy for the diseases most incident to Republican Government. And according to the degree of pleasure and pride, we feel in being Republicans, ought to be our zeal in cherishing the spirit, and supporting the character of Federalists.

PUBLIUS

51

James Madison
February 6, 1788

To the People of the State of New York

To what expedient then shall we finally resort for maintaining in practice the necessary partition of power among the several departments, as laid down in the constitution? The only answer that can be given is, that as all these exterior provisions are found to be inadequate, the defect must be supplied, by so contriving the interior structure of the government, as that its several constituent parts may, by their mutual relations, be the means of keeping each other in their proper places. Without presuming to undertake a full development of this important idea, I will hazard a few general observations, which may perhaps place it in a clearer light, and enable us to form a more correct judgment of the principles and structure of the government planned by the convention.

In order to lay a due foundation for that separate and distinct exercise of the different powers of government, which to a certain extent, is admitted on all hands to be essential to the preservation of liberty, it is evident that each department should have a will of its own; and consequently should be so constituted, that the members of each should have as little agency as possible in the appointment of the members of the others. Were this principle rigorously adhered to, it would require that all the appointments for the supreme executive, legislative, and judiciary magistracies, should be drawn from the same fountain of authority, the people, through channels, having no communication whatever with one another. Perhaps such a plan of constructing the several departments would be less difficult in practice than it may in contemplation appear. Some difficulties however, and some additional expense, would attend the execution of it. Some deviations therefore from the principle must be admitted. In the constitution of the judiciary department in particular, it might be inexpedient to insist rigorously on the principle; first, because peculiar qualifications being essential in the members, the primary consideration ought to be to select that mode of choice, which best secures these qualifications; secondly, because the permanent tenure by which the appointments are held in that department, must soon destroy all sense of dependence on the authority conferring them.

It is equally evident that the members of each department should be as little dependent as possible on those of the others, for the emoluments annexed to their offices. Were the executive magistrate, or the judges, not independent of the legislature in this particular, their independence in every other would be merely nominal.

But the great security against a gradual concentration of the several powers in the same department, consists in giving to those who administer each department, the necessary constitutional means, and personal motives, to resist encroachments of the others. The provision for defense must in this, as in all other cases, be made commensurate to the danger of attack. Ambition must be made to counteract ambition. The interest of the man must be connected with the constitutional rights of the place. It may be a reflection on human nature, that such devices should be necessary to control the abuses of government. But what is government itself but the greatest of all reflections on human nature? If men were angels, no government would be necessary. If angels were to govern men, neither external nor internal controls on government would be necessary. In framing a government which is to be administered by men over men, the great difficulty lies in this: You must first enable the government to control the governed; and in the next place, oblige it to control itself. A dependence on the people is no doubt the primary control on the government; but experience has taught mankind the necessity of auxiliary precautions.

This policy of supplying by opposite and rival interests, the defect of better motives, might be traced through the whole system of human affairs, private as well as public. We see it particularly displayed in all the subordinate distributions of power; where the constant aim is to divide and arrange the several offices in such a manner as that each may be a check on the other; that the private interest of every individual, may be a sentinel over the public rights. These inventions of prudence cannot be less requisite in the distribution of the supreme powers of the state.

But it is not possible to give each department an equal power of self defense. In republican government the legislative authority, necessarily, predominates. The remedy for this inconveniency is, to divide the legislature into different branches; and to render them by different modes of election, and different principles of action, as little connected with each other, as the nature of their common functions, and their common dependence on the society, will admit. It may even be necessary to guard against dangerous encroachments by still further precautions. As the weight of the legislative authority requires that it should be thus divided, the weakness of the executive may require, on the other hand, that it should be fortified. An absolute negative, on the legislature, appears at first view to be the natural defense with which the executive magistrate should be armed. But perhaps it would be neither altogether safe, nor alone sufficient. On ordinary occasions, it might not be exerted with the requisite firmness; and on extraordinary occasions, it might be prefidiously abused. May not this defect of an absolute negative be supplied, by some qualified connection between this weaker department, and the weaker branch of the stronger department, by which the latter may be led to support the constitutional rights of the former, without being too much detached from the rights of its own department?

If the principles on which these observations are founded be just, as I persuade myself they are, and they be applied as a criterion, to the several state constitutions, and to the federal constitution, it will be found, that if the latter does not perfectly correspond with them, the former are infinitely less able to bear such a test.

There are moreover two considerations particularly applicable to the federal system of America, which place that system in a very interesting point of view.

First. In a single republic, all the power surrendered by the people, is submitted to the administration of a single government; and usurpations are guarded against by a division of the government into distinct and separate departments. In the compound republic of America, the power surrendered by the people, is first divided between two distinct governments, and then the portion allotted to each, subdivided among distinct and separate departments. Hence a double security arises to the rights of the people. The different governments will control each other; at the same time that each will be controlled by itself.

Second. It is of great importance in a republic, not only to guard the society against the oppression of its rulers; but to guard one part of the society against the injustice of the other part. Different interests necessarily exist in different classes of citizens. If a majority be united by a common interest, the rights of the minority will be insecure. There are but two methods of providing against this evil: The one by creating a will in the community independent of the majority, that is, of the society itself, the other by comprehending in the society so many separate descriptions of citizens, as will render an unjust combination of a majority of the whole, very improbable, if not impracticable. The first method prevails in all governments possessing an hereditary or self appointed authority. This at best is but a precarious security; because a power independent of the society may as well espouse the unjust views of the major, as the rightful interests, of the minor party, and may possibly be turned against both parties. The second method will be exemplified in the federal republic of the United States. While all authority in it will be derived from and dependent on the society, the society itself will be broken into so many parts, interests and classes of citizens, that the rights of individuals or of the minority, will be in little danger from interested combinations of the majority. In a free government, the security for civil rights must be the same as for religious rights. It consists in the one case in the multiplicity of interests, and in the other, in the multiplicity of sects. The degree of security in both cases will depend on the number of interests and sects; and this may be presumed to depend on the extent of country and number of people comprehended under the same government. This view of the subject must particularly recommend a proper federal system to all the sincere and considerate friends of republican government: Since it shows that in exact proportion as the territory of the union may be formed into more circumscribed confederacies or states, oppressive combinations of a majority will be facilitated, the best security under the republican form, for the rights of every class of citizens, will be diminished; and consequently, the stability and independence of some member of the government, the only other security, must be proportionally increased. Justice is the end of government. It is the end of civil society. It ever has been, and ever will be pursued, until it be obtained, or until liberty be lost in the pursuit. In a society under the forms of which the stronger faction can readily unite and oppress the weaker, anarchy may as truly be said to reign, as in a state of nature where the weaker individual is not secured against the violence of the stronger: And as in the latter state even the stronger individuals are prompted by the uncertainty of their condition, to submit to a government which may protect the weak as well as themselves: So in the former state, will the more powerful factions or parties be gradually induced by a like motive, to wish for a government which will protect all parties, the weaker as well as the more powerful. It can be little doubted, that if the state of Rhode Island was separated from the confederacy, and left to itself, the insecurity of rights under the popular form of government within such narrow limits, would be displayed by such reiterated oppressions of factious majorities, that some power altogether independent of the people would soon be called for by the voice of the very factions whose misrule had proved the necessity of it. In the extended republic of the United States, and among the great variety of interests, parties and sects which it embraces, a coalition of a majority of the whole society could seldom take place on any other principles than those of justice and the general good; and there being thus less danger to a minor from the will of the major party, there must be less pretext also, to provide for the security of the former, by introducing into the government a will not dependent on the latter; or in other words, a will independent of the society itself. It is no less certain than it is important, notwithstanding the contrary opinions which have been entertained, that the larger the society, provided it lie within a practicable sphere, the more duly capable will be of self government. And happily for the *republican cause,* the practicable sphere may be carried to a very great extent, by a judicious modification and mixture of the *federal principle.*

PUBLIUS

Glossary

501(c)(3) organizations: Tax-exempt groups that are prohibited from lobbying or campaigning for a party or candidate. (Chapter 8)

501(c)(4) organizations: Tax-exempt groups that exist to promote social welfare and can advocate for specific policy issues. (Chapter 8)

A

actual malice: Supreme Court test for libel of a public figure, in which the plaintiff must prove that the publisher knew the material was false or acted with reckless disregard of whether it was true or false. (Chapter 7)

agenda setting: Ability of the media to affect the way people view issues, people, or events by controlling which stories are shown and which are not. (Chapter 7)

amendment: Formal process of changing the Constitution. (Chapter 2)

Antifederalists: Those who opposed the new proposed Constitution during the ratification period. (Chapter 2)

appropriate: Congress's power to allocate a set amount of federal dollars for a specific program or agency. (Chapter 12)

approval rating: Job performance evaluation for the president, Congress, or other public official or institution that is generated by public opinion polls and is typically reported as a percentage. (Chapter 6)

Articles of Confederation: Initial governing authority of the United States, 1781–88. (Chapter 2)

Australian ballot: Voting system in which state governments run elections and provide voters the option of choosing candidates from multiple parties; also called the secret ballot. (Chapter 9)

authorize: Congress's power to create a federal program or agency and set levels of federal funds to support that program or agency. (Chapter 12)

autocracy: System of government in which the power to govern is concentrated in the hands of an individual ruler. (Chapter 1)

B

ballot: List of candidates who are running for elected office; used by voters to make their choice. (Chapter 9)

battleground state: State in which the outcome of the presidential election is uncertain and in which candidates invest much time and money, especially if its votes are vital for a victory in the Electoral College. (Chapter 10)

Bill of Rights: First ten amendments to the Constitution, which provide basic political rights. (Chapter 2)

Bill of Rights: First ten amendments to the Constitution, which provide basic political rights. (Chapter 4)

Black Lives Matter: Movement that grew out of the perceived discounting of black lives by police and juries. (Chapter 5)

Brown v. Board of Education: The 1954 Supreme Court decision striking down segregated schools. (Chapter 5)

bully pulpit: Nickname for the power of the president to use the attention associated with the office to persuade the media, Congress, and the public to support his policy positions. (Chapter 13)

bureaucracy: Executive branch departments, agencies, boards, and commissions that carry out the responsibilities of the federal government. (Chapter 14)

C

cabinet secretaries: Heads of cabinet departments and chief advisers to the president on the issues under their jurisdiction. (Chapter 14)

cabinet: Set of executive departments responsible for carrying out federal policy in specific issue areas. (Chapter 14)

capitalism: Economic system in which businesses and key industries are privately owned and in which individuals, acting on their own or with others, are free to create businesses. (Chapter 1)

career civil servants: Federal employees who are hired through a merit based system to implement federal programs and who are expected to be neutral in their political affiliations. (Chapter 14)

caucus: Meeting of party members in town halls, schools, and private homes to select a presidential nominee. (Chapter 9)

censorship: The suppression of words, images, or ideas that are considered "offensive" or "dangerous" by a government or private group. Protection from being censored is guaranteed by the First Amendment. (Chapter 7)

checks and balances: Government structure that authorizes each branch of government (executive, legislative, and judicial) to share powers with the other branches, thereby holding some scrutiny of and control over the other branches. (Chapter 2)

checks and balances: Government structure that authorizes each branch of government (executive, legislative, and judicial) to share powers with the other branches, thereby holding some scrutiny of and control over the other branches. (Chapter 1)

chief of staff: Person who coordinates and oversees interactions among the president, his personal staff, and his cabinet secretaries. (Chapter 13)

citizens' groups: Groups that form to draw attention to purely public issues that affect all citizens equally. (Chapter 8)

citizenship: Full-fledged membership in a nation. (Chapter 5)

civic duty: Social force that binds a person to actively participate in public and political life. (Chapter 11)

civic interest: Concern for the well-being of society and the nation as a whole. (Chapters 1, 11)

civil liberties: Those rights, such as freedom of speech and religion, that are so fundamental that they are outside the authority of government to regulate. (Chapter 4)

Civil Rights Act: Prohibits discrimination in employment, education, and places of public accommodation (1964). (Chapter 5)

civil rights: Set of rights centered around the concept of equal treatment that government is obliged to protect. (Chapter 5)

Civil Service Commission: Created by the Pendleton Act to administer entrance exams for the federal civil service and set standards for promotion based on merit. (Chapter 14)

civil service: The nonpartisan federal workforce employed to carry out government programs and policies. (Chapter 14)

civil society: Voluntary organizations that allow communities to flourish. (Chapter 1)

clear and present danger test: First Amendment test that requires the state to prove there is a high likelihood that the speech in question would lead to a danger that Congress has a right to prevent. (Chapter 4)

cloture: Vote that can stop a filibuster and bring debate on a bill to end. (Chapter 12)

commander in chief: Head of the armed forces of the United States. (Chapter 13)

commerce clause: Gives Congress the power to regulate commerce with foreign nations, with Indian tribes, and among the various states (Article I, Section 8). (Chapter 3)

compelling interest test: Standard frequently used by the Supreme Court in civil liberties cases to determine whether a state has a compelling interest for infringing on a right and whether the law is narrowly drawn to meet that interest. (Chapter 4)

compulsory voting: Practice that requires citizens to vote in elections or face punitive measures such as community service, fines, or imprisonment. (Chapter 11)

concurrent budget resolution: Congressional blueprint outlining general amounts of funds that can be spent on federal programs. (Chapter 12)

concurrent powers: Powers held by both the national and state governments in a federal system. (Chapter 3)

confederal system: System of government in which ultimate authority rests with the regional (for example, state) governments. (Chapter 3)

confidence interval: Statistical range with a given probability that takes random error into account. (Chapter 6)

Connecticut Compromise: Compromise on legislative representation whereby the lower chamber is based on population, and the upper chamber provides equal representation to the states. (Chapter 2)

conservatives: Individuals who distrust government, believing that free markets offer better ways than government involvement to improve people's livelihood. In the social sphere, conservatives have more faith in government's ability to enforce traditional values. (Chapters 1, 6)

constitution: Document or set of documents that establishes the basic rules and procedures for how a society shall be governed. (Chapter 2)

Constitutional Convention: Meeting in 1787 at which twelve states intended to revise the Articles of Confederation but ended up proposing an entirely new Constitution. (Chapter 2)

constitutional system: System of government in which people set up and agree on the basic rules and procedures that will govern them. (Chapter 1)

content-neutral: Free speech doctrine that allows certain types of regulation of speech, as long as the restriction does not favor one side or another of a controversy. (Chapter 4)

continuing resolution: Measure passed to fund federal programs when the appropriations process has not been completed by September 30, the end of the fiscal year. (Chapter 12)

Court-packing plan: President Franklin Roosevelt's proposal to add new justices to the Supreme Court so that the Court would uphold his policies. (Chapter 3)

D

Declaration of Independence: The 1776 document declaring American independence from Great Britain and calling for equality, human rights, and citizen participation. (Chapter 2)

democracy: System of government in which the supreme power is vested in the people and exercised by them either directly or indirectly through elected representatives. (Chapter 1)

direct democracy: Form of democracy in which political power is exercised directly by citizens. (Chapters 1, 3)

divided government: Situation in which one party controls the executive branch and the other party controls one or both parts of the legislative branch. (Chapter 12)

Dred Scott v. Sandford: The 1857 Supreme Court decision declaring that blacks could not be citizens and Congress could not ban slavery in the territories. (Chapter 5)

dual federalism: Doctrine holding that state governments and the federal government have almost completely separate functions. (Chapter 3)

E

earmark: Federal dollars devoted specifically to a local project in a congressional district or state. (Chapter 12)

economic interest group: Group formed to advance the economic status of its members. (Chapter 8)

efficacy: Extent to which people believe their actions can affect public affairs and the actions of government. (Chapter 6)

efficacy: Extent to which people believe their actions can affect public affairs and the actions of government. (Chapter 11)

egalitarianism: Belief in human equality that disdains inherited titles of nobility and inherited wealth. (Chapter 1)

Electoral College: The presidential electors, selected every four years to represent the votes of their respective states, who meet to cast the electoral votes for president and vice president. (Chapters 2, 10)

entitlement programs: Federal programs, such as Social Security, Medicare, or Medicaid, that pay out benefits to individuals based on a specified set of eligibility criteria. (Chapter 13)

enumerated powers: Powers expressly granted to Congress by the Constitution. (Chapters 2, 3)

Equal Pay Act: Prohibits different pay for males and females for the same work (1963). (Chapter 5)

equal protection clause: Prevents states from denying any person the equal protection of the laws (Fourteenth Amendment). (Chapter 5)

equality of opportunity: Expectation that citizens may not be discriminated against based on race, gender, or national background and that every citizen should have an equal chance to succeed in life. (Chapters 1, 5)

equality of outcome: Expectation that equality is achieved if results are comparable for all citizens regardless of race, gender, or national background or that such groups are proportionally represented in measures of success in life. (Chapters 1, 5)

equality: Idea that all individuals are equal in their moral worth and so must be equal in treatment under the law and have equal access to the decision-making process. (Chapter 1)

establishment clause: First Amendment clause prohibiting governmental establishment of religion. (Chapter 4)

exclusionary rule: Supreme Court rule declaring that evidence found in violation of the Fourth Amendment cannot be used at trial. (Chapter 4)

executive branch: The branch of the federal government that executes the laws. (Chapter 1)

executive order: Presidential directive that usually involves implementing a specific law. (Chapter 13)

executive privilege: President's right to engage in confidential communications with his advisers. (Chapter 13)

exit polls: Polls that survey a sample of voters immediately after exiting the voting booth to predict the outcome of the election before the ballots are officially counted. (Chapter 6)

expectation of privacy test: Supreme Court test for whether Fourth Amendment protections apply. (Chapter 4)

F

faction: Defined by James Madison as any group that places its own interests above the aggregate interests of society. (Chapters 1, 8)

fake news: Fabricated news that has no basis in evidence and is often designed to mimic traditional news sources, but is not factually accurate. (Chapter 7)

federal budget deficit: Difference between the amount of money the federal government spends in outlays and the amount of money it receives from revenues. (Chapter 12)

Federal Register: Official published record of all executive branch rules, regulations, and orders. (Chapter 14)

federal regulatory commission: Federal agency typically run by a small number of officials, known as commissioners, who are appointed by the president for fixed terms and oversee economic or political issues. (Chapter 14)

federalism: System of government in which sovereignty is constitutionally divided between national and state governments. (Chapters 1, 2, and 3)

Federalist Papers: Series of essays written by James Madison, Alexander Hamilton, and John Jay arguing for the ratification of the Constitution; today a leading source for understanding the Constitution. (Chapter 7)

Federalists: Initially, those who supported the Constitution during the ratification period; later, the name of the political party established by supporters of Alexander Hamilton. (Chapter 2)

filibuster: Tactic of extended speech designed to delay or block passage of a bill in the Senate. (Chapter 12)

Founders: The people who were involved in establishing the United States, whether at the time of the Declaration of Independence or the writing of the Constitution. (Chapter 1)

Framers: The people who were involved in writing the Constitution. (Chapter 1)

framing: Ability of the media to influence public perception of issues by constructing the issue or discussion of a subject in a certain way. (Chapter 7)

franchise: Right to vote; also called suffrage. (Chapter 11)

free exercise clause: First Amendment clause protecting the free exercise of religion. (Chapter 4)

free rider problem: Problem faced by interest groups when a collective benefit they provide is so widespread and diffuse that members and nonmembers alike receive it, reducing the incentive for joining the group. (Chapter 8)

fugitive slave clause: Required states to return runaway slaves; negated by the Thirteenth Amendment (Article IV, Section 2). (Chapter 3)

G

gender gap: Differences in the political attitudes and behavior of men and women. (Chapter 6)

general election: Election in which voters choose their elected officials. (Chapter 9)

general welfare clause: Gives Congress the power to tax to provide for the general welfare (Article I, Section 8). (Chapter 2)

Generation Z: Generation born from 1997, onward. (Chapters 1, 6)

generational replacement: Cycle whereby younger generations replace older generations in the electorate. (Chapter 11)

gerrymandering: Redistricting that blatantly benefits one political party over the other or concentrates (or dilutes) the voting impact of racial and ethnic groups. (Chapter 10)

grandfather clauses: Election rules that exempted people from difficult literacy and interpretation tests for voting if their grandfathers had been eligible to vote. (Chapter 11)

grassroots movement: Group that forms in response to an economic or political event but does not focus on only one issue. (Chapter 8)

graveyard voting: Corrupt practice of using a dead person's name to cast a ballot in an election. (Chapter 11)

Great Society: Lyndon Johnson's program for expanding the federal social welfare programs in health care, education, and housing and for ending poverty. (Chapter 13)

H

hard news: Political news coverage, traditionally found in the printed press, that is more fact-based, opposed to more interpretive narratives and commentary. (Chapter 7)

head of state: Title given to the president as national leader. (Chapter 13)

hold: Power available to a senator to prevent the unanimous consent that allows a bill or presidential nomination to come to the Senate floor, which can be broken by invoking cloture (currently sixty votes on most items). (Chapter 12)

home style: The way in which incumbents portray themselves to constituents. (Chapter 12)

House majority leader: Leader of the majority party in the House and second in command to the Speaker. (Chapter 12)

House minority leader: Leader of the minority party in the House. (Chapter 12)

I

ideological interest groups: Groups that form among citizens with the same beliefs about a specific issue. (Chapter 8)

impeachment: Process whereby the House brings charges against the president or another federal official that will, upon conviction by the Senate, remove him or her from office. (Chapter 13)

imperial presidency: Power of the president to speak for the nation on the world stage and to set the policy agenda at home. (Chapter 13)

implied powers: Powers not expressly granted to Congress but added through the necessary and proper clause. (Chapters 2, 3)

incorporate: To apply provisions of the Bill of Rights to the states. (Chapter 4)

independent agency: Federal organization that has independent authority and does not operate within a cabinet department. (Chapter 14)

Independents: Individuals who do not affiliate with either of the major political parties. (Chapter 6)

individualism: Set of beliefs holding that people, and not government, are responsible for their own well-being. (Chapter 1)

inside strategy: A strategy employed by interest groups to pursue a narrow policy change and influence legislators directly rather than using a wider grassroots approach. (Chapter 8)

institutional model: Model of voting that focuses on the context of the election, including whether it is close and whether the rules encourage or discourage participation. (Chapter 11)

interest groups: Groups of citizens who share a common interest—a political opinion, religious or ideological belief, a social goal, or an economic characteristic—and try to influence public policy to benefit themselves. (Chapter 8)

invisible primary: Period just before the primaries begin during which candidates attempt to capture party support and media coverage. (Chapters 9, 10)

iron law of oligarchy: Theory that leaders in any organization eventually behave in their own self-interest, even at the expense of rank-and-file members; the larger the organization, the greater the likelihood that the leader will behave this way. (Chapter 8)

iron triangle: Insular and closed relationship among interest groups, members of Congress, and federal agencies. (Chapter 8)

issue network: View of the relationship among interest groups, members of Congress, and federal agencies as more fluid, open, and transparent than that described by the term iron triangle. (Chapter 8)

J

Jim Crow laws: Southern laws that established strict segregation of the races and gave their name to the segregation era. (Chapters 5, 11)

judicial branch: The branch of the federal government that interprets the laws. (Chapter 1)

judicial review: Authority of courts to declare laws passed by Congress and acts of the executive branch to be unconstitutional. (Chapter 2)

L

lame duck: Term-limited official in his or her last term of office. (Chapter 13)

Lawrence v. Texas: 2003 Supreme Court case extending the right to privacy to homosexual behavior. (Chapter 4)

legislative branch: The branch of the federal government that makes the laws. (Chapter 1)

Lemon test: Test for determining whether aid to religion violates the establishment clause. (Chapter 4)

levels of conceptualization: Measure of how ideologically coherent individuals are in their political evaluations. (Chapter 6)

libel: Publishing false and damaging statements about another person. (Chapter 7)

liberals: Individuals who have faith in government to improve people's lives, believing that private efforts are insufficient. In the social sphere, liberals usually support diverse lifestyles and tend to oppose any government action that seeks to shape personal choices. (Chapters 1, 6)

libertarians: Those who generally believe that government should refrain from acting to regulate either the economy or moral values. (Chapter 1)

liberty: Political value that cherishes freedom from an arbitrary exercise of power that constricts individual choice. (Chapter 1)

literacy tests: Tests requiring reading and interpretation skills in order to vote. (Chapter 11)

lobbying: Act of trying to persuade elected officials to adopt a specific policy change or maintain the status quo. (Chapter 8)

M

majoritarian: System of policy making in which those with a numerical majority hold authority. (Chapter 1)

majority rule: Idea that a numerical majority of a group should hold the power to make decisions binding on the whole group; a simple majority. (Chapter 1)

majority vote: Vote in which the winner needs to win 50 percent plus 1 of the votes cast. (Chapter 9)

marketplace of ideas: Idea that the government should not restrict the expression of ideas because the people are capable of accepting good ideas and rejecting bad ones. (Chapter 4)

markup: Process by which bills are literally marked up, or written, by the members of the committee. (Chapter 12)

mass media: News sources, including newspapers, television, radio, and the Internet, whose purpose is to provide a large audience with information about the nation and the world. (Chapter 7)

McCulloch v. Maryland: The 1819 Supreme Court decision upholding the right of Congress to create a bank. (Chapter 3)

median voter theorem: Theory that, in a two-party race, if voters select candidates on the basis of ideology and everyone participates equally, the party closer to the middle will win. (Chapter 9)

merit system: System of employment under which employees are chosen and promoted based on merit. (Chapter 14)

microtargeting: A marketing technique that employs user data to identify interests of specific individuals or groups and inform advertisers what message is most effective for those users. Used by politicians in campaigning to target ads to certain groups. (Chapter 7)

microtargeting: Gathering detailed information on cross sections of the electorate to track potential supporters and tailor political messages for them; also called narrowcasting. (Chapter 10)

midterm elections: Congressional elections held between the presidential elections. (Chapter 10)

Millennials: Generation born between 1981 and 1996. (Chapters 1, 6)

Miller test: Supreme Court test for determining whether material is obscene. (Chapter 4)

minimal effects model: View of the media's impact as marginal because most people seek news reports to reinforce beliefs already held rather than to develop new ones. (Chapter 7)

minority rights: Idea that the majority should not be able to take certain fundamental rights away from those in the minority. (Chapter 1)

Missouri Plan: Process for selecting state judges whereby the original nomination is by appointment, and subsequent retention is by a retention election. (Chapter 3)

moderates: Individuals who are in the middle of the ideological spectrum and do not hold consistently strong views about whether government should be involved in people's lives. (Chapters 1, 6)

monarchy: System of government that assigns power to a single person who inherits that position and rules until death. (Chapter 1)

muckraking: Journalistic practice of investigative reporting that seeks to uncover corruption and wrongdoing. (Chapter 7)

N

national committee: Top level of national political parties; coordinates national presidential campaigns. (Chapter 9)

national debt: Sum of loans and interest that the federal government has accrued over time to pay for the federal deficit. (Chapter 12)

natural (unalienable) rights: Rights that every individual has and that government cannot legitimately take away. (Chapters 1, 4)

necessary and proper clause: Gives Congress the power to pass all laws necessary and proper to the powers enumerated in Article I, Section 8. (Chapters 2, 3)

negativity: Campaign strategy of telling voters why they should not vote for the opponent and of highlighting information that raises doubts about the opponent. (Chapter 10)

New Deal: Franklin Delano Roosevelt's program for ending the Great Depression through government intervention in the economy and development of a set of safety-net programs for individuals. (Chapter 13)

news media: Subset of the mass media that provides the news of the day, gathered and reported by journalists. (Chapter 7)

nonattitudes: Sources of error in public opinion polls in which individuals feel obliged to give opinions when they are unaware of the issue or have no opinions about it. (Chapter 6)

nongovernmental organizations (NGOs): Organizations independent of governments that monitor and improve political, economic, and social conditions throughout the world. (Chapter 8)

not-so-minimal effects model: View of the media's impact as substantial, occurring by agenda setting, framing, and priming. (Chapter 7)

nullification: Right of states to invalidate acts of Congress they believe to be illegal. (Chapter 3)

O

Office of Management and Budget (OMB): Federal agency that oversees the federal budget and all federal regulations. (Chapter 14)

oligarchy: System of government in which the power to govern is concentrated in the hands of a powerful few, usually wealthy individuals. (Chapter 1)

omnibus bill: One very large bill that encompasses many separate bills. (Chapter 13)

order: Political value in which the rule of law is followed and does not permit actions that infringe on the well-being of others. (Chapter 1)

override: Congress's power to overturn a presidential veto with a two-thirds vote in each chamber. (Chapter 12)

oversight: Powers of Congress to monitor how the executive branch implements the laws. (Chapter 14)

P

pardon: Full forgiveness for a crime. (Chapter 13)

party alignment: Voter identification with a political party in repeated elections. (Chapter 9)

party caucus: Group of party members in a legislature. (Chapter 9)

party identification: Psychological attachment to a political party; partisanship. (Chapters 1, 6)

party platform: Document that lays out a party's core beliefs and policy proposals for each presidential election. (Chapters 9, 10)

patronage system: Political system in which government programs and benefits are awarded based on political loyalty to a party or politician. (Chapter 9)

Pendleton Act: 1883 act that established a merit- and performance-based system for federal employment. (Chapter 14)

penny press: Newspapers sold for a penny, initiating an era in which the press began to rely on circulation and advertising for income and not on political parties. (Chapter 7)

permanent campaign: Charge that presidents and members of Congress focus more on winning the next election than on governing. (Chapter 10)

pluralist: View of democratic society in which interest groups compete over policy goals, and elected officials are mediators of group conflict. (Chapters 1, 8)

plurality vote: Vote in which the winner needs to win more votes than any other candidate. (Chapter 9)

pocket veto: Automatic veto that occurs when Congress goes out of session within ten days of submitting a bill to the president and the president has not signed it. (Chapter 13)

polarization: Condition in which differences between parties and/or the public are so stark that disagreement breaks out, fueling attacks and controversy. (Chapter 6)

political action committees (PACs): Groups formed to raise and contribute funds to support electoral candidates and that are subject to campaign finance laws. (Chapter 8)

political appointees: Federal employees appointed by the president with the explicit task of carrying out his political and partisan agenda. (Chapter 14)

political culture: A shared way of thinking about community and government and the relationship between them. (Chapter 1)

political equality: The idea that people should have equal amounts of influence in the political system. (Chapter 1)

political ideology: Set of coherent political beliefs that offers a philosophy for thinking about the scope of government. (Chapters 1, 6)

political parties: Broad coalitions of interests organized to win elections in order to enact a commonly supported set of public policies. (Chapters 2, 9)

political parties: Broad coalitions of interests organized to win elections in order to enact a commonly supported set of public policies. (Chapter 1)

political tolerance: Willingness of people to put up with ideas with which they disagree. (Chapter 4)

political trust: Extent to which people believe the government acts in their best interests. (Chapter 6)

politics: Process by which people make decisions about who gets what, when, and how. (Chapter 1)

poll taxes: Tax on voting; prohibited by the Twenty-Fourth Amendment (1964). (Chapters 5, 11)

popular vote: Tally of total votes from individual citizens, as opposed to the electoral vote. (Chapter 10)

populists: Those who oppose concentrated wealth and adhere to traditional moral values. (Chapter 1)

position issues: Political issues that offer specific policy choices and often differentiate candidates' views and plans of action. (Chapter 10)

power elite: Small handful of decision makers who hold authority over a large set of issues. (Chapter 1)

presidential coattails: Effect of a popular president or presidential candidate on congressional elections, boosting votes for members of his or her party. (Chapter 10)

presidential directive: Official instructions from the president regarding federal policy. (Chapter 13)

primary election: Election in which voters select the candidates who will run on the party label in the general election; also called direct primary. (Chapter 9)

priming: Process whereby the media influence the criteria the public uses to make decisions. (Chapter 7)

prior restraint: Government restrictions on freedom of the press that prevent material from being published. (Chapter 4)

private discrimination: Discrimination by private individuals or businesses. (Chapter 5)

private goods: Goods or benefits provided by government in which most of the benefit falls to the individuals, families, or companies receiving them. (Chapter 1)

propaganda model: Extreme view of the media's role in society, arguing that the press serves the interest of the government only, driving what the public thinks about important issues. (Chapter 7)

proportional representation: An electoral system that assigns party delegates according to vote share in a presidential primary election or that assigns seats in the legislature according to vote share in a general election. (Chapter 9)

public discrimination: Discrimination by national, state, or local governments. (Chapter 5)

public goods: Goods or benefits provided by government from which everyone benefits and from which no one can be excluded. (Chapters 1, 8)

public opinion: Aggregate of individual attitudes or beliefs about certain issues or officials. (Chapter 6)

public policy: Intentional actions of government designed to achieve a goal. (Chapter 1)

push polls: Polls that are designed to manipulate the opinions of those being polled. (Chapter 6)

R

random sample: Method of selection that gives everyone who might be selected to participate in a poll an equal chance to be included. (Chapter 6)

ranking member: Leader of the minority-party members of a committee. (Chapter 12)

rational voting: Economic model of voting wherein citizens weigh the benefits of voting against the costs in order to take the most personally beneficial course of action. (Chapter 11)

rationality: Acting in a way that is consistent with one's self-interest. (Chapter 6)

realignment: Long-term shift in voter allegiance from one party to another. (Chapter 9)

reconciliation: A measure used to bring all bills that contain changes in the tax code or entitlement programs in line with the congressional budget. (Chapter 12)

Reconstruction: The period from 1865 to 1877 in which the former Confederate states gained readmission to the Union and the federal government passed laws to help the emancipated slaves. (Chapter 5)

redistricting: Process whereby state legislatures redraw the boundaries of congressional districts in the state to make them equal in population size. (Chapter 10)

regulations: Guidelines issued by federal agencies for administering federal programs and implementing federal law. (Chapter 14)

representative democracy: Form of democracy in which citizens elect public officials to make political decisions and formulate laws on their behalf. (Chapter 1)

representative sample: Method of selection that allows a sample to be representative of the entire population, ensuring that key groups are accurately reflected in the sample. (Chapter 6)

republic: Form of government in which power derives from citizens, but public officials make policy and govern according to existing law. (Chapters 1, 2)

reserve powers: Powers retained by the states under the Constitution. (Chapter 3)

responsible parties: Parties that take responsibility for offering the electorate a distinct range of policies and programs, thus providing a clear choice. (Chapter 9)

responsiveness: Idea that government should implement laws and policies that reflect the wishes of the public and any changes in those wishes. (Chapter 1)

revolving door: Movement of members of Congress, lobbyists, and executive branch employees into paid positions in each other's organizations. (Chapter 8)

right of association: Right to freely associate with others and form groups, as protected by the First Amendment. (Chapter 8)

right of petition: Right to ask the government for assistance with a problem or to express opposition to a government policy, as protected by the First Amendment. (Chapter 8)

right to privacy: Constitutional right inferred by the Supreme Court that has been used to protect unlisted rights such as sexual privacy and reproductive rights, plus the right to end life-sustaining medical treatment. (Chapter 4)

Roe v. Wade: The 1973 Supreme Court case extending the right to privacy to abortion. (Chapter 4)

rule of law: Legal system with known rules that are enforced equally against all people. (Chapter 1)

rule: Guidelines issued by the House Rules Committee that determine how many amendments may be considered for each bill. (Chapter 12)

S

safe seat: Seat in Congress considered to be reliably held by one party or the other. (Chapter 10)

Same-day voter registration: Practice allows voters to register and cast a vote on the same day. (Chapter 11)

sanctuary jurisdiction: A state or local government that enacts laws or policies that limit its cooperation with federal immigration enforcement officials. (Chapter 3)

Schedule C appointees: Federal employees appointed by the president to oversee civil service employees. (Chapter 14)

secede: To formally withdraw from a nation-state. (Chapter 3)

seditious libel: Conduct or language that incites rebellion against the authority of a state. (Chapter 7)

selective benefits: Benefits offered exclusively to members of an interest group. (Chapter 8)

selective exposure: Process whereby people secure information from sources that agree with them, thus reinforcing their beliefs. (Chapter 7)

selective incorporation: Doctrine used by the Supreme Court to make those provisions of the Bill of Rights that are fundamental rights binding on the states. (Chapter 4)

selective perception: Process whereby partisans interpret the same information differently. (Chapter 7)

self-government: Rule by the people. (Chapters 1, 3)

self-interest: Concern for one's own advantage and well-being. (Chapters 1, 6, and 11)

Senate majority leader: Leader of the majority party in the Senate. (Chapter 12)

Senate minority leader: Leader of the minority party in the Senate. (Chapter 12)

Senior Executive Service (SES): Senior management personnel in the federal government appointed by the president. (Chapter 14)

separate-but-equal doctrine: Supreme Court doctrine that upheld segregation as long as there were equivalent facilities for blacks. (Chapter 5)

separation of powers: Government structure in which authority is divided among branches (executive, legislative, and judicial), with each holding separate and independent powers and areas of responsibility. (Chapters 1, 2)

signing statements: Written remarks issued by the president when signing a bill into law that often reflect his interpretation of how the law should be implemented. (Chapter 13)

single-issue groups: Groups that form to present one view on a highly salient issue that is intensely important to members, such as gun control or abortion. (Chapter 8)

single-member plurality system: Electoral system that assigns one seat in a legislative body to represent citizens who live in a defined area (a district) based on which candidate wins the most votes. (Chapter 9)

social contract: Theory that government has only the authority accorded it by the consent of the governed. (Chapter 1)

socialism: Economic system in which the government owns major industries. (Chapter 1)

socialization: Impact and influence of one's social environment on the views and attitudes one carries in life, a primary source of political attitudes. (Chapter 6)

soft news: News stories focused less on facts and policies than on sensationalizing secondary issues or on less serious subjects of the entertainment world. (Chapter 7)

Speaker of the House: Constitutional and political leader of the House. (Chapter 12)

special interests: Set of groups seeking a particular benefit for themselves in the policy process. (Chapter 8)

state action: Action by a state, as opposed to a private person, that constitutes discrimination and therefore is an equal protection violation. (Chapter 5)

State of the Union address: Speech on the condition of the country given by the president to Congress every January. (Chapter 13)

states' rights: View that states have strong independent authority to resist federal rules under the Constitution (Chapter 3)

Stonewall riots: Street protest in 1969 by gay patrons against a police raid of a gay bar in New York; the protest is credited with launching the gay rights movement. (Chapter 5)

strategic politician hypothesis: Effect that the strength of the economy and the popularity of the sitting president have on the decision to run for Congress. (Chapter 10)

suffrage: Right to vote; also called franchise. (Chapter 11)

Super PACs: Independent groups that can raise unlimited amounts of money from individuals, labor unions, and corporations and can spend it to support or oppose political candidates but cannot coordinate directly with candidates or political parties. (Chapter 10)

supremacy clause: Makes federal law supreme over state laws (Article VI). (Chapter 3)

swing states: States that are not clearly pro-Republican or pro-Democrat and therefore are of vital interest to presidential candidates, as they can determine election outcomes. (Chapter 10)

swing voters: Voters who are neither reliably Republican nor reliably Democratic and who are pursued by each party during an election, as they can determine which candidate wins. (Chapter 10)

symbolic speech: Actions, such as burning the flag, that convey a political message without spoken words. (Chapter 4)

T

term limits: Rule restricting the number of terms an elected official can serve in a given office. (Chapter 10)

third parties: Minor political parties that present a third alternative to the two dominant political parties in the American political system. (Chapter 9)

three-fifths compromise: Compromise over slavery at the Constitutional Convention that granted states extra representation in the House of Representatives based on their number of slaves at the ratio of three-fifths. (Chapter 2)

tracking polls: Polls that seek to gauge changes of opinion of the same sample size over a period of time; they are common during the closing months of presidential elections. (Chapter 6)

turnout: Share of all eligible voters who actually cast ballots. (Chapter 11)

U

unanimous consent agreement: Agreement among all 100 senators on how a bill or presidential nomination will be debated, changed, and voted on in the Senate. (Chapter 12)

unions: Interest groups of individuals who share a common type of employment and seek better wages and working conditions through collective bargaining with employers. (Chapter 8)

unitary system: System of government in which ultimate authority rests with the national government. (Chapter 3)

U.S. Census: Article 1, Section 2 of the Constitution mandates that the United States population be counted every 10 years to determine the number of seats each state gets in the House of Representatives and how to distribute federal funds. (Chapter 10)

V

valence issues: Noncontroversial or widely supported campaign issues that are unlikely to differ among candidates. (Chapter 10)

valid secular purpose: Supreme Court test that allows states to ban activities that infringe on religious practices as long as the state has a nonreligious rationale for prohibiting the behavior. (Chapter 4)

vanishing marginals: Trend marking the decline of competitive congressional elections. (Chapter 10)

veto: Authority of the president to block legislation passed by Congress. Congress can override a veto by a two-thirds majority in each chamber. (Chapters 2, 13)

vote-by-mail (VBM) system: Method of voting in an election whereby ballots are distributed to voters by mail, and voters complete and return the ballots by mail. (Chapter 11)

voter apathy: Lack of interest in voting and in politics generally. (Chapter 11)

voter registration: Enrollment required prior to voting to establish eligibility. (Chapter 11)

Voting Rights Act: Gives the federal government the power to prevent discrimination in voting rights (1965). (Chapter 5)

voting-age population (VAP): Used to calculate the rate of participation by dividing the number of voters by the number of people in the country who are 18 and over. (Chapter 11)

voting-eligible population (VEP): Used to calculate the rate of participation by dividing the number of voters by the number of people in the country who are eligible to vote rather than just of voting age. (Chapter 11)

W

War Powers Act: The 1973 act that provides that the president cannot send troops into military conflict for more than a total of ninety days without seeking a formal declaration of war, or authorization for continued military action, from Congress. (Chapter 13)

watchdog: Role of the press in monitoring government actions. (Chapter 7)

wedge issue: Divisive issue focused on a particular group of the electorate that candidates use to gain more support by taking votes away from their opponents. (Chapter 10)

whistleblowers: Employees who report mismanagement, corruption, or illegal activity within their agencies. (Chapter 14)

white primary: Election rules that prohibited blacks from voting in Democratic primaries. (Chapter 11)

winner-take-all system: Electoral system in which whoever wins the most votes in an election wins the election. (Chapter 9)

women's suffrage movement: Movement to grant women the right to vote. (Chapter 5)

writ of habeas corpus: Right of individuals who have been arrested and jailed to go before a judge, who determines whether their detention is legal. (Chapter 4)

Y

yellow journalism: Style of journalism in the late-nineteenth century characterized by sensationalism intended to capture readers' attention and increase circulation. (Chapter 7)

Endnotes

Chapter 1

1. February 5, 2008 speech, http://www.nytimes.com/2008/02/05/us/politics/05text-obama.html?_r=0.

2. International Social Survey Program, as cited in Russell Dalton, *The Good Citizen* (Washington, D.C.: CQ Press, 2007), 144; Morley Winograd and Michael D. Hais, *Millennial Makeover: MySpace, YouTube and the Future of American Politics* (New Brunswick, NJ: Rutgers University Press, 2008), 260–63. The caption for the photo on page 5 is drawn from this source.

3. Larry Bartels, *Unequal Democracy* (Princeton, NJ: Princeton University Press, 2008); David Cay Johnston, "The Gap Between Rich and Poor Grows in the United States," *New York Times,* March 29, 2007. The caption for the photo on page 5 is drawn from these sources: U.S. census data; Merrill Goozner, "Top 1 Percent Got Lion's Share of Income," *Fiscal Times,* March 5, 2012, http://www.thefiscaltimes.com/Blogs/Gooz-News/2012/03/05/Top-1-Percent-Got-Lions-Share-of-Income-Gains-in-2010.aspx; and Emmanuel Saez, "Striking It Richer: The Evolution of Top Incomes in the United States (Updated with 2009 and 2010 Estimates)," *Pathways Magazine* (Winter 2008): 6–7, http://www.stanford.edu/group/scspi/_media/pdf/pathways/winter_2008/Saez.pdf.

4. "Americans' Approval of Congress Drops to Single Digits," *New York Times,* October 25, 2011, http://www.nytimes.com/interactive/2011/10/25/us/politics/approval-of-congress-drops-to-single-digits.html.

5. Kerem Ozan Kalkan, Geoffrey C. Layman, and Eric M. Uslaner, "Attitudes Toward Muslims in Contemporary American Society," *Journal of Politics* 69 (2009): 847–62; Brett Benson, Jennifer Merolla, and John Geer, "Two Steps Forward, One Step Back?" *Electoral Studies* 30 (2011): 607–20.

6. "Obama Ratings Historically Polarized," *Gallup Politics,* January 27, 2012, accessed April 10, 2012, http://www.gallup.com/poll/152222/Obama-Ratings-Historically-Polarized.aspx.

7. See http://www.usdebtclock.org, accessed March 28, 2020.

8. Charles Beard, *American Government and Politics* (New York: Macmillan Company, 1915), 18.

9. Edmund Burke, "Reflections on the Revolution in France," in *The Portable Edmund Burke,* ed. Isaac Kramnick (New York: Viking, 1999), 32.

10. John Adams to John Taylor, April 15, 1814, in *The Political Writings of John Adams: Representative Selections,* ed. George Peek Jr. (New York: Hackett Publishing, 2003), 67.

11. Quoted in David McCullough, *John Adams* (New York: Simon and Schuster, 2001), 68.

12. Jonathan Grossman, "Fair Labor Standards Act of 1938: Maximum Struggle for a Minimum Wage," U.S. Department of Labor, accessed April 1, 2014, http://www.dol.gov/dol/aboutdol/history/flsa1938.htm.

13. U.S. Department of Labor, "Minimum Wage," https://www.dol.gov/general/topic/wages/minimumwage.

14. Kelsey Snell, "What's Inside the Senate's $2 Trillion Coronavirus Aid Package," *NPR News,* accessed March 28, 2020, https://www.npr.org/2020/03/26/821457551/whats-inside-the-senate-s-2-trillion-coronavirus-aid-package.

15. Josiah Ober, *Mass and Elite in Democratic Athens: Rhetoric, Ideology and the Power of the People* (Princeton, NJ: Princeton University Press, 1991).

16. Harold Lasswell, *Politics: Who Gets What, When, How* (New York: McGraw-Hill, 1936).

17. See Noor Wazwaz, "It's Official: The U.S. Is Becoming a Minority-Majority Nation," *U.S. News & World Report,* http://www.usnews.com/news/articles/2015/07/06/its-official-the-us-is-becoming-a-minority-majority-nation.

18. Danielle Allen, quoted in "Here's Why Voters Are So Anxious This Election," *NPR News,* January 25, 2016, accessed January 25, 2016, http://www.npr.org/2016/01/25/464217330/heres-why-voters-are-so-anxious-this-election.

19. Hannah Knowles, "Federal Judge Will Not Reverse Georgia's Decision to Purge 100,000 Voters," *Washington Post,* December 28, 2019, accessed February 11, 2020, https://www.washingtonpost.com/politics/2019/12/28/federal-judge-will-not-reverse-georgias-decision-purge-voters/.

20. *Obergefell v. Hodges,* 576 U.S. ___ (2015).

21. David Remnick, "The President's Hero," *New Yorker,* February 2, 2009, http://www.newyorker.com/talk/comment/2009/02/02/090202taco_talk_remnick.

22. *Garner v. Louisiana,* 368 U.S. 157 (1961), reversing convictions over attempts to desegregate a lunch counter in Baton Rouge, Louisiana; *Browder v. Gayle,* 142 F. Supp. 707 (1956), ending segregated buses in Montgomery, Alabama; and *Cooper v. Aaron* 358 U.S. 1 (1958), ordering the desegregation of Central High School in Little Rock, Arkansas.

23. Winograd and Hais, *Millennial Makeover;* Morley Winograd and Michael D. Hais, "The Boomers Had Their Day. Make Way for the Millennials," *Washington Post,* February 3, 2008, http://www.washingtonpost.com/wp-dyn/content/article/2008/02/01/AR2008020102826.html; Corey Seemiller, *Generation Z Goes to College* (San Francisco: Jossey-Bass, 2016).

24. See https://www2.ed.gov/about/overview/budget/budget20/justifications/n-sao.pdf.

25. Darrell M. West, Grover J. Whitehurst, and E. J. Dionne Jr., "Invisible: 1.4 Percent Coverage for Education Is Not Enough," *The Brookings Institution,* December 2, 2009, accessed April 10, 2012, http://www.brookings.edu/research/reports/2009/12/02-education-news-west.

26. See http://www.usdebtclock.org, accessed February 11, 2020.

27. James Madison to W. T. Barry, "Epilogue: Securing the Republic," August 4, 1822, in *The Founders' Constitution,* ed. Philip B. Kurland and Ralph Lerner (Chicago, IL: University of Chicago Press, 1986), accessed April 25, 2012, http://press-pubs.uchicago.edu/founders documents/v1ch18s35.html.

Chapter 2

1. Cited in Lupe S. Salinas, "Gus Garcia and Thurgood Marshall: Two Legal Giants Fighting for Justice," *Thurgood Marshall Law Review* 28 (2003): 145–73.

2. *Delgado et al. v. Bastrop Independent School District,* Civil No. 388, W.D. Texas (1948).

3. Michael A. Olivas (ed.), *Colored Men and Hombres Aqui:* Hernandez v. Texas *and the Emergence of Mexican-American Lawyering* (Houston, Tex.: Arte Público Press, 2006).

4. *Hernandez v. Texas,* 347 U.S. 475 (1954).

5. *Hernandez v. Texas,* at 475.

6. *Hernandez v. Texas,* at 479.

7. Gordon S. Wood, *The American Revolution* (New York: Modern Library Chronicles, 2002), 39.

8. Edmund Burke, "Speech to the Electors of Bristol," November 3, 1774, in *The Founders' Constitution,* ed. Philip B. Kurland and Ralph Lerner (Chicago, IL: University of Chicago Press, 1986), accessed

April 25, 2012, http://press-pubs.uchicago.edu/founders/documents /v1ch13s7.html.

9. Robert Middlekauff, *The Glorious Cause: The American Revolution, 1763–1789* (New York: Oxford University Press, 1982), 231.

10. Thomas Paine, *Common Sense* (Philadelphia, PA, 1776), *USHistory.org*, accessed April 10, 2012, http://www.ushistory.org/paine/commonsense /sense4.htm.

11. Articles of Confederation, Article IX, Paragraph 5, *U.S. Constitution Online*, accessed April 10, 2012, http://www.usconstitution.net /articles.html#Article9.

12. Thomas Jefferson, "Notes on the State of Virginia," 1784, in *The Founders' Constitution*, ed. Philip B. Kurland and Ralph Lerner (Chicago, IL: University of Chicago Press, 1986), accessed April 25, 2012, http:// press-pubs.uchicago.edu/founders/documents/v1ch10s9.html.

13. Historical Census Browser, University of Virginia, *Geospatial and Statistical Data Center*, accessed April 10, 2012, http://mapserver.lib .virginia.edu/.

14. Middlekauff, *The Glorious Cause*, 624.

15. William Riker, "The Heresthetics of Constitution Making," *American Political Science Review* 78 (1984): 1–16.

16. "Variant Texts of the Plan Presented by William Patterson," in *Debates in the Federal Convention of 1787 Reported by James Madison*, ed. Gaillard Hunt and James B. Scott (New York: 1920), 102–4, quoted by the Avalon Project, Yale University, Lillian Goldman Law Library, accessed April 10, 2012, http://avalon.law.yale.edu/18th_century /patexta.asp.

17. "1790 Census of Slave and Free Population," U.S. Census of Population and Housing, Historical Census Browser, University of Virginia, Geospatial and Statistical Data Center, accessed April 10, 2012, http://mapserver.lib.virginia.edu/.

18. Quoted in Max Farrand, *The Framing of the Constitution of the United States* (New Haven, Conn.: Yale University Press, 1913), 1:486–7.

19. Garry Wills, *Negro President: Jefferson and the Slave Power* (Boston, MA: Houghton Mifflin, 2003), 5–6.

20. James Madison, *Letters and Other Writings of James Madison: 1769–1793* (New York: Worthington, 1884), 1:186.

21. Quoted in Max Farrand, ed., *The Records of the Federal Convention of 1787* (New Haven, Conn.: Yale University Press, 1911), 3:359.

22. Wendy J. Schiller and Charles Stewart III, *Electing the Senate: Indirect Democracy before the 17th Amendment* (Princeton, NJ: Princeton University Press, 2014).

23. See https://www.fairvote.org/faithless_electors_fizzle.

24. See Allison M. Martens, "Reconsidering Judicial Supremacy: From the Counter-Majoritarian Difficulty to Constitutional Transformations," *Perspectives on Politics* 5 (2007): 447–59.

25. Marco Rubio, "Convention Can Restore Limited Government," *USA Today*, January 6, 2016, accessed February 8, 2016, http://www .usatoday.com/story/opinion/2016/01/06/marco-rubio-constitutional -convention-editorials-debates/78368672/.

26. James Madison, "Federalist 47," in *The Federalist Papers*, U.S. Constitution Online, accessed April 10, 2012, http://www.constitution .org/fed/federa47.htm.

27. James Madison, "Federalist 39," in *The Federalist Papers*, U.S. Constitution Online, accessed May 3, 2012, http://www.constitution .org/fed/federa39.htm.

28. Brutus, "Antifederalist 1," *U.S. Constitution Online*, accessed May 10, 2012, http://www.constitution.org/afp/brutus01.htm.

29. Ibid.

30. See http://www.constitution.org/rc/rat_va_08.txt.

31. James Madison, "Federalist 41," in *The Federalist Papers*, U.S. Constitution Online, accessed April 10, 2012, http://www.constitution .org/fed/federa41.htm.

32. "June 16, 1788: Patrick Henry Demands and Gets a Bill of Rights," *Free Republic*, accessed May 10, 2012, http://www.freerepublic.com /focus/f-news/1003306/posts.

33. Equal Rights Amendment, "History of the Equal Rights Amendment," accessed February 17, 2020, https://www.equalrightsamendment .org/the-equal-rights-amendment.

34. *Wickard v. Filburn,* 317 U.S. 111 (1942).

35. *National Federation of Independent Business v. Sebelius*, 11–393 (2012).

36. Derived by authors from https://www.archives.gov/open/dataset -amendments.html, accessed February 17, 2020.

37. *Furman v. Georgia*, 408 U.S. 238 (1972).

38. *Gregg v. Georgia*, 428 U.S. 153 (1976).

39. "States With and Without the Death Penalty," Death Penalty Information Center, accessed January 16, 2016, http://www.death penaltyinfo.org/states-and-without-death-penalty.

40. *Hurst v. Florida*, 193 L. Ed. 2d 504 (2016).

41. "Federal Death Penalty," Death Penalty Information Center, accessed April 10, 2012, http://www.deathpenaltyinfo.org/federal -death-penalty?scid=29&did=147.

42. Alan Yuhas, "Dzhokhar Tsarnaev Sentenced to Death for Boston Marathon Bombing—As It Happened," *The Guardian*, May 15, 2015, accessed January 16, 2016, http://www.theguardian.com/us-news /live/2015/may/15/dzhokhar-tsarnaev-boston-marathon-bombing.

43. David Baldus, Charles A. Pulaski Jr., and George Woodworth, *Equal Justice and the Death Penalty* (Boston, MA: Northeastern University Press, 1990).

44. *McCleskey v. Kemp*, 481 U.S. 279 (1987).

45. *Roper v. Simmons*, 543 U.S. 551 (2005); *Kennedy v. Louisiana,* 554 U.S. 407 (2008).

46. See http://www.innocenceproject.org/know/, accessed January 16, 2016.

47. *District Attorney's Office v. Osborne*, 557 U.S. 52 (2009).

48. Daryl J. Levinson and Richard H. Pildes, "Separation of Parties, Not Powers," *Harvard Law Review* 119 (2006): 2311.

49. Alexander Keyssar, *The Right to Vote* (New York: Basic Books, 2000), 17.

Chapter 3

1. Marissa Evans, "The 25 Most Influential Women in State Politics, Kate Brown: 'A Voice for Those That Don't Have One'," *Roll Call*, February 8, 2016, accessed February 8, 2016, http://blogs.rollcall.com/news /influential-women-kate-brown/.

2. "Gays in Politics: Uncommon Clout," Summary: Oregon's gay and lesbian activists have forged one of the country's strongest political alliances, *The Oregonian*, April 11, 1994.

3. "Essay by Kate Brown" for *Out and Elected in the USA*, accessed January 24, 2016, http://outhistory.org/exhibits/show/out-and-elected/1992 /kate-brown.

4. Jeremy W. Peters, "Openly Gay, and Openly Welcomed in Congress," *New York Times*, January 25, 2016, accessed February 6, 2016, http:// www.nytimes.com/2013/01/26/us/politics/gay-lawmakers-growing -presence-suggests-shift-in-attitudes.html?pagewanted=all&_r=0; Christin Marcos, "115th Congress Will Be Most Racially Diverse in History," *The Hill*, November 17, 2016, accessed January 24, 2018, http://thehill.com/homenews/house/306480-115th-congress-will -be-most-racially-diverse-in-history.

5. "Women Who Lead: Governor Kate Brown," Equity Foundation, March 2015, accessed January 26, 2016, http://www.equityfoundation.org/blog/women-who-lead-governor-kate-brown/.

6. Kate Brown, "2016 Policy Agenda," prepared remarks, January 20, 2016, accessed January 30, 2016, http://www.oregon.gov/gov/media/Pages/speeches/2016-Policy-Agenda.aspx.

7. Colin Bonwick, *The American Revolution* (Charlottesville: University of Virginia Press, 1991), 194.

8. "The First Political Cartoons," Archiving Early America, accessed July 7, 2016, http://www.earlyamerica.com/earlyamerica/firsts/cartoon/.

9. William Riker, *Federalism: Origin, Operation, Significance* (Boston, MA: Little Brown, 1964), 11.

10. Article 6, the Virginia Plan, accessed August 7, 2014, http://avalon.law.yale.edu/18th_century/vatexta.asp.

11. James Madison, "*Federalist 39*," in *The Federalist Papers, U.S. Constitution Online,* accessed April 13, 2012, http://www.constitution.org/fed/federa39.htm.

12. *Revenues and Expenditures for Public Elementary and Secondary Education: School Year 2011–12 (Fiscal Year 2012)* (Washington, D.C.: National Center for Education Statistics, January 2015), accessed January 25, 2016, http://nces.ed.gov/pubs2014/2014303.pdf.

13. Michael B. Berkman and Eric Plutzer, *Ten Thousand Democracies* (Washington D.C.: Georgetown University Press, 2005).

14. *Brown v. The Board of Education*, 247 U.S. 483 (1954).

15. *Cisneros v. Corpus Christi*, 404 U.S. 1211 (1971).

16. Joy Resmovits, "No Child Left Behind Waivers Granted to 33 U.S. States, Some with Strings Attached," *Huffington Post*, July 19, 2012, accessed July 20, 2012, http://www.huffingtonpost.com/2012/07/19/no-child-left-behind-waiver_n_1684504.html.

17. Fundamental Change, Innovation in America's Schools Under Race to the Top, November 2015, accessed January 25, 2016, http://www2.ed.gov/programs/racetothetop/rttfinalrpt1115.pdf.

18. Fundamental Change, Innovation in America's Schools Under Race to the Top, November 2015, accessed January 25, 2016, http://www2.ed.gov/programs/racetothetop/rttfinalrpt1115.pdf; American Recovery and Reinvestment Act of 2009. Pub. L. 111–5. 123 Stat. 115 17 February 2009, sections 14005–14007.

19. *Cohens v. Virginia*, 19 U.S. 264 (1821).

20. "Sanctuary Cities: What and Where Are They?" *DOPPLR*, April 27, 2017, accessed March 8, 2020, https://www.dopplr.com/sanctuary-city-list/; Conrad Wilson, "30 Years Later, Oregon's 'Sanctuary State' Law Serves as a Model for Others," OPB, April 17, 2017, accessed March 8, 2020, https://www.opb.org/news/article/oregon-sanctuary-city-state-donald-trump-immigration/; Justin Wingerter, "Denver Mayor Says Immigrants 'Not Pawns' after Trump Threatens Sanctuary Cities," *Denver Post*, April 12, 2019, accessed March 8, 2020, https://www.denverpost.com/2019/04/12/denver-mayor-immigrants-trump-sanctuary-cities/.

21. *Chisolm v. Georgia*, 2 U.S. 419 (1793).

22. Elinor Ostrom, *Governing the Commons: The Evolution of Institutions for Collective Action* (New York: Cambridge University Press, 1990), 106–10.

23. *United States v. Windsor*, 133 S. Ct. 2675 (2013).

24. Patrick Henry, Speech at the Virginia Ratifying Convention, June 4, 1788, http://press-pubs.uchicago.edu/founders/documents/v1ch8s38.html.

25. Christopher M. Parker, "Ideological Voting in Supreme Court Federalism Cases, 1953–2007," *Justice System Journal* 32, 2 (2011): 206–34.

26. See http://www.azleg.gov/DocumentsForBill.asp?Bill_Number=HB2201&Session_ID=115, accessed February 22, 2016; Robby Korth and Jessica Boehm, "Butt Out: State Legislatures Move to Nullify Federal Gun Laws," *NBC News,* August 21, 2014, accessed January 24, 2018, https://www.nbcnews.com/news/investigations/butt-out-state-leg islatures-move-nullify-federal-gun-laws-n185326; Justine McDaniel, Robby Korth, and Jessica Boehm, "Eight States Have Passed Laws Voiding Federal Firearms Regulations," *GUNWARS*, August 16, 2014, accessed March 8, 2020, http://gunwars.news21.com/2014/eight-states-have-passed-laws-voiding-federal-firearms-regulations/; "State Firearm Preemption Laws Fact Sheet," Everytown for Gun Safety, February 20, 2018, accessed March 8, 2020, https://everytownresearch.org/fact-sheet-preemption-laws/.

27. *McCulloch v. Maryland*, 17 U.S. 316 (1819).

28. *Gibbons v. Ogden*, 22 U.S. 1 (1824).

29. Daniel Webster's statement is from his Senate debate with Robert Y. Hayne of South Carolina, January 27, 1830. The Jefferson Day dinner took place on April 13, 1830. See Richard B. Morris and Jeffrey B. Morris, eds., *Encyclopedia of American History*, 7th ed. (New York: HarperCollins, 1996), 189–90.

30. *Dred Scott v. Sandford*, 60 U.S. 393 (1857).

31. "Confederate States of America—Declaration of the Immediate Causes Which Induce and Justify Secession of South Carolina from the Federal Union," December 24, 1860, Avalon Project, Yale University, Lillian Goldman Law Library, accessed April 30, 2012, http://avalon.law.yale.edu/19th_century/csa_scarsec.asp.

32. See http://www.civil-war.net/pages/ordinances_secession.asp.

33. Andrew Johnson, "Veto of the Civil Rights Bill," March 27, 1866, Teaching American History, accessed April 13, 2012, http://teachingamericanhistory.org/library/document/veto-of-the-civil-rights-bill/.

34. Morton Grodzins, *The American System: A New View of the Government of the United States* (New York: Rand McNally, 1966), 8.

35. Wendy J. Schiller, "Building Careers and Courting Constituents: U.S. Senate Representation, 1889–1924," *Studies in American Political Development* 20 (2006): 1.

36. *National Labor Relations Board v. Jones & Laughlin Steel Corporation*, 301 U.S. 1 (1937).

37. *United States v. Darby Lumber Company*, 312 U.S. 100 (1941).

38. *Wickard v. Filburn*, 317 U.S. 111 (1942).

39. Grodzins, *in American System*, 8–9.

40. "American Independent Party Platform of 1968," October 13, 1968, Gerhard Peters and John Woolley, *The American Presidency Project,* accessed April 13, 2012, http://www.presidency.ucsb.edu/ws//index.php?pid=29570#axzz1rwnAcK5P.

41. Sean Nicholson-Crotty, "Rational Election Cycles and the Intermittent Political Safeguards of Federalism," *Publius: The Journal of Federalism* 38 (2008): 295–314.

42. Timothy Conlon, *New Federalism: Intergovernmental Reform from Nixon to Reagan* (Washington D.C.: Brookings Institution, 1988).

43. Bill Clinton, "The Era of Big Government Is Over," radio address, *CNN,* January 27, 1996, accessed April 13, 2012, http://www.cnn.com/US/9601/budget/01-27/clinton_radio/.

44. Tim Conlan and John Dinan, "Federalism, the Bush Administration, and the Transformation of American Conservatism," *Publius: The Journal of Federalism* 37 (2007): 279–303.

45. Scott F. Abernathy, *No Child Left Behind and the Public Schools* (Ann Arbor: University of Michigan Press, 2007), 23.

46. John Schwartz, "Obama Seems to Be Open to a Broader Role for States," *New York Times,* January 29, 2009, http://www

.nytimes.com/2009/01/30/us/politics/30federal.html/; "DEA Pot Raids Go On; Obama Opposes," *Washington Times,* February 5, 2009, http://www.washingtontimes.com/news/2009/feb/05/dea-led-by-bush-continues-pot-raids/?page=1.

47. Juliet Eilperin and Brady Dennis, "Trump Administration to Revoke California's Power to Set Stricter Auto Emissions Standards," *New York Times,* September 17, 2019.

48. *Younger v. Harris,* 401 U.S. 37 (1971).

49. *United States v. Lopez,* 514 U.S. 549 (1995).

50. *South Dakota v. Dole,* 483 U.S. 203 (1987) at 211.

51. *National Federation of Independent Business v. Sebelius,* 132 S. Ct. 2566 (2012).

52. *National Federation of Independent Business v. Sebelius,* 183 L. Ed 2d 450 (2012).

53. "READ: Appeals Court Ruling on Affordable Care Act," *CNN,* December 18, 2019, https://www.cnn.com/2019/12/18/politics/ruling-on-aca-5th-circuit/index.html.

54. Frances E. Lee, "Bicameralism and Geographic Politics: Allocating Funds in the House and Senate," *Legislative Studies Quarterly* 29 (2004): 185–213.

55. Per capita figures derived by authors from United States Census, "2018 Annual Survey of State Government Finances Tables," https://www.census.gov/data/tables/2018/econ/state/historical-tables.html and United States Census, "Population, Population Change, and Estimated Components of Population Change: April 1, 2010 to July 1, 2019," https://www.census.gov/data/datasets/time-series/demo/popest/2010s-state-total.html.

56. John Hudak, *Presidential Pork: White House Influence over the Distribution of Federal Grants* (Washington D.C.: Brookings, 2014).

57. *The Partial Veto in Wisconsin,* Information Bulletin 04-1 (Madison: State of Wisconsin Legislative Reference Bureau, 2004), http://legis.wisconsin.gov/lrb/pubs/ib/04ib1.pdf.

58. Michael Cooper, "Budget Is Job of Governor, Judges Rule," *New York Times,* December 17, 2004.

59. The Federal Reserve, "State and Local Government Pension Funding Status, 2002–2017," Accessed March 3, 2020, https://www.federalreserve.gov/releases/z1/dataviz/pension/funding_status/table/.

60. Michael Lewis, "California *and* Bust," *Vanity Fair,* November 2011, http://www.vanityfair.com/business/features/2011/11/michael-lewis-201111; Scott Malone, "Rhode Island's Central Falls Files for Bankruptcy," *Reuters,* August 1, 2011, accessed May 11, 2012, http://www.reuters.com/article/2011/08/01/us-rhodeisland-centralfalls-idUSTRE7703ID20110801; Michael Cooper and Mary Williams Walsh, "Alabama Town's Failed Pension Is a Warning," *New York Times,* December 23, 2010, http://www.nytimes.com/2010/12/23/business/23prichard.html?pagewanted=print.

61. Rae Hodge, "How Kentucky Became a Surprising Leader in Flattening the Curve on COVID-19," *CNET,* March 25, 2020, accessed March 25, 2020, https://www.cnet.com/news/how-kentucky-became-a-surprising-leader-in-flattening-the-curve-on-covid-19/; David Mattingly, "Graph Comparing Ky. and Tenn. Coronavirus Responses Goes Viral," *WAVE Louisville,* March 25, 2020, accessed March 31, 2020, https://www.msn.com/en-us/travel/news/graph-comparing-ky-and-tenn-coronavirus-responses-goes-viral/ar-BB11EEmv.

62. Center for American Women and Politics, Rutgers University, *Eagleton Institute of Politics,* "History of Women Governors," accessed January 26, 2016, http://www.cawp.rutgers.edu/history-women-governors.

63. Julie Dolan, Melissa Deckman, and Michele Swers, *Women and Politics: Paths to Power and Political Influence* (Upper Saddle River, NJ: Pearson Prentice Hall, 2007) and Richard Herrera and Karen Shafer,

"Women in the Governor's Mansion," in *Women & Executive Office,* ed. Melody Rose (Boulder, Col.: Lynn Reiner, 2013).

64. Gary C. Jacobson, "Strategic Politicians and the Dynamics of U.S. House Elections, 1946–86," *American Political Science Review* 83 (1989): 773–93.

65. T. S. Last, "Voters Choose not to Retain Judge," *Albuquerque Journal North,* November 5, 2015, accessed January 25, 2016, http://www.abqjournal.com/491897/abqnewsseeker/voters-choose-not-to-retain-judge-raphaelson.html.

66. *Republican Party of Minnesota v. White,* 536 U.S. 765 (2002).

67. *Pay to Play: How Big Money Buys Access to the Texas Supreme Court* (Austin, Tex.: Texans for Public Justice, 2001), http://info.tpj.org/docs/2001/04/reports/paytoplay/paytoplay.pdf.

68. *Caperton v. Massey Coal Co.* 556 U.S. 868 (2009).

69. Governing, "The Number of Local Governments by State," May 31, 2019, accessed March 5, 2020, https://www.governing.com/gov-data/number-of-governments-by-state.html.

70. U.S. Senate elections are staggered according to Article I, Section 3, of the Constitution, resulting in a third of U.S. Senate seats up for election in any federal election.

71. Recall that Nebraska has a unicameral legislature, resulting in a total of ninety-nine legislative chambers in the fifty states. See also National Conference of State Legislatures, https://www.ncsl.org/research/elections-and-campaigns/2020-legislative-races-by-state-and-legislative-chamber.aspx, accessed March 8, 2020.

72. The New American Leaders Project, "States of Inclusion," accessed January 24, 2016, http://www.newamericanleaders.org/states_of_inclusion_2016_report.html.

73. Frank M. Bryan, *Real Democracy: The New England Town Meeting and How It Works* (Chicago, IL: University of Chicago Press, 2003), 65–79.

74. See http://www.washingtonpost.com/blogs/the-fix/post/arizona-recall-why-russell-pearce-lost/2011/11/09/gIQALj6a5M_blog.html.

75. National Conference of State Legislatures, "Initiative, Referendum, and Recall," *NCSL.org,* http://www.ncsl.org/legislatures-elections/elections/initiative-referendum-and-recall-overview.aspx.

76. *Hollingsworth v. Perry,* 133 S. Ct. 2652 (2013).

77. http://www.iandrinstitute.org/BW%202015-2%20Results%20(v1).pdf, accessed January 25, 2016.

78. http://www.iandrinstitute.org/BW%202014-2%20Election%20results%20(v1)%202014-11-04.pdf, and http://www.iandrinstitute.org/BW%202014-1%20Preview%20(v1)%202014-10-15.pdf, accessed November 5, 2014; and http://www.wcvb.com/news/massachusetts-minimum-wage-set-to-increase-in-2016/37147868, accessed February 8, 2016.

79. "Colorado Marijuana-Legalization Amendment Spending Tops $3 Million," *Denver Post,* accessed April 6, 2014, http://www.denverpost.com/ci_21820068/colorado-marijuana-legalization-amendment-spending-tops-3-million.

80. National Institute for Money in State Politics, accessed January 25, 2016, http://www.followthemoney.org/media-room/news-releases/show/275.

81. Andrew Oxford, "Arizona Lawmakers May Ask Voters to Give Up Some of Their Power over Ballot Measures," *Arizona Republic,* February 27, 2020, accessed February 27, 2020, https://www.azcentral.com/story/news/politics/legislature/2020/02/27/ballot-measures-arizona-could-face-restrictions-under-gop-proposals/4801111002/; Bob Christie, "Arizona House OKs Initiative Signature Collection Changes," *Houston Chronical,* March 4, 2020, accessed March 6, 2020, https://www.chron.com/news/article/Arizona-House-OKs-initiative-signature-collection-15106048.php.

Chapter 4

1. Brutus, "*Antifederalist 2*," U.S. Constitution Online, accessed May 9, 2012, http://www.constitution.org/afp/brutus02.htm.

2. *West Virginia Board of Education v. Barnette*, 319 U.S. 624 (1943).

3. Annals of Congress, H439 (June 8, 1789), American Memory, *Library of Congress,* accessed May 18, 2012, http://memory.loc.gov/cgi-bin/ampage?collId=llac&fileName=001/llac001.db&recNum=221.

4. *Schenck v. United States,* 249 U.S. 47 (1919).

5. *Barron v. Baltimore*, 32 U.S. 243 (1833); Zechariah Chafee Jr., *Free Speech in the United States* (Cambridge, Mass.: Harvard University Press, 1967); *Gilbert v. Minnesota*, 254 U.S. 325 (1920).

6. *Ex Parte Starr*, 263 F. 145 (1920).

7. Judith A. Baer, *Equality Under the Constitution* (Ithaca, N.Y.: Cornell University Press, 1983).

8. *Chicago B & Q Railway Company v. Chicago*, 166 U.S. 226 (1897).

9. *Gitlow v. New York*, 268 U.S. 652 (1925).

10. *Palko v. Connecticut*, 302 U.S. 319 (1937).

11. Abraham Lincoln, "July 4th Message to Congress (July 4, 1861)," Miller Center, *University of Virginia,* accessed May 18, 2012, http://millercenter.org/president/speeches/detail/3508.

12. *Ex parte Milligan*, 71 U.S. 2 (1866).

13. *Ex parte McCardle*, 74 U.S. 506 (1868).

14. *Schenck v. United States*, 249 U.S. 47 (1919); *Debs v. United States,* 249 U.S. 211 (1919).

15. *Abrams v. United States,* 250 U.S. 616 (1919).

16. David Cole, "Enemy Aliens," *Stanford Law Review* 54 (2002): 953.

17. Bernard A. Weisberger, "Terrorism Revisited," *American Heritage* 44 (November 1993), accessed June 4, 2014, http://www.americanheritage.com/content/terrorism-revisited.

18. John Earl Haynes and Harvey Klehr, *Venona: Decoding Soviet Espionage in America* (New Haven, Conn.: Yale University Press, 1999).

19. *Watkins v. United States*, 354 U.S. 178 (1957).

20. *Barenblatt v. United States*, 360 U.S. 109 (1959).

21. Ellen Schrecker, *Many Are the Crimes: McCarthyism in America* (Boston, MA: Little, Brown, 1998), xiii.

22. Select Committee to Study Governmental Operations, *Intelligence Activities and the Rights of Americans*, Book II, accessed May 18, 2012, http://www.intelligence.senate.gov/pdfs94th/94755_II.pdf, p. 213.

23. Zachary Fagenson, "U.S. Judge Re-sentences Jose Padilla to 21 Years on Terrorism Charges," *Reuters*, September 9, 2014, accessed February 7, 2016, http://www.reuters.com/article/us-usa-florida-padilla-idUSKBN0H41TW20140909.

24. *Hirota v. MacArthur*, 338 U.S. 197 (1948).

25. *Hamdan v. Rumsfeld,* 548 U.S. 557 (2006).

26. *Brandenburg v. Ohio*, 395 U.S. 444 (1969).

27. *Chaplinsky v. New Hampshire*, 315 U.S. 568 (1942).

28. David L. Hudson Jr., "Hate Speech and Campus Speech Codes," *First Amendment Center,* September 13, 2002, accessed May 9, 2012, http://www.firstamendmentcenter.org/hate-speech-campus-speech-codes.

29. *UWM Post v. Board of Regents of the University of Wisconsin*, 774 F. Supp. 1163 (1991).

30. Foundation for Individual Rights in Education (FIRE), "Speech Codes: Alive and Well, 10 Years Later," accessed June 4, 2014, http://www.thefire.org/speech-codes-alive-and-well-10-years-later/.

31. Alan Charles Kors and Harvey Silvergate, *The Shadow University: The Betrayal of Liberty on America's Campuses* (New York: Free Press, 1998).

32. *John Doe. v. University of Michigan*, 721 F. Supp. 852 (1989).

33. Ibid.

34. *UWM Post v. Board of Regents of the University of Wisconsin*, 774 F. Supp. 1163 (1991).

35. See https://www.thefire.org/10-worst-colleges-for-free-speech-2020/.

36. "Warning: College Students, This Editorial May Upset You," *Los Angeles Times*, March 31, 2014, http://www.latimes.com/opinion/editorials/la-ed-trigger-warnings-20140331,0,6700908.story#ixzz2yaSoYsXi.

37. See http://chronicle.com/blogs/conversation/2014/03/10/trigger-warnings-trigger-me.

38. Anemona Hartocollis, "Yale Lecturer Resigns After Email on Halloween Costumes," *New York Times*, December 7, 2015, A21.

39. Jonathan H. Adler, "Suzanne Venker is Unwelcome at Williams College," *Washington Post*, October 28, 2015, accessed February 16, 2016, https://www.washingtonpost.com/news/volokh-conspiracy/wp/2015/10/22/suzanne-venker-is-unwelcome-at-williams-college/.

40. *Virginia v. Black*, 538 U.S. 343 (2003).

41. See http://www.fas.org/irp/agency/doj/fisa/#rept.

42. Robin Toner and Neil A. Lewis, "A Nation Challenged: Congress; House Passes Terrorism Bill Much Like Senate's, but With 5-Year Limit," *New York Times,* October 12, 2011, accessed April 27, 2014, http://www.nytimes.com/2001/10/13/us/nation-challenged-congress-house-passes-terrorism-bill-much-like-senate-s-but.html.

43. Robert McMillan, "Obama Administration Defends Bush Wiretapping," *PCWorld,* July 15, 2009, http://www.pcworld.com/article/168502/obama_administration_defends_bush_wiretapping.html.

44. *Al Haramain Islamic Foundation v. Obama*, 690 F.3d 1089 (2012), accessed April 28, 2014, http://cdn.ca9.uscourts.gov/datastore/opinions/2012/08/07/11-15468.pdf.

45. *Smith v. Maryland*, 442 U.S. 735 (1979).

46. See http://www.nytimes.com/2013/06/08/us/mining-of-data-is-called-crucial-to-fight-terror.html?nl=todaysheadlines&emc=edit_th_20130608&_r=0.

47. Charlie Savage, "Judge Questions Legality of N.S.A. Phone Records," *New York Times*, December 16, 2013, accessed February 7, 2016, http://www.nytimes.com/2013/12/17/us/politics/federal-judge-rules-against-nsa-phone-data-program.html.

48. See http://www.nytimes.com/2014/03/25/us/obama-to-seek-nsa-curb-on-call-data.html.

49. Charlie Savage, "Judge Deals a Blow to N.S.A. Data Collection Program," *New York Times*, November 9, 2015, accessed February 7, 2016, http://www.nytimes.com/2015/11/10/us/politics/judge-deals-a-blow-to-nsa-phone-surveillance-program.html.

50. See http://epic.org/privacy/wiretap/stats/fisa_stats.html.

51. See http://afgeneralcounsel.dodlive.mil/2014/01/14/u-s-judiciary-weighs-in-on-special-advocates-before-fisa-court/; http://www.opencongress.org/bill/s990-112/show; http://www.nytimes.com/interactive/2015/06/01/us/elections/presidential-candidates-on-nsa-and-patriot-act.html?_r=0.

52. *Tinker v. Des Moines School District,* 393 U.S. 503 (1969). The quotation in the caption on page 121 is from this decision, at 506.

53. *Bland et al. v. Roberts*, E.D. Va. (April 24, 2012).

54. *United States v. O'Brien*, 391 U.S. 367 (1968).

55. *Hill v. Colorado*, 530 U.S. 703 (2000).

56. *McCullen v. Coakley*, 134 S. Ct. 2518 (2014).

57. *West Virginia Board of Education v. Barnette*, 319 U.S. 624 (1943).

58. *Texas v. Johnson*, 491 U.S. 397 (1989).

59. *Morse v. Frederick*, 551 U.S. 393 (2007).

60. *Walker v. Sons of Confederate Veterans*, 135 S. Ct. 2239 (2015).

61. *ACLU of N.C. v. Conti*, 912 F. Supp. 2d 262 (2012).

62. *Grayned v. City of Rockford*, 408 U.S. 104 (1972).

63. *National Socialist Party of America v. Village of Skokie*, 432 U.S. 43 (1977).

64. William Blackstone, *Commentaries on the Laws of England*, 1769 (Chicago, IL: University of Chicago Press, 2002), 4: 151–53.

65. *New York Times v. United States*, 403 U.S. 713 (1971).

66. *United States v. Progressive*, 467 F. Supp. 990 (1979).

67. See http://www.wikileaks.org.

68. Adam Liptak and Brad Stone, "Judge Shuts Down Web Site Specializing in Leaks," *New York Times*, February 20, 2008.

69. *Hustler Magazine v. Falwell*, 485 U.S. 46 (1988).

70. Anna Badkhen, "Web Can Ruin Reputation with Stroke of a Key," *San Francisco Chronicle*, May 6, 2007.

71. *Miller v. California*, 413 U.S. 15 (1973).

72. *Jenkins v. Georgia*, 418 U.S. 153 (1974).

73. *New York v. Ferber*, 458 U.S. 747 (1982).

74. *Ashcroft v. Free Speech Coalition*, 535 U.S. 234 (2002).

75. *Reno v. American Civil Liberties Union*, 521 U.S. 844 (1997).

76. *Brown v. Entertainment Merchants Association*, 131 S. Ct. 2729 (2011).

77. *United States v. Stevens*, 559 U.S. 460 (2010).

78. *Roberts v. United States Jaycees*, 468 U.S. 609 (1984).

79. *Boy Scouts v. Dale*, 530 U.S. 640 (2000).

80. Todd Leopold, "Boy Scouts Change Policy on Gay Leaders," *CNN*, July 28, 2015, accessed February 17, 2016, http://www.cnn.com/2015/07/27/us/boy-scouts-gay-leaders-feat/.

81. Edward Hart, "Remonstrance of the Inhabitants of the Town of Flushing to Governor Stuyvesant," December 27, 1657, Flushing Monthly Meeting of the Religious Society of Friends, accessed May 10, 2012, http://www.nyym.org/flushing/remons.html.

82. Henry J. Abraham and Barbara A. Perry, *Freedom and the Court*, 6th ed. (New York: Oxford University Press, 1994), 223.

83. Ontario Consultants on Religious Tolerance, "Religious Laws," *ReligiousTolerance.org*, accessed May 9, 2012, http://www.religioustolerance.org/lawmenu.htm.

84. *Rosenberger v. University of Virginia*, 515 U.S. 819 (1995).

85. *Church of Lakumi Babalu Aye v. City of Hialeah*, 508 U.S. 520 (1993).

86. *Reynolds v. United States*, 98 U.S. 145 (1878).

87. Bill Mears, "Judge Strikes Down Part of Utah Polygamy Law in 'Sister Wives' Case," *CNN*, December 16, 2013, http://www.cnn.com/2013/12/14/justice/utah-polygamy-law/.

88. Dustin Gardiner, "Phoenix Council Favors Silence Over Satanists—For Now," *Arizona Republic*, February 18, 2016, accessed February 25, 2016, http://www.azcentral.com/story/news/local/phoenix/2016/02/17/phoenix-council-favors-silence-over-satanists--now/80430980/.

89. *Clay, aka Ali, v. United States*, 403 U.S. 698 (1971).

90. *Employment Division v. Smith*, 494 U.S. 872 (1990).

91. *City of Boerne v. Flores*, 521 U.S. 507 (1997), at 536.

92. *Hosanna-Tabor Evangelical Lutheran Church and School v. Equal Employment Opportunity Commission*, 132 S. Ct. 694 (2012).

93. "Rethinking the Incorporation of the Establishment Clause: A Federalist View," *Harvard Law Review* 105 (1992): 1700.

94. *Everson v. Board of Education*, 330 U.S. 1 (1947).

95. *Lemon v. Kurtzman*, 403 U.S. 602 (1971).

96. *Engel v. Vitale*, 370 U.S. 421 (1962) (prayer); *Abington School District v. Schempp*, 374 U.S. 203 (1963) (Bible reading).

97. *Epperson v. Arkansas*, 393 U.S. 97 (1968).

98. *Edwards v. Aguillard*, 482 U.S. 578 (1987).

99. *Kitzmiller v. Dover Area School District*, 400 F. Supp. 2d 707 (2005).

100. See http://www.slate.com/articles/health_and_science/science/2014/01/creationism_in_public_schools_mapped_where_tax_money_supports_alternatives.html.

101. *Lee v. Weisman*, 505 U.S. 577 (1992).

102. *Santa Fe Independent School District v. Doe*, 530 U.S. 290 (2000).

103. *Board of Education v. Allen*, 392 U.S. 236 (1968).

104. *Meek v. Pittenger*, 421 U.S. 349 (1975).

105. *District of Columbia v. Heller*, 554 U.S. 570 (2008).

106. *McDonald v. Chicago*, 561 U.S. 3025 (2010).

107. See http://www.scribd.com/doc/133630146/NRA-s-National-School-Shield-Report.

108. See http://smartgunlaws.org/summary-of-enacted-laws-since-newtown.

109. See http://www.nytimes.com/2014/01/01/nyregion/federal-judge-upholds-majority-of-new-york-gun-law.html.

110. See http://www.cnn.com/2014/04/23/us/georgia-governor-signs-gun-bill/.

111. Manny Fernandez and Dave Montgomery, "Texas Lawmakers Pass a Bill Allowing Guns at Colleges," *New York Times*, June 2, 2015, A11.

112. *Florence v. County of Burlington*, 10-945 (2012).

113. *Riley v. California*, 134 S. Ct. 999 (2014).

114. *Schneckloth v. Bustamonte*, 412 U.S. 218 (1973).

115. *Missouri v. McNeely* 133 S. Ct. 1552 (2013).

116. *Maryland v. King*, 133 S. Ct. 1958 (2013).

117. Jeffrey A. Segal, "Predicting Supreme Court Decisions Probabilistically: The Search and Seizure Cases, 1962–1981," *American Political Science Review* 78 (1984): 801.

118. *California v. Ciraolo*, 476 U.S. 207 (1986).

119. *Florida v. Jardines*, 133 S. Ct. 1409 (2013).

120. *Kyllo v. United States*, 533 U.S. 27 (2001).

121. *Virginia v. Moore*, 553 U.S. 164 (2008).

122. *Prado Navarette v. California*, accessed April 28, 2014, http://www.supremecourt.gov/opinions/13pdf/12-9490_3fb4.pdf.

123. *United States v. Jones*, 132 S. Ct. 945 (2012).

124. *Vernonia School District 47J v. Acton*, 515 U.S. 646 (1995); *National Treasury Union v. Von Raab*, 489 U.S. 656 (1989); *Chandler v. Miller*, 520 U.S. 305 (1997).

125. *Mapp v. Ohio*, 367 U.S. 643 (1961).

126. Priscilla H. Machado Zotti, *Injustice for All: Mapp v. Ohio and the Fourth Amendment* (New York: Peter Lang, 2005).

127. *United States v. Leon*, 468 U.S. 897 (1984).

128. *Nix v. Williams*, 467 U.S. 431 (1984).

129. *Miranda v. Arizona*, 384 U.S. 436 (1966).

130. *Dickerson v. United States*, 530 U.S. 428 (2000).

131. *Powell v. Alabama*, 287 U.S. 45 (1932).

132. *Gideon v. Wainwright*, 372 U.S. 335 (1963).

133. *Argersinger v. Hamlin*, 407 U.S. 25 (1972).

134. *Ramos v. Louisiana* (2020) https://www.supremecourt.gov/opinions/19pdf/18-5924_n6io.pdf.

135. *Georgia v. McCollum*, 505 U.S. 42 (1992); *J. E. B. v. Alabama*, 511 U.S. 127 (1994).

136. Seehttp://www.justice.gov/opa/pr/federal-officials-close-investigation-death-trayvon-martin.

137. Matt Apuzzo, "Dylann Roof, Charleston Shooting Suspect, Is Indicted on Federal Hate Crime Charges," *New York Times*, July 22, 2015, A12.

138. Akhil Amar, *The Bill of Rights* (New Haven, Conn.: Yale University Press, 1998), 82.

139. *Rummel v. Estelle*, 445 U.S. 263 (1980).

140. *Furman v. Georgia*, 408 U.S. 238 (1972).

141. *Gregg v. Georgia*, 428 U.S. 153 (1976).

142. *District Attorney's Office v. Osborne*, 557 U.S. 52 (2009).

143. *Herrera v. Collins*, 506 U.S. 390 (1993).

144. *Griswold v. Connecticut*, 381 U.S. 479 (1965).

145. *Eisenstadt v. Baird*, 405 U.S. 438 (1972).

146. Gerald Rosenberg, *The Hollow Hope* (Chicago, IL: University of Chicago Press, 1991), 262.

147. *Roe v. Wade*, 410 U.S. 113 (1973).

148. *Planned Parenthood of Southeastern Pennsylvania v. Casey*, 505 U.S. 833 (1992).

149. *Stenberg v. Carhart*, 530 U.S. 914 (2000).

150. *Gonzalez v. Carhart*, 550 U.S. 124 (2007).

151. See https://www.guttmacher.org/state-policy/explore/state-policies-later-abortions, accessed March 2, 2020.

152. *Whole Woman's Health et al. v. Hellerstedt* (2016). See http://www.guttmacher.org/statecenter/updates/2015/statetrends42015.html.

153. Lori A. Ringhand and Paul M. Collins Jr., "May It Please the Senate: An Empirical Analysis of the Senate Judiciary Committee Hearings of Supreme Court Nominees, 1939–2009" (University of Georgia School of Law Research Paper Series, Paper No. 10-12, 2010).

154. *Bowers v. Hardwick*, 478 U.S. 186 (1986).

155. National Opinion Research Center, General Social Survey, University of Chicago.

156. *Lawrence v. Texas*, 539 U.S. 558 (2003).

157. *Cruzan v. Director, Missouri Department of Health*, 497 U.S. 261 (1990), at 278.

158. *Washington v. Glucksberg*, 521 U.S. 702; *Vacco v. Quill*, 521 U.S. 793 (1997).

159. *Village of Belle Terre v. Boraas*, 416 U.S. 1 (1974).

160. *West Virginia State Board of Education v. Barnette*, 319 U.S. 624 (1943).

161. Robert Dahl, "Decision-Making in a Democracy: The Supreme Court as a National Policy-Maker," *Journal of Public Law* 6 (1957): 279–95.

162. Anthony Lewis, *Freedom for the Thought That We Hate: A Biography of the First Amendment* (New York: Basic Books, 2007).

163. John L. Sullivan, James Pierson, and George Marcus, *Political Tolerance and American Democracy* (Chicago, IL: University of Chicago Press, 1973); James L. Gibson, "Enigmas of Intolerance: Fifty Years After Stouffer's *Communism, Conformity, and Civil Liberties*," *Perspectives on Politics* 4 (March 2006): 22.

164. August 2007 Freedom Forum Survey, retrieved May 13, 2012, from the iPOLL Databank, The Roper Center for Public Opinion Research, University of Connecticut.

Chapter 5

1. Information for this vignette came from Anna Fifield, "Tough Talk over Illegal Immigrants Leaves 'Dreamers' Disillusioned," *Financial Times*, February 27, 2012, accessed April 29, 2014 via LexisNexis Academic Universe; Lawrence Downes, "Questions for a Young Immigration-Rights Activist," *New York Times*, April 10, 2013, http://www.nytimes.com/2013/04/11/opinion/questions-for-a-young-immigration-rights-activist.html?_r=0; http://www.youtube.com/watch?v=FVZKfoXsMxk; http://freedomfromfearaward.com/celebrate/erikaandiola; http://www.facebook.com/erika.andiola; http://unitedwedream.org/press-releases/dream-youth-and-supporters-denounce-home-raid-and-detention-of-erika-andiolas-family-by-ice/; Julia Preston, "Report Finds Deportation Focus on Criminal Records, *New York Times*, April 29, 2014, p. A16, http://www.nytimes.com/2014/04/30/us/report-finds-deportations-focus-on-criminal-records.html?_r=0; "Erika Andiola Slams Obama over Deportations," accessed April 30, 2014, http://video.foxnews.com/v/3430812515001/erika-andiola-slams-obama-over-deportations/#sp=show-clips.

2. Paulina Firozi, "Listen To 4 Interviews From NPR's March 8 Live Special," *NPR*, March 9, 2016, accessed March 15, 2016, http://www.npr.org/2016/03/09/469566893/listen-to-4-interviews-from-nprs-march-8-live-special.

3. See Alexander Keyssar, *The Right to Vote* (New York: Basic Books, 2000), 17 (women) and 164 (Indians).

4. Senator Lyman Trumbull, quoted in Judith Baer, *Equality under the Constitution* (Ithaca, N.Y.: Cornell University Press, 1983), 96.

5. https://hbr.org/2020/05/the-disproportionate-impact-of-covid-19-on-black-health-care-workers-in-the-u-s

6. Quoted in Steven M. Gillon and Cathy D. Matson, *The American Experiment*, 2nd ed. (Boston, MA: Houghton Mifflin, 2006), 61.

7. *Dred Scott v. Sandford*, 60 U.S. 393 (1857).

8. Peter H. Schuck and Rogers M. Smith, *Citizenship Without Consent* (New Haven, Conn.: Yale University Press, 1985), 1–2.

9. *Johnson v. M'Intosh*, 21 U.S. 543 (1823), at 569.

10. *Elk v. Wilkins*, 112 U.S. 94 (1884).

11. Institute for Texan Cultures, *The Tejanos*, accessed June 3, 2014, http://www.texancultures.com/assets/1/15/Texans_One_and_All%20-%20The%20Tejanos.pdf.

12. Kevin R. Johnson, "The Forgotten Repatriation of Persons of Mexican Ancestry and Lessons for the War on Terror," *Pace Law Review* 26, 1 (2005): 104.

13. Texas State Historical Association, *Operation Wetback*, accessed June 3, 2014, http://www.tshaonline.org/handbook/online/articles/pqo01.

14. Johnson, 111.

15. Johnson, 110.

16. California Alien Land Law (1913).

17. *Korematsu v. United States*, 323 U.S. 214 (1944).

18. Anne McDermott, "Orphans Tell of World War II Internment," March 24, 1997, *CNN,* http://www.cnn.com/US/9703/24/interned.orphans.

19. Immigration Act of 1907, 43 Statutes at Large 153.

20. Rogers M. Smith, *Civic Ideals* (New Haven, Conn.: Yale University Press, 1997), 16; Siobhan B. Sommerville, "Queer Alienage: The Racial and Sexual Logic of the 1952 U.S. Immigration and Nationality Act," Working Paper Series on Historical Systems, *Peoples and Cultures* (No. 12), 2002, 8, accessed June 6, 2014, http://www2.bgsu.edu /downloads/cas/file46880.pdf.

21. "Immigration Restriction," eHistory @ The Ohio State University, accessed May 12, 2012, http://ehistory.osu.edu/osu/mmh/clash /Imm_KKK/Immigration%20Pages/Immigration-page1.htm.

22. Smith, *Civic Ideals,* 17.

23. Immigration Act of 1924, 43 Statutes at Large 153.

24. *United States v. Cruikshank*, 92 U.S. 542 (1876).

25. Ronald Walters, "'The Association Is for the Direct Attack': The Militant Context of the NAACP Challenge to *Plessy*," *Washburn Law Journal* 43 (Winter 2004): 329.

26. *Plessy v. Ferguson,* 163 U.S. 537 (1896).

27. Vicki L. Ruiz, "South by Southwest: Mexican Americans and Segregated Schooling, 1900–1950," *OAH Magazine of History* 15 (Winter 2001): 23–27.

28. *Westminster School District v. Mendez*, 161 F.2d 774 (1947).

29. Ruiz, "South by Southwest."

30. Quoted in Renata Fengler, "Abigail and John Adams Discuss Women and Republican Government: 1776," part of the "Documenting American History" project, University of Wisconsin–Green Bay, last modified July 29, 2009, accessed April 25, 2012, http://www.historytools .org/sources/Abigail-John-Letters.pdf.

31. Keyssar, *Right to Vote.*

32. *Minor v. Happersett*, 88 U.S. 162 (1874).

33. Justice Bradley, concurring in *Bradwell v. Illinois*, 83 U.S. 130 (1872), at 142.

34. Judith A. Baer, *The Chains of Protection* (Westport, Conn.: Greenwood Press, 1978), 6–10.

35. E. Susan Barber, comp., "One Hundred Years Toward Suffrage: An Overview," Library of Congress, *National American Woman Suffrage Association Collection,* accessed May 14, 2012, http://memory.loc .gov/ammem/naw/nawstime.html.

36. Survey conducted by the Office of Public Opinion Research, July 1945, retrieved May 14, 2012, from the iPOLL Databank, The Roper Center for Public Opinion Research, University of Connecticut.

37. "The Law: Up from Coverture," *Time Magazine,* March 20, 1972, http://www.time.com/time/magazine/article/0,9171,942533,00 .html.

38. *Kirchberg v. Feenstra*, 450 U.S. 455 (1981), at 456.

39. Richard Kluger, *Simple Justice* (New York: Knopf, 1975), 376.

40. See Laurence H. Tribe, *American Constitutional Law* (Mineola, N.Y.: Foundation Press, 1988), 1561–65.

41. See https://obamawhitehouse.archives.gov/sites/default/files/dear _colleague_sexual_violence.pdf.

42. Ibid.

43. Ibid.

44. See https://www.nytimes.com/2017/09/22/us/devos-colleges-sex -assault.html.

45. Ibid.

46. Data gathered from https://www.nytimes.com/interactive/2019/us /politics/2020-presidential-candidates.html.

47. Nicole Brown, "Here's Everyone Donald Trump's Insulted in November," *MSNBC,* November 30, 2015, accessed March 15, 2016, http://www.msnbc.com/msnbc/heres-everyone-donald-trump -has-insulted-november; see http://www.washingtonpost.com /wp-srv/special/politics/2012-exit-polls/table.html.

48. Staff, "National Exit Polls: How Different Groups Voted," *New York Times,* November 4, 2020, accessed November 12, 2020, https:// www.nytimes.com/interactive/2020/11/03/us/elections/exit-polls -president.html.

49. *Civil Rights Cases*, 109 U.S. 3 (1883); *Shelley v. Kraemer*, 334 U.S. 1 (1948).

50. *Missouri ex rel. Gaines v. Canada*, 305 U.S. 337 (1938); *Sipuel v. Board of Regents of University of Oklahoma*, 332 U.S. 631 (1948); *Sweatt v. Painter*, 339 U.S. 629 (1950).

51. *Bolling v. Sharpe*, 347 U.S. 497 (1954).

52. *Brown v. Board of Education*, 349 U.S. 294 (1955).

53. *Cooper v. Aaron*, 358 U.S. 1 (1958).

54. Gerald N. Rosenberg, *The Hollow Hope: Can Courts Bring About Social Change* (Chicago, IL: University of Chicago Press, 1991), 46–54.

55. *Alexander v. Holmes County Board of Education*, 396 U.S. 1218 (1969).

56. *Browder v. Gayle*, 352 U.S. 903 (1956).

57. *Jackson v. Alabama*, 348 U.S. 888 (1954).

58. Quoted in Walter F. Murphy, *Elements of Judicial Strategy* (Chicago, IL: University of Chicago Press, 1964), 193.

59. *Loving v. Virginia*, 388 U.S. 1 (1967).

60. David Fankhauser, "Freedom Rides: Recollections by David Fankhauser," last modified May 13, 2011, accessed April 25, 2012, http:// biology.clc.uc.edu/fankhauser/society/freedom_rides/freedom _ride_dbf.htm.

61. Martin Luther King Jr., "Letter from Birmingham Jail," April 16, 1963, *The King Center,* accessed April 25, 2012, http://www.thekingcenter .org/archive/document/letter-birmingham-city-jail-0.

62. Martin Luther King Jr., "The I Have a Dream Speech," August 28, 1963, *U.S. Constitution Online,* accessed April 25, 2012, http://www .usconstitution.net/dream.html.

63. *Heart of Atlanta Motel v. United States*, 379 U.S. 241 (1964); *Katzenbach v. McClung*, 379 U.S. 294 (1964).

64. *Griggs v. Duke Power Co.*, 401 U.S. 424 (1971).

65. *Wards Cove Packing Co. v. Antonio*, 490 U.S. 642 (1989).

66. *Ricci v. DeStefano,* 557 U.S. 557 (2009).

67. *Guinn v. United States*, 238 U.S. 347 (1915); *Smith v. Allwright*, 321 U.S 649 (1944).

68. Martin Luther King Jr., "Civil Right No. 1: The Right to Vote," *New York Times Magazine,* March 14, 1965, 26.

69. Pew Hispanic Center, "Dissecting the 2008 Electorate: Most Diverse in U.S. History," *Pew Research Center,* April 30, 2009, accessed April 25, 2012, http://www.pewhispanic.org/2009/04/30/dissecting-the-2008 -electorate-most-diverse-in-us-history/.

70. *Northwest Austin Municipal Utility District No. One v. Holder*, 557 U.S. 193 (2009).

71. Rachel Weiner, "Black Voters Turned Out at Higher Rate Than White Voters in 2012 and 2008," *Washington Post,* April 29, 2013, http://www.washingtonpost.com/blogs/the-fix/wp/2013/04/29 /black-turnout-was-higher-than-white-turnout-in-2012-and-2008.

72. *Shelby County v. Holder*, 133 S. Ct. 2612 (2013).

73. Adam Liptak, "Supreme Court Invalidates Key Part of Voting Rights," *New York Times*, June 25, 2013, http://www.nytimes.com/2013/06/26/us/supreme-court-ruling.html?pagewanted=all&_r=0>.

74. See blacklivesmatter.com/about.

75. https://www.law.com/dailyreportonline/2020/05/08/lawyers-for-ahmaud-arberys-family-have-more-questions-following-arrests-for-his-killing/?slreturn=20200506220943

76. Conor Friedersdorf, "'It's Time for Good Cops to Do Something About Bad Cops'," *The Atlantic*, June 27, 2015, accessed March 15, 2016, http://www.theatlantic.com/politics/archive/2015/06/its-time-for-good-cops-to-do-something-about-bad-cops/396890/.

77. Ralph Ellis, Holly Yan, and Pat St. Claire, "After Fatal Shootings by Police, Chicago Mayor Calls for Changes in Officer Training," *CNN*, December 27, 2015, accessed March 15, 2016, http://www.cnn.com/2015/12/27/us/chicago-police-shooting/.

78. *Hernandez v. Texas*, 347 U.S. 475 (1954).

79. *Cisneros v. Corpus Christi Independent School District*, 404 U.S. 1211 (1970).

80. Reynaldo Contreras and Leonard A. Valverde, "The Impact of *Brown* on the Education of Latinos," *Journal of Negro Education* 63 (1994): 471–72.

81. *Plyler v. Doe*, 457 U.S. 202 (1982).

82. *San Antonio Independent School District v. Rodriguez*, 411 U.S. 1 (1973).

83. *Edgewood Independent School District v. Kirby*, 777 S.W.2d 391, 392 (Tex. 1989).

84. Library of Congress. *Hispanic Americans in Congress, 1822–1995*, http://www.loc.gov/rr/hispanic/congress/gonzalez.html; Molly Ivins, November 30, 2000, http://www.creators.com/opinion/molly-ivins/molly-ivins-november-30-2000-11-30.html.

85. *Katzenbach v. Morgan*, 384 U.S. 641 (1966); *Cardona v. Power*, 384 U.S. 672 (1966).

86. 42 USC sec. 203 (1975).

87. *White v. Regester*, 412 U.S. 755 (1973). See also *Graves v. Barnes*, 405 U.S. 1201 (1972).

88. Charles L. Cotrell and R. Michael Stevens, "The 1975 Voting Rights Act and San Antonio, Texas: Toward a Federal Guarantee of a Republican Form of Government," *Publius* (1977): 79–99; United States Commission on Civil Rights, "Using the Voting Rights Act" (Washington, D.C.: U.S. Government Printing Office, 1975).

89. Cotrell and Stevens, 87.

90. Guadalupe San Miguel, Jr., *"Let All of Them Take Heed": Mexican Americans and the Campaign for Educational Equality in Texas, 1910–1981* (Austin: University of Texas Press, 1987).

91. See http://svrep.org/.

92. National Conference of State Legislatures, February 24, 2020, *Voter Identification Requirements, Voter Laws*, http://www.ncsl.org/research/elections-and-campaigns/voter-id.aspx.

93. *Johnson v. DeGrandy*, 512 U.S. 997 (1994).

94. United Farm Workers, "Successes Through the Years," http://www.ufw.org/_page.php?menu=research&inc=history/02.html.

95. Steven Yaccino and Lizette Alvarez, "New G.O.P. Bid to Limit Voting in Swing States," *New York Times*, March 29, 2014, http://www.nytimes.com/2014/03/30/us/new-gop-bid-to-limit-voting-in-swing-states.html?hp&_r=1&assetType=nyt_now.

96. Cesar Chavez, *1984 Commonwealth Club Address*, http://www.ufw.org/_page.php?menu=research&inc=history/12.html.

97. Juilana Barrera, "Immigration Activist Erika Andiola Joins Bernie Sanders Campaign," *Latin Times*, November 3, 2015, accessed March 15, 2016, http://www.latintimes.com/immigration-activist-erika-andiola-joins-bernie-sanders-campaign-351134.

98. Rachel Bachman, "U.S. Women's Soccer Games Outearned Men's Games," *The Wall Street Journal*, July 17, 2019, accessed March 29, 2020, https://www.wsj.com/articles/u-s-womens-soccer-games-out-earned-mens-games-11560765600.

99. See https://www.documentcloud.org/documents/6807392-USSF summaryjudgment.html, accessed February 17, 2020.

100. U.S. Bureau of Labor Statistics, *Highlights of Women's Earnings in 2016* (Washington, D.C., November 2015), Table 1, accessed March 29, 2020,

101. https://www.bls.gov/opub/reports/womens-earnings/2018/home.htm.

102. *Burlington Northern and Santa Fe Railway Co. v. White*, 548 U.S. 53 (2006).

103. *Ledbetter v. Goodyear Tire and Rubber Co.*, 550 U.S. 618 (2007).

104. Ibid., at 645.

105. Lilly Ledbetter Fair Pay Act of 2009, Pub. L. No. 111-2, 42 USC 2000e-5 (2009), http://www.gpo.gov/fdsys/pkg/PLAW-111publ2/html/PLAW-111publ2.htm.

106. ABA Section of Labor & Employment Law, *Survey of Recent Cases Under the Lily Ledbetter Fair Pay Act*, March 2011, accessed May 23, 2012, http://www2.americanbar.org/calendar/ll0322-2011-midwinter-meeting/Documents/08_complexlitigation.pdf (on new cases), and U.S. Bureau of Labor Statistics, *Highlights of Women's Earnings*, on continuing pay disparity.

107. See http://beta.congress.gov/bill/113th-congress/senate-bill/84, accessed April 29, 2014.

108. Wesley Lowery, "Senate Falls Six Votes Short of Passing Paycheck Fairness Act," *Washington Post*, April 9, 2014, http://www.washingtonpost.com/blogs/post-politics/wp/2014/04/09/senate-falls-six-votes-short-of-passing-paycheck-fairness-act/.

109. Juliet Eilpern, "Obama to Sign Two Executive Orders Aimed at Narrowing Gender Gap in Wages," *Washington Post*, April 7, 2014, http://www.washingtonpost.com/politics/obama-to-sign-two-executive-orders-aimed-at-narrowing-gender-gap-in-wages/2014/04/07/3f0ce4a8-be74-11e3-bcec-b71ee10e9bc3_story.html.

110. See https://www.congress.gov/bill/114th-congress/house-bill/1619.

111. *Bowers v. Hardwick*, 478 U.S. 186 (1986).

112. *Romer v. Evans*, 517 U.S. 620 (1996).

113. *Lawrence v. Texas*, 539 U.S. 558 (2003).

114. See http://www.gallup.com/poll/183332/majority-say-gays-lesbians-born-not-made.aspx.

115. See http://www.apd.army.mil/pdffiles/ad2013_24.pdf.

116. Steven Beardsley, "Overseas Benefits Elusive for Same-Sex Military Couples," February 6, 2015, accessed March 15, 2016, http://www.stripes.com/news/overseas-benefits-elusive-for-same-sex-military-couples-1.328129.

117. 570 U.S. 744.

118. A September 2015 Quinnipiac University poll found by a 55–38 margin that Americans support allowing same-sex couples to get married; data accessed February 22, 2016, from http://www.pollingreport.com/civil.htm.

119. U.S. Equal Employment Opportunity Commission, *The Americans with Disabilities Act: A Primer for Small Business*, last modified February 4, 2004, accessed May 15, 2012, http://www.eeoc.gov/eeoc/publications/adahandbook.cfm.

120. See http://www.charlotteobserver.com/news/politics-government/article68401147.html, accessed May 21, 2016.

121. Seehttp://www.esquire.com/news-politics/news/a43931/north-carolina-anti-lgbt-law-boycott/, accessed May 21, 2016.

122. Bostock v. Clayton County, Georgia, https://www.supremecourt.gov/opinions/19pdf/17-1618_hfci.pdf.

123. See https://www.today.com/video/transgender-student-athletes-speak-out-on-title-ix-debate-64626245731, accessed February 26, 2020.

124. See https://adflegal.blob.core.windows.net/mainsite-new/docs/default-source/documents/legal-documents/selina-soule---title-ix-complaint/selina-soule---title-ix-complaint---complaint-filed-with-u-s-doe-office-for-civil-rights-(2019-06-17).pdf?sfvrsn=4e2231c5_4, accessed February 26, 2020.

125. See http://www.eeoc.gov/eeoc/publications/fs-bathroom-access-transgender.cfm, accessed May 23, 2016.

126. See http://www.nytimes.com/2016/05/14/us/transgender-students-and-new-rules-in-public-schools.html, accessed May 21, 2016.

127. Abby Goodnough, Erica L. Green, and Margot Sanger-Katz, "Trump Administration Proposes Rollback of Transgender Protections," The New York Times, May 24, 2019, accessed February 26, 2020, https://www.nytimes.com/2019/05/24/us/politics/donald-trump-transgender-protections.html.

128. U.S. Equal Employment Opportunity Commission, The Americans with Disabilities Act: A Primer for Small Business, last modified February 4, 2004, accessed May 15, 2012, http://www.eeoc.gov/eeoc/publications/adahandbook.cfm.

129. "Employers Say OFCCP Disabilities Proposal Would Be Overly Burdensome," Bloomberg BNA, April 16, 2012, accessed May 14, 2012, http://www.bna.com/employers-say-ofccp-n12884908933.

130. David A. Harris, "Driving While Black: Racial Profiling on Our Nation's Highways," June 7, 1999, American Civil Liberties Union, accessed April 25, 2012, http://www.aclu.org/racial-justice/driving-while-black-racial-profiling-our-nations-highways.

131. United States v. Travis, 837 F. Supp. 1386 (1993); Derricott v. State of Maryland 611 A.2d 592 (1992).

132. "6 Men of Iraqi Descent Sue Over Detention," Chicago Tribune, November 2, 2007.

133. See http://www.nytimes.com/2014/04/16/nyregion/police-unit-that-spied-on-muslims-is-disbanded.html.

134. Krishnadev Calamur, "NYPD Settles Pair of Lawsuits Over Muslim Surveillance," The Atlantic, January 7, 2016, accessed February 22, 2016, http://www.theatlantic.com/national/archive/2016/01/nypd-surveillance-muslims-settlement/423174/.

135. "State Felon Voting Laws," Procon.org, last modified February 9, 2016, accessed February 22, 2016, http://felonvoting.procon.org/view.resource.php?resourceID=000286#washington.

136. Christopher Uggen, Sarah Shannon, and Jeff Manza, "State-Level Estimates for Felon Disenfranchisement in the United States, 2010," The Sentencing Project, July 2012, accessed April 5, 2014, http://www.sentencingproject.org/doc/publications/fd_State_Level_Estimates_of_Felon_Disen_2010.pdf.

137. Seehttps://www.pewresearch.org/fact-tank/2019/12/13/19-striking-findings-from-2019/, accessed March 18, 2020.

138. United States v. Texas 195 L Ed. 2d 638 (2016).

139. Department of Homeland Security v. Regents of the University of California, https://www.supremecourt.gov/opinions/19pdf/18-587_5ifl.pdf.

140. MSNBC/Telemundo/Marist Poll, August 2015. USMARIST.091415MT.R01. Marist College Institute for Public Opinion. Storrs, CT: Roper Center for Public Opinion Research, iPOLL [distributor], accessed February 26, 2016.

141. Robert Farley, "Trump Challenges Birthright Citizenship," FactCheck, accessed March 16, 2016, http://www.factcheck.org/2015/11/trump-challenges-birthright-citizenship/.

142. Plyler v. Doe, 457 U.S. 202 (1982).

143. King, "Civil Right No. 1."

144. See https://www.census.gov/quickfacts/table/PST045215/48.

145. M. V. Hood, Quentin Kidd, and Irwin L. Morris, "The Key Issue: Constituency Effects and Southern Senators' Roll-Call Voting on Civil Rights," Legislative Studies Quarterly 26 (2001): 599–621.

146. Royce Carroll, Jeff Lewis, James Lo, Nolan McCarty, Keith Poole, and Howard Rosenthal, "'Common Space' DW-NOMINATE Scores with Bootstrapped Standard Errors (Joint House and Senate Scaling)," Voteview.com, last modified January 22, 2011, accessed May 14, 2012, http://www.voteview.com/dwnomjoint.asp.

147. Wallace Witkowski, "Nike Drops Pacquiao Endorsement Deal After Anti-gay Comments," Morningstar, February 17, 2016, accessed March 15, 2016, http://www.morningstar.com/news/market-watch/TDJNMW_20160217498/nike-drops-pacquiao-endorsement-deal-after-antigay-comments.html.

Chapter 6

1. "2011 Women Business Owner of the Year—J. Ann Selzer," Business Record, July 29, 2011, http://www.businessrecord.com/Content/OUR-EVENTS/Upcoming-Business-Record-Events/Article/2011-Women-Business-Owner-of-the-Year-J-Ann-Selzer/153/758/53853.

2. "2011 Women Business Owner of the Year—J. Ann Selzer," Business Record, July 29, 2011, http://www.businessrecord.com/Content/OUR-EVENTS/Upcoming-Business-Record-Events/Article/2011-Women-Business-Owner-of-the-Year-J-Ann-Selzer/153/758/53853.

3. "2011 Women Business Owner of the Year—J. Ann Selzer," Business Record, July 29, 2011, http://www.businessrecord.com/Content/OUR-EVENTS/Upcoming-Business-Record-Events/Article/2011-Women-Business-Owner-of-the-Year-J-Ann-Selzer/153/758/53853.

4. Ibid.

5. Molly Ball, "Friday Interview: The Polling Guru of the Iowa Caucuses," The Atlantic, November 25, 2011, http://www.theatlantic.com/politics/archive/2011/11/friday-interview-the-polling-guru-of-the-iowa-caucuses/249036/.

6. Ibid.

7. "2011 Women Business Owner of the Year," Business Record.

8. Austin Cannon, "Polling Power: J. Ann Selzer and the Iowa Poll," Iowa Caucus Project, October 25, 2015, http://iowacaucusproject.org/2015/10/polling-power-j-ann-selzer-and-the-iowa-poll/.

9. Steven Shepard, "Ann Selzer's Secret Sauce," Politico, December 12, 2015, http://www.politico.com/story/2015/12/ann-selzer-iowa-pollster-216151.

10. Cannon, "Polling Power."

11. Lisa Lerer, Johnathan Martin, and Michael M. Grynbaum, "Des Moines Register Poll of Iowa Caucusgoers Abruptly Shelved," The New York Times, February 1, 2020, https://www.nytimes.com/2020/02/01/us/politics/des-moines-register-polls-iowa-caucus.html.

12. Carol Hunter, "From the Editor: Des Moines Register, Partners Cancel Release of Iowa Poll after Respondent Raises Concerns," Des Moines Register, February 1, 2020, https://www.desmoinesregister.com/story/news/2020/02/01/des-moines-register-cnn-cancels-release-iowa-poll-over-respondent-concerns/4637168002/.

13. Quoted in Harry Jaffa, *The Crisis of the House Divided*, 2nd ed. (Chicago, IL: University of Chicago Press, 1959), 10.

14. James Bryce, *The American Commonwealth* (New York: Macmillan, 1895), 239.

15. The first scholar to discuss how the public rallies to support the president in time of trouble was John Mueller, *War, Presidents, and Public Opinion* (New York: Wiley, 1970).

16. "Presidential Approval Ratings - - Donald Trump," *Gallup*, https://news.gallup.com/poll/203198/presidential-approval-ratings-donald-trump.aspx.

17. Methodology: Conducted by Quinnipiac University Polling Institute, January 19–January 23, 2018, and based on 1,245 telephone interviews. Sample: National registered voters. The interviews included landlines and cell phones. [USQUINN.012418.R22.]

18. See https://today.yougov.com/topics/politics/articles-reports/2020/04/27/americans-trust-local-governments; https://www.upi.com/Top_News/US/2020/04/23/Poll-Americans-trust-governors-most-when-it-comes-to-COVID-19-crisis/6381587664674/.

19. See http://www.people-press.org/2015/11/23/public-trust-in-government-1958-2015/. See 2012 American National Election Studies, http://electionstudies.org/.

20. Barack Obama, Inaugural Address, January 20, 2009, http://www.whitehouse.gov/blog/inaugural-address.

21. *Pew Research Center*, "Most Americans Say the U.S. is Among the Greatest Countries in the World," accessed May 9, 2018, http://www.pewresearch.org/fact-tank/2017/06/30/most-americans-say-the-u-s-is-among-the-greatest-countries-in-the-world/.

22. Jeffrey M. Jones "Sharply Fewer Democrats Say They Are Proud to Be Americans," *Gallup*, April 3, 2017, http://news.gallup.com/poll/207614/sharply-fewer-democrats-say-proud-americans.aspx.

23. Megan Brenan, "American Pride Hits New Low; Few Proud of Political System," *Gallup*, July 2, 2019, https://news.gallup.com/poll/259841/american-pride-hits-new-low-few-proud-political-system.aspx.

24. It is hard to know the exact share of people who would support overthrowing the American government because pollsters almost never ask that question. In our search of questions asked over the past seventy-five years, we have not found one such question. A database at the Roper Center at the University of Connecticut contains nearly five hundred thousand questions, allowing a detailed search.

25. Quoted in Francis B. Carpenter, *Six Months at the White House: The Story of a Picture* (New York: Hurd and Houghton, 1866), 218. See also Mario Cuomo, *Lincoln on Democracy* (New York: Harper, 1990).

26. Robert Hilderbrand, *Power and the People* (Chapel Hill: University of North Carolina Press, 1981).

27. Eli Saslow, *Ten Letters: The Stories Americans Tell Their President* (New York: Doubleday, 2011).

28. Quoted in John Geer, *From Tea Leaves to Opinion Polls* (New York: Columbia University Press, 1996), 50–51.

29. Benjamin Ginsberg, *The Captive Public* (New York: Basic Books, 1986).

30. Robert Erikson and Kent Tedin, *American Public Opinion*, 6th ed. (New York: Longman, 2003), 7.

31. V. O. Key, *Public Opinion and American Democracy* (New York: Knopf, 1961), 536.

32. George Gallup, *The Pulse of Democracy* (New York: Simon and Schuster, 1940).

33. Seymour Sudman and Norman M. Bradburn, "The Organizational Growth of Public Opinion Research in the United States," *Public Opinion Quarterly* 51, pt. 2, Supplement: 50th Anniversary Issue (1987): S67–S78.

34. Franklin Roosevelt made occasional use of polls. Truman had no use for polls, but Eisenhower's advisers clearly paid attention to them. For the best scholarly account of the presidential use of polls, see Robert Eisinger, *The Evolution of Presidential Polling* (New York: Cambridge University Press, 2003).

35. Erikson and Tedin, *American Public Opinion*, 8th ed. 26–33.

36. Joshua D. Clinton and Steven Rogers, "Robo-Polls: Taking Cues from Traditional Sources?" *PS: Political Science & Politics* 46, 2 (2013): 333–37.

37. Ibid.

38. Giovanni Russonello and Sarah Lyall, "Surprising Poll Results: People Are Now Happy to Pick Up the Phone," *The New York Times*, April 17, 2020, EndNotes.docxhttps://www.nytimes.com/2020/04/17/us/politics/polling-coronavirus.html.

39. Alicia C. Shepard, "How They Blew It," *American Journalism Review* (January/February 2001).

40. Steven Shepard, "Is This the Beginning of the End of the Exit Poll?" *Politico*, December 17, 2019, https://www.politico.com/story/2017/12/09/exit-polls-election-day-frustration-287913.

41. Nick Gass and Burgess Everett, "Cruz Denies Trump Accusations Over 'Push Polls,'" *Politico*, February 11, 2016, http://www.politico.com/story/2016/02/donald-trump-ted-cruz-south-carolina-push-polls-219158.

42. These data come from 2003 polls retrieved April 15, 2012, from the iPOLL Databank, the Roper Center for Public Opinion Research, University of Connecticut.

43. Philip E. Converse, "Nonattitudes and American Public Opinion: Comment: The Status of Nonattitudes," *American Political Science Review* 68 (June 1974): 650–60.

44. Claudia Deane, Courtney Kennedy, and Scott Keeter, "A Field Guide to Polling: Election 2020 Edition," *Pew Research Center*, November 19, 2019, https://www.pewresearch.org/methods/2019/11/19/a-field-guide-to-polling-election-2020-edition/.

45. Pew Research Center for People & the Press, "Cell Phones and the 2008 Vote: An Update," *Pew Research Center*, July 17, 2008, accessed April 27, 2012, http://pewresearch.org/pubs/901/cell-phones-polling-election-2008.

46. Deane, Kennedy, and Keeter, "A Field Guide to Polling."

47. Erikson and Tedin, *American Public Opinion*, 6th ed. 121.

48. M. Kent Jennings, Laura Stoker, and Jake Bowers, "Politics Across Generations," *Journal of Politics* 71 (July 2009): 782–99.

49. John Alford and John Hibbing, "Biology and Rational Choice," *Political Economy Newsletter*, Fall 2005.

50. Shankar Vedantam, "Nature, Nurture and Your Politics," Hidden Brain, *NPR*, October 8, 2018, https://www.npr.org/2018/10/03/654127241/nature-nurture-and-your-politics.

51. Amy Lavoie, "The Genes in Your Congeniality: Researchers Identify Genetic Influence in Social Networks," *Harvard Science: Culture + Society*, January 26, 2009.

52. Peter Hatemi, Nathan A. Gillespie, Lindon J. Eaves, Brion S. Maher, Sarah E. Medland, David C. Smyth, Harry N. Beeby, Scott D. Gordon, Grant W. Montgomery, Ghu Zhu, Enda M. Byrne, Bradley T. Webb, Andrew C. Heath, and Nicholas G. Martin, "A Genome-Wide Analysis of Liberal and Conservative Political Attitudes," *Journal of Politics* 73 (2011): 1–15.

53. John R. Alford, John Hibbing, and Carolyn L. Funk, "Twin Studies, Molecular Genetics, Politics, and Tolerance," *Perspectives on Politics* 6 (December 2008); John Hibbing, John R. Alford, and Carolyn L. Funk, "Beyond Liberals and Conservatives to Political Genotypes and Phenotypes," *Perspectives on Politics* 6 (June 2008): 321–28.

54. Pew Research Center for the People & the Press, "Young Voters in the 2008 Election," *Pew Research Center,* November 12, 2008, accessed April 27, 2012, http://pewresearch.org/pubs/1031 /young-voters-in-the-2008-election.

55. See http://www.huffingtonpost.com/2012/11/07/youth-vote-2012 -turnout-exit-polls_n_2086092.html.

56. Tyler Kingkade. "Youth Vote 2012 Turnout: Exit Polls Show Greater Share of Electorate Than In 2008," *The Huffington Post,* November 7, 2012, http://www.huffingtonpost.com/2012/11/07 /youth-vote-2012-turnout-exit-polls_n_2086092.html; *New York Times,* "Election 2016: Exit Polls," accessed November 12, 2016, http:// www.nytimes.com/interactive/2016/11/08/us/politics/election -exit-polls.html?_r=0.

57. Pew Internet & American Life Project, "Millennials Will Benefit and Suffer Due to Their Interconnected Lives," *Pew Research Center,* February 29, 2012, accessed April 27, 2012, http://www.pewinter-net.org/Reports/2012/Hyperconnected-lives.aspx?src=prc-headline.

58. Robert Erikson and Kent Tedin, *American Public Opinion,* 8th ed. (New York: Longman, 2010).

59. This theory comes out of the work of John Zaller, *Nature of Mass Beliefs* (New York: Cambridge University Press, 1992).

60. Poll conducted by *NBC News/Wall Street Journal,* October 25–28, 1997, and January 17–20, 2007, retrieved April 15, 2012, from the iPOLL Databank, the Roper Center for Public Opinion Research, University of Connecticut.

61. Fox News Polls conducted in June 2015 and 2017, accessed through Roper Center at Cornell University on February 25, 2018.

62. Matthew Goldberg, Abel Gustafson, Seth Rosenthal, John Kotcher, Edward Maibach, and Anthony Leiserowitz, "For the First Time, the Alarmed Are Now the Largest of Global Warming's Six Americas," Yale Program on Climate Change Communication, January 16, 2020, https://climatecommunication.yale.edu/publications/for-the-first -time-the-alarmed-are-now-the-largest-of-global-warmings-six -americas/.

63. The classic book that lays out the argument about party identifica-tion is Angus Campbell, Philip Converse, Warren Miller, and Donald Stokes, *The American Voter* (New York: Wiley, 1960).

64. See https://news.gallup.com/poll/203198/presidential-approval-ratings -donald-trump.aspx.

65. See American National Election Studies, "Party Identification 7-Point Scale 1952–2008," *ANES Guide to Public Opinion and Electoral Behavior,* last modified August 5, 2010, accessed April 27, 2012, http://www.electionstudies.org/nesguide/toptable/tab2a_1.htm.

66. David Brooks, "What Independents Want," *New York Times,* November 5, 2009, A31.

67. John Sides, "Three Myths About Political Independents," *The Monkey Cage* (blog), December 17, 2009, http://www.themonkeycage.org /blog/2009/12/17/three_myths_about_political_in/.

68. John Laloggia, "6 Facts about U.S. Political Independents," *Pew Research Center,* May 15, 2019, https://www.pewresearch.org /fact-tank/2019/05/15/facts-about-us-political-independents/.

69. See https://news.gallup.com/poll/275792/remained-center-right -ideologically-2019.aspx.

70. This way of thinking about the public comes from Philip Converse, "Nature of Belief Systems in Mass Publics," in *Ideology and Discontent,* ed. David Apter (New York: Free Press, 1964).

71. The exact percentage of the public that was literate at the time of the founding is unclear. This percentage reflects the best guess of some historians.

72. *CIA World Factbook,* https://www.cia.gov/library/publications /the-world-factbook/geos/us.html.

73. Paul Lazarsfeld, Bernard Berelson, and Helen Gaudet, *The People's Choice* (New York: Duell, Sloane, Pearce, 1944).

74. Bernard Berelson, Paul F. Lazarsfeld, and William N. McPhee, *Voting: A Study of Opinion Formation in a Presidential Campaign* (Chicago, IL: University of Chicago Press, 1954).

75. Converse, "Nature of Belief Systems in Mass Publics."

76. These data all come from Erikson and Tedin, *American Public Opinion,* 8th ed., 61.

77. John Zaller, "Monica Lewinsky and the Mainsprings of American Politics," in *Mediated Politics: Communication in the Future of Democracy,* ed. W. Lance Bennett and Robert M. Entman (Cambridge, U.K.: Cambridge University Press, 2001).

78. Stanley Kelley, *Interpreting Elections* (Princeton, NJ: Princeton University Press, 1983).

79. Christopher Achen, "Mass Political Attitudes and the Survey Response," *American Political Science Review* 69 (1975): 1218–31.

80. Jennifer Hochschild, *What's Fair* (New Haven, CT.: Yale University Press, 1980).

81. Sam Popkin developed this concept in his book *The Reasoning Voter* (Chicago: University of Chicago Press, 1991).

82. "The Polarization of the Congressional Parties," *Voteview.com,* last modified March 6, 2012, accessed April 27, 2012, http://voteview .com/political_polarization.asp.

83. For a comprehensive account of these data, see Alan Abramowitz and Kyle Saunders, "Is Polarization a Myth?" *Journal of Politics* 70 (2008): 542–55.

84. "The Polarization of the Congressional Parties."

85. *Pew Research Center,* "Beyond Distrust: How Americans View Their Government," November 23, 2015, http://www.people -press.org/2015/11/23/beyond-distrust-how-americans-view -their-government/.

86. Alan Abramowitz, *The Disappearing Center* (New Haven, CT.: Yale University Press, 2010).

87. "The Abu Ghraib Files," *Salon,* March 14, 2006, http://www.salon .com/2006/03/14/introduction_2/.

88. Sarah Mendelson, "The Guantanamo Countdown," *Foreign Affairs,* October 1, 2009.

89. See https://www.realclearpolitics.com/docs/CNN_RV_.pdf.

90. Alexa Lardieri, "Nearly Half of Americans Support Airstrike that Killed Iranian Leader, Poll Finds," *U.S. News & World Report,* January 8, 2020, https://www.usnews.com/new/politics/articles/2020-01-08 /poll-nearly-half-of-americans-support-airstrike-that-killed-top-iranian -military-leader.

91. Survey conducted by Quinnipiac University Polling Institute, January 4–7, 2014, retrieved May 4, 2014, from the iPOLL Databank, the Roper Center for Public Opinion Research, University of Connecticut.

92. Surveys conducted by AP-NORC Center, August 12–29, 2013, and *Associated Press/National Opinion Research Center,* December 10–13, 2015, retrieved March 17, 2016, from the iPOLL Databank, the Roper Center for Public Opinion Research, University of Connecticut.

93. Data come from polling data from the *Pew Research Center* in 2002, 2013, and 2016.

94. The data from 2000 are from the *CBS/New York Times* polls conducted during the presidential campaigns and available through the iPOLL Databank, the Roper Center for Public Opinion Research, University of Connecticut.

95. *CBS News/New York Times* Poll, November 2016 [survey question]. USCBSNYT.110716.R01. *CBS News/New York Times* [producer].

Cornell University, Ithaca, NY: Roper Center for Public Opinion Research, iPOLL [distributor], accessed November 12, 2016.

96. Drew Desilver, "U.S. Trails Most Developed Countries in Voter Turnout," *Pew Research Center,* May 21, 2018, https://www.pewresearch.org/fact-tank/2018/05/21/u-s-voter-turnout-trails-most-developed-countries/.

97. Erikson and Tedin, *American Public Opinion,* 8th ed., 193.

98. Jenifer De Pinto, "Support for Marijuana Legalization Hits New High, CBS News Poll Finds," *CBS News,* April 19, 2919, https://www.cbsnews.com/news/support-for-marijuana-legalization-hits-new-high-cbs-news-poll-finds/.

99. Survey conducted for *CBS News/New York Times,* February 19–23, 2014, retrieved April 7, 2014, from the iPOLL Databank, the Roper Center for Public Opinion Research, University of Connecticut.

100. *Pew Research Center,* "Party Affiliation among Jews," *Pew Research Center,* accessed March 2, 2020, https://www.pewforum.org/religious-landscape-study/religious-tradition/jewish/party-affiliation/.

101. *Pew Research Center,* "Muslim Americans: Middle Class and Mostly Mainstream," *Pew Research Center,* May 22, 2007, accessed April 27, 2012, http://pewresearch.org/pubs/483/muslim-americans.

102. Erikson and Tedin, *American Public Opinion,* 6th ed., 215.

103. *New York Times,* "Election 2016: Exit Polls," accessed November 12, 2016, http://www.nytimes.com/interactive/2016/11/08/us/politics/election-exit-polls.html?_r=0.

104. Center for American Women and Politics, Eagleton Institute of Politics, Rutgers University, "The Gender Gap: Voting Choices in Presidential Elections," December 2008, accessed May 23, 2012, http://www.cawp.rutgers.edu/fast_facts/voters/documents/GGPresVote.pdf.

105. "Women Voters Propel Democratic Takeover of U.S. House of Representatives; Large Gender Gaps Apparent in Most 2018 Senate and Gubernatorial Races," Center for American Women and Politics, Rutgers Eagleton Institute of Politics, November 8, 2018, http://cawp.rutgers.edu/sites/default/files/resources/press-release-women-voters-2018_0.pdf.

106. See http://www.pewresearch.org/fact-tank/2017/12/11/for-the-first-time-more-americans-say-2010-health-care-law-has-had-a-positive-than-negative-impact-on-u-s/.

107. John Gramlich and Katherine Schaeffer, "7 Facts About Guns in the U.S.," *Pew Research Center,* October 22, 2019, https://www.pewresearch.org/fact-tank/2019/10/22/facts-about-guns-in-united-states/.

108. Data from American National Election Studies, "Aid to Blacks/Minorities 1970–2008," *ANES Guide to Public Opinion and Electoral Behavior,* last modified August 5, 2010, accessed May 12, 2012, http://www.electionstudies.org/nesguide/2ndtable/t4b_4_1.htm.

109. *Pew Research Center,* "The Partisan Divide on Political Values Grows Even Wider," October 5, 2017, http://www.people-press.org/2017/10/05/the-partisan-divide-on-political-values-grows-even-wider/.

110. Victor Rubin, et al., "Counting a Diverse Nation: Disaggregating Data on Race and Ethnicity to Advance a Culture of Health," PolicyLink, 2018, https://www.policylink.org/sites/default/files/Counting_a_Diverse_Nation_08_15_18.pdf.

111. Jens Manuel Krogstad, "After Decades of GOP Support, Cubans Shifting Toward the Democratic Party," *Pew Research Center,* June 24, 2016, http://www.pewresearch.org/fact-tank/2014/06/24/after-decades-of-gop-support-cubans-shifting-toward-the-democratic-party; *Pew Research Center,* "Latino Support for Democrats Falls, but Democratic Advantage Remains: Immigration Not a Deal-Breaker Issue for Half of Latino Voters," October 29, 2014, http://www.pewhispanic.org/files/2014/10/2014-10-29_NSL-latino-politics.pdf.

112. Rodolfo De la Garza, Louis DeSipio, F. Chris Garcia, John Garcia, and Angelo Falcon, *Latino Voices: Mexican, Puerto Rican, and Cuban Perspectives on American Politics* (Boulder, CO.: Westview Press, 1992).

113. See http://www.pewresearch.org/fact-tank/2016/11/29/hillary-clinton-wins-latino-vote-but-falls-below-2012-support-for-obama/.

114. Luis Noe-Bustamante, Abby Budiman, and Mark Hugo Lopez, "Where Latinos Have the Most Eligible Voters in the 2020 Election," *Pew Research Center,* January 31, 2020, https://www.pewresearch.org/fact-tank/2020/01/31/where-latinos-have-the-most-eligible-voters-in-the-2020-election/.

115. Abby Budiman, Luis Noe-Bustamante, and Mark Hugo Lopez, "Naturalized Citizens Make Up Record One-in-Ten U.S. Eligible Voters in 2020," *Pew Research Center,* February 26, 2020, https://www.pewresearch.org/hispanic/2020/02/26/naturalized-citizens-make-up-record-one-in-ten-u-s-eligible-voters-in-2020/.

116. Alexander Kuo, Neil Malhotra, and Cecilia Hyunjung Mo, "Why Do Asian Americans Identify as Democrats? Testing Theories of Social Exclusion and Intergroup Solidarity," working paper, Vanderbilt University, February 25, 2014, accessed November 12, 2016, http://www.nytimes.com/interactive/2016/11/08/us/politics/election-exit-polls.html?_r=0.

117. That figure combines Democratic identifiers with "leaners."

118. Pew Research Hispanic Trends Project, December 28, 2011, http://www.pewhispanic.org/2011/12/28/vii-views-of-the-political-parties-and-party-identification.

119. Jens Manuel Krogstad, Antonio Flores, and Mark Hugo Lopez, "Key Takeaways About Latino Voters in the 2018 Midterm Elections," *Pew Research Center,* November 18, 2018, https://www.pewresearch.org/fact-tank/2018/11/09/how-latinos-voted-in-2018-midterms/.

120. Jens Manuel Krogstad, Ana Gonzalez-Barrera, and Christine Tamir, "Latino Democratic Voters Place High Importance on 2020 Presidential Election," *Pew Research Center,* January 17, 2020, https://www.pewresearch.org/fact-tank/2020/01/17/latino-democratic-voters-place-high-importance-on-2020-presidential-election/.

121. Efrén O. Pérez, 2015, "Xenophobic Rhetoric and Its Political Effects on Immigrants and Their Co-Ethnics," *American Journal of Political Science* 59(3): 549–564.

122. Krogstad, Flores, and Lopez, "Key Takeaways About Latino Voters in the 2018 Midterm Elections."

123. "Record Numbers of Latinos Sworn in to 116th Congress," *NALEO Educational Fund,* January 3, 2019, https://naleo.org/wp-content/uploads/2019/06/1_3_19-NEF-Release-on-116th-Congress-Final.pdf.

124. *Pew Research Center* for the People & the Press, "Where the Public Stands on Immigration Reform," *Pew Research Center,* November 23, 2009, accessed April 27, 2012, http://pewtrusts.org/our-work-report-detail.aspx?id=56203.

125. Norman H. Nie, Jane Junn, and Kenneth Stehlik-Barry, *Education and Democratic Citizenship in America* (Chicago, IL: University of Chicago Press, 1996).

126. V. O. Key, *The Responsible Electorate* (Cambridge, MA.: Harvard University Press, 1966), 1.

127. Robert S. Erikson, Michael B. MacKuen, and James A. Stimson, *The Macro Polity* (Cambridge, U.K.: Cambridge University Press, 2002).

128. See Key, *Public Opinion and American Democracy,* and Douglas Arnold, *Logic of Congressional Action* (New Haven, CT.: Yale University Press, 1991).

Chapter 7

1. House.gov, "Congresswoman Alexandria Ocasio-Cortez," accessed February 17, 2020, https://ocasio-cortez.house.gov.

2. *Knock Down the House,* directed by Rachel Lears. Jubilee Films in association with Atlas Films and Artemis Rising, 2019, *Netflix,* https://www.netflix.com/watch/81080637?trackId=14277281&tctx=0%2C0%2C93e2992a-e49c-4a36-987b-3a8d2654a9c3-746502541%2C%2C.

3. Eliza Relman, "THE TRUTH ABOUT ALEXANDRIA OCASIO-CORTEZ: The Inside Story of How, in Just One Year, Sandy the Bartender Became a Lawmaker Who Triggers Both Parties," *Insider,* January 6, 2019, accessed February 17, 2020, https://www.insider.com/alexandria-ocasio-cortez-biography-2019-1.

4. Charlotte Alter, "'Change Is Closer Than We Think.' Inside Alexandria Ocasio-Cortez's Unlikely Rise," *Time,* March 21, 2019, accessed February 17, 2020, https://time.com/longform/alexandria-ocasio-cortez-profile/.

5. *Knock Down the House,* 2019.

6. Relman, "THE TRUTH ABOUT ALEXANDRIA OCASIO-CORTEZ."

7. Herbert Gans, *Democracy and the News* (New York: Oxford University Press, 2003), 1.

8. Thomas Jefferson to Edward Carrington, "Volume 5, Amendment I (Speech and Press), Document 8," January 16, 1787, *The Founders' Constitution,* ed. Philip B. Kurland and Ralph Lerner (Chicago, IL: University of Chicago Press, 1986), accessed May 27, 2012, http://press-pubs.uchicago.edu/founders/documents/amendI_speechs8.html.

9. *Pew Research Center's* Project for Excellence in Journalism, "A Year in the News," *The State of the News Media 2009: An Annual Report on American Journalism,* accessed May 27, 2012, http://stateofthemedia.org/2009/a-year-in-the-news. See especially the section titled "The Economy Finally Emerges as a Major Story."

10. Bob Woodward and Carl Bernstein, *All the President's Men* (New York: Simon and Schuster, 1994).

11. Thomas E. Patterson, *Out of Order* (New York: Knopf, 1993), 82.

12. *Near v. Minnesota,* 283 U.S. 697 (1931).

13. *New York Times Co. v. United States,* 403 U.S. 713 (1971).

14. *Obsidian Finance Group, LLC and Kevin D. Padrick v. Crystal Cox* (2014).

15. "iHeartMedia", accessed March 6, 2018, http://www.iheartmedia.com/iheartmedia/index.

16. Associated Press, "Gannett Co. Acquires Midwest South Newspapers for $280 M," *GazetteXtra,* October 8, 2015, http://www.gazettextra.com/20151008/gannett_co_acquires_midwest_south_newspapers_for_280m.

17. Jeremy D. Mayer, *American Media Politics in Transition* (New York: McGraw-Hill, 2007), 76.

18. *Federal Communications Commission v. Pacifica Foundation,* 438 U.S. 726 (1978).

19. *FCC v. Fox Television Stations,* 173 L. Ed. 2d 738 (2009).

20. Emma Llansó and Mark Stanley, "Communications Decency Act," Center for Democracy & Technology, September 21, 2011, accessed June 25, 2014, https://cdt.org/blog/shielding-the-messengers-section-230-and-free-speech-online/.

21. Electronic Frontier Foundation, "CDA 230: The Most Important Law Protecting Internet Speech," accessed March 16, 2020, https://www.eff.org/issues/cda230.

22. Liberty Counsel, "Legislative History of COPA," *LC.org,* accessed June 4, 2012, http://www.lc.org/profamily/copa.pdf.

23. Federal Trade Commission, "Facts for Consumers," 2007. See http://ftc.gov/ for all available information collected by the FTC for consumers.

24. Library of Congress, "An Act to Prevent Child Abduction and the Sexual Exploitation of Children," see http://thomas.loc.gov/.

25. Federal Trade Commission, "Computers and the Internet: Privacy and Security." See http://www.ftc.gov for information on this issue and others.

26. Benjamin Franklin, "An Apology for Printers," *Pennsylvania Gazette,* May 27, 1731, reprinted as *An Apology for Printers* (Washington, D.C.: Acropolis Books, 1973).

27. Mayer, *American Media Politics in Transition,* 81.

28. Michael Schudson and Susan Tifft, "American Journalism in Historical Perspective," in *The Press,* ed. Geneva Overholser and Kathleen Hall Jamieson (New York: Oxford University Press, 2005), 19.

29. Michael Schudson, *Discovering the News: A Social History of American Newspapers* (New York: Basic Books, 1978).

30. William Riker, *The Strategy of Rhetoric: Campaigning for the American Constitution* (New Haven, CT.: Yale University Press, 1996).

31. David McCullough, *John Adams* (New York: Simon and Schuster, 2001).

32. Sedition Act, July 14, 1798, U.S. Constitution Online, accessed June 4, 2012, http://www.constitution.org/rf/sedition_1798.htm.

33. John Geer, *In Defense of Negativity: Attack Ads in Presidential Campaigns* (Chicago, IL: University of Chicago Press, 2006).

34. Michael Schudson, *The Sociology of News* (New York: W. W. Norton, 2003), 75.

35. Melvin Laracey, "Who Listened? Political Media Communications by 'Pre-Modern' Presidents" (paper presented at the annual meeting of the Midwest Political Science Association, Chicago, IL., 2004).

36. James Hamilton, *All the News That's Fit to Sell: How the Market Transforms Information into News* (Princeton, NJ: Princeton University Press, 2006).

37. Ibid., 53.

38. See Great Projects Film Company, "Yellow Journalism," *Public Broadcast System* (*PBS*), 1999, accessed May 15, 2012, http://www.pbs.org/crucible/journalism.html.

39. As quoted by Matt Drudge in "Anyone with a Modem Can Report on the World" (address before the National Press Club, June 2, 1998).

40. Jon Blackwell, "1906: Rumble over 'The Jungle,'" *Trentonian,* http://www.capitalcentury.com/1906.html.

41. Schudson and Tifft, "American Journalism in Historical Perspective," 17–46.

42. Rose McDermott, *Presidential Leadership, Illness, and Decision Making* (New York: Cambridge University Press, 2007).

43. Iyengar, *Media Politics;* American National Election Studies, *ANES Guide to Public Opinion and Electoral Behavior,* http://www.electionstudies.org/nesguide/nesguide.htm.

44. Brian Stelter, "Lester Holt Gets Anchor Chair in Moment for Black Journalists," *CNN Money,* June 18, 2015, http://money.cnn.com/2015/06/18/media/lester-holt-nbc-promotion.

45. Data retrieved May 1, 2012, from the iPOLL Databank, the Roper Center for Public Opinion Research, University of Connecticut.

46. Theodore H. White, *The Making of the President, 1960* (New York: Atheneum Publishers, 1961).

47. Sidney Krause, *The Great Debates: Kennedy v. Nixon, 1960* (Bloomington: Indiana University Press, 1977). The quotation is from Kennedy's telegram to the NBC board chair, accepting the invitation to debate, quoted in the *Tri City Herald,* July 28, 1960.

48. Robert Farley, "Survey Says: Trump Misleads on Debate Performances," *FactCheck.org,* February 21, 2020, https://www.factcheck.org/2020/02/survey-says-trump-misleads-on-debate-performances/.

49. Schudson and Tifft, "American Journalism in Historical Perspective," 26.

50. Susannah Fox and Lee Rainie, "About This Report," *Pew Research Center, Internet, Science and Technology: The Web at 25 in the U.S.*, February 27, 2014, accessed April 20, 2014, http://www.pewinternet.org/2014/02/27/summary-of-findings-3/.

51. Charlie Sorrel, "Apple's iPad Sales Accelerate: Three Million Sold in 80 Days," *Gadget Lab* (blog), Wired, June 23, 2010, http://www.wired.com/gadgetlab/2010/06/apples-ipad-sales-accelerate-three-million-sold-in-80-days.

52. See https://www.omnicoreagency.com/twitter-statistics/.

53. Shea Bennett, "How Many Millennials, Gen-Xers and Baby Boomers Use Facebook, Twitter and Instagram," *Ad Week: Social Times*, June 3, 2014, accessed March 27, 2016, http://www.adweek.com/socialtimes/millennials-gen-x-baby-boomers-social-media/499110.

54. "60 Incredible and Interesting Twitter Stats and Statistics," *Brandwatch*, January 2, 2020, https://www.brandwatch.com/blog/twitter-stats-and-statistics/.

55. Data available at "Report: Community Journalism in the United States," Bill Lane Center for the American West, Stanford University, last modified August 7, 2011, accessed May 27, 2012, http://www.stanford.edu/group/ruralwest/cgi-bin/drupal/projects/newspapers.

56. For data on news consumption, see *The State of the News Media 2014* report available from the *Pew Research Center's* Project for Excellence in Journalism at http://www.journalism.org/packages/state-of-the-news-media-2014/.

57. Alex Jones, *Losing the News* (New York: Oxford University Press, 2009).

58. The data come from a study conducted for the Newspaper Association of America. See "Study: Newspapers Attract 102.8 million U.S. Internet Users," *SFN Blog*, World Association of Newspapers and News Publishers, http://www.sfnblog.com/2010/10/14/study-newspapers-attract-1028-million-us-internet-users.

59. Geoffrey Cowan, "Leading the Way to Better News" (Discussion Paper Series, Joan Shorenstein Center on the Press, Politics, and Public Policy, Harvard University, 2008), 7.

60. See http://www.journalism.org/fact-sheet/newspapers/, accessed March 6, 2018.

61. See https://www.poynter.org/business-work/2020/advance-local-to-lay-off-the-last-four-reporters-at-the-plain-dealer/.

62. Michael Barthel, "Newspaper: Fact Sheet," *State of the News Media 2015*, Pew Research Center, April 29, 2015, accessed March 23, 2016, http://www.journalism.org/2015/04/29/newspapers-fact-sheet.

63. Ibid.

64. Nancy Vogt, "Audio: Fact Sheet," *State of the News Media 2015*, Pew Research Center, April 29, 2015, http://www.journalism.org/2015/04/29/audio-fact-sheet.

65. David Barker, *Rushed to Judgment* (New York: Columbia University Press, 2002).

66. *Pew Research Center's* Project for Excellence in Journalism, "Talk Radio," *The State of the News Media 2012*, Pew Research Center, accessed May 28, 2012, http://stateofthemedia.org/2012/audio-how-far-will-digital-go/#talk-radio.

67. No one has studied reasons why liberal talk radio has failed, but we offer some hypotheses here. Thank you to Markus Prior of Princeton University for brainstorming with us on this topic.

68. See http://www.adweek.com/tvnewser/evening-news-ratings-week-of-may-22-2/330626, accessed March 6, 2018.

69. Katerina Eva Masta, "Fewer Americans Rely on TV News; What Type They Watch Varies by Who They Are," *Pew Research Center*, January 5, 2018, https://www.pewresearch.org/fact-tank/2018/01/05/fewer-americans-rely-on-tv-news-what-type-they-watch-varies-by-who-they-are/.

70. See http://tvbythenumbers.zap2it.com/2016/01/14/late-night-ratings-jan-4-8-2016-daily-show-and-nightly-show-start-2016-on-upswing/.

71. See http://www.hollywoodreporter.com/news/john-olivers-talk-show-ratings-735187.

72. Toni Fitzgerald, "How Many Viewers Watched Eddie Murphey Host 'Saturday Night Live?," *Forbes*, December 22, 2019, https://www.forbes.com/sites/tonifitzgerald/2019/12/22/how-many-viewers-watched-eddie-murphy-host-saturday-night-live/#6f8bf65f47ba.

73. eBizMBA's ranking of the top fifteen blogs is available at http://www.ebizmba.com/articles/blogs. The rankings shown here were retrieved in March 2020.

74. Eric Lawrence, John Sides, and Henry Farrell, "Self-Segregation or Deliberation? Blog Readership, Participation, and Polarization in American Politics," *Perspectives on Politics* 8, 1 (2010): 146.

75. See http://www.drudgereport.com and http://www.rushlimbaugh.com/.

76. Dylan Tweney, "Controlled Chaos: An Interview with Kos," *Epicenter* (blog), *Wired*, May 8, 2007, http://blog.wired.com/business/2007/05/controlled_chao.html.

77. Michael M. Grynbaum. "White House Grants Press Credentials to a Pro-Trump Blog," *The New York Times*, February 13, 2017, accessed March 6, 2018, https://www.nytimes.com/2017/02/13/business/the-gateway-pundit-trump.html; https://www.washingtonpost.com/?utm_term=.7eb825a190b8.

78. "The Podcast Consumer 2019," *Edison Research*, April 5, 2019, https://www.edisonresearch.com/the-podcast-consumer-2019/.

79. Nic Newman, "Inpsired by The Daily, Dozens of Daily News Podcasts Are Punching above Their Weight Worldwide," *Nieman Lab*, December 3, 2019, https://www.niemanlab.org/2019/12/inspired-by-the-daily-dozens-of-daily-news-podcasts-are-punching-above-their-weight-worldwide/.

80. Elisa Shearer and Katerina Eva Matsa, "News Use Across Social Media Platforms 2018," *Pew Research Center*, September 10, 2018, https://www.journalism.org/2018/09/10/news-use-across-social-media-platforms-2018/.

81. See https://www.washingtonpost.com/?utm_term=.7eb825a190b8.

82. See https://zephoria.com/top-15-valuable-facebook-statistics/.

83. Kevin Granville, "Facebook and Cambridge Analytica: What You Need to Know as Fallout Widens," *The New York Times*, March 19, 2018, https://www.nytimes.com/2018/03/19/technology/facebook-cambridge-analytica-explained.html.

84. See https://zephoria.com/top-15-valuable-facebook-statistics/.

85. Chris O'Brien, "CEO Mark Zuckerberg Predicts 5 Billion Facebook Users by 2030," *Vulture Beat*, July 4, 2016, http://venturebeat.com/2016/02/04/ceo-mark-zuckerberg-predicts-5b-facebook-users-by-2030.

86. See https://blog.hubspot.com/marketing/snapchat-vs.-tiktok.

87. See https://twitter.com/realDonaldTrump.

88. "2018 Congressional Social Media Report," Quorum, 2018, https://www.quorum.us/data-driven-insights/congress-social-media-2018/412/.

89. See https://twitter.com/SpeakerPelosi and https://twitter.com/senatemajldr.

90. Jacob R. Straus, "Social Media Adoption by Members of Congress; Trends and Congressional Considerations," Congressional Research Service, October 9, 2018, https://fas.org/sgp/crs/misc/R45337.pdf.

91. "National Politics on Twitter: Small Share of U.S. Adults Produce Majority of Tweets," *Pew Research Center*, October 23, 2019, https://www.people-press.org/2019/10/23/national-politics-on-twitter-small-share-of-u-s-adults-produce-majority-of-tweets/.

92. Christina Pazzanese, "Danger in the Internet Echo Chamber," *Harvard Law Today,* March 24, 2017, https://today.law.harvard.edu/danger-internet-echo-chamber/.

93. Elisa Shearer and Katerina Eva Matsa, "News Use Across Social Media Platforms 2018," *Pew Research Center,* September 10, 2018, https://www.journalism.org/2018/09/10/news-use-across-social-media-platforms-2018/.

94. AJ Willingham, "Slacktivism Is Over. The #NeverAgain Movement Is about What's Next," *CNN,* March 25, 2018, https://www.cnn.com/2018/03/25/us/march-for-our-lives-slacktivism-trnd/index.html.

95. Harmeet Kaur, "10 Petitions That Made the Biggest Impact This Decade," *CNN,* December 31, 2019, https://www.cnn.com/2019/12/22/us/top-petitions-decade-change-trnd/index.html.

96. See https://www.pewresearch.org/fact-tank/2020/06/10/black livesmatter-surges-on-twitter-after-george-floyds-death/, accessed June 27, 2020.

97. Jeff Brady, "Teen Climate Activist Greta Thunberg Arrives In New York After Sailing the Atlantic," *NPR,* August 28, 2019, https://www.npr.org/2019/08/28/754818342/teen-climate-activist-greta-thunberg-arrives-in-new-york-after-sailing-the-atlan.

98. Monica Anderson, Skye Toor, Lee Rainie, and Aaron Smith, "Activism in the Social Media Age," *Pew Research Center,* July 11, 2018, https://www.pewresearch.org/internet/2018/07/11/activism-in-the-social-media-age/.

99. "Election 2016: Campaigns as a Direct Source of News," *Pew Research Center,* July 18, 2016, https://www.journalism.org/2016/07/18/candidates-differ-in-their-use-of-social-media-to-connect-with-the-public/.

100. Sue Halpern, "The Problem of Political Advertising on Social Media," *The New Yorker,* October 24, 2019, https://www.newyorker.com/tech/annals-of-technology/the-problem-of-political-advertising-on-social-media.

101. See https://www.congress.gov/bill/115th-congress/senate-bill/1989/text.

102. See https://www.warner.senate.gov/public/index.cfm/the-honest-ads-act.

103. Zach Montellaro, "The Honest Ads Act Returns," *Politico,* May 19, 2019, https://www.politico.com/newsletters/morning-score/2019/05/09/the-honest-ads-act-returns-615586.

104. Niam Yaraghi, "Twitter's Ban on Political Advertisements Hurts Our Democracy," *The Brookings Institution,* January 8, 2020, https://www.brookings.edu/blog/techtank/2020/01/08/twitters-ban-on-political-advertisements-hurts-our-democracy/.

105. Ann M. Ravel, "Facebook, Google and Twitter's Political Ad Policies Are Bad for Democracy," *CNN Business,* December 18, 2019, https://www.cnn.com/2019/12/18/perspectives/facebook-google-twitter-political-ads/index.html.

106. See Halpern's *The New Yorker* article.

107. Rachel Frazin, "2020 Democrats Adapt to Changing Social Media Landscape," *The Hill,* July 18, 2019, https://thehill.com/homenews/campaign/453636-2020-democrats-adapt-to-changing-social-media-landscape.

108. Juana Summers, "Bloomberg Has Already Spent $450 Million On Ads Since Launching His Campaign," *NPR,* February 21, 2020, https://www.npr.org/2020/02/21/808163144/bloomberg-has-already-spent-450-million-on-ads-since-launching-his-campaign.

109. Paige Leskin, "Inside Mike Bloomberg's Bizarre Strategy to Dominate Social Media That's Dwarfed Trump's 2016 Efforts by Millions of Dollars," *Business Insider,* February 20, 2020, https://www.business insider.com/mike-bloomberg-presidential-campaign-social-media-strategy-millennials-memes-influencers-2020-2.

110. Maggie Koerth, "Bloomberg's Money Bought Him Something – Just Not The Nomination," FiveThirtyEight, March 5, 2020, https://fivethirtyeight.com/features/bloombergs-money-bought-him-something-just-not-the-nomination/.

111. See http://tvbythenumbers.zap2it.com/2013/05/22/telemundo-delivers-best-season-ever-up-9-vs-2011-2012-season/183980 and http://www.deadline.com/2013/05/cbs-wins-season-abc-tops-adults-18-49-in-seasons-final-week.

112. Nick Corasaniti, "Univision Aims to Make Hispanic Voting Bloc Even More Formidable," *New York Times,* February 22, 2016, accessed November 12, 2016, http://www.nytimes.com/2016/02/23/us/politics/univision-hispanic-voting.html?smprod=nytcore-iphone&smid=nytcore-iphone-share&_r=0; https://www.washingtonpost.com/news/monkey-cage/wp/2016/11/11/in-record-numbers-latinos-voted-overwhelmingly-against-trump-we-did-the-research.

113. Jens Manuel Krogstad, Antonio Flores and Mark Hugo Lopez, "Key Takeaways about Latino Voters in the 2018 Midterm Elections," *Pew Research Center,* November 9, 2018, https://www.pewresearch.org/fact-tank/2018/11/09/how-latinos-voted-in-2018-midterms/.

114. "Record Number of Latinos Sworn in to 116th Congress," *NALEO,* January 3, 2019, https://naleo.org/wp-content/uploads/2019/06/1_3_19-NEF-Release-on-116th-Congress-Final.pdf.

115. Jens Manuel Krogstad, Ana Gonzalez-Barrera, and Christine Tamir, "Latino Democratic Voters Place High Importance on 2020 Presidential Election," *Pew Research Center,* January 17, 2020, https://www.pewresearch.org/fact-tank/2020/01/17/latino-democratic-voters-place-high-importance-on-2020-presidential-election/.

116. Thomas E. Patterson, *Young People and News* (Cambridge, MA: Joan Shorenstein Center on the Press, Politics, and Public Policy, Harvard University, July 2007).

117. Morley Winograd and Michael D. Hais, *Millennial Makeover: MySpace, YouTube and the Future of American Politics* (New Brunswick, NJ: Rutgers University Press, 2008); Jaime Fuller, "Iowa Dem Senate Hopeful Dismisses Grassley as 'Farmer from Iowa Who Never Went to Law School,'" *Washington Post,* March 25, 2014, accessed July 28, 2014.

118. See https://www.foia.gov/faq/html.

119. Ted Bridis, "US Sets New Record for Censoring, Withholding Government Files," *Associated Press,* March 12, 2018, https://apnews.com/714791d91d7944e49a284a51fab65b85/US-sets-new-record-for-censoring,-withholding-gov%27t-files.

120. Paul Lazarsfeld, Bernard Berelson, and Hazel Gaudet, *The People's Choice* (New York: Columbia University Press, 1944). It is worth noting that the 1940 campaign was probably the worst campaign in which to look for possible media effects. It was the only presidential election in U.S. history in which a sitting president, Franklin Roosevelt, was running for a third term. The stability of preference surely reflected the fact that people had opinions about Roosevelt and that not much would change them one way or the other. In contrast, Senator Obama was not a well-known figure in the 2008 presidential campaign.

121. Angus Campbell, Philip Converse, Warren Miller, and Donald Stokes, *The American Voter* (New York: Wiley, 1960).

122. Andrew Dugan, "Despite Enrollment Success, Healthcare Law Still Unpopular," *Gallup,* May 29, 2014, http://www.gallup.com/poll/170750/despite-enrollment-success-healthcare-law-remains-unpopular.aspx.

123. Bernard Cohen, *The Press and Foreign Policy* (Princeton, NJ: Princeton University Press, 1963), 13.

124. Darrell M. West, Grover J. Whitehurst, and E. J. Dionne Jr., "Invisible: 1.4 Percent Coverage for Education Is Not Enough," *The Brookings Institution,* December 2, 2009, accessed May 28, 2012, http://www.brookings.edu/research/reports/2009/12/02-education-news-west.

125. Shanto Iyengar and Jennifer A. McGrady, *Media Politics: A Citizen's Guide* (New York: W.W. Norton, 2007), 216.

126. These scholars have reshaped how we think about framing. In fact, Kahneman won a Nobel Prize for this work in 2003. See http://psych .hanover.edu/classes/cognition/papers/tversky81.pdf.

127. W. Lance Bennett, Regina C. Lawrence, and Steven Livingston, *When the Press Fails: Political Power and the News Media from Iraq to Katrina* (Chicago, IL: University of Chicago Press, 2007).

128. Jonathan Ladd, *Why Americans Hate the Media* (Princeton, NJ: Princeton University Press, 2012).

129. Ibid. Ladd also kindly provided us updated figures for this trend line.

130. "Trust in Government," *Gallup*, accessed March 10, 2020, https:// news.gallup.com/poll/5392/trust-government.aspx.

131. See https://www.forbes.com/sites/niallmccarthy/2020/05/20/where -trust-in-the-medias-covid-19-coverage-is-highest--lowest-around -the-world-infographic/#4f65372552c5.

132. Schudson, *The Sociology of News*, 33.

133. Paola Chavez and Veronica Stracqualursi, "The History of the Donald Trump–Megyn Kelly Feud," *ABC News*, March 3, 2016, http://abcnews .go.com/Politics/history-donald-trump-megyn-kelly-feud /story?id=36526503.

134. See the Accuracy in Media website at http://www.aim.org.

135. Conducted by *Gallup* Organization, March 9–29, 2017, and based on 789 telephone interviews. Sample: National adult. Interviews were conducted with respondents on landline telephones and cellular phones. The sample includes 30 percent landline and 70 percent cell phone respondents, http://news.gallup.com/poll/207794/six-partisan -bias-news-media.aspx.

136. Thomas Patterson, "Political Roles of the Journalist," in *The Politics of the News*, ed. Doris Graber, Denis McQuail, and Pippa Norris (Washington, D.C.: CQ Press, 2000), 3.

137. For a thoughtful discussion of soft news, see Matthew Baum, *Soft News Goes to War: Public Opinion and American Foreign Policy in the New Media Age* (Princeton, NJ: Princeton University Press, 2003), 6–7.

138. Schudson and Tifft, "American Journalism in Historical Perspective," 28.

139. Douglas Craig, *Fireside Politics* (Baltimore, MD.: Johns Hopkins University Press, 2000).

140. Gary Bunker, *From Rail-Splitter to Icon: Lincoln's Image in Illustrated Periodicals, 1860–1865* (Kent, OH.: Kent State University Press, 2001).

141. CB Presidential Research Services, "Presidential Campaign Slogans," PresidentsUSA.net, accessed May 28, 2012, http://www.presidents usa.net/campaignslogans.html.

142. *Pew Research Center* for the People & the Press, "Public Knowledge of Current Affairs Little Changed by News and Information Revolutions," *Pew Research Center*, April 15, 2007, accessed May 28, 2012, http:// www.people-press.org/2007/04/15/public-knowledge-of-current -affairs-little-changed-by-news-and-information-revolutions/.

143. Kari Paul, "False News Stories Are 70% More Likely to be Retweeted on Twitter Than True Ones," *MarketWatch*, October 25, 2018, https:// www.marketwatch.com/story/fake-news-spreads-more-quickly-on -twitter-than-real-news-2018-03-08.

144. Soroush Vosoughi, Deb Roy and Sinan Aral, "The Spread of True and False News Online," *Science*, March 9, 2018, https://science.science mag.org/content/359/6380/1146.

145. Jeffrey Gottfried et al, "Trust the News Media in the Trump Era," *Pew Research Center*, December 12, 2019, https://www.journalism .org/2019/12/12/trusting-the-news-media-in-the-trump-era/.

146. Dorothy Wickenden, "How Facebook Continues to Spread Fake News," *The Political Scene, The New Yorker* podcast, November 7, 2019, https://www.newyorker.com/podcast/political-scene/how -facebook-continues-to-spread-fake-news

147. Sarah Perez, "Facebook Launches a Digital Literacy Library Aimed at Educators," *TechCrunch*, August 2, 2018, https://tech-crunch.com/2018/08/02/facebook-launches-a-digital-literacy -library-aimed-at-educators/?guccounter=1&guce_referrer =aHR0cHM6Ly93d3cuZ29vZ2xlLmNvbS8&guce_referrer_sig=AQA AADg74RYnWMFCOe_dBktLUDlqEGyknrFqeF1CNtPunWBUCJyp 9KNF0EW6MkyQ-8aG_HSS5FZYuNN3FsXYWwE0bNkgPGmcPWmV extp7n5cNVz58gN4vX9FbMMhuyGb4ri20reP8wk3Y9zVhb6Q7nAW OdLV-elPHBLoqDFtAPnsHJ5N.

148. Ronan Costello, "Twitter Builds Partnership with UNESCO on Media and Information Literacy," Twitter, October 24, 2019, https://blog .twitter.com/en_us/topics/company/2019/twitter-launches-new-media -literacy-handbook-for-schools.html.

149. Jacob Poushter, "Smartphone Ownership Rates Skyrocket in Many Emerging Economics, but Digital Divide Remains," *Pew Research Center*, February 22, 2016, http://www.pewglobal .org/2016/02/22/smartphone-ownership-rates-skyrocket-in-many -emerging-economies-but-digital-divide-remains; see https:// www.politico.com/magazine/story/2016/12/fake-news-history -long-violent-214535; https://www.nytimes.com/2017/01/11/upshot /the-real-story-about-fake-news-is-partisanship.html; and https://www.brookings.edu/research/how-to-combat-fake-news-and -disinformation/.

150. Andrew Perrin and Maeve Duggan, "American's Internet Access: 2000–2015," *Pew Research Center*, June 26, 2015, accessed April 3, 2016, http://www.pewinternet.org/2015/06/26/americans-internet-access -2000-2015.

151. *Pew Research Center*, "Cell Phone and Smartphone Ownership Demographics," accessed April 21, 2014, http://www.pewinternet .org/data-trend/mobile/cell-phone-and-smartphone-ownership -demographics.

152. The argument presented over the next few paragraphs is inspired by the work of Markus Prior, *Post Broadcast Democracy* (New York: Cambridge University Press, 2007).

153. Ibid.

154. Kate Sullivan, "Here Are the 4 Congresswomen Known as 'The Squad' Targeted by Trump's Racist Tweets," *CNN*, July 16, 2019, https:// www.cnn.com/2019/07/15/politics/who-are-the-squad/index.html.

155. See http://www.politifact.com/truth-o-meter/statements/2012/sep/18 /mitt-romney/romney-says-47-percent-americans-pay-no-income -tax/, accessed March 6, 2018.

156. See http://www.politifact.com/personalities/donald-trump/, accessed March 6, 2018.

Chapter 8

1. This vignette relies on the following sources: Dana Bash, "'Stronger, Better, Tougher: Giffords Improves, but She'll Never Be the Same," April 10, 2013, accessed March 13, 2018, https:// www.cnn.com/2013/04/09/politics/giffords-health/index.html; Center for Responsible Politics, Opensecrets.org, "Americans for Responsible Solutions," accessed March 13, 2018, https://www .opensecrets.org/pacs/lookup2.php?strID=C00540443&cycle =2014; The Giffords Law Center, "History," accessed March 13, 2018, http://lawcenter.giffords.org/about/history/; quote taken from Giffords.org, accessed March 13, 2018, https://giffords .org/2018/02/2018-political-program/; "Gabrielle Giffords Biography," accessed March 13, 2018, https://www.biography .com/people/gabrielle-giffords-20550593.

2. Alexis de Tocqueville, *Democracy in America*, ed. J. P. Mayer, trans. George Lawrence (New York: Doubleday & Company, 1969), 193.

3. William C. DiGiacomantonio, "Petitioners and Their Grievances," in *The House and Senate in the 1790s: Petitioning, Lobbying, and Institutional Development*, ed. Kenneth R. Bowling and Donald R. Kennon (Columbus: Ohio University Press, 2002), 29–56.

4. Interest groups at the state level have even been involved in elections for state judges. See Clive S. Thomas, Michael L. Boyer, and Ronald J. Hrebenar, "Interest Groups and State Court Elections: A New Era and Its Challenges," *Judicature* 87 (2003): 135–49.

5. Elizabeth Cady Stanton, Susan B. Anthony, and Matilda J. Gage, eds., *History of Woman Suffrage* (Rochester, N.Y.: Charles Mann Publishers, 1887), 1:70.

6. "141 Men and Girls Die in Waist Factory Fire; Trapped High Up in Washington Place Building; Street Strewn with Bodies; Piles of Dead Inside," *New York Times*, March 26, 1911, 1.

7. Office of the Secretary, United States Department of Labor, "Our Mission," accessed May 23, 2012, http://www.dol.gov/opa/aboutdol/mission.htm.

8. National Labor Relations Act, 29 U.S.C. §§ 151–169 (1935), http://www.nlrb.gov/national-labor-relations-act.

9. Beth L. Leech, Frank R. Baumgartner, Timothy M. La Pira, and Nicholas A. Semanko, "Drawing Lobbyists to Washington: Government Activity and the Demand for Advocacy," *Political Research Quarterly* 58, no. 1 (2005): 19–30.

10. Anita Snow and Terry Tang, "Arizona Teachers End Walkout after Governor Signs Off on 20 Percent Raise," *Associated Press*, May 3, 2018, accessed March 11, 2010, https://www.chicagotribune.com/nation-world/ct-arizona-teacher-protests-20180503-story.html; Monte Whaley, "Pueblo Teachers Reach Tentative Agreement with District for 2 Percent Pay Hike," *The Denver Post*, May 12, 2018, accessed March 11, 2020, https://www.denverpost.com/2018/05/12/pueblo-teacher-strike-is-over/; Gregory Krieg, "Is the West Virginia Teachers' Strike the Future of American Labor?" *CNN.com*, accessed March 11, 2020, https://www.cnn.com/2018/03/05/politics/west-virginia-teachers-strike-future-unions/index.html; Howard Blume and Sonali Kohli, "LAUSD Teachers' Strike Ends. Teachers to Return to Work Wednesday," *Los Angeles Times*, January 1, 2020, accessed March 11, 2020, https://www.latimes.com/local/education/la-me-edu-lausd-teachers-strike-negotiations-20190122-story.html; Dana Goldstein and Elizabeth Dias, "Oklahoma Teachers End Walkout After Winning Raises and Additional Funding," *New York Times*, April 12, 2018, accessed March 11, 2020, https://www.nytimes.com/2018/04/12/us/oklahoma-teachers-strike.html.

11. National Nurses United. Accessed March 26, 2020, https://www.nationalnursesunited.org/.

12. Amnesty International. "Exposed, Silenced, Attacked: Failures to Protect Health and Essential Workers During the COVID-19 Pandemic." July, 2020. Accessed August 22, 2020 at https://www.amnesty.org/download/Documents/POL4025722020ENGLISH.PDF, see pp. 5, 14.

13. United Automobile, Aerospace and Agricultural Implement Workers of America, accessed February 17, 2016, uaw.org/about.

14. Keith Laing and Ian Thibodeau, "UAW Membership Dropped by 35,000 in 2018," *The Detroit News*, March 29, 2019, accessed March 8, 2020, https://www.detroitnews.com/story/business/autos/2019/03/29/uaw-membership-dropped-last-year/3314861002/.

15. Brent Snavely, "UAW Membership Tops 400,000 for First Time Since '08," *Detroit Free Press*, March 31, 2015, accessed February 17, 2016, https://www.usatoday.com/story/money/cars/2015/03/31/uaw-membership-tops-first-time-since/70753012/; Pheobe Wall Howard. "Many of UAW's newest members aren't traditional autoworkers." *Detroit Free Press*. April 14, 2020, accessed May 12, 2020 https://www.freep.com/story/money/cars/2020/04/14/uaw-membership-2019/2923908001/

16. National Right to Work Legal Defense Foundation, Inc., "Right to Work States," accessed March 1, 2018, http://www.nrtw.org/rtws.htm.

17. U.S. Bureau of Labor Statistics, "Union Members Summary," January 22, 2020, accessed March 10, 2020, https://www.bls.gov/news.release/union2.nr0.htm.

18. MoveOn.org, http://front.moveon.org/.

19. MoveOn.org, https://front.moveon.org/a-short-history/.

20. American Israel Public Affairs Committee, accessed June 4, 2014, http://www.aipac.org/.

21. Mark R. Amstutz, "Faith-Based NGOs and U.S. Foreign Policy," in *The Influence of Faith: Religious Groups and Foreign Policy,* ed. by Elliot Abrams (Lanham, Md.: Rowman and Littlefield Publishers, 2001), 175–87; National Council of the Churches of Christ in the USA, http://www.ncccusa.org.

22. http://www.amnestyusa.org/our-work/countries/middle-east-and-north-africa/syria; *Human Rights Watch,* accessed February 8, 2016, https://www.hrw.org.

23. http://www.rescue.org/crisis-syria.

24. Coral Davenport, "Citing Climate Change, Obama Rejects Construction of Keystone XL Oil Pipeline, *New York Times*, November 6, 2015, http://www.nytimes.com/2015/11/07/us/obama-expected-to-reject-construction-of-keystone-xl-oil-pipeline.html?R=0; Sierra Club, accessed February 8, 2016, http://content .sierraclub.org/press-releases/2015/11/how-sierra-club-and-its -allies-beat-keystone-xl-pipeline.

25. Sierra Club, "Sierra Club and DTE Reach Agreement for Ground breaking Energy Efficiency Pilot Program to Minimize Utility Shut-offs," March 5, 2020, accessed March 10, 2020, https://www.sierraclub.org/press-releases/2020/03/sierra-club-and-dte-reach-agreement-for-groundbreaking-energy-efficiency.

26. Kay Brilliant, "NEA's Response to Race to the Top," National Education Association, August 21, 2008, accessed May 23, 2012, http://www.nea.org/home/35447.htm.

27. League of United Latin American Citizens, accessed February 8, 2016, http://lulac.org/about/history/milestones.

28. League of United Latin American Citizens. "LULAC Historic Court Win Forces Pesticide Off Market," February 11, 2020, accessed March 8, 2020, https://lulac.org/news/pr/LULAC_Historic_Court_Win_Forces_Pesticide_Off_Market/.

29. League of United Latin American Citizens, https://lulac.org/news/pr/LULAC_Launches_Website_To_Help_The_Latino_Community_Access_Critical_COVID-19_Information_And_Resources/.

30. For more information on general lobbying, see Anthony J. Nownes, *Total Lobbying* (New York: Cambridge University Press, 2006).

31. Center for Responsive Politics, "Lobbying Database," *OpenSecrets.org,* accessed January 22, 2020 https://www.opensecrets.org/federal-lobbying/summary.

32. Ibid.

33. Bureau of the Census, "NAIS 2011—Oil and Gas Extraction," http://thedataweb.rm.census.gov/TheDataWeb_HotReport2/econsnapshot/snapshot.hrml?NAICS=211&IND=%3DCOMP%28C2 %2FC3*1000%29&STATE=ALL&COUNTY=ALL.

34. Environmental Protection Agency, "EPA's Study of Hydraulic Fracturing and Its Potential Impact on Drinking Water Resources," accessed June 4, 2014, http://www2.epa.gov/hfstudy.

35. Environmental Protection Agency, "EPA's Draft Assessment of the Potential Impacts of Hydraulic Fracturing for Oil and Gas on Drinking Water Resources," accessed January 24, 2016, http://www.epa.gov/sites/production/files/2015-06/documents/draft_hf_assessment_fs_6_3_15_508_km_0.pdf.

36. ANGA, "About Us," http://anga.us/about-us#.UycJCfldWCk; NRDC "Consolidated Financial Statements," June 30, 2013, http://www.nrdc.org/about/NRDC_auditedfinancialstatements_FY2013.pdf.

37. ANGA, "Washington County Pennsylvania Retrospective Case Study Characterization Report," February 2013, http://anga.us/media/content/F7BDA298-DFF6-686B-2DF23939F9838B75/files/13%20Feb%2022%20FinalWashingtonCountyReport_clean%2021.pdf.

38. Reid Frazier, "$3 Million Settlement Reached in High-Profile Fracking Case," *NPR*, June 4, 2019, accessed March 10, 2020, https://www.npr.org/2019/06/04/729370149/-3-million-settlement-revealed-in-high-profile-fracking-case.

39. Natural Resources Defense Council, "Fracking: Community Defense," http://www.nrdc.org/land/fracking-community-defense/.

40. Ibid.

41. Natural Resources Defense Council, accessed January 24, 2016, http://switch-board.nrdc.org/blogs/bmordick/independent_expert_scientists.html.

42. Bart Jansen, "Legislative Summary: Congressional Affairs: Lobbying Practices and Disclosures," *CQ Weekly Online*, January 7, 2008, 39.

43. Citizens for Responsibility and Ethics in Washington, "About CREW," accessed March 14, 2014, http://www.citizensforethics.org/pages/about; http://www.citizensforethics.org/pages/under-investigation/.

44. U.S. Internal Revenue Service, "Exemption Requirements—Section 501(c)(3) Organizations," accessed June 4, 2014, http://www.irs.gov/Charities-&-Non-Profits/Charitable-Organizations/Exemption-Requirements-Section-501(c)(3)-Organizations.

45. James Oliphant, "Remember the IRS Tea-Party Scandal? Get Ready for Round Two," *National Journal*, February 5, 2014, accessed March 14, 2014, http://www.nationaljournal.com/white-house/remember-the-irs-tea-party-scandal-get-ready-for-round-two-20140205.

46. Patricia Cohen, Kenneth P. Vogel, and Jim Tankersley, "I.R.S. Will No Longer Force Kochs and Other Groups to Disclose Donors," *New York Times*, July 17, 2018, accessed March 11, 2020, https://www.nytimes.com/2018/07/17/us/politics/irs-will-no-longer-force-kochs-and-other-groups-to-disclose-donors.html.

47. *Buckley v. Valeo*, 424 U.S. 1 (1976).

48. See www.thelibreinitiative.com/about/us, accessed February 8, 2016.

49. Jens Manuel Krogstad and Mark Hugo Lopez, "Hillary Clinton Won Latino Vote but Fell below 2012 Support for Obama," *Pew Research Center*, November 29, 2016, accessed March 1, 2018, http://www.pewresearch.org/fact-tank/2016/11/29/hillary-clinton-wins-latino-vote-but-falls-below-2012-support-for-obama/.

50. See www.thelibreinitiative.com/faqs; http://latino.foxnews.com/latino/politics/2015/09/29/conservative-group-libre-quietly-but-diligently-making-inroads-into-latino/, accessed February 8, 2016.

51. Jens Manuel Krogstad and Mark Hugo Lopez, "Hillary Clinton Won Latino Vote but Fell below 2012 Support for Obama," *Pew Research Center*, November 29, 2016, accessed March 1, 2018, http://www.pewresearch.org/fact-tank/2016/11/29/hillary-clinton-wins-latino-vote-but-falls-below-2012-support-for-obama/.

52. Brian Latimer, "Latinos' Presence in State Capitols Grows, Expands with Election," *NBC News*, November 15, 2016, accessed March 11, 2020, https://www.nbcnews.com/storyline/2016-election-day/record-number-latino-state-legislature-wins-bolsters-dem-succession-n684371.

53. Suzanne Gamboa, "Latinos Show Record Gains in Congress, Though Numbers Are Still Low," *NBC News*, November 15, 2018, accessed March 11, 2020, https://www.nbcnews.com/news/latino/latinos-show-record-gains-congress-though-numbers-are-still-low-n936781.

54. Staff, "National Exit Polls: How Different Groups Voted," *New York Times*, November 4, 2020, accessed November 12, 2020, https://www.nytimes.com/interactive/2020/11/03/us/elections/exit-polls-president.html.

55. See John R. Wright, *Interest Groups and Congress: Lobbying, Contributions, and Influence* (Boston, MA: Allyn & Bacon, 1995, reprinted in Longman Classics Series, 2009); Michelle L. Chin, Jon R. Bond, and Nehemia Geva, "A Foot in the Door: An Experimental Study of PAC and Constituency Effects on Access," *Journal of Politics* 62 (2000): 534–49.

56. *Federal Election Commission v. Wisconsin Right to Life, Inc.*, 551 U.S. 449 (2007).

57. *McCutcheon et al. v. Federal Election Commission*, decided April 2, 2014, http://www.supremecourt.gov/opinions/13pdf/12-536_e1pf.pdf.

58. Tocqueville, *Democracy in America*, 514.

59. David Truman, *The Governmental Process: Political Interests and Public Opinion* (New York: Alfred Knopf, 1971).

60. Mancur Olson, *The Logic of Collective Action* (Cambridge, MA, Mass.: Harvard University Press, 1971).

61. Robert Dahl, *A Preface to Democratic Theory* (Chicago, IL: University of Chicago Press, 1956). Also see Robert Dahl, *Who Governs?*, 2nd ed. (New Haven, Conn.: Yale University Press, 2005).

62. C. Wright Mills, *The Power Elite* (New York: Oxford University Press, 1956).

63. Theodore J. Lowi, *The End of Liberalism: Ideology, Policy, and the End of Public Authority* (New York: Norton, 1969).

64. Larry M. Bartels, *Unequal Democracy, 2nd ed.* (Princeton, NJ: Princeton University Press, 2016); Martin Gilens, *Affluence and Influence* (Princeton, NJ: Princeton University Press, 2012).

65. E. E. Schattschneider, *The Semi-Sovereign People* (New York: Holt, Rinehart, and Winston, 1960). Also see E. E. Schattschneider, *Politics, Pressures, and the Tariff* (New York: Prentice Hall, 1935).

66. Anna North, "7 Positive Changes That Have Come from the #MeToo Movement," Vox, October 4, 2019, accessed March 11, 2020, https://www.vox.com/identities/2019/10/4/20852639/me-too-movement-sexual-harassment-law-2019; Jan Ranson, "Harvey Weinstein's Stunning Downfall: 23 Years in Prison," *New York Times*, March 11, 2020, accessed March 26, 2020, https://www.nytimes.com/2020/03/11/nyregion/harvey-weinstein-sentencing.html.

67. National Highway Traffic Safety Administration, accessed January 24, 2016, http:/www.nhtsa.gov/fuel-economy.

68. Coral Davenport, "Trump Administration Unveils Its Plan to Relax Car Pollution Rules," *New York Times*, August 2, 2018, accessed March 11, 2020, https://www.nytimes.com/2018/08/02/climate/trump-auto-emissions-california.html.

69. Coral Davenport, "Trump's Path to Weaker Fuel Efficiency Rules May Lead to a Dead End," *New York Times*, February 13, 2020, accessed March 11, 2020, https://www.nytimes.com/2020/02/13/climate/trump-fuel-economy-rollback.html; Department of Transportation, "The Safer Affordable Fuel-Efficient (SAFE) Vehicles Rule for Model Years 2021–2026, Passenger Cars and Light Trucks," accessed April 3, 2020, https://www.nhtsa.gov/sites/nhtsa.dot.gov/files/documents/final_safe_preamble_web_version_200330.pdf; Anna M. Phillips and Russ Mitchell. "Trump Weakens Fuel Economy Standards, Rolling Back Key U.S. Effort Against Climate Change," *Los Angeles Times*, March 31, 2020, accessed April 3, 2020, https://www.latimes.com/politics/story/2020-03-31/trump-rolls-back-fuel-economy-standards.

70. Dwight D. Eisenhower, "Farewell Radio and Television Address to the American People," January 17, 1961; Gerhard Peters and John T. Woolley, The American Presidency Project, accessed May 23, 2012, http://www.presidency.ucsb.edu/ws/index.php?pid=12086&st=&st1=#axzz1uPYslFQG.

71. Thom Shankar and Helene Cooper, "Pentagon Plans to Shrink Army to Pre-World War II Level," *New York Times*, February 23, 2014, http://www.nytimes.com/2014/02/24/us/politics/pentagon-plans-to-shrink-army-to-pre-world-war-ii-level.html.

72. Hugh Heclo, "Issue Networks and the Executive Establishment," in *The New American Political System*, ed. Anthony King (Washington, D.C.: American Enterprise Institute, 1978), 87–124.

73. Lauren French, Anna Palmer, and Jake Sherman, "GOP Lawmakers Confront DeMint Over Ratings," *Politico.com*, January 28, 2015, accessed January 24, 2016, http://www.politico.com/story/2015/01/gop/lawmakers-jim-deimint-heritage-foundation-ratings-114672; Elania Johnson and Nancy Cook, "The Real Reason Jim DeMint Got the Boot." *Politico.com*, May 2, 2017, accessed March 1, 2018, http://www.politico.com/story/2017/05/02/why-jim-demint-was-ousted-from-heritage-237876.

74. Americans for Tax Reform, "About Americans for Tax Reform," accessed May 23, 2012, http://www.atr.org/about.

75. Robert H. Salisbury, "An Exchange Theory of Interest Groups," *Midwest Journal of Political Science* 13 (1969): 1–32.

76. In *Logic of Collective Action*, Olson labels these *selective incentives* (p. 51).

77. Ibid, pp. 50–51.

78. National Rifle Association, Membership, accessed March 8, 2020, https://membership.nra.org/FAQ; Asher Stockler, "The National Rifle Association Is Laying Off Staff, Cutting Salaries and Reducing Hours Amid COVID-19 Outbreak," *Newsweek.com*, March 23, 2020, accessed March 26, 2020, https://www.newsweek.com/national-rifle-association-covid-19-wayne-lapierre-1493853.

79. AARP, 2018 AARP Annual Report, https://www.aarp.org/content/dam/aarp/about_aarp/annual_reports/2019/822801-internal-2018-annual-report-web.pdf, p. 36.

80. Ibid.

81. James Hohmann, "Club for Growth Plots Role as 2016 Kingmaker, But Will It Find 'the One'," *Politico.com*, March 3, 2015, accessed February 8, 2016, http://www.politico.com/story/2015/03/club-for-growth-2016-candidate-115633.

Chapter 9

1. V. O. Key Jr., *Politics, Parties, and Pressure Groups*, 5th ed. (New York: Thomas Y. Crowell Company, 1964).

2. Center for Responsive Politics, "Political Parties," accessed November 9, 2016, https://www.opensecrets.org/parties.

3. Ibid.

4. For more information on the informal networking that occurs among party activists, see Gregory Koger, Seth Masket, and Hans Noel, "Partisan Webs: Information Exchange and Party Networks," *British Journal of Political Science* 39 (2009): 633–53.

5. Marjorie Hershey, *Party Politics in America*, 12th ed. (New York: Pearson-Longman, 2007), 159.

6. Byron E. Shafer, *Quiet Revolution: The Struggle for the Democratic Party & The Shaping of Post-Reform Politics* (New York: Russell Sage Foundation, 1983), 172.

7. In the 2016 Democratic nomination contest between former Secretary of State Hillary Clinton and Senator Bernie Sanders (I-VT), superdelegates played a very important role, as they had in the 2008 contest between then-Senator Barack Obama (D-IL) and then-Senator Hilary Clinton (D-NY). Almost from the start of the 2016 presidential nomination phase of the process, Secretary Clinton led Senator Sanders among superdelegates by large margins. Heading into the Democratic national party convention, Clinton had secured the pledges of 572 superdelegates out of a total of 713, or 80 percent. (David Chalian, "How CNN's Count Puts Clinton Over the Top," *CNN Politics*, June 6, 2016, http://www.cnn.com/2016/06/06/politics/superdelegates-hillary-clinton-nomination.)

8. Republican National Committee, "New Timing Rules for 2012 Republican Presidential Nominating Schedule," as cited by Josh Putnam; "An Update on the 2012 Republican Delegate Selection Rules," *FrontloadingHQ* (blog), February 27, 2011, http://frontloading.blogspot.com/2011/02/update-on-2012-republican-delegate.html.

9. Peter Hamby, "GOP Adopts Changes to 2016 Presidential Primary Process," *CNN.com*, January 24, 2014, accessed April 3, 2014, http://politicalticker.blogs.cnn.com/2014/01/24/gop-adopts-changes-to-2016-presidential-primary-process/; Election Central, 2016 Primary Election Schedule, http://www.uspresidentialelectionnews.com/2016-presidential-primary-schedule-calendar; Jake Miller, "How Many GOP Presidential Debates Is Too Many?" *CBS News*, January 16, 2015, http://www.cbsnews.com/news/how-many-gop-presidential-debates-is-too-many/; https://www.gop.com/2016-gophq/event_schedule/?schedule_type=debate; Marty Cohen, David Karol, Hans Noel, and John Zaller, *The Party Decides: Presidential Nominations Before and After Reform* (Chicago, IL: University of Chicago Press, 2008).

10. Arthur T. Hadley, *The Invisible Primary* (New York: Prentice Hall, 1976); Marty Cohen, David Karol, Hans Noel, and John Zaller, *The Party Decides: Presidential Nominations Before and After Reform* (Chicago, IL: University of Chicago Press, 2008).

11. George Washington, "Washington's Farewell Address," reprinted in Randall E. Adkins, *The Evolution of Political Parties, Campaigns, and Elections* (Washington, D.C.: CQ Press, 2008), 47–50

12. John F. Bibby and Brian F. Schaffner, *Politics, Parties and Elections in America*, 6th ed. (Boston, MA: Thomson-Wadsworth, 2008), 24.

13. U.S. Senate, Office of the Historian, *Biographical Directory of the United States Congress*, http://bioguide.congress.gov.

14. U.S. Senate, Office of the Historian, *Senate History*, http://www.senate.gov/artandhistory/history/minute/Nominating_presidents.htm.

15. Martin Van Buren, "Letter to Thomas Ritchie," 1827, reprinted in *The Evolution of Political Parties, Campaigns, and Elections: Landmark Documents, 1787–2007*, ed. Randall E. Adkins (Washington, D.C.: CQ Press, 2008), 65–69.

16. U.S. Census Bureau, "1990 Population and Housing Unit Counts: United States," Table 2, in *1990 Census of Population and Housing*, accessed May 31, 2012, http://www.census.gov/population/www/censusdata/files/table-2.pdf.

17. Quoted in James L. Sundquist, *Dynamics of the Party System* (Washington, D.C.: Brookings Institution Press, 1973), 65.

18. Sean M. Theriault, *The Power of the People* (Columbus: Ohio State University Press, 2005), Chapter 3.

19. Douglas W. Jones, "The Australian Paper Ballot," in "A Brief Illustrated History of Voting," University of Iowa, Department of Computer Science, 2003, accessed May 31, 2012, http://www.divms.uiowa.edu/~jones/voting/pictures/.

20. Erik J. Engstrom and Samuel Kernell, "Manufactured Responsiveness: The Impact of State Electoral Laws on Unified Party Control of the Presidency and the House of Representatives, 1840–1940," *American Journal of Political Science* 49 (July 2005): 531–49, see 535.

21. Anthony Downs, *An Economic Theory of Democracy* (New York: Harper, 1957).

22. Stuart Elaine Macdonald and George Rabinowitz, "Solving the Paradox of Nonconvergence: Valence, Position, and Direction in Democratic Politics," *Electoral Studies* 17, no. 3 (1998): 281–300.

23. Maurice Duverger, "Public Opinion and Political Parties in France," *American Political Science Review* 46, no. 4 (1952): 1069–78, especially 1071.

24. James R. Whitson, "President Elect: The Unofficial Homepage of the Electoral College," PresidentElect.org, accessed February 18, 2016, http://presidentelect.org/e1892.html.

25. See https://my.lp.org/elected-officials/?page=CiviCRM&q=civicrm/profile&gid=38&force=1&crmRowCount=100&reset=1, accessed April 5, 2020.

26. Texas State Historical Association, *Raza Unida Party*, http://www.tshaonline.org/handbook/online/articles/war01.

27. Kate Zernike, Kitty Bennett, Ford Fessenden, Kevin Quealy, Amy Schoenfeld, Archie Tse, and Derek Willis, "Where Tea Party Candidates Are Running," *New York Times*, October 14, 2010, accessed April 4, 2014, http://www.nytimes.com/interactive/2010/10/15/us/politics/tea-party-graphic.html.

28. For an expanded analysis of the Tea Party, see Theda Skocpol and Vanessa Williams, *The Tea Party and the Remaking of Republican Conservatism* (New York: Oxford University Press, 2013).

29. John Terbush, "How the Tea Party Lost the 2014 Election," *The Week*, November 5, 2016, accessed February 18, 2016, http://www.nytimes.com/interactive/2010/10/15/us/politics/tea-party-graphic.html.

30. Jonathan Martin, "For Many Republican Incumbents, Challenge from Right Fizzles," *New York Times*, April 4, 2014, http://www.nytimes.com/2014/04/05/us/politics/tea-party-challenge-to-republican-incumbents-fizzles.html.

31. Russell Berman, "The Class of 2010 Heads Home," *The Atlantic*, February 22, 2016, accessed February 6, 2018, https://www.theatlantic.com/politics/archive/2016/02/house-republican-tea-party-class-2010-leaves-congress/463227/; Rachel Bade and Elena Schneider, "GOP Establishment Trounces Tea Party in Congressional Primaries," *Politico*, August 31, 2016, accessed February 6, 2018, https://www.politico.com/story/2016/08/congress-primaries-establishment-trounces-tea-party-227609.

32. For a detailed discussion of how interest groups interact with parties in campaigning, see Matthew J. Burbank, Ronald J. Hrebenar, and Robert C. Benedict, *Parties, Interest Groups, and Political Campaigns* (Boulder, Colo.: Paradigm Publishers, 2008).

33. Katherine Schaeffer, "Share of Americans Who Favor Stricter Gun Laws Has Increased Since 2017," accessed April 5, 2020, https://www.pewresearch.org/fact-tank/2019/10/16/share-of-americans-who-favor-stricter-gun-laws-has-increased-since-2017/.

34. Ibid.

35. Ibid.

36. Democratic National Committee, "The 2016 Democratic Party Platform," https://www.democrats.org/party-platform#gun-violence.

37. Republican National Committee, "The 2016 Republican Party Platform," https://prod-static-ngop-pbl.s3.amazonaws.com/media/documents/DRAFT_12_FINAL[1]-ben_1468872234.pdf.

38. Center for Responsive Politics, "Political Action Committees," accessed April 5, 2020, http://www.opensecrets.org/pacs/.

39. "Election Results 2008," *New York Times*, December 9, 2008, http://elections.nytimes.com/2008/results/president/map.html.

40. Becca Stanek, "3 Charts Show How American Voted in the Midterm Election," November 4, 2014, accessed February 6, 2016, http://mic.com/articles/103422/3-charts-show-how-america-voted-in-this-year-s-midterm-elections#.qVc99SKQ6.

41. Alec Tyson and Shiva Maniam, "Behind Trump's Victory: Divisions by Race, Gender, Education," *Pew Research Center*, November 9, 2016, http://www.pewresearch.org/fact-tank/2016/11/09/behind-trumps-victory-divisions-by-race-gender-education; Jon Huang,

Samuel Jacoby, K. K. Rebecca Lai, and Michael Strickland, "Election 2016: Exit Polls," *New York Times*, November 8, 2016, http://www.nytimes.com/interactive/2016/11/08/us/politics/election-exit-polls.html.

42. Staff, "National Exit Polls: How Different Groups Voted," New York Times, November 4, 2020, https://www.nytimes.com/interactive/2020/11/03/us/elections/exit-polls-president.html.

43. Staff, "National Exit Polls: How Different Groups Voted," New York Times, November 4, 2020, https://www.nytimes.com/interactive/2020/11/03/us/elections/exit-polls-president.html.

44. David Damore and Matt Barreto, "The Latino Threshold to Win in 2016," July 17, 2015, accessed February 19, 2016, http://www.latinodecisions.com/blog/2015/07/17/the-latino-threshold-in-2016-to-win/.

45. Alec Tyson and Shiva Maniam, "Behind Trump's Victory: Divisions by Race, Gender, Education," *Pew Research Center*, November 9, 2016, http://www.pewresearch.org/fact-tank/2016/11/09/behind-trumps-victory-divisions-by-race-gender-education/; Roper Center for Public Opinion Research, "How Groups Voted 2016," accessed February 6, 2018, https://ropercenter.cornell.edu/polls/us-elections/how-groups-voted/groups-voted-2016/.

46. Jens Manuel Krogstag, Mark Hugo Lopez, Gustavo Lopez, Jeffrey S. Passel, and Eileen Patten, "Millennials Make Up Almost Half of Latino Eligible Voters In 2016," January 19, 2016, *Pew Research Center*, http://www.pewhispanic.org/2016/01/19/millennials-make-up-almost-half-of-latino-eligible-voters-in-2016/.

47. "Donald Trump Doubles Down on Mexico 'Rapists' Comments Despite Outrage," *Guardian*, July 2, 2015, accessed March 1, 2016, http://www.theguardian.com/us-news/2015/jul/02/donald-trump-racist-claims-mexico-rapes; Albert R. Hunt, "Republicans Risk Repeating Mistake on Hispanic Vote," *New York Times*, January 24, 2016, accessed March 1, 2016, http://www.nytimes.com/2016/01/25/us/politics/republicans-risk-repeating-mistake-on-hispanic-vote.html?ref=politics&_r=0.

48. Mark Hugo Lopez, Ana Gonzalez-Barrera and Jens Manuel Krogstad, "More Latinos Have Serious Concerns About Their Place in America Under Trump," October 25, 2018, accessed March 10, 2020, https://www.pewresearch.org/hispanic/2018/10/25/views-of-president-donald-trump/.

49. *Engel v. Vitale*, 370 U.S. 421 (1962).

50. Scholar Tasha Philpot pointed to underlying shifts as early as 2004. See Tasha S. Philpot, "A Party of a Different Color? Race, Campaign Communication, and Party Politics," *Political Behavior* 26 (2004): 249–70.

51. Greg Giroux, "Final Tally Shows Obama First Since '56 to Win 51% Twice," *Bloomberg News*, accessed April 4, 2014, http://www.bloomberg.com/news/2013-01-03/final-tally-shows-obama-first-since-56-to-win-51-twice.html; Roper Center, accessed April 28, 2014, http://www.ropercenter.uconn.edu/elections/how_groups_voted/voted_12.html.

52. Steven Shepard, "Poll: Voters Oppose Straight Obamacare Repeal," *Politico*, July 7, 2017, accessed February 10, 2018, https://www.politico.com/story/2017/07/25/poll-obamacare-repeal-no-replace-240937; Jonathan Easley, "Poll: Majority Oppose GOP Tax Bill," *The Hill*, December 13, 2017, accessed February 10, 2018, http://thehill.com/homenews/administration/364781-poll-majority-oppose-gop-tax-bill; Brett Samuels, "Poll: Most Americans Support DACA," January 14, 2018, accessed, February 10, 2018, http://thehill.com/homenews/administration/368959-poll-most-americans-support-daca.

53. Jeffrey M. Jones, "Democratic Edge in Party Affiliation Up to Seven Points," *Gallup.com*, accessed April 6, 2020, http://www.gallup.com/poll/211817/party-affiliation.aspx.

Chapter 10

1. See Michael Barone and Chuck McCutcheon, "Arizona," in *The Almanac of American Politics 2014* (Chicago, IL: University of Chicago Press, 2013). Also, "Kyrsten Sinema's Biography," *Project Vote Smart*, accessed April 20, 2014, http://votesmart.org/candidate/biography/28338/kyrsten-sinema#.U1SPgscmCZw.

2. Manuel Roig-Franzia, "Kyrsten Sinema: A Success Story Like Nobody Else's," *Washington Post*, January 2, 2013, accessed May 16, 2014, http://www.washingtonpost.com/lifestyle/style/kyrsten-sinema-a-success-story-like-nobody-elses/2013/01/02/d31fadaa-5382-11e2-a613-ec8d394535c6_story.html.

3. Ibid.

4. Barone and McCutcheon, "Arizona."

5. Ronald J. Hansen, "Senate Candidates Martha McSally, Kyrsten Sinema Separating Themselves in Money Race" *AZ Central*, February 5, 2018, accessed March 6, 2018, https://www.azcentral.com/story/news/politics/elections/2018/02/05/senate-candidates-martha-mcsally-kyrsten-sinema-separating-themselves-money-race/1089119001/; Amber Phillips, "Kyrsten Sinema's Decision to Run for Senate in Arizona Is Welcome News for Democrats," *Washington Post*, September 29, 2017, accessed March 6, 2018, https://www.washingtonpost.com/news/the-fix/wp/2017/09/29/kyrsten-sinemas-decision-to-run-for-senate-in-arizona-is-welcome-news-for-democrats/?utm_term=.2e56e328993a; "Sinema: A Record of Accomplishment," http://kyrstensinema.com/record/, accessed May 15, 2014.

6. Quoted in Jeff Broadwater, *George Mason, Forgotten Founder* (Chapel Hill: University of North Carolina Press, 2006), 178.

7. *Presidential Elections, 1789–2004* (Washington, D.C.: CQ Press, 2005), 179.

8. "Faithless Elector State Laws," Fair Vote, accessed February 13, 2020, https://www.fairvote.org/faithless_elector_state_laws.

9. "Faithless Electors," Fair Vote, accessed February 13, 2020, https://www.fairvote.org/faithless_electors.

10. For more on the differences between indirect and direct elections of U.S. senators, see Wendy J. Schiller and Charles Stewart III, *Electing the Senate: Indirect Democracy before the 17th Amendment* (Princeton, NJ: Princeton University Press, 2014).

11. Abigail Abrams, "Here's What We Know So Far About Russia's 2016 Meddling," *Time*, April 18, 2019, accessed February 13, 2020, https://time.com/5565991/russia-influence-2016-election/.

12. For a longer discussion of redistricting, see Bernard Grofman, Lisa Handley, and Richard G. Niemi, *Minority Representation and the Quest for Voting Equality* (New York: Cambridge University Press, 1992).

13. Editorial Board, "A Flurry of Courts Have Ruled on Election Maps. Here's What They've Said," *New York Times*, January 29, 2018, accessed March 6, 2018, https://www.nytimes.com/2018/01/29/us/politics/gerrymandering-election-maps.html.

14. Stephen Nicholson, *Voting by Agenda* (Princeton, NJ: Princeton University Press, 2005).

15. Adam Liptak, "Supreme Court Bars Challenges to Partisan Gerrymandering," *New York Times*, June 29, 2019, accessed February 14, 2020, https://www.nytimes.com/2019/06/27/us/politics/supreme-court-gerrymandering.html.

16. See http://www.americanbar.org/content/dam/aba/migrated/leadership/fact_sheet.authcheckdam.pdf, accessed May 4, 2014.

17. Susan Hyde and Nikolay Marinov, "National Elections Across Democracy and Autocracy: Which Elections Can Be Lost?" (manuscript, Yale University, 2010), accessed June 1, 2012, http://hyde.research.yale.edu/nelda.

18. Robert A. Dahl, "What Political Institutions Does Large-Scale Democracy Require?," *Political Science Quarterly* 120 (2005): 187–98.

19. *Pew Research Center*, "Election 2016: 2016 Campaign: Strong Interest, Widespread Dissatisfaction," accessed November 2, 2016, http://www.people-press.org/2016/07/07/1-campaign-engagement-and-interest.

20. Michael McGerr, *The Decline of Popular Politics* (New York: Oxford University Press, 1986).

21. Nathan Martin and Maggie Haberman, "Ted Cruz Hopes Early Campaign Entry Will Focus Voters' Attention," *New York Times*, March 22, 2015.

22. Sidney Blumenthal, *The Permanent Campaign* (New York: Simon and Schuster, 1982).

23. Marty Cohen, David Karol, Hans Noel, and John Zaller, *The Party Decides: Presidential Nominations Before and After Reform* (Chicago, IL: University of Chicago Press, 2008).

24. United States Elections Project, "2016 Presidential Nomination Contest Turnout Rates," http://www.electproject.org/2016P.

25. Natasha Koreck, David Siders, and Alex Thompson, "'It's a Total Meltdown': Confusion Grips Iowa with No Official Results in Sight," *Politico*, February 4, 2020, accessed February 14, 2020, https://www.politico.com/news/2020/02/03/iowa-caucus-2020-election-110600.

26. Domenico Montanaro, "Super Tuesday Was Created To Nominate Someone Moderate. It Backfired," *NPR*, February 29, 2020, https://www.npr.org/2016/02/29/468253626/a-history-of-super-tuesday.

27. Domenico Montanaro, "Your State-By-State Guide To Super Tuesday," *NPR*, March 2, 2020, https://www.npr.org/2020/03/02/811028381/your-state-by-state-guide-to-super-tuesday.

28. "What Went Down On Super Tuesday," FiveThirtyEight, March 4, 2020, https://fivethirtyeight.com/live-blog/super-tuesday/.

29. Jasmine C. Lee, Annie Daniel, Rebecca Lieberman, Blacki Migliozzi, Alexander Burns, and Sarah Almukhtar, "Which Democrats Are Leading the 2020 Presidential Race?," *New York Times*, March 6, 2020, https://www.nytimes.com/interactive/2020/us/elections/democratic-polls.html.

30. Aaron Bycoffe, "The Endorsement Primary," FiveThirtyEight, accessed November 2, 2016, http://projects.fivethirtyeight.com/2016-endorsement-primary."

31. Cynthia Littleton and Oriana Schwindt, "Final Ratings for Third Donald Trump-Hillary Clinton Debate: 71.6 Million," *Variety*, October 20, 2016, accessed November 2, 2016, http://variety.com/2016/tv/news/tv-ratings-donald-trump-hillary-clinton-final-debate-1201895174.

32. Sidney Krause, *The Great Debates: Kennedy v. Nixon 1960* (Bloomington: Indiana University Press, 1977).

33. Federal Election Commission, "The FEC and Federal Campaign Finance Law: Historical Background," February 2004, accessed June 4, 2012, http://www.fec.gov/pages/brochures/fecfeca.shtml.

34. "Contribution Limits for 2019–2020 Federal Elections," https://www.fec.gov/updates/contribution-limits-2019-2020/.

35. Ibid.

36. See https://www.opensecrets.org/pres16/raised-summ.

37. See https://www.opensecrets.org/2020-presidential-race/candidate/bernie-sanders?id=N00000528.

38. See https://www.opensecrets.org/2020-presidential-race.

39. See https://www.commondreams.org/news/2020/02/06/sanders-25-million-january-haul-more-any-other-democrat-raised-any-full-quarter-2019.

40. Richard Briffault, "Super PACs" (Working Paper 12-298, Columbia Law School, April 16, 2012).

41. Beatrice Jin, Zach Montellaro, and Maggie Severns, "The Money: Who's Winning – and Losing – the Great 2020 Money Chase," *Politico*, accessed February 15, 2020, https://www.politico.com/2020-election/president/democratic-primary/candidates/fundraising-and-campaign-finance-tracker/.

42. See https://www.opensecrets.org/2020-presidential-race.

43. Matea Gold and Anu Narayanswamy, "41% of All Super PAC Money Comes From Donors," *Boston Globe*, April 17, 2016, https://www.bostonglobe.com/news/nation/2016/04/16/all-super-pac-money-comes-from-donors/5TJLQ5gxHMRclXlhAVVK2H/story.html.

44. See https://www.opensecrets.org/outsidespending/summ.php?cycle=2016&chrt=V&disp=O&type=S.

45. Alyson Hurt and Sean McMinn, "Tracking The Money Race Behind The Presidential Campaign," *NPR*, February 12, 2020, accessed February 15, 2020, https://www.npr.org/2019/04/16/711812314/tracking-the-money-race-behind-the-presidential-campaign.

46. See https://www.opensecrets.org/outsidespending/summ.php?cycle=2016&chrt=V&disp=O&type=S.

47. Steven J. Rosenstone and John Mark Hansen, Mobilization, Participation, and Democracy in America (New York: Macmillan, 1993).

48. "2016 Outside Spending, by Super PAC," *OpenSecrets.org,* accessed November 2, 2016, https://www.opensecrets.org/outsidespending/summ.php?chrt=V&type=S.

49. Nate Silver, "Election Update: Where Are the Undecided Voters?" FiveThirtyEight, accessed November 10, 2016, http://fivethirtyeight.com/features/election-update-where-are-the-undecided-voters.

50. See https://www.usatoday.com/story/news/politics/elections/2020/10/18/donald-trumps-toughest-hurdle-2020-election-win-few-undecideds/3654305001/.

51. The best book on "swing states" is still Daron R. Shaw, *The Race to 270: The Electoral College and the Campaign Strategies of 2000 and 2004* (Chicago, IL: University of Chicago Press, 2006).

52. The Battleground States Project, *Politico.com*, accessed November 2, 2016, http://www.politico.com/2016-election/swing-states.

53. Mark J. Penn with E. Kinney Zalesne, *Microtrends: The Small Forces Behind Tomorrow's Big Changes* (New York: Twelve, Hatchett Book Group USA, 2007), xiii.

54. "Identifying the 2020 Battleground States," accessed February 16, 2020, https://electoralvotemap.com/2020-battleground-states/.

55. Thomas B. Edsall, "Let the Nanotargeting Begin," *Campaign Stops* (blog), *New York Times*, April 15, 2012, http://campaignstops.blogs.nytimes.com/2012/04/15/let-the-nanotargeting-begin/.

56. See http://www.thevictorylab.com/for an account of the revolution in campaigns that is often called "microtargeting."

57. Darren Samuelsohn, "Inside Clinton's Plan to Win Over Millennials," *Politico,* accessed November 12, 2016, http://www.politico.com/story/2016/06/hillary-clinton-millennials-young-voters-224507.

58. Katie Kuehner-Hebert, "Cover Story: The Direct Marketing Election," *Target Marketing*, November 1, 2012, http://www.targetmarketingmag.com/article/election-2012-barack-obama-mitt-romney-microtargeting-retargeting-mobile-marketing-social-media-voter-databases/1, accessed May 2, 2014.

59. John G. Geer, *In Defense of Negativity* (Chicago, IL: University of Chicago Press, 2006), 59–60.

60. Lynn Vavreck, *The Message Matters* (Princeton, NJ: Princeton University Press, 2009).

61. Meg Anderson, "From the Economy to Race, See Where the Candidates Stand on the Big Issues," *NPR*, accessed November 12, 2016, http://www.npr.org/2016/10/18/496926243/from-the-economy-to-race-see-where-the-candidates-stand-on-the-big-issues.

62. Donald Stokes, "Spatial Models of Party Competition," *American Political Science Review* 57 (1963): 368–77.

63. Geer, *In Defense of Negativity*, 105.

64. Sunshine Hillygus and Todd Shields, *The Persuadable Voter* (Princeton, NJ: Princeton University Press, 2008), 36.

65. Emily Cadei, "How Donald Trump Made Race the Wedge Issue of 2016," *Newsweek*, accessed November 12, 2016, http://www.newsweek.com/trump-race-wedge-issue-494601.

66. Kathleen Jamieson, *Dirty Politics* (New York: Oxford University Press, 1992).

67. Erika Franklin Fowler and Travis N. Ridout, "Negative, Angry and Ubiquitous: Political Advertising in 2012," *The Forum, A Journal of Applied Research in Contemporary Politics* 10, no. 4 (2012): 51–61.

68. Wesleyan Media Project, "Advertising Analysis," accessed November 10, 2016, http://mediaproject.wesleyan.edu.

69. Geer, *In Defense of Negativity*.

70. Zachary Karabell, *The Last Campaign* (New York: Vintage, 2001).

71. Geer, *In Defense of Negativity*, 9–10.

72. *The Fiscal Times*, "Most Forecasters Predict a Win for Clinton, Except for Two," accessed November 12, 2016, http://www.thefiscaltimes.com/2016/09/04/Most-Forecasters-Predict-Win-Clinton-Except-Two.

73. Ibid.

74. Anthony Downs, *An Economic Theory of Democracy* (New York: Harper, 1957).

75. Mark C. Westlye, *Senate Elections and Campaign Intensity* (Baltimore, MD.: Johns Hopkins University Press, 1991).

76. Federal Election Commission, *Federal Election Campaign Laws* (Washington, D.C.: Federal Election Commission, April 2008), 56–60, http://www.fec.gov. Note that the contribution levels have been increased slightly to adjust for inflation.

77. See https://www.opensecrets.org/races, accessed November 12, 2016; Albert Cover, "One Good Term Deserves Another: The Advantage of Incumbency in Congressional Elections," *American Journal of Political Science* 21, no. 3 (1977): 523–41.

78. Gary C. Jacobson, *The Politics of Congressional Elections*, 8th ed. (Upper Saddle River, NJ: Prentice Hall, 2012).

79. Richard F. Fenno Jr., *Home Style: Home Members in Their Districts* (Boston, MA: Little, Brown, 1978).

80. "Longest Serving Senators," accessed February 15, 2020, https://www.senate.gov/senators/longest_serving_senators.htm; "Members With 40 Years or More House Experience," accessed February 15, 2020, https://history.house.gov/Institution/Seniority/40-Years/.

81. Jacobson, *The Politics of Congressional Elections*.

82. ABC News Poll, November 2016 [survey question]. USABC.110616. R05. *ABC News* [producer]. Cornell University, Ithaca, NY: Roper Center for Public Opinion Research, iPOLL [distributor], accessed November 12, 2016.

83. John Zaller, "Politicians as Prize Fighters," in *Politicians and Party Politics,* ed. John G. Geer (Baltimore, MD.: Johns Hopkins University Press, 1998), 128–85.

84. Bruce Oppenheimer, "Deep Red and Blue Congressional Districts: The Causes and Consequences of Declining Party Competitiveness," in *Congress Reconsidered*, 8th ed., ed. Lawrence Dodd and Bruce Oppenheimer (Washington, D.C.: CQ Press, 2005), 135–58.

85. Jacobson, *The Politics of Congressional Elections*.

86. "Voter Turnout," FairVote, accessed February 15, 2020, https://www.fairvote.org/voter_turnout#voter_turnout_101.

87. Tracy Sulkin, "Promises Made and Promises Kept," in *Congress Reconsidered*, ed. Lawrence Dodd and Bruce Oppenheimer (Washington, D.C.: CQ Press, 2009), 119–40.

88. Tracy Sulkin and Nathaniel Swigger, "Is There Truth in Advertising?" *Journal of Politics* 70 (2008): 232–44.

89. Gary C. Jacobson and Samuel Kernell, *Strategy and Choice in Congressional Elections* (New Haven, Conn.: Yale University Press, 1983).

90. Jacobson, *The Politics of Congressional Elections*.

91. Gerald M. Pomper, *Elections in America* (New York: Longman, 1980), 161.

92. Poll conducted by The Roper Center for Public Opinion Research, February 9–23, 1980, retrieved June 9, 2012, from the iPOLL Databank, The Roper Center for Public Opinion Research, University of Connecticut.

93. Poll conducted by Penn and Schoen Associates, October 10–12, 1984, retrieved June 9, 2012, from the iPOLL Databank, The Roper Center for Public Opinion Research, University of Connecticut.

94. Poll conducted by Greenberg Quinlan Rosner Research, October 30–November 2, 2008, retrieved June 9, 2012, from the iPOLL Databank, The Roper Center for Public Opinion Research, University of Connecticut.

95. *NBC News/Wall Street Journal* Poll, November 2016 [survey question]. USNBCWSJ.110616.R04A. Hart Research Associates/Public Opinion Strategies [producer]. Cornell University, Ithaca, NY: Roper Center for Public Opinion Research, iPOLL [distributor], accessed November 12, 2016.

96. V. O. Key, *The Responsible Electorate* (Cambridge, Mass.: Harvard University Press, 1966).

97. See https://www.realclearpolitics.com/epolls/other/direction_of_country-902.html.

98. Ibid.

Chapter 11

1. Ta-Nehisi Coates, "There is No Post-Racial America," *The Atlantic*, July /August 2015, http://www.theatlantic.com/magazine/archive/2015/07/post-racial-society-distant-dream/395255/.

2. This story has been compiled from the following sources: Benjamin Wallace-Wells, "The Hard Truths of Ta-Nehisi Coates," *New York Magazine*, July 12, 2015, http://nymag.com/daily/intelligencer/2015/07/ta-nehisi-coates-between-the-world-and-me.html; NPR, "Ta-Nehisi Coates on His Work and the Painful Process of Getting Conscious," November 21, 2015, http://www.npr.org/2015/11/21/456879598/ta-nehisi-coates-on-his-work-and-the-painful-process-of-getting-conscious; Ta-Nehisi Coates, "The Case for Reparations," *The Atlantic*, June 2014; Michelle Alexander, "Ta-Nehisi Coates's 'Between the World and Me,'" *New York Times*, August 17, 2015, http://www .nytimes.com/2015/08/17/books/review/ta-nehisi-coates-between-the-world-and-me.html?_r=0; Ta-Nehisi Coates, *Between the World and Me* (New York: Spiegel & Grau, 2015).

3. "Ta-Nehisi Coates on His Work and the Painful Process of Getting Conscious," *NPR* interview, *All Things Considered*, November 21, 2015, http://www.npr.org/2015/11/21/456879598/ta-nehisi-coates-on-his-work-and-the-painful-process-of-getting-conscious.

4. Wallace-Wells, "The Hard Truths of Ta-Nehisi Coates."

5. Alexander, "Ta-Nehisi Coates's 'Between the World and Me.'"

6. "Ta-Nehisi Coates on His Work and the Painful Process of Getting Conscious," NPR interview.

7. Kevin Corder and Christina Wolbrecht, "Political Context and the Turnout of New Women Voters After Suffrage," *Journal of Politics* 68 (2006): 34–49.

8. Samuel Huntington, "The United States," in *The Crisis of Democracy*, ed. Michael Crozier, Samuel Huntington, and Joji Watanuki (New York: NYU Press, 1975), 59–115.

9. Steven E. Finkel "Reciprocal Effects of Participation and Political Efficacy: A Panel Analysis," *American Journal of Political Science* 29, no. 4 (1985): 891–913; Steven E. Finkel, "The Effects of Participation on Political Efficacy and Political Support: Evidence from a West German Panel," *Journal of Politics* 49, no. 2 (1987): 441–64. These articles provide empirical evidence that supports the arguments of Carol Pateman, *Participation and Democratic Theory* (New York: Cambridge University Press, 1970).

10. This section draws heavily on Alexander Keyssar, *The Right to Vote: The Contested History of Democracy in the United States* (New York: Basic Books, 2001).

11. Washington actually won 132 of the 135 Electoral College votes in 1792. Three electors—one from Vermont and two from Maryland—did not cast ballots.

12. Keyssar, *The Right to Vote*, 10–21.

13. For detailed data on the 1824 presidential election, see John T. Woolley and Gerhard Peters, "Election of 1824," The American Presidency Project, accessed June 7, 2012, http://www.presidency.ucsb.edu/showelection.php?year=1824.

14. Some now question the claims of a "corrupt bargain." See Jeffrey A. Jenkins and Brian R. Sala, "The Spatial Theory of Voting and the Presidential Election of 1824," *American Journal of Political Science* 42, no. 4 (1998): 1157–79.

15. Elisabeth Griffith, *In Her Own Right: The Life of Elizabeth Cady Stanton* (New York: Oxford University Press, 1984), 153–54. See also Doug Linder, "The Trial of Susan B. Anthony for Illegal Voting," 2001, accessed June 7, 2012, http://www.law.umkc.edu/faculty/projects/ftrials/anthony/sbaaccount.html.

16. Harold Gosnell, *Getting Out the Vote* (Chicago, IL: University of Chicago Press, 1927).

17. Corder and Wolbrecht, "Political Context," 46.

18. Ibid.

19. Measuring turnout can be done a number of different ways, and each way can yield different estimates. If you ask people if they voted, many will say yes even if they did not. "Self-reports" inflate turnout numbers. The numbers used in the paragraph are simply the reported vote in the election divided by the number of people eligible to vote—or what is called voting-age population (VAP).

20. Harold W. Stanley and Richard Niemi, *Vital Statistics on American Politics 2013–2014* (Thousand Oaks, CA: CQ Press, 2013); Hannah Hartig, "In Year of Record Midterm Turnout, Women Continued to Vote at Higher Rates Than Men," *Pew Research Center,* May 3, 2019, accessed April 29, 2020, https://www.pewresearch.org/fact-tank/2019/05/03/in-year-of-record-midterm-turnout-women-continued-to-vote-at-higher-rates-than-men/.

21. Ronald L. F. Davis, "Creating Jim Crow: In-Depth Essay," The History of Jim Crow, http://www.jimcrowhistory.org/history/creating2.htm.

22. This figure underestimates the true cost of the poll tax in today's dollars. We divided $2 by $86 to arrive at 2.3 percent. We then multiplied the 2.3 percent by $43,000, the median income in the United States in 2000. The precise dollar estimate is $989. But the average income of blacks in the South was surely less than $86, and that ignores the issue that African Americans would rarely have that much cash available to them.

23. J. Morgan Kousser, "Poll Tax," in *The International Encyclopedia of Elections* (Washington, D.C.: CQ Press, 1999), 208–09.

24. *Smith v. Allwright,* 321 U.S. 649 (1944).

25. Sarah A. Binder and Steven S. Smith, *Political or Principle: Filibustering in the United States Senate* (Washington, D.C.: Brookings Institution Press, 1996).

26. The term *negroes* was commonly used at the time. Poll conducted by Opinion Research Corporation, October 15–November 15, 1963, retrieved June 21, 2012, from the iPOLL Databank, The Roper Center for Public Opinion Research, University of Connecticut.

27. Voting and Registration in the Election of November 2016. United States Census, accessed, February 23, 2018. https://www.census.gov/data/tables/time-series/demo/voting-and-registration/p20-580.html.

28. Thomas Rochon and Ikuo Kabashima, "Movement and Aftermath," in *Politicians and Party Politics*, ed. John G. Geer (Baltimore, MD.: Johns Hopkins University Press, 1998), 102–21.

29. Paul Taylor and Mark Hugo Lopez, "Six Take-Aways from the Census Bureau's Voting Report," *Pew Research Center*, May 8, 2013, http://www.pewresearch.org/fact-tank/2013/05/08/six-take-aways-from-the-census-bureaus-voting-report/; Tami Luhby, "How Hillary Clinton Lost," *CNN Politics*, November 9, 2016, http://www.cnn.com/2016/11/09/politics/clinton-votes-african-americans-latinos-women-white-voters/index.html?curator=MediaREDEF.

30. Even as of 2013, the U.S. Census estimated that over 25 percent of Americans aged 5 and over speak a language other than English at home. U.S. Census, "Detailed Languages Spoken at Home and Ability to Speak English for the Population 5 Years and Over: 2009–2013," October 2015, http://www.census.gov/data/tables/2013/demo/2009-2013-lang-tables.html. In 2009, among Latinos, the average across all groups was 76 percent. Tallese D. Johnson, Merarys Rios, Malcolm P. Drewery, Sharon R. Ennis, and Myoung Ouk Kim, U.S. Department of Commerce, U.S. Bureau of the Census, "People Who Spoke a Language Other than English at Home by Ethnic Origin and Race: 2009," 2010.

31. *Katzenbach v. Morgan*, 384 U.S. 641 (1966).

32. 42 USC 203 §1973 to 1973bb.

33. Voting Rights Act Language Assistance Amendments of 1992: Hearings on S. 2236 before the Subcomm. on the Constitution of the Senate Comm. on the Judiciary [1992 hearings], 102d Cong., 2d Sess., S. Hrg. 102-1066, at 134 (1992).

34. Luis Noe-Bustamante, Abby Budiman and Mark Hugo Lopez, "Where Latinos Have the Most Eligible Voters in the 2020 Election," *Pew Research Center*, January 31, 2020, https://www.pewresearch.org/fact-tank/2020/01/31/where-latinos-have-the-most-eligible-voters-in-the-2020-election/.

35. Marisa Abrajano and Michael Alvarez, *New Faces, New Voices: The Hispanic Electorate in America* (Princeton, NJ: Princeton University Press, 2010); Matt A. Barreto, Gary M. Segura, and Nathan D. Woods, "The Mobilizing Effect of Majority-Minority Districts on Latino Turnout," *American Political Science Review* 98, no. 1 (2004): 65–75; Matt A. Barreto, Loren Collingwood, and Sylvia Manzano, "A New Measure of Group Influence in Presidential Elections: Assessing Latino Influence in 2008," *Political Research Quarterly* 63 (2010): 908–21.

36. National Conference of State Legislatures, January 5, 2018, *Voter Identification Requirements, Voter Laws*, http://www.ncsl.org/research/elections-and-campaigns/voter-id.aspx.

37. *Crawford v. Marion County Election Board*, 553 U.S. 181 (2008). See also Bill Mears, "High Court Upholds Indiana's Voter ID Law," *CNN*, April 28, 2008, http://articles.cnn.com/2008-04-28/politics/scotus.voter.id_1_voter-impersonation-voter-id-laws-voter-fraud?_s=PM:POLITICS; Linda Greenhouse, "In a 6-to-3 Vote, Justices Uphold a Voter ID Law," *New York Times*, April 29, 2008.

38. American Civil Liberties Union, "*Applewhite et al. v. Commonwealth of Pennsylvania*, et al.," accessed May 19, 2012, http://www.aclupa.org/our-work/legal/legaldocket/applewhite-et-al-v-commonwealth-pennsylvania-et-al/; Rick Lyman, "Pennsylvania Voter ID Law Struck Down as Judge Cites Burden on Citizens," *New York Times*, January 17, 2014, http://www.nytimes.com/2014/01/18/us/politics/pennsylvania-voter-id-law-struck-down.html.

39. Wade Goodwin, "Texas Voter ID Law Creates a Problem for Some Women," October 20, 2013, http://www.npr.org/2013/10/30/241891800/texas-voter-id-law-creates-a-problem-for-some-women.

40. Matt A. Barreto and Gabriel R. Sanchez, "Accepted Photo Identification and Different Subgroups in the Eligible Voter Population, State of Texas," Expert Report Submitted on Behalf of Plaintiffs in *Veasey v. Perry*, Case 2:13-cv-00193, June 27, 2014, http://www.latinodecisions.com/blog/wp-content/uploads/2014/10/Texas-Voter-ID-Expert-Report_Barreto_Sanchez.pdf.

41. 42 USC 203 §1973 to 1973bb.

42. Zoltan Hajnal, Nazita Lajevardi, and Lindsay Nielsen, "Voter Identification Laws and the Suppression of Minority Votes," *The Journal of Politics*, 79 (2017): 363–79; Justin Grimmer, Eitan Hersh, Marc Meredith, Jonathan Mummolo, and Clayton Nall, "Obstacles to Estimating Voter ID Laws' Effect on Turnout," *The Journal of Politics*, 80 (2018): 1045–51.

43. There were four exceptions: the voting age was 18 in Georgia and Kentucky, 19 in Alaska, and 20 in Hawaii.

44. Thom File, "Voting in America: A Look at the 2016 Presidential Election," United States Census, May 10, 2017, https://www.census.gov/newsroom/blogs/random-samplings/2017/05/voting_in_america.html

45. Michael P. McDonald, "2020 Presidential Nomination Contest Turnout Rates," U.S. Elections Project, accessed April 10, 2020, http://www.electproject.org/2020P.

46. Jan Leighley, "Attitudes, Opportunities, and Incentives," *Political Research Quarterly* 48 (1995): 184.

47. United State Census, Voting and Registration in the Election of November 2016, accessed February 23, 2018, https://www.census.gov/data/tables/time-series/demo/voting-and-registration/p20-580.html.

48. File, "Voting in America."

49. Jan E. Leighley and Jonathan Nagler, *Who Votes Now?* (Princeton, NJ: Princeton University Press, 2014).

50. File, "Voting in America"; Richard Fry, "Millennials and Gen Xers outvoted Boomers and Older Generations in 2016 Election," *Pew Research Center*, July 31, 2017, accessed February 20, 2018, http://www.pewresearch.org/fact-tank/2017/07/31/millennials-and-gen-xers-outvoted-boomers-and-older-generations-in-2016-election/

51. Mark Hugo Lopez and Paul Taylor, "Latino Voters in the 2012 Election," *Pew Research Center*, November 7, 2012, http://www.pewhispanic.org/2012/11/07/latino-voters-in-the-2012-election/; Jens Manuel Krogstag and Mark Hugo Lopez, "Hilary Clinton Wins Latino Vote, but Falls Below 2012 Support for Obama," *Pew Research Center*, November 9, 2016, accessed November 10, 2016, http://www.pewresearch.org/fact-tank/2016/11/09/hillary-clinton-wins-latino-vote-but-falls-below-2012-support-for-obama/.

52. See, for instance, Raymond Wolfinger and Steven Rosenstone, *Who Votes?* (New Haven, Conn.: Yale University Press, 1980). There has been much research since the publication of this book, but it remains a leading source on this topic.

53. U.S. Census, *Voting and Registration in the Election of 2012*, https://www.census.gov/data/tables/time-series/demo/voting-and-registration/p20-580.html.

54. Cindy D. Kam and Carl L. Palmer, "Reconsidering the Effects of Education on Political Participation," *Journal of Politics* 70, no. 3 (2008): 612–31; Rachel Milstein Sondheimer and Donald Green, "Using Experiments to Estimate the Effects of Education on Voter

55. Turnout," *American Journal of Political Science* 54, no. 1 (2010): 174–89.

55. Anthony Downs, *An Economic Theory of Democracy* (New York: Harper, 1957).

56. Howard Gillman, *The Votes That Counted* (Chicago, IL: University of Chicago Press, 2001), 77.

57. William Riker and Peter Ordeshook, "A Theory of the Calculus of Voting," *American Political Science Review* 62 (1968): 25–42.

58. For other efforts to solve this problem, see John H. Aldrich, "Rational Choice and Turnout," *American Journal of Political Science* 37, no. 1 (1993): 246–78; Robert Grafstein, "An Evidential Decision Theory of Turnout," *American Journal of Political Science* 35 (1991): 989–1010.

59. The Public, the Political System and American Democracy, April 26, 2018, accessed April 10, 2020, https://www.people-press.org/2018/04/26/9-the-responsibilities-of-citizenship/.

60. Allyson L. Holbrook and Jon A. Krosnick, "Social Desirability Bias in Voter Turnout Reports: Tests Using the Item Count Technique," *Public Opinion Quarterly* 74 (2010): 37–67.

61. David Campbell, *Why We Vote* (Princeton, NJ: Princeton University Press, 2006).

62. G. Bingham Powell Jr., "American Voter Turnout in Comparative Perspective," *American Political Science Review* 80 (1986): 17–43; Henry Brady, Sidney Verba, and Kay Schlozman, "Beyond SES: A Resource Model of Political Participation," *American Political Science Review* 89 (1995): 271–94.

63. John Zipp, "Perceived Representativeness and Voting: An Assessment of the Impact of 'Choices' vs. 'Echoes,'" *American Political Science Review* 79 (1985): 50–61.

64. Alan S. Gerber, Donald P. Green, and David W. Nickerson, "Getting Out the Vote in Local Elections: Results from Six Door-to-Door Canvassing Experiments," *Journal of Politics* 65 (2003): 4; Donald P. Green and Alan S. Gerber, *Get Out the Vote, 2015* (Washington, DC: Brookings Institution Press); Alan S. Gerber and Donald P. Green, "The Effects of Canvassing, Telephone Calls, and Direct Mail on Voter Turnout: A Field Experiment," *American Political Science Review* (2000) 94: 653–663.

65. Allison Dale and Aaron Strauss, "Don't Forget to Vote: Text Message Reminders as a Mobilization Tool," *American Journal of Political Science* 53 (2009): 787–804.

66. Steven J. Rosenstone and John Mark Hansen, *Mobilization, Participation, and Democracy in America* (New York: Macmillan, 1993).

67. James H. Fowler, Laura A. Baker, and Christopher T. Dawes, "Genetic Variation in Political Participation," *American Political Science Review* 102, no. 2 (2008): 233–48.

68. James H. Fowler and Christopher T. Dawes, "Two Genes Predict Voter Turnout," *Journal of Politics* 70 (2008): 579–94.

69. Evan Charney and William English, "Candidate Genes and Political Behavior," *American Political Science Review* 106 (2012): 1–34.

70. Brad T. Gomez, Thomas G. Hansford, and George A. Krause, "The Republicans Should Pray for Rain: Weather, Turnout, and Voting in U.S. Presidential Elections," *Journal of Politics* 69 (2007): 649–63; Bernard Fraga and Eitan Hersh, "Voting Costs and Voter Turnout in Competitive Elections," *Quarterly Journal of Political Science*, 5 (2011): 339–356.

71. Frances Fox Piven and Richard A. Cloward, *Why Americans Still Don't Vote: And Why Politicians Want It That Way* (Boston, MA: Beacon Press, 2000); Martin P. Wattenberg, *Where Have All the Voters Gone?* (Boston: Harvard University Press, 2002); Thomas E. Patterson, *The Vanishing Voter: Public Involvement in an Age of Uncertainty* (New York: Alfred A. Knopf, 2003).

72. Michael P. McDonald, "2014 Presidential Nomination Contest Turnout Rates," U.S. Elections Project, accessed April 2, 2016, http://www.electproject.org/2014g; Michael P. McDonald, "2018 November General Election Turnout Rates," U.S. Elections Project, accessed April 10, 2020, http://www.electproject.org/2018g.

73. "2016 November General Election Turnout Rates," United States Election Project, accessed November 15, 2016, http://www.electproject.org/2016g.

74. "2016 November General Election Turnout Rates," United States Election Project, accessed November 15, 2016, http://www.electproject.org/2016g; "National General Election VEP Turnout Rates, 1789–Present," United States Election Project, accessed November 15, 2016, http://www.electproject.org/national-1789-present.

75. Powell, "American Voter Turnout in Comparative Perspective," 17–37.

76. This "puzzle of participation" was first discussed by Richard Brody in *The New American Political System,* ed. Anthony King (Washington, D.C.: American Enterprise Institute for Public Policy Research, 1978).

77. Warren Miller, "Puzzle Transformed," *Political Behavior* 14 (1992): 1–43.

78. Rosenstone and Hansen, *Mobilization, Participation, and Democracy in America.*

79. Ibid.

80. Keena Lipsitz, Christine Trost, Matthew Grossman, and John Sides, "What Voters Want from Campaign Communication," *Political Communication* 22 (2005): 337–54.

81. Steven Ansolabehere and Shanto Iyengar, *Going Negative* (New York: Free Press, 1995).

82. John G. Geer, *In Defense of Negativity* (Chicago, IL: University of Chicago Press, 2006).

83. See, for example, Joshua Clinton and John Lapinski, "'Targeted' Advertising and Voter Turnout: An Experimental Study of the 2000 Presidential Election," *Journal of Politics* 66 (2004): 69–96.

84. Richard R. Lau, Lee Sigelman, and Ivy Brown Rovner, "A New Meta-Analysis," *Journal of Politics* 69 (2007): 176–209.

85. Jens Manuel Krogstag, Jeffrey S. Passel, and D'Vera Cohn, "5 Facts About Illegal Immigration in the U.S.," *Pew Research Center,* June 12, 2019, https://www.pewresearch.org/fact-tank/2019/06/12/5-facts-about-illegal-immigration-in-the-u-s/.

86. U.S. Department of Justice, Bureau of Justice Statistics, "Jail Inmates in 2018," March 2020, accessed April 10, 2020, https://www.bjs.gov/content/pub/pdf/ji18_sum.pdf.

87. Michael P. McDonald and Samuel L. Popkin, "The Myth of the Vanishing Voter," *American Political Science Review* 95 (2001): 963–74.

88. *Evenwel v. Abbott,* 578 U.S. (2016).

89. Larry Bartels, *Unequal Democracy* (Princeton, NJ: Princeton University Press, 2008).

90. Task Force on American Inequality, "American Democracy in an Age of Rising Inequality," American Political Science Association, 2004.

91. Bartels, *Unequal Democracy.*

92. See http://www.slate.com/blogs/weigel/2014/04/24/gilens_and_page_find_that_rich_americans_rule_politics_but_despair_the_fact.html, accessed June 3, 2014.

93. See Dayton McKean, *The Boss: The Hague Machine in Action* (New York: Russell and Russell Publishers, 1967), for an account of the corrupt practices of machine politicians.

94. See James Bryce, *The American Commonwealth* (New York: Macmillan, 1895).

95. For the best account of the importance and impact of registration, see Benjamin Highton, "Voter Registration and Turnout in the United States," *Perspectives on Politics* 2 (2004): 507–15.

96. National Conference of State Legislatures, *Same-Day Voter Registration*, June 2, 2015, http://www.ncsl.org/research/elections -and-campaigns/same-day-registration.aspx. The states are Colorado, Connecticut, Idaho, Illinois, Iowa, Maine, Minnesota, Montana, New Hampshire, Wisconsin, and Wyoming.

97. Karyn Rotker, "State History and Immigrant Voting," *Milwaukee Journal Sentinel*, October 29, 2006.

98. Highton, "Voter Registration and Turnout."

99. Read about the National Voter Registration Act of 1993 at http:// www.justice.gov/crt/about/vot/nvra/activ_nvra.php.

100. U.S. Election Assistance Commission, accessed April 29, 2020, https://www.eac.gov/about_the_eac/help_america_vote_act.aspx.

101. Texas Secretary of State Carlos H. Cascos' official website, http:// www.sos.state.tx.us/ and http://www.votetexas.gov/.

102. United States Election Project, 2016 November General Election Turnout Rates, accessed February 20, 2018, http://www.electproject .org/2016g, United States Election Project, 2018 November General Election Turnout Rates, accessed April 15, 2020, http://www.electproject .org/2018g.

103. See https://www.sos.state.co.us/pubs/rule_making/written_comments /2009/111009_commoncause_votebymailproject.pdf, accessed June 30, 2014.

104. National Conference of State Legislatures, *Absentee and Early Voting*, March 24, 2016, http://www.ncsl.org/research/elections-and-campaigns /absentee-and-early-voting.aspx.

105. Paul Gronke, Eva Galanes-Rosenbaum, and Peter A. Miller, "Early Voting and Turnout," *PS: Political Science and Politics* (October 2003): 639–45.

106. Steven Yaccino and Lizette Alvarez, "New G.O.P. Bid to Limit Voting in Swing States," *New York Times*, March 29, 2014.

107. Christopher Ingraham, "Universal Vote-by-Mail Doesn't Benefit Any Political Party, Study Finds," *Washington Post*, April 16, 2020, accessed, April 16, 2020, https://www.washingtonpost.com /business/2020/04/16/universal-vote-by-mail-doesnt-benefit-any-political -party-study-finds/.

108. "Same Day Voter Registration," National Conference of State Legislatures, June 28, 2019, accessed April 15, 2020, https://www .ncsl.org/research/elections-and-campaigns/same-day-registration .aspx; "New Report Ranks 2016 Voter Turnout for 50 States," CISION PR Newswire, March 16, 2017, accessed February 24, 2018, https:// www.prnewswire.com/news-releases/new-report-ranks-2016-voter -turnout-for-50-states-300424504.html.

109. Jeffrey Gottfried, "When Discussing Politics, Family Plays Larger Role for Women than for Men," *Pew Research Center,* August 5, 2015, http://www.pewresearch.org/fact-tank/2015/08/05/when-discussing -politics-family-plays-larger-role-for-women-than-for-men/.

110. Vietnam War Protests, accessed April 4, 2016, http://www.history .com/topics/vietnam-war/vietnam-war-protests.

111. See some of the following literature on social movements and protest behavior: David S. Meyer and Sidney Tarrow, eds., *The Social Movement Society: Contentious Politics for a New Century* (Lanham, MD: Rowman & Littlefield, 1998); Sidney Tarrow, *Power in Movement: Social Movements, Collective Action and Politics* (Cambridge, U.K.: Cambridge University Press, 1994); Russell J. Dalton, *Citizen Politics: Public Opinion and Political Parties in Advanced Industrial Democracies*, 6th ed. (Washington, DC: CQ Press, 2013); M. Kent Jennings, "Residues of a Movement: The Aging of the American Protest Generation," *American Political Science Review* 81 (1987): 367–82; Neal Caren, Andrew Raj Ghoshal, and Vanesa Ribas, "A Social Movement Generation: Cohort and Period Trends in Protest Attendance and Petition Signing," *American Sociological Review*, 76 (2011): 125–51.

112. Ellen Bara Stolzenberg, Kevin Eagan, Edgar Romo, Elaine Jessica Tamargo, Melissa C. Aragon, Madeline Luedke, and Nathaniel Kang, *The American Freshman: National Norms Fall 2018* (Higher Education Research Institute: University of California, Los Angeles).

113. Stolzenberg, et al., *The American Freshman, 2018*; Kevin Egan, Ellen Bara Stolzenberg, Joseph J. Ramirez, Melissa C. Aragon, Maria Ramirez Suchard, and Sylvia Hurtado, *The American Freshman: National Norms Fall 2014* (Higher Education Research Institute: University of California, Los Angeles); Kevin Egan, Ellen Bara Stolzenberg, Abigail K. Bates, Melissa C. Aragon, Maria Ramirez Suchard, and Cecilia Rios-Aguilar, *The American Freshman: National Norms Fall 2015* (Higher Education Research Institute: University of California, Los Angeles).

114. John Eligon and Richard Perez-Pena, "University of Missouri Protests Spur Day of Change," *New York Times*, November 9, 2015, http://www.nytimes .com/2015/11/10/us/university-of-missouri-system -president-resigns.html.

115. Ibid.

116. Billy Goodykoontz, "Florida School Shooting: Teenagers Are Changing the Conversation on Gun Control," *Arizona Republic*, February 25, 2018, accessed February 25, 2018, https://www.azcentral.com/story /entertainment/media/2018/02/25/florida-school-shooting-teenagers -changing-conversation-gun-control/371158002/; Wesley Lowery, "He Survived the Florida School Shooting: He Vows Not to Return to Classes until Gun Laws Change," *Washington Post*, February 18, 2018, accessed February 18, 2018, https://www.washingtonpost .com/news/post-nation/wp/2018/02/18/students-organize-to-fight -for-gun-law-changes/?utm_term=.536e1d8431de.

117. 530 U.S. 703 (2000).

118. 134 S. Ct. 2518 (2014).

119. "Going Too Far: The American Public's Attitudes Toward Protest Movements," The Roper Center for Public Opinion Research, http:// ropercenter.cornell.edu/going-too-far-the-american-publics-attitudes -toward-protest-movements/. Figures based on a 2013 poll con-ducted by AP/Gfk Knowledge Networks, accessed April 24, 2016.

120. Alia Wong and Adrienne Green, "Campus Politics: A Cheat Sheet," *The Atlantic*, April 4, 2016, accessed April 24, 2016, http://www. theatlantic.com/education/archive/2016/04/campus-protest -roundup/417570/.

121. Steven Goff, "Nurses to Protest at White House and Demand Protective Equipment," *The Washington Post*, April 20, 2020, accessed April 29, 2020, https://www.washingtonpost.com/world/2020 /04/20/coronavirus-latest-news/#link-Q5FWCTHXZZBXLASV V6EPDAUKIU; Perry Vandell and Richard Ruelas, "Protesters Rally at Arizona Capitol, Calling for End of Stay-at-Home Order," *The Arizona Republic*, April 20, 2020, accessed April 20, 2020, https:// www.azcentral.com/story/news/local/phoenix-breaking/2020 /04/20/rally-reopen-economy-planned-near-arizona-capitol /5165957002/.

122. Dennis Johnson, "Communicating with Congress," in *Congress and the Internet*, ed. James A. Thurber and Colton C. Campbell (New York: Prentice Hall, 2003).

123. Congressional Management Foundation. "Communicating with Congress: How Capitol Hill is Coping with the Surge in Citizen Advocacy," accessed April 2, 2016, http://www.congressfoundation .org/component/content/article/68. Data derived from the Office of Chief Administrative Office of the House of Representatives and the U.S. Senate Sergeant at Arms.

124. For one example, see Congresswoman Lizzie Fletcher's official web-site at https://fletcher.house.gov/.

125. Shannon Greenwod, Andrew Perrin, and Maeve Duggan, "Social Media Update 2016," *Pew Research Center*, accessed February 15, 2018, http://www.pewinternet.org/2016/11/11 /social-media -update-2016/.

126. See http://swampland.time.com/2012/11/15/exclusive-obamas-2012 -digital-fundraising-outperformed-2008, accessed June 3, 2014.

127. Paul Blumenthal, "Election 2012: Fundraising Year-End Totals Reveal Obama Record, GOP Disparity, Rich Super PACs," *Huffington Post*, February 1, 2012, http://www.huffingtonpost.com/2012/02/01 /election-2012/02/01/election-2012-fundraising-obama-romney -super-pacs_n_1247228.html; Paul Blumenthal and Aaron Bycoffe, "Here Are the Top Super PAC Mega-Donors in 2014 Elections," *Huffington Post*, November 3, 2014, accessed November 5, 2014.

128. Anu Narayanswamy, Aaron Williams, and Matea Gold, "Meet the Wealthy Donors Who Are Pouring Millions in the 2016 Elections," *Washington Post*, November 2, 2016. https://www.washingtonpost .com/graphics/politics/superpac-donors-2016/; "Election 2016: Money Raised as of October 19," *Washington Post*, accessed November 11, 2016, https://www.washingtonpost.com/graphics/politics /superpac-donors-2016/.

129. Center for Responsive Politics, "2020 election to cost $14 billion, blowing away spending records," *OpenSecrets.org*, October 28, 2020, https://www.opensecrets.org/news/2020/10/cost-of-2020-election -14billion-update.

130. National Council of State Legislatures, "Felon Voting Rights," October 14, 2019, accessed April 15, 2020; Jeff Manza and Christopher Ugge, *Locked Out: Felon Disenfranchisement and American Democracy* (Oxford, U.K.: Oxford University Press, 2007).

Chapter 12

1. This story was compiled from information on Representative Joaquín Castro's congressional website, http://castro.house.gov/; Georgia Park, "Castro Highlights Importance of Public Service Work, Leadership," *The Chronicle*, April 2, 2014, http://www.dukechronicle .com/articles/2014/04/02/castro-highlights-importance-public -service-work-leadership; "Interview with Representative Joaquin Castro," *The Situation Room*, CNN, January 4, 2013, http://www .realclearpolitics.com/articles/2013/01/04/interview_with _representative_joaquin_castro_116607. html#ixzz2yDth5yUN; Office of the Secretary of State of Texas, "Race Summary Report, 2012 General Election," November 6, 2012, http://elections.sos.state .tx.us; "Congressman Castro Visits Afghanistan," KSAT-San Antonio, April 7, 2014, http://www.ksat.com/news/Congressman-Castro -visits-Afghanistan/25370616; https://castro.house.gov/media-center /press-releases/castro-coffman-denham-introduce-bipartisan -legislation-supporting-women, accessed February 17, 2016; mysanan tonio.com Staff, "2016 Election Winners in Bexar County and Texas," accessed November 9, 2016, http://www.mysanantonio .com/news/local/politics/electionresults/us_house_by_texas _county; "Joaquin Castro," Bill Track, https://www.billtrack50.com /LegislatorDetail/19152; "Congressmen Castro, Taylor Introduce the Feeding Hungry Students in School Act," *Van Taylor*, May 14, 2019, https://vantaylor.house.gov/news/documentsingle.aspx? DocumentID=2240; Spencer Hsu, "A Sense of Place," *Stanford Magazine*, July/August 2015, accessed May 18, 2020, https://stanfordmag.org /contents/a-sense-of-place; Staff, "U.S. House Election Results," *New York Times*, accessed November 12, 2020, https://www.nytimes. com/interactive/2020/11/03/us/elections/results-house.html ?action=click&pgtype=Article&state=default&module=styln-elec tions-2020&region=TOP_BANNER&context=election_recirc.

2. Totals do not include House Delegates or the Resident Commissioner; see Jennifer E. Manning, *Membership of the 114th Congress: A Profile*, CRS Report for Congress, R43869 (Washington, D.C.: Congressional Research Service), October 31, 2015, accessed February 17, 2016, http://www.fas.org/sgp/crs/misc/R3869.pdf; *Census.gov*, "Annual Estimates of the Resident Population for Selected Age Groups by Sex for the United States, States, Counties, and Puerto Rico Commonwealth and Municipios: April 1, 2010 to July 1, 2014," accessed February 17, 2016, http://factfinder.census.gov/faces /tableservices/jsf/pages/productview.xhtml?src=bkmk.

3. Manning, *Membership*.

4. Ibid. For a broader discussion of the careers of women legislators in the House, see Jennifer Lawless and Sean Theriault, "Will She Stay or Will She Go? Career Ceilings and Women's Retirement from the U.S. Congress," *Legislative Studies Quarterly* 30 (2005): 581–96.

5. Letter from a Federal Farmer to a Republican, October 9, 1787; John DeWitt III, Boston, *American Herald*, November 5, 1787; Brutus III, *New York Journal*, November 15, 1787, http://csac.history.wisc.edu /house_of_representatives.htm.

6. See Wendy J. Schiller and Charles Stewart III, *Electing the Senate: Indirect Democracy Before the Seventeenth Amendment* (Princeton, NJ: Princeton University Press, 2015), and Lana R. Slack, *Senate Manual: Standing Rules, Orders, Laws, and Resolutions Affecting the Business of the United States Senate* (Washington, D.C.: U.S. Government Printing Office, 1988), 684–85.

7. U.S. Senate, "Senate Classes," Senate.gov, accessed June 21, 2012, http://www.senate.gov/artandhistory/history/common/briefing /Constitution_Senate.htm#3.

8. In rare cases in which a senator dies or resigns, an interim replacement is typically chosen by the governor of the state until an election is held to fill the seat.

9. U.S. Census Bureau, Kristen D. Burnett, "Congressional Apportionment," November 2011, accessed February 17, 2016, http://www.census.gov /prod/cen2010/briefs/c2010br-08.pdf; *Census.gov*, "Annual Population Estimates," http://www.census.gov/popclock/.

10. Based on calculations of 2020 population. Sandra L. Colby and Jennifer M. Ortman, "Projections of the Size and Composition of the U.S. Population: 2014–2060," Current Population Reports: U.S. Census Bureau, accessed May 12, 2020, https://www.census.gov/content /dam/Census/library/publications/2015/demo/p25-1143.pdf.

11. After the first census of the new federal government under the Constitution, Congress grew to 105 members in 1792. See Brian Frederick, *Congressional Representation and Constituents: The Case for Increasing the Size of the U.S. House of Representatives* (New York: Routledge, 2010), 23–24.

12. U.S. House of Representatives, "Historical Highlights: The Permanent Apportionment Act of 1929," June 11, 1929, accessed June 21, 2012, http://artandhistory.house.gov/highlights.aspx?action=view&intID =200.

13. Ally Mutnick, "Epic Redistricting Battles Loom in States Poised to Gain, Lose House Seats," Politico.com, December 30, 2019, accessed May 11, 2020, https://www.politico.com/news/2019/12/30/redistricting -house-2020-091451.

14. For a discussion of representation by Latino members, see Jason P. Casellas, "The Institutional and Demographic Determinants of Latino Representation," *Legislative Studies Quarterly* 34, no. 3 (2009): 399–426; see also David Leal and Frederick M. Hess, "Who Chooses Experience? Examining the Use of Veteran Staff by House Freshmen," *Polity* 36 (2004): 651–64.

15. U.S. Bureau of the Census, "Fast Facts for Congress," My Congressional District (the American Community Survey), accessed March 19, 2020, http://www.census.gov/fastfacts/.

16. See *Shaw v. Reno*, 509 U.S. 630 (1993); *Miller v. Johnson*, 515 U.S. 900 (1995); and *Easley v. Cromartie*, 532 U.S. 234 (2001). *Thornburg v. Gingles*, 478 U.S. 30 (1986), provides plaintiffs with a right to force a

state to create a majority-minority district if the minority community is large and concentrated enough to form a potential voting majority in the district, the minority community votes cohesively, but the white voting prevents the minority community from electing its preferred candidate. For a longer discussion of redistricting, see Bernard Grofman, Lisa Handley, and Richard G. Niemi, *Minority Representation and the Quest for Voting Equality* (New York: Cambridge University Press, 1992).

17. Frances E. Lee and Bruce I. Oppenheimer, *Sizing up the Senate: The Unequal Consequences of Equal Representation* (Chicago, IL: University of Chicago Press, 1999).

18. Two prominent works on this point are Richard F. Fenno Jr., *The Power of the Purse: Appropriations Politics in Congress* (Boston, MA: Little, Brown, 1966), and Aaron B. Wildavsky, *The New Politics of the Budgetary Process* (Boston, MA: Addison-Wesley Educational, 1992).

19. Fiona McGillivray, "Trading Free and Opening Markets," in *International Trade and Political Institutions,* ed. Fiona McGillivray, Iain McLean, Robert Pahre, and Cheryl Schonhardt-Bailey (Cheltenham, U.K.: Edward Elgar, 2001), 80–98.

20. *Wickard v. Filburn*, 317 U.S. 111 (1942).

21. U.S. Courts: Federal Courts, http://www.uscourts.gov/FederalCourts .aspx.

22. Sarah A. Binder and Forrest Maltzman, "Senatorial Delay in Confirming Federal Judges, 1947–1998," *American Journal of Political Science* 46, no. 1 (2002): 190–99.

23. Supremecourt.gov, accessed August 31, 2020, https://www.supreme court.gov/opinions/19pdf/19-715_febh.pdf.

24. Sarah A. Binder, *Majority Rights, Minority Rule* (New York: Cambridge University Press, 1997); Eric Schickler, *Disjointed Pluralism: Institutional Innovation and the Development of the U.S. Congress* (Princeton, NJ: Princeton University Press, 2001).

25. Sean Gailmard and Jeffery A. Jenkins, "Minority-Party Power in the Senate and the House of Representatives," in *Why Not Parties? Party Effects in the United States Senate*, ed. Nathan W. Monroe, Jason M. Roberts, and David W. Rohde (Chicago, IL: University of Chicago Press, 2008), 181–97.

26. Randall Strahan, *Leading Representatives: The Agency of Leaders in the Politics of the U.S. House* (Baltimore, MD: Johns Hopkins University Press, 2007).

27. Ibid., 79–126.

28. David W. Rohde, *Parties and Leaders in the Postreform House* (Chicago, IL: University of Chicago Press, 1991).

29. Gary W. Cox and Mathew D. McCubbins, *Legislative Leviathan: Party Government in the House* (Berkeley, CA: University of California Press, 1993).

30. Jennifer Steinhauer, "John Boehner, House Speaker, Will Resign from Congress," *New York Times*, September 25, 2015, accessed February 17, 2016, http://www.nytimes.com/2015/09/26/us/john-boehner-to -resign-from-congress.html?_r=0; Mike DeBonis, "Paul Ryan Elected House Speaker," *Washington Post*, October 29, 2015, accessed February 17, 2016, https://www.washingtonpost.com/news/powerpost/wp/2015/10/29/paul -ryan-set-to-be-elected-62nd-house-speaker/.

31. Gallup.com, "Congressional Job Approval at 12% in February," accessed April 16, 2014, http://www.gallup.com/poll/167375 /congressional-job-approval-february.aspx.

32. Gallup.com, "Congressional Approval," accessed March 13, 2018, http://news.gallup.com/poll/1600/congress-public.aspx.

33. Justin McCarthy, "Trump's Job Rating Slides; U.S. Satisfaction Tumbles," *Gallup.com*, April 16, 2020, accessed May 11, 2020, https:// news.gallup.com/poll/308675/trump-job-rating-slides-satisfaction -tumbles.aspx.

34. Barry C. Burden and Tammy M. Frisbee, "Preferences, Partisanship, and Whip Activity in the U.S. House of Representatives," *Legislative Studies Quarterly* 29 (2004): 569–90.

35. Ralph Huitt, "Democratic Party Leadership in the Senate," *American Political Science Review* 55 (1961): 333–44.

36. E. Scott Adler and John Wilkerson, "Intended Consequences: Jurisdictional Reform and Issue Control in the U.S. House of Representatives," *Legislative Studies Quarterly* 33, no. 1 (2008): 85–112.

37. Abby Livingston, "How Joe Barton's Downfall Led to Two Competitive Texas Races," *The Texas Tribune,* May 9, 2018, accessed May 12, 2020, https://www.texastribune.org/2018/05/09/north -texas-voters-begin-consider-future-without-joe-barton/.

38. David W. Rohde, "Committee Reform in the House of Representatives and the Subcommittee Bill of Rights," *Annals of the American Academy of Political and Social Science* 411, no. 1 (1974): 39–47.

39. For a list of current caucuses, see Committee on House Administration, "112th Congress Congressional Member Organizations (CMO)," updated April 11, 2012, accessed June 21, 2012, http://cha.house .gov/sites/republicans.cha.house.gov/files/documents/cmo_cso _docs/cmo_112th_congress.pdf.

40. U.S. Senate, Statistics and Lists, *Resume of Congressional Activity,* various years, 2017–2018, accessed August 31, 2020, https://www .senate.gov/reference/resources/pdf/Resumes/115_2.pdf.

41. For an extended discussion of the right of recognition and the powers it affords senators, see Floyd Riddick, *Senate Procedure*, ed. Alan Frumin (Washington D.C.: U.S. Government Printing Office, 1992), 1091–99.

42. Sarah A. Binder and Steven S. Smith, *Politics or Principle: Filibustering in the U.S. Senate* (Washington, D.C.: Brookings Institution Press, 1997). For a discussion of the use of the filibuster by retiring senators, see Martin Overby, L. Overby, and Lauren Bell, "Rational Behavior or the Norm of Cooperation? Filibustering Among Retiring Senators," *Journal of Politics* 66 (2004): 906–24.

43. For more details on the cloture rules and other changes, see Valerie Heitshusen, Congressional Research Service, "Majority Cloture for Nominations: Implications and the 'Nuclear' Proceedings," December 6, 2013, R43331, accessed April 16, 2014, http://www.fas.org/sgp /crs/misc/R43331.pdf.

44. American Constitution Society, "Judicial Nominations," accessed May 11, 2020, https://www.acslaw.org/judicial-nominations/.

45. David Stout, Carl Hulse, and Sheryl Gay Stolberg, "Senate Backs Disputed Judicial Nomination," *New York Times*, October 27, 2007, A21; Robert Barnes, "Scalia's Death Plunges Court, National Politics into Turmoil," *Washington Post,* February 13, 2016 accessed February 17, 2016, https://www.washingtonpost.com /national/scalias-death-plunges-court-national-politics-into-turmoil /2016/02/13/136c0590-d2a4-11e5-b2bc-988409ee911b_story .html.

46. Wendy J. Schiller, "Resolved the Filibuster Should Be Abolished— Con," in *Debating Reform*, 4th ed., ed. Richard J. Ellis and Michael Nelson (Washington, D.C.: CQ Press, 2020).

47. Justin Wise, "First Responder Swipes at Rand Paul, Mike Lee After Senate Passes 9/11 Victims Fund Extension," *The Hill,* July 23, 2019, accessed May 14, 2020, https://thehill.com/homenews/senate /454388-first-responder-swipes-at-rand-paul-mike-lee-in-speech -celebrating-9-11.

48. Wendy J. Schiller, "Senators as Political Entrepreneurs: Using Bill Sponsorship to Shape Legislative Agendas," *American Journal of Political Science* 1 (1995): 186–203.

49. Glen Krutz, *Hitching a Ride: Omnibus Legislating in the U.S. Congress* (Columbus: Ohio State University Press, 2001).

50. For a general discussion on committees, see Keith R. Krehbiel, *Information and Legislative Organization* (Ann Arbor: University of Michigan Press, 1991).

51. For a few examples of this work, see Aage Clausen, *How Congressmen Decide* (New York: St. Martin's Press, 1973); John Kingdon, *Congressmen's Voting Decisions* (New York: Harper & Row, 1989); David W. Brady, *Critical Elections and Congressional Policy Making* (Stanford, Calif.: Stanford University Press, 1988); Stanley Bach and Steven S. Smith, *Managing Uncertainty in the U.S. House of Representatives* (Washington, D.C.: Brookings Institution Press, 1989). For examples of the ideological examination of roll call voting, see Keith T. Poole and Howard Rosenthal, *Ideology and Congress* (New Brunswick, NJ: Transaction Publishers, 2009).

52. Jonathan Miller, "Party Unity on Congressional Votes Takes a Dive: CQ Vote Studies," *Rollcall.com*, February 28, 2019, accessed May 9, 2020, https://www.rollcall.com/2019/02/28/party-unity-on-congressional-votes-takes-a-dive-cq-vote-studies/.

53. C. Lawrence Evans and Walter J. Oleszek, "Message Politics and Senate Procedure," in *The Contentious Senate: Partisanship, Ideology and the Myth of Cool Judgment*, ed. Colton C. Campbell and Nicol C. Rae (Lanham, Md.: Rowman and Littlefield, 2000).

54. Barbara Sinclair, *Unorthodox Lawmaking: New Legislative Processes in the U.S. Congress*, 4th ed. (Washington, D.C.: CQ Press, 2011).

55. Staff AP, "US Unemployment Surges to a Depression-era Level of 14.7%," *AP.com*, accessed May 9, 2020, https://apnews.com/908d7a004c316baceb916112c0a35ed0

56. Bureau of Labor Statistics, "Labor Force Statistics from the Current Population Survey," http://data.bls.gov/timeseries/LNS14000000.

57. Department of Labor, "Unemployment Insurance 75th Anniversary," accessed April 17, 2014, http://www.dol.gov/ocia/pdf/75th-Anniversary-Summary-FINAL.pdf.

58. Staff, Department of Labor, "Chronology of Federal Unemployment Compensation Laws, February 2014," accessed April 17, 2014, http://workforcesecurity.doleta.gov/unemploy/pdf/chronfedlaws.pdf.

59. Congressional Budget and Impoundment Control Act of 1974 (Public Law 93-344). For additional background on budget history, see the Senate Budget Committee's website, http://www.budget.senate.gov/democratic/public/index.cfm/history-of-the-budget-committee.

60. Balanced Budget and Emergency Deficit Control Act of 1985 (Public Law 99-177). For historical tables on the U.S. federal budget, see Congressional Budget Office, "The Budget and Economic Outlook Fiscal Years 2012 to 2022," January 31, 2012, accessed June 21, 2012, http://www.cbo.gov/publication/42905. The Fiscal 1985 budget deficit number is taken from Table F-1, http://www.cbo.gov/publication/42911.

61. Walter J. Oleszek, *Congressional Procedures and the Policy Process*, 6th ed. (Washington, D.C: CQ Press, 2004), especially 63–69. For a more comprehensive look at the history of budget politics and deficits, see Jasmine Farrier, *Passing the Buck: Congress, Budgets, and Deficits* (Lexington: University of Kentucky Press, 2004).

62. Molly E. Reynolds, "Four Lessons from the Senate Tax Bill," *Brookings*, https://www.brookings.edu/blog/fixgov/2017/12/02/four-lessons-from-the-senate-tax-bill/.

63. Charles M. Cameron, *Veto Bargaining: Presidents and the Politics of Negative Power* (New York: Cambridge University Press, 2000).

64. Albert D. Cover and Bruce S. Brumberg, "Baby Books and Ballots: The Impact of Congressional Mail on Constituent Opinion," *American Political Science Review* 76 (1982): 347–59.

65. Richard L. Hall, *Participation in Congress* (New Haven, Conn.: Yale University Press, 1998).

66. Tracy Sulkin, *Issue Politics in Congress* (New York: Cambridge University Press, 2005).

67. U.S. Senate, Statistics and Lists, *Final Resume of Congressional Activity*, 2017–2018, https://www.senate.gov/reference/resources/pdf/Resumes/115_1.pdf, https://www.senate.gov/reference/resources/pdf/Resumes/115_2.pdf.

68. For a comprehensive look at this congressional activity, see Diana Evans, *Greasing the Wheels: Using Pork Barrel Projects to Build Majority Coalitions in Congress* (New York: Cambridge University Press, 2004).

69. Richard F. Fenno Jr., *Home Style: House Members in Their Districts* (Boston, MA: Little, Brown, 1978).

70. David R. Mayhew, *Congress: The Electoral Connection* (New Haven, Conn.: Yale University Press, 1974).

71. For an extended discussion of how senators from the same state interact, see Schiller, *Partners and Rivals*.

72. Kyle Kondik and Geoffrey Skelley, "Incumbent Reelection Rates Higher Than Average in 2016," accessed March 13, 2018, http://www.rasmussenreports.com/public_content/political_commentary/commentary_by_kyle_kondik/incumbent_reelection_rates_higher_than_average_in_2016.

73. Jordan Misra, U.S. Census Bureau, "Voter Turnout Rates Among All Voting Age and Major Racial and Ethnic Groups Were Higher Than in 2014," April 23, 2019, accessed May 11, 2020, https://www.census.gov/library/stories/2019/04/behind-2018-united-states-midterm-election-turnout.html.

Chapter 13

1. Sylvia Mathews Burwell, "Testimony before the Senate Health, Education, Labor, and Pensions Committee," May 8, 2014, accessed May 15, 2014, http://www.help.senate.gov/imo/media/doc/Burwell.pdf.

2. This story was compiled from the Office of Management and Budget's website, http://www.whitehouse.gov/omb; President Barack Obama, transcript of "Remarks by the President in Nominating Sylvia Mathews Burwell as Secretary of Health and Human Services," October 9, 2013, http://www.whitehouse.gov; Dylan Matthews, "Sylvia Mathews Burwell: Six Things to Know about the New White House Budget Director," Wonkblog, *Washington Post*, March 3, 2013; "Q&A: Sylvia Mathews, President of the Gates Foundation Global Development Program," *Seattle Times*, March 17, 2007; Jennifer Haberkorn, "Sylvia Mathews Burwell's Hurdles," *Politico*, April 11, 2014; Sarah Plummer, "Obama Taps Hinton Native for Budget Chief," *The Register-Herald*, March 5, 2013.

3. Hedrick Smith, "Bush Says He Sought to Avoid Acting Like Surrogate President," *New York Times*, April 12, 1981, A1, http://www.nytimes.com/1981/04/12/us/bush-says-he-sought-to-avoid-acting-like-surrogate-president.html.

4. Bruce G. Peabody and Scott E. Grant, "The Twice and Future President: Constitutional Interstices and the Twenty-Second Amendment," *Minnesota Law Review* 83 (1999): 565–94.

5. "The Presidents," The White House, accessed June 22, 2012, http://www.whitehouse.gov/about/presidents.

6. Arthur Schlesinger Jr., *The Imperial Presidency* (New York: Mariner Books, 2004; first published 1973).

7. U.S. Department of Justice, Office of the Pardon Attorney, "Clemency Statistics," accessed September 1, 2020, https://www.justice.gov/pardon/clemency-statistics.

8. Neil A. Lewis, "Delay Denied, Libby Is Seen as Weeks From Prison," *New York Times*, June 15, 2007, www.nytimes.com/2007/06/15/washington/15libby.html.

9. Nora V. Demleitner, "Don't Be Fooled by Slick Ad. Most People Given Clemency by Trump Don't Look Like Alice Marie Johnson," *USAToday*, February 13, 2020, accessed June 1, 2020, https://www.usatoday.com/story/opinion/policing/spotlight/2020/02/13/most-people-given-clemency-trump-dont-look-like-alice-marie-johnson/4671405002/.

10. Robert Wielaard, "Kosovo Recognition Irritates Russia and China," *Herald-Tribune*, February 19, 2008, A11, http://www.heraldtribune.com/article/20080219/NEWS/802190626.

11. Kathryn Dunn Tenpas, "Tracking Turnover in the Trump Administration," *Brookings Institution*, May 2020, accessed May 23, 2020, https://www.brookings.edu/research/tracking-turnover-in-the-trump-administration/.

12. Charles M. Cameron, *Veto Bargaining: Presidents and the Politics of Negative Power* (New York: Cambridge University Press, 2000).

13. Glenn S. Krutz, *Hitching a Ride: Omnibus Legislating in the U.S. Congress* (Columbus: Ohio State University Press, 2001). Also see Cameron, *Veto Bargaining*.

14. William W. Lammers and Michael A. Genovese, *The Presidency and Domestic Policy* (Washington, D.C.: CQ Press, 2000), 315–24.

15. John Burnett, "$11 Billion and Counting: Trump's Border Wall Would Be the World's Most Costly," *National Public Radio*, January 20, 2020, accessed May 24, 2020, https://www.npr.org/2020/01/19/797319968/-11-billion-and-counting-trumps-border-wall-would-be-the-world-s-most-costly.

16. Wilson delivered the speech on December 2, 1913. See John T. Woolley and Gerhard Peters, "Length of State of the Union Messages and Addresses (in words), Washington–Obama," The American Presidency Project, accessed June 22, 2012, http://www.presidency.ucsb.edu/sou_words.php#axzz1yaTY1UIo.

17. Jeff Cummins, "State of the Union Addresses and the President's Legislative Success," *Congress and the Presidency* 37 (2010): 176–99.

18. The chronology that follows is taken from the *Washington Post*'s history of Watergate, available online at http://www.washingtonpost.com/wp-srv/onpolitics/watergate/chronology.htm.

19. Ibid.

20. William G. Howell, *Power Without Persuasion: The Politics of Direct Presidential Action* (Princeton, NJ: Princeton University Press, 2003).

21. Harold C. Relyea, *Presidential Directives: Background and Overview*, CRS Report for Congress, 98-611 (Washington, D.C.: Congressional Research Service, 2007).

22. Kenneth R. Mayer, "Executive Orders and Presidential Power," *Journal of Politics* 61 (1999): 445–66, especially 448.

23. Ibid.

24. Harry S. Truman, "Memo 'Concerning the Interpretation of the President's Order . . . ,'" Harry S. Truman Library & Museum, ca. 1948, accessed June 22, 2012, http://www.trumanlibrary.org/whistlestop/study_collections/desegregation/large/documents/index.php?documentdate=1948-00-00&documentid=5-20&studycollectionid=&pagenumber=1&sortorder=.

25. "Executive Order 10730, Providing Assistance for the Removal of an Obstruction of Justice within the State of Arkansas," news release, September 24, 1957, Dwight D. Eisenhower Presidential Library & Museum, http://www.eisenhower.archives.gov/research/online_documents/civil_rights_little_rock/Press_Release_EO_10730.pdf.

26. Staff, "Trump Travel Ban: What Does This Ruling Mean?" *BBCnews.com*, June 26, 2018, accessed May 25, 2020, https://www.bbc.com/news/world-us-canada-39044403; Oyez.com, "Trump v. Hawaii," accessed May 27, 2020, https://www.oyez.org/cases/2017/17-965.

27. Gerhard Peters and John T. Woolley, "Executive Orders," The American Presidency Project, ed. John T. Woolley and Gerhard Peters (Santa Barbara, CA, 1999–2020), accessed September 1, 2020, https://www.presidency.ucsb.edu/statistics/data/executive-orders.

28. Christopher S. Kelley and Bryan W. Marshall, "The Last Word: Presidential Power and the Role of Signing Statements," *Presidential Studies Quarterly* 38 (2008): 248–67; Michael J. Berry, "Controversially Executing the Law: George W. Bush and the Constitutional Signing Statement," *Congress and the Presidency* 36 (2009): 244–71.

29. The White House, "Memorandum for the Heads of Executive Departments and Agencies: Subject: Presidential Signing Statements," news release, March 9, 2009, http://www.whitehouse.gov/the-press-office/memorandum-presidential-signing-statements.

30. Gerhard Peters and John T. Woolley, "Signing Statements," *The American Presidency Project*, ed. John T. Woolley and Gerhard Peters (Santa Barbara, CA, 1999–2020), accessed September 1, 2020, https://www.presidency.ucsb.edu/.

31. Joseph A. Pika and John Anthony Maltese, *The Politics of the Presidency*, 8th ed. (Washington, D.C.: CQ Press, 2012), 14–16.

32. "Bully Pulpit," C-SPAN Congressional Glossary, accessed June 22, 2012, http://legacy.c-span.org/guide/congress/glossary/alphalist.htm.

33. George C. Edwards III, *On Deaf Ears: The Limits of the Bully Pulpit* (New Haven, Conn.: Yale University Press, 2006).

34. John T. Woolley and Gerhard Peters, "Presidential News Conferences, Hoover–Obama," The American Presidency Project, accessed November 7, 2016, http://www.presidency.ucsb.edu/news_conferences.php.

35. Zachary A. Goldfarb and Juliet Eilperin, "White House Looking for New Ways to Penetrate Polarized Media," *Washington Post*, May 6, 2014, accessed online May 7, 2014, http://www.washingtonpost.com/politics/white-house-looking-for-new-ways-to-penetrate-polarized-media/2014/05/06/ebd39b6c-d532-11e3-aae8-c2d44bd79778_story.html; Melvin C. Laracey, *Presidents and People: The Partisan Story of Going Public* (College Station: Texas A&M University Press, 2002); Reed L. Welch, "Presidential Success in Communicating with the Public Through Televised Addresses," *Presidential Studies Quarterly* 33 (2003): 347–65; Samuel Kernell and Laurie L. Rice, "Cable and the Partisan Polarization of the President's Audience," *Presidency Studies Quarterly* 41, no. 4 (2011): 693–711.

36. Richard E. Neustadt, *Presidential Power and the Modern Presidents* (New York: Free Press, 1990).

37. Jon R. Bond, Richard Fleisher, and B. Dan Wood, "The Marginal and Time Varying Effect of Public Approval on Presidential Success in Congress," *Journal of Politics* 65 (2003): 92–110.

38. Andrew Barrett and Matthew Eshbaugh-Soha, "Presidential Success on the Substance of Legislation," *Political Research Quarterly* 60 (2007): 100–12.

39. Emily Jane Charnock, James A. McCann, and Kathryn D. Tenpas, "Presidential Travel from Eisenhower to George W. Bush: An Electoral College Strategy," *Political Science Quarterly* 124 (2009): 323–39.

40. Joint Resolution of Congress, House Joint Resolution 1145, August 7, 1964, *Department of State Bulletin*, August 24, 1964, reprinted in Henry Steele Commager and Milton Cantor, eds., *Documents of American History*, 10th ed. (Englewood Cliffs, NJ: Prentice Hall, 1988), 2: 690.

41. Louis Fisher, *Presidential War Power*, 2nd ed. (Lawrence: University Press of Kansas, 2004), 128–33.

42. Ibid., 144–51.

43. For a longer discussion of this struggle for power over the conduct of war, see William G. Howell and Jon C. Pevenhouse, *Congressional Checks on Presidential War Powers* (Princeton, NJ: Princeton University Press, 2007).

44. For more on presidential decisions to engage in military conflicts, see James Meernick, "Domestic Politics and the Political Use of Military

Force by the United States," *Political Research Quarterly* 54 (2001): 889–904.

45. U.S. House of Representatives, House Joint Resolution, 114 Section 3(a)1, Library of Congress, http://thomas.loc.gov.

46. John J. Kruzel, "Afghanistan Troop Level to Eclipse Iraq by Midyear," United States Army, March 25, 2010, http://www.army.mil/article /36297/.

47. Greg Jaffe and Missy Ryan, "Up to 1,000 More U.S. Troops Could Be Headed to Afghanistan This Spring", *Washington Post*, January 21, 2018, accessed March 15, 2018, https://www.washingtonpost.com /world/national-security/up-to-1000-more-us-troops-could-be-headed -to-afghanistan-this-spring/2018/01/21/153930b6-fd1b-11e7 -a46b-a3614530bd87_story.html?utm_term=.b8d844515cfe.

48. Kathy Gannon. "Number of American troops in Afghanistan drops to 8,600 as Taliban make big changes ahead of expected talks." *Associated Press.* July 19, 2020, accessed September 1, 2020, https:// www.militarytimes.com/news/your-military/2020/07/19/number -of-american-troops-in-afghanistan-drops-to-8600-as-taliban-make -big-changes-ahead-of-expected-talks/.

49. This paragraph is based on "Libya", *New York Times,* updated June 7, 2016, http://www.nytimes.com/topic/destination/libya.

50. This section is based on "Syria," *New York Times,* updated June 7, 2016, http://www.nytimes.com/topic/destination/syria.

51. Julia Manchester, "Poll: Voters Back Trump's Decision Not to strike Iran," *The Hill.com,* July 2, 2019, accessed May 24, 2020, https:// thehill.com/homenews/administration/451396-poll-voters-back -trumps-decision-not-to-strike-iran.

52. *Hamdi v. Rumsfeld,* 542 U.S. 507 (2004).

53. *Rasul v. Bush*, 542 U.S. 466 (2004).

54. *Hamdan v. Rumsfeld*, 548 U.S. 557 (2006).

55. Scott Shane and Thom Shanker, "Yemen Strike Reflects U.S. Shift to Drones as Cheaper War Tool," October 2, 2011, *New York Times*, accessed May 6, 2014, http://www.nytimes.com/2011/10/02/world /awlaki-strike-shows-us-shift-to-drones-in-terror-fight.html?_r=0.

56. Craig Whitlock, "U.S. Airstrike that Killed American Teen in Yemen Raises Legal, Ethical Questions," *Washington Post*, October 22, 2011, accessed May 6, 2014, http://www.washingtonpost.com/world /national-security/us-airstrike-that-killed-american-teen-in-yemen -raises-legal-ethical-questions/2011/10/20/gIQAdvUY7L_story .html.

57. White House, Office of the Press Secretary, "Remarks by the President at the National Defense University, May 23, 2013," http://www .whitehouse.gov/the-press-office/2013/05/23/remarks-president -national-defense-university.

58. Staff, "Public Continues to Back U.S. Drone Attacks," *Pew Research Center,* May 28, 2015, accessed March 4, 2016, http:// www.people-press.org/2015/05/28/public-continues-to-back-u -s-drone-attacks/.

59. *Boumediene v. Bush*, 553 U.S. 723 (2008).

60. James P. Pfiffner, *The Modern Presidency,* 6th ed. (Boston, MA: Wadsworth Cengage Learning, 2011), 99; White House, "The Executive Branch: Executive Office of the President," accessed May 15, 2014, http://www.whitehouse.gov/our-government/executive-branch #eop.

61. Fred I. Greenstein, *Presidential Difference,* 3rd ed. (Princeton, NJ: Princeton University Press, 2009).

62. Mondale wrote a detailed memorandum to President Carter outlining his views of the office of vice president. For a broader discussion of Mondale's vice presidential tenure, see Richard Moe, "The Making of the Modern Vice Presidency: A Personal Reflection," *Minnesota History* 60 (2006): 88–99.

63. Joel K. Goldstein, "The Rising Power of the Modern Vice Presidency," *Presidential Studies Quarterly* 38, no. 3 (2008): 389.

64. For background on the story of Marian Anderson, see Raymond Arsenault, *Sound of Freedom: Marian Anderson, the Lincoln Memorial, and the Concert That Awakened America* (New York: Bloomsbury Press, 2009).

65. Stephen Skowronek, *The Politics Presidents Make: Leadership from John Adams to Bill Clinton* (Cambridge, Mass.: Harvard University Press, 1997). Also see Stephen Skowronek, *Presidential Leadership in Political Time: Reprise and Reappraisal* (Lawrence: University Press of Kansas, 2008).

66. Aaron Wildavsky, "The Two Presidencies" in *The Presidency*, ed. Aaron Wildavsky (Boston, MA: Little, Brown, 1969), 231–43.

67. For a test of this theory, see Brandes Canes-Wrone, William G. Howell, and David E. Lewis, "Toward a Broader Understanding of Presidential Power: A Reevaluation of the Two Presidencies Thesis," *Journal of Politics* 69 (2007): 1–16.

68. Lammers and Genovese, *Presidency and Domestic Policy*. See also Neustadt, *Presidential Power and the Modern Presidents*.

69. Samuel Kernell, *Going Public: New Strategies of Presidential Leadership*, 4th ed. (Washington, D.C.: CQ Press, 2007), 131.

70. Ibid., 87–88.

71. Lammers and Genovese, *Presidency and Domestic Policy*.

72. Robert A. Caro, *The Years of Lyndon Johnson: The Passage of Power* (New York: Alfred A. Knopf, 2012), 487. Also see Lyndon Johnson's commencement address at Howard University, "To Fulfill These Rights," June 4, 1965, accessed June 22, 2012, http://www .lbjlib.utexas.edu/johnson/archives.hom/speeches.hom/650604.asp.

73. Lynn Rosellini, "'Honey, I Forgot to Duck,' Injured Reagan Tells Wife," *New York Times*, March 21, 1981, http://www.nytimes .com/1981/03/31/us/honey-i-forgot-to-duck-injured-reagan-tells -wife.html.

74. American Rhetoric, "Top 100 Speeches," accessed June 22, 2012, http://www.americanrhetoric.com/newtop100speeches.htm.

75. Hank C. Jenkins-Smith, Carol L. Silva, and Richard W. Waterman, "Micro- and Macro-level Models of the Presidential Expectations Gap," *Journal of Politics* 67 (2005): 690–715.

Chapter 14

1. Jon Cohen, "'I'm Going to Keep Pushing.' Anthony Fauci Tries to Make the White House Listen to Facts of the Pandemic," *Science*, March 22, 2020, accessed March 23, 2020, https://www.sciencemag.org /news/2020/03/i-m-going-keep-pushing-anthony-fauci-tries-make -white-house-listen-facts-pandemic.

2. This profile was compiled from the National Institute of Allergy and Infectious Dis-eases, https://www.niaid.nih.gov/; Natalie Angier, "SCIENTIST AT WORK: Anthony S. Fauci; Consummate Politician on the AIDS Front," *New York Times,* February 15, 1994, accessed March 23, 2020, https://www.nytimes.com/1994/02/15/science /scientist-at-work-anthony-s-fauci-consummate-politician-on-the -aids-front.html?searchResultPosition=3; Denise Grady, "Not His First Epidemic: Dr. Anthony Fauci Sticks to the Facts," *New York Times,* March 8, 2020, accessed March 23, 2020, https://www.nytimes .com/2020/03/08/health/fauci-coronavirus.html?searchResult Position=5; Staff, MMWR, "Epidemiology of HIV/AIDS --- United States, 1981–2005," June 1, 2006, accessed Mach 23, 2020, https://www .cdc.gov/mmwr/preview/mmwrhtml/mm5521a2.htm#tab;Staff; HIV. gov, "Fast Facts," accessed March 23, 2020, https://www.hiv.gov /hiv-basics/overview/data-and-trends/statistics.

3. Max Weber, *Economy and Society,* ed. Guenther Roth and Claus Wittich (Berkeley: University of California Press, 1978).

4. FY2021 Budget, Table 5-2: Total Federal Employment, https://www.whitehouse.gov/wp-content/uploads/2020/02/ap_5_strengthening_fy21.pdf P. 53.

5. "President Jefferson in the White House," Eyewitness to History, 2006, accessed June 27, 2012, http://www.eyewitnesstohistory.com/jeffersonwhitehouse.htm.

6. "The Cabinet," The White House, accessed September 1, 2020, http://www.whitehouse.gov/administration/cabinet.

7. *Fiscal Year 2021 Analytical Perspectives, Budget*, Table 21-11, "Budget Authority by Agency in the Adjusted Baseline," p. 285, accessed February 16, 2020, https://www.whitehouse.gov/wp-content/uploads/2020/02/spec_fy21.pdf; FY2021 Budget, Table 5-1 Federal Civilian Employment in the Executive Branch, https://www.whitehouse.gov/wp-content/uploads/2020/02/ap_5_strengthening_fy21.pdf p. 52.

8. Department of Health and Human Services, "HHS Programs and Services," accessed February 17, 2016, http://www.hhs.gov/about/programs/index.html.

9. FY2021 Budget, Table 5-1: Federal Civilian Employment in the Executive Branch, https://www.whitehouse.gov/wp-content/uploads/2020/02/ap_5_strengthening_fy21.pdf p. 52.

10. U.S. Department of Health and Human Services, "About HHS," http://www.hhs.gov/about/.

11. James Q. Wilson, *Bureaucracy* (New York: Basic Books, 1989), 91.

12. Donald F. Kettl, *System Under Stress: Homeland Security and American Politics*, 2nd ed. (Washington, D.C.: CQ Press, 2007), 37–39.

13. Tom Krisher, "Takata Recalls 10 Million More Airbags from 14 Automakers including Subaru, Ford, GM and Toyota," *USA Today*, January 8, 2020, accessed February 17, 2020, https://www.usatoday.com/story/money/cars/2020/01/08/takata-airbag-recall-2020-more-airbags-recalled-explosion-risk/2848334001/.

14. Benjamin Zhang, "There's No Way Volkswagen Will Pay the US $18 Billion in Fines for Cheating on Emissions Tests," *Business Insider*, September 21, 2015, accessed April 4, 2016, http://www.businessinsider.com/theres-no-way-volkswagen-is-going-to-pay-the-us-18-billion-in-fines-for-cheating-on-emissions-tests-2015-9; Russell Hotten, "Volkswagen: The Scandal Explained," *BBC News*, December 10, 2015, accessed April 4, 2016, http://www.bbc.com/news/business-34324772; Staff, "FTC Sues Volkswagen over 'Clean Diesel' Claims; VW Could Face Billions in Fines," *Chicago Tribune* News Services, March 30, 2016, accessed April 4, 2016, http://www.chicagotribune.com/business/ct-ftc-sues-vw-emissions-20160329-story.html; US Environmental Protection Agency, "Volkswagen Clean Air Act Partial Settlement," June 28, 2016, https://www.epa.gov/enforcement/volkswagen-clean-air-act-partial-settlement.

15. Staff, Johns Hopkins University, "COVID-19 Global Cases by the Center for Systems Science and Engineering (CSSE) at Johns Hopkins University," accessed March 12, 2020, https://gisanddata.maps.arcgis.com/apps/opsdashboard/index.html#/bda7594740fd40299423467b48e9ecf6.

16. Aaron Blake, "GOP Congressman—Who Warned Trump about Pandemics—Offers Pointed Criticism of Proposed CDC Cuts," Washington Post, March 10, 2020, accessed March 13, 2020, https://www.washingtonpost.com/politics/2020/03/10/conservative-congressman-who-warned-trump-about-pandemics-offers-pointed-criticism-proposed-cdc-cuts/.

17. Mike Arnot, "What the New European Travel Ban Means for Air Travelers," The *New York Times*, March 13, 2020, accessed March 13, 2020, https://www.nytimes.com/2020/03/13/travel/european-travel-ban-flights.html.

18. Staff, "Coronavirus: US Is Failing on Testing, Says Fauci," BBC News U.S. and Canada, accessed March 11, 2020, https://www.bbc.com/news/world-us-canada-51860529.

19. Wilson, *Bureaucracy*, 69–70.

20. Daniel P. Carpenter, *The Forging of Bureaucratic Autonomy: Reputations, Networks, and Policy Innovation in Executive Agencies, 1862–1928* (Princeton, NJ: Princeton University Press, 2001).

21. U.S. Postal Service, Office of the Postmaster, *The United States Postal Service: An American History, 1775–2006* (Washington, D.C.: Government Relations, U.S. Postal Service, 2007), 6–7, http://about.usps.com/publications/pub100.pdf.

22. Federal Communications Commission, "What We Do," accessed June 9, 2018, https://www.fcc.gov/about-fcc/what-we-do.

23. Keith Collins, "Why Net Neutrality Was Repealed and How it Affects You," *New York Times*, December 14, 2017, accessed June 9, 2018, https://www.nytimes.com/2017/12/14/technology/net-neutrality-rules.html.

24. Cecilia Kang, "Ajit Pai Nears His Biggest Win with Net Neutrality Repeal," *New York Times*, December 13, 2017, accessed June 9, 2018, https://www.nytimes.com/2017/12/13/technology/net-neutrality-fcc-ajit-pai.html.

25. Letter from Ellen Rosenblum, Attorney General of Oregon, to the FCC Commissioners, December 13, 2017. Signed by seventeen attorneys general from CA, DE, DC, HI, IL, IA, MA, KY, ME, MD, MS, NC, PA, RI, VT, VA, WA, accessed June 9, 2018, https://www.doj.state.or.us/wp-content/uploads/2017/12/ag_letter_12-13-2017.pdf.

26. Cecilia Kang, "California Lawmakers Pass Nation's Toughest Net Neutrality Law," *New York Times*, August 31, 2018, accessed February 18, 2020, https://www.nytimes.com/2018/08/31/technology/california-net-neutrality-bill.html.

27. Michael Moss, "*E. coli* Path Shows Flaws in Beef Inspection," *New York Times*, October 3, 2009, A1; Michael Moss, "*E. coli* Outbreak Traced to Company That Halted Testing of Ground Beef Trimmings," *New York Times*, November 12, 2009, A16; Bill Tomson, "Tuna Blamed in Salmonella Outbreak Is Recalled," *Wall Street Journal*, April 17, 2012, A3.

28. U.S. Consumer Product Safety Commission, http://www.cpsc.gov.

29. "The Consumer Financial Protection Bureau," The White House, September 17, 2010, http://www.whitehouse.gov/photos-and-video/video/2010/09/17/consumer-financial-protection-bureau.

30. Kate Berry, "Dems Unload on CFPB's Kraninger: 'You Are Absolutely Worthless,'" *American Banker*, October 16, 2019, accessed February 21, 2020, https://www.americanbanker.com/news/dems-unload-on-cfpbs-kraninger-you-are-absolutely-worthless.

31. David E. Lewis, *Politics of Presidential Appointments: Political Control and Bureaucratic Performance* (Princeton, NJ: Princeton University Press, 2008), 12–13.

32. Theda Skocpol, *Protecting Soldiers and Mothers* (Cambridge, Mass.: Harvard University Press, 1992).

33. Sean M. Theriault, *The Power of the People* (Columbus: Ohio State University Press, 2005), Chapter 3.

34. Lewis, *Politics of Presidential Appointments*, 19–20, especially Figure 2.1.

35. U.S. Office of Personnel Management, "Federal Employment Statistics: Federal Civilian Employment," September 2013, accessed April 1, 2016, http://www.opm.gov/feddata/html/geoagy10.asp.

36. Department of Labor, Bureau of Labor Statistics, accessed April 1, 2016, http://www.bls.gov/ooh/about/ooh-faqs.htm.

37. For more on political appointees, see Jeff Gill and Richard Waterman, "Solidary and Functional Costs: Explaining the Presidential Appointment Contradiction," *Journal of Public Administration Research and Theory* 14 (2004): 547–69.

38. Lewis, *Politics of Presidential Appointments*, 11.

39. Ibid., 100, Figure 4.3.

40. United States Office of Personnel Management Annual Report to the President, Hispanic Employment in the Federal Government Fiscal Year 2017, https://www.opm.gov/policy-data-oversight/diversity-and-inclusion/reports/hispanic-2017.pdf; United States Office of Personnel Management, 2017 Common Characteristics of the Government, https://www.opm.gov/policy-data-oversight/data-analysis-documentation/federal-employment-reports/common-characteristics-of-the-government/ccog2017.pdf.

41. Juliet Eilperin, "Obama Cabinet Picks Add Diversity, But Still Frustrate White House Allies," *Washington Post,* March 4, 2013, http://www.washingtonpost.com/national/health-science/obama-cabinet-picks-add-diversity-but-still-frustrate-white-house-allies/2013/03/04/7e2030a6-84fe-11e2-98a3-b3db6b9ac586_story.html.

42. For an in-depth example of private contracting in Medicaid in New York State, see Nina Bernstein, "Medicaid Shift Sees Rush for Profitable Clients," *New York Times,* May 8, 2014, http://www.nytimes.com/2014/05/09/nyregion/medicaid-shift-fuels-rush-for-profitable-clients.html.

43. U.S. Office of Special Counsel, "Hatch Act," updated October 6, 2011, http://www.osc.gov/hatchact.htm, and "Political Activity and the Federal Employee," http://www.osc.gov/documents/hatchact/ha_fed.pdf, both accessed June 27, 2012.

44. For more on the relationships among bureaucrats, members of Congress, and interest groups, see Anthony M. Bertelli and Christian R. Grose, "Secretaries of Pork? A New Theory of Distributive Public Policy," *Journal of Politics* 71 (2009): 926–45; and Sanford C. Gordon and Catherine Hafer, "Corporate Influence and the Regulatory Mandate," *Journal of Politics* 69 (2007): 300–19.

45. For in-depth studies of congressional oversight, see Charles R. Shipan, "Regulatory Regimes, Agency Actions, and the Conditional Nature of Congressional Influence," *American Political Science Review* 9 (2004): 467–80; Keith W. Smith, "Congressional Use of Authorization and Oversight," *Congress and the Presidency* 37 (2010): 45–63.

46. Daniel P. Carpenter, "Groups, the Media, Agency Waiting Costs, and FDA Drug Approval," *American Journal of Political Science* 46, no. 3 (2002): 490–505. Also see Susan L. Moffitt, "Promoting Agency Reputation Through Public Advice: Advisory Committee Use in the FDA," *Journal of Politics* 72, no. 3 (2010): 1–14. For a longer discussion of the history and effectiveness of the FDA, see Daniel P. Carpenter, *Reputation and Power: Organizational Image and Pharmaceutical Regulation at the FDA* (Princeton, N.J.: Princeton University Press, 2010).

47. U.S. Food and Drug Administration, "FDA Safety Communication: Shasta Technologies GenStrip Blood Glucose Test Strips May Report False Results," issued April 29, 2014, accessed May 8, 2014, http://www.fda.gov/MedicalDevices/Safety/AlertsandNotices/ucm395180.htm.

48. L. Paige Whitaker, "The Whistleblower Protection Act: An Overview," CRS Report for Congress, RL33918 (Washington, D.C.: Congressional Research Service, March 12, 2007).

49. Kevin Liptak, Paul LeBlanc, and Olanma Mang. "Whistleblower Timeline: Team Trump Contacts and Ukraine," *CNN.com,* November 13, 2019, accessed March 24, 2020, cnn.com/2019/09/20/politics/whistleblower-timeline-ukraine-team-trump/index.html.

50. Adam Goldman, Julian E. Barnes, Maggie Haberman, and Nicholas Fandos, "Lawmakers Are Warned That Russia Is Meddling to Re-elect Trump," *New York Times,* February 20, 2020, https://www.nytimes.com/2020/02/20/us/politics/russian-interference-trump-democrats.html.

Chapter 15

1. Material for this vignette taken from Justice Sotomayor's memoir, *My Beloved World* (2013); the Supreme Court case *Schuette v. Coalition to Defend Affirmative Action*, 134 S.Ct. 1623 (2014), http://www.supremecourt.gov/opinions/13pdf/12-682_j4ek.pdf; and an interview on National Public Radio (http://www.npr.org/2013/01/14/167699633/a-justice-deliberates-sotomayor-on-love-health-and-family).

2. "Federal Judgeships," Administrative Office of the United States Courts, accessed Apri 14, 2020, 2014, https://www.uscourts.gov/judges-judgeships/authorized-judgeships.

3. Federal litigation data can be found at "Federal Judicial Caseload Statistics 2015," Administrative Office of the U.S. Courts, accessed June 6, 2016, http://www.uscourts.gov/statistics-reports/analysis-reports/federal-judicial-caseload-statistics.

4. *Steelworkers v. Weber*, 443 U.S. 193 (1979).

5. *Firefighters Local Union No. 1784 v. Stotts,* 467 U.S. 561 (1984).

6. *Johnson v. Transportation Agency*, 480 U.S. 616 (1987).

7. *Fullilove v. Klutznick*, 448 U.S. 448 (1980).

8. *Richmond v. J. A. Croson Co.*, 488 U.S. 469 (1989).

9. *Metro Broadcasting, Inc. v. FCC*, 497 U.S. 547 (1990); *Adarand Constructors, Inc. v. Pena,* 515 U.S. 200 (1995).

10. *Regents v. Bakke,* 438 U.S. 265 (1978).

11. *Hopwood v. Texas*, 78 F.3d 932 (1996).

12. See http://www.nbcnews.com/news/latino/more-latinos-whites-admitted-university-california-n85511, accessed June 5, 2014.

13. *Schuette v. BAMN*, 134 S.Ct. 1623 (2014).

14. *Fisher v. University of Texas at Austin*, 133 S. Ct. 2411 (2013).

15. *Fisher v. University of Texas*, 136 S. Ct. 2198 (2016).

16. Civil Rights Act 78 Stat. 252, 42 U.S.C. 2000d.

17. Federal litigation data, Adminstrative Office of the U.S. Courts.

18. Paul M. Collins Jr., "Friends of the Court: Examining the Influence of *Amicus Curiae* Participation in U.S. Supreme Court Litigation," *Law and Society Review* 38 (2004): 807–32.

19. Rebecca Salokar, *The Solicitor General: The Politics of Law* (Philadelphia, PA: Temple University Press, 1992).

20. Lisa Solowiej and Paul Collins Jr., "Counteractive Lobbying in the U.S. Supreme Court," *American Politics Research* 37 (2009): 670–99.

21. *Regents of the University of California v. Bakke,* 438 U.S. 265 (1978).

22. Federal Bureau of Investigation, *Crime in the United States 2014,* Fall 2015, accessed March 4, 2016, http://www.fbi.gov/about-us/cjis/ucr/crime-in-the-u.s/2014/crime-in-the-u.s.-2014/offenses-known-to-law-enforcement/clearances/main.

23. Mark Motivans, "Federal Justice Statistics 2010," U.S. Department of Justice, Office of Justice Programs, Bureau of Justice Statistics, accessed May 7, 2014, http://www.bjs.gov/content/pub/pdf/fjs10.pdf.

24. Gregory Caldeira and John R. Wright, "Organized Interests and Agenda Setting in the U.S. Supreme Court," *American Political Science Review* 82 (1988): 1109–28.

25. Adam Bonica, Adam S. Chilton, Jacob Goldin, Kyle Rozema, and Maya Sen, "Legal Rasputins? Law Clerk Influence on Voting at the U.S. Supreme Court," June 14, 2018. Available at SSRN: https://ssrn.com/abstract=2815545 or http://dx.doi.org/10.2139/ssrn.2815545.

26. *Hopwood v. Texas*, 78 F.3d 932 (1996).

27. *Obergefell v. Hodges,* 135 S. Ct. 2071 (2015).

28. Nina Totenberg, "Record Number Of Amicus Briefs Filed In Same-Sex-Marriage Cases," *NPR*, April 28, 2015, accessed March 4, 2016, http://www.npr.org/sections/itsallpolitics/2015/04/28/402628280/record-number-of-amicus-briefs-filed-in-same-sex-marriage-cases.

29. Timothy Johnson, Paul Wahlbeck, and James Spriggs, "The Influence of Oral Arguments on the U.S. Supreme Court," *American Political Science Review* 100 (2006): 99–113.

30. Greg Stohr, *A Black and White Case* (Princeton, N.J.: Bloomberg Press, 2006), 277.

31. Timothy Johnson, Paul Wahlbeck, and James Spriggs, "The Influence of Oral Arguments on the U.S. Supreme Court," *American Political Science Review* 100 (2006): 99–113.

32. See *Marks v. United States* 430 U.S. 188 (1977).

33. Alexander Bickel, *The Least Dangerous Branch: The Supreme Court at the Bar of Politics* (Indianapolis: Bobbs-Merrill, 1963).

34. Harold J. Spaeth, Sara Benesh, Lee Epstein, Andrew D. Martin, Jeffrey A. Segal, and Theodore J. Ruger, Supreme Court Database, Version 2020, Release 01, accessed October 12, 2020, http://supremecourt database.org.

35. *Gonzalez v. Raich*, 545 U.S. 1 (2005).

36. Jeffrey A. Segal and Harold J. Spaeth, *The Supreme Court and the Attitudinal Model Revisited* (New York: Cambridge University Press, 2002).

37. Ibid.

38. Lee Epstein and Jack Knight, *The Choices Justices Make* (Washington, D.C.: CQ Press, 1998); Forrest Maltzman, James F. Spriggs II, and Paul J. Wahlbeck, *Crafting Law on the Supreme Court: The Collegial Game* (New York: Cambridge University Press, 2000).

39. Jan Crawford, "Roberts Switched Views to Uphold Health Care Law," *Face the Nation, CBS News,* July 1, 2012, http://www.cbsnews.com/8301-3460_162-57464549/roberts-switched-views-to-uphold-health-care-law/.

40. See Lawrence Baum, *The Puzzle of Judicial Behavior* (Ann Arbor: University of Michigan Press, 1997).

41. Jeffrey A. Segal and Robert M. Howard, "How Supreme Court Justices Respond to Litigant Requests to Overturn Precedent," *Judicature* 85 (2001): 148–57.

42. Jeffrey A. Segal and Robert M. Howard, "A Preference for Deference? The Supreme Court and Judicial Review," *Political Research Quarterly* 57 (2004): 131–43. See also Lori Ringhand, "The Changing Face of Judicial Activism: An Empirical Examination of Voting Behavior on the Rehnquist Natural Court," *Constitutional Commentary* 24 (2007): 43.

43. Gerald Rosenberg, *The Hollow Hope* (Chicago, IL: University of Chicago Press, 1991).

44. *United States v. Nixon,* 418 U.S. 683 (1974).

45. *Reynolds v. Sims*, 377 U.S. 533 (1964).

46. *Roe v. Wade*, 410 U.S. 113 (1973).

47. "Samuel Chase—The Samuel Chase Impeachment Trial," Law Library, accessed May 10, 2012, http://law.jrank.org/pages/5151/Chase-Samuel-Chase-Impeachment-Trial.htm.

48. Lee Epstein and Jeffrey A. Segal, *Advice and Consent: The Politics of Judicial Appointments* (New York: Oxford University Press, 2006).

49. Denis Steven Rutkus and Mitchel A. Sollenberger, *Judicial Nomination Statistics: U.S. District and Circuit Courts, 1977–2003*, CRS Report for Congress, RL31635 (Washington, D.C.: Congressional Research Service, February 23, 2004), Table 2(b), accessed July 1, 2014, http://www.senate.gov/reference/resources/pdf/RL31635.pdf.

50. Barry J. McMillion "Judicial Nomination Statistics and Analysis: U.S. District and Circuit Courts, 1977–2018." *Congressional Research Service*, https://crsreports.congress.gov/product/pdf/R/R45622, accessed November 9, 2020.

51. Carrie Severino, "Democrats Obscuring Judicial Facts," *USA Today*, June 7, 2013, http://www.judicialnetwork.com/democrats-obscuring-judicial-facts/.

52. Denis Steven Rutkus and Mitchel A. Sollenberger, *Judicial Nomination Statistics: U.S. District and Circuit Courts, 1977–2003*, CRS Report for Congress, RL31635 (Washington, D.C.: Congressional Research Service, February 23, 2004), Table 2(b), accessed July 1, 2014, http://www.senate.gov/reference/resources/pdf/RL31635.pdf.

53. "Florence E. Allen Named Federal Judge; First Woman to Get Place on Circuit Bench," *New York Times*, March 7, 1934, p. 9.

54. See http://www.blackpast.org/aah/hastie-william-henry-1904-1976, accessed March 4, 2016.

55. See http://www.jtb.org/index.php?src=directory&view=biographies&srctype=detail&refno=98&category=Hispanic%20Judges, accessed March 4, 2016.

56. All data here are from Barry J. McMillion, "U.S. Circuit and District Court Judges: Profile of Select Characteristics," Congressional Research Service, March 19, 2014, accessed March 28, 2016, https://www.fas.org/sgp/crs/misc/R43426.pdf.

57. Christina L. Boyd, Lee Epstein, and Andrew D. Martin, "The Causal Effects of Sex on Judging," *American Journal of Political Science* 54 (2010): 389–411.

58. Adam N. Glynn and Maya Sen, "Identifying Judicial Empathy: Does Having Daughters Cause Judges to Rule for Women's Issues," *American Journal of Political Science* 59 (2015): 37–54.

59. Ibid., 38.

60. Kenneth L. Manning, "¿Como Decide?: Decision-Making by Latino Judges in the Federal Courts," accessed March 4, 2016, http://citation.allacademic.com/meta/p_mla_apa_research_citation/0/8/3/3/9/pages83393/p83393-1.php.

61. Susan B. Haire and Laura P. Moyer, *Diversity Matters: Judicial Policy Making in the U.S. Courts of Appeals* (Charlottesville: University of Virginia Press, 2015).

62. Richard Nixon, "Transcript of President's Announcement," *New York Times*, October 22, 1971.

63. David Yalof, *Pursuit of Justices: Presidential Politics and the Pursuit of Supreme Court Nominees* (Chicago, IL: University of Chicago Press, 1999).

64. Information is from Democratic strategy memos obtained and quoted in part by *USA Today. See* Severino, "Democrats Obscuring Judicial Facts."

65. Lee Epstein, Jeffrey A. Segal, Harold J. Spaeth, and Thomas G. Walker, *The Supreme Court Compendium*, 6th ed. (Washington D.C.: CQ Press, 2015).

66. Jonathan P. Kastellec, Jeffrey R. Lax, and Justin H. Phillips, "Public Opinion and Senate Confirmation of Supreme Court Nominees," *Journal of Politics* 72 (2010): 767–84; *District of Columbia v. Heller*, 554 U.S. 570 (2008); *McDonald v. Chicago*, 561 U.S. 742 (2010); *Citizens United v. FEC*, 558 U.S. 310 (2010); *Printz v. United States*, 521 U.S. 898 (1997); *Friedrichs v. California Teachers Association*, 136 S.Ct. 1083 (2016).

67. Charlie Savage, "A Judge's View of Judging Is on the Record," *New York Times*, May 14, 2009, p. A21, http://www.nytimes.com/2009/05/15/us/15judge.html.

68. Charles M. Cameron, Albert D. Cover, and Jeffrey A. Segal, "Senate Voting on Supreme Court Nominees: A Neoinstitutional Model," *American Political Science Review* 84 (1990): 525–34.

69. Christina Boyd, Lee Epstein, and Andrew D. Martin, "Untangling the Causal Effects of Sex on Judging," *American Journal of Political Science* 54 (2010): 389–411.

70. See, e.g., Karen O'Connor and Jeffrey A. Segal, "Justice Sandra Day O'Connor and the Supreme Court's Reaction to Its First Female Member," *Women and Politics* 10 (1990): 95–104.

71. John J. Szmer, Tammy A. Sarver, and Erin B. Kaheny, "Have We Come a Long Way, Baby? The Influence of Attorney Gender on Supreme Court Decision Making," *Politics and Gender* 6 (2010): 1–36.

72. *McCulloch v. Maryland,* 4 Wheaton 316 (1819); *Gibbons v. Ogden,* 9 Wheaton 1 (1824); and *Cohens v. Virginia,* 6 Wheaton 264 (1821).

73. 60 U.S. 393 (1857).

74. *Slaughterhouse Cases,* 83 U.S. 36 (1873).

75. *United States v. Cruikshank,* 92 U.S. 542 (1876).

76. *Civil Rights Cases,* 109 U.S. 3 (1883).

77. *Brandenburg v. Ohio*, 395 U.S. 444 (1969) (speech rights); *New York Times v. Sullivan*, 376 U.S. 254 (1964) (press rights); *Memoirs v. Massachusetts*, 383 U.S. 413 (1966) (obscenity); and *Engel v. Vitale*, 370 U.S. 421 (1962); *Abington Township School District v. Schempp*, 374 U.S. 203 (1963) (prayer and Bible reading).

78. *Brown v. Board of Education*, 347 U.S. 483 (1954); *Wesberry v. Sanders*, 376 U.S. 1 (1964); *Reynolds v. Sims*, 377 U.S. 533 (1964).

79. *Griswold v. Connecticut*, 381 U.S. 479 (1965) (birth control); *Roe v. Wade*, 410 U.S. 113 (1973).

80. *Mapp v. Ohio*, 367 U.S. 643 (1961); *Miranda v. Arizona*, 384 U.S. 436 (1966).

81. *Swann v. Charlotte-Mecklenburg Board of Education*, 402 U.S. 1 (1971) (busing); *Roe v. Wade*, 410 U.S. 113 (1973) (abortion); *Furman v. Georgia*, 408 U.S. 238 (1972) (death penalty); *Reed v. Reed*, 404 U.S. 71 (1971) (sex discrimination); and *Regents of the University of California v. Bakke*, 438 U.S. 265 (1978) (affirmative action).

82. *San Antonio Independent School District v. Rodriguez*, 411 U.S. 1 (1973) (school funding); *United States v. Leon*, 468 U.S. 897 (1984) (limiting the exclusionary rule); and *New York v. Quarles*, 467 U.S. 649 (1984) (limiting *Miranda*).

83. *Lawrence v. Texas*, 539 U.S. 558 (2003).

84. *Planned Parenthood v. Casey*, 505 U.S. 833 (1992); *United States v. Lopez*, 514 U.S. 549 (1995); *Gratz v. Bollinger*, 539 U.S. 244 (2003); and *Grutter v. Bollinger*, 539 U.S. 306 (2003).

85. *Bush v. Gore,* 531 U.S. 98 (2000).

86. Adam Liptak, "Justices Offer Receptive Ear to Business Interests," *New York Times*, December 19, 2010, p. A1.

87. *Wal-mart Stores v. Dukes*, 131 S. Ct. 2541 (2011).

88. *Citizens United v. Federal Election Commission*, 558 U.S. 310 (2010).

89. *National Federation of Independent Business et al. v. Sebelius*, 132 S. Ct. 2566 (2012).

90. *Obergefell v. Hodges*, 135 S. Ct. 2584 (2015).

91. *Schuette v. Coalition to Defend Affirmative Action*, 133 S. Ct. 1653 (2014).

92. Robert Dahl, "Decision Making in a Democracy: The Supreme Court as a National Policy-Maker," *Journal of Public Law* 6 (1957): 179–295.

93. Herbert M. Kritzer, "Federal Judges and Their Political Environments: The Influence of Public Opinion," *American Journal of Political Science* 23 (1979): 194–207.

94. *West Virginia State Board of Education v. Barnette*, 319 U.S. 624 (1943), 638.

Chapter 16

1. Lori Lightfoot for Chicago. "A Strategy for Public Safety in Every Neighborhood," accessed October 20, 2020, https://lightfoot forchicago.com/wp-content/uploads/2019/01/LL-Position-paper _StrategyPublicSafety.pdf.

2. Kim Kozlowski and Sarah Rahal (2019), "UM alum Lightfoot to be Chicago's 1st black female mayor," Detroit News, archived from the original on April 4, 2019, retrieved April 4, 2019; Maudlyne Ihejirika (2016), "The woman at the center of Rahm Emanuel's efforts to reform the police," *Chicago Sun-Times,* archived from the original on April 4, 2019, accessed April 4, 2019; Curtis Black (2019), "Is Lori Lightfoot really the progressive candidate?" *Chicago Reader,* archived from the original on February 19, 2019, accessed February 18, 2019; "Former federal prosecutor picked to run Chicago Police Board," *Chicago Sun-Times,* May 31, 2015, archived from the original on February 27, 2019, accessed February 27, 2019; Curtis Black (2019), "Lightfoot's long, complicated record on policing easy to distort," *Chicago Reporter,* archived from the original on April 1, 2019, accessed April 1, 2019; Greg Hinz (2019), "Lightfoot panel to rewrite city's affordable housing law," *Crain's Chicago Business,* archived from the original on November 23, 2019, accessed November 26, 2019, https://msmag azine.com/2020/06/03/black-women-mayors-healing-and-leading -their-communities/; Fran Spielman (2020), "Lightfoot poll shows strong support for her and the police reforms she champions," *Chicago Sun-Times,* accessed July 17, 2020; Mayer Brown, "Congratulations to Chicago Mayor and Former Mayer Brown Partner Lori Lightfoot," accessed October 19, 2020, https://www.mayerbrown.com/en /perspectives-events/publications/2019/05/congratulations-to -chicago-mayor-lori-lightfoot; Ballotpedia; "Mayoral election in Chicago, Illinois (2019)," accessed October 19, 2020, https://ballot pedia.org/Mayoral_election_in_Chicago,_Illinois_(2019)#Election_history.

3. Bryan D. Jones and Frank M. Baumgartner, *The Politics of Attention* (Chicago, IL: University of Chicago Press, 2005).

4. Mary Emily O'Hara, "LGBTQ Advocates Say Trump's New Executive Order Makes Them Vulnerable to Discrimination." March 29, 2017, accessed June 9, 2018, https://www.nbcnews.com/feature/nbc -out/lgbtq-advocates-say-trump-s-news-executive-order-makes -them-n740301.

5. Kate Sheppard, "North Carolina Coal Ash Spill Renews Push for Long-Delayed Federal Regulations," *HuffPost.com,* February 5, 2014, accessed May 24, 2014, http://www.huffingtonpost.com /2014/02/05/coal-ash-spill-north-carolina_n_4733164.html; U.S. Government Printing Office, July 2, 2015, *Federal Register*, https:// www.gpo.gov/fdsys/pkg/FR-2015-07-02/pdf/2015-15913.pdf.

6. *New State Ice Co. v. Liebmann,* 285 U.S. 262 (1932) at 311. See Andrew Karch, *Democratic Laboratories: Policy Diffusion Among the American States* (Ann Arbor: University of Michigan Press, 2007).

7. NORML: Working to Reform Marijuana Laws, "State Laws," accessed May 1, 2020, https://norml.org/laws.

8. Craig Volden, "States as Policy Laboratories: Emulating Success in the Children's Health Insurance Program," *American Journal of Political Science* 50 (2006): 294–312.

9. Chris Koski, "Greening America's Skylines: The Diffusion of Low-Salience Policies," *Policy Studies Journal* 38 (2010): 93–117.

10. Michael Mintron and Sandra Vergari, "Policy Networks and Innovations Diffusion: The Case of State Education Reforms," *Journal of Politics* 60 (1998): 126–48.

11. Christopher Stream, "Health Reform in the States: A Model of State Small Group Health Insurance Market Reforms," *Political Research Quarterly* 52 (1999): 499–525.

12. Frederick J. Boehmke and Richard Witmer, "Disentangling Diffusion: The Effects of Social Learning and Economic Competition on State Policy Innovation and Expansion," *Political Research Quarterly* 57 (2004): 39–51.

13. Charles R. Shipan and Craig Volden, "Bottom-Up Federalism: The Diffusion of Antismoking Policies from U.S. Cities to States," *American Journal of Political Science* 50 (2006): 825–43.

14. Robert R. Preuhs, "State Policy Components of Interstate Migration in the United States," *Political Research Quarterly* 52 (1999): 527–47.

15. David M. Konisky, "Regulatory Competition and Environmental Enforcement: Is There a Race to the Bottom?" *American Journal of Political Science* 51 (2003): 853.

16. *Shapiro v. Thompson*, 394 U.S. 618 (1969); *Saenz v. Roe*, 526 U.S. 489 (1999).

17. Craig Volden, "The Politics of Competitive Federalism: A Race to the Bottom in Welfare Benefits?" *American Journal of Political Science* 46 (2006): 352–63.

18. Department of Housing and Urban Development, "HUD Historical Background," http://portal.hud.gov/hudportal/HUD.

19. For details on these programs, see the U.S. Department of Health and Human Services, Centers for Medicare and Medicaid Services (CMS), http://www.cms.hhs.gov.

20. See http://portal.hud.gov/hudportal/documents/huddoc?id=HUD Programs2016.pdf; also see Center on Budget and Policy Priorities, "Policy Basics: Section 8 Project-Based Rental Assistance," accessed March 22, 2014, http://www.cbpp.org/cms/?fa=view&id=3891.

21. Social Security Administration, "FY 2021 President's Budget: Key Tables," Table 5, p. 6 accessed March 31, 2020, https://www.ssa.gov/budget/FY21Files/2021BST.pdf. Calculation based on $4.7 trillion budget; Congressional Budget Office, "Budget and Economic Data: 10 year Budget Projections," Table 1, accessed on March 31, 2020, https://www.cbo.gov/about/products/budget-economic-data#3.

22. Centers for Disease Control and Prevention, "Early Release of Selected Estimates Based on Data from the 2010 National Health Interview Survey," *CDC.gov*, updated and accessed June 14, 2016, http://www.cdc.gov/nchs/nhis/released201106.htm#1.

23. Reed Abelson, Abby Goodnough, and Robert Pear, "What Happens If Obamacare Is Struck Down?" *New York Times*, March 26, 2019, accessed March 31, 2020, https://www.nytimes.com/2019/03/26/health/obamacare-trump-health.html.

24. Samantha Artiga and Kendal Orgera, "Key Facts on Health and Health Care by Race and Ethnicity." *Henry J. Kaiser Foundation*, November 12, 2019, accessed March 31, 2020, https://www.kff.org/report-section/key-facts-on-health-and-health-care-by-race-and-ethnicity-coverage-access-to-and-use-of-care/.

25. Mary Agnes Carey, "Burwell Says 'Beat Goes On' As HHS Seeks To Expand Health Law's Influence" February 5, 2016, *Kaiser Health News*, accessed April 20, 2016, http://khn.org/news/burwell-says-beat-goes-on-as-hhs-seeks-to-expand-health-laws-influence/.

26. Kaiser Family Foundation, "Status of State Action on the Medicaid Expansion Decision," March 13, 2020, accessed March 31, 2020, https://www.kff.org/health-reform/state-indicator/state-activity-around-expanding-medicaid-under-the-affordable-care-act/?currentTimeframe=0&sortModel=%7B%22colId%22:%22Location%22,%22sort%22:%22asc%22%7D.

27. Marybeth Musumeci, "Explaining Texas v. U.S.: A Guide to the Case Challenging the ACA," *Kaiser Family Foundation*, September 17, 2020, accessed September 17, 2020, https://www.kff.org/health-reform/issue-brief/explaining-texas-v-u-s-a-guide-to-the-case-challenging-the-aca/.

28. Centers for Medicare and Medicaid Services, "Affordable Care Act," http://www.medicaid.gov/AffordableCareAct/Affordable-Care-Act.html.

29. Department of Health and Human Services, "The Affordable Care Act and Latinos," accessed March 10, 2014, http://www.hhs.gov/health-care/facts/factsheets/2012/04/aca-and-latinos04102012a.html; Tamara Keith, "Obama Pitches Health Care Law to Latinos in a Bid to Boost Enrollment," *National Public Radio*, March 6, 2014, http://www.npr.org/blogs/codeswitch/2014/03/06/286859961/obama-pitches-health-care-law-to-latinos-in-bid-to-boost-enrollment.

30. Bryan Baker, "Estimates of the Lawful Permanent Resident Population in the United States: January 2015," Office of Immigration Statistics, Department of Homeland Security, May 2019, accessed March 31, 2020, https://www.dhs.gov/sites/default/files/publications/lpr_population_estimates_january_2015.pdf.

31. U.S. Citizenship and Immigration Services, "About Us," accessed May 31, 2012, http://www.uscis.gov/aboutus.

32. Staff, Department of Homeland Security, "Infographics 2016: Lawful Permanent Residents 2016," accessed June 9, 2018, https://www.dhs.gov/immigration-statistics/visualization/2016.

33. Staff, Department of Homeland Security, "Legal Immigration and Adjustment of Status Report Fiscal Year 2019, Quarter 4," March 4, 2020, accessed March 31, 2020, https://www.dhs.gov/immigration-statistics/special-reports/legal-immigration.

34. Caitlin Oprysko, Anita Kumar, and Nahal Toosi, "Trump Administration Expands Travel Ban," *Politico.com*, January 31, 2020 accessed April 7, 2020, https://www.politico.com/news/2020/01/31/trump-administration-expands-travel-ban-110005.

35. Ibid; Staff, Department of Homeland Security, "Legal Immigration and Adjustment of Status Report Quarterly Data," July 2, 2018, accessed April 7, 2020, https://www.dhs.gov/immigration-statistics/readingroom/special/LIASR.

36. U.S. Citizenship and Immigration Services, "Statement from Secretary of Homeland Security Janet Napolitano on July 1, 2013," accessed June 13, 2014, http://www.uscis.gov/family/same-sex-marriages.

37. U.S. Citizenship and Immigration Services, "A Guide to Naturalization," http://www.uscis.gov/us-citizenship/citizenship-through-naturalization/guide-naturalization.

38. Bryan Baker and Nancy Rytina, "Estimates of the Unauthorized Immigrant Population Residing in the United States: January 2012," Office of Immigration Statistics Department of Homeland Security, March 2013, https://www.dhs.gov/sites/default/files/publications/ois_ill_pe_2012_2.pdf.

39. Anita Kumar. "After Delays, Trump on Track to Build More Than 450 Miles of Border Wall," *Politico.com*, February 14, 2020 accessed April 7, 2020, https://www.politico.com/news/2020/02/14/trump-450-miles-border-wall-115339; U.S. Customs and Border Protection, "Border Wall System," https://www.cbp.gov/border-security/along-us-borders/border-wall-system.

40. U.S. Immigration Support, "Your Online Guide to U.S. Visas, Green Cards and Citizenship," http://www.usimmigrationsupport.org.

41. Luis Miranda, "Get the Facts on the DREAM Act," *White House Blog*, December 1, 2010, http://www.whitehouse.gov/blog/2010/12/01/get-facts-dream-act.

42. The White House, Office of the Press Secretary, "Remarks by the President on Immigration," last modified on June 15, 2012, accessed July 2, 2012, http://www.whitehouse.gov/the-press-office/2012/06/15/remarks-president-immigration.

43. Adam Liptak and Michael D. Shear, "Obama Immigration Plan Seems to Divide Supreme Court," *New York Times*, April 18, 2016, accessed April 20, 2016, http://www.nytimes.com/2016/04/19/us/politics/supreme-court-immigration.html.

44. The United States Supreme Court, *Department of Homeland Security v. Regents of University of California*, decided June 18, 2020, https://www.supremecourt.gov/opinions/19pdf/18-587_5ifl.pdf.

45. Anita Kumar, "Trump Struggles to Win over Republicans on Immigration," *Politico.com*, February 15, 2020, accessed April 7, 2020, https://www.politico.com/news/2020/02/15/immigration-infrastructure-week-trump-administration-114913.

46. Randal C. Archibold, "Arizona Enacts Stringent Law on Immigration," *New York Times*, April 23, 2010, A1.

47. *Kansas v. Garcia, Oyez.com,* accessed on April 13, 2020, https://www.oyez.org/cases/2019/17-834; Andrew Chung, "U.S. Supreme Court Gives States Latitude to Prosecute Illegal Immigrants," *Reuters.com,* March 3, 2020, accessed April 13, 2020, https://www.reuters.com/article/u.s-usa-court-immigration/us-supreme-court-gives-states-latitude-to-prosecute-illegal-immigrants-idUSKBN20Q26S.

48. Bryan Griffith and Jessica Vaughan, "Maps: Sanctuary Cities, Counties, and States," *Center for Immigration Studies,* July 27, 2017, accessed June 9, 2018, https://cis.org/Map-Sanctuary-Cities-Counties-and-States.

49. Jack Lewis, "The Birth of the EPA," *EPA Journal* (Washington, D.C.: U.S. Environmental Protection Agency, 1985), http://www.epa.gov.

50. Bruce Jones, "Despite Growing Energy Independence, U.S. Cannot Escape Global Risks," *Brookings Institution,* May 27, 2014, accessed July 2, 2014, http://www.brookings.edu/blogs/planetpolicy/posts/2014/05/27-energy-independence-us-global-risks-jones.

51. U.S. Energy Information Administration, "International Energy Outlook 2016," May 11, 2016, http://www.eia.gov/forecasts/ieo/.

52. U.S. Census Bureau, "Quick Facts: Flint City, Michigan," accessed April 26, 2016, http://www.census.gov/quickfacts/table/PST045215/2629000.

53. Much of this paragraph and the next one is based on the timeline reported by Merritt Kennedy in "Lead-Laced Water in Flint: A Step-By-Step Look at the Makings of a Crisis," *www.npr.com,* April 20, 2016, accessed April 21, 2016, http://www.npr.org/sections/thetwo-way/2016/04/20/465545378/lead-laced-water-in-flint-a-step-by-step-look-at-the-makings-of-a-crisis. Also see Staff, "6 Michigan Employees Indicted in Flint Water Crisis: Report," *Jurist,* July 29, 2016, accessed August 29, 2016, http://www.jurist.org/paperchase/2016/07/6-michigan-employees-indicted-in-flint-water-crisis.php.

54. CNN Editorial Research, Flint Water Crisis Fast Facts, *CNN.com,* December 13, 2019, accessed April 13, 2020, https://www.cnn.com/2016/03/04/us/flint-water-crisis-fast-facts/index.html; Staff, "Whitmer: Update on Flint Water Crisis Investigation Coming Soon," Grand Rapids Press MLive.com, December 22, 2019, accessed April 13, 2020, https://www.detroitnews.com/story/news/michigan/flint-water-crisis/2019/12/22/whitmer-flint-water-crisis-investigation-update/40872845/.

55. United States Bureau of Labor Statistics, "Employment Situation Summary Table A. Household Data, Seasonally Adjusted," June 5, 2020, https://www.bls.gov/news.release/empsit.a.htm.

56. Kate Lobosco, "When Will You Get Your Stimulus Cash, and How?" *CNN.com,* April 2, 2020, accessed April 13, 2020, https://www.cnn.com/2020/04/01/politics/stimulus-money-distribution-individuals/index.html.

57. Chuck DeVore, "The Trump Tax Cut Is Two Years Old, Where Are the Jobs Being Created?" *Forbes.com,* March 5, 2020, accessed April 13, 2020, https://www.forbes.com/sites/chuckdevore/2020/03/05/the-trump-tax-cut-is-two-years-old-where-are-the-jobs-being-created/#566d31a62bfe.

58. Lachlan Markay and Jay Lucas, "Timeline: Keystone's Three Years in Limbo," *The Foundry* (blog), January 19, 2012, http://blog.heritage.org/2012/01/19/timeline-keystones-three-years-in-limbo/.

59. "Keystone XL Pipeline Project," TransCanada, accessed May 22, 2012, http://www.transcanada.com/keystone.html.

60. House Energy and Commerce Committee, "Keystone XL Review=Anything but Ordinary," accessed June 14, 2016, https://energycommerce.house.gov/news-center/news/keystone-xl-review-anything-ordinary.

61. Pierre Bertrand, "Keystone Pipeline: 5 Things You Need to Know," *International Business Times,* January 19, 2012, http://www.ibtimes.com/keystone-pipeline-5-things-you-need-know-397928.

62. John M. Broder, "TransCanada Renewing Request to Build Keystone Pipeline," *New York Times,* February 27, 2012, http://www.nytimes.com/2012/02/28/science/earth/keystone-pipeline-permit-request-to-be-renewed.html?_r=2&hp.

63. President Barack Obama, "Statement by the President on the Keystone XL Pipeline," November 6, 2015, accessed April 21, 2016, https://www.whitehouse.gov/the-press-office/2015/11/06/statement-president-keystone-xl-pipeline; *Associated Press,* "Trump Administration Approves Keystone XL Pipeline," Fortune.com, March 24, 2017, accessed June 9, 2018, http://fortune.com/2017/03/24/trump-keystone-xl-pipeline-approved/.

64. Nina Lakhani. "Major Blow to Keystone XL Pipeline as Judge Revokes Key Permit," *The Guardian,* April 15, 2020, accessed May 1, 2020, https://www.theguardian.com/environment/2020/apr/15/keystone-xl-pipeline-montana-judge-environment.

65. Bloomberg News. "Keystone XL pipeline remains blocked in Supreme Court order." *Los Angeles Times,* July 6, 2020, accessed September 17, 2020, https://www.latimes.com/business/story/2020-07-06/supreme-court-keystone-xl-oil-pipeline-project.

66. The Brookings Institution, "Webinar: Federal Reserve Chair Jerome Powell on COVID-19 and the Economy," April 9, 2020, accessed April 18, 2020, https://www.brookings.edu/events/webinar-federal-reserve-chair-jerome-powell-on-covid-19-and-the-economy/; also see The Federal Reserve, https://www.federalreserve.gov/.

67. D. Andrew Austin, *The Debt Limit: History and Recent Increases,* CRS Report for Congress, RL31967 (Washington, D.C.: Congressional Research Service, October 1, 2015), http://www.fas.org/sgp/crs/misc/RL31967.pdf.

68. The White House, Office of Management and Budget, Historical Tables, Table 1.1—Summary of Receipts, Outlays, and Surpluses or Deficits (–): 1789–2017; The White House, Office of Management and Budget, Historical Tables, Table 7.1—Federal Debt at the End of Year:—2017. Both tables are available at http://www.whitehouse.gov/omb/budget/Historicals/.

69. Andrew Restuccia, Burgess Everett, and Heather Caygle, "Longest Shutdown in History Ends after Trump Relents on Wall: Congress Quickly Passed Legislation to End the Shutdown, but It's Unclear If Lawmakers Can Reach an Agreement by Feb. 15," *Politico.com,* January 25, 2019, accessed April 18, https://www.politico.com/story/2019/01/25/trump-shutdown-announcement-1125529.

70. Grace Segers and Emily Tillett, "Trump Signs Budget Deal and Suspends Debt Ceiling," August 2, 2019, *CBS News.com,* accessed April 18, 2020, https://www.cbsnews.com/news/whats-in-the-budget-deal-negotiated-by-congress-and-the-white-house/.

71. Office of the U.S. Trade Representative, "UNITED STATES–MEXICO–CANADA TRADE FACT SHEET Modernizing NAFTA into a 21st Century Trade Agreement," accessed April 18, 2020, https://ustr.gov/trade-agreements/free-trade-agreements/united-states-mexico-canada-agreement/fact-sheets/modernizing.

72. "2017: U.S. Trade in Goods with China," *U.S. Census Bureau,* accessed June 9, 2018, https://www.census.gov/foreign-trade/balance/c5700.html.

73. Information in this paragraph is from World Trade Organization, http://www.wto.org.

74. "World Trade Organization Adopts Report Ruling in Favor of the United States in Chicken Products Trade Dispute with China," September 25, 2013, https://ustr.gov/about-us/policy-offices/press-office/press-releases/2013/september/WTO-ruling-favor-US-chicken-China.

75. Europa: Gateway to the European Union, http://europa.eu/.

76. British Broadcasting Company (BBC), Staff, "Brexit: All You Need to Know about the UK Leaving the EU," February 17, 2020, accessed April 20, 2020, https://www.bbc.com/news/uk-politics-32810887.

77. "Washington's Farewell Address," 1796, Yale Law School Avalon Project, http://avalon.law.yale.edu.

78. Woodrow Wilson, "Address to Congress Requesting a Declaration of War against Germany," April 2, 1917, http://www.millercenter.org.

79. Staff, Radio Free Europe, "Zelenskiy Declares February 26 Memorial Day to Mark Annexation of Crimea," February 26, 2020, accessed April 20, 2020, https://www.rferl.org/a/zelenskiy-february-26-crimea -memorial-day-annexation-russia/30456329.html.

80. Barbara Salazar Torreon and Sofia Plagakis, "Instances of Use of United States Armed Forces Abroad, 1798–2020," January 13, 2020, accessed April 20, 2020, https://fas.org/sgp/crs/natsec/R42738.pdf.

81. John Mueller, *War, Presidents, and Public Opinion* (New York: Wiley, 1970).

82. Presidential Approval Ratings, *Gallup Historical Statistics,* accessed May 12, 2012, http://www.gallup.com/poll/124922/presidential -approval-center.aspx.

83. "Presidential Approval Ratings," George W. Bush, *Gallup.com,* accessed May 12, 2012, http://www.gallup.com/poll/124922/presidential -approval-center.aspx.

84. United Nations, "Treaty on the Non-Proliferation of Nuclear Weapons (NPT)," https://www.un.org/disarmament/wmd/nuclear /npt/.

85. Staff, *The Washington Post,* "Full Text of the Iran Nuclear Deal," accessed April 21, 2016, http://apps.washingtonpost.com/g/documents /world/full-text-of-the-iran-nuclear-deal/1651/.

86. President Barack Obama, "Implementation Day," accessed April 21, United States Agency for International Development, http://www .usaid.gov.

87. David E. Sanger and William J. Broad, "Iran Crosses a Key Threshold: It Again Has Sufficient Fuel for a Bomb," *New York Times,* March 3, 2020, accessed April 20, 2020, https://www.nytimes .com/2020/03/03/world/middleeast/iran-nuclear-weapon-trump .html.

88. United States Agency for International Development, http://www .usaid .gov.

89. USAID, https://www.usaid.gov/results-and-data/budget-spending /congressional-budget-justification/fy2021.

90. World Bank, http://www.worldbank.org.

91. Michael W. Doyle, "Liberalism and World Politics," *American Political Science Review* 80 (1986): 1151–69.

92. World Bank, Archives, http://www.worldbank.org.

93. The World Bank, "Fiscal Year 2019 Data: World Bank Group Financing for Partner Countries," in Annual Report, https://www.worldbank .org/en/about/annual-report/fiscal-year-data.

94. Information in this and the next paragraphs from International Monetary Fund, http://www.imf.org.

95. International Monetary Fund, "IMF Members' Quotas and Voting Power, and IMF Board of Governors," February 20, 2018," accessed June 9, 2018; "IMF Lending: Fact Sheet," March 27, 2020, accessed April 21, 2020, http://www.imf.org/external/np/sec/memdir/members .aspx#3https://www.imf.org/en/About/Factsheets/IMF-Lending.

96. Peace Corps, "Fast-Facts," September 30, 2019, accessed April 21, 2020, https://www.peacecorps.gov/news/fast-facts/.

97. National Peace Corps Association, "Level Peace Corps Funding Approved for FY2020," December 17, 2019, accessed April 21, 2020, https://www.peacecorpsconnect.org/articles/congress-set-to -approve-level-peace-corps-funding.

Index

Note: Page numbers followed by *f* and *t* indicate figures and tables, respectively.